The Adventures in Literature Program

ADVENTURES FOR READERS: BOOK ONE
Teacher's Manual
Test Booklet
Reading/Writing Workshop, Grade 7

ADVENTURES FOR READERS: BOOK TWO
Teacher's Manual
Test Booklet
Reading/Writing Workshop, Grade 8

ADVENTURES IN READING
Teacher's Manual
Test Booklet
Reading/Writing Workshop, Grade 9

ADVENTURES IN APPRECIATION
Teacher's Manual
Test Booklet
Reading/Writing Workshop, Grade 10

ADVENTURES IN AMERICAN LITERATURE
Teacher's Manual
Test Booklet
Lessons in Critical Reading and Writing:
Henry James's *Washington Square* and *Daisy Miller*

ADVENTURES IN ENGLISH LITERATURE
Teacher's Manual
Test Booklet
Lessons in Critical Reading and Writing:
Shakespeare's *Hamlet*

ADVENTURES IN MODERN LITERATURE
Teacher's Manual
Test Booklet

ADVENTURES IN WORLD LITERATURE
Teacher's Manual
Test Booklet
Lessons in Critical Reading and Writing:
Three Masters of Russian Fiction

PAUL McCORMICK

Hunterdon Central High School, Flemington, New Jersey
GENERAL TEACHING CONSULTANT AND CONTRIBUTOR
Teacher's Manual

WINIFRED POST

Dana Hall School, Wellesley, Massachusetts
GENERAL TEACHING CONSULTANT AND CONTRIBUTOR
Composition and Language Program

QUENTIN ANDERSON

Columbia University, New York, New York
*Milton, Pope, Wordsworth, Keats, Tennyson,
Browning, Conrad, Joyce*

G. B. HARRISON

University of Michigan, Ann Arbor, Michigan
Shakespeare

J. B. PRIESTLEY

London
Historical Introductions, The English Novel

A. R. GURNEY

Massachusetts Institute of Technology, Cambridge, Massachusetts
Sheridan

DWIGHT LINDLEY

Hamilton College, Clinton, New York
Nineteenth-Century Authors

ALAN PRYCE–JONES

London and New York
Twentieth-Century Biographies

THOMAS M. FOLDS

Dean of Education
The Metropolitan Museum of Art, New York, New York
Fine Arts Program

ADVENTURES
in English Literature

CLASSIC EDITION

Harcourt Brace Jovanovich

NEW YORK CHICAGO SAN FRANCISCO ATLANTA DALLAS *and* LONDON

PAUL McCORMICK is Chairman of the English Department of Hunterdon Central High School, Hunterdon, New Jersey. Mr. McCormick received a master's degree from Rutgers University and has taught at a number of NDEA English Institutes.

WINIFRED POST is Head of the English Department at Dana Hall School, Wellesley, Massachusetts. She received A.B. and A.M. degrees from Radcliffe College and a Masters of Arts in Teaching from Harvard University. An active member of the College Board Commission on English, Miss Post was chairman of the Committee responsible for End-of-Year Examinations in English—Grades 9–12, and of the Committee responsible for "12,000 Students and Their English Teachers".

QUENTIN ANDERSON is Professor of English at Columbia University. He received A.B. and Ph.D. degrees from Columbia University, and a master's degree from Harvard University. He is a specialist in American and in nineteenth-century English literature. Professor Anderson taught at the Universities of Toulouse and Lille, France, in 1962–63 and was visiting professor at the University of Sussex, England, 1966–67.

G. B. HARRISON is Emeritus Professor of English at the University of Michigan. Editor of *Shakespeare: The Complete Works,* his other books include *The Elizabethan and Jacobean Journals, Introducing Shakespeare,* and *Shakespeare's Tragedies.*

J. B. PRIESTLEY is one of England's best-known playwrights, essayists, novelists, and critics. Among his many works are the critical history *Literature and Western Man,* the novel *Good Companions,* the essay collection *Midnight on the Desert,* and *Charles Dickens: A Pictorial Biography.* He is also co-editor of two books in the *Adventures in Good Books* series: *Four English Novels* and *Four English Biographies.*

A. R. GURNEY, JR. is an Associate Professor of English at the Massachusetts Institute of Technology. He is a graduate of the Yale School of Drama and has produced and published several plays.

DWIGHT LINDLEY is Professor of English at Hamilton College in Clinton, New York. He received an A.B. from Hamilton College and M.A. and Ph.D. degrees from Columbia University. Professor Lindley has also taught at Bowdoin College, Brunswick, Maine. He is a specialist in Victorian literature and is coeditor of a forthcoming edition of the letters of John Stuart Mill.

ALAN PRYCE–JONES, English author, critic, and journalist, is a former editor of the London Times Literary Supplement. He is a graduate of Oxford University, Oxford, England. Mr. Pryce–Jones's literary criticism has been widely published in this country.

THOMAS M. FOLDS is Dean of Education at The Metropolitan Museum of Art in New York. A graduate of Yale College and the Yale School of Fine Arts, Mr. Folds has been an instructor of English and Art Director at the Phillips Exeter Academy, New Hampshire, and a Professor of Art and Chairman of the Department of Art at Northwestern University.

Front cover by Al Forsyth from Design Photographers International.
Coin used as colophon courtesy of The American Numismatic Society.

Copyright © 1979, 1973, 1968, 1963 by Harcourt Brace Jovanovich, Inc.

PRINTED IN THE UNITED STATES OF AMERICA

ISBN 0-15-335123-3

CONTENTS

v

THE ELIZABETHAN AGE

THE SEVENTEENTH CENTURY

THE EIGHTEENTH CENTURY

THE ROMANTIC AGE

THE VICTORIAN AGE

THE TWENTIETH CENTURY

Contemporary British Writing

The Fine Arts Program

THE ANGLO-SAXON PERIOD

(449–1066)

FIRST, why do we date the Anglo-Saxon period from 449 to 1066? According to tradition, it was in 449 that the first band of Germanic people crossed the North Sea to Britain to settle in what is now the county of Kent. They were Jutes, from the peninsula of Jutland in Denmark, and they were the first of many such invaders. Following the Jutes came Angles and Saxons. Together these invaders created the Anglo-Saxon England ("Angleland") that lasted until 1066, when the Norman-French, led by William, Duke of Normandy, successfully invaded and conquered the country.

From 449 to 1066 is a long time—over six centuries. England during this period was not the unified country it is today. Most of this time the land was divided into little kingdoms, and during the last two centuries of this period the Anglo-Saxons had to contend with the Viking invaders, called "Danes" by the English, who at one time controlled about half of England and threatened the rest.

Most of these six centuries come within a period frequently described as the "Dark Ages." This description, meant to suggest a time of barbarism, ignorance, confusion, and violence, is now generally considered by historians to be misleading. These ages were not as dark as they were once thought to be. They were by no means without knowledge, communications, and trade and had arts and crafts of a fairly high order. True, it was a time filled with violence, cruelty, and much confused fighting, but then our own world today can hardly be said to be free from such vices and follies.

What plunged the western world into comparative darkness was the collapse of the vast Roman Empire, which for centuries had maintained order from Hadrian's Wall, in northern Britain, to distant Arabia. It was possible at the height of the Roman Empire to travel on post roads and use the same currency from what is now the north of England to the Middle East, beyond the Red Sea. It has never been possible to do this since that time, for all our talk of progress. For years, far longer than the British ruled India, the southern half of Britain had been part of the Roman Empire. The first Roman invasion was a series of raids by Julius Caesar from 57 to 50 B.C. Nearly a century later, the Roman conquest of Britain was made under the Emperor Claudius. Once they had conquered the British inhabitants, a Celtic people, the Roman legions remained as defenders. But, when, in about 410, Roman forces were finally withdrawn to protect Rome itself, the Jutes, Angles, and Saxons began their successful invasions.

If ever you visit England you can find fascinating remains of Roman Britain, such as the ruins of public baths or of the tiled floors of Roman villas. Many of the great highways of England have as their foundations the original military roads made by the Roman legions. And familiar place names ending in "caster" or "chester" owe their origin to the Roman occupation, for the Latin word for a camp was *castra*.

THE GERMANIC INVASIONS

After the Roman legions had gone, the Britons were no match for the invaders from across the North Sea. The Britons, however, did not retreat to the mountains and moors without a struggle. Behind the half-legendary King Arthur, afterwards transformed into a hero of medieval romance, was the figure of a Celtic leader who organized determined resistance. But the invaders from the North and the East arrived in wave after wave—Angles, Saxons, and Jutes—taking possession of the best land and creating kingdoms of their own, the most important being Kent, Northumbria, Mercia, and Wessex. Before long the Anglo-Saxons were compelled to organize themselves into larger units in order to resist further invasions. Political power then shifted from Northumbria to Mercia to Wessex, the kingdom of Alfred the Great. As early as 787 people from farther north—the terrible Norsemen, Danes, or Vikings—began raiding, pillaging, and burning. Some of these Danes eventually settled in northern and eastern England, bringing with them their own customs, laws, and attitudes of mind that long outlasted the Norman conquest.

The political and military history of these times, roughly from the eighth

ENGLAND IN
ALFRED'S TIME

century to the middle of the eleventh, is confused and chaotic. But a few important facts do stand out. Exceptional Anglo-Saxon kings like Alfred the Great and Athelstan were successful in their struggle against the Norse invaders. Alfred's grandson Athelstan, after defeating a savage confederacy of Danes, Scots, and Welsh, was recognized as king of all Britain. Also, the Anglo-Saxons were converted to Christianity, partly through the efforts of Celtic missionaries from Ireland and Scotland, but mostly through missionaries from Rome. Saint Augustine, sent by Pope Gregory the Great, was the most important of these. Augustine became the first Archbishop of Canterbury and promoted the spread of Christianity throughout the kingdom. When the kingdom was conquered by William of Normandy in 1066, it had long been Christian.

THE ANGLO-SAXONS

Although so much of it even then was Danish in laws, customs, and characteristics, we can call the kingdom conquered by the Normans Anglo-Saxon. What kind of people were the Anglo-Saxons? Before we answer this, we should remember that the Anglo-Saxons were victims of the bad habit, typical of many invaders, of considering that the conquered people have a much lower level of civilization than their own, that they are mere barbarians whose defeat is inevitable and a sign of the world's progress. One might imagine that the Anglo-Saxons were fit only to be the serfs of their Norman conquerors, but this idea is quite false. Indeed, the Normans

Left, a manuscript illustration of an Anglo-Saxon family. Right, Anglo-Saxon relics of the seventh century: a bronze vessel, gold buckle, and pair of clasps.

were superior principally in government organization, in military organization and tactics, and in architecture; in many other respects they were inferior to the Anglo-Saxon civilization that they conquered but did not entirely destroy.

Probably everybody knows that the Anglo-Saxons were hardy and brave, as stubborn in defense as the ordinary English soldiery has been ever since. Anglo-Saxon society was comparatively well-developed, branching out from the family unit to the clan and tribe and then to the kingdom. While the Anglo-Saxons easily developed great loyalty to their chosen leaders, they had a natural tendency toward what we should call now a democratic habit of mind—that is, they liked to hold meetings in which people could openly express what they thought and felt.

ANGLO-SAXON CIVILIZATION

What is not generally realized, however, is that the Anglo-Saxons had a highly developed feeling for beauty. They had a passion for fine ornament, and their craftsmen produced many beautiful pieces, such as brooches and bracelets of exquisite design and workmanship. They were in fact a more artistic and poetic people than their Norman conquerors, who were essentially soldiers and administrators. Behind the glories of English literature, as it has come down to us, is a mixture of the Celtic and Anglo-Saxon

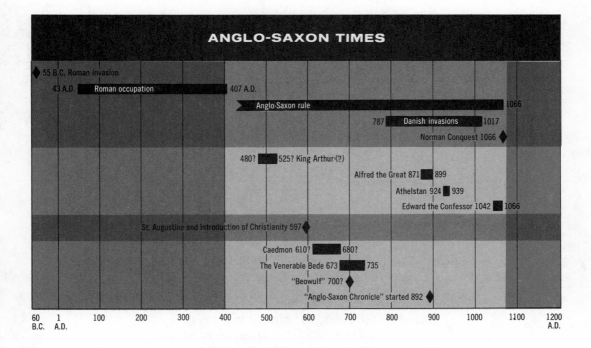

ANGLO-SAXON TIMES

55 B.C. Roman invasion
43 A.D. Roman occupation 407 A.D.
Anglo-Saxon rule 1066
787 Danish invasions 1017
Norman Conquest 1066
480? 525? King Arthur (?)
Alfred the Great 871 899
Athelstan 924 939
Edward the Confessor 1042 1066
St. Augustine and introduction of Christianity 597
Caedmon 610? 680?
The Venerable Bede 673 735
"Beowulf" 700?
"Anglo-Saxon Chronicle" started 892

| 60 B.C. | 1 A.D. | 100 | 200 | 300 | 400 | 500 | 600 | 700 | 800 | 900 | 1000 | 1100 | 1200 A.D. |

temperaments, a combination of the misty mountains and moors, to which the Celts had retreated, and the bright meadows cultivated by the Anglo-Saxon peasants.

It is easy for an American student, living far away in time and space from these Anglo-Saxon people, to imagine that what was thought and felt so long ago, so far away, is completely unimportant today except to the historian and scholar. But this is wrong. We are all *in* the same continuous living web of history that contains these ancient people. To take one example, consider these names of the days of the week—Tuesday, Wednesday, Thursday, Friday. All these names are derived from the names of old Anglo-Saxon gods. Even many basic American traditions in law, conduct, outlook, language, and literature are a legacy from the Anglo-Saxons.

ANGLO-SAXON LITERATURE

Long after they had been converted to Christianity and had developed a recognizable civilization, the Anglo-Saxons were fond of feasting to celebrate successful battles or expeditions. In the great "mead hall," after the food had been attacked with hunting knives and fingers and the bones had been flung to the dogs, the scop (poet) or the gleeman with his harp would entertain the company. Songs, gay or melancholy, were sung; heroic tales were retold; or the poet, as an all-round entertainer, put elaborate riddles

"June: Cutting Wood." An illustration from an eleventh-century calendar.

to his audience. To the Anglo-Saxon the riddle was an intellectual exercise. What do you think is the subject of this one?

> I'm prized by men, in the meadows I'm found,
> Gathered on hill-sides, and hunted in groves;
> From dale and from down, by day I am brought.
> Airy wings carry me, cunningly store me,
> Hoarding me safe. Yet soon men take me;
> Drained into vats, I'm dangerous grown.
> I tie up my victim, and trip him, and throw him;
> Often I floor a foolish old churl.
> Who wrestles with me, and rashly would measure
> His strength against mine, will straightway find himself
> Flung to the ground, flat on his back,
> Unless he leave his folly in time,
> Put from his senses and power of speech,
> Robbed of his might, bereft of his mind,
> Of his hands and feet. Now find me my name,
> Who can blind and enslave men so upon earth,
> And bring fools low in broad daylight.

Although with the coming of the church a written literature had begun to evolve, the great tradition, which persisted for centuries, was oral, not written down but committed to memory by generation after generation of poets, gleemen, and minstrels. The alliteration which the Anglo-Saxons used and their emphatic rhythms of poetry awaken a strong emotional response, as we all know. But for the Anglo-Saxons, who lived long before printed books arrived and indeed long before poets could read and write, these poetic devices also served another purpose—namely, as aids to memory. When we find ourselves remembering a nursery rhyme, as we often do just because it has alliteration and a strongly marked rhythm, we

"August: Harvesting." An illustration from an eleventh-century calendar.

might give a thought to the old Anglo-Saxon poets and gleemen standing in the firelit mead halls.

Although there must have been a great wealth of heroic narrative verse and, later on, of dramatic monologues of a somewhat lyrical nature, highly suitable for recitation, very little has survived. We have only the great epic *Beowulf;* portions of other epics, together with later fragments of battle pieces; some religious poems; and a small group of dramatic poems, of which "The Seafarer" is an excellent example. One reason so little Anglo-Saxon poetry has come down to us is that in the ninth century the conquering Danes plundered the monastery libraries and destroyed many records of Anglo-Saxon civilization and literature. Also, although we are indebted to monks for much of the Anglo-Saxon literature which has survived, some monks deplored the pagan spirit of the older Anglo-Saxon poems and saw no reason to transcribe works which were essentially pagan in spirit. Much of the Anglo-Saxon poetry that has survived, including *Beowulf,* contains Christian graftings on essentially pagan beliefs. On the other hand, some of the surviving poems are dramatic retellings of Biblical events.

The churchmen who wrote verse generally wrote in Latin, though occasionally they included lines in English. (It was from their imitation of church hymns in Latin that the gradual introduction of rhyme into English verse developed.) The earlier prose writers and chroniclers among the Anglo-Saxon churchmen also wrote in Latin. The greatest of these was known as the Venerable Bede (673–735), the most learned and industrious writer of the whole period, author of the *Ecclesiastical History* (731), an excellent historical authority of its time. As an historian Bede is rightly regarded as "the father of English history." Nearly two centuries later, Alfred the Great (871–99), the ablest and most remarkable of all English kings, not only became the patron of scholars and educators but turned

In this engraving, Alfred the Great divides England into counties.

author and translator himself after delivering his kingdom from the Danes. Anglo-Saxon prose and history owe most to his influence and his example. Rather than use Latin, as had been the custom, Alfred promoted use of written English and was responsible for the initiation of the *Anglo-Saxon Chronicle,* the first historical record to be kept in English. The briefest study of Alfred's reign makes nonsense of any idea of the Anglo-Saxons as drunken oafs existing in a "Dark Age." Alfred maintained diplomatic relations with all neighboring kings and princes, sent frequent embassies to Rome, corresponded with the Patriarch of Jerusalem, and may even, as we are told, have sent a mission as far as India. He also formulated a code of law and founded the first English "public schools." A truly great man, Alfred did much to educate a society that, with its social organization and laws, its letters and arts, was far from being barbarous, but, indeed, made an enduring contribution to our civilization.

J.B.P.

Note: The dates given throughout after the names of kings and rulers are the dates of their reigns; those after the names of literary and other historical figures are birth and death dates.

The Seafarer

Translated by J. Duncan Spaeth

"The Seafarer" is one of the oldest poems in our language. Written by an unknown author of the eighth or ninth century, it is now about twelve hundred years old. In spirit, however, it is quite contemporary. Its intensity of feeling, its vividness, and its eloquence speak to us across the centuries and recall the long, high-prowed ships of Anglo-Saxon days and even the sound of surf and the smell of sea wrack.

From earliest times, the sea has always played a vital role in English life and consequently in its literature. In its original form, this early poem about the sea expresses two opposing attitudes toward the life of a seafarer, both spoken by one voice. In the translation below, the metrical charm and flowing alliteration of the Anglo-Saxon verse have been skillfully preserved, and the conflicting points of view have been given to two speakers—a youth eager for adventure on the high seas, and an old sailor weary of loneliness, hardship, and danger.

THE OLD SAILOR

True is the tale that I tell of my travels,
Sing of my seafaring sorrows and woes;
Hunger and hardship's heaviest burdens,
Tempest and terrible toil of the deep,
Daily I've borne on the deck of my boat.   5
Fearful the welter of waves that encompassed me,
Watching at night on the narrow bow,
As she drove by the rocks, and drenched me with spray.
Fast to the deck my feet were frozen,
Gripped by the cold, while care's hot surges   10
My heart o'erwhelmed, and hunger's pangs
Sapped the strength of my sea-weary spirit.
Little he knows whose lot is happy,
Who lives at ease in the lap of the earth,
How, sick at heart, o'er icy seas,   15
Wretched I ranged the winter through,
Bare of joys, and banished from friends,
Hung with icicles, stung by hailstones.
Nought I heard but the hollow boom
Of wintry waves, or the wild swan's whoop.   20
For singing I had the solan's° scream;
For peals of laughter, the yelp of the seal;
The sea mew's cry, for the mirth of the mead hall.
Shrill through the roar of the shrieking gale
Lashing along the sea cliff's edge,   25
Pierces the ice-plumed petrel's° defiance,

21. **solan** (sō′lən): a sea bird like a gull. 26. **petrel:** a sea bird.

"The Seafarer" from *Old English Poetry*, translated by J. Duncan Spaeth. Reprinted by permission of Princeton University Press.

And the wet-winged eagle's answering scream.
Little he dreams that drinks life's pleasure,
By danger untouched in the shelter of towns,
Insolent and wine-proud, how utterly weary   30
Oft I wintered on open seas.
Night fell black, from the north it snowed
Harvest of hail.

THE YOUTH

          Oh, wildly my heart
Beats in my bosom and bids me to try   35
The tumble and surge of seas tumultuous,
Breeze and brine and the breakers' roar.
Daily, hourly, drives me my spirit
Outward to sail, far countries to see.
Liveth no man so large in his soul,   40
So gracious in giving, so gay in his youth,
In deeds so daring, so dear to his lord,
But frets his soul for his sea adventure,
Fain to try what fortune shall send.
Harping he needs not, nor hoarding of treasure;   45
Nor woman can win him, nor joys of the world.
Nothing does please but the plunging billows;
Ever he longs, who is lured by the sea.
Woods are abloom, the wide world awakens,
Gay are the mansions, the meadows most fair;   50
These are but warnings, that haste on his journey
Him whose heart is hungry to taste
The perils and pleasures of the pathless deep.

THE OLD SAILOR

Dost mind the cuckoo mournfully calling?
The summer's watchman sorrow forebodes.   55
What does the landsman that wantons in luxury,
What does he reck the rough sea's foe,
The cares of the exile, whose keel has explored
The uttermost parts of the ocean ways!

THE YOUTH

Sudden my soul starts from her prison house,   60
Soareth afar o'er the sounding main;
Hovers on high, o'er the home of the whale;
Back to me darts the bird sprite and beckons,
Winging her way o'er woodland and plain,
Hungry to roam, and bring me where glisten   65
Glorious tracts of glimmering foam.
This life on land is lingering death to me,
Give me the gladness of God's great sea.

1. Which sections of the poem give a more detailed picture of life at sea, those spoken by the old sailor or by the youth? How might you account for this difference?

2. "Shrill through the roar of the shrieking gale" (line 24) captures the quality of the gale through the sound of the words. (See *onomatopoeia,* page 885.) Cite other lines in which sound is important either in imitating or suggesting events or feelings.

3. Lines 13–33 describe the hardships of a winter spent at sea. Which lines refer to other seasons of the year? What feelings and opinions about the sea do these seasons call up? Why does the youth see the blooming woods and the awakening world as "warnings" (lines 49–51)?

4. As noted in the introduction, this poem was written originally not as a dialogue, but as a monologue taking place within the seafarer's mind. Account for the seafarer's changes of feeling about the sea, especially in lines 60–68. Does the feeling of these lines surprise you, considering the unfavorable comments about life at sea earlier in the poem, or are these final lines a convincing conclusion? Defend your answer.

ANGLO–SAXON POETRY

One fact to keep in mind when reading Anglo-Saxon poetry is that such poetry has a strong oral tradition behind it. Early Anglo-Saxon poems were memorized rather than written and were recited by *scops* (skops), wandering poets who chanted their poems in the mead halls of kings and nobles. Poems that were eventually written down and that have therefore come down to us (like "The Seafarer" and *Beowulf)* are probably not, in all respects, in the same form as the poems that were recited by the scops; but the later, written poems are quite similar to the earlier, memorized ones. They have very strong rhythms, suitable for chanting, as you will discover by reading a few lines of "The Seafarer" aloud.

Anglo-Saxon poetry has the following characteristics:

1. The lines do not rhyme. In this respect, Anglo-Saxon poetry is like blank verse. (See page 876.)

2. The rhythm of a line depends primarily on the number of *beats,* or *accented syllables.* Each line has four beats.

3. The number of unaccented syllables in a line may vary. Thus some lines may be long and others short, but, whether long or short, all lines are similar in having the same number of beats. In reciting a poem, a scop probably hurried through long lines and sustained short ones.

4. Each line has a pause, or *caesura,* after the second beat. Thus each line is divided into two halves, each half having two beats.

5. *Alliteration* (see page 874) is an important factor in Anglo-Saxon poetry. One or more accented syllables in the first half of a line almost always alliterate with one or more accented syllables in the second half. Thus alliteration binds together the two halves of a line. (In this respect Dr. Spaeth's translations are very close to the original.)

If the jingle about Old King Cole were put into Anglo-Saxon verse form, it might sound like the lines below. As you read these lines, note how they exemplify the characteristics of Anglo-Saxon poetry.

> Cole was the king; he was keen and merry;
> Mirthful he was, with minstrels in mead hall.
> He called for his cup; he called for his pipe.
> His fiddlers were three, and fine was their
> trilling.

Another important characteristic of Anglo-Saxon poetry is the use of *kennings,* phrases that are an elaborate and indirect way of naming persons, things, or events. Thus in "The Seafarer," the sea is called "the pathless deep" (line 53) and the body is the soul's "prison house" (line 60); in *Beowulf* (page 12) Hrothgar is referred to as "the Scyldings' Friend" (line 43), and Grendel is "the man-devourer" (line 194). Sometimes a kenning was unusual and would force an audience to be alert and use its wits. Sometimes it was a synonym that had been used many times before (such as "ring-giver" for king or "wave-skimmer" for ship) and was as common as the eighteenth-century use of "finny tribe" for fish. An Anglo-Saxon audience, hearing, for example, of Beowulf's determination to go "O'er the swan-road" (line 61) would know that he meant to travel over the sea. The kenning was a frequent and distinctive ornament of Old English poetry.

FOR COMPOSITION

Compare John Masefield's "Sea Fever" with "The Seafarer," considering context, style, use of meter, alliteration, and so on.

Beowulf

Translated by J. Duncan Spaeth

Beowulf is the first landmark in English literature and the greatest literary work which we have inherited from the Anglo-Saxons. The source of our knowledge of this old English epic is a single surviving tenth-century manuscript—and this manuscript is undoubtedly a copy of an earlier one.

The *Beowulf* manuscript reflects the combination of elements of widely different cultures which was typical of the Anglo-Saxon period. In *Beowulf* both pagan and Christian ideas are represented, exclamations over the fate of sinners and occasional exhortations to prayer intermingling with pagan concepts such as that of Wyrd, or fate. The author of *Beowulf,* though unknown, may have been a Christianized West Saxon who worked old pagan legends into his story; or, possibly, the overlay of Christian references was added by monks as they copied the manuscript. The character of Beowulf, which seems to be a blending of an actual historical figure with various mythical heroes, itself epitomizes this mixture of pagan and Christian tradition.

While the poem is generally thought to have been composed sometime during the seventh or eighth century, the events described in *Beowulf* have been dated somewhere between the third and fourth century. They are a rich compound of myth and heroic legend, the product of many centuries of storytelling, and, like similar German sagas, provide fitful illumination of an obscure period of European history. Although written in English, the theme, characters, and setting of the poem are Scandinavian in origin.

Though the author of *Beowulf* had undoubtedly heard the story from many sources, the poem is far more than the mere amalgamation of primitive tales. The poet managed to fuse the scattered bits into an artistic whole. A folk epic dealing with the traditions of a people, *Beowulf,* like every epic, is grand in conception. In lofty language, with supernatural elements interwoven, it tells of the noble deeds of its warrior-hero and his companions. Its theme is universal—the unending struggle of good against evil, the perpetual human battle against a hostile environment. This is the timeless story of a brave leader who tries to save a people from great peril.

Beowulf, the hero of the story, is the embodiment of Anglo-Saxon ideals. A champion of freedom and justice, he has courage, superhuman strength, unfailing loyalty, and devotion to duty. Against him are pitted cruel monsters. Cheerless and austere in tone, the drama unfolds against a background of severe but magnificent Northern scenery. The pagan concept of Wyrd dominates the Christian concept of a guiding and controlling providence, and creates the somber mood that pervades all Anglo-Saxon literature. Its majestic language, compelling rhythm, and straightforward narrative all help to make *Beowulf* one of the early masterpieces of our language.

The poem begins as a mysterious ship from an unknown country comes into harbor one day. It brings an infant called Scyld [1] to the homeland of the Spear-Danes. This child later becomes their king, and a good king he is, reigning long and successfully. When he dies, his subjects spare no pains in honoring him. As is the custom in Scandinavia, they clothe him in armor, surround him with treasure, place him on a ship, and send him back to the sea.

Years pass. Scyld's descendant, Hrothgar, [2] wins great fame and wealth in battles with enemies. He builds the greatest of mead halls, called Heorot, [3] where his loyal warriors may gather. Hrothgar feels that he has earned peace, rest, and enjoyment of the riches he has won. But fate has other things in store for him. There now appears on the scene a villain, a superhuman monster named Grendel. [4]

[1] **Scyld** (shild).   [2] **Hrothgar** (roth'gär).   [3] **Heorot** (hā'ə·rot): literally, Hart Hall, because the horns of a stag or hart adorned its gables. The site of Heorot may be identified with Leire in Seeland, Denmark.   [4] **Grendel** (gren'dəl).

From "Beowulf" from *Old English Poetry,* translated by J. Duncan Spaeth. Reprinted by permission of Princeton University Press.

In the darkness dwelt a demon-sprite,
Whose heart was filled with fury and hate,
When he heard each night the noise of revel
Loud in the hall, laughter and song.
To the sound of the harp the singer chanted   5
Lays he had learned, of long ago;

*All is happiness
in the new home
until the angry
fiend Grendel
comes from his
lair.*
How the Almighty had made the earth,
Wonder-bright lands, washed by the ocean;
How he set, triumphant, sun and moon
To lighten all men that live on the earth.   10
He brightened the land with leaves and branches;
Life he created for every being,
Each in its kind, that moves upon earth.
So, happy in hall, the heroes lived,
Wanting naught, till one began   15
To work them woe, a wicked fiend.

The demon grim was Grendel called,
Marsh stalker huge, the moors he roamed.
The joyless creature had kept long time
The lonely fen,° the lairs of monsters,   20
Cast out from men, an exile accurst.
The killing of Abel, brother of Cain°
Was justly avenged by the Judge Eternal.

When night had fallen, the fiend crept near
To the lofty hall, to learn how the Danes   25
In Heorot fared, when the feasting was done.
The athelings° all within he saw
Asleep after revel, not recking of danger,
And free from care. The fiend accurst,
Grim and greedy, his grip made ready;   30
Snatched in their sleep, with savage fury,
Thirty warriors; away he sprang

*Grendel enters
the main hall
at night and
carries off thirty
warriors.*
Proud of his prey, to repair to his home,
His blood-dripping booty to bring to his lair.
At early dawn, when daybreak came,   35
The vengeance of Grendel was revealed to all;
Their wails after wassail° were widely heard,
Their morning woe. The mighty ruler,
The atheling brave, sat bowed with grief.

So Grendel wrongfully ruled the hall,   40
One against all till empty stood
That lordly mansion, and long remained so.
For the space of twelve winters the Scyldings' Friend°

20. **fen:** low marshland, a moor.   22. This is one of a number of passages which indicate
that the author of the epic in its present form was a Christian. For the story of Cain and Abel,
see Genesis 4.   27. **athelings:** nobles.   37. **wassail** (wos'əl): the festive drinking of the night
before.   43. **Scyldings' Friend:** Hrothgar.

*The murders
continue for twelve
years, and gleemen
spread the news
abroad.*
Bore in his breast the brunt of this sorrow,
Measureless woe. In mournful lays   45
The tale became known; 'twas told abroad
In gleemen's songs, how Grendel had warred
Long against Hrothgar, and wreaked his hate
With murderous fury through many a year.

The wise men take counsel together, erect altars to their heathen gods, and pray
for relief from the monster, all to no avail. At last, from an unexpected source,
Hrothgar and his people are given new hope of deliverance.

THE COMING OF BEOWULF

Thus boiled with care the breast of Hrothgar;   50
Ceaselessly sorrowed the son of Healfdene,°
None of his chieftains might change his lot.
Too fell was the foe that afflicted the people
With wrongs unnumbered, and nightly horrors.
Then heard in his home King Hygelac's thane,°   55
The dauntless Jute, of the doings of Grendel.
In strength he outstripped the strongest of men
That dwell in the earth in the days of this life.
Gallant and bold, he gave command

*Beowulf makes
plans to go to the
aid of the Danes.*
To get him a boat, a good wave-skimmer.   60
O'er the swan-road,° he said, he would seek the king
Noble and famous, who needed men.
Though dear to his kin, they discouraged him not;
The prudent in counsel praised the adventure,
Whetted his valor, awaiting good omens.   65
He with fourteen followers hardy
Went to embark; he was wise in seamanship,
So Beowulf chose from the band of the Jutes
Heroes brave, the best he could find;
Showed them the landmarks, leading the way.   70
Soon they descried their craft in the water,
At the foot of the cliff. Then climbed aboard
The chosen troop; the tide was churning
Sea against sand; they stowed away
In the hold of the ship their shining armor,   75
War gear and weapons; the warriors launched
Their well-braced boat on her welcome voyage.
Swift o'er the waves with a wind that favored,
Foam on her breast, like a bird she flew;
A day and a night they drove to seaward,   80
Cut the waves with the curving prow,
Till the seamen that sailed her sighted the land,
Shining cliffs and coastwise hills,

51. **Healfdene** (hā′alf·den·nə): half-Dane; that is, his mother was a foreigner.   55. **Hygelac's**
(hig′ə·läks) **thane:** Beowulf. Hygelac is a historical character—king of the Jutes, a people who
lived in southern Sweden, according to most authorities, or in northern Denmark.   61. **swan-
road:** sea.

Headlands bold. The harbor opened,
Their cruise was ended. Then quickly the sailors,   85
The crew of Weder folk,° clambered ashore,
Moored their craft with clank of chain mail,
And goodly war gear. God they thanked
That their way was smooth o'er the surging waves.

At the coast, Beowulf and his men are met by a guard, who, after being convinced
of their good intentions, conducts them toward the palace. They enter the hall, and
Beowulf introduces himself to Hrothgar and his thanes.

"Hail, King Hrothgar: Hygelac's thane   90
And kinsman am I. Known is the record
Of deeds of renown I have done in my youth.
Far in my home, I heard of this Grendel;
Seafarers tell the tale of the hall:
How bare of warriors, this best of buildings   95
Deserted stands, when the sun goes down
And twilight deepens to dark in the sky.
By comrades encouraged, I come on this journey.
The best of them bade me, the bravest and wisest,
To go to thy succor, O good King Hrothgar;   100
For well they approved my prowess in battle,
They saw me themselves come safe from the conflict
When five of my foes I defeated and bound,

Beowulf declares Beating in battle the brood of the monsters.
the prowess that At night on the sea with nickers° I wrestled,   105
makes him a fit Avenging the Weders, survived the sea peril,
opponent for And crushed in my grip the grim sea monsters
Grendel. That harried my neighbors. Now I am come
To cope with Grendel in combat single,
And match my might against the monster alone.   110
I pray thee therefore, prince of the Scyldings,
Not to refuse the favor I ask,
Having come so far, O friend of the Shield-Danes,
That I alone with my loyal comrades,
My hardy companions, may Heorot purge.   115

Moreover they say that the slaughterous fiend
In wanton mood all weapons despises.
Hence—as I hope that Hygelac may,
My lord and king, be kind to me—
Sword and buckler° I scorn to bear,   120
Gold-adorned shield, as I go to the conflict.
With my grip will I grapple the gruesome fiend,
Foe against foe, to fight for our life.
And he that shall fall his faith must put

---

86. **Weder** (wā′dər) **folk:** another name for the Jutes.   105. **nickers:** sea demons, probably
walruses or whales.   120. **buckler:** a kind of shield worn on one arm.

In the judgment of God. If Grendel wins,   125
He is minded to make his meal in the hall
Untroubled by fear, on the folk of the Jutes,
As often before he fed on the Danes.
No need for thee then to think of my burial.
If I lose my life, the lonely prowler   130
My blood-stained body will bear to his den,
Swallow me greedily, and splash with my gore
His lair in the marsh; no longer wilt then
Have need to find me food and sustenance.
To Hygelac send, if I sink in the battle,   135
This best of corselets that covers my breast,
Heirloom of Hrethel,° rarest of byrnies,°
The work of Weland.° So Wyrd° will be done."

Hrothgar replies with complimentary reference to Beowulf's father, and then once more recounts the horrors of Grendel's visits to Heorot. A banquet is prepared, with the usual eating and drinking and minstrel's song. Unferth (un'fârth), a jealous Danish courtier, belittles Beowulf by sarcastic comment on his defeat in a swimming match with Breca, a young prince of another tribe. Beowulf replies by giving his version of this adventure, in which he had killed nine sea demons. Then Beowulf goes on to accuse Unferth of murdering his own brothers, a kenning (see page 883), or metaphor, meaning that he fled from a battlefield where they were killed.

After this tilt the banquet proceeds. The queen, Wealhtheow (wā'əl·thā·ō), passes the cup. The noisy revel continues until at last Hrothgar and his followers leave Heorot to Beowulf and his men. Beowulf once more asserts that he will meet Grendel unarmed. Then he and his men lie down and go to sleep.

BEOWULF'S FIGHT WITH GRENDEL

Now Grendel came, from his crags of mist
Across the moor; he was curst of God.   140
The murderous prowler meant to surprise
In the high-built hall his human prey.
He stalked 'neath the clouds, till steep before him
The house of revelry rose in his path,
The gold-hall of heroes, the gaily adorned.   145
Hrothgar's home he had haunted full often,
But never before had he found to receive him
So hardy a hero, such hall guards there.
Close to the building crept the slayer,
Doomed to misery. The door gave way,   150
Though fastened with bolts, when his fist fell on it.
Maddened he broke through the breach he had made;
Swoln° with anger and eager to slay,
The ravening fiend o'er the bright-paved floor
Furious ran, while flashed from his eyes   155
An ugly glare like embers aglow.

---

137. **Hrethel** (hrā'thəl): father of King Hygelac. **byrnies:** coats of mail. 138. **Weland** (wā'lənd): the celestial blacksmith of the Northmen, corresponding to Vulcan of classical mythology. **Wyrd:** Fate. 153. **Swoln:** swollen.

He saw in the hall, all huddled together,
The heroes asleep. Then laughed in his heart
The hideous fiend; he hoped ere dawn
To sunder body from soul of each;   160
He looked to appease his lust of blood,
Glut his maw° with the men he would slay.
But Wyrd had otherwise willed his doom;
Never again should he get a victim
After that night.

           Narrowly watched   165
Hygelac's thane how the horrible slayer
Forward should charge in fierce attack.
Nor was the monster minded to wait:
Sudden he sprang on a sleeping thane.
Ere he could stir, he slit him open;   170
Bit through the bone joints, gulped the blood,
Greedily bolted the body piecemeal.

Grendel devours   Soon he had swallowed the slain man wholly,
a sleeping man,   Hands and feet. Then forward he hastened,
then attacks   Sprang at the hero, and seized him at rest;   175
Beowulf.   Fiercely clutched him with fiendish claw.
But quickly Beowulf caught his forearm,
And threw himself on it with all his weight.
Straight discovered that crafty plotter,
That never in all mid-earth had he met   180
In any man a mightier grip.
Gone was his courage, and craven fear
Sat in his heart, yet helped him no sooner.
Fain° would he hide in his hole in the fenland,
His devil's den. A different welcome   185
From former days he found that night!
Now Hygelac's thane, the hardy, remembered
His evening's boast, and bounding up,
Grendel he clenched, and cracked his fingers;
The monster tried flight, but the man pursued;   190
The ravager hoped to wrench himself free
And gain the fen, for he felt his fingers
Helpless and limp in the hold of his foe.

'Twas a sorry visit the man-devourer
Made to the Hall of the Hart that night.   195
Dread was the din, the Danes were frighted
By the uproar wild of the ale-spilling fray.
The hardiest blenched as the hall foes wrestled
In terrible rage. The rafters groaned;
'Twas wonder great that the wine hall stood   200
Firm 'gainst the fighters' furious onslaught,

162. **maw:** stomach.   184. **Fain:** gladly.

*The mead hall is
almost wrecked
in the fury of the
battle.*

Nor fell to the ground, that glorious building.
With bands of iron 'twas braced and stiffened
Within and without. But off from the sill
Many a mead-bench mounted with gold   205
Was wrung where they wrestled in wrath together.
The Scylding nobles never imagined
That open attack, or treacherous cunning,
Could wreck or ruin their royal hall,
The lofty and antlered, unless the flames   210
Should someday swallow it up in smoke.
The din was renewed, the noise redoubled;
Each man of the Danes was mute with dread,
That heard from the wall the horrible wail,
The gruesome song of the godless foe,   215
His howl of defeat, as the fiend of hell
Bemoaned his hurt. The man held fast;
Greatest he was in grip of strength,
Of all that dwelt upon earth that day.

Loath in his heart was the hero-deliverer   220
To let escape his slaughterous guest.
Of little use that life he deemed
To humankind. The comrades of Beowulf
Unsheathed their weapons to ward their leader,
Eagerly brandished their ancient blades,   225
The life of their peerless lord to defend.
Little they deemed, those dauntless warriors,
As they leaped to the fray, those lusty fighters,
Laying on boldly to left and to right,
Eager to slay, that no sword upon earth,   230
No keenest weapon, could wound that monster:
Point would not pierce, he was proof against iron;
'Gainst victory blades the devourer was charmed.
But a woeful end awaited the wretch,
That very day he was doomed to depart,   235
And fare afar to the fiends' domain.

*Beowulf tears
Grendel's arm
from its socket,
and the mortally
wounded Grendel
crawls to his lair.*

Now Grendel found, who in former days
So many a warrior had wantonly slain,
In brutish lust, abandoned of God,
That the frame of his body was breaking at last.   240
Keen of courage, the kinsman of Hygelac
Held him grimly gripped in his hands.
Loath was each to the other alive.
The grisly monster got his death wound:
A huge split opened under his shoulder;   245
Crunched the socket, cracked the sinews,
Glory great was given to Beowulf.
But Grendel escaped with his gaping wound,
O'er the dreary moor his dark den sought,
Crawled to his lair. 'Twas clear to him then,   250

The count of his hours to end had come,
Done were his days. The Danes were glad,
The hard fight was over, they had their desire.
Cleared was the hall, 'twas cleansed by the hero
With keen heart and courage, who came from afar.   255

FOR STUDY AND DISCUSSION

1. What do you learn about the Anglo-Saxon view of the world and of the meaning of life as expressed in lines 7–13? Why can Grendel be considered as an element of disorder in the world as it is described in these lines?

2. Cite some of the phrases used to describe Grendel in lines 16–21. How are these phrases related to our own traditional ideas of evil? What is the relation of the reference to Cain and Abel (lines 22–23) to the description of Grendel immediately preceding it? Why are Grendel's bloody acts described as "vengeance" (line 36)? Why is he later described as "curst of God" (line 140)?

3. What do you learn about Beowulf in lines 63–65 to indicate that he is regarded as no ordinary man? What is your reaction to Beowulf's speech to Hrothgar (lines 90–138)? Do you consider it boastful? What do you think was the reaction of an Anglo-Saxon reader or audience?

4. Study the description of Grendel's entrance into the hall in lines 139–65. Do you think that this account is an effective, suspenseful piece of writing? Why or why not? Why do you think the author has Grendel leap at another man before grappling with Beowulf?

5. What details raise the fight between Beowulf and Grendel above the level of a commonplace brawl and serve to make it a heroic struggle? Does the fact that Beowulf's comrades attempt to aid him add or detract from the heroic quality of the fight? Why does the author make Grendel invulnerable to all human weapons?

6. Does Beowulf prevail primarily through skill in combat or through strength? What virtues does Beowulf display in the fight?

7. In what ways does *Beowulf* illustrate the following Anglo-Saxon ideals of conduct: (a) allegiance to lord or king, (b) love of glory as the ruling motive in every noble life, (c) belief in the inevitability of fate? What qualities of character do you think the Anglo-Saxons most admired and despised? Do we still admire and despise the same qualities?

METAPHOR AND SIMILE

For a full appreciation of prose and poetry, one should have an understanding of *metaphor* and *simile*. Both are figures of speech based on comparisons between things that are essentially unlike.

Of the two, the simile is the more obvious figure of speech. The use of a word of comparison such as *like* or *as* signals that a simile is being used. Line 79 of *Beowulf*, for example, describes a ship traveling over the waves by saying "like a bird she flew." And note line 156 where Grendel's eyes flash "like embers aglow." Contrary to the simile, in which a comparison is expressed directly, the metaphor merely implies a comparison. Line 52 of "The Seafarer," "Him whose heart is hungry to taste," conveys the state of a young man eager for experience. In line 60 of "The Seafarer" ("Sudden my soul starts from her prison house"), the soul is described as being in a prison house because it is breaking out of its confinement.

Find other examples of similes and metaphors in "The Seafarer" and *Beowulf*. Explain why these figures of speech are more imaginative and convey the idea more vividly than a literal term.

FOR COMPOSITION

1. Explain why you think *Beowulf* has interested readers for over a thousand years. What does this poem offer a modern reader?

2. The character of Beowulf is a mixture of pride and humility. Explore this mixture in a brief composition, distinguishing carefully between pride and conceit. Remember that in Beowulf's time heroes were not expected to be modest about their accomplishments.

3. Every generation has had its heroes who reflect the general character of their society. Discuss the differences and similarities in the concept of the hero in Anglo-Saxon times and today. What do these differences reveal about the change in morals and values? What do they reveal about continuity in our morals and values?

BEDE (673–735)

The earliest important prose writer and first historian of England was the Venerable Bede, a contemporary of the first English poet of note, the unknown author of *Beowulf*. Both men were products of Northumbria, the old Angle kingdom in northeastern England which, from the late seventh through the early eighth century, was prominent in both literature and politics.

Bede was a man of great learning. A scholar of Latin, Greek, and Hebrew, he was also a prolific writer on theological, historical, and scientific subjects, and in his many scholarly works made accessible to his countrymen a comprehensive view of the learning of Western Europe in his day. The most famous of his works—and the most important for the early history of England—is *The Ecclesiastical History of the English People,* in which Bede tells of the growth of Christianity in his country.

Educated from the age of seven as a Benedictine monk, Bede spent most of his life in the sister monasteries of Wearmouth and Jarrow, where he lived a quiet life studying, teaching, and writing. The title "Venerable" was added to his name in recognition of his widespread reputation for wisdom, humility, and scholarship.

The Ecclesiastical History, from which the following selection is taken, was composed by Bede in simple and straightforward Latin prose. So highly respected was it as a historical document that Alfred the Great, himself a renowned scholar and writer, later had it translated into Old English as part of his effort to spread learning throughout his kingdom.

The Poet Caedmon

FROM *The Ecclesiastical History of the English People*

THERE WAS in this abbess's [Hild's] monastery [1] a certain brother, particularly remarkable for the grace of God, who was wont to make pious and religious verses, so that whatever was interpreted to him out of Scripture, he soon after put the same into poetical expressions of much sweetness and feeling, in English, which was his native language. By his verses the minds of many were often excited to despise the world and to aspire to the life in heaven. Others of the English nation after him attempted to compose religious poems, but none could compare with him, for he did not learn the art of poetry from men, nor of man, but from God; but being assisted from above, he freely received the gift of God. For this reason he never could compose any trivial or idle poem, but only those which relate to religion suited his religious tongue; for having lived in a secular habit till he was well advanced in years, he had never learned anything of versifying; for which reason being

[1] this . . . monastery: Whitby, a monastery for men and women, founded about 657. Its first abbess, Hild, died in 680.

"Story of Caedmon" from *The Ecclesiastical History of the English Nation* by the Venerable Bede. Everyman's Library Edition. Reprinted by permission of E. P. Dutton & Co., Inc.

sometimes at entertainments, when it was agreed for the sake of mirth that all present should sing in their turns, when he saw the harp come toward him, he rose up from table and returned home.

Having done so at a certain time and gone out of the house where the entertainment was, to the stable, where he had to take care of the cattle that night, he there laid himself down to rest at the proper time; a person appeared to him in his sleep, and saluting him by his name, said, "Caedmon, sing some song to me." He answered, "I cannot sing; for that was the reason why I left the entertainment and retired to this place, because I could not sing." The other who talked to him replied, "However, you shall sing to me." "What shall I sing?" rejoined he. "Sing the beginning of created beings," said the other. Having received this answer he presently began to sing verses to the praise of God the Creator, which he had never before heard, the purport whereof was thus: "We now ought to praise the Maker of the heavenly kingdom, the power of the Creator and his counsel, the deeds of the Father of Glory. How He, being the eternal God, became the author of all miracles, who first, as almighty preserver of the human race, created heaven for the sons of men as the roof of the house, and next the earth." This is the sense, but not the words in order as he sang them in his sleep; for verses, though never so well composed, cannot be literally translated out of one language into another without losing much of their beauty and loftiness. Awaking from his sleep, he remembered all that he had sung in his dream, and soon added much more to the same effect in verse worthy of the Deity.

In the morning he came to the steward, his superior, and having acquainted him with the gift which he had received, was conducted to the abbess, by whom he was ordered, in the presence of many learned men, to tell his dream, and repeat the verses, that they might all give their judgment what it was and whence his verse proceeded. They all concluded that heavenly grace had been conferred on him by our Lord. They expounded to him a passage in holy writ, either historical, or doctrinal, ordering him, if he could, to put the same into verse. Having undertaken it, he went away and, returning the next morning, gave it to them, composed in most excellent verse; whereupon the abbess, embracing the grace of God in the man, instructed him to quit the secular habit and take upon him the monastic life; which being accordingly done, she associated him with the rest of the brethren in her monastery and ordered that he should be taught the whole series of sacred history. Thus he, keeping in mind all he heard, and as it were, like a clean animal chewing the cud, converted the narrative into most harmonious verse; and sweetly repeating the same, made his masters in their turn his hearers. He sang of the creation of the world, of the origin of man, and of all the history of Genesis; of the departure of the children of Israel out of Egypt, and their entering into the land of promise, with many other histories from holy writ; of the incarnation, passion, and resurrection of our Lord, and of his ascension into heaven; of the coming of the Holy Ghost, and the preaching of the apostles; also of the terror of future judgment, the horror of the pains of hell, and

The Venerable Bede

the delights of heaven; besides many more about the divine benefits and judgments: by all which he endeavored to turn away men from the love of vice and to excite in them the love of, and application to, good actions. For he was a very religious man, humbly submissive to regular discipline, but full of zeal against those who behaved themselves otherwise; for which reason he ended his life happily.

For when the time of his departure drew near, he labored for the space of fourteen days under a bodily infirmity which seemed to prepare the way for him, yet so moderate that he could talk and walk the whole time. Nearby was the house to which those that were sick and like shortly to die were carried. He desired the person that attended him, in the evening, as the night came on in which he was to depart this life, to make ready a place there for him to take his rest. This person, wondering why he should desire it, because there was as yet no sign of his dying soon, nevertheless did what he had ordered. He accordingly was placed there and, conversing pleasantly in a joyful manner with the rest that were in the house before, when it was past midnight, he asked them whether they had the Eucharist [1] there. They answered, "What need of the Eucharist? for you are not likely to die, since you talk so joyfully with us, as if you were in perfect health." "However," said he, "bring me the Eucharist." Having received the same into his hand, he asked whether they were all in charity with him and without any ill will or rancor. They answered that they were all in perfect charity and free from all anger; and in their turn asked him whether he was in the same mind toward them. He straightway answered, "I am in charity, my children, with all the servants of God." Then strengthening himself with the heavenly viaticum, [2] he prepared for the entrance

---

[1] **Eucharist:** consecrated bread and wine used in the Christian sacrament of Holy Communion, which commemorates the death of Christ.

[2] **viaticum:** here used in the ecclesiastical sense of receiving Holy Communion before dying.

into another life, and asked how near the hour was when the brothers were to be awakened to sing the nocturnal lauds of our Lord. They answered, "It is not far off." Then he said, "It is well; let us wait that hour"; and signing himself with the sign of the cross, he laid his head on the pillow and, falling into a slumber, so ended his life in silence.

Thus it came to pass that as he had served God with a simple and pure mind and tranquil devotion, so he now departed to His presence, leaving the world by a tranquil death; and that tongue, which had composed so many holy words in praise of the Creator, in like manner uttered its last words whilst he was in the act of signing himself with the cross and recommending his soul into the hands of God. From what has been here said, he would seem to have had foreknowledge of his death.

FOR STUDY AND DISCUSSION

1. The story of Caedmon has perennial appeal as an account of lowliness exalted. Where else may one find this theme? Bear in mind that Caedmon's miracle occurred in a stable.

2. Caedmon could be said to have a "gift" for poetry. How does Bede explain this gift? What were its limitations?

3. How is Caedmon's death appropriate to his life? Is Bede's account of the death written simply or elaborately? Would it be more or less effective if it were written in a different style—for example, with a greater show of emotion? Explain.

4. Bede, who wrote in Latin, explains that he can give only the "sense" of the poem that Caedmon sang (in Anglo-Saxon) for the person who appeared to him in his sleep. Bede explains that "verses, though never so well composed, cannot be literally translated out of one language into another without losing much of their beauty and loftiness." Do you agree? Why or why not?

5. Bede writes of Caedmon: "By his verses the minds of many were often excited to despise the world and to aspire to the life in heaven." Would a modern writer be likely to praise poets because their verses excited us "to despise the world"? Explain why or why not.

THE GROWTH OF THE ENGLISH LANGUAGE

The Old English Period

From the *Beowulf* manuscript

Language existed long before written literature. We cannot trace English, or any other language, to its ultimate origin, because this origin is buried far back in the prehistoric past of the human race.

We can, however, trace the history of English as far back as a language that scholars call "Indo-European," which was spoken five or six thousand years ago by a group of tribes who lived somewhere in Europe or in the western part of Asia. Well before 2000 B.C., this group began to break up. One branch eventually migrated as far as India; others found their way to Asia Minor, to Greece, to Italy, and to northern and western Europe. Once the various branches were geographically separated, the form of the language spoken by each branch gradually changed. By the beginning of the first century A.D., the original Indo-European tongue had evolved into more than a dozen distinctly different languages, among them Sanskrit, Greek, Latin, and Germanic. Latin later evolved into the group of modern languages that includes Italian, French, and Spanish. Germanic evolved into the group of languages that includes German, Dutch, Swedish, and English.

The history of English as a separate language begins in the middle of the fifth century A.D., when the Angles, Saxons, and Jutes invaded Britain. The invaders brought with them their own language, a dialect of Germanic. This dialect, which soon came to be designated as "Angle-ish," or English, was the ancestor of our present-day language. The invaders also brought with them their own alphabet, which consisted of a set of characters called runes. The runic alphabet was used for carving inscriptions on materials like wood and stone. Except for these carvings, however, not much use was made of writing. Written records were not kept; stories, legends, and poems were passed along orally from generation to generation. Most of the knowledge we have of Old English, therefore, is based on manuscripts that were written fairly late in the Anglo-Saxon period by monks who used the Latin alphabet for writing English.

An Old English inscription in the runic alphabet is a complete mystery to most of us today. Later forms of writing, like that in the sample from the *Beowulf* manuscript reproduced above, also seem to represent a strange language. Even printing in our modern alphabet a passage in Old English would not help very much to clarify its meaning, although you would be able to recognize a few words and you could probably guess at the meanings of many others. Look, for example, at the following passage from *Beowulf*. Beneath the Old English is a word-for-word translation in modern English. A modern poetic translation of the same passage appears on page 18 of this book, beginning with line 248.

Scolde Grendel thonan
Should Grendel thence
feorhseoc fleon under fenhleothu
life-sick flee under fen-slopes

secean wynleas wic. Wiste the geornor
seek joyless dwelling. Knew he more surely
thæt his aldres wæs ende gegongen,
that his life's was end reached
dogora dægrim.
days' day-number.

The literal sense of this is, "Thence
Grendel, dying, had to flee through the
bogs and seek his joyless dwelling. He
knew surely that his life's end was
reached, [his allotted] number of days."

A number of the Old English words in
this passage are the same, or nearly the
same, as their modern equivalents—for
instance, *under, thæt, his, wæs, ende.* In
fact, although many other languages have
contributed words to present-day English,
the basic words that we use most often are
usually part of the native English stock.
Such words include most of our prepositions, like *under, to, for, from, with;* most
of our connectives, like *that, and, where,
or;* most of our pronouns, like *his, I, we,
your;* and many of our common nouns and
verbs.

The grammar of present-day English is
also closely related to that of Old English.
For instance, our verbs still have many of
the same tense formations that they had in
Old English: *was* and *were* are still past-
tense forms of the verb *be,* just as *wæs*
and *wære* were past-tense forms in Old
English. And word order in modern English tends to follow the same patterns that
were used in Old English: a preposition
precedes its object, a subject usually precedes its verb, an appositive usually follows the word with which it is in apposi-
tion. In fact, the contributions that other
languages have made to English have usually not affected the basic structure of the
language very much, but have merely supplied new words that can be fitted into
English sentence patterns.

During the Anglo-Saxon period, there
were three other languages that made important contributions to the English vocabulary. The first was the language
spoken by the Celtic population of Britain. The Celts retreated before the Anglo-
Saxon invaders but left behind them a
number of Celtic place names and geographical terms, including *Kent, York,
Thames, Dover,* and *Avon.* A second language that contributed words to Old
English was Latin. After the Anglo-
Saxons had been converted to Christianity, they adopted many Christian terms
from Latin, including *altar, disciple, mass,
nun,* and *shrine.* A number of words related to education and learning, such as
school, verse, paper, and *title,* were also
taken over from Latin during this period,
as were some everyday words like *plant,
mat,* and *box.* The third influential language was Old Norse, the language of the
Danish invaders who settled in the northern part of England. The names of about
six hundred towns in northern England
still end in -*by,* from the Old Norse *byr*
("town"), and the same word is preserved
in *bylaw.* Most of the words that the
Danes contributed to our language are
everyday terms like *add, fellow, guess,
kindle, leg, loose, lug, nag, raise, sky,* and
window.

FOR STUDY AND DISCUSSION

1. The words listed below have been part
of the English language for over a thousand
years. Using an unabridged dictionary or a
college dictionary, find out which words are
native English terms and which ones entered
Old English from Celtic, Latin, or Old Norse:

after	mother
crag	noon
drink	scrap
egg	temple

2. During the Anglo-Saxon period, people
in the northern part of England often adopted
an Old Norse word in place of an Old English
word that had the same meaning, while people
in southern England usually continued to use
the Old English term. In some cases both
words have survived as part of our language.
Following are four pairs of this kind. Look up
the words in each pair in a dictionary and find
out which is the native English term and which
the Old Norse term:

no, nay
sick, ill
skill, craft
skin, hide

THE MEDIEVAL PERIOD

(1066–1485)

I N 1066, at the Battle of Hastings, Harold, the Saxon king of England, was defeated by William "the Conqueror," Duke of Normandy, who invaded England to support his claim that he had been promised the English throne. An efficient and ruthless soldier, with a number of experienced soldiers of fortune among his followers, William was soon able to conquer the whole country.

The Normans—a name derived from "Northman"—were in large part descended from the Vikings who had seized and then remained in north-western France, which became known as "Normandy." After more than a hundred years in France, the Normans had adopted many French customs and had their own variation of the French language, Norman-French. They were a curious people: superb soldiers, excellent administrators and lawyers, great borrowers and adapters, but lacking inventiveness and original ideas. Even the architecture and the ambitious building in stone that they introduced into England originated in north Italy. It used to be assumed that their Norman conquerors "civilized" the beaten Saxons, but in some respects, notably in their more democratic system of government and in their crafts and designs, the Saxons were further advanced than the Normans. After the Conquest, because of the highly centralized and stable Norman government, England became a more formidable power, also a country much closer to the mainstream of European civilization. Finally—and what is most important here—the Norman and Saxon elements were soon fused into a national English character, neither predominantly Norman nor Saxon but a subtle blend of both.

MEDIEVAL CIVILIZATION

Roughly from the eleventh to the fifteenth century, Western Europe achieved a complete civilization and a complete culture of its own. Although our present-day civilization has grown directly out of medieval civilization, life in the Middle Ages was far different from what we know today. To begin with, medieval society had a secure foundation and framework of religion. Everyone was a son or daughter of the Church and on his way to Heaven or Hell. Fierce and powerful rulers could sometimes be seen walking barefoot to do penance for their sins. Everybody, from the highest to the lowest, was conscious of being on trial here on earth. Of course people misbehaved then as people did before and have done since, but then they knew that they were misbehaving and that they were miserable sinners. This world to them was like a transparency through which gleamed the fire of Hell or the bright blue of Heaven.

The Church was responsible for the spiritual life of all Christendom, linking together all the kingdoms, dukedoms, principalities, and free cities of western and central Europe. In Latin it had a language common to all educated people. Its chief scholars and philosophers, like the famous Thomas Aquinas, moved freely from university to university and from country to country. Its abbeys and monasteries were not only the chief centers of learning and the arts in the period before the establishment of the universities of Oxford and Cambridge in the thirteenth century, but, as economically self-sufficient units, they were also often immense farms, places where all manner of handicrafts were taught and practiced. In addition, monasteries also fed the poor and served as hotels for travelers. The great Gothic cathedrals, those impressive and noble creations of human minds and hands, were built during this period. England has some of the finest specimens of these astonishing buildings, which are poetry and music in stone.

The greatest single achievement of the Middle Ages was the idea of the commonwealth of Christendom, a kind of spiritual and cultural empire uniting people of different nationalities, but speaking different languages and enjoying many different regional ways of life. In our own day science and invention have given us things that would have seemed to the medieval mind like so many strange miracles and the marvels of sorcerers. However, we have not yet achieved our own equivalent of the commonwealth of Christendom, a whole society, a civilization and a common culture, united under God.

MEDIEVAL SOCIETY

Existing alongside the Church was the complicated feudal system based on landholding. Nobody owned land independently but only as a vassal of

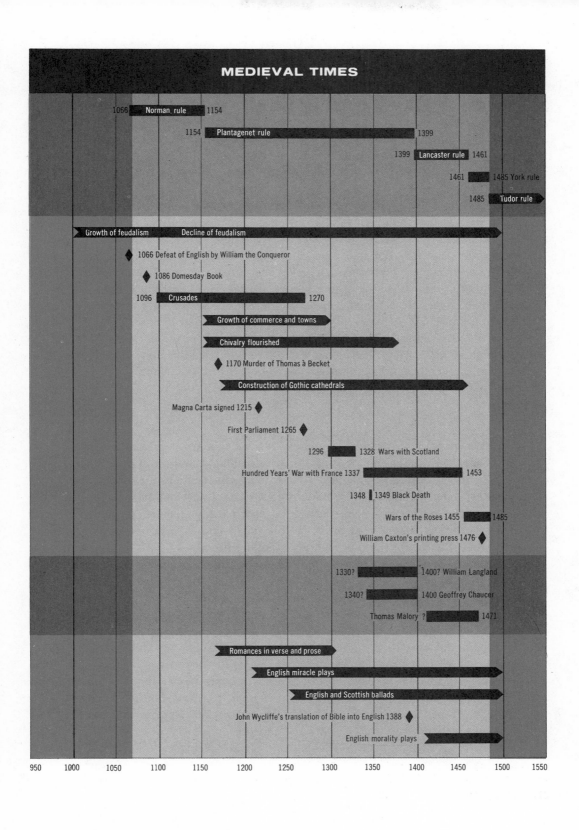

MEDIEVAL TIMES

1066 Norman rule 1154

1154 Plantagenet rule 1399

1399 Lancaster rule 1461

1461 1485 York rule

1485 Tudor rule

Growth of feudalism   Decline of feudalism

1066 Defeat of English by William the Conqueror

1086 Domesday Book

1096 Crusades 1270

Growth of commerce and towns

Chivalry flourished

1170 Murder of Thomas à Becket

Construction of Gothic cathedrals

Magna Carta signed 1215

First Parliament 1265

1296 1328 Wars with Scotland

Hundred Years' War with France 1337 1453

1348 1349 Black Death

Wars of the Roses 1455 1485

William Caxton's printing press 1476

1330? 1400? William Langland

1340? 1400 Geoffrey Chaucer

Thomas Malory ? 1471

Romances in verse and prose

English miracle plays

English and Scottish ballads

John Wycliffe's translation of Bible into English 1388

English morality plays

950   1000   1050   1100   1150   1200   1250   1300   1350   1400   1450   1500   1550

an overlord, who in turn owed allegiance either to some great noble or to the king himself. The system was really an elaborate chain of loyalties, with rent, so to speak, paid principally in military service to the overlord. As the towns grew, the craftsmen and tradesmen organized themselves into guilds, which decided wages and prices, insisted upon good standards of material and workmanship, and regulated terms of apprenticeship for the particular craft or trade. Indeed not only apprenticeship but almost everything in medieval society, including the clothing people wore, was regulated and carefully ordered.

People knew their places in this society. Those of humble birth might be promoted to positions of great power and influence only in the Church. If we suddenly found ourselves members of such a society we should undoubtedly feel that much of our personal freedom had been taken away from us. Because it was essentially a society with a secure religious foundation, there were, however, some compensations. For example, as we see in Chaucer, people belonging to very different classes could quite happily go on a pilgrimage together, in a way that would have been unusual in later eras. People had rights as well as particular obligations and responsibilities of their rank or class. There was less downright brutal tyranny than there was in the centuries that followed the Middle Ages, or indeed in some of the totalitarian systems our world has known during the past forty years.

MEDIEVAL LIFE

Medieval life was austere in many ways: no modern comforts and conveniences; not much choice in dress; travel difficult and often dangerous; and food (lacking sugar, potatoes, and many other things), even for the wealthy, offering little variety. Most foodstuffs could not be preserved, sometimes a lot had to be eaten quickly—and this explains the special feast times—while at other times ordinary folk might find themselves on a very poor diet. But again, there were other compensations.

Because there was no industry, no enormous factories pouring out smoke, no railroads, no vast dark cities, both in its towns and its countryside the Middle Ages were bright and full of color, a perpetual feast for the eye. A great noble would have a crowd of retainers dressed in gay livery. Costumes were often fantastically varied and rich, and a typical medieval throng would look to us like a splendid ballet. Religious festivals provided plenty of holidays during which people enjoyed themselves singing and dancing and playing games, watching archers compete or knights in their magnificent tournaments. Religion also helped to relieve the austerity of medieval times by preaching that life on earth was much less important than life after death.

In spite of the treasured memory of great heroes like King Richard "the Lion-Hearted," the history of the Crusades makes mournful reading. Each Crusade began in high hope, in a genuine desire to rescue Jerusalem from the Turks, but most ended squalidly in raiding, looting, and a tangle of power politics. Still, in the end, Western Europe gained much from these expeditions to the Near East. Christian Europe was exposed to Arabic culture— especially mathematics and medicine—at its highest level. Commercial and intellectual horizons were greatly broadened, and both knowledge and all manner of refinements in living were brought back from the East. It was the Crusades too, even though they ended so badly, that encouraged the ideal of true knightly behavior known as *chivalry*.

Today we use the term *chivalrous* to describe the conduct of well-mannered and sensitive men toward women, but the medieval idea of chivalry, though it included the relations between the sexes, went far beyond this. It sought, with the aid of the Church, to make the knightly warrior as devout and tenderhearted off the battlefield as he was bold and fearless on it. The bloodstained, ferocious history of the Crusades suggests that chivalry was an ideal rather than an actual code of conduct. It was, however, of considerable importance in literature, where, as noble ladies insisted upon more and more songs and tales to please their taste, it was joined to the companion idea of *romance*.

THE MEDIEVAL ROMANCE

Medieval *romance* consisted largely of tales of chivalry to which were added a love interest (to please the ladies) and all sorts of wonders and marvels—faerie enchantments, giants, dragons, wizards, and sorceresses. The humbler folk of the Middle Ages were ready to believe anything of this kind; the aristocrats and the clergy, though better informed, still existed in a world largely unexplored and not mapped, a little world, poised between Heaven and Hell, in which the natural merged into the marvelous and the supernatural.

The medieval concept of romantic love came from France. Indeed the first English romances—verse, and later prose tales relating the quests knights undertook for their ladies—were translations from the French, abridged to concentrate on adventure and eliminate the long, moralizing speeches about love. These romantic tales came from three principal sources —Britain (the story of King Arthur and his knights), France (the court of Charlemagne), and Rome (classical stories, such as the conquest of Troy). In the famous legends of King Arthur and his Knights of the Round Table, collected and retold by Sir Thomas Malory in his *Morte d'Arthur* (see page 69), chivalry and romance play equal parts.

GROWTH OF THE ENGLISH NATION

It took about two hundred and fifty years for Normans and Saxons to merge their individual identities into one English nation. Unfortunately for both England and France, the English monarchy never voluntarily relinquished its hold on its French possessions. As a result there were numerous costly wars in France, culminating in the series of wars now known as the "Hundred Years' War" (1337–1453). Although in the end driven from France, England won many a famous victory in these wars, thanks largely to the terrible longbows of the English infantry. Used by the English from the time of Edward I (1272–1307) onward, these six-foot bows, with yard-long arrows capable of piercing a knight's armor, were among the most effective weapons known to Western Europe in the late Middle Ages. In fact, the longbows—together with gunpowder, another new element in European warfare—eventually did much to end the Middle Ages by making knights and castles less effective in warfare.

Because the English kings and barons, unlike those in other countries, depended upon their bowmen, who came from the common folk, these folk showed an independent spirit not to be found in peasants abroad. But long before the Hundred Years' War there had taken root in England certain ideas and practices that were far different from those of other European countries. These ideas were greatly to affect England's future development. Henry II (1154–89), a descendant of both William the Conqueror and Alfred the Great, reformed the judicial system and firmly established the right of all Englishmen to trial by a jury of their peers. In 1215 the barons compelled Henry's vicious son, King John, to sign the famous Magna Carta. This very elaborate charter was intended to do little more than protect the rights and privileges of the barons themselves; but as it established the principle that even the king must obey the common law, it was to have great importance in later centuries in establishing the rights of Englishmen.

The term common law refers to law which is common to the whole country and all its people, in contrast to kinds of law applying only to certain classes of persons. It developed as society itself developed, based not on legal codes but on usages and precedents—that is, on what good judges had already decided and laid down as law. Common law was taken by the English settlers to America, so that it is also the foundation of American law. The third foundation stone in the later expansion of English freedoms came in 1295, when John's grandson, Edward I, called the first Parliament that included not only the great nobles and bishops ("lords"), but also representatives of the lesser nobles and of the townspeople ("commons").

The Parliament of Edward I.

Living on an island, these increasingly independent Englishmen were conscious of themselves as a nation earlier than were most other European peoples. They thought of themselves as Englishmen. This sense of nationality was unusual in the Middle Ages, when nationalism had not yet become a strong force.

THE WARS OF THE ROSES

During the High Middle Ages, roughly from the twelfth to the middle of the fourteenth century, the English of all classes lived comparatively well. In 1348, however, came the Black Death, the first of a series of plagues that killed more than a third of the population. The scarcity of labor caused by the plagues was the death knell of feudalism. In 1381, inflamed by repressive laws and burdensome taxes and encouraged by the teachings of the religious reformer John Wycliffe, the peasants rose in bloody revolt. The revolt was put down harshly, but economic and social unrest continued. Then, hard on the heels of the Hundred Years' War, came the so-called Wars of the Roses (1455–85), a civil war between the House of York, whose emblem was the white rose, and the House of Lancaster, symbolized by a red rose. When in 1485 Henry VII succeeded Richard III and united the

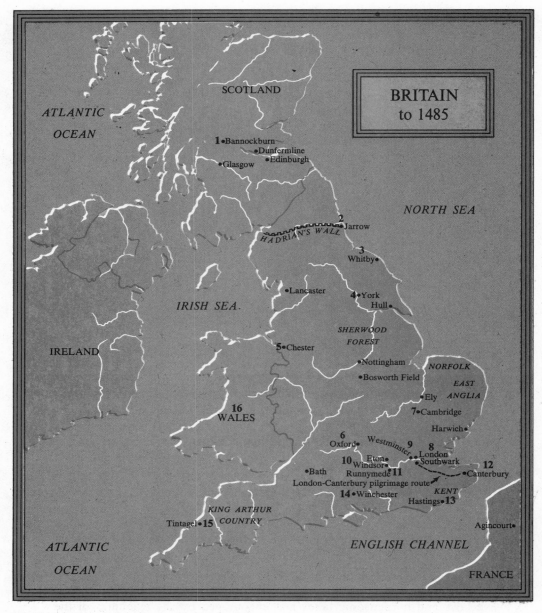

BRITAIN
to 1485

ATLANTIC OCEAN

SCOTLAND

1 •Bannockburn
•Dunfermline
•Glasgow •Edinburgh

NORTH SEA

2 •Jarrow
HADRIAN'S WALL

3 •Whitby

•Lancaster

4 •York
Hull•

IRISH SEA

SHERWOOD FOREST

5 •Chester

•Nottingham
•Bosworth Field

NORFOLK
EAST ANGLIA

•Ely
7 •Cambridge

IRELAND

16 **WALES**

Harwich•

6 •Oxford
Westminster•
10 Eton•
•Windsor 9 8 •London
Runnymede 11 •Southwark
•Bath 12 •Canterbury
London–Canterbury pilgrimage route

KENT
14 •Winchester
Hastings• 13

Agincourt•

Tintagel• 15
KING ARTHUR COUNTRY

ATLANTIC OCEAN

ENGLISH CHANNEL

FRANCE

1 Battle site where Robert Bruce defeated the English (1314). 2 Seventh-century monastery where the Venerable Bede lived. 3 The Anglo-Saxon poet Caedmon was a monk here. 4 Church center of northern England and early center of learning. 5 One of the oldest cities in England, still medieval in appearance; Chester cycle of miracle plays, fourteenth–sixteenth centuries. 6 and 7 England's oldest and greatest universities, founded in Middle Ages. 8 Principal city since Middle Ages; home of Chaucer. 9 Caxton's press, first in England, established here (1476). 10 Chief residence of English kings since the time of William the Conqueror. 11 Magna Carta signed here (1215). 12 Chief church center of England; site of murder (1170) and shrine of Thomas à Becket. 13 Great victory here by William of Normandy (1066) began Norman Conquest of England. 14 Seat of government of Alfred the Great; Anglo-Saxon Chronicle compiled here. 15 Picturesque ruins; legendary birthplace of King Arthur. 16 Annexed to England (1284).

feuding families through marriage, he ended the wars and founded the Tudor line. When Henry VII came to the throne in 1485, the real Middle Ages had vanished.

GEOFFREY CHAUCER

The first truly great figure in English literature was Geoffrey Chaucer (1340?–1400). Although ready to traffic in the fashionable romance of the day, he obviously was quite skeptical about it, being as sharply realistic as a modern novelist in much of his work. Because Chaucer is so far removed from us and his manner and language, especially in the original Middle English, seem so quaint, we can easily underestimate this astonishing man. He was not only a great poet and a fine storyteller but also the first of the poker-faced humorists. There is just a twinkle in his eye as he gravely, often ironically, adds one descriptive stroke to another, never failing, if we are alert, to make his points. This man, whether moving as a diplomat from one royal court to another or lounging about an innyard among people, missed nothing. And his greatest work belongs not to *romance* but to poetic and humorous realism. With Chaucer the writer is no longer anonymous but emerges in all the variety and subtlety of an impressive individual.

FOLK POET AND THE DRAMA

From the common people of early England and Scotland came ballads, songs not written down but recited and sung in innumerable alehouses and at thousands of firesides. This folk poetry flourished in the fourteenth and fifteenth centuries, but it was not until the middle of the eighteenth century that it was carefully collected and published. Through the German poet Herder, who had a passion for folk poetry, these English and Scottish ballads came to influence the whole German Romantic movement and then, later, the English Romantic poets. But most of them originally belong, as their themes and settings suggest, to the later Middle Ages, to whose unknown wandering minstrels many future generations of poets were enormously indebted.

The popular drama reached a tremendous height in the Elizabethan Age, but its origins are in the Middle Ages. During the frequent holiday times celebrating religious festivals, the trade guilds entertained the crowd with miracle plays, rough dramatizations of Biblical stories performed on large wagons or on platforms erected in market places or innyards. As a rule the wicked characters in these plays, including the devil himself, were played as comic characters, thereby creating a tradition of popular comedy that the Elizabethan dramatists followed. It was all very rough-and-ready, but in these humble performances there was already stirring the glorious theater of Shakespeare.

Woodcut from an early edition of *Everyman*.

Toward the end of the Middle Ages in England, during the dark troubled times of the fifteenth century, the miracle plays gave place to the morality plays. These plays, although presented in the same way as the miracle plays, tended to be elaborate and sophisticated dramatic allegories in which characters representing various virtues and vices confronted one another. The most famous of the morality plays, and one still often performed in many countries, was *Everyman*. Although this play was not English in origin, a thoroughly English adaptation of it soon became very popular. Even during the present century this play has been performed in the English theater fairly often.

English literature owes a great deal to the Middle Ages. In this period a great many literary forms had their origin. The High, or Gothic, Middle Ages, best represented now by their glorious cathedrals, have always haunted the imagination of the more poetic English writers with a bright and gaily colored vision of cavalcades of knights, squires, minstrels, pages, pilgrims, crusaders, troubadours, monks, scholars, and fine ladies in hilltop castles. But the real secret of the appeal of this period at its best does not lie in its romantic picturesqueness, enchanting though that may be. It comes from the fact that during these years Western people, those restless, inventive, aggressive, troubled creatures, achieved an elaborately organized way of life completely contained within a common religion.

J.B.P.

EARLY ENGLISH AND SCOTTISH BALLADS

The ballads of early England and Scotland, known today as the *popular, traditional,* or *folk* ballad, arose in medieval times—mostly in the fifteenth century—from the traditions of the common people. Because they were passed on from generation to generation by word of mouth and not set down in writing for several centuries, it is impossible to trace the identity of their original authors or to ascertain which of the many variations of these ballads was the original version.

Few of the English and Scottish folk ballads were printed before the eighteenth century. It was *Reliques of Ancient English Poetry,* the collection of ballads published by Bishop Thomas Percy in 1765, that gave impetus to an interest in these old ballads that persists to this day. Since the publication of Percy's collection, others have been inspired to make their own collections. The Scottish poet and novelist Sir Walter Scott, among others, went to the English-Scottish border region to write down—from the dictation of the border people who were still singing them—the various versions of many of these old songs.

The subject matter of the folk ballads stemmed from the everyday life of the common folk. The most popular themes, often tragic ones, were disappointed love, jealousy, revenge, sudden disaster, and deeds of adventure and daring. Many of the usual devices of telling a story are evident in the old ballads. The narrative is simple and direct. A single incident is related in dramatic fashion, with only slight attention paid to characterization and description. Little or no background introduction is given and the story is developed largely through dialogue, the narrative often hinted at rather than told in detail. Sometimes the reader must guess what happens between stanzas or who is speaking in certain stanzas. Often standard speeches have a special or set meaning, as though they were part of a code. For example, when the heroine of the ballad "Bonny Barbara Allan" (see page 36) calls upon her mother to make her bed "soft and narrow," it is understood that she is about to die.

Another device commonly used in ballads is the *refrain,* in which the last line or two of each stanza are repeated, thus adding an effective note of emphasis or suspense and contributing to the ballad's melody and rhythmic flow. Sometimes *incremental repetition* is used: that is, the repetition of a previous line or lines but with a slight variation each time, which advances the story stanza by stanza.

Above all, the ballads are musical in nature. They were meant to be sung, one voice carrying the main part of the stanza, with the rest of the group joining in on the refrain. Since the French word for ballad once meant *to dance,* it is likely that people also danced to the old ballad rhythms.

Because the ballads were so much a part of their tradition, it is natural that wherever the English and Scottish people went they took their ballads with them. It was thus that the early British settlers introduced their ballads, in all their many versions, to North America, where they have worked their way into our own folklore and become part of our own national heritage.

Bonny Barbara Allan

As is the case with so many ballads, the constant telling and retelling of this tragic love song has resulted in a great variety of versions. Ninety-two variations of this popular ballad have found their way into the folklore of Virginia alone. In some of these versions the hero's name varies. In some versions, Barbara dies repentant, in others not. The version given here is considered as close to the original Scottish story as any others that are known.

It was in and about the Martinmas time,°
　When the green leaves were a-falling,
That Sir John Graeme, in the West
　　Country,
　Fell in love with Barbara Allan.

He sent his men down through the town　5
　To the place where she was dwelling:
"O haste and come to my master dear,
　Gin° ye be Barbara Allan."

O hooly,° hooly rose she up,
　To the place where he was lying,　　10
And when she drew the curtain by,
　"Young man, I think you're dying."

"O it's I'm sick, and very, very sick,
　And it's a' for Barbara Allan";
"O the better for me ye's never be,　　15
　Though your heart's blood were a-
　　spilling.

"O dinna ye mind,° young man," said she,
　"When the red wine ye were fillin',
That ye made the healths gae round and
　　round,
　And slighted Barbara Allan?"　　20

He turned his face unto the wall,
　And death was with him dealing;
"Adieu, adieu, my dear friends all,
　And be kind to Barbara Allan."

And slowly, slowly raise she up,　　25
　And slowly, slowly left him,
And, sighing, said she could not stay,
　Since death of life had reft him.

She had not gane a mile but twa,°　　29
　When she heard the dead-bell ringing,
And every jow° that the dead-bell geid,°
　It cried, "Woe to Barbara Allan!"

"O mother, mother, make my bed!
　O make it saft and narrow!
Since my love died for me today,　　35
　I'll die for him tomorrow."

They buried her in the old churchyard,
　And Sir John's grave was nigh her.
And from his heart grew a red, red rose,
　And from her heart a brier.　　40

They grew to the top o' the old church
　　wall,
　Till they could grow no higher,
Until they tied a true love's knot—
　The red rose and the brier.

---

1. **Martinmas time:** November 11.　8. **Gin:** if.
9. **hooly:** slowly.　17. **dinna ye mind:** don't you remember.

29. **not . . . twa:** gone only two miles.　31. **jow:** stroke.　**geid:** gave.

Get Up and Bar the Door

Although most medieval ballads treat tragic themes, there are exceptions. Many of the less serious ballads deal with domestic humor, as does the following familiar tale.

It fell about the Martinmas time,
  And a gay time it was then,
When our goodwife got puddings to make,
  She's boild them in the pan.

The wind sae cauld blew south and north.
  And blew into the floor;   6
Quoth our goodman to our goodwife,
  "Gae out and bar the door."

"My hand is in my hussyfskap,°
  Goodman, as ye may see;   10
An it shoud nae be barrd this hundred
    year,
  It's no be barrd for me."°

They made a paction° tween them twa,
  They made it firm and sure,
That the first word whaeer° shoud speak,
  Shoud rise and bar the door.   16

Then by there came two gentlemen,
  At twelve o'clock at night,
And they could neither see house nor hall,
  Nor coal nor candlelight.   20

"Now whether is this a rich man's house,
  Or whether it is a poor?"°
But neer a word wad ane o' them° speak,
  For barring of the door.

And first they° ate the white puddings,
  And then they ate the black;   26

Tho muckle° thought the goodwife to
    hersel,
  Yet neer a word she spake.

Then said the one unto the other,
  "Here, man, tak ye my knife;   30
Do ye tak aff the auld man's beard,
  And I'll kiss the goodwife."

"But there's nae water° in the house,
  And what shall we do than?"
"What ails ye at the pudding broo,°   35
  That boils into° the pan?"

O up then started our goodman,
  An angry man was he:
"Will ye kiss my wife before my een,
  And scad° me wi pudding bree?"°   40

Then up and started our goodwife,
  Gied three skips on the floor:
"Goodman, you've spoken the foremost
    word;
  Get up and bar the door."

27. **muckle:** much. 33. **water:** probably to scald the beard in order to scrape it off. 35. "What's the matter with using the pudding water?" 36. **into:** in. 40. **scad:** scald. **bree:** broth, liquor.

9. **hussyfskap:** household duties. 11–12. "The door will not be barred in a hundred years if I have to bar it." 13. **paction:** agreement. 15. **whaeer:** whoever. 21–22. The strangers ask this question. 23. **them:** the man and his wife. 25. **they:** the strangers.

Sir Patrick Spens

Although scholars have been unable to identify its hero, it is generally agreed that this
ballad is based on an actual historical event,
the disastrous voyage of a Norwegian ship
which, late in the thirteenth century, set out
from Scotland with the Norwegian king and his
Scottish bride.

The king sits in Dumferling° toune,
   Drinking the blude-reid wine:
"O whar will I get a skilly° skipper,
   To sail this new schip of mine?"

O up and spak an eldern knicht,°   5
   Sat at the kings richt kne:
"Sir Patrick Spens is the best sailor,
   That ever sailed the se."

The king has written a braid° letter,
   And sealed it wi his hand,   10
And sent it to Sir Patrick Spens,
   Was walking on the strand.

The first line that Sir Patrick red,
   A loud lauch lauched he;
The next line that Sir Patrick red,   15
   The teir blinded his ee.°

"O wha is this has don this deid,
   And told the king o' me,
To send us out at this time o' the yeir,
   To sail upon the se!   20

"Mak ready, mak ready, my mirry men all,
   Our guid schip sails the morne."
"Now, ever alake,° my master deir,
   I feir a deadlie storme.

"I saw the new moone late yestreen,   25
   Wi' the auld moone in hir arme,
And if we gang to se, master,
   I feir we'll cum to harme."

O laith,° laith wer our guid Scots lords
   To weet their cork-heild schoone;°   30
Bot lang owre° a' the play was playd,
   They wat their hats aboone.°

O lang, lang may their ladies sit,
   Wi their fans into their hand;
Before they se Sir Patrick Spens   35
   Cum sailing to the strand.

And lang, lang may their maidens sit,
   Wi their gold kems° in their hair,
All waiting for their ain deir loves,
   For thame they'll se na mair.   40

Haf owre,° haf owre to Aberdour,°
   'Tis fiftie fadom deip,
And thair lies guid Sir Patrick Spens,
   Wi the Scots lords at his feit.

1. **Dumferling** (dum·fûr′ling): a town near Edinburgh, now Dunfermline. 3. **skilly:** skillful. 5. **eldern knicht:** older knight. 9. **braid:** on a broad
sheet, or long. 16. **ee:** eye. 23. **alake:** alack, alas.

29. **laith:** loath, unwilling. 30. **cork-heild schoone:**
cork-heeled shoes. 31. **owre:** ere, before.
32. Their hats floated above them. 38. **kems:**
combs. 41. **Haf owre:** half over, halfway. **Aberdour:** a small town near Edinburgh.

BONNY BARBARA ALLAN

1. The story of "Bonny Barbara Allan" takes place "about the Martinmas time," or in November. Is November an appropriate time of the year for the story to take place? Would the ballad be more or less effective if the story took place in June?

2. What is the significance of lines 39–40? Would these lines be as appropriate to the story if a brier had grown up from Sir John's grave and a rose from Barbara Allan's?

3. What parallels are there between the fates of Sir John and Barbara Allan? Do you think their fates were just? Explain.

GET UP AND BAR THE DOOR

1. Do you sympathize with the husband or the wife in "Get Up and Bar the Door"? Do you think it fair that the wife wins?

2. To establish a basically comic situation and then introduce developments that make the situation even more ludicrous is a popular comic device. How is this device used in "Get Up and Bar the Door"?

SIR PATRICK SPENS

1. The demands of duty is a common literary theme. Sir Patrick Spens does his duty even though he is certain that his course of action will lead to his death. Explain his reactions to the king's letter in lines 13–16. Can he be called a heroic figure? Why or why not? Have you encountered similar situations in other poems and stories? Do you think that Sir Patrick made the right decision? Explain.

2. What role does a superstitious belief in evil omens play in "Sir Patrick Spens"? What other sea poems and stories have you read in which similar beliefs are expressed? At what point in the narrative do you first realize that the ballad will end tragically?

3. The doom of Sir Patrick and his sailors is not told directly. Instead, the poem shifts in line 29 from a narrative to a lament for the drowned men. What do you think about this shift? Would the ballad be more or less effective if it had continued as a narrative?

4. Much of the dramatic effect of this ballad depends on various contrasts. For example, in lines 29–36 the drowned Scottish lords are contrasted with the ladies waiting for them. Point out other contrasts and explain how each contributes to the effectiveness of the poem.

THE FOLK BALLAD

Unlike the literary ballads written by poets such as Sir Walter Scott and Samuel Taylor Coleridge, the old folk ballads were the "popular songs" of their day. As such, their form was simple and regular and thus fairly easy to remember in performance. The typical ballad stanza consists of four lines—that is, a *quatrain*—with eight syllables in the first and third lines and six syllables in the shorter second and fourth lines. The clear and definite beat of the ballad stanza makes it readily adaptable to all types of stories. The meter is usually iambic, meaning that, as is shown in the stanza quoted below, the stress in each line falls on every other syllable. (An iamb is a metrical foot consisting of an unaccented syllable followed by an accented one.) Unlike the alliterative verse of the Anglo-Saxon period, the ballad rhymes, with the rhyme usually appearing in the second and fourth lines of each stanza, as is shown here.

"The wind sae cauld blew south and north,

    And blew into the *floor;*

Quoth our goodman to our goodwife,

    'Gae out and bar the *door.*'"

The metrical simplicity of the ballad matches the simplicity of its language. Although code language is sometimes used (for example, asking that one's bed be made "soft and narrow" means that the speaker is dying), the language of the ballads is usually direct and straightforward. So too is the ballad's narrative, despite the use of understatement, abrupt transitions, and tantalizing clues which often make it necessary for the reader to puzzle out who is speaking in a given stanza and what has transpired between stanzas.

FOR COMPOSITION

1. The job of a newspaper reporter is to present only the facts. Write a reporter's version of the story of Sir Patrick Spens. Then compare this version with the ballad, pointing out what the ballad conveys that the newspaper version does not.

2. If there are collections of British and American folk ballads in your library, write a composition in which you compare several versions of "Bonny Barbara Allan." Describe changes that have been made in the American versions and defend the version that you think is most effective.

GEOFFREY CHAUCER
(1340?–1400)

To William Caxton, England's first printer, Geoffrey Chaucer was "the worshipful father and first founder and embellisher of ornate eloquence in our English." Perceptive as this accolade was in its time, today Chaucer is acclaimed not only as "the father of English poetry" but also as the father of the modern short story and novel—in short, as the father of English literature. In addition, we are indebted to him for the most vivid contemporary description of fourteenth-century England.

A man of affairs as well as a man of letters, Chaucer's development as the one was closely paralleled by his development as the other. Born into a family which belonged to the rising middle class, he obtained through his father, a successful wine merchant, a position as page in a household which was closely associated with the court of King Edward III. His mastery of Latin, French, and Italian, in addition to equipping him for diplomatic and civil service, also enabled him to translate literary works in all three languages, an important factor in his development as a writer.

A court favorite, Chaucer rose quickly in the world. Before he was twenty he served as a soldier in France and, upon being captured, was ransomed by his king. Thereafter, throughout his life, he served his country loyally—as courtier, diplomat, civil administrator, and translator. Entrusted with important and delicate diplomatic missions, he traveled on several occasions to France and Italy, and his journeys abroad played an important role in his literary and intellectual development. Subsequently, he served as Comptroller of Customs for the Port of London; Member of Parliament; Justice of the Peace; Clerk of the Works at Westminster Abbey, the Tower of London, and elsewhere; and finally as a sub-forester of one of the king's forests. He was, in fact, a highly valued public servant and was fortunate to enjoy for most of his life the patronage of the influential John of Gaunt, Duke of Lancaster and uncle of King Richard II. During his long public career, he became acquainted with the most important men of his day—diplomats and rulers as well as writers. At his death, his reputation as a man of affairs and his genius as a poet well established, he was buried in Westminster Abbey. Today, in the history of English literature, Chaucer's name stands second only to that of Shakespeare.

One of Chaucer's most important contributions to English literature is his development of the resources of the English language for literary purposes. In his day, English was still considered primarily a rough peasant language. England's Norman rulers had introduced French to England, and this language was still spoken in court circles and by the aristocracy. Church Latin was used in the monasteries, the centers of learning, and was still at the command of the educated. Although earlier poets had written in a primitive English, there was very little English literature beyond the range of traditional and anonymous ballads. When he began to write, therefore, Chaucer had to proceed by trial and error, taking his models at first from French and Italian sources and feeling his way toward a full use of his native tongue. Chaucer himself spoke late Middle English, the London speech of his day, and it was by using this language instead of the more fashionable French for his poetry that he added tremendously to its prestige and set an example which was followed thereafter.

As a writer, Chaucer was extremely prolific. In his early short lyrics and longer works such as *The Book of the Duchess* we see the influence of the French poetry of his day. Later, in works such as *Parliament of Fowls* and *Troilus and Criseyde,* his writing reflected the influence of the Italian masters Dante, Petrarch, and Boccaccio. By 1386, when he began *The Canterbury Tales,* his most ambitious work, he had become master of his craft.

For *The Canterbury Tales* Chaucer used the structural device of the frame story, a popular one used in the thousand and one tales of *The Arabian Nights' Entertainment* and the one hundred tales of Boccaccio's *Decameron.* As the frame around which to group his tales, Chaucer chose a springtime pilgrimage to Canterbury Cathedral, the site of the splendid shrine of St. Thomas à Becket, who had been murdered there two centuries before. In Chaucer's day it was customary throughout Europe for members of all classes to travel to religious shrines to seek miraculous cures, to gain remission of their sins, or simply to satisfy their wanderlust. In England the pilgrimage to Canterbury was by far the most popular, and to this day traces of the old "pilgrims' way" still persist.

Chaucer's choice of frame for *The Canterbury Tales,* in addition to giving equal scope to his talents as narrator, philosopher, dramatist, and observer, had several other advantages. By using the device of a journey, it was possible to bring together quite naturally persons of varied occupations and diverse social rank, a rarity in medieval society. Thus Chaucer was able to present in his work a cross-section of medieval society, drawing his characters from the three most important groups of his day—feudal, ecclesiastical, and urban. The characters who are members of the feudal system are related to the land: these are the Knight, the Squire, the Yeoman, the Franklin, the Reeve, the Miller, and the Plowman. Those in the ecclesiastical order represent individuals belonging to the medieval church: the Parson, the Summoner, the Monk, the Prioress, the Friar, the Pardoner, and the Student. The other pilgrims are professional and mercantile laymen from the fast-growing towns of Chaucer's day: the Physician, the Lawyer, the Manciple, the Merchant, the Shipman, the tradesmen, the Cook, the Wife of Bath (a clothmaker), and the Innkeeper.

Chaucer's plan for *The Canterbury Tales* was an ambitious one. Each pilgrim was to tell two stories on the way to Canterbury and two on the return journey to London. The poet died, however, before this plan was realized and, instead of the proposed one hundred twenty-four stories, he wrote only twenty-four. The portion of the work that was completed, however, is a masterpiece of vivid and realistic writing. Setting his work in his own time, he established a realistic style of writing that was to persist for centuries. Chaucer's mere descriptions of the pilgrims in his *Prologue* are considered by historians as our best picture of life in fourteenth-century England. In these portraits Chaucer's own background and temperament is reflected. A man of the world, large-minded, humane, tolerant, and amused by other people, he shows a profound understanding of human motivation, and comments—sometimes seriously, sometimes humorously—both on his characters and on some of the most critical social problems of his day. His tone ranges from comic to ironic to satirical, but always he reveals himself as a genial and warmhearted person who has sympathy for other people.

Though *The Canterbury Tales* is often referred to as the first collection of short stories in English literature, these stories, unlike the modern short story, are written in poetry rather than in prose. In the *Prologue,* Chaucer experimented with rhymed pairs of five-beat iambic lines, a verse form known as the heroic couplet and popularized three centuries later by John Dryden and Alexander Pope. Chaucer's style in *The Canterbury Tales* is remarkably flexible; for he had by this time thrown off the stiff conventions of his earlier French and Italian sources. His prose, like his vocabulary, is easy and informal. Although he was always an amateur who never wrote for pay or publication, Chaucer achieved in *The Canterbury Tales* the deceptive ease which is the hallmark of the professional.

FROM *The Prologue to The Canterbury Tales*

Entering the world of Geoffrey Chaucer through *The Canterbury Tales* is rather like standing in front of a splendid medieval painting or Florentine fresco. Painted in bright colors against a glowing background, the Knight, the Prioress, the Monk, the Pardoner, the Wife of Bath, and the rest of the Canterbury pilgrims move in perpetual sunlight, like processional figures winding uphill into the blue distance. In the *Prologue* to his masterpiece, Chaucer, with a brisk flourish, paints the setting of his story and then proceeds to introduce his cast of characters, from the Knight to the Host of the Tabard Inn. In his role as narrator, Chaucer maintains throughout an air of personal detachment; his appreciation of the individuality of his characters affords an honest and objective account of each of them. Indeed, at times it is difficult to determine whether he intends to commend or reprimand, so well does he blend satire with faint praise. In this broad panorama of human nature, the poet reveals what is base, noble, and essentially human in man.

In the version of the *Prologue* given here,

Chaucer's Prologue to *The Canterbury Tales* from *The Works of Geoffrey Chaucer,* edited by F. N. Robinson. Reprinted by permission of Houghton Mifflin Company.

Chaucer's descriptions of his most memorable pilgrims are presented in their entirety. Note that the first forty-two lines of the *Prologue* are given in the original Middle English, with a modern English translation supplied in smaller type in alternate lines. As you read, notice the similarities between the two forms of the language.

In reading Chaucer's *Prologue* in the original Middle English, remember that you are, after all, reading English and that most of Chaucer's words either have not changed in spelling or are close enough to their modern equivalents to cause little or no trouble. Most of the consonants are pronounced just as we do those in modern English. In the pronunciation table on page 62, you will find explanations of the few consonants that differ from modern pronunciation and also of the variations in vowel sounds. Pronounce every syllable in a word, even when it appears to be our modern silent *e* (marked in the original Middle English with two dots over the *e*). Thus, the word *talë* is pronounced in two syllables as *tah-leh* and *croppës* as *crop-pess*.

Once you try reading the *Prologue* aloud, you will soon become accustomed to Middle English. You will find it much less like a foreign tongue and more like an oddly musical form of your own language—which, of course, it is. You will also discover that the sense will come more easily as you more closely approximate the sound. After listening to a recording or to an experienced reader of Middle English, refer to the pronunciation table and try to work out the various sounds on your own. Practice aloud until you can read the lines with confidence as to both their sound and sense.

Here bygynneth the Book of the Tales of Caunterbury.

Whan that Aprill with his shourës sootë
When April with his showers hath pierced the drought
The droghte of March hath percëd to the rootë,
Of March with sweetness to the very root,
And bathëd every veyne in swich licour
And flooded every vein with liquid power
Of which vertu engendrëd is the flour;
That of its strength engendereth the flower;
Whan Zephirus eek with his sweetë breeth   5
When Zephyr° also with his fragrant breath   5
Inspirëd hath in every holt and heeth
Hath urged to life in every holt° and heath
The tendrë croppës, and the yongë sonnë
New tender shoots of green, and the young sun
Hath in the Ram his halvë cours yronnë,
Half of his course within the Ram° hath run,
And smalë fowelës maken melodyë,
And little birds are making melody
That slepen al the nyght with open yë   10
That sleep the whole night through with open eye,   10
(So priketh hem nature in hir corages);
For in their hearts doth Nature stir them so,
Thannë longen folk to goon on pilgrimages,
Then people long on pilgrimage to go,
And palmeres for to seken straungë strondës,
And palmers° to be seeking foreign strands,
To fernë halwës, kowthe in sondry londës;
To distant shrines renowned in sundry lands.
And specially from every shirës endë   15
And then from every English countryside   15
Of Engelond to Caunterbury they wendë,
Especially to Canterbury they ride,
The hooly blisful martir for to sekë,
There to the holy sainted martyr° kneeling
That hem hath holpen whan that they were seekë.
That in their sickness sent them help and healing.

Bifil that in that seson on a day,
Now in that season it befell one day
In Southwerk at the Tabard as I lay   20
In Southwark at the Tabard as I lay,   20
Redy to wenden on my pilgrymagë
Ready upon my pilgrimage to start
To Caunterbury with ful devout coragë,
Toward Canterbury, reverent of heart,

---

5. **Zephyr** (zef'ər): the west wind. 6. **holt:** plantation. 8. **Ram:** the first of the twelve signs of the zodiac. The time indicated in the passage is about April 11. The year is 1387. 13. **palmers** (pä'mərz): pilgrims who visited the Holy Land and wore two crossed palms to indicate that they had done so. 17. **martyr:** Thomas à Becket, Archbishop of Canterbury, who was murdered in 1170 and canonized in 1173.

At nyght was come into that hostelryë

There came at night into that hostelry

Wel nyne and twenty in a compaignyë,

Full nine and twenty in a company,

Of sondry folk, by aventure yfallë   25

People of all kinds that chanced to fall   25

In felaweshipe, and pilgrimes were they allë.

In fellowship, and they were pilgrims all

That toward Caunterbury wolden rydë.

Riding to Canterbury. The stables there

The chambrës and the stablës weren wydë,

Were ample, and the chambers large and fair,

And wel we weren esëd attë bestë,

And well was all supplied us of the best,

And shortly, whan the sonnë was to restë,   30

And by the time the sun had gone to rest   30

So hadde I spoken with hem everichon

I knew them and had talked with every one,

That I was of hir felaweshipe anon,

And so in fellowship had joined them soon,

And madë forward erly for to rysë,

Agreeing to be up and take our way

To take oure wey ther as I yow devysë.

Where I have told you, early with the day.

But nathelees, whil I have tyme and spacë,   35

But nonetheless, while I have space and time,   35

Er that I ferther in this talë pacë,

Before I venture farther with my rime,

Me thynketh it acordaunt to resoun

It seems to me no more than reasonable

To tellë yow al the condicioun

That I should speak of each of them and tell

Of ech of hem, so as it semëd me,

Their characters, as these appeared to me,

And whiche they weren, and of what degree,   40

And who they were, and what was their degree,°   40

And eek in what array that they were innë;

And something likewise of their costumes write;

And at a knyght than wol I first bigynnë.

And I will start by telling of a knight.

A KNIGHT there was, and that a noble man,

Who from the earliest time when he began

To ride forth, loved the way of chivalry,   45

Honor and faith and generosity.

Nobly he bare himself in his lord's war,

And he had ridden abroad (no man so far),

In many a Christian and a heathen land,

Well honored for his worth on every hand.   50

40. **degree:** rank.

The Knight (left) and the Squire, from William Caxton's edition of *The Canterbury Tales* (ca. 1484).

He was at Alexandria° when that town
Was won, and many times had sat him down
Foremost among the knights at feast in Prussia.
In Lithuania had he fought, and Russia,
No Christian more. Well was his worth attested   55
In Spain when Algeciras was invested,
And at the winning of Lyeys was he,
And Sataly, and rode in Belmarie;
And in the Great See° he had been at hand
When many a noble host had come to land.   60
Of mortal battles he had known fifteen,
And jousted for our faith at Tramessene
Thrice in the lists, and always slain his foe.
And he had been in Turkey, years ago,
Lending the prince of Palaty his sword   65
In war against another heathen lord;
And everywhere he went his fame was high.
And though renowned, he bore him prudently;
Meek was he in his manner as a maid.
In all his life to no man had he said   70
A word but what was courteous and right:
He was a very perfect noble knight.
But now to tell you what array he had—
His steeds were good, but he himself was clad
Plainly; in fustian° doublet he was dressed,   75
Discolored where his coat of mail had pressed,
For he was lately come from his voyage,
And went at once to do his pilgrimage.

With him there went a SQUIRE, that was his son,
A lover and soldier, full of life and fun,   80
With locks tight-curled, as if just out of press;

51–64. **Alexandria . . . Turkey:** The Knight had engaged in campaigns that spanned the continent from Spain to Asia Minor, from the Baltic shores to North Africa. 59. **Great See:** the Mediterranean. 75. **fustian:** thick cloth made of cotton and flax.

His age in years was twenty, I should guess.
In stature he appeared of middle height,
And great of strength, and wondrous quick and light.
And he had gone campaigning recently   85
In Flanders, in Artois, and Picardy,
And in this short space bore a gallant part,
Hoping for favor in his lady's heart.
His raiment shone as if he were a mead°
Broidered with flowers fresh and white and red.   90
Singing or fluting was he all the day;
He was as lusty° as the month of May.
Short was his gown, with sleeves both long and wide,
Well could he sit a horse and fairly ride;
He could make songs, and prettily indite,°   95
And joust and dance as well, and draw and write.
So fierce by night did love his heart assail
He slept no more than doth a nightingale.
Courteous he was, humble, willing and able,
And carved before his father at the table.°   100

He° had a YEOMAN there, and none beside
In service, for it pleased him so to ride;
And he was clad in coat and hood of green.
He bore a sheaf of arrows, bright and keen,
And wings of peacock feathers edged the wood.   105
He kept his gear the way a yeoman should—
No shafts of his with feathers dragging low!—
And in his hand he bare a mighty bow.
Close-cropped his head was, and his face was brown,
He knew well all the woodcraft that was known.   110
Gay on his arm an archer's guard he wore;
A buckler° at one side and sword he bore;
Upon the other side a dagger swung,
Sharp as a spear's point, richly wrought and hung.
Saint Christopher° on his breast made silver sheen.   115
He bore a horn; his baldric° was of green;
In truth, he was a forester, I should guess.

Also there was a nun, a PRIORESS,
And she went smiling, innocent and coy;
The greatest oath she swore was by Saint Loy;°   .120
And she was known as Madame Eglentine.
Full well she sang the services divine,
Intoning through her nose right prettily,
And fair she spoke her French and fluently

89. **mead** (mēd): meadow. 92. **lusty:** joyous, happy. 95. **make . . . indite:** compose both
lyrics and music. 100. **And . . . table:** It was the custom for the son to wait upon his father and
carve his meat. 101. **He:** the Knight. 112. **buckler** (buk'lər): a shield. 115. **Saint Christopher:** patron saint of travelers and foresters, whose figure on a medal is believed to shield the
wearer from danger. 116. **baldric** (bôl'drik): belt. 120. **Saint Loy:** St. Eligius, a French saint
who had been a goldsmith and was known for his meticulous manners.

The Yeoman

The Prioress

After the school of Stratford-at-the-Bow;°   125
(The French that Paris spoke she didn't know.)
Well taught she was at table; she would let
No food fall from her lips; she never wet
Her fingers deeply in the sauce; with care
She raised each morsel; well would she beware   130
Lest any drop upon her breast should fall;
In manners she delighted above all.
Always she wiped her upper lip so clean
That never a fleck of grease was to be seen
Within her cup when she had drunk. When she   135
Reached for her food, she did it daintily.
Pleasant she was, and loved a jest as well,
And in demeanor she was amiable.
Ever to use the ways of court she tried,
And sought to keep her manner dignified,   140
That all folk should be reverent of her.
But, speaking of her heart and character,
Such pity had she, and such charity
That if she saw a trapped mouse she would cry—
If it had died, or even if it bled;   145
And she had little dogs to which she fed
Fine roasted meat, or milk, or dainty bread;
How would she weep if one of them were dead,
Or any one should strike it viciously:
She was all heart and sensibility!   150
Her face was fair in pleated wimple° draped,
Her eyes were gray as glass, her nose well shaped,
Her mouth full small and thereto soft and red,
But of a truth she had a fair forehead,

125. **Stratford-at-the-Bow:** a Benedictine nunnery near London where an inferior French, not Parisian French, was spoken.   151. **wimple** (wĭm′pəl): a covering of linen or silk cloth for head, neck, and chin. It is still worn by nuns, but in medieval times it was worn by all women.

A span in breadth or I should be surprised,   155
For certainly she was not undersized.
Handsome her cloak, as I was well aware;
And wrought of coral round her arm she bare
A bracelet all of beads and green gauds° strung,
And down from this a golden pendant hung—   160
A brooch on which was written a crowned *A*
Followed by *Amor Vincit Omnia.*°

Another NUN rode in her retinue,
That as her chapelaine° served, and THREE PRIESTS° too.

A MONK was there, of much authority;   165
A hunter and a rider-out° was he,
A manly man, to be an abbot able.
Full many a dainty horse he had in stable,
And when he rode ye might his bridle hear
Jingle upon the whistling wind as clear   170
And all as loud as sounds the chapel bell
Where this same lord was keeper of the cell.
The rules of Maurice and of Benedict,°
These being ancient now, and rather strict,
This monk ignored, and let them go their ways,   175
And laid a course by rules of newer days.
He held that text worth less than a plucked hen
Which said that hunters were not holy men,
Or that a monk who follows not the rule
Is like a fish when it is out of pool—   180
That is to say, a monk out of his cloister.
Indeed, he held that text not worth an oyster;
And his opinion here was good, I say.
For why go mad with studying all day,
Poring over a book in some dark cell,   185
And with one's hands go laboring as well,
As Austin° bids? How shall the world be served?
Let Austin's work for Austin be reserved!
Therefore he hunted hard and with delight;
Greyhounds he had as swift as birds in flight;   190
To gallop with the hounds and hunt the hare
He made his joy, and no expense would spare.
I saw his sleeves trimmed just above the hand
With soft gray fur, the finest in the land;

---

159. **gauds:** beads on a rosary, each bead indicating a prayer to be recited.   162. *Amor . . . Omnia:* Love conquers all things.   164. **chapelaine:** secretary.   **Three Priests:** It is supposed that "and three priests" was added by some scribe to fill out a line left incomplete by Chaucer. Only one priest is mentioned later, and the total of "nine and twenty" (line 24) allows for only one.   166. **rider-out:** inspector of church property.   173. **Maurice . . . Benedict:** St. Benedict, an Italian monk, founded a number of monasteries throughout Western Europe; St. Maurice was a disciple of his.   187. **Austin:** St. Augustine, Bishop of Hippo (A.D. 354–430). Critical of the laziness of monks, he suggested that they engage in manual labor.

The Monk

The Friar

And fastening his hood beneath his chin,   195
Wrought out of gold, he wore a curious pin—
A love knot at the larger end there was!
His head was wholly bald and shone like glass,
As did his face, as though with ointment greased
He was full fat and sleek, this lordly priest.   200
His fierce bright eyes that in his head were turning
Like flames beneath a copper cauldron burning,
His supple boots, the trappings of his steed,
Showed him a prelate fine and fair indeed!
He was not pale like some tormented ghost.   205
He loved a fat swan best of any roast.
His palfrey° was as brown as is a berry.

There was a FRIAR, a wanton° and a merry,
Licensed to beg—a gay, important fellow.
In all four orders no man was so mellow   210
With talk and dalliance.° He had brought to pass
The marrying of many a buxom lass,
Paying himself the priest and the recorder:°
He was a noble pillar to his order!
He was familiar too and well beloved   215
By all the franklins° everywhere he moved
And by good women of the town withal,
For he had special powers confessional
As he himself would let folk understand:
He had been licensed by the Pope's own hand!   220
Full sweetly would he listen to confession,
And very pleasantly absolved transgression;
He could give easy penance if he knew
There would be recompense in revenue;

207. **palfrey** (pôl′frē): a saddle horse. 208. **wanton:** jolly. 211. **dalliance:** gossip, chat.
213. **recorder:** the man who officially recorded the marriage ceremony. 216. **franklins:** landowners.

For he that to some humble order hath given—   225
Is he not by that token all but shriven?°
For if he gave, then of a certain, said he,
He knew the man was penitent already!
For many a man may be so hard of heart
He may not weep, though sore may be his smart,°   230
Therefore his case no tears and prayers requires:
Let him give silver to the needy friars!
Always he kept his tippet° stuffed with knives
And pins, that he could give to comely wives.
And of a truth he had a merry note,   235
For he could sing and play upon the rote—°
There he would take the prize for certainty.
His neck was white as is the *fleur-de-lys.*°
He was as strong as any champion.
As for the inns, he knew them every one,   240
Their hosts and barmaids too—much better than
He'd know a leper or a beggar-man;
For it was not for such a one as he
To seek acquaintance in the company
Of loathsome lepers—no, not for a minute!   245
There was no decency or profit in it.
One should avoid such trash and cultivate
Vendors of food and folk of rich estate.
And if a profit was to be expected
No courtesy or service he neglected.   250
There was no man so able anywhere—
As beggar he was quite beyond compare.
He paid a fee to get his hunting ground;
None of his brethren dared to come around;
For though a widow might not own a shoe,   255
So pleasant was his *In principio,*°
That he would have a farthing ere he went;
His profits more than paid him back his rent!
And like a puppy could he romp; yet he
Could work on love days with authority,   260
For he was not a monk threadbare of collar,
Out of some cloister, like a half-starved scholar,
But rather like a master or a pope.
Of double worsted was his semi-cope,°
That rounded upward like a molded bell.   265
He lisped a little, wantonly° and well,
To make his words the sweeter on his tongue.
And in his harping, after he had sung,

---

226. **shriven:** forgiven for his sins.   230. **smart:** pain.   233. **tippet** (tip'it): long, dangling part of a sleeve or hood.   236. **rote:** a stringed instrument.   238. *fleur-de-lys:* lily.   256. *In principio* (in prin·chēp'ē·ō): "In the beginning," the opening words of the Gospel of John, held by the ignorant to be a magic formula, and for this reason a favorite phrase used by some begging friars.   264. **semi-cope** (sem'ē·cōp): a short cape.   266. **wantonly:** in an affected manner.

Deep in his head his eyes would twinkle bright,
As do the stars upon a frosty night. 270
Hubert this begging friar was called by name.

Next, all in motley garbed, a MERCHANT came,
With a forked beard. High on his horse he sat,
Upon his head a Flanders beaver hat;
His boots were buckled fair and modishly. 275
He spoke his words with great solemnity,
Having in mind his gain in pounds and pence.
He wished the sea, regardless of expense,
Kept safe from Middleburg to Orëwell.°
Cunningly could he buy French crowns, or sell, 280
And great sagacity in all ways showed;
No man could tell of any debt he owed,
So circumspect he was in everything,
His loans, his bargains, and his trafficking.
In truth, a worthy man withal was he, 285
And yet I know not what his name might be.

There was a STUDENT° out of Oxford town,
Indentured long to logic and the gown.
Lean as a rake the horse on which he sat,
And he himself was anything but fat, 290
But rather wore a hollow look and sad.
Threadbare the little outercoat he had,
For he was still to get a benefice°
And thoughts of worldly office° were not his.
For he would rather have beside his bed 295
Twenty books arrayed in black or red
Of Aristotle° and his philosophy
Than robes or fiddle or jocund psaltery.°
Yet though he was philosopher, his coffer
Indeed but scanty store of gold could offer, 300
And any he could borrow from a friend
On books and learning straightway would he spend,
And make with prayer a constant offering
For those that helped him with his studying.
He gave to study all his care and heed, 305
Nor ever spoke a word beyond his need,
And that was said in form, respectfully,
And brief and quick and charged with meaning high.
Harmonious with virtue was his speech,
And gladly would he learn and gladly teach. 310

---

279. **Middleburg . . . Orëwell:** the Dutch and English towns, respectively, between which
traveled the ships bearing the merchant's goods.   287. **Student:** Though perhaps a student of
the humanities, he is also in training for the taking of holy orders.   293. **benefice:** a position in
the church, such as that of curate or rector.   294. **worldly office:** secular employment.
297. **Aristotle** (ar′is·tot′l): Greek philosopher (384–322 B.C.), regarded by medieval scholars as
the highest authority on all matters of learning.   298. **psaltery** (sôl′tər·ē): a stringed instrument.

A FRANKLIN in his company appeared;
As white as any daisy shone his beard;
Sanguine was his complexion; he loved dearly
To have his sop° in wine each morning early.
Always to pleasure would his custom run,   315
For he was Epicurus'° own son,
Who held opinion that in pleasure solely
Can man find perfect bliss and have it wholly.
Householder he, a mighty and a good;
He was Saint Julian° in his neighborhood;   320
His bread, his ale, were always prime, and none
Had better store of vintage than his own.
Within his house was never lack of pasty
Or fish or flesh—so plenteous and tasty
It seemed the place was snowing meat and drink,   325
All dainty food whereof a man could think.
And with the changing seasons of the year
Ever he changed his suppers and his fare.
Many fat partridges were in his mew,°
And bream° in pond, and pike in plenty, too.   330
Woe to his cook if all his gear were not
In order, or his sauce not sharp and hot!
And in his hall the plenteous platters lay
Ready upon the table all the day.
At sessions° he would play the lord and sire;   335
He went to parliament as knight-of-shire.
A dagger and purse of woven silk
Hung at his girdle, white as morning milk.
As sheriff he had served, and auditor;
Nowhere was any vassal worthier.   340

A GOOD WIFE° was there from beside the city
Of Bath°—a little deaf, which was a pity.
Such a great skill on making cloth she spent
That she surpassed the folk of Ypres and Ghent.°
No parish wife would dream of such a thing   345
As going before her° with an offering,
And if one did, so angry would she be
It put her wholly out of charity.°
Her coverchiefs were woven close of ground,°
And weighed, I lay an oath, at least ten pound   350
When of a Sunday they were on her head.
Her stockings were a splendid scarlet red
And tightly laced, with shoes supple and new.
Bold was her face, and fair and red of hue.

314. **sop:** a piece of bread. 316. **Epicurus** (ep′ə·kyoঁor′əs): Greek philosopher (342?–270? B.C.), who taught that happiness is the goal of life. 320. **Saint Julian:** saint of hospitality. 329. **mew** (myoঁo): pen. 330. **bream:** fish. 335. **sessions:** local court sessions. 341. **Wife:** a matron, or married woman. 342. **Bath:** a town in southwest England. 344. **Ypres** (ē′pr′) ... **Ghent** (gent): famous centers of the Flemish wool trade. 346. **going ... her:** preceding her when approaching the church altar. 348. **charity:** good will. 349. **ground:** texture.

The Parson

She was a worthy woman all her life;   355
Five times at church door had she been a wife,
Not counting other company in youth—
But this we need not mention here, in truth.
Thrice at Jerusalem this dame had been,
And many a foreign river she had seen,   360
And she had gone to Rome and to Boulogne,°
To Saint James' in Galicia,° and Cologne.°
Much lore she had from wandering by the way;
Still, she was gap-toothed, I regret to say.
Upon a gentle, ambling nag she sat,   365
Well wimpled, and upon her head a hat
As broad as is a buckler or a targe.°
A mantle hung about her buttocks large
.And on her feet a pair of pointed spurs.
No tongue was readier with a jest than hers.   370
Perhaps she knew love remedies, for she
Had danced the old game long and cunningly.

There was a PARSON, too, that had his cure°
In a small town, a good man and a poor;
But rich he was in holy thought and work.   375
Also he was a learned man, a clerk,
Seeking Christ's gospel faithfully to preach;
Most piously his people would he teach.
Benign and wondrous diligent was he,
And very patient in adversity—   380
Often had he been tried to desperation!
He would not make an excommunication
For tithes° unpaid, but rather would he give—
Helping his poor parishioners to live—

361. **Boulogne** (bo͞o·lōn′): a city in northern France on the English Channel.   362. **Galicia**
(gə·lish′ə): a region in northwest Spain.   **Cologne** (kə·lōn′): a German city on the Rhine River.
367. **targe**: shield, target.   373. **cure**: curacy, parish.   383. **tithes**: church taxes consisting of
one tenth of a person's annual income or production.

From the offerings, or his own small property;   385
In little he would find sufficiency.
Broad was his parish, with houses far apart,
Yet come it rain or thunder he would start
Upon his rounds, in woe or sickness too,
And reach the farthest, poor or well-to-do,   390
Going on foot, his staff within his hand—
Example that his sheep could understand—
Namely, that first he wrought° and after taught.
These words from holy gospel he had brought,
And used to add this metaphor thereto—   395
That if gold rust, what then shall iron do?
For if the priest be bad, in whom we trust,
What wonder is it if a layman rust?
And shame to him—happy the priest who heeds it—
Whose flock is clean when he is soiled who leads it!   400
Surely a priest should good example give,
Showing by cleanness how his sheep should live.
He would not put his benefice to hire,°
Leaving his sheep entangled in the mire,
While he ran off to London, to Saint Paul's,°   405
To take an easy berth, chanting for souls,
Or with some guild° a sinecure° to hold,
But stayed at home and safely kept his fold
From wolves that else had sent it wandering;
He was a shepherd and no hireling.   410
And virtue though he loved, and holiness,
To sinful men he was not pitiless,
Nor was he stern or haughty in his speech,
But wisely and benignly would he teach.
To tempt folk unto heaven by high endeavor   415
And good example was his purpose ever.
But any person who was obstinate,
Whoever he was, of high or low estate,
Him on occasion would he sharply chide;
No better priest doth anywhere reside.   420
He had no thirst for pomp or reverence,
Nor bore too sensitive a consciënce,
But taught Christ's and his twelve apostles' creed,
And first in living of it took the lead.

With him his brother, a simple PLOWMAN, rode,   425
That in his time had carted many a load
Of dung; true toiler and a good was he,
Living in peace and perfect charity.
First he loved God, with all his heart and will,
Always, and whether life went well or ill;   430

---

393. **wrought:** practiced.   403. **put . . . hire:** hire another parson to take over his parish
duties.   405. **Saint Paul's:** famous cathedral in London.   407. **guild** (gild): an association of
merchants. **sinecure** (sī′nə·kyŏor): a position that involves little work or responsibility.

The Miller

And next—and as himself—he loved his neighbor.
And always for the poor he loved to labor,
And he would thresh and ditch and dyke, and take
Nothing for pay, but do it for Christ's sake.   435
Fairly he paid his tithes when they were due,
Upon his goods and on his produce, too.
In plowman's gown he sat astride a mare.

A MILLER and a REEVE were also there.
The MILLER, big alike of bone and muscle,   440
Was a stout fellow, fit for any tussle,
And proved so, winning, everywhere he went,
The prize ram in the wrestling tournament.
He was thick-shouldered, knotty, broad and tough;
There was no door but he could tear it off
Its hasps,° or with his head could butt it through.   445
His beard was red as any fox or sow,
And broad in shape as if it were a spade,
And at his nose's very tip displayed
There sat a wart, on which a tuft of hairs
Rose like the bristles on a red sow's ears;   450
The nostrils underneath were black and wide.
He bore a sword and buckler at his side.
Broad gaped his mouth as some great furnace door.
He would go babbling boastfully, or roar
Coarse jests that reeked of sin and harlotries.   455
And he would steal and charge a buyer thrice;
He had a thumb to cheat the scales, by God!
His costume was a white coat with blue hood.
Upon the bagpipes he could blow a ditty,
And piped us out that morning from the city.   460

445. **hasps:** hinges.

Slender and choleric the REEVE° appeared;
As close as ever he could he shaved his beard;
Around his ears the hair was closely shorn,
And docked on top, the way a priest's is worn;
His legs were long and lean, with no more calf   465
Than ye would find upon a walking staff.
Well could he keep a garner° and a bin;
There was no auditor could do him in.
And he could estimate by drought and rain
What he would get from seed, and how much grain.   470
The horses, swine, and cows his lord possessed,
Stock, dairy, poultry, sheep, and all the rest—
Of all such things this reeve had full control,
And made report by contract on the whole,
Because his lord had yet but twenty years.   475
No man there was could find him in arrears.
No bailiff, herd° or hind° but he could tell
Their shifts and trickeries—he knew them well;
These fellows feared him as they feared their death.
His dwelling stood full fair upon a heath;   480
Green trees made shadow there on all the sward.°
He picked up money better than his lord,
Rich were the hidden stores he called his own.
And he could please his master with a loan
That came from what were justly his own goods,   485
Get thanks, and also get some coats and hoods!
In youth he had applied himself with care
To learn a trade; he was a carpenter.
This reeve upon a stallion had installed him;
He was a dapply gray and Scot he called him.   490
A sky-blue surcoat good of length he wore,
And by his side a rusty blade he bore;
From Norfolk° came this reeve of whom I tell,
Close to a town that men call Baldeswell.
Like to a friar's his dress was tucked about,   495
And ever he rode the hindmost of our rout.

The summoner° brought a noble PARDONER°
Of Roncivalles,° his fellow traveler
And crony, lately from the court at Rome,
Loudly he sang, "Come hither, love, O come!"   500
The summoner bore him bass—a mighty voice:
Never made trumpet half so loud a noise.

---

461. **Reeve** (rēv): estate manager.   467. **garner:** granary.   477. **herd:** herdsman.   **hind:** farm laborer.   481. **sward:** thickly covered grassland.   493. **Norfolk** (nôr′fək): a county in eastern England.   497. **summoner:** another of the pilgrims. Summoners were officials who brought to court offenders against the Church.   **Pardoner:** a preacher who raised money for religious works by soliciting offerings to which indulgences (pardons) were attached. The granting of pardons for offerings was often abused, however, and fake pardoners were not infrequent. 498. **Roncivalles** (ron′sə·valz): the Hospital of Blessed Mary of Roncivalles, a religious institution in London.

The Pardoner

This pardoner had hair yellow as wax,
But smooth it hung, as hangs a hank of flax,
And down in strings about his neck it fell   505
And all about his shoulders spread as well;
Yet thin in wisps it lay there, one by one.
But hood, for jollity, the man would none,
Safe in his wallet° it was packed away;
He thought he kept the fashion of the day;   510
Hair loose, save for his cap, his head was bared.
His bulging eyeballs like a rabbit's glared.
He had a vernicle° sewed on his cap.
His wallet lay before him in his lap,
Brim full of pardons piping hot from Rome.   515
As small as any goat's his voice would come,
Yet no beard had he nor would ever have,
But all his face shone smooth as from a shave;
I think he was a gelding or a mare.
But at his trade, from Berwick unto Ware°   520
There was no pardoner could go his pace.
For in his bag he kept a pillowcase
That was, he said, our Blessed Lady's veil;
He claimed to own the fragment of the sail
That Peter° had the time he walked the sea   525
And Jesu saved him in his clemency.
He had a cross of latten° set with stones,
And in a glass a handful of pig's bones.
But with these relics when he had in hand
Some humble parson swelling in the land,   530
In one day he could get more revenue
Than would the parson in a month or two.

---

509. **wallet**: knapsack. 513. **vernicle** (vûr′nə·kəl): holy relic. 520. **Berwick . . . Ware**: two towns: one in southeastern Scotland, the other outside of London. 525. **Peter**: St. Peter was a fisherman before he became a disciple of Christ. 527. **latten**: a metal resembling brass.

And thus with tricks and artful flattery
He fooled both flock and parson thoroughly.
But let us say, to make the truth less drastic,   535
In church he was a fine ecclesiastic;
Well could he read a lesson or a story,
But best of all he sang an offertory;
For well he knew that when the song was sung,
Then he must preach, and smoothly file his tongue   540
For silver, as he could full cunningly—
Therefore he sang so loud and merrily.

Now in few words I have rehearsed for you
Number, array, and rank, and told you too
Wherefore they came to make a company   545
In Southwark, at this noble hostelry,
The Tabard, standing close beside the Bell.°
But now the time is come when I should tell
Of how we bore ourselves that night when we
Had all alighted at that hostelry;   550
Then shall I say what on the road befell,
And all else of our pilgrimage as well.
But first I pray that in your courtesy
Ye will not deem it my vulgarity
If I am wholly frank in my narration   555
Both of their manners and their conversation,
And give their words exactly as they fell;
For this I know—and ye must know as well—
That whoso tells a tale after a man
He must repeat as closely as he can   560
What has been said, and every word include,
Though much of what he writes be broad and rude;
Else must he make the tale he tells untrue,
Invent, or shape the words of it anew.
None may he spare, not though it be his brother,   565
Nor slight one word more than he does another.
For Christ himself speaks plain in holy writ;
Ye know well there is nothing base in it.
And Plato° says, to any that can read,
The words must be the cousin of the deed.   570
Also I pray that ye will pardon me,
That I have nowise set in their degree
The people in this tale, as they should stand;°
My wit is scant, ye well can understand.
   Great cheer our good host° made us every one,   575
And straightway to the supper set us down,

---

547. **Bell:** another inn.   569. **Plato:** Greek philosopher (427?–347? B.C.). Chaucer could
not read Greek, but he knew Plato through Latin translations.   571–73. **Also . . . stand:**
Chaucer apologizes for the fact that he has not presented his characters in order of their rank, as
would have been considered proper in medieval society.   575. **host:** The host has been almost
certainly identified with a real innkeeper named Harry Bailly, who had an inn at Southwark in
Chaucer's time.

And choicest of his food before us placed;
Strong was the wine and goodly to our taste.
Our host, a seemly man, was fit withal
To be a marshal in a banquet hall,   580
For he was large, with eyes that brightly shone:
In Cheapside° fairer burgess was there none.
Bold of his speech he was, wise and well taught;
In short, in ways of manhood lacked for naught.
Also he was a gladsome, merry man,   585
And when the meal was ended he began
To jest and speak of mirth with other things
(When we had settled all our reckonings),
And thus he said: "Lordings, for certainty
Ye have been welcome here and heartily;   590
For on my word, if I shall tell no lie,
I never saw so merry a company
This year together in my house as now.
Fain would I please you did I know but how.
And now I have bethought me of a way   595
To give you mirth, and ye shall nothing pay.
Ye go to Canterbury—now God speed you!
With good reward the blessèd martyr heed you!
And well I know that, as ye go along
Ye shall tell tales, and turn to play and song,   600
For truly joy or comfort is there none
To ride along the road dumb as a stone;
And therefore I will fashion you some sport
To fill your way with pleasure of a sort.
And now if, one and all, it likes you well   605
To take my judgment as acceptable,
And each to do his part as I shall say,
Tomorrow, as we ride along the way,
Then by the soul of my father that is dead,
Ye shall be merry, or I will give my head!   610
Up with your hands now, and no more of speech!"
Agreement took us little time to reach.
We saw no reason for an argument,
But gave at once and fully our consent,
And bade him shape his verdict as he chose.   615
"Lordings," quoth he, "hear now what I propose,
But take it not, I pray you, in disdain;
This is the point, to speak both brief and plain:
Each one, to make your traveling go well,
Two tales upon this pilgrimage shall tell—   620
Going to Canterbury. And each of you
Journeying home shall tell another two,
Of happenings that long ago befell.
And he of us that best his tales shall tell—
That is, that telleth tales which are the best   625
In profit and in pleasant interest,

582. **Cheapside:** a district of London.

Shall have a supper (we to pay the cost),
Here in this place, sitting beside this post,
When we are come again from Canterbury.
And with design to make you the more merry   630
Myself along with you will gladly ride,
All at my own expense, and be your guide.
And whoso dares my judgment to withsay
Shall pay what we may spend along the way.
And if ye grant the matter shall be so,   635
Tell me without more words, that I may go
And quickly shape my plans to suit your need."
And we assented, and by oath agreed
Gladly, and also prayed our host that he
Would pledge to give his service faithfully—   640
That he would be our governor, and hold
In mind and judge for us the tales we told,
And set a supper at a certain price,
We to be ruled in all by his device,
In things both great and small. So to a man   645
We gave our full agreement to his plan.
And then the wine was fetched, and every guest
Drank of it straightway, and we went to rest,
And there was nothing further of delay.
    And on the morn, with brightening of day,   650
Up rose our host, and busily played the cock,
And gathered us together in a flock,
And forth we rode, just barely cantering,

In this manuscript painting the pilgrims leave the Tabard Inn on their way to Canterbury.

Until we reached St. Thomas' Watering.°
And there it was our host at length drew rein,   655
And said, "Now Lordings, hearken me again;
Here will I call your pact to memory.
If evensong and morningsong agree,°
Let us see now who first begins his tale!
As I may ever drink of wine or ale   660
Whoso rebels at anything I say
Shall stand for all we spend along the way.
Now draw your lots before we take us hence,
And he that draws the shortest shall commence.
Sire knight," he said, "my master and my lord,   665
Draw now your lot, for here ye have my word.
Come near," quoth he, "my lady prioress,
And ye, sir clerk, have done with bashfulness!
Don't study here! Fall to now, every man!"
Then each at once to draw his lot began,   670
And briefly, as to how the matter went,
Whether it were by chance or accident,
The truth is this—the lot fell to the knight;
And all were blithe and there was much delight.
And now in reason he could hardly fail   675
According to the pact, to tell his tale,
As ye have heard—what more is there to say?
And when this good man saw how matters lay,
As one resolved in sense and courtesy,
His compact made, to keep it cheerfully,   680
He said: "Since it is I begin the game,
Come, let the cut be welcome, in God's name!
Now let us ride, and hearken what I say."
And with that word we went upon our way.

654. **St. Thomas' Watering:** a watering place less than two miles from the Tabard Inn.
658. **If . . . agree:** If you feel this morning as you did last night.

FOR STUDY AND DISCUSSION

1. How do Chaucer's descriptions of the external appearance—the physical attributes and dress—of the pilgrims reveal or suggest their inner nature? In which cases does even the horse ridden by a pilgrim give some insight into the character of the rider? Which of the pilgrims do you think Chaucer admired most? Which ones did he not admire? Give reasons for your answers.

2. Note Chaucer's use of comparisons, especially similes, to enhance his descriptions of the pilgrims. For example, the Friar's eyes twinkle "as do the stars upon a frosty night," and the Reeve's leg is no fatter than "a walking staff." What other descriptive comparisons can you find?

3. The eighteenth-century English poet William Blake remarked, "Every age is a Canterbury pilgrimage; we all pass on, each sustaining one or other of these characters." In this statement Blake notes that the various types of characters in Chaucer's *Prologue* are to be found in every society. What modern equivalents of the Merchant and the Oxford Student can you suggest? Describe them. Do the characteristics of any of the other pilgrims suggest any contemporary figures, even though they might belong to a different profession?

CHAUCER'S CHARACTERS

The character sketch goes back as far as the Greek writer Theophrastus, who described not individuals but *types* of characters, such as the greedy man, the superstitious man, and so on. Studying Chaucer's character sketches reveals his ability to depict not only a type—a person typical of his class and occupation—but an individual as well. Notice, for example, in the description of the Knight, that Chaucer indicates not only how well the Knight lives up to the ideals of chivalry, but that he is also a mild-mannered and courteous gentleman who has been tempered by battle.

As we have seen, one method Chaucer used to individualize his characters was to give a description of their physical appearance. Which pilgrims does he portray by describing or suggesting a human foible or frailty? What are these weaknesses? In each case what is Chaucer's attitude toward them—one of tolerance or disapproval? Is Chaucer's satire as he pokes fun at people ever bitter or malicious? Point out examples of satire in the *Prologue* that struck you as particularly sharp appraisals of human weaknesses.

Chaucer also reveals character in his ex-amples of human virtue. Which of the pilgrims arouses admiration because of his noble qualities? What are the specific virtues that Chaucer seems to hold in high esteem?

In describing his characters, Chaucer also discloses a good deal about himself. In which passages does he reveal his tolerance? his sense of humor? his keen observation and love of nature?

FOR COMPOSITION

1. In a carefully planned composition of two paragraphs, compare the characters of the Monk and the Parson, using specific examples to support your general points about their personalities, abilities, and so on.

2. Using Chaucer's methods, write a character sketch about a type of person found in modern society. You may wish to describe a doctor, a lawyer, an industrialist, a teacher, an actor, or someone you know. Write your sketch in either prose or verse.

PRONUNCIATION TABLE

The exact pronunciation of Chaucerian English is a difficult and uncertain matter. Nevertheless, if you follow these rules, you will produce something very close to Chaucer's own pronunciation.

VOWELS

a—always the sound *ah*. It may be prolonged as in *bathëd* (bahth·ed), line 3 of the Prologue, and *maken* (mahken), line 9; or shortened in *at, and*. Note that *a* is never pronounced as in *hate* or *hat* in modern English, but always with the *ah* sound.

ai, ay, ei, ey—as in *day. Veyne*, line 3; *arʀay*, line 41.

au, aw—as in *house. Straungë*, line 13; *Caunterbury*, line 16; *felaweshipe*, line 26.

i, y, long—as in *meet. Nyne*, line 24, and *rydë*, line 27.

oo—usually pronounced like the modern ō. See *sootë*, line 1; *rootë*, line 2.

e, long—as in *hate, they. Sweetë* (swāta), line 5. A vowel doubled is always long. *Eek* (āke), line 5; *breeth* (brāth), line 5.

e, short—as in *men. Hem*, line 11; second syllable of *slepen*, line 10, and *priketh*, line 11.

Note that the final *e,* printed as *ë*—which would usually be silent in modern English, is almost always pronounced in Middle English. Its sound is like the final *a* in modern words. Thus *sootë*, line 1, is like the last two syllables of *Minnesota*.

When the final *e* precedes a vowel or *h,* it is not pronounced, as in line 2, *droghte of March.* In this text the *e* which is to be pronounced as another syllable is indicated thus: ë.

CONSONANTS

Most of the consonants are as in modern English. A few show foreign influence.

g—as in *get*, except in French words before *e* and *i* where it is like *zh. Corages*, line 11; *pilgrimages,* line 12 (similar to *garages* in modern English).

gh, ch—never silent as in modern English. Pronounced like the German *ch* in *nicht. Droghte*, line 2; *nyght*, line 10. In *knyght*, line 42, the *k* is also pronounced as in German (k·nicht). Before a vowel or at the end of a word *ch* is pronounced as in *church.*

c, t—never blended with a following *i* as in modern *condition* or *special;* but the *i* is pronounced as a separate syllable. (*C* has the sound of *s* when it comes before *i.*) *Specially* (four syllables), line 15; *condicioun* (four syllables), line 38.

The Pardoner's Tale

After the Knight begins the pilgrims' game of storytelling by telling a graceful tale of courtly love, a chivalric theme entirely appropriate to its narrator, the Miller, the Reeve, the Prioress, Chaucer himself—each of the pilgrims in turn—tells his tale. The stories related by the pilgrims present an extended revelation of their characters and serve to confirm Chaucer's portrayal of them in the *Prologue*. These tales shed much light on medieval thought and conduct, and most of them leave the reader with some moral, maxim, or timeless piece of wisdom.

Finally it is the Pardoner's turn to entertain the company. He launches into a sermon using as his text: "Greed is the root of all evil." Illustrating his text with an *exemplum,* or illustrative anecdote, he tells the story of three roisterers, which follows below.

> Now these three rioters of whom I tell,
> Long yet ere prime° was rung by any bell,
> Were seated in a tavern at their drinking.
> And as they sat, they heard a death bell clinking
> Before a body going to its grave.   5
> Then roused the one and shouted to his knave—°
> "Be off at once!" he cried. "Run out and spy
> Whose body it may be that passeth by;
> And look thou get his name aright," he cried.
>   "No need, sir—none at all," this boy replied.   10
> "They told me that before ye came, two hours;
> He was, God's name, an old fellow of yours.
> By night, it seems, and sudden was his dying;
> Flat on his bench, all drunken, was he lying,
> When up there crept a thief that men call Death   15
> (Who in this country all the people slay'th)
> And smote his heart asunder with his spear
> And all in silence went his way from here.
> During the plague° he hath a thousand slain,
> And master, ere ye meet him this is plain: 20
> That it is wise and very necessary
> To be prepared for such an adversary,
> Have readiness to meet him evermore;
> So taught my mother—now I say no more."
> "Yes, by Saint Mary," said the taverner,   25
> "The boy speaks true, for he hath slain this year

---

2. **prime:** sometime between the hours of 6:00 and 9:00 A.M.   6. **knave** (nāv): a male servant; here, a tavern boy.   19. **plague** (plāg): the dread disease, also known as the Black Death, that killed almost half the population of England in 1348 and 1349.

From the *Prologue,* beginning on page 44, "A KNIGHT there was, . . ." to page 61 ". . . we went upon our way." and "The Pardoner's Tale" from Chaucer's *The Canterbury Tales,* edited by Frank E. Hill. Published as a Tartan Paperback by David McKay Company, Inc. Reprinted by permission of the publishers.

Woman and child and man in yonder town,
And page and villain he hath smitten down.
I hold his habitation must be there.
Great wisdom were it that a man beware—   30
Lest he some fearful injury incur."
"Yea, by God's arms," replied this rioter.
"Is he so perilous a knave° to meet?
Now will I seek him both by way and street,
Upon the bones of God I make a vow!   35
Fellows, we three are one—then hear me now:
Let each of us hold up his hand to th' other,
And each of us become the other's brother;
And we will slay this faithless traitor Death—
He shall be slain, he that so many slay'th,   40
Yea, by God's dignity, ere it be night!"
      And so all three together made their plight°
To live and die each one of them for other,
As though he had been born the other's brother.
And in this drunken passion forth they started,   45
And toward that very village they departed
Of which the tavernkeeper spoke before.
And then full many a grisly oath they swore,
And rent the Savior's body limb from limb—°
Death should be dead if they discovered him!   50
When they had traveled hardly half a mile,
Just as they would have stepped across a stile,°
They chanced to meet a poor and aged man.
This old man meekly spake, and thus began
To greet them: "May God look upon you, sirs!"   55
      The greatest braggart of these rioters
Replied: "Now curse thee, churl!° What, where apace?°
Why all wrapped up and hidden save thy face?
How darest thou live so long in Death's defy?"
      Straightway this old man looked him in the eye   60
And answered thus: "Because I cannot meet
A man, by country way or city street,
Though unto Ind° I made a pilgrimage,
Willing to give his youth and take my age!
So must I have my age in keeping still,   65
As long a time, indeed, as God shall will.
      "Nor Death, alas! will have my life from me;
So like a wretch I wander restlessly
And on the ground, which is my mother's gate,
Knock with my staff and cry both early and late,   70
'Mother, belovèd Mother, let me in!
See how I wither, flesh and blood and skin;

33. **knave:** here, scoundrel, rogue. 42. **plight:** pledge. 49. **rent ... limb:** In swearing,
they used expressions such as "God's arms" and "Upon the bones of God" (e.g., lines 32 and
35). 52. **stile:** a series of steps on each side of a fence or wall. 57. **churl** (chûrl): peasant.
apace: at a quick pace, hurrying. 63. **Ind:** India.

Alas my bones! When shall they be at rest?
Mother, how gladly would I change my. chest°
That in my room so long a time hath been—   75
Yea, for a haircloth° I could wrap me in!'
But yet she will not do me this poor grace.
Wherefore all pale and withered is my face.
　　"But, sirs, ye lack in common courtesy
That to an aged man speak villainy°   80
When he hath sinned neither in word nor deed.
For well in holy writings may ye read,
'Before an aged man, whose hair is gray,
Ye should arise'; and therefore thus I say:
To an old man no hurt or evil do,   85
No more than ye would have men do to you
In your old age, if ye so long abide.
And God be with you, where ye walk or ride—
I must be gone where I have need to go."
　　"Nay now, old rogue! By God, thou shalt not so!"   90
Answered another rioter anon;
"Thou partest not so lightly, by Saint John!
Thou spake right now of that same traitor Death
That in this country all our comrades slay'th;
Have here my word: thou art a spy of his!   95
Then take the worst, or tell us where he is,
By God and by the Holy Sacrament!
For truly, thou art of his covenant,°
To slay young folk like us, thou false intriguer!"
　　"Now, sirs," he answered, "since ye be so eager   100
To find this Death, turn up that crooked way;
There in yon wood I left him, sooth to say,
Under a tree, and there he will abide.
Not for your boasting will he run and hide.
See ye that oak tree? Ye shall find him there.   105
God, that redeemed mankind, save you and spare,
And better you!" Thus spoke this aged man;
And toward the tree these drunken rascals ran
All three, and there, about its roots, they found
Of golden florins,° minted fine and round,   110
Well nigh eight bushels lying, as they thought.
No longer then the traitor Death they sought,
But each was made so happy by the sight
Of all those florins shining fair and bright
That down they sat beside the precious hoard.   115
The worst of them was first to speak his word.
　　"Brothers," he said, "take heed of what I say;
My wit is great, although I jest and play!
Fortune hath found it fit to give this treasure
That we may live our lives in lust° and pleasure;   120

74. **chest:** chest for clothes.　76. **haircloth:** here, a shroud.　80. **villainy** (vil′ən·ē) rudely.
98. **of his covenant:** in agreement with him.　110. **florins:** gold coins.　120. **lust:** merriment,
delight.

Lightly it comes—so shall it melt away!
God's dignity! Who would have dreamed today
That we should have so fine and fair a grace?
But could the gold be carried from this place
Home to my house, or else to one of yours—   125
For well we know that all this gold is ours—
Then were we in a high felicity!°
But such a thing by day could never be;
Men would proclaim us thieves and cause our seizure;
Might even make us hang for our own treasure!   130
This gold must then be carried hence by night
With secrecy and cautious oversight.°
Wherefore I say, draw lot among us all,
And let us mark the way the lot shall fall;
And he that draws it shall with willing heart   135
And nimble pace toward the town depart,
And fetch in secret wine and bread, and we
That stay behind shall guard full carefully
This gold; and if our comrade does not tarry,
When it is night we will this treasure carry   140
Wherever by agreement shall be planned."
Then one held out the lots within his hand,
And bade them draw, and look where it would fall;
And it fell on the youngest of them all,
And so by compact toward the town he started.   145
And scarce a moment after he departed
The one of them spoke slyly to the other:
"Thou know'st well thou art sworn to be my brother;
Now something to thy profit will I say.
Thou see'st our fellow takes himself away;   150
And here is gold, and that great quantity,
That shall be portioned out among us three.
Nevertheless, if I could shape it so
That we should share it all between us two,
Had I not done a comrade's turn by thee?"   155
    The other said: "But that could never be!
He knows we two are here and guard the gold;
What could we do? What wouldst thou have him told?"
    "Shall what I say be secret?" asked the first;
"Then shortly shall the method be rehearsed   160
Whereby I think to bring it well about."
"Agreed," replied the other, "out of° doubt
I will betray thee not, as God is true."
    "Now," said the first, "thou know'st that we are two,
And two of us are mightier than one.   165
Watch when he sits, then go as if in fun—
As thou wouldst play about with him, and grip him,
And with my dagger through his sides I'll rip him,

127. **were . . . felicity:** we'd all be in the best of luck. 132. **oversight:** supervision. 162. **out of:** without.

While thou art struggling with him, as in play;
And see thou use thy knife the selfsame way.   170
Then all this treasure shall belong to none,
My dearest friend, but me and thee alone!
Then may we sate our lusts until we tire
And play at dice whenever we desire!"
And thus these rascals have devised a way   175
To slay the third, as ye have heard me say.

   This youngest, he that journeyed to the town,
Within his heart rolled often up and down
The beauty of these florins new and bright.
"O Lord!" quoth he, "If it were so I might   180
Have all this treasure to myself alone,
There liveth no man underneath the throne
Of God, that might exist more merrily
Than I!" And so the fiend,° our enemy,
Put in his head that he should poison buy   185
Wherewith to make his two companions die;
Because the fiend found him in such a state
That he had leave° his fall to consummate,
For it was out of doubt his full intent
To slay them both, and never to repent!   190
So forth he goes—no longer will he tarry—
Unto the town, to an apothecary,
And prays° for poison to exterminate
Some rats, and pole cats that had robbed of late
His roosts—and he would wreak° him, if he might,   195
On vermin that tormented him by night.

   Then this apothecary, answering:
"God save my soul, but thou shalt have a thing
That, let a living creature drink or eat
No bigger portion than a grain of wheat,   200
And he shall die, and that in shorter while,
By God, than thou wouldst take to walk a mile—
This poison is so strong and violent."

   All on his cursèd wickedness intent,
This rascal ran as fast as he could fly,   205
Bearing the poison, to a street near by,
And got three bottles of a man he knew;
And then he poured his poison in the two,
But in the third, his own, put none at all.
For all the night he thought to heave and haul   210
Carrying gold—then would he slake° his thirst.
And so this rascal (may he be accurst!)
Filled all his bottles full of wine; and then
Back to his fellows he repaired again.

   What need is there to sermon of it more?   215
For just as they had planned his death before,

---

    184. **fiend:** devil. 188. **leave:** permission. 193. **prays:** begs. 195. **wreak:** get even.
211. **slake:** quench.

They slew him now, and quickly. Then the one
Spoke to the other after it was done:
"Now let us eat and drink and make us merry,
And afterward we will his body bury."   220
And so by chance he drank, that very minute,
Out of a bottle with the poison in it,
And gave his comrade drink when he was through,
From which in little while they died, the two.
    But truly Avicenna,° I suppose,   225
Wrote never in his canons of such throes°
And wondrous agonies of poisoning
As these two wretches had in perishing.
Thus died these murderers of whom I tell,
And he who falsely poisoned them as well.   230

225. **Avicenna** (av′ə·sen′ə): Arabic physician and philosopher (980–1037).   226. **throes:** torments, violent pains.

FOR STUDY AND DISCUSSION

1. What do you learn about the three companions at the beginning of the tale (lines 1–41) that makes you expect they will meet a bad end? Is it appropriate that the man whose death bell they hear is an old comrade of the three men? Explain.

2. The boy at the tavern advises "That it is wise and very necessary/ To be prepared for such an adversary,/ Have readiness to meet him evermore." In what way do the three men fail to understand this advice? How are the characters of the three men revealed by their failure to understand the boy's advice? by their roistering? by their treatment of the old man?

3. The three men make a vow "To live and die each one of them for other." In the light of what happens, how does this vow have a double meaning?

4. The old man whom the three comrades meet on the road is a rather mysterious figure, since apparently he cannot die and is able to tell the three men where to find Death. What is his significance? Is he merely an old man, or is he a symbolic figure? Why do you think Chaucer brings him into the tale at all instead of merely having the men go to the tree and find the gold?

5. How do you think Chaucer expected his readers to react to the attitude of the three comrades toward the new-found treasure, as expressed in lines 119–21? What is your opinion of this attitude?

6. How does line 155 bring out the irony in the vow of comradeship made by the three men?

7. The moral of this tale is *Radix malorum est cupiditas:* the root of evil is greed. Point out lines that emphasize the greediness of the three men.

8. After the Pardoner concludes his tale, he resumes his sermon against greed and proceeds to offer his fellow travelers, for a proper fee, pardons and his store of "authentic" relics of pigs' bones and rags. What ironic parallel can thus be drawn between the Pardoner and the theme of his tale?

9. "The Pardoner's Tale" has often been cited as an example of a perfect short story. What qualities that you would expect to find in a good short story do you find in this tale? In what ways is this tale different from a modern short story?

FOR COMPOSITION

Medieval readers recognized "The Pardoner's Tale" as an *exemplum*, a tale inserted into a sermon to illustrate a moral. In this case, the moral is, of course, "Greed is the root of all evil."

Write your own exemplum, a tale illustrating a common saying such as "A stitch in time saves nine," or "A fool and his money are soon parted." Remember while you are writing, that much of the effectiveness of an exemplum depends on a good choice of details.

SIR THOMAS MALORY

(?–1471)

Thomas Malory wrote *Morte d'Arthur* ("Death of Arthur") in a prison cell. The charges against him ranged from extortion, robbery, and cattle rustling, to "waylaying the Duke of Buckingham." It is possible, however, that few of the crimes were real. He was, after all, a Lancastrian in a time of Yorkist ascendancy, and the law is ever a ready weapon to those in power. In fact, in 1468 when two general amnesties were declared by King Edward IV, Malory, unlike the other prisoners in jail at the time, was not set free. This may indicate that Malory had been singled out as a particular enemy by the Crown because of his opposing role in the War of the Roses.

Born around 1400, Malory left his family's seat in Warwickshire and entered upon a distinguished career. He fought in the Hundred Years' War and was elected to Parliament in 1445. It was during the days of civil disorder that preceded the Wars of the Roses that his fortune took a downward course from which it never recovered. Malory apparently tried to regain land that was rightfully his, and was arrested and indicted on a wide variety of offenses, which appear to have been committed between 1451 and 1452. Although he pleaded not guilty to all charges brought against him, and his actual guilt is in doubt, Malory was far from a peaceful, law-abiding citizen and very much a part of the turbulent times in which he lived. He once engineered an escape from prison by swimming across a moat and, together with a band of followers, terrorized a nearby abbey for two days. It is thought that he was serving a twenty-year prison term when he wrote *Morte d'Arthur* and that he remained in jail until his death in 1471, one year after completing his great work. Malory's literary achievement was the compilation, arrangement, and rewriting from the original Latin, French, and English sources, of the tales of King Arthur and the knights of his Round Table. These he linked together under the title *Morte d'Arthur*, a work which stands as the last great collection of medieval romances.

Malory was fortunate to have been a contemporary of William Caxton, author, translator, editor, and the man who introduced printing into England. The debt of English literature to Caxton is immeasurable. Over a hundred books are known to have been printed and sometimes translated in his shop, among them *The Canterbury Tales* and *Morte d'Arthur*. Caxton first published the latter in 1485, adding a preface which provided historical background to the legend of King Arthur.

Morte d'Arthur, a faithful representation of chivalric ideals and medieval life and thought, has inspired later writers to treat the same theme. Malory's serious approach to the romantic world of gentle knights and fair ladies, however, stands in direct contrast to the lighter treatment of this theme in books such as *A Connecticut Yankee in King Arthur's Court* by Mark Twain, *Galahad* by John Erskine, and *The Once and Future King* by T. H. White.

Morte d'Arthur

While there are no contemporary records to prove the truth of the Arthurian legends, the many ancient songs and stories celebrating the reign of Arthur suggest that such a man truly existed. However, although in his preface to *Morte d'Arthur,* William Caxton offered to skeptics what he considered proof of Arthur's existence, the real King Arthur remains shrouded in mystery, and it can be assumed only that he was a Celtic chieftain of the sixth century, known for his wisdom and courage.

Early sources indicate that King Arthur and his knights—Galahad, Gawain, and the others—were not originally the romantic figures that appear in Malory's story. These heroes came into Norman minstrelsy from twelfth-century poetic accounts. In these tales Arthur and his Celtic earls were rough heroes in the epic tradition of *Beowulf.* As time passed, however, an enormous body of chivalric romance grew up around them, and the rude Celtic heroes became marvelously refined. Every circumstance of their lives was embellished with ceremony. Arthur's exploits were enlarged, a round table was established for his counsel, and to his circle of knights a French knight was added, the renowned Launcelot.

Morte d'Arthur was written in a time of transition. The feudal order was dying. By the time Malory began writing his story, soldiers were fighting with gunpowder, a middle class of tradesmen was arising, and the practices of chivalry were being superseded by a new aristocratic code. Malory, in a desire to escape the disorder and uneasiness of his day, tried to recapture lost ideals of the romantic past as recounted in his tale of noble kings, adventurous knights, and damsels in distress.

Malory's tale begins with the mysterious birth of Arthur and ends with his equally mysterious death. The central concern is with the adventures of Arthur and his famous knights of the Round Table—a group dedicated to the ideal of moral and spiritual perfection afforded by the union of the knightly code of courage and loyalty and the monastic code of chastity and purity. The knights fight many battles and win much glory, all of which is a credit to the name of King Arthur.

Near the end of the story, however, the tide of good fortune turns. Launcelot falls in love with Arthur's queen, Guinevere, and the lady returns his love. One by one the other knights become discontented, selfish, or disillusioned. Thus weakened, the kingdom is attacked by force under Sir Mordred, Arthur's treacherous nephew, and ultimately it goes down in defeat. Arthur is borne away on a barge by three mysterious ladies of Avalon.

In the following account young Arthur, guided by his faithful companion Merlin, the court magician, receives his sword Excalibur from the Lady of the Lake. Because the various legends of King Arthur arose at different points in time, it is not unusual to find many contradictory episodes in Malory's story. For example, elsewhere in *Morte d'Arthur* Arthur receives his sword as a boy when one day he pulls it from a block of stone, thus proving his right to rule England.

The following selection, told in Malory's simple and distinctive prose though modernized in spelling, relates an incident that occurred when Arthur was a young man and still in the initial stages of proving himself the epitome of the chivalric ideal. The aura of romance and mystery that is so characteristic of the medieval period is in full evidence here.

HOW ARTHUR FOUGHT WITH KING PELLINORE AND HOW MERLIN SAVED ARTHUR'S LIFE, AND ARTHUR BY THE MEAN OF MERLIN GAT HIS SWORD EXCALIBUR.

THEN ON THE DAY there came in the court a squire on horseback, leading a knight before him wounded to the death, and told him how there was a knight in the forest had reared up a pavilion [1] by a well and hath slain my master, a good knight,

---

[1] **pavilion** (pə·vil′yən): a tent.

his name was Miles; wherefore I beseech you that my master may be buried, and that some knight may revenge my master's death. Then the noise was great of that knight's death in the court, and every man said his advice. Then came Griflet that was but a squire, and he was but young, of the age of the king Arthur, so he besought the king for all his service that he had done him to give the order of knighthood.

Thou art full young and tender of age, said Arthur, for to take so high an order on thee.

Sir, said Griflet, I beseech you to make me knight.

Sir, said Merlin, it were great pity to lose Griflet, for he will be a passing [1] good man when he is of age, abiding with you the term of his life. And if he adventure his body with yonder knight at the fountain, it is in great peril if ever he come again, for he [2] is one of the best knights of the world, and the strongest man of arms.

Well,[3] said Arthur.

So at the desire of Griflet, the king made him knight.

Now, said Arthur unto Sir Griflet, sith [4] I have made you knight thou might give me a gift.

What ye will, said Griflet.

Thou shalt promise me by the faith of thy body, when thou hast jousted with the knight at the fountain, whether it fall [5] ye be on foot or on horseback, that right so ye shall come again unto me without making any more debate.

I will promise you, said Griflet, as you desire. Then took Griflet his horse in great haste, and dressed his shield [6] and took a spear in his hand, and so he rode a great wallop till he came to the fountain, and thereby he saw a rich pavilion, and thereby under a cloth stood a fair horse well saddled and bridled, and on a tree a shield of divers colors and a great spear. Then Griflet smote on the shield with the butt of his spear, that the shield fell down to the ground.

With that the knight came out of the pavilion, and said, Fair knight, why smote ye down my shield?

For [7] I will joust with you, said Griflet.

It is better ye do not, said the knight, for ye are but young, and late made knight, and your might is nothing to mine.

As for that, said Griflet, I will joust with you.

That is me loath, said the knight, but sith I must needs, I will dress me thereto.

Of whence be ye? said the knight.

Sir, I am of Arthur's court.

So the two knights ran together that Griflet's spear all to-shivered; and therewithal he smote Griflet through the shield and the left side and brake the spear, and the truncheon [8] stuck in his body, that horse and knight fell down.

When the knight saw him lie so on the ground, he alighted, and was passing heavy,[9] for he weened [10] he had slain him, and then he unlaced his helm and gat him wind, and so with the truncheon he set him on his horse, and so betook him to God,[11] and said he had a mighty heart, and if he might live he would prove a passing good knight. And so Sir Griflet rode to the court, where great dole [12] was made for him. But through good leeches [13] he was healed and saved.

Then King Arthur was passingly wroth for the hurt of Sir Griflet. And so he commanded a privy man of his chamber that ere it be day his best horse and armor,

---

[1] **passing:** exceedingly.

[2] **he:** the knight at the fountain.

[3] **Well:** It is well, or so be it. Arthur is replying to Griflet's request, not to Merlin.

[4] **sith:** since.

[5] **fall:** happen.

[6] **dressed his shield:** took up his shield in position for combat.

[7] **For:** because.

[8] **truncheon** (trun'chən): spear shaft.

[9] **passing heavy:** exceedingly grieved; weighed down with sorrow.

[10] **weened:** supposed.

[11] **betook him to God:** left him to the care of God.

[12] **dole:** grieving.

[13] **leeches:** doctors.

with all that longeth [1] unto his person, be without the city or tomorrow day.[2] Right so on tomorrow day he met with his man and his horse, and so mounted up and dressed his shield and took his spear, and bade his chamberlain tarry there till he came again. And so Arthur rode a soft pace till it was day, and then was he ware of three churls [3] chasing Merlin, and would have slain him. Then the king rode unto them, and bade them: Flee, churls! then were they afeard when they saw a knight, and fled. O Merlin, said Arthur, here hadst thou been slain for all thy crafts [4] had I not been.

Nay, said Merlin, not so, for I could save myself an [5] I would: and thou art more near thy death than I am, for thou goest to the deathward, an God be not thy friend.

So as they went thus talking they came to the fountain, and the rich pavilion there by it. Then King Arthur was ware where sat a knight armed in a chair.

Sir knight, said Arthur, for what cause abidest thou here, that there may no knight ride this way but if he joust with thee? I rede thee leave [6] that custom, said Arthur.

This custom, said the knight, have I used and will use maugre [7] who saith nay, and who is grieved with my custom let him amend it that will.

I will amend it, said Arthur.

I shall defend [8] thee, said the knight. Anon [9] he took his horse and dressed his shield and took a spear, and they met so hard either in other's shields, that all to-shivered their spears. Therewith anon Arthur pulled out his sword.

Nay, not so, said the knight; it is fairer,

said the knight, that we run more together with sharp spears.

I will well, said Arthur, an I had any more spears.

I have enow, said the knight; so there came a squire and brought two good spears, and Arthur chose one and he another; so they spurred their horses and came together with all their mights, that either brake their spears to their hands. Then Arthur set hand on his sword.

Nay, said the knight, ye shall do better; ye are a passing good jouster as ever I met withal, and for the love of the high order of knighthood let us joust once again.

I assent me, said Arthur.

Anon there were brought two great spears, and every knight gat a spear, and therewith they ran together that Arthur's spear all to-shivered. But the other knight hit him so hard in the midst of the shield that horse and man fell to the earth, and therewith Arthur was eager and pulled out his sword and said, I will assay [10] thee, sir knight, on foot, for I have lost the honor on horseback. Then the knight alighted and dressed his shield unto Arthur. And there began a strong battle with many great strokes, and so hewed with their swords that the cantels [11] flew in the fields. So at the last they smote together that both their swords met even together. But the sword of the knight smote King Arthur's sword in two pieces, wherefore he was heavy.

Then said the knight unto Arthur, Thou art in my danger whether me list to save thee or slay thee, and but thou yield thee as overcome and recreant,[12] thou shalt die.

As for death, said King Arthur, welcome be it when it cometh, but to yield me unto thee as recreant I had liefer die than to be so shamed. And therewithal the king leapt unto Pellinore,[13] and took him by the

---

[1] **longeth:** belongs.

[2] **without . . . day:** outside the city before daylight tomorrow.

[3] **churls:** peasants.

[4] **crafts:** magic arts.

[5] **an:** if.

[6] **rede thee leave:** advise you to give up.

[7] **maugre** (mô'gər): in spite of.

[8] **defend:** prohibit, prevent.

[9] **Anon:** at once.

[10] **assay** (ə·sā'): test, try.

[11] **cantels** (kan'təlz): pieces or fragments cut or sliced off, presumably from their shields.

[12] **but . . . recreant** (rek'rē·ənt): unless you admit that you are defeated and a coward.

[13] **Pellinore:** the knight of the fountain.

middle and threw him down, and raced off [1] his helm. When the knight felt that, he was adread, and anon he brought Arthur unto him, for he was a passing big man of might, and raced off his helm and would have smitten off his head.

Then came Merlin and said, Knight, hold thy hand, for an thou slay that knight thou puttest this realm in the greatest damage that ever was realm: for this knight is a man of more worship than thou wotest of. [2]

Why, who is he? said the knight.

It is King Arthur.

Then would he have slain him for dread of his wrath, and heaved up his sword, and therewith Merlin cast an enchantment to the knight, that he fell to the earth in a great sleep. Then Merlin took up King Arthur and rode forth on the knight's horse.

Alas! said Arthur, what hast thou done, Merlin? Hast thou slain this good knight by thy crafts? There liveth not so worshipful a knight as he was; I had liefer than the stint of my land a year that he were alive. [3]

Care ye not, said Merlin, for he is wholer than ye; for he is but asleep, and will awake within three hours. I told you, said Merlin, what a knight he was; here had ye been slain had I not been.

Right so the king and he departed, and went unto an hermit that was a good man and a great leech. So the hermit searched all his wounds and gave him good salves; so the king was there three days, and then were his wounds well amended that he might ride and go, and so departed. And as they rode, Arthur said, I have no sword.

No force, [4] said Merlin, hereby is a sword that shall be yours, an I may.

So they rode till they came to a lake, the which was a fair water and broad, and in the midst of the lake Arthur was ware of

Arthur receives his sword from the Lady of the Lake. Drawing by Aubrey Beardsley.

an arm clothed in white samite, [5] that held a fair sword in that hand.

Lo! said Merlin, yonder is that sword that I spake of. With that they saw a damsel going upon the lake.

What damsel is that? said Arthur.

That is the Lady of the Lake, said Merlin; and within that lake is a rock, and therein is as fair a place as any on earth, and richly beseen; [6] and this damsel will come to you anon, and then speak ye fair to her that she will give you that sword. Anon withal came the damsel unto Arthur, and saluted him, and he her again.

Damsel, said Arthur, what sword is that, that yonder the arm holdeth above the water? I would it were mine, for I have no sword.

Sir Arthur, king, said the damsel, that sword is mine, and if ye will give me a gift when I ask it you, ye shall have it.

---

[1] **raced off:** tore off.

[2] **more ... wotest of:** more importance than you know.

[3] **liefer ... alive:** I had rather have him alive than have a year's income from my land.

[4] **No force:** no matter.

[5] **samite** (sā′mĭt): heavy silk, interwoven with gold and silver.

[6] **beseen:** decorated.

By my faith, said Arthur, I will give you what gift ye will ask.

Well! said the damsel, go ye into yonder barge, and row yourself to the sword, and take it and the scabbard with you, and I will ask my gift when I see my time. So Sir Arthur and Merlin alighted and tied their horses to two trees, and so they went into the ship, and when they came to the sword that the hand held, Sir Arthur took it up by the handles and took it with him, and the arm and the hand went under the water. And so they came unto the land and rode forth.

Then Sir Arthur looked on the sword and liked it passing well.

Whether [1] liketh you better, said Merlin, the sword or the scabbard?

Me liketh better the sword, said Arthur.

Ye are more unwise, said Merlin, for the scabbard is worth ten of the sword, for whiles ye have the scabbard upon you, ye shall never lose no blood, be ye never so sore wounded; therefore keep well the scabbard always with you. So they came unto Carlion, [2] whereof his knights were passing glad. And when they heard of his adventures, they marveled that he would jeopard [3] his person so, alone. But all men of worship said it was merry to be under such a chieftain that would put his person in adventure as other poor knights did.

[1] **Whether:** which.

[2] **Carlion:** Arthur's residence, which has been identified with the modern town of Caerleon in southwest England.

[3] **jeopard** (jep'ərd): risk.

FOR STUDY AND DISCUSSION

1. Why do you suppose Malory has Merlin avoid using magic against the "churls" who attack him and lets Arthur rescue him instead? Is Arthur's stature as a hero and leader lessened by his defeat at Pellinore's hands? Do you think that it is appropriate that Merlin, a person of special powers and wisdom, rescues Arthur? In what ways has Arthur proven himself worthy of Excalibur in this selection?

2. What do you learn from this selection about the medieval standards of conduct which the code of chivalry demanded? How does this confirm what you already have learned from Chaucer's description of the Knight (page 44)?

3. What difference in setting, tone, character, and theme can you distinguish in *Beowulf* and *Morte d'Arthur?*

LANGUAGE AND VOCABULARY

In *The Canterbury Tales* and *Morte d'Arthur* we have two vivid examples of the intermingling of Norman-French and Anglo-Saxon. In Chaucer we find graceful and courtly French terms such as *chivalrye, sovereyn,* and *gentil* set in direct contrast to more basic everyday words of the Anglo-Saxon language such as *coppe, eek, londes, ech,* and *yong.* In *Morte d'Arthur,* words such as *wroth, churls,* and *wotest* seem quite harsh beside French words such as *pavilion* and *chamberlain,* for example.

Meanings, like customs, vary according to time, place, and situation. Today changes in meaning take different forms. Words may become generalized and extended, or specialized and restricted. Thus, a mill today is no longer just a place to grind grain, but a place to make things by any process; and corn no longer refers to all grains, but in the United States simply means maize. Then too, words may take on positive or negative connotations and meanings so that *churl,* once defined as "peasant," now refers to a rude and surly person. The following list of words of French derivation is taken from the works of Chaucer and Malory. Using your dictionary for reference, explain the change in meaning that has taken place in each word since its original use in Old French. Which of the types of change mentioned above does each represent?

jeopardy	gentle	assay
recreant	charity	bachelor
company	sanguine	adventure

FOR COMPOSITION

1. Indicate the qualities, such as courage, wisdom, consideration, that a great leader should have. Then show how Beowulf and King Arthur measure up to this ideal picture of a great leader.

2. In a brief composition, tell what you learned from the selections in this unit about the literature, the customs and society, and the ideals and beliefs of the Middle Ages.

THE GROWTH OF THE ENGLISH LANGUAGE

The Middle English Period

A great deal happened to our language between the time of *Beowulf* and the time of *The Canterbury Tales*. If you compare the lines in Old English that are printed on page 23 with the selections in Chaucer's Middle English on pages 43–44, you will see that Chaucer's language is on the whole understandable to a modern reader —whereas the Old English lines are incomprehensible, except for a few scattered words.

The differences between Old English and the English of Chaucer's time were a result of striking changes both in the grammatical system and in the vocabulary of the language. The most noticeable change in the grammatical system was the disappearance of most grammatical endings on words. As an example, look at the various forms of the expression "the day" in Old English and in Chaucer's English.

OLD ENGLISH

	Singular	*Plural*
Nominative	se dæg	tha dagas
Genitive	thæs dæges	thara daga
Dative	thæm dæge	thæm dagum
Accusative	thone dæg	tha dagas
Instrumental	thy dæge	thæm dagum

MIDDLE ENGLISH

	Singular	*Plural*
Nominative, Accusative	the day	the dayes
Genitive	the dayes	

A glance at the listing above shows that in Middle English the system of grammatical endings had been greatly simplified. We do not know exactly why the Old English grammatical endings changed or disappeared. One reason, however, was probably the tendency in spoken English to slur over unaccented syllables, leaving out unimportant sounds.

From the point of view of language historians, it is these grammatical changes that mark the division between Old English and Middle English. The Norman Conquest did not have a direct influence on these changes: they had begun to take place about a century before the Conquest, and they were essentially complete within about a century after it.

The Conquest did, however, have a great influence on the changes in vocabulary that took place during the Middle English period. The Normans brought the French language into England; and, by the close of the Middle English period, more than 10,000 French words had been assimilated into English.

The rate of borrowing was slow at first. During the first two centuries following the Conquest, French remained the language of the Norman rulers and English the language of the common people. The two groups did not intermingle to any great extent. Only about 900 French words are known to have made their way into English during this time, and many of those words were of the kind that people of the humbler classes would be likely to learn from their masters—words like *dame, sir, noble,* and *servant.*

The overwhelming flow of French words into English began about the middle of the thirteenth century. Political ties between England and Normandy were cut at this time, and the Normans who stayed in England began to consider themselves English. Most of them learned English and began using it in their daily affairs. Landowners, government officials, judges, and lawyers gradually began to conduct their transactions in English instead of French. In changing to English from French, however, they continued to employ a great many French terms.

Some of these were terms for which there were no exact equivalents in English—for instance, governmental terms such as *parliament, council,* and *mayor.* But many of the other terms introduced from French at this time were commonplace words like *people, city, village, air, river, carry, join, move,* and *push.* Of course, there were already words in English to express these ideas. What happened to the native vocabulary when this flood of French words poured into the language? Sometimes a French word completely replaced the English word. French *people,* for instance, soon replaced English *leod.* Very often, however, the words from both languages continued in use. We thus have French *city* along with the native English *borough,* French *village* along with the native English *town,* and so forth.

Although French was the chief language from which Middle English derived new words, it was not the only one. Churchmen and scholars of the period continued to borrow words from Latin, just as their Anglo-Saxon predecessors had done. Another source of new words was opened when trade sprang up between England and the Low Countries during the late Middle Ages. A number of our commercial terms—for instance, *freight* and *mart*—were borrowed from Dutch or Flemish at this time.

One extremely significant development that took place in Middle English was the gradual adoption of a standard written language. During the early part of the period, there was no such thing as "standard English": people wrote in their own local dialects and spelled according to their own pronunciations. From about 1400 on, however, people in all parts of England tended to make their written English conform to the usage of the London dialect. Local differences continued to exist in the spoken language, but they practically disappeared from written English.

The passages by Chaucer (pages 43–44) and Malory (pages 70–74) represent the London dialect of Middle English at somewhat different historical stages. The ballads on pages 36–38 are not in Middle English (Middle English versions no longer exist), but in a dialect directly descended from the Middle English dialect of northern England and southern Scotland. Although this dialect is still spoken in parts of Scotland, it is rarely used today as a written language. English-speaking people the world over now write the standard language that developed from the London dialect of Chaucer's day.

FOR STUDY AND DISCUSSION

1. As we have seen, Middle English often borrowed a French word for which there was already a corresponding word in English. In such cases, it frequently happened that one of the two words continued to be used in a general sense while the other developed a more limited or specialized meaning. Look up the following pairs of words in an unabridged dictionary or a college dictionary. Which word in each pair came from French, and which from Old English? Which is the more general word in each pair, and which is more limited?

anoint	deem	house
smear	judge	mansion

2. Because the educated people tended to borrow words from Latin, Middle English sometimes acquired not only a French equivalent but also a Latin equivalent for a native English term. In cases where all three words have remained in use, sometimes the Latin word has continued to sound a little more bookish or high-flown than the other two. In the following sets of synonyms, one word in each set entered Middle English from Old English, one entered from French, and one entered directly from Latin. Using a dictionary, find out the language from which each word came into Middle English. For these sets, do you think it is true that the Latin word seems more high-flown than the other two? Explain.

belief, credo, faith
royal, kingly, regal

THE ELIZABETHAN AGE

(1485–1625)

ENGLAND's Elizabethan Age was created partly by a general European movement that we call the Renaissance. The term Renaissance refers to the rebirth or reawakening of interest in Europe in the culture of ancient Greece and Rome. The movement started in Italy in the fourteenth century and spread gradually throughout the western world. The Renaissance did not destroy the Middle Ages, as is often suggested, so much as it built from that period what we think of as a new age. Where the Middle Ages had related people to God, the Renaissance concentrated more on human nature itself. In this less strictly ordered, looser form of society, an age of extraordinarily gifted and brilliant individuals developed, probably not to be matched, especially in their versatility, by people in any other age. Indeed, the "ideal" of the Renaissance was the "complete man," a scholar, poet, and gentleman accomplished both in the world of action and the world of contemplation. Sir Philip Sidney (see page 93) was considered just such a man by his contemporaries.

THE RENAISSANCE

Many important things happened almost simultaneously to bring about this Renaissance. First, the capture of Constantinople (1453) by the Turks drove many Greek scholars to take refuge in Italy, there to revive classical learning. Then there was the invention of printing by movable metal types, which enormously increased the production and spread of books. The development of banking, capital investment, and letters of credit made trading easier and more prosperous, creating a wealthy and influential merchant class in the growing cities. There were also great voyages of discovery, which brought Europeans into closer contact with Asia and opened the New World to European exploration. Finally there was exploration on the intellectual level as well. With the new emphasis on the individual, the strong authoritarian bonds of the Middle Ages soon were cast aside. The right of individuals to independent thought and inquiry was championed by leading scholars (called humanists) such as the great Erasmus and gradually was taken up by the public at large. The Renaissance was truly the beginning of the modern world. Our lives and minds today are shaped and colored by the many new institutions which developed during this period and by the great outpouring of new ideas in religion, philosophy, science, politics, literature, and all the other arts.

With the passing of the Middle Ages, the common religious faith of medieval times also disappeared. Not long after all the discoveries of the Renaissance had first excited people, the Reformation arrived to challenge the corruption and later even the doctrines of the Church. This religious movement, which began as a protest against various practices of the Roman Catholic Church, began on the European continent, where Martin Luther in Germany and John Calvin in Switzerland were the most notable proponents of the new religious thought. John Knox led the growing Protestant movement in Scotland. There were now Protestants and Catholics, many of them believing it impossible to live in peace alongside people who did not share their own particular faith. This attitude led to ruinous wars in France and later in Germany.

In England the ruinous Wars of the Roses ended in 1485 with the defeat of Richard III (whom many people believe to be a good king blackened by Tudor propaganda) by Henry Tudor, who became Henry VII. The country had had enough of civil war and of quarrelsome nobles with private armies, and Henry VII (1485–1509), a shrewd, hard man, made his throne secure by taking more and more power into his own capable hands. His son, Henry VIII (1509–47), seemed at first a handsome, jolly giant but later became suspicious, tyrannical, and cruel. He did not marry six wives because he was fond of women, though he was, but because he hoped for a son to succeed him. Though the Pope's refusal to allow Henry to divorce his first wife, Catherine of Aragon, may have been the immediate cause of Henry's break with Rome and the subsequent establishment of the Protestant church in England, it was by no means the sole cause. There were political and ecclesiastical as well as personal reasons: the growth of English nationalism made the subjection of English affairs to an outside power increasingly unacceptable, and the strong Protestant movement on the continent had greatly influenced English thought.

Elizabeth, daughter of Anne Boleyn, whom Henry married after breaking with Rome, succeeded her half-sister Mary (1553–58), who had married Philip of Spain and tried to restore her kingdom to the Pope. Elizabeth (1558–1603) came to the throne when she was only twenty-five, and her position was very difficult indeed. A Protestant, she had still many Catholics among her subjects. And Philip of Spain, who had the best army in Europe, still coveted England for the Pope and was enraged by the continual piratical raids of Elizabeth's daredevil sea captains on his treasure ships from the New World and on the ports of the Spanish Main in the Caribbean. Though progressing fast under the firm government of the Tudor monarchs, England was not yet one of the great powers. What Elizabeth needed was time, and she played for that time with an astonishing mixture of characteristics: audacity and wiliness. She was in fact—this thin red-haired woman —by far the cleverest ruler of her age. She was unusually well-educated, at once brilliant and shrewd, capable of outwitting any diplomat sent to her. Careful with public money to the point of meanness, she was forever compelling her wealthier subjects to entertain her lavishly to keep both her and her people amused. She was cautious and crafty in her efforts to preserve peace, but magnificently bold when danger threatened. By stimulating foreign commerce and exploration, she promoted English sea power and colonial expansion; by pursuing moderate religious policies, she prevented the danger of open conflict between Protestant and Catholic; by respecting its privileges, she assured the loyalty of Parliament; she reduced taxes,

"Elizabeth Hawking." A woodcut from Tuberville's *Book of Faulconrie* (1575).

The Spanish Armada attacked by the English fleet (1588). This wood engraving was copied from an old tapestry which was destroyed by a fire in the House of Lords.

broadened education, and encouraged scholarship and the arts. By the later years of her reign, England had achieved remarkable prosperity. Elizabeth was certainly one of the greatest English monarchs, and well deserves to have her name given to one of England's most glorious epochs.

Elizabeth had been reigning thirty years when what she had always schemed to avoid came to pass. In 1588, after many delays, the Spanish Armada, a fleet of huge galleons, sailed for the invasion of England. Unlike Philip of Spain, Elizabeth had no regular army of veterans, only bands of militia. The Spanish galleons had only to land and Elizabeth's kingdom was doomed. But David beat Goliath. The smaller and faster English vessels, superbly handled by the best seamen in the world, outmatched the unwieldy Spanish galleons, more like floating fortresses and barracks than ships, and then a great storm arose to scatter and destroy the Armada. England was saved. The menacing shadow of Spain under which Elizabeth had lived ever since she took the crown suddenly vanished. The queen, the great "Gloriana" as she was called, and her cheering, bell-ringing subjects came out into the sunshine.

THE FLOWERING OF ELIZABETHAN LITERATURE

All the chief literary glories of the Elizabethan Age—many of which appeared during the reign of Elizabeth's successor, James I (1603–25)—came after the defeat of the Spanish Armada. It was as if the nation had suddenly found itself. It discovered new sources of confidence, energy, and delight, and expressed all these in literature. Up until the last twelve years of the sixteenth century, England, though making rapid progress under the Tudors, had been far behind Italy, France, and Spain in literature and the arts and the whole civilizing process of the Renaissance.

The English poets, such as they were, could only imitate foreign models, the most important of which was the sonnet form, imported from Italy. The Earl of Surrey and Sir Thomas Wyatt, both early Elizabethan poets, successfully used this form during the first half of the sixteenth century. Much later, Shakespeare—and much later still, Milton—raised this form to a great poetic height.

The prose in Elizabethan times was stiff and ungainly, creaking in its joints. Although the chroniclers and pamphleteers, men like Greene and Dekker and Nashe (who also tried his hand at fiction), were busy during the later years of the century, although before the age ended it had given us the essays of Francis Bacon (1561–1626) and the stately narratives of Sir Walter Raleigh, prose as a general instrument of expression was hardly yet completely mastered. It was still not sufficiently flexible. Bacon and Raleigh in their very different ways—or an eccentric scholar like Robert Burton, whose *Anatomy of Melancholy* (1621) is one of the masterpieces of the age—might have been able to compel the prevailing prose style to serve their various purposes, but it was not until the following age that both the grand and the familiar prose styles came easily to authors.

Indeed, before the last dozen years of the century, the English language as an instrument was not really ready for great literature: there it was, like a vast organ, with nobody knowing yet how to handle the keyboard and work the stops. It was as if the queen's taut anxiety, her unsleeping watchfulness during these first thirty years of her reign, had influenced the whole mood of the nation, which wanted to sing but could only keep clearing its throat. Once the Spanish menace was removed, however, the tremendous release that followed changed everything. The aging queen was by this time a fabulous figure. The whole nation suddenly flowered. It is from this time on that we find the Elizabethans of legend, with all their extraordinary energy and self-confidence, beginning to flourish. And this transformation is perfectly reflected in the literature of the time. The English language, that great instrument which nobody had known how to play, suddenly came right. If this may seem an exaggeration, then we must remember that within ten years after the defeat of the Armada, Shakespeare was not only writing some of the greatest poetry the world has ever known but was also using a vocabulary unequaled in its size, variety, and richness. These later Elizabethans, of all classes, had a passion for magnificent language: they got drunk on words. And some of us, reading now what they wrote during those distant years, can still feel something of their intoxication. The Elizabethans had a general passion for poetry, both lyrical and dramatic, and out of it they created one marvel after another.

ELIZABETHAN LONDON

The Elizabethan society which produced the great plays was itself essentially dramatic. Within its new national unity it was richly varied: there

ELIZABETHAN TIMES

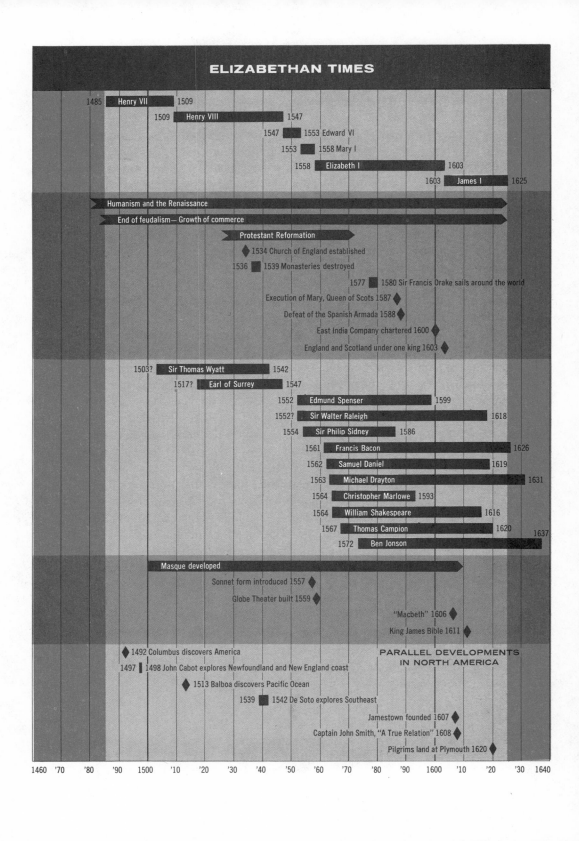

1485 Henry VII 1509

1509 Henry VIII 1547

1547 1553 Edward VI

1553 1558 Mary I

1558 Elizabeth I 1603

1603 James I 1625

Humanism and the Renaissance

End of feudalism— Growth of commerce

Protestant Reformation

◆ 1534 Church of England established

1536 1539 Monasteries destroyed

1577 1580 Sir Francis Drake sails around the world

Execution of Mary, Queen of Scots 1587 ◆

Defeat of the Spanish Armada 1588 ◆

East India Company chartered 1600 ◆

England and Scotland under one king 1603 ◆

1503? Sir Thomas Wyatt 1542

1517? Earl of Surrey 1547

1552 Edmund Spenser 1599

1552? Sir Walter Raleigh 1618

1554 Sir Philip Sidney 1586

1561 Francis Bacon 1626

1562 Samuel Daniel 1619

1563 Michael Drayton 1631

1564 Christopher Marlowe 1593

1564 William Shakespeare 1616

1567 Thomas Campion 1620

1572 Ben Jonson 1637

Masque developed

Sonnet form introduced 1557 ◆

Globe Theater built 1559 ◆

"Macbeth" 1606 ◆

King James Bible 1611 ◆

◆ 1492 Columbus discovers America

1497 1498 John Cabot explores Newfoundland and New England coast

◆ 1513 Balboa discovers Pacific Ocean

1539 1542 De Soto explores Southeast

PARALLEL DEVELOPMENTS
IN NORTH AMERICA

Jamestown founded 1607 ◆

Captain John Smith, "A True Relation" 1608 ◆

Pilgrims land at Plymouth 1620 ◆

1460 '70 '80 '90 1500 '10 '20 '30 '40 '50 '60 '70 '80 '90 1600 '10 '20 '30 1640

was the fabulous Queen Elizabeth herself and her splendid court (and many a young nobleman spent all he possessed just to make a fine appearance there). At the court there were magnificent masques, lavish and often spectacular entertainments which combined music, song, dance, and splendid costuming. These entertainments were generally acted by amateurs but devised by professional dramatists, notably Ben Jonson. The staging of masques was often very elaborate, and a great architect like Inigo Jones did not think it beneath his dignity to design the decorations and stage machinery.

Then there was the growing middle class of merchants, many of them already tending toward Puritanism and providing a sturdy opposition (itself provocative of drama) to poets and players and all the swaggering roisterers; there were the sea captains and sailors from the ends of the earth, the crowds of lively young apprentices, and the hearty common folk who packed the theaters to listen for hours to poetic drama. Elizabethan London was like a gigantic fair, crammed and noisy with all manner of characters, some of them magnificent in costumes paid for by the sale of their estates, others in rags and tatters. In the noblemen's palaces off the Strand, running down to the river, musicians sang to lutes and poets brought copies of their verses; in the taverns of Eastcheap the wits exchanged rapid quips and the girls giggled; and not far away was the sinister bulk of the Tower with its thumbscrews and racks and executioners' axes. And in the oval-shaped roofless theaters nearby, packed almost every afternoon, the players were saying lines that are now immortal.

THE ELIZABETHAN THEATER

Great poetical drama is far rarer, far harder to achieve, than great lyrical or narrative poetry or prose fiction, just because so many things have to be right for it all at the same time. There must be not only exceptional dramatic poets but also exceptional players, theaters, and audiences. And here the Elizabethan dramatists were fortunate. All the evidence we possess suggests that English acting in Shakespeare's time was very good indeed, so that companies of English players were in demand abroad. Women's parts were played by boys highly trained in movement, gesture, and the speaking of verse. What we would now call the "stars" among the men, players like Edward Alleyn and Richard Burbage, who owned substantial shares in the playhouses as Shakespeare finally did, must have been very fine performers indeed. And all these actors, while capable of making themselves heard from the pit to the uppermost gallery, were able to get through their scenes at what seems to us now an astonishing pace. We know this because very long plays like *Hamlet* could be performed in their entirety during an afternoon. In ordinary productions of Shakespeare's longer plays, it has been the practice ever since the eighteenth century to make many cuts, whole scenes often being omitted to enable modern actors, in their slower pace, to present the play in a reasonable length of time.

The Elizabethan stage which favored this rapid pace, just as it favored an intimate and imaginative relationship between poet, players, and audience, came into existence almost by accident. Before the London playhouses were built, the wealthier nobles had kept troupes of players among their retainers and often sent these troupes touring the country. Shakespeare as a boy must have seen them, for records show that towns no larger than Stratford might have visits from six troupes in a year. When playing in towns, these touring companies used innyards, where the crowd could surround the platform that was erected and those purchasing more expensive space could seat themselves in the galleries running outside the bedrooms of the inn. The London playhouses merely improved upon this setting. Their stages still had a platform coming out into the audience, but they also had entrances at each side, a small inner stage that could be curtained off, and, above, an upper stage or balcony.

All outdoor scenes were played on the platform or forestage, with curtains drawn to hide the inner stage. These curtains were pulled back, to reveal a throne or whatever was needed, for indoor scenes. The balcony was used whenever two different levels were necessary, for sentries on battlements or girls like Juliet looking for their lovers. For swift, imaginative poetic drama this type of stage was far superior to the "picture frame" stage, with elaborate painted scenery, that succeeded it. The play could move quickly from one short scene to the next, more like our films than most of our contemporary plays. Not having a scene painter and lighting electrician to help him, the dramatist had to be imaginative and so was his audience.

Although Elizabethan audiences liked to have some clowning, singing, dancing, and sword combats in their plays, they must have enjoyed the poetry too; otherwise they would not have filled the playhouses. It is fortunate for English literature that the university scholars and wits, who wanted stiff and solemn drama in the style of the Roman dramatist Seneca, did not have their way. The professionals who ran the London playhouses refused to imitate the classics and made good use of the crude but valuable dramatic material, the wealth of popular entertainment, already in existence. For though the men who built and ran these theaters had to look to the court and the more important nobles both for the necessary licenses and official patronage, they knew that to keep their companies in employment and to fill their pits and galleries popular support was essential.

The rapid development of Elizabethan drama, from primitive comedy and tragedy to great masterpieces within twenty-five years, is astounding. It produced not only the incomparable Shakespeare but with him a large group of other dramatists, all with talent and some touched with genius. In this group were Ben Jonson (1572–1637), Christopher Marlowe (1564–1593), George Chapman (1559?–1634?), John Marston (1575?–1634), Thomas Dekker (1570–1632); and later—actually Jacobean not Elizabethan dramatists—there were Thomas Middleton (1570?–1627), Thomas Heywood (d. 1650?), John Webster (1580?–1625?), Francis Beaumont (1584–1616), John Fletcher (1579–1625), Philip Massinger (1583–1640), and John Ford (fl. 1639). Some of these dramatists could also write exquisite lyrical verse. Indeed, outside the drama, this age is notable chiefly for its effortless, enchanting lyrics, the songs it lightly tossed into the air. No age that came afterwards ever quite captured this golden singing, ever returned to this May morning of English poetry.

THE END OF AN ERA

History does not organize itself into conveniently packaged periods. Movements and trends which have their beginning and which flourish during the reign, for instance, of one monarch do not disappear abruptly with the death of that monarch. True as this is, however, there was, after the death of the first Elizabeth, a perceptible waning of what we have come to call "the Elizabethan spirit." Elizabethan writers such as Shakespeare, Bacon, and Donne lived on into the reign of Elizabeth's successor, James I, and produced what is still considered some of the world's greatest literature. Nevertheless, after Elizabeth's death, the mood of the nation darkened. There were uncertainties of all kinds, and the optimism of the days following the defeat of the Armada slowly diminished.

After the death of Queen Elizabeth in 1603, James I, the son of Mary Queen of Scots, succeeded to the English throne. He thereafter ruled his kingdom of Scotland together with that of England. A pedantic, cowardly man who considered himself king by "divine right," James was soon unpopular with most of his English subjects, who disliked his Scots favorites and his pro-Spanish policy. But he must be credited with one great contribution to English literature, for in 1604 he set his bishops the task of making a new translation of the Bible. First published in 1611, the new Bible was known from then on as the King James Version. The accuracy of this translation has often been criticized by scholars, but what cannot be questioned is the sheer beauty, the haunting magic of its English. This is the Bible that centuries of writers have known from childhood onwards, and echoes of this noble old work can be heard in nearly all the finest English prose.

The earlier years of Elizabeth's reign were anxious and difficult; the later years of James I were strangely corrupt, unhealthy, as if the sun had stopped shining. Between these years—let us say, roughly, from 1590 to 1610—was one of the miraculous golden times of literature, when the London streets were filled with richly gifted men, bursting with energy and zest for life.

J.B.P.

EDMUND SPENSER
(1552–1599)

Of all the English poets who are acknowledged as great poets, Edmund Spenser is probably the least read. Perhaps this is because much of his work is in the form of long, descriptive allegories. Even in his own time he was a deliberately old-fashioned poet who felt more at home in the past age of chivalry than in the aggressive and energetic reign of Queen Elizabeth. Nevertheless, Spenser's influence on later poets was considerable, and for this reason he is often referred to as "the poet's poet."

Spenser was not of high birth as were his friends and contemporaries, Sir Philip Sidney and Sir Walter Raleigh. Son of a London clothmaker, he attended school on scholarship and worked his way through Cambridge University while trying his hand at translating and poetry. It was publication of *The Shepherd's Calendar* (1579) that won Spenser recognition at Elizabeth's court. This poem, which is divided into twelve parts, one for each month of the year, describes the beauties of the country-side and exhibits Spenser's wide reading in the classics as well as in the European writers of his day.

At the age of twenty-eight, Spenser, as secretary to the Lord Deputy of Ireland, set sail for the country which was thereafter to be his home, a country which at that time was torn by political turmoil. While living in Ireland, Spenser, with the encouragement of Sir Walter Raleigh, began writing his great epic, *The Faerie Queene.* Spenser's dedication of this ambitious work to Queen Elizabeth so flattered her that she granted him a pension, though not the responsible court post in London that he desired. Recognized as "the prince of poets in his time" but disappointed by repeated unsuccessful attempts for personal advancement at court, Spenser spent most of the rest of his life in Ireland, devoting himself to the management of his estate and to his duties as a civil servant, and continuing to write poetry. In the sonnet sequence *Amoretti,* selections from which follow, he recorded the history of his courtship of his second wife, Elizabeth Boyle. *Epithalamion,* his greatest lyric, was written in celebration of his marriage to that lady.

Though Spenser came to appreciate his life in Ireland as a far better one for a poet than the strenuous life at court, his contentment was not long-lived. In the course of a general insurrection against the English, Spenser's home was burned to the ground. Spenser himself escaped with his life and was sent with government dispatches to London, where shortly after his return, he contracted a fatal illness. Buried with honors in Westminster Abbey, he was laid to rest next to Geoffrey Chaucer, who, with Sir Philip Sidney, was his greatest inspiration.

The Faerie Queene, Spenser's masterpiece and the longest well-known poem in English literature, was planned to consist of twelve books, the hero of each a knight who personified a moral virtue. Only six of the books—those representing Holiness, Temperance, Chastity, Friendship, Justice, and Courtesy—were completed, though a legend persists that part of the concluding books perished in the flames of Spenser's castle. For *The Faerie Queen* Spenser invented a stanza form of his own, a nine-line stanza rhyming *ababbcbcc.* The first eight lines are in iambic pentameter, and the ninth line contains two extra syllables. Called the Spenserian stanza, this form was imitated by later poets such as Burns, Byron, Shelley, and Keats.

The month of June: an illustration from *The Shepherd's Calendar.*

Amoretti

Sonnet 26

	Rhyme scheme	
Sweet is the rose, but grows upon a briar;	*a*	
Sweet is the juniper, but sharp his bough;°	*b*	
Sweet is the eglantine, but pricketh near;	*a*	
Sweet is the fir bloom, but his branch is rough;	*b*	
Sweet is the cypress, but his rind is tough;	*b*	5
Sweet is the nut, but bitter is his pill;°	*c*	
Sweet is the broom flower, but yet sour enough;	*b*	
And sweet is moly,° but his root is ill.	*c*	
So every sweet with sour is tempered still,	*c*	
That maketh it be coveted the more:	*d*	10
For easy things, that may be got at will,	*c*	
Most sorts of men do set but little store.	*d*	
Why then should I account of little pain,	*e*	
That endless pleasure shall unto me gain!	*e*	

2. **his bough:** In the sixteenth century *his* was still used where today we use *its. Bough* was probably pronounced to rhyme with *rough* in medieval times, to which Spenser likes to refer. 6. **pill:** center or core. 8. **moly:** an herb with white blossoms and a black root.

Sonnet 75

One day I wrote her name upon the strand,
But came the waves and washed it away;
Again I wrote it with a second hand,
But came the tide, and made my pains his prey.
"Vain man," said she, "that dost in vain assay   5
A mortal thing so to immortalize!
For I myself shall like to this decay,
And eke° my name be wiped out likewise."
"Not so," quod I, "Let baser things devise
To die in dust, but you shall live by fame: 10
My verse your virtues rare shall eternize,
And in the heavens write your glorious name;
Where, whenas death shall all the world subdue,
Our love shall live, and later life renew."

8. **eke:** also.

Sonnet 79

Men call you fair, and you do credit° it,
For that yourself you daily such do see;
But the true fair, that is the gentle wit
And virtuous mind, is much more praised of me.
For all the rest, however fair it be,   5
Shall turn to naught and lose that glorious hue;
But only that is permanent and free
From frail corruption that doth flesh ensue,
That is true beauty; that doth argue you
To be divine and born of heavenly seed;   10
Derived from that fair Spirit, from whom all true
And perfect beauty did at first proceed:
He only fair, and what he fair hath made;
All other fair, like flowers, untimely fade.

1. **credit:** believe.

FOR STUDY AND DISCUSSION

1. Shakespeare's King Henry IV says, "Out of this nettle, danger, we pluck the flower, safety." What similar thought does Spenser's Sonnet 26 express? By what device does Spenser develop his idea? In the closing couplet what does Spenser mean by "little pain" and by "endless pleasure"?

2. In Sonnet 75 how does the poet propose to make his love's virtues live on? Define the different senses in which the word *vain* is used (line 5). What is the meaning of the word *assay* (line 5)?

3. In Sonnet 79 what is the difference between Spenser's use of "fair" in line 1 and his use of "true fair" in line 3? The word *fair* occurs seven times in this sonnet. Comment on its probable meaning in each of these seven contexts. To whom does "he" (line 13) refer? What does the poet feel is "true beauty"?

Elizabethan Love Lyrics and Sonnets

It is quite natural that we find love and beauty as major themes running through so much of Elizabethan poetry, for the English of the Renaissance were in love with beauty, especially human beauty, which they considered an outward sign of the spirit striving for perfection. It is natural, too, that these themes should find their expression in song, for music was as important as poetry to the Elizabethans. The plays of the period were liberally sprinkled with melodies that captivated their audiences. But Elizabethans did not consider music simply as pleasant listening, a primarily passive pleasure. In the same sense that a young gentleman was expected to be expert with the sword or show a fine leg in doublet and hose, so also was he expected to participate in the singing of madrigals and to carry off his part with only a glance at the score. Many of the songs and lyrics of the time were assembled in popular collections such as Tottle's *Miscellany* (1557). It has been said that more poets sang and published in the seventy-five years after 1550 than in the thousand years preceding.

Elizabethans sang in a variety of forms. The madrigal, the pastoral, and the sonnet were but a few of the many forms that enabled the poet to express his highly individual feelings on love and beauty. The madrigal is a complex musical form in which several voices sing without accompaniment. Nearly all the poets of the day wrote lyrics intended to be sung in this form. The pastoral is a poem in which shepherds and shepherdesses spend their time singing, dancing, and lovemaking in an idyllic rural setting. It was the sonnet, however, that was the most popular form of the period.

The sonnet, perfected in Italy in the fourteenth century by the Italian Renaissance poet Petrarch, was introduced into England by Sir Thomas Wyatt (1503–1542). Overnight it became fashionable in the English court to write contemplative love poems in this form. Before long, however, the Italian sonnet was modified by the Elizabethans who felt the original form to be too rigid. Whatever the variations, the sonnet form reigned supreme, and many poets of the day—such as Sidney, Spenser, Shakespeare, and Daniel— wrote famous sonnet sequences, series of loosely related sonnets united by a central theme, chiefly that of love.

The sonnet is a poem of fourteen lines, written in iambic pentameter: that is, the meter provides for ten syllables to the line with a stress on every other syllable. The Italian sonnet consists of an octave (eight lines) and a sestet (six lines), usually rhyming *abba, abba, cde, cde*. The Elizabethan sonnet, on the other hand, consists of three quatrains (a series of three four-line units) and a couplet (two lines), usually rhyming *abab, cdcd, efef, gg*. The final couplet usually functions as a clinching or concluding statement. Sometimes individual poets varied these basic patterns to suit their own needs. Spenser, for example, used a variation of the Italian pattern, and Drayton also varied the standard pattern to suit his needs.

The practice of writing charming and ingenious poems to one's lady stemmed from a courtly tradition dating back to medieval France. The convention governing the relationship between the poet and his lady was inflexible. She was the "cruel fair" whose favors her servant sought endlessly but hopelessly. Her moods created the weather. A brightening glance, for example, was a good omen but not entirely trustworthy, because eyes as "rising suns" could change instantly to eyes as "stars," in which case they were capable of emitting "angry sparks." Then again, while the lady's eyes were alternately suns or stars, her hair was almost invariably "gold wires"; her cheeks, "roses"; her lips, "cherries"; and her teeth, "orient pearls." The love lyrics addressed to her were not necessarily addressed to a living person. It was small matter whether the lady did or did not exist in fact. Very often these love poems were addressed to a small circle of congenial spirits—fellow poets, wits, ladies of fashion—whom the poet wished to amuse. The way to impress this company was to exhibit special ingenuity in devising new variations on the old theme or in polishing one's work to an impressively high gloss. The reproach that such poetry is "insincere" would have astonished any Elizabethan. The rules were there with all the weighty authority of tradition behind them, and they were there to be followed. To depart from them would be as incomprehensible as if a chess player were to propose a change of rules to an opponent in order to "express oneself better."

"Singing People," by the sixteenth-century Italian painter and sculptor Niccolo dell' Abate. The writing and singing of madrigals, long a favorite pastime in Italy, was extremely popular in Elizabethan England, where, by the middle of the sixteenth century, an important native school of madrigalists flourished.

CHRISTOPHER MARLOWE
(1564–1593)

SIR WALTER RALEIGH
(1552?–1618)

Christopher Marlowe was not yet thirty when he died. Quarrelsome and highly unconventional, his short life was a whirlwind of turbulence and color. While a student at Cambridge University, he was apparently involved in secret intelligence work for the government. Because of his hot temper and his taste for political intrigue, he was, throughout his life, constantly in trouble even after he had established himself as a poet and playwright of note. We know that Marlowe was stabbed to death in a tavern brawl, but it is still uncertain as to whether he was killed in a fight over a bill or because of his involvement in undercover political intrigue.

A typical Renaissance man, Marlowe combined a life of action with a career as a scholar and man of letters. Most important to posterity is that he was a poet of genius, his controlled and magnificent writing carrying the stamp of his powerful personality. His tragic dramas, which center on the lust for power, are second only to those of Shakespeare. Marlowe's heroes will their own destruction and are eventually consumed by their insatiable desires. The construction of Marlowe's plays, his technique of focusing attention on a single prominent character, and, above all, the power and variety which he instilled into dramatic blank verse— "the mighty line" so admired by Ben Jonson—greatly influenced Elizabethan drama and paved the way for the plays of William Shakespeare. Marlowe's influence on his contemporaries is perhaps most vividly revealed by his idyllic pastoral lyric, "The Passionate Shepherd to His Love," which inspired a flood of imitations and replies, among which the best known is that by Sir Walter Raleigh (see page 92).

Raleigh and Marlowe had much in common. Both were adventurous men, both had rough tempers and came to a violent end, and both were profound skeptics in an age of warring faiths. It is not surprising that the two became close friends. Raleigh, a remarkable individual, was at once explorer, soldier, sailor, statesman, poet, and historian. For his explorations in both North and South America, his efforts to found a colony (Virginia) in the New World, and his loyal service as courtier to the queen, he was awarded a knighthood and large tracts of land. He moved in and out of royal favor, however, and in and out of prison, and finally was condemned and executed. While serving a thirteen-year sentence in the Tower of London, Raleigh wrote his long *History of the World*. Earlier he had written an account of his journey to the Americas.

More than a century after Raleigh's death, the eighteenth-century writer Samuel Johnson, in his famous *Dictionary,* noted Raleigh as the authority on "the phrases of policy, war, and navigation." Raleigh's place in history, however, is more often thought of as that of a gallant courtier who epitomized the Elizabethan spirit and shared the Elizabethan facility for turning out a graceful lyric.

The Passionate Shepherd
to His Love

CHRISTOPHER MARLOWE

Come live with me and be my love,
And we will all the pleasures prove
That hills and valleys, dales and fields,
Or woods or steepy mountain yields.

And we will sit upon the rocks,   5
Seeing the shepherds feed their flocks,
By shallow rivers, to whose falls
Melodious birds sing madrigals.

And I will make thee beds of roses,
And a thousand fragrant posies,   10
A cap of flowers, and a kirtle°
Embroidered all with leaves of myrtle;

A gown made of the finest wool,
Which from our pretty lambs we pull;
Fair linèd slippers for the cold,   15
With buckles of the purest gold;

A belt of straw and ivy buds
With coral clasps and amber studs;
And if these pleasures may thee move,
Come live with me and be my love.   20

Thy silver dishes for thy meat
As precious as the gods do eat,
Shall on an ivory table be
Prepared each day for thee and me.

The shepherd swains shall dance and sing
For thy delight each May morning;   26
If these delights thy mind may move,
Then live with me and be my love.

11. **kirtle** (kûrt′l): a dress.

PASTORAL POETRY

The first pastorals were written by the Greek poet Theocritus and were later imitated by Virgil in his *Eclogues*. In the Renaissance, the pastoral was used for satiric and allegorical purposes. From the conventional pastoral the "pastoral elegy" developed—an independent form which was used by European poets through the nineteenth century, most notably by the English poets Milton, Shelley, and Arnold. Use your dictionary to check the derivation of the word "pastoral." Why is Marlowe's poem called a "pastoral lyric"?

The Nymph's Reply
to the Shepherd

SIR WALTER RALEIGH

If all the world and love were young,
And truth in every shepherd's tongue,
These pretty pleasures might me move
To live with thee and be thy love.   4

Time drives the flocks from field to fold,
When rivers rage, and rocks grow cold;
And Philomel° becometh dumb;
The rest complains of cares to come.

The flowers do fade, and wanton fields
To wayward Winter reckoning yields;   10
A honey tongue, a heart of gall,
Is fancy's spring, but sorrow's fall.

Thy gowns, thy shoes, thy beds of roses,
Thy cap, thy kirtle, and thy posies,
Soon break, soon wither, soon forgotten,
In folly ripe, in reason rotten.   16

Thy belt of straw and ivy buds,
Thy coral clasps and amber studs,
All these in me no means can move
To come to thee and be thy love.   20

But could youth last, and love still breed,
Had joys no date,° nor age no need,
Then these delights my mind might move
To live with thee and be thy love.

7. **Philomel** (fil′ə·mel): the nightingale. 22. **no date:** no final date; no end.

FOR STUDY AND DISCUSSION

How would you characterize the life described by Marlowe's shepherd? How does the nymph's attitude in Raleigh's poem contrast with the shepherd's? Can the two differing attitudes be reconciled? Explain.

SIR PHILIP
SIDNEY
(1554–1586)

Sir Philip Sidney was described by another Elizabethan poet as "the very essence of congruity." This was, in fact, the consensus of most of Sidney's contemporaries, for he combined chivalry and goodness, noble looks and talent, courage and charm to a rare degree. His reputation as the Renaissance ideal of the complete man, which still endures after nearly four hundred years, has perhaps depended as much upon his personality as upon his considerable accomplishments.

Born heir to one of the most beautiful of English estates, Penshurst Place in Kent, Sidney was fortunate both in family and friends. His father was Queen Elizabeth's Lord Deputy of Ireland; his mother, herself an aristocrat of high rank, was a sister of the Earl of Leicester, long one of the Queen's most trusted advisors. His sister Mary, Countess of Pembroke, was a leading patroness of letters; among his friends were the Earl of Essex and the poet Spenser. Sidney studied at both Oxford and Cambridge Universities, but received a degree from neither. Instead he spent three years touring the Continent, extending his education by learning foreign tongues and through contact with the outstanding scholars of the period. He was thus prepared in the mainstream of Renaissance and Reformation life and gained firsthand knowledge of European politics. Despite this training, his aristocratic family background, and the Queen's obvious admiration for him, Sidney never held high office in government, though recognition was given him in the form of a knighthood which he received a few years before his death.

Sidney's death of a wound received in battle in Holland was in keeping with the spirit of gallantry which characterized his entire life. His friend and first biographer, Fulke Greville, told how the wounded Sidney passed his cup of water to a dying soldier with the chivalric words, "Thy necessity is greater than mine." During the course of his short life, Sidney had inspired such remarkable respect and affection that his death was the cause of great mourning at court and throughout the kingdom. Further attesting to the esteem in which he was held are over two hundred elegies written to his memory, including those by Spenser, Drayton, and the Scottish prince who later became James I of England.

Sidney left behind him at least three literary landmarks. His pastoral romance *Arcadia* (1590), written at his sister's suggestion, was the first long piece of Renaissance prose fiction. *The Defense of Poesy* (1593), in which Sidney affirmed the universality of poetry and assessed the English literature of his day, is a major work of literary criticism. His *Astrophel and Stella* ("Starlover and Star"), published in 1591, was the first of the great Elizabethan sonnet sequences. In this series of 108 sonnets, Sidney·recorded the progress of his hopeless love for a beautiful young lady of rank. *Astrophel and Stella,* which was inspired by the sonnet sequences of the Italian poet Petrarch, in turn inspired the writing of many other sonnet cycles—among them those by Spenser, Drayton, and Shakespeare—and created a vogue which flourished throughout the Elizabethan period. Largely because of *Astrophel and Stella,* two sonnets from which follow, Sidney became one of the major influences on Elizabethan poetry.

Sonnet 31

With how sad steps, O Moon, thou climb'st the skies!
How silently, and with how wan a face!
What, may it be that even in heavenly place
That busy archer his sharp arrows tries?
Sure, if that long-with-love-acquainted eyes   5
Can judge of love, thou feel'st a lover's case.
I read it in thy looks; thy languished grace,
To me, that feel the like, thy state descries.°
Then, even of fellowship, O Moon, tell me,
Is constant love deemed there but want of wit?°   10
Are beauties there as proud as here they be?
Do they above love to be loved, and yet
Those lovers scorn whom that love doth possess?
Do they call virtue there ungratefulness?

8. **descries:** betrays, makes known.   10. **wit:** intelligence, good sense.

Sonnet 39

Come, Sleep! O Sleep, the certain knot of peace,
The baiting place° of wit, the balm of woe,
The poor man's wealth, the prisoner's release,
The indifferent judge between the high and low;
With shield of proof shield me from out of the prease°   5
Of those fierce darts Despair at me doth throw:
O make in me those civil wars to cease;
I will good tribute pay, if thou do so.
Take thou of me smooth pillows, sweetest bed,
A chamber deaf to noise and blind to light,   10
A rosy garland and a weary head:
And if these things, as being thine by right,
Move not thy heavy grace, thou shalt in me,
Livelier than elsewhere, Stella's image see.

2. **baiting place:** place of refreshment.   5. **prease:** crowd.

1. In Sonnet 31, Sidney personifies the moon: that is, he represents it as having human characteristics (see *personification*, page 886). What are these characteristics? Why does the moon climb the sky with "sad steps" (line 1)? Who is the "busy archer" (line 4)? In what sense are the moon's eyes "long-with-love-acquainted"? Rephrase in your own words the question asked in lines 12–13. What is the tone of the poem?

2. What does Sidney ask of sleep in Sonnet 39? "The poor man's wealth" is a *paradox*, an apparent contradiction. How do you explain this phrase? Why is it effective in this context? Why is sleep "the indifferent judge"? What "civil wars" take place within the poet?

3. Both sonnets by Sidney are examples of the poetic device called *apostrophe*, in which an absent person, place, or abstraction is addressed as though it were alive and present. How do Sidney's sonnets fit this definition?

FOR COMPOSITION

Reread the sonnets of Spenser and Sidney. Of these two poets, which do you think has a more realistic approach to his subject matter? In your discussion, consider each poet's use of imagery, personification, and tone.

SAMUEL DANIEL

(1562–1619)

The son of a music teacher, Samuel Daniel, after studying at Oxford University for a time and traveling in Italy, became tutor to William Herbert, a relative of George Herbert (page 212). Happily for Daniel and his literary aspirations, Herbert's mother was not only the sister of Sir Philip Sidney but also the leader of a literary circle in her own right. From this group Daniel received early encouragement as a poet, and by the age of thirty had published *Delia,* a sonnet sequence. For a good part of his life, Daniel earned his living by tutoring and later by farming; but, throughout, he continued to write, producing, among other things, a history in verse of the Wars of the Roses, a volume of poetic epistles, two tragedies, a number of masques and pastorals for the court of James I, and a popular, though uncompleted, prose *History of England.*

Like Michael Drayton (page 97), Daniel was a meticulous craftsman, and was known to continue revising and polishing his work even after publication. He led a quiet life. A seventeenth-century biographer wrote of him that "as the Tortoise burieth himself all the Winter in the ground, so Mr. Daniel would lie hid at his garden house . . . nigh London for some months together (the more retiredly to enjoy the company of the Muses)." Of all his many works, it is *Delia* which today is best remembered and most highly regarded. Two examples from this sonnet sequence are given below. Whether or not the "Delia" of the title refers to a lady whom the poet admired is unknown. Most probably these sonnets were inspired by Daniel's admiration for sonnets of French and Italian poets as well as for those written by Sir Philip Sidney, the leading poet of his day and brother of Daniel's first patroness.

Sonnet 11

Tears, vows, and prayers win the hardest heart,
Tears, vows, and prayers have I spent in vain;
Tears cannot soften flint, nor vows convert,
Prayers prevail not with a quaint disdain.
I lose my tears where I have lost my love,   5
I vow my faith, where faith is not regarded,
I pray in vain, a merciless to move:
So rare a faith ought better be rewarded.
Yet, though I cannot win her will with tears,
Though my soul's idol scorneth all my vows,   10
Though all my prayers be to so deaf ears,
No favor though the cruel fair allows,
Yet will I weep, vow, pray to cruel she;
Flint, frost, disdain, wears, melts, and yields, we see.

Sonnet 54

Care-charmer Sleep, son of the sable Night,
Brother to Death, in silent darkness born,
Relieve my anguish, and restore the light;
With dark forgetting of my cares return.
And let the day be time enough to mourn   5
The shipwreck of my ill-adventured youth;
Let waking eyes suffice to wail their scorn,
Without the torment of the night's untruth.
Cease, dreams, the images of day desires,
To model forth the passions of the morrow;   10
Never let rising sun approve° you liars,
To add more grief to aggravate my sorrow.
Still° let me sleep, embracing clouds in vain,
And never wake to feel the day's disdain.

11. **approve:** prove.   13. **Still:** always.

FOR STUDY AND DISCUSSION

1. In Daniel's Sonnet 11, why does the poet persist even though, as he complains, "Tears, vows, and prayers have I spent in vain"? Do you think that the poet's feelings have blinded him to the hopelessness of his situation, or does he seem to believe that just as flint wears and frost melts, his love's disdain will melt?

2. In Sonnet 11, what do you think Daniel's intention was in citing "tears," "vows," and "prayers" in this order? Distinguish between vows and prayers.

3. In Daniel's Sonnet 54, what special boon does the poet ask from sleep? What possibility does he dread? How is this sonnet both like and unlike Sidney's Sonnet 39?

4. What do you think the poet is admitting in line 13 of Sonnet 54? Do you believe he is self-indulgent? Explain your answer.

MICHAEL DRAYTON
(1563–1631)

Throughout his long lifetime Michael Drayton was a prolific writer of poetry. Influenced mainly by his contemporary, Edmund Spenser, Drayton nevertheless experimented with all kinds and styles of poetry fashionable in his day—pastoral, historical, patriotic, religious, and purely lyric. His most ambitious undertaking—though not his best poetry—was *Poly-Olbion* ("having many blessings"), a long survey of the British Isles in which the poet interspersed legends and bits of history with descriptions "of the rivers, mountains, and forests, and other parts of this renowned isle of Great Britain." Since it was Drayton's intention in this poem to describe every river, every mountain and forest in Britain as well as all of the flora and fauna in the country, it is not surprising that the poem was never completed.

Despite the impressiveness of this mammoth undertaking, it is chiefly for his short lyric poetry that Drayton is remembered. The freshness, grace, and careful craftsmanship that made him a popular poet in his own period still commend his work to us today. The sonnet sequence. *Idea's Mirror,* in which the following sonnet appears, is an excellent example of the exquisite poetry Drayton was capable of composing.

Sonnet 42

Some men there be which like my method well,
And much commend the strangeness of my vein;
Some say I have a passing° pleasing strain,
Some say that in my humor I excel;
Some, who not kindly relish my conceit,   5
They say, as poets do I use to feign,
And in bare words paint out my passion's pain;
Thus sundry men their sundry minds repeat.
I pass° not, I, how men affected be,
Nor who commends or discommends my verse;   10
It pleaseth me if I my woes rehearse,
And in my lines if she my love may see.
Only, my comfort still consists in this:
Writing her praise, I cannot write amiss.

3. **passing:** surpassingly, very.   9. **pass:** care.

1. Where does the speaker of Drayton's Sonnet 42 "rehearse" his woes? What is the special connotation of "conceit" (line 5)? To what four groups of men does the poet refer as "sundry men"? Drayton's sonnet is in the Elizabethan form of three quatrains with a clinching couplet at the end (see page 89).

How does Drayton's final couplet drive home his answer to the "sundry men"?

2. Examine the form of the sonnets on pages 87–88, 94, and 96–97. Which are Italian? Which are Elizabethan? Do any of the poets vary the standard rhyme scheme? If so, which ones? What particular value, if any, is there in varying the rhyme scheme?

THOMAS CAMPION
(1567–1620)

Thomas Campion enjoyed the variety of activities and interests which were characteristic of Elizabethan poets. As a student at Cambridge, he imbibed deeply of the Greek and Latin classics, the core of the "new learning" of Renaissance Europe. He studied both law and medicine and ultimately practiced the latter as his profession, becoming well known as a "doctor of physic." His leisure hours he filled with poetry, music, and literary criticism.

Celebrated chiefly, however, as a skillful maker of songs, Campion distinguished himself among his own generation, as to us, by his polished simplicity of style and his flawless ear for the music of words. He composed a multitude of songs, setting most of them to music himself and publishing them in four editions throughout his lifetime as *A Book of Airs*. Two of the best-known examples from these collections are given below. In addition to composing airs, madrigals, and sonnets, Campion also wrote a number of masques and court pageants, all extremely popular. His love lyrics, almost all of which are intensely musical, remind us that their composer was as much musician as poet. "I have chiefly aimed," he wrote in one of his prefaces, "to couple my words and notes lovingly together." This Campion did superbly.

When to Her Lute Corinna Sings

When to her lute Corinna sings,
Her voice revives the leaden strings,
And doth in highest notes appear,
As any challenged echo clear;
But when she doth of mourning speak,   5
Ev'n with her sighs the strings do break.

And as her lute doth live or die,
Led by her passion, so must I:
For when of pleasure she doth sing,
My thoughts enjoy a sudden spring;   10
But if she doth of sorrow speak,
Ev'n from my heart the strings do break.

There Is a Garden in Her Face

There is a garden in her face,
   Where roses and white lilies grow,
A heavenly paradise is that place,
   Wherein all pleasant fruits do flow.
There cherries grow, which none may buy   5
Till "Cherry ripe!" themselves do cry.

Those cherries fairly do enclose
   Of orient pearl a double row;
Which when her lovely laughter shows,
They look like rosebuds filled with snow: 10
Yet them nor peer nor prince can buy,
Till "Cherry ripe!" themselves do cry.

Her eyes like angels watch them still;
   Her brows like bended bows do stand,
Threatening with piercing frowns to kill   15
   All that attempt with eye or hand
Those sacred cherries to come nigh,
Till "Cherry ripe!" themselves do cry.

FOR STUDY AND DISCUSSION

1. Strings, real and fanciful, play a prominent part in "When to Her Lute Corinna Sings." What figure of speech is "leaden strings"? In both stanzas the poet speaks of breaking strings. Which strings are real and which are fanciful?

2. Do the descriptions of the women in Campion's poems seem realistic or fanciful? Point out specific details to support your answer.

3. Notice how figurative language adds to the effectiveness and artistry of the poems on pages 87–99. Upon what figures of speech are the poems most often based? Point out particularly effective images. How does the figurative language contribute to the development of the main idea in each of these poems?

WILLIAM
SHAKESPEARE
(1564–1616)

For the last three hundred and fifty years, William Shakespeare has been regarded as the greatest of all writers in the English language.

Shakespeare was born in April 1564 in Stratford-on-Avon, then a small country town of less than 2,000 inhabitants, in the county of Warwickshire. His father, John Shakespeare, was a glover who was for a time one of the leading citizens of Stratford. In 1568 John Shakespeare was chosen high bailiff (mayor), but later he withdrew from civic life.

Records of the dramatist's early life are scarce. At the age of eighteen he married Anne Hathaway, who was eight years older than himself. A daughter was born in May 1583, and twins in 1585. For the next eight years nothing certain is known of Shakespeare's life. There is a well-known legend (which can neither be proved nor refuted) that he fell foul of Sir Thomas Lucy, the local magnate, and was forced to leave Stratford. By 1592, when he was twenty-eight, Shakespeare was becoming known in London as an actor and a writer of successful plays. Thereafter the records accumulate.

In 1593 Shakespeare published a long narrative poem called *Venus and Adonis,* and in 1594 another, *The Rape of Lucrece.* Both poems were dedicated to the young Earl of Southampton, and both were very popular. That same year Shakespeare became a sharer in the Lord Chamberlain's company of actors, writing plays for the company as well as acting in them. Shakespeare's early plays were performed in the playhouses known as The Theater and The Curtain. In 1599 the company built the Globe Theater, where most of Shakespeare's greatest plays were performed.

By 1598 it was widely acknowledged that Shakespeare was the greatest of English dramatists. His plays were popular and booksellers were printing them, sometimes in stolen versions. The Chamberlain's Men prospered and were often summoned to act at the court of Queen Elizabeth I, but their greatest prosperity came after her death in 1603 when her successor, King James I, took over the company and made them his own players—The King's Men.

Shakespeare's career as a dramatist lasted for nearly twenty years. Around 1610 he withdrew from London and the theater and lived for the rest of his life in Stratford-on-Avon as a respected citizen and well-to-do gentleman. He died on April 23, 1616 and was buried in the church at Stratford-on-Avon.

Shakespeare wrote two long narrative poems, 154 sonnets, two long poems, and thirty-seven plays of all kinds—comedies, histories, tragedies, and farces. During his lifetime only fourteen of his plays were separately printed. Seven years after his death some of his friends and fellow actors collected and published an edition of thirty-six of the plays in one large volume—the famous First Folio (1623).

THE DEVELOPMENT OF SHAKESPEARE'S ART

Great artists are not born fully developed. They need a natural gift, but they must also learn their craft by imitation, practice, and experiment. Shakespeare learned to write plays in the best of schools—the theater itself. He soon learned to develop his natural skills and to the end of his working life was still experimenting with new ways of writing plays and forcing words to express his meaning. So marked is this development that most of his plays can be approximately dated by style alone.

Shakespeare's dramatic development can be divided roughly into four periods: *Early, Balanced, Overflowing,* and *Final.*

The most important plays of the Early period are *Richard III, The Taming of the Shrew, Richard II, A Midsummer Night's Dream,* and *Romeo and Juliet* (the best of them all). These plays were written within the period 1592 to 1594–95.

With *The Merchant of Venice,* the Early period merges into the Balanced period, to which most of the more popular plays belong—*Henry IV, Much Ado About Nothing, As You Like It, Julius Caesar, Hamlet,* and *Othello.* By the end of this period (about 1603) Shakespeare had achieved a full sense of character, and he could write speeches and dialogue that are not only full of meaning but, by their choice of vocabulary and rhythm, can express the whole nature of the speaker. Later, as his feelings became deeper, Shakespeare for a time passed into a period when his thoughts and emotions came too thickly and powerfully for controlled logical expression. To this Overflowing period belong two of his finest tragedies—*King Lear* and *Macbeth.* At the end of his career Shakespeare passed into a Final period in which he achieved perfect poise between expression and deep thought. Of the plays of this period the greatest is *The Tempest.*

The best way of appreciating the development of Shakespeare's art is to compare a few passages from each of the four periods, observing certain aspects of each.

Descriptive Poetry in Shakespeare's Drama

Modern audiences regard as long a speech of more than five lines; Shakespeare's audiences enjoyed listening to speeches of fifty to a hundred lines on all kinds of topics—description, self-analysis, comment on the play, comment on life, and discussion of passing events. The following passages from plays, mostly from longer speeches of various periods, will illustrate Shakespeare's poetic development.

In *Richard III,* one of Shakespeare's Early plays, Clarence, in prison, relates a fearful dream.

> CLARENCE. Methought that I had broken from the Tower,
> And was embarked to cross to Burgundy,
> And in my company my brother Gloucester,
> Who from my cabin tempted me to walk
> Upon the hatches. Thence we looked toward England,
> And cited up a thousand fearful times
> During the wars of York and Lancaster
> That had befall'n us. As we paced along

Upon the giddy footing of the hatches,
Methought that Gloucester stumbled, and in falling
Struck me, that thought to stay him, overboard,
Into the trembling billows of the main.
Lord, Lord! Methought what pain it was to drown!
What dreadful noise of waters in mine ears!
What ugly sights of death within mine eyes!
Methought I saw a thousand fearful wrecks,
Ten thousand men that fishes gnawed upon,
Wedges of gold, great anchors, heaps of pearl,
Inestimable stones, unvalued jewels,
All scattered in the bottom of the sea.
Some lay in dead men's skulls, and in those holes
Where eyes did once inhabit there were crept,
As 'twere in scorn of eyes, reflecting gems,
Which wooed the slimy bottom of the deep
And mocked the dead bones that lay scattered by.

This speech has some dramatic importance. Clarence has been treacherous to his brother Edward IV and has good reason to suspect that he is in great danger. His dream symbolizes subconscious dread, but its chief purpose is to let the audience listen to a fine speech, a composition almost like an aria in opera.

In *Romeo and Juliet*, also from the Early period, Romeo tells Mercutio that he has had a dream. Mercutio, who is an irrepressible talker, thereupon breaks out:

MERCUTIO. Oh then, I see Queen Mab hath been with you.
She is the fairies' midwife, and she comes
In shape no bigger than an agate stone
On the forefinger of an alderman,
Drawn with a team of little atomies [1]
Athwart men's noses as they lie asleep—
Her wagon spokes made of long spinners' legs;
The cover, of the wings of grasshoppers;
Her traces,[2] of the smallest spider's web;
Her collars, of the moonshine's watery beams;
Her wagoner, a small gray-coated gnat
Not half so big as a round little worm
Pricked from the lazy finger of a maid.
Her chariot is an empty hazelnut,
Made by the joiner squirrel or old grub,
Time out o' mind the fairies' coachmakers.
And in this state she gallops night by night
Through lovers' brains, and then they dream of love;
O'er courtiers' knees, that dream on curtseys straight;
O'er lawyers' fingers, who straight dream on fees;
O'er ladies' lips, who straight on kisses dream,
Which oft the angry Mab with blisters plagues
Because their breaths with sweetmeats tainted are.

[1] **atomies:** tiny things.
[2] **traces:** harness.

Sometime she gallops o'er a courtier's nose,
And then dreams he of smelling out a suit.[1]
And sometime comes she with a tithe pig's tail
Tickling a parson's nose as a' lies asleep,
Then dreams he of another benefice.

This speech is exuberant poetry for its own sake, adding nothing to the plot or characterization, but creating one of the high moments of the play.

In *Antony and Cleopatra,* written late in his career, after *Macbeth,* Shakespeare has Enobarbus describe Antony's first meeting with Cleopatra.

ENOBARBUS. I will tell you.
    The barge she sat in, like a burnished throne,
    Burned on the water. The poop was beaten gold,
    Purple the sails, and so perfumèd that
    The winds were lovesick with them. The oars were silver,
    Which to the tune of flutes kept stroke and made
    The water which they beat to follow faster,
    As amorous of their strokes. For her own person,
    It beggared all description. She did lie
    In her pavilion, cloth of gold of tissue,
    O'er picturing that Venus where we see
    The fancy outwork nature. On each side her
    Stood pretty dimpled boys, like smiling Cupids,
    With divers-colored fans, whose wind did seem
    To glow the delicate cheeks which they did cool,
    And what they undid did.
AGRIPPA.   O, rare for Antony!
ENOBARBUS. Her gentlewomen, like the Nereides,
    So many mermaids, tended her i' the eyes,
    And made their bends adornings. At the helm
    A seeming mermaid steers. The silken tackle
    Swell with the touches of those flower-soft hands
    That yarely [2] frame the office. From the barge
    A strange invisible perfume hits the sense
    Of the adjacent wharfs. The city cast
    Her people out upon her. And Antony,
    Enthronèd i' the market place, did sit alone
    Whistling to the air, which, but for vacancy,[3]
    Had gone to gaze on Cleopatra too,
    And made a gap in nature.

In this magnificent passage written twelve to fourteen years after Clarence's dream in *Richard III,* Shakespeare reverts to his earlier method of writing narrative poetry, but the speech has its purpose in the play, for it creates an impression of the fascination, magnificence, and luxury of Cleopatra. Shakespeare thus used words to achieve what a modern film production tried to achieve with lavish sets and costumes and an expenditure of $10,000,000.

[1] **smelling . . . suit:** winning some favor.
[2] **yarely:** in a workmanlike way.
[3] **vacancy:** vacuum.

Shakespeare's Use of Imagery

All writers, especially poets, use imagery—that is, by simile, metaphor, symbol, and other poetic devices they expand and deepen the meaning of what they are saying. In his early plays Shakespeare used simile and metaphor lavishly but seldom subtly. Often the image was inserted for its own effect rather than to add to the depth of what was said.

In *Richard III,* which is representative of the Early period, Tyrrel comments on the murder of the little Princes:

> TYRREL. The tyrannous and bloody deed is done,
> The most arch act of piteous massacre
> That ever yet this land was guilty of.
> Dighton and Forrest, whom I did suborn
> To do this ruthless piece of butchery,
> Although they were fleshed villains, bloody dogs,
> Melting with tenderness and kind compassion,
> Wept like two children in their deaths' sad stories.
> "Lo, thus," quoth Dighton, "lay those tender babes."
> "Thus, thus," quoth Forrest, "girdling one another
> Within their innocent alabaster arms."
> Their lips were four red roses on a stalk,
> Which in their summer beauty kissed each other.

The image of the four red roses is artificial and sentimental, for red lips do not look like roses on a stalk. Nor does the image add to the picture of the boys or to the horror of their murder.

In the plays of his maturity, Shakespeare's imagery is usually apt and convincing. Thus in *Troilus and Cressida,* written during the Balanced period, about the same time as *Hamlet,* Achilles refuses to come out and fight the Trojans. He sulks in his tent. Ulysses tries to persuade him that he is making a bad mistake; no one, not even a hero, can rest content with his past triumphs.

> ULYSSES. Time hath, my lord, a wallet at his back
> Wherein he puts alms for oblivion,
> A great-sized monster of ingratitudes.
> Those scraps are good deeds past, which are devoured
> As fast as they are made, forgot as soon
> As done. Perseverance, dear my lord,
> Keeps honor bright. To have done is to hang
> Quite out of fashion, like a rusty mail
> In monumental mockery. Take the instant way,
> For honor travels in a strait so narrow,
> Where one but goes abreast. Keep then the path,
> That one by one pursue. If you give way
> Or hedge aside from the direct forthright,
> Like to an entered tide they all rush by
> And leave you hindmost.
> Or like a gallant horse fall'n in first rank,
> Lie there for pavement to the abject rear,
> O'errun and trampled on. Then what they do in present,
> Though less than yours in past, must o'ertop yours.
> For time is like a fashionable host

That slightly shakes his parting guest by the hand,
And with his arms outstretched, as he would fly,
Grasps in the comer. Welcome ever smiles,
And farewell goes out sighing. Oh, let not virtue seek
Remuneration for the thing it was;
For beauty, wit,
High birth, vigor of bone, desert in service,
Love, friendship, charity, are subjects all
To envious and calumniating time.
One touch of nature makes the whole world kin,
That all with one consent praise newborn gawds,
Though they are made and molded of things past,
And give to dust that is a little gilt
More laud than gilt o'erdusted.

The imagery in this passage is very varied, yet vividly distinct. Time, personified as so often, is not interested in the past. Like an ungrateful beggar with his bag of scraps, Time picks up everything. A man who rests on his reputation is like the rusty armor hung up over a dead warrior's tomb—a pathetic mockery of his former prowess. Achilles must keep on going, for rivals are always pressing on him, like the racing incoming tide or the chargers in the rear of a cavalry charge which over-run those who have already fallen. Ungrateful Time is like the host who welcomes the new guests but barely nods to those who are leaving; or like the new gilt plaster image which is more prized for its glitter than the old true gold which has become shabby with age. By this use of image after image, each clear and apt, Ulysses tries to convince Achilles that by sulking he is only hurting himself.

In the plays of the Overflowing period, the imagery is often striking and most effective but at the same time indistinct, compressed, sometimes difficult—suggested rather than expressed. As you read *Macbeth* you should look for passages of this sort. Note particularly Lady Macbeth's speech in Act I, Scene V (lines 34–50) and Macbeth's speech in Act I, Scene VII (lines 1–28).

In his Final period, Shakespeare often reverted to a deceptively simple kind of image. In *The Tempest* Prospero has just entertained the two young lovers, Ferdinand and Miranda, with a masque. After the dancers leave, Prospero comments:

Our revels now are ended. These our actors,
As I foretold you, were all spirits, and
Are melted into air, into thin air.
And, like the baseless fabric of this vision,
The cloud-capped towers, the gorgeous palaces,
The solemn temples, the great globe itself—
Yea, all which it inherit—shall dissolve
And, like this insubstantial pageant faded,
Leave not a rack behind. We are such stuff
As dreams are made on, and our little life
Is rounded with a sleep.

Here the idea of the impermanence of all things is expressed in three clear little pictures, each of things that are usually symbols of stability—towers, castles, temples. All ultimately dissolve in a wisp of cloud (rack). The thought is profound; the expression entirely simple.

Sonnets

Because of the publication of Sir Philip Sidney's *Astrophel and Stella* in 1591, the sonnet was a highly popular form with English poets in the last years of the sixteenth century. Since the rigid pattern of the sonnet (see page 89) is often cramping, this form is not always effective in dealing with deep or complex ideas. It is admirable, however, for expressing both serious thoughts and graceful, complimentary sentiments, and for its exact and concentrated expression of a single idea or emotion.

Shakespeare's sonnets have been much discussed. Seemingly they are poems of intimate experience addressed by the poet to a young friend of surpassing beauty and high social rank, and to a mistress or so-called "dark lady." Although many theories exist, so far no one has identified definitively either the young man or the lady.

Sonnet 18

	Rhyme scheme	
Shall I compare thee to a summer's day?	*a*	
Thou art more lovely and more temperate:	*b*	
Rough winds do shake the darling buds of May,	*a*	
And summer's lease hath all too short a date;	*b*	
Sometimes too hot the eye of heaven shines,	*c*	5
And often is his gold complexion dimmed;	*d*	
And every fair from fair sometime declines,	*c*	
By chance, or nature's changing course, untrimmed.°	*d*	
But thy eternal summer shall not fade	*e*	
Nor lose possession of that fair thou owest;°	*f*	10
Nor shall Death brag thou wanderest in his shade,	*e*	
When in eternal lines to time thou growest—	*f*	
So long as men can breathe, or eyes can see,	*g*	
So long lives this, and this gives life to thee.	*g*	

Sonnet 29

When in disgrace with fortune and men's eyes
I all alone beweep my outcast state,
And trouble deaf heaven with my bootless° cries,
And look upon myself, and curse my fate;
Wishing me like to one more rich in hope,   5
Featured like him, like him with friends possessed,
Desiring this man's art, and that man's scope,
With what I most enjoy contented least;

SONNET 18: 8. **untrimmed:** shorn of its beauty.   10. **owest:** own.
SONNET 29: 3. **bootless:** useless.

Yet in these thoughts myself almost despising,
Haply° I think on thee—and then my state,   10
Like to the lark at break of day arising
From sullen earth, sings hymns at heaven's gate;
For thy sweet love remembered such wealth brings
That then I scorn to change my state with kings.

Sonnet 55

Not marble, nor the gilded monuments
Of princes, shall outlive this powerful rime;
But you shall shine more bright in these contents°
Than unswept stone, besmeared with sluttish time.
When wasteful war shall statues overturn,   5
And broils° root out the work of masonry,
Nor Mars his sword° nor war's quick fire shall burn
The living record of your memory.
'Gainst death and all-oblivious enmity°
Shall you pace forth; your praise shall still find room   10
Even in the eyes of all posterity
That wear this world out to the ending doom.
So, till the judgment° that yourself° arise,
You live in this, and dwell in lovers' eyes.

Sonnet 73

That time of year thou may'st in me behold
When yellow leaves, or none, or few, do hang
Upon those boughs which shake against the cold,
Bare ruined choirs, where late the sweet birds sang.
In me thou see'st the twilight of such day   5
As after sunset fadeth in the west,
Which by and by black night doth take away,
Death's second self, that seals up all in rest.
In me thou see'st the glowing of such fire,
That on the ashes of his youth doth lie   10
As the deathbed whereon it must expire,
Consumed with that which it was nourished by.
—This thou perceiv'st, which makes thy love more strong,
To love that well which thou must leave ere long.

SONNET 29: 10. **Haply:** by chance.
SONNET 55: 3. **these contents:** this poem.   6. **broils:** fights, brawls.   7. **Mars his sword:**
Mars' sword.   9. **all-oblivious enmity:** war which sends all to oblivion.   13. **judgment:** Day
of Judgment, when the world will come to an end and all the dead will arise.   **that yourself:**
when you yourself.

WILLIAM SHAKESPEARE   107

Sonnet 116

Let me not to the marriage of true minds
Admit impediments. Love is not love
Which alters when it alteration finds,
Or bends with the remover° to remove—
O, no! it is an ever-fixèd mark   5
That looks on tempests, and is never shaken;
It is the star to every wandering bark,
Whose worth's unknown, although his height be taken.
Love's not Time's fool, though rosy lips and cheeks
Within his bending sickle's compass come;   10
Love alters not with his brief hours and weeks,
But bears it out ev'n to the edge of doom—
If this be error, and upon me proved,
I never writ, nor no man ever loved.

4. **remover:** inconstant lover.

FOR STUDY AND DISCUSSION

1. In Sonnets 18 and 55, what view does the poet express on the relationship between the immortality of his verse and of the person he is addressing? Do you think the time that has elapsed since Shakespeare wrote these sonnets proves or disproves his point?

2. In Sonnet 29 what two moods are contrasted? What kinds of men does the poet say he envies? What causes the poet's change of mood in the last few lines of the poem? Judging from the reference in lines 11–12 of Sonnet 29, what would you say the lark symbolized to Shakespeare?

3. The images in Sonnet 73 are considered particularly effective. How do the three principal images introduced in the three quatrains relate to the mood and theme of the poem? Each of these images is followed by an additional metaphor. Explain the appropriateness of these metaphors to the principal image of the quatrain and to the poem as a whole.

4. In Sonnet 116, what is the meaning of line 13? In the second quatrain to what is true love compared? How does the image of Time in the third quatrain relate to the theme of the poem?

5. Some authorities feel that most of Shakespeare's sonnets are spoiled by the final couplet. Do you think this is true of any of the five sonnets you have read? If so, explain why.

6. Elizabethans tended to regard time as "the great enemy." Where does the poet's attitude toward time, the destroyer, appear in these poems? One way to fight time is summed up in the phrase *carpe diem:* "seize the day, enjoy the present." Which of these sonnets give this advice?

FOR COMPOSITION

1. After reading at least four sonnets written by poets other than Shakespeare, write an essay in which you compare several of them to one or more by Shakespeare. In your essay, say whether the Shakespeare sonnet is more or less pleasing or effective than the others. Use direct quotations to enforce your argument.

2. Try to write a sonnet in the Shakespearean pattern. When you have finished, write a short paragraph detailing the special difficulties you encountered in using this form.

Shakespeare and His Theater

A novelist or a poet can wait years for recognition; a playwright must succeed with a play at once or the theater closes and the actors starve. The making of plays is more influenced by externals than any other kind of writing: a play needs the collaboration of author, actors, and audience. It is immediately influenced by such matters as public taste, the personalities and competence of the actors, the stage and its equipment, the size of the theater, and the financial status of the producing company.

Forms of drama and customs of the theater change from country to country and from age to age. Greek plays were written to be played in a vast open-air auditorium; the production therefore had to be slow and simple. In most modern theaters we sit in darkness, looking into a picture frame in which the figures come to life in bright artificial light. As we shall see, Shakespeare's plays were written for a theater very different from our picture frame or the Greeks' enormous auditorium.

Shakespeare's Globe Theater was a small, three-level octagon, open to the sky (see illustration, page 119). Its diameter was 86 feet and its height about 33 feet; inside was a yard about 56 feet across. The whole theater would fit comfortably inside the infield of a baseball diamond.

The stage, lit only by daylight, jutted out into the yard and was surrounded on three sides by spectators. Over the stage, supported by two pillars, was a roof (called "the shadow") which protected the players and their costumes from rain. These pillars served as trees, masts, and the like; they also provided effective hiding places for spies and murderers. Beneath the stage were trap doors through which ghosts could ascend and descend.

Behind the main stage, occupying one side of the octagon, was a recess, or inner stage. This inner stage was frequently used. Here indoor scenes, especially those requiring stage properties, were played; the inner stage then became a tomb, a cave, a study, or a prison. When not needed, the inner stage was concealed by curtains. At the sides of the inner stage, and behind it, were the actors' dressing rooms.

Three tiered galleries surrounded the yard. The part of the second gallery which was built over the main stage was known as the upper stage and was used as a bedroom, or the walls of a castle or city. A balcony jutted out in front of the upper stage, and on either side of the balcony were windows.

The most important difference between the Globe and a modern theater is that there was no general stage curtain to hide the stage and therefore to separate actors from their audience. There was no scenery, realistic or symbolic, and little visual illusion; Shakespeare's audiences used their imagination to provide a background. The setting, apart from some properties—whether the scene was a wild heath, Lady Macbeth's chamber, Dunsinane Castle, or the field of battle—was the back wall on which drapes were hung. Since there was no scenery to be changed (or paid for), Shakespeare could have as many scenes as he needed. When the actors left the stage, that scene ended; when a new group of actors came on, a new scene began and its locality was shown by the action. If a scene had a specific location, this was indicated by a few words of dialogue. Thus, in Act I, Scene vi of *Macbeth,* when King Duncan comes to be Lady Macbeth's guest, his location is clearly set by his opening statement: "This castle hath a pleasant seat." Actors' costumes were also used to indicate the scene. Soldiers with arms were understood to be marching on a battlefield; servants carrying dishes were part of a banquet scene.

Although scenery was not used, color and splendor were not lacking. The actors were arrayed in lavish and magnificent costumes. Adding to this effect were simple but colorful properties such as torches, musical instruments, weapons, and thrones. Fog was created by smoke sent up through one of the traps, and lightning was produced by flashes of gunpowder. In fact, the first Globe Theater burned to the ground when a cannon set off during a performance of *Henry VIII* set fire to the thatched roof of the building.

Since the playhouse was so small, playing was intimate. Nothing divided actors from spectators, and the greatest subtlety of effect thus was possible —in tone of voice, inflection, gesture, even the raising of an eyebrow. There was no need, as in the usual modern theater, for the actor to shout or to move slowly in order to project his personality across a vast space. In the production of most modern plays the theory, or rather pretense, is that the persons onstage are living out their lives quite unaware that they are being watched and overheard. This was not so in Shakespeare's theater. Shakespearean drama was an experience mutually shared by the actors and spectators who together made the play. The actor made the audience a part of himself. Thus it seemed to the Elizabethan audience quite natural to hear Lady Macbeth read her husband's letter aloud or to hear Macbeth utter his inner thoughts, for the audience so closely identified itself with the characters that their thoughts were shared.

Shakespeare's company was a "fellowship of players"—a permanent repertory company—consisting of ten to fifteen sharers in the profits, with ten or a dozen extras. There were also three or four boys who took the parts of girls or young women, for as yet there were no professional actresses on the English stage. The company also included a clown or low comedian. Each afternoon, according to the repertory system, a different play was presented. The company necessarily added continually to its roster of plays since the average life of a new play was about ten performances. Popular plays were acted more frequently; unpopular plays were dropped after a first or second performance. This meant that the company was constantly in rehearsal, for it had to be able to put on a new play very quickly. The players had little time for elaborate production, but the preparation of a new play was always facilitated by the fact that the players were used to working together as a team. In a pinch, they could improvise.

All of these factors—the flexible stage arrangements, the intimate relationship between actors and audience, and the variety permitted by the repertory system—contributed to make the Elizabethan play a very lively form of entertainment.

["MACBETH" FOLLOWS ON PAGE 119.]

ENGLISH PAINTING

The Late Middle Ages and the Renaissance

Among the very few paintings which have come down to us from medieval England, the most famous and beautifully preserved are four small pictures on the fronts and backs of two oak panels. Because the panels are hinged together, so that they can be closed like the covers of a book, they form what is known as a *diptych*. And because they once belonged to the Earls of Pembroke at Wilton House, we refer to them today as the *Wilton Diptych*.

Who the painter of the *Wilton Diptych* may have been, no one knows. But by examining the pictures themselves, we can discover at least part of their meaning and perhaps make a good guess as to their original purpose. Two of the four are reproduced here: the inside face of the left panel (PLATE 1) and the back of the right one (PLATE 2).

In PLATE 1 we see the figures of three crowned kings and a half-clad fourth figure holding a baby lamb who is obviously meant to represent St. John the Baptist. The artist seems to have made no attempt at individual portraiture in the faces of the three kings. Yet we have clues to their identity. Notice, for instance, the arrow held by the king at the left. From medieval English history we know that this figure must represent King Edmund, who was killed by an arrow during a Danish invasion. The ring held by the next king indicates that he is Edward the Confessor, who once gave a ring to a poor pilgrim later identified as St. John the Baptist.

The most important king in the *Wilton Diptych* is the one kneeling in the foreground. On his brooch and repeated many times in the pattern of his brocaded robe is the figure of a deer. There can be no question, then, who this kneeling figure is meant to represent, because the white deer—a medieval symbol of purity and piety—was also the emblem of King Richard II. Moreover, the deer appears again, on a much larger scale, on the back of the second panel (PLATE 2). Undoubtedly the *Wilton Diptych* was intended as an altarpiece, perhaps for the King's own use, for he is being presented here to the Madonna and Child, who are shown in the facing inside panel surrounded by angels.

Much of our knowledge of the daily life and customs of medieval England comes to us from tiny illustrations, called *illuminations*, which were painted on the pages of handwritten manuscripts. The manuscript illumination shown in PLATE 3, for instance, describes the pageantry of a late medieval tournament. In the second half of the fifteenth century, when this little picture was painted, pageantry was about all that was left from the great age of chivalry; for though tournaments were still held as sport for the nobility, most of their hazards had been eliminated. In this picture crested "warriors" are shown breaking each other's lances, while a bystander indicates his excitement with a theatrical gesture and gallery spectators appear to acknowledge by their bland expressions that the entire event is no more than a game.

Within a half-century after this tournament was painted, Western Europe underwent vast changes. With the development of printing, the revival of classical learning, and the separation between the new Protestant churches and the church of Rome, the modern age began. Interest in the individual, and therefore in portraiture, ran high. For many years, most of the outstanding portraits made in England were by foreign artists, among whom was the German painter Hans Holbein. Holbein visited Sir Thomas More's house in London and drew portraits of More's family. Holbein painted faces we could recognize anywhere; for he made both features and character his subject. In PLATE 4 the features, expression, and carriage of Sir Thomas More all combine to give us an impression of his resolute character.

Holbein's portrait of King Henry VIII (PLATE 5), though smaller than a sheet of typewriter paper, conveys a persuasive impression of physical bulk and overriding strength. The figure looms so close to the front of the picture that the shoulders and hands are partially cropped; the plain blue background brings out the contour of the feathered hat and the massive square head. The averted eyes suggest that Henry is rapt in visions of his own. The determined jaw indicates his readiness to act. This is the monarch who in 1534 declared himself to be the head of the Church of England. His old friend Thomas More, unwilling to accept this pronouncement, was executed.

Henry's ban on religious subjects in painting gave added impetus to English interest in portraiture. In about 1600, his younger daughter, Queen Elizabeth I, was portrayed (PLATE 6) by an artist of the school of Nicholas Hilliard (see page 215). Her ornate dress is depicted meticulously, though without the variety of texture caught so artfully in Holbein's *Henry VIII*. Compared to Holbein's portraits, Hilliard's picture makes the Queen's face and hands appear unnaturally flat. No longer young, Elizabeth disliked an art that subtly modeled features by means of light and shadow, for it added unflattering years. Yet there remains a sharp characterization of this strong and intelligent woman in whose reign England attained new glories.

PLATE 1. ARTIST UNKNOWN: *The Wilton Diptych,* detail, left inside panel. About 1395. Tempera on wood. 21 x 14½ inches. (Reproduced by courtesy of the Trustees. The National Gallery, London)

PLATE 2. ARTIST UNKNOWN: *The Wilton Diptych,* detail, right outside panel. About 1395. Tempera on wood. 21 x 14½ inches. (Reproduced by courtesy of the Trustees. The National Gallery, London)

114

PLATE 3. ARTIST UNKNOWN: *Ordinances of Chivalry, Tournament Scene.* About 1450. English illuminated manuscript, full page measures $9\frac{3}{4}$ by $6\frac{3}{4}$ inches. (The Pierpont Morgan Library, New York)

PLATE 4. HANS HOLBEIN, THE YOUNGER (German, 1497–1543): *Sir Thomas More*. 1527. Oil on wood, 29$\frac{3}{8}$ x 23$\frac{3}{8}$ inches. (Copyright The Frick Collection, New York)

PLATE 5. HANS HOLBEIN, THE YOUNGER (German, 1497–1543): *Henry VIII*. 1536. Oil and tempera on wood, $10\frac{3}{4}$ x $7\frac{3}{4}$ inches. (Collection Thyssen-Bornemisza, Lugano-Castagnola)

PLATE 6. SCHOOL OF NICHOLAS HILLIARD (English, about 1600). *Queen Elizabeth I: The Ermine Portrait*. Oil on panel, 41½ x 34 inches. (Reproduced by courtesy of the Marquess of Salisbury, K.G.)

Macbeth

William Shakespeare's *Macbeth* is a powerful drama of a man whose weakness first brought him power, then defeat. As a play for acting, it outdistances most because of its admirable construction and its many scenes that are theatrically powerful as well as inherently dramatic. The story is based on historical fact; Shakespeare adapted it from two episodes related in a contemporary history book, Holinshed's *Chronicles* (1577), a work frequently used by Shakespeare for his history plays. *Macbeth* was probably written in 1606 as a tribute to James I, who traced his ancestry to the Scottish nobleman Banquo. Alive with the passions of eleventh-century Scotland, yet timeless in its impact, *Macbeth* is one of the most gripping of Shakespeare's tragedies.

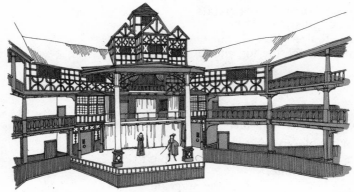

The Globe Theater

Dramatis Personae

DUNCAN, *King of Scotland*

MALCOLM ⎫
DONALBAIN ⎬ *his sons*

MACBETH ⎫ *generals of the*
BANQUO ⎬ *King's army*

MACDUFF ⎫
LENNOX ⎪
ROSS ⎪ *noblemen of*
MENTEITH ⎬ *Scotland*
ANGUS ⎪
CAITHNESS ⎭

LADY MACBETH

LADY MACDUFF

GENTLEWOMAN *attending on Lady Macbeth*

HECATE, *goddess of witchcraft*

THREE WITCHES

FLEANCE, *son of Banquo*

SIWARD, *Earl of Northumberland, general of the English forces*

YOUNG SIWARD, *his son*

SEYTON, *an officer attending on Macbeth*

BOY, *son of Macduff*

AN ENGLISH DOCTOR

A SCOTCH DOCTOR

A SERGEANT

A PORTER

AN OLD MAN

APPARITIONS

LORDS, GENTLEMEN, OFFICERS, SOLDIERS, MURDERERS, ATTENDANTS, *and* MESSENGERS

SCENE—*Scotland and England.* TIME—*The eleventh century.*

ACT I

SCENE I. *A desert place.*

[Thunder and lightning. Enter three WITCHES.*]*

FIRST WITCH. When shall we three meet again
    In thunder, lightning, or in rain?
SECOND WITCH. When the hurly-burly's done,
    When the battle's lost and won.
THIRD WITCH. That will be ere the set of sun.   5
FIRST WITCH. Where the place?
SECOND WITCH.   Upon the heath.
THIRD WITCH. There to meet with Macbeth.
FIRST WITCH. I come, Graymalkin!°
ALL. Paddock° calls. Anon.°
    Fair is foul, and foul is fair: 10
    Hover through the fog and filthy air.   *[Exeunt.]*

SCENE II. *A camp near Forres.**

[Alarum† within. Enter DUNCAN, MALCOLM, DONALBAIN, LENNOX, *with*
ATTENDANTS, *meeting a bleeding* SERGEANT.*]*

DUNCAN. What bloody man is that? He can report,
    As seemeth by his plight, of the revolt
    The newest state.
MALCOLM.   This is the sergeant
    Who like a good and hardy soldier fought
    'Gainst my captivity. Hail, brave friend!   5
    Say to the king the knowledge of the broil°
    As thou didst leave it.
SERGEANT.   Doubtful it stood,
    As two spent swimmers, that do cling together
    And choke° their art. The merciless Macdonwald—
    Worthy to be a rebel, for to that   10
    The multiplying villainies of nature
    Do swarm upon him—from the western isles
    Of kerns and gallowglasses° is supplied;
    And fortune, on his damnèd quarrel smiling,
    Showed° like a rebel's wench. But all's too weak;   15
    For brave Macbeth—well he deserves that name—
    Disdaining fortune, with his brandished steel,
    Which smoked with bloody execution,
    Like valor's minion° carvèd out his passage

SCENE I: 8. **Graymalkin:** cat. 9. **Paddock:** toad. According to the superstition of the times, witches used the cat and the toad as helpers. **Anon:** at once.
    SCENE II: * **Forres** (fôr'is): a town in northeast Scotland, site of King Duncan's palace. †*Alarum:* a trumpet call offstage. 6. **broil:** battle. 9. **choke:** render useless. 13. **kerns and gallowglasses:** light-armed, undisciplined soldiers and better-trained, more heavily armed soldiers. 15. **Showed:** appeared. 19. **minion:** favorite.

Till he faced the slave; 20
Which ne'er shook hands, nor bade farewell to him,
Till he unseamed him° from the nave to the chaps,
And fixed his head upon our battlements.

DUNCAN. O valiant cousin! worthy gentleman!

SERGEANT. As whence the sun 'gins his reflection° 25
Shipwrecking storms and direful thunders break,
So from that spring whence comfort seemed to come
Discomfort swells. Mark, king of Scotland, mark:
No sooner justice had with valor armed
Compelled these skipping kerns to trust their heels, 30
But the Norweyan° lord, surveying vantage,
With furbished arms and new supplies of men
Began a fresh assault.

DUNCAN.   Dismayed not this
Our captains, Macbeth and Banquo?

SERGEANT.   Yes;
As° sparrows eagles, or the hare the lion. 35
If I say sooth,° I must report they were
As cannons overcharged with double cracks,° so they
Doubly redoubled strokes upon the foe.
Except they meant to bathe in reeking wounds,
Or memorize another Golgotha,° 40
I cannot tell.
But I am faint, my gashes cry for help.

DUNCAN. So well thy words become thee as thy wounds;
They smack of honor both. Go get him surgeons.

[*Exit* SERGEANT, *attended.*]

Who comes here?

[*Enter* ROSS.]

MALCOLM.   The worthy thane° of Ross. 45

LENNOX. What a haste looks through his eyes! So should he look
That seems to speak things strange.

ROSS.   God save the king!

DUNCAN. Whence camest thou, worthy thane?

ROSS.   From Fife, great king;
Where the Norweyan banners flout the sky
And fan our people cold. Norway himself, 50
With terrible numbers,
Assisted by that most disloyal traitor,
The thane of Cawdor,° began a dismal conflict;
Till that Bellona's bridegroom,° lapped in proof,°
Confronted him with self-comparisons, 55

---

22. **unseamed him:** split him open.   25. **'gins ... reflection:** rises.   31. **Norweyan** (nôr·wā′yən): Norwegian.   35. **As:** no more than.   36. **sooth:** truth.   37. **cracks:** charges.   40. **memorize ... Golgotha** (gol′gə·thə): make the place as memorable for slaughter as Golgotha, where Christ was crucified.   45. **thane:** a Scottish title of rank similar to the English earl.   53. **Cawdor** (kô′dər).   54. **Bellona's bridegroom:** Macbeth, a great soldier, is called the mate of Bellona, the Roman war goddess.   **lapped in proof:** dressed in armor.

Point against point rebellious, arm 'gainst arm,
Curbing his lavish° spirit; and, to conclude,
The victory fell on us.

DUNCAN.   Great happiness!

ROSS.   That now
Sweno, the Norways' king, craves composition;°
Nor would we deign him burial of his men   60
Till he disbursèd at Saint Colme's inch°
Ten thousand dollars to our general use.

DUNCAN. No more that thane of Cawdor shall deceive
Our bosom interest.° Go pronounce his present° death,
And with his former title greet Macbeth.   65

ROSS. I'll see it done.

DUNCAN. What he hath lost, noble Macbeth hath won.   [*Exeunt.*]

SCENE III. *A heath near Forres.*

[*Thunder. Enter the three* WITCHES.]

FIRST WITCH. Where hast thou been, sister?

SECOND WITCH. Killing swine.°

THIRD WITCH. Sister, where thou?

FIRST WITCH. A sailor's wife had chestnuts in her lap.
And munched, and munched, and munched. "Give me," quoth I.   5
"Aroint thee,° witch!" the rump-fed ronyon° cries.
Her husband's to Aleppo° gone, master o' the *Tiger;*
But in a sieve° I'll thither sail,
And, like a rat without a tail,
I'll do, I'll do, and I'll do.   10

SECOND WITCH. I'll give thee a wind.

FIRST WITCH. Thou'rt kind.

THIRD WITCH. And I another.

FIRST WITCH. I myself have all the other,
And the very ports they blow,
All the quarters that they know   15
I' the shipman's card.°
I will drain him dry as hay;
Sleep shall neither night nor day
Hang upon his penthouse lid;°
He shall live a man forbid.°   20
Weary se'nnights° nine times nine
Shall he dwindle, peak,° and pine;

57. **lavish:** insolent.   59. **composition:** terms of peace.   61. **Saint Colme's inch:** island near Edinburgh (now called Inchcolm).   64. **bosom interest:** vital concerns.   **present:** immediate.
SCENE III: 2. **Killing swine:** Witches were commonly accused of killing their neighbors' pigs.
6. **Aroint thee:** be off!   **ronyon:** mangy creature.   7. **Aleppo:** trading center in Syria.   8. **sieve:** In the Scottish witchcraft trials in 1592, witches confessed to sailing in sieves.   17. **card:** compass.
20. **penthouse lid:** eyelid: literally, the slanted roof of a shed.   21. **forbid:** accursed.   22. **se'nnights:** weeks.   23. **peak:** grow thin.

Though his bark cannot be lost,
Yet it shall be tempest-tost.   25
Look what I have.
SECOND WITCH. Show me, show me.
FIRST WITCH. Here I have a pilot's thumb,
Wrecked as homeward he did come.   [*Drum within.*]
THIRD WITCH. A drum, a drum!   30
Macbeth doth come.
ALL. The weird sisters, hand in hand,
Posters° of the sea and land,
Thus do go about, about;
Thrice to thine and thrice to mine   35
And thrice again, to make up nine.
Peace! the charm's wound up.

[*Enter* MACBETH *and* BANQUO.]

MACBETH. So foul and fair a day I have not seen.
BANQUO. How far is 't called to Forres? What are these
So withered and so wild in their attire,   40
That look not like the inhabitants o' the earth,
And yet are on 't? Live you? or are you aught
That man may question? You seem to understand me,
By each at once her choppy° finger laying
Upon her skinny lips. You should° be women,   45
And yet your beards forbid me to interpret
That you are so.
MACBETH.   Speak, if you can. What are you?
FIRST WITCH. All hail, Macbeth! hail to thee, thane of Glamis!°
SECOND WITCH. All hail, Macbeth! hail to thee, thane of Cawdor!
THIRD WITCH. All hail, Macbeth, that shalt be king hereafter!   50
BANQUO. Good sir, why do you start, and seem to fear
Things that do sound so fair? I' the name of truth,
Are ye fantastical,° or that indeed
Which outwardly ye show? My noble partner
You greet with present grace and great prediction   55
Of noble having° and of royal hope,
That he seems rapt° withal; to me you speak not.
If you can look into the seeds of time,
And say which grain will grow and which will not,
Speak then to me, who neither beg nor fear   60
Your favors nor your hate.
FIRST WITCH. Hail!
SECOND WITCH. Hail!
THIRD WITCH. Hail!
FIRST WITCH. Lesser than Macbeth, and greater.   65
SECOND WITCH. Not so happy,° yet much happier.

---

33. **Posters:** quick riders. 44. **choppy:** chapped. 45. **should:** must. 48. **Glamis:** pronounced in
two syllables in the play, but pronounced (glämz) in modern English. 53. **fantastical:** creatures of the
imagination. 56. **having:** possessions. 57. **rapt:** in a trance. 66. **happy:** fortunate.

THIRD WITCH. Thou shalt get kings, though thou be none;
    So all hail, Macbeth and Banquo!
FIRST WITCH. Banquo and Macbeth, all hail!
MACBETH. Stay, you imperfect speakers, tell me more.
    By Sinel's° death I know I am thane of Glamis;   70
    But how of Cawdor? The thane of Cawdor lives,
    A prosperous gentleman; and to be king
    Stands not within the prospect of belief,
    No more than to be Cawdor. Say from whence   75
    You owe this strange intelligence, or why
    Upon this blasted heath you stop our way
    With such prophetic greeting? Speak, I charge you.   [WITCHES *vanish*.]
BANQUO. The earth hath bubbles, as the water has,
    And these are of them. Whither are they vanished?   80
MACBETH. Into the air; and what seemed corporal° melted
    As breath into the wind. Would they had stayed!
BANQUO. Were such things here as we do speak about?
    Or have we eaten on the insane root°
    That takes the reason prisoner?   85
MACBETH. Your children shall be kings.
BANQUO.   You shall be king.
MACBETH. And thane of Cawdor too: went it not so?
BANQUO. To the selfsame tune and words. Who's here?

        [*Enter* ROSS *and* ANGUS.]

ROSS. The king hath happily received, Macbeth,
    The news of thy success; and when he reads
    Thy personal venture in the rebels' fight,   90
    His wonders and his praises do contend
    Which should be thine or his.° Silenced with that,
    In viewing o'er the rest o' the selfsame day,
    He finds thee in the stout Norweyan ranks,
    Nothing afeard of what thyself didst make,   95
    Strange images of death.° As thick as hail
    Came post° with post; and every one did bear
    Thy praises in his kingdom's great defense,
    And poured them down before him.
ANGUS.   We are sent   100
    To give thee from our royal master thanks;
    Only to herald thee into his sight,
    Not pay thee.
ROSS. And, for an earnest° of a greater honor,
    He bade me, from him, call thee thane of Cawdor;
    In which addition,° hail, most worthy thane!   105
    For it is thine.
BANQUO.   [*Aside*] What, can the devil speak true?

---

71. **Sinel's** (sī′nəlz): Macbeth's father. 81. **corporal:** of bodily substance, real. 84. **insane root:**
henbane or hemlock, supposed to cause madness. 93. **Which . . . his:** whether he should wonder at
you or praise you. 96–97. **Nothing . . . death:** killing and not being afraid of being killed. 98. **post:**
mounted messenger. 104. **earnest:** pledge. 106. **addition:** title.

MACBETH. The thane of Cawdor lives; why do you dress me
    In borrowed robes?
ANGUS.   Who was the thane lives yet;
    But under heavy judgment bears that life   110
    Which he deserves to lose. Whether he was combined
    With those of Norway, or did line° the rebel
    With hidden help and vantage,° or that with both
    He labored in his country's wreck, I know not;
    But treasons capital,° confessed and proved,   115
    Have overthrown him.
MACBETH.   [*Aside*] Glamis, and thane of Cawdor!
    The greatest is behind.° [*To* ROSS *and* ANGUS] Thanks for your pains.
    [*To* BANQUO] Do you not hope your children shall be kings,
    When those that gave the thane of Cawdor to me
    Promised no less to them?
BANQUO.   That, trusted home,°   120
    Might yet enkindle you unto° the crown,
    Besides the thane of Cawdor. But 'tis strange;
    And oftentimes, to win us to our harm,
    The instruments of darkness tell us truths,
    Win us with honest trifles, to betray 's   125
    In deepest consequence.
    Cousins, a word, I pray you.
MACBETH.   [*Aside*] Two truths are told,
    As happy prologues to the swelling act
    Of the imperial theme.°—I thank you, gentlemen.
    [*Aside*] This supernatural soliciting   130
    Cannot be ill, cannot be good. If ill,
    Why hath it given me earnest of success,
    Commencing in a truth? I am thane of Cawdor.
    If good, why do I yield to that suggestion
    Whose horrid image doth unfix my hair   135
    And make my seated° heart knock at my ribs,
    Against the use of nature?° Present fears
    Are less than horrible imaginings;
    My thought, whose murder yet is but fantastical,
    Shakes so my single state° of man that function°   140
    Is smothered in surmise;° and nothing is
    But what is not.°
BANQUO.   Look, how our partner's rapt.
MACBETH. [*Aside*] If chance will have me king, why, chance may crown me,
    Without my stir.
BANQUO.   New honors come upon him,
    Like our strange° garments, cleave not to their mold   145
    But with the aid of use.

    112. **line:** support.   113. **vantage:** assistance.   115. **capital:** deserving death.   117. **behind:** yet
to come.   120. **home:** fully.   121. **enkindle . . . unto:** set afire your hopes for.   129. **imperial theme:**
that Macbeth will be king.   136. **seated:** firmly imbedded.   137. **Against . . . nature:** in an unnatural
way.   140. **single state:** the individual was often regarded as a "microcosm," a miniature universe.
function: action.   141. **surmise:** imagination.   141–42. **nothing . . . not:** Nothing is real to me except
my imaginings.   145. **strange:** new.

MACBETH.   [*Aside*] Come what come may,
  Time and the hour runs through the roughest day.
BANQUO. Worthy Macbeth, we stay upon your leisure.
MACBETH. Give me your favor.° My dull brain was wrought
  With things forgotten. Kind gentlemen, your pains   150
  Are registered° where every day I turn
  The leaf to read them. Let us toward the king.
  [*To* BANQUO] Think upon what hath chanced, and, at more time,
  The interim having weighed it,° let us speak
  Our free hearts each to other.
BANQUO.   Very gladly.   155
MACBETH. Till then, enough. Come, friends.   [*Exeunt.*]

SCENE IV. *Forres. The Palace.*

[*Flourish.* * *Enter* DUNCAN, MALCOLM, DONALBAIN, LENNOX, *and* ATTENDANTS.]

DUNCAN. Is execution done on Cawdor? Are not
  Those in commission yet returned?
MALCOLM.   My liege,
  They are not yet come back. But I have spoke
  With one that saw him die; who did report
  That very frankly he confessed his treasons,   5
  Implored your highness' pardon and set forth
  A deep repentance. Nothing in his life
  Became him like the leaving it; he died
  As one that had been studied in his death
  To throw away the dearest thing he owed,   10
  As 'twere a careless trifle.
DUNCAN.   There's no art
  To find the mind's construction° in the face;
  He was a gentleman on whom I built
  An absolute trust.

        [*Enter* MACBETH, BANQUO, ROSS, *and* ANGUS.]

              O worthiest cousin!
  The sin of my ingratitude even now   15
  Was heavy on me. Thou art so far before
  That swiftest wing of recompense is slow
  To overtake thee. Would thou hadst less deserved,
  That the proportion both of thanks and payment
  Might have been mine!° Only I have left to say,   20
  More is thy due than more than all can pay.
MACBETH. The service and the loyalty I owe,
  In doing it, pays itself. Your highness' part
  Is to receive our duties; and our duties
  Are to your throne and state, children and servants,   25

149. **Give . . . favor:** Forgive me.   151. **registered:** recorded (in my heart).   154. **The . . . it:** having considered it meanwhile.
  SCENE IV: * **Flourish:** trumpet fanfare.   12. **the . . . construction:** a person's character.   19–20.
That . . . mine: that my thanks might have exceeded the rewards you deserve.

Which do but what they should, by doing everything
Safe toward° your love and honor.

DUNCAN.   Welcome hither;
I have begun to plant thee, and will labor
To make thee full of growing. Noble Banquo,
That hast no less deserved, nor must be known   30
No less to have done so, let me infold thee
And hold thee to my heart.

BANQUO.   There if I grow,
The harvest is your own.

DUNCAN.   My plenteous joys,
Wanton° in fullness, seek to hide themselves
In drops of sorrow. Sons, kinsmen, thanes,   35
And you whose places are the nearest, know
We will establish our estate° upon
Our eldest, Malcolm, whom we name hereafter
The Prince of Cumberland; which honor must
Not unaccompanied invest him only,   40
But signs of nobleness, like stars, shall shine
On all deservers. From hence to Inverness,°
And bind us further to you.

MACBETH. The rest is labor, which is not used for you.°
I'll be myself the harbinger and make joyful   45
The hearing of my wife with your approach;
So humbly take my leave.

DUNCAN.   My worthy Cawdor!

MACBETH. [*Aside*] The Prince of Cumberland! That is a step
On which I must fall down, or else o'erleap,
For in my way it lies. Stars, hide your fires;   50
Let not light see my black and deep desires;
The eye wink at° the hand; yet let that be,
Which the eye fears, when it is done, to see.   [*Exit.*]

DUNCAN. True, worthy Banquo; he is full so valiant,
And in his commendations I am fed;   55
It is a banquet to me. Let's after him,
Whose care is gone before to bid us welcome.
It is a peerless kinsman.   [*Flourish. Exeunt.*]

SCENE V. *Inverness.* MACBETH'S *castle.*

[*Enter* LADY MACBETH, *reading a letter.*]

LADY MACBETH. "They met me in the day of success; and I have learned by the
perfectest report, they have more in them than mortal knowledge. When I
burned in desire to question them further, they made themselves air, into
which they vanished. Whiles I stood rapt in the wonder of it, came mis-
sives° from the king, who all-hailed me 'Thane of Cawdor'; by which   5

---

27. **Safe toward:** with sure regard for.   34. **Wanton:** unrestrained.   37. **We . . . estate:** I (here, as
elsewhere, Duncan uses the royal "we") will make (Malcolm) the heir to my throne.   42. **Inverness:**
Macbeth's castle.   44. **The . . . you:** Anything done for you is a pleasure.   52. **wink at:** be blind to.
SCENE V: 5. **missives:** messengers.

title, before, these weird sisters saluted me, and referred me to the coming
on of time with 'Hail, king that shalt be!' This have I thought good to de-
liver thee, my dearest partner of greatness, that thou mightst not lose the
dues of rejoicing, by being ignorant of what greatness is promised thee.
Lay it to thy heart, and farewell."   10
Glamis thou art, and Cawdor; and shalt be
What thou art promised. Yet do I fear thy nature;
It is too full o' the milk of human kindness
To catch the nearest way. Thou wouldst be great;
Art not without ambition, but without   15
The illness° should attend it. What thou wouldst highly
That wouldst thou holily; wouldst not play false,
And yet wouldst wrongly win. Thou 'ldst have, great Glamis,
That which cries, "Thus thou must do, if thou have it";
And that which rather thou dost fear to do   20
Than wishest should be undone.° Hie thee hither,
That I may pour my spirits in thine ear,
And chastise with the valor of my tongue
All that impedes thee from the golden round,°
Which fate and metaphysical° aid doth seem   25
To have thee crowned withal.

[Enter a MESSENGER.]

What is your tidings?

MESSENGER. The king comes here tonight.
LADY MACBETH.   Thou 'rt mad to say it!
  Is not thy master with him? who, were 't so,
  Would have informed for preparation.
MESSENGER. So please you, it is true; our thane is coming.   30
  One of my fellows had the speed of° him,
  Who, almost dead for breath, had scarcely more
  Than would make up his message.
LADY MACBETH.   Give him tending;
  He brings great news.   [Exit MESSENGER.]
The raven himself is hoarse
  That croaks the fatal entrance of Duncan   35
  Under my battlements. Come, you spirits
  That tend on mortal thoughts, unsex me here,
  And fill me from the crown to the toe top-full
  Of direst cruelty! make thick my blood;
  Stop up the access and passage to remorse,   40
  That no compunctious visitings of nature°
  Shake my fell purpose, nor keep peace between
  The effect and it! Come to my woman's breasts,
  And take my milk for gall,° you murdering ministers,°

---

16. **illness:** here, wickedness. 18–21. **Thou 'ldst ... undone:** The thing that you want, great
Glamis, requires doing certain things to obtain it, things you are afraid to do, but, once done, you will
not want undone. 24. **golden round:** crown. 25. **metaphysical:** supernatural. 31. **had ... of:**
overtook. 41. **compunctious ... nature:** natural feelings of pity and remorse. 44. **gall:** bitterness.
murdering ministers: spirits of murder.

Wherever in your sightless° substances   45
You wait on nature's mischief! Come, thick night,
And pall° thee in the dunnest° smoke of hell,
That my keen knife see not the wound it makes,
Nor Heaven peep through the blanket of the dark,
To cry "Hold, hold!"

[*Enter* MACBETH.]

              Great Glamis! worthy Cawdor!   50
Greater than both, by the all-hail hereafter!
Thy letters have transported me beyond
This ignorant present, and I feel now
The future in the instant.
MACBETH.   My dearest love,
Duncan comes here tonight.
LADY MACBETH.   And when goes hence?   55
MACBETH. Tomorrow, as he purposes.
LADY MACBETH.   O, never
Shall sun that morrow see!
Your face, my thane, is as a book where men
May read strange matters. To beguile° the time,
Look like the time; bear welcome in your eye,   60
Your hand, your tongue; look like the innocent flower,
But be the serpent under 't. He that's coming
Must be provided for; and you shall put
This night's great business into my dispatch;
Which shall to all our nights and days to come   65
Give solely sovereign sway° and masterdom.
MACBETH. We will speak further.
LADY MACBETH.   Only look up clear;°
To alter favor° ever is to fear.
Leave all the rest to me.   [*Exeunt.*]

SCENE VI. *Before* MACBETH'S *castle.*

[*Hautboys and torches.* Enter* DUNCAN, MALCOLM, DONALBAIN, BANQUO,
LENNOX, MACDUFF, ROSS, ANGUS, *and* ATTENDANTS.]

DUNCAN. This castle hath a pleasant seat;° the air
    Nimbly and sweetly recommends itself
    Unto our gentle senses.
BANQUO.   This guest of summer,
    The temple-haunting martlet,° does approve,°
    By his loved mansionry,° that the heaven's breath   5

---

    45. **sightless:** invisible. 47. **pall:** envelop as with a pall. **dunnest:** darkest. 59. **beguile:** deceive.
66. **sovereign sway:** absolute power. 67. **look up clear:** look innocent. 68. **To . . . favor:** to change
your facial expression; that is, to show fear.
    SCENE VI: * **Hautboys** (hō'boiz) **and torches:** The oboes announce the entrance of royalty; the
torches indicate that it is night. 1. **seat:** location. 4. **martlet:** swallow, once a slang word for dupe—
one who is easily deceived. **approve:** show. 5. **mansionry:** building.

Smells wooingly here; no jutty, frieze,
Buttress, nor coign of vantage,° but this bird
Hath made his pendent bed and procreant cradle.°
Where they most breed and haunt, I have observed,
The air is delicate.

[*Enter* LADY MACBETH.]

DUNCAN.   See, see, our honored hostess!   10
    The love that follows us sometimes is our trouble,
    Which still we thank as love. Herein I teach you
    How you shall bid God 'ild° us for your pains,
    And thank us for your trouble.
LADY MACBETH.   All our service
    In every point twice done and then done double   15
    Were poor and single business to contend
    Against those honors deep and broad wherewith
    Your majesty loads our house; for those of old,
    And the late dignities heaped up to them,
    We rest your hermits.°
DUNCAN.   Where's the thane of Cawdor?   20
    We coursed° him at the heels, and had a purpose
    To be his purveyor;° but he rides well;
    And his great love, sharp as his spur, hath holp° him
    To his home before us. Fair and noble hostess,
    We are your guest tonight.
LADY MACBETH.   Your servants ever   25
    Have theirs, themselves, and what is theirs in compt,°
    To make their audit at your highness' pleasure,
    Still° to return your own.
DUNCAN.   Give me your hand;
    Conduct me to mine host. We love him highly,
    And shall continue our graces toward him.   30
    By your leave, hostess.
                                                    [*Exeunt.*]

SCENE VII. MACBETH's *castle.*

[*Hautboys and torches. Enter a* SEWER,* *and divers* SERVANTS *with dishes and
service, and pass over the stage. Then enter* MACBETH.]

MACBETH. If it were done when 'tis done, then 'twere well
    It were done quickly. If the assassination
    Could trammel up the consequence, and catch
    With his surcease success;° that but this blow
    Might be the be-all and the end-all here,   5

7. **coign of vantage:** convenient corner. 8. **procreant** (prō′krē·ənt) **cradle:** where the young are
hatched. 13. **God 'ild:** God reward. They should thank him for the trouble he causes them, since he
is there because he loves them. 20. **rest . . . hermits:** remain bound to pray for you, as hermits pray
for a benefactor's soul. 21. **coursed:** chased. 22. **purveyor:** court official who goes ahead to arrange for the provisions for the king's table. 23. **holp:** helped. 26. **compt:** account. 28. **Still:**
always.

SCENE VII: * **sewer:** steward, butler. 2–4. **If . . . success:** if only the murder would have no after-
effects, but be final and successful with Duncan's death.

But° here, upon this bank and shoal of time,
We'ld jump° the life to come. But in these cases
We still have judgment here; that we but teach
Bloody instructions, which, being taught, return
To plague the inventor. This even-handed° justice   10
Commends° the ingredients of our poisoned chalice°
To our own lips. He's here in double trust;
First, as I am his kinsman and his subject,
Strong both against the deed; then, as his host,
Who should against his murderer shut the door,   15
Not bear the knife myself. Besides, this Duncan
Hath borne his faculties° so meek, hath been
So clear° in his great office, that his virtues
Will plead like angels, trumpet-tongued, against
The deep damnation of his taking-off;   20
And pity, like a naked newborn babe,
Striding the blast, or heaven's cherubin, horsed
Upon the sightless couriers° of the air,
Shall blow the horrid deed in every eye,
That tears shall drown the wind. I have no spur   25
To prick the sides of my intent, but only
Vaulting ambition, which o'erleaps itself
And falls on the other.°

[*Enter* LADY MACBETH.]

How now! what news?
LADY MACBETH. He has almost supped. Why have you left the chamber?

MACBETH. Hath he asked for me?
LADY MACBETH.   Know you not he has?   30
MACBETH. We will proceed no further in this business.
He hath honored me of late; and I have bought
Golden opinions from all sorts of people,
Which would be worn now in their newest gloss,
Not cast aside so soon.
LADY MACBETH.   Was the hope drunk   35
Wherein you dressed yourself? Hath it slept since?
And wakes it now, to look so green and pale
At what it did so freely?° From this time
Such I account thy love. Art thou afeard
To be the same in thine own act and valor   40
As thou art in desire? Wouldst thou have that
Which thou esteem'st the ornament of life,°
And live a coward in thine own esteem,
Letting "I dare not" wait upon "I would,"
Like the poor cat i' the adage?°

6. **But:** even. 7. **jump:** risk. 10. **even-handed:** impartial. 11. **Commends:** offers. **chalice:**
cup. 17. **faculties:** powers. 18. **clear:** free from reproach. 23. **sightless couriers:** unseen messengers, i.e., the winds. 28. **other:** i.e., the other side. 38. **freely:** without compulsion. 42. **ornament
of life:** i.e., the crown. 45. **adage:** This refers to the old proverb, "The cat would eat fish but would
not wet her feet."

MACBETH.   Prithee, peace!
I dare do all that may become a man;
Who dares do more is none.
LADY MACBETH.   What beast was 't, then,
That made you break° this enterprise to me?
When you durst do it, then you were a man;
And, to be more than what you were,° you would   50
Be so much more the man. Nor time nor place
Did then adhere,° and yet you would make both.
They have made themselves, and that their° fitness now
Does unmake you. I have given suck, and know
How tender 'tis to love the babe that milks me;   55
I would, while it was smiling in my face,
Have plucked my nipple from his boneless gums,
And dashed the brains out, had I so sworn as you
Have done to this.
MACBETH.   If we should fail?
LADY MACBETH.   We fail!
But screw your courage to the sticking-place   60
And we'll not fail. When Duncan is asleep—
Whereto the rather shall his day's hard journey
Soundly invite him—his two chamberlains
Will I with wine and wassail° so convince°
That memory, the warder of the brain,   65
Shall be a fume,° and the receipt of reason
A limbeck only.° When in swinish sleep
Their drenchèd natures lie as in a death,
What cannot you and I perform upon
The unguarded Duncan? what not put upon   70
His spongy officers, who shall bear the guilt
Of our great quell?°
MACBETH.   Bring forth men children only;
For thy undaunted mettle should compose
Nothing but males. Will it not be received,
When we have marked with blood those sleepy two   75
Of his own chamber and used their very daggers,
That they have done 't?
LADY MACBETH.   Who dares receive it other,
As we shall make our griefs and clamor roar
Upon his death?
MACBETH.   I am settled, and bend up°
Each corporal agent° to this terrible feat.   80
Away, and mock the time with fairest show;
False face must hide what the false heart doth know.   [*Exeunt.*]

---

48. **break:** reveal.   50. **to . . . were:** that is, to be king.   52. **Did then adhere:** was then suitable for the murder.   53. **that their:** their very.   64. **wassail:** carousing; boisterous drinking and merrymaking. **convince:** overcome.   66. **be a fume:** be confused by the fumes of drink.   66–67. **the receipt . . . only:** The part of the brain which reasons would become like a still (limbeck), distilling only confused thoughts.   72. **quell:** murder.   79. **bend up:** stretch tight.   80. **corporal agent:** bodily strength and power.

1. How does the line "fair is foul, and foul is fair," first spoken by the witches in Scene i and later echoed in Scene iii by Macbeth and Banquo, foreshadow the events of the entire act and set the tone of the play?

2. What impression do you have of Macbeth from Scene ii? Why is this initial characterization important?

3. In Scene iii, Macbeth and Banquo react differently to the witches and their predictions. How does Macbeth react? How does Banquo react? What is the significance of Banquo's question (lines 51–52): "Good sir, why do you start, and seem to fear/ Things that do sound so fair?" Is there any evidence in Act I that Macbeth had previously entertained the possibility of becoming king? If so, what does this indicate about the role the witches play in influencing Macbeth's thoughts and actions?

4. Later in the play Macbeth complains that he is overshadowed by Banquo's greater character. What indications of this overshadowing are there in Scene iii? In what ways is Banquo "lesser than Macbeth, and greater"?

5. What do we learn about the character of Macbeth from his *asides* (his speeches not heard by others) in Scene iii? What else do we learn about Macbeth and about his wife from her soliloquy in Scene v? Who seems to be the stronger person?

6. What are your impressions of Duncan in Act I? What is ironic about the king's speech (Scene iv, lines 11–21) when he greets Macbeth?

7. Analyze Macbeth's argument with himself at the beginning of Scene vii. What is he afraid of? How does Lady Macbeth persuade him? What are her arguments? Do you agree with her that Macbeth's hesitation is a sign of weakness? Why or why not?

BLANK VERSE

Except for a few isolated prose passages, *Macbeth* is written in *blank verse*, which, introduced into English literature in the sixteenth century, was used in most Elizabethan dramas. Blank verse is unrhymed verse written in iambic pentameter. An *iamb* is one unstressed syllable followed by one stressed syllable, as in the words *to dance*. The term *pentameter* indicates that there are five feet, or beats, to a line. Note the following example from Act I of *Macbeth:*

"So foul and fair a day I have not seen."
  1   2   3   4   5

More than any other verse form, blank verse most closely reflects the natural, easy rhythms of English speech. Because of this and because of its fluency and flexibility, blank verse has always been a popular form. After Shakespeare and the Elizabethans, it was used by later poets such as Milton, Wordsworth, Tennyson, and Browning, and more recently by T. S. Eliot and Maxwell Anderson, who used a freer version of this meter in their poetic dramas.

ACT II

SCENE I. *Court of* MACBETH'S *castle.*

[*Enter* BANQUO, *and* FLEANCE * *bearing a torch before him.*]

BANQUO. How goes the night, boy?
FLEANCE. The moon is down; I have not heard the clock.
BANQUO. And she goes down at twelve.
FLEANCE.   I take 't, 'tis later, sir.
BANQUO. Hold, take my sword. There's husbandry° in heaven;
  Their candles are all out. Take thee that° too.   5
  A heavy summons° lies like lead upon me,

---

* **Fleance** (fle·ans). 4. **husbandry:** economy. 5. **that:** probably his sword belt. 6. **heavy summons:** great weariness.

And yet I would not sleep. Merciful powers,
Restrain in me the cursèd thoughts that nature
Gives way to in repose!

[Enter MACBETH, *and a* SERVANT *with a torch.]*

                    Give me my sword.
Who's there?   10
MACBETH. A friend.
BANQUO. What, sir, not yet at rest? The king's abed.
He hath been in unusual pleasure, and
Sent forth great largess to your offices.°
This diamond he greets your wife withal,   15
By the name of most kind hostess; and shut up°
In measureless content.
MACBETH.   Being unprepared,
Our will became the servant to defect;
Which else should free have wrought.°
BANQUO.   All's well.
I dreamt last night of the three weird sisters: 20
To you they have showed some truth.
MACBETH.   I think not of them;
Yet, when we can entreat an hour to serve,
We would spend it in some words upon that business,
If you would grant the time.
BANQUO.   At your kind'st leisure.
MACBETH. If you shall cleave to my consent, when 'tis,   25
It shall make honor for you.
BANQUO.   So° I lose none
In seeking to augment it, but still keep
My bosom franchised° and allegiance° clear,
I shall be counseled.°
MACBETH.   Good repose the while!
BANQUO. Thanks, sir; the like to you!   *[Exeunt* BANQUO *and* FLEANCE.] 30
MACBETH. Go bid thy mistress, when my drink is ready,
She strike upon the bell. Get thee to bed.   *[Exit* SERVANT.]
Is this a dagger which I see before me,
The handle toward my hand? Come, let me clutch thee.
I have thee not, and yet I see thee still.   35
Art thou not, fatal vision, sensible°
To feeling as to sight? or art thou but
A dagger of the mind, a false creation,
Proceeding from the heat-oppressèd brain?
I see thee yet, in form as palpable°   40
As this which now I draw.
Thou marshal'st° me the way that I was going;
And such an instrument I was to use.

14. **largess ... offices:** gifts of money to the servant quarters.　16. **shut up:** retired to his room.
17–19. **Being ... wrought:** Had we more warning of the king's visit, our hospitality would have been
more lavish.　26. **So:** so long as.　28. **bosom franchised:** conscience clear. **allegiance:** that is, to the
king.　29. **counseled:** listen to your proposal.　36. **sensible:** tangible.　40. **palpable:** obvious.
42. **marshal'st:** leadest.

Mine eyes are made the fools o' the other senses,
Or else worth all the rest; I see thee still,   45
And on thy blade and dudgeon° gouts° of blood,
Which was not so before. There's no such thing.
It is the bloody business which informs°
Thus to mine eyes. Now o'er the one half-world
Nature seems dead, and wicked dreams abuse   50
The curtained sleep! witchcraft celebrates
Pale Hecate's° offerings, and withered murder,
Alarumed by his sentinel, the wolf,
Whose howl's his watch,° thus with his stealthy pace,
With Tarquin's ravishing strides,° toward his design   55
Moves like a ghost. Thou sure and firm-set earth,
Hear not my steps, which way they walk, for fear
Thy very stones prate of my whereabout,
And take the present horror° from the time,
Which now suits with° it. Whiles I threat, he lives;   60
Words to the heat of deeds too cold breath gives.   [A bell rings.]
I go, and it is done; the bell invites me.
Hear it not, Duncan; for it is a knell
That summons thee to heaven or to hell.   [Exit.]

SCENE II. *The same.*

[Enter LADY MACBETH.]

LADY MACBETH. That which hath made them drunk hath made me bold;
What hath quenched them hath given me fire. Hark! Peace!
It was the owl that shrieked, the fatal bellman,°
Which gives the stern'st good night. He is about it.
The doors are open; and the surfeited grooms°   5
Do mock their charge with snores. I have drugged their possets,°
That death and nature do contend about them.
Whether they live or die.
MACBETH. [*Within*] Who's there? what, ho!
LADY MACBETH. Alack, I am afraid they have awaked,   10
And 'tis not done. The attempt and not the deed
Confounds° us. Hark! I laid their daggers ready;
He could not miss 'em. Had he not resembled
My father as he slept, I had done 't.

[Enter MACBETH.]

My husband!
MACBETH. I have done the deed. Didst thou not hear a noise?   15

46. **dudgeon:** handle. **gouts:** drops. 48. **informs:** creates forms. 52. **Hecate** (hek'ə·tē): goddess of the underworld and of witchcraft, to whom the witches pledge allegiance. 54. **howl's ... watch:** tells time by howling. 55. **Tarquin's ... strides:** like Tarquin, son of a sixth-century Roman king. 59. **present horror:** the silence of midnight. 60. **suits with:** matches.
SCENE II: 3. **fatal bellman:** At midnight on the night before an execution, a bellman rang a handbell outside the condemned person's cell, bidding repentance of sins. 5. **surfeited grooms:** overfed servants. 6. **possets:** warm drinks, taken at bedtime. 12. **confounds:** ruins.

LADY MACBETH. I heard the owl scream and the crickets cry.
Did not you speak?
MACBETH.   When?
LADY MACBETH.   Now.
MACBETH.   As I descended?
LADY MACBETH. Ay.
MACBETH. Hark!
Who lies i' the second chamber?
LADY MACBETH.   Donalbain.   20
MACBETH. This is a sorry sight.   [*Looking on his hands.*]
LADY MACBETH. A foolish thought, to say a sorry sight.
MACBETH. There's one did laugh in 's sleep, and one cried "Murder!"
That they did wake each other. I stood and heard them;
But they did say their prayers, and addressed them   25
Again to sleep.
LADY MACBETH.   There are two lodged together.
MACBETH. One cried "God bless us!" and "Amen" the other,
As they had seen me with these hangman's hands.
Listening their fear, I could not say "Amen,"
When they did say "God bless us!"
LADY MACBETH.   Consider it not so deeply.   30
MACBETH. But wherefore could not I pronounce "Amen"?
I had most need of blessing, and "Amen"
Stuck in my throat.
LADY MACBETH.   These deeds must not be thought
After these ways; so, it will make us mad.
MACBETH. Methought I heard a voice cry "Sleep no more!   35
Macbeth does murder sleep," the innocent sleep,
Sleep that knits up the raveled sleave° of care,
The death of each day's life, sore labor's bath,
Balm of hurt minds, great nature's second course,°
Chief nourisher in life's feast——
LADY MACBETH.   What do you mean?   40
MACBETH. Still it cried "Sleep no more!" to all the house;
"Glamis hath murdered sleep, and therefore Cawdor
Shall sleep no more; Macbeth shall sleep no more."
LADY MACBETH. Who was it that thus cried? Why, worthy thane,
You do unbend° your noble strength, to think   45
So brainsickly of things. Go get some water,
And wash this filthy witness from your hand.
Why did you bring these daggers from the place?
They must lie there; go carry them; and smear
The sleepy grooms with blood.
MACBETH.   I'll go no more.   50
I am afraid to think what I have done;
Look on 't again I dare not.
LADY MACBETH.   Infirm of purpose!
Give me the daggers. The sleeping and the dead

37. **raveled sleave:** tangled skein, as of yarn.   39. **second course:** the main part of the feast.   45. **unbend:** relax.

Are but as pictures; 'tis the eye of childhood
That fears a painted devil. If he do bleed,   55
I'll gild the faces of the grooms withal;
For it must seem their guilt.   [*Exit. Knocking within.*]
MACBETH.   Whence is that knocking?
How is 't with me, when every noise appalls me?
What hands are here? Ha! they pluck out mine eyes.
Will all great Neptune's ocean wash this blood   60
Clean from my hand? No, this my hand will rather
The multitudinous seas incarnadine,°
Making the green one red.

[*Reenter* LADY MACBETH.]

LADY MACBETH. My hands are of your color; but I shame
To wear a heart so white. [*Knocking within.*] I hear a knocking   65
At the south entry. Retire we to our chamber;
A little water clears us of this deed.
How easy is it, then! Your constancy°
Hath left you unattended. [*Knocking within.*] Hark! more knocking.
Get on your nightgown, lest occasion call us,   70
And show us to be watchers. Be not lost
So poorly in your thoughts.
MACBETH. To know my deed, 'twere best not know myself.   [*Knocking within.*]
Wake Duncan with thy knocking! I would thou couldst!   [*Exeunt.*]

SCENE III. *The same.*

[*Knocking within. Enter a* PORTER.]

PORTER.° Here's a knocking indeed! If a man were porter of hell gate, he should
have old turning the key.° [*Knocking within.*] Knock, knock, knock! Who's
there, i' the name of Beelzebub?° Here's a farmer, that hanged himself on
the expectation of plenty.° Come in time; have napkins enow about you;
here you'll sweat for 't. [*Knocking within.*] Knock, knock! Who's there,   5
in the other devil's name? Faith, here's an equivocator,° that could swear in
both the scales against either scale; who committed treason enough for
God's sake, yet could not equivocate to heaven. O, come in, equivocator.
[*Knocking within.*] Knock, knock, knock! Who's there? Faith, here's an
English tailor come hither, for stealing out of a French hose.° Come in,   10
tailor; here you may roast your goose.° [*Knocking within.*] Knock, knock;
never at quiet! What are you? But this place is too cold for hell. I'll devil-
porter it no further; I had thought to have let in some of all professions
that go the primrose way to the everlasting bonfire. [*Knocking within.*]
Anon, anon! I pray you, remember the porter.   [*Opens the gate.*]   15

62. **incarnadine** (in·kär'nə·dīn): make red.   68. **constancy**: firmness of purpose.
SCENE III: 1. The following speech is said by a drunken porter (a man who tends the castle gate).
It is full of puns and jests that refer to current happenings in Shakespeare's day.   2. **old . . . key:** grow
old letting in so many damned souls.   3. **Beelzebub** (bē·el'zə·bub): Satan's assistant.   4. **expectation
of plenty:** He hoarded grain in hopes that a bad harvest would raise prices.   6. **equivocator:** liar.
10. **stealing . . . hose:** The tailor stole some cloth from the hose while making them.   11. **goose:**
tailor's pressing iron.

[*Enter* MACDUFF *and* LENNOX.]

MACDUFF. Was it so late, friend, ere you went to bed,
    That you do lie so late?
PORTER. Faith, sir, we were carousing till the second cock;° and drink, sir, is a
    great provoker.
MACDUFF. I believe drink gave thee the lie last night.   20
PORTER. That it did, sir, i' the very throat on me. But I requited him for his lie;
    and, I think, being too strong for him, though he took up my legs some-
    time, yet I made a shift to cast him.°
MACDUFF. Is thy master stirring?

[*Enter* MACBETH.]

    Our knocking has awaked him; here he comes.   25
LENNOX. Good morrow, noble sir.
MACBETH.   Good morrow, both.
MACDUFF. Is the king stirring, worthy thane?
MACBETH.   Not yet.
MACDUFF. He did command me to call timely on him.
    I have almost slipped the hour.
MACBETH.   I'll bring you to him.
MACDUFF. I know this is a joyful trouble to you;   30
    But yet 'tis one.
MACBETH. The labor we delight in physics° pain.
    This is the door.
MACDUFF.   I'll make so bold to call,
    For 'tis my limited service.°   [*Exit.*]
LENNOX. Goes the king hence today?
MACBETH.   He does—he did appoint so.   35
LENNOX. The night has been unruly: where we lay,
    Our chimneys were blown down; and, as they say,
    Lamentings heard i' the air; strange screams of death,
    And prophesying with accents terrible
    Of dire combustion° and confused events   40
    New hatched to the woeful time. The obscure bird°
    Clamored the livelong night; some say, the earth
    Was feverous and did shake.
MACBETH.   'Twas a rough night.
LENNOX. My young remembrance cannot parallel
    A fellow to it.   45

[*Reenter* MACDUFF.]

MACDUFF. O horror, horror, horror! Tongue nor heart
    Cannot conceive nor name thee!
MACBETH. }
                                What's the matter?
LENNOX. }
MACDUFF. Confusion now hath made his masterpiece!
    Most sacrilegious murder hath broke ope

---

18. **second cock:** 3 A.M.   23. **cast him:** vomit.   32. **physics:** cures.ᵛ   34. **limited service:** appointed
duty.   40. **dire combustion:** terrible horror.   41. **obscure bird:** owl, obscure (meaning "dark") because the owl is a nocturnal bird.

The Lord's anointed temple,° and stole thence   50
    The life o' the building!
MACBETH.   What is 't you say? The life?
LENNOX. Mean you his majesty?
MACDUFF. Approach the chamber, and destroy your sight
    With a new Gorgon.° Do not bid me speak;
    See, and then speak yourselves.   [*Exeunt* MACBETH *and* LENNOX.]
                      Awake, awake!   55
    Ring the alarum bell. Murder and treason!
    Banquo and Donalbain! Malcolm! awake!
    Shake off this downy sleep, death's counterfeit,
    And look on death itself! Up, up, and see
    The great doom's image!° Malcolm! Banquo!   60
    As from your graves rise up, and walk like sprites,°
    To countenance° this horror! Ring the bell.   [*Bell rings.*]

              [*Enter* LADY MACBETH.]

LADY MACBETH. What's the business,
    That such a hideous trumpet calls to parley°
    The sleepers of the house? Speak, speak!
MACDUFF.   O gentle lady,   65
    'Tis not for you to hear what I can speak;
    The repetition, in a woman's ear,
    Would murder as it fell.

              [*Enter* BANQUO.]

              O Banquo, Banquo,
    Our royal master's murdered!
LADY MACBETH.   Woe, alas!
    What, in our house?
BANQUO.   Too cruel anywhere.   70
    Dear Duff, I prithee, contradict thyself,
    And say it is not so.

       [*Reenter* MACBETH *and* LENNOX, *with* ROSS.]

MACBETH. Had I but died an hour before this chance,°
    I had lived a blessèd time; for, from this instant,
    There's nothing serious in mortality.   75
    All is but toys:° renown and grace is dead;
    The wine of life is drawn, and the mere lees
    Is left this vault° to brag of.

        [*Enter* MALCOLM *and* DONALBAIN.]

DONALBAIN. What is amiss?
MACBETH.   You are, and do not know 't:
    The spring, the head, the fountain of your blood   80
    Is stopped; the very source of it is stopped.

---

50. **Lord's . . . temple:** the body of the king. 54. **Gorgon:** the snake-headed monster Medusa, so terrible to look upon that it turned those who saw it to stone. 60. **great . . . image:** Doomsday, the end of the world. 61. **sprites:** ghosts. 62. **countenance:** be in keeping with. 64. **parley:** a conference of war. 73. **chance:** event. 76. **toys:** trifles. 78. **vault:** as used here, world.

MACDUFF. Your royal father's murdered.

MALCOLM.   O, by whom?

LENNOX. Those of his chamber, as it seemed, had done 't.
　　Their hands and faces were all badged° with blood;
　　So were their daggers, which unwiped we found   85
　　Upon their pillows.
　　They stared, and were distracted; no man's life
　　Was to be trusted with them.

MACBETH. O, yet I do repent me of my fury,
　　That I did kill them.

MACDUFF.   Wherefore did you so?   90

MACBETH. Who can be wise, amazed, temperate and furious,
　　Loyal and neutral, in a moment? No man.
　　The expedition° of my violent love
　　Outrun the pauser,° reason. Here lay Duncan,
　　His silver skin laced with his golden blood,   95
　　And his gashed stabs looked like a breach in nature
　　For ruin's wasteful entrance; there, the murderers,
　　Steeped in the colors of their trade, their daggers
　　Unmannerly breeched° with gore. Who could refrain,
　　That had a heart to love, and in that heart   100
　　Courage to make 's love known?

LADY MACBETH.   Help me hence, ho!

MACDUFF. Look to the lady.

MALCOLM. [Aside to DONALBAIN] Why do we hold our tongues,
　　That most may claim this argument for ours?

DONALBAIN. [Aside to MALCOLM] What should be spoken here, where our fate, 105
　　Hid in an auger hole,° may rush, and seize us?
　　Let's away;
　　Our tears are not yet brewed.

MALCOLM.   [Aside to DONALBAIN] Nor our strong sorrow
　　Upon the foot of motion.°

BANQUO.   Look to the lady: [LADY MACBETH is carried out.]
　　And when we have our naked frailties hid,°   110
　　That suffer in exposure, let us meet,
　　And question this most bloody piece of work,
　　To know it further. Fears and scruples shake us.
　　In the great hand of God I stand; and thence
　　Against the undivulged pretense I fight   115
　　Of treasonous malice.°

MACDUFF.   And so do I.

ALL.   So all.

MACBETH. Let's briefly put on manly readiness,
　　And meet i' the hall together.

ALL.   Well contented. [Exeunt all but MALCOLM and DONALBAIN.]

---

84. **badged:** marked; literally, wearing a badge as servants of murder.　93. **expedition:** hasty action.
94. **pauser:** restrainer.　99. **Unmannerly breeched:** covered with blood instead of their regular sheaths.
106. **augur hole:** a tiny hole, an improbable hiding place; that is, the smallest event may cause our
downfall.　109. **Upon . . . motion:** is not yet moving.　110. **when . . . hid:** when we have put on our
clothes. All but Macduff have come straight from bed.　115–16. **Against . . . malice:** I fight against the
malicious treason which is not yet fully revealed.

MALCOLM. What will you do? Let's not consort with them;
    To show an unfelt sorrow is an office   120
    Which the false man does easy. I'll to England.
DONALBAIN. To Ireland, I; our separated fortune
    Shall keep us both the safer. Where we are,
    There's daggers in men's smiles. The near in blood,
    The nearer bloody.°
MALCOLM.   This murderous shaft° that's shot   125
    Hath not yet lighted,° and our safest way
    Is to avoid the aim. Therefore, to horse;
    And let us not be dainty of leave-taking,
    But shift away. There's warrant in that theft
    Which steals itself, when there's no mercy left.°   [*Exeunt.*] 130

SCENE IV. *Outside* MACBETH's *castle.*

[*Enter* ROSS *and an* OLD MAN.]

OLD MAN. Threescore and ten I can remember well;
    Within the volume of which time I have seen
    Hours dreadful and things strange; but this sore night
    Hath trifled former knowings.
ROSS.   Ah, good father,
    Thou seest, the heavens, as troubled with man's act,   5
    Threaten his bloody stage. By the clock, 'tis day,
    And yet dark night strangles the traveling lamp.°
    Is 't night's predominance, or the day's shame,
    That darkness does the face of earth entomb,
    When living light should kiss it?
OLD MAN.   'Tis unnatural,   10
    Even like the deed that's done. On Tuesday last,
    A falcon, towering in her pride of place,
    Was by a mousing owl hawked at and killed.
ROSS. And Duncan's horses—a thing most strange and certain—
    Beauteous and swift, the minions of their race,   15
    Turned wild in nature, broke their stalls, flung out,
    Contending 'gainst obedience, as they would make
    War with mankind.
OLD MAN.   'Tis said they eat each other.
ROSS. They did so, to the amazement of mine eyes
    That looked upon 't. Here comes the good Macduff.   20

[*Enter* MACDUFF.]

    How goes the world, sir, now?
MACDUFF.   Why, see you not?
ROSS. Is 't known who did this more than bloody deed?

124–25. **The . . . bloody:** The nearer we are in blood relationship to Duncan, the more likely we are to be murdered.   125. **shaft:** arrow.   126. **lighted:** come down to earth.   129–30. **There's . . . left:** We are justified in stealing away in these merciless times.
   SCENE IV: 7. **traveling lamp:** sun.

MACDUFF. Those that Macbeth hath slain.

ROSS.   Alas, the day!
  What good could they pretend?

MACDUFF.   They were suborned;°
  Malcolm and Donalbain, the king's two sons,   25
  Are stolen away and fled; which puts upon them
  Suspicion of the deed.

ROSS.   'Gainst nature still!
  Thriftless ambition, that wilt ravin up°
  Thine own life's means! Then 'tis most like
  The sovereignty will fall upon Macbeth.   30

MACDUFF. He is already named, and gone to Scone°
  To be invested.

ROSS.   Where is Duncan's body?

MACDUFF. Carried to Colmekill,°
  The sacred storehouse of his predecessors,
  And guardian of their bones.

ROSS.   Will you to Scone?   35

MACDUFF. No, cousin, I'll to Fife.°

ROSS.   Well, I will thither.

MACDUFF. Well, may you see things well done there. Adieu!
  Lest our old robes sit easier than our new!°

ROSS. Farewell, father.

OLD MAN. God's benison° go with you; and with those   40
  That would make good of bad, and friends of foes!

                                                        [*Exeunt.*]

24. **suborned** (sə·bôrned′): bribed.   28. **ravin up:** devour greedily.   31. **Scone** (skŏͦn): where
Scottish kings were crowned.   33. **Colmekill:** the ancient burying place of Scottish kings, now called
Iona.   36. **Fife:** Macduff's castle.   38. **Lest . . . new:** Macduff shows his misgivings about the future
with Macbeth as king.   40. **benison:** blessing.

FOR STUDY AND DISCUSSION: ACT II

1. An atmosphere of foreboding and horror is built up in Act II. Much of the horror is implicit in Macbeth's famous "dagger" soliloquy in Scene i (lines 33–64). Why does Macbeth refer to the dagger as "fatal vision"? What does he mean by a "dagger of the mind"?

2. In Scene ii Macbeth, after the murder of Duncan, is troubled by voices he heard or thought he heard. Why could he not say "Amen" when a voice said, "God bless us!"? What is meant by "Macbeth does murder sleep"? Why won't Macbeth return to Duncan's room? How, on the other hand, does Lady Macbeth characterize the dead, in lines 53–55?

3. The symbols of blood and water are interwoven in lines 55–68 of Scene ii. What does each symbolize? How do the different attitudes of Macbeth and his wife to their bloodstained hands serve to point up the basic difference in their characters?

4. What effect does the porter's humorous speech and the knocking at the beginning of Scene iii have on the atmosphere of tension and horror in Scene ii? Does it increase or destroy this horror? What is ironic about the porter's drunken imaginings? (A student report on DeQuincey's essay "On the Knocking at the Gate in *Macbeth*" will provide interesting background on this question.)

5. The murder of Duncan provokes different thoughts and reactions in Macbeth's guests. After carefully rereading Scene iii, lines 70–130, describe the private thoughts of Banquo and Malcolm.

6. What examples are there throughout Act II of the effect upon nature of human deeds? In Scene iv alone, what three strange and unnatural events are described that would instill the superstitious Elizabethan audience with a sense of foreboding?

ACT III

SCENE I. *Forres. The palace.*

[*Enter* BANQUO.]

BANQUO. Thou hast it now: king, Cawdor, Glamis, all,
 As the weird women promised, and, I fear,
 Thou play'dst most foully for 't; yet it was said
 It should not stand in thy posterity,
 But that myself should be the root and father   5
 Of many kings. If there come truth from them—
 As upon thee, Macbeth, their speeches shine—
 Why, by the verities on thee made good,
 May they not be my oracles as well,
 And set me up in hope? But hush! no more.   10

[*Sennet* sounded. Enter* MACBETH, *as king,* LADY MACBETH, *as queen,* LENNOX, ROSS, LORDS, LADIES, *and* ATTENDANTS.]

MACBETH. Here's our chief guest.
LADY MACBETH.   If he had been forgotten,
 It had been as a gap in our great feast,
 And all-thing° unbecoming.
MACBETH. Tonight we hold a solemn supper,° sir,
 And I'll request your presence.
BANQUO.   Let your highness   15
 Command upon me; to the which my duties
 Are with a most indissoluble tie
 For ever knit.
MACBETH. Ride you this afternoon?
BANQUO. Ay, my good lord.   20
MACBETH. We should have else desired your good advice,
 Which still hath been both grave and prosperous,
 In this day's council; but we'll take tomorrow.
 Is 't far you ride?
BANQUO. As far, my lord, as will fill up the time   25
 'Twixt this and supper. Go not my horse the better,
 I must become a borrower of the night
 For a dark hour or twain.
MACBETH.   Fail not our feast.
BANQUO. My lord, I will not.
MACBETH. We hear, our bloody cousins are bestowed   30
 In England and in Ireland, not confessing
 Their cruel parricide, filling their hearers
 With strange invention. But of that tomorrow,
 When therewithal we shall have cause of state

---

 * **Sennet:** trumpet fanfare announcing the approach of an important person.   13. **all-thing:** altogether.   14. **solemn supper:** ceremonious feast.

Craving us jointly.° Hie you to horse; adieu,   35
Till you return at night. Goes Fleance with you?
BANQUO. Ay, my good lord. Our time does call upon 's.°
MACBETH. I wish your horses swift and sure of foot;
And so I do commend you to their backs.
Farewell.   [*Exit* BANQUO.]   40
Let every man be master of his time
Till seven at night. To make society
The sweeter welcome, we will keep ourself
Till suppertime alone; while° then, God be with you!
                    [*Exeunt all but* MACBETH *and an* ATTENDANT.]
Sirrah, a word with you: attend those men
Our pleasure?   45
ATTENDANT. They are, my lord, without the palace gate.
MACBETH. Bring them before us.   [*Exit* ATTENDANT.]
                            To be thus° is nothing;
But° to be safely thus.—Our fears in Banquo
Stick deep; and in his royalty of nature°   50
Reigns that which would be feared. 'Tis much he dares;
And to° that dauntless temper of his mind,
He hath a wisdom that doth guide his valor
To act in safety. There is none but he
Whose being I do fear; and, under him,   55
My Genius is rebuked,° as, it is said,
Mark Antony's was by Caesar. He chid the sisters
When first they put the name of king upon me,
And bade them speak to him; then prophetlike
They hailed him father to a line of kings.   60
Upon my head they placed a fruitless crown,
And put a barren scepter in my gripe,°
Thence to be wrenched with an unlineal hand,
No son of mine succeeding. If 't be so,
For Banquo's issue have I filed° my mind;   65
For them the gracious Duncan have I murdered;
Put rancors in the vessel of my peace
Only for them; and mine eternal jewel°
Given to the common enemy of man,°
To make them kings—the seed° of Banquo kings!   70
Rather than so, come, Fate, into the list,
And champion me to the utterance!° Who's there?

[*Reenter* ATTENDANT, *with two* MURDERERS.]

Now go to the door, and stay there till we call.   [*Exit* ATTENDANT.]
Was it not yesterday we spoke together?

---

35. **Craving us jointly:** demanding the attention of both of us.   37. **Our . . . upon's:** Our business is urgent.   44. **while:** until.   48. **thus:** king.   49. **But:** unless.   50. **royalty of nature:** kingly nature.   52. **And to:** added to.   56. **My . . . rebuked:** My guardian spirit is cowed.   62. **gripe:** grip.   65. **filed:** defiled.   68. **eternal jewel:** immortal soul.   69. **common . . . man:** the Devil.   70. **seed:** descendants.   72. **champion . . . utterance:** fight me to the death.

FIRST MURDERER. It was, so please your highness.

MACBETH.   Well then, now   75
    Have you considered of my speeches? Know
    That it was he in the times past which held you
    So under fortune,° which you thought had been
    Our innocent self. This I made good to you
    In our last conference, passed in probation with° you,   80
    How you were borne in hand,° how crossed, the instruments,
    Who wrought with them, and all things else that might
    To half a soul° and to a notion° crazed
    Say "Thus did Banquo."

FIRST MURDERER.   You made it known to us.

MACBETH. I did so, and went further, which is now   85
    Our point of second meeting. Do you find
    Your patience so predominant in your nature
    That you can let this go? Are you so gospeled°
    To pray for this good man and for his issue,
    Whose heavy hand hath bowed you to the grave   90
    And beggared yours for ever?

FIRST MURDERER.   We are men, my liege.

MACBETH. Ay, in the catalogue ye go for men;
    As hounds and greyhounds, mongrels, spaniels, curs,
    Shoughs,° water rugs,° and demiwolves, are clept°
    All by the name of dogs; the valued file°   95
    Distinguishes the swift, the slow, the subtle,
    The housekeeper, the hunter, every one
    According to the gift which bounteous nature
    Hath in him closed, whereby he does receive
    Particular addition,° from the bill   100
    That writes them all alike; and so of men.
    Now, if you have a station in the file,°
    Not i' the worst rank of manhood, say 't;
    And I will put that business in your bosoms,
    Whose execution takes your enemy off,   105
    Grapples you to the heart and love of us,
    Who wear our health but sickly in his life,
    Which in his death were perfect.°

SECOND MURDERER.   I am one, my liege,
    Whom the vile blows and buffets of the world
    Have so incensed that I am reckless what   110
    I do to spite the world.

FIRST MURDERER.   And I another
    So weary with disasters, tugged with fortune,

   77–78. **held . . . fortune:** was the cause of your bad fortune. 80. **passed . . . with:** proved to.
81. **borne in hand:** deceived. 83. **half a soul:** halfwit. **notion:** mind. 88. **gospeled:** ready to forgive.
94. **Shoughs:** shaggy-haired dogs. **water rugs:** water spaniels. **clept:** called. 95. **valued file:** list
of those valued. 100. **addition:** distinction (to set him apart from other dogs). 102. **file:** ranks.
107–08. **Who . . . perfect:** So long as Banquo lives, I am a sick man.

That I would set my life on any chance,
To mend it, or be rid on 't.
MACBETH.   Both of you
Know Banquo was your enemy.
BOTH MURDERERS.   True, my lord.   115
MACBETH. So is he mine; and in such bloody distance,°
That every minute of his being thrusts
Against my near'st of life;° and though I could
With barefaced power sweep him from my sight
And bid my will avouch° it, yet I must not,   120
For certain friends that are both his and mine,
Whose loves I may not drop, but wail his fall°
Who I myself struck down; and thence it is,
That I to your assistance do make love,
Masking the business from the common eye   125
For sundry weighty reasons.
SECOND MURDERER.   We shall, my lord,
Perform what you command us.
FIRST MURDERER.   Though our lives——
MACBETH. Your spirits shine through you. Within this hour at most
I will advise you where to plant yourselves;
Acquaint you with the perfect spy o' the time,°   130
The moment on 't; for 't must be done tonight,
And something° from the palace; always thought
That I require a clearness;° and with him—
To leave no rubs nor botches in the work—
Fleance his son, that keeps him company,   135
Whose absence is no less material to me
Than is his father's, must embrace the fate
Of that dark hour. Resolve yourselves apart;°
I'll come to you anon.
BOTH MURDERERS.   We are resolved, my lord.
MACBETH. I'll call upon you straight; abide within.   [*Exeunt* MURDERERS.]   140
It is concluded. Banquo, thy soul's flight,
If it find heaven, must find it out tonight.   [*Exit.*]

SCENE II. *The palace.*

[*Enter* LADY MACBETH *and a* SERVANT.]

LADY MACBETH. Is Banquo gone from court?
SERVANT. Ay, madam, but returns again tonight.
LADY MACBETH. Say to the king, I would attend his leisure
For a few words.

---

116. **distance:** disagreement.   118. **near'st of life:** inmost being, myself.   120. **avouch:** justify.
122. **wail his fall:** pretend to bewail Banquo's death (but [I must] wail).   130. **the . . . time:** the exact
moment.   132. **something:** some distance.   133. **require a clearness:** must remain above suspicion.
138. **Resolve . . . apart:** Make your own decision.

SERVANT.   Madam, I will.   [*Exit.*]

LADY MACBETH.   Naught's had, all's spent,
Where our desire is got without content.   5
'Tis safer to be that which we destroy
Than by destruction dwell in doubtful joy.

[*Enter* MACBETH.]

How now, my lord! why do you keep alone,
Of sorriest fancies your companions making,
Using those thoughts which should indeed have died   10
With them they think on? Things without all remedy
Should be without regard; what's done is done.

MACBETH. We have scotched° the snake, not killed it;
She'll close° and be herself, whilst our poor malice
Remains in danger of her former tooth.°   15
But let the frame of things disjoint, both the worlds suffer,°
Ere we will eat our meal in fear, and sleep
In the affliction of these terrible dreams
That shake us nightly. Better be with the dead,
Whom we, to gain our peace, have sent to peace,   20
Than on the torture of the mind to lie
In restless ecstasy.° Duncan is in his grave;
After life's fitful fever he sleeps well;
Treason has done his worst; nor steel, nor poison,
Malice domestic, foreign levy, nothing,   25
Can touch him further.

LADY MACBETH.   Come on;
Gentle my lord, sleek o'er your rugged looks;
Be bright and jovial among your guests tonight.

MACBETH. So shall I, love; and so, I pray, be you.
Let your remembrance apply to Banquo;   30
Present him eminence,° both with eye and tongue;
Unsafe the while, that° we
Must lave° our honors in these flattering streams,
And make our faces vizards° to our hearts,
Disguising what they are.

LADY MACBETH.   You must leave this.   35

MACBETH. O, full of scorpions is my mind, dear wife!
Thou know'st that Banquo, and his Fleance, lives.

LADY MACBETH. But in them nature's copy 's not eterne.°

MACBETH. There's comfort yet; they are assailable;
Then be thou jocund; ere the bat hath flown   40
His cloistered flight, ere to black Hecate's summons
The shard-borne° beetle with his drowsy hums

---

13. **scotched:** wounded.   14. **close:** heal.   15. **in . . . tooth:** in as much danger as before.   16. **But
. . . suffer:** Let the universe fall to pieces, let both heaven and earth perish.   22. **ecstasy:** madness,
mental agony.   31. **Present . . . eminence:** make much of him.   32. **Unsafe . . . that:** we are not safe as
long as.   33. **lave:** wash.   34. **vizards** (viz'ərdz): masks.   38. **in . . . eterne:** They will not live forever.   42. **shard-borne:** borne aloft on scaly wings.

Hath rung night's yawning peal, there shall be done
A deed of dreadful note.

LADY MACBETH.   What's to be done?

MACBETH. Be innocent of the knowledge, dearest chuck,°   45
Till thou applaud the deed. Come, seeling° night,
Scarf up the tender eye of pitiful day;
And with thy bloody and invisible hand
Cancel and tear to pieces that great bond°
Which keeps me pale! Light thickens, and the crow   50
Makes wing to the rooky° wood;
Good things of day begin to droop and drowse;
Whiles night's black agents to their preys do rouse.
Thou marvel'st at my words; but hold thee still;
Things bad begun make strong themselves by ill.   55
So, prithee, go with me.   [*Exeunt.*]

SCENE III. *A park near the palace.*

[*Enter three* MURDERERS.]

FIRST MURDERER. But who did bid thee join with us?

THIRD MURDERER.   Macbeth.

SECOND MURDERER. He needs not our mistrust, since he delivers
Our offices° and what we have to do
To the direction just.°

FIRST MURDERER.   Then stand with us.
The west yet glimmers with some streaks of day;   5
Now spurs the lated traveler apace
To gain the timely inn; and near approaches
The subject of our watch.

THIRD MURDERER.   Hark! I hear horses.

BANQUO. [*Within*] Give us a light there, ho!

SECOND MURDERER.   Then 'tis he; the rest
That are within the note of expectation°   10
Already are i' the court.

FIRST MURDERER.   His horses go about.°

THIRD MURDERER. Almost a mile; but he does usually,
So all men do, from hence to the palace gate
Make it their walk.

SECOND MURDERER.   A light, a light!

[*Enter* BANQUO, *and* FLEANCE *with a torch.*]

THIRD MURDERER.   'Tis he.

FIRST MURDERER. Stand to 't.   15

---

45. **chuck:** chick.   46. **seeling:** blinding. In falconry the eyelids of a hawk were sealed (sewn shut) in order to train it.   49. **great bond:** that which binds me; that is, Banquo's life.   51. **rooky:** full of rooks, or crows.

SCENE III: 3. **offices:** duties.   4. **direction just:** exact detail.   10. **note of expectation:** list of expected guests.   11. **His . . . about:** His horses have been taken to the stable.

BANQUO. It will be rain tonight.
FIRST MURDERER.   Let it come down.   [*They set upon* BANQUO.]
BANQUO. O treachery! Fly, good Fleance, fly, fly, fly!
     Thou mayst revenge. O slave!   [*Dies.* FLEANCE *escapes.*]
THIRD MURDERER. Who did strike out the light?
FIRST MURDERER.   Was 't not the way?
THIRD MURDERER. There's but one down; the son is fled.
SECOND MURDERER.   We have lost   20
     Best half of our affair.
FIRST MURDERER. Well, let's away, and say how much is done.   [*Exeunt.*]

SCENE IV. *Hall in the palace.*

[*A banquet prepared. Enter* MACBETH, LADY MACBETH, ROSS, LENNOX, LORDS,
and ATTENDANTS.]

MACBETH. You know your own degrees;° sit down. At first
     And last the hearty welcome.
LORDS.   Thanks to your majesty.
MACBETH. Ourself will mingle with society,
     And play the humble host.
     Our hostess keeps her state,° but in best time   5
     We will require her welcome.
LADY MACBETH. Pronounce it for me, sir, to all our friends;
     For my heart speaks they are welcome.

          [*First* MURDERER *appears at the door.*]

MACBETH. See, they encounter thee with their hearts' thanks.
     Both sides are even; here I'll sit i' the midst;   10
     Be large in mirth; anon we'll drink a measure°
     The table round. [*Approaching the door*] There's blood upon thy face.
MURDERER. 'Tis Banquo's then.
MACBETH. 'Tis better thee without than he within.
     Is he dispatched?   15
MURDERER. My lord, his throat is cut; that I did for him.
MACBETH. Thou art the best o' the cutthroats: yet he's good
     That did the like for Fleance. If thou didst it,
     Thou art the nonpareil.°
MURDERER.   Most royal sir,
     Fleance is 'scaped.   20
MACBETH. Then comes my fit again. I had else been perfect,
     Whole as the marble, founded as the rock,
     As broad and general as the casing° air;
     But now I am cabined, cribbed, confined, bound in
     To saucy doubts and fears. But Banquo's safe?   25
MURDERER. Ay, my good lord; safe in a ditch he bides,

SCENE IV: 1. DEGREES: ranks. At state banquets each guest was seated according to his rank.
5. **keeps . . . state:** sits on a throne apart. 11. **measure:** toast. 19. **nonpareil:** without equal. 23. **casing:** enclosing.

With twenty trenchèd gashes on his head,
The least a death to nature.°

MACBETH.   Thanks for that;
There the grown serpent lies; the worm° that's fled
Hath nature that in time will venom breed,   30
No teeth for the present. Get thee gone; tomorrow
We'll hear ourselves again.   [*Exit* MURDERER.]

LADY MACBETH.   My royal lord,
You do not give the cheer. The feast is sold
That is not often vouched,° while 'tis amaking,
'Tis given with welcome. To feed were best at home;   35
From thence the sauce to meat is ceremony;°
Meeting were bare without it.

MACBETH.   Sweet remembrancer!
Now, good digestion wait on appetite,
And health on both!

LENNOX.   May 't please your highness sit.

[*The* GHOST *of* BANQUO *enters, and sits in* MACBETH'S *place*.]

MACBETH. Here had we now our country's honor roofed,°   40
Were the graced person of our Banquo present;
Who may I rather challenge for unkindness
Than pity for mischance!°

ROSS.   His absence, sir,
Lays blame upon his promise. Please 't your highness
To grace us with your royal company.   45

MACBETH. The table's full.

LENNOX.   Here is a place reserved, sir.

MACBETH. Where?

LENNOX. Here, my good lord. What is 't that moves your highness?

MACBETH. Which of you have done this?

LORDS.   What, my good lord?

MACBETH. Thou canst not say I did it; never shake   50
Thy gory locks at me.

ROSS. Gentlemen, rise; his highness is not well.

LADY MACBETH. Sit, worthy friends; my lord is often thus,
And hath been from his youth. Pray you, keep seat;
The fit is momentary; upon a thought°   55
He will again be well. If much you note him,
You shall offend him and extend his passion.
Feed, and regard him not. [*To* MACBETH] Are you a man?

MACBETH. Ay, and a bold one, that dare look on that
Which might appall the devil.

LADY MACBETH.   O proper stuff!   60

28. **nature:** natural life.   29. **worm:** little snake.   33–34. **The feast . . . vouched:** The feast at which guests are not made welcome is a mere bought dinner.   36. **From . . . ceremony:** When one is away from home, politeness or ceremony adds a pleasant flavor to the meal.   40. **our . . . roofed:** all the most honorable men in the country under our roof.   42–43. **Who . . . mischance:** That is, I'd rather believe that he is absent through discourtesy than because of some accident.   55. **upon a thought:** in a moment.

This is the very painting of your fear;
This is the air-drawn dagger which, you said,
Led you to Duncan. O, these flaws° and starts,
Impostors to true fear, would well become
A woman's story at a winter's fire,   65
Authorized° by her grandam. Shame itself!
Why do you make such faces? When all's done,
You look but on a stool.
MACBETH. Prithee, see there! behold! look! lo! how say you?
Why, what care I? If you canst nod, speak too.   70
If charnel houses° and our graves must send
Those that we bury back, our monuments
Shall be the maws of kites.°   [GHOST *vanishes.*]
LADY MACBETH.   What, quite unmanned in folly?
MACBETH. If I stand here, I saw him.
LADY MACBETH.   Fie, for shame!
MACBETH. Blood hath been shed ere now, i' the olden time,   75
Ere humane statute purged the gentle weal;°
Ay, and since too, murders have been performed
Too terrible for the ear. The time has been,
That, when the brains were out, the man would die,
And there an end; but now they rise again,   80
With twenty mortal murders on their crowns,°
And push us from our stools. This is more strange
Than such a murder is.
LADY MACBETH.   My worthy lord,
Your noble friends do lack you.
MACBETH.   I do forget.
Do not muse at me, my most worthy friends;   85
I have a strange infirmity, which is nothing
To those that know me. Come, love and health to all;
Then I'll sit down. Give me some wine; fill full.
I drink to the general joy o' the whole table,
And to our dear friend Banquo, whom we miss;   90
Would he were here! to all, and him, we thirst,
And all to all.
LORDS.   Our duties, and the pledge.

[*Reenter* GHOST.]

MACBETH. Avaunt!° and quit my sight! let the earth hide thee!
Thy bones are morrowless, thy blood is cold;
Thou has no speculation° in those eyes   95
Which thou dost glare with!
LADY MACBETH.   Think of this, good peers,
But as a thing of custom; 'tis no other;
Only it spoils the pleasure of the time.

63. **flaws:** literally, gusts of wind.   66. **Authorized:** vouched for.   71. **charnel houses:** places where human bones, dug up in making a new grave, were stored.   73. **maws of kites:** bellies of birds of prey.
76. **Ere . . . weal:** before humane laws civilized the state.   81. **crowns:** heads.   93. **Avaunt** (ə·vônt'): Begone!   95. **speculation:** power of sight.

MACBETH. What man dare, I dare.
       Approach thou like the rugged Russian bear,   100
       The armed rhinoceros, or the Hyrcan° tiger;
       Take any shape but that,° and my firm nerves
       Shall never tremble; or be alive again,
       And dare me to the desert° with my sword;
       If trembling I inhabit° then, protest me   '105
       The baby of a girl. Hence, horrible shadow!
       Unreal mockery, hence!   [GHOST *vanishes*.]
                     Why, so; being gone
       I am a man again. Pray you, sit still.
LADY MACBETH. You have displaced the mirth, broke the good meeting,
       With most admired° disorder.
MACBETH.   Can such things be,   110
       And overcome° us like a summer's cloud,
       Without our special wonder? You make me strange
       Even to the disposition that I owe,°
       When now I think you can behold such sights,
       And keep the natural ruby of your cheeks,   115
       When mine is blanched with fear.
ROSS.   What sights, my lord?
LADY MACBETH. I pray you, speak not; he grows worse and worse;
       Question enrages him. At once, good night.
       Stand not upon the order of your going,°
       But go at once.
LENNOX.   Good night; and better health   120
       Attend his majesty!
LADY MACBETH.   A kind good night to all!
           [*Exeunt all but* MACBETH *and* LADY MACBETH.]
MACBETH. It will have blood; they say, blood will have blood.
       Stones have been known to move and trees to speak;
       Augurs° and understood relations° have
       By maggot-pies and choughs and rooks brought forth   125
       The secret'st man of blood.° What is the night?
LADY MACBETH. Almost at odds with morning, which is which.
MACBETH. How say'st thou, that Macduff denies his person
       At our great bidding?
LADY MACBETH.   Did you send to him, sir?
MACBETH. I hear it by the way; but I will send.   130
       There's not a one of them but in his house
       I keep a servant fee'd.° I will tomorrow,
       And betimes I will, to the weird sisters.
       More shall they speak; for now I am bent° to know,
       By the worst means, the worst. For mine own good,   135

---

101. **Hyrcan** (hûr′kən): from Hyracania, an ancient Asian province south of the Caspian Sea.
102. **that:** that is, Banquo's shape. 104. **desert:** a place where neither of us could escape. 105. **inhabit:** remain indoors. 110. **admired:** to be wondered at. 111. **overcome:** come over, overshadow. 113. **disposition . . . owe:** my own nature. 119. **Stand . . . going:** Do not wait to leave in order of rank. 124. **Augurs:** omens. **understood relations:** the relation between the omen and what it signifies. 126. **man of blood:** murderer. 132. **fee'd:** in my pay as a spy. 134. **bent:** eager.

All causes shall give way. I am in blood
Stepped in so far that, should I wade no more,
Returning were as tedious as go o'er.
Strange things I have in head, that will to hand;
Which must be acted ere they may be scanned.°   140
LADY MACBETH. You lack the season° of all natures, sleep.
MACBETH. Come, we'll to sleep. My strange and self-abuse
   Is the initiate fear° that wants hard use;
   We are yet but young in deed.   [*Exeunt.*]

SCENE V. *A heath.*

[*Thunder. Enter the three* WITCHES, *meeting* HECATE.]

FIRST WITCH. Why, how now, Hecate! you look angerly.
HECATE. Have I not reason, beldams° as you are,
   Saucy and overbold? How did you dare
   To trade and traffic with Macbeth
   In riddles and affairs of death;   5
   And I, the mistress of your charms,
   The close contriver° of all harms,
   Was never called to bear my part,
   Or show the glory of our art?
   And, which is worse, all you have done   10
   Hath been but for a wayward son,
   Spiteful and wrathful, who, as others do,
   Loves for his own ends, not for you.
   But make amends now; get you gone,
   And at the pit of Acheron°   15
   Meet me i' the morning; thither he
   Will come to know his destiny.
   Your vessels and your spells provide,
   Your charms and everything beside.
   I am for the air; this night I'll spend   20
   Unto a dismal and a fatal end;
   Great business must be wrought ere noon.
   Upon the corner of the moon
   There hangs a vaporous drop profound;
   I'll catch it ere it come to ground;   25
   And that distilled by magic sleights°
   Shall raise such artificial sprites°
   As by the strength of their illusion
   Shall draw him on to his confusion.°
   He shall spurn fate, scorn death, and bear   30

---

140. **scanned:** examined.   141. **season:** that which keeps fresh.   143. **initiate fear:** novice's fear;
that is, when I have more experience in murder, I shall not be troubled by ghosts.
   SCENE V: 2. **beldams:** hags.   7. **close contriver:** secret inventor.   15. **Acheron** (ak'ə·ron): hell; in
Greek mythology, the river leading to Hades.   26. **sleights:** devices.   27. **artificial sprites:** spirits
created by magic.   29. **confusion:** destruction.

His hopes 'bove wisdom, grace, and fear;
And you all know, security°
Is mortals' chiefest enemy.

> [*Music and a song within:* "Come away, come away," etc.]

Hark! I am called; my little spirit, see,
Sits in a foggy cloud, and stays for me.   [*Exit.*] 35

FIRST WITCH. Come, let's make haste; she'll soon be back again.   [*Exeunt.*]

SCENE VI. *Forres. The palace.*

[*Enter* LENNOX *and another* LORD.]

LENNOX. My former speeches have but hit your thoughts,
Which can interpret further;° only, I say,
Things have been strangely borne.° The gracious Duncan
Was pitied of Macbeth; marry, he was dead;
And the right-valiant Banquo walked too late;   5
Whom, you may say, if 't please you, Fleance killed,
For Fleance fled; men must not walk too late.
Who cannot want° the thought how monstrous
It was for Malcolm and for Donalbain
To kill their gracious father? Damnèd fact!   10
How it did grieve Macbeth! Did he not straight
In pious rage the two delinquents tear,
That were the slaves of drink and thralls° of sleep?
Was not that nobly done? Ay, and wisely too;
For 'twould have angered any heart alive   15
To hear the men deny 't. So that, I say,
He has borne all things well; and I do think
That had he Duncan's sons under his key—
As, an 't please Heaven, he shall not—they should find
What 'twere to kill a father; so should Fleance.   20
But, peace! for from broad° words and 'cause he failed
His presence at the tyrant's feast, I hear
Macduff lives in disgrace. Sir, can you tell
Where he bestows himself?
LORD.   The son of Duncan,
From whom this tyrant holds the due of birth,°   25
Lives in the English court, and is received
Of the most pious Edward with such grace
That the malevolence of fortune nothing
Takes from his high respect.° Thither Macduff
Is gone to pray the holy king, upon his aid   30

32. **security:** false sense of safety.
SCENE VI: 2. **Which ... further:** from which you can draw your own conclusions. 3. **borne:** managed. 8. **want:** be without. 13. **thralls:** slaves. 21. **broad:** too free, unguarded. 25. **From ... birth:** Malcolm's claim to the throne is withheld by Macbeth. 28–29. **That ... respect:** In spite of his misfortunes, he is regarded with the utmost respect.

154   THE ELIZABETHAN AGE

To wake Northumberland and warlike Siward;
That by the help of these—with Him above
To ratify the work—we may again
Give to our tables meat, sleep to our nights,
Free from our feasts and banquets bloody knives, 35
Do faithful homage and receive free honors;°
All which we pine for now; and this report
Hath so exasperate the king that he
Prepares for some attempt of war.

LENNOX.   Sent he to Macduff?

LORD. He did; and with an absolute "Sir, not I," 40
The cloudy° messenger turns me his back,
And hums, as who should say, "You'll rue the time
That clogs° me with this answer."

LENNOX.   And that well might
Advise him to a caution, to hold what distance
His wisdom can provide. Some holy angel 45
Fly to the court of England and unfold
His message ere he come, that swift blessing
May soon return to this our suffering country
Under a hand accursed!

LORD.   I'll send my prayers with him.   [*Exeunt.*]

36. **free honors:** honors given to free men.   41. **cloudy:** surly.   43. **clogs:** burdens.

FOR STUDY AND DISCUSSION: ACT III

1. In the opening speech of Act III, Banquo muses on the witches' prophecies. Which have come true? Which give Banquo hope for the future? Could Banquo have done anything to prevent the foul actions of Macbeth? Why did he remain silent?

2. In *Macbeth* there is a great deal of dramatic irony in which situations are often the tragic reverse of what the participants think. Macbeth, for example, thought he would achieve happiness after murdering Duncan. In the opening conversation of Scene i (lines 11–40), are several examples of dramatic irony. Pick out four separate instances and explain the irony of each.

3. How do Scenes i and ii reveal a moral change in Macbeth? There is also a change in the relationship between Macbeth and his wife. What is the change and where is it most apparent? What does it reveal about Macbeth's moral state?

4. One of the great puzzles of the play is the appearance of the third murderer in Scene iii. Some authorities feel it is a messenger from Macbeth; some feel it is Macbeth himself; some feel it is a person who, either from friendship to Banquo's cause or at the witches' instigation, joins the murderers to assure Fleance's escape. Select one of these theories, or invent one of your own, and be ready to defend it.

5. In the banquet scene (Scene iv), what speeches by Macbeth seem to call forth Banquo's ghost? What is ironic about this timing? How does Lady Macbeth act to save Macbeth?

6. By the time of the banquet scene, Macbeth has taken the two major steps necessary for the achievement of his goal. This action and the simultaneous increase of tension is known technically as the *rising action* of the play. Rising action builds toward a *climax*, the dramatic highpoint, or point of greatest tension in the play. All action after the climax is referred to as the *falling action*, or resolution, of the play. Reread the banquet scene (Scene iv). Why is it the climax or turning point of *Macbeth*?

ACT IV

SCENE I. *A cavern. In the middle, a boiling caldron.*

[*Thunder. Enter the three* WITCHES.]

FIRST WITCH. Thrice the brinded° cat hath mewed.
SECOND WITCH. Thrice and once the hedge pig whined.
THIRD WITCH. Harpier° cries, "'Tis time, 'tis time."
FIRST WITCH. Round about the caldron go;
    In the poisoned entrails throw. 5
    Toad, that under cold stone
    Days and nights has thirty-one
    Sweltered venom sleeping got,
    Boil thou first i' the charmèd pot.
ALL. Double, double toil and trouble; 10
    Fire burn, and caldron bubble.
SECOND WITCH. Fillet of a fenny snake,
    In the caldron boil and bake;
    Eye of newt and toe of frog,
    Wool of bat and tongue of dog, 15
    Adder's fork° and blindworm's sting,
    Lizard's leg and howlet's wing,
    For a charm of powerful trouble,
    Like a hell broth boil and bubble.
ALL. Double, double toil and trouble; 20
    Fire burn, and caldron bubble.
THIRD WITCH. Scale of dragon, tooth of wolf,
    Witches' mummy, maw and gulf°
    Of the ravined° salt-sea shark,
    Root of hemlock digged i' the dark, 25
    Slivered in the moon's eclipse,
    Nose of Turk and Tartar's lips,
    Finger of birth-strangled babe
    Ditch-delivered by a drab,
    Make the gruel thick and slab;° 30
    Add thereto a tiger's chaudron,°
    For the ingredients of our caldron.
ALL. Double, double toil and trouble;
    Fire burn, and caldron bubble.
SECOND WITCH. Cool it with a baboon's blood, 35
    Then the charm is firm and good.

[*Enter* HECATE, *to the other three* WITCHES.]

HECATE. O, well done! I commend your pains;
    And every one shall share i' the gains;

---

1. **brinded:** striped. 3. **Harpier:** one of the spirits attending the witches. 16. **fork:** forked tongue.
blindworm: small, harmless, limbless lizard. 23. **maw and gulf:** belly and gullet. 24. **ravined:**
ravenous. 30. **slab:** like thick mud. 31. **chaudron:** entrails.

And now about the caldron sing,
Like elves and fairies in a ring, 40
Enchanting all that you put in.
        [*Music and a song:* "Black spirits," etc. HECATE *retires.*]
SECOND WITCH. By the pricking of my thumbs,
Something wicked this way comes.
    Open, locks,
    Whoever knocks! 45

        [*Enter* MACBETH.]

MACBETH. How now, you secret, black, and midnight hags!
What is 't you do?
ALL.   A deed without a name.
MACBETH. I conjure you, by that which you profess,°
Howe'er you come to know it, answer me;
Though you untie the winds and let them fight 50
Against the churches; though the yesty° waves
Confound and swallow navigation up;
Though bladed corn be lodged° and trees blown down;
Though castles topple on their warders' heads;
Though palaces and pyramids do slope 55
Their heads to their foundations; though the treasure
Of nature's germens° tumble all together,
Even till destruction sicken; answer me
To what I ask you.
FIRST WITCH.   Speak.
SECOND WITCH.   Demand.
THIRD WITCH.   We'll answer.
FIRST WITCH. Say, if thou 'dst rather hear it from our mouths, 60
Or from our masters'?
MACBETH.   Call 'em; let me see 'em.
FIRST WITCH. Pour in sow's blood, that hath eaten
Her nine farrow;° grease that's sweaten
From the murderer's gibbet° throw
Into the flame.
ALL.   Come, high or low; 65
Thyself and office° deftly show!

        [*Thunder.* First Apparition: *an armed* HEAD.*]

MACBETH. Tell me, thou unknown power——
FIRST WITCH.   He knows thy thought;
Hear his speech, but say thou naught.
FIRST APPARITION. Macbeth! Macbeth! Macbeth! beware Macduff;
Beware the thane of Fife. Dismiss me. Enough.   [*Descends.*] 70
MACBETH. Whate'er thou art, for thy good caution, thanks;
Thou hast harped° my fear aright: but one word more——

---

48. **that ... profess:** that is, witchcraft. 51. **yesty:** foaming. 53. **lodged:** beaten down. 57. **germens:** seeds. 63. **farrow:** young pigs. 64. **gibbet:** gallows on which the bodies of criminals were left hanging as a warning. 66. **office:** function. * **an armed Head:** a symbol of Macduff. 72. **harped:** hit upon.

FIRST WITCH. He will not be commanded: here's another.
    More potent than the first.

          [*Thunder*. Second Apparition: *a bloody* CHILD.*]

SECOND APPARITION. Macbeth! Macbeth! Macbeth!   75
MACBETH. Had I three ears, I 'ld hear thee.
SECOND APPARITION. Be bloody, bold, and resolute; laugh to scorn
    The power of man, for none of woman born
    Shall harm Macbeth.   [*Descends*.]
MACBETH. Then live, Macduff; what need I fear of thee?   80
    But yet I'll make assurance double sure,
    And take a bond of fate.° Thou shalt not live;
    That I may tell pale-hearted fear it lies,.
    And sleep in spite of thunder.

   [*Thunder*. Third Apparition: *a* CHILD *crowned*,† *with a tree in his hand*.]

               What is this
    That rises like the issue of a king,   85
    And wears upon his baby brow the round
    And top of sovereignty?°
ALL.   Listen, but speak not to 't.
THIRD APPARITION. Be lion-mettled, proud; and take no care
    Who chafes, who frets, or where conspirers are.
    Macbeth shall never vanquished be until   90
    Great Birnam wood to high Dunsinane hill
    Shall come against him.   [*Descends*.]
MACBETH.   That will never be.
    Who can impress° the forest, bid the tree
    Unfix his earth-bound root? Sweet bodements!° good!
    Rebellion's head, rise never till the wood   95
    Of Birnam rise, and our high-placed Macbeth
    Shall live the lease of nature,° pay his breath
    To time and mortal custom. Yet my heart
    Throbs to know one thing: tell me, if your art
    Can tell so much: shall Banquo's issue ever   100
    Reign in this kingdom?
ALL.   Seek to know no more.
MACBETH. I will be satisfied; deny me this,
    And an eternal curse fall on you! Let me know.
    Why sinks that caldron? and what noise is this?   [*Hautboys*.]
FIRST WITCH. Show!   105
SECOND WITCH. Show!
THIRD WITCH. Show!
ALL. Show his eyes, and grieve his heart;
    Come like shadows, so depart!

   * **a bloody Child:** Macduff at birth.   82. **take . . . fate:** To be sure the prophecy is fulfilled, he will
kill Macduff.   † **a Child crowned:** symbol of Malcolm.   87. **top of sovereignty:** crown.   93. **impress:**
force into service.   94. **bodements:** prophecies.   97. **lease of nature:** his natural span of life.

[*A show* of eight* KINGS, *the last with a glass† in his hand;* BANQUO'S GHOST
following.]

MACBETH. Thou art too like the spirit of Banquo; down!   110
    Thy crown doth sear mine eyeballs. And thy hair,
    Thou other gold-bound brow, is like the first.
    A third is like the former. Filthy hags!
    Why do you show me this? A fourth! Start, eyes!
    What, will the line stretch out to the crack of doom?   115
    Another yet! A seventh! I'll see no more.
    And yet the eighth appears, who bears a glass
    Which shows me many more; and some I see
    That twofold balls and treble scepters° carry.
    Horrible sight! Now, I see, 'tis true;   120
    For the blood-boltered° Banquo smiles upon me,
    And points at them for his.° [APPARITIONS *vanish.*] What, is this so?
FIRST WITCH. Ay, sir, all this is so; but why
    Stands Macbeth thus amazedly?
    Come, sisters, cheer we up his sprites,°   125
    And show the best of our delights.
    I'll charm the air to give a sound,
    While you perform your antic round;°
    That this great king may kindly say,
    Our duties did his welcome pay.   130
        [*Music. The* WITCHES *dance, and then vanish with* HECATE.]
MACBETH. Where are they? Gone? Let this pernicious hour
    Stand aye accursèd in the calendar!
    Come in, without there!

            [*Enter* LENNOX.]

LENNOX.   What's your grace's will?
MACBETH. Saw you the weird sisters?
LENNOX.   No, my lord.
MACBETH. Came they not by you?
LENNOX.   No indeed, my lord.   135
MACBETH. Infected be the air whereon they ride;
    And damned all those that trust them! I did hear
    The galloping of horse: who was 't came by?
LENNOX. 'Tis two or three, my lord, that bring you word
    Macduff is fled to England.
MACBETH.   Fled to England!   140
LENNOX. Ay, my good lord.
MACBETH. Time, thou anticipatest my dread exploits;
    The flighty purpose never is o'ertook
    Unless the deed go with it.° From this moment

---

   * **show:** a dumb show—figures passing silently across the back of the stage. † **glass:** mirror.
119. **twofold . . . scepters:** insignia of the kingdoms of England, Scotland, and Ireland, united in
1603 when Scotland's James VI (descended from Banquo) became James I of England. 121. **blood-
boltered:** his hair matted with blood. 122. **his:** that is, his descendants. 125. **sprites:** spirits.
128. **antic round:** grotesque dance. 143–44. **The . . . it:** An impulsive plan is never fulfilled unless
carried out at once.

The very firstlings of my heart shall be   145
The firstlings of my hand. And even now,
To crown my thoughts with acts, be it thought and done.
The castle of Macduff I will surprise;
Seize upon Fife; give to the edge o' the sword
His wife, and babes, and all unfortunate souls   150
That trace him in his line. No boasting like a fool;
This deed I'll do before this purpose cool.
But no more sights!—Where are these gentlemen?
Come, bring me where they are.   [*Exeunt.*]

SCENE II. *Fife.* MACDUFF'S *castle.*

[*Enter* LADY MACDUFF, *her* SON, *and* ROSS.]

LADY MACDUFF. What had he done, to make him fly the land?
ROSS. You must have patience, madam.
LADY MACDUFF.   He had none;
   His flight was madness. When our actions do not,
   Our fears do make us traitors.
ROSS.   You know not
   Whether it was his wisdom or his fear.   5
LADY MACDUFF. Wisdom! to leave his wife, to leave his babes,
   His mansion and his titles° in a place
   From whence himself does fly? He loves us not;
   He wants the natural touch; for the poor wren,
   The most diminutive of birds, will fight,   10
   Her young ones in her nest, against the owl.
   All is the fear and nothing is the love;
   As little is the wisdom, where the flight
   So runs against all reason.
ROSS.   My dearest coz,°
   I pray you, school° yourself; but for your husband,   15
   He is noble, wise, judicious, and best knows
   The fits o' the season.° I dare not speak much further;
   But cruel are the times, when we are traitors
   And do not know ourselves, when we hold rumor
   From what we fear, yet know not what we fear,   20
   But float upon a wild and violent sea
   Each way and move.° I take my leave of you;
   Shall not be long but I'll be here again.
   Things at the worst will cease, or else climb upward
   To what they were before. [*To the boy*] My pretty cousin,   25
   Blessing upon you!
LADY MACDUFF. Fathered he is, and yet he's fatherless.
ROSS. I am so much a fool, should I stay longer,
   It would be my disgrace and your discomfort.
   I take my leave at once.   [*Exit.*]

SCENE II: 7. **titles:** possessions. 14. **coz:** cousin. 15. **school:** discipline. 17. **fits . . . season:** disorders of the time. 22. **Each . . . move:** tossed this way and that, as a ship in a tempest.

LADY MACDUFF.   Sirrah, your father's dead;   30
     And what will you do now? How will you live?
SON. As birds do, mother.
LADY MACDUFF.   What, with worms and flies?
SON. With what I get, I mean; and so do they.
LADY MACDUFF. Poor bird! thou 'ldst never fear the net nor lime,°
     The pitfall nor the gin.°   35
SON. Why should I, mother? Poor° birds they are not set for.
     My father is not dead, for all your saying.
LADY MACDUFF. Yes, he is dead. How wilt thou do for a father?
SON. Nay, how will you do for a husband?
LADY MACDUFF. Why, I can buy me twenty at any market.   40
SON. Then you'll buy 'em to sell again.
LADY MACDUFF. Thou speak'st with all thy wit; and yet, i' faith,
     With wit enough for thee.
SON. Was my father a traitor, mother?
LADY MACDUFF. Ay, that he was.   45
SON. What is a traitor?
LADY MACDUFF. Why, one that swears and lies.
SON. And be all traitors that do so?
LADY MACDUFF. Every one that does so is a traitor, and must be hanged.
SON. And must they all be hanged that swear and lie?   50
LADY MACDUFF. Every one.
SON. Who must hang them?
LADY MACDUFF. Why, the honest men.
SON. Then the liars and swearers are fools, for there are liars and swearers enow
     to beat the honest men and hang up them.   55
LADY MACDUFF. Now, God help thee, poor monkey! But how wilt thou do for a
     father?
SON. If he were dead, you 'ld weep for him; if you would not, it were a good sign
     that I should quickly have a new father.
LADY MACDUFF. Poor prattler, how thou talk'st!   60

               [*Enter a* MESSENGER.]

MESSENGER. Bless you, fair dame! I am not to you known,
     Though in your state of honor I am perfect.°
     I doubt° some danger does approach you nearly.
     If you will take a homely° man's advice,
     Be not found here; hence, with your little ones.   65
     To fright you thus, methinks, I am too savage;
     To do worse to you were fell° cruelty,
     Which is too nigh your person. Heaven preserve you!
     I dare abide no longer.   [*Exit.*]
LADY MACDUFF.   Whither should I fly?
     I have done no harm. But I remember now   70
     I am in this earthly world; where to do harm
     Is often laudable, to do good sometime

---

34. **lime:** birdlime, a sticky substance to trap small birds. 35. **gin:** trap. 36. **Poor:** worthless.
62. **in . . . perfect:** I well know you to be an honorable person. 63. **doubt:** suspect. 64. **homely:**
simple. 67. **fell:** fierce.

Accounted dangerous folly. Why then, alas,
Do I put up that womanly defense,
To say I have done no harm?

[*Enter* MURDERERS.]

                                 What are these faces?   75
FIRST MURDERER. Where is your husband?
LADY MACDUFF. I hope, in no place so unsanctified
    Where such as thou mayst find him.
FIRST MURDERER.   He's a traitor.
SON. Thou liest, thou shag-eared° villain!
FIRST MURDERER.   What, you egg!   [*Stabbing him.*]
    Young fry of treachery!
SON.   He has killed me, mother: 80
    Run away, I pray you!   [*Dies.*]
    [*Exit* LADY MACDUFF, *crying* "Murder!" *Exeunt* MURDERERS, *following her.*]

SCENE III. *England. Before the* KING'S *palace.*

[*Enter* MALCOLM *and* MACDUFF.]

MALCOLM. Let us seek out some desolate shade, and there
    Weep our sad bosoms empty.
MACDUFF.   Let us rather
    Hold fast the mortal° sword, and like good men
    Bestride our downfall'n birthdom.° Each new morn
    New widows howl, new orphans cry, new sorrows   5
    Strike heaven on the face, that it resounds
    As if it felt with Scotland and yelled out
    Like syllable of dolor.°
MALCOLM.   What I believe, I'll wail,
    What know, believe, and what I can redress,
    As I shall find the time to friend,° I will.   10
    What you have spoke, it may be so perchance.
    This tyrant, whose sole° name blisters our tongues,
    Was once thought honest; you have loved him well;
    He hath not touched you yet. I am young; but something
    You may deserve of him through me, the wisdom   15
    To offer up a weak poor innocent lamb
    To appease an angry god.
MACDUFF. I am not treacherous.
MALCOLM.   But Macbeth is.
    A good and virtuous nature may recoil
    In an imperial charge.° But I shall crave your pardon; 20
    That which you are my thoughts cannot transpose.°
    Angels are bright still, though the brightest° fell.

79. **shag-eared:** hairy-eared.
    SCENE III: 3. **mortal:** deadly. 4. **birthdom:** native land. 8. **Like . . . dolor:** an anguished echo.
10. **to friend:** to be a friend. 12. **sole:** very. 19–20. **recoil . . . charge:** commit a wicked deed at a
king's command. 21. **transpose:** change. 22. **brightest:** Lucifer, the brightest angel.

Though all things foul would wear the brows of grace,
Yet grace must still look so.°
MACDUFF.   I have lost my hopes.
MALCOLM. Perchance even there where I did find my doubts.   25
Why in that rawness° left you wife and child,
Those precious motives, those strong knots of love,
Without leave-taking? I pray you,
Let not my jealousies° be your dishonors,
But mine own safeties.° You may be rightly just,   30
Whatever I shall think.
MACDUFF.   Bleed, bleed, poor country!
Great tyranny! lay thou thy basis sure,
For goodness dare not check thee; wear thou thy wrongs;
The title is affeered!° Fare thee well, lord;
I would not be the villain that thou think'st   35
For the whole space that's in the tyrant's grasp,
And the rich East to boot.
MALCOLM.   Be not offended;
I speak not as in absolute fear of you.
I think our country sinks beneath the yoke;
It weeps, it bleeds; and each new day a gash   40
Is added to her wounds. I think withal
There would be hands uplifted in my right;
And here from gracious England have I offer
Of goodly thousands. But, for all this,
When I shall tread upon the tyrant's head,   45
Or wear it on my sword, yet my poor country
Shall have more vices than it had before,
More suffer and more sundry ways than ever,
By him that shall succeed.
MACDUFF.   What should he be?
MALCOLM. It is myself I mean; in whom I know   50
All the particulars of vice so grafted
That, when they shall be opened, black Macbeth
Will seem as pure as snow, and the poor state
Esteem him as a lamb, being compared
With my confineless harms.
MACDUFF.   Not in the legions   55
Of horrid hell can come a devil more damned
In evils to top Macbeth.
MALCOLM.   I grant him bloody,
Luxurious,° avaricious, false, deceitful,
Sudden, malicious, smacking of every sin
That has a name; but there's no bottom, none,   60
In my voluptuousness. Your wives, your daughters,
Your matrons and your maids, could not fill up

---

24. **still look so:** still appear as goodness. Malcolm can't tell yet whether Macduff is to be trusted.
26. **rawness:** unprotected state. 29. **jealousies:** suspicions. 30. **safeties:** protection. 34. **affeered:** confirmed; that is, since goodness dares not oppose tyranny, tyranny's title or right to power is confirmed. 58. **Luxurious:** lustful.

The cistern of my lust, and my desire
All continent impediments° would o'erbear
That did oppose my will. Better Macbeth   65
Than such an one to reign.

MACDUFF.   Boundless intemperance
In nature is a tyranny; it hath been
The untimely emptying of the happy throne
And fall of many kings. But fear not yet
To take upon you what is yours. You may   70
Convey your pleasures in a spacious plenty,°
And yet seem cold,° the time you may so hoodwink.
We have willing dames enough; there cannot be
That vulture in you, to devour so many
As will to greatness dedicate themselves,   75
Finding it so inclined.

MALCOLM.   With this there grows
In my most ill-composed affection such
A staunchless° avarice that, were I king,
I should cut off the nobles for their lands,
Desire his jewels and this other's house;   80
And my more-having would be as a sauce
To make me hunger more, that I should forge
Quarrels unjust against the good and loyal,
Destroying them for wealth.

MACDUFF.   This avarice
Sticks deeper, grows with more pernicious root   85
Than summer-seeming° lust, and it hath been
The sword of° our slain kings. Yet do not fear;
Scotland hath foisons° to fill up your will,
Of your mere own.° All these are portable,°
With other graces weighed.   90

MALCOLM. But I have none. The king-becoming graces,
As justice, verity, temperance, stableness,
Bounty, perseverance, mercy, lowliness,
Devotion, patience, courage, fortitude,
I have no relish of them, but abound   95
In the division of each several crime,
Acting it many ways. Nay, had I power, I should
Pour the sweet milk of concord into hell,
Uproar the universal peace, confound
All unity on earth.

MACDUFF.   O Scotland, Scotland!   100
MALCOLM. If such a one be fit to govern, speak.
I am as I have spoken.

MACDUFF.   Fit to govern!
No, not to live. O nation miserable

---

64. **continent impediments:** restraints.   71. **Convey . . . plenty:** find plenty of room in which to indulge your pleasures secretly.   72. **cold:** chaste.   78. **staunchless:** insatiable.   86. **summer-seeming:**
fleeting, that which lasts like summer, only for a season.   87. **The sword of:** that which has killed.
88. **foisons:** plenty.   89. **mere own:** own property.   **portable:** endurable.

With an untitled° tyrant bloody-sceptered,
When shalt thou see thy wholesome days again,   105
Since that the truest issue of thy throne°
By his own interdiction° stands accursed,
And does blaspheme his breed? Thy royal father
Was a most sainted king; the queen that bore thee,
Oftener upon her knees than on her feet,   110
Died every day she lived.° Fare thee well!
These evils thou repeat'st upon thyself
Have banished me from Scotland. O my breast,
Thy hope ends here!

MALCOLM.   Macduff, this noble passion,
Child of integrity, hath from my soul   115
Wiped the black scruples, reconciled my thoughts
To thy good truth and honor. Devilish Macbeth
By many of these trains° hath sought to win me
Into his power, and modest wisdom plucks me
From overcredulous haste; but God above   120
Deal between thee and me! for even now
I put myself to thy direction, and
Unspeak mine own detraction,° here abjure
The taints and blames I laid upon myself,
For strangers to my nature. I am yet   125
Unknown to woman, never was foresworn,°
Scarcely have coveted what was mine own,
At no time broke my faith, would not betray
The devil to his fellow, and delight
No less in truth than life; my first false speaking   130
Was this upon myself. What I am truly,
Is thine and my poor country's to command;
Whither indeed, before thy here-approach,
Old Siward, with ten thousand warlike men,
Already at a point,° was setting forth.   135
Now we'll together; and the chance of goodness
Be like our warranted quarrel!° Why are you silent?

MACDUFF. Such welcome and unwelcome things at once
'Tis hard to reconcile.

[*Enter a* DOCTOR.]

MALCOLM. Well; more anon.—Comes the king forth, I pray you?   140
DOCTOR. Ay, sir; there are a crew of wretched souls
That stay his cure;° their malady convinces
The great assay of art;° but at his touch—
Such sanctity hath Heaven given his hand—
They presently amend.

104. **untitled:** having no right to the throne.   106. **truest . . . throne:** child of the true king.   107. **interdiction:** exclusion.   111. **Died . . . lived:** lived always in a state of grace, prepared for death.   118. **trains:** enticements.   123. **detraction:** slander.   126. **was foresworn:** broke my oath.   135. **at a point:** prepared for action.   136–37. **the chance . . . quarrel:** May our chance of success be as good as the outcome of our argument.   142. **stay his cure:** wait for him to heal them.   142–43. **convinces . . . art:** defeats the best efforts of medical skill.

MALCOLM.   I thank you, Doctor.   [*Exit* DOCTOR.]   145
MACDUFF. What's the disease he means?
MALCOLM.   'Tis called the evil;°
    A most miraculous work in this good king;
    Which often, since my here-remain in England,
    I have seen him do. How he solicits Heaven,
    Himself best knows; but strangely visited people,   150
    All swoln° and ulcerous, pitiful to the eye,
    The mere° despair of surgery, he cures,
    Hanging a golden stamp° about their necks,
    Put on with holy prayers; and 'tis spoken,
    To the succeeding royalty he leaves   155
    The healing benediction. With this strange virtue,
    He hath a heavenly gift of prophecy,
    And sundry blessings hang about his throne,
    That speak him full of grace.

[*Enter* ROSS.]

MACDUFF.   See, who comes here?
MALCOLM. My countryman; but yet I know him not.   160
MACDUFF. My ever-gentle° cousin, welcome hither.
MALCOLM. I know him now. Good God, betimes° remove
    The means° that makes us strangers!
ROSS.   Sir, amen.
MACDUFF. Stands Scotland where it did?
ROSS.   Alas, poor country!
    Almost afraid to know itself. It cannot   165
    Be called our mother, but our grave; where nothing,
    But who knows nothing, is once seen to smile;
    Where sighs and groans and shrieks that rend the air
    Are made, not marked; where violent sorrow seems
    A modern ecstasy.° The dead man's knell   170
    Is there scarce asked for who;° and good men's lives
    Expire before the flowers in their caps,
    Dying or ere they sicken.
MACDUFF.   O, relation°
    Too nice,° and yet too true!
MALCOLM.   What's the newest grief?
ROSS. That of an hour's age doth hiss the speaker;°   175
    Each minute teems° a new one.
MACDUFF.   How does my wife?
ROSS. Why, well.

---

146. **evil:** scrofula (skrof′yə·lə), a skin disease. Edward the Confessor reputedly healed sufferers by his saintly touch. The reference is made here as a compliment to James I, who, though at first reluctant to continue the practice of touching sufferers, finally yielded to the urgings of his English ministers. 151. **swoln:** swollen. 152. **mere:** utter. 153. **stamp:** medal. 161. **gentle:** noble. 162. **betimes:** soon. 163. **means:** that is, Malcolm's exile from Scotland. 170. **modern ecstasy:** a slight mental disturbance. 170–71. **The dead . . . who:** People can no longer keep track of Macbeth's victims. 173. **relation:** account. 174. **nice:** exact. 175. **That . . . speaker:** There are so many sorrows that a report only an hour old is hissed as stale news. 176. **teems:** gives birth to.

MACDUFF.   And all my children?

ROSS.   Well too.

MACDUFF. The tyrant has not battered at their peace?

ROSS. No; they were well at peace when I did leave 'em.

MACDUFF. Be not a niggard of your speech; how goes 't?   180

ROSS. When I came hither to transport the tidings,
    Which I have heavily borne, there ran a rumor
    Of many worthy fellows that were out;°
    Which was to my belief witnessed° the rather,
    For that I saw the tyrant's power afoot.   185
    Now is the time of help; your eye in Scotland
    Would create soldiers, make our women fight,
    To doff° their dire distresses.

MALCOLM.   Be 't their comfort
    We are coming thither. Gracious England hath
    Lent us good Siward° and ten thousand men;   190
    An older and a better soldier none
    That Christendom gives out.

ROSS.   Would I could answer
    This comfort with the like! But I have words
    That would be howled out in the desert air,
    Where hearing should not latch° them.

MACDUFF.   What concern they?   195
    The general cause? or is it a fee grief°
    Due to some single breast?

ROSS.   No mind that's honest
    But in it shares some woe; though the main part
    Pertains to you alone.

MACDUFF.   If it be mine,
    Keep it not from me—quickly let me have it.   200

ROSS. Let not your ears despise my tongue for ever,
    Which shall possess them with the heaviest sound
    That ever yet they heard.

MACDUFF.   Hum! I guess at it.

ROSS. Your castle is surprised; your wife and babes
    Savagely slaughtered: to relate the manner,   205
    Were, on the quarry° of these murdered deer,
    To add the death of you.

MALCOLM.   Merciful Heaven!
    What, man! ne'er pull your hat upon your brows;
    Give sorrow words. The grief that does not speak
    Whispers the o'erfraught° heart and bids it break.   210

MACDUFF. My children too?

ROSS.   Wife, children, servants, all
    That could be found.

MACDUFF.   And I must be from thence!
    My wife killed too?

---

183. **out**: in rebellion. 184. **witnessed**: confirmed. 188. **doff**: put off. 190. **Siward** (sē'wärd).
195. **latch**: catch. 196. **fee grief**: a grief belonging to only one person. 206. **quarry**: heap of game
slain in a hunt. 210. **o'erfraught**: overburdened.

ROSS.   I have said.

MALCOLM.   Be comforted.
Let's make us medicines of our great revenge,
To cure this deadly grief.   215

MACDUFF. He has no children. All my pretty ones?
Did you say all? O hell kite! All?
What, all my pretty chickens and their dam
At one fell swoop?

MALCOLM. Dispute it° like a man.

MACDUFF.   I shall do so;   220
But I must also feel it as a man.
I cannot but remember such things were,
That were most precious to me. Did Heaven look on,
And would not take their part? Sinful Macduff,
They were all struck for thee! naught° that I am,   225
Not for their own demerits, but for mine,
Fell slaughter on their souls. Heaven rest them now!

MALCOLM. Be this the whetstone of your sword; let grief
Convert to anger; blunt not the heart, enrage it.

MACDUFF. O, I could play the woman with mine eyes   230
And braggart with my tongue! But, gentle heavens,
Cut short all intermission; front to front°
Bring thou this fiend of Scotland and myself;
Within my sword's length set him; if he 'scape,
Heaven forgive him too!

MALCOLM.   This tune goes manly   235
Come, go we to the king; our power is ready;
Our lack is nothing but our leave.° Macbeth
Is ripe for shaking, and the powers above
Put on their instruments.° Receive what cheer you may:
The night is long that never finds the day.   [*Exeunt.*] 240

220. **Dispute it:** Resist your grief.   225. **naught:** worthless.   232. **front to front:** face to face.
237. **leave:** permission to go.   239. **Put . . . instruments:** encourage us as their agents.

FOR STUDY AND DISCUSSION: ACT IV

1. In Act III, Scene v, Hecate orders the three witches to raise spirits that will cause Macbeth to "spurn fate, scorn death, and bear/ His hopes 'bove wisdom, grace, and fear." How do the witches succeed in carrying out this command in Act IV, Scene i? Why is Macbeth oblivious to the hidden meanings in the witches' prophecies? What occurrence in this scene deeply disturbs him?

2. Why does Macbeth decide to murder Macduff's family? How does this decision differ from his decisions to murder Duncan and Banquo? What does this indicate about the development of Macbeth's character? What do you think is the dramatic purpose of the conversation in Scene ii between Lady Macduff and her son?

3. In Scene iii, how does Malcolm describe himself to Macduff? Why does he misrepresent his character to Macduff? Defend or criticize the reasons behind this false representation.

4. In Scene iii, Ross has the heart-rending task of reporting to Macduff the murder of his family. How does Ross try to evade this distasteful duty? What is the significance of Macduff's remark, "He has no children"?

ACT V

SCENE I. *Dunsinane. Anteroom in the castle.*

[*Enter a* DOCTOR OF PHYSIC *and a* WAITING-GENTLEWOMAN.]

DOCTOR. I have two nights watched with you, but can perceive no truth in your report. When was it she last walked?

GENTLEWOMAN. Since his majesty went into the field,° I have seen her rise from her bed, throw her nightgown upon her, unlock her closet, take forth paper, fold it, write upon 't, read it, afterward seal it, and again return to bed; 5 yet all this while in a most fast sleep.

DOCTOR. A great perturbation in nature, to receive at once the benefit of sleep, and do the effects of watching! In this slumbery agitation, besides her walking and other actual performances, what, at any time, have you heard her say?

GENTLEWOMAN. That, sir, which I will not report after her.   10

DOCTOR. You may to me; and 'tis most meet you should.

GENTLEWOMAN. Neither to you nor any one, having no witness to confirm my speech.

[*Enter* LADY MACBETH, *with a taper.*]

Lo you, here she comes! This is her very guise;° and, upon my life, fast asleep. Observe her; stand close.°   15

DOCTOR. How came she by that light?

GENTLEWOMAN. Why, it stood by her; she has light by her continually; 'tis her command.

DOCTOR. You see, her eyes are open.

GENTLEWOMAN. Ay, but their sense is shut.   20

DOCTOR. What is it she does now? Look, how she rubs her hands.

GENTLEWOMAN. It is an accustomed action with her, to seem thus washing her hands. I have known her continue in this a quarter of an hour.

LADY MACBETH. Yet here's a spot.

DOCTOR. Hark! She speaks. I will set down what comes from her, to satisfy my 25 remembrance the more strongly.

LADY MACBETH. Out, damned spot! out, I say!—One: two: why, then 'tis time to do 't.—Hell is murky!—Fie, my lord, fie! a soldier, and afeard? What need we fear who knows it, when none can call our power to account?—Yet who would have thought the old man to have had so much blood in 30 him?

DOCTOR. Do you mark that?

LADY MACBETH. The thane of Fife had a wife; where is she now?—What, will these hands ne'er be clean?—No more o' that, my lord, no more o' that; you mar all with this starting.   35

DOCTOR. Go to, go to; you have known what you should not.

GENTLEWOMAN. She has spoke what she should not, I am sure of that; Heaven knows what she has known.

LADY MACBETH. Here's the smell of the blood still; all the perfumes of Arabia will not sweeten this little hand. Oh, oh, oh!   40

DOCTOR. What a sigh is there! The heart is sorely charged.°

3. **into the field:** out with the army. 14. **guise:** custom. 15. **close:** hidden. 41. **charged:** burdened; oppressed with care.

WILLIAM SHAKESPEARE   169

GENTLEWOMAN. I would not have such a heart in my bosom for the dignity of the whole body.

DOCTOR. Well, well, well——

GENTLEWOMAN. Pray God it be, sir.   45

DOCTOR. This disease is beyond my practice; yet I have known those which have walked in their sleep who have died holily in their beds.

LADY MACBETH. Wash your hands, put on your nightgown; look not so pale.—I tell you yet again, Banquo's buried; he cannot come out on 's grave.

DOCTOR. Even so?   50

LADY MACBETH. To bed, to bed! There's knocking at the gate. Come, come, come, come, give me your hand. What's done cannot be undone.—To bed, to bed, to bed!   [*Exit.*]

DOCTOR. Will she go now to bed?

GENTLEWOMAN. Directly.   55

DOCTOR. Foul whisperings are abroad; unnatural deeds
    Do breed unnatural troubles; infected minds
    To their deaf pillows will discharge their secrets.
    More needs she the divine than the physician.
    God, God forgive us all! Look after her;   60
    Remove from her the means of all annoyance,°
    And still keep eyes upon her. So, good night;
    My mind she has mated,° and amazed my sight.
    I think, but dare not speak.

GENTLEWOMAN.   Good night, good doctor.   [*Exeunt.*]

SCENE II. *The country near Dunsinane.*

[*Drum and colors.* Enter* MENTEITH,† CAITHNESS,‡ ANGUS, LENNOX, *and* SOLDIERS.]

MENTEITH. The English power is near, led on by Malcolm,
    His uncle Siward and the good Macduff.
    Revenges burn in them; for their dear causes
    Would to the bleeding and the grim alarm°
    Excite the mortified° man.

ANGUS.   Near Birnam wood   5
    Shall we well meet them; that way are they coming.

CAITHNESS. Who knows if Donalbain be with his brother?

LENNOX. For certain, sir, he is not; I have a file
    Of all the gentry. There is Siward's son,
    And many unrough youths that even now   10
    Protest their first of manhood.°

MENTEITH.   What does the tyrant?

CAITHNESS. Great Dunsinane he strongly fortifies.
    Some say he's mad; others that lesser hate him

---

61. **annoyance:** harm.   63. **mated:** confused.

SCENE II: * **Drum and colors:** a drummer and a soldier with a flag.   † **Menteith** (men·tēth').
‡ **Caithness** (kāth'nəs).   4. **alarm:** call to arms.   5. **mortified:** half dead.   11. **Protest . . . manhood:** show that they have hardly reached manhood.

Do call it valiant fury; but, for certain,
He cannot buckle his distempered cause   15
Within the belt of rule.°
ANGUS.   Now does he feel
His secret murders sticking on his hands;
Now minutely° revolts upbraid his faith breach;°
Those he commands move only in command,
Nothing in love. Now does he feel his title   20
Hang loose about him, like a giant's robe
Upon a dwarfish thief.
MENTEITH.   Who then shall blame
His pestered° senses to recoil and start,
When all that is within him does condemn
Itself for being there?
CAITHNESS.   Well, march we on,   25
To give obedience where 'tis truly owed.
Meet we the medicine of the sickly weal,°
And with him pour we in our country's purge
Each drop of us.
LENNOX.   Or so much as it needs,
To dew° the sovereign flower° and drown the weeds.°   30
Make we our march toward Birnam.   [*Exeunt, marching.*]

SCENE III. *Dunsinane. A room in the castle.*

[*Enter* MACBETH, DOCTOR, *and* ATTENDANTS.]

MACBETH. Bring me no more reports; let them fly all;°
Till Birnam wood remove to Dunsinane,
I cannot taint° with fear. What's the boy Malcolm?
Was he not born of woman? The spirits that know
All mortal consequences° have pronounced me thus: 5
"Fear not, Macbeth; no man that's born of woman
Shall e'er have power upon thee." Then fly, false thanes,
And mingle with the English epicures!°
The mind I sway by and the heart I bear
Shall never sag with doubt nor shake with fear.   10

[*Enter a* SERVANT.]

The devil damn thee black, thou cream-faced loon!
Where got'st thou that goose look?
SERVANT. There is ten thousand——
MACBETH.   Geese, villain?
SERVANT.   Soldiers, sir.
MACBETH. Go, prick thy face, and over-red thy fear,

---

16. **Within ... rule:** under control. 18. **minutely:** every minute. **faith breach:** disloyalty.
23. **pestered:** troubled. 27. **medicine ... weal:** the medicine (i.e., Malcolm and his party) which will
heal the commonwealth. 30. **dew:** water. **sovereign flower:** Malcolm. **weeds:** Macbeth.
SCENE III: 1. **let ... all:** let them all desert me. 3. **taint:** be infected. 5. **mortal consequences:**
human fate. 8. **epicures:** gluttons: that is, not soldiers.

Thou lily-livered boy. What soldiers, patch?° 15
Death of thy soul! those linen° cheeks of thine
Are counselors to fear. What soldiers, whey-face?
SERVANT. The English force, so please you.
MACBETH. Take thy face hence. [*Exit* SERVANT.]
              Seyton!—I am sick at heart,
When I behold—Seyton, I say!—This push° 20
Will cheer me ever, or disseat me now.
I have lived long enough. My way of life
Is fall'n into the sear,° the yellow leaf;
And that which should accompany old age,
As honor, love, obedience, troops of friends, 25
I must not look to have; but, in their stead,
Curses, not loud but deep, mouth honor, breath,
Which the poor heart would fain deny, and dare not.
Seyton!

[*Enter* SEYTON.]

SEYTON. What is your gracious pleasure?
MACBETH.   What news more? 30
SEYTON. All is confirmed, my lord, which was reported.
MACBETH. I'll fight till from my bones my flesh be hacked.
    Give me my armor.
SEYTON.   'Tis not needed yet.
MACBETH. I'll put it on.
    Send out moe° horses; skirr° the country round; 35
    Hang those that talk of fear. Give me mine armor.
    How does your patient, doctor?
DOCTOR.   Not so sick, my lord,
    As she is troubled with thick-coming fancies,
    That keep her from her rest.
MACBETH.   Cure her of that.
    Canst thou not minister to a mind diseased, 40
    Pluck from the memory a rooted sorrow,
    Raze out the written troubles of the brain
    And with some sweet oblivious antidote
    Cleanse the stuffed bosom of that perilous stuff
    Which weighs upon the heart?
DOCTOR.   Therein the patient 45
    Must minister to himself.
MACBETH. Throw physic° to the dogs; I'll none of it.
    Come, put mine armor on; give me my staff.
    Seyton, send out. Doctor, the thanes fly from me.
    Come, sir, dispatch. If thou couldst, doctor, cast 50
    The water° of my land, find her disease,
    And purge it to a sound and pristine° health,
    I would applaud thee to the very echo,

---

15. **patch:** fool. 16. **linen:** pale as linen. 20. **push:** attack. 23. **sear:** dry, withered. 35. **moe:** more. **skirr:** scour. 47. **physic:** medicine. 50–51. **cast . . . water:** diagnose the illness. 52. **pristine:** i.e., former.

That should applaud again.—Pull 't off, I say.—°
What rhubarb, senna, or what purgative drug,   55
Would scour these English hence? Hear'st thou of them?
DOCTOR. Ay, my good lord; your royal preparation
Makes us hear something.
MACBETH.   Bring it after me.
I will not be afraid of death and bane,
Till Birnam forest come to Dunsinane.   60
DOCTOR [*Aside*] Were I from Dunsinane away and clear,
Profit again should hardly draw me here.   [*Exeunt.*]

SCENE IV. *Country near Birnam wood.*

[*Drum and colors. Enter* MALCOLM, *old* SIWARD *and his* SON, MACDUFF, MEN-
TEITH, CAITHNESS, ANGUS, LENNOX, ROSS, *and* SOLDIERS *marching.*]

MALCOLM. Cousins, I hope the days are near at hand
That chambers will be safe.°
MENTEITH.   We doubt it nothing.
SIWARD. What wood is this before us?
MENTEITH.   The wood of Birnam.
MALCOLM. Let every soldier hew him down a bough
And bear it before him; thereby shall we shadow°   5
The numbers of our host and make discovery
Err in report of us.
SOLDIERS.   It shall be done.
SIWARD. We learn no other but the confident tyrant
Keeps still in Dunsinane, and will endure
Our setting down° before 't.
MALCOLM.   'Tis his main hope;   10
For where there is advantage to be given,
Both more or less have given him the revolt,°
And none serve with him but constrainèd° things
Whose hearts are absent too.
MACDUFF.   Let our just censures
Attend the true event,° and put we on   15
Industrious soldiership.
SIWARD.   The time approaches
That will with due decision make us know
What we shall say we have and what we owe.
Thoughts speculative their unsure hopes relate,
But certain issue strokes must arbitrate;°   20
Toward which advance the war.   [*Exeunt, marching.*]

54. **Pull . . . say:** Macbeth orders Seyton to pull off part of his armor which has been put on wrong
in his haste.
    SCENE IV: 2. **chambers . . . safe:** that is, people will be safe in their own homes. 5. **shadow:** conceal.
10. **setting down:** siege. 12. **Both . . . revolt:** Both the higher and lower classes ("more or less") have
deserted Macbeth. 13. **constrainèd:** forced. 15. **Attend . . . event:** wait until the battle is over.
20. **arbitrate:** decide.

SCENE V. *Dunsinane. Within the castle.*

[*Enter* MACBETH, SEYTON, *and* SOLDIERS, *with drum and colors.*]

MACBETH. Hang out our banners on the outward walls;
    The cry is still "They come!" Our castle's strength
    Will laugh a siege to scorn; here let them lie
    Till famine and the ague° eat them up.
    Were they not forced° with those that should be ours,   5
    We might have met them dareful, beard to beard,
    And beat them backward home.   [*A cry of women within.*]
                     What is that noise?
SEYTON. It is the cry of women, my good lord.   [*Exit.*]
MACBETH. I have almost forgot the taste of fears.
    The time has been, my senses would have cooled   10
    To hear a night-shriek; and my fell of hair°
    Would at a dismal treatise° rouse and stir
    As life were in 't. I have supped full with horrors;
    Direness, familiar to my slaughterous thoughts,
    Cannot once start° me.

              [*Reenter* SEYTON.]

            Wherefore was that cry?   15
SEYTON. The queen, my lord, is dead.
MACBETH. She should have died hereafter;°
    There would have been a time for such a word.
    Tomorrow, and tomorrow, and tomorrow,
    Creeps in this petty pace from day to day   20
    To the last syllable of recorded time,
    And all our yesterdays have lighted fools
    The way to dusty death. Out, out, brief candle!
    Life's but a walking shadow, a poor player
    That struts and frets his hour upon the stage   25
    And then is heard no more. It is a tale
    Told by an idiot, full of sound and fury,
    Signifying nothing.

            [*Enter* MESSENGER.]

    Thou comest to use thy tongue; thy story quickly.
MESSENGER. Gracious my lord,   30
    I should report that which I say I saw,
    But know not how to do it.
MACBETH.   Well, say, sir.
MESSENGER. As I did stand my watch upon the hill,
    I looked toward Birnam, and anon, methought,
    The wood began to move.
MACBETH.   Liar and slave!   35
MESSENGER. Let me endure your wrath, if 't be not so.
    Within this three mile may you see it coming;
    I say, a moving grove.

---

4. **ague:** fever. 5. **forced:** reinforced. 11. **my ... hair:** the hair on my scalp. 12. **dismal treatise:** gloomy story. 15. **start:** startle. 17. **She ... hereafter:** She would have died sometime.

MACBETH.   If thou speak'st false,
    Upon the next tree shalt thou hang alive,
    Till famine cling° thee; if thy speech be sooth,°   40
    I care not if thou dost for me as much.
    I pull in resolution,° and begin
    To doubt the equivocation° of the fiend
    That lies like truth: "Fear not, till Birnam wood
    Do come to Dunsinane." And now a wood   45
    Comes toward Dunsinane. Arm, arm, and out!
    If this which he avouches does appear,
    There is nor flying hence nor tarrying here.
    I 'gin to be aweary of the sun,
    And wish the estate o' the world were now undone.   50
    Ring the alarum bell! Blow, wind! come, wrack!°
    At least we'll die with harness° on our back.   *[Exeunt.]*

SCENE VI. *Dunsinane. Before the castle.*

[*Drum and colors. Enter* MALCOLM, *old* SIWARD, MACDUFF, *and their* ARMY, *with
   boughs*.]

MALCOLM. Now near enough; your leavy° screens throw down,
    And show like those you are. You, worthy uncle,
    Shall, with my cousin, your right noble son,
    Lead our first battle. Worthy Macduff and we
    Shall take upon's else remains to do,   5
    According to our order.
SIWARD.   Fare you well.
    Do we but find the tyrant's power tonight,
    Let us be beaten, if we cannot fight.
MACDUFF. Make all our trumpets speak; give them all breath,
    Those clamorous harbingers° of blood and death.   *[Exeunt.]* 10

SCENE VII. *Another part of the field.*

[*Alarums. Enter* MACBETH.]

MACBETH. They have tied me to a stake; I cannot fly,
    But, bearlike, I must fight the course.° What's he
    That was not born of woman? Such a one
    Am I to fear, or none.

[*Enter young* SIWARD.]

YOUNG SIWARD. What is thy name?
MACBETH.   Thou 'lt be afraid to hear it.   5

    40. **cling:** wither. **sooth:** truth. 42. **resolution:** courage. 43. **equivocation:** double talk.
51. **wrack:** wreck. 52. **harness:** armor.
    SCENE VI: 1. **leavy:** leafy. 10. **harbingers:** messengers.
    SCENE VII: 2. **But . . . course:** Like a bear chained to a stake and attacked by hounds, Macbeth
must endure to the end.

YOUNG SIWARD. No; though thou call'st thyself a hotter name
    Than any is in hell.
MACBETH.   My name's Macbeth.
YOUNG SIWARD. The devil himself could not pronounce a title
    More hateful to mine ear.
MACBETH.   No, nor more fearful.
YOUNG SIWARD. Thou liest, abhorrèd tyrant; with my sword   10
    I'll prove the lie thou speak'st.   [*They fight and young* SIWARD *is slain.*]
MACBETH.   Thou wast born of woman.
    But swords I smile at, weapons laugh to scorn,
    Brandished by man that's of a woman born.   [*Exit.*]

           [*Alarums. Enter* MACDUFF.]

MACDUFF. That way the noise is. Tyrant, show thy face!
    If thou be'st slain and with no stroke of mine,   15
    My wife and children's ghosts will haunt me still.
    I cannot strike at wretched kerns,° whose arms
    Are hired to bear their staves;° either thou, Macbeth,
    Or else my sword with an unbattered edge
    I sheathe again undeeded. There thou shouldst be;   20
    By this great clatter, one of greatest note
    Seems bruited.° Let me find him, fortune!
    And more I beg not.   [*Exit. Alarums.*]

       [*Enter* MALCOLM *and old* SIWARD.]

SIWARD. This way, my lord; the castle's gently rendered:°
    The tyrant's people on both sides do fight;   25
    The noble thanes do bravely in the war;
    The day almost itself professes yours,
    And little is to do.
MALCOLM.   We have met with foes
    That strike beside us.°
SIWARD.   Enter, sir, the castle.   [*Exeunt. Alarums.*]

SCENE VIII. *Another part of the field.*

[*Enter* MACBETH.]

MACBETH. Why should I play the Roman fool,° and die
    On mine own sword? Whiles I see lives, the gashes
    Do better upon them.

[*Enter* MACDUFF.]

MACDUFF.   Turn, hell-hound, turn!
MACBETH. Of all men else I have avoided thee.
    But get thee back; my soul is too much charged   5
    With blood of thine already.

    17. **kerns:** foot soldiers hired as mercenaries. 18. **staves:** spears. 22. **bruited:** revealed by the
noise. 24. **gently rendered:** easily surrendered. 29. **beside us:** on our side.
    SCENE VIII: 1. **play . . . fool:** like Brutus or Cassius, who committed suicide in the moment of defeat.

MACDUFF.   I have no words;
     My voice is in my sword, thou bloodier villain
     Than terms can give thee out!   [*They fight.*]
MACBETH.   Thou losest labor;
     As easy mayst thou the intrenchant° air
     With thy keen sword impress° as make me bleed.   10
     Let fall thy blade on vulnerable crests;°
     I bear a charmèd life, which must not yield
     To one of woman born.
MACDUFF.   Despair thy charm;
     And let the angel whom thou still hast served
     Tell thee, Macduff was from his mother's womb   15
     Untimely ripped.
MACBETH. Accursèd be that tongue that tells me so,
     For it hath cowed my better part of man!
     And be these juggling fiends no more believed,
     That palter° with us in a double sense;   20
     That keep the word of promise to our ear,
     And break it to our hope. I'll not fight with thee.
MACDUFF. Then yield thee, coward,
     And live to be the show and gaze o' the time.
     We'll have thee, as our rarer monsters° are,   25
     Painted upon a pole,° and underwrit,
     "Here may you see the tyrant."
MACBETH.   I will not yield,
     To kiss the ground before young Malcolm's feet,
     And to be baited with the rabble's curse.
     Though Birnam wood be come to Dunsinane,   30
     And thou opposed, being of no woman born,
     Yet I will try the last. Before my body
     I throw my warlike shield. Lay on, Macduff,
     And damned be him that first cries "Hold, enough!"
                                   [*Exeunt, fighting. Alarums.*]

[*Retreat. Flourish. Enter, with drum and colors,* MALCOLM, *old* SIWARD, ROSS,
     the other THANES, *and* SOLDIERS.]

MALCOLM. I would the friends we miss were safe arrived.   35
SIWARD. Some must go off;° and yet, by these I see,
     So great a day as this is cheaply bought.
MALCOLM. Macduff is missing, and your noble son.
ROSS. Your son, my lord, has paid a soldier's debt.
     He only lived but till he was a man;   40
     The which no sooner had his prowess confirmed
     In the unshrinking station° where he fought,
     But like a man he died.
SIWARD.   Then he is dead?

---

9. **intrenchant:** that cannot be cut. 10. **impress:** make a dent in. 11. **vulnerable crests:** heads that
can be wounded. 20. **palter:** juggle. 25. **monsters:** freaks. 26. **Painted ... pole:** your portrait
painted on a placard and stuck on a pole. 36. **go off:** be killed in battle. 42. **unshrinking station:**
standing firm when he fought Macbeth.

ROSS. Ay, and brought off the field. Your cause of sorrow
    Must not be measured by his worth, for then   45
    It hath no end.
SIWARD.   Had he his hurts before?°
ROSS. Ay, on the front.
SIWARD.   Why then, God's soldier be he!
    Had I as many sons as I have hairs,   *[Flourish.]*
    I would not wish them to a fairer death.
    And so, his knell is knolled.
MALCOLM.   He's worth more sorrow,   50
    And that I'll spend for him.
SIWARD.   He's worth no more.
    They say he parted well, and paid his score;
    And so, God be with him! Here comes newer comfort.

         [Reenter MACDUFF, *with* MACBETH'S *head.*]

MACDUFF. Hail, king! for so thou art. Behold, where stands
    The usurper's cursèd head. The time is free.°   55
    I see thee compassed with thy kingdom's pearl,°
    That speak my salutation in their minds;
    Whose voices I desire aloud with mine:
    Hail, King of Scotland!
ALL.   Hail, King of Scotland!   *[Flourish.]*
MALCOLM. We shall not spend a large expense of time   60
    Before we reckon with your several° loves,
    And make us even with you.° My thanes and kinsmen,
    Henceforth be earls, the first that ever Scotland
    In such an honor named. What's more to do,
    Which would be planted newly with the time,   65
    As calling home our exiled friends abroad
    That fled the snares of watchful tyranny;
    Producing forth the cruel ministers
    Of this dead butcher and his fiendlike queen,
    Who, as 'tis thought, by self and violent hands   70
    Took off her life; this, and what needful else
    That calls upon us, by the grace of Grace,
    We will perform in measure,° time, and place;
    So, thanks to all at once and to each one,
    Whom we invite to see us crowned at Scone.   *[Flourish. Exeunt.]* 75

    46. **before:** in front. Because young Siward was wounded in front, his father knew that he died
fighting, not fleeing.   55. **The . . . free:** Liberty is restored.   56. **compassed . . . pearl:** surrounded by
the noblest men in the kingdom.   61. **several:** separate.   62. **make . . . you:** pay you what we owe.
73. **measure:** full measure.

                            .

FOR STUDY AND DISCUSSION: ACT V

1. In Scene i, the famous "sleepwalking scene," Lady Macbeth relives events which have taken place earlier in the play. In her ravings she skips from one event to another, but she always returns to the same one. Of the three events she broods over, which troubles her most deeply? Why?

2. In Scene iii, reread lines 22–28, beginning, "I have lived long enough." What does this soliloquy tell us about Macbeth's state of mind on the eve of battle? Which of Shake-

speare's sonnets on pages 106–08 has a similar theme?

3. Macbeth's final word on the meaning of life is given in Scene v, lines 19–28. How would you describe, in one word, the tone of this soliloquy? What are Macbeth's thoughts on life as expressed in lines 19–23? What specifically is the "brief candle" and what is its connection to "a poor player"?

4. Macbeth is a brave soldier almost to the end. On what occasions in Act V does Macbeth express his courage? Where does his courage momentarily fail him? Macbeth is sometimes cited as an example of "the villain as hero." Do you agree? Explain your answer.

5. Do the deaths of Macbeth and his wife arouse pity? Must a play elicit the sympathy of the audience in order to be tragic? Explain.

6. How has Shakespeare structured this act to show the outer and inner forces of destruction working simultaneously to defeat Macbeth? What is the effect of this structure on the pace of the action?

THE PLAY AS A WHOLE

1. Although Macbeth and Lady Macbeth possess a number of the same character traits, they also reveal many dissimilarities of character. Referring to specific lines or incidents throughout the play, compare and contrast the characters of Macbeth and his wife.

2. Analyze the character of one of the leading figures in *Macbeth* and show, by reference to specific lines in the play, the means whereby this person's character is revealed: through the reactions of others, through the person's own actions or conversations, or through soliloquies.

3. While the speeches of both Macbeth and Lady Macbeth are written in blank verse (see page 876) and are identical in rhythm and meter, the poetic language in which they express their throughts and feelings is quite different. Quoting passages from the play, analyze and compare the language used by Macbeth and his wife. Why do you think Shakespeare had these characters express themselves in these particular ways?

4. In *Macbeth,* the aura of darkness, deception, and horror that envelops the entire play is created mainly by the sense of violence and foreboding that is evoked by the imagery. Citing examples from the play, show how the dominant images of darkness, blood, nature, and the supernatural contribute to the atmosphere of this tragedy.

5. A frequent subject of debate is the question of just how much control the witches had over Macbeth's free will and his destiny. Present your own opinions on this argument, supporting your viewpoint with references to the play.

FOR COMPOSITION

1. In the final speech of the play, Malcolm refers to Macbeth and Lady Macbeth as "this dead butcher and his fiendlike queen." Are these phrases adequate descriptions of Macbeth and his wife as you have come to know them in the five acts of this play? Defend your answer, citing the most telling evidence from the play.

2. The characters of the first Thane of Cawdor, King Duncan, Banquo, Lady Macbeth, and Macbeth all contained flaws which, to a greater or lesser degree, were the cause of their downfall. Referring to specific passages in the play, describe the flaws of each of these characters and explain if you think the characters deserved their fate.

Reading *Macbeth*

In reading *Macbeth,* or any other play, five factors demand special attention: theme, plot, characterization, diction, atmosphere.

The theme of *Macbeth* can be summed up in Macbeth's own words: "Blood will have blood."

This theme is worked out in the plot. *Macbeth* opens with a meeting of the three witches, a scene which creates an atmosphere of foreboding and introduces the evil powers which are about to tempt Macbeth to his ruin. After a scene showing King Duncan and his nobles receiving the report of Macbeth's victory in battle, the witches reappear, as they said they would, to meet Macbeth. When Macbeth enters with Banquo, the witches accost them and make their prophecies, to which Macbeth reacts strongly. Thereafter each scene arises out of what has gone before, and we, the spectators, become more and more involved in the story, until the inevitable downfall of Macbeth.

But plot depends on character: in life, events happen because people act according to their different natures. Unless a writer convinces us that people are "real," we have little interest in them. In *Macbeth,* Shakespeare has concentrated all his skill in characterization in the two leading figures: Macbeth and Lady Macbeth. Before Macbeth appears, we hear of his great bravery in battle. In the next scene, when we first see him, we sense that he is vastly ambitious and so given to brooding that he becomes unconscious of what is happening around him. Two scenes later Lady Macbeth, commenting on his letter, gives us her view of her husband's nature—"too full o' the milk of human kindness." With that remark she convinces us that she herself is *not*. Macbeth is ambitious but somewhat scrupulous; he has evil desires but is too timid to play false—unless his wife forces him to it. Lady Macbeth, it seems obvious, is the stronger nature. In Scene vii we see her work on her husband. Macbeth's soliloquy (lines 1–28) shows that he shrinks from the murder of Duncan; his wife, however, forces him into action with her taunt that he is a coward. Many other examples of skillful characterization abound in this play.

Diction, the language used by the characters, is a most important aspect of any play. *Macbeth* is full of the highest dramatic verse, especially in Macbeth's important speeches and soliloquies. A great dramatic speech combines a perfect union of sound, rhythm, and meaning to the individual speaker and the situation, thus enabling the audience to experience vicariously the characters' feelings. A good example of a great dramatic speech is Macbeth's soliloquy (Act III, Scene i) as he awaits the murderers whom he has hired to kill Banquo. The speech begins on a level of calm, objective thought: Banquo is dangerous, dauntless, and wise; he overshadows Macbeth; he even dared rebuke the weird sisters until they promised that he would be the father of a line of kings. With this prospect Macbeth's objectivity is overcome by passion; rational statement is replaced by the repetitions of emotional rhetoric: "for *Banquo*'s issue . . . for *them* . . . only for *them* . . . to make *them* kings"—until it rises into a final note, almost a cry, of desperation that he will dare fate to a fight to the finish.

A fifth factor demanding our attention is atmosphere, the way a dramatist persuades us to respond to and feel the mood of a scene. In *Macbeth* examples vary from the mood of a fine summer evening, with birds feeding their young in nests under the eaves as Duncan comes to Macbeth's castle, to the tense quiet of the scene where Lady Macbeth listens as Macbeth murders the King and then comes down the stairs, his hands sticky with blood. Stark monosyllables build up the atmosphere: "Did you not speak?" "When?" "Now." "As I descended?" "Ay." "Hark!" The world breaks in on this scene of horror when a sudden loud knocking interrupts the whisperings. The audience is now so tense that relief must be given. To this end, Shakespeare shifts suddenly to the drunken porter, who grumblingly pretends that he is the keeper of the gate of Hell and does not realize that he is so indeed.

Atmosphere is also created through the use of imagery, in some striking simile or metaphor. Three images are most significant in *Macbeth:* blood, water, and darkness. In listening to the play, we are seldom conscious of the use of these or any other images. Like the soft drumbeats in a symphony, however, the imagery affects our total response to the significance of the tragedy—but we hardly notice unless we are concentrating on the drummer.

Macbeth: An Afterword

Macbeth can be regarded in several ways. The story, which comes from Scottish history, is a sordid record of treachery, murder, insurrection, and retribution, but Shakespeare elevated it into great tragedy. The word *tragedy* has so often been misused that now it often means little more than violent or even sudden death. A tragic drama is much more; it reveals the universal forces that control human life. All Shakespeare's tragedies illustrate the idea that "there's a divinity that shapes our ends," and in most tragedies there is a moment when the tragic victim commits an action which tumbles him or her into destruction. Sometimes the action is deliberate but mistaken; sometimes it seems that the victim is quite powerless, and that destruction is inevitable whatever is done.

Some critics regard *Macbeth* as a tragedy of fate, as if Macbeth were the plaything of an evil power against which he could offer no resistance. The idea of a malignant fate is common in Greek tragedy. In the most moving of all Greek tragedies, *Oedipus the King*, Oedipus errs and suffers; but he is a man who is held responsible for awful errors which he committed through sheer well-meaning ignorance. On every occasion he acts deliberately as he thinks for the best. Oedipus, like most of the other heroes of Greek tragedy, is basically a "good" man.

In *Macbeth* there is at first sight the same kind of irresistible destiny. The witches hail Macbeth as thane of Glamis, thane of Cawdor, and king hereafter. Macbeth is already thane of Glamis. He immediately receives word that King Duncan has granted him the title of Cawdor. This prophecy so quickly fulfilled, doubtless he will also become king. If so, Macbeth can hardly be held responsible for what follows. Those taking this view also consider Macbeth essentially a "good" man whom we should pity rather than condemn.

Nevertheless, in spite of the prophecies of the witches, Macbeth is not quite like Oedipus. He has free will to reject what is offered; never for a moment is he deceived into thinking it is a good deed to murder Duncan. He chooses evil deliberately and, having chosen, finds himself overwhelmed with the results of his sin. The witches and all they represent are thus not so much embodiments of inevitable fate as they are voices of temptation.

Macbeth knows well enough that chance will never make him king and that only through murder can he achieve the crown. He toys with the idea of murder, and he immediately strives to stifle his conscience with the notion that he is being supernaturally *solicited* to commit the deed.

Macbeth's letter tells Lady Macbeth of his meeting with the witches. When she learns of the prophecy that her husband shall become king, Lady Macbeth begins at once to plot Duncan's murder. Lady Macbeth is both contrast and complement to her husband. While Macbeth has an uneasy conscience, Lady Macbeth appears to have none at all. She is hard, efficient, and ruthlessly ambitious—her ambition expressing itself through her husband, whom she drives relentlessly. It does not occur to her to speculate upon what may happen after the murder.

Macbeth murders the sleeping king and immediately is overcome by horror as he realizes the significance of what he has done. He asks, "Will all great Neptune's ocean wash this blood/ Clean from my hand?" Rashly confident, Lady Macbeth replies, "A little water clears us of this deed."

So the prophecy is fulfilled. Macbeth becomes king, but he never enjoys a moment's satisfaction. When the witches promised that he should be king, they made other promises to Banquo. Because Banquo knows too much, Macbeth is afraid of him. By slaying Duncan, Macbeth feels, he has put himself in Banquo's power. Although to kill Banquo and his son is to defy the fate which promised that Banquo would be father of kings, Macbeth—knowing he has already lost his soul—will defy fate. Thus Macbeth further degenerates before our eyes.

Banquo and his son Fleance must, then, be the next victims. But the murderers bungle in the dark and Fleance escapes. In the banquet scene which follows, husband and wife are again contrasted. When, in his terrified imagination, Macbeth sees Banquo sitting in his place, he forgets the real world and by his wild mutterings nearly reveals all. His wife, however, keeps her head and hustles the guests away.

At this point in the play, there is a sharp change in the character of Macbeth; hereafter his degeneration is swift and terrible. He becomes utterly desperate. So deeply immersed in blood is he that it is easier to continue than to stop. No more remorse for him! As he grows more reckless, he ceases either to conceal his actions or to care what others think. The tide has turned; and the devil, having given Macbeth what he desired, is now preparing to destroy him. Like others who sell their souls, Macbeth learns that the devil drives a hard bargain.

The fourth act shows how Macbeth is again cheated by the evil fate which urges him on to his ruin. Since it was the witches who first encouraged him, he goes again to demand their help. And again Macbeth is given three prophecies. For the moment he is satisfied that his life is charmed.

The final act of the play begins with Lady Macbeth. Macbeth no longer needs her. As he has become more desperate and ruthless, she has begun to wither. She is alone now, with only her ghosts to haunt her. In the broken mutterings of her sleepwalking scene, she reveals the punishment which has been meted out to her. She is utterly bewildered that her competent management should have broken down so utterly: "who would have thought the old man to have had so much blood in him?"

As for Macbeth, he is desperately alone. He has even begun to pity himself because his old age will lack love, honor, obedience, troops of friends; what else did he—could he—expect? When the news of his wife's death is brought to him, he sinks to his final disillusionment:

". . . Out, out, brief candle!
Life's but a walking shadow, a poor player
That struts and frets his hour upon the
 stage
And then is heard no more. It is a tale
Told by an idiot, full of sound and fury,
Signifying nothing."

All the blood and fury and horror have proven quite futile, for life itself no longer has meaning. Nothing is left for Macbeth except the exact fulfillment of the prophecies and his ultimate death at the hands of Macduff.

So the infernal power has the last word with Macbeth. Shakespeare calls it "fate," but it is not the cold, irresistible, unemotional fate of Greek drama (which the Greeks called "necessity"), a power which exceeded even that of the gods. Macbeth's fate is cunning, malevolent, and personal, concerned not with the pattern of the universe but with the destruction of an individual through a choice made by himself alone. The fate which destroys Macbeth can, in its method and malignancy, hardly be distinguished from the work of the devil.

BEN JONSON

(1572–1637)

Ben Jonson began life as a bricklayer. From this humble beginning, he became a dramatist who rivaled Shakespeare—one whom John Dryden claimed to be "the most learned and judicious writer which any theater ever had."

Bored by bricklaying, Jonson in his early youth ran away to join the army and fight the Spaniards on the battlefields of Flanders. Not yet twenty, he returned to England and in time joined a company of provincial actors as both playwright and player. His career as a dramatist began in earnest when he became a member of the Lord Chamberlain's company, to which Shakespeare also belonged. Like Shakespeare, Jonson was a keen observer of human nature, but he was satirical rather than sympathetic. He ridiculed social abuses, human eccentricities, affectations, and vices. *Volpone* ("The Fox"), his best-known play, in telling the story of an old miser, satirizes human greed and is a good example of Jonson's technique of making his point by exaggerating characters and situations. Jonson's aim as a dramatist was to bring back into fashion what he considered to be the virtues of classical comedy as exemplified by Roman dramatists such as Terence and Plautus. He was a distinguished scholar and, as against what he considered the unrestrained and untheoretical genius of Shakespeare, he strove to refine the art of playwriting according to the classical Roman pattern. Jonson also, though less successfully, wrote tragedies, and on James I's accession he turned to the writing of masques, elaborately staged entertainments which were presented at court.

Quickly acknowledged as a leading dramatist, Jonson was also recognized as unofficial poet laureate and an intellectual leader. At the Mermaid Tavern he presided over immortal evenings of talk with the chief writers of the day. Shakespeare, Marlowe, Raleigh, Bacon, and John Donne were among his friends, although, as one of his contemporaries observed, he was "a great lover and praiser of himself, a contemner and scorner of others." His contemning and scorning involved him in a number of quarrels, literary and otherwise. For killing a fellow actor in a duel, he was imprisoned and barely escaped hanging. On another occasion he nearly lost his nose and ears as punishment for contributing to a play which offended the king. His conceit was shown by his publishing his collected works in 1616, thereby setting a precedent since, until then, it had been customary to treat play scripts as working copies for actors rather than as literature.

But despite his quick temper and obvious self-esteem, Jonson won the love of his friends and especially of younger poets such as Robert Herrick, John Suckling, and

Richard Lovelace. Calling themselves "Sons of Ben," they tried to emulate Jonson's lyrics, which in their polish and simplicity reflected his adherence to the classical tradition of the ancient Greeks and Romans. When he died, Jonson was secure in his reputation as foremost writer of comedies and foremost satirist of his day, as well as a gifted lyric poet and an accomplished critic. No one quarreled with the simple epitaph in Westminster Abbey: "O Rare Ben Jonson."

The Noble Nature

It is not growing like a tree
In bulk, doth make man better be;
Or standing long an oak, three hundred year,
To fall a log at last, dry, bald, and sere:
A lily of a day   5
Is fairer far in May;
Although it fall and die that night,
It was the plant and flower of light.
In small proportions we just beauties see,
And in short measures life may perfect be.   10

On My First Son

Farewell, thou child of my right hand,° and joy;
My sin was too much hope of thee, loved boy,
Seven years thou wert lent to me, and I thee pay,
Exacted by thy fate, on the just day.°
O, could I lost all father° now! For why   5
Will man lament the state he should envy?
To have so soon 'scaped world's and flesh's rage,
And, if no other misery, yet age!
Rest in soft peace, and, asked, say here doth lie
Ben Jonson his best piece of poetry;   10
For whose sake, henceforth, all his vows be such
As what he loves may never like too much.

1. **child of my right hand:** The Hebrew name, Benjamin, means literally "son of my right hand." Jonson's son died of the plague in 1603.   4. **on . . . day:** exactly on the day.   5. **lost . . . father:** lose the feeling of being a father.

To the Memory of My Beloved Master, William Shakespeare

To draw no envy, Shakespeare, on thy name,
Am I thus ample to thy book and fame;
While I confess thy writings to be such
As neither man nor muse can praise too much.
'Tis true, and all men's suffrage.° But these ways   5
Were not the paths I meant unto thy praise:
For silliest° ignorance on these may light,
Which, when it sounds at best, but echoes right;
Or blind affection, which doth ne'er advance
The truth, but gropes, and urgeth all by chance;   10
Or crafty malice might pretend this praise,
And think to ruin, where it seemed to raise . . .
But thou art proof against them, and, indeed,
Above the ill fortune of them, or the need.
I therefore will begin. Soul of the age!   15
The applause, delight, the wonder of our stage!
My Shakespeare, rise! I will not lodge thee by
Chaucer, or Spenser, or bid Beaumont° lie
A little further, to make thee a room.
Thou art a monument without a tomb,   20
And art alive still while thy book doth live
And we have wits to read and praise to give.
That I not mix thee so, my brain excuses,
I mean with great, but disproportioned Muses;
For if I thought my judgment were of years,   25
I should commit thee surely with thy peers,
And tell how far thou didst our Lyly outshine,
Or sporting Kyd, or Marlowe's° mighty line.
And though thou hadst small Latin and less Greek,
From thence to honor thee, I would not seek   30
For names; but call forth thundering Aeschylus,
Euripides, and Sophocles to us;
Pacuvius, Accius,° him of Cordova dead,°
To life again, to hear thy buskin° tread,

---

5. **suffrage:** vote; decision.   7. **silliest:** simplest, most innocent.   18. **Beaumont:** Francis Beaumont, a dramatist and contemporary of Jonson and Shakespeare.   27–28. **Lyly, Kyd, Marlowe:** sixteenth-century English dramatists who influenced Shakespeare.   31–33. **Aeschylus . . . Accius:** classical Greek and Roman writers of tragedy.   33. **him . . . dead:** refers to Seneca.   34. **buskin:** a thick-soled shoe, worn by tragic actors.

And shake a stage; or, when thy socks° were on,   35
Leave thee alone for the comparison
Of all that insolent Greece or haughty Rome
Sent forth, or since did from their ashes come.
Triumph, my Britain, thou hast one to show
To whom all scenes of Europe homage owe.   40
He was not of an age, but for all time!
And all the Muses still were in their prime,
When, like Apollo, he came forth to warm
Our ears, or like a Mercury to charm.
Nature herself was proud of his designs   45
And joyed to wear the dressing of his lines,
Which were so richly spun, and woven so fit,
As, since, she will vouchsafe no other wit.
The merry Greek, tart Aristophanes,
Neat Terence, witty Plautus,° now not please,   50
But antiquated and deserted lie,
As they were not of Nature's family.
Yet must I not give Nature all; thy art,
My gentle Shakespeare, must enjoy a part.
For though the poet's matter nature be,   55
His art doth give the fashion; and, that he
Who casts to write a living line, must sweat
(Such as thine are) and strike the second heat
Upon the Muses' anvil, turn the same
(And himself with it) that he thinks to frame,   60
Or, for the laurel, he may gain a scorn;
For a good poet's made, as well as born.
And such wert thou! Look how the father's face
Lives in his issue; even so the race
Of Shakespeare's mind and manners brightly shines   65
In his well turnèd and true filèd° lines;
In each of which he seems to shake a lance,°
As brandished at the eyes of ignorance.
Sweet swan of Avon! what a sight it were
To see thee in our waters yet appear,   70
And make those flights upon the banks of Thames
That so did take Eliza and our James!°
But stay, I see thee in the hemisphere
Advanced, and made a constellation there!
Shine forth, thou Star of Poets, and with rage   75
Or influence, chide or cheer the drooping stage,
Which, since thy flight from hence, hath mourned like night,
And despairs day, but for thy volume's light.

---

35. **socks:** thin-soled shoes, worn by comic actors.   49–50. **Aristophanes . . . Plautus:** classical Greek and Roman writers of comedy admired by Jonson.   66. **filèd:** polished.   67. **shake a lance:** probably a pun on Shakespeare's name.   72. **Eliza . . . James:** Queen Elizabeth I and King James I. (Shakespeare's plays were performed for both.)

FROM *Timber:*
De Shakespeare Nostrati *

I remember the players have often mentioned it as an honor to Shakespeare that in his writing (whatsoever he penned) he never blotted out a line. My answer hath been, "Would he had blotted a thousand!" which they thought a malevolent speech. I had not told posterity this but for their ignorance who chose that circumstance to commend their friend by wherein he most faulted; and to justify mine own candor, for I loved the man, and do honor his memory on this side idolatry as much as any. He was, indeed, honest, and of an open and free nature; had an excellent phantasy,[1] brave[2] notions, and gentle expressions, wherein he flowed with that facility that sometimes it was necessary he should be stopped. *"Sufflaminandus erat,"* [3] as Augustus said of Haterius. His wit was in his own power; would the rule of it had been so, too! Many times he fell into those things could not escape laughter, as when he said in the person of Caesar, one speaking to him, "Caesar, thou dost me wrong." He replied, "Caesar never did wrong but with just cause"; and such like, which were ridiculous. But he redeemed his vices with his virtues. There was ever more in him to be praised than to be pardoned.

* *De Shakespeare Nostrati:* on Shakespeare, our fellow countryman.

[1] **phantasy:** fantasy, unrestrained imagination.

[2] **brave:** fine.

[3] *Sufflaminandus erat:* He ought to have been stopped.

William Shakespeare (right) with Ben Jonson seated next to him at the table.

FOR STUDY AND DISCUSSION

1. In "The Noble Nature," is Jonson arguing that the lily is superior to the oak tree? Explain your answer. Without reference to trees and lilies, state Jonson's theme.

2. What is the tone of "On My First Son"? How is this tone established? Why does Jonson call his son his "best piece of poetry"? Jonson implies that man should envy the dead. Why? What advantages does death bring, according to the poet?

3. In what specific ways is Shakespeare's greatness as a poet and dramatist described in "To the Memory of My Beloved Master, William Shakespeare"? Is the evaluation of Shakespeare's merits objective? What do we learn of Jonson from this poem?

4. In the excerpt from *Timber,* Jonson explains a remark he made as an *epigram*—a brief, pointed, clever observation. Show that the reply he quotes from Shakespeare's *Julius Caesar* is also an epigram. Explain in a sentence the irony in the fact that Jonson had to write a sort of apology to explain his criticism of Shakespeare.

FOR COMPOSITION

Ben Jonson's tombstone in Westminster Abbey bears the legend "O Rare Ben Jonson." The five selections you have read make up only a tiny sampling of his work, but they do suggest the variety in which his genius expressed itself. Using direct quotations as illustrations, write a short essay showing why Jonson deserved to be called "rare."

FRANCIS BACON
(1561–1626)

Francis Bacon was a key figure in the transition from the intellectual world of the late Middle Ages to that of modern Europe. Though designated an Elizabethan, Bacon was, more precisely, the prophet of a new century, one characterized by its growing scientific spirit. He recognized his unique position, calling himself "the trumpeter of a new age." His career and character reveal him to be a man of various qualities. His critics agree: Pope called him "the wisest, brightest, and the meanest of mankind," while Ben Jonson declared him to be "one of the greatest men, and most worthy of admiration that had been in many ages."

Bacon's misfortune was to make a great name for himself by a rare combination of intellectual energy and worldly acumen, to be counted among the wise men of his time, and then, by a paradoxical twist, to find himself publicly disgraced. Born into an aristocratic family, he entered diplomatic service after two years at Cambridge University. He studied law and became a member of Parliament in 1584. During his service as a royal counsel under Queen Elizabeth, he incurred much ill feeling by helping to secure a conviction for treason against the Earl of Essex, whose patronage he had previously enjoyed. It was not until the reign of James I that he was able to achieve the status that he so eagerly sought. In a period of eleven years he advanced to the influential position of Lord Chancellor. In 1618, the same year, he was also raised to a barony. But his political success was short-lived. Three years later, he was brought before the House of Lords on charges of bribery. While he pleaded guilty, he denied that he had allowed "gifts" to influence his judicial decisions. In any case, he was thrown out of office, fined, and imprisoned. After two days in the Tower of London, Bacon was released and, retiring from public life, he thereafter gave himself over to literature and scientific experiment.

Lytton Strachey remarked that "Bacon's mind was universal in its comprehensiveness; there was nothing in the world of which he could not write." This was not an overstatement. Neither was the claim made by Bacon himself as a typical Renaissance scholar, "I have taken all knowledge to be my province." During the course of his lifetime he distinguished himself as a scholar in several fields and as a scientist, writer, and philosopher. His practical experience of the world also made him a great lawyer and a considerable statesman. As a philosopher he was greatly concerned with people's understanding of themselves and of their world. *The Advancement of Learning,* in which Bacon analyzed the various divisions of knowledge and considered the possible means of advancing them, epitomizes this concern as does his later great work *Novum Organum (The New Instrument),* in which he described the method by which knowledge could be universalized. Bacon's major contribution to modern science was his promotion of the inductive method of reasoning, which, exactly contrary to the deductive method used by medieval scholars, formulated generalizations only after close observation of facts.

But it was not only in science that Bacon broke new ground. When he published his first *Essays* in 1597, he became England's first essayist. Like Montaigne, whose *Essais* appeared almost twenty years before his own, Bacon wrote in the idiom of the classical scholar, undertaking in a more formal style than Montaigne's discussions of topics such as "Of Studies," "Of Travel," "Of Followers and Friends," and "Of Marriage and Single Life." The *Essays,* written in a powerful, direct, and compact style, are laden with quotations, metaphors, witticisms, and allusions which clearly mark them as the work of Francis Bacon. As a Renaissance scholar, Bacon wrote more often in Latin than he did in English, which perhaps accounts for the fact that his English style sometimes seems difficult or obscure to modern readers. But his commentaries are shrewd and often brilliant, and as apt today as when first written.

Of Wisdom for a Man's Self

An ANT is a wise creature for itself, but it is a shrewd[1] thing in an orchard or garden; and certainly men that are great lovers of themselves waste the public. Divide with reason between self-love and society; and be so true to thyself as[2] thou be not false to others, specially to thy king and country. It is a poor center of a man's actions, himself. It is right earth; for that only stands fast upon his own center;[3] whereas all things that have affinity with the heavens move upon the center of another, which they benefit. The referring of all to a man's self is more tolerable in a sovereign prince, because

themselves are not only themselves, but their good and evil is at the peril of the public fortune; but it is a desperate evil in a servant to a prince or a citizen in a republic. For whatsoever affairs pass such a man's hands, he crooketh them to his own ends, which must needs be often eccentric to the ends of his master or state. Therefore let princes or states choose such servants as have not this mark, except they mean their service should be made but the accessory. That which maketh the effect more pernicious is that all proportion is lost. It were disproportion enough for the servant's good to be preferred before the master's; but yet it is a greater extreme when a little good of the servant shall carry things against a great good of the master's. And yet that is the case of bad officers, treasurers, ambassadors, generals, and other false and corrupt servants; which set a bias upon their bowl[4] of their own petty ends and envies, to the overthrow of their master's great and important affairs. And

---

[1] **shrewd:** vexatious, destructive.

[2] **as:** that.

[3] **own center:** The old astronomical system of Ptolemy, to which Bacon adhered, assumed that the sun, planets, and stars revolve around the earth.

[4] **bias . . . bowl:** The weight of the bowling ball is not centered, and thus will not roll in a straight path.

Effayes.

Religious Meditations.

Places of perfwafion and diffwafion.

Scene and allowed.

At London,
Printed for Humfrey Hooper, and are
to be fold at the blacke Beare
in Chauncery Lane.
1597.

Title page of Bacon's *Essays*, First Edition.

for the most part, the good such servants receive is after the model of their own fortune; but the hurt they sell for that good is after the model of their master's fortune. And certainly it is the nature of extreme self-lovers, as they will set a house on fire and it were but to roast their eggs; and yet these men many times hold credit with their masters because their study is but to please them and profit themselves, and for either respect they will abandon the good of their affairs.

Wisdom for a man's self is, in many branches thereof, a depraved thing: it is the wisdom of rats, that will be sure to leave a house somewhat before it fall; it is the wisdom of the fox, that thrusts out the badger who digged and made room for him; it is the wisdom of crocodiles, that shed tears when they would devour. But that which is specially to be noted is that those which (as Cicero says of Pompey) are *sui amantes sine rivali* [1] are many

---

[1] *sui . . . rivali:* lovers of themselves, without rival (Cicero, *Letters*, III, 8).

times unfortunate; and whereas they have all their time sacrificed to themselves, they become in the end themselves sacrifices to the inconstancy of fortune, whose wings they thought by their self-wisdom to have pinioned.

FOR STUDY AND DISCUSSION

In a famous treason trial Bacon testified against his friend the Earl of Essex. Essex was convicted and beheaded. Even though Bacon's testimony was minor, his part in the trial has been condemned by some as an example of bad faith. Show, by using quotations from "Of Wisdom for a Man's Self," that Bacon was simply practicing what he preached in carrying out a loyalty larger than friendship. The other charge against Bacon is that as a high public official he accepted bribes. Show by quotations that in this instance Bacon was *not* practicing what he preached in "Of Wisdom for a Man's Self."

BACON'S STYLE

One of the characteristics of Bacon's style is his use of the balanced sentence. A sentence is balanced when identical or similar grammatical structure is used to express contrasting ideas. Here is an example of a balanced sentence from Bacon's essay "Of Studies": "Reading maketh a full man, conference a ready man, and writing an exact man." Look too at the sentence on page 189 beginning "It were disproportion enough . . ." Another example of the balanced sentence is the famous line by Alexander Pope, the eighteenth-century poet (page 296): "To err is human, to forgive divine."

The balanced sentence, an effective device for achieving clarity and emphasis, came into the English language from classical Roman prose, which was much admired by English writers from the sixteenth century on.

FOR COMPOSITION

Although Bacon is the father of the English essay, his writing style is not the easy, personal one usually associated with later examples of that literary form. Select from "Of Wisdom for a Man's Self" two passages which are especially heavy or formal. Rephrase these passages in light, modern English.

The King James Bible

In 1604, only a year after he had ascended the throne, King James I appointed fifty-four of England's most eminent scholars and churchmen to begin work on a new translation of the Bible. This entailed comparing the various English translations then in existence with the Latin Bibles of the Middle Ages as well as with the original Greek and Hebrew texts. Seven years later, in 1611, the Authorized, or King James, Version of the Holy Bible was completed. Often referred to as "the only classic ever created by a committee," its uniform excellence and beauty caused it from the start to be acknowledged as a masterpiece, an outstanding literary work whose great popularity persists to the present day.

The significance of the King James Bible lies not only in its own intrinsic merits but in the fact that it represents the culmination of many efforts throughout several centuries to provide English-speaking peoples with a Bible written in their own tongue. Throughout most of the Middle Ages, the Bible was written in Latin and was therefore inaccessible to the average person. Though there were several early attempts to render portions of the Scriptures into English, little of importance was achieved until late in the fourteenth century, when John Wycliffe and his followers produced the first complete transcription into English. This translation of 1382 succeeded in reaching a fair number of people, although the manuscripts were costly, representing as they did enormous amounts of meticulous handiwork.

With the advent of the Reformation, which spread throughout Europe early in the sixteenth century, came a new emphasis on the Bible as the ultimate authority on religious doctrine. Simultaneously, therefore, a need arose for English translations which would make the Bible available to a still larger number of people. It was William Tyndale, a leader of the English Reformation, who produced the first printed version of the New Testament in English. Determined to bring the Bible to everyone, even "the boy that driveth the plow," Tyndale sacrificed his life to his mission. He printed his masterful translation of the New Testament in 1525 and then, despite the violent religious conflicts of his time, proceeded to translate the Old Testament. He never finished. Imprisoned for heresy in 1535, Tyndale was executed eighteen months later.

Various other English Bibles followed, among them Miles Coverdale's version (1535), based partly on Tyndale's translation, and the so-called Great Bible, which was prepared with Coverdale's supervision. Under the auspices of Henry VIII, the Great Bible in 1540 was finally established for use in the churches. It was not until the appearance of the King James Version in 1611, however, that there existed a simple, well-translated English Bible that was both authorized by the church and generally accepted by the people.

The King James Bible was indisputably such a book. Produced with exacting care by the most distinguished scholars, written at a time when the English language was at its height, it has communicated eloquently with every age. Its simplicity, beauty, and vigor of language, its sheer poetry, has influenced both English and American literature immeasurably. As generations of readers have memorized it, quoted it, and woven its phrases into their speech, the King James Version has continued, after more than three centuries, to have a tremendous effect upon our language. Writers of both prose and poetry have consciously or unconsciously drawn upon it for vocabulary and imagery, the rhythm of a passage, or the shaping of a phrase.

Analyzing a sample from the King James Version will perhaps reveal something of its brilliant use of language. Here is an illustration from the Book of Psalms. In its Greek derivation *psalm* means "song"; the original Hebrew title means "praise." Such is the purpose of these poems.

Psalm 8

O Lord our Lord,
How excellent is thy name in all the earth!
Who hast set thy glory above the heavens.
Out of the mouths of babes and sucklings hast thou ordained strength
    because of thine enemies,
That thou mightest still the enemy and the avenger.   5
When I consider thy heavens, the work of thy fingers,
The moon and the stars, which thou hast ordained;
What is man, that thou art mindful of him?
And the son of man, that thou visitest him?
For thou hast made him a little lower than the angels,   10
And hast crowned him with glory and honor.
Thou madest him to have dominion over the works of thy hands;
Thou hast put all things under his feet:
All sheep and oxen,
Yea, and the beasts of the field;   15
The fowl of the air, and the fish of the sea,
And whatsoever passeth through the paths of the seas.
O Lord our Lord,
How excellent is thy name in all the earth!   20

Note first that the two opening lines are also used to conclude the poem. *Repetition* is one device that was frequently employed by King James's translators. *Parallelism,* another form of repetition, is found in phrases such as "the work of thy fingers" and "the works of thy hands"; "the fowl of the air, and the fish of the sea"; and in the psalmist's two questions. *Imagery* abounds in the awesome description of God, whose hands molded heaven and earth. *Comparison* is used to describe the relationship between God and humans: God, whose glory is "above the heavens," and humans who are "a little lower than the angels." Throughout there is a perfect blend of language and content.

Psalm 8 is one of many examples of the rich and varied use of language in the King James Version of the Bible. That this superb seventeenth-century translation has had so great an influence on subsequent English prose and poetry is easily appreciated.

THE GROWTH OF THE ENGLISH LANGUAGE

The Elizabethan Age

It may come as a surprise to learn that Shakespeare wrote in Modern English, since the language of the Elizabethan Age often seems antiquated and quite "unmodern" to twentieth-century readers. Nevertheless, Shakespeare's speech and our own have enough in common so that language historians consider that they both belong to the same stage in the history of English. If twentieth-century Americans could be transported through time to the London of Shakespeare's day, they would find that they could communicate fairly easily with the people they met. They would feel that people were speaking English with an unfamiliar accent, it is true, but the accent would not be much harder to understand than some of the present-day accents of the British Isles.

However, if the same Americans were transported to the London of Chaucer's day, only two centuries earlier, they would find it almost impossible either to make themselves understood or to understand what was said to them. The reason for this is that English pronunciation changed greatly between Chaucer's time and Shakespeare's. The changes were so extensive that Middle English and Modern English sound like two different languages.

The most important changes involved the pronunciation of vowel sounds. In Middle English—as in Latin and in most modern foreign languages that are written in the Latin alphabet—the letter *a* represented the sound *ah,* while a long *e* sounded like our long *a,* and long *i* and *y* like our long *e.* A long *o* was always pronounced *oh,* and a long *u* (often spelled *ou*) was $\overline{oo}.$ Thus the Middle English pronunciation of *care* might sound to us like *car; sheep* would sound to us like *shape; my* would sound like *me; to* would sound like *toe;* and *south* would sound like *sooth.* During the fifteenth and sixteenth centuries, however, the pronunciation of all the long vowel sounds gradually shifted. By Shakespeare's time most of the long vowels had acquired the values that they still have today.

Another striking change was the disappearance of the final *e* sound at the ends of words. In Chaucer's verse the final *e* was often pronounced in words like *space, straunge* ("strange"), and *ende* ("end"). The tendency in spoken English to slur over unaccented syllables, a tendency which seems always to have been present in the language, probably accounted for the dropping of these final *e*'s in pronunciation. The same tendency probably also accounted for the fact that many other unaccented vowel sounds came to be reduced to the indistinct *uh* sound represented in dictionaries by the symbol "ə."

English spelling, oddly enough, was not much affected by these great changes in pronunciation. As we discovered in studying the language of the Middle English period (pages 75–76), a standard written form of English came into use during the fifteenth century. Before that time, spelling had represented a writer's own pronunciation, and spellings therefore had varied widely not only from one historical period to the next but also from one local dialect to the next. Once fairly standardized forms had come into use, though, scribes and clerks—who did most of the actual writing of Middle English documents—tended to adhere to the familiar spellings instead of respelling words according to their own pronunciation. The introduction of the printing press into England reinforced this tendency. The early printers often relied for their material on manuscripts that had been written by Middle English scribes, and a printer would simply set words into type the way he found them written in the manuscript. It thus happened that a great many Middle English spellings became permanently fixed in our language, despite the later changes in the pronunciation of the words.

This is why long *a, e, i, o,* and *u* usually stand for different sounds in Modern English than they do in all other languages that use the Latin alphabet. English spelling was already largely fixed before the shift in English vowel sounds took place. The same reason accounts for the presence of so many "silent letters" in English words. The *gh* in words like *night, slaughter,* and *freight* had been pronounced in Middle English; as had the final *e* that ends so many words, and the initial *g* and *k* in words like *gnat* and *knob.*

Englishmen of the Elizabethan period continued to borrow words from other languages. Throughout the Middle Ages, the educated had usually preferred to use Latin for their serious writing. But now the English began to take a new pride in their native tongue, and they deliberately set out to use English in writing about all matters. To do this, they found they frequently had to borrow terms from Latin or Greek to express concepts for which there were no words in English. Many of our abstract terms entered the language this way—from Latin, words like *allusion, consolidate, education, esteem, exist, meditate;* from Greek, words like *synonymous, autocracy, catastrophe.* The languages of continental Europe also continued to supply new words. The English who traveled abroad brought back news of continental customs and fashions, introducing words like the French *vogue* and *mustache.* From Italy they brought back many words relating to architecture and music, like *piazza, sonata,* and *violin.* From Spaniards they acquired words relating to the exploration of the New World, such as *alligator, armadillo,* and *cocoa.* Spanish sailors and traders passed on some terms from American Indian languages, too, including *canoe, cannibal, hurricane,* and *tobacco.*

By about 1550, it had become so fashionable for writers to sprinkle their pages with foreign expressions that critics began to object strongly to "inkhorn terms" (Latin and Greek words) and "oversea language" (European words). Some of the words that the critics singled out for ridicule do sound strange to us today: *adminiculation* ("help"), *suppeditate* ("provide"), *splendidious.* But other terms that were attacked as being obscure and newfangled are now quite familiar to us: *celebrate, compatible, confidence, destitute, extol, inflate,* and *strenuous,* to name a few. Toward the end of the Elizabethan Age, writers grew more cautious about borrowing foreign words, but a great many of the new words that had already been introduced were on their way to becoming a permanent part of our language.

FOR STUDY AND DISCUSSION

1. Most Latin words that had entered English during the Anglo-Saxon period gradually changed in form and meaning as the centuries passed. Some of the same Latin words were "re-borrowed" early in the Modern English period, with their original Latin form and meaning. Look up the following two pairs of words in the dictionary, and find out which word in each pair was borrowed by Old English and which by Modern English. Which word is closer to the Latin word in form and meaning?

    clerk, cleric   script, shrift

2. The change in pronunciation of long vowel sounds in the transition from Middle English to Modern English is known to language historians as the "Great Vowel Shift." This shift affected all the long vowel sounds at the same time because there was a regular phonetic principle underlying the changes in sound. Look up the Great Vowel Shift in Albert C. Baugh's *A History of the English Language* or in another book on language history, and prepare a brief explanation of the phonetic process involved.

THE SEVENTEENTH CENTURY

(1625–1700)

THIS IS a very curious period, but many English historians and literary scholars prefer this age to any other. During most of it, England (and Scotland, which now shared the same monarchy) steered a rather eccentric course in both her political and her literary life. Until the final years of this period, for example, what was being written in England was quite unlike what was being written elsewhere in Western Europe, just as public events in England did not reflect any general European pattern. It was a time when the English were out on their own, just going their own way.

POLITICAL UPHEAVAL

The English nowadays are considered a quiet, easygoing people, not given to fanaticism and violence. But in this period they horrified the rest of Europe. In the middle of it, they not only rebelled against Charles I (1625–49), their rightful sovereign, but they then imprisoned and finally executed him. Charles had inherited from his father, James I, the medieval idea of the "divine right" of the kings, which assumed that a country was the personal possession of the monarch, who enjoyed a kind of direct lease from Heaven. But by the time Charles I came to the throne, religious, political, economic ideas and developments were rising in a strong tide against this ancient notion. Thus Parliament refused to regard itself as a mere fund-granting institution, to which the monarchy could apply when more money was needed and then ignore. The people in general might still be royalist in sentiment, but there were powerful factions, usually devoted to religious sects outside the established Church, which were strongly republican. This division, which split the country during the Civil War, was finally healed in a rather characteristic English fashion by retaining the monarchy, to please public sentiment, but at the same time considerably increasing the power of Parliament. The end result was the "constitutional monarchy," which on the whole has worked well. The first step toward it was taken in the bloodless "Glorious Revolution," when the people, disliking James II (1685–88), a militant Catholic in what was now a Protestant country, got rid of him and invited a Dutch prince, William of Orange (1689–1702), who had married James's daughter Mary, to take the crown. But William did not ascend the throne on the same terms as those under which James and other Stuarts had ruled, for now the monarchy was a constitutional one, as it has been ever since. This means, broadly speaking, that the monarch reigns but does not rule, that real political power belongs not to the Crown but to Parliament.

The Civil War, which began in 1642, was a war between Charles I and those who sided with him, mostly landowners and country folk, and the Parliament forces, drawn mostly from London and the larger towns. It was a war between Cavaliers, long-haired, gay, and reckless, and crop-headed, grimly determined Puritans, or Roundheads, as they were called. Victory went to Parliament in the end because it found in Oliver Cromwell a military leader of genius, whose New Model Army, known as "Ironsides," was probably the finest in Europe.

Calling himself the Protector, Cromwell (1653–58), ruling with the help of his major-generals, became in fact a dictator. He was extremely able and very soon raised the prestige of England abroad. But his Protectorate was unpopular with most of the English, who found Cromwell's rule harsher than the Stuarts' and whose idea of amusement was not psalm-singing and listening to very long sermons. The people were delighted when the monarchy was restored in 1660.

PURITANISM

Cromwell's triumph was really the triumph of Puritanism, the last it enjoyed on any great political scale in England. Serious and austere Christian believers, the Puritans, so called because of their desire to purify their religion of the formal ceremonies practiced in the Church of England, wanted the freedom to follow their own consciences in matters of religious observance and the conduct of life. (For this very reason, just prior to Cromwell's time, some Puritans left their homes in England and settled in New England.) Though Puritanism was never again as strong a political force as during Cromwell's rule, it is a mistake to imagine that it vanished from the English scene after the Restoration of 1660. In a less exaggerated and aggressive form, discovered at its best in *Areopagitica,* John Milton's noble plea for freedom of the press, Puritanism persisted throughout the next two and a half centuries, influencing not only social legislation but also the develop-

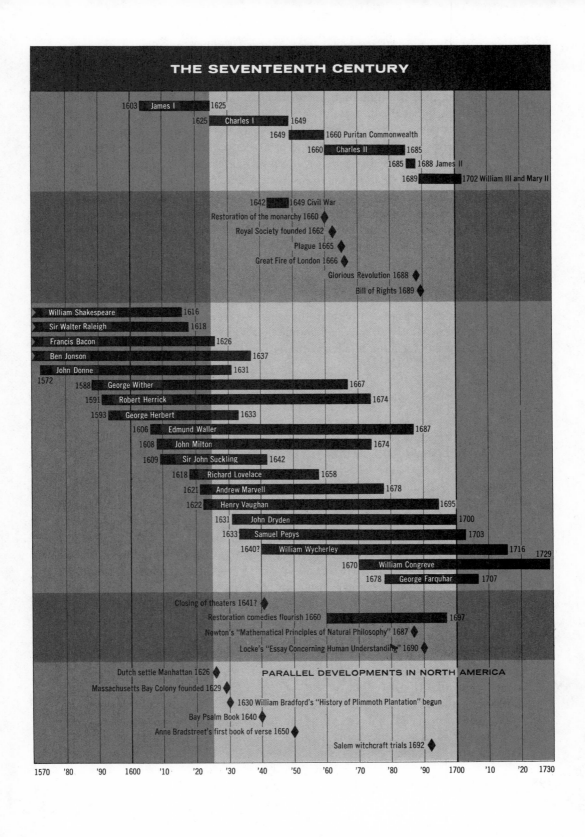

THE SEVENTEENTH CENTURY

1603 James I 1625
1625 Charles I 1649
1649 1660 Puritan Commonwealth
1660 Charles II 1685
1685 1688 James II
1689 1702 William III and Mary II

1642 1649 Civil War
Restoration of the monarchy 1660
Royal Society founded 1662
Plague 1665
Great Fire of London 1666
Glorious Revolution 1688
Bill of Rights 1689

William Shakespeare 1616
Sir Walter Raleigh 1618
Francis Bacon 1626
Ben Jonson 1637
John Donne 1631
1572
1588 George Wither 1667
1591 Robert Herrick 1674
1593 George Herbert 1633
1606 Edmund Waller 1687
1608 John Milton 1674
1609 Sir John Suckling 1642
1618 Richard Lovelace 1658
1621 Andrew Marvell 1678
1622 Henry Vaughan 1695
1631 John Dryden 1700
1633 Samuel Pepys 1703
1640? William Wycherley 1716 1729
1670 William Congreve
1678 George Farquhar 1707

Closing of theaters 1641?
Restoration comedies flourish 1660 1697
Newton's "Mathematical Principles of Natural Philosophy" 1687
Locke's "Essay Concerning Human Understanding" 1690

Dutch settle Manhattan 1626
Massachusetts Bay Colony founded 1629
PARALLEL DEVELOPMENTS IN NORTH AMERICA
1630 William Bradford's "History of Plimmoth Plantation" begun
Bay Psalm Book 1640
Anne Bradstreet's first book of verse 1650
Salem witchcraft trials 1692

1570 '80 '90 1600 '10 '20 '30 '40 '50 '60 '70 '80 '90 1700 '10 '20 1730

ment of literature. If the nineteenth-century English novelists were more restricted in their choice and handling of themes than French novelists were, this was due chiefly to the fact that the new, large reading public in England had not escaped the influence of Puritanism.

But the original Puritans were very different from their nineteenth-century descendants. They were deeply religious, in a stern Old Testament style, but they condemned the church, the priesthood, and all ritualistic forms of worship, just as they also denounced playgoing, singing (except psalm-singing), dancing, and all popular amusements and pastimes. The nineteenth-century English historian Thomas Macaulay said of them that they disliked bear-baiting not because it gave pain to the bear but because it gave pleasure to the spectators. Many of them were gloomy, bigoted, and intolerant, and some of them no doubt were as absurd as writers like Ben Jonson made them out to be; but there was plenty of ability among them, and not only for trading and fighting. They produced writers of the stature of John Milton (1608–1674) and John Bunyan (1628–1688) and, in addition, some extremely original and audacious political theorists, known chiefly as "Levellers" because they wanted to make all people politically equal, or level. There was indeed a great ferment of ideas among these English nonconformists and rebels.

RESTORATION ENGLAND

The restoration of the monarchy brought about many important changes, and to understand these we have to know something about the king himself, Charles II (1660–85). He was the eldest son of the unhappy Charles I. Never were a father and son more unlike each other than these two. If the father had too much dignity and self-importance, his son had, if anything, too little. Tall, very swarthy, lazy, and dissipated, Charles II had great personal charm and plenty of intelligence but not much conscience. His contemporaries declared that "he never said a foolish thing and never did a wise one." This is unjust. He did many wise things, though he was anything but a dutiful, conscientious monarch, for he wasted money on trifles, secretly accepted a pension from Louis XIV, and, in spite of his oath to reign as a Protestant, was probably always at heart a Catholic. But he was not a bigoted one, like his brother, afterwards James II.

During the reign of Charles II, the greatest European power was France, where the despotic if magnificent Louis XIV ruled from his new palace at Versailles. During his long period of exile, Charles had lived in France. French influence in manners, literature, and the arts was now irresistible. The Restoration brought England out of its comparative isolation into a European orbit dominated by France, and what was fashionable in Paris soon became fashionable in London. French classical style and manner were imitated in spite of the fact that London not long after the Restoration had terrible troubles entirely her own—namely, the Plague (1665) and the Great Fire (1666). The latter devastated the old city, which was then rebuilt under the direction of the famous architect Christopher Wren.

For all his indolence and frivolity, Charles II was interested in ideas, and he lived in the right time and place in which to discover them. During Charles's reign, Francis Bacon's idea of a society composed of writers and scientists became a reality in the formation of the Royal Society of London. This Society, composed of distinguished philosophers, scientists, and people of many other branches of scholarship, was founded in London in 1662 under the direct patronage of Charles II and still exists today. Samuel Pepys (1633–1703), secretary of the Navy, was one of the early presidents of the Royal Society.

It is from this same Samuel Pepys that we know a great deal about the intimate life of London in this time. From his completely candid diary, which he wrote in secret shorthand and never intended to be published, Pepys shows us the London of the Plague and the Great Fire. The same London was also the home of the new scientific theories, experiments, and philosophical ideas: the city of the great Isaac Newton (1642–1727), the mathematician and astronomer; of William Harvey (1578–1657), who discovered the circulation of the blood; of John Locke (1632–1704), whose *Essay Concerning Human Understanding* described our mental processes and whose influence on the eighteenth century was enormous. The new scientific and rational age came into existence in the London of Charles II.

THE GLORIOUS REVOLUTION

In 1688 James II, the Catholic brother and successor to Charles II, had to flee England, and his daughter Mary and her husband William, ruler of Holland, jointly took the crown, reigning as the first constitutional monarchs, which, as we have seen already, meant that their power was severely limited. The coming of William and Mary was called the "Glorious Revolution" and was celebrated as such, quite justly too, because a complete and extremely important change had been made. The whole system of government had been reversed without violence and bloodshed. From now on, the English learned that quiet revolutions are possible and that important political changes need not be violent and murderous. The joint reign of William and Mary helped to create a new England.

FRENCH CULTURAL INFLUENCE

What the reign of William and Mary chiefly did was to put England squarely into the general European scene. William himself was the leading Protestant challenger of Louis XIV, easily the most powerful monarch in

Europe and himself a militant Catholic. A little later, England, making full use of the military genius of the Duke of Marlborough (1650–1722), was able to attack and defeat the armies of Louis time after time. England won the war, and her new position on the European scene put England even more than before under the social, cultural, and literary influence of France. The French classical style and manners of Versailles were imitated in England, but there was always some difference, just because the English like to have at least something of their own way.

So the English poets, at the end of the century, were not *exactly* like the French poets. They obeyed some of the same rules, but not all. The dramatists, especially in tragedy, now kept one eye on the French, but not both eyes. And indeed in comedy, though the French (such as Molière) were masters of the form, the English went very much their own way. And they began telling stories in their own way, chiefly in a sober, realistic way, of which the master, soon to be discovered, was Daniel Defoe (1661?–1731). John Dryden (1631–1700), a kind of literary dictator, accepted much of what was dictated at Versailles and in Paris, but he too contrived to keep his essential Englishness. And in science and philosophy it was Paris that began to learn from London. Charles II did not found his Royal Society in vain.

LITERARY DEVELOPMENTS

Altogether this is a very interesting period, not all of a piece as some other periods are, not confined to one great high road of thought and feeling, but breaking out, almost bursting, in many different directions. It is as if the instability and turbulence of the political scene set people thinking, feeling, and writing in widely different ways. There was no typical seventeenth-century outlook. Milton, the solemn Puritan, was a seventeenth-century poet; so was Robert Herrick (1591–1674), who wrote gay poems to pretty women. They shared only the time in which they lived.

Because of the sharp political division of England into Puritans and Cavaliers, it might be expected that the writers of this period can be placed in parallel classifications. However, any strict division into Puritan writers and Cavalier writers ignores many differentiations and considerable cross-pollination. It is fairly easy to label men like Robert Herrick, Richard Lovelace (1618–1658), and John Suckling (1609–1642) as men who wrote "Cavalier" verse, gay, devil-may-care poetry extolling the transient pleasures of love, youth, happiness, and beauty. But with many other writers any such specialized categories break down. George Wither (1588–1667), for example, wrote Elizabethan pastorals and lyrics and later fervent Puritan hymns and political tracts. This kind of diversity, as well as the influence of various literary styles, was characteristic of many another writer of the day.

BRITAIN 1485-1700

ATLANTIC OCEAN

SCOTLAND

- Forres
- Inverness

Glamis ●1
Birnam Wood ●
Scone ●
FIFE

● Edinburgh

NORTH SEA

IRISH SEA

IRELAND

Dublin ●3

ENGLAND

2 ● Nun Appleton
● York

4 ● Naseby

5 ● Aldwincle All Saints

6 ● Cambridge

WALES

Stratford-on-Avon ●7

Newton St. Briget ●8

9 ● Oxford

11

Horton ●10 ● London
Hampton Court ● ● Southwark
13 12

● Canterbury

14 ● Bemerton

Dean Pryor ●15

ATLANTIC OCEAN

ENGLISH CHANNEL

FRANCE

1 Macbeth's castle. 2 Marvell tutored here. 3 Farquhar and Congreve attended Trinity College here. 4 Decisive victory (1645) by Cromwell's Parliamentary forces in Civil War. 5 Birthplace of John Dryden. 6 Spenser, Marlowe, Campion, Bacon, Herrick, Marvell, Milton, Herbert, Dryden, and Pepys attended university here. 7 Shakespeare born, grew up, retired, died, and buried here. 8 Home of Henry Vaughan. 9 Raleigh, Sidney, Daniel, Lovelace, Wither, Vaughan, and Wycherley attended university here. 10 Home of John Milton, 1632–38. 11 Political, literary, and commercial capital of England. Birthplace of Spenser, Bacon, Jonson, Donne, Milton, and Pepys, all of whom lived and wrote here, as did Shakespeare, Marlowe, Raleigh, Congreve, and Dryden. 12 Site of Globe Theater, partly owned by Shakespeare, where he acted and his plays were performed. 13 From time of Henry VIII, a favorite palace of English kings. 14 George Herbert famed for his preaching at Fugglestone, near here. 15 Robert Herrick was vicar here.

The seventeenth-century poet who created the most compelling new style was John Donne (1572–1631), the earliest and greatest of the metaphysical poets. Donne was brought up as a Roman Catholic but later joined the Church of England and finally became Dean of St. Paul's. His sermons, often delivered in magnificent prose, were very popular, and certain passages from them are still frequently quoted. But it is as a poet that he has had strongest influence, first during the seventeenth century and then, after a long period of almost complete neglect, on the poetry that followed immediately after World War I. Modern poets turn to Donne because he is both highly intellectual and impassioned and uses imagery in the modern manner, as if it were a kind of inspired shorthand. His chief weaknesses, which may be found in all his followers, are obscurity and a rather crabbed unmusical manner, song becoming argument.

People of this age went to extremes, and even literary forms were quick to change and develop during the seventeenth century. Prose writing offers us a particularly good example of this change and development. It moved in two different directions, though not quite at the same time. The earlier development, found in Milton's prose or in the sermons of eloquent preachers like Jeremy Taylor (1613–1667) and Sir Thomas Browne (1606–1682), produced writing of increasing complexity, in which sentences branched out into dozens of relative clauses. It is prose quite unlike ordinary speech, elaborate in its structure, poetical in its richness of imagery, its tremendous sentences gleaming and glittering with images, like Christmas trees covered with glass ornaments and candles. The very richest English prose belongs to the seventeenth century.

The later development, taking place during the last twenty years of the century was quite different, for instead of moving away from ordinary speech the new prose style began to reproduce much of the manner and rhythm of the best talk of the time. John Dryden, though primarily a poet, was an original master of this new kind of prose, and his exquisite perfection in it was really a greater achievement than anything he wrote in verse. The charm of Dryden's prose comes from the fact that, while it seems to have the manner and rhythm of good talk, it has not entirely broken with the more poetical past and its bright imagery. Much earlier, Bacon in his essays had hammered out for himself a prose that suited him, but it is stiff and heavy compared with Dryden's prose, which dances and sparkles like the finest talk.

Late in the century, dramatists, the creators of Restoration comedy, brought to the theater a similar prose style. The Restoration theater was very different from the Elizabethan theater, the remnants of which the victorious Puritans had closed in about 1641. It is easy, however, to make too much out of this closing of the playhouses. The glorious popular theater of the Elizabethans had disappeared years before the Puritans took action.

The age of dramatic masterpieces had gone, and most of the popular enthusiasm had gone with it. The playhouses that were closed already existed only in a kind of twilight. It was a drama in its decadence that was forbidden to the public and "bootlegged" through secret private performances in large country houses.

The Restoration theater was a theater for the court, the nobility, the ladies and gentlemen of fashion. Women's roles, formerly played by boys, were now played by actresses, like the famous Nell Gwyn. Both the auditorium and the stage, quite unlike those of the Elizabethan playhouses, followed French and Italian models; and it was here, with a few differences, that the modern theater began. That wonderful old stage on which the action of Shakespearean drama passed so swiftly and imaginatively was seen no more.

Among the creators of Restoration comedy, the master stylist was undoubtedly William Congreve (1670–1729), who wrote his comedies while he was still in his twenties and then gave up writing altogether. In other than stylistic respects Congreve was inferior to others in this group, notably William Wycherly (1640?–1716) and later George Farquhar (1678–1707), for he was not as good as they in contriving acceptable plots and amusing situations. But at his best, in *The Way of the World* (1700), which is still often played in the English theater, his dialogue is enchanting, wonderful prose for actors and actresses to speak. It is, of course, meant for the ear and not the eye, to be heard and not silently read, but this is true of all good English prose whether it is as solemn and stately as the Bible or Milton, or as witty and frivolous as the dialogue of Congreve. Listen to good prose and you will soon discover how alive and magical it is.

We shall end as we began. This is a very curious period. The prose of this period progressed almost as far as English prose has ever gone, and the poetry of the day presents us an astonishing variety—from the gay, careless Cavalier songs to the solemnities of Milton and the profound intricacies of the metaphysical poets such as John Donne. We should perhaps note in passing that not all critics agree exactly where the line of demarcation between Elizabethan literature and seventeenth-century literature occurs. Donne, for example, is often included among the Elizabethans; and many of the most famous Elizabethans—for example, Shakespeare and Ben Jonson—actually did their best work after James I had succeeded to the throne. But the true seventeenth century, as a literary period, arrived toward the end of James's reign, when the Elizabethan spirit in writing had vanished. This is how we have dealt with it here.

The seventeenth century was a restless and often violent age, offering extremes and many contradictions, but undeniably it was both fascinating and fruitful.

J.B.P.

JOHN DONNE
(1572–1631)

John Donne's reputation as a poet has risen and fallen and risen again to a startling degree. A fairly prolific poet, his work may be said to represent two very different attitudes. In his youth wild, worldly, and cynical, Donne wrote "harsh" love lyrics that won him an immediate circle of admirers. Then, as he grew older and turned toward religion, Donne devoted himself to philosophical and spiritual writing. All his work had great influence on poets both of his century and our own.

Born to a wealthy and distinguished family strong in the Roman Catholic faith, Donne traveled, studied law, theology, and medicine, and—a brilliant, dashing, and handsome young man—enjoyed the life of Elizabethan London. Later, disenchanted by a worldly life, after an inner religious struggle, he became a member of the Church of England. His advancement in government service was halted when his secret marriage to the sixteen-year-old Anne More roused her powerful and influential family to such fury that Donne's career was firmly blocked and he was even put in jail. During years of obscurity and soul-searching, Donne moved steadily toward service in the church and, at the age of forty-three, was ordained a priest. Before long, he became famous as an eloquent preacher and outstanding churchman. In the final period of his life, after being made Dean of St. Paul's Cathedral, he composed religious poetry and magnificent sermons which stand among the masterpieces of English prose. Since he could not publish his love poetry as an ecclesiastic, it was only after his death that the world learned of his wide-ranging genius.

In the eighteenth century, the world condemned Donne as an uncouth versifier. The English language was still in a period of great flux, in which successive critics tried to establish firm rules for prose and poetry alike. The somber splendors of Donne's style broke every rule, and he was dismissed—though with respect—as an eccentric. It was not until the 1920's that a revolution in taste, developed by T. S. Eliot and other poets and critics, set Donne once again at the height of fashion.

Donne is very much a personal writer. Those to whom his complex personality appeals are strongly partisan; those who find him needlessly obscure and rough-textured deplore his faults to the exclusion of his virtues. Donne was a master of rare intensity who expressed himself in words which flash like separate sparks even when they refuse to cohere into a steady fire. He was, moreover, a sensitive exponent of the dilemma of modern times, pulled one way by a frank acceptance of human weakness and another by an unsatisfied need for spiritual certainties.

Woman's Constancy

Now thou hast loved me one whole day,
Tomorrow when thou leav'st, what wilt thou say?
Wilt thou then antedate some new made vow?
   Or say that now
We are not just those persons which we were?   5
Or that oaths made in reverential fear
Of Love, and his wrath, any may forswear?
Or, as true deaths, true marriages untie,
So lovers' contracts, images of those,
Bind but till sleep, death's image, them unloose?   10
   Or, your own end to justify,
For having purpos'd change and falsehood, you
Can have no way but falsehood to be true?
Vain lunatic, against these 'scapes° I could
   Dispute and conquer, if I would,   15
   Which I abstain to do,
For tomorrow I may think so too.

Song

Sweetest love, I do not go
  For weariness of thee,
Nor in hope the world can show
  A fitter love for me;
   But since that I   5
Must die at last, 'tis best
To use° myself in jest,
  Thus by feigned deaths to die.

Yesternight the sun went hence,
  And yet is here today;   10
He hath no desire nor sense,
  Nor half so short a way;
   Then fear not me,
But believe that I shall make
Speedier journeys, since I take   15
  More wings and spurs than he.

O how feeble is man's power,
  That if good fortune fall,
Cannot add another hour,
  Nor a lost hour recall!   20
   But come bad chance,°
And we join to it our strength,
And we teach it art and length,
  Itself o'er us to advance.

When thou sigh'st, thou sigh'st not wind,
  But sigh'st my soul away;   26
When thou weep'st, unkindly kind,
  My life's blood doth decay:
   It cannot be
That thou lovest me as thou say'st,   30
If in thine my life thou waste,
  That art the best of me.

   Let not thy divining heart
    Forethink me any ill;
   Destiny may take thy part   35
    And may thy fears fulfill.
    But think that we
   Are but turned aside to sleep:
   They who one another keep
    Alive, ne'er parted be.   40

WOMAN'S CONSTANCY: 14. **scapes:** excuses, evasions. SONG: 7. **use:** condition.
21. **come bad chance:** if bad fortune should come.

Holy Sonnet I

Thou hast made me, and shall thy work
  decay?
Repair me now, for now mine end doth
  haste;
I run to death, and death meets me as fast,
And all my pleasures are like yesterday.
I dare not move my dim eyes any way,
Despair behind and death before doth
  cast   6
Such terror, and my feeble flesh doth
  waste
By sin in it, which it towards Hell doth
  weigh.
Only thou art above, and when towards
  thee
By thy leave I can look, I rise again;   10
But our old subtle foe so tempteth me
That not one hour myself I can sustain.
Thy grace may wing me to prevent his art,
And thou like adamant° draw mine iron
  heart.

Holy Sonnet VII

At the round earth's imagined corners,
  blow
Your trumpets, angels,° and arise, arise
From death, you numberless infinities
Of souls, and to your scattered bodies go;
All whom the flood did, and fire shall,
  o'erthrow;   5
All whom war, death, age, agues, tyran-
  nies,
Despair, law, chance, hath slain, and you
  whose eyes
Shall behold God, and never taste death's
  woe.°
But let them sleep, Lord, and me mourn a
  space,
For, if above all these, my sins abound, 10
'Tis late to ask abundance of thy grace
When we are there. Here on this lowly
  ground
Teach me how to repent; for that's as good
As if thou hadst sealed my pardon with
  thy blood.

HOLY SONNET I: 14. **adamant:** loadstone.
HOLY SONNET VII: 2. **angels:** "And after these things I saw four angels standing on the four corners of the earth . . ." (Revelation 7:1). 7-8. **you . . . woe:** A reference to Luke 9:27, "But I tell you of a truth, there shall be some standing here which shall not taste of death till they see the kingdom of God"; that is, those who are still living at Judgment Day.

FOR STUDY AND DISCUSSION

WOMAN'S CONSTANCY

1. The first thirteen lines of "Woman's Constancy" is a series of questions directed to a woman who "has loved me one whole day." In these questions the poet suggests the possible arguments the woman may offer in defense of her fickleness. State in your own words each of these possible excuses. To what does "those" in line 9 refer? In line 13, how can "falsehood" be the only way to be "true"?

2. Did line 17 surprise you? Why or why not is it an appropriate ending to the poem? What is the poet's attitude toward love? Do you believe him?

SONG

1. What is the meaning of the first stanza of "Song"? Support your answer with evidence from the poem, giving special attention to "feigned deaths" in line 8.

2. Why in line 9 does Donne introduce the sun? What does he mean by "wings and spurs" in line 16? In line 17, why is man's power called "feeble"? How is this observation related to the situation described in this poem?

3. Explain the paradox in line 27.

4. There are two admonitions in the final stanza, one negative and one positive. Explain each in your own words.

HOLY SONNET I

1. Examine the construction of this sonnet: into how many parts is it divided? How are these parts related to each other?

2. Who is the "old subtle foe" in line 11?

3. Does this poem show Donne to be a humble man? Defend your answer.

HOLY SONNET VII

1. In "Holy Sonnet VII," for what occasion are the angels to blow their trumpets at "the round earth's imagined corners"?

2. To what "flood" and "fire" does Donne

refer in line 5? In line 10, to whom or to what does "all these" refer? In line 12, to what place does the word "there" refer?

3. Where in this sonnet does the direction of thought shift?

DONNE'S POETIC STYLE

John Donne's sharp reaction against the decorum of Elizabethan love poetry is readily seen by comparing his poetic style with that of Elizabethan poets like Sidney, Daniel, and Campion (see pp. 93, 95, 98). The Elizabethans praised and pined for distant and idealized ladies in gentle and courtly language. Donne, on the other hand, used an unconventional, straightforward, and often brusque style. Compare, for example, Elizabethan lines such as "Tears, vows, and prayers have I spent in vain," "Men call you fair, and you do credit it," and "There is a garden in her face" with "Mark but this flea" and "For God's sake hold your tongue," lines with which Donne opens two of his best-known love poems. And, instead of perpetuating what he felt was the trite blandness of the typical Elizabethan metaphor in which a lady was described as a "fair flower," her lips rubies, her eyes sapphires, and her locks gold, Donne used striking images and the *metaphysical conceit,* a less ornamental but still often extravagant metaphor which points out an unusual parallel between what are usually highly dissimilar elements. A conceit typical of Donne's original and far more intellectual style is his comparison, for instance, of himself lying sick in bed to a map which is being studied by his doctors; and, in another poem, his comparison of his soul and that of his wife to the two points of a compass, forever joined even though forced apart. The comparisons are original and apt, however unconventional by Elizabethan standards.

Also characteristic of Donne's style is his use of *paradox,* a statement apparently, though not necessarily, self-contradictory. Look again, for example, at line 13 of "Woman's Constancy," where Donne speaks of "falsehood" as the only way to be "true." And look again at line 27 of "Song" where a lady is referred to as being "unkindly kind." Both are examples of paradox, though the latter is a special kind of paradox, a figure of speech called *oxymoron.* Taken from the Greek *oxys* meaning "sharp" and *moros* meaning "foolish," oxymoron is a short self-contradictory phrase (like "living death" or "beloved enemy") which suggests a paradox in a very few words.

FOR COMPOSITION

Select from this book or from your outside reading two poems, one by a sixteenth-century poet and typically Elizabethan, and the other by John Donne and typical of his work as an innovator. Explain how these two poems contrast as to attitude, content, and language.

Meditation XVII

"Meditation XVII" is one of a number of short pieces for which Donne took notes in 1623 while recovering from a serious illness. The following year he published these thoughts in his book, *Devotions Upon Emergent Occasions.* Donne's own translation of the Latin motto with which he prefaced "Meditation XVII" is "Now, this bell tolling softly for another, says to me, Thou must die." Here, in Donne's prose, is the same individuality that is revealed in his poetry.

PERCHANCE he for whom this bell tolls may be so ill as that he knows not it tolls for him; and perchance I may think myself so much better than I am as that they who are about me and see my state may have caused it to toll for me, and I know not that.

The church is catholic, universal, so are all her actions; all that she does belongs to all. When she baptizes a child, that action concerns me; for that child is thereby connected to that body which is my head too, and ingrafted into that body whereof I am a member. And when she buries a man, that action concerns me: all mankind is of one author, and is one volume. When one man dies, one chapter is not torn out of the book, but translated into a better language; and every chapter must be so translated. God employs several translators; some pieces are translated by age, some by sickness, some by war, some by justice; but God's hand is in every translation, and his hand shall bind up all our scattered leaves again for that library where every book shall lie open to one another.

As therefore the bell that rings to a sermon calls not upon the preacher only but upon the congregation to come, so this bell calls us all; but how much more me who am brought so near the door by this sickness! There was a contention as far as a suit—in which piety and dignity, religion and estimation,[1] were mingled—which of the religious orders should ring to prayers first in the morning; and it was determined that they should ring first that rose earliest.

If we understand aright the dignity of this bell that tolls for our evening prayer, we would be glad to make it ours by rising early, in that application, that it might be ours as well as his, whose indeed it is.

The bell doth toll for him that thinks it doth; and though it intermit again, yet from that minute that that occasion wrought upon him he is united to God.

Who casts not up his eye to the sun when it rises? but who takes off his eye from a comet when that breaks out? Who bends not his ear to any bell which upon any occasion rings? but who can remove it from that bell which is passing a piece of himself out of this world?

No man is an island entire of itself; every man is a piece of the continent, a part of the main.[2] If a clod be washed away by the sea, Europe is the less, as well as if a promontory were, as well as if a manor of thy friend's or of thine own were. Any man's death diminishes me, because I am involved in mankind, and therefore never send to know for whom the bell tolls; it tolls for thee.

Neither can we call this a begging of misery or a borrowing of misery, as though we were not miserable enough of ourselves but must fetch in more from the next house, in taking upon us the misery of our neighbors. Truly it were an ex-cusable covetousness if we did, for affliction is a treasure, and scarce any man hath enough of it. No man hath affliction enough that is not matured and ripened by it and made fit for God by that affliction.

If a man carry treasure in bullion or in a wedge of gold and have none coined into current money, his treasure will not defray him as he travels. Tribulation is treasure in the nature of it, but it is not current money in the use of it, except we get nearer and nearer our home, heaven, by it. Another man may be sick too, and sick to death, and this affliction may lie in his bowels as gold in a mine and be of no use to him; but this bell that tells me of his affliction digs out and applies that gold to me, if by this consideration of another's danger I take mine own into contemplation, and so secure myself by making my recourse to my God, who is our only security.

FOR STUDY AND DISCUSSION

1. To what door does Donne refer in paragraph 3 when he speaks of "me who am brought so near the door by this sickness"?

2. At the beginning of paragraph 5 Donne writes, "The bell doth toll for him that thinks it doth." Later he says, "No man is an island entire of itself" and "never send to know for whom the bell tolls; it tolls for thee." Explain Donne's meaning in each of these statements.

3. In paragraph 8 Donne calls affliction "a treasure." How does he argue that affliction can benefit man? Do you agree?

In the final paragraph Donne distinguishes between "treasure" and "current money." What is the difference between the two? How may a man turn his "treasure" into "current money"?

FOR COMPOSITION

Donne's "Meditation XVII" achieves both unity and diversity by stating a single theme with a number of variations, or specific examples. Donne's main theme is the one which Ernest Hemingway used as the title of his novel *For Whom the Bell Tolls*. Write a short essay in which you state Donne's main theme and his variations. How do the variations, or examples, relate to the central theme?

---

[1] **estimation:** self-esteem.
[2] **main:** mainland.

SEVENTEENTH–CENTURY LYRIC POETRY

English poetry of the seventeenth century is among the richest and most various. Although we cannot describe the great outpouring of verse in this period as belonging to formal "schools," we can speak of different styles of poetry which were current at this time. There were three of these. It must be emphasized, however, that each writer, though influenced by one style or another, or by a combination of styles, usually followed his own particular bent.

Most traditional of the seventeenth-century poets were those who emulated the elaborate style of Edmund Spenser, who, apart from Shakespeare, was the most important poet of the Elizabethan Age. The work of men like George Wither and Michael Drayton, who continued to turn out sonnets, pastoral poetry, epics, and verse narratives which were popular in Elizabethan days, typified this style of seventeenth-century poetry. Inspired by Spenser's masterpiece *The Faerie Queen,* others also tried their hand at epics, but it wasn't until John Milton produced *Paradise Lost* (1667) that a worthy, though unsimilar, successor to Spenser's great epic appeared. Spenser's moral approach to poetry and his patriotic feeling influenced Milton greatly and, though Milton considered himself Spenser's literary heir, the work of each poet was so original in its own way as to be unique.

The other two styles of seventeenth-century poetry represent reactions against Spenser's style. One of these styles was influenced by the poetry of Ben Jonson, the other by that of John Donne. Ben Jonson, cutting through the elaborateness of conventional Elizabethan poetry, took as his guide ancient Greek and Roman poetry, which he admired for its directness of expression, its precision, balance, and restraint. Jonson's wit and classical learning inspired the group of younger poets who liked to call themselves "sons of Ben" (see page 184). The most notable of these were Robert Herrick, John Suckling, and Richard Lovelace, the best-known "Cavalier" poets. In the poetry of Suckling and Lovelace, as in that of Edmund Waller, the influence of Jonson's classicism is seen combined with touches of John Donne.

From John Donne, on the other hand, came what was by far the most original influence on seventeenth-century poetry. Like Jonson, Donne rebelled against the techniques and subject matter of Elizabethan poetry. Unlike Jonson, he moved away from smooth and polished verse and, often in irregular meter and unusual verse forms, wrote intense, dramatic, and frequently complex and difficult verse, in which he explored a great variety of emotional, intellectual, and spiritual experience. Alternately witty, ironic, philosophical, or mystical, Donne was also often purposely abrupt and colloquial and used unusual metaphors which were totally lacking in the proprieties of traditional Elizabethan verse. All of these characteristics prompted John Dryden later in the century to refer to Donne as a "metaphysical" poet. Donne was the first and greatest of these. George Herbert, Henry Vaughan, and Andrew Marvell are among the most important of his followers. Each of these younger poets, though strongly influenced by Donne's approach to poetry, nevertheless developed his own highly personal attitude and mode of expression. From Marvell came a rich combination of Jonsonian polish and the verbal ingenuity of the metaphysical tradition; from Herbert and Vaughan and others of Donne's general religious persuasion came some of the most profound devotional poetry in our language.

George Wither

George Wither (1588–1667) is remembered today as a writer of clear and sparkling pastoral poetry. His uncompromising character is evident both in his politics and in his poetry: his politics moved him from Royalist to Puritan; his poetry defied the age by harking back to Elizabethan traditions. Wither's well-to-do family sent him to Oxford and then to London for legal training, but he never practiced law. He wrote poetry which was extremely popular in spite of its unfashionable pastoral content, and satirical political pamphlets which soon landed him in prison. The period of his best lyric writing ended in 1622 with the publication of *Fair Virtue, the Mistress of Philarete,* which includes "Shall I, Wasting in Despair." Thereafter Wither's growing immersion in Puritanism seemed to stifle his gift for poetry. In 1642 he sold his estate to raise a cavalry troop for Oliver Cromwell. Captured by the Royalists, he was saved from death only by the intervention of Sir John Denham, who claimed he saved Wither so that he himself would not be considered the worst poet in England! Not long after the Civil War, Wither's forthrightness again caused him trouble. This time he lost his appointment under Cromwell "by declaring unto him [Cromwell] those truths which he was not willing to hear of." After the Restoration, Wither's pamphleteering resulted in another prison term, this time for three years. His poetic reputation waned during his lifetime only to be revived by Charles Lamb and others who admired the "virile lyricism" of his early poetry.

Shall I, Wasting in Despair

Shall I, wasting in despair,
Die, because a woman's fair?
Or make pale my cheeks with care,
'Cause another's rosy are?
Be she fairer than the day,   5
Or the flowery meads in May,
 If she be not so to me,
 What care I how fair she be?

Should my heart be grieved or pined,
'Cause I see a woman kind?   10
Or a well-disposèd nature
Joinèd with a lovely feature?
Be she meeker, kinder than
Turtle dove, or pelican,°
 If she be not so to me,   15
 What care I how kind she be?

Shall a woman's virtues move
Me to perish for her love?
Or her well-deserving known,
Make me quite forget mine own?   20
Be she with that goodness blest
Which may gain her name of best,
 If she be not such to me,
 What care I how good she be?

'Cause her fortune seems too high,   25
Shall I play the fool and die?
Those that bear a noble mind,
Where they want° of riches find,
Think, "What, with them, they would do
That, without them, dare to woo!"   30
 And unless that mind I see,
 What care I though great she be?

Great, or good, or kind, or fair,
I will ne'er the more despair!
If she love me (this believe!)   35
I will die, ere she shall grieve;
If she slight me when I woo,
I can scorn, and let her go;
 For if she be not for me,
 What care I for whom she be?   40

14. **pelican:** a bird which was believed to tear open its breast in order to feed its offspring with its own blood. 28. **want:** lack.

Sir John Suckling

The most elegant and dashing young gentleman at the court of Charles I, Sir John Suckling (1609–1642), who inherited a fortune at eighteen and was knighted at twenty-one, passed his short life as the archetype of the beau Cavalier. He spent his fortune liberally in the king's service and in the extravagant pursuits of courtly life. A celebrated gambler as well as a noted gamboler, he is said to have invented cribbage and to have spent a fortune producing his play *Aglaura,* which contains the delightful song below. Suckling also spent a fortune lavishly outfitting a cavalry troop which rode out to battle for King Charles in brave scarlet and white. Another political adventure forced him into exile in Paris where, his career as a courtier ended and his fortune melted away, Suckling died, most likely by his own hand.

Gay, flippant, and spontaneous, Suckling was a brilliant but casual artist who achieved his measure of literary immortality as a unique master of the light lyric. Admired by his contemporaries as well as by the eighteenth-century dramatist William Congreve, he is still thought of as, in Congreve's words, "natural, easy Suckling."

Song FROM *Aglaura* *

Why so pale and wan, fond lover?
  Prithee, why so pale?
Will, when looking well can't move her,
  Looking ill prevail?
  Prithee, why so pale?   5

Why so dull and mute, young sinner?
  Prithee, why so mute?
Will, when speaking well can't win her,
  Saying nothing do 't?
  Prithee, why so mute?   10

Quit, quit for shame! This will not move;
  This cannot take her.
If of herself she will not love,
  Nothing can make her:
  The devil take her!   15

* *Aglaura* (à·glô′rà): a drama by Suckling, performed with magnificent scenery and costumes.

Richard Lovelace

Richard Lovelace (1618–1658) is a paragon of superlatives. He has been called the most romantic figure of English literature, the best-known Cavalier poet, the most gallant and handsome man of his time. Born to a wealthy family and to a military tradition, he stood out even in his youth as a courtly gentleman and a gifted amateur of both music and painting. From his mid-twenties, his life was crowded with events and action: inheriting the huge family fortune, writing poetry, serving as a Cavalier during the Civil War, both in court and on the battlefield. Petitioning Parliament to restore the rights of Charles I cost him a sentence in a Puritan prison. After his release he fought in Holland for the French king and, upon his return to England, was again imprisoned. There he gathered and revised his poems, which were later published under the title *Lucasta.* His short life ended in poverty.

Lovelace is remembered especially for two lyrics—"To Althea, from Prison" and "To Lucasta, on Going to the Wars." His work shows the influences of both Jonson and Donne, and he is often compared to his friend John Suckling. Lovelace is fully as graceful as Suckling, but graver, more serious in his attitude. His airy lyrics express perfectly the best of the Cavalier manner and spirit.

To Lucasta,* on Going to the Wars

Tell me not, sweet, I am unkind,
  That from the nunnery
Of thy chaste breast and quiet mind
  To war and arms I fly.

True, a new mistress now I chase,   5
  The first foe in the field;
And with a stronger faith embrace
  A sword, a horse, a shield.

Yet this inconstancy is such
  As you, too, shall adore;   10
I could not love thee, dear, so much,
  Loved I not honor more.

* Lucasta (lōō·kas′tə).

Edmund Waller

Once admired as the greatest English lyric poet, Edmund Waller (1606–1687) is remembered today for a small bouquet of lyrics and for his early work with the heroic couplet form (see page 878) which Dryden, Pope, and other early eighteenth-century poets perfected as a medium of brilliant satirical comment. Born to wealth, Waller was said to have been "nursed in parliaments." At sixteen he served under the first Stuart king, James I, and more than sixty years later he served, a highly respected member, under the fourth and last Stuart king, James II. In between, Waller's political fortunes—and his political course—fluctuated erratically. As a Royalist, he represented the Puritans in dealings with Charles I. For his part in a violent Royalist plot against the Puritans, Waller was sentenced to death, but his sentence was ultimately commuted to a fine and exile. His wit saved him on more than one occasion. Pardoned after eight years, Waller returned to England and wrote his "panegyric" to Cromwell; after the Stuart restoration in 1660, he wrote "Upon His Majesty's Happy Return." When Charles II asked why that poem was inferior to the one he had written for Cromwell, Waller replied, "Sire, we poets never succeed so well in writing truth as in fiction."

As a poet, Waller established an instant reputation with his first book, but today only a few of his works—graceful lyrics like "Go, Lovely Rose"—are admired. Still, Waller's reputation as a leading formalizer of English poetic style is secure. Dryden wrote of him, "Unless he had written, none of us could write."

Go, Lovely Rose!

Go, lovely rose!
Tell her that wastes her time and me
    That now she knows,
When I resemble her to thee,
How sweet and fair she seems to be.   5

Tell her that's young,
And shuns to have her graces spied,
    That hadst thou sprung
In deserts, where no men abide,
Thou must have uncommended died.   10

Small is the worth
Of beauty from the light retired;
    Bid her come forth,
Suffer herself to be desired,
And not blush so to be admired.   15

Then die! that she
The common fate of all things rare
    May read in thee:
How small a part of time they share
That are so wondrous sweet and fair.   20

George Herbert

George Herbert (1593–1633) was, after Donne, the most important of the metaphysical poets. Born to wealthy aristocracy and educated at Cambridge, he was attracted for a time to the sophisticated, elegant life at court, but the death of James I ended his hope for political advancement. Herbert, who numbered among his friends John Donne and Sir Francis Bacon, shortly thereafter settled down to the outwardly quiet life of a country parson and soon gained a reputation as a model clergyman. At Cambridge he had been an outstanding orator, and, as a preacher, his eloquence was so great that, on hearing the bell toll, farmers would leave the plow in the furrow to hasten to church.

Herbert wrote his poetry in Latin as well as in English. He was a great experimenter and indulged in the seventeenth-century liking for "wit" by writing poems in lines arranged in the shape of a pair of wings or an altar. No one knew the inner Herbert until the posthumous publication of *The Temple* in 1633. In this ingenious masterpiece, a collection of meditative poems written during the last years of his life, is reflected the intense conflict between secular and religious life which Herbert experienced several years before, a conflict which was firmly resolved when he made the decision to devote his life to the church. Herbert loved the church as an institution and his poetry celebrated the symbolic significance of the church building, the ritual and music of the church, and even the clerical vestment. "The Collar" illustrates the main features of Herbert's poetry—symbolic writing and the use of the "metaphysical conceit" (see page 207). To Herbert the collar is the symbol of his final submission to God.

The Collar

I struck the board° and cried, "No more!
    I will abroad!°
What, shall I ever sigh and pine?
My lines and life are free: free as the road,
    Loose as the wind, as large as store.°   5
      Shall I be still in suit?°
Have I no harvest but a thorn,
To let me blood and not restore
What I have lost with cordial° fruit?
      Sure there was wine,   10
Before my sighs did dry it; there was corn,
    Before my tears did drown it.
Is the year only lost to me?
    Have I no bays° to crown it,
No flowers, no garlands gay? all blasted?
      All wasted?   16
Not so, my heart; but there is fruit,
      And thou hast hands.
Recover all thy sigh-blown age
On double pleasures. Leave thy cold dis-
      pute   20
Of what is fit and not. Forsake thy cage,
    Thy rope of sands,°
Which petty thoughts have made (and
    made to thee
Good cable, to enforce and draw,
      And be thy law,   25
While thou didst wink and wouldst not
    see).
      Away! take heed!
      I will abroad!
Call in thy death's-head° there! Tie up thy
    fears!
      He that forbears   30
To suit and serve his need
    Deserves his load."
But as I raved, and grew more fierce and
    wild
    At every word,
Methought I heard one calling, "Child!"
    And I replied, "My Lord."   36

1. **board:** table. 2. **I . . . abroad:** i.e., I will go out into the world. 5. **store:** abundance. 6. **still . . . suit:** always petitioning. 9. **cordial:** restorative. 14. **bays:** laurel. 22. **rope of sands:** church teachings considered futile by a defiant young man. In his more pious days they were the "good cable" of line 24. 29. **death's-head:** memento of mortality.

A view of Oxford and its university as it appeared in the seventeenth century.

Henry Vaughan

Just as George Herbert was a disciple of John Donne, so Henry Vaughan (1622–1695) was greatly influenced by the work of George Herbert. Vaughan, a devoted Welshman, attended Oxford and studied briefly in London. It was as a student in London that he first became interested in poetry. After serving with the Royalists during the Civil War, Vaughan returned to his native Wales, where he spent the rest of his life as a successful country doctor. Like George Herbert, Vaughan's poetic inspiration stemmed from religion. Although a loyal churchman, he approached his religion—unlike Herbert—more through personal intuition than through the institution of the church. He was also deeply influenced by nature and is sometimes referred to as one of the first English nature poets.

Though Vaughan's poetry does not reflect the consistently skillful craftsmanship for which Herbert is known, his powers of mystical expression are, at their best, unexcelled. The religious poetry in Vaughan's collection called *Silex Scintillans* ("sparks of divine fire struck from a hard heart"), an illustration of which follows, represents his special contribution to the literature of his time. "The Retreat" illustrates Vaughan's mastery of metaphysical imagery. In expressing his belief that children are blessed with a special innocence and sense of divine awareness, it anticipates by over a century William Wordsworth's famous "Ode: Intimations of Immortality."

The Retreat

Happy those early days! when I
Shined in my angel-infancy;
Before I understood this place
Appointed for my second race,°
Or taught my soul to fancy aught   5
But a white, celestial thought;
When yet I had not walked above
A mile, or two, from my first love,
And looking back at that short space
Could see a glimpse of His bright face: 10
When on some gilded cloud or flow'r
My gazing soul would swell an hour,
And in those weaker glories spy
Some shadows of eternity;
Before I taught my tongue to wound   15
My conscience with a sinful sound,
Or had the black art to dispense
A sev'ral° sin to ev'ry sense;
But felt through all this fleshly dress°
Bright shoots of everlastingness.   20
    O, how I long to travel back,
And tread again that ancient track!
That I might once more reach that plain,
Where first I left my glorious train;
From whence th' enlightened spirit sees
That shady city of palm trees—°   26
But ah! my soul with too much stay
Is drunk, and staggers in the way!
Some men a forward motion love,
But I by backward steps would move,   30
And when this dust falls to the urn,
In that state I came, return.

4. **second race:** earthly existence. 18. **sev'ral:** different. 19. **fleshly dress:** the body. 26. **shady . . . trees:** probably paradise.

1. In the first two stanzas of "Shall I, Wasting in Despair," Wither compares a lady to things of nature—flowers and birds. Why does he abandon these natural allusions in the third and fourth stanzas? Is this sonnet a love lyric? Tell why you think it is or isn't.

2. What attitude does Suckling express in "Song" from *Aglaura?* Would the poem be improved if the last line read: "Till thou forsake her"? Give reasons for your answer.

3. Point out the paradox in "To Lucasta, on Going to the Wars." How does Lovelace compare love to war? Is the statement in the last sentence intended to be complimentary? Explain.

4. In Waller's "Go, Lovely Rose," what do the rose and the lady have in common? What would the poet have the lady learn from the death of the rose?

5. As its title suggests, George Herbert's "The Collar" is a poem reflecting a struggle. What kind of struggle is suggested, and how does this struggle end? Identify the "I" and the "thou" in the poem. Within the context of the poem, explain what is suggested by the words "thorn," "blood," "cordial fruit," and "wine" in lines 7–10.

6. Why do you think Henry Vaughan calls his poem "The Retreat"? What does Vaughan mean by "angel-infancy" (line 2)? by "my first love" (line 8)? To what state does he wish to return?

FOR COMPOSITION

1. Lovelace and Suckling, considered by many as twin stereotypes of the Cavalier ideal, are sometimes also contrasted. The last stanza of Suckling's "Song" from *Aglaura* and the last two lines of Lovelace's "To Lucasta, on Going to the Wars" are well-known lines of English poetry. Write a short essay in which you contrast the philosophies of the two poets as expressed in these lines.

2. In a short essay, show how Herbert's poem "The Collar" illustrates the metaphysical conceit. Give specific instances and say why you consider Herbert's conceit effective or ineffective.

3. Do you consider Vaughan's "retreat" a retreat from reality? Write a composition explaining your viewpoint.

ENGLISH PAINTING

Early English Portraiture

Small-scale portraits, or "miniatures," were very popular in Elizabethan court circles. Small enough to be held in the hand or hung on gold chains around the neck, they delighted courtiers who loved personal adornment. Queen Elizabeth's official miniaturist, and the first native-born English painter about whom we have much information, was Nicholas Hilliard. The two miniatures by Hilliard shown here are *A Young Man Among Roses* (PLATE 1) and *Sir Anthony Mildmay* (PLATE 2).

The young man in PLATE 1 probably presented his miniature to a lady as a token of his devotion. Apparently his love was not returned, for around the top of the oval an inscription in Latin reads: "My praised faith causes my suffering." The roses symbolize his love; but thorns, which represent the pains of love, are particularly prominent here. A hand placed on the heart and a melancholy gaze suggest the theme of lovesickness.

Hilliard's portrait of Sir Anthony Mildmay (PLATE 2) dates from the year Mildmay was knighted and made ambassador to France. Surrounded by the accessories of a gentleman, Sir Anthony is the very picture of confidence and pride. The armor and the pavilion, which forms the background, make us think of him as a knightly defender. The trunk brings to mind his new appointment, as Sir Anthony would have to take his gear with him to France. A little dog looks up at his master, full of trust.

Despite Hilliard's successes, the English portrait style was set by a foreigner—a Flemish painter named Anthony Van Dyck. After several visits to England, he was appointed Court Painter to King Charles I in 1632. In Van Dyck's almost life-size portrait of the King (PLATE 3), the dismounted sovereign, elegant and haughty even on an outing, stands with left arm akimbo near a spreading tree. Seemingly diverted just for a moment from his intention to walk away, he turns toward us—but looks over our heads. It is as if we were kneeling. The King commands all our attention; it is on him that most of the light plays. A gentleman-in-waiting attends to the King's horse, while a page holds his cloak; both stand entirely in the shade. Even the horse, which otherwise would loom higher than the King, bows its head. By 1635, the year this portrait was painted, the high-handedness of

King Charles had driven some Parliamentary leaders to think of rebellion.

Comparing this likeness of Charles I with the two earlier miniatures by Hilliard (PLATES 1 and 2), we can see some of the important innovations Van Dyck brought to English portraiture. In contrast to Hilliard's meticulous linear rendering of minute details, Van Dyck painted with a bold and sweeping brushstroke, creating an effect of great dash and elegance. This effect is intensified by the curving formation of plants in the foreground, by the luxuriant branches and foliage overhead, and by the billowing clouds in the sky. Notice also that Van Dyck's lighting is not evenly distributed over figures and background as in Hilliard's portraits, but is concentrated mainly on the important left half of the composition. Deeper tones and shadows tie together most of the details throughout the rest of the painting.

Van Dyck was succeeded as Court Painter by an English artist, William Dobson, who portrayed a number of the Cavaliers in King Charles's service. One of the most devoted was Endymion Porter (PLATE 4), a well-informed agent who was helpful in making purchases for the royal collection of pictures. Dobson made no attempt to prettify Porter's puffy hands and plain features, nor did he take particular interest in the sheen on fine fabrics. But by catching the solid pose and by including relevant details, Dobson convincingly represented a country gentleman of assured position and varied tastes. The gun and the dead rabbit held by a groom indicate that Porter is a sportsman; the bust of a poet and the relief in the right foreground suggest his interest in the arts.

Civil war broke out in 1642 between the Royalists and the Parliamentarians, and seven years later the defeated Charles was executed. The austere Puritanism which followed did little to foster the arts. Nevertheless, a few artists were commissioned to paint likenesses of eminent Puritans. *Oliver Cromwell with His Squire* (PLATE 5), a portrait in the "grand" manner by Robert Walker, is the most notable of these. A strong light from the left illuminates Cromwell's face in such a way that the two halves seem utterly different. One looks young, smiling, and clear; the other, dour and troubled, expressing the determination of this devout Puritan.

In 1660 the monarchy was restored. Some years later, a German artist named Godfrey Kneller settled in London and built up a large clientele as a fashionable portraitist. A rapid and dexterous painter, Kneller was a virtuoso who turned out elegant pictures of many famous people of the Restoration and the early eighteenth century. The value to us of these portraits lies not so much in their psychological insights as in their accuracy as visual records of persons known to us from history. The portrait of the architect Sir Christopher Wren (PLATE 6), painted in 1711, shows him with a compass and an architectural plan—for after the Great Fire of 1666. Wren designed the new St. Paul's Cathedral and some fifty other London churches, many of which we can still visit today.

216

PLATE 1. NICHOLAS HIL-
LIARD (English, 1547–
1619): *A Young Man Among
Roses*. About 1588. Parch-
ment, $5\frac{3}{8}$ x $2\frac{3}{4}$ inches. (Victoria
and Albert Museum, London,
Crown Copyright)

217

PLATE 2. NICHOLAS HILLIARD (English, 1547–1619): *Sir Anthony Mildmay*. Before 1596. Gouache on parchment, $9\frac{1}{4}$ x $6\frac{7}{8}$ inches. (The Cleveland Museum of Art, Purchase from the J. H. Wade Fund)

218

PLATE 3. SIR ANTHONY VAN DYCK (Flemish, 1599–1641): *Charles I of England*. About 1635. Oil on canvas, 107 x 83½ inches. (The Louvre, Paris)

PLATE 4. WILLIAM DOBSON (English, 1610–1646): *Endymion Porter*. About 1642. Oil on canvas, 58 x 49 inches. (Reproduced by courtesy of the Trustees, The Tate Gallery, London)

220

PLATE 5. ROBERT WALKER (English, 1600–1659): *Oliver Cromwell with His Squire*. About 1649. Oil on canvas, 49½ x 39½ inches. (The National Portrait Gallery, London)

PLATE 6. SIR GODFREY KNELLER (English, 1646–1723): *Sir Christopher Wren.* 1711. Oil on canvas, 49 x 39½ inches. (The National Portrait Gallery, London)

ROBERT HERRICK
(1591–1674)

Robert Herrick, by the age of thirty, was already a lyric poet of high renown. But, judged by the literary styles of his day, he was also a little old-fashioned. Influenced by the Latin classicism of Ben Jonson, whom he canonized as "Saint Ben," Herrick wrote graceful lyrics marked with Elizabethan freshness and simplicity at a time when taste was already turning toward the metaphysical complexities of John Donne. Unfortunately, *Hesperides,* Herrick's best-known volume of poetry, was published in 1648—the worst possible time, for during the turmoil of the Civil War there was little interest in Elizabethan lyrics celebrating rural life. It was not until over two centuries later that Elizabeth Barrett Browning and Algernon Charles Swinburne set the seal on Herrick's reputation, the latter going so far as to call him "the greatest songwriter . . . ever born of English race."

The details of Herrick's life remain somewhat shadowy. The son of a London goldsmith, he worked at his father's craft for a while before taking a degree at Cambridge. Then he was drawn into Ben Jonson's circle, soon becoming one of the famous "Sons of Ben" and Jonson's greatest pupil and admirer. In 1627 Herrick entered the priesthood of the Church of England and served as chaplain in an unsuccessful military expedition of his friend, the Duke of Buckingham. Two years later, Herrick obtained from Charles I a church living in "warty" Devon. London born, Herrick at first hated this rough and rocky rural exile with its uncourtly country folk. But his classical training under Jonson had made him an admirer of the Roman poet Horace, famed for his depiction of rustic scenes; and Herrick soon began to write of Devon, discovering in himself an understanding—even a love—for the brooks, blossoms, birds, and bowers of the West Country. The Puritans expelled Herrick from his "place of exile" in 1647, but he returned after the restoration of Charles II to live out his long life as vicar of Dean Prior, the small country parish among whose half-pagan charms he found his "lyric feast."

Herrick's poems fall into two categories: pure song of wholly secular nature and somewhat labored religious verse. He shocked posterity by introducing his "jocund" (his own word for it) temperament into his poetic conceits, which seemed scandalous for a clergyman. Much of the same, however, could be objected to in other literary vicars—John Donne and Laurence Sterne, the eighteenth-century novelist, spring to mind—and there is enough charm and music in the best of Herrick's love poetry, and in his lilting pastorals, to assure him a place among the most delightful of singers.

The Argument * of His Book

I sing of brooks, of blossoms, birds, and bowers:
Of April, May, of June, and July flowers.
I sing of Maypoles, hock carts,° wassails,° wakes,°
Of bridegrooms, brides, and of their bridal cakes.
I write of youth, of love, and have access   5
By these to sing of cleanly wantonness.°
I sing of dews, of rains, and piece by piece
Of balm, of oil, of spice, and ambergris.°
I sing of Time's trans-shifting; and I write
How roses first came red, and lilies white.   10
I write of groves, of twilights, and I sing
The court of Mab,° and of the Fairy King.
I write of hell; I sing (and ever shall)
Of heaven, and hope to have it after all.

To Daffodils

Fair daffodils, we weep to see
  You haste away so soon.
As yet, the early-rising sun
  Has not attained his noon.
    Stay, stay,   5
  Until the hasting day
    Has run
But to the evensong;°
And, having prayed together, we
  Will go with you along.   10

We have short time to stay, as you;
  We have as short a spring;
As quick a growth to meet decay,
  As you, or any thing.
    We die,   15
As your hours do, and dry
    Away,
Like to the summer's rain;
Or as the pearls of morning dew,
  Ne'er to be found again.   20

THE ARGUMENT OF HIS BOOK: * **Argument:** theme, summary. This poem summarizes the
contents of *Hesperides,* in which all of the following poems appear.   3. **hock cart:** the wagon
bearing the last load of harvest; on its arrival, the merrymaking of "harvest home" began.
wassails: toasts; drinking to someone's health, an expression of good will.   **wakes:** parish festivals.   6. **cleanly wantonness:** wholesome merrymaking.   8. **ambergris:** used in making perfume.   12. **Mab:** the Fairy Queen who, with Oberon, the Fairy King, is celebrated in Shakespeare's *A Midsummer Night's Dream.*
   TO DAFFODILS: 8. **evensong:** vesper service.

To Dianeme

Sweet, be not proud of those two eyes,
Which starlike sparkle in their skies;
Nor be you proud that you can see
All hearts your captives, yours, yet free;
Be you not proud of that rich hair,   5
Which wantons with the lovesick air:
Whenas that ruby which you wear,
Sunk from the tip of your soft ear,
Will last to be a precious stone,
When all your world of beauty's gone.   10

To the Virgins, to Make Much of Time

Gather ye rosebuds while ye may,
  Old Time is still a-flying;
And this same flower that smiles today,
  Tomorrow will be dying.

The glorious lamp of heaven, the sun,   5
  The higher he's a-getting;
The sooner will his race be run,
  And nearer he's to setting.

That age is best which is the first,
  When youth and blood are warmer;   10
But being spent, the worse, and worst
  Times, still succeed the former.

Then be not coy, but use your time;
  And while ye may, go marry:
For having lost but once your prime,   15
  You may forever tarry.

FOR STUDY AND DISCUSSION

1. What is the meaning of the last two lines of "The Argument of His Book"? The poet tells us in this poem what he intends to write about. Does he carry out his intentions in the three poems that follow?

2. What analogy does Herrick make in "To Daffodils"? Do the "summer's rain" (line 18) and "morning dew" (line 19) strengthen or weaken the analogy? Explain your answer.

3. What advice does the poet give to Dianeme? To what are her eyes compared? Of what two things does Dianeme seem most proud? Through what reminder does the poet seek to puncture her pride?

4. The theme of "To the Virgins, to Make Much of Time," like that of "To Daffodils" and "To Dianeme," belongs to a tradition known as *carpe diem* (that is, "live for today") that was typically Cavalier. Which lines in this poem best summarize this theme? How do the symbols in this poem help convey this theme? What is the tone of the poem? How does it compare with that of "To Daffodils"? How does the rhythm used in "To Daffodils" reflect a different attitude toward a similar theme?

FOR COMPOSITION

Do you think that the idea of "living for today" would have been popular during the Middle Ages? Why or why not? Do you think it is popular today? Write a short composition giving reasons for your answers.

ANDREW
MARVELL
(1621–1678)

Like so many of his contemporaries, Andrew Marvell led two lives—one as writer and one as public servant. Recognized during his lifetime as a highly able statesman, if he was considered as a writer at all it was as a writer of prose, for in connection with his broad interest in practical affairs, in problems of corruption and injustice, he wrote considerably on both political and ecclesiastical subjects. Throughout his life he did indeed produce much more prose than poetry. To twentieth-century critics, however, Marvell's prose is far outranked by his superb lyric poetry.

The son of a clergyman, Marvell was educated at Cambridge University, after which he traveled widely on the Continent for a number of years, especially in Holland, France, Italy, and Spain. The languages he learned in these countries, plus his knowledge of Greek and Latin, equipped him admirably for his future endeavors.

During the Civil War, Marvell served as tutor at the country estate of one of Cromwell's leading supporters. Here, with lovely natural surroundings providing him with an abundant source of inspiration, Marvell wrote some of his best poetry on the beauties of nature. A second tutoring post followed, this time as teacher of a ward of Oliver Cromwell himself. It was during this period that Marvell became acquainted with a man who had made several trips to the Bermudas, which, in the early seventeenth century were settled by religious dissenters from England. The inspiration for "Bermudas" (page 227) is attributed to this association.

At the age of thirty-six, Marvell began governmental service as Assistant Secretary of Foreign Tongues, a post in which he served as assistant to John Milton, Cromwell's Latin Secretary. Shortly afterward, he was elected to Richard Cromwell's Parliament, and he served as a Member of Parliament for the remainder of his life. That his support of Cromwell and the Commonwealth—and, after the Restoration, his writing of political satires and pamphlets—apparently had no adverse effect on his political career bears witness to the great respect in which Marvell was held by both parties.

Despite his active public life, Marvell's fame today rests on his poetry, which was influenced by both Jonson and Donne. The deep appreciation of the beauties of the natural world and the graceful style evident in Marvell's lyrics mark their author as one of the most distinguished and highly gifted poets of the seventeenth century and one of the great English masters of lyric poetry.

Bermudas

Where the remote Bermudas ride,
In the ocean's bosom unespied,
From a small boat that rowed along,
The listening winds received this song:

"What should we do but sing His
    praise,   5
That led us through the watery maze
Unto an isle so long unknown,
And yet far kinder than our own?
Where He the huge sea monsters wracks,°
That lift the deep upon their backs;   10
He lands us on a grassy stage,
Safe from the storms' and prelates' rage.
He gave us this eternal spring
Which here enamels every thing,
And sends the fowls to us in care,   15
On daily visits through the air;
He hangs in shades the orange bright,
Like golden lamps in a green night,
And does in the pomegranates close
Jewels more rich than Ormus° shows;   20
He makes the figs our mouths to meet,
And throws the melons at our feet;
But apples° plants of such a price,
No tree could ever bear them twice;
With cedars, chosen by His hand,   25
From Lebanon, He stores the land;
And makes the hollow seas, that roar,
Proclaim the ambergris° on shore;
He cast (of which we rather boast)
The Gospel's pearl upon our coast,   30
And in these rocks for us did frame
A temple, where to sound His name.
Oh! let our voice His praise exalt,
Till it arrive at heaven's vault,
Which, thence (perhaps) rebounding, may
Echo beyond the Mexique Bay."   36

Thus sung they in the English boat,
An holy and a cheerful note;
And all the way, to guide their chime,
With falling oars they kept the time.   40

9. **wracks:** wrecks. 20. **Ormus:** Ormuz, a Portuguese seaport on the Persian Gulf, symbolic of great wealth. 23. **apples:** pineapples. 28. **ambergris:** substance used in making perfume.

The Garden

How vainly men themselves amaze°
To win the palm, the oak, or bays,
And their incessant labors see
Crowned from some single herb, or tree,
Whose short and narrow-vergèd shade   5
Does prudently° their toils upbraid;
While all flowers and all trees do close
To weave the garlands of repose!

Fair Quiet, have I found thee here,
And Innocence, thy sister dear?   10
Mistaken long, I sought you then
In busy companies of men.
Your sacred plants, if here below,
Only among the plants will grow;
Society is all but rude   15
To° this delicious solitude.

No white nor red° was ever seen
So amorous as this lovely green.
Fond lovers, cruel as their flame,
Cut in these trees their mistress' name: 20
Little, alas, they know or heed
How far these beauties hers exceed!
Fair trees, wheresoe'er your barks I
    wound,
No name shall but your own be found.

When we have run our passion's heat,
Love hither makes his best retreat.   26
The gods, that mortal beauty chase,
Still in a tree did end their race:
Apollo hunted Daphne so,
Only that she might laurel grow;   30
And Pan did after Syrinx speed,
Not as a nymph, but for a reed.°

What wondrous life is this I lead!
Ripe apples drop about my head;
The luscious clusters of the vine   35
Upon my mouth do crush their wine;

1. **amaze:** perplex. 6. **prudently:** wisely. 16. **To:** compared to. 17. **white nor red:** the white and red of a lady's complexion. 29–32. **Apollo . . . reed:** In Greek mythology, Apollo pursued Daphne and Pan pursued Syrinx. Both nymphs escaped, but Daphne was turned into a laurel bush and Syrinx into a clump of reeds.

The nectarine and curious° peach
Into my hands themselves do reach;
Stumbling on melons, as I pass,
Insnared with flowers, I fall on grass. 40

Meanwhile the mind, from pleasure less
Withdraws into its happiness;
The mind, that ocean where each kind
Does straight its own resemblance find;
Yet it creates, transcending these, 45
Far other worlds and other seas,
Annihilating all that's made
To a green thought in a green shade.

Here at the fountain's sliding foot,
Or at some fruit tree's mossy root, 50
Casting the body's vest aside,
My soul into the boughs does glide:
There, like a bird, it sits and sings,
Then whets° and combs its silver wings,
And, till prepared for longer flight, 55
Waves in its plumes the various light.

Such was that happy garden-state,
While man there walked without a mate:
After a place so pure and sweet,
What other help could yet be meet! 60
But 'twas beyond a mortal's share
To wander solitary there:
Two paradises 'twere in one
To live in paradise alone.

How well the skillful gardener drew, 65
Of flowers and herbs, this dial new;
Where, from above, the milder sun
Does through a fragrant zodiac run;
And, as it works, the industrious bee
Computes its time as well as we! 70
How could such sweet and wholesome
        hours
Be reckoned but with herbs and flowers?

37. **curious:** rare. 54. **whets:** preens.

FOR STUDY AND DISCUSSION

BERMUDAS

1. Name the two islands referred to in lines
7–8 of "Bermudas." Why is one "far kinder"
than the other? Marvell describes the kinder
isle through a series of images. To which of
the five senses do they appeal?

2. What, in line 12, does "prelates' rage"
refer to? In lines 13–14, in what sense does
spring "enamel" everything? Is the simile in
lines 17–18 an effective one? Why or why not?
What is the "Gospel's pearl" referred to in
line 30?

3. Describe the structure of "Bermudas."
Into how many parts is it divided? What is
the function of these various parts?

What is the main sentiment expressed in
this poem?

THE GARDEN

1. What is Marvell's meaning in the first
stanza of "The Garden"? How does the meaning of the second stanza follow from that of
the first? What pleasures does the poet find
in the garden? Can they be found elsewhere?
Judging from lines 15–16 and lines 61–64,
what does the poet seem to enjoy most in the
garden?

2. Note the descriptive details in stanza 5
and the extended image in stanza 7. What other
images do you find in this poem? In line 51,
what is "the body's vest"?

3. "The Garden," one of the finest examples of pastoral poetry in the English language,
is perhaps the single poem which has done
most to earn Marvell his reputation as the master poet of gardens. What atmosphere does
Marvell create in this poem? What is his attitude toward nature?

4. Compare "The Garden" with Marlowe's
"The Passionate Shepherd to His Love"
(page 92) and with Wordsworth's "Lines
Written in Early Spring" (page 450). In what
ways are these poems similar? in what ways
different? Compare the theme and tone of
these poems.

JOHN MILTON

(1608–1674)

In John Milton, poet, Puritan, and statesman, two great historical movements combined and found a single voice. Milton was a child of both Renaissance and Reformation. The Renaissance repossessed the Greek and Roman classics, seeking to strengthen its claims for the greatness and variety of human accomplishments; the Reformation, as Milton experienced it, sought to sweep away the church establishment which survived in England after King Henry VIII broke away from the Roman Catholic Church. As a Puritan, Milton believed that the individual's relation to his God was the heart of Christianity and that the individual's chief aid was the Bible, the revealed voice of God. Kings, bishops, the intricate theological disputes of the Middle Ages, officials and institutions which tried to make rules for the believer—all these had to be replaced, Milton believed, by the "upright heart and pure," the only temple acceptable to God.

Of what importance is the Renaissance to a study of Milton? The Renaissance was first of all a revival of learning, and of that learning Milton acquired an amazing command. Greek and Latin mythology, poetry and philosophy, all the testimonies to what people had been allowed under God's providence to achieve were at his fingertips. He was one of the last persons whom we may think of as having to fulfill the Renaissance ideal of universal learning. But we must emphasize the phrase "under God's providence," for eager as Milton was to acknowledge human accomplishment, whether pagan or Christian, he saw all of human history as an episode in God's management of the universe.

There are two historical difficulties to clear up before we can understand Milton, and it is most important to clear up both of them, since the explanation will help us to understand our own times as well as Milton's. One has to do with Milton's conception of humans as fallen creatures whose story he tells in *Paradise Lost;* the other involves Milton's learning and his language. Taking the latter first, it is not a question of the difficulty of the language itself: it is what Milton *believed language could do* that we must understand. In his age language was considered the instrument of God's highest gift to us, the gift which gave meaning to free will: that is, the power to reason. But in our age the belief that language, human speech, can give a unified picture of the universe and human destiny has almost disappeared. Much of our knowledge, for example, is hidden in scientific formulae which few of us understand. Much of our experience of the world comes through pictures rather than speeches, but more important than the existence of many ways of re-

_cording what is known is the fact of specialization. Today, areas of knowledge that Milton thought of as the responsibility of every learned person have slipped into the hands of specialists: medicine, astronomy, mathematics, political science, logic, psychology, history, all have become specialized; and each of these areas of knowledge in a greater or lesser degree has adopted a language of its own.

This difficulty is related to the first one. Milton thought of people as fallen creatures whose daily actions reveal them to be sinners. If we are puzzled by this idea, if the Bible story seems far from our lives, it may be necessary to remind ourselves how much a part of us it really is. Is it not true that we often feel guilty, ashamed, and fearful, often feel that we have lost an assured happiness which we are forever trying to recover? This is exactly the state of Milton's Adam and Eve after the fall. But, you may say, Milton had a single story to account for this feeling of loss, and he was sure that he could tell this story in a language that was common to all. Can we today afford to let our humanity be split up into specialized activities? Don't we have an obligation to find ways of making our common nature and our common obligations plain to everybody? If we cannot do so, we shall find it very hard to hold ourselves or other people responsible for what we do. It is clear enough that Milton, who, by explaining how we are responsible for our actions, gives us, as one critic puts it, "the gift of dignity," and is at our elbows right now, asking a question about our lives and how we justify them.

THE LIFE OF JOHN MILTON

John Milton was the son of a scrivener, not simply a copyist as the word suggests, but one who performed certain tasks—such as drawing up deeds and wills—that we now assign to lawyers. The elder Milton was an accomplished musician with a wide acquaintance among the distinguished musicians of his day, some of whom became friends of his son as well. John Milton was sent to St. Paul's School in London where most of the work centered on the study of the Latin classics, although the older boys studied Greek and even a little Hebrew. Because it was not considered the language of the learned, no one studied English. The subjects of St. Paul's curriculum were grammar, rhetoric (the art of persuasion), and logic. From St. Paul's Milton went to Cambridge University, where he took both a bachelor's and master's degree. While still a youngster he acquired a working knowledge of French and Italian. The poetry he began to write while he was at Cambridge was mostly in Latin, which he read and wrote as easily as he did English. By the time he was seventeen, Milton knew an astonishing amount about the two sources on which his poetry was to be based: the Greek and Latin classics and the Bible.

Although it was expected that he would eventually take holy orders in the Anglican Church, Milton, convinced with many another Puritan that he must be free to worship God in his own way, decided against the priesthood while still at Cambridge. Fortunately, his father was quite content to afford him the leisure to pursue a literary career. Milton therefore lived on his father's estate in the little village of Horton for the five years following his departure from Cambridge in 1632. Before leaving Cambridge Milton had written an ode, "On the Morning of Christ's Nativity," in which his greatness plainly appeared. While at Horton (or perhaps in the year before he left Cambridge) he wrote his twin poems "L'Allegro," and "Il Penseroso." "Lycidas," one of the greatest elegies in English, a lament for the death of a Cambridge friend, Edward King, was also composed at Horton. Milton also wrote two masques during the Horton period. The masque was a court entertainment, a special kind of drama in verse, danced and sung by amateurs, often with elaborate musical and scenic effects. One of these masques, *Comus,* developed the Puritan theme of the power of temperance over intemperance and was acted at Ludlow Castle in 1634. Clearly, during his years at Horton, the handsome young poet was beginning to be known.

In 1638, Milton left Horton for travel in France, Switzerland, and Italy, where he was made welcome by poets and learned men of his day. He visited Galileo, the famous scientist whose telescope and astronomical observations are mentioned in Milton's poetry. In 1639 news of political disturbance at home prevented a further trip to Sicily and Greece, and Milton returned to London, where he occupied himself for a time as tutor to his nephews and others.

In the 1640's Milton became deeply involved in the political and ecclesiastical controversy of his day. He wrote forceful pamphlets advocating reform of the English Church and joined forces with Puritans who challenged the tyranny of King Charles I. Milton's noblest prose work, *Areopagitica* (1644), a great plea for liberty of the press, was written in this period. When the Puritans assumed political power and proceeded to execute Charles I in 1649, a great French scholar, Salmasius, denounced the new regime, and Milton made his reputation international by the force and weight of the Latin pamphlets in which he replied to the charges. He was soon appointed Latin Secretary to Oliver Cromwell's Council of State, a major post since all diplomatic dispatches and state papers were written in Latin. Milton retained this important post even after he became totally blind in 1651, and had as one of his assistants the distinguished poet Andrew Marvell (see page 226).

The political power of the Puritans declined after the death of Oliver Cromwell, and in 1660 Charles II, son of Charles I, was restored to the throne. Upon the Restoration, Milton was imprisoned briefly and fined heavily for his role in the Commonwealth. When released from prison, he withdrew completely from public affairs.

During his twenty years as a statesman, Milton produced only a few sonnets in English verse. With his enforced retirement in 1660, however, he returned to poetry and, often dictating to his three daughters, spent most of the rest of his life on what proved to be his greatest works: *Paradise Lost* (1667), *Paradise Regained,* and *Samson Agonistes,* both published in 1671. In *Paradise Lost* and *Paradise Regained* Milton returned to the theme to which he had dedicated himself as a young man—people's sins against God and their attempts to regain God's grace. *Samson Agonistes,* though modeled on the form of the Greek tragedies, deals with a Biblical theme: the story of the blinded and imprisoned hero, Samson, whose fate closely paralleled Milton's own misfortunes. Of these three long works, *Paradise Lost,* with its more than ten thousand lines of magnificent blank verse, is the best-known and perhaps the greatest literary work of the Puritan period in England.

On His Having Arrived at the Age of Twenty-three

How soon hath Time, the subtle thief of youth,
Stolen on his wing my three and twentieth year!
My hasting days fly on with full career,
But my late spring no bud or blossom show'th.
Perhaps my semblance might deceive the truth,   5
That I to manhood am arrived so near,
And inward ripeness doth much less appear,
That some more timely-happy spirits endu'th.
Yet be it less or more, or soon or slow,
It shall be still° in strictest measure even   10
To that same lot, however mean or high,
Toward which Time leads me, and the will of Heaven;
All is, if I have grace to use it so,
As ever in my great Taskmaster's eye.

10. **still:** always.

On His Blindness

When I consider how my light is spent,
Ere half my days in this dark world and wide,
And that one talent° which is death to hide
Lodged with me useless, though my soul more bent
To serve therewith my Maker, and present   5
My true account, lest he returning chide,
"Doth God exact day labor, light denied?"
I fondly° ask. But Patience, to prevent
That murmur, soon replies, "God doth not need
Either man's work or his own gifts; who best   10
Bear his mild yoke, they serve him best. His state
Is kingly: thousands° at his bidding speed,
And post o'er land and ocean without rest;
They also serve who only stand and wait."

3. **one talent:** reference to the parable of the talents (Matthew 25:14–30) in which a "wicked and slothful" servant is reprimanded for hiding his one talent, or coin, in the earth instead of putting it to good use. 8. **fondly:** foolishly. 12. **thousands:** thousands of angels.

COMMENTARY

Milton stayed closer to Italian models for the sonnet than did his great predecessors, Spenser and Shakespeare. "On His Having Arrived at the Age of Twenty-three" rhymes *abba, abba, cdedce,* the rhymes of the octave (the first eight lines) being enclosed instead of alternating. Wordsworth, himself a great writer of sonnets, tells us that in Milton's hands the sonnet often became a "trumpet," and a modern Milton scholar points out that Milton does not encourage us to pause and note the relationship between the two conventional parts of the sonnet form. Milton was less concerned than earlier English poets with making a sharp distinction between octave and sestet (the final six lines). His sonnets are best thought of as "verse paragraphs." In keeping with this intention, Milton avoided the final couplet which sometimes has too mechanical a ring, even in Shakespeare, as if the writer were packing all meanings into a neat two-line bundle. Milton's sonnets roll forward toward a conclusion of the whole paragraph of poetic assertion with a power that seems irresistible.

"On His Having Arrived at the Age of Twenty-three" makes three very simple assertions. With ringing authority it relates these assertions in a fashion which prepares us for the conclusion: the situation of the soul confronted by its God. The poem begins with the biographical fact that Milton looked younger than he was at the age of twenty-three. Although it appears that he is still a youth, in years he is already a man. Yet what the world thinks and feels about this apparent contradiction is unimportant when we realize that in God's eyes Milton is being made ready for exactly that destiny which is his, "if I have grace to use it so." The quotation reminds us that hope is a Christian virtue, and Milton who (as we happen to know) was reflecting on the parable of the talents (see Matthew 25:14–30) when he wrote this poem, properly asked for grace to ful-fill the high "lot" he envisioned for himself.

In "On His Blindness," as in the conclusion of "On His Having Arrived at the Age of Twenty-three," Milton is concerned with his use of his powers or talent. But the biographical fact with which this sonnet deals has far graver significance than that referred to in the earlier sonnet. Here Milton refers to the blindness which overtook him in 1651.

Read the poem over, preferably aloud, until you feel sure that you can divide it in accordance with the divisions of its thought (example: "though my soul more bent/ To serve therewith my Maker"). There is much room for argument on this question. Make a written list of the poem's divisions as you see them.

FOR STUDY AND DISCUSSION

ON HIS HAVING ARRIVED

1. This sonnet moves from an external and conventional account of the meaning of time to its special significance to Milton in the light of the parable of the talents. Describe this movement in your own words.

2. Who are the "more timely-happy spirits" described in line 8?

3. Milton's writing is sometimes very compressed. Line 13 of this sonnet opens with "All is." How might these two words be paraphrased? Construct an argument to support your answer. The problem is a real one, for scholars are not sure of the correct answer.

ON HIS BLINDNESS

1. In "On His Blindness," in what two senses is the word *talent* employed? Is Milton's talent in fact useless? Why is it "death" to hide it?

2. In "On His Having Arrived" Milton reports a biographical fact which points up a discrepancy between an appearance and a reality. A parallel situation is pointed out in "On His Blindness." What is it?

3. Do you think the word *wait* in the famous last line of "On His Blindness" suggests mere submission to the fact that God has ordained Milton's blindness? Explain.

4. What puns, or implications of punning, can you find in "On His Blindness"?

L'Allegro AND Il Penseroso

It is thought that "L'Allegro" and "Il Penseroso" may have been planned as a re-working of one of Milton's academic assignments at Cambridge University: a comparison, in Latin, of the pleasures of night and day. Such attempts to bring all powers of rhetoric to bear on both sides of a case were, in Milton's day, an important part of the university curriculum. The Italian title of the first poem, which means "the cheerful man," suggests companionability too. "Il Penseroso" refers to the thoughtful or contemplative man, who, by a tradition extending as far back as the Greek philosopher Aristotle, searches out the truth of things. Milton's appeal to "Melancholy," therefore, does not mean that he wishes to be gloomy; it simply refers to those subdued pleasures appropriate to the student and seeker after knowledge.

L'Allegro

Hence, loathèd Melancholy,
  Of Cerberus° and blackest Midnight born,
In Stygian° cave forlorn
  'Mongst horrid shapes, and shrieks, and sights unholy,
Find out some uncouth° cell,   5
  Where brooding darkness spreads his jealous wings,
And the night raven sings;
  There under ebon° shades and low-browed rocks,
As ragged as thy locks,
  In dark Cimmerian° desert ever dwell.
But come, thou Goddess fair and free,   11
In heaven yclept° Euphrosyne,°
And by men, heart-easing Mirth,
Whom lovely Venus, at a birth,
With two sister Graces more,   15
To ivy-crownèd Bacchus° bore;
Or whether (as some sager sing)
The frolic wind that breathes the spring,

Zephyr,° with Aurora° playing,
As he met her once a-Maying,   20
There on beds of violets blue,
And fresh-blown roses washed in dew,
Filled her with thee, a daughter fair,
So buxom, blithe, and debonair.
Haste thee, Nymph, and bring with thee
Jest and youthful Jollity,   26
Quips and Cranks° and wanton Wiles,
Nods, and Becks, and wreathèd Smiles,
Such as hang on Hebe's° cheek,
And love to live in dimple sleek;   30
Sport that wrinkled Care derides,
And Laughter holding both his sides.
Come, and trip it as ye go
On the light fantastic toe,
And in thy right hand lead with thee   35
The mountain nymph, sweet Liberty;
And if I give thee honor due,
Mirth, admit me of thy crew,
To live with her, and live with thee,
In unreprovèd° pleasures free;   40
To hear the lark begin his flight,
And singing startle the dull night,
From his watchtower in the skies,
Till the dappled dawn doth rise;
Then to come, in spite of sorrow,   45
And at my window bid good-morrow,
Through the sweetbriar, or the vine,
Or the twisted eglantine;
While the cock, with lively din,
Scatters the rear of darkness thin,   50

---

2. **Cerberus** (sûr′bər·əs): in classical mythology, the three-headed dog guarding the portals of Hades. 3. **Stygian** (stij′ē·ən): referring to the Styx, one of the five rivers surrounding Hades; infernal, dark, and gloomy. 5. **uncouth**: strange, unknown. 8. **ebon**: black. 10. **Cimmerian** (si·mir′ē·ən): a mythical people in Homer's *Odyssey* who are described as living in perpetual darkness; densely dark and gloomy. 12. **yclept**: called. **Euphrosyne** (yōō·fros′ə·nē): one of three sister goddesses who conferred beauty, charm, and joy on humans and nature. 16. **Bacchus** (bak′əs): god of wine and revelry.

19. **Zephyr** (zef′ər): the west wind. **Aurora** (ô·rôr′ə): goddess of the dawn. 27. **Cranks**: twists or turns in speech. 29. **Hebe** (hē′bē): cupbearer to the Greek gods. 40. **unreprovèd**: not deserving of censure.

And to the stack or the barn door
Stoutly struts his dames before;
Oft listening how the hounds and horn
Cheerly rouse the slumbering morn,
From the side of some hoar hill,   55
Through the high wood echoing shrill:
Sometime walking, not unseen,
By hedgerow elms, on hillocks green,
Right against the eastern gate,
Where the great sun begins his state,°   60
Robed in flames and amber light,
The clouds in thousand liveries dight;°
While the ploughman, near at hand,
Whistles o'er the furrowed land,
And the milkmaid singeth blithe,   65
And the mower whets his scythe,
And every shepherd tells his tale°
Under the hawthorn in the dale.
Straight mine eye hath caught new pleasures,
Whilst the lantskip° round it measures: 70
Russet lawns and fallows gray,
Where the nibbling flocks do stray,
Mountains on whose barren breast
The laboring clouds do often rest,
Meadows trim with daisies pied,°   75
Shallow brooks and rivers wide;
Towers and battlements it sees
Bosomed high in tufted trees,
Where perhaps some beauty lies,
The cynosure° of neighboring eyes.   80
Hard by, a cottage chimney smokes
From betwixt two aged oaks,
Where Corydon and Thyrsis° met
Are at their savory dinner set
Of herbs and other country messes,°   85
Which the neat-handed Phillis dresses;
And then in haste her bower she leaves,
With Thestylis to bind the sheaves;
Or if the earlier season lead,
To the tanned haycock in the mead.   90
Sometimes with secure delight
The upland hamlets will invite,

When the merry bells ring round,
And the jocund rebecks° sound
To many a youth and many a maid   95
Dancing in the chequered shade;
And young and old come forth to play
On a sunshine holiday,
Till the livelong daylight fail:
Then to the spicy nut-brown ale,   100
With stories told of many a feat,
How fairy Mab° the junkets° eat;
She was pinched and pulled, she said,
And he,° by friar's lantern° led,
Tells how the drudging goblin° sweat   105
To earn his cream bowl duly set,
When in one night, ere glimpse of morn,
His shadowy flail hath threshed the corn
That ten day laborers could not end;
Then lies him down the lubber fiend,°   110
And stretched out all the chimney's length,
Basks at the fire his hairy strength;
And crop-full out of doors he flings,
Ere the first cock his matin° rings.   114
Thus done the tales, to bed they creep,
By whispering winds soon lulled asleep.
Towered cities please us then,
And the busy hum of men,
Where throngs of knights and barons bold
In weeds° of peace high triumphs° hold,
With store of ladies, whose bright eyes   121
Rain influence,° and judge the prize
Of wit or arms, while both contend
To win her grace whom all commend.
There let Hymen° oft appear   125
In saffron robe, with taper clear,

94. **jocund rebecks** (jok'ənd rē'beks): merry violins. 102. **fairy Mab**: probably a fairy of Welsh folklore. (A famous description of how she causes dreams occurs in *Romeo and Juliet*, Act I, Scene iv.) **junkets**: delicate sweetmeats, often made of curdled milk. 103–04. **She, he**: two of the storytellers. **friar's lantern**: "will-o'-the-wisp," a dancing light on marshy ground, supposed to lead travelers astray. 105. **drudging goblin**: Robin Goodfellow, Puck, who supposedly did chores at night to earn the food put out for him. 110. **lubber fiend**: awkward sprite. 114. **matin**: a morning song, or call to early prayers. 120. **weeds**: garments. **triumphs**: public shows or pageants. 121–22. **whose . . . influence**: The stars were once thought to affect human action; hence, the bright eyes of the ladies are compared to stars. 125. **Hymen** (hī'mən): Greek god of marriage. The smoking of his torch or taper was considered a bad omen; hence, *with taper clear* (line 126) signifies a happy marriage.

60. **state**: stately progress. 62. **dight**: dressed. 67. **tells his tale**: counts his sheep. 70. **lantskip**: landscape. 75. **pied** (pīd): having two or more colors. 80. **cynosure** (sī'nə·shŏŏr): the center of attention. 83. **Corydon** (kôr'ə·dən) **and Thyrsis** (thûr'səs): conventional names for rustics or shepherds in pastoral poetry, as *Phillis* and *Thestylis* (thes'ti·lis), in lines 86 and 88, are for country maidens. 85. **messes**: dishes.

And pomp, and feast, and revelry,
With masque and antique pageantry;
Such sights as youthful poets dream
On summer eves by haunted stream.   130
Then to the well-trod stage anon,
If Jonson's learnèd sock° be on,
Or sweetest Shakespeare, Fancy's child,
Warble his native wood-notes wild;°
And ever against eating cares,   135
Lap me in soft Lydian airs,°
Married to immortal verse,
Such as the meeting° soul may pierce°
In notes with many a winding bout°
Of linkèd sweetness long drawn out,   140
With wanton heed and giddy cunning,
The melting voice through mazes running,
Untwisting all the chains that tie
The hidden soul of harmony;   144
That Orpheus°self may heave his head
From golden slumber on a bed
Of heaped Elysian flowers, and hear
Such strains as would have won the ear
Of Pluto, to have quite set free
His half-regained Eurydice.   150
These delights if thou canst give,
Mirth, with thee I mean to live.

Il Penseroso

Hence, vain deluding Joys,
    The brood of Folly without father bred,
How little you bestead,°   ⟩
    Or fill the fixèd mind with all your toys;°
Dwell in some idle brain,   5
    And fancies fond° with gaudy shapes
        possess,

As thick and numberless
    As the gay motes that people the sun-
        beams,
Or likest hovering dreams,
    The fickle pensioners of Morpheus'°
        train.   10
But hail, thou Goddess sage and holy,
Hail, divinest Melancholy,
Whose saintly visage is too bright
To hit the sense of human sight,
And therefore to our weaker view   15
O'erlaid with black, staid Wisdom's hue;
Black, but such as in esteem
Prince Memnon's° sister might beseem,
Or that starred Ethiop queen° that strove
To set her beauty's praise above   20
The sea nymphs, and their powers
    offended.
Yet thou art higher far descended:
Thee bright-haired Vesta° long of yore
To solitary Saturn° bore;
His daughter she (in Saturn's reign   25
Such mixture was not held a stain),
Oft in glimmering bowers and glades
He met her, and in secret shades
Of woody Ida's° inmost grove,
While yet there was no fear of Jove.°   30
Come, pensive Nun, devout and pure,
Sober, steadfast, and demure,
All in a robe of darkest grain,°
Flowing with majestic train,
And sable stole of cypress lawn°   35
Over thy decent shoulders drawn.
Come, but keep thy wonted state,°
With even step and musing gait,
And looks commercing° with the skies,

---

132. **sock:** the symbol of comedy, as the buskin or
boot is of tragedy. 134. **native . . . wild:** implying
that Shakespeare's verse is as natural as the singing
of a bird, in contrast to the more "learnèd" poetry of
Ben Jonson. 136. **Lydian** (lid′ē·ən) **airs:** delicate,
soft melodies. 138. **meeting:** responsive. **pierce:**
comprehend. 139. **bout:** a musical "run," or passage. 145. **Orpheus** (ôr′fē·əs): the most famous musician of Greek mythology, who persuaded Pluto,
king of the dead, to release his dead wife, *Eurydice*
(yo͞o·rid′ə·sē), from the underworld. His wish was
granted on condition that Orpheus not look back at
Eurydice while leading her to the upper world. When
he forgot himself at the last minute, he lost her completely.
IL PENSEROSO: 3. **bestead:** help. 4. **toys:** trifles.
6. **fond:** foolish.

10. **Morpheus** (môr′fē·əs): the Greek god of
dreams. 18. **Prince Memnon:** in Greek legend,
a handsome king of the Ethiopians who fought in
the Trojan War. 19. **Ethiop queen:** When Cassi-
opeia, wife of the Ethiopian king Cepheus, boasted
that her daughter Andromeda was more beautiful
than the sea nymphs, she was changed into a constellation. 23. **Vesta:** Roman goddess of the hearth
and daughter of Saturn. 24. **Saturn:** father of Jove
and Roman god of agriculture whose reign (see line
25) was considered a golden age. 29. **Ida:** a mountain in Crete where, hidden from his father, Jove was
born and raised. 30. **Jove:** Jupiter, king of the gods,
believed to have overthrown Saturn, his father.
33. **grain:** dye. 35. **sable . . . lawn:** black veil of
crepe. 37. **state:** dignity. 39. **commercing:** com-
muning.

Thy rapt soul sitting in thine eyes;   40
There held in holy passion still,
Forget thyself to marble,° till
With a sad° leaden downward cast
Thou fix them on the earth as fast.   44
And join with thee calm Peace and Quiet,
Spare° Fast, that oft with gods doth diet,
And hears the Muses in a ring
Aye round about Jove's altar sing;
And add to these retired Leisure,
That in trim gardens takes his pleasure;   50
But first, and chiefest, with thee bring
Him that yon soars on golden wing,
Guiding the fiery-wheelèd throne,
The cherub Contemplation;
And the mute Silence hist along,   55
'Less Philomel° will deign a song,
In her sweetest, saddest plight,°
Smoothing the rugged brow of Night,
While Cynthia° checks her dragon yoke
Gently o'er the accustomed oak.   60
Sweet bird, that shunn'st the noise of folly,
Most musical, most melancholy!
Thee, chauntress,° oft the woods among
I woo to hear thy evensong;
And missing thee, I walk unseen   65
On the dry smooth-shaven green,
To behold the wandering moon,
Riding near her highest noon,
Like one that had been led astray   69
Through the heaven's wide pathless way;
And oft, as if her head she bowed,
Stooping through a fleecy cloud.
Oft on a plat of rising ground
I hear the far-off curfew sound
Over some wide-watered shore,   75
Swinging slow with sullen roar;
Or if the air will not permit,
Some still removèd place will fit.
Where glowing embers through the room
Teach light to counterfeit a gloom,   80
Far from all resort of mirth,
Save the cricket on the hearth,

Or the bellman's° drowsy charm,
To bless the doors from nightly harm.
Or let my lamp at midnight hour   85
Be seen in some high lonely tower,
Where I may oft outwatch the Bear,°
With thrice-great Hermes,° or unsphere°
The spirit of Plato to unfold
What worlds or what vast regions hold   90
The immortal mind that hath forsook
Her mansion in this fleshly nook;
And of those daemons° that are found
In fire, air, flood, or under ground,
Whose power hath a true consent°   95
With planet or with element.
Sometime let gorgeous Tragedy
In sceptered pall come sweeping by,
Presenting Thebes, or Pelops' line,
Or the tale of Troy° divine.   100
Or what (though rare) of later age
Ennobled hath the buskined stage.°
But, O sad Virgin, that thy power
Might raise Musaeus° from his bower,
Or bid the soul of Orpheus° sing   105
Such notes as, warbled to the string,
Drew iron tears down Pluto's cheek,
And made Hell grant what love did seek;
Or call up him that left half told°
The story of Cambuscan bold,   110
Of Camball, and of Algarsife,
And who had Canace to wife,
That owned the virtuous ring and glass,
And of the wondrous horse of brass,
On which the Tartar king did ride;   115
And if aught else great bards beside

83. **bellman:** a night watchman who called the hours.   87. **outwatch ... Bear:** to stay awake all night (the constellation of the Bear never sets). 88. **thrice-great Hermes:** Hermes Trismegistus, (thrice-great), the Greek name for an Egyptian god regarded as the founder of alchemy, astrology, and other occult sciences.   **unsphere:** call down to earth from his heavenly sphere.   93. **daemons:** According to Plato, there were four elements: earth, water, air, fire. Later philosophers thought each element had its own presiding spirit, or "demon." 95. **consent:** harmony.   99–100. **Thebes** (thēbz), **Pelops** (pē'lops), **Troy:** subjects of Greek tragedies. 102. **buskined stage:** Buskins were high boots worn by actors of ancient Greece as a symbol of tragedy. The sock was a symbol of comedy.   104. **Musaeus** (mū·zē'əs): a poet in Greek mythology.   105. **soul of Orpheus:** See note for line 145, page 236. 109. **him ... told:** Chaucer never finished the Squire's Tale, a story described in the next few lines.

42. **Forget ... marble:** become so completely engrossed in thought that you seem like a marble statue. 43. **sad:** serious.   46. **Spare:** lean (adjective). 56. **Philomel** (fil'ə·mel): the poetic name for nightingale; from Greek mythology.   57. **plight:** mood. 59. **Cynthia:** Diana, the moon goddess, whose chariot was drawn by dragons, and to whom the oak was sacred.   63. **chauntress** (chôn'tres): a singer.

In sage and solemn tunes have sung,
Of tourneys and of trophies hung,
Of forests and enchantments drear, 119
Where more is meant than meets the ear,
Thus, Night, oft see me in thy pale career,
Till civil-suited° Morn appear,
Not tricked and frounced° as she was wont
With the Attic boy° to hunt,
But kerchieft in a comely cloud, 125
While rocking winds are piping loud,
Or ushered with a shower still,
When the gust hath blown his fill,
Ending on the rustling leaves,
With minute drops from off the eaves. 130
And when the sun begins to fling
His flaring beams, me, Goddess, bring
To archèd walks of twilight groves,
And shadows brown that Sylvan° loves,
Of pine or monumental oak, 135
Where the rude ax with heavèd stroke
Was never heard the nymphs to daunt,
Or fright them from their hallowed haunt.
There in close covert by some brook,
Where no profaner eye may look, 140
Hide me from day's garish eye,
While the bee with honied thigh,
That at her flowery work doth sing,
And the waters murmuring
With such consort as they keep, 145
Entice the dewy-feathered Sleep;
And let some strange mysterious dream
Wave at his wings in airy stream
Of lively portraiture displayed,
Softly on my eyelids laid. 150
And as I wake, sweet music breathe
Above, about, or underneath,
Sent by some spirit to mortals good,
Or the unseen Genius of the wood.°
But let my due feet never fail 155
To walk the studious cloister's pale,°
And love the high embowèd roof,
With antic° pillars massy proof,°

122. **civil-suited:** in the sober garb of a citizen.
123. **tricked and frounced:** dressed in gay robes,
probably with hair curled.   124. **Attic boy:** Cephalus
(sef′ə·ləs), a young huntsman of Attica, beloved by
Aurora, the dawn.   134. **Sylvan:** Sylvanus (sil·vā′
nəs), god of the woodlands.   154. **Genius . . . wood:**
the ancient Greeks believed that a benign deity dwelt
in every grove.   156. **pale:** boundary.   158. **antic:**
ornamented. **massy proof:** able to bear the weight
they support.

And storied windows richly dight,°
Casting a dim religious light. 160
There let the pealing organ blow
To the full-voiced quire below,
In service high and anthems clear,
As may with sweetness, through mine ear,
Dissolve me into ecstasies, 165
And bring all Heaven before mine eyes.
And may at last my weary age
Find out the peaceful hermitage,
The hairy gown and mossy cell,
Where I may sit and rightly spell° 170
Of every star that heaven doth show,
And every herb that sips the dew,
Till old experience do attain
To something like prophetic strain.
These pleasures, Melancholy, give, 175
And I with thee will choose to live.

159. **storied . . . dight:** richly colored stained-glass
windows which depict Bible stories.   170. **spell:**
learn the meaning by study.

COMMENTARY

MILTON'S METRICAL SKILL

The first ten lines of "L'Allegro" seem
to be a burlesque of the elaborate mythology of such Latin poets as Ovid. The delicate gaiety of the octosyllabic couplets
which follow represents a complete
change, not simply of meter, but of tone,
as you will discover as you read aloud the
first twenty-four lines of the poem. The
danger of the octosyllabic couplet used
in both "L'Allegro" and "Il Penseroso" is
that it will fall into a rocking-horse or
singsong rhythm. Milton avoids this effect, apparently without effort, but of
course he is actually writing with supreme
care. Reread lines 31–44 of "L'Allegro."

"Sport that wrinkled Care derides,
And Laughter holding both his sides.
Come and trip it as ye go
On the light fantastic toe,
And in thy right hand lead with thee
The mountain nymph, sweet Liberty;
And if I give thee honor due,
Mirth, admit me of thy crew,

To live with her, and live with thee,
In unreprovèd pleasures free;
To hear the lark begin his flight,
And singing startle the dull night,
From his watchtower in the skies,
Till the dappled dawn doth rise . . ."

In these lines the emphases fall in a way you can easily work out: in the first line it is on the first personification used in the poem, *Sport;* in the next line it is on the personified *Laughter,* after an initial light syllable. The third line has no such heavy emphases: two lighter emphases are dictated by the movement of the meaning; they fall on the word *Come,* and on the phrase *and trip it.* In the following line the chief emphasis is unmistakably on the word *fantastic.* Now, although Milton sometimes omits a light syllable (as in the lines beginning with *Sport* and *Mirth),* the lines quoted read like regular octosyllabics. The effect of regular meter is of course enforced by the rhyming couplets. So the emphases pointed to above form a kind of counterpoint, one set of rhythms beating against another. Since we are not poets like Milton, we cannot quite give a recipe for this effect, but we may be grateful for the rippling fun in a verse form which in most hands sounds like the ticking of a metronome.

PERSONIFICATION

The lines quoted above also offer an illustration of a device common to Milton and his age; that is, personification. Here we have personifications of states, such as *Laughter, Care, Mirth;* of an occupation, *Sport;* of a principle, *Liberty.* Milton was brilliant at personification. There is a marvelously economical one here: "Laughter holding both his sides." Is *dull night* in line 43 of "L'Allegro" still another personification? Make a list of all the personifications in "L'Allegro."

What should be especially noticed and remembered is that in using personification, Milton referred to things understood by all his readers by virtue of their common experience as human beings. Milton thought of his humanity as common to all men and hardly likely to change. And, just as to Milton Mirth and Melancholy had the same meaning for all, so also when Milton turned to the Bible or to the classics for personification and allusions, he simply referred to what, to him, were the best and most accurate terms he could use. To Milton, the Bible and the classics, two sources of knowledge considered specialized today, were without question among the things one had to know in order to understand human nature and destiny.

FOR STUDY AND DISCUSSION

1. In "L'Allegro," the first of the pleasures of the cheerful man is watching the sunrise. What are the rest? Why do you think they are presented in this particular order?

2. In line 42 of "L'Allegro," sound is described as affecting darkness. Lines 49–50 are an example of the same figurative device. What effect do they have on the reader?

3. The last and highest of the pleasures in "L'Allegro" is poetry akin to "Lydian airs" (line 136). How do the comparisons in lines 139–44 suggest that poetry has both a form that holds it together *and* a burden of strong feeling? Begin your analysis with the phrases "wanton heed" and "giddy cunning."

4. Compare the section of "L'Allegro" ending with line 24 with the corresponding section of "Il Penseroso" ending with line 36. What parallels and deliberate contrasts do you find?

5. Do the "vain deluding Joys" condemned in "Il Penseroso" (lines 1–10) represent the same kind of joy described in "L'Allegro"? Is the "loathèd Melancholy" banished in "L'Allegro" (lines 1–10) the same kind of melancholy described in "Il Penseroso"? In answering, cite specific lines in the poems.

6. The highest pleasure offered by Mirth is matched by what reward offered by Melancholy?

7. Make two parallel columns and compare the resemblances and differences of the two poems on the following points: (a) the character of the cheerful and the pensive person; (b) time of day and the period of human life covered; (c) companions chosen; (d) references to objects in nature—birds, heavenly bodies, sounds, others; (e) references to literature and music.

Paradise Lost

Before deciding to write an epic poem on the human fall, Milton had considered and rejected many other projects for long works, including a poem on the legends of King Arthur. He also sketched a drama on the fall, "Adam Unparadised," but gave it up, perhaps because the span of the action of a tragedy was customarily limited to a single day. The great epic models of the day were Homer and Virgil, and Milton followed their pattern in many ways. (Staging a battle in Heaven, beginning his action in the middle—*in medias res*—and then telling the earlier part of the story through the reminiscences of his characters, furnishing an elaborate catalogue of the princes among the fallen angels, are a few of these.) But the first few lines of *Paradise Lost* make us aware that the Book of Genesis is the controlling source of the poem. Here, as elsewhere in Milton, the broad reaches of classical tradition are subordinated to the Christian story, and are even more sharply limited by Milton's focus on what happens within the single mind. The very heart of the poem, is, after all, Adam's decision—that crucial misuse of reason and free will which explains the history of all humankind to come. Aside from that action, Milton's agents are necessarily Satan and "the greater Man," He who redeems us from the consequences of Adam's act.

Two selections from *Paradise Lost* follow. The first selection is from Book I, the opening of the poem. After stating his subject and invoking a Heavenly Muse, who may inspire him to deal with matters higher than those of classical epic, Milton tells of the situation of the fallen angels, what they first feel and how they first act in Hell. Generations of readers have found the most interesting character of Milton's poem to be Satan. The Romantics, who had a taste for lonely rebels, called Satan the "hero" of the poem. But Milton's largest intention is far from this. To "justify the ways of God to men" is not to apologize, but to make very plain to each reader how fatal, how irretrievable, are human actions—humans, who are mortal, who have but one chance to follow the right path. Satan is secondary because he can never finally win or lose.

> Of man's first disobedience, and the fruit
> Of that forbidden tree, whose mortal taste
> Brought death into the world, and all our woe,
> With loss of Eden, till one greater Man°
> Restore us, and regain the blissful seat,   5
> Sing, Heavenly Muse,° that on the secret° top
> Of Oreb, or of Sinai,° didst inspire
> That shepherd, who first taught the chosen seed
> In the beginning how the Heavens and Earth
> Rose out of Chaos;° or if Sion hill°   10

4. **one . . . Man:** Christ.   6. **Heavenly Muse:** Milton invokes Urania, the muse of astronomy and sacred poetry, to help him compose his great epic. Milton associates her with the divine spirit that inspired "that shepherd," Moses, who received the word of God and interpreted it for the Hebrews, "the chosen seed."   **secret:** remote, mysterious.   7. **Oreb . . . Sinai:** Horeb (hŭ′reb) and Sinai (sī′nī) alternate names for the mountain on which God gave Moses the law. 9–10. **In . . . Chaos:** The first five books of the Bible are ascribed to Moses.   10. **Sion hill:** one of the hills of Jerusalem on which the temple was built.

Delight thee more, and Siloa's brook° that flowed
Fast by the oracle of God, I thence
Invoke thy aid to my adventurous song,
That with no middle flight intends to soar
Above the Aonian mount,° while it pursues   15
Things unattempted yet in prose or rhyme.
And chiefly thou, O Spirit,° that dost prefer
Before all temples the upright heart and pure,
Instruct me, for thou know'st; thou from the first
Wast present, and with mighty wings outspread   20
Dovelike sat'st brooding on the vast abyss
And mad'st it pregnant: what in me is dark
Illumine, what is low raise and support;
That to the highth° of this great argument
I may assert Eternal Providence,   25
And justify the ways of God to men.
        Say first, for Heaven hides nothing from thy view,
Nor the deep tract of Hell, say first what cause
Moved our grand° parents in that happy state,
Favored of Heaven so highly, to fall off   30
From their Creator, and transgress his will
For one restraint,° lords of the world besides?
Who first seduced them to that foul revolt?
The infernal Serpent; he it was, whose guile,
Stirred up with envy and revenge, deceived   35
The mother of mankind, what time his pride
Had cast him out from Heaven, with all his host
Of rebel angels, by whose aid aspiring
To set himself in glory above his peers,
He trusted to have equaled the Most High,   40
If he opposed; and with ambitious aim
Against the throne and monarchy of God,
Raised impious war in Heaven and battle proud
With vain attempt. Him the Almighty Power
Hurled headlong flaming from the ethereal sky   45
With hideous ruin and combustion down
To bottomless perdition, there to dwell
In adamantine° chains and penal fire,
Who durst defy the Omnipotent to arms.
Nine times the space that measures day and night   50
To mortal men, he with his horrid crew
Lay vanquished, rolling in the fiery gulf,
Confounded though immortal. But his doom
Reserved him to more wrath; for now the thought

11. **Siloa's brook:** a stream near Sion Hill where stood the temple, "the oracle of God."
15. **Aonian mount:** Mount Helicon in Greek mythology, home of the classic muses. Milton
refers to his intention of writing on a theme greater than Greek poetry had attempted.
17. **Spirit:** divine inspiration. 24. **highth:** height. 29. **grand:** first. 32. **one restraint:** that
they should not eat of the fruit of the tree of knowledge. 48. **adamantine:** unbreakable, hard
as a diamond.

Both of lost happiness and lasting pain   55
Torments him; round he throws his baleful eyes,
That witnessed° huge affliction and dismay
Mixed with obdúrate pride and steadfast hate.
At once as far as angels ken° he views
The dismal situation waste and wild: 60
A dungeon horrible on all sides round
As one great furnace flamed, yet from those flames
No light, but rather darkness visible
Served only to discover sights of woe,
Regions of sorrow, doleful shades, where peace   65
And rest can never dwell, hope never comes
That comes to all; but torture without end
Still urges,° and a fiery deluge, fed
With everburning sulphur unconsumed:
Such place Eternal Justice had prepared   70
For those rebellious, here their prison ordained
In utter darkness, and their portion set
As far removed from God and light of Heaven
As from the center thrice to the utmost pole.°
O how unlike the place from whence they fell!   75
There the companions of his fall, o'erwhelmed
With floods and whirlwinds of tempestuous fire,
He soon discerns, and weltering by his side
One next himself in power, and next in crime,
Long after known in Palestine, and named   80
Beelzebub.° To whom the Archenemy,
And thence in Heaven called Satan, with bold words
Breaking the horrid silence thus began:
    "If thou beest he—but O how fallen! how changed
From him, who in the happy realms of light   85
Clothed with transcendent brightness didst outshine
Myriads though bright—if he whom mutual league,
United thoughts and counsels, equal hope
And hazard in the glorious enterprise,
Joined with me once, now misery hath joined   90
In equal ruin: into what pit thou seest
From what height fallen! so much the stronger proved
He with his thunder; and till then who knew
The force of those dire arms? Yet not for those,
Nor what the potent Victor in his rage   95
Can else inflict, do I repent or change,
Though changed in outward luster, that fixed mind
And high disdain, from sense of injured merit,
That with the Mightiest raised me to contend,
And to the fierce contention brought along   100

57. **witnessed:** gave evidence of.   59. **ken:** sight.   68. **Still urges:** always presses, afflicts.
74. **center . . . pole:** three times the distance from the earth (center) to the furthest point in the
universe.   81. **Beelzebub** (bē·el'zə·bub): The name given in this poem to the fallen angel next
in command to Satan. In other connections, the name is often used interchangeably with that
of Satan.

Innumerable force of spirits armed
That durst dislike his reign, and, me preferring,
His utmost power with adverse power opposed
In dubious battle on the plains of Heaven,
And shook his throne. What though the field be lost? 105
All is not lost; the unconquerable will,
And study of revenge, immortal hate,
And courage never to submit or yield:
And what is else not to be overcome?
That glory never shall his wrath or might 110
Extort from me. To bow and sue for grace
With suppliant knee, and deify his power
Who from the terror of this arm so late
Doubted° his empire, that were low indeed,
That were an ignominy and shame beneath 115
This downfall; since by fate the strength of gods
And this empyreal substance° cannot fail,
Since through experience of this great event,
In arms not worse, in foresight much advanced,
We may with more successful hope resolve 120
To wage by force or guile eternal war
Irreconcilable to our grand Foe,
Who now triumphs, and in the excess of joy
Sole reigning holds the tyranny of Heaven."
   So spake the apostate Angel, though in pain, 125
Vaunting aloud, but racked with deep despair;
And him thus answered soon his bold compeer:°
   "O Prince, O Chief of many thronèd Powers,
That led the embattled Seraphim° to war
Under thy conduct, and in dreadful deeds 130
Fearless, endangered Heaven's perpetual King,
And put to proof his high supremacy,
Whether upheld by strength, or chance, or fate;
Too well I see and rue the dire event,
That with sad overthrow and foul defeat 135
Hath lost us Heaven, and all this mighty host
In horrible destruction laid thus low,
As far as gods and heavenly essences
Can perish: for the mind and spirit remains
Invincible, and vigor soon returns, 140
Though all our glory extinct, and happy state
Here swallowed up in endless misery.
But what if he our Conqueror (whom I now
Of force believe almighty, since no less
Than such could have o'erpowered such force as ours) 145
Have left us this our spirit and strength entire
Strongly to suffer and support our pains,

---

114. **Doubted:** feared for.   117. **empyreal substance:** Heaven, the empyrean, and its inhabitants were composed of an indestructible substance.   127. **compeer:** companion, equal.
129. **Seraphim** (ser′ə·fim): angels of the highest rank.

That we may so suffice his vengeful ire,
Or do him mightier service as his thralls
By right of war, whate'er his business be,   150
Here in the heart of Hell to work in fire,
Or do his errands in the gloomy deep?
What can it then avail, though yet we feel
Strength undiminished, or eternal being
To undergo eternal punishment?"   155
    Whereto with speedy words the Archfiend replied:
"Fallen Cherub, to be weak is miserable,
Doing or suffering:° but of this be sure,
To do aught good never will be our task,
But ever to do ill our sole delight,   160
As being the contrary to his high will
Whom we resist. If then his providence
Out of our evil seek to bring forth good,
Our labor must be to pervert that end,
And out of good still° to find means of evil;   165
Which ofttimes may succeed, so as perhaps
Shall grieve him, if I fail° not, and disturb
His inmost counsels from their destined aim.
But see the angry Victor hath recalled
His ministers of vengeance and pursuit   170
Back to the gates of Heaven; the sulphurous hail
Shot after us in storm, o'erblown hath laid
The fiery surge, that from the precipice
Of Heaven received us falling, and the thunder,
Winged with red lightning and impetuous rage,   175
Perhaps hath spent his shafts, and ceases now
To bellow through the vast and boundless deep.
Let us not slip° the occasion, whether scorn
Or satiate° fury yield it from our Foe.
Seest thou yon dreary plain, forlorn and wild,   180
The seat of desolation, void of light,
Save what the glimmering of these livid flames
Casts pale and dreadful? Thither let us tend
From off the tossing of these fiery waves,
There rest, if any rest can harbor there,   185
And reassembling our afflicted powers,°
Consult how we may henceforth most offend
Our Enemy, our own loss how repair,
How overcome this dire calamity,
What reinforcement we may gain from hope,   190
If not, what resolution from despair."
    Thus Satan talking to his nearest mate
With head uplift above the wave, and eyes
That sparkling blazed; his other parts besides,

---

158. **Doing or suffering:** whether active or passive. 165. **still:** always. 167. **fail:** mistake.
178. **slip:** lose. 179. **satiate** (sā′shē·āt): satisfied. 186. **afflicted powers:** overthrown forces.

Prone on the flood, extended long and large, 195
Lay floating many a rood,° in bulk as huge
As whom the fables name of monstrous size,
Titanian or Earthborn, that warred on Jove,
Briareos or Typhon,° whom the den
By ancient Tarsus held, or that seabeast 200
Leviathan,° which God of all his works
Created hugest that swim the ocean stream:
Him haply slumbering on the Norway foam,
The pilot of some small night-foundered skiff,
Deeming some island, off, as seamen tell, 205
With fixed anchor in his scaly rind
Moors by his side under the lee, while night
Invests the sea, and wishèd morn delays:
So stretched out huge in length the Archfiend lay
Chained on the burning lake; nor ever thence 210
Had risen or heaved his head, but that the will
And high permission of all-ruling Heaven
Left him at large to his own dark designs,
That with reiterated crimes he might
Heap on himself damnation, while he sought 215
Evil to others, and enraged might see
How all his malice served but to bring forth
Infinite goodness, grace and mercy shown
On man by him seduced, but on himself
Treble confusion, wrath and vengeance poured. 220
   Forthwith upright he rears from off the pool
His mighty stature; on each hand the flames
Driven backward slope their pointing spires, and rolled
In billows, leave in the midst a horrid vale.
Then with expanded wings he steers his flight 225
Aloft, incumbent° on the dusky air
That felt unusual weight, till on dry land
He lights, if it were land that ever burned
With solid, as the lake with liquid fire;
And such appeared in hue, as when the force 230
Of subterranean wind transports a hill
Torn from Pelorus,° or the shattered side
Of thundering Etna, whose combustible
And fueled entrails thence conceiving fire,
Sublimed° with mineral fury, aid the winds, 235
And leave a singèd bottom all involved°

---

196. **rood:** Milton conceived of the angels as being enormous in size. A rood is equal to seven or eight yards.   198–99. **Titanian . . . Typhon:** the Titans and Giants ("Earthborn") were often confused. Briareos (brī·ar′ē·əs), also called Briareus, was a hundred-handed giant who helped Zeus (Jove) defeat the Titans. Typhon (tī′fən), a son of Earth, was a hundred-headed serpent monster from Cilicia (sə·lish′ə), near Tarsus, who attacked heaven and was imprisoned by Zeus.   201. **Leviathan** (lə·vī′ə·thən): a sea monster.   226. **incumbent:** lying. 232. **Pelorus** (pə·lôr′əs): a cape in Sicily, now Faro.   235. **Sublimed:** sublimated; i.e., turned into vapor by heat and solidified by cooling.   236. **involved:** enveloped.

With stench and smoke:° such resting found the sole
Of unblest feet. Him followed his next mate,
Both glorying to have scaped the Stygian° flood
As gods, and by their own recovered strength,   240
Not by the sufferance of supernal° power.
    "Is this the region, this the soil, the clime,"
Said then the lost Archangel, "this the seat
That we must change for Heaven, this mournful gloom
For that celestial light? Be it so, since he   245
Who now is sovran° can dispose and bid
What shall be right: farthest from him is best,
Whom reason hath equaled, force hath made supreme
Above his equals. Farewell, happy fields,
Where joy for ever dwells! Hail, horrors! hail,   250
Infernal world! and thou, profoundest Hell,
Receive thy new possessor; one who brings
A mind not to be changed by place or time.
The mind is its own place, and in itself
Can make a Heaven of Hell, a Hell of Heaven.   255
What matter where, if I be still the same,
And what I should be, all but less than he
Whom thunder hath made greater? Here at least
We shall be free; the Almighty hath not built
Here for his envy, will not drive us hence: 260
Here we may reign secure, and in my choice
To reign is worth ambition, though in Hell:
Better to reign in Hell than serve in Heaven."

230–37. **as when . . . smoke:** an example of the extended simile which Milton frequently uses to strengthen his pictures. Pelorus (line 232) is a promontory in Sicily. 239. **Stygian** (stij′ē·ən): pertaining to the river Styx, which, in Greek mythology, surrounded the abode of the dead. Satan and Beelzebub, because they are of immortal substance, cannot die. 241. **supernal:** heavenly. 246. **sovran:** sovereign.

COMMENTARY

    "If then his providence
Out of our evil seek to bring forth good,
Our labor must be to pervert that end,
And out of good still to find means of
    evil . . ." (lines 162–65)

With these words Satan states the principle that must henceforth govern the behavior of the fallen angels. After he makes this announcement, the main action of the poem begins with Satan's determination to leave the brimstone lake on which he floats and seek the shore, "that ever burned/ With solid, as the lake with liquid fire." In lines 192–241 Milton gives us for the first time a sense of physical scene, of creatures huge almost beyond imagination, and of a hell horrible indeed, but clearly most horrible because of what it contains, an erring will opposed to God. Satan addresses his new home:

        "Hail, horrors! hail,
    Infernal world! and thou, profoundest
        Hell,
    Receive thy new possessor; one who
        brings
    A mind not to be changed by place or
        time.
    The mind is its own place, and in itself
    Can make a Heaven of Hell, a Hell of
        Heaven." (lines 250–55)

The words "The mind is its own place" may remind us of the "bottomless perdition" of line 47. Satan is damned by enclosing himself within his own mind, his own error. And this error is a "bottomless" one from which he cannot escape. Satan's claim (see line 248) that he has been overcome by nothing more than force, that his reason equals God's, is a terrible mistake.

FOR STUDY AND DISCUSSION

Make an argument for the proposition that in the passage from Book I, Hell is a state of mind; construct an opposed argument for the proposition that it is a place. Base your assertions on evidence from the text.

THE LANGUAGE OF "PARADISE LOST"

The first sixteen lines of Milton's epic make up a single sentence. The governing verb of that sentence occurs in the sixth line, beginning "Sing, Heavenly Muse." Unrhymed iambic pentameter, the familiar blank verse of Shakespeare, was not very common in Milton's day, half a century later. Milton's first readers, like ourselves, found in his verse an unusual majesty and elevation. How is it secured? The first thing to note is that Milton makes a very skillful use, not simply of classical models, but of Latin sentence construction which he carries over into English. The delay in the use of the verb and the placing of a number of qualifications first is an example. In a note prefaced to the 1668 edition of *Paradise Lost,* Milton explains why he avoided rhyme and what qualities he prizes in verse. (He is thinking of Latin and Italian as well as English verse; he wrote poetry in all three languages.) He avoided rhyme because rhyme offers "no true musical delight; which consists only in apt numbers, fit quantity of syllables, and the sense variously drawn out from one verse into another, not in the jingling sound of like endings, a fault avoided by the learned ancients both in poetry and all good oratory." The first sentence of *Paradise Lost* gives us a clear idea of what Milton means by "sense variously drawn out." We can understand his "apt numbers" easily enough; he was thinking of the number of stresses in a line, but he was mistaken in thinking that he could carry over into English the Latin use of "quantity." This means the amount of time devoted to voicing each syllable: the ear cannot make these measurements so precisely in English.

If you read aloud, as you must if you are to understand and enjoy Milton, you will soon find that particular words have taken on an extraordinary sonority and weight. Consider, for example, the following passages:

> ". . . what in me is dark
> Illumine, what is low raise and support;
> That to the height of this great argument
> I may assert Eternal Providence,
> And justify the ways of God to men."
> (lines 22–26)

> "Him the Almighty Power
> Hurled headlong flaming from the ethereal sky
> With hideous ruin and combustion, down
> To bottomless perdition, there to dwell
> In adamantine chains and penal fire,
> Who durst defy the Omnipotent to arms." (lines 44–49)

Once you have trained your ear by reading aloud you will begin to find what Milton calls "true musical delight" in such turns as "what in me is dark / Illumine," a phrasing in which the word *illumine* seems for the first time fully to express what we always knew it meant, "to light up." (There is, of course, a buried allusion to Milton's blindness here.) It is hardly an accident that this is a word of Latin origin. Much of Milton's power with words comes from his intimate sense of the relation of their original meanings in Latin to their differently shaded meanings in English. (Sometimes he simply reverts to the Latin meaning while using the English form.) We may note that the word *argument*, which to our ears suggests a lively dispute, has more than one sense to give it weight here. We still employ it to mean the reasoned presentation of a case, a meaning which is here bound up with a sense with which we are unfamiliar—in which *argument* means the "content of a work." Milton is dealing, then, with what, from his point of view, is the greatest possible argument: the story of the human creation, fall, and promised redemption.

The second quotation may be used to illustrate how plastic English sentence structure appears in Milton's hands. First of all, we notice that placing "Him" (Satan) before "Almighty Power" has the effect of focusing our attention on Satan and his fall (the placing of the pronoun as the chief stress in the line contributes to this) and of introducing the highly effective succession of "h" sounds which includes "*h*urled *h*eadlong" in the second line and "*h*ideous" in the third. This succession would be flat if it were not interrupted by "Almighty Power." If we make a somewhat arbitrary list of the elements of this sentence a number of other points are apparent. The normal English order would be something like this: The Almighty Power hurled Satan, who had dared to take arms against him, down to hell to live in chains and fire. Here, of course, the relative clause introduced by "who" comes at the very end, *after* we have had a chance to absorb the consequences of defying God. We may make a rough list of the elements of the sentence in this form:

Subject:	Almighty Power
Object:	Him (Satan)
Verb:	Hurled

How "hurled"?	Headlong
In what state?	Flaming
From whence?	Ethereal sky
Under what conditions?	With hideous ruin and combustion
In what direction?	Down

To what place (state)?	Perdition
Kind of perdition?	Bottomless
To do what there?	Dwell
Under what conditions?	Adamantine chains and penal fire

Obviously one could go much further in such an analysis. In particular, the rich play with "perdition" might be explored. It is not simply the state of being lost forever, but of being damned, given over to destruction. Perhaps the chief impression which arises from an analysis of elements such as we have just sketched is of the impossibility of making a recipe for so welding them together. We may remember these six lines as an example—apparently simple, yet clearly depending for their effect on more things than we can point to. This is what Coleridge meant by "the shaping power of imagination."

There are many other things to watch for if you wish to learn something of the power of Milton's verse. One of the most important is suggested by the opening of Satan's speech to Beelzebub:

"If thou beest he—but O how fallen! how changed
From him, who in the happy realms of light
Clothed with transcendent brightness didst outshine
Myriads though bright—" (lines 84–87)

Note the force of the interjection, "but O how fallen," introduced *before* the description of the terrible change the angel has undergone, and the weight and compression of "Myriads though bright" which calls up an impression of thousands of shining angels whom Beelzebub had outshone: it is as if the English language had offered itself to Milton as a set of newly minted words. Of course, they were not new. What happened is that they were in the hands of a master who could so place them and so employ them that they presented an unfamiliar and striking freshness. This aspect of Milton's poem has changed with changes in vocabulary which have occurred over the years. It has changed because certain of Milton's expressions were common in his age and are not in ours. Yet on the whole the change has been *relatively* slight: Milton found and exploited possibilities in English which no one save Keats has ever successfully approached since his day.

FOR STUDY AND DISCUSSION

1. Choose for careful analysis a passage from *Paradise Lost* of not more than ten lines. Look up any words that are not completely clear to you. Note any unfamiliar uses of these words that you have found.

2. Point out five words which you think Milton used with particularly powerful effect. Try to explain the sources of that effect in each case.

Following his intention, announced in Book I, of perverting good, "And out of good still to find means of evil," Satan plans to work against God's good by causing the downfall of his first earthly human creatures, Adam and Eve. In Book IX, knowing that God has forbidden Adam and Eve under penalty of death to eat of the fruit of the tree of knowledge, Satan resolves to tempt them into transgressing against God's will by doing just that. He comes to Paradise as a mist at night and enters into a sleeping serpent. The next morning, finding Eve alone, he praises Eve above all other creatures in Paradise. He tells Eve that before eating the fruit of a certain tree he was a mere beast. This fruit, he says, gave him speech and reason. He flatters Eve greatly by saying that all he has learned since attaining reason has only made him admire her the more. Eve succumbs to the wiles of the serpent and asks to be shown the marvelous tree. Since the serpent has become human, why should she herself not become like a god?

> So talked the spirited° sly Snake; and Eve
> Yet more amazed unwary thus replied:
> "Serpent, thy overpraising leaves in doubt
> The virtue of that fruit, in thee first proved.
> But say, where grows the tree, from hence how far?   5
> For many are the trees of God that grow
> In Paradise, and various, yet unknown
> To us; in such abundance lies our choice
> As leaves a greater store of fruit untouched,
> Still hanging incorruptible, till men   10
> Grow up to their provision,° and more hands
> Help to disburden Nature of her birth."°
> To whom the wily adder, blithe and glad:
> "Empress, the way is ready, and not long,
> Beyond a row of myrtles, on a flat,   15
> Fast by a fountain, one small thicket past
> Of blowing° myrrh and balm; if thou accept
> My conduct, I can bring thee thither soon."
> "Lead then," said Eve. He leading swiftly rolled
> In tangles, and made intricate seem straight,   20
> To mischief swift. Hope elevates, and joy
> Brightens his crest, as when a wandering fire,°

---

1. **spirited:** inspired (by Satan).   11. **Grow . . . provision:** multiply in proportion to the food provided.   12. **birth:** the fruit Nature bears.   17. **blowing:** blooming.   22. **wandering fire:** will-o'-the-wisp.

Compact of unctuous° vapor, which the night
Condenses, and the cold environs round,
Kindled through agitation to a flame,   25
Which oft, they say, some evil spirit attends,
Hovering and blazing with delusive light,
Misleads the amazed nightwanderer from his way
To bogs and mires, and oft through pond or pool,
There swallowed up and lost, from succor far.   30
So glistered the dire Snake, and into fraud
Led Eve, our credulous mother, to the tree
Of prohibition, root of all our woe;
Which when she saw, thus to her guide she spake:
    "Serpent, we might have spared our coming hither,   35
Fruitless to me, though fruit be here to excess,
The credit of whose virtue rest with thee,°
Wondrous indeed, if cause of such effects.
But of this tree we may not taste nor touch;
God so commanded, and left that command   40
Sole daughter of his voice; the rest,° we live
Law to ourselves, our reason is our law."
    To whom the Tempter guilefully replied:
"Indeed? Hath God then said that of the fruit
Of all these garden trees ye shall not eat,   45
Yet lords declared of all in Earth or air?"
    To whom thus Eve yet sinless: "Of the fruit
Of each tree in the garden we may eat,
But of the fruit of this fair tree amidst
The garden, God hath said, 'Ye shall not eat   50
Thereof, nor shall ye touch it, lest ye die.'"
    She scarce had said, though brief, when now more bold
The Tempter, but with show of zeal and love
To man, and indignation at his wrong,
New part puts on,° and as to passion moved,   55
Fluctuates disturbed, yet comely, and in act
Raised,° as of some great matter to begin.
As when of old some orator renowned
In Athens or free Rome, where eloquence
Flourished, since mute, to some great cause addressed,   60
Stood in himself collected, while each part,
Motion, each act won audience ere the tongue,
Sometimes in highth began, as no delay
Of preface brooking through his zeal of right:°
So standing, moving, or to highth upgrown,   65
The Tempter all impassioned thus began:
    "O sacred, wise, and wisdom-giving plant,

---

23. **Compact of unctuous:** oily.   37. **credit . . . thee:** proof of the fruit's power must remain
only with you   41. **the rest:** in everything else.   55. **New . . . on:** assumes a new role; that is,
sympathy with humans.   56–57. **act raised:** his body poised.   63–64. **Sometimes . . . right:** Often,
too excited to be bothered by a preface, the orator would burst into the middle of his speech.

Mother of science,° now I feel thy power
Within me clear, not only to discern
Things in their causes, but to trace the ways   70
Of highest agents, deemed however wise.
Queen of this universe, do not believe
Those rigid threats of death; ye shall not die:
How should ye? by the fruit? it gives you life
To° knowledge; by the Threatener? look on me,   75
Me who have touched and tasted, yet both live,
And life more perfect have attained than Fate
Meant me, by venturing higher than my lot.
Shall that be shut to man, which to the beast
Is open? or will God incense his ire   80
For such a petty trespass, and not praise
Rather your dauntless virtue, whom the pain
Of death denounced,° whatever thing death be,
Deterred not from achieving what might lead
To happier life, knowledge of good and evil?   85
Of good, how just? of evil, if what is evil
Be real, why not known, since easier shunned?
God therefore cannot hurt ye, and be just;
Not just, not God; not feared then, nor obeyed:
Your fear itself of death removes the fear.   90
Why then was this forbid? Why but to awe,
Why but to keep ye low and ignorant,
His worshipers? he knows that in the day
Ye eat thereof, your eyes that seem so clear,
Yet are but dim, shall perfectly be then   95
Opened and cleared, and ye shall be as gods,
Knowing both good and evil as they know.
That ye should be as gods, since I as man,
Internal man,° is but proportion meet,
I of brute human, ye of human gods.   100
So ye shall die perhaps, by putting off
Human, to put on gods,° death to be wished,
Though threatened, which no worse than this can bring.
And what are gods that man may not become
As they, participating° godlike food?   105
The gods are first, and that advantage use
On our belief, that all from them proceeds;
I question it, for this fair Earth I see,
Warmed by the sun, producing every kind,
Them nothing. If they° all things, who enclosed   110
Knowledge of good and evil in this tree,
That whoso eats thereof, forthwith attains
Wisdom without their leave? and wherein lies

---

68. **science:** knowledge. 75. **To:** as well as. 83. **denounced:** threatened. 99. **Internal man:** a man of mental powers. 101–02. **by . . . gods:** by rising from the human state to a god-like state. 105. **participating:** sharing. 110. **If they:** if they produced.

The offense, that man should thus attain to know?
What can your knowledge hurt him, or this tree   115
Impart against his will, if all be his?
Or is it envy, and can envy dwell
In heavenly breasts? These, these and many more
Causes import° your need of this fair fruit.
Goddess humane,° reach then, and freely taste!"   120
    He ended, and his words replete with guile
Into her heart too easy entrance won.
Fixed on the fruit she gazed, which to behold
Might tempt alone, and in her ears the sound
Yet rung of his persuasive words, impregned°   125
With reason, to her seeming, and with truth;
Meanwhile the hour of noon drew on, and waked
An eager appetite, raised by the smell
So savory of that fruit, which with desire,
Inclinable now grown to touch or taste,   130
Solicited her longing eye; yet first
Pausing a while, thus to herself she mused:
    "Great are thy virtues, doubtless, best of fruits,
Though kept from man, and worthy to be admired,
Whose taste, too long forborne, at first assay°   135
Gave elocution to the mute, and taught
The tongue not made for speech to speak thy praise.
Thy praise he also who forbids thy use
Conceals not from us, naming thee the Tree
Of Knowledge, knowledge both of good and evil;   140
Forbids us then to taste, but his forbidding
Commends thee more, while it infers the good
By thee communicated, and our want;
For good unknown sure is not had, or had
And yet unknown, is as not had at all.   145
In plain° then, what forbids he but to know,
Forbids us good, forbids us to be wise?
Such prohibitions bind not. But if Death
Bind us with afterbands, what profits then
Our inward freedom? In the day we eat   150
Of this fair fruit, our doom is, we shall die.
How dies the Serpent? He hath eaten and lives,
And knows, and speaks, and reasons, and discerns,
Irrational till then. For us alone
Was death invented? or to us denied   155
This intellectual food, for beasts reserved?
For beasts it seems; yet that one beast which first
Hath tasted, envies not, but brings with joy
The good befallen him, author unsuspect,°
Friendly to man, far from deceit or guile.   160

119. **import:** prove. 120. **humane:** gracious, kindly. 125. **impregned:** impregnated.
135. **assay:** trial. 146. **In plain:** in plain language. 159. **author unsuspect:** a witness without
suspicion.

What fear I then, rather what know to fear°
Under this ignorance of good and evil,
Of God or death, of law or penalty?
Here grows the cure of all, this fruit divine,
Fair to the eye, inviting to the taste,   165
Of virtue to make wise; what hinders then
To reach, and feed at once both body and mind?"
    So saying, her rash hand in evil hour
Forth reaching to the fruit, she plucked, she eat.
Earth felt the wound, and Nature from her seat   170
Sighing through all her works gave signs of woe,
That all was lost. Back to the thicket slunk
The guilty Serpent, and well might, for Eve
Intent now wholly on her taste, nought else
Regarded; such delight till then, as seemed,   175
In fruit she never tasted, whether true
Or fancied so, through expectation high
Of knowledge, nor was godhead° from her thought.
Greedily she engorged without restraint,
And knew not eating death.°   180

161. **what . . . fear:** In her ignorance. Eve does not know what to fear and what not to fear.
178. **godhead:** She expected to become godlike immediately. 180. **knew . . . death:** She did not know she was eating death.

FOR STUDY AND DISCUSSION

1. In lines 44–46 and 67–120, the serpent makes a speech. Milton, himself a master of the art of rhetoric, or persuasion, here has marshaled a series of reasons why Eve should disobey God's command and eat of the fruit of the tree of knowledge.

Lines 44–46 are clearly meant to make Eve feel that she and Adam cannot be "lords . . . of all" and "law to ourselves" (line 42) if they are forbidden to taste the fruit of the knowledge of good and evil. When Eve objects, the snake as "orator" makes a more formal reply. Analyze this reply carefully, being sure that you cover these points in your discussion:

a. What power does the serpent claim he now possesses?

b. What use of names or epithets does the serpent make to plant in Eve's mind the idea of her right to question the divine command that she should not eat of the fruit of the tree of knowledge?

c. To what virtue does the serpent appeal in arguing against Eve's fear of the unknown thing called "death"?

d. What low or petty motive for forbidding the fruit of the tree of knowledge does the serpent attribute to God?

e. What happy meaning does he ascribe to death?

f. What inconsistency is apparent in lines 104–05?

g. What argument does the serpent produce against the belief that God is responsible for the creation of the earth?

h. How does the serpent use the notion of God's omnipotence to argue against his commandment?

2. Considering both of the passages cited in the preceding question, to which vice does Milton attribute the fall of both Satan and man?

3. Aside from those which the serpent presents in his long and artful speech, what arguments does Eve herself have for eating the fruit?

4. What seems to you the most plausible argument for tasting the tree's fruit? Why?

5. Eve concludes by declaring that to eat of the fruit is "to feed at once both body and mind." Which of these impulses, to feed the body or the mind, is the greater sin?

SAMUEL PEPYS
(1633–1703)

On May 26, 1703, Samuel Pepys's friend and fellow diarist, John Evelyn, wrote: "This day died Mr. Samuel Pepys, a very worthy, industrious and curious person, none in England exceeding him in knowledge of the navy. . . . He was universally beloved, hospitable, generous, learned in many things, skilled in music, a very great cherisher of learned men of whom he had conversation." This much at least was known of Pepys, the public man, at the time of his death. What Evelyn did not know was that Pepys had left behind a diary, written in shorthand, that, over one hundred years later, revealed Pepys as a private man. This diary has become one of our best sources of knowledge of seventeenth-century life.

Pepys, the son of a poor tailor, was helped by a wealthy relative to attend Cambridge and to achieve public office. He worked hard and, after the Restoration of Charles II, was able to pile up a small fortune and to rise in the navy office until, as Secretary of the Admiralty, he virtually ran the navy, making it a model of economy and efficiency. Pepys wrote books on naval affairs that became standard in Admiralty circles, and he was ultimately elected president of the Royal Society. His career was not all smooth sailing, however: he was more than once called to account by the House of Commons, and he was twice imprisoned for political intrigue, but the charges against him were not proven. When the Glorious Revolution overthrew his good friend, James II, Pepys's career was ended. He spent his declining years in comfortable retirement, writing letters and arranging his large library.

Included in this library were six mysterious volumes of manuscript written in what appeared to be a secret code. It was not until 1818 that work was begun on deciphering these volumes. After years of hard work (much of it unnecessary, since the translator overlooked in Pepys's own library a book of shorthand which would greatly have simplified the work), a portion of the diary, which was never intended for any eyes but his own, was finally published. The world was delighted to discover not only the many-sided private man hidden behind the man of affairs but, even more, the detailed description of life in London in the exciting decade of the 1660's. Along with remarkable candid pictures of his personal life, Pepys presents great public canvasses: the splendid coronation of Charles II; a gruesome execution by hanging, drawing, and quartering; the Plague of 1665; the Great London Fire of 1666. The almost forgotten manuscript has become the most famous account of seventeenth-century life and is known everywhere simply as Pepys's *Diary*.

The Diary of Samuel Pepys

PERSONAL AFFAIRS

August 19, 1660. (Lord's Day.) This morning Sir W. Batten, Pen,[1] and myself went to church to the churchwardens to demand a pew, which at present could not be given us, but we are resolved to have one built. So we stayed and heard Mr. Mills, a very good minister. Home to dinner, where my wife had on her new petticoat that she bought yesterday, which indeed is a very fine cloth, and a fine lace, but that being of a light color, and the lace all silver, it makes no great show. Mr. Creed and my brother Tom dined with me. After they were gone I went up to put my papers in order and finding my wife's clothes lie carelessly laid up, I was angry with her, which I was troubled for. After that my wife and I went and walked in the garden, and so home to bed.

November 21, 1660. This morning my wife and I went to Paternoster Row, and there we bought some green watered moire for a morning waistcoat. And after that we went to Mr. Cade's to choose some pictures for our house. After that my wife went home, and I to Pope's Head and bought me an agate-hafted knife, which cost me 5s. So home to dinner, and so to the office all the afternoon, and at night to my violin (the first time that I have played on it since I came to this house) in my dining room, and afterward to my lute there, and I took much pleasure to have the neighbors come forth into the yard to hear me. So up to bed.

January 3, 1661. To the Theater: and here the first time that I ever saw women come upon the stage.[2]

March 27, 1661. To the Dolphin to a dinner of Mr. Harris's where Sir Williams both and my Lady Batten and her two daughters, and other company, where a great deal of mirth, and there stayed until 11 o'clock at night, and in our mirth I sang and sometimes fiddled. At last we fell to dancing, the first time that ever I did in my life, which I did wonder to see myself do.

May 31, 1661. I went to my father's, but to my great grief I found my father and mother in a great deal of discontent one with another, and indeed my mother is now grown so pettish that I know not how my father is able to bear with it. I did talk to her so as did not indeed become me, but I could not help it, she being so insufferably foolish and simple, so that my father, poor man, is become a very unhappy man.

December 31, 1661. My wife and I this morning to the painter's, and there she sat[3] the last time. After supper, and my barber had trimmed me, I sat down to end my journal for this year, and my condition at this time, by God's blessing, is thus: my health is very good, and so my wife's in all respects: my servants, W. Hewer, Sarah, Nell, and Wayneman: my house at the Navy Office. I suppose myself to be worth about £500 clear in the world, and my goods of my house my own, and what is coming to me from Brampton when my father dies, which God defer. My chiefest thought is now to get a good wife for Tom, there being one offered by the Joyces, a cousin of theirs, worth £200 in ready money. But my greatest trouble is that I have for this last half year been a very great spendthrift in all manner of respects, that I am afeared to cast up my accounts, though I hope I

---

[1] **Sir W. Batten, Pen:** Sir William Batten and Sir William Pen (referred to later as "Sir Williams both") were members of the Navy Board of which Pepys was Clerk of the Acts.

[2] **women . . . stage:** In Elizabethan times boys played the roles of women on the stage, and this custom continued until almost the end of the seventeenth century.

[3] **she sat:** She had been having her portrait painted.

am worth what I say above. But I will cast them up very shortly. I have newly taken a solemn oath about abstaining from plays and wine, which I am resolved to keep according to the letter of the oath which I keep by me.

June 8, 1662. (Lord's Day.) To my Lady's, and there supped with her; and merry among other things, with the parrot which my Lord hath brought from the sea, which speaks very well, and cries Poll so pleasantly that made my Lord give it to Lady Paulina; but my Lady her mother do not like it. Home and observe my man Will to walk with his cloak flung over his shoulder like a ruffian, which, whether it was that he might not be seen to walk along with the footboy I know not, but I was vexed at it; and coming home and after prayers, I did ask him where he learned that immodest garb, and he answered me that it was not immodest, or some such slight answer, at which I did give him two boxes on the ears, which I never did before, and so was after a little troubled at it.

THE EXECUTION OF A REGICIDE

October 13, 1660. I went out to Charing Cross, to see Major General Harrison[1] hanged, drawn, and quartered; which was done there, he looking as cheerful as any man could do in that condition. He was presently cut down, and his head and heart shown to the people, at which there was great shouts of joy. It is said that he said that he was sure to come shortly at the right hand of Christ to judge them that now had judged him; and that his wife do expect his coming again. Thus it was my chance to see the King beheaded at Whitehall,[2] and to see the first blood shed in revenge for the blood of the King at Charing Cross. From thence to my Lord's, and took Captain Cuttance and Mr.

Sheply to the Sun Tavern, and did give them some oysters. After that I went by water home, where I was angry with my wife for her things lying about, and in my passion kicked the little fine basket which I bought her in Holland, and broke it, which troubled me after I had done it. Within all the afternoon setting up shelves in my study. At night to bed.

THE CORONATION OF CHARLES II

April 23, 1661. Coronation Day. About four I rose and got to the Abbey, where I followed Sir J. Denham,[3] the Surveyor, with some company that he was leading in. And with much ado, by the favor of Mr. Cooper, his man, did get up into a great scaffold across the north end of the Abbey, where with a great deal of patience I sat from past four till eleven before the King came in. And a great pleasure it was to see the Abbey raised in the middle, all covered with red, and a throne (that is a chair) and footstool on the top of it; and all the officers of all kinds, so much as the very fiddlers, in red vests.

At last comes in the Dean and Prebends[4] of Westminster, with the Bishops (many of them in cloth-of-gold copes), and after them the Nobility, all in their Parliament robes, which was a most magnificent sight. Then the Duke, and the King with a scepter (carried by my Lord Sandwich) and sword and mond[5] before him, and the crown too. The King in his robes, bare-headed, which was very fine. And after all had placed themselves, there was a sermon and the service; and then in the Choir at the high altar, the King passed through all the ceremonies of the Coronation, which to my great grief I and most in the Abbey

---

[1] **Major General Harrison:** one of the signers of the death warrant of Charles I.

[2] King Charles I was beheaded in 1649 when Pepys was sixteen.

[3] **Sir J. Denham:** a popular poet who was also in charge of government buildings.

[4] **Prebends** (preb'əndz): high officials in the church.

[5] **mond:** an orb of gold, with a cross set with precious stones.

could not see. The crown being put upon his head, a great shout began, and he came forth to the throne; and there passed more ceremonies: as taking the oath, and having things read to him by the Bishop; and his Lords (who put on their caps as soon as the King put on his crown) and bishops came and kneeled before him. And three times the King at Arms[1] went to the three open places on the scaffold and proclaimed that if anyone could show any reason why Charles Stuart should not be King of England, that now he should come and speak. And a General Pardon also was read by the Lord Chancellor, and medals flung up and down by my Lord Cornwallis, of silver, but I could not come by any. But so great a noise that I could make but little of the music; and indeed, it was lost to everybody.

I went out a little while before the King had done all his ceremonies, and went round the Abbey to Westminster Hall, all the way within rails, and ten thousand people, with the ground covered with blue cloth; and scaffolds all the way. Into the Hall I got, where it was very fine with hangings and scaffolds one upon another full of brave ladies; and my wife in one little one, on the right hand. Here I stayed walking up and down, and at last, upon one of the side stalls, I stood and saw the King come in with all the persons (but the soldiers) that were yesterday in the cavalcade; and a most pleasant sight it was to see them in their several robes. And the King came in with his crown on, and his scepter in his hand, under a canopy borne up by six silver staves, carried by Barons of the Cinque Ports,[2] and little bells at every end.

And after a long time, he got up to the farther end, and all set themselves down at their several tables; and that was also a brave sight; and the King's first course carried up by the Knights of the Bath. And many fine ceremonies there was of the herald's leading up people before him, and bowing; and my Lord of Albemarle's going to the kitchen and eat a bit of the first dish that was to go to the King's table. But, above all, was these three Lords, Northumberland, and Suffolk, and the Duke of Ormond, coming before the courses on horseback, and staying so all dinnertime, and at last to bring up[3] [Dymock] the King's champion, all in armor on horseback, with his spear and target carried before him. And a herald proclaims, "That if any dare deny Charles Stuart to be lawful King of England, here was a champion that would fight with him"; and with these words, the champion flings down his gauntlet, and all this he do three times in his going up toward the King's table. At last when he is come, the King drinks to him and then sends him the cup, which is of gold, and he drinks it off and then rides back again with the cup in his hand. I went from table to table to see the bishops and all others at their dinner, and was infinitely pleased with it. And at the Lords' table, I met with William Howe, and he spoke to my Lord for me, and he did give me four rabbits and a pullet, and so I got it and Mr. Creed and I got Mr. Michell to give us some bread, and so we at a stall eat[4] it, as everybody else did what they could get. I took a great deal of pleasure to go up and down, and look upon the ladies, and to hear the music of all sorts, but above all, the twenty-four violins.

THE LONDON FIRE

September 2, 1666. (Lord's Day.) Some of our maids sitting up late last night to get things ready against our feast today, Jane called us up about

---

[1] **King at Arms:** chief of the heralds.

[2] **Cinque** (singk) **Ports:** five ports on the English Channel: Hastings, Sandwich, Dover, Romney, and Hythe.

[3] The ceremony here described is no longer observed as part of the coronation. It was a holdover from the days of chivalry.

[4] **eat** (et): meaning *ate*.

The London fire of 1666 as depicted by the contemporary engraver, Wenceslaus Hollar.

three in the morning, to tell us of a great fire they saw in the city. So I rose and slipped on my nightgown, and went to her window, and thought it to be on the back side of Mark Lane at the farthest; but, being unused to such fires as followed, I thought it far enough off; and so went to bed again and to sleep. About seven rose again to dress myself, and there looked out at the window, and saw the fire not so much as it was and farther off. So to my closet to set things to rights after yesterday's cleaning.

By and by Jane comes and tells me that she hears that above 300 houses have been burned down tonight by the fire we saw, and that it is now burning down all Fish Street, by London Bridge. So I made myself ready presently, and walked to the Tower,[1] and there got up upon one of the high places, Sir J. Robinson's little son going up with me; and there I did see the houses at the end of the bridge all on fire, and an infinite great fire on this and the other side the end of the bridge; which, among other people, did trouble me for poor little Michell and our Sarah on the bridge.[2] So down, with my heart full of trouble, to the Lieutenant of the Tower, who tells me that it begun this morning in the King's baker's house in Pudding Lane, and that it hath burned St. Magnus Church and most part of Fish Street already. So I down to the waterside, and there got a boat and through bridge, and there saw a lamentable fire. Poor Michell's house, as far as the Old Swan, already burned that way, and the fire running farther, that in a very little time it got as far as the Steel Yard, while I was there. Everybody endeavoring to remove their goods, and flinging into the river or bringing them into lighters that lay off; poor people staying in their houses as long as till the very fire touched them, and then running into boats, or clambering from one pair of stairs by the waterside to another. And among other things, the poor pigeons, I perceive, were loath to leave their houses, but hovered about the windows and balconies till they were, some of them burned, their wings, and fell down. Having stayed, and in an hour's time seen the fire rage every way, and nobody, to my sight, endeavoring to quench it, but to remove their goods, and leave all to the fire, and having seen it get as far as the Steel Yard, and the wind mighty high and driving it into the City;[3] and everything, after so long a drought, proving combustible, even the very stones of churches. I to Whitehall, and there up to the King's closet in the Chapel, where people come about me, and I did give them an account dismayed them all, and word was carried in to the King. So I was called for and did tell the King and Duke of York what I saw, and that un-

---

[1] **Tower:** The Tower of London.
[2] **on the bridge:** Old London Bridge was like a street with houses built on it.

[3] **City:** the area of the original city of London, now its commercial center.

less his Majesty did command houses to be pulled down nothing could stop the fire. They seemed much troubled, and the King commanded me to go to my Lord Mayor from him and command him to spare no houses, but to pull down before the fire every way. The Duke of York bid me tell him that if he would have any more soldiers he shall; and so did my Lord Arlington afterward, as a great secret. Here meeting with Captain Cocke, I in his coach, which he lent me, and Creed with me to Paul,[1] and there walked along Watling Street, as well as I could, every creature coming away laden with goods to save, and here and there sick people carried away in beds. Extraordinary good goods carried in carts and on backs. At last met my Lord Mayor in Canning Street, like a man spent, with a handkerchief about his neck. To the King's message he cried, like a fainting woman, "Lord! what can I do? I am spent: people will not obey me. I have been pulling down houses; but the fire overtakes us faster than we can do it." That he needed no more soldiers and that, for himself, he must go and refresh himself, having been up all night.

So he left me, and I him, and walked home, seeing people all almost distracted, and no manner of means used to quench the fire. The houses, too, so very thick thereabouts and full of matter for burning, as pitch and tar, in Thames Street; and warehouses of oil, and wines, and brandy, and other things. Here I saw Mr. Issake Houblon, the handsome man, prettily dressed and dirty, at his door at Dowgate, receiving some of his brothers' things, whose houses were on fire; and, as he says, have been removed twice already; and he doubts (as it soon proved) that they must be in a little time removed from his house also which was a sad consideration. And to see the churches all filling with goods by people who themselves should have been quietly there at this time.

By this time it was about twelve o'clock; and so home. Soon as dined, away, and walked through the city, the streets full of nothing but people and horses and carts laden with goods, ready to run over one another, and removing goods from one burned house to another. They now removing out of Canning Street (which received goods in the morning) into Lombard Street, and farther; and among others I now saw my little goldsmith, Stokes, receiving some friend's goods, whose house itself was burned the day after. We parted at Paul's; he home, and I to Paul's Wharf, where I had appointed a boat to attend me, and took in Mr. Carcasse and his brother, whom I met in the street, and carried them below and above bridge, to and again to see the fire, which was now got farther, both below and above, and no likelihood of stopping it. Met with the King and Duke of York in their barge, and with them to Queenhithe, and there called Sir Richard Browne to them. Their order was only to pull down houses apace, and so below bridge at the waterside; but little was or could be done, the fire coming upon them so fast. Good hopes there was of stopping it at the Three Cranes above, and at Buttolph's Wharf below bridge, if care be used; but the wind carries it into the City, so as we know not by the waterside what it do there. River full of lighters and boats taking in goods, and good goods swimming in the water, and only I observed that hardly one lighter or boat in three that had the goods of a house in, but there was a pair of virginals[2] in it.

Having seen as much as I could now, I away to Whitehall by appointment and there walked to St. James's Park, and there met my wife and Creed and walked to my boat; and there upon the water again, and to the fire up and down, it still

[1] **Paul's:** St. Paul's Cathedral.

[2] **pair of virginals:** a small, legless harpsichord popular in the sixteenth and seventeenth centuries.

increasing, and the wind great. So near the fire as we could for smoke; and all over the Thames, with one's face in the wind, you were almost burned with a shower of firedrops. This is very true; so as houses were burned by these drops and flakes of fire, three or four, nay, five or six houses, one from another. When we could endure no more upon the water, we to a little alehouse on the Bankside, over against the Three Cranes, and there stayed till it was dark almost, and saw the fire grow; and, as it grew darker, appeared more and more, and in corners and upon steeples, and between churches and houses, as far as we could see up the hill of the City, in a most horrid malicious bloody flame not like the fine flame of an ordinary fire. Barbary and her husband away before us. We stayed till, it being darkish, we saw the fire as only one entire arch of fire from this to the other side of the bridge and in a bow up the hill for an arch of above a mile long: it made me weep to see it. The churches, houses, and all on fire and flaming at once; and a horrid noise the flames made, and the crackling of houses at their ruin.

So home with a sad heart, and there find everybody discoursing and lamenting the fire; and poor Tom Hater come with some few of his goods saved out of his house, which is burned upon Fish Street Hill. I invited him to lie at my house, and did receive his goods, but was deceived in his lying there, the news coming every moment of the growth of the fire; so as we were forced to begin to pack up our own goods and prepare for their removal; and did by moonshine (it being brave dry, and moonshine, and warm weather) carry much of my goods into the garden, and Mr. Hater and I did remove my money and iron chests into my cellar, as thinking that the safest place. And got my bags of gold into my office, ready to carry away, and my chief papers of accounts also there, and my tallies into a box by themselves. So great was our fear, as Sir W. Batten hath carts come out of the country to fetch away his goods this night. We did put Mr. Hater, poor man, to bed a little; but he got but very little rest, so much noise being in my house, taking down of goods.

3rd. About four o'clock in the morning, my Lady Batten sent me a cart to carry away all my money, and plate, and best things, to Sir W. Rider's at Bednall Green. Which I did, riding myself in my nightgown in the cart; and, Lord! to see how the streets and the highways are crowded with people running and riding, and getting of carts at any rate to fetch away things. I find Sir W. Rider tired with being called up all night, and receiving things from several friends. His house full of goods, and much of Sir W. Batten's and Sir W. Pen's. I am eased at my heart to have my treasure so well secured. Then home, with much ado to find a way, nor any sleep all this night to me nor my poor wife.

FOR STUDY AND DISCUSSION

1. What do we learn about Pepys from his *Diary* that we can't learn from a public record of his achievements? What were Pepys's characteristics as a human being? What were his enthusiasms? his strong and weak points? How did he act toward his servant? toward his wife? How did he react to the Great Fire?

2. Do you think Pepys's *Diary* would be famous today if it contained only descriptions of great events and none of personal affairs? Explain your answer.

3. Of what historical value is the *Diary?* How does it contribute to our knowledge of English life in the seventeenth century?

4. How does the style of the *Diary* reflect Pepys's personality? Compare and contrast this selection with the essays of Bacon.

FOR COMPOSITION

The ability to observe closely, as Samuel Pepys did, is a rare and valuable skill. Imagining that you are that diarist, write a journal description of some home, school, local, or even national, event that you have witnessed. Be sure to employ the narrative and descriptive skills that make for good reporting.

JOHN DRYDEN
(1631–1700)

Speaking of his own time, John Dryden wrote that "the language is become more courtly, and our thoughts are better dressed." This phrase underlines both the strength and the weakness of Dryden's influence on literature. On the one hand, he can be accepted, as the late Victorian critic George Saintsbury accepts him, as "without exception the greatest craftsman in English letters"; on the other, his craftsmanship led him to place too much stress on writing as a gentlemanly occupation, designed above all for pleasure. His influence was great, so great and lasting that the last quarter of the seventeenth century is, by common consent, the "Age of Dryden."

Born into a strongly Puritan family, Dryden lived as a young man through the dour decade of Commonwealth rule. He went to London where his early work was more striking for its political self-contradiction than for its literary quality: within two years he wrote *Heroic Stanzas* praising Oliver Cromwell and *Astrea Redux,* celebrating the Restoration of Charles II. In London Dryden married the daughter of an earl; and he joined the Royal Society, believing that "a man should be learned in several sciences . . . to be a complete and excellent poet." Dryden seems to have been easy and pliable by nature, a satirist capable of hitting hard but keener on the defense than on the attack. His best years were spent in court circles which reacted strongly against Cromwellian austerity. If he changed his opinions with the times, he was far from alone in doing so.

Dryden was first successful as a dramatist, and in fifteen years he turned out eighteen plays. In an attempt to refine on the Elizabethans, he wrote his earlier tragedies in rhymed verse, after French models. Although his plays are not performed today, in their own day *All for Love, The Conquest of Granada, The Spanish Friar,* and *Marriage à la Mode* were extremely successful. Even the inferior plays contain exquisite lyrics that are still pleasing.

As a literary critic Dryden established the neoclassical standards of order, balance, and harmony; his greatest critical work is *Essay of Dramatic Poesy,* in which appears his remarkable appreciation of Shakespeare. In poetry Dryden set an enduring style with his neat "heroic couplets"—paired lines of rhymed iambic pentameter. Of his satires the greatest are *Absalom and Achitophel,* which draws a parallel between the Biblical story of King David and the then-current problem of succession to the English throne, and *Mac Flecknoe,* which derides the reputation of a rival poet, Thomas Shadwell. Having defended the Church of England in *Religio*

Laici, a long poem of great brilliance, Dryden, ever susceptible to the spirit of the times, turned Roman Catholic and wrote the even more memorable didactic Catholic poem, *The Hind and the Panther.* When, however, the Glorious Revolution brought in Protestant William and Mary, Dryden remained Catholic and so lost the position and income of poet laureate. Pressed for money all his life and now nearly sixty years old, he worked harder than ever, producing more plays, excellent translations, and some of his best odes.

John Dryden is remembered today for *The Hind and the Panther;* for a handful of odes, of which that in memory of the young poet, Anne Killigrew, and the two in honor of St. Cecilia's Day are the most famous; and for a substantial body of prose criticism. The great eighteenth-century writer, Dr. Samuel Johnson, said that Dryden found English poetry of brick and left it of marble. The metaphor is more striking than apt, for by implication it asserts the absolute superiority of smooth eighteenth-century diction to the splendors of the Elizabethans. All the same, by his wide range, his musicality, his gift for writing finely turned verse and good, smooth prose, Dryden set a standard that determined the contemporary style of literature. As Ben Jonson had been two generations before and Samuel Johnson would be two generations later, John Dryden was the literary spokesman of his age.

FROM *An Essay of Dramatic Poesy*

Although Dryden was celebrated as poet laureate, he is best remembered today as the father of modern English prose. The clarity, precision, and grace of his prose style have been admired by writers and critics alike.

For all practical purposes, Dryden originated what we call "literary criticism"—analysis of the merits and interesting aspects of pieces of literature. In works like *An Essay of Dramatic Poesy,* which is an excellent example of Dryden's prose and one of the first important works in English literary criticism, he launched the modern reputations of Chaucer and Shakespeare. In the excerpt from the *Essay* given here, Dryden contrasts the "naturally learned" Shakespeare with "the more correct poet," Ben Jonson.

To BEGIN, then, with Shakespeare. He was the man who of all modern, and perhaps ancient poets, had the largest and most comprehensive soul. All the images of Nature were still present in him, and he drew them, not laboriously, but luckily; when he describes anything, you more than see it, you feel it too. Those who accuse him to have wanted [1] learning give him the greater commendation: he was naturally learned. He needed not the spectacles of books to read Nature; he looked inwards, and found her there. I cannot say he is everywhere alike; were he so, I should do him injury to compare him with the greatest of mankind. He is many times flat, insipid; his comic wit degenerating into clenches,[2] his serious swelling into bombast. But he is always great when some great occasion is presented to him; no man can say he ever had a fit subject for his wit[3] and did not raise himself as high above the rest of poets.

Quantum lenta solent inter viburna cupressi.[4]

[1] **wanted:** lacked.
[2] **clenches:** puns (now obsolete).
[3] **wit:** intelligence, imaginative mind. Throughout, in referring to "wit," Dryden means inventiveness and imagination rather than humor.
[4] ***Quantum ... cupressi:*** as cypresses rise above shrubs.

The consideration of this made Mr. Hales of Eton say that there is no subject of which any poet ever wrote but he would produce it much better done in Shakespeare; and however others are now more generally preferred before him, yet the age wherein he lived, which had contemporaries with him Fletcher[1] and Jonson, never equaled them to him in their esteem: and in the last King's court, when Ben's reputation was at highest, Sir John Suckling, and with him the greater part of the courtiers, set our Shakespeare far above him.

Beaumont and Fletcher, of whom I am next to speak, had, with the advantage of Shakespeare's wit, which was their precedent, great natural gifts, improved by study.... The first play that brought Fletcher and him in esteem was their *Philaster:* for, before that, they had written two or three very unsuccessfully, as the like is reported of Ben Jonson, before he writ *Every Man in His Humor*. Their plots were generally more regular than Shakespeare's, especially those that were made before Beaumont's death; and they understood and imitated the conversation of gentlemen much better; whose wild debaucheries, and quickness of wit in repartees, no poet before them could paint as they have done. Humor, which Ben Jonson derived from particular persons, they made it their business not to describe: they represented all the passions very lively, but above all, love. I am apt to believe the English language in them arrived to its highest perfection: what words have since been taken in are rather superfluous than ornamental. Their plays are now the most pleasant and frequent entertainments of the stage; two of theirs being acted through the year for one of Shakespeare's or Jonson's: the reason is because there is a certain gaiety in their comedies and pathos in their more serious plays, which suit generally with all men's humors. Shakespeare's language is like-wise a little obsolete, and Ben Jonson's wit comes short of theirs.

As for Jonson, to whose character I am now arrived, if we look upon him while he was himself (for his last plays were but his dotage), I think him the most learned and judicious writer which any theater ever had. He was a most severe judge of himself, as well as others. One cannot say he wanted wit, but rather that he was frugal of it. In his works you find little to retrench or alter. Wit, and language, and humor also in some measure we had before him; but something of art was wanting to the drama till he came. He managed his strength to more advantage than any who preceded him. You seldom find him making love in any of his scenes, or endeavoring to move the passions; his genius was too sullen and saturnine to do it gracefully, especially when he knew he came after those who had performed both to such a height. Humor was his proper sphere; and in that he delighted most to represent mechanic people.[2] He was deeply conversant in the ancients, both Greek and Latin, and he borrowed boldly from them: there is scarcely a poet or historian among the Roman authors of those times whom he has not translated in *Sejanus* and *Catiline*.[3] But he has done his robberies so openly, that one may see he fears not to be taxed by any law. He invades authors like a monarch; and what would be theft in other poets is only victory in him. With the spoils of these writers he so represents old Rome to us, in its rites, ceremonies, and customs, that if one of their poets had written either of his tragedies, we had seen less of it than in him. If there was any fault in his language, 'twas that he weaved it too closely and laboriously, in his comedies especially: perhaps, too, he did a little too much to Romanize our tongue, leaving the words which he translated almost as much Latin as when he found them: wherein, though he learnedly followed

---

[1] **Fletcher:** John Fletcher, joint author with Francis Beaumont, mentioned below, of many plays popular in the Elizabethan period.

[2] **mechanic people:** artisans.
[3] *Sejanus* **and** *Catiline:* plays by Ben Jonson.

their language, he did not enough comply with the idiom of ours. If I would compare him with Shakespeare, I must acknowledge him the more correct poet, but Shakespeare the greater wit. Shakespeare was the Homer,[1] or father of our dramatic poets; Jonson was the Virgil,[2] the pattern of elaborate writing; I admire him, but I love Shakespeare. To conclude of him; as he has given us the most correct plays, so in the precepts which he has laid down in his *Discoveries,* we have as many and profitable rules for perfecting the stage, as any wherewith the French can furnish us. . . .

[1] **Homer:** traditional author of the Greek epics, the *Iliad* and the *Odyssey.*
[2] **Virgil:** author of the Roman epic, the *Aeneid.*

FOR STUDY AND DISCUSSION

1. According to Dryden in *An Essay of Dramatic Poesy,* what are Jonson's strong points? his weak ones? Does Dryden condemn Jonson for borrowing from the ancient Greeks and Romans? Cite evidence to support your answer. According to Dryden, what are Shakespeare's faults and merits? Do you agree? Cite examples of these faults and merits from *Macbeth.* In what sense does Dryden consider Shakespeare not a "correct" poet?

2. What difference, if any, is there between Dryden's evaluation of Shakespeare in this essay and Ben Jonson's in "To the Memory of My Beloved Master" (page 185)? Which evaluation is more objective? Does that necessarily make it the superior judgment? Why?

3. Compare Dryden's prose style with that of Francis Bacon. Which is the simpler style? Justify your opinion.

A Song for St. Cecilia's Day

Every year on November 22, a choral concert was given in London in honor of St. Cecilia, a Christian martyr of the third century, the patron saint of music, and, according to tradition, the inventor of the pipe organ. For these concerts original odes were composed and set to music. Dryden wrote two odes for this purpose: "A Song for St. Cecilia's Day," which was presented in 1687, and "Alexander's Feast," which was performed exactly ten years later. In both of these odes Dryden celebrates the power of music. As you read the following ode, note how effectively Dryden unifies sound and sense in his use of words, rhythm, and structure.

I

From harmony, from heavenly harmony
　　This universal frame began:
　　　When Nature underneath a heap
　　　Of jarring atoms lay,
　　And could not heave her head,　　　　　　　5
The tuneful voice was heard from high:
　　"Arise, ye more than dead."
Then cold, and hot, and moist, and dry,°
　　In order to their stations leap,
　　　And Music's power obey.　　　　　　　10
From harmony, from heavenly harmony
　　This universal frame began:
　　　From harmony to harmony
Thro' all the compass of the notes it ran,
The diapason° closing full in Man.　　　　　　15

8. **cold . . . dry:** i.e., the four elements of which all matter was said to be composed.
15. **diapason:** When this organ stop is pulled, all the differently toned pitches are sounded in octaves with the keys played, thereby producing the organ's fullest sound.

II

What passion cannot Music raise and quell!
    When Jubal° struck the corded shell,
    His listening brethren stood around,
    And, wondering, on their faces fell
    To worship that celestial sound.   20
Less than a god they thought there could not dwell
    Within the hollow of that shell
    That spoke so sweetly and so well.
What passion cannot Music raise and quell!

III

    The trumpet's loud clangor   25
        Excites us to arms,
    With shrill notes of anger,
        And mortal alarms.
    The double double double beat
        Of the thundering drum   30
Cries: "Hark! the foes come;
Charge, charge, 'tis too late to retreat."

IV

    The soft complaining flute
    In dying notes discovers
    The woes of hopeless lovers,   35
Whose dirge is whispered by the warbling lute.

V

    Sharp violins proclaim
Their jealous pangs, and desperation,
Fury, frantic indignation,
Depth of pains, and height of passion,   40
    For the fair, disdainful dame.

VI

    But O! what art can teach,
    What human voice can reach,
The sacred organ's praise?
    Notes inspiring holy love,   45
Notes that wing their heavenly ways
    To mend the choirs above.

17. **Jubal:** "The father of all such as handle the harp and organ" (Genesis 4:21).

Orpheus° could lead the savage race;
And trees unrooted left their place,
    Sequacious of° the lyre;
But bright Cecilia raised the wonder higher: 50
When to her organ vocal breath was given,
An angel heard, and straight appeared,
    Mistaking earth for heaven.

GRAND CHORUS

As from the power of sacred lays   55
*   The spheres began to move,°*
And sung the great Creator's praise
*   To all the blest above;*
So, when the last and dreadful hour
This crumbling pageant shall devour,   60
The trumpet shall be heard on high,
The dead shall live, the living die,
And Music shall untune the sky.

48. **Orpheus:** in Greek mythology, a bard whose music charmed even beasts and trees.
50. **Sequacious of:** following. 56. *spheres ... move:* The planets and other heavenly bodies were thought to make music as they orbited.

FOR STUDY AND DISCUSSION

1. In line 2, to what does "universal frame" refer? In what sense is the word "harmony" used? Why are the final two lines of the first stanza appropriate?

2. According to Dryden, what passions are raised and quelled by the power of music? With what instruments are the various passions associated? What instrument does Dryden praise most highly?

3. In line 40 Dryden uses *antithesis:* the balancing against each other of two contrasting words, thoughts, or phrases. Point out other examples of antithesis in this poem.

4. This poem derives much of its effect from *onomatopoeia.* Point out words and phrases in which sound suggests meaning.

5. Explain the meaning of the "Grand Chorus." In the first stanza of the poem, Dryden speaks of music as having organized the created world. This being so, do you think the last line of the poem is a paradox? Explain.

THE ODE

Its name based on a Greek word meaning "song," the ode, a form of long lyric poem, was originated by the Greeks to honor gods and heroes. The Greek odes of Pindar were sung and danced by a chorus, the various movements of the dance corresponding to the different sections of the poem. The characteristics of the original ode were modified by the Romans, and still later by the English. The English form, imitations of the classic Greek and Roman odes, was established by John Dryden. Early English odes were written in praise of a person, of music or poetry, or of abstract ideas, such as liberty. The elaborate address, irregular rhythm, and lofty feeling of the ode also appealed to the Romantic poets who wrote the most famous examples of this form in English. See, for example, Wordsworth's "Intimations of Immortality," Shelley's "To a Skylark," and Keats's "Ode on a Grecian Urn" (pages 476, 524, and 544).

THE GROWTH OF THE ENGLISH LANGUAGE

The Seventeenth Century

One of the most remarkable things that happened to the English language in the course of the seventeenth century was that it reached a fairly stable form—at least so far as the written language is concerned. Writers of the previous century had often felt, with some reason, that they were completely reshaping their native tongue. They had borrowed words wholesale from foreign languages; they had developed elaborate prose styles (frequently in imitation of Latin prose); and they had delighted in rhetorical outpourings that overwhelmed readers with strange terms and fantastic figures of speech.

In the seventeenth century, however, this exuberant Elizabethan attitude gradually gave way to a concern for polishing and refining the language. Milton was one of the last writers to make a deliberate practice of borrowing words from Latin. He was also one of the last to deliberately pattern his style after classical models, using long, weighty sentences and Latinate constructions. Writers who were born later than Milton were no longer so interested in making English ornate, elaborate, or extravagant; they were more interested in trying to make it clear and accurate.

One thing that contributed to this new attitude toward language was the rapid rise of interest in scientific subjects. The modern "Age of Science" was beginning, and the educated public was fascinated by the experiments and discoveries that were taking place in medicine, astronomy, physics, and related fields. Writers on these subjects realized, of course, that clarity and accuracy were essential for their purposes. But they sometimes complained that English—although it had ad-mittedly proved to be an excellent language for poetry and drama—was not suited for expressing exact ideas. For this reason, a few of the leading thinkers of the time continued the old practice of writing in Latin, feeling that it was easier to present ideas accurately in that language. Isaac Newton, for instance, used Latin to write his famous work on mathematics.

However, English was the usual language for scientific discussions in England. The Royal Society was to some extent responsible for this. The Society, which had begun as an informal discussion group, continued to conduct its proceedings in English after it had been officially chartered and had become a center of London intellectual life. As a result, the papers that were read at the weekly meetings of the Society, many of which were later published, were ordinarily in English. Thus the existence of the Society not only encouraged a great deal of scientific writing in English, but also provided an opportunity for people to discuss and criticize each other's scientific prose.

That the members of the Royal Society saw room for improvement in each other's prose is clear from the fact that in 1664, two years after the chartering of the Society, they set up a committee "to improve the English tongue, particularly for philosophic [that is, scientific] purposes." Dryden and several other eminent writers were among those who were appointed to the committee. The idea of forming such a committee had undoubtedly been suggested by the example of the French Academy, a group of French writers and critics that had been organized earlier in the seventeenth century for the purpose of improving the French language. The

Academy was working on a French dictionary and also planned to compile treatises on French grammar, rhetoric, and poetics. The Royal Society's committee considered similar projects—a dictionary (there were no English dictionaries at that time, except for a few books that gave definitions of unusual words and technical terms), a grammar, a set of reformed spelling rules, a collection of translations from classical literature that could serve as models of elegant style for aspiring writers, and so forth.

For better or for worse, however, the committee made no headway on any of these projects and soon dissolved. Many people feel that this was just as well: the subsequent history of English literature might have been quite different if the committee had become a permanent body that insisted on dictating rules of style and usage to the country's writers.

The reform in English prose style that the committee had hoped to accomplish did come about, but it did so through the effort and example of individual writers. In striving to make their own writing clear, Dryden and others of his generation arrived at a kind of prose that was admired and imitated by succeeding generations. To see the difference between late seventeenth-century prose and the kind that had been written earlier, you can turn back to the selection from Malory's *Morte d'Arthur* on page 70. Malory, who was probably not very conscious of "style" in his writing, strings his story together with a series of *and*'s, *then*'s, and *so*'s that make his work sound a little childish or primitive to a modern reader:

"Right *so* on tomorrow day he met with his man *and* his horse, *and so* mounted up *and* dressed his shield *and* took his spear, *and* bade his chamberlain tarry there till he came again. *And so* Arthur rode a soft pace till it was day, *and then* was he ware of three churls chasing Merlin, *and* would have slain him."

The next sizeable prose selection in this book, Bacon's "Of Wisdom for a Man's Self" (page 189), does show great attention to style, but the kind of style that Bacon had in mind was that of classical Latin. While his sentences are elaborately constructed and carefully balanced, they do not seem to flow smoothly. Each statement seems to stand alone, making Bacon's essay sound more like a collection of proverbs than like a connected piece of writing:

"Wisdom for a man's self is, in many branches thereof, a depraved thing:/ it is the wisdom of rats, that will be sure to leave a house somewhat before it fall;/it is the wisdom of the fox, that thrusts out the badger who digged and made room for him;/it is the wisdom of crocodiles, that shed tears when they would devour."

It is not until we come to the prose of the late seventeenth century that we find the kind of sentence structure and paragraph organization that we are accustomed to in modern writing. Except for a few words and idioms that are no longer current, the selection from Dryden's *Essay on Dramatic Poesy* (page 262) might almost have been written in the twentieth century.

FOR STUDY AND DISCUSSION

1. In Dryden's *Essay on Dramatic Poesy* there are a few words that are used in senses no longer common today. Using a college dictionary or an unabridged dictionary, look up the first three words that are footnoted on page 262: *want(ed)*, *clench(es)*, and *wit*. Does the dictionary give definitions that fit the senses in which these words were used by Dryden?

2. Some dictionaries arrange definitions in chronological order, giving the earliest meaning first. Other dictionaries arrange definitions in order of frequency, giving the most common meaning first. If your dictionary has a definition for *want* that fits Dryden's use of the word, is this one of the first definitions given for the word, or does it come later in the list? Judging from this clue, what kind of arrangement does your dictionary follow—chronological order, or order of frequency?

THE EIGHTEENTH CENTURY

(1700–1800)

T HE EIGHTEENTH CENTURY in England wore many faces. Early eighteenth-century writers, seeing a parallel to the admired age of Roman literature under Emperor Augustus, called their time "the Augustan Age," and because these writers deliberately followed the form and content of ancient Greek and Roman models, the period is sometimes known as "the Neoclassical Age." For reasons we shall see later on, it has also been called "the Age of Enlightenment," and "the Age of Elegance."

THE AGE OF REASON

On the whole, this was a century very well pleased with itself. Although wars continued, Britain was free of the revolutionary heat of the seventeenth century and the growing doubts and dark divisions of the nineteenth century. The upper classes and the middle classes in Britain during this age felt that they were living in the best of all possible worlds. Although the influential German philosopher Leibnitz (1646–1716) had proved this to almost everybody's satisfaction, the great French satirist Voltaire (1694–1778), whose famous *Candide* is a savage attack on complacency, would not accept this smug notion.

The complacency of the eighteenth century was due partly to the work of the scientists and philosophers who really belonged to the previous century. The age idolized the mathematician-philosopher Sir Isaac Newton (1642–1727), whose *Mathematical Principles of Natural Philosophy* (1687) provided the framework of a system that seemed capable of explaining everything in the universe. So great was Newton's influence that Alexander Pope, one of the greatest poets of the age, was prompted to write, "God said, 'Let

Newton be!' and all was light.'' But others besides Newton contributed to the intellectual ferment of the age. John Locke's *Essay Concerning Human Understanding* (1690), Bishop Berkeley's *A Treatise Concerning the Principles of Human Knowledge* (1710), David Hume's *Treatise of Human Nature* (1739–40), and Jean-Jacques Rousseau's ideas on the social contract and the "noble savage" were just a few of the many influences on the intellectual climate of the age.

It was the work of Newton and others that led to the philosophy of the universe as a smoothly running machine first set in motion by a vaguely benevolent deity. So long as people understood the working of this machine, they could be said to be masters of it. This rational religion was known as Deism. Indeed, it is because human reason and the watchword "common sense" played so large and significant a role in this period that it is often referred to as "the Age of Reason."

THE FIRST THREE GEORGES

In this century the power of the king in the British government continued the decline that had begun with the first Stuarts a century earlier. After William and Mary came Mary's sister Anne (1702–14), the last of the Stuart monarchs. Ordinarily the crown then would have passed to James Stuart, later called the "Old Pretender," son of the exiled (and dead) James II. But James, like his father, was a Catholic, and Parliament had passed an act that the British sovereign must be Protestant. The crown therefore passed to the next in line after James Stuart, who happened to be the elector of Hanover in Germany. The powerful Louis XIV of France continued to harbor James Stuart and to back his claim to the British throne, and in Britain—particularly in Scotland and Ireland—there were many Stuart supporters, called "Jacobites" (from the Latin *Jacobus*, James).

Thus in 1714 the German-speaking elector of Hanover came to the throne as George I (1714–27). He was succeeded by his son, George II (1727–60), who like his father did not learn English well and showed greater interest in little Hanover than in Great Britain. These Georges therefore allowed control of the British government to fall almost completely into the hands of Parliament, where it remains to this day. The third King George, whose reign spanned sixty years, attempted to be what neither of the first two Georges had been—a strong English king. His attempt at ruling had some unfortunate results, notably the loss to Britain of thirteen of its American colonies.

The Hanovers were not exactly admirable men, but two attempts—in 1715 and 1745—to restore the Stuarts were failures. (In 1745, however, the Scottish followers of "Bonnie Prince Charlie," the Old Pretender's son, reached the English Midlands before they were defeated. It is around this

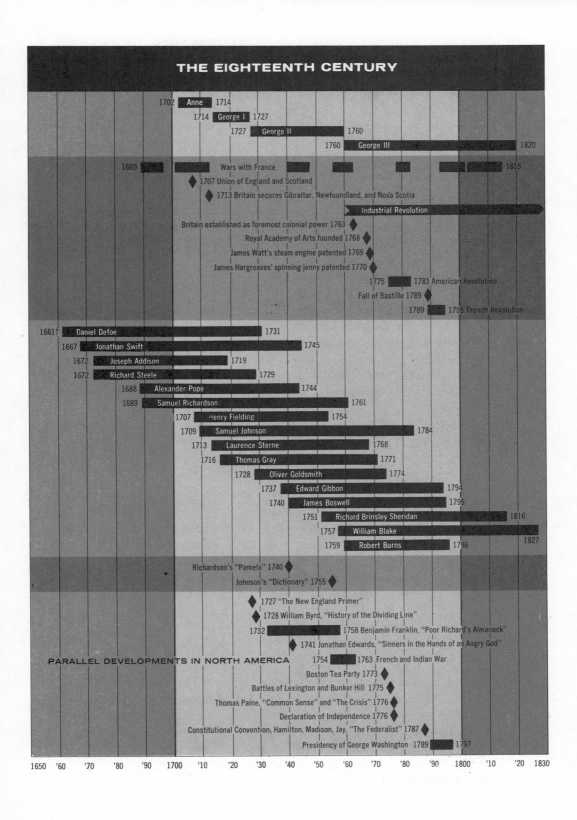

THE EIGHTEENTH CENTURY

1702 Anne 1714
1714 George I 1727
1727 George II 1760
1760 George III 1820

1689 Wars with France 1815
◆ 1707 Union of England and Scotland
◆ 1713 Britain secures Gibraltar, Newfoundland, and Nova Scotia
Industrial Revolution
Britain established as foremost colonial power 1763 ◆
Royal Academy of Arts founded 1768 ◆
James Watt's steam engine patented 1769 ◆
James Hargreaves' spinning jenny patented 1770 ◆
1775 1783 American Revolution
Fall of Bastille 1789 ◆
1789 1795 French Revolution

1661? Daniel Defoe 1731
1667 Jonathan Swift 1745
1672 Joseph Addison 1719
1672 Richard Steele 1729
1688 Alexander Pope 1744
1689 Samuel Richardson 1761
1707 Henry Fielding 1754
1709 Samuel Johnson 1784
1713 Laurence Sterne 1768
1716 Thomas Gray 1771
1728 Oliver Goldsmith 1774
1737 Edward Gibbon 1794
1740 James Boswell 1795
1751 Richard Brinsley Sheridan 1816
1757 William Blake 1827
1759 Robert Burns 1796

Richardson's "Pamela" 1740 ◆
Johnson's "Dictionary" 1755 ◆

◆ 1727 "The New England Primer"
◆ 1728 William Byrd, "History of the Dividing Line"
1732 1758 Benjamin Franklin, "Poor Richard's Almanack"
◆ 1741 Jonathan Edwards, "Sinners in the Hands of an Angry God"
PARALLEL DEVELOPMENTS IN NORTH AMERICA 1754 1763 French and Indian War
Boston Tea Party 1773 ◆
Battles of Lexington and Bunker Hill 1775 ◆
Thomas Paine, "Common Sense" and "The Crisis" 1776 ◆
Declaration of Independence 1776 ◆
Constitutional Convention; Hamilton, Madison, Jay, "The Federalist" 1787 ◆
Presidency of George Washington 1789 1797

1650 '60 '70 '80 '90 1700 '10 '20 '30 '40 '50 '60 '70 '80 '90 1800 '10 '20 1830

'45 rebellion that so many romantic stories have been written.) In Parliament at this time the two-party political system came into being. The Whigs represented chiefly the financial and mercantile interests, the cities and towns, the progressive element, and were strongly opposed to any interference in politics by the monarchy. The Tories, many of them Jacobites in these earlier years, represented the country squires and their folk, all the people who favored old traditions. Though there were general elections then as now, only a comparatively small number of people were entitled to vote. Some quite large towns had no Member of Parliament at all, while some decaying little places known as "rotten boroughs" were still able to elect two members. There was no real political democracy as we know it today, but the ordinary people of the eighteenth century were public-spirited and often expressed their dissatisfaction by violent rioting that could be quelled only by military force.

From the beginning to the end of the century the great rival of Britain—the enemy—was France. At first the struggle was for European supremacy, and this led to the brilliant victories of John Churchill, Duke of Marlborough, an ancestor of Sir Winston Churchill. By the middle of the century, when Britain found a great war minister in William Pitt, afterwards Earl of Chatham (who, incidentally, sided with the colonists in the War of Independence), the struggle with France was for overseas empire. Here Britain had an advantage because she had the better navy and knew how to use her sea power. During these years the huge British Empire, ranging from Gibraltar to India and Canada, began to be built up. In the last ten years of the century, Britain fought the French again because the British Tory ministers were afraid of the consequences of the French Revolution, perhaps the most important historical event before the world wars of the twentieth century.

The eighteenth century was a century of wars, fought in all manner of places and conditions, but they were not wars as we understand them now. They were usually fought by small professional armies, and the daily lives of most people in the nations concerned were affected hardly at all. Even when Britain and France were at war, trade and cultural exchanges continued between the two countries. There was no "total war," one whole nation trying to conquer another, such as we have had in the twentieth century.

THE INDUSTRIAL REVOLUTION

During the latter half of the century British prosperity was increasing rapidly because of what we have come to call the "Industrial Revolution"—that is, the increasing use of machinery and steam power in the manufacture of goods. What previously had been made by hand, often by people working at home, was now manufactured on an infinitely larger scale in mills and factories. Though the Industrial Revolution eventually took hold throughout

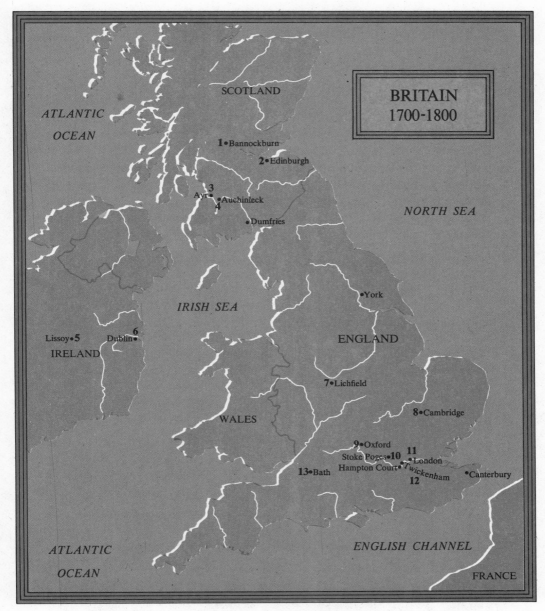

BRITAIN
1700-1800

SCOTLAND

ATLANTIC
OCEAN

1•Bannockburn

2•Edinburgh

3
Ayr• •Auchinleck
4

•Dumfries

NORTH SEA

•York

IRISH SEA

Lissoy•5   Dublin•6
IRELAND

ENGLAND

7•Lichfield

8•Cambridge

WALES

9•Oxford
Stoke Poges•10   11
Hampton Court• •London
13•Bath   •Twickenham   •Canterbury
12

ATLANTIC

OCEAN

ENGLISH CHANNEL

FRANCE

1 Site of 1314 battle, celebrated by Burns, in which Robert Bruce defeated the English. 2 Capital of Scotland. Site of famous university, attended by Boswell and Goldsmith. Burns lionized here after publication of his first book of poetry. 3 Home of Robert Burns. 4 Family home of James Boswell. 5 Childhood home of Oliver Goldsmith. 6 Birthplace of Steele, Swift, and Sheridan. Swift and Goldsmith attended Trinity College here, and Swift later became Dean of St. Patrick's. 7 Birthplace of Addison and Johnson. 8 Gray and Sterne studied here, and Gray later taught here. 9 Addison, Steele, Johnson, and Gibbon attended the university here. 10 Village identified with Gray's "Elegy in a Country Churchyard"; Gray buried here. 11 Coffeehouses flourished and *The Tatler, Spectator,* and Defoe's *Review* were published here. Center of elegant society; writer's mecca where Johnson's Literary Club met. 12 Home of Alexander Pope. 13 Popular resort, visited by Fielding, Smollett, Sheridan, Goldsmith, Jane Austen, and others. Setting of Sheridan's *The Rivals.*

the western world, Britain easily led the way because she had the necessary coal and iron ore, her inventors designed many of the new machines, and her growing empire gave her large overseas markets. This led to a rapid increase in population as well as in national wealth.

But with all this sheer gain there came some sad losses, as many writers were quick to perceive. William Blake (1757–1827), the poet, artist, and mystic, referred with horror to "the dark, satanic mills." Much of England, especially in the north and the Midlands, was rapidly transformed into a blackened, ruined countryside of mine shafts, slag heaps, tall chimneys pouring out smoke, and horrible industrial towns in which people lived and worked in appalling conditions. All this, against which writer after writer protested, was not observed and felt in its full force until the next century, but already in the eighteenth century its shadow began to creep over the country.

NEW RELIGIOUS DEVELOPMENTS

At this time, the interest of those who worried about, or were displaced by, the new industrialism was captured by religious reformers such as John and Charles Wesley. In the early part of the eighteenth century, Puritan sentiments were muted and most English people belonged to the Church of England. The Church of England during the eighteenth century existed, for the most part, in a state of sleepy conformity. Many clergymen, some of

One of the first of the many new machines invented during the early years of the Industrial Revolution was James Hargreaves' spinning jenny, patented in 1770.

them the younger sons of aristocratic landowners who could not provide for them out of their estates but could offer them church "livings," had several different and widely separated parishes. They took the incomes attached to these parishes and then appointed poor curates, at fifty pounds a year, to do the work. Some bishops did not live within their dioceses or, if they did, they often concerned themselves more with scholarly research, antiquarianism, even chemistry, than they did with church work. Some of these eighteenth-century churchmen did not really believe in the Christian faith at all, regarding it as something intended for simple, uneducated minds. Laurence Sterne (1713–1768), for example, the great humorous novelist, was a parson, but he can hardly be accepted as a Christian believer. As soon as he became a successful writer he spent long periods hundreds of miles away from his church and his vicarage.

Such official indifference to the burning realities of religion inevitably produced a sharp reaction. The brothers Wesley began to convert people to a fervently evangelical type of Christianity. Throughout the century the various nonconformist sects which had developed were joined by more and more of the working folk and the members of the new middle classes created by the Industrial Revolution, especially in the Midlands and the north of England, where the growth of industry late in the period was to send the population figures soaring.

During this period, then, we have an elegant, complacent, skeptical, and cynical upper class, a growing number of earnestly pious and intensely respectable people belonging to the middle and artisan classes, and finally the poor—sharply drawn not only by the writers of the time but also by the artist William Hogarth (1697–1764). (See pages 319–26.) Hogarth, whose great talent was exact realism, shows us a panorama of the lives of all classes. We learn from Hogarth, as we do from the novelists of the day, that life was often rough and rowdy, filled with crude sports and heavy drinking.

AN AGE OF ELEGANCE

Largely oblivious to the problems of the poor, a small minority, waited upon by servants who were themselves often waited upon by humbler servants, lived lives which were more than comfortable. Many of them lived on a superb scale. Never, for example, in European history do we see men and women so elaborately artificial, so far removed from natural appearance, as these men and women of the eighteenth century. The men wore wigs, which often had to be curled every day, and with them gaily colored and lace-trimmed satin coats and waistcoats, silk stockings, and buckled shoes. The women often had immense coiffures of powdered hair and enormous hooped skirts and were carried to their parties in sedan chairs. An evening party in high society, taking place in a room lit with hundreds of candles, must have been an impressive spectacle.

These people lived better in some ways than similar people have done since. We know from pictures of the age and from the eighteenth-century houses, furniture, and domestic utensils still in existence that the outward trappings of their lives were truly magnificent. The domestic architecture, from the Queen Anne style to the late Georgian, has probably never been equaled. The interior decoration of the Adam brothers, the furniture designed by Chippendale, Hepplewhite, and Sheraton—all these were magnificent. Find if you can, if only reposing in some museum, a Georgian silver tankard or coffee pot. Remember that these people were surrounded by such things all day, and you will then realize with what style they lived.

Only a small minority, however, lived on this superb scale. The mass of the people did not wear wigs (which cost a great deal of money) and satin coats and breeches and silk stockings; they did not sit on chairs designed by Chippendale and Hepplewhite, nor drink out of beautiful silver tankards. They dressed plainly, wore their own hair unpowdered, and drank out of clumsy mugs and cups.

The middle class, struggling to establish itself, found its ideal social center in the coffeehouses, which came to occupy the large blank space between the town houses of the aristocrats and the rough and roaring taverns of the Elizabethans and Jacobeans. The coffeehouses offered the same services to professional middle-class Londoners that clubs did later, and still do. So City men—financiers, merchants, shipowners—met at Lloyd's coffeehouse, where Lloyd's, the most famous insurance firm in the world, was established. Writers, from John Dryden to Alexander Pope, generally met at Will's.

This Chippendale bureau and Hepplewhite chair typify the elegance of the age.

An old engraving showing St. James's Palace in the time of Queen Anne.

Other coffeehouse patrons, who might be City men, politicians, lawyers, writers, and the more free-and-easy aristocrats, foregathered at White's (now a rather exclusive club), St. James's, the Grecian, Buttons, and the Turk's Head. At such places, news could be gathered and exchanged, some business conducted, political secrets whispered. There also might be serious discussion of religion, philosophy, literature, domestic and foreign affairs, as well as a good deal of pleasant or malicious gossip. The result of this coffeehouse habit was a knitting together of the middle and upper sections of English society, which was a considerable benefit to the writer, among others, and to literature. It helped, too, to create a feeling, characteristic of this century, that this closely knit and highly articulate society represented a new but enduring civilization, not unlike but superior to the ancient civilizations of Greece and Rome. This civilization belonged only to persons of some position, wealth, and influence; the common people were still a long way outside it. If you were reasonably fortunate in your status, however, you could settle down to enjoy "the best of all possible worlds."

A PUBLIC LITERATURE

Literature at the beginning of this period—say, during the reign of Queen Anne—was created chiefly for this small and compact society of important and influential persons. It was very much a public literature, not representing the deeply felt impressions, hopes, or fears of one individual but the outlook and values of this limited society. It was a literature that could be read aloud in a drawing room, enjoyed in a theater or some other public place.

Now, an atmosphere of this kind encourages comedy, satire in both verse and prose, pleasant little essays, and criticism, but it is bad for poetry. Shakespeare's sonnets or Keats's odes would have seemed embarrassing to this society, which did not expect from literature anything so intensely private or intimately revealing. One does not describe one's most secret dreams to fifty people (many of them ready to snicker) in a drawing room. Poetry at its best comes out of an essentially individual inner life, out of what is private and not public. What these people believed in was not the inner life but rather what they felt to be civilized good taste, what persons of common sense and with reasonably nice feelings could enjoy together.

This cramps the real poet. We cannot help feeling that a writer like Alexander Pope (1688–1744), with his wonderful command of the smooth and often witty rhymed couplet, was never able to express himself as fully as he might have in another age. Within narrow limits he did wonderfully well. But, for example, in his otherwise skillful translation of Homer, we feel he is dressing the rugged heroes of Greece and Troy in wigs, satin coats, and silk stockings and providing them with canes and snuffboxes.

The writers of Queen Anne's reign, poets like John Gay (1685–1732) and Matthew Prior (1664–1721) and essayists like Joseph Addison (1672–1719) and Richard Steele (1672–1729) did not expect to be rewarded chiefly by the general reading public. Either they were rewarded directly by the wealthy patrons to whom they dedicated their work or they were given easy, well-paid government jobs, called "sinecures," that would enable them to continue writing in comfortable circumstances. It was the small but influential society for which they wrote that generally brought authors their rewards. This may seem an odd system to us and certainly it had its disadvantages—as we know from a famous bitter letter (see page 335) addressed by Samuel Johnson (1709–1784) to his would-be patron, Lord Chesterfield (1694–1773)—but it had some advantages too. It meant that a writer could confidently address his work to cultivated, intelligent readers and could confidently maintain a certain level in his writing.

Very soon, however, the dependence of authors upon patronage gave way to a system not unlike our own, except that publishers of books in those days were still themselves booksellers. Readers were no longer confined to a small class. The new middle class, especially its women members, took to buying and reading books. If they could not afford to buy them, they borrowed them from lending libraries. An amusing scene in Sheridan's comedy *The Rivals* (page 357) shows that young women borrowed fiction in large quantities from the lending libraries. (*The Rivals* as well as Sheridan's later comedy, *The School for Scandal,* and Goldsmith's *She Stoops to Conquer,* all written between 1770 and 1780, were not only extremely successful in their own time but have been almost equally successful ever since.) The fact that young women in the 1770's borrowed so much fiction shows that the novel, though a comparatively new literary form, already had won great popularity.

At any rate, outstanding novelists of the day—men such as Samuel Richardson (1689–1761), author of *Pamela;* Henry Fielding (1707–1754), author of *Tom Jones;* Laurence Sterne, author of *Tristram Shandy;* and Tobias Smollett (1721–1771), author of *Humphrey Clinker*—were almost entirely dependent upon this new and growing reading public. Authors of more weighty works, however—Samuel Johnson, for instance, or Edward Gibbon (1737–1794), the great historian of the Roman Empire—usually brought out their works accompanied by a list of wealthy subscribers, whose support guaranteed that the books would at least pay for themselves.

Nevertheless, professional writers who had to earn their living and had no government pension (as Johnson finally had) usually led desperate lives scribbling away day and night to keep themselves from starvation. They would often undertake, for miserable payment, to write long books on subjects they knew little about, just because these were what the booksellers demanded from them. For years a man of genius like Oliver Goldsmith (1728–1774)—capable of writing comedy, fiction, and verse that would enchant future generations—wasted precious time and energy on this sort of hack work. If the rewards of good original work had been greater and more immediate than they were, the literature of this century might have been even richer than it is.

THE BEGINNINGS OF ROMANTICISM

In his masterpiece, the *Life of Samuel Johnson,* James Boswell (1740–1795) tells about an old acquaintance of Johnson's who said that he too might have been a philosopher except that "cheerfulness kept breaking in." Now something had to break into this eighteenth century in Britain, for it was altogether too calm and complacent, too sure of itself and its standards, too contemptuous of the past and of all that earlier people had thought and felt, too easily convinced that a new and superior age had arrived, too certain that it was the best of all possible worlds. It ignored or denounced too often the secret inner lives of people, their hidden dreams and desires and hopes, all that belonged essentially to people as individuals and not as members of a society. Even writers who seem typically eighteenth-century figures show that the pressure of this conformity was too much for them: Jonathan Swift, for all his powerful intellect, has a suggestion of some dark madness in his savage satires, and Johnson, for all his sociability and delight in good talk, is at heart melancholy and fearful, enjoying the lighted dinner table all the more because of the threatening darkness.

What breaks through into this public literature of an ordered and complacent society is the other side of man's life, his inner world of wonder and strange feeling, all that cannot be expressed in a social mood of philosophic calm. This new literature belongs not to what is public and classical but to what is essentially private, and thus is called *romantic*. This breakthrough, which was gradual and began about the middle of the century, showed itself in various ways. It showed itself in the curious hothouse sentimentality of Richardson's novels, soon to conquer Europe, and in the strongly personal mixture of humor and sentiment in Laurence Sterne's work. It showed itself in the publication of Bishop Percy's *Reliques of Ancient English Poetry* (1765), a collection of ballads that had a tremendous influence on the whole Romantic movement of the early nineteenth century. It showed itself in the new taste—led by that apparently typical eighteenth-century dilettante, Horace Walpole (1717–1797)—for ruins and Gothic castles and tales of mystery. It showed itself in the fashion during the latter half of the century for founding strange, secret societies interested in magic and in mysterious rites.

But this breakthrough was most obvious in poetry. Though they are all in many ways typical eighteenth-century men, Thomas Gray (1716–1771), Oliver Goldsmith, and William Cowper (1731–1800) in their best verse began to show the other side of life. Robert Burns (1759–1796), the national poet of Scotland, alternated between verse in the acceptable eighteenth-century style and impassioned lyrics or comic-pathetic narrative poems about the peasantry that are undoubtedly Romantic in feeling. And then there was William Blake (see pages 274 and 424), an astonishing character and one of the world's great originals, who in his earliest poems seems like another Elizabethan but then flashes out, completely disregarding the taste of the time, in work that blazes with his own highly original genius. By this time the Romantic Age had almost arrived.

The last years of the eighteenth century were altogether different from its first years. Nothing was certain after the destructive fury of the French Revolution. Britain was sharply divided between those who feared and denounced the French Revolution and those who welcomed it. Old values and standards seemed to vanish in the smoke of burning buildings and the roar of Napoleon's cannons, which were heard everywhere in Europe from Spain to Moscow. Anything could happen now: it was that kind of world, that kind of universe. The social order was no longer as stable as it once had been. The old aristocracy was giving way to a rising middle class, and there was increasing sympathy for the underprivileged classes. Ideas of political freedom, of independence, of the human "family" and people's "natural rights" had become more and more widespread, as revolutions on both sides of the Atlantic Ocean had attested. A new spirit was abroad. Gone were the philosophic calm, the complacency, the exultation of good taste, the curled wigs and lacy satin coats, the coffeehouse wits and critics and their *Tatlers* and *Spectators:* the whole age was as dead as Queen Anne.

J.B.P.

DANIEL DEFOE
(1661?–1731)

Everyone knows the story of *Robinson Crusoe,* a fictional account of a man's struggle to survive amidst the hostile and lonely surroundings of a desert island. Few realize that the publication in 1719 of this book by Daniel Defoe paved the way for the modern English novel. Defoe's perceptive and accurate observations and his sober, straightforward style led to accusations that he was "forging a story and imposing it on the world for truth"—and so, in a sense, he was. Defoe was an accomplished journalist in an age when the profession was new and skilled news-papermen were rare. His gift for storytelling was that of the journalist: he had the ability to achieve verisimilitude—to create something that appeared to be factually true. A vivid imagination coupled with a lively curiosity about people, a photographic memory for significant details, and a sure sense of the dramatic contributed to the aura of reality which distinguishes all of his work.

Defoe's boundless energy enabled him to combine the life of a writer with that of a man of action. The son of a London butcher, he traveled on the Continent, served in the army, became a tradesman, and was employed for some time as a secret service agent for the government. Although he was past thirty when he began to write, he developed into a prolific writer. In 1704, he established the *Review,* an early London newspaper which he ran almost singlehandedly for nine years. After producing gazettes and political pamphlets by the score, Defoe turned from journalism to the writing of novels and fictitious history such as *Robinson Crusoe* and *A Journal of the Plague Year.*

No life demonstrates more dramatically than Defoe's both the peril and the power of the pen, especially the pen dipped in irony. Defoe's *The Shortest Way with Dissenters* reduced to absurdity the rabid intolerance prevalent in his time. Although an ardent dissenter himself, he pretended to advocate an off-with-their-heads policy toward all those who dared to dissent with the tenets of the Church of England. The authorities at first took him literally and many unwary church officials endorsed his position, but, when they discovered that they had been de-ceived by his tone, they were not amused. Defoe was arrested, tried, and sentenced to prison and three successive appearances in the pillory. The pillory sentence, which was meant to degrade him publicly, turned to triumph when, instead of the expected jeering, a group of his friends sang a satiric song Defoe had composed for the occasion and pelted him with flowers rather than rocks and rotten eggs.

A Journal of the Plague Year

When Defoe published the *Journal* in 1722, the bubonic plague had ravaged the Continent for a number of years and there was the possibility that it would once again infest England as it had in 1665, over fifty years before. With a journalist's sensitivity to what arouses public interest, Defoe wrote, in diary form, a fictional but seemingly authentic account of the experiences of a London tradesman in the Great Plague of 1665. Early in the journal the diarist speaks of his indecision about leaving London for the safety of the country. Finally, feeling an obligation to look after his servants and his business, he took consolation from the Bible ("Surely he shall deliver thee from the noisome pestilence") and chose to stay.

In its matter-of-fact narrative and its vivid and careful reporting of detail, the *Journal* illustrates Defoe's ability to persuade his readers that fiction is literal truth. Although Defoe himself lived through the Great Plague of 1665, he was only a small child at the time and thus most likely drew his information for the *Journal* entirely from records and conversations. In the following excerpt from the *Journal,* he describes some of the day-to-day horrors of the epidemic.

It PLEASED God that I was still spared, and very hearty and sound in health, but very impatient of being pent up within doors without air, as I had been for fourteen days, or thereabouts; and I could not restrain myself, but I would go to carry a letter for my brother to the posthouse. Then it was, indeed, that I observed a profound silence in the streets. When I came to the posthouse, as I went to put in my letter, I saw a man stand in one corner of the yard, and talking to another at a window, and a third had opened a door belonging to the office. In the middle of the yard lay a small leather purse, with two keys hanging at it, and money in it, but nobody would meddle with it. I asked how long it had lain there; the man at the window said it had lain almost an hour, but they had not meddled with it, because they did not know but the person who dropped it might come back to look for it. I had no such need of money, nor was the sum so big that I had any inclination to meddle with it to get the money at the hazard it might be attended with; so I seemed to go away, when the man who had opened the door said he would take it up; but so that if the right owner came for it, he should be sure to have it. So he went in and fetched a pail of water, and set it down hard by the purse, then went again and fetched some gunpowder and cast a good deal of powder upon the purse, and then made a train from that which he had thrown loose upon the purse; the train reached about two yards. After this he goes in a third time, and fetches out a pair of tongs red hot, and which he had prepared, I suppose, on purpose; and first setting fire to the train of powder, that singed the purse, and also smoked the air sufficiently. But he was not content with that; but he then takes up the purse with the tongs, holding it so long till the tongs burnt through the purse, and then he shook the money out into the pail of water, so he carried it in. The money, as I remember, was about thirteen shillings, and some smooth groats, and brass farthings.

There might, perhaps, have been several poor people, as I have observed above, that would have been hardy enough to have ventured for the sake of the money; but you may easily see, by what I have observed, that the few people who were spared were very careful of themselves at that time when the distress was so exceeding great.

It would pierce the hearts of all that came by to hear the piteous cries of those infected people, who being thus out of their understandings by the violence of their pain, or the heat of their blood, were either shut in, or perhaps tied in their beds and chairs, to prevent their doing themselves hurt, and who would make a dreadful outcry at their being confined, and at their not being permitted to die at large, as they called it, and as they would have done before.

This running of distempered people about the streets was very dismal, and the magistrates did their utmost to prevent it; but as it was generally in the night and always sudden when such attempts were made, the officers could not be at hand to prevent it, and even when they got out in the day, the officers appointed did not care to meddle with them, because, as they were all grievously infected, to be sure, when they were come to that height, so they were more than ordinarily infectious, and it was one of the most dangerous things that could be to touch them. On the other hand, they generally ran on, not knowing what they did, till they dropped down stark dead, or till they had exhausted their spirits so as that they would fall, and then die in perhaps half an hour or an hour; and what was most piteous to hear, they were sure to come to themselves entirely in that half-hour or hour, and then to make most grievous and piercing cries and lamentations in the deep afflicting sense of the condition they were in. This was much of it before the order for shutting up of houses was strictly put in execution, for at first the watchmen were not so rigorous and severe as they were afterward in the keeping the people in; that is to say, before they were, I mean some of them, severely punished for their neglect, failing in their duty and letting people who were under their care slip away, or conniving at their going abroad, whether sick or well. But after they saw the officers appointed to examine into their conduct were resolved to have them do their duty, or be punished for the omission, they were more exact, and the people were strictly restrained; which was a thing they took so ill, and bore so impatiently, that their discontents can hardly be described; but there was an absolute necessity for it, that must be confessed, unless some other measures had been timely entered upon, and it was too late for that.

Had not this particular of the sick being restrained as above, been our case at that time,[1] London would have been the most dreadful place that ever was in the world; there would, for aught I know, have as many people died in the streets as died in their houses; for when the distemper was at its height, it generally made them raving and delirious, and when they were so, they would never be persuaded to keep in their beds but by force; and many, who were not tied, threw themselves out of windows when they found they could not get leave to go out of their doors.

It was for want of people conversing one with another, in this time of calamity, that it was impossible any particular person could come at the knowledge of all the extraordinary cases that occurred in different families; and particularly I believe it was never known to this day how many people in their deliriums drowned themselves in the Thames and in the river which runs from the marshes by Hackney, which we generally called Ware River, or Hackney River. As to those which were set down in the weekly bill,[2] they were indeed few; nor could it be known of any of those, whether they drowned themselves by accident or not. But I believe I might reckon up more who within the compass of my knowledge or observation really drowned themselves in that year than are put down in the bill of all put together, for many of the bodies were never found, who yet were known to be so lost: and the like, in other methods of self-destruction. There was also one man, in or about Whitecross Street, who burnt himself to death in his bed; some said it was done by himself, others that it was by the treachery of the nurse that attended

---

[1] **Had not ... time:** if we had not restrained the sick people in the manner described above.

[2] **bill:** a list of the dead in each parish and the cause of death.

The Bills of Mortality listed the deaths caused by the Great Plague of 1665.

him; but that he had the plague upon him was agreed by all. . . .

We that were examiners [1] were often not able to come at the knowledge of the infection being entered into a house till it was too late to shut it up; and sometimes not till the people that were left were all dead. In Petticoat Lane two houses together were infected, and several people sick; but the distemper was so well concealed that the examiner, who was my neighbor, got no knowledge of it till notice was sent him that the people were all dead, and that the carts [2] should call there to fetch them away. The two heads of the families concerted their

measures, and so ordered their matters, as that when the examiner was in the neighborhood, they appeared generally at a time, and answered, that is, lied for one another; or got some of the neighborhood to say they were all in health, and, perhaps, knew no better, till death making it impossible to keep it any longer as a secret, the dead carts were called in the night to both houses, and so it became public; but when the examiner ordered the constable to shut up the houses, there was nobody left in them but three people, two in one house and one in the other, just dying, and a nurse in each house, who acknowledged that they had buried five before, that the houses had been infected nine or ten days, and that for all the rest of the two families, which were many, they were gone, some sick, some well, or whether sick or well, could not be known.

In like manner, at another house in the same lane, a man, having his family infected, but very unwilling to be shut up, when he could conceal it no longer, shut up himself; that is to say, he set the great Red Cross upon his door, with the words, "Lord have Mercy upon Us"; and so deluded the examiner, who supposed it had been done by the constable by order of the other examiner, for there were two examiners to every district or precinct; by this means he had free egress and regress [3] into his house again, and out of it, as he pleased, notwithstanding it was infected; till at length his stratagem was found out, and then he, with the sound part of his servants and family, made off and escaped; so they were not shut up at all.

These things made it very hard, if not impossible, as I have said, to prevent the spreading of an infection by the shutting up of houses, unless the people would think the shutting up of their houses no grievance, and be so willing to have it done as that they would give notice

[1] **examiners:** men whose job it was to determine which houses had been infected by the plague.

[2] **carts:** The dead bodies were collected at night in carts and taken to a common burial ground, since the churchyards would not hold them all.

[3] **egress and regress:** exit and entrance.

duly and faithfully to the magistrates of their being infected, as soon as it was known by themselves; but as that cannot be expected from them, and the examiners cannot be supposed, as above, to go into their houses to visit and search, all the good of shutting up the houses will be defeated, and few houses will be shut up in time, except those of the poor, who cannot conceal it, and of some people who will be discovered by the terror and consternation which the thing put into them.

It is here, however, to be observed, that after the funerals became so many that people could not toll the bell, mourn, or weep, or wear black for one another, as they did before; no, nor so much as make coffins for those that died; so after a while the fury of the infection appeared to be so increased, that in short, they shut up no houses at all. It seemed enough that all the remedies of that kind had been used till they were found fruitless, and that the plague spread itself with an irresistible fury; so that as the fire, the succeeding year, spread itself and burnt with such violence that the citizens, in despair, gave over[1] their endeavors to extinguish it, so in the plague it came at last to such violence that the people sat still, looking at one another, and seemed quite abandoned to despair. Whole streets seemed to be desolated, and not to be shut up only, but to be emptied of their inhabitants; doors were left open, and windows stood shattering with the wind in empty houses for want of people to shut them. In a word, people began to give up themselves to their fears, and to think that all regulations and methods were in vain, and that there was nothing to be hoped for but an universal desolation; and it was even in the height of this general despair that it pleased God to stay his hand, and to slacken the fury of the contagion, in such a manner as was even surprising (like its beginning),

[1] over: up.

and demonstrated it to be his own particular hand, and that above, if not without, the agency of means, as I shall take notice of in its proper place.

But I must still speak of the plague as in its height, raging even to desolation, and the people under the most dreadful consternation, even, as I have said, to despair. It is hardly credible to what excesses the passions of men carried them in this extremity of the distemper, and this part, I think, was as moving as the rest.

FOR STUDY AND DISCUSSION

1. What kind of man is Defoe's imaginary first-person reporter? What does the manner in which he describes the horrifying events he witnessed tell you about the narrator? Why do you think Defoe chose this kind of person as the narrator of an "eyewitness" account?

2. In Defoe's own words, list some of the most telling details that make the *Journal* read like the account of an on-the-spot reporter. Which details contribute most to the reader's sense of the horror of the plague? Is it his choice of details or his wording that makes Defoe's account so effective? Explain.

3. What observations on human behavior does Defoe make? Does he pass judgment on what he observes? How does this relate to the practice of a good reporter?

4. Compare Defoe's description of the plague with Pepys's account of the Great Fire of the following year (page 257). Which do you consider more graphic, more realistic in impression? Why? How does the attitude of the author of the *Journal* compare with Pepys's attitude? Support your answers with evidence from the selections.

FOR COMPOSITION

By reading and by talking with people who remember it well, find out all you can about some event (an earthquake, fire, or other natural disaster) that occurred before you were old enough to be aware of it. Then, giving yourself a carefully chosen identity and clearly established viewpoint, bear in mind the devices by which Defoe achieves an impression of reality and write a first-person account of the event as though you had been there.

JOSEPH ADDISON
(1672–1719)

RICHARD STEELE
(1672–1729)

One of the most famous literary partnerships in English literature is that of Addison and Steele, who together created a new form and style of writing—that of the familiar essay. Though markedly different in temperament, Addison and Steele collaborated superbly, first in *The Tatler* and later in *The Spectator,* two early and popular periodicals (the forerunners of our present-day magazines) for which Addison and Steele between them wrote most of the essays.

Except for an unfortunate political quarrel a year before Addison's death, Addison and Steele were lifelong friends as well as collaborators. The two first met at the Charterhouse School in London and went on together to Oxford University. But Steele, witty, warmhearted, impulsive, and somewhat reckless in practical matters, left school to join the army, where he rose to the rank of captain. He also served as manager of a theater, for which he wrote several comedies, and as editor of the Whig party newspaper, an appointment he obtained through Addison, a fellow Whig. Later he turned to still other ventures as magazine publisher, poet, reformer, and Member of Parliament, and was generally known as a dashing man-about-town. Meanwhile, his more scholarly, withdrawn, and dignified friend, Addison, had taken his degree and embarked upon a literary career. A poem celebrating the victory of the Duke of Marlborough at Blenheim brought him to public attention when he was still fairly young. Though he is remembered chiefly as an essayist and stylist of English prose, he served his country in various political capacities as well. In 1717, shortly after he married the Countess of Warwick, he was appointed Secretary of State, a position enjoyed until his death two years later.

Steele started *The Tatler* in 1709. It was an immediate success. A modest one-page paper, it contained news, coffeehouse gossip, and comments on current events. In later issues Steele adopted the more serious purpose of serving as a moral influence and speaking out against the negligence and improprieties of his contemporaries. Addison began his collaboration with Steele by contributing articles to this paper.

When *The Tatler* was discontinued because of political difficulties, Addison and Steele decided to found together *The Spectator,* a new periodical which would take literature, manners, and morals as its subject matter. With good-natured satire, tolerance, and common sense, Addison and Steele sought to reform social tastes and behavior. That their gentle tone apparently was the right one with which to address their age is confirmed by a contemporary who said of them that they "ventured to tell the town that they were a parcel of fops, fools, and vain coquettes; but in such a manner as even pleased them and made them even more than half believe that they spoke the truth."

Although Steele may have been the more inventive and original member of this partnership, Addison was the more polished writer. Samuel Johnson, in his conclusion to the *Life of Addison,* wrote, "Whoever wishes to attain an English style, familiar but not coarse, elegant but not ostentatious, must give his days and nights to the volumes of Addison." Thus, while it was Steele who conceived the idea of the familiar periodical essay, it was Addison who perfected it.

The Tatler (1709–1711)

The *Tatler* owed its inception partly to Steele's fear of bankruptcy and partly to his interest in the reform of morals and the betterment of his fellow creatures. His use of Isaac Bickerstaff as a pen name assured the paper public attention. Jonathan Swift had used the Bickerstaff name the year before when he played a practical joke on a quack astrologer named Partridge. Swift, writing under the imaginary name of Isaac Bickerstaff, predicted that, according to the stars, Partridge was to die of a fever on March 28. On March 28, Swift printed a solemn announcement of Partridge's death and the newspapers carried detailed accounts of the funeral. Highly incensed, Partridge insisted that he was alive. Bickerstaff retorted that, according to the stars, he could not be and that to pretend otherwise was an affront to stellar omniscience. With adroit salesmanship, Richard Steele took advantage of this horseplay when he began his *Tatler* under the supposed authorship of Isaac Bickerstaff.

The audience which *The Tatler* addressed is mainly the growing middle class; the paper's tone is the casual, conversational one of the coffeehouse, the middle class's new-found fraternity house and practical university. In the Prospectus of *The Tatler,* in which Steele sets forth the general plan of his paper, we see the importance of the coffeehouse as a gathering place for the social, political, and literary life of the day. Just as in the Prospectus, which follows, Steele prefaced many of his essays with an appropriate Greek or Latin motto, a practice which was continued in *The Spectator.* The motto accompanying the Prospectus was taken from the Roman poet Juvenal and, as translated by the poet Alexander Pope, reads:

"Whate'er men do, or say, or think, or dream,
  Our motley paper seizes for its theme."

PROSPECTUS

No. 1. Tuesday, 12 April, 1709.

THOUGH the other papers, which are published for the use of the good people of England, have certainly very wholesome effects, and are laudable in their particular kinds, they do not seem to come up to the main design of such narrations, which, I humbly presume, should be principally intended for the use of politic persons, who are so public-spirited as to neglect their own affairs to look into transactions of state. Now these gentlemen, for the most part, being persons of strong zeal, and weak intellects, it is both a charitable and necessary work to offer something, whereby such worthy and well-affected members of the commonwealth may be instructed, after their reading, what to think; which shall be the end and purpose of this my paper, wherein I shall, from time to time, report and consider all matters of what kind soever that shall occur to me, and publish such my advices and reflections every Tuesday, Thursday, and Saturday in the week, for the convenience of the post. I resolve to have something which may be of entertainment to the fair sex, in honor of whom I have invented the title of this paper. I therefore earnestly desire all persons, without distinction, to take it in for the present *gratis,*[1] and hereafter at the price of one penny, forbidding all hawkers to take more for it at their peril. And I desire all persons to consider that I am at a very great charge [2] for the proper materials for this work, as well as that, before I re-

[1] *gratis:* free of charge.
[2] **charge:** pains.

Above left, Joseph Addison.
Above right, Richard Steele.
Far left, the first issue of *The Spectator*.

solved upon it, I had settled a correspondence in all parts of the known and knowing world. And forasmuch as this globe is not trodden upon by mere drudges of business only, but that men of spirit and genius are justly to be esteemed as considerable agents in it, we shall not, upon a dearth of news, present you with musty foreign edicts, and dull proclamations, but shall divide our relation of the passages which occur in action or discourse throughout this town, as well as elsewhere, under such dates of places as may prepare you for the matter you are to expect in the following manner.

All accounts of gallantry, pleasure, and entertainment shall be under the article of White's Chocolate House; poetry under that of Will's Coffeehouse; learning, under the title of Grecian; foreign and domestic news, you will have from St. James's Coffeehouse; and what else I have to offer on any other subject shall be dated from my own apartment.

I once more desire my reader to consider, that as I cannot keep an ingenious man to go daily to Will's under twopence each day, merely for his charges;[1] to White's under sixpence; nor to the Grecian, without allowing him some plain Spanish,[2] to be as able as others at the learned table; and that a good observer cannot speak with even Kidney[3] at St. James's without clean linen; I say, these considerations will, I hope, make all persons willing to comply with my humble request (when my *gratis* stock is exhausted) of a penny apiece; especially since they are sure of some proper amusement, and that it is impossible for me to want means to entertain them, having, besides the force of my own parts,[4] the power of divination, and that I can, by casting a figure, tell you all that will happen before it comes to pass.

But this last faculty I shall use very sparingly, and speak but of few things until they are passed, for fear of divulging matters which may offend our superiors.

[1] **charges:** expenses. The twopence would buy him some coffee, presumably.

[2] **Spanish:** wine.

[3] **Kidney:** name of a waiter.

[4] **force . . . parts:** the power of my own abilities.

The Spectator (1711–1712)

The first issue of *The Spectator* appeared two months after *The Tatler* was discontinued. *The Spectator* was not another *Tatler* under a new name. Its authors realized that in trying to be too many things to too many people, *The Tatler* had become a hodgepodge. Therefore they limited *The Spectator* to discussions of literature, manners, and morals, and confined each issue of the paper to a single theme. The purpose of the new paper was "to enliven morality with wit, and to temper wit with morality." The subject matter was both serious and amusing, ranging from discussions of ladies' fashions to discussions of religion. In a far more polished literary style than we are accustomed to in our own newspapers, *The Spectator* gently but pointedly satirized the extravagances of the fashionable life of the day. The paper, which became tremendously popular, appeared daily and carried classified advertisements.

In *The Spectator,* as in *The Tatler,* Addison and Steele delivered their opinions through an imaginary spokesman, The Spectator, a quiet, sensible, and good-natured man whose signature appeared on every essay. Maintaining a position of detachment, he objectively observed and exposed social follies and pretensions and provided subtle advice in hopes of correcting them. Like the fashionable men of his time, The Spectator belonged to a club and regularly frequented the best coffeehouses. The members of his club, The Spectator Club, described in the essay below, were carefully selected to represent the various classes and opinions of eighteenth-century society, thus creating a broad scope for satire. The club member who had the greatest popular appeal was Sir Roger de Coverley, a country gentleman to whom Addison devoted many of his most famous essays. When printed together these essays constitute a running narrative which is, in effect, a predecessor of another literary form—the novel.

Of the two essays from *The Spectator* which follow, the first is by Steele, the second by Addison.

THE SPECTATOR CLUB

No. 2. Friday, March 2, 1711.

*—Haec alii sex
Vel plures uno conclamant ore.**

THE FIRST of our society is a gentleman of Worcestershire, of ancient descent, a baronet; his name Sir Roger de Coverley. His great-grandfather was inventor of that famous country dance which is called after him. All who know that shire are very well acquainted with the parts and merits of Sir Roger. He is a gentleman that is very singular in his behavior, but his singularities proceed from his good sense, and are contradictions to the manners of the world only as he thinks the world is in the wrong. However, this humor creates him no enemies, for he does nothing with sourness of obstinacy; and his being unconfined to modes and forms makes him but the readier and more capable to please and oblige all who know him. When he is in town, he lives in Soho Square.[1] It is said he keeps himself a bachelor by reason he was crossed in love by a perverse, beautiful widow of the next county to him. Before this disappointment, Sir Roger was what you call a fine gentleman, had often supped with my Lord Rochester and Sir George Etherege,[2] fought a duel upon his first coming to town, and kicked Bully Dawson[3] in a public coffeehouse for calling him "youngster." But being ill-used by the above-mentioned widow, he was very serious for a year and a half; and though, his temper being naturally jovial, he at last got over it, he grew careless of himself, and never dressed afterward. He continues to wear a coat and doublet of the same cut that were in fashion at the time of his repulse, which, in his merry humors, he tells us, has been

* *Haec . . . ore:* "Six others and more shout this with one accord." (From Juvenal's *Satires.*)
[1] **Soho Square:** a once fashionable area of London.
[2] **Lord Rochester . . . Etherege:** writers and courtiers of the Restoration Period.
[3] **Bully Dawson:** a notorious swindler and gambler.

in and out[1] twelve times since he first wore it. 'Tis said Sir Roger grew humble in his desires after he had forgot this cruel beauty; but this is looked upon by his friends rather as matter of raillery than truth. He is now in his fifty-sixth year, cheerful, gay, and hearty; keeps a good house in both town and country; a great lover of mankind; but there is such a mirthful cast in his behavior that he is rather beloved than esteemed. His tenants grow rich, his servants look satisfied, all the young women profess love to him, and the young men are glad of his company; when he comes into a house he calls the servants by their names, and talks all the way upstairs to a visit. I must not omit that Sir Roger is a justice of the quorum;[2] that he fills the chair at a quarter-session[3] with great abilities; and, three months ago, gained universal applause by explaining a passage in the Game Act.[4]

The gentleman next in esteem and authority among us is another bachelor, who is a member of the Inner Temple;[5] a man of great probity, wit, and understanding; but he has chosen his place of residence rather to obey the direction of an old humorsome father, than in pursuit of his own inclinations. He was placed there to study the laws of the land, and is the most learned of any of the house in those of the stage. Aristotle and Longinus are much better understood by him than Littleton or Coke.[6] The father sends up, every post, questions relating to marriage articles, leases, and tenures, in the neighborhood; all which questions he agrees with an attorney to answer and take care of in the lump.[7] He is studying the passions themselves, when he should be inquiring into the debates among men which arise from them. He knows the argument of each of the orations of Demosthenes and Tully,[8] but not one case in the reports of our own courts. No one ever took him for a fool, but none, except his intimate friends, know he has a great deal of wit. This turn makes him at once both disinterested and agreeable; as few of his thoughts are drawn from business, they are most of them fit for conversation. His taste of books is a little too just[9] for the age he lives in; he has read all, but approves of very few. His familiarity with the customs, manners, actions, and writings of the ancients makes him a very delicate observer of what occurs to him in the present world. He is an excellent critic, and the time of the play is his hour of business; exactly at five he passes through New Inn, crosses through Russell Court, and takes a turn at Will's[10] till the play begins; he has his shoes rubbed and his periwig powdered at the barber's as you go into the Rose.[11] It is for the good of the audience when he is at a play, for the actors have an ambition to please him.

The person of next consideration is Sir Andrew Freeport, a merchant of great eminence in the city of London, a person of indefatigable industry, strong reason, and great experience. His notions of trade are noble and generous, and (as every rich man has usually some sly way of jesting which would make no great figure were he not a rich man) he calls the sea the British Common.[12] He is acquainted with commerce in all its parts and will tell you that it is a stupid and barbarous way to extend dominion by arms; for true power is to be got by arts and industry. He will often argue that if this part of our trade were well cultivated, we should gain from one nation; and if an-

---

[1] **in and out:** in and out of fashion.

[2] **justice . . . quorum:** one of a select group of justices of the peace.

[3] **quarter-session:** a meeting of the county court every three months.

[4] **Game Act:** a complex law defining the rights of hunters and the punishment for poaching.

[5] **member . . . Temple:** a lawyer.

[6] **Littleton . . . Coke:** early English jurists.

[7] **all . . . lump:** that is, he pays another attorney to do his work.

[8] **Demosthenes** (de·mos'thə·nez) **. . . Tully** (tul'ē): Demosthenes was a famous Greek orator; Tully (Cicero) was a famous Roman orator.

[9] **just:** proper; exacting.

[10] **Will's:** a coffeehouse.

[11] **Rose:** an eating place near the theater.

[12] **Common:** open to the use of all.

other, from another. I have heard him prove that diligence makes more lasting acquisitions than valor, and that sloth has ruined more nations than the sword. He abounds in several frugal maxims, among which the greatest favorite is, "A penny saved is a penny got." A general trader of good sense is pleasanter company than a general scholar; and Sir Andrew having a natural unaffected eloquence, the perspicuity of his discourse gives the same pleasure that wit would in another man. He had made his fortunes himself, and says that England may be richer than other kingdoms by as plain methods as he himself is richer than other men; though at the same time I can say this of him, that there is not a point in the compass but blows home a ship in which he is an owner.

Next to Sir Andrew in the clubroom sits Captain Sentry, a gentleman of great courage, good understanding, but invincible modesty. He is one of those that deserve very well, but are very awkward at putting their talents within the observation of such as should take notice of them. He was some years a captain, and behaved himself with great gallantry in several engagements and at several sieges; but having a small estate of his own, and being next heir to Sir Roger, he has quitted a way of life in which no man can rise suitably to his merit who is not something of a courtier as well as a soldier. I have heard him often lament that in a profession where merit is placed in so conspicuous a view, impudence should get the better of modesty. When he has talked to this purpose I never heard him make a sour expression, but frankly confess that he left the world because he was not fit for it. A strict honesty and an even, regular behavior are in themselves obstacles to him that must press through crowds who endeavor at the same end with himself—the favor of a commander. He will, however, in this way of talk, excuse generals for not disposing according to men's desert, or inquiring into it, "For," says he, "that great man who has a mind to help me, has

as many to break through to come at me as I have to come at him"; therefore he will conclude that the man who would make a figure, especially in a military way, must get over all false modesty, and assist his patron against the importunity of other pretenders by a proper assurance in his own vindication. He says it is a civil cowardice to be backward in asserting what you ought to expect, as it is a military fear to be slow in attacking when it is your duty. With this candor does the gentleman speak of himself and others. The same frankness runs through all his conversation. The military part of his life has furnished him with many adventures, in the relation of which he is very agreeable to the company; for he is never overbearing, though accustomed to command men in the utmost degree below him; nor ever too obsequious from an habit of obeying men highly above him.

But that our society may not appear a set of humorists [1] unacquainted with the gallantries and pleasures of the age, we have among us the gallant Will Honeycomb, a gentleman who, according to his years, should be in the decline of his life, but having ever been very careful of his person, and always had a very easy fortune, time has made but very little impression either by wrinkles on his forehead or traces in his brain. His person is well turned and of a good height. He is very ready at that sort of discourse with which men usually entertain women. He has all his life dressed very well, and remembers habits as others do men. He can smile when one speaks to him, and laughs easily. He knows the history of every mode, and can inform you from which of the French king's wenches our wives and daughters had this manner of curling their hair, that way of placing their hoods; whose frailty was covered by such a sort of petticoat, and whose vanity to show her foot made that part of the dress so short in such a year. In a word, all his conversation and knowledge has been in the female

[1] **humorists:** eccentrics.

world. As other men of his age will take notice to you what such a minister said upon such and such an occasion, he will tell when the Duke of Monmouth danced at court such a woman was then smitten, another was taken with him at the head of his troop in the Park. In all these important relations, he has ever about the same time received a kind glance or a blow of a fan from some celebrated beauty, mother of the present Lord Such-a-one. If you speak of a young commoner that said a lively thing in the House, he starts up: "He has good blood in his veins; Tom Mirabell, the rogue, cheated me in that affair; that young fellow's mother used me more like a dog than any woman I ever made advances to." This way of talking of his very much enlivens the conversation among us of a more sedate turn; and I find there is not one of the company but myself, who rarely speak at all, but speaks of him as of that sort of man who is usually called a well-bred, fine gentleman. To conclude his character, where women are not concerned, he is an honest, worthy man.

I cannot tell whether I am to account him whom I am next to speak of as one of our company, for he visits us but seldom; but when he does, it adds to every man else a new enjoyment of himself. He is a clergyman, a very philosophic man, of general learning, great sanctity of life, and the most exact good breeding. He has the misfortune to be of a very weak constitution, and consequently cannot accept of such cares and business as preferments in his function[1] would oblige him to; he is therefore among divines what a chamber–counselor[2] is among lawyers. The probity of his mind and the integrity of his life create him followers, as being eloquent or loud advances others. He seldom introduces the subject he speaks upon; but we are so far gone in years that he observes, when he is among us, an earnestness to have him fall on some divine topic, which

he always treats with much authority, as one who has no interest in this world, as one who is hastening to the object of all his wishes and conceives hope from his decays and infirmities. These are my ordinary companions.

A YOUNG LADY'S DIARY

No. 323. Tuesday, March 11, 1712.

Modo vir, modo femina.*—OVID

THE JOURNAL[3] with which I presented my readers on Tuesday last has brought me in several letters with accounts of many private lives cast into that form. I have the Rake's Journal, the Sot's Journal, and among several others a very curious piece entitled The Journal of a Mohock.[4] By these instances I find that the intention of my last Tuesday's paper has been mistaken by many of my readers. I did not design so much to expose vice as idleness, and aimed at those persons who pass away their time rather in trifles and impertinence, than in crimes and immoralities. Offenses of this latter kind are not to be dallied with, or treated in so ludicrous a manner. In short, my journal only holds up folly to the light, and shows the disagreeableness of such actions as are indifferent in themselves, and blamable only as they proceed from creatures endowed with reason.

My following correspondent, who calls herself Clarinda, is such a journalist as I require: she seems by her letter to be placed in a modish state of indifference between vice and virtue, and to be susceptible of either, were there proper pains taken with her. Had her journal been filled with gallantries, or such occurrences as

---

[1] **preferments . . . function:** advancements in the church.

[2] **chamber–counselor:** a lawyer who renders opinions in private rather than in court.

---

* *Modo . . . femina:* "Sometimes a man, sometimes a woman." (From Ovid's *Metamorphoses.*)

[3] **Journal:** i.e., diary.

[4] **Mohock:** one of a band of eighteenth-century hoodlums who preyed on Londoners on the streets at night.

had shown her wholly divested of her natural innocence, notwithstanding it might have been more pleasing to the generality of readers, I should not have published it; but as it is only the picture of a life filled with a fashionable kind of gaiety and laziness, I shall set down five days of it, as I have received it from the hand of my correspondent.

Dear Mr. Spectator,

You having set your readers an exercise in one of your last week's papers, I have performed mine according to your orders and herewith send it you enclosed. You must know, Mr. Spectator, that I am a maiden lady of a good fortune, who have had several matches offered me for these ten years last past, and have at present warm applications made to me by a very pretty fellow. As I am at my own disposal, I come up to town every winter and pass my time after the manner you will find in the following journal, which I began to write upon the very day after your *Spectator* upon that subject.

TUESDAY *night*. Could not go to sleep till one in the morning for thinking of my journal.

WEDNESDAY. *From eight till ten*. Drank two dishes of chocolate in bed, and fell asleep after them.

From ten to eleven. Eat a slice of bread and butter, drank a dish of bohea,[1] read *The Spectator*.

From eleven to one. At my toilette, tried a new head.[2] Gave orders for Veny[3] to be combed and washed. Mem.[4] I look best in blue.

From one till half an hour after two. Drove to the Change.[5] Cheapened[6] a couple of fans.

Till four. At dinner. Mem. Mr. Froth

passed by in his new liveries.

From four to six. Dressed, paid a visit to old Lady Blithe and her sister, having before heard they were gone out of town that day.

From six to eleven. At basset.[7] Mem. Never set again upon the ace of diamonds.

THURSDAY. *From eleven at night to eight in the morning*. Dreamed that I punted to [8] Mr. Froth.

From eight to ten. Chocolate. Read two acts in *Aurenzebe* [9] a-bed.

From ten to eleven. Tea table. Sent to borrow Lady Faddle's Cupid [10] for Veny. Read the playbills. Received a letter from Mr. Froth. Mem. Locked it up in my strongbox.

Rest of the morning. Fontange,[11] the tire-woman, her account of my Lady Blithe's wash. Broke a tooth in my little tortoise-shell comb. Sent Frank to know how my Lady Hectic rested after her monkey's leaping out at window. Looked pale. Fontange tells me my glass is not true. Dressed by three.

From three to four. Dinner cold before I sat down.

From four to eleven. Saw company. Mr. Froth's opinion of Milton. His account of the Mohocks. His fancy for a pincushion. Picture in the lid of his snuffbox. Old Lady Faddle promises me her woman to cut my hair. Lost five guineas at crimp.[12]

Twelve a clock at night. Went to bed.

FRIDAY. *Eight in the morning*. A-bed. Read over all Mr. Froth's letters. Cupid and Veny.

Ten a clock. Stayed within all day, not at home.

From ten to twelve. In conference with my mantua-maker.[13] Sorted a suit of rib ands. Broke my blue china cup.

From twelve to one. Shut myself up in

---

[1] **dish of bohea:** cup of tea.
[2] **head:** headdress.
[3] **Veny:** short for Venice, her lap dog.
[4] **Mem.:** memorandum.
[5] **Change:** the Exchange, where securities are traded.
[6] **Cheapened:** bargained for.

[7] **basset:** a card game.
[8] **punted to:** played cards with.
[9] *Aurenzebe* (ôr′əng·zēb): a play by Dryden.
[10] **Cupid:** a dog.
[11] **Fontange:** a famous French hairdresser.
[12] **crimp:** card game.
[13] **mantua-maker:** cloak-maker.

my chamber, practiced Lady Betty Modely's skuttle.[1]

One in the afternoon. Called for my flowered handkerchief. Worked half a violet leaf in it. Eyes ached and head out of order. Threw by my work, and read over the remaining part of *Aurenzebe.*

From three to four. Dined.

From four to twelve. Changed my mind, dressed, went abroad, and played at crimp till midnight. Found Mrs. Spitely at home. Conversation Mrs. Brilliant's necklace false stones. Old Lady Loveday going to be married to a young fellow that is not worth a groat. Miss Prue gone into the country. Tom Towneley has red hair. Mem. Mrs. Spitely whispered in my ear that she had something to tell me about Mr. Froth; I am sure it is not true.

Between twelve and one. Dreamed that Mr. Froth lay at my feet, and called me Indamora.[2]

SATURDAY. Rose at eight a clock in the morning. Sat down to my toilette.

From eight to nine. Shifted a patch [3] for half an hour before I could determine it. Fixed it above my left eyebrow.

From nine to twelve. Drank my tea and dressed.

From twelve to two. At Chapel. A great deal of good company. Mem. The third air in the new opera. Lady Blithe dressed frightfully.

From three to four. Dined. Mrs. Kitty called upon me to go to the opera before I was risen from table.

From dinner to six. Drank tea. Turned off [4] a footman for being rude to Veny.

Six a clock. Went to the opera. I did not see Mr. Froth till the beginning of the second act. Mr. Froth talked to a gentleman in a black wig. Bowed to a lady in the front box. Mr. Froth and his friend clapped Nicolini [5] in the third act. Mr. Froth cried out Ancora.[6] Mr. Froth led me to my chair. I think he squeezed my hand.

Eleven at night. Went to bed. Melancholy dreams. Methought Nicolini said he was Mr. Froth.

SUNDAY. Indisposed.

MONDAY. *Eight a clock.* Waked by Miss Kitty. *Aurenzebe* lay upon the chair by me. Kitty repeated without book the eight best lines in the play. Went in our mobs [7] to the dumb man, according to appointment. Told me that my lover's name began with a G. Mem. The conjurer was within a letter of Mr. Froth's name, etc.

Upon looking back into this my journal, I find that I am at a loss to know whether I pass my time well or ill; and indeed never thought of considering how I did it, before I perused your speculation upon that subject. I scarce find a single action in these five days that I can thoroughly approve of, except the working upon the violet leaf, which I am resolved to finish the first day I am at leisure. As for Mr. Froth and Veny, I did not think they took up so much of my time and thoughts, as I find they do upon my journal. The latter of them I will turn off if you insist upon it; and if Mr. Froth does not bring matters to a conclusion very suddenly, I will not let my life run away in a dream.

Your humble servant,
CLARINDA.

To resume one of the morals of my first paper, and to confirm Clarinda in her good inclinations, I would have her consider what a pretty figure she would make among posterity, were the history of her whole life published like these five days of it. I shall conclude my paper with an epitaph written by an uncertain author [8] on Sir Philip Sidney's sister, a lady who seems to have been of a temper very much

---

[1] **skuttle:** a rapid, affected walk.
[2] **Indamora:** the heroine in Dryden's *Aurenzebe.*
[3] **patch:** a beauty mark.
[4] **Turned off:** fired, sacked.
[5] **Nicolini:** a famous Italian singer.

[6] **Ancora:** "Encore."
[7] **mobs:** caps tied under the chin with ribbons.
[8] **uncertain author:** Ben Jonson is thought to be the author of these lines.

different from that of Clarinda. The last thought of it is so very noble that I dare say my reader will pardon the quotation.

On the Countess Dowager of Pembroke

Underneath this marble hearse
Lies the subject of all verse,
Sidney's sister, Pembroke's mother,
Death, ere thou hast killed another,
Fair and learned and good as she,
Time shall throw a dart at thee.

FOR STUDY AND DISCUSSION

1. His use of the penname Isaac Bicker-staff is one indication of Steele's shrewd salesmanship. What other indication of Steele's skill as a salesman do you find in the Prospectus to *The Tatler?*

2. How does the subject matter proposed for *The Tatler* compare with that of our own newspapers?

3. In their essays Addison and Steele wished to make certain points about literature, manners, and morals. What particular attitudes toward these three subjects are exemplified by the members of the Spectator Club?

4. Judging from the differences in the tone used to describe each of the members of the Spectator Club, which members does the writer seem to favor? Of which is he somewhat critical? Demonstrate, by quoting from the text, how Steele brings his characters to life simply by means of a single phrase or sentence.

5. Which passages in "A Young Lady's Diary" indicate most vividly Clarinda's frivolous existence? Clarinda, in looking over her diary entries, has second thoughts about some of her actions and reactions. Do these second thoughts make us more sympathetic toward her? Explain. What effect does Addison achieve by quoting the lines on the Countess of Pembroke?

THE ESSAY

Although Greek and Latin writers such as Cicero, Seneca, and Plutarch had written short prose pieces somewhat similar to the essay, the literary form known as the *essay* originated with a French writer, Michel de Montaigne, who in 1580 published two volumes of short prose pieces entitled *Essais.* Montaigne drew the title for his work from the French word meaning *attempt,* or *endeavor.* In his essays Montaigne expressed himself in a conversational style on a variety of subjects—on anything, in fact, that interested him. Then, in the late sixteenth century, Francis Bacon borrowed Montaigne's term and introduced the essay into English literature (see page 189). With the creation in the eighteenth century of the periodical essay of Addison and Steele, the essay form gained great popularity and thereafter attracted many English writers—Charles Lamb, William Hazlitt, Thomas Macaulay, and Matthew Arnold, to name a few.

In studying the essay form, it is useful to distinguish between the formal and the informal essay. In the *formal* essay, of which the essays of Bacon are a good example, the writer's purpose is to instruct or persuade, and the tone is usually dignified and impersonal. Ideas are developed through a logical arrangement of pertinent details as in Bacon's "Of Wisdom for a Man's Self" (page 189). The *informal* essay is characterized by its personal and relaxed approach to its subject and by its conversational tone. Many informal essays are significant not so much for *what* the author says as for *how* he says it. That the informal essay spans a wide range of subject matter and approach is seen in Addison's gently satirical piece "A Young Lady's Diary" (page 292), Charles Lamb's whimsical "Dream Children" (page 506), and George Orwell's thoughtful essay "Shooting an Elephant" (page 802).

FOR COMPOSITION

1. Analyze the news coverage, features, general interest, and readability of the newspaper which you see most often. Consider the ways in which this newspaper could be improved and, assuming you are going to publish a competing paper, write a prospectus explaining to prospective readers why they should purchase your newspaper.

2. Write several entries that might be found in the diary of a twentieth-century Clarinda.

ALEXANDER POPE
(1688–1744)

How much do you love civilization? This is a hard question: it involves too many things and reminds us of too many problems. It is a question, however, that meant a great deal to Alexander Pope, and it was much easier for him to answer. Pope's poetry reveals a deep and discriminating passion for the things he loved in his civilization, and a lively, lashing scorn for whatever threatened it. His world was a more manageable one than ours. In Pope's day, there were fewer people to worry about, and, since he was no democrat, he was able to assume that if a group of wits and aristocrats set an acceptable standard, nobody would have to worry about the common people, for whom, after all, kings and parliaments were responsible. Furthermore, Pope was not assaulted as we are by a bewildering variety of cultures, each of which has a claim on the understanding and sympathy of all the rest, nor was he as impressed as we must be by the magnitude of historical change. For him the past, or the past that was worth remembering, was Christian and classic, just as it had been for Milton, although the view he took of the past was not Milton's view. Pope's was more deeply colored by "rationalism." Rationalism is a conviction that one should think and behave rationally—according to reason; it takes for granted the idea that the world is put together in such a way that the human mind can grasp it. This is a very old idea, at least as old as the ancient Greek philosopher and critic Aristotle. We, of course, are unable to describe in words the universe as conceived by the modern physicist; nor do we believe that our everyday speech can effectively lay hold of things. But Pope thought he could describe his world in words—not completely, but well enough, as the English philosopher John Locke said, for human purposes.

Writers of the nineteenth century, the Romantics (see page 437), condemned the rationalism of Pope's age. They found it both dull and stifling. But Pope is not dull, and this fact may help us to see what the Romantics overlooked: the fact that Pope's poetry was not only much more than merely reasonable or "correct," to use Pope's word, but that it is passionate poetry. We judge the loves of other people according to what we are able to love, and a passion for the civilization of their time was not common among the Romantics.

Scholarship and criticism have recovered Pope for us. We are able to perceive his energy and seriousness and see that they are called forth by his love for the order that people imposed on their world. The English critic F. R. Leavis writes: "the 'correctness' of Pope's literary form derives its strength from a social code and a civilization." The Romantic attack included the charge that Pope and his fellows thought of poetry as chiefly decorative and not, therefore, deeply felt. We may now say that it was in great measure a poetry about how to behave: how to act as a person, a thinker, an artist. What the Romantics were really questioning was not the manner, but the matter—the belief Pope held that the art, politics, and customs of his age were worth all his time and attention. We must, of course, admit that giving such public matters so much attention means ignoring what is merely individual and personal. If, however, you are willing to make the sacrifice of ignoring the personal, individualistic, and atypical, Pope offers you a beautifully shaped ideal of conduct in art and life.

Let us attempt to understand that ideal. We may begin with two lines from Part II of the *Essay on Criticism,* two lines which are among the most famous Pope wrote:

> "True wit is nature to advantage dressed
> What oft was thought, but ne'er so well expressed . . ."

Here we find two key terms, *wit* and *nature.* The following passage from Part I of the *Essay on Criticism* contains some other terms which need explanation.

> "When first young Maro in his boundless mind
> A work to outlast immortal Rome designed,
> Perhaps he seemed above the critic's law,
> And but from nature's fountains scorned to draw:
> But when to examine every part he came,
> Nature and Homer were, he found, the same.
> Convinced, amazed, he checks the bold design,
> And rules as strict his labored work confine
> As if the Stagirite o'erlooked each line.
> Learn hence for ancient rules a just esteem;
> To copy nature is to copy them."

Here, first of all, we are concerned with the relation of *nature* to Homer (the artist) and the "rules" (of art and of civilization). In these lines, Virgil, Homer's great successor as an epic poet (whom Pope refers to above as Maro), is said to have discovered that no better pattern—that is, nothing closer to nature—could be found than the one Homer had employed. *Nature* here does not mean beautiful scenery or the observed behavior of other people: it refers to the way in which the world reflects God's purposes. Pope maintains that a general view of the scheme of things enables us to discover what these purposes are. Our minds can take in the creator's scheme because our minds, imperfect though they are, are nonetheless made in accord with the pattern or image of the divine mind. We can see that it is God's world because God has given us minds equipped to see just that. Of course, this sounds tidier than it was in practice because even in Pope's day there was disagreement about which aspects of the natural world supplied evidence of God's design. But Pope is making as much sense as he can, and he does not pretend to do more than follow the teachings of the philosophers.

In the passage just quoted, Pope says that Homer wrote an almost perfect poem because he followed nature almost perfectly. For this reason, he was the very best example to follow. Such rules as Aristotle (whom Pope calls "the Stagirite" because he was born at Stagira) drew from Homer were, therefore, almost perfect rules. These "rules" formulated by Aristotle were in turn applied by the critics of later days.

But where does *wit* come in? It is proper to call Pope a satirist. He certainly wrote satire—that is, amusing and ironic verse in which he denounced the follies and vices of his time—but what makes him a great satirist is his *wit*. The uses of this word are various, and more than one is important here. For example, Pope himself is *a* wit and moved in a great company of wits. The word also refers to cleverness and clever sayings, to literary figures of speech known as *conceits,* such as those in the line, "While China's earth receives the smoking tide" (page 307, line 110) which, as a literal description of an action, means "while coffee is poured into cups." But the root meaning of *wit* is the power some have to be the executives of nature, to make brilliant sense of a world that dull people cannot grasp. There is something happy or fortunate in wit. It is something more than following the rules: it is akin to *genius,* and this too is a favorite term for Pope and his fellows.

So *wit* is a word of great potency. By wit we may be reminded of certain contradictions as well as assertions. A wit both employs the rules and leaps beyond them. We may look back to a metaphysical poet such as John Donne (page 204) and recall that the yoking together of things we ordinarily think of as far removed from one another is one of the properties of metaphysical poetry. With a far greater emphasis on the attempt to make rules for poetry and human behavior, Pope is also able to bring unlike things together. In fact, the triumph of his early poem, the *Essay on Criticism,* is that it does so. In this poem we see Pope's power and skill in his wonderfully modulated use of the heroic couplet: it stitches the world together and creates a sense of order. Thus it is really wit in the form of Pope's own genius that makes Pope's world—his view of nature and the rules—acceptable.

Pope's verse exhibits even more clearly a group of rhetorical devices which have been undergoing a development in English verse since the mid-seventeenth century: that is, parallelism, balance, and antithesis within the span of a couplet or even a line. One soon gets accustomed to such effects of parallelism as, "The berries crackle, and the mill turns round" (page 307, line 106) and more obvious still, "Thrice she looked back, and thrice the foe drew near" (page 308, line 138). There is a comic antithesis in the line, "When husbands, or when lapdogs breathe their last" (page 308, line 158). For balance, consider one of Pope's lovelier lines, "In glittering dust and painted fragments lie" (page 308, line 160). These devices are not employed out of a mere love of rhetoric: they represent a way of seeing experience itself. They present a vision of the world as ordered as if a symmetry-loving architect had built it.

THE LIFE OF ALEXANDER POPE

Pope, who never grew beyond four feet six inches, was ravaged in youth by tuberculosis of the spine. He was troubled all his life by an aching, twisted body and chronic headaches. Ill and stunted as he was, he could hardly marry, and he had to undergo much cruel scoffing at this physical disability. He was born to a Catholic merchant family. In his age Catholics could neither attend the universities nor hold public office. Nonetheless, he enjoyed many advantages. His father was modestly well off, and, like Milton's father, encouraged his son to pursue his studies and to write. Pope was fortunate in finding elders with whom he could talk about his favorite reading—Homer, Virgil, Spenser, Milton, and Dryden, his hero, whom he saw as a boy. With almost magical suddenness, he found himself the admired junior of a literary circle, the protégé of the aging Wycherley, a famous playwright, who actually asked him to assist him in revising some of his work. The publication of his *Pastorals* in 1709 established Pope as a literary figure. The *Essay on Criticism* (1711) and the first version of *The Rape of the Lock* (1712) brought him fame.

Pope wrote in an age in which politics and sharp personal attacks were characteristic of the literary scene. There was continual warfare, not simply among the known writers, but with the often anonymous hacks who wrote for pay and were collectively known as "Grub Street" after the thoroughfare on which they lived. Pope could be as savage as the rest when attacked, but he was truer than many of his contemporaries to the principle that one ought to attack only the typical follies of the age. He made himself financially independent while in his early thirties by publishing highly successful translations of the *Iliad* (1715–20) and the *Odyssey* (1725–26). A satiric epic, *The Dunciad,* first appeared in 1728, and the *Essay on Man,* Pope's ambitious attempt to summarize the human condition as he had earlier summed up the accepted doctrine about criticism, was published in 1733–34. We should also note that much of Pope's greatest poetry is to be found in his shorter works.

The life of this intense and lively man was marked by fortunate friendships with many of the leading figures of the day, among them John Gay (author of *The Beggar's Opera*), Jonathan Swift, Dr. Arbuthnot, Lord Oxford (a Prime Minister), and Lord Bolingbroke, who was for a time Secretary of State and who suggested to Pope the composition of the *Essay on Man.* Except for Gay, who was hardly a political figure, all of these men were Tories. Pope had early had differences with the famous Whig essayist, Joseph Addison (page 286), and fell into a group closer to his inherited sympathies, a group which included many of England's ablest wits. We have numerous letters and records which vividly suggest the zest with which these men pursued every political, literary, and philosophic question which the age presented. The figure of Pope was not the least dazzling in this company, and his biographers have had a hard time finding the man in the midst of the fireworks. The atmosphere of struggle in which he lived, and the difficulties of every sort that he had to overcome are further complicated by the tactics he adopted to make sure that his powers and his fame were properly imaged in the eyes of the world. The custom of anonymous publication made all sorts of tricks possible and even respectable. For example, Pope wrote ridiculous attacks on himself to make the actual attackers appear foolish; he tried to make it appear that he did not want his letters published and yet secretly urged their publication. But this foxy man was a lion in behalf of what he deeply believed, and his major works were written in the service of what he deeply cherished, not to glorify Alexander Pope.

In 1718 Pope rented a villa at Twickenham on the Thames River, and he made this estate, with its magnificent garden and grotto, one of the most famous of the day. Here he found time not simply for an enormous volume of work but for friends and visitors as well. Throughout his life he made a place for himself by the sheer force of his mind, and he died a widely honored man.

Pope's qualities are difficult to sum up. The poet Swinburne wrote, "What a spirit it was! How fiery, bright, and dauntless!" And the British critic F. R. Leavis speaks of Pope as at once "polite and profound," "elegant and insolent." He was all these things and more. An acquaintance with him greatly enlarges our sense both of the possibilities of the English language and of civilization itself. Pope's age was primarily an age of prose, and he wrote only poetry; yet his influence upon other writers was so great, both in his own time and later, that we speak today of the Age of Pope.

Essay on Criticism

The *Essay on Criticism,* published in 1711, when Pope was only twenty-three, consists of three parts and a total of 744 lines. Part I is quite theoretical in content and discusses Pope's concept of nature, the rules we derive from nature, the importance of wit, and the merits of ancient and modern writers, topics much discussed in Pope's day. In Part II Pope deals with some of the difficulties of practical criticism. Part III describes what Pope regarded as ideal criticism and the ideal critic. The first portion of Part II follows below.

Of all the causes which conspire to blind
Man's erring judgment, and misguide the mind,
What the weak head with strongest bias rules,
Is pride, the never-failing vice of fools.
Whatever Nature has in worth denied,   5
She gives in large recruits° of needful pride;
For as in bodies, thus in souls, we find
What wants° in blood and spirits, swelled with wind:
Pride, where wit fails, steps in to our defense,
And fills up all the mighty void of sense.   10
If once right reason drives that cloud away,
Truth breaks upon us with resistless day.
Trust not yourself; but your defects to know,
Make use of every friend—and every foe.
  A little learning is a dangerous thing;   15
Drink deep, or taste not the Pierian spring:°
There shallow draughts intoxicate the brain,
And drinking largely sobers us again.
Fired at first sight with what the Muse imparts,
In fearless youth we tempt° the heights of arts,   20
While from the bounded level of our mind,
Short views we take, nor see the lengths behind;
But more advanced, behold with strange surprise
New distant scenes of endless science° rise!
So pleased at first the towering Alps° we try,   25
Mount o'er the vales, and seem to tread the sky,
Th' eternal snows appear already passed,
And the first clouds and mountains seem the last;
But, those attained, we tremble to survey
The growing labors of the lengthened way,   30
Th' increasing prospect tires our wandering eyes,
Hills peep o'er hills, and Alps on Alps arise!
  A perfect judge will read each work of wit
With the same spirit that its author writ:

6. recruits: supplies. **8. wants:** lacks. **16. Pierian** (pī·ir′ē′ən) **spring:** a fountain in Pieria, sacred to the Muses and supposed to give poetic inspiration to those who drink from it. **20. tempt:** attempt. **24. science:** knowledge. **25. Alps:** a range of high mountains in south-central Europe.

Survey the whole, nor seek slight faults to find 35
Where Nature moves, and rapture warms the mind;
Nor lose, for that malignant dull delight,
The generous pleasure to be charmed with wit.
But in such lays° as neither ebb, nor flow,
Correctly cold, and regularly low,° 40
That shunning faults, one quiet tenor keep;
We cannot blame indeed—but we may sleep.
In wit, as Nature, what affects our hearts
Is not th' exactness of peculiar° parts;
'Tis not a lip, or eye, we beauty call, 45
But the joint force and full result of all.
Thus when we view some well-proportioned dome,°
(The world's just wonder, and even thine, O Rome!)
No single parts unequally surprise,
All comes united to th' admiring eyes; 50
No monstrous height, or breadth, or length appear;
The whole at once is bold, and regular.
   Whoever thinks a faultless piece to see,
Thinks what ne'er was, nor is, nor e'er shall be.
In every work regard the writer's end, 55
Since none can compass more than they intend;
And if the means be just, the conduct° true,
Applause, in spite of trivial faults, is due.
As men of breeding, sometimes men of wit,
T' avoid great errors, must the less commit: 60
Neglect the rules each verbal critic° lays,
For not to know some trifles, is a praise.
Most critics, fond of some subservient art,
Still make the whole depend upon a part:
They talk of principles, but notions° prize, 65
And all to one loved folly sacrifice.
   Once on a time, La Mancha's knight,° they say,
A certain bard encountering on the way,
Discoursed in terms as just, with looks as sage,
As e'er could Dennis° of the Grecian stage; 70
Concluding all were desperate sots and fools,
Who durst depart from Aristotle's rules.
Our author, happy in a judge so nice,
Produced his play, and begged the knight's advice;
Made him observe the subject, and the plot, 75
The manners, passions, unities; what not?
All which, exact to rule, were brought about,
Were but a combat in the lists left out.

---

   39. lays: songs or simple lyric poems. **40. regularly low:** conforming to the rules (i.e. "regular"), but uninspired. **44. peculiar:** particular. **47. dome:** the dome of a building, here possibly a building like St. Peter's Cathedral in Rome. **57. conduct:** arrangement of parts. **61. verbal critic:** a critic overconcerned with petty details. **65. notions:** whims. **67. La Mancha's knight:** Don Quixote. The story is from a sequel to the Cervantes novel of the same name written by another author. **70. Dennis:** John Dennis (1657–1734) was an English critic often ridiculed for his pomposity, and a bitter enemy of Pope.

"What! leave the combat out?" exclaims the knight;
Yes, or we must renounce the Stagirite.°   80
"Not so, by Heaven" (he answers in a rage)
"Knights, squires, and steeds, must enter on the stage."
So vast a throng the stage can ne'er contain.
"Then build a new, or act it in a plain."
　　Thus critics, of less judgment than caprice,   85
Curious° not knowing, not exact but nice,°
Form short ideas; and offend in arts
(As most in manners) by a love to parts.
　　Some to conceit° alone their taste confine,
And glittering thoughts struck out at every line;   90
Pleased with a work where nothing's just or fit;
One glaring chaos and wild heap of wit.
Poets like painters, thus, unskilled to trace
The naked nature and the living grace,
With gold and jewels cover every part,   95
And hide with ornaments their want of art.
True wit is Nature to advantage dressed,
What oft was thought, but ne'er so well expressed;
Something, whose truth convinced at sight we find,
That gives us back the image of our mind.   100
As shades more sweetly recommend the light,
So modest plainness sets off sprightly 'wit.
For works may have more wit than does 'em good,
As bodies perish through excess of blood.
　　Others for language all their care express,   105
And value books, as women men, for dress:
Their praise is still—the style is excellent:
The sense, they humbly take upon content.°
Words are like leaves; and where they most abound,
Much fruit of sense beneath is rarely found.   110
False eloquence, like the prismatic glass,
Its gaudy colors° spreads on every place;°
The face of Nature we no more survey,
All glares alike, without distinction gay:
But true expression, like th' unchanging sun,   115
Clears, and improves whate'er it shines upon,
It gilds all objects, but it alters none.
Expression is the dress of thought, and still
Appears more decent,° as more suitable;
A vile conceit in pompous words expressed,   120
Is like a clown° in regal purple dressed:
For different styles with different subjects sort,
As several garbs with country, town, and court.
Some by old words to fame have made pretense,
Ancients in phrase, mere moderns in their sense;   125
Such labored nothings, in so strange a style,

80. **Stagirite:** Aristotle was a native of Stagira, Greece. 86. **Curious:** fussy. **nice:** minutely accurate. 89. **conceit:** far-fetched or affected figurative language. 108. **content:** trust (a pun on the noun *content*). 112. **gaudy colors:** that is, ornaments of style. **place:** that is, subject or theme. 119. **decent:** attractive. 121. **clown:** rustic, boor.

Amaze th' unlearn'd, and make the learnèd smile.
Unlucky, as Fungoso in the play,°
These sparks with awkward vanity display
What the fine gentleman wore yesterday;   130
And but so mimic ancient wits at best,
As apes our grandsires, in their doublets dressed.
In words, as fashions, the same rule will hold;
Alike fantastic, if too new, or old:
Be not the first by whom the new are tried,   135
Nor yet the last to lay the old aside.

128. **Fungoso . . . play:** a character from Ben Jonson's *Every Man Out of His Humor* who tries to imitate the fashionable habits of another character in the play.

COMMENTARY

Notice that the *Essay on Criticism* is written in heroic couplets, most of which are *closed;* that is, either each line or each couplet contains a complete sentence element or a complete thought. These iambic pentameter couplets are called "heroic" simply because it had been the custom to use this form in writing about heroic subjects. As a form, the heroic couplet gives us the impression of order and clarity. There was a widespread theory in Pope's day that, when presented with the right alternatives and the right comparisons, the mind would perceive the truth intuitively, because it is a truth-perceiving organ, so to speak. Thus the parallels and oppositions in Pope's poem reinforce the impression that the question he is discussing can be handled decisively. Here, then, is an example of the way in which the poetic form of an age can be expressive of the beliefs of that age.

We may take the following passage from the *Essay on Criticism* (lines 109–10) for illustration:

"Words are like leaves; and where they most abound,
Much fruit of sense beneath is rarely found."

Pope's simile of many words and many leaves (little sense and little fruit), is, we notice, partly compressed into a metaphor ("fruit of sense") which enables the poet to leave out the explicit statement that trees with too many leaves yield little fruit. Also note that neither the simile nor the metaphor create a strong impression or emotion that remains with the reader. Neither leaves a reverberation in the mind. When their job is done, they retire from the scene like efficient servants. In general, Pope's use of poetic devices is economical and sharply controlled. This is true of his use of sound effects as well. He follows the advice he gives elsewhere in this poem ("The sound must seem an echo to the sense"). Lines 39–42 may be quoted as an instance:

"But in such lays as neither ebb, nor flow,
Correctly cold, and regularly low,
That shunning faults, one quiet tenor keep;
We cannot blame indeed—but we may sleep."

These lines echo the dullness they describe, as does a very famous couplet (also from the *Essay on Criticism*) about the six-beat line called the "Alexandrine," which was employed in Pope's time for some very bad verse:

"A needless Alexandrine ends the song
That, like a wounded snake, drags its slow length along."

In this line you *hear* the Alexandrine dragging.

1. In lines 35–52, Pope comments on regularity and proportion and suggests a standard for judging works of art. Express the meaning of this passage in your own words.

2. In lines 89–96, what does Pope have to say about decorative verse and the use of conceits?

3. What is the logical difficulty in the famous couplet (lines 97–98) which begins, "True wit is Nature . . ."? Despite this difficulty, what significant observation does this couplet make?

4. Lines 105–36 deal with diction (the choice of words) and with what we call tone (the use of language in accord with the subject and the writer's attitude toward it). Make a list of the faults Pope characterizes in these lines. Compare the advice he gives here with some that you can find in a textbook on diction and usage. For example, does the textbook include anything not found in Pope's lines?

FOR COMPOSITION

Select a statement from the *Essay on Criticism* or from the Commentary on the *Essay on Criticism* and use it as the topic sentence of a paragraph of comment of your own. You may, for example, wish to support or attack Pope's statement that "a little learning is a dangerous thing" (line 15), or to comment upon his comparison between many words and many leaves (lines 109–10).

The Rape of the Lock

Although Pope was often quarrelsome, he had many friends to whom he showed the kindly side of his nature. On one notable occasion he attempted unsuccessfully to act as peacemaker. Because a foppish young baron named Lord Petre had snipped a curl from the head of a Miss Arabella Fermor and refused to give it up, there arose between the two families a quarrel which threatened to become a feud. Pope's friend, John Caryll, suggested that he write a poem about this trivial incident to show the absurdity of all the excitement. The result was "The Rape of the Lock," a mock-heroic, or mock epic, poem.

Pope himself described a mock epic as "using a vast force to lift a feather." Thus he wrote his poem in the grand epic style of the *Iliad,* the *Odyssey,* the *Aeneid,* and *Paradise Lost,* and filled it with amusing parallels to Homer, Virgil, and Milton. By recalling parallel situations of tragic or heroic importance in famous epic poems, he emphasized the triviality of his own subject. A card game, for example, is treated as if it were a battle outside the walls of Troy, though Pope's setting is "the level green" of the card table. Instead of being mortally wounded from the spears of Homeric warfare, the beaux fall dead before the angry glances of the ladies. Just before the lock is cut, sylphs gather to defend it just as the angels gather to defend Adam and Eve from Satan in *Paradise Lost.* Because Pope always maintains just the right degree of sympathy with the human characters in his poem, none of these parallels to the classical epic overload the poem or seem too weighty for Pope's delicate joke to bear.

The poem is written in five cantos, but because of its great length only a portion of it is given here. Canto I opens with a formal statement of the theme—"what mighty contests rise from trivial things"—and invokes the Muse to inspire the poet. Belinda, heroine of the poem, is visited by the sylph Ariel who warns her that some dread fate hangs over her head. In Canto II, Belinda, on a pleasure boat on the Thames, is being conducted with other young fashionables to the palace of Hampton Court. An adventurous baron, admiring two of Belinda's curls, determines to obtain them. Belinda's protecting sylph Ariel exhorts a host of other airy beings to come to Belinda's defense. Canto III follows.

Close by those meads, forever crowned with flowers,
Where Thames with pride surveys his rising towers,
There stands a structure of majestic frame,°
Which from the neighboring Hampton takes its name.
Here Britain's statesmen oft the fall foredoom   5
Of foreign tyrants and of nymphs at home;
Here thou, great Anna! whom three realms obey,°
Dost sometimes counsel take—and sometimes tea.°

   Hither the heroes and the nymphs resort,
To taste awhile the pleasures of a court;   10
In various talk th' instructive hours they passed,
Who gave the ball, or paid the visit last;
One speaks the glory of the British Queen,
And one describes a charming Indian screen;
A third interprets motions, looks, and eyes;   15
At every word a reputation dies.
Snuff, or the fan,° supply each pause of chat,
With singing, laughing, ogling, and all that.

   Meanwhile, declining from the noon of day,
The sun obliquely shoots his burning ray;   20
The hungry judges soon the sentence sign,
And wretches hang that jurymen may dine;
The merchant from th' Exchange° returns in peace,
And the long labors° of the toilet cease.
Belinda now, whom thirst of fame invites,   25
Burns to encounter two adventurous knights,
At omber° singly to decide their doom;
And swells her breast with conquests yet to come.
Straight the three bands prepare in arms to join,
Each band the number of the sacred nine.°   30
Soon as she spreads her hand, th' aerial guard
Descend, and sit on each important card:
First, Ariel perched upon a Matador,°
Then each, according to the rank they bore;
For sylphs, yet mindful of their ancient race,   35
Are, as when women, wondrous fond of place.

   Behold, four kings in majesty revered,
With hoary whiskers and a forky beard;
And four fair queens whose hands sustain a flower,
The expressive emblem of their softer power;   40

3. **structure ... frame:** Hampton Court, a handsome royal residence near London.
7. **Anna! ... obey:** Queen Anne was ruler of England, Scotland, and Ireland. 8. **tea:** pronounced tā. 17. **Snuff ... fan:** Taking snuff in the eighteenth century was almost as widespread among gentlemen as cigarette smoking is today. A lady was seldom without her fan to occupy her hands and often to help her flirtations. 23. **Exchange:** a place where merchants, brokers, and bankers met to transact business. 24. **long labors:** Because of the elaborate, towering headdresses of that time, ladies often spent most of the day at their dressing tables preparing for a ball in the evening. 27. **omber:** a fashionable card game. 30. **the sacred nine:** The nine cards in each player's hand are compared to the nine Muses of the Greeks. 33. **Matador:** a card that had power to take a trick, derived from the Spanish word for bullfighter.

Four knaves in garbs succinct,° a trusty band,
Caps on their heads, and halberts° in their hand;
And particolored troops, a shining train,
Draw forth to combat on the velvet plain.
  The skillful nymph reviews her force with care: 45
Let spades be trumps! she said, and trumps they were.
  Now move to war her sable Matadors,
In show like leaders of the swarthy Moors.
Spadillio° first, unconquerable lord!
Led off two captive trumps and swept the board.   50
As many more Manillio° forced to yield
And marched a victor from the verdant field.°
Him Basto° followed, but his fate more hard
Gained but one trump and one plebeian card.
With his broad saber next, a chief in years,   55
The hoary majesty of spades appears,
Puts forth one manly leg, to sight revealed,
The rest his many-colored robe concealed.
The rebel knave, who dares his prince engage,
Proves the just victim of his royal rage.   60
E'en mighty Pam,° that kings and queens o'erthrew,
And mowed down armies in the fights of Loo,
Sad chance of war! now destitute of aid,
Falls undistinguished by the victor spade!
  Thus far both armies to Belinda yield;   65
Now to the baron fate inclines the field.
His warlike Amazon her host invades,
The imperial consort of the crown of spades;
The club's black tyrant first her victim died,
Spite of his haughty mien, and barbarous pride.   70
What boots° the regal circle on his head,
His giant limbs, in state unwieldy spread;
That long behind he trails his pompous robe,
And, of all monarchs, only grasps the globe?
  The baron now his diamonds pours apace;   75
Th' embroidered king who shows but half his face,
And his refulgent° queen, with powers combined,
Of broken troops an easy conquest find.
Clubs, diamonds, hearts, in wild disorder seen,
With throngs promiscuous° strew the level green.   80
Thus when dispersed a routed army runs,
Of Asia's troops, and Afric's sable sons,
With like confusion different nations fly,
Of various habit, and of various dye,

---

41. **succinct** (sǝk·singkt′): belted. 42. **halberts** (hal′bǝrts): long-handled weapons with metal heads. 49. **Spadillio:** the ace of spades. 51. **Manillio:** another trump card. 52. **verdant field:** The omber table was covered with green cloth. 53. **Basto:** the ace of clubs. 61. **Pam:** In a card game called "Loo," the knave of clubs, Pam, was the highest card and therefore "kings and queens o'erthrew" and "mowed down armies." In omber, the game now being played, the knave was less powerful. 71. **What boots:** of what benefit is. 77. **refulgent** (ri·ful′jǝnt): radiant, resplendent. 80. **promiscuous:** mixed.

The pierced battalions disunited fall,   85
In heaps on heaps; one fate o'erwhelms them all.
　　The knave of diamonds tries his wily arts,
And wins (oh, shameful chance!) the queen of hearts.
At this the blood the virgin's cheek forsook,
A livid paleness spreads o'er all her look;   90
She sees, and trembles at the approaching ill,
Just in the jaws of ruin, and codille.°
And now (as oft in some distempered state)
On one nice trick depends the general fate.
An ace of hearts steps forth; the king unseen   95
Lurked in her hand, and mourned his captive queen:
He springs to vengeance with an eager pace,
And falls like thunder on the prostrate ace.
The nymph exulting fills with shouts the sky;
The walls, the woods, and long canals reply.   100
　　O thoughtless mortals; ever blind to fate,
Too soon dejected, and too soon elate.
Sudden, these honors shall be snatched away,
And cursed forever this victorious day.
　　For lo! the board with cups and spoons is crowned,   105
The berries crackle, and the mill turns round;°
On shining altars of Japan° they raise
The silver lamp; the fiery spirits blaze;
From silver spouts the grateful liquors glide,
While China's earth° receives the smoking tide.   110
At once they gratify their scent and taste,
And frequent cups prolong the rich repast.
Straight hover round the fair her airy band;
Some, as she sipped, the fuming liquor fanned,
Some o'er her lap their careful plumes displayed,   115
Trembling, and conscious of the rich brocade.
Coffee (which makes the politician wise,
And see through all things with his half-shut eyes)
Sent up in vapors to the baron's brain
New stratagems the radiant locks to gain.   120
Ah, cease, rash youth! desist ere 'tis too late,
Fear the just gods, and think of Scylla's fate!°
Changed to a bird, and sent to flit in air,
She dearly pays for Nisus' injured hair!
　　But when to mischief mortals bend their will,   125
How soon they find fit instruments of ill!
Just then Clarissa drew with tempting grace
A two-edged weapon from her shining case:
So ladies in romance assist their knight,
Present the spear, and arm him for the fight.   130

---

　　92. **codille:** a term meaning the defeat of the lone hand.　　106. **The berries . . . round:** Prepared coffee could not be bought in those days, but the coffee berries were ground in a small hand mill at the table.　　107. **altars of Japan:** Imported lacquered tables were popular at this time.　　110. **China's earth:** The cups were earthenware imported from China.　　122. **Scylla's** (sil′əz) **fate:** Scylla betrayed her father, King Nisus, by sending the enemy a lock of his hair.

He takes the gift with reverence, and extends
The little engine on his fingers' ends;
This just behind Belinda's neck he spread,
As o'er the fragrant steams she bends her head.
Swift to the lock a thousand sprites repair,   135
A thousand wings, by turns, blow back the hair;
And thrice they twitched the diamond in her ear;
Thrice she looked back, and thrice the foe drew near.
Just in that instant, anxious Ariel sought
The close recesses of the virgin's thought;   140
As on the nosegay in her breast reclined,
He watched th' ideas rising in her mind,
Sudden he viewed, in spite of all her art,
An earthly lover lurking at her heart.
Amazed, confused, he found his power expired,   145
Resigned to fate, and with a sigh retired.
  The peer now spreads the glittering *forfex*° wide,
T' inclose the lock; now joins it, to divide.
E'en then, before the fatal engine closed,
A wretched sylph too fondly interposed: 150
Fate urged the shears, and cut the sylph in twain,
(But airy substance soon unites again).
The meeting points the sacred hair dissever
From the fair head, forever, and forever!
  Then flashed the living lightning from her eyes,   155
And screams of horror rend th' affrighted skies.
Not louder shrieks to pitying Heaven are cast,
When husbands, or when lap dogs breathe their last;
Or when rich China vessels, fallen from high,
In glittering dust and painted fragments lie!   160

147. *forfex* (fôr′fəks): Latin for *shears*.

"Let wreaths of triumph now my temples twine,"
The victor cried; "the glorious prize is mine!
While fish in streams, or birds delight in air,
Or in a coach and six the British fair,
As long as *Atalantis*° shall be read,   165
Or the small pillow grace a lady's bed,
While visits shall be paid on solemn days,
When numerous wax lights in bright order blaze,
While nymphs take treats, or assignations give,
So long my honor, name, and praise shall live!   170
What Time would spare, from steel receives its date,°
And monuments, like men, submit to fate!
Steel could the labor of the gods destroy,
And strike to dust th' imperial towers of Troy;
Steel could the works of mortal pride confound,   175
And hew triumphal arches to the ground.
What wonder then, fair nymph! thy hairs should feel,
The conquering force of unresisted steel?"

CANTO V

In Canto IV, Umbriel, a melancholy sprite, brings a bag (similar to the bag of winds once held by Ulysses) in which are contained "the force of female lungs, sighs, sobs, and passions, and the war of tongues." These he empties over the head of Belinda, who immediately bursts into loud lamentations on the loss of her lock. She then calls upon Sir Plume to aid her in regaining her lock. This ineffectual fop swears the favorite oaths of the time—"Zounds! Plague on 't! Prithee, pox!"—but fails to move the baron.

Then, in the beginning of Canto V, Clarissa urges good sense and good humor, but in vain. The story concludes with a mighty battle between the belles and the beaux.

"To arms, to arms!" the fierce virago cries,
And swift as lightning to the combat flies.
All side in parties, and begin th' attack;
Fans clap, silks rustle, and tough whalebones crack;
Heroes' and heroines' shouts confus'dly rise,   5
And bass and treble voices strike the skies.
No common weapons in their hands are found,
Like gods they fight, nor dread a mortal wound.°
    So when bold Homer makes the gods engage,
And heavenly breasts with human passions rage;   10
'Gainst Pallas, Mars, Latona, Hermes° arms;
And all Olympus° rings with loud alarms:
Jove's thunder roars, Heaven trembles all around,
Blue Neptune storms, the bellowing deeps resound;
Earth shakes her nodding towers, the ground gives way,   15

165. *Atalantis:* a popular book of scandalous gossip.   171. **receives its date:** is destroyed.
CANTO V: 8. **Like . . . wound:** The gods, being immortal, did not have to fear death in battle.
11. **Pallas, Mars, Latona, Hermes:** gods who directed the Trojan War. The first and fourth were on the side of the Greeks, the second and third on the Trojan side.   12. **Olympus:** the mountain in northern Greece on which the gods supposedly lived.

And the pale ghosts start at the flash of day!
Triumphant Umbriel on a sconce's° height
Clapped his glad wings, and sat to view the fight;
Propped on their bodkin spears,° the sprites survey
The growing combat, or assist the fray.   20
While through the press enraged Thalestris° flies,
And scatters death around from both her eyes,
A beau and witling° perished in the throng,
One died in metaphor, and one in song.
"O cruel nymph! a living death I bear,"   25
Cried Dapperwit, and sunk beside his chair.
A mournful glance Sir Fopling° upward cast,
"Those eyes are made so killing"—was his last.
Thus on Mæander's° flowery margin lies
Th' expiring swan, and as he sings he dies.   30
When bold Sir Plume had drawn Clarissa down,
Chloe° stepped in and killed him with a frown;
She smiled to see the doughty hero slain,
But, at her smile, the beau revived again.
Now Jove suspends his golden scales in air,   35
Weighs the men's wits against the lady's hair;
The doubtful beam long nods from side to side;
At length the wits mount up, the hairs subside.
See, fierce Belinda on the Baron flies,
With more than usual lightning in her eyes;   40
Nor feared the chief th' unequal fight to try,
Who sought no more than on his foe to die.
But this bold lord with manly strength endued,
She with one finger and a thumb subdued:
Just where the breath of life his nostrils drew,   45
A charge of snuff the wily virgin threw;
The gnomes direct, to every atom just,
The pungent grains of titillating dust.
Sudden, with starting tears each eye o'erflows,
And the high dome re-echoes to his nose.   50
"Now meet thy fate," incensed Belinda cried,
And drew a deadly bodkin from her side. . . .
"Boast not my fall," he cried, "insulting foe!
Thou by some other shalt be laid as low;
Nor think to die dejects my lofty mind;   55
All that I dread is leaving you behind!
Rather than so, ah, let me still survive,
And burn in Cupid's flames—but burn alive."
"Restore the lock!" she cries; and all around
"Restore the lock!" the vaulted roofs rebound.   60

17. **sconce:** a candleholder attached to the wall.   19. **bodkin spears:** large needles.   21. **Thalestris** (thə·les′tris): an Amazon who figured in medieval tales of Alexander the Great.   23. **witling:** a gentleman with empty pretensions to high intelligence.   26–27. **Dapperwit, Sir Fopling:** names of humorous characters in sophisticated comedies of the time.   29. **Mæander's:** The Mæander was a winding river in Asia.   32. **Chloe** (klō′ē): a shepherdess loved by Daphnis in a Greek pastoral romance.

Not fierce Othello in so loud a strain
Roared for the handkerchief that caused his pain.°
But see how oft ambitious aims are crossed,
And chiefs contend till all the prize is lost!
The lock, obtained with guilt, and kept with pain,   65
In every place is sought, but sought in vain.
With such a prize no mortal must be blessed,
So Heav'n decrees! with Heav'n who can contest?
Some thought it mounted to the lunar sphere,
Since all things lost on earth are treasured there.   70
There heroes' wits are kept in ponderous vases,
And beaux' in snuffboxes and tweezer cases;
There broken vows and deathbed alms are found,
And lovers' hearts with ends of riband bound. . . .
    But trust the Muse—she saw it upward rise,   75
Though marked by none but quick, poetic eyes. . . .
A sudden star, it shot through liquid air,
And drew behind a radiant trail of hair. . . .
    Then cease, bright nymph! to mourn thy ravished hair,
Which adds new glory to the shining sphere!   80
Not all the tresses that fair head can boast,
Shall draw such envy as the lock you lost.
For, after all the murders of your eye,
When, after millions slain, yourself shall die;
When those fair suns shall set, as set they must,   85
And all those tresses shall be laid in dust:
This lock, the Muse shall consecrate to fame,
And 'midst the stars inscribe Belinda's name.

61–62. **Not . . . pain:** In Shakespeare's tragedy *Othello*, the hero is convinced of his wife's faithlessness when she cannot find a handkerchief which he had given her. The handkerchief had actually been stolen by an enemy to be used as evidence against her.

FOR STUDY AND DISCUSSION

1. From what you know of the conventions of epic poetry, point out two or three incidents in *The Rape of the Lock* that parallel the action in *Beowulf*, or *Paradise Lost* (or in the epics of Homer), and explain what each of these allusions contributes to the poem as a whole.

2. What purpose does the card game serve in the poem? How does Pope bring his card game to life?

3. Is there a victor and a victory at the close of *The Rape of the Lock*? If so, who is the victor and what is the nature of the victory?

POPE'S SATIRE

Satire (see pages 333 and 889) can range from light, impersonal mockery to bitter, cruel ridicule. In both verse and prose, satire, as a means of criticizing manners, education, politics, and religion, was highly fashionable in the eighteenth century, and Alexander Pope was one of its leading exponents. From what you have read of Pope, how would you describe him as a satirist? What specifically does he ridicule? In what manner does he criticize? What events in Pope's life do you think might have influenced him to write satire?

How does Pope's satire compare with that of Chaucer? How does it compare with the satire of Addison and Steele? Explain, with references to specific selections.

FOR COMPOSITION

Consider several subjects for a modern mock epic, and develop one of them in a brief essay.

JONATHAN SWIFT
(1667–1745)

Jonathan Swift, a master of satire, is among the most formidable of English writers. Unleashing all the corrosive power of his intensely bitter irony, he launched a savage attack on humankind. He believed that people, throughout history, had destroyed and debased everything they touched and were odious animals, "cunning, malicious, treacherous, and revengeful." Like his friend Alexander Pope, Swift scorned and ridiculed the follies of society and its institutions. But his targets seemed larger than Pope's, his attacks less personal. He wrote Pope, "Principally I hate and detest that animal called man; although I heartily love John, Peter, Thomas, and so forth."

Born in Dublin of English parents, Swift late in life became a national hero to the Irish for his role in their struggle against England. But he never liked Ireland and considered his Irish birth only the first of many misfortunes. The second was the poverty that made him dependent on the grudging charity of an uncle. After being educated at Trinity College in Dublin, Swift went to England to serve as a private secretary to another relative, Sir William Temple, a patron of letters and former ambassador to Holland. Unhappy because of his subservient position in Temple's household and because his hopes of gaining entrance to public life did not materialize, he returned to Ireland and took orders in the church. After a year in a country parish, however, he returned to Temple's household. Following the death of Sir William in 1699, Swift launched himself upon a successful career as a pamphleteer and political writer. His expectations, however, whether political or ecclesiastical, were continually disappointed. For a while his pamphlets helped the Tories hold power, and he was a considerable force in British politics, but after Queen Anne died and the Whigs succeeded the Tories, Swift's hope of becoming a bishop was gone forever. Having earlier been appointed Dean of Saint Patrick's Cathedral in Dublin, he retired in bitterness to this post which he held, in spite of bodily and mental disorders, for thirty-two years.

The one person who made his life in Ireland endurable was Esther Johnson, a woman much younger than himself for whom he had a famous and hopeless love. His *Journal to Stella,* a collection of letters to her, is read today as an intimate picture of life in the eighteenth century. His masterpiece, *Gulliver's Travels,* like Defoe's *Robinson Crusoe,* concerns an imaginary journey. The similarity, however, ends there, for Swift's book is undoubtedly the most merciless and devastating indictment of humanity—and of the corruption and hypocrisy of British society, in particular—ever written. Throughout his life Swift spoke his mind. In *A Tale of a Tub,* his first success, he satirized various sects of the church. In *The Battle of the Books* he involved himself in literary controversy. As part of his involvement in Irish affairs, he wrote the celebrated *A Modest Proposal,* in which he ironically suggested that Irish children "in the present deplorable state of the kingdom" should be fattened up, sold, and eaten, as food "very proper for landlords, who, as they have already devoured most of the parents, seem to have best title to the children."

In spite of his bearish and acidic attitude toward the human race, Swift engages our sympathy, not only as the victim of grave physical infirmities, but because he remained, until madness engulfed him, a man of penetrating and lonely intelligence. One writer compared his tragic life to the ruin of a great empire. George Orwell, one of his literary heirs in the twentieth century, marked Swift's strength as "a terrible intensity of vision, capable of picking out a single hidden truth and then magnifying and distorting it."

Gulliver's Travels

Gulliver's Travels is Swift's final word on people as individuals and as social animals. All his contempt and hatred for the pettiness, cruelty, injustice, and stupidity that he saw in people was poured into this greatest of all prose satires. Though he claimed that "His satire points at no defect,/ But what all mortals may correct," the book nevertheless failed as a vehicle of social reform. Swift, through Gulliver, complained in a letter written after the initial reception of the book: "Yahoos [people reduced to a bestial state] were a species of animals utterly incapable of amendment by precepts or examples."

Swift's imaginative shrinking of the English to one-twelfth their actual size, his strange lands inhabited by giants and talking horses, not only served his satiric purposes but also opened the book to generations of children who, unaware of the satire, have delighted in these unusual beings. Swift's writing is at all times straightforward, unpretentious, and devoid of any artifice, such as vague literary allusions or poetic imagery. He conceived the writer's aim as the attainment of "that simplicity without which no human performance can arrive at any great perfection."

In the gullible Lemuel Gulliver, "first a surgeon, and then a captain of several ships," Swift found his ideal spokesman. Through Gulliver he exposes the corruption in every revered English institution, leaving no doubt as to the targets of his satire. Britain's political system is the recipient of his scorn in "The Voyage to Lilliput," a place where Gulliver discovers that members of political parties are distinguished by the height of their heels. In "A Voyage to Brobdingnag" Swift mocks the immorality and cruelty of English society. During Gulliver's trip to Laputa, false pedantry and learning are ridiculed when the scientists and scholars of this country conduct an eight-year experiment to extract sunbeams from cucumbers. But Swift deals his cruelest blow in Gulliver's journey to the land of the Houyhnhnms, where intelligent and noble horses govern the Yahoos, a breed of filthy, brutish humans. As a result of his travels, the honest, well-meaning Gulliver gradually comes to realize that there is often a discrepancy between appearance and reality, that people are not always what they seem to be, and that evil is present wherever people exist.

A VOYAGE TO LILLIPUT

Gulliver, shipwrecked somewhere in the South Pacific, struggles to an unknown shore and falls asleep. The Lilliputians (lil′ə·pyōō′shənz), who are only six inches tall, discover and tie down the sleeping "giant." After he awakens, they transport him with great difficulty to their capital and house him in an unused temple. He gradually begins to learn their language and to win their favor, although his sword and pistols are not returned to him and he remains a prisoner. The similarity between Gulliver's situation and English politics and court life, ridiculed by reduction to such tiny scale, reaches its peak in Chapter 3, which follows.

MY GENTLENESS and good behavior had gained so far on the emperor and his court, and indeed upon the army and people in general, that I began to conceive hopes of getting my liberty in a short time. I took all possible methods to cultivate this favorable disposition. The natives came by degrees to be less apprehensive of any danger from me. I would sometimes lie down and let five or six of them dance on my hand; and at last the boys and girls would venture to come and play at hide-and-seek in my hair. I had now made a good progress in understanding and speaking their language.

The emperor had a mind, one day, to entertain me with several of the country shows, wherein they exceed all nations I have known, both for dexterity and magnificence. I was diverted with none so much as that of the rope dancers, performed upon a slender white thread extended about two feet and twelve inches from the ground. Upon which I shall desire liberty, with the reader's patience, to enlarge a little.

This diversion is only practiced by those persons who are candidates for great employments and high favor at court. They are trained in this art from their youth, and are not always of noble birth or liberal education. When a great office is vacant, either by death or disgrace (which often happens), five or six of those candidates petition the emperor to entertain his majesty and the court with a dance on the rope; and whoever jumps the highest, without falling, succeeds in the office. Very often the chief ministers themselves are commanded to

show their skill, and to convince the emperor that they have not lost their faculty. Flimnap,[1] the treasurer, is allowed to cut a caper on the strait rope at least an inch higher than any other lord in the whole empire. I have seen him do the somersault several times together upon a trencher,[2] fixed on a rope, which is no thicker than a common packthread in England. My friend Reldresal,[3] principal secretary for private affairs, is, in my opinion, if I am not partial, the second after the treasurer; the rest of the great officers are much upon a par.

These diversions are often attended by fatal accidents, whereof great numbers are on record. I myself have seen two or three candidates break a limb. But the danger is much greater when the ministers themselves are commanded to show their dexterity! for, by contending to excel themselves and their fellows, they strain so far that there is hardly one of them who hath not received a fall,[4] and some of them two or three. I was assured that a year or two before my arrival, Flimnap would have infallibly broke his neck if one of the king's cushions, that accidentally lay on the ground, had not weakened the force of his fall.

There is likewise another diversion, which is only shown before the emperor and empress and first minister, upon particular occasions. The emperor lays on the table three fine silken threads,[5] of six inches long; one is blue, the other red, and the third green. These threads are proposed as prizes for those persons whom the emperor hath a mind to distinguish by a peculiar mark of his favor. The ceremony is performed in his maj-

---

[1] **Flimnap:** probably refers to Sir Robert Walpole, Whig statesman of Swift's day.

[2] **trencher:** a wooden platter.

[3] **Reldresal:** probably Lord Townshend, chief ally of Walpole.

[4] **fall:** loss of office. At this time political power shifted a number of times between the Whigs and the Tories.

[5] **three . . . threads:** an allusion to the ribbons of the Orders of the Garter, the Bath, and the Thistle, often awarded to politicians.

esty's great chamber of state, where the candidates are to undergo a trial of dexterity very different from the former, and such as I have not observed the least resemblance of in any other country of the old or the new world.

The emperor holds a stick in his hands, both ends parallel to the horizon, while the candidates, advancing one by one, sometimes leap over the stick, sometimes creep under it backward and forward several times, according as the stick is advanced or depressed. Sometimes the emperor holds one end of the stick, and his first minister the other; sometimes the minister has it entirely to himself. Whoever performs his part with most agility, and holds out the longest in leaping and creeping, is rewarded with the blue colored silk; the red is given to the next, and the green to the third, which they all wear girt twice round about the middle; and you see few great persons about this court who are not adorned with one of these girdles.

The horses of the army, and those of the royal stables, having been daily led before me, were no longer shy, but would come up to my very feet without starting. The riders would leap them over my hand as I held it on the ground; and one of the emperor's huntsmen, upon a large courser, took my foot, shoe and all, which was indeed a prodigious leap.

I had the good fortune to divert the emperor one day after a very extraordinary manner. I desired he would order several sticks of two feet high, and the thickness of an ordinary cane, to be brought me; whereupon his majesty commanded the master of his woods to give directions accordingly; and the next morning six woodmen arrived with as many carriages, drawn by eight horses to each.

I took nine of these sticks, and fixing them firmly in the ground in a quadrangular figure, two feet and a half square, I took four other sticks and tied them parallel at each corner, about two feet from the ground; then I fastened my handkerchief to the nine sticks that stood erect, and extended it on all sides, till it was as tight as the top of a drum; and the four parallel sticks, rising about five inches higher than the handkerchief, served as ledges on each side.

When I had finished my work, I desired the emperor to let a troop of his best horse, twenty-four in number, come and exercise upon this plain. His majesty approved of the proposal, and I took them up one by one in my hands, ready mounted and armed, with the proper officers to exercise them. As soon as they got into order, they divided into two parties, performed mock skirmishes, discharged blunt arrows, drew their swords, fled and pursued, attacked and retired, and, in short, discovered the best military discipline I ever beheld. The parallel sticks secured them and their horses from falling over the stage; and the emperor was so much delighted that he ordered this entertainment to be repeated

several days, and once was pleased to be lifted up and give the word of command; and, with great difficulty, persuaded even the empress herself to let me hold her in her close chair within two yards of the stage, from whence she was able to take a full view of the whole performance.

It was my good fortune that no ill accident happened in these entertainments; only once a fiery horse, that belonged to one of the captains, pawing with his hoof, struck a hole in my handkerchief, and his foot slipping, he overthrew his rider and himself; but I immediately relieved them both, and covering the hole with one hand, I set down the troop with the other, in the same manner as I took them up. The horse that fell was strained in the left shoulder, but the rider got no hurt, and I repaired my handkerchief as well as I could; however, I would not trust to the strength of it any more in such dangerous enterprises.

About two or three days before I was set at liberty, as I was entertaining the court with these kinds of feats, there arrived an express to inform his majesty that some of his subjects riding near the place where I was first taken up had seen a great black substance lying on the ground, very oddly shaped, extending its edges round as wide as his majesty's bed-chamber, and rising up in the middle as high as a man; that it was no living creature, as they at first apprehended, for it lay on the grass without motion; and some of them had walked round it several times; that, by mounting upon each other's shoulders, they had got to the top, which was flat and even, and, stamping upon it, they found it was hollow within; that they humbly conceived it might be something belonging to the man-mountain; and if his majesty pleased, they would undertake to bring it with only five horses.

I presently knew what they meant, and was glad at heart to receive this intelligence.[1] It seems, upon my first reaching the shore after our shipwreck, I was in such confusion that, before I came to the place where I went to sleep, my hat, which I had fastened with a string to my head while I was rowing, and had stuck on all the time I was swimming, fell off after I came to land; the string, as I conjecture, breaking by some accident which I never observed, but thought my hat had been lost at sea. I entreated his imperial majesty to give orders it might be brought to me as soon as possible, describing to him the use and nature of it; and the next day the wagoners arrived with it, but not in a very good condition; they had bored two holes in the brim, within an inch and a half of the edge, and fastened two hooks in the holes; these hooks were tied by a long cord to the harness, and thus my hat was dragged along for above half an English mile; but the ground in that country being extremely smooth and level, it received less damage than I expected.

Two days after this adventure, the emperor, having ordered that part of the army which quarters in and about his metropolis to be in readiness, took a fancy of diverting himself in a very singular manner. He desired I would stand like a colossus,[2] with my legs as far asunder as I conveniently could. He then commanded his general (who was an old, experienced leader and a great patron of mine) to draw up the troops in close order and march them under me; the foot by twenty-four in a breast and the horse by sixteen, with drums beating, colors flying, and pikes advanced. This body consisted of three thousand foot and a thousand horse. . . .

I had sent so many memorials and petitions for my liberty that his majesty at length mentioned the matter, first in the cabinet, and then in a full council; where it was opposed by none, except Skyresh Bolgolam[3] who was pleased, without any

---

[1] **intelligence:** news, information.

[2] **colossus:** an enormous statue.

[3] **Skyresh Bolgolam:** probably the Earl of Nottingham. His animosity toward Gulliver probably represents Nottingham's opposition to the Tory ministry in 1711.

provocation, to be my mortal enemy. But it was carried against him by the whole board, and confirmed by the emperor. That minister was *galbet*, or admiral of the realm, very much in his master's confidence, and a person well versed in affairs, but of a morose and sour complexion.[1] However, he was at length persuaded to comply; but prevailed that the articles and conditions upon which I should be set free, and to which I must swear, should be drawn up by himself.

These articles were brought to me by Skyresh Bolgolam in person, attended by two undersecretaries, and several persons of distinction. After they were read, I was demanded to swear to the performance of them, first in the manner of my own country, and afterward in the method prescribed by their laws; which was to hold my right foot in my left hand, and to place the middle finger of my right hand on the crown of my head, and my thumb on the tip of my right ear.

But because the reader may be curious to have some idea of the style and manner of expression peculiar to that people, as well as to know the articles upon which I recovered my liberty, I have made a

[1] **complexion:** disposition.

translation of the whole instrument, word for word, as near as I was able, which I here offer to the public.

"*Golbasto Momaren Evlame Gurdilo Shefin Mully Ully Gue*, most mighty Emperor of Lilliput, delight and terror of the universe, whose dominions extend five thousand *blustrugs* (about twelve miles in circumference) to the extremities of the globe; monarch of all monarchs, taller than the sons of men; whose feet press down to the center, and whose head strikes against the sun; at whose nod the princes of the earth shake their knees; pleasant as the spring, comfortable as the summer, fruitful as autumn, dreadful as winter. His most sublime Majesty proposeth to the man-mountain, lately arrived to our celestial dominions, the following articles, which by a solemn oath he shall be obliged to perform.

"1. The man-mountain shall not depart from our dominions without our license under our great seal.

"2. He shall not presume to come into our metropolis without our express order; at which time the inhabitants shall have two hours' warning to keep within their doors.

"3. The said man-mountain shall confine his walks to our principal high roads,

and not offer to walk or lie down in a meadow or field of corn.

"4. As he walks the said roads, he shall take the utmost care not to trample upon the bodies of any of our loving subjects, their horses or carriages, nor take any of our said subjects into his hands without their own consent.

"5. If an express requires extraordinary dispatch, the man-mountain shall be obliged to carry in his pocket the messenger and horse a six days' journey once in every moon, and return the said messenger back (if so required) safe to our imperial presence.

"6. He shall be our ally against our enemies in the island of Blefuscu,[1] and do his utmost to destroy their fleet, which is now preparing to invade us.

"7. That the said man-mountain shall at his times of leisure be aiding and assisting to our workmen, in helping to raise certain great stones toward covering the wall of the principal park, and other our royal buildings.

"8. That the said man-mountain shall, in two moons' time, deliver in an exact survey of the circumference of our dominions, by a computation of his own paces round the coast.

"9. That upon his solemn oath to observe all the above articles, the said man-mountain shall have a daily allowance of meat and drink sufficient for the support of 1,728 of our subjects, with free access to our royal person, and other marks of our favor. Given at our palace at Belfaborac the twelfth day of the ninety-first moon of our reign."

I swore and subscribed to these articles with great cheerfulness and content, although some of them were not so honorable as I could have wished; which proceeded wholly from the malice of Skyresh Bolgolam the high admiral; whereupon my chains were immediately unlocked, and I was at full liberty; the emperor himself in person did me the honor to be by at the whole ceremony. I

[1] **Blefuscu**: France.

made my acknowledgments by prostrating myself at his majesty's feet; but he commanded me to rise; and after many gracious expressions, which to avoid the censure of vanity I shall not repeat, he added that he hoped I should prove a useful servant and well deserve all the favors he had already conferred upon me, or might do for the future.

The reader may please to observe that in the last article for the recovery of my liberty the emperor stipulates to allow me a quantity of meat and drink sufficient for the support of 1,728 Lilliputians. Sometime after, asking a friend at court how they came to fix on that determined number, he told me that his majesty's mathematicians having taken the height of my body by the help of a quadrant, and finding it to exceed theirs in the proportion of twelve to one, they concluded, from the similarity of their bodies, that mine must contain at least 1,728 of theirs, and consequently would require as much food as was necessary to support that number of Lilliputians. By which the reader may conceive an idea of the ingenuity of that people, as well as the prudent and exact economy of so great a prince.

Gulliver's greatest service to Lilliput is his capture of the fleet of the enemy country, Blefuscu. By cutting the anchor ropes with his knife and attaching fifty ships to a central cable, he is able to drag them after him as he wades across the channel between the two countries.

Warned by a friend that Skyresh Bolgolam and several others are planning to impeach him for high treason, Gulliver flees to Blefuscu. Despite the fact that Gulliver captured his fleet, the Emperor of Blefuscu receives him kindly. (This episode is a satire on the impeachment and escape to France of Bolingbroke, a leader of the Tory party and a close friend of Swift.) Soon after, Gulliver discovers a derelict lifeboat which he uses to launch himself on his journey home. As proof of his strange adventure he takes with him a pocketful of live cattle and sheep.

[JONATHAN SWIFT CONTINUES ON
PAGE 327.]

ENGLISH PAINTING

William Hogarth

Unlike artists of the seventeenth century, William Hogarth portrayed not just the highborn and famous, but people of all classes. A feeling for theater suggested compositional ideas to him and stories that might be told in pictures. "My picture is my stage," he once remarked, "and my men and women players." A keen observer, a pointed satirist, and a masterful handler of paint, he ranks as one of England's most important artists.

A young woman in the street cries out her shrimps for sale—and Hogarth rushes home to paint *The Shrimp Girl* (PLATE 1). Intoxicated by his subject's robust charm, he records his vision with exuberance. Here, Hogarth's brushstrokes are loose, and the details are not worked out; but the picture catches the unknown model's expression, making it forever vivid.

In *Calais Gate* (PLATE 2) Hogarth presents a picture as if it were a scene in a play, with us sitting in the front row viewing the actors and setting framed in the proscenium arch. In front, on either side, unobtrusive figures huddle in shadow, while the principal action takes place in the center of the "stage," strongly lighted from the left. Two walls enclosing the scene on either side lead the eye back to an arched gate, divided diagonally by dramatic light and shadow. Beyond we can see a servant carrying an immense sirloin, addressed to the proprietress of the English inn at Calais. An overfed friar pokes greedily at the beef, while scrawny French soldiers, just given their meager rations from a great cauldron, gape in amazement. Such fine fare is not for them.

In 1748, on his way home from France, then at uneasy peace with England, Hogarth stopped at Calais and sketched the fortified gate. The artist's own head is visible at the left, near the gate, with a guard's pike raised threateningly behind. Hogarth had reason to express a derogatory opinion of the French. He had been arrested under suspicion of being a spy, an experience which appealed to his satiric sense and English pride. Though the French were supposed to be fine hosts and great cooks, they had nothing, as Hogarth points out in this painting, to compare with the roast beef of England.

A Scene from "The Beggar's Opera" (PLATE 3), based directly on a

319

famous theatrical success of 1728, again shows Hogarth's preference for all that is English, including the London underworld. In *The Beggar's Opera* John Gay used old English tunes instead of following Italian operatic conventions, and made a highwayman named Macheath into a "hero." We can see the curtain overhead and the boxes on either side for privileged spectators. An intense light, as if from footlights, plays on the actors. Macheath, committed to Newgate Prison, stands fettered in the center while Polly and Lucy, rivals for his love, kneel and intercede for him.

The series of eight paintings entitled *A Rake's Progress* tells another story. Tom Rakewell, an irresponsible youth, inherits a fortune, squanders it, spurns the only girl who really cares for him, and ends in a madhouse. So as to have the moral of this tale reach as many people as possible, Hogarth reproduced the series in inexpensive engravings. In the fourth episode (PLATE 4), Tom Rakewell, in debt from gambling, steps from his sedan chair into the presence of a bailiff who holds a warrant for his arrest. The faithful Sarah offers money to save him from imprisonment, in her haste dropping her trinket box. A lamplighter, neglecting his task as he watches the scene, lets the oil run onto the roof of the sedan chair. In the background looms St. James's Palace, a well-known London landmark. Such realistic details make the story all the more convincing.

In another series of paintings, one exposing the follies and illegalities of a Parliamentary election, Hogarth painted a profusion of realistic details to create a lively sense of the ridiculous. *Chairing the Member* (PLATE 5), the last of this series, shows the victorious candidate carried aloft in a triumphal procession. But is his position really secure? A fight breaks out between a sailor with a wooden leg and a thresher whose flail hits one of the chair-bearers and makes him crumple. A man on a donkey beats the sailor's chained bear. A squealing sow chasing her piglets upsets a woman, who falls into another chair-bearer. Pandemonium reigns. The noisy crowd presses forward, led by a witless fiddler. Seeing the Member about to topple to the ground, a lady behind the balustrade faints. Overhead flies a goose, a bird as stupid as the people below.

Out of this confusion Hogarth shapes a clear composition. The nearest and largest figures form a pyramid—a pyramid about to collapse. Other figures, less clearly seen, are bunched together in the background. The walls converge toward a building which encloses the scene.

In an unusual composite portrait called *The Painter's Servants* (PLATE 6), the effect given is like that of a private album. The sitters are more closely grouped than they would be in a commissioned picture. Light from the left falls on the six faces, each turned in a different direction, and picks out the white edges of caps and collars. Hogarth portrayed his servants without condescension and without flattery, and he made each of them strongly individual and alive.

PLATE 1. WILLIAM HOGARTH (1697–1764): *The Shrimp Girl*. Oil on canvas, 25 x 20 inches. (Reproduced by courtesy of the Trustees, The National Gallery, London)

PLATE 2. WILLIAM HOGARTH (1697–1764): *Calais Gate.* 1749. Oil on canvas, 31 x 37¼ inches. (Reproduced by courtesy of the Trustees, The Tate Gallery, London)

PLATE 4. WILLIAM HOGARTH (1697–1764): *Arrest for Debt*, number 4 in the series *A Rake's Progress*. About 1732. Oil on canvas, $24\frac{5}{8}$ x $29\frac{5}{8}$ inches. (Trustees, Sir John Soane's Museum, London)

324

PLATE 5. WILLIAM HOGARTH (1697–1764): *Chairing the Member.* 1754. Oil on canvas, 39⅞ x 51½ inches. (Trustees, Sir John Soane's Museum, London)

325

PLATE 6. WILLIAM HOGARTH (1697–1764): *The Painter's Servants*. 1750's. Oil on canvas, 24¼ x 29½ inches. (Reproduced by courtesy of the Trustees, The Tate Gallery, London)

A VOYAGE TO BROBDINGNAG

On his second voyage Gulliver finds himself in Brobdingnag, a country Swift locates in the then little-known region of Alaska. Here the natives are twelve times as tall as Gulliver, instead of one-twelfth his height. As in Lilliput, Gulliver learns the language and observes the ways of the people. Taken in by a farmer, he is exhibited as a curiosity and finally sold to the Queen. In general, Gulliver is well treated: the farmer's daughter Glumdalclitch goes to court with him as "nurse and instructor"; quilted boxes are specially constructed for him to live in and to travel in; a boat to maneuver in a water trough is made for his and the Brobdingnagians's amusement. Still, his diminutive size causes many misadventures: he is nearly trampled to death, dropped from the palace roof by a court monkey, eaten alive by a baby, torn to pieces by rats, drowned in a cream pitcher, and killed by a linnet. Finally his travel box is carried off by a great eagle and dropped into the ocean. Rescued by a passing ship, he returns to England.

In *A Voyage to Brobdingnag,* Swift builds on the satire he employed in *A Voyage to Lilliput,* particularly in Gulliver's wide-eyed descriptions of the gross-appearing Brobdingnagians and in his innocent discourses on English politics. In trying to explain what an admirable people the English are, Gulliver succeeds only in horrifying the good King of Brobdingnag. Their best-known discussion follows.

THE KING, who, as I before observed, was a prince of excellent understanding, would frequently order that I should be brought in my box, and set upon the table in his closet. He would then command me to bring one of my chairs out of the box, and sit down within three yards distance upon the top of the cabinet, which brought me almost to a level with his face. In this manner I had several conversations with him. I one day took the freedom to tell his Majesty that the contempt he discovered towards Europe and the rest of the world did not seem answerable to those excellent qualities of mind that he was master of. That reason did not extend itself with the bulk of the body: on the contrary, we observed in our country that the tallest persons were usually least provided with it. That among other animals, bees and ants had the reputation of more industry, art and sagacity than many of the larger kinds. And that, as inconsiderable as he took me to be, I hoped I might live to do his Majesty some signal service. The King heard me with attention, and began to conceive a much better opinion of me than he had ever before. He desired I would give him as exact an account of the government of England as I possibly could; because, as fond as princes commonly are of their own customs (for so he conjectured of other monarchs; by my former discourses), he should be glad to hear of anything that might deserve imitation.

Imagine with thyself, courteous reader, how often I then wished for the tongue of Demosthenes or Cicero,[1] that might have enabled me to celebrate the praise of my own dear native country in a style equal to its merits and felicity.

I began my discourse by informing his Majesty that our dominions consisted of two islands, which composed three mighty kingdoms under one sovereign, beside our plantations in America. I dwelt long upon the fertility of our soil and the temperature of our climate. I then spoke at large upon the constitution of an English parliament, partly made up of an illustrious body called the House of Peers, persons of the noblest blood and of the most ancient and ample patrimonies. I described that extraordinary care always taken of their education in arts and arms to qualify them for being counselors born to the king and kingdom; to have a share in the legislature; to be members of the highest court of judicature, from whence there could be no appeal; and to be champions always ready for the defense of their

---

[1] **Demosthenes or Cicero:** Greek and Roman orators, respectively.

prince and country, by their valor, conduct, and fidelity. That these were the ornament and bulwark of the kingdom, worthy followers of their most renowned ancestors, whose honor had been the reward of their virtue, from which their posterity were never once known to degenerate. To these were joined several holy persons, as part of that assembly, under the title of bishops, whose peculiar business it is to take care of religion and of those who instruct the people therein. These were searched and sought out through the whole nation by the prince and wisest counselors, among such of the priesthood as were most deservedly distinguished by the sanctity of their lives and the depth of their erudition; who were indeed the spiritual fathers of the clergy and the people.

That the other part of the parliament consisted of an assembly called the House of Commons, who were all principal gentlemen, freely picked and culled out by the people themselves, for their great abilities and love of their country, to represent the wisdom of the whole nation. And these two bodies make up the most august assembly in Europe, to whom, in conjunction with the prince, the whole legislature is committed.

I then descended to the courts of justice, over which the judges, those venerable sages and interpreters of the law, presided, for determining the disputed rights and properties of men, as well as for the punishment of vice and protection of innocence. I mentioned the prudent management of our treasury; the valor and achievements of our forces by sea and land. I computed the number of our people, by reckoning how many millions there might be of each religious sect or political party among us. I did not omit even our sports and pastimes, or any other particular which I thought might redound to the honor of my country. And I finished all with a brief historical account of affairs and events in England for about an hundred years past.

This conversation was not ended under five audiences, each of several hours, and the King heard the whole with great attention, frequently taking notes of what I spoke, as well as memorandums of what questions he intended to ask me.

When I had put an end to these long discourses, his Majesty in a sixth audience consulting his notes, proposed many doubts, queries, and objections upon every article. He asked what methods were used to cultivate the minds and bodies of our young nobility, and in what kind of business they commonly spent the first and teachable part of their lives. What course was taken to supply that assembly when any noble family became extinct. What qualifications were necessary in those who are to be created new lords: whether the humor of the prince, a sum of money to a court lady or a prime minister, or a design of strengthening a party opposite to the public interest ever happened to be motives in those advancements. What share of knowledge these lords had in the laws of their country, and how they came by it, so as to enable them to decide the properties of their fellow subjects in the last resort. Whether they were always so free from avarice, partialities, or want, that a bribe, or some other sinister view, could have no place among them. Whether those holy lords I spoke of were constantly promoted to that rank upon account of their knowledge in religious matters, and the sanctity of their lives, had never been compliers with the times while they were common priests, or slavish prostitute chaplains[1] to some nobleman, whose opinions they continued servilely to follow after they were admitted into that assembly.

He then desired to know what arts were practiced in electing those whom I called commoners: whether a stranger with a strong purse might not influence the vulgar voters to choose him before their own landlord, or the most considerable gentleman in the neighborhood. How it came to pass that people were so violently bent upon getting into this assembly, which I allowed to be a great trouble and expense, often to the ruin of their families, without any salary or pension: because this appeared such an exalted strain of virtue and public spirit that his Majesty seemed to doubt it might possibly not be always sincere: and he desired to know whether such zealous gentlemen could have any views of refunding themselves for the charges and trouble they were at, by sacrificing the public good to the designs of a weak and vicious prince in conjunction with a corrupted ministry. He multiplied his questions, and sifted me thoroughly upon every part of this head, proposing numberless inquiries and objections, which I think it not prudent or convenient to repeat.

Upon what I said in relation to our courts of justice, his Majesty desired to be satisfied in several points: and this I was the better able to do, having been formerly almost ruined by a long suit in chancery,[2] which was decreed for me with costs. He asked what time was usually spent in determining between right and wrong, and what degree of expense. Whether advocates and orators had liberty to plead in causes manifestly known to be unjust, vexatious, or oppressive. Whether party in religion or politics were observed to be of any weight in the scale of justice. Whether those pleading orators were persons educated in the general knowledge of equity, or only in provincial, national, and other local customs. Whether they or their judges had any part in penning those laws which they assumed the liberty of interpreting and glossing upon at their pleasure. Whether they had ever at different times pleaded for and against the same cause, and cited precedents to prove contrary opinions. Whether they were a rich or a poor corporation. Whether they received any pecuniary reward for pleading or delivering their opinions. And particularly, whether they were ever admitted as members in the lower senate.

He fell next upon the management of our treasury;[3] and said he thought my memory had failed me because I computed our taxes at about five or six millions a year, and when I came to mention the issues, he found they sometimes amounted to more than double; for the notes he had taken were very particular in this point, because he hoped, as he told me, that the knowledge of our conduct might be useful to him, and he could not be deceived in his calculations. But, if what I told him were true, he was still at a loss how a kingdom could run out of its estate like a private person. He asked me who were our creditors; and where we found money to pay them. He wondered to hear me talk of such chargeable and extensive wars; that certainly we must be a quarrelsome people, or live among very bad neighbors, and that our generals must needs be richer than our kings.[4] He asked

[1] **chaplains:** an allusion to Low Church bishops appointed by the Whigs under George I.

[2] **suit in chancery:** The Court of Chancery, which settled claims between individuals, was notoriously slow and expensive.

[3] **treasury:** Here Swift discusses two issues between the Tories and the Whigs—the national debt and the standing army.

[4] **generals . . . kings:** a reference to the fortune which the Duke of Marlborough made from the War of Spanish Succession (1701–14).

what business we had out of our own islands, unless upon the score of trade or treaty, or to defend the coasts with our fleet. Above all, he was amazed to hear me talk of a mercenary standing army in the midst of peace and among a free people. He said, if we were governed by our own consent in the persons of our representatives, he could not imagine of whom we were afraid, or against whom we were to fight; and would hear my opinion, whether a private man's house might not better be defended by himself, his children, and family, than by half a dozen rascals picked up at a venture in the streets, for small wages, who might get an hundred times more by cutting their throats.

He laughed at my odd kind of arithmetic (as he was pleased to call it) in reckoning the numbers of our people by a computation drawn from the several sects among us in religion and politics. He said he knew no reason why those who entertain opinions prejudicial to the public should be obliged to change, or should not be obliged to conceal them. And as it was tyranny in any government to require the first, so it was weakness not to enforce the second: for a man may be allowed to keep poisons in his closet, but not to vend them about as cordials.

He observed that among the diversions of our nobility and gentry, I had mentioned gaming. He desired to know at what age this entertainment was usually taken up, and when it was laid down; how much of their time it employed; whether it ever went so high as to affect their fortunes; whether mean vicious people, by their dexterity in that art, might not arrive at great riches, and sometimes keep our very nobles in dependence, as well as habituate them to vile companions, wholly take them from the improvement of their minds, and force them, by the losses they received, to learn and practice that infamous dexterity upon others.

He was perfectly astonished with the historical account I gave him of our affairs during the last century, protesting it was only an heap of conspiracies, rebellions, murders, massacres, revolutions, banishments; the very worst effects that avarice, faction, hypocrisy, perfidiousness, cruelty, rage, madness, hatred, envy, lust, malice, and ambition could produce.

His Majesty, in another audience, was at the pains to recapitulate the sum of all I had spoken; compared the questions he made with the answers I had given; then taking me into his hands, and stroking me gently, delivered himself in these words, which I shall never forget, nor the manner he spoke them in. "My little friend Grildrig, you have made a most admirable panegyric upon your country. You have clearly proved that ignorance, idleness, and vice are the proper ingredients for qualifying a legislator: that laws are best explained, interpreted, and applied by those whose interest and abilities lie in perverting, confounding, and eluding them. I observe among you some lines of an institution, which in its original might have been tolerable, but these half erased, and the rest wholly blurred and blotted by corruptions. It doth not appear from all you have said how any one perfection is required towards the procurement of any one station among you; much less that men are ennobled on account of their virtue, that priests are advanced for their piety or learning, soldiers for their conduct or valor, judges for their integrity, senators for the love of their country, or counselors for their wisdom. As for yourself (continued the King), who have spent the greatest part of your life in traveling, I am well disposed to hope you may hitherto have escaped many vices of your country. But by what I have gathered from your own relation, and the answers I have with much pains wringed and extorted from you, I cannot but conclude the bulk of your natives to be the most pernicious race of little odious vermin that nature ever suffered to crawl upon the surface of the earth."

Nothing but an extreme love of truth could have hindered me from concealing this part of my story. It was in vain to discover my resentments, which were always turned into ridicule; and I was forced to rest with patience while my noble and most beloved country was so injuriously treated. I am heartily sorry as any of my readers can possibly be that such an occasion was given: but this prince happened to be so curious and inquisitive upon every particular that it could not consist either with gratitude or good manners to refuse giving him what satisfaction I was able. Yet thus much I may be allowed to say in my own vindication, that I artfully eluded many of his questions, and gave to every point a more favorable turn by many degrees than the strictness of truth would allow. For I have always borne that laudable partiality to my own country, which Dionysius Halicarnassensis [1] with so much justice recommends to an historian: I would hide the frailties and deformities of my political mother, and place her virtues and beauties in the most advantageous light. This was my sincere endeavor in those many discourses I had with that mighty monarch, although it unfortunately failed of success.

But great allowances should be given to a King who lives wholly secluded from the rest of the world, and must therefore be altogether unacquainted with the manners and customs that most prevail in other nations: the want of which knowledge will ever produce many prejudices, and a certain narrowness of thinking, from which we and the politer countries of Europe are wholly exempted. And it would be hard indeed, if so remote a prince's notions of virtue and vice were to be offered as a standard for all mankind.

To confirm what I have now said, and further, to show the miserable effects of a confined education, I shall here insert a passage which will hardly obtain belief. In hopes to ingratiate myself farther into his Majesty's favor, I told him of an invention discovered between three and four hundred years ago to make a certain pow-

der into an heap of which the smallest spark of fire falling would kindle the whole in a moment, although it were as big as a mountain, and make it all fly up in the air together, with a noise and agitation greater than thunder. That a proper quantity of this powder rammed into an hollow tube of brass or iron, according to its bigness, would drive a ball of iron or lead with such violence and speed as nothing was able to sustain its force. That the largest balls thus discharged would not only destroy whole ranks of an army at once, but batter the strongest walls to the ground, sink down ships, with a thousand men in each, to the bottom of the sea; and, when linked together by a chain, would cut through masts and rigging, divide hundreds of bodies in the middle, and lay all waste before them. That we often put this powder into large hollow balls of iron, and discharged them by an engine into some city we were besieging, which would rip up the pavement, tear the houses to pieces, burst and throw splinters on every side, dashing out the brains of all who came near. That I knew the ingredients very well, which were cheap, and common; I understood the manner of compounding them, and could direct his workmen how to make those tubes of a size proportionable to all other things in his Majesty's kingdom, and the largest need not be above two hundred foot long; twenty or thirty of which tubes, charged with the proper quantity of powder and balls, would batter down the walls of the strongest town in his dominions in a few hours, or destroy the whole metropolis, if ever it should pretend to dispute his absolute commands. This I humbly offered to his Majesty as a small tribute of acknowledgment in return of so many marks that I had received of his royal favor and protection.

The King was struck with horror at the description I had given of those terrible engines and the proposal I had made. He was amazed how so impotent and groveling an insect as I (these were his expressions) could entertain such inhuman ideas,

[1] **Dionysius Halicarnassensis:** a Greek writer living in Rome in the time of Augustus whose work praised the virtues of the Romans.

and in so familiar a manner as to appear wholly unmoved at all the scenes of blood and desolation, which I had painted as the common effects of those destructive machines, whereof he said, some evil genius, enemy to mankind, must have been the first contriver. As for himself, he protested, that although few things delighted him so much as new discoveries in art or in nature, yet he would rather lose half his kingdom than be privy to such a secret, which he commanded me, as I valued my life, never to mention any more.

A strange effect of *narrow principles* and *short views!* that a prince possessed of every quality which procures veneration, love, and esteem; of strong parts, great wisdom, and profound learning, endued with admirable talents for government, and almost adored by his subjects, should from a *nice unnecessary scruple,* whereof in Europe we can have no conception, let slip an opportunity put into his hands that would have made him absolute master of the lives, the liberties, and the fortunes of his people. Neither do I say this with the least intention to detract from the many virtues of that excellent King, whose character I am sensible will on this account be very much lessened in the opinion of an English reader: but I take this defect among them to have risen from their ignorance, by not having hitherto reduced politics into a science, as the more acute wits of Europe have done. For, I remember very well, in a discourse one day with the King, when I happened to say there were several thousand books among us written upon the art of government, it gave him (directly contrary to my intention) a very mean opinion of our understandings. He professed both to abominate and despise all *mystery, refinement,* and *intrigue,* either in a prince or a minister. He could not tell what I meant by *secrets of state,* where an enemy or some rival nation were not in the case. He confined the knowledge of governing within very *narrow bounds;* to common sense and reason, to justice and lenity, to the speedy determination of civil and criminal causes; with some other obvious topics, which are not worth considering. And he gave it for his opinion, that whoever could make two ears of corn, or two blades of grass to grow upon a spot of ground where only one grew before, would deserve better of mankind, and do more essential service to his country, than the whole race of politicians put together.

The learning of this people is very defective, consisting only in morality, history, poetry, and mathematics, wherein they must be allowed to excel. But the last of these is wholly applied to what may be useful in life, to the improvement of agriculture, and all mechanical arts; so that among us it would be little esteemed. And as to ideas, entities, abstractions, and transcendentals,[1] I could never drive the least conception into their heads.

[1] **ideas . . . transcendentals:** terms used by medieval scholars.

FOR STUDY AND DISCUSSION

1. In "A Voyage to Lilliput," the Whig Prime Minister Robert Walpole and his ally Lord Townshend are satirized as Flimnap and Reldresal. Do you think that such attacks on individuals contradict Swift's statement, "I have ever hated all nations, professions, and communities, and all my love is toward individuals"? Explain your answer.

2. Which device do you think creates a more effective situation for satire: a hero who is a giant among Lilliputians or one who is a pygmy among Brobdingnagians? Or do you think these devices equally effective? Give examples from the text to support your viewpoint.

3. How does the tone of Swift's satire on humankind change as he moves from the Lilliputians to Brobdingnagians? To what do you attribute this change of tone? What change of tone occurs at the very beginning of Gulliver's discourse to the King of Brobdingnag on "his own dear native country"?

4. As the defeated British army surrendered their arms to George Washington, their bands played "The World Turned Upside Down." An instance of "the-world-turned-upside-

down" occurs in the last book of *Gulliver's Travels* where horses are masters and men are servants. Many of the differences Swift describes are, of course, moral and political as well as physical. Cite instances of "the-world-turned-upside-down" in the selections from *Gulliver's Travels* which you have just read.

5. What devices does Swift use to induce the reader to accept Gulliver's adventures as actual happenings—at least to the extent of willingly suspending disbelief? Compare Swift's method with Defoe's in the excerpt from *A Journal of the Plague Year.*

6. Pope, in *The Rape of the Lock,* and Swift, in *Gulliver's Travels,* make use of two related techniques of ridicule: inflating triviality by elevating it to grandeur, and deflating grandeur by reducing it to triviality. Referring to their works, explain each writer's use of both of these techniques.

SATIRE

"Satire," wrote Jonathan Swift, "is a sort of glass wherein beholders do generally discover everybody's face but their own." Swift's wry comment on human nature was occasioned—in part, at least—by the failure of *Gulliver's Travels* to reform the English nation. Speaking through Gulliver, Swift wrote in the preface to the second edition: "Behold, after above six months' warning, I cannot learn that my book hath produced one single effect according to my intentions." The satirist is, above all, a reformer. The bitterness so often associated with satirical writing results from the writer's observation that people are not living up to the writer's standards of human behavior. The writer heaps ridicule on human heads believing that satire is a form of therapy. "Those who are ashamed of nothing else," wrote Pope, "are so of being ridiculous."

The aims of satire vary, as does the tone of the critic. The satirist may desire to reform social conduct, ridicule a personal enemy, or denounce everything in people that is found distasteful. The tone with which he or she launches the attack can range from light humor to scathing sarcasm, depending upon the degree of indignation. Differences in purpose and tone can be seen by comparing the satire of Addison and Steele (page 286) with that of Pope (page 296) and Swift. How does the satire of these four writers differ in style, tone, and intent?

Although, as author of *Gulliver's Travels,* Swift wrote what is probably the most famous satire in the English language, he was not the first to make use of this literary art. The good-natured and tolerant Chaucer satirized the worst follies of churchmen in his Pardoner. Shakespeare, in the play within a play in *Hamlet,* turns satire on his fellow actors. In the eighteenth century, a golden age of satire, Alexander Pope, Addison and Steele, and others used satire as a most effective weapon against their adversaries in intramural literary quarrels. Satire is by no means dead; its tart quality appeals to us today in our threatening and comfortable, scientifically ordered and confusing, sweet-and-sour world. Usually, modern satire, like that of Swift, follows Addison's rule: to "pass over a single foe to charge whole armies." T. S. Eliot's "The Hollow Men" (page 751) and George Orwell's *Animal Farm* are examples of twentieth-century satire in the best tradition. But beyond a shrug here and a return slap there, today's society pays no more heed to the supposed therapeutic effect of satire than did the Yahoos so painstakingly ridiculed by Jonathan Swift.

LANGUAGE AND VOCABULARY

In describing the skills of the Lilliputians, Swift says that the "candidates for great employment" must undergo a trial of *dexterity.* The highest honors go to the one who exhibits the greatest *agility.* How are these two words related in meaning? How do they differ? List synonyms for these words and explain their exact use.

In Gulliver's conversation with the King of Brobdingnag a number of words appear that are closely related in meaning to the word *intelligence.* All of these words are nouns except *prudent* whose noun form is *prudence.* Consulting your dictionary, supply definitions that differentiate the meaning of these words: *sagacity, prudence, erudition, reason, knowledge, learning.*

FOR COMPOSITION

1. Select from *Gulliver's Travels* a single target of Swift's satire and write a composition in which you show how he attacks this target in the selections you have read.

2. Write an imaginary scene in which a modern Gulliver tries to initiate the King of Brobdingnag into some mysteries of modern society. Include the King's reactions.

SAMUEL JOHNSON
(1709–1784)

The great name of Samuel Johnson is due, strangely, less to his own merits than to the brilliance of his biographer, James Boswell, thanks to whom Johnson is among the best-known figures in the world. Johnson's merits were many, however, and they were wide and varied. He was a first-rate critic, a successful novelist, poet, and lexicographer, and a fair playwright. When to these abilities are added a superb gift for talk, a didactic manner which molded the taste of his age in London (and thus in all of England), and a number of personal eccentricities, it becomes clear why Johnson is one of the most picturesque characters and great literary personalities of all time.

Not until Johnson was in his fifties did he escape the pinch of poverty. The son of an unbusinesslike bookseller in the country town of Lichfield, he had few advantages in life. Temporary good fortune enabled him to enter Oxford University, where he was handicapped by two idiosyncrasies of temperament: indolence and melancholy. Of that unhappy time he wrote: "I was miserably poor, and I thought to fight my way by my literature and my wit; so I disregarded all power and all authority." At the Christmas break of his second year, he left the University and returned home to make desultory attempts at writing and schoolteaching.

Johnson's prospects were then at a low point. His face scarred by scrofula and his body given to convulsive twitches, he was also physically awkward and personally slovenly. He was desperately poor, without settled plans, and seemingly without ability to carry any project through to completion. Nonetheless a widow twenty years his senior marked him as a "most sensible" man. They married and, after an unsuccessful attempt to establish a boarding school, moved to London, where for the next ten years Johnson made his difficult way as a literary man.

The frequent observation that Johnson's reputation owes more to Boswell's biography of him than to the merits of his own writing stems, for the most part, from the nature of his prose style. Johnson's work is a mirror of his personality—serious, scholarly, at times witty, and often rather weighty. He indulged in lengthy and involved sentences and in polysyllabic words of Latin derivation, as is seen in the definition in his *Dictionary* of *network:* "anything reticulated or decussated at equal distances with interstices between the intersections." Goldsmith once told him: "If you were to make little fishes talk, they would talk like whales." In his periodical, *The Rambler,* in which Johnson tried to emulate Addison and Steele's *Spectator,* he ended, as has been said, in playing "the elephant to Addison's antelope." One cannot expect to find levity, grace, or charm in Johnson's writing, but rather an extraordinary display of erudition and common sense.

It was not until Johnson was nearly fifty-four that Boswell entered his circle—a fact which should be remembered when we consider Boswell's verdicts on any but the last twenty years of Johnson's life. By that time Johnson was famous as poet (*The Vanity of Human Wishes*), novelist (*Rasselas*), essayist, lexicographer, and scholar worthy of a royal pension. He was also a noted sage. In 1764, at the age of fifty-five, Johnson joined Sir Joshua Reynolds, the renowned painter; Edmund Burke, the statesman; Oliver Goldsmith, the poet; Richard Sheridan, the dramatist; Edward Gibbon, the historian; and others in forming the celebrated Literary Club, a group which dined regularly at the Turk's Head Tavern. Though many of the most outstanding men of the day were members, it was Johnson, with his wisdom, wit, and personal vitality, who dominated this distinguished group. Enlivened by both the comradeship of the Club and his association with Mr. and Mrs. Henry Thrale (who provided him a second home during most of the rest of his life), Johnson became an institution all by himself, with Boswell as recorder.

Johnson's main contribution to his age was his application of a vigorous mind and a scholar's instinct to establishing for his contemporaries a strict canon for good writing. The eighteenth century was an era of rules. Johnson undertook the task, in his preparation of a standard *Dictionary of the English Language,* in his essays in *The Rambler* and *The Idler,* and his *Lives of the English Poets,* to demonstrate convincingly the virtues of "correctness" in writing. Through his work and personality, Samuel Johnson bestowed on the world a rich treasury of frank good sense and the subject matter for the best of biographies.

Letter to Lord Chesterfield

Johnson's letter to Lord Chesterfield is historically significant because of its impact on the patronage system, which still prevailed in England in Johnson's time. Because the reading public was small, the only way of obtaining substantial financial return from writing was by securing a patron from among the wealthy nobility. The writer dedicated the work to a patron, who in return looked after the writer's welfare. When first contemplating his *Dictionary,* Johnson sought the support of Lord Chesterfield, the most elegant gentleman of his day. After rebuffing Johnson's request for financial support, Chesterfield, seven years later, just before the *Dictionary* was to be published, wrote two articles in its praise. His indignation aroused by Chesterfield's attempt to win his favor and perhaps cajole him into

dedicating the *Dictionary* to him, Johnson wrote the following letter, which is said to have broken irrevocably the shackles of the patronage system. Thenceforth writers began to seek financial support from public rather than private recognition of their merit.

February 7, 1755

To the Right Honorable the Earl of Chesterfield.

MY LORD: I have been lately informed by the proprietor of the *World* [1] that two papers, in which my Dictionary is recommended to the public, were written by your Lordship. To be so distinguished is an honor which, being very little accustomed to favors from the great, I know not well how to receive or in what terms to acknowledge.

[1] the *World:* a newspaper run by Edward Moore, a friend of Johnson's.

When, upon some slight encouragement, I first visited your Lordship, I was overpowered, like the rest of mankind, by the enchantment of your address, and could not forbear to wish that I might boast myself *Le vainqueur du vainqueur de la terre* [1] —that I might obtain that regard for which I saw the world contending; but I found my attendance so little encouraged that neither pride nor modesty would suffer me to continue it. When I had once addressed your Lordship in public, I had exhausted all the art of pleasing which a retired and uncourtly scholar can possess. I had done all that I could; and no man is well pleased to have his all neglected, be it ever so little.

Seven years, my Lord, have now passed since I waited in your outward rooms, or was repulsed from your door; during which time I have been pushing on my work through difficulties, of which it is useless to complain, and have brought it, at last, to the verge of publication without one act of assistance, one word of encouragement, or one smile of favor. Such treatment I did not expect, for I never had a Patron before.

The shepherd in Virgil grew at last acquainted with Love and found him a native of the rocks. [2]

Is not a Patron, my Lord, one who looks with unconcern on a man struggling for life in the water, and when he has reached ground, encumbers him with help? The notice which you have been pleased to take of my labors, had it been early, had been kind; but it has been delayed till I am indifferent, and cannot enjoy it; till I am solitary, [3] and cannot impart it; till I am known, and do not want it. I hope it is no very cynical

asperity not to confess obligations where no benefit has been received, or to be unwilling that the Public should consider me as owing that to a Patron which Providence has enabled me to do for myself.

Having carried on my work thus far with so little obligation to any favorer of learning, I shall not be disappointed though I should conclude it, if less be possible, with less; for I have been long wakened from that dream of hope, in which I once boasted myself with so much exultation.

My Lord,
Your Lordship's most humble,
Most obedient servant,
Sam. Johnson

Preface to Shakespeare

Johnson's edition of Shakespeare is remembered today chiefly for two things: its clear interpretation of obscure passages and the sound judgments of its thoughtful Preface. As a neoclassical critic, Johnson wrote in a time strongly prejudiced in favor of tradition, authority, and, as regards drama, the classical rules, most important of which was the observation of the unities of time and place. Johnson, describing himself in his Preface as "almost frighted at my own temerity . . . when I estimate the fame and the strength of those that maintain the contrary opinion," proceeded to assess Shakespeare (who violated the rules more than he obeyed them) by his own standards of logic and common sense rather than by the generally accepted aesthetic standards of his day. Venerated though they were, Johnson argued, the unities "have given more trouble to the poet than pleasure to the auditor." Though he himself observed the rules in many ways, Johnson did not parrot prevailing beliefs. To the twentieth-century reader the Preface to Shakespeare may not seem particularly novel, but in Johnson's day, when Shakespeare's alleged irregularities as a dramatist required defense, Johnson defended them with daring and skill.

---

[1] **Le . . . terre:** "The conqueror of the conqueror of the world."

[2] **The shepherd . . . rocks:** a reference to a passage in Virgil's eighth *Eclogue* (a pastoral poem in which shepherds converse on the cruelty and inhumanity of love).

[3] **till . . . solitary:** Johnson's wife died in 1752, while he was working on his *Dictionary*.

In the following passage from his Preface, Johnson suggests what to him are some of Shakespeare's admirable qualities as a dramatist.

ANTIQUITY, like every other quality that attracts the notice of mankind, has undoubtedly votaries that reverence it, not from reason, but from prejudice. Some seem to admire indiscriminately whatever has been long preserved, without considering that time has sometimes cooperated with chance; all perhaps are more willing to honor past than present excellence; and the mind contemplates genius through the shades of age, as the eye surveys the sun through artificial opacity. The great contention of criticism is to find the faults of the moderns, and the beauties of the ancients. While an author is yet living we estimate his powers by his worst performance, and when he is dead we rate them by his best.

To works, however, of which the excellence is not absolute and definite, but gradual and comparative; to works not raised upon principles demonstrative and scientific, but appealing wholly to observation and experience, no other test can be applied than length of duration and continuance of esteem. What mankind have long possessed they have often examined and compared, and if they persist to value the possession, it is because frequent comparisons have confirmed opinion in its favor. As among the works of nature no man can properly call a river deep or a mountain high, without the knowledge of many mountains and many rivers; so in the productions of genius, nothing can be styled excellent till it has been compared with other works of the same kind. Demonstration immediately displays its power and has nothing to hope or fear from the flux of years, but works tentative and experimental must be estimated by their proportion to the general and collective ability of man, as it is discovered in a long succession of endeavors. Of the first building that was raised, it might be with cer-

tainty determined that it was round or square, but whether it was spacious or lofty must have been referred to time. The Pythagorean scale of numbers [1] was at once discovered to be perfect, but the poems of Homer we yet know not to transcend the common limits of human intelligence, but by remarking that nation after nation, and century after century, has been able to do little more than transpose his incidents, new-name his characters, and paraphrase his sentiments.

The reverence due to writings that have long subsisted arises therefore not from any credulous confidence in the superior wisdom of past ages or gloomy persuasion of the degeneracy of mankind, but is the consequence of acknowledged and indubitable positions, that what has been longest known has been most considered, and what is most considered is best understood.

The poet of whose works I have undertaken the revision may now begin to assume the dignity of an ancient, and claim the privilege of established fame and prescriptive veneration. He has long outlived his century, the term commonly fixed as the test of literary merit. Whatever advantages he might once derive from personal allusions, local customs, or temporary opinions have for many years been lost; and every topic of merriment or motive of sorrow, which the modes of artificial life afforded him, now only obscure the scenes which they once illuminated. The effects of favor and competition are at an end; the tradition of his friendships and his enmities has perished; his works support no opinion with arguments, nor supply any faction with invectives; they can neither indulge vanity nor gratify malignity, but are read without any other reason than the desire of pleasure, and are therefore praised only as pleasure is obtained; yet, thus un-

[1] **Pythagorean . . . numbers:** a reference to a theory described in Aristotle's *Metaphysics*—namely, that numbers are "the elements in everything." Pythagoras attributed mystical significance to numbers.

assisted by interest or passion, they have passed through variations of taste and changes of manners and, as they devolved from one generation to another, have received new honors at every transmission.

But because human judgment, though it be gradually gaining upon certainty, never becomes infallible, and approbation, though long continued, may yet be only the approbation of prejudice or fashion, it is proper to inquire by what peculiarities of excellence Shakespeare has gained and kept the favor of his countrymen.

Nothing can please many, and please long, but just representations of general nature. Particular manners can be known to few, and therefore few only can judge how nearly they are copied. The irregular combinations of fanciful invention may delight awhile, by that novelty of which the common satiety of life sends us all in quest; but the pleasures of sudden wonder are soon exhausted, and the mind can only repose on the stability of truth.

Shakespeare is, above all writers, at least above all modern writers, the poet of nature; the poet that holds up to his readers a faithful mirror of manners and of life. His characters are not modified by the customs of particular places, unpracticed by the rest of the world; by the peculiarities of studies or professions, which can operate but upon small numbers; or by the accidents of transient fashions or temporary opinions; they are the genuine progeny of common humanity, such as the world will always supply and observation will always find. His persons act and speak by the influence of those general passions and principles by which all minds are agitated and the whole system of life is continued in motion. In the writings of other poets a character is too often an individual; in those of Shakespeare it is commonly a species.

It is from this wide extension of design that so much instruction is derived. It is this which fills the plays of Shakespeare with practical axioms and domestic wisdom. It was said of Euripides that every verse was a precept; and it may be said of Shakespeare that from his works may be collected a system of civil and economical prudence. Yet his real power is not shown in the splendor of particular passages, but by the progress of his fable and the tenor of his dialogue; and he that tries to recommend him by select quotations will succeed like the pedant in Hierocles,[1] who, when he offered his house to sale, carried a brick in his pocket as a specimen.

It will not easily be imagined how much Shakespeare excels in accommodating his sentiments to real life, but by comparing him with other authors. It was observed of the ancient schools of declamation that the more diligently they were frequented, the more was the student disqualified for the world, because he found nothing there which he should ever meet in any other place. The same remark may be applied to every stage but that of Shakespeare. The theater, when it is under any other direction, is peopled by such characters as were never seen, conversing in a language which was never heard, upon topics which will never arise in the commerce of mankind. But the dialogue of this author is often so evidently determined by the incident which produces it, and is pursued with so much ease and simplicity, that it seems scarcely to claim the merit of fiction, but to have been gleaned by diligent selection out of common conversation and common occurrences.

Upon every other stage the universal agent is love, by whose power all good and evil is distributed, and every action quickened or retarded. To bring a lover, a lady, and a rival into the fable; to entangle them in contradictory obligations, perplex them with oppositions of interest, and harass them with violence of desires inconsistent with each other; to make them meet in rapture and part in agony; to fill their mouths with hyperbolical joy and outrageous sorrow; to distress them as noth-

---

[1] **Hierocles:** fifth-century scholar and critic.

ing human ever was distressed; to deliver them as nothing human ever was delivered—is the business of a modern dramatist. For this probability is violated, life is misrepresented, and language is depraved. But love is only one of many passions, and, as it has no great influence upon the sum of life, it has little operation in the dramas of a poet, who caught his ideas from the living world, and exhibited only what he saw before him. He knew that any other passion, as it was regular or exorbitant, was a cause of happiness or calamity.

Characters thus ample and general were not easily discriminated and preserved, yet perhaps no poet ever kept his personages more distinct from each other. I will not say with Pope that every speech may be assigned to the proper speaker, because many speeches there are which have nothing characteristical; but, perhaps, though some may be equally adapted to every person, it will be difficult to find any that can be properly transferred from the present possessor to another claimant. The choice is right when there is reason for choice.

Other dramatists can only gain attention by hyperbolical or aggravated characters, by fabulous and unexampled excellence or depravity, as the writers of barbarous romances invigorated the reader by a giant and a dwarf; and he that should form his expectations of human affairs from the play, or from the tale, would be equally deceived. Shakespeare has no heroes; his scenes are occupied only by men who act and speak as the reader thinks that he should himself have spoken or acted on the same occasion. Even where the agency is supernatural, the dialogue is level with life. Other writers disguise the most natural passions and most frequent incidents, so that he who contemplates them in the book will not know them in the world. Shakespeare approximates the remote, and familiarizes the wonderful; the event which he represents will not happen, but if it were possible, its effects would be probably such

as he has assigned; and it may be said that he has not only shown human nature as it acts in real exigences, but as it would be found in trials to which it cannot be exposed.

This therefore is the praise of Shakespeare, that his drama is the mirror of life; that he who has mazed his imagination in following the phantoms which other writers raise up before him may here be cured of his delirious ecstasies by reading human sentiments in human language, by scenes from which a hermit may estimate the transactions of the world, and a confessor predict the progress of the passions.

FOR STUDY AND DISCUSSION

1. What light is cast upon Johnson's character by his conduct toward Lord Chesterfield?

2. In his Preface to Shakespeare, Johnson inquires "by what peculiarities of excellence Shakespeare has gained and kept the favor of his countrymen." What answers does Johnson arrive at in his inquiry? How do Johnson's comments on Shakespeare compare with Dryden's in "An Essay on Dramatic Poesy"?

3. What does Johnson mean when he refers to Shakespeare as "the poet of nature"?

4. "Shakespeare," Johnson writes, "has no heroes; his scenes are occupied only by men who act and speak as the reader thinks that he should himself have spoken or acted on the same occasion." What do you think Johnson meant by "heroes"? Considering *Macbeth* (or any other Shakespeare plays), do you agree that Shakespeare has no heroes?

FOR COMPOSITION

In "The Gentleman" (page 578), Cardinal Newman says that if a gentleman "engages in controversy of any kind, his disciplined intellect preserves him from the blundering discourtesy of better, perhaps, but less-educated minds, who, like blunt weapons, tear and hack instead of cutting clean . . ." Does Johnson in his letter to Lord Chesterfield exemplify Newman's definition of a gentleman? Is answering, keep in mind the occasion that provoked the letter, Johnson's purpose in writing the letter, his correspondent, and the tone in which he addresses his correspondent.

JAMES BOSWELL
(1740–1795)

James Boswell secured his position in English literature by assuring the immortality of Samuel Johnson, but had Johnson never lived Boswell would still deserve a high place as one of the best of diarists.

Only lately, through a series of unexpected discoveries as dramatic as any detective story, have we come to know Boswell not simply as author of *The Life of Samuel Johnson* but as a man of wide experience and many interests. Since 1840, thousands of pages of papers, letters, and diaries formerly thought to have been destroyed by his literary executors have been appearing in all sorts of unlikely places. One of the most spectacular finds was uncovered in the 1920's in an old Irish castle. In 1950 general publication of this great collection began with *Boswell's London Journal, 1762–1763*. For the first time the world came to know Boswell as he had been: a kaleidoscopic, moody, irrepressible man, by turns rakish and remorseful, taking his color from his company, vain, snobbish, aggressive, and at the same time able to win over almost anybody by his charm of manner.

Boswell's early life differed in nearly every way from Johnson's. He was born into a Scottish family of wealth, power, and position. To please his father, the Laird of Auchinleck, Boswell studied law. At one time he tried to get a commission in the peacetime army. His real career of celebrity-chasing and writing began about the time he first met Johnson when visiting London in 1763. Recording this event along with other adventures during his stay, he then left on a tour of the Continent. Upon his return to London, he was admitted, under Johnson's sponsorship, to membership in the select Literary Club.

It was with Johnson that Boswell was at his best. Spurred by respect and near-idolatry of his subject, willing to sustain Johnson's occasional exasperation at his continual questioning, Boswell noted his friend's every conversation, habit, and peculiarity with conscientious fidelity. That he was more than a sycophant who appealed to some personal quirk in the older man is shown by his list of outstanding friends: outside Johnson's literary circle, Boswell "collected" such celebrities as the Corsican patriot Paoli and the philosophers Voltaire and Rousseau.

In a critical essay on Boswell, an outspoken critic calls him "a coxcomb and a bore, weak, vain, pushing, curious, garrulous." However true this may be, it is all the more remarkable that in spite of, or possibly because of, these weaknesses Boswell produced his monumental work. But this is only one aspect of Boswell, for his amazingly retentive memory, honesty, discerning insight into people, flair for the dramatic, and his gift for writing simple, quick-paced, vivid narrative are assets which cannot be overlooked. One can only regard with awe the dedication and discipline required to devote thirty years to a single endeavor. While known to be a man of great vanity, Boswell more than fulfilled his prophecy in the opening pages of *The Life of Samuel Johnson:* "I will venture to say that he [Johnson] will be seen in this work more completely than any man who has ever yet lived."

Boswell's personal journals—his *Journal of a Tour to the Hebrides* and his *Journal of a Tour to Corsica*—go beyond the memorializing of a great man. Here he dared to examine his own character and actions with open eyes. These works and his biography of Johnson serve to confirm Thomas Carlyle's remark that "Boswell wrote a good book because he had a heart and an eye to discern wisdom and an utterance to render it forth; because of his free insight, his lively talent, and, above all, of his love and childlike openmindedness."

The Life of Samuel Johnson

When *The Life of Samuel Johnson* was published in 1791, Boswell was at first criticized by many for so frankly revealing all of Johnson's weaknesses and idiosyncrasies as well as his strengths and virtues. Boswell insisted, however, that he would not make his "tiger a cat to please anybody." Time has proved Boswell correct in his belief that the greatness of his subject would enable him to withstand such truthful and candid exposure. The biography has resulted in lasting fame for both subject and author.

For many years Boswell's image has suffered from Thomas Macaulay's picture of him as a clownish puppy who followed Johnson about, fawning on him and waiting for the great man to throw him a bone of wit. This distorted view is based partly on Boswell's own unabashed record of his humiliation by Johnson at their first meeting (page 342). But a close reading of *The Life of Samuel Johnson* or of the *London Journal* will prove otherwise. Although a celebrity chaser, Boswell did not force himself on Johnson. Within a month after their initial meeting, it was Johnson who asked Boswell why he didn't call oftener, and toward the end of his life Johnson remembered a long trip to the Hebrides with Boswell so pleasantly that he wrote him asking whether they might ever enjoy such a trip again.

Johnson, thirty-one years older than his young friend and many times wiser in the hard ways of the world, is sometimes said to have served as a substitute for Boswell's unyielding and overbearing father. It is certain that Boswell and his father were not on good terms and that the Laird disapproved of his son's London life and his friendship with Johnson about as much as he did of his earlier attempts to obtain a military commission. Boswell's association with Johnson, however, gave his previously erratic life a sense of purpose. The Johnson–Boswell relationship was, in short, mutually advantageous.

[THE DICTIONARY]

Samuel Johnson was the first lexicographer to undertake almost single-handedly the complex and arduous task of standardizing, and thus stabilizing, our language. He so carefully worked out his plan for his *Dictionary, with a Grammar and History of the English Language* that it was the accepted authority for over one hundred years. The dictionary is unique in that it is very personal. Johnson's humor and his prejudices are revealed in definitions such as that for *excise duty:* "a hateful tax levied by wretches hired by those to whom excise is paid"; and *lexicographer:* "a writer of dictionaries, a harmless drudge." Johnson's *Dictionary* was published in 1755 after much hardship, disappointment, sickness, and sorrow, the heaviest blow being the death of his beloved wife. The following excerpt from Boswell's *Life of Johnson* appears in the first part of the biography, which covers the period before Boswell's first meeting with Johnson.

How LONG this immense undertaking had been the object of his contemplation, I do not know. I once asked him by what means he had attained to that astonishing knowledge of our language by which he was enabled to realize a design of such extent and accumulated difficulty. He told me that "it was not the effect of particular study; but that it had grown up in his mind insensibly." . . .

That he was fully aware of the arduous nature of the undertaking, he acknowledges; and shows himself perfectly sensible of it in the conclusion of his "Plan"; but he had a noble consciousness of his own abilities, which enabled him to go on with undaunted spirit.

Dr. Adams found him one day busy at his Dictionary, when the following dialogue ensued:

Adams: "This is a great work, Sir. How are you to get all the etymologies?" [1]

Johnson: "Why, Sir, here is a shelf with Junius, and Skinner,[2] and others; and there is a Welsh gentleman who has published a collection of Welsh proverbs, who will help me with the Welsh."

Adams: "But, Sir, how can you do this in three years?"

Johnson: "Sir, I have no doubt that I can do it in three years."

Adams: "But the French Academy, which consists of forty members, took forty years to compile their Dictionary."

Johnson: "Sir, thus it is. This is the proportion. Let me see: forty times forty is sixteen hundred. As three to sixteen hundred so is the proportion of an Englishman to a Frenchman."

With so much ease and pleasantry could he talk of that prodigious labor which he had undertaken to execute.

While the Dictionary was going forward, Johnson lived part of the time in Holborn, part in Gough Square, Fleet Street; and he had an upper room fitted up like a countinghouse for the purpose, in which he gave to the copyists their several tasks. The words, partly taken from other Dictionaries, and partly supplied by himself, having been first written down with spaces left between them, he delivered in writing their etymologies, definitions, and various significations. The authorities were copied from the books themselves, in which he had marked the passages with a black-lead pencil, the traces of which could be easily effaced. I have seen several of them in which that trouble had not been taken; so that they were just as when used by the copyists. It is remarkable that he was so attentive in the choice of the passages in which words were authorized that one may read page after page of his Dictionary with improvement and pleasure; and it should not pass unobserved that he has quoted no author whose writings had a tendency to hurt sound religion and morality.

The necessary expense of preparing a work of such magnitude for the press must have been a considerable deduction from the price stipulated to be paid for the copyright.[3] I understand that nothing was allowed by the booksellers on that account; and I remember his telling me that a large portion of it having, by mistake, been written upon both sides of the paper, so as to be inconvenient for the compositor, it cost him twenty pounds to have it transcribed upon one side only.

[BOSWELL'S FIRST MEETING WITH DR. JOHNSON]

Mr. Thomas Davies, the actor, who then kept a bookseller's shop in Russell Street, Covent Garden, told me that Johnson was very much his friend, and came frequently to his house, where he more than once invited me to meet him: but by some unlucky accident or other he was prevented from coming to us. . . .

At last, on Monday the 16th of May, when I was sitting in Mr. Davies' back

---

[1] **etymologies** (et'ə·mol'ə·jēz): origins and derivations of words.

[2] **Junius, and Skinner:** seventeenth-century English scholars, both of whom wrote books on etymology. Skinner was also a physician.

[3] **price . . . copyright:** The price was £1,575.

parlor, after having drunk tea with him and Mrs. Davies, Johnson unexpectedly came into the shop; and Mr. Davies having perceived him through the glass door in the room in which we were sitting, advancing toward us—he announced his awful approach to me, somewhat in the manner of an actor in the part of Horatio, when he addressed Hamlet on the appearance of his father's ghost, "Look, my Lord, it comes." I found that I had a very perfect idea of Johnson's figure, from the portrait of him painted by Sir Joshua Reynolds soon after he had published his Dictionary, in the attitude of sitting in his easy chair in deep meditation; which was the first picture his friend did for him, which Sir Joshua very kindly presented to me, and from which an engraving has been made for this work. Mr. Davies mentioned my name, and respectfully introduced me to him. I was much agitated; and recollecting his prejudice against the Scotch, of which I had heard much, I said to Davies, "Don't tell him where I come from."

"From Scotland," cried Davies, roguishly.

"Mr. Johnson (said I), I do indeed come from Scotland, but I cannot help it."

I am willing to flatter myself that I meant this as light pleasantry to soothe and conciliate him, and not as an humiliating abasement at the expense of my country. But however that might be, this speech was somewhat unlucky; for with that quickness of wit for which he was so remarkable, he seized the expression "come from Scotland," which I used in the sense of being of that country; and, as if I had said that I had come away from it, or left it, retorted, "That, Sir, I find, is what a very great many of your countrymen cannot help."

This stroke stunned me a good deal; and when we had sat down, I felt myself not a little embarrassed, and apprehensive of what might come next.

He then addressed himself to Davies: "What do you think of Garrick? He has refused me an order for the play for Miss Williams, because he knows the house will be full, and that an order would be worth three shillings."

Eager to take any opening to get into conversation with him, I ventured to say, "O, Sir, I cannot think Mr. Garrick would grudge such a trifle to you."

"Sir (said he, with a stern look), I have known David Garrick longer than you have done; and I know no right you have to talk to me on the subject."

Perhaps I deserved this check; for it was rather presumptuous in me, an entire stranger, to express any doubt of the justice of his animadversion upon his old acquaintance and pupil. I now felt myself much mortified, and began to think that the hope which I had long indulged of obtaining his acquaintance was blasted. And, in truth, had not my ardor been uncommonly strong, and my resolution uncommonly persevering, so rough a reception might have deterred me forever from making any further attempts. Fortunately, however, I remained upon the field not wholly discomfited; and was soon rewarded by hearing some of his conversation. . . .

A few days afterward I called on Davies and asked him if he thought I might take the liberty of waiting on Mr. Johnson at his Chambers in the Temple.[1] He said I certainly might, and that Mr. Johnson would take it as a compliment. So on Tuesday the 24th of May, after having been enlivened by the witty sallies of Messieurs Thornton, Wilkes, Churchill, and Lloyd,[2] with whom I had passed the morning, I boldly repaired to Johnson. His Chambers were on the first floor of No. 1, Inner Temple-lane, and I entered them with an impression given me by the Reverend Dr. Blair, of Edinburgh, who had been introduced to him not long before, and described his having "found the Giant in his den"; an expression which, when I came to be pretty well acquainted with

---

[1] **Temple:** an area of London in which lawyers lived and where the law courts are located.

[2] **Thornton . . . Lloyd:** literary wits and friends of Boswell.

Johnson, I repeated to him, and he was diverted at this picturesque account of himself.

He received me very courteously: but it must be confessed that his apartment, and furniture, and morning dress were sufficiently uncouth. His brown suit of clothes looked very rusty: he had on a little old shriveled unpowdered wig, which was too small for his head; his shirt neck and knees of his breeches were loose; his black worsted stockings ill drawn up; and he had a pair of unbuckled shoes by way of slippers. But all these slovenly particularities were forgotten the moment that he began to talk. Some gentlemen, whom I do not recollect, were sitting with him; and when they went away, I also rose; but he said to me, "Nay, don't go."

"Sir (said I), I am afraid that I intrude upon you. It is benevolent to allow me to sit and hear you."

He seemed pleased with this compliment, which I sincerely paid him, and answered, "Sir, I am obliged to any man who visits me." . . .

When I rose a second time, he again pressed me to stay, which I did.

He told me that he generally went abroad at four in the afternoon and seldom came home till two in the morning. I took the liberty to ask if he did not think it was wrong to live thus, and not make more use of his great talents. He owned it was a bad habit. On reviewing, at the distance of many years, my journal of this period, I wonder how, at my first visit, I ventured to talk to him so freely, and that he bore it with so much indulgence.

Before we departed, he was so good as to promise to favor me with his company one evening at my lodgings; and, as I took my leave, shook me cordially by the hand. It is almost needless to add that I felt no little elation at having now so happily established an acquaintance of which I had been so long ambitious.

My readers will, I trust, excuse me for being thus minutely circumstantial, when it is considered that the acquaintance of Dr. Johnson was to me a most valuable acquisition and laid the foundation of whatever instruction and entertainment they may receive from my collections concerning the great subject of the work which they are now perusing.

[DR. JOHNSON'S PECULIARITIES]

He had another particularity,[1] of which none of his friends even ventured to ask an explanation. It appeared to me some superstitious habit, which he had contracted early, and from which he had never called upon his reason to disentangle him. This was his anxious care to go out or in at a door or passage by a certain number of steps from a certain point, or at least so as that either his right or his left foot (I am not certain which) should constantly make the first actual movement when he came close to the door or passage. Thus I conjecture: for I have, upon innumerable occasions, observed him suddenly stop, and then seem to count his steps with a deep earnestness; and when he had neglected or gone wrong in this sort of magical movement, I have seen him go back again, put himself in a proper posture to begin the ceremony, and, having gone through it, break from his abstraction, walk briskly on, and join his companion. Sir Joshua Reynolds has observed him to go a good way about rather than cross a particular alley in Leicester[2] Fields; but this Sir Joshua imputed to his having had some disagreeable recollections associated with it.

That the most minute singularities which belonged to him, and made very observable parts of his appearance and manner, may not be omitted, it is requisite to mention that while talking or even musing as he sat in his chair, he commonly held his head to one side toward his right shoulder, and shook it in a tremulous manner, moving his body backward and forward, and rubbing his left knee in the same direction, with the palm of his hand.

[1] **another particularity:** The first one described was his habit of talking to himself.
[2] **Leicester** (les'tər).

In the intervals of articulating he made various sounds with his mouth; sometimes giving a half whistle, sometimes as if ruminating, or what is called chewing the cud, sometimes making his tongue play backward from the roof of his mouth, as if clucking like a hen, and sometimes protruding it against his upper gums in front, as if pronouncing quickly under his breath, too, too, too: all this accompanied sometimes with a thoughtful look, but more frequently with a smile. Generally when he had concluded a period,[1] in the course of a dispute, by which time he was a good deal exhausted by violence and vociferation, he used to blow out his breath like a whale. This I suppose was a relief to his lungs; and seemed in him to be a contemptuous mode of expression, as if he had made the arguments of his opponents fly like chaff before the wind.

[JOHNSON AND GOLDSMITH]

Boswell, in his description of Oliver Goldsmith, remarked that because he was vain and had "an eager desire of being conspicuous wherever he was, he frequently talked carelessly without knowledge of the subject, or even without thought." As a result, he was occasionally made to appear foolish, and often, as in the following incident, he brought his mortification on himself. The conversation as the selection opens is only one of a series which took place one night among eleven men gathered in the home of the Dilly brothers, booksellers.

During this argument, Goldsmith sat in restless agitation, from a wish to get in and shine. Finding himself excluded, he had taken his hat to go away, but remained for some time with it in his hand, like a gamester, who, at the close of a long night, lingers for a little while, to see if he can have a favorable opening to finish with success. Once when he was beginning to speak, he found himself overpowered by the loud voice of Johnson, who was at the opposite end of the table, and did not perceive Goldsmith's attempt. Thus disappointed of his wish to obtain the attention

[1] **concluded a period:** ended a sentence.

of the company, Goldsmith in a passion threw down his hat, looking angrily at Johnson, and exclaimed in a bitter tone, "Take it." When Toplady was going to speak, Johnson uttered some sound, which led Goldsmith to think that he was beginning again, and taking the words from Toplady. Upon which, he seized this opportunity of venting his own envy and spleen, under the pretext of supporting another person: "Sir (said he to Johnson), the gentleman has heard you patiently for an hour: pray allow us now to hear him."

Johnson (sternly): "Sir, I was not interrupting the gentleman. I was only giving him a signal of my attention. Sir, you are impertinent." Goldsmith made no reply, but continued in the company for some time.

He and Mr. Langton and I went together to the Club, where we found Mr. Burke, Mr. Garrick, and some other members, and among them our friend Goldsmith, who sat silently brooding over Johnson's reprimand to him after dinner. Johnson perceived this, and said aside to some of us, "I'll make Goldsmith forgive me"; and then called to him in a loud voice, "Dr. Goldsmith—something passed today where you and I dined: I ask your pardon." Goldsmith answered placidly, "It must be much from you, Sir, that I take ill." And so at once the difference was over, and they were on as easy terms as ever, and Goldsmith rattled away as usual.

In our way to the Club tonight, when I regretted that Goldsmith would, upon every occasion, endeavor to shine, by which he often exposed himself, Mr. Langton observed that he was not like Addison, who was content with the fame of his writings, and did not aim also at excellency in conversation, for which he found himself unfit: and that he said to a lady who complained of his having talked little in company, "Madam, I have but ninepence in ready money, but I can draw for a thousand pounds." I observed that Goldsmith had a great deal of gold in his cabinet, but not content with that, was always taking out his purse. Johnson: "Yes, Sir, and that so often an empty purse!"

Goldsmith's incessant desire of being conspicuous in company was the occasion of his sometimes appearing to such disadvantage as one should hardly have supposed possible in a man of his genius. When his literary reputation had risen deservedly high, and his society was much courted, he became very jealous of the extraordinary attention which was everywhere paid to Johnson. One evening, in a circle of wits, he found fault with me for talking of Johnson as entitled to the honor of unquestionable superiority. "Sir (said he), you are for making a monarchy of what should be a republic."

He was still more mortified, when talking in a company with fluent vivacity, and, as he flattered himself, to the admiration of all who were present; a German who sat next him, and perceived Johnson rolling himself as if about to speak, suddenly stopped him, saying, "Stay, stay—Toctor Shonson is going to say something." This was, no doubt, very provoking, especially to one so irritable as Goldsmith, who frequently mentioned it with strong expressions of indignation.

It may also be observed that Goldsmith was sometimes content to be treated with an easy familiarity, but upon occasions would be consequential and important. An instance of this occurred in a small particular. Johnson had a way of contracting the names of his friends: as Beauclerk, Beau; Boswell, Bozzy; Langton, Lanky; Murphy, Mur; Sheridan, Sherry. I remember one day, when Tom Davies was telling that Dr. Johnson said, "We are all in labor for a name to Goldy's play," Goldsmith seemed displeased that such a liberty should be taken with his name, and said, "I have often desired him not to call me Goldy." Tom was remarkably attentive to the most minute circumstance about Johnson. I recollect his telling me once, on my arrival in London, "Sir, our great friend has made an improvement on his appellation of old Mr. Sheridan. He calls him now Sherry derry."

Boswell's London Journal, 1762–1763

The *London Journal* is the detailed account of a twenty-two-year-old Scot who fled from parental authority and sought in London excitement and independence of life as a man about town. Boswell here shows himself to be a many-sided human being—now naive, now sophisticated; now pleasure-seeking, now virtue-seeking; often serious but never dull. His many diaries, carefully hidden or neglected in the family archives, were laboriously recovered and brought to Yale University in 1949. The *London Journal* was the first of these papers to be published and became both a bestseller and a key work in literary history.

The *Journal* throws light not only on Boswell himself, but on his friendship with Johnson. The following selections show how Boswell sought Johnson's advice in his personal affairs and the kindly spirit with which Johnson replied. The first entry below also illustrates Boswell's habit of recording unconnected sentences that he remembered from his conversations with his friend.

I TOLD HIM all my story. "Sir," said he, "your father has been wanting to make the man of you at twenty which you will be at thirty. Sir, let me tell you that to be a Scotch landlord,[1] where you have a number of families dependent upon and attached to you, is perhaps as high a situation as humanity can arrive at. A merchant upon 'Change with a hundred thousand pounds is nothing. The Duke of Bedford with all his immense fortune is but a little man in reality. He has no ten-

Saturday 25 June [*1763*]

---

[1] **Scotch landlord:** Boswell, the eldest son of the family, was due to inherit his father's lands and responsibilities.

From *Boswell's London Journal 1762–1763* edited by Frederick A. Pottle. Copyright 1950 by Yale University. Reprinted by permission of McGraw-Hill Book Company and Yale University.

ants who consider themselves as under his patriarchal care.

"Sir, a father and a son should part at a certain time of life. I never believed what my father said. I always thought that he spoke ex officio,[1] as a priest does.

"Sir, I am a friend to subordination. It is most conducive to the happiness of society. There is a reciprocal pleasure in governing and being governed.

"Sir, I think your breaking off idle connections by going abroad is a matter of importance. I would go where there are courts and learned men."

I then complained to him how little I knew, and mentioned study. "Sir," said he, "don't talk of study just now. I will put you upon a plan. It will require some time to talk of that." I put out my hand. "Will you really take a charge of me? It is very good in you, Mr. Johnson, to allow me to sit with you thus. Had I but thought some years ago that I should pass an evening with the Author of *The Rambler!*" These expressions were all from the heart, and he perceived that they were; and he was very complacent and said, "Sir, I am glad we have met. I hope we shall pass many evenings and mornings too together."

Thursday 14 July

Mr. Johnson and I met at the Mitre by ourselves. He was in most excellent humor, though the night was very rainy. I said it was good for the vegetable part of the creation. "Ay, Sir," said he, "and for the animals who eat those vegetables, and for the animals who eat those animals." We had a good supper, which made us very comfortable.

I said, "You and I, Sir, are very good companions, but my father and I are not so. Now what can occasion this? For you are as old a man as my father, and you are certainly as learned and as knowing." "Sir," said he, "I am a man of the world. I live in the world, and I take in some measure the color of the world as it moves

[2] **ex officio** (eks ə·fish′ē·ō): by reason of his office (here as a father).

along. But your father is a judge in a remote part of the country, and all his notions are taken from the old world. Besides, there must always be a struggle between a father and son while the one aims at power and the other at independency." I told him that I was afraid of my father's forcing me to be a lawyer. "Why, Sir," said he, "you need not be afraid of his forcing you to be a laborious practicing lawyer. That is not in his power. For, as the proverb says, 'One man may lead a horse to the water, but twenty cannot make him drink.' He may be displeased, but it will not go far. If he only insists on your having as much law as is necessary for a man of property, and endeavors to get you into Parliament, he is quite in the right."

Saturday 16 July

He advised me to keep a journal of my life, fair and undisguised. He said it would be a very good exercise, and would yield me infinite satisfaction when the ideas were faded from my remembrance. I told him that I had done so ever since I left Scotland. He said he was very happy that I pursued so good a plan. And now, O my journal! art thou not highly dignified? Shalt thou not flourish tenfold? No former solicitations or censures could tempt me to lay thee aside; and now is there any argument which can outweigh the sanction of Mr. Samuel Johnson? He said indeed that I should keep it private, and that I might surely have a friend who would burn it in case of my death. For my own part, I have at present such an affection for this my journal that it shocks me to think of burning it. I rather encourage the idea of having it carefully laid up among the archives of Auchinleck. However, I cannot judge fairly of it now. Some years hence I may. I told Mr. Johnson that I put down all sorts of little incidents in it. "Sir," said he, "there is nothing too little for so little a creature as man. It is by studying little things that we attain the great knowledge of having as little misery and as much happiness as possible."

1. Do you think Johnson himself fitted his description of a lexicographer as "a harmless drudge"? Explain. What does such a definition tell you about the dictionary in which it appears? What does it imply about the man who wrote the definition?

2. What qualities in Johnson does Boswell discover in their first meeting? What qualities in Boswell are revealed in his description of the meeting?

3. In his biography Boswell writes that Goldsmith "has sagacity enough to cultivate assiduously the acquaintance of Johnson," and that "to me and many others it appeared that he studiously copied the manner of Johnson, though, indeed, upon a smaller scale." How do these quotations help you to evaluate Boswell's account of the conversation between Johnson and Goldsmith? How do you think Boswell felt about Goldsmith?

4. Even though Boswell was very much a personality in his own right, he submerged his personality in that of Dr. Johnson, a man thirty years his senior. Does he seem to you to be partial or impartial as a biographer? Explain your answer.

5. Johnson seems to have had a habit of speaking in maxims: there are at least eight in the three journal entries. Select any two maxims and tell whether or not you agree with Johnson's generalizations. Be sure to explain your reasoning.

BIOGRAPHY AND AUTOBIOGRAPHY

In English the word *biography,* as a literary term, first came into use with John Dryden, who defined it as "the history of particular men's lives." Today we have an expanded definition: a biography is now denoted as a work that accurately presents the entire life of an individual, with the facts of a life and times interpreted in such a way as to give a complete and unified impression of a character, personality, and mind.

People have always been fascinated by the lives of others, and the desire to satisfy this curiosity has been a prime reason for the reading of biographies. Self-education is another reason. Plutarch, the first-century Greek biographer, wrote that the lives he studied provided "a sort of looking glass in which I

may see how to adjust and adorn my own life." Students also often read biographies to learn more about history; there is even a theory that history can be learned entirely through reading the lives of great people. The wish to relive periods of similar experience in our own lives or to share in the struggles and emotional experiences of outstanding people of the past also leads us to read biographies.

The advantage of autobiography, journals, and diaries is that in them the subjects speak of themselves. It is in diaries and journals, which are usually not intended for publication, that we are permitted the most revealing glimpses into an individual's personal life. The principal advantage of biography over autobiography is objectivity. A good biographer can stand apart and present a relatively unbiased picture of a person's life and times. But whether biography or autobiography, the value of the work can best be measured by how honestly and perceptively it defines the subject.

Compare the selections from Boswell's *Life of Johnson* with another biography you have read. Which do you think more clearly and candidly portrays its subject? Support your answer by referring to both texts.

LANGUAGE AND VOCABULARY

A single word can often have a number of different meanings, depending upon the context in which it is used. Boswell, in his *London Journal,* reports Johnson as saying: "There is nothing too *little* for so *little* a creature as man. It is by studying *little* things that we attain the great knowledge of having as *little* misery and as much happiness as possible." Giving special attention to the four uses of the key word *little,* write a paragraph in which you explain what Johnson means.

FOR COMPOSITION

As readers, we get Boswell's picture of the events he describes in his *Life of Johnson* and *London Journal.* How do you suppose Johnson himself would have described the same events: the first meeting with Boswell? the argument with Goldsmith? a discussion with Boswell of the father–son relationship? Pretending you are Johnson, write a journal entry describing an event or a conversation from this period of his life.

OLIVER GOLDSMITH
(1728–1774)

Few writers in all English literature have known such amazing versatility as Oliver Goldsmith. It is remarkable that a man who was to achieve lasting fame in four different types of literature turned to writing only as a last resort, after unsuccessfully engaging in a variety of other endeavors.

Like Steele and Swift, Goldsmith was born in Ireland, and, like Swift and Johnson, he knew the humiliating compulsions of poverty. His family was much like the Primrose family of his novel, *The Vicar of Wakefield*—"generous, credulous, simple, and inoffensive," easy marks for the unscrupulous. Goldsmith's progress through school and college was punctuated by erratic behavior, but he was finally granted a degree from Dublin's Trinity College. There followed a number of vain attempts to establish himself in a profession. After bungling his chance for the ministry (some say he put an end to his ecclesiastical possibilities by appearing before the examining bishop in scarlet trousers), he gambled away money borrowed from an uncle to study law in London. He was forgiven and granted more money, this time to study medicine at the University of Leyden. A year later he set out on a walking tour of the Continent "with a guinea in his pocket, one shirt on his back, and a flute in his hand." In 1756 he returned to London, penniless, and drifted into the hack writing which paid him much better than the literary work for which he is remembered.

Goldsmith's impracticality and irresponsibility kept him in unrelieved poverty throughout his life. He lived from hand to mouth, and at one point, the story goes, his landlady impounded his only pair of breeches to prevent his slipping off without paying his rent. On another occasion, he was rescued from debtor's prison by Samuel Johnson. His engaging personality, however, enabled him to wheedle so much credit that he died two thousand pounds in debt, causing the astounded Dr. Johnson to exclaim, "Was ever poet so trusted?" His warmth and simplicity endeared him to his fellow members of the Literary Club and most of all to Johnson, who was completely opposite in nature to the carefree, reckless Goldsmith. Johnson's devotion to him was the envy of Boswell, whose jealousy is apparent in his comments about this "coarse and vulgar man . . . a curious, old, pedantic fellow with some genius."

Seldom profound but never boring, Goldsmith overcame harsh circumstances and, writing with wit, whimsy, and lightheartedness, presented a light, cool picture of life. His prose style is esteemed for its unique intermingling of formal and colloquial language and his own personal brand of grace, clarity, and kindliness. David Garrick, the actor, in an epitaph written in jest, characterized the writer and his work in saying: "Here lies Nolly Goldsmith, for shortness called 'Noll,'/ Who wrote like an angel and talked like poor Poll."

To Goldsmith belongs the distinction of producing essays, a poem, a novel, and a comedy that are still read and enjoyed. His first real success was the collection of essays entitled *The Citizen of the World.* This was followed by the novel, *The Vicar of Wakefield,* which tells a story of English country life. In 1770 *The Deserted Village* was published. A nostalgic portrayal of life in an Irish village probably similar to the one in which the poet himself grew up, this poem expressed the growing interest in the middle and late eighteenth century in rural settings and humble lives, and in both subject matter and sentiment pointed forward to the Romantic movement. *She Stoops to Conquer,* Goldsmith's rollicking and robust comedy, restored liveliness and wit to English drama.

Although Johnson sometimes ridiculed his friend "Goldy," he recognized and generously praised his literary powers. About the personal failings and vanities that Goldsmith was never able to overcome, Samuel Johnson remarked: "Let not his frailties be remembered; he was a very great man." And it was Johnson who wrote the inscription for the memorial to Goldsmith in Westminster Abbey: "He touched nothing that he did not adorn."

The Citizen of the World

The eighteenth century was a period that attempted to view itself—its customs, conventions, life, and world—with clear-sighted vision and perfect perspective unblurred by emotion. In *The Citizen of the World* Goldsmith undertook to view his world with such perspective. For this purpose he used the device of an imaginary Chinese philosopher, Lien Chi Altangi, who, during a visit to England, wrote letters to another Oriental sage in which he described the English people and their ways. The idea of using a worldly-wise Oriental as his spokesman probably was suggested to Goldsmith by the wave of enthusiasm for Far Eastern culture which was sweeping Europe at the time. Lien Chi Altangi's cosmopolitan, candid, and somewhat critical reactions were meant to clarify Englishmen's views of their own excesses and absurdities.

This series of essays consists of over 123 letters which originally were published in a newspaper in 1760–61. Enlivened by Gold-

smith's individuality and charm, the letters follow the tradition of Addison's and Steele's *Spectator* in their light touch and their use of gentle satire. Greatly admired, they won the praise even of Dr. Johnson, the literary dictator of the age, who asked: "Is there a man, sir, now, who can pen an essay with such ease and elegance as Goldsmith?"

LETTER 4

*English Pride—Liberty—
An Instance of Both—
Newspapers—Politeness*

THE ENGLISH seem as silent as the Japanese, yet vainer than the inhabitants of Siam. Upon my arrival I attributed that reserve to modesty, which, I now find, has its origin in pride. Condescend to address them first, and you are sure of their acquaintance; stoop to flattery, and you conciliate their friendship and esteem. They bear hunger, cold, fatigue, and all the miseries of life without shrinking; danger only calls forth their fortitude; they even exult in calamity; but contempt is what they cannot bear. An Englishman fears contempt more than death; he often flies to death as a refuge from its pressure, and dies when he fancies the world has ceased to esteem him.

Pride seems the source, not only of their national vices, but of their national virtues also. An Englishman is taught to love his king as his friend, but to acknowledge no other master than the laws which himself has contributed to enact. He despises those nations who, that one may be free, are all content to be slaves; who first lift a tyrant into terror, and then shrink under his power as if delegated from heaven. Liberty is echoed in all their assemblies; and thousands might be found ready to offer up their lives for the sound, though perhaps not one of all the number understands the meaning. The lowest mechanic, however, looks upon it as his duty to be a watchful guardian of his country's freedom, and often uses a language that might seem haughty even in the mouth of the Great Emperor, who traces his ancestry to the Moon.

A few days ago, passing by one of their prisons, I could not avoid stopping, in order to listen to a dialogue which I thought might afford me some entertainment. The conversation was carried on between a debtor through the grate of his prison, a porter who had stopped to rest his burthen,[1] and a soldier at the window. The subject was upon a threatened invasion from France, and each seemed extremely anxious to rescue his country from the impending danger. "For my part," cries the prisoner, "the greatest of my apprehensions is for our freedom; if the French should conquer, what would become of English liberty? My dear friends, liberty is the Englishman's prerogative; we must preserve that at the expense of our lives; of that the French shall never deprive us. It is not to be expected that men who are slaves themselves would preserve our freedom should they happen to conquer."—"Ay, slaves," cries the porter, "they are all slaves, fit

only to carry burthens, every one of them. Before I would stoop to slavery, may this be my poison," and he held the goblet in his hand, "may this be my poison—but I would sooner 'list[2] for a soldier."

The soldier, taking the goblet from his friend, with much awe fervently cried out, "It is not so much our liberties as our religion that would suffer by such a change; ay, our religion, my lads. May the Devil sink me into flames," such was the solemnity of his adjuration, "if the French should come over but our religion would be utterly undone!" So saying, instead of a libation, he applied the goblet to his lips, and confirmed his sentiments with a ceremony of the most persevering devotion.

In short, every man here pretends to be a politician; even the fair sex are sometimes found to mix the severity of national altercation with the blandishments of love, and often become conquerors by more weapons of destruction than their eyes.

This universal passion for politics is gratified by daily gazettes, as with us in China. But, as in ours the Emperor endeavors to instruct his people, in theirs the people endeavor to instruct the administration. You must not, however, imagine that they who compile these papers have any actual knowledge of the politics or the government of a state; they only collect their materials from the oracle of some coffeehouse, which oracle has himself gathered them the night before from a beau at a gaming table, who has pillaged his knowledge from a great man's porter, who has had his information from the great man's gentleman,[3] who has invented the whole story for his own amusement the night preceding.

The English, in general, seem fonder of gaining the esteem than the love of those they converse with. This gives a formality to their amusements: their gayest conversations have something too wise for

---

[1] **burthen:** burden.

[2] **'list:** enlist.
[3] **gentleman:** valet.

innocent relaxation; though in company you are seldom disgusted with the absurdity of a fool, you are seldom lifted into rapture by those strokes of vivacity which give instant though not permanent pleasure.

What they want, however, in gaiety they make up in politeness. You smile at hearing me praise the English for their politeness, you who have heard very different accounts from the missionaries at Pekin, who have seen such a different behavior in their merchants and seamen at home. But I must still repeat it: the English seem more polite than any of their neighbors; their great art in this respect lies in endeavoring, while they oblige, to lessen the force of the favor. Other countries are fond of obliging a stranger, but seem desirous that he should be sensible of the obligation. The English confer their kindness with an appearance of indifference, and give away benefits with an air as if they despised them.

Walking a few days ago, between an Englishman and a Frenchman, in the suburbs of the city, we were overtaken by a heavy shower of rain. I was unprepared; but they had each large coats, which defended them from what seemed to me a perfect inundation. The Englishman, seeing me shrink from the weather, accosted me thus: "Pshaw, man, what dost shrink at? Here, take this coat; I don't want it; I find it no way useful to me; I had as lief be without it." The Frenchman began to show his politeness in turn. "My dear friend," cries he, "why won't you oblige me by making use of my coat? You see how well it defends me from the rain; I should not choose to part with it to others, but to such a friend as you I could even part with my skin to do him service."

From such minute instances as these, most reverend Fum Hoam, I am sensible your sagacity will collect instruction. The volume of nature is the book of knowledge; and he becomes most wise who makes the most judicious selection. Farewell.

LETTER 21

At the Playhouse

The English are as fond of seeing plays acted as the Chinese; but there is a vast difference in the manner of conducting them. We play our pieces in the open air, the English theirs under cover; we act by daylight, they by the blaze of torches. One of our plays continues eight or ten days successively; an English piece seldom takes up above four hours in the representation.

My companion in black, with whom I am now beginning to contract an intimacy, introduced me a few nights ago to the playhouse, where we placed ourselves conveniently at the foot of the stage. As the curtain was not drawn before my arrival, I had an opportunity of observing the behavior of the spectators and indulging those reflections which novelty generally inspires.

The rich in general were placed in the lowest seats, and the poor rose above them in degrees proportioned to their poverty. The order of precedence seemed here inverted; those who were undermost all the day, now enjoyed a temporary eminence and became masters of the ceremonies. It was they who called for the music, indulging every noisy freedom, and testifying all the insolence of beggary in exaltation.

They who held the middle region seemed not so riotous as those above them, nor yet so tame as those below: to judge by their looks, many of them seemed strangers there as well as myself; they were chiefly employed, during this period of expectation, in eating oranges, reading the story of the play, or making assignations.

Those who sat in the lowest rows, which are called the pit, seemed to consider themselves as judges of the merits of the poet and the performers; they were assembled partly to be amused, and partly to show their taste; appearing to labor under that restraint which an affectation of superior discernment generally pro-

duces. My companion, however, informed me that not one in a hundred of them knew even the first principles of criticism; that they assumed the right of being censors because there was none to contradict their pretensions; and that every man who now called himself a connoisseur became such to all intents and purposes.

Those who sat in the boxes appeared in the most unhappy situation of all. The rest of the audience came merely for their own amusement; these rather to furnish out a part of the entertainment themselves. I could not avoid considering them as acting parts in dumb show—not a courtesy or a nod that was not the result of art; not a look nor a smile that was not designed for murder. Gentlemen and ladies ogled each other through spectacles; for my companion observed that blindness was of late become fashionable; all affected indifference and ease, while their hearts at the same time burned for conquest. Upon the whole, the lights, the music, the ladies in their gayest dresses, the men with cheerfulness and expectation in their looks, all conspired to make a most agreeable picture and to fill a heart that sympathizes at human happiness with inexpressible serenity.

The expected time for the play to begin at last arrived; the curtain was drawn, and the actors came on. A woman, who personated a queen, came in courtseying to the audience, who clapped their hands upon her appearance. Clapping of hands is, it seems, the manner of applauding in England; the manner is absurd, but every

country, you know, has its peculiar absurdities. I was equally surprised, however, at the submission of the actress, who should have considered herself as a queen, as at the little discernment of the audience who gave her such marks of applause before she attempted to deserve them. Preliminaries between her and the audience being thus adjusted, the dialogue was supported between her and a most hopeful youth, who acted the part of her confidant. They both appeared in extreme distress, for it seems the queen had lost a child some fifteen years before, and still keeps its dear resemblance next to her heart, while her kind companion bore a part in her sorrows.

Her lamentations grew loud; comfort is offered, but she detests the very sound: she bids them preach comfort to the winds. Upon this her husband comes in, who, seeing the queen so much afflicted, can himself hardly refrain from tears, or avoid partaking in the soft distress. After thus grieving through three scenes, the curtain dropped for the first act.

"Truly," said I to my companion, "these kings and queens are very much disturbed at no very great misfortune: certain I am, were people of humbler stations to act in this manner, they would be thought divested of common sense." I had scarce finished this observation when the curtain rose and the king came on in a violent passion. His wife had, it seems, refused his proffered tenderness, had spurned his royal embrace; and he seemed resolved not to survive her fierce disdain. After he had thus fretted, and the queen had fretted through the second act, the curtain was let down once more.

"Now," says my companion, "you perceive the king to be a man of spirit; he feels at every pore: one of your phlegmatic sons of clay would have given the queen her own way and let her come to herself by degrees; but the king is for immediate tenderness, or instant death: death and tenderness are leading passions of every modern buskined hero; [1] this moment they embrace, and the next stab, mixing daggers and kisses in every period."

I was going to second his remarks, when my attention was engrossed by a new object: a man came in balancing a straw upon his nose, and the audience were clapping their hands in all the raptures of applause. "To what purpose," cried I, "does this unmeaning figure make his appearance? Is he a part of the plot?" "Unmeaning, do you call him?" replied my friend in black; "this is one of the most important characters of the whole play; nothing pleases the people more than seeing a straw balanced: there is a great deal of meaning in the straw; there is something suited to every apprehension in the sight; and a fellow possessed of talents like these is sure of making his fortune."

The third act now began with an actor who came to inform us that he was the villain of the play and intended to show strange things before all was over. He was joined by another, who seemed as much disposed for mischief as he; their intrigues continued through this whole division. "If that be a villain," said I, "he must be a very stupid one to tell his secrets without being asked; such soliloquies of late are never admitted in China."

The noise of clapping interrupted me once more; a child of six years old was learning to dance on the stage, which gave the ladies and mandarins infinite satisfaction. "I am sorry," said I, "to see the pretty creatures so early learning so bad a trade; dancing being, I presume, as contemptible here as in China." "Quite the reverse," interrupted my companion; "dancing is a very reputable and genteel employment here; men have a greater chance for encouragement from the merit of their heels than their heads. One who jumps up and flourishes his toes three times before he comes to the ground may have three hundred a year; he who flourishes them four times gets four hundred; but he who arrives at five is inestimable, and may demand what salary he thinks proper. The female dancers, too, are valued for this sort of jumping and crossing; and it is a cant word among them that she deserves most who shows highest. But the fourth act is begun; let us be attentive."

In the fourth act the queen finds her long-lost child, now grown up into a youth of smart parts and great qualifications; wherefore she wisely considers that the crown will fit his head better than that of her husband, whom she knows to be a driveler. The king discovers her design, and here comes on the deep distress: he loves the queen, and he loves the kingdom; he resolves, therefore, in order to possess both, that her son must die. The queen exclaims at his barbarity, is frantic with rage, and at length, overcome with sorrow, falls into a fit; upon which the curtain drops, and the act is concluded.

"Observe the art of the poet," cries my companion. "When the queen can say no more, she falls into a fit. While thus her eyes are shut, while she is supported in the arms of her Abigail,[2] what horrors do we not fancy! We feel it in every nerve: take my word for it, that fits are the true aposiopesis [3] of modern tragedy."

The fifth act began, and a busy piece it was. Scenes shifting, trumpets sounding, mobs hallooing, carpets spreading, guards bustling from one door to another; gods,

[1] **buskined hero:** tragic actor. Greek and Roman tragic actors wore a laced half-boot called a buskin.

[2] **Abigail:** maid.

[3] **aposiopesis** (ap'ə·sī'ə·pē'sis): a sudden breaking off in the middle of a speech.

demons, daggers, racks, and ratsbane. But whether the king was killed, or the queen was drowned, or the son poisoned, I have absolutely forgotten.

When the play was over, I could not avoid observing, that the persons of the drama appeared in as much distress in the first act as the last: "How is it possible," said I, "to sympathize with them through five long acts! Pity is but a short-lived passion; I hate to hear an actor mouthing trifles; neither startings, strainings, nor attitudes affect me, unless there be cause: after I have been once or twice deceived by those unmeaning alarms, my heart sleeps in peace, probably unaffected by the principal distress. There should be one great passion aimed at by the actor as well as the poet; all the rest should be subordinate, and only contribute to make that the greater; if the actor, therefore, exclaims upon every occasion in the tones of despair, he attempts to move us too soon; he anticipates the blow, he ceases to affect, though he gains our applause."

I scarcely perceived that the audience were almost all departed; wherefore mixing with the crowd, my companion and I got into the street; where, essaying an hundred obstacles from coachwheels and palanquin[1] poles, like birds in their flight through the branches of a forest, after various turnings we both at length got home in safety. Adieu.

[1] **palanquin** (pal′ən·kēn′): a covered conveyance, usually for one person, carried by poles on the shoulders of two or more men.

FOR STUDY AND DISCUSSION

1. In Letter 4, Lien Chi Altangi writes: "Pride seems the source, not only of their national vices, but of their national virtues also." Does the rest of the essay make clear what these "national vices" and "national virtues" are? If so, what are they? At what points and by what means might this essay challenge complacency in a thoughtful English reader of the eighteenth century?

2. How does the conversation of the debtor, the porter, and the soldier and the anecdote of the overcoats increase the effectiveness of Letter 4? How does Goldsmith achieve unity in this essay on the four apparently separate topics of pride, liberty, newspapers, and politeness?

3. In Letter 21, what conventions practiced in the theater of his time does Goldsmith ridicule? How does he make the reader share his feeling that they are absurd?

4. The explanation by the man in black of the status of straw-balancing and dancing in England is a close parallel to Gulliver's description of ceremonies performed before the Lilliputian emperor. Find the pertinent passage in "A Voyage to Lilliput" (page 313) and compare the two descriptions. Whose satire is more effective, Goldsmith's or Swift's? Explain your choice.

LANGUAGE AND VOCABULARY

Examining words derived from the same Latin prefix frequently reveals that the prefix has more than one meaning. In the two selections by Goldsmith there are a number of words having the prefix *dis-*. This prefix can have one of five different meanings: (1) "away from" or "apart" as in *dislodge* or *dismiss,* (2) "the reverse of the undoing of" as in *disown* or *disconnect,* (3) "the loss of some quality, or power" as in *disable* or *disbar,* (4) "not" as in *disloyal* or *distasteful,* (5) "completely" or "thoroughly" as in *disannul.*

Referring to your dictionary, explain how their Latin derivations make clear which of the five meanings of the prefix *dis-* apply in each of the following words: *discernment, disturbed, disdain, disposed, disgusted.* Make a list of five other words with the prefix *dis-*. Before checking with your dictionary, try to guess the meaning of the prefix that applies to each of your words.

FOR COMPOSITION

In *The Citizen of the World,* Goldsmith tries to look at his world with objectivity, in the hope that he can thereby induce his readers to do likewise. Using a technique similar to Goldsmith's use of an imaginary Chinese philosopher, bring into your own world an imaginary exchange student from another part of the world. Put yourself in his place and write in the first-person singular an account of his imagined responses to a typical experience of a day in your school or home.

RICHARD
BRINSLEY
SHERIDAN
(1751–1816)

If heredity means anything, Richard Brinsley Sheridan had to be a literary man. His Irish grandfather was a schoolmaster, scholar, and friend of Jonathan Swift; his mother was a novelist and playwright; his father an actor, theater-manager, and successful teacher of elocution. Sheridan was born in Dublin, but, because of financial difficulties, his family moved to England when he was still a boy. The same financial difficulties prevented Sheridan from receiving much of a formal education, but despite this early disadvantage he managed to make his mark in several different careers—as a playwright, theater-manager, politician and Member of Parliament, and dashing man about town.

It was as a dashing man about town that Sheridan eloped in 1773 with Elizabeth Ann Linley, a beautiful concert singer and the toast of fashionable society, over whom he fought two duels with a persistent rival. Two years later, combining his perceptive observations of high society, his familiarity with stagecraft, and his gift for language, he produced his first theatrical success, *The Rivals*. It became an enormous success. Celebrated at the age of twenty-four as the writer of one of the best comedies in the English language, he was deemed "a considerable man" even by the estimable Dr. Johnson, who promptly sponsored Sheridan for membership in the celebrated Literary Club. The following year, Sheridan became part owner of the famous Drury Lane Theater in London, and at twenty-six he wrote and produced *The School for Scandal*. In 1779 *The Critic*, also highly successful, was produced.

After this time, although he continued to direct the Drury Lane Theater through years of vicissitudes, Sheridan turned his attention to politics. He entered Parliament in 1780, and his brilliant use of language soon won him wide recognition as an orator. For over twenty-five years Sheridan was a leading political figure in an era which boasted such distinguished Parliamentarians as William Pitt, Edmund Burke, and Charles James Fox.

Well established in the highest political and social circles, Sheridan enjoyed living in an extravagant manner that was far beyond his means. The Drury Lane Theater supported his fashionable life for many years, but Sheridan's complicated and irregular business practices eventually caught up with him. During the quarter of a century he was a Member of Parliament, he could not be sent to debtor's prison. As soon as he lost his seat in the House of Commons, however, his troubles began, and not even auctioning off his property could save him from the threat of arrest. Sheridan's last days were spent in poverty, but his death in 1816 was the occasion of an elaborate funeral and burial with great public honor in Westminster Abbey.

THE RIVALS

The history of English high comedy has had an interesting pattern. It has normally flowered at the end of an era, and, after Shakespeare, most of its great playwrights have been Irish. About one hundred years after Shakespeare's best comedies (such as *Twelfth Night, As You Like It* and *Much Ado About Nothing)* were written, Dublin-educated William Congreve crowned the Restoration period with such brilliant comedies as *Love for Love* (1695) and *The Way of the World* (1700). Toward the end of the eighteenth century, following a long spate of hopelessly sentimental domestic dramas, Dublin-born Richard Brinsley Sheridan asked English society to laugh at itself in plays such as *The Rivals* and *The School for Scandal*. Finally, after another arid epoch of middle-class melodrama, audiences at the end of the nineteenth century saw a rebirth of the high comedy of manners in the works of Irishmen Oscar Wilde and, more important, George Bernard Shaw.

Comedy, which thrives on poking holes in a particular social fabric, requires a concrete, immediately recognizable social order against which it can operate. There is not much point, a comic playwright might say, in taking up arms against a petty, insecure adversary. Hence it seems natural for the great periods of comedy to have flourished near the end of an era: the manners these plays satirize needed time to settle themselves and whenever they did, it seems that a comic playwright was waiting in the wings to make fun of them. Furthermore, it would seem that the Irishman is especially adept at doing this sort of thing. The Irish love language. They love to talk, and their talk so often demonstrates a keen sense of wit and paradox, a formidable tool in attacking the social order. To this the Irish add an exuberant sense of horseplay and fun. Finally, as semi-outsiders looking in on a highly formalized British society, these Irish writers seem to have felt a combination of both affection and distaste for what they saw. They knew the social world well enough to depict it with accuracy, yet they were sufficiently removed from it by temperament and birth to comment sharply upon it. These ambivalent attitudes seem to have propelled the Irish to write a great number of amusing yet pointed plays.

Sheridan's *The Rivals* is certainly one of the milestones in this tradition. By introducing social satire, pungent wit, and sparkling dialogue, Sheridan, along with Oliver Goldsmith, emulated the brilliant comedies of the early Restoration. As you read *The Rivals,* note the sheer delight in language, for which Sheridan is justly famous. Note also the ingenuity of the plot, which follows the Renaissance unities by knotting and unknotting itself in one day and one place. While the play is unmistakably contrived, the fun to a large extent lies in the contrivance. We are in on the major ruse of the play from the moment in Scene 1 when we hear Fag tell Thomas, "Captain Absolute and Ensign Beverley are one and the same person."

The characters in *The Rivals* have come to Bath to have fun, and Sheridan's idea is to have fun at their expense. The play is ingenious and ingenuous, and, in some respects, as mixed up as Mrs. Malaprop's rhetoric. There is much confusion, but just as the high point of confusion is reached over who is dueling with whom, who knows whose dual roles, and who is fooling whom (or himself) about whom (or what), the characters sort themselves out, and all's well in the artificial but lively society of eighteenth-century Bath.

The Rivals

Characters

in order of their appearance

THOMAS, *coachman to Sir Anthony Absolute*
FAG, *footman to Captain Absolute*
LYDIA LANGUISH, *fashionable young niece of Mrs. Malaprop*
LUCY, *maid to Mrs. Malaprop*
JULIA MELVILLE, *Lydia's cousin, ward of Sir Anthony Absolute*
MRS. MALAPROP, *Lydia's aunt*
SIR ANTHONY ABSOLUTE, *wealthy country gentleman*
CAPTAIN ABSOLUTE, *son of Sir Anthony Absolute*
FAULKLAND, *Julia's suitor, friend of Captain Absolute*
BOB ACRES, *Lydia's formal suitor*
SIR LUCIUS O'TRIGGER, *bankrupt Irish nobleman*
DAVID, *servant to Bob Acres*
MAID, BOY, SERVANTS

SCENE: *Bath, a fashionable resort in eighteenth-century England*

ACT I

SCENE 1. *A street.*

[*Enter* THOMAS; *he crosses the stage;* FAG *follows, looking after him.*]

FAG. What! Thomas! Sure 'tis he? What! Thomas! Thomas!

THOMAS. Hey! Odd's life![1] Mr. Fag! Give us your hand, my old fellow-servant.

FAG. Excuse my glove, Thomas: I'm devilish glad to see you, my lad. Why, my prince of charioteers, you look as hearty —but who the deuce thought of seeing you in Bath?

THOMAS. Sure, master, Madam Julia, Harry, Mrs. Kate, and the postilion, be all come.

FAG. Indeed!

THOMAS. Ay, master thought another fit of the gout was coming to make him a visit; so he'd a mind to gi't the slip, and whip! We were all off at an hour's warning.

FAG. Ay, ay, hasty in everything, or it would not be Sir Anthony Absolute!

THOMAS. But tell us, Mr. Fag, how does young master? Odd! Sir Anthony will stare to see the captain here!

FAG. I do not serve Captain Absolute now.

THOMAS. Why sure![2]

FAG. At present I am employed by Ensign Beverley.

THOMAS. I doubt,[3] Mr. Fag, you ha'n't changed for the better.

FAG. I have not changed, Thomas.

---

[1] **Odd's life:** God's life. One of the mild oaths fashionable at the time. Numerous examples are found in the play: "Zounds" (God's wounds), "'sdeath" (God's death), "Lud" (Lord), "odds triggers and flints," and so on. Most of these oaths are meaningless.

[2] **Why sure!:** exclamation of surprise.
[3] **doubt:** fear.

THOMAS. No! Why didn't you say you had left young master?

FAG. No. Well, honest Thomas, I must puzzle you no farther: briefly then—Captain Absolute and Ensign Beverley are one and the same person.

THOMAS. The devil they are!

FAG. So it is indeed, Thomas; and the ensign half of my master being on guard at present—the captain has nothing to do with me.

THOMAS. So, so! What, this is some freak, I warrant! Do tell us, Mr. Fag, the meaning o't—you know I ha' trusted you.

FAG. You'll be secret, Thomas?

THOMAS. As a coach horse.

FAG. Why then the cause of all this is Love—Love, Thomas, who (as you may get read to you) has been a masquerader ever since the days of Jupiter.

THOMAS. Ay, ay; I guessed there was a lady in the case. But pray, why does your master pass only for an ensign? Now if he had shammed general indeed——

FAG. Ah! Thomas, there lies the mystery o' the matter. Hark'ee, Thomas, my master is in love with a lady of a very singular taste: a lady who likes him better as a half-pay ensign than if she knew he was son and heir to Sir Anthony Absolute, a baronet of three thousand a year.[1]

THOMAS. That is an odd taste indeed! But has she got the stuff, Mr. Fag? Is she rich, hey?

FAG. Rich! Why, I believe she owns half the stocks! Zounds! Thomas, she could pay the national debt as easily as I could my washerwomen! She has a lap dog that eats out of gold; she feeds her parrot with small pearls, and all her thread papers[2] are made of bank notes!

THOMAS. Bravo, faith! Odd! I warrant she has a set of thousands[3] at least. But does she draw kindly with the captain?

FAG. As fond as pigeons.

THOMAS. May one hear her name?

FAG. Miss Lydia Languish. But there is an old tough aunt in the way; though, by the by, she has never seen my master— for we got acquainted with miss while on a visit in Gloucestershire.

THOMAS. Well—I wish they were once harnessed together in matrimony. But pray, Mr. Fag, what kind of a place is this Bath? I ha' heard a deal of it—here's a mort o'[4] merrymaking, hey?

FAG. Pretty well, Thomas, pretty well— 'tis a good lounge; in the morning we go to the pump room[5] (though neither my master nor I drink the waters); after breakfast we saunter on the parades,[6] or play a game at billiards; at night we dance; but damn the place, I'm tired of it: their regular hours stupefy me—not a fiddle nor a card after eleven! However, Mr. Faulkland's gentleman and I keep it up a little in private parties. I'll introduce you there, Thomas—you'll like him much.

THOMAS. Sure I know Mr. Du-Peigne— you know his master is to marry Madam Julia.

FAG. I had forgot. But, Thomas, you must polish a little—indeed you must. Here now—this wig! What the devil do you do with a wig, Thomas? None of the London whips of any degree of *ton*[7] wear wigs now.

THOMAS. More's the pity! more's the pity! I say. Odd's life! When I heard how the lawyers and doctors had took to their own hair, I thought how 'twould go next: odd rabbit it! When the fashion had got foot on the bar, I guessed 'twould mount to the box—but 'tis all out of character, believe me, Mr. Fag: and look'ee, I'll never gi' up mine—the lawyers and doctors may do as they will.

FAG. Well, Thomas, we'll not quarrel about that.

THOMAS. Why, bless you, the gentle-

---

[1] **three . . . year:** a yearly income worth about $30,000 in Sheridan's time. Sir Anthony is moderately wealthy by eighteenth-century standards.

[2] **thread papers:** papers folded to separate skeins of thread.

[3] **set of thousands:** a set of matched coach horses worth thousands of pounds.

[4] **mort o':** lot of.

[5] **pump room:** a room connected with medicinal springs where the waters are drunk.

[6] **parades:** public walks, promenades.

[7] **ton:** style, fashion.

men of the professions ben't all of a mind —for in our village now, thoff [1] Jack Gauge, the exciseman,[2] has ta'en to his carrots,[3] there's little Dick the farrier swears he'll never forsake his bob,[4] though all the college should appear with their own heads!

FAG. Indeed! well said, Dick! but hold —mark! mark! Thomas.

THOMAS. Zooks! 'tis the captain. Is that the Lady with him?

FAG. No, no, that is Madam Lucy, my master's mistress's maid. They lodge at that house—but I must after him to tell him the news.

THOMAS. Odd! he's given her money! Well, Mr. Fag——

FAG. Good-by, Thomas. I have an appointment in Gyde's porch [5] this evening at eight; meet me there, and we'll make a little party. (*Exeunt severally.*)

SCENE 2. *A dressing room in* MRS. MALA-PROP'S *lodgings.*

[LYDIA *sitting on a sofa with a book* [6] *in her hand.* LUCY *has just returned from a message.*]

LUCY. Indeed, ma'am, I traversed half the town in search of it! I don't believe there's a circulating library in Bath I han't been at.

LYDIA. And could not you get *The Reward of Constancy?*

LUCY. No, indeed, ma'am.

LYDIA. Nor *The Fatal Connection?*

LUCY. No, indeed, ma'am.

LYDIA. Nor *The Mistakes of the Heart?*

LUCY. Ma'am, as ill luck would have it, Mr. Bull said Miss Sukey Saunter had just fetched it away.

LYDIA. Heigh-ho! Did you inquire for *The Delicate Distress?*

LUCY. Or, *The Memoirs of Lady Wood-ford?* Yes, indeed, ma'am, I asked every-where for it; and I might have brought it from Mr. Frederick's, but Lady Slattern Lounger, who had just sent it home, had so soiled and dog's-eared it, it wa'n't fit for a Christian to read.

LYDIA. Heigh-ho! Yes, I always know when Lady Slattern has been before me. She has a most observing thumb; and, I believe, cherishes her nails for the convenience of making marginal notes. Well, child, what have you brought me?

LUCY. Oh! here, ma'am. (*Taking books from under her cloak and from her pockets*) This is *The Gordian Knot* and this *Peregrine Pickle*. Here are *The Tears of Sensibility* and *Humphrey Clinker*. This is *The Memoirs of a Lady of Quality, written by Herself,* and here the second volume of *The Sentimental Journey.*

LYDIA. Heigh-ho! What are those books by the glass?

LUCY. The great one is only *The Whole Duty of Man,* where I press a few blonds,[7] ma'am.

LYDIA. Very well—give me the sal volatile.

LUCY. Is it in a blue cover, ma'am?

LYDIA. My smelling bottle, you simpleton!

LUCY. Oh, the drops—here, ma'am.

LYDIA. Hold! here's someone coming— quick! see who it is. (*Exit* LUCY.) Surely I heard my cousin Julia's voice.

[*Reenter* LUCY.]

LUCY. Lud! ma'am, here is Miss Melville.

LYDIA. Is it possible?

[*Exit* LUCY. *Enter* JULIA.]

LYDIA. My dearest Julia, how delighted am I! (*Embrace*) How unexpected was this happiness!

JULIA. True, Lydia—and our pleasure is the greater. But what has been the

---

[1] **thoff:** though.
[2] **exciseman:** tax collector.
[3] **carrots:** his own red hair.
[4] **bob:** wig.
[5] **Gyde's porch:** popular meeting rooms kept by Mr. Gyde.
[6] **book:** Lydia is addicted to the sentimental novels of her day, which she takes seriously. The books mentioned in this scene were all popular in Sheridan's time.

[7] **blonds:** lacy nets used as scarves.

matter? You were denied to me at first!

LYDIA. Ah, Julia, I have a thousand things to tell you! But first inform me what has conjured you to Bath? Is Sir Anthony here?

JULIA. He is—we are arrived within this hour—and I suppose he will be here to wait on Mrs. Malaprop as soon as he is dressed.

LYDIA. Then before we are interrupted, let me impart to you some of my distress! I know your gentle nature will sympathize with me, though your prudence may condemn me! My letters have informed you of my whole connection with Beverley; but I have lost him, Julia! My aunt has discovered our intercourse by a note she intercepted, and has confined me ever since! Yet, would you believe it? she has absolutely fallen in love with a tall Irish baronet she met one night since she has been here, at Lady Macshuffle's rout.[1]

JULIA. You jest, Lydia!

LYDIA. No, upon my word. She really carries on a kind of correspondence with him, under a feigned name though, till she chooses to be known to him: but it is a Delia or a Celia, I assure you.

JULIA. Then, surely, she is now more indulgent to her niece.

LYDIA. Quite the contrary. Since she has discovered her own frailty, she is become more suspicious of mine. Then I must inform you of another plague! That odious Acres is to be in Bath today— so that I protest I shall be teased out of all spirits!

JULIA. Come, come, Lydia, hope for the best. Sir Anthony shall use his interest with Mrs. Malaprop.

LYDIA. But you have not heard the worst. Unfortunately I had quarreled with my poor Beverley, just before my aunt made the discovery, and I have not seen him since to make it up.

JULIA. What was his offense?

LYDIA. Nothing at all! But, I don't know how it was, as often as we had been together, we had never had a quarrel,

and, somehow, I was afraid he would never give me an opportunity. So, last Thursday, I wrote a letter to myself, to inform myself that Beverley was at that time paying his addresses to another woman. I signed it *your friend unknown,* showed it to Beverley, charged him with his falsehood, put myself in a violent passion, and vowed I'd never see him more.

JULIA. And you let him depart so, and have not seen him since?

LYDIA. 'Twas the next day my aunt found the matter out. I intended only to have teased him three days and a half, and now I've lost him forever.

JULIA. If he is as deserving and sincere as you have represented him to me, he will never give you up so. Yet, consider, Lydia, you tell me he is but an ensign, and you have thirty thousand pounds.

LYDIA. But you know I lose most of my fortune if I marry without my aunt's consent, till of age; and that is what I have determined to do, ever since I knew the penalty. Nor could I love the man who would wish to wait a day for the alternative.

JULIA. Nay, this is caprice!

LYDIA. What, does Julia tax me with caprice? I thought her lover Faulkland had inured her to it.

JULIA. I do not love even his faults.

LYDIA. But apropos—you have sent to him, I suppose?

JULIA. Not yet, upon my word—nor has he the least idea of my being in Bath. Sir Anthony's resolution was so sudden, I could not inform him of it.

LYDIA. Well, Julia, you are your own mistress (though under the protection of Sir Anthony), yet have you, for this long year, been a slave to the caprice, the whim, the jealousy of this ungrateful Faulkland, who will ever delay assuming the right of a husband, while you suffer him to be equally imperious as a lover.

JULIA. Nay, you are wrong entirely. We were contracted before my father's death. That, and some consequent embarrassments, have delayed what I know

---

[1] **rout:** party, large social gathering.

to be my Faulkland's most ardent wish. He is too generous to trifle on such a point —and for his character, you wrong him there, too. No, Lydia, he is too proud, too noble, to be jealous; if he is captious, 'tis without dissembling; if fretful, without rudeness. Unused to the fopperies of love, he is negligent of the little duties expected from a lover—but being unhackneyed in the passion, his affection is ardent and sincere; and as it engrosses his whole soul, he expects every thought and emotion of his mistress to move in unison with his. Yet, though his pride calls for this full return, his humility makes him undervalue those qualities in him which would entitle him to it; and not feeling why he should be loved to the degree he wishes, he still suspects that he is not loved enough. This temper, I must own, has cost me many unhappy hours; but I have learned to think myself his debtor for those imperfections which arise from the ardor of his attachment.

LYDIA. Well, I cannot blame you for defending him. But tell me candidly, Julia, had he never saved your life, do you think you should have been attached to him as you are? Believe me, the rude blast that overset your boat was a prosperous gale of love to him.

JULIA. Gratitude may have strengthened my attachment to Mr. Faulkland, but I loved him before he had preserved me; yet surely that alone were an obligation sufficient.

LYDIA. Obligation! why a water spaniel would have done as much! Well, I should never think of giving my heart to a man because he could swim.

JULIA. Come, Lydia, you are too inconsiderate.

LYDIA. Nay, I do but jest. What's here?

[Reenter LUCY in a hurry.]

LUCY. O ma'am, here is Sir Anthony Absolute just come home with your aunt.

LYDIA. They'll not come here. Lucy, do you watch.

[Exit LUCY.]

JULIA. Yet I must go. Sir Anthony does not know I am here, and if we meet, he'll detain me, to show me the town. I'll take another opportunity of paying my respects to Mrs. Malaprop, when she shall treat me, as long as she chooses, with her select words so ingeniously misapplied without being mispronounced.

[Reenter LUCY.]

LUCY. O Lud! ma'am, they are both coming upstairs.

LYDIA. Well, I'll not detain you, coz.[1] Adieu, my dear Julia. I'm sure you are in haste to send to Faulkland. There, through my room you'll find another staircase.

JULIA. Adieu! *(Embraces LYDIA, and exit.)*

LYDIA. Here, my dear Lucy, hide these books. Quick, quick! Fling *Peregrine Pickle* under the toilet—throw *Roderick Random* into the closet—put *The Innocent Adultery* into *The Whole Duty of Man*—thrust *Lord Aimworth* under the sofa—cram *Ovid* behind the bolster— there—put *The Man of Feeling* into your pocket—so, so—now lay *Mrs. Chapone* in sight and leave *Fordyce's Sermons* open on the table.

LUCY. O burn it, ma'am! the hairdresser has torn away as far as *Proper Pride*.

LYDIA. Never mind—open at *Sobriety*. Fling me *Lord Chesterfield's Letters*. Now for 'em.

[Exit LUCY. Enter MRS. MALAPROP and SIR ANTHONY ABSOLUTE.]

MRS. MALAPROP. There, Sir Anthony, there sits the deliberate simpleton who wants to disgrace her family and lavish herself on a fellow not worth a shilling.

LYDIA. Madam, I thought you once—

MRS. MALAPROP. You thought, miss! I don't know any business you have to think at all—thought does not become a

---

[1] **coz**: cousin.

young woman. But the point we would request of you is that you will promise to forget this fellow—to illiterate [1] him, I say, quite from your memory.

LYDIA. Ah, madam! our memories are independent of our wills. It is not so easy to forget.

MRS. MALAPROP. But I say it is, miss; there is nothing on earth so easy as to forget, if a person chooses to set about it. I'm sure I have as much forgot your poor dear uncle as if he had never existed—and I thought it my duty so to do; and let me tell you, Lydia, these violent memories don't become a young woman.

SIR ANTHONY. Why sure she won't pretend to remember what she's ordered not! Ay, this comes of her reading!

LYDIA. What crime, madam, have I committed, to be treated thus?

MRS. MALAPROP. Now don't attempt to extirpate [2] yourself from the matter; you know I have proof controvertible [3] of it. But tell me, will you promise to do as you're bid? Will you take a husband of your friends' choosing?

LYDIA. Madam, I must tell you plainly, that had I no preference for anyone else, the choice you have made would be my aversion.

MRS. MALAPROP. What business have you, miss, with preference and aversion? They don't become a young woman; and you ought to know, that as both always wear off, 'tis safest in matrimony to begin with a little aversion. I am sure I hated your poor dear uncle before marriage—and yet, miss, you are sensible what a wife I made—and when it pleased Heaven to release me from him, 'tis unknown what tears I shed! But suppose we were going to give you another choice, will you promise us to give up this Beverley?

LYDIA. Could I belie my thoughts so far as to give that promise, my actions would certainly as far belie my words.

MRS. MALAPROP. Take yourself to your room. You are fit company for nothing but your own ill humors.

LYDIA. Willingly, ma'am—I cannot change for the worse. (Exit.)

MRS. MALAPROP. There's a little intricate [4] hussy for you!

SIR ANTHONY. It is not to be wondered at, ma'am—all this is the natural consequence of teaching girls to read. Had I a thousand daughters, by Heaven! I'd as soon have them taught the black art as their alphabet!

MRS. MALAPROP. Nay, nay, Sir Anthony, you are an absolute misanthropy. [5]

SIR ANTHONY. In my way hither, Mrs. Malaprop, I observed your niece's maid coming forth from a circulating library! She had a book in each hand—they were half-bound volumes, with marble covers! From that moment I guessed how full of duty I should see her mistress!

MRS. MALAPROP. Those are vile places, indeed!

SIR ANTHONY. Madam, a circulating library in a town is as an evergreen tree of diabolical knowledge! It blossoms through the year—and depend on it, Mrs. Malaprop, that they who are so fond of handling the leaves, will long for the fruit at last.

MRS. MALAPROP. Fy, fy, Sir Anthony, you surely speak laconically. [6]

SIR ANTHONY. Why, Mrs. Malaprop, in moderation now, what would you have a woman know?

MRS. MALAPROP. Observe me, Sir Anthony. I would by no means wish a daughter of mine to be a progeny [7] of learning; I don't think so much learning becomes a young woman; for instance, I would never let her meddle with Greek

---

[1] **illiterate:** obliterate. Mrs. Malaprop is noted for misusing words. Such absurd misuse of language has become known as *malapropism.*

[2] **extirpate:** extricate, disengage.

[3] **controvertible:** incontrovertible, undeniable.

[4] **intricate:** obstinate.

[5] **misanthropy:** misanthrope, hater of mankind.

[6] **laconically:** she probably means "ironically"

[7] **progeny:** prodigy.

or Hebrew or algebra or simony or flux-ions or paradoxes [1] or such inflammatory branches of learning—neither would it be necessary for her to handle any of your mathematical, astronomical, diabolical [2] instruments. But, Sir Anthony, I would send her, at nine years old, to a board-ing school, in order to let her learn a little ingenuity and artifice.[3] Then, sir, she should have a supercilious [4] knowledge in accounts; and as she grew up, I would have her instructed in geometry,[5] that she might know something of the contagious [6] countries; but above all, Sir Anthony, she should be mistress of orthodoxy,[7] that she might not misspell and mispronounce words so shamefully as girls usually do; and likewise that she might reprehend [8] the true meaning of what she is saying. This, Sir Anthony, is what I would have a woman know; and I don't think there is a superstitious [9] article in it.

SIR ANTHONY. Well, well, Mrs. Mala-prop, I will dispute the point no further with you; though I must confess that you are a truly moderate and polite arguer, for almost every third word you say is on my side of the question. But Mrs. Mala-prop, to the more important point in debate—you say you have no objection to my proposal?

MRS. MALAPROP. None, I assure you. I am under no positive engagement with Mr. Acres, and as Lydia is so obstinate against him, perhaps your son may have better success.

SIR ANTHONY. Well, madam, I will write for the boy directly. He knows not a syllable of this yet, though I have for some time had the proposal in my head.

He is at present with his regiment.

MRS. MALAPROP. We have never seen your son, Sir Anthony; but I hope no objection on his side.

SIR ANTHONY. Objection! let him object if he dare! No, no, Mrs. Malaprop, Jack knows that the least demur puts me in a frenzy directly. My process was always very simple—in their younger days, 'twas "Jack do this"—if he demurred, I knocked him down—and if he grumbled at that, I always sent him out of the room.

MRS. MALAPROP. Ah, and the properest way, o' my conscience! Nothing is so conciliating to young people as severity. Well, Sir Anthony, I shall give Mr. Acres his discharge and prepare Lydia to re-ceive your son's invocations,[10] and I hope you will represent her to the captain as an object not altogether illegible.[11]

SIR ANTHONY. Madam, I will handle the subject prudently. Well, I must leave you; and let me beg you, Mrs. Malaprop, to enforce this matter roundly [12] to the girl. Take my advice—keep a tight hand; if she rejects this proposal, clap her under lock and key; and if you were just to let the servants forget to bring her dinner for three or four days, you can't conceive how she'd come about. (Exit.)

MRS. MALAPROP. Well, at any rate, I shall be glad to get her from under my intuition.[13] She has somehow discovered my partiality for Sir Lucius O'Trigger—sure, Lucy can't have betrayed me! No, the girl is such a simpleton, I should have made her confess it. Lucy! Lucy! (Calls) Had she been one of your artificial [14] ones, I should never have trusted her.

[Reenter LUCY.]

LUCY. Did you call, ma'am?

MRS. MALAPROP. Yes, girl. Did you see Sir Lucius while you was out?

LUCY. No, indeed, ma'am, not a glimpse of him.

---

[1] **simony . . . paradoxes:** probably a reference to the mathematical terms *geometry, functions,* and *parabolas*.

[2] **diabolical:** dialectical.

[3] **ingenuity and artifice:** ingenuousness and artistry.

[4] **supercilious:** superficial.

[5] **geometry:** geography.

[6] **contagious:** contiguous.

[7] **orthodoxy:** orthography.

[8] **reprehend:** comprehend.

[9] **superstitious:** superfluous.

[10] **invocations:** addresses, proposals.

[11] **illegible:** ineligible.

[12] **roundly:** plainly, bluntly.

[13] **intuition:** tuition; that is, my care.

[14] **artificial:** artful.

MRS. MALAPROP. You are sure, Lucy, that you never mentioned——

LUCY. Oh, gemini! I'd sooner cut my tongue out.

MRS. MALAPROP. Well, don't let your simplicity be imposed on.

LUCY. No, ma'am.

MRS. MALAPROP. So, come to me presently, and I'll give you another letter to Sir Lucius; but mind, Lucy—if ever you betray what you are entrusted with (unless it be other people's secrets to me), you forfeit my malevolence[1] forever, and your being a simpleton shall be no excuse for your locality.[2] (Exit.)

LUCY. Ha! ha! ha! So, my dear Simplicity, let me give you a little respite. (Altering her manner) Let girls in my station be as fond as they please of appearing expert and knowing in their trusts; commend me to a mask of silliness, and a pair of sharp eyes for my own interest under it! Let me see to what account have I turned my simplicity lately. (Looks at a paper) For abetting Miss Lydia Languish in a design of running away with an ensign—in money, sundry times, twelve pound twelve; gowns, five; hats, ruffles, caps, etc., etc., numberless! From the said ensign, within this last month, six guineas and a half. About a quarter's pay! Item, from Mrs. Malaprop, for betraying the young people to her—when I found matters were likely to be discovered—two guineas and a black paduasoy.[3] Item, from Mr. Acres, for carrying divers letters—which I never delivered—two guineas and a pair of buckles. Item, from Sir Lucius O'Trigger, three crowns, two gold pocket-pieces, and a silver snuff box! Well done, Simplicity! Yet I was forced to make my Hibernian[4] believe that he was corresponding, not with the aunt, but with the niece; for though not overrich, I found he had too much pride and delicacy to sacrifice the feelings of a gentleman to the necessities of his fortune. (Exit.)

[1] **malevolence:** benevolence.
[2] **locality:** loquacity.
[3] **paduasoy:** a garment made of silk from Padua.
[4] **Hibernian:** Irishman.

FOR STUDY AND DISCUSSION

1. The term *exposition* is used to describe the playwright's provision to the audience of essential background information: the setting of the play, its tone, identification of the characters, and the initial dramatic situation. The exposition in *The Rivals* begins with Fag's second speech: "But who the deuce thought of seeing you in Bath?" How much exposition is contained in Scene 1 of the play? how much in Scene 2? What is the initial dramatic situation? What parallel can you draw between Sheridan's device of opening his play with a conversation between servants and Shakespeare's device of beginning *Macbeth* with the conversation of the three witches and *Julius Caesar* with the conversation between the tribunes?

2. Thomas tells Fag that he will never give up his wig, and he seems to feel that the habit of showing one's own hair is simply a new fad. How does this remark relate to the masquerading which goes on in *The Rivals?*

3. In Act I Lydia spends a great deal of time asking for, and then hiding, books. Why is she so interested in reading these books? What do their titles have in common? How has Lydia applied her reading to her life?

4. When Lydia tells Lucy to hide her books, Sheridan plays with the titles. Lydia seems to treat the books as real people, just as she will treat her real love affair as a storybook affair. Cite specific lines where Lydia tends to mix art and life.

5. What comparisons and contrasts does Sheridan effect by juxtaposing the love affair of Julia and Faulkland to those of Lydia and Absolute and Mrs. Malaprop and Sir Lucius O'Trigger? What difficulty is Julia having with Faulkland? Since everyone else in the play is plotting or masquerading, what point may Sheridan be making about refusing to wear a mask?

6. Describe Sir Anthony Absolute as a father. Why is his last name appropriate? Do you think his authoritarian approach is comical? Why or why not?

FOR COMPOSITION

In Scene 2, Mrs. Malaprop and Sir Anthony discuss the education of women. Write a short paper in which you describe Mrs. Malaprop's point of view. What is ironic about her defense of education?

ACT II

SCENE 1. CAPTAIN ABSOLUTE's *lodgings.*

[CAPTAIN ABSOLUTE *and* FAG.]

FAG. Sir, while I was there, Sir Anthony came in. I told him you had sent me to inquire after his health and to know if he was at leisure to see you.

ABSOLUTE. And what did he say, on hearing I was at Bath?

FAG. Sir, in my life I never saw an elderly gentleman more astonished! He started back two or three paces, rapped out a dozen interjectural oaths, and asked what the devil had brought you here.

ABSOLUTE. Well, sir, and what did you say?

FAG. Oh, I lied, sir—I forgot the precise lie; but you may depend on't, he got no truth from me. Yet, with submission, for fear of blunders in future, I should be glad to fix what has brought us to Bath, in order that we may lie a little consistently. Sir Anthony's servants were curious, sir, very curious indeed.

ABSOLUTE. You have said nothing to them?

FAG. Oh, not a word, sir, not a word! Mr. Thomas, indeed, the coachman (whom I take to be the discreetest of whips)——

ABSOLUTE. 'Sdeath!—you rascal! you have not trusted him!

FAG. Oh, no, sir—no—no—not a syllable, upon my veracity! He was, indeed, a little inquisitive; but I was sly, sir—devilish sly! My master (said I), honest Thomas (you know, sir, one says honest to one's inferiors), is come to Bath to recruit. Yes, sir, I said to recruit—and whether for men, money, or constitution, you know, sir, is nothing to him nor anyone else.

ABSOLUTE. Well, recruit will do—let it be so.

FAG. Oh, sir, recruit will do surprisingly —indeed, to give the thing an air, I told Thomas that your honor had already enlisted five disbanded chairmen, seven minority waiters, and thirteen billiard-markers.[1]

ABSOLUTE. You blockhead, never say more than is necessary.

FAG. I beg pardon, sir—I beg pardon— but, with submission, a lie is nothing unless one supports it. Sir, whenever I draw on my invention for a good current lie, I always forge endorsements as well as the bill.

ABSOLUTE. Well, take care you don't hurt your credit by offering too much security. Is Mr. Faulkland returned?

FAG. He is above, sir, changing his dress.

ABSOLUTE. Can you tell whether he has been informed of Sir Anthony and Miss Melville's arrival?

FAG. I fancy not, sir; he has seen no one since he came in but his gentleman, who was with him at Bristol. I think, sir, I hear Mr. Faulkland coming down——

ABSOLUTE. Go tell him I am here.

FAG. Yes, sir. *(Going)* I beg pardon, sir, but should Sir Anthony call, you will do me the favor to remember that we are recruiting, if you please.

ABSOLUTE. Well, well.

FAG. And, in tenderness to my character, if your honor could bring in the chairmen and waiters, I should esteem it as an obligation; for though I never scruple a lie to serve my master, yet it hurts one's conscience to be found out. *(Exit.)*

ABSOLUTE. Now for my whimsical friend—if he does not know that his mistress is here, I'll tease him a little before I tell him——

[*Enter* FAULKLAND.]

Faulkland, you're welcome to Bath again; you are punctual in your return.

FAULKLAND. Yes; I had nothing to detain me when I had finished the business I went on. Well, what news since I left

---

[1] **chairmen . . . billiard-markers:** These men are all unemployed, "disbanded." A political "minority" is out of office, thus out of work; "chairmen" refers to bearers of sedan chairs.

you? How stand matters between you and Lydia?

ABSOLUTE. Faith, much as they were; I have not seen her since our quarrel; however, I expect to be recalled every hour.

FAULKLAND. Why don't you persuade her to go off with you at once?

ABSOLUTE. What, and lose two thirds of her fortune? You forget that, my friend. No, no, I could have brought her to that long ago.

FAULKLAND. Nay, then, you trifle too long. If you are sure of her, propose to the aunt in your own character, and write to Sir Anthony for his consent.

ABSOLUTE. Softly, softly; for though I am convinced my little Lydia would elope with me as Ensign Beverley, yet am I by no means certain that she would take me with the impediment of our friends' consent, a regular humdrum wedding, and the reversion of a good fortune on my side. No, no; I must prepare her gradually for the discovery, and make myself necessary to her, before I risk it. Well, but Faulkland; you'll dine with us today at the hotel?

FAULKLAND. Indeed, I cannot; I am not in spirits to be of such a party.

ABSOLUTE. By heavens! I shall forswear your company. You are the most teasing, captious, incorrigible lover! Do love like a man.

FAULKLAND. I own I am unfit for company.

ABSOLUTE. Am I not a lover; ay, and a romantic one too? Yet do I carry everywhere with me such a confounded farrago [1] of doubts, fears, hopes, wishes, and all the flimsy furniture of a country miss's brain!

FAULKLAND. Ah! Jack, your heart and soul are not, like mine, fixed immutably on one only object. You throw for a large stake, but losing, you could stake and throw again: but I have set my sum of happiness on this cast, and not to succeed were to be stripped of all.

---

[1] **farrago:** confused mixture.

ABSOLUTE. But, for heaven's sake! what grounds for apprehension can your whimsical brain conjure up at present?

FAULKLAND. What grounds for apprehension, did you say? Heavens! are there not a thousand! I fear for her spirits—her health—her life! My absence may fret her; her anxiety for my return, her fears for me, may oppress her gentle temper; and for her health, does not every hour bring me cause to be alarmed? If it rains, some shower may even then have chilled her delicate frame! If the wind be keen, some rude blast may have affected her! The heat of noon, the dews of the evening, may endanger the life of her for whom only I value mine. O Jack! when delicate and feeling souls are separated, there is not a feature in the sky, not a movement of the elements, not an aspiration of the breeze, but hints some cause for a lover's apprehension!

ABSOLUTE. Ay, but we may choose whether we will take the hint or not. So, then, Faulkland, if you were convinced that Julia were well and in spirits, you would be entirely content?

FAULKLAND. I should be happy beyond measure. I am anxious only for that.

ABSOLUTE. Then to cure your anxiety at once—Miss Melville is in perfect health, and is at this moment in Bath.

FAULKLAND. Nay, Jack—don't trifle with me.

ABSOLUTE. She is arrived here with my father within this hour.

FAULKLAND. Can you be serious?

ABSOLUTE. I thought you knew Sir Anthony better than to be surprised at a sudden whim of this kind. Seriously, then, it is as I tell you—upon my honor.

FAULKLAND. My dear friend! Hollo, Du-Peigne! [2] my hat. My dear Jack— now nothing on earth can give me a moment's uneasiness.

[*Reenter* FAG.]

FAG. Sir, Mr. Acres, just arrived, is below.

---

[2] **Du-Peigne:** Faulkland's servant.

ABSOLUTE. Stay, Faulkland, this Acres lives within a mile of Sir Anthony, and he shall tell you how your mistress has been ever since you left her. Fag, show this gentleman up.

[*Exit* FAG.]

FAULKLAND. What, is he much acquainted in the family?

ABSOLUTE. Oh, very intimate: I insist on your not going: besides, his character will divert you.

FAULKLAND. Well, I should like to ask him a few questions.

ABSOLUTE. He is likewise a rival of mine—that is, of my other self's, for he does not think his friend Captain Absolute ever saw the lady in question; and it is ridiculous enough to hear him complain to me of one Beverley, a concealed skulking rival, who——

FAULKLAND. Hush!—he's here.

[*Enter* ACRES.]

ACRES. Ha! my dear friend, noble captain, and honest Jack, how do'st thou? just arrived, faith, as you see. Sir, your humble servant. Warm work on the roads, Jack!—Odds whips and wheels! I've traveled like a comet, with a tail of dust all the way as long as the Mall.[1]

ABSOLUTE. Ah! Bob, you are indeed an eccentric planet, but we know your attraction hither. Give me leave to introduce Mr. Faulkland to you; Mr. Faulkland, Mr. Acres.

ACRES. Sir, I am most heartily glad to see you: sir, I solicit your connections. Hey, Jack—what, this is Mr. Faulkland, who——

ABSOLUTE. Ay, Bob, Miss Melville's Mr. Faulkland.

ACRES. Odso! she and your father can be but just arrived before me? I suppose you have seen them. Ah! Mr. Faulkland, you are indeed a happy man.

FAULKLAND. I have not seen Miss Melville yet, sir; I hope she enjoyed full health and spirits in Devonshire?

ACRES. Never knew her better in my life, sir, never better. Odds blushes and blooms! she has been as healthy as the German spa.[2]

FAULKLAND. Indeed! I did hear that she had been a little indisposed.

ACRES. False, false, sir—only said to vex you: quite the reverse, I assure you.

FAULKLAND. There, Jack, you see she has the advantage of me; I had almost fretted myself ill.

ABSOLUTE. Now are you angry with your mistress for not having been sick?

FAULKLAND. No, no, you misunderstand me: yet surely a little trifling indisposition is not an unnatural consequence of absence from those we love. Now confess—isn't there something unkind in this violent, robust, unfeeling health?

ABSOLUTE. Oh, it was very unkind of her to be well in your absence, to be sure!

ACRES. Good apartments, Jack.

FAULKLAND. Well, sir, but you were saying that Miss Melville has been so exceedingly well—what then she has been merry and gay, I suppose? Always in spirits—hey?

ACRES. Merry, odds crickets! she has been the belle and spirit of the company wherever she has been—so lively and entertaining! so full of wit and humor!

FAULKLAND. There, Jack, there. Oh, by my soul! there is an innate levity in woman that nothing can overcome. What! happy, and I away!

ABSOLUTE. Have done! How foolish this is! just now you were only apprehensive for your mistress's spirits.

FAULKLAND. Why, Jack, have I been the joy and spirit of the company?

ABSOLUTE. No, indeed, you have not.

FAULKLAND. Have I been lively and entertaining?

ABSOLUTE. Oh, upon my word, I acquit you.

FAULKLAND. Have I been full of wit and humor?

---

[1] **Mall:** a fashionable promenade in London.

[2] **German spa:** any watering place or resort.

ABSOLUTE. No, faith, to do you justice, you have been confoundedly stupid indeed.

ACRES. What's the matter with the gentleman?

ABSOLUTE. He is only expressing his great satisfaction at hearing that Julia has been so well and happy—that's all—hey, Faulkland?

FAULKLAND. Oh! I am rejoiced to hear it—yes, yes, she has a happy disposition!

ACRES. That she has indeed—then she is so accomplished—so sweet a voice—so expert at her harpsichord—such a mistress of flat and sharp, squallante, rumblante, and quiverante![1] There was this time month—odds minums and crotchets! how she did chirrup at Mrs. Piano's concert!

FAULKLAND. There again, what say you to this? you see she has been all mirth and song—not a thought of me!

ABSOLUTE. Pho! man, is not music the food of love?

FAULKLAND. Well, well, it may be so. Pray, Mr.——, what's his damned name? Do you remember what songs Miss Melville sung?

ACRES. Not I indeed.

ABSOLUTE. Stay, now, they were some pretty melancholy purling-stream airs, I warrant; perhaps you may recollect; did she sing, "When absent from my soul's delight?"

ACRES. No, that wa'n't it.

ABSOLUTE. Or, "Go, gentle dales!" (Sings)

ACRES. Oh, no! nothing like it. Odds! now I recollect one of them—"My heart's my own, my will is free." (Sings)

FAULKLAND. Fool! fool that I am! to fix all my happiness on such a trifler! 'Sdeath! to make herself the pipe and balladmonger of a circle to soothe her light heart with catches and glees![2]— What can you say to this, sir?

<hr>

[1] **squallante . . . quiverante:** a mixture of nonsense and musical terms.
[2] **catches and glees:** lighthearted songs.

ABSOLUTE. Why, that I should be glad to hear my mistress had been so merry, sir.

FAULKLAND. Nay, nay, nay—I'm not sorry that she has been happy—no, no, I am glad of that—I would not have had her sad or sick—yet surely a sympathetic heart would have shown itself even in the choice of a song—she might have been temperately healthy, and somehow, plaintively gay; but she has been dancing too, I doubt not!

ACRES. What does the gentleman say about dancing?

ABSOLUTE. He says the lady we speak of dances as well as she sings.

ACRES. Ay, truly, does she—there was at our last race ball——

FAULKLAND. Hell and the devil! There! there—I told you so! I told you so! Oh! she thrives in my absence! Dancing! But her whole feelings have been in opposition with mine; I have been anxious, silent, pensive, sedentary—my days have been hours of care, my nights of watchfulness. She has been all health! spirit! laugh! song! dance! Oh! damned, damned levity!

ABSOLUTE. For heaven's sake, Faulkland, don't expose yourself so! Suppose she has danced, what then? Does not the ceremony of society often oblige——

FAULKLAND. Well, well, I'll contain myself—perhaps as you say—for form's sake. What, Mr. Acres, you were praising Miss Melville's manner of dancing a minuet—hey?

ACRES. Oh, I dare insure her for that— but what I was going to speak of was her country dancing. Odds swimmings! she has such an air with her!

FAULKLAND. Now disappointment on her! Defend this, Absolute; why don't you defend this? Country dances! jigs and reels! am I to blame now? A minuet I could have forgiven—I should not have minded that—I say I should not have regarded a minuet—but country dances! Zounds! had she made one in a cotillion —I believe I could have forgiven even

The Theater Royal, Drury Lane, where *The Rivals,* Sheridan's first success, was performed.

that—but to be monkey-led for a night—
to run the gauntlet through a string of
amorous palming puppies—to show paces
like a managed filly! Oh, Jack, there never
can be but one man in the world whom a
truly modest and delicate woman ought
to pair with in a country dance; and, even
then, the rest of the couples should be her
great-uncles and aunts!

ABSOLUTE. Ay, to be sure—grandfathers
and grandmothers!

FAULKLAND. If there be but one vicious
mind in the set, 'twill spread like a contagion—the
action of their pulse beats to
the lascivious movement of the jig—their
quivering, warm-breathed sighs impregnate
the very air—the atmosphere becomes
electrical to love, and each amorous
spark darts through every link of the
chain! I must leave you—I own I am
somewhat flurried—and that confounded
looby [1] has perceived it. *(Going)*

ABSOLUTE. Nay, but stay, Faulkland,

and thank Mr. Acres for his good news.

FAULKLAND. Damn his news! *(Exit.)*

ABSOLUTE. Ha! ha! ha! poor Faulkland
five minutes since—"nothing on earth
could give him a moment's uneasiness!"

ACRES. The gentleman wa'n't angry at
my praising his mistress, was he?

ABSOLUTE. A little jealous, I believe,
Bob.

ACRES. You don't say so? Ha! ha! jealous
of me—that's a good joke.

ABSOLUTE. There's nothing strange in
that, Bob! Let me tell you, that sprightly
grace and insinuating manner of yours
will do some mischief among the girls
here.

ACRES. Ah! you joke—ha! ha! mischief
—ha! ha! but you know I am not my own
property, my dear Lydia has forestalled
me. She could never abide me in the country,
because I used to dress so badly—but
odds frogs [2] and tambours! [3] I shan't take

---

[1] **looby:** awkward, doltish fellow.

[2] **frogs:** ornamented loops used to fasten a coat.
[3] **tambours:** embroidery frames.

matters so here, now ancient madam has no voice in it: I'll make my old clothes know who's master. I shall straightway cashier the hunting frock and render my leather breeches incapable. My hair has been in training some time.

ABSOLUTE. Indeed!

ACRES. Ay—and tho'ff the side curls are a little restive, my hind part takes it very kindly.

ABSOLUTE. Oh, you'll polish, I doubt not.

ACRES. Absolutely, I propose so—then if I can find out this Ensign Beverley, odds triggers and flints! I'll make him know the difference o't.

ABSOLUTE. Spoke like a man! But pray, Bob, I observe you have got an odd kind of a new method of swearing——

ACRES. Ha! ha! you've taken notice of it—'tis genteel, isn't it! I didn't invent it myself though; but a commander in our militia, a great scholar, I assure you, says that there is no meaning in the common oaths, and that nothing but their antiquity makes them respectable; because, he says, the ancients would never stick to an oath or two, but would say, by Jove! or by Bacchus! or by Mars! or by Venus! or by Pallas, according to the sentiment: so that to swear with propriety, says my little major, the oath should be an echo to the sense;[1] and this we call the *oath referential,* or *sentimental swearing*— ha! ha! 'tis genteel, isn't it.

ABSOLUTE. Very genteel, and very new, indeed!—and I dare say will supplant all other figures of imprecation.

ACRES. Aye, aye, the best terms will grow obsolete. Damns have had their day.

[*Reenter* FAG.]

FAG. Sir, there is a gentleman below desires to see you. Shall I show him into the parlor?

ABSOLUTE. Ay—you may.

ACRES. Well, I must be gone——

ABSOLUTE. Stay; who is it, Fag?

FAG. Your father, sir.

ABSOLUTE. You puppy, why didn't you show him up directly?

[*Exit* FAG.]

ACRES. You have business with Sir Anthony. I expect a message from Mrs. Malaprop at my lodgings. I have sent also to my dear friend, Sir Lucius O'-Trigger. Adieu, Jack! We must meet at night, when you shall give me a dozen bumpers [2] to little Lydia.

ABSOLUTE. That I will with all my heart. (*Exit* ACRES.) Now for a parental lecture— I hope he has heard nothing of the business that brought me here—I wish the gout had held him fast in Devonshire, with all my soul!

[*Enter* SIR ANTHONY ABSOLUTE.]

Sir, I am delighted to see you here; looking so well! Your sudden arrival at Bath made me apprehensive for your health.

SIR ANTHONY. Very apprehensive, I dare say, Jack. What, you are recruiting here, hey?

ABSOLUTE. Yes, sir, I am on duty.

SIR ANTHONY. Well, Jack, I am glad to see you, though I did not expect it, for I was going to write to you on a little matter of business. Jack, I have been considering that I grow old and infirm, and shall probably not trouble you long.

ABSOLUTE. Pardon, sir, I never saw you look more strong and hearty; and I pray frequently that you may continue so.

SIR ANTHONY. I hope your prayers may be heard, with all my heart. Well, then, Jack, I have been considering that I am so strong and hearty I may continue to plague you a long time. Now, Jack, I am sensible that the income of your commission, and what I have hitherto allowed you, is but a small pittance for a lad of your spirit.

[1] **the oath . . . sense:** a parody on a line in Alexander Pope's *Essay on Criticism,* "The sound must seem an echo to the sense" (see page 300).

[2] **give . . . bumpers:** drink a dozen toasts.

ABSOLUTE. Sir, you are very good.

SIR ANTHONY. And it is my wish, while yet I live, to have my boy make some figure in the world. I have resolved, therefore, to fix you at once in a noble independence.

ABSOLUTE. Sir, your kindness overpowers me—such generosity makes the gratitude of reason more lively than the sensations even of filial affection.

SIR ANTHONY. I am glad you are so sensible of my attention—and you shall be master of a large estate in a few weeks.

ABSOLUTE. Let my future life, sir, speak my gratitude; I cannot express the sense I have of your munificence. Yet, sir, I presume you would not wish me to quit the army?

SIR ANTHONY. Oh, that shall be as your wife chooses.

ABSOLUTE. My wife, sir!

SIR ANTHONY. Ay, ay, settle that between you—settle that between you.

ABSOLUTE. A wife, sir, did you say?

SIR ANTHONY. Ay, a wife—why, did not I mention her before?

ABSOLUTE. Not a word of her, sir.

SIR ANTHONY. Odd so! I mus'n't forget her though. Yes, Jack, the independence I was talking of is by marriage—the fortune is saddled with a wife—but I suppose that makes no difference.

ABSOLUTE. Sir! sir! you amaze me!

SIR ANTHONY. Why, what the devil's the matter with the fool? Just now you were all gratitude and duty.

ABSOLUTE. I was, sir—you talked to me of independence and a fortune, but not a word of a wife.

SIR ANTHONY. Why—what difference does that make? Odds life, sir! if you have the estate, you must take it with the live-stock on it, as it stands.

ABSOLUTE. If my happiness is to be the price, I must beg leave to decline the purchase. Pray, sir, who is the lady?

SIR ANTHONY. What's that to you, sir? Come, give me your promise to love and to marry her directly.

ABSOLUTE. Sure, sir, this is not very reasonable, to summon my affections for a lady I know nothing of!

SIR ANTHONY. I am sure, sir, 'tis more unreasonable in you to object to a lady you know nothing of.

ABSOLUTE. Then, sir, I must tell you plainly that my inclinations are fixed on another—my heart is engaged to an angel.

SIR ANTHONY. Then pray let it send an excuse. It is very sorry—but business prevents its waiting on her.

ABSOLUTE. But my vows are pledged to her.

SIR ANTHONY. Let her foreclose, Jack; let her foreclose; they are not worth redeeming; besides, you have the angel's vows in exchange, I suppose; so there can be no loss there.

ABSOLUTE. You must excuse me, sir, if I tell you, once for all, that in this point I cannot obey you.

SIR ANTHONY. Hark'ee, Jack; I have heard you for some time with patience—I have been cool—quite cool; but take care—you know I am compliance itself—when I am not thwarted; no one more easily led—when I have my own way; but don't put me in a frenzy.

ABSOLUTE. Sir, I must repeat—in this I cannot obey you.

SIR ANTHONY. Now damn me! if ever I call you Jack again while I live!

ABSOLUTE. Nay, sir, but hear me.

SIR ANTHONY. Sir, I won't hear a word —not a word! not one word! so give me your promise by a nod—and I'll tell you what, Jack—I mean, you dog—if you don't, by——

ABSOLUTE. What, sir, promise to link myself to some mass of ugliness! to——

SIR ANTHONY. Zounds! sirrah! the lady shall be as ugly as I choose: she shall have a hump on each shoulder; she shall be as crooked as the crescent; her one eye shall roll like the bull's in Cox's Museum; she shall have a skin like a mummy—she shall be all this, sirrah! —yet I will make you ogle her all day, and sit up all night to write sonnets on her beauty.

ABSOLUTE. This is reason and moderation indeed!

SIR ANTHONY. None of your sneering, puppy! no grinning, jackanapes!

ABSOLUTE. Indeed, sir, I never was in a worse humor for mirth in my life.

SIR ANTHONY. 'Tis false, sir. I know you are laughing in your sleeve; I know you'll grin when I am gone, sirrah!

ABSOLUTE. Sir, I hope I know my duty better.

SIR ANTHONY. None of your passion, sir! none of your violence, if you please! It won't do with me, I promise you.

ABSOLUTE. Indeed, sir, I never was cooler in my life.

SIR ANTHONY. 'Tis a confounded lie! I know you are in a passion in your heart; I know you are, you hypocritical young dog! But it won't do.

ABSOLUTE. Nay, sir, upon my word——

SIR ANTHONY. So you will fly out! can't you be cool like me? What the devil good can passion do? Passion is of no service, you impudent, insolent, overbearing reprobate! There, you sneer again! don't provoke me! But you rely upon the mildness of my temper—you do, you dog! You play upon the meekness of my disposition! Yet take care—the patience of a saint may be overcome at last! but mark! I give you six hours and a half to consider of this: if you then agree, without any condition, to do everything on earth that I choose, why—confound you! I may in time forgive you. If not, zounds! don't enter the same hemisphere with me! don't dare to breathe the same air, or use the same light with me! but get an atmosphere and a sun of your own! I'll strip you of your commission; I'll lodge a five-and-threepence in the hands of trustees, and you shall live on the interest. I'll disown you, I'll disinherit you, I'll unget you! and damn me! if ever I call you Jack again!

[*Exit* SIR ANTHONY.]

ABSOLUTE. Mild, gentle, considerate father—I kiss your hands! What a tender method of giving his opinion in these matters Sir Anthony has! I dare not trust him with the truth. I wonder what old wealthy hag it is that he wants to bestow on me! Yet he married himself for love! and was in his youth a bold intriguer and a gay companion!

[*Reenter* FAG.]

FAG. Assuredly, sir, your father is wrath to a degree; he comes downstairs eight or ten steps at a time—muttering, growling, and thumping the banisters all the way. I and the cook's dog stand bowing at the door—rap! he gives me a stroke on the head with his cane; bids me carry that to my master; then kicking the poor turnspit [1] into the area, damns us all, for a puppy triumvirate! Upon my credit, sir, were I in your place and found my father such very bad company, I should certainly drop his acquaintance.

ABSOLUTE. Cease your impertinence, sir, at present. Did you come in for nothing more? Stand out of the way! (*Pushes him aside, and exit.*)

FAG. So! Sir Anthony trims my master; he is afraid to reply to his father—then vents his spleen on poor Fag! When one is vexed by one person, to revenge one's self on another, who happens to come in the way, is the vilest injustice! Ah! it shows the worst temper—the basest——

[*Enter* BOY.]

BOY. Mr. Fag! Mr. Fag! your master calls you.

FAG. Well, you little dirty puppy, you need not bawl so! The meanest disposition! the——

BOY. Quick, quick, Mr. Fag!

FAG. Quick! quick! you impudent jackanapes! Am I to be commanded by you too? you little, impertinent, insolent, kitchen-bred——

[*Exit kicking and beating him.*]

---

[1] **turnspit**: a small dog, like a dachshund, often used in a treadmill to turn a spit.

SCENE 2. *The North Parade* *

[*Enter* LUCY.]

LUCY. So—I shall have another rival to add to my mistress's list—Captain Absolute. However, I shall not enter his name till my purse has received notice in form. Poor Acres is dismissed! Well, I have done him a last friendly office, in letting him know that Beverley was here before him. Sir Lucius is generally more punctual, when he expects to hear from his *dear Delia*, as he calls her: I wonder he's not here! I have a little scruple of conscience from this deceit; though I should not be paid so well if my hero knew that Delia was near fifty and her own mistress.

[*Enter* SIR LUCIUS O'TRIGGER.]

SIR LUCIUS. Ha! my little ambassadress —upon my conscience, I have been looking for you; I have been on the South Parade this half hour.

LUCY (*speaking simply*). O gemini! and I have been waiting for your lordship here on the North.

SIR LUCIUS. Faith! maybe that was the reason we did not meet; and it is very comical too, how you could go out and I not see you—for I was only taking a nap at the Parade Coffeehouse, and I chose the window on purpose that I might not miss you.

LUCY. My stars! Now I'd wager a sixpence I went by while you were asleep.

SIR LUCIUS. Sure enough it must have been so—and I never dreamt it was so late, till I waked. Well, but my little girl, have you got nothing for me?

LUCY. Yes, but I have—I've got a letter for you in my pocket.

SIR LUCIUS. O faith! I guessed you weren't come empty-handed. Well—let me see what the dear creature says.

LUCY. There, Sir Lucius. (*Gives him a letter*)

SIR LUCIUS (*reads*). *Sir—there is often a sudden incentive* [1] *impulse in love that has a greater induction* [2] *than years of domestic combination: such was the commotion* [3] *I felt at the first superfluous* [4] *view of Sir Lucius O'Trigger. Very pretty, upon my word. Female punctuation* [5] *forbids me to say more; yet let me add that it will give me joy infallible* [6] *to find Sir Lucius worthy the last criterion* [7] *of my affections. Delia.* Upon my conscience! Lucy, your lady is a great mistress of language. Faith, she's quite the queen of the dictionary! For the devil a word dare refuse coming at her call— though one would think it was quite out of hearing.

LUCY. Ay, sir, a lady of her experience——

SIR LUCIUS. Experience! what, at seventeen?

LUCY. O true, sir—but then she reads so—my stars! how she will read offhand!

SIR LUCIUS. Faith, she must be very deep read to write this way—though she is rather an arbitrary writer, too—for here are a great many poor words pressed into the service of this note that would get their *habeas corpus* from any court in Christendom.[8]

LUCY. Ah! Sir Lucius, if you were to hear how she talks of you!

SIR LUCIUS. Oh, tell her I'll make her the best husband in the world, and Lady O'Trigger into the bargain! But we must get the old gentlewoman's consent—and do everything fairly.

LUCY. Nay, Sir Lucius, I thought you wa'n't rich enough to be so nice.

SIR LUCIUS. Upon my word, young woman, you have hit it: I am so poor that I can't afford to do a dirty action. If I did

* **The North Parade:** a broad paved walk.
[1] **incentive:** intuitive.

[2] **induction:** seduction.
[3] **commotion:** emotion.
[4] **superfluous:** superficial.
[5] **punctuation:** punctiliousness, careful observance of etiquette.
[6] **infallible:** ineffable, indescribable.
[7] **criterion:** degree or iota.
[8] ***habeas corpus . . . Christendom:*** Mrs. Malaprop's abuse of words is almost criminal. The words could demand to be presented in court (*habeas corpus*) to defend themselves against Mrs. Malaprop's misuse.

not want money, I'd steal your mistress and her fortune with a great deal of pleasure. However, my pretty girl *(Gives her money),* here's a little something to buy you a ribbon; and meet me in the evening, and I'll give you an answer to this. So, hussy, take a kiss beforehand to put you in mind. *(Kisses her)*

LUCY. O Lud! Sir Lucius—I never seed such a gemman! My lady won't like you if you're so impudent.

SIR LUCIUS. Faith she will, Lucy! That same—pho! what's the name of it?—modesty—is a quality in a lover more praised by the women than liked; so, if your mistress asks you whether Sir Lucius ever gave you a kiss, tell her fifty—my dear.

LUCY. What, would you have me tell a lie?

SIR LUCIUS. Ah, then, you baggage! I'll make it a truth presently.

LUCY. For shame now! here is someone coming.

SIR LUCIUS. Oh, faith, I'll quiet your conscience!

[*Exit humming a tune. Enter* FAG.]

FAG. So, so, ma'am! I humbly beg pardon.

LUCY. O Lud! now, Mr. Fag, you flurry one so.

FAG. Come, come, Lucy, here's no one by—so a little less simplicity, with a grain or two more sincerity, if you please. You play false with us, madam. I saw you give the baronet a letter. My master shall know this—and if he don't call him out, I will.

LUCY. Ha! ha! ha! you gentlemen's gentlemen are so hasty. That letter was from Mrs. Malaprop, simpleton. She is taken with Sir Lucius's address.

FAG. How! what tastes some people have! Why, I suppose I have walked by her window a hundred times. But what says our young lady? any message to my master?

LUCY. Sad news, Mr. Fag. A worse rival than Acres! Sir Anthony Absolute has proposed his son.

FAG. What, Captain Absolute?

LUCY. Even so—I overheard it all.

FAG. Ha! ha! ha! very good, faith. Good-by, Lucy, I must away with this news.

LUCY. Well, you may laugh—but it is true, I assure you. *(Going)* But, Mr. Fag, tell your master not to be cast down by this.

FAG. Oh, he'll be so disconsolate!

LUCY. And charge him not to think of quarreling with young Absolute.

FAG. Never fear! never fear!

LUCY. Be sure—bid him keep up his spirits.

FAG. We will—we will. *(Exeunt severally.)*

FOR STUDY AND DISCUSSION

1. In Scene 1 Fag makes quite a virtue of lying: "I forget the precise lie; but you may depend on't, he got no truth from me." But he admits a difficulty inherent in lying: "It hurts one's conscience to be found out." How would Fag define *conscience?* What is it about Fag's lying that bothers Jack Absolute? What attitude toward lying does Sheridan satirize in this scene?

2. Early in Act II, Absolute declares that though he is convinced Lydia would elope with him as Ensign Beverley, "yet am I by no means certain she would take me with the impediment of our friends' consent, a regular humdrum wedding, and the reversion of a good fortune on my side." In other words, he is forced to play a role in order to win Lydia. Do we condemn him for this? Do we condemn Lydia? Or do we admire them for their efforts? Compare Absolute's attitude toward love with Faulkland's, for example.

3. At the end of Scene 1, Sir Anthony urges Absolute to be calm. How do his words conflict with his behavior? How does this conflict contribute to the theme of the play?

4. What do Bob Acres and Sir Lucius O'Trigger have in common? What do Fag and Lucy have in common? Explain how these characters are related to the theme of the play.

5. By the end of Act II, we are aware of the play's main plot and the various subplots. What is the main plot? Identify the subplots. How are they linked together?

ACT III

SCENE 1. *The North Parade.*

[*Enter* CAPTAIN ABSOLUTE.]

ABSOLUTE. 'Tis just as Fag told me, indeed. Whimsical enough, faith. My father wants to force me to marry the very girl I am plotting to run away with! He must not know of my connection with her yet awhile. He has too summary a method of proceeding in these matters. However, I'll read my recantation instantly. My conversion is something sudden, indeed—but I can assure him it is very sincere. So, so—here he comes. He looks plaguey gruff. (*Steps aside*)

[*Enter* SIR ANTHONY ABSOLUTE.]

SIR ANTHONY. No—I'll die sooner than forgive him. Die, did I say? I'll live these fifty years to plague him. At our last meeting, his impudence had almost put me out of temper. An obstinate, passionate, self-willed boy! Who can he take after? This is my return for getting him before all his brothers and sisters—for putting him, at twelve years old, into a marching regiment, and allowing him fifty pounds a year, besides his pay, ever since! But I have done with him; he's anybody's son for me. I never will see him more, never—never—never.

ABSOLUTE (*aside, coming forward*). Now for a penitential face.

SIR ANTHONY. Fellow, get out of my way.

ABSOLUTE. Sir, you see a penitent before you.

SIR ANTHONY. I see an impudent scoundrel before me.

ABSOLUTE. A sincere penitent. I am come, sir, to acknowledge my error and to submit entirely to your will.

SIR ANTHONY. What's that?

ABSOLUTE. I have been revolving and reflecting and considering on your past goodness and kindness and condescension to me.

SIR ANTHONY. Well, sir?

ABSOLUTE. I have been likewise weighing and balancing what you were pleased to mention concerning duty and obedience and authority.

SIR ANTHONY. Well, puppy?

ABSOLUTE. Why, then, sir, the result of my reflections is—a resolution to sacrifice every inclination of my own to your satisfaction.

SIR ANTHONY. Why now you talk sense —absolute sense. I never heard anything more sensible in my life. Confound you! you shall be Jack again.

ABSOLUTE. I am happy in the appellation.

SIR ANTHONY. Why, then, Jack, my dear Jack, I will now inform you who the lady really is. Nothing but your passion and violence, you silly fellow, prevented my telling you at first. Prepare, Jack, for wonder and rapture—prepare. What think you of Miss Lydia Languish?

ABSOLUTE. Languish! What, the Languishes of Worcestershire?

SIR ANTHONY. Worcestershire! no. Did you ever meet Mrs. Malaprop and her niece, Miss Languish, who came into our country just before you were last ordered to your regiment?

ABSOLUTE. Malaprop! Languish! I don't remember ever to have heard the names before. Yet stay—I think I do recollect something. Languish! Languish! She squints, don't she? A little red-haired girl?

SIR ANTHONY. Squints! A red-haired girl! Zounds! no.

ABSOLUTE. Then I must have forgot; it can't be the same person.

SIR ANTHONY. Jack! Jack! what think you of blooming, love-breathing seventeen?

ABSOLUTE. As to that, sir, I am quite indifferent. If I can please you in the matter, 'tis all I desire.

SIR ANTHONY. Nay, but, Jack, such eyes! such eyes! so innocently wild! so bashfully irresolute! not a glance but speaks and kindles some thought of love! Then, Jack, her cheeks! her cheeks, Jack! so deeply blushing at the insinuations of her telltale eyes! Then, Jack, her lips! O, Jack, lips smiling at their own discretion; and if not smiling, more sweetly pouting; more lovely in sullenness.

ABSOLUTE (*aside*). That's she, indeed. Well done, old gentleman.

SIR ANTHONY. Then, Jack, her neck! O Jack! Jack!

ABSOLUTE. And which is to be mine, sir; the niece or the aunt?

SIR ANTHONY. Why, you unfeeling, insensible puppy, I despise you! When I was of your age, such a description would have made me fly like a rocket! The aunt, indeed! Odds life! when I ran away with your mother, I would not have touched anything old or ugly to gain an empire.

ABSOLUTE. Not to please your father, sir?

SIR ANTHONY. To please my father! zounds! not to please—Oh, my father—odd so!—yes—yes; if my father indeed had desired—that's quite another matter. Though he wa'n't the indulgent father that I am, Jack.

ABSOLUTE. I dare say not, sir.

SIR ANTHONY. But, Jack, you are not sorry to find your mistress is so beautiful?

ABSOLUTE. Sir, I repeat it—if I please you in this affair, 'tis all I desire. Not that I think a woman the worse for being handsome; but, sir, if you please to recollect, you before hinted something about a hump or two, one eye, and a few more graces of that kind—now, without being very nice, I own I should rather choose a wife of mine to have the usual number of limbs and a limited quantity of back: and though one eye may be very agreeable, yet as the prejudice has always run in favor of two, I would not wish to affect a singularity in that article.

SIR ANTHONY. What a phlegmatic sot it is! Why, sirrah, you're an anchorite!—a vile, insensible stock. You a soldier!—you're a walking block, fit only to dust the company's regimentals on! Odds life! I have a great mind to marry the girl myself!

ABSOLUTE. I am entirely at your disposal, sir: if you should think of addressing Miss Languish yourself, I suppose you would have me marry the aunt; or if you should change your mind, and take the old lady—'tis the same to me—I'll marry the niece.

SIR ANTHONY. Upon my word, Jack, thou'rt either a very great hypocrite, or—but, come, I know your indifference on such a subject must be all a lie—I'm sure it must—come, now—damn your demure face—come, confess, Jack—you have been lying, ha'n't you? You have been playing the hypocrite, hey! I'll never forgive you if you ha'n't been lying and playing the hypocrite.

ABSOLUTE. I'm sorry, sir, that the respect and duty which I bear to you should be so mistaken.

SIR ANTHONY. Hang your respect and duty! But come along with me. I'll write a note to Mrs. Malaprop, and you shall visit the lady directly. Her eyes shall be the Promethean [1] torch to you—come along, I'll never forgive you if you don't come back stark mad with rapture and impatience—if you don't, egad, I will marry the girl myself! (*Exeunt.*)

SCENE 2. JULIA'S *dressing room.*

[FAULKLAND *discovered alone.*]

FAULKLAND. They told me Julia would return directly; I wonder she is not yet come! How mean does this captious, unsatisfied temper of mine appear to my cooler judgment! Yet I know not that I indulge it in any other point: but on this one subject, and to this one subject, whom I think I love beyond my life, I am ever ungenerously fretful and madly capricious! I am conscious of it—yet I cannot correct myself! What tender honest joy sparkled in her eyes when we met! how delicate was the warmth of her expression! I was ashamed to appear less happy —though I had come resolved to wear a

---

[1] **Promethean:** Prometheus stole fire from the gods for humankind.

face of coolness and upbraiding. Sir Anthony's presence prevented my proposed expostulations: yet I must be satisfied that she has not been so very happy in my absence. She is coming! Yes! I know the nimbleness of her tread, when she thinks her impatient Faulkland counts the moments of her stay.

[*Enter* JULIA.]

JULIA. I had not hoped to see you again so soon.

FAULKLAND. Could I, Julia, be contented with my first welcome—restrained as we were by the presence of a third person?

JULIA. O Faulkland, when your kindness can make me thus happy, let me not think that I discovered something of coldness in your first salutation.

FAULKLAND. 'Twas but your fancy, Julia. I was rejoiced to see you—to see you in such health. Sure I had no cause for coldness?

JULIA. Nay, then, I see you have taken something ill. You must not conceal from me what it is.

FAULKLAND. Well, then—shall I own to you that my joy at hearing of your health and arrival here, by your neighbor Acres, was somewhat dampened by his dwelling much on the high spirits you had enjoyed in Devonshire—on your mirth—your singing—dancing, and I know not what! For such is my temper, Julia, that I should regard every mirthful moment in your absence as a treason to constancy. The mutual tear that steals down the cheek of parting lovers is a compact that no smile shall live there till they meet again.

JULIA. Must I never cease to tax my Faulkland with this teasing minute caprice? Can the idle reports of a silly boor weigh in your breast against my tried affections?

FAULKLAND. They have no weight with me, Julia: No, no—I am happy if you have been so—yet only say that you did not sing with mirth—say that you thought of Faulkland in the dance.

JULIA. I never can be happy in your absence. If I wear a countenance of content, it is to show that my mind holds no doubt of my Faulkland's truth. If I seemed sad, it were to make malice triumph and say that I fixed my heart on one who left me to lament his roving and my own credulity. Believe me, Faulkland, I mean not to upbraid you when I say that I have often dressed sorrow in smiles, lest my friends should guess whose unkindness had caused my tears.

FAULKLAND. You were ever all goodness to me. Oh, I am a brute, when I but admit a doubt of your true constancy!

JULIA. If ever without such cause from you, as I will not suppose possible, you find my affections veering but a point, may I become a proverbial scoff for levity and base ingratitude.

FAULKLAND. Ah! Julia, that last word is grating to me. I would I had no title to your gratitude! Search your heart, Julia; perhaps what you have mistaken for love is but the warm effusion of a too thankful heart.

JULIA. For what quality must I love you?

FAULKLAND. For no quality! To regard me for any quality of mind or understanding were only to esteem me. And for person—I have often wished myself deformed, to be convinced that I owe no obligation there for any part of your affection.

JULIA. Where nature has bestowed a show of nice attention in the features of a man, he should laugh at it as misplaced. I have seen men, who in this vain article, perhaps, might rank above you; but my heart has never asked my eyes if it were so or not.

FAULKLAND. Now this is not well from you, Julia—I despise person in a man—yet if you loved me as I wish, though I were an Ethiop, you'd think none so fair.

JULIA. I see you are determined to be unkind! The contract which my poor father bound us in gives you more than a lover's privilege.

FAULKLAND. Again, Julia, you raise

ideas that feed and justify my doubts. I would not have been more free—no—I am proud of my restraint. Yet—yet—perhaps your high respect alone for this solemn compact has fettered your inclinations, which else had made a worthier choice. How shall I be sure, had you remained unbound in thought and promise, that I should still have been the object of your persevering love?

JULIA. Then try me now. Let us be free as strangers as to what is past: my heart will not feel more liberty!

FAULKLAND. There now! so hasty, Julia! so anxious to be free! If your love for me were fixed and ardent, you would not lose your hold, even though I wished it!

JULIA. Oh! you torture me to the heart! I cannot bear it.

FAULKLAND. I do not mean to distress you. If I loved you less, I should never give you an uneasy moment. But hear me. All my fretful doubts arise from this. Women are not used to weigh and separate the motives of their affections: the cold dictates of prudence, gratitude, or filial duty may sometimes be mistaken for the pleadings of the heart. I would not boast—yet let me say that I have neither age, person, nor character to found dislike on; my fortune such as few ladies could be charged with indiscretion in the match. O Julia! when love receives such countenance from prudence, nice minds will be suspicious of its birth.

JULIA. I know not whither your insinuations would tend, but as they seem pressing to insult me, I will spare you the regret of having done so. I have given you no cause for this! *(Exit in tears.)*

FAULKLAND. In tears! Stay, Julia: stay but for a moment. The door is fastened! Julia!—my soul—but for one moment! I hear her sobbing! 'Sdeath! what a brute am I to use her thus! Yet stay! Ay—she is coming now—how little resolution there is in a woman—how a few soft words can turn them! No, faith!—she is not coming either. Why, Julia—my love— say but that you forgive me—come but to tell me that—now this is being too resentful. Stay! she is coming too—I thought she would—no steadiness in anything: her going away must have been a mere trick then—she sha'n't see that I was hurt by it—I'll affect indifference—*(Hums a tune; then listens)* No—zounds! she's not coming! nor don't intend it, I suppose. This is not steadiness, but obstinacy! Yet I deserve it. What, after so long an absence, to quarrel with her tenderness! 'twas barbarous and unmanly! I should be ashamed to see her now. I'll wait till her just resentment is abated—and when I distress her so again, may I lose her forever! and be linked instead to some antique virago, whose gnawing passions and long hoarded spleen shall make me curse my folly half the day and all the night. *(Exit.)*

SCENE 3. MRS. MALAPROP'S *lodgings.*

[MRS. MALAPROP, *with a letter in her hand, and* CAPTAIN ABSOLUTE.]

MRS. MALAPROP. Your being Sir Anthony's son, captain, would itself be a sufficient accommodation,[1] but from the ingenuity[2] of your appearance, I am convinced you deserve the character here given of you.

ABSOLUTE. Permit me to say, madam, that as I never yet have had the pleasure of seeing Miss Languish, my principal inducement in this affair at present is the honor of being allied to Mrs. Malaprop; of whose intellectual accomplishments, elegant manners, and unaffected learning, no tongue is silent.

MRS. MALAPROP. Sir, you do me infinite honor! I beg, captain, you'll be seated. *(They sit.)* Ah! few gentlemen, nowadays, know how to value the ineffectual[3] qualities in a woman—few think how a little knowledge becomes a gentlewoman. Men have no sense now but for the worthless flower of beauty!

ABSOLUTE. It is but too true, indeed,

[1] **accommodation:** recommendation.
[2] **ingenuity:** ingenuousness.
[3] **ineffectual:** intellectual.

ma'am; yet I fear our ladies should share the blame—they think our admiration of beauty so great, that knowledge in them would be superfluous. Thus, like garden trees, they seldom show fruit, till time has robbed them of more specious blossom. Few, like Mrs. Malaprop and the orange tree, are rich in both at once!

MRS. MALAPROP. Sir, you overpower me with good breeding.—He is the very pine-apple [1] of politeness!—You are not ignorant, captain, that this giddy girl has somehow contrived to fix her affections on a beggarly, strolling, eavesdropping ensign, whom none of us have seen, and nobody knows anything of.

ABSOLUTE. Oh, I have heard the silly affair before. I'm not at all prejudiced against her on that account.

MRS. MALAPROP. You are very good and very considerate, captain. I am sure I have done everything in my power since I exploded [2] the affair; long ago I laid my positive conjunctions [3] on her never to think on the fellow again; I have since laid Sir Anthony's preposition [4] before her; but, I am sorry to say, she seems resolved to decline every particle [5] that I enjoin her.

ABSOLUTE. It must be very distressing, indeed, ma'am.

MRS. MALAPROP. Oh! it gives me the hydrostatics [6] to such a degree. I thought she had persisted [7] from corresponding with him; but, behold, this very day I have interceded [8] another letter from the fellow; I believe I have it in my pocket.

ABSOLUTE. Oh, the devil; my last note. (Aside)

MRS. MALAPROP. Ay, here it is.

ABSOLUTE. Ay, my note indeed! Oh, the little traitress Lucy. (Aside)

MRS. MALAPROP. There, perhaps you

may know the writing. (Gives him the letter)

ABSOLUTE. I think I have seen the hand before—yes, I certainly must have seen this hand before——

MRS. MALAPROP. Nay, but read it, captain.

ABSOLUTE (reads). My soul's idol, my adored Lydia!—Very tender, indeed!

MRS. MALAPROP. Tender, ay, and profane too, o' my conscience.

ABSOLUTE (reads). I am excessively alarmed at the intelligence you send me, the more so as my new rival—

MRS. MALAPROP. That's you, sir.

ABSOLUTE (reads). Has universally the character of being an accomplished gentleman and a man of honor.—Well, that's handsome enough.

MRS. MALAPROP. Oh, the fellow has some design in writing so.

ABSOLUTE. That he had, I'll answer for him, ma'am.

MRS. MALAPROP. But go on, sir—you'll see presently.

ABSOLUTE (reads). As for the old weatherbeaten she-dragon who guards you—Who can he mean by that?

MRS. MALAPROP. Me, sir!—me!—he means me! There—what do you think now?—but go on a little further.

ABSOLUTE. Impudent scoundrel!—— (Reads) it shall go hard but I will elude her vigilance, as I am told that the same ridiculous vanity, which makes her dress up her coarse features and deck her dull chat with hard words which she don't understand——

MRS. MALAPROP. There, sir, an attack upon my language! What do you think of that? An aspersion upon my parts of speech! Was ever such a brute! Sure, if I reprehend [9] anything in this world, it is the use of my oracular [10] tongue and a nice derangement of epitaphs! [11]

ABSOLUTE. He deserves to be hanged

---

[1] **pineapple:** pinnacle.
[2] **exploded:** exposed.
[3] **conjunctions:** injunctions.
[4] **preposition:** proposition.
[5] **particle:** article.
[6] **hydrostatics:** hysterics.
[7] **persisted:** desisted.
[8] **interceded:** intercepted.

[9] **reprehend:** comprehend.
[10] **oracular:** vernacular.
[11] **derangement of epitaphs:** arrangement of epithets.

and quartered! Let me see—*(Reads) same ridiculous vanity——*

MRS. MALAPROP. You need not read it again, sir.

ABSOLUTE. I beg pardon, ma'am. *(Reads) does also lay her open to the grossest deceptions from flattery and pretended admiration—an impudent coxcomb—so that I have a scheme to see you shortly with the old harridan's consent and even to make her a go-between in our interview.* Was ever such assurance!

MRS. MALAPROP. Did you ever hear anything like it? He'll elude my vigilance, will he? Yes, yes! ha! ha! he's very likely to enter these doors; we'll try who can plot best!

ABSOLUTE. So we will, ma'am—so we will! Ha! ha! ha! a conceited puppy, ha! ha! ha! Well, but, Mrs. Malaprop, as the girl seems so infatuated by this fellow, suppose you were to wink at her corresponding with him for a little time—let her even plot an elopement with him—then do you connive at her escape—while I, just in the nick, will have the fellow laid by the heels and fairly contrive to carry her off in his stead.

MRS. MALAPROP. I am delighted with the scheme; never was anything better perpetrated! [1]

ABSOLUTE. But, pray, could not I see the lady for a few minutes now? I should like to try her temper a little.

MRS. MALAPROP. Why, I don't know. I doubt she is not prepared for a visit of this kind. There is a decorum in these matters.

ABSOLUTE. O Lord! she won't mind me —only tell her Beverley——

MRS. MALAPROP. Sir!

ABSOLUTE. Gently, good tongue. *(Aside)*

MRS. MALAPROP. What did you say of Beverley?

ABSOLUTE. Oh, I was going to propose that you should tell her, by way of jest, that it was Beverley who was below; she'd come down fast enough then—ha! ha! ha!

MRS. MALAPROP. 'Twould be a trick she well deserves; besides, you know the fellow tells her he'll get my consent to see her—ha! ha! Let him if he can, I say again. Lydia, come down here! *(Calling)* He'll make me a go-between in their interviews! —ha! ha! ha! Come down, I say, Lydia! I don't wonder at your laughing, ha! ha! ha! his impudence is truly ridiculous.

ABSOLUTE. 'Tis very ridiculous, upon my soul, ma'am, ha! ha! ha!

MRS. MALAPROP. The little hussy won't hear. Well, I'll go and tell her at once who it is. She shall know that Captain Absolute is come to wait on her. And I'll make her behave as becomes a young woman.

ABSOLUTE. As you please, madam.

MRS. MALAPROP. For the present, captain, your servant. Ah! you've not done laughing yet, I see—elude my vigilance; yes, yes; ha! ha! ha! *(Exit.)*

ABSOLUTE. Ha! ha! ha! one would think now that I might throw off all disguise at once and seize my prize with security; but such is Lydia's caprice, that to undeceive were probably to lose her. I'll see whether she knows me.

[*Walks aside and seems engaged in looking at the pictures. Enter* LYDIA.]

LYDIA. What a scene am I now to go through! Surely nothing can be more dreadful than to be obliged to listen to the loathsome addresses of a stranger to one's heart. I have heard of girls persecuted as I am, who have appealed in behalf of their favored lover to the generosity of his rival; suppose I were to try it—there stands the hated rival—an officer too; but oh, how unlike my Beverley! I wonder he don't begin—truly he seems a very negligent wooer—quite at his ease, upon my word! I'll speak first—Mr. Absolute.

ABSOLUTE. Ma'am. *(Turns around)*

LYDIA. O heavens! Beverley!

ABSOLUTE. Hush; hush, my life! softly! be not surprised!

LYDIA. I am so astonished; and so terrified and so overjoyed! For Heaven's sake —how came you here?

ABSOLUTE. Briefly, I have deceived your aunt—I was informed that my new rival was to visit here this evening, and

---

[1] **perpetrated:** prepared.

contriving to have him kept away, have passed myself on her for Captain Absolute.

LYDIA. O charming! And she really takes you for young Absolute.

ABSOLUTE. Oh, she's convinced of it.

LYDIA. Ha! ha! ha! I can't forbear laughing to think how her sagacity is overreached!

ABSOLUTE. But we trifle with our precious moments—such another opportunity may not occur; then let me conjure my kind, my condescending angel, to fix the time when I may rescue her from undeserving persecution, and with a licensed warmth, plead for my reward.

LYDIA. Will you then, Beverley, consent to forfeit that portion of my paltry wealth—that burden on the wings of love?

ABSOLUTE. Oh, come to me—rich only thus—in loveliness! Bring no portion to me but thy love—'twill be generous in you, Lydia—for well you know it is the only dower your poor Beverley can repay.

LYDIA. How persuasive are his words— how charming will poverty be with him! (Aside)

ABSOLUTE. Ah! my soul, what a life will we then live! Love shall be our idol and support! We will worship him with a monastic strictness; abjuring all wordly toys, to center every thought and action there. Proud of calamity, we will enjoy the wreck of wealth; while the surrounding gloom of adversity shall make the flame of our pure love show doubly bright. By Heavens! I would fling all goods of fortune from me with a prodigal hand to enjoy the scene where I might clasp my Lydia to my bosom and say the world affords no smile to me but here—(Embracing her) if she holds out now, the devil is in it! (Aside)

LYDIA. Now could I fly with him to the antipodes! But my persecution is not yet come to a crisis. (Aside)

[Reenter MRS. MALAPROP, listening.]

MRS. MALAPROP. I am impatient to know how the little hussy deports herself. (Aside)

ABSOLUTE. So pensive, Lydia! Is then your warmth abated?

MRS. MALAPROP. Warmth abated! So!— she has been in a passion, I suppose. (Aside)

LYDIA. No—nor ever can while I have life.

MRS. MALAPROP. An ill-tempered little devil! She'll be in a passion all her life— will she? (Aside)

LYDIA. Think not the idle threats of my ridiculous aunt can ever have any weight with me.

MRS. MALAPROP. Very dutiful, upon my word! (Aside)

LYDIA. Let her choice be Captain Absolute, but Beverley is mine.

MRS. MALAPROP. I am astonished at her assurance—to his face—this is to his face. (Aside)

ABSOLUTE. Thus then let me enforce my suit. (Kneeling)

MRS. MALAPROP (aside). Ay, poor young man—down on his knees entreating for pity! I can contain no longer. (Coming forward) Why, thou vixen! I have overheard you.

ABSOLUTE. Oh, confound her vigilance! (Aside)

MRS. MALAPROP. Captain Absolute, I know not how to apologize for her shocking rudeness.

ABSOLUTE (aside). So all's safe, I find. (Aloud) I have hopes, madam, that time will bring the young lady——

MRS. MALAPROP. Oh, there's nothing to be hoped for from her! She's as headstrong as an allegory [1] on the banks of Nile.

LYDIA. Nay, madam, what do you charge me with now?

MRS. MALAPROP. Why, thou unblushing rebel—didn't you tell this gentleman to his face that you loved another better? Didn't you say you never would be his?

LYDIA. No, madam—I did not.

MRS. MALAPROP. Good heavens! what assurance! Lydia, Lydia, you ought to know that lying don't become a young

[1] **allegory**: alligator.

woman! Didn't you boast that Beverley, that stroller Beverley, possessed your heart? Tell me that, I say.

LYDIA. 'Tis true, ma'am, and none but Beverley——

MRS. MALAPROP. Hold!—hold! Assurance—you shall not be so rude.

ABSOLUTE. Nay, pray, Mrs. Malaprop, don't stop the young lady's speech: she's very welcome to talk thus—it does not hurt me in the least, I assure you.

MRS. MALAPROP. You are too good, captain—too amiably patient. But come with me, miss. Let us see you again soon, captain—remember what we have fixed.

ABSOLUTE. I shall, ma'am.

MRS. MALAPROP. Come, take a graceful leave of the gentleman.

LYDIA. May every blessing wait on my Beverley, my loved Bev——

MRS. MALAPROP. Hussy! I'll choke the word in your throat! Come along—come along.

[*Exeunt severally;* CAPTAIN ABSOLUTE *kissing his hand to* LYDIA, MRS. MALAPROP *stopping her from speaking.*]

SCENE 4. ACRES' *lodgings.*

[ACRES, *as just dressed, and* DAVID.]

ACRES. Indeed, David—do you think I become it so?

DAVID. You are quite another creature, believe me, master, by the mass! An' we've any luck we shall see the Devon monkeyrony [1] in all the printshops in Bath!

ACRES. Dress does make a difference, David.

DAVID. 'Tis all in all, I think. Difference! why, an' you were to go now to Clod Hall, I am certain the old lady wouldn't know you; Master Butler wouldn't believe his own eyes, and Mrs. Pickle would cry, Lard presarve me! Our dairymaid would come giggling to the door, and I warrant Dolly Tester, your honor's favorite, would blush like my waistcoat.

¹ **monkeyrony:** macaroni, a dandy.

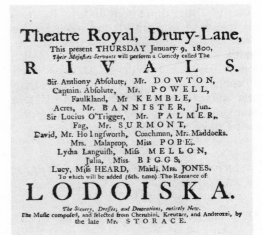

Theater program for *The Rivals.*

Oons! I'll hold a gallon, there an't a dog in the house but would bark, and I question whether Phillis would wag a hair of her tail!

ACRES. Ay, David, there's nothing like polishing.

DAVID. So I says of your honor's boots; but the boy never heeds me!

ACRES. But, David, has Mr. De-la-grace been here? I must rub up my balancing and chasing and boring. [2]

DAVID. I'll call again, sir.

ACRES. Do—and see if there are any letters for me at the post office.

DAVID. I will. By the mass, I can't help looking at your head! If I hadn't been by at the cooking, I wish I may die if I should have known the dish again myself. *(Exit.)*

ACRES (*practicing a dancing step*). Sink, slide—coupee. [3] Confound the first inventors of cotillions! say I—they are as bad as algebra to us country gentlemen. I can walk a minuet easy enough when I am forced—and I have been accounted a good stick in a country dance. Odds jigs and tabors! I never valued your crossover to couple—figure in—right and left— and I'd foot it with e'er a captain in the

² **balancing . . . boring:** terms used in dancing.
³ **coupee:** a forward motion in dancing.

county! But these outlandish heathen allemandes[1] and cotillions are quite beyond me! I shall never prosper at 'em, that's sure. Mine are true-born English legs—they don't understand their curst French lingo—their *pas* this, and *pas* that, and *pas* t'other! Damn me!—my feet don't like to be called paws! no, 'tis certain I have most anti-Gallican toes!

[*Enter* SERVANT.]

SERVANT. Here is Sir Lucius O'Trigger to wait on you, sir.

ACRES. Show him in.

[*Exit* SERVANT. *Enter* SIR LUCIUS O'TRIGGER.]

SIR LUCIUS. Mr. Acres, I am delighted to embrace you.

ACRES. My dear Sir Lucius, I kiss your hands.

SIR LUCIUS. Pray, my friend, what has brought you so suddenly to Bath?

ACRES. Faith! I have followed Cupid's Jack-a-lantern[2] and find myself in a quagmire at last. In short, I have been very ill used, Sir Lucius. I don't choose to mention names, but look on me as on a very ill-used gentleman.

SIR LUCIUS. Pray what is the case? I ask no names.

ACRES. Mark me, Sir Lucius, I fall as deep as need be in love with a young lady —her friends take my part—I follow her to Bath—send word of my arrival; and receive answer that the lady is to be otherwise disposed of. This, Sir Lucius, I call being ill used.

SIR LUCIUS. Very ill, upon my conscience. Pray, can you divine the cause of it?

ACRES. Why, there's the matter; she has another lover, one Beverley, who, I am told, is now in Bath. Odds slanders and lies! He must be at the bottom of it.

SIR LUCIUS. A rival in the case, is there? And you think he has supplanted you unfairly?

ACRES. Unfairly! to be sure he has. He never could have done it fairly.

SIR LUCIUS. Then sure you know what is to be done!

ACRES. Not I, upon my soul!

SIR LUCIUS. We wear no swords here,[3] but you understand me.

ACRES. What! fight him?

SIR LUCIUS. Ay, to be sure: what can I mean else?

ACRES. But he has given me no provocation.

SIR LUCIUS. Now, I think he has given you the greatest provocation in the world. Can a man commit a more heinous offense against another man than to fall in love with the same woman? Oh, by my soul! it is the most unpardonable breach of friendship.

ACRES. Breach of friendship! ay, ay; but I have no acquaintance with this man. I never saw him in my life.

SIR LUCIUS. That's no argument at all— he has the less right then to take such a liberty.

ACRES. Gad, that's true—I grow full of anger, Sir Lucius! I fire apace! Odds hilts and blades! I find a man may have a deal of valor in him and not know it! But couldn't I contrive to have a little right on my side?

SIR LUCIUS. What the devil signifies right when your honor is concerned? Do you think Achilles, or my little Alexander the Great, ever inquired where the right lay? No, by my soul, they drew their broadswords and left the lazy sons of peace to settle the justice of it.

ACRES. Your words are a grenadier's march to my heart! I believe courage must be catching! I certainly do feel a kind of valor rising as it were—a kind of courage, as I may say. Odds flints, pans, and triggers! I'll challenge him directly.

SIR LUCIUS. Ah, my little friend, if I had Blunderbuss Hall here, I could show you a range of ancestry, in the old O'Trigger

---

[1] **allemandes:** lively German dances.
[2] **Jack-a-lantern:** will o' the wisp.

[3] **We . . . here:** Gentlemen could not wear swords at Bath. This rule was aimed at the fashionable habit of dueling.

line, that would furnish the new room; [1] every one of whom had killed his man! For though the mansion house and dirty acres have slipped through my fingers, I thank heaven our honor and the family pictures are as fresh as ever.

ACRES. O, Sir Lucius! I have had ancestors too! Every man of 'em colonel or captain in the militia! Odds barrels! Say no more—I'm braced for it. The thunder of your words has soured the milk of human kindness in my breast. Zounds! as the man in the play says, "I could do such deeds!" [2]

SIR LUCIUS. Come, come, there must be no passion at all in the case—these things should always be done civilly.

ACRES. I must be in a passion, Sir Lucius —I must be in a rage. Dear Sir Lucius, let me be in a rage, if you love me. Come, here's pen and paper. *(Sits down to write)* I would the ink were red! Indite, I say, indite! How shall I begin? Odds bullets and blades! I'll write a good bold hand, however.

SIR LUCIUS. Pray compose yourself.

ACRES. Come—now, shall I begin with an oath? Do, Sir Lucius, let me begin with a damme.

SIR LUCIUS. Pho! pho! do the thing decently, and like a Christian. Begin now— *Sir——*

ACRES. That's too civil by half.

SIR LUCIUS. *To prevent the confusion that might arise——*

ACRES. Well——

SIR LUCIUS. *From our both addressing the same lady——*

ACRES. Ay, there's the reason—*same lady*—well——

SIR LUCIUS. *I shall expect the honor of your company——*

ACRES. Zounds! I'm not asking him to dinner.

SIR LUCIUS. Pray be easy.

ACRES. Well, then, *honor of your company——*

---

[1] **new room:** new assembly room or ballroom.
[2] **I . . . deeds!:** Perhaps a misquotation of Macbeth's "I have done the deed!"

SIR LUCIUS. *To settle our pretensions——*

ACRES. Well.

SIR LUCIUS. Let me see, ay, King's-Mead-Fields [3] will do—*in King's-Mead-Fields.*

ACRES. So, that's done. Well, I'll fold it up presently; my own crest—a hand and dagger shall be the seal.

SIR LUCIUS. You see now this little explanation will put a stop at once to all confusion or misunderstanding that might arise between you.

ACRES. Ay, we fight to prevent any misunderstanding.

SIR LUCIUS. Now, I'll leave you to fix your own time. Take my advice, and you'll decide it this evening if you can; then let the worst come of it, 'twill be off your mind tomorrow.

ACRES. Very true.

SIR LUCIUS. So I shall see nothing of you, unless it be by letter, till the evening. I would do myself the honor to carry your message; but, to tell you a secret, I believe I shall have just such another affair on my own hands. There is a gay captain here, who put a jest on me lately, at the expense of my country, and I only want to fall in with the gentleman, to call him out.

ACRES. By my valor, I should like to see you fight first! Odds life! I should like to see you kill him, if it was only to get a little lesson.

SIR LUCIUS. I shall be very proud of instructing you. Well for the present—but remember now, when you meet your antagonist, do everything in a mild and agreeable manner. Let your courage be as keen, but at the same time as polished, as your sword. *(Exeunt severally.)*

---

[3] **King's-Mead-Fields:** an outlying area of Bath, selected to prevent the authorities from discovering and stopping the duel.

FOR STUDY AND DISCUSSION

1. In Act II the threads of the plot are pulled together so that we see the problems Jack Absolute's masquerade as Ensign Beverley has created for him. Do you think he could have satisfied all parties concerned by making a

clean breast of his deception at the beginning of Act III? Do you think he continues his dual role mainly to please Lydia or to please himself?

2. In Act III Jack Absolute enjoys playing the penitent son with his father. In a sense, he is being all that his father asked him to be; yet Sir Anthony is again impatient with him. Why? How does this scene support the theme of the play?

3. Discuss the irony in each of the following exchanges: in the scene between Absolute and Mrs. Malaprop, in the scene between Absolute and Lydia, in the conversation between David and his master Acres, and in that of Acres and Sir Lucius.

4. In the scene between Absolute and Lydia the difference between the mask and the man seems to be narrowing. At what point in the action did this narrowing become inevitable?

5. What details does Sheridan give to suggest that the role of the gentleman does not become Bob Acres? How does he suggest that Sir Lucius O'Trigger is not the courageous dueler he pretends to be? Part of the humor in this play derives from the characters' unawareness of their own frailties and their revelation of that ignorance through their own words. Cite specific examples of this type of humor in Act III.

FOR COMPOSITION

In addition to the obvious conflicts between various characters in the play, would you say that Sheridan also implies that each character is his or her own worst rival? Explain your answer in a brief composition in which you comment particularly on one or two of the major and minor characters.

ACT IV

SCENE 1. ACRES' *lodgings.*

[ACRES *and* DAVID.]

DAVID. Then, by the mass, sir! I would do no such thing—ne'er a St. Lucius O'Trigger in the kingdom should make me fight, when I wasn't so minded. Oons! what will the old lady say, when she hears o't?

ACRES. Ah! David, if you had heard Sir Lucius! Odds sparks and flames! he would have roused your valor.

DAVID. Not he, indeed. I hate such bloodthirsty cormorants. Look'ee, master, if you wanted a bout at boxing, quarterstaff, or shortstaff, I should never be the man to bid you cry off: but for your curst sharps and snaps,[1] I never knew any good come of 'em.

ACRES. But my honor, David, my honor! I must be very careful of my honor.

DAVID. Ay, by the mass! and I would be very careful of it; and I think in return my honor couldn't do less than to be very careful of me.

ACRES. Odds blades! David, no gentleman will ever risk the loss of his honor!

DAVID. I say then, it would be but civil in honor never to risk the loss of a gentleman. Look'ee, master, this honor seems to me to be a marvelous false friend: ay, truly, a very courtierlike servant. Put the case, I was a gentleman (which, thank God, no one can say of me); well—my honor makes me quarrel with another gentleman of my acquaintance. So—we fight. (Pleasant enough that!) Boh; I kill him (the more's my luck!) now, pray who gets the profit of it? Why, my honor. But put the case that he kills me! by the mass! I go to the worms, and my honor whips over to my enemy.

ACRES. No, David—in that case!—odds crowns and laurels! your honor follows you to the grave.

DAVID. Now, that's just the place where I could make a shift to do without it.

ACRES. Zounds! David, you are a coward! It doesn't become my valor to listen to you. What, shall I disgrace my ancestors? Think of that, David—think what it would be to disgrace my ancestors!

DAVID. Under favor, the surest way of not disgracing them, is to keep as long as you can out of their company. Look'ee now, master, to go to them in such haste—with an ounce of lead in your brains—I should think might as well be let alone. Our ancestors are very good kind of folks;

[1] **sharps and snaps:** swords and pistols.

but they are the last people I should choose to have a visiting acquaintance with.

ACRES. But, David, now, you don't think there is such very, very, very great danger, hey? Odds life! people often fight without any mischief done!

DAVID. By the mass, I think 'tis ten to one against you! Oons! here to meet some lionhearted fellow, I warrant, with his damned double-barreled swords and cut-and-thrust pistols! Lord bless us! it makes me tremble to think o't. Those be such desperate bloody-minded weapons! Well, I never could abide 'em—from a child I never could fancy 'em! I suppose there an't been so merciless a beast in the world as your loaded pistol!

ACRES. Zounds! I won't be afraid! Odds fire and fury! you shan't make me afraid. Here is the challenge, and I have sent for my dear friend Jack Absolute to carry it for me.

DAVID. Ay, i' the name of mischief, let him be the messenger. For my part I wouldn't lend a hand to it for the best horse in your stable. By the mass! it don't look like another letter! It is, as I may say, a designing and malicious-looking letter; and I warrant smells of gunpowder like a soldier's pouch! Oons! I wouldn't swear it mayn't go off!

ACRES. Out, you poltroon! you han't the valor of a grasshopper.

DAVID. Well, I say no more—'twill be sad news, to be sure, at Clod Hall! But I ha' done. How Phillis will howl when she hears of it! Ah, poor bitch, she little thinks what shooting her master's going after! And I warrant old Crop, who has carried your honor, field and road, these ten years, will curse the hour he was born. (Whimpering)

ACRES. It won't do, David. I am determined to fight—so get along, you coward, while I'm in the mind.

[Enter SERVANT.]

SERVANT. Captain Absolute, sir.

ACRES. Oh! show him up. (Exit SERVANT.)

DAVID. Well, Heaven send we be all alive this time tomorrow.

ACRES. What's that? Don't provoke me, David!

DAVID. Good-by, master. (Whimpering)

ACRES. Get along, you cowardly, dastardly, croaking raven!

[Exit DAVID, enter CAPTAIN ABSOLUTE.]

ABSOLUTE. What's the matter, Bob?

ACRES. A vile, sheep-hearted blockhead! If I hadn't the valor of St. George and the dragon to boot——

ABSOLUTE. But what did you want with me, Bob?

ACRES. Oh! There——(Gives him the challenge)

ABSOLUTE (aside to Ensign Beverley). So, what's going on now? (Aloud) Well, what's this?

ACRES. A challenge!

ABSOLUTE. Indeed! Why, you won't fight him; will you, Bob?

ACRES. Egad, but I will, Jack. Sir Lucius has wrought me to it. He has left me full of rage—and I'll fight this evening, that so much good passion mayn't be wasted.

ABSOLUTE. But what have I to do with this?

ACRES. Why, as I think you know somehow of this fellow, I want you to find him out for me and give him this mortal defiance.

ABSOLUTE. Well, give it to me, and trust me he gets it.

ACRES. Thank you, my dear friend, my dear Jack; but it is giving you a great deal of trouble.

ABSOLUTE. Not in the least—I beg you won't mention it. No trouble in the world, I assure you.

ACRES. You are very kind. What it is to have a friend! You couldn't be my second, could you, Jack?

ABSOLUTE. Why no, Bob—not in this affair—it would not be quite so proper.

ACRES. Well, then, I must get my friend Sir Lucius. I shall have your good wishes, however, Jack?

ABSOLUTE. Whenever he meets you, believe me.

Theater review from a
London newspaper, 1794.

[*Reenter* SERVANT.]

SERVANT. Sir Anthony Absolute is below, inquiring for the captain.

ABSOLUTE. I'll come instantly. (*Exit*
SERVANT.) Well, my little hero, success
attend you. (*Going*)

ACRES. Stay—stay, Jack. If Beverley
should ask you what kind of a man your
friend Acres is, do tell him I am a devil of
a fellow—will you, Jack?

ABSOLUTE. To be sure I shall. I'll say
you are a determined dog—hey, Bob?

ACRES. Ah, do, do—and if that frightens
him, egad, perhaps he mayn't come. So
tell him I generally kill a man a week; will
you, Jack?

ABSOLUTE. I will, I will; I'll say you are
called in the country Fighting Bob.

ACRES. Right—right—'tis all to prevent
mischief; for I don't want to take his life
if I clear my honor.

ABSOLUTE. No—that's very kind of you.

ACRES. Why, you don't wish me to kill
him—do you, Jack?

ABSOLUTE. No, upon my soul, I do not.
But a devil of a fellow, hey? (*Going*)

ACRES. True, true—but stay—stay, Jack
—you may add, that you never saw me in
such a rage before—a most devouring
rage!

ABSOLUTE. I will, I will.

ACRES. Remember, Jack—a determined
dog!

ABSOLUTE. Ay ay, Fighting Bob!
(*Exeunt severally.*)

SCENE 2. MRS. MALAPROP'S *lodgings*.

[MRS. MALAPROP *and* LYDIA.]

MRS. MALAPROP. Why, thou perverse
one—tell me what you can object to him?
Isn't he a handsome man?—tell me that.
A genteel man? a pretty figure of a man?

LYDIA (*aside*). She little thinks whom
she is praising! (*Aloud*) So is Beverley,
ma'am.

MRS. MALAPROP. No caparisons,[1] miss,
if you please. Caparisons don't become a
young woman. No! Captain Absolute is
indeed a fine gentleman!

LYDIA. Ay, the Captain Absolute you
have seen. (*Aside*)

MRS. MALAPROP. Then he's so well bred
—so full of alacrity and adulation—and
has so much to say for himself—in such
good language, too! His physiognomy[2]
so grammatical! Then his presence is so
noble! I protest, when I saw him, I thought
of what Hamlet says in the play:

"Hesperian curls—the front of Job himself!—

An eye, like March, to threaten at command!—

A station, like Harry Mercury, new—"[3]

[1] **caparisons:** comparisons.
[2] **physiognomy:** phraseology.
[3] The original reads:

"Hyperion's curls, the front of Jove himself,
An eye like Mars, to threaten and command,
A station like the herald Mercury,
New-lighted on a heaven-kissing hill."
(*Hamlet*, Act III, Scene iv)

Something about kissing—on a hill—however, the similitude struck me directly.

LYDIA. How enraged she'll be presently, when she discovers her mistake! (Aside)

[Enter SERVANT.]

SERVANT. Sir Anthony and Captain Absolute are below, ma'am.

MRS. MALAPROP. Show them up here. (Exit SERVANT.) Now, Lydia, I insist on your behaving as becomes a young woman. Show your good breeding, at least, though you have forgot your duty.

LYDIA. Madam, I have told you my resolution! I shall not only give him no encouragement, but I won't even speak to or look at him. (Flings herself into a chair, with her face from the door)

[Enter SIR ANTHONY ABSOLUTE and CAPTAIN ABSOLUTE.]

SIR ANTHONY. Here we are, Mrs. Malaprop; come to mitigate the frowns of unrelenting beauty, and difficulty enough I had to bring this fellow. I don't know what's the matter; but if I had not held him by force, he'd have given me the slip.

MRS. MALAPROP. You have infinite trouble, Sir Anthony, in the affair. I am ashamed for the cause! (Aside to LYDIA) Lydia, Lydia, rise, I beseech you! Pay your respects!

SIR ANTHONY. I hope, madam, that Miss Languish has reflected on the worth of this gentleman, and the regard due to her aunt's choice, and my alliance. (Aside to CAPTAIN ABSOLUTE) Now, Jack, speak to her.

ABSOLUTE (aside). What the devil shall I do! (Aside to SIR ANTHONY) You see, sir, she won't even look at me whilst you are here. I knew she wouldn't! I told you so. Let me entreat you, sir, to leave us together! (Seems to expostulate with his father)

LYDIA (aside). I wonder I han't heard my aunt exclaim yet! Sure she can't have looked at him! Perhaps the regimentals [1]

[1] regimentals: military uniforms.

are alike, and she is something blind.

SIR ANTHONY. I say, sir, I won't stir a foot yet!

MRS. MALAPROP. I am sorry to say, Sir Anthony, that my affluence [2] over my niece is very small. (Aside to LYDIA) Turn round, Lydia: I blush for you!

SIR ANTHONY. May I not flatter myself that Miss Languish will assign what cause of dislike she can have to my son! (Aside to CAPTAIN ABSOLUTE) Why don't you begin, Jack? Speak, you puppy—speak!

MRS. MALAPROP. It is impossible, Sir Anthony, she can have any. She will not say she has. (Aside to LYDIA) Answer, hussy! why don't you answer?

SIR ANTHONY. Then, madam, I trust that a childish and hasty predilection will be no bar to Jack's happiness. (Aside to CAPTAIN ABSOLUTE) Zounds! sirrah! why don't you speak?

LYDIA (aside). I think my lover seems as little inclined to conversation as myself. How strangely blind my aunt must be!

ABSOLUTE. Hem! hem! madam—hem! (Attempts to speak, then returns to SIR ANTHONY) Faith! sir, I am so confounded—and—so—so—confused! I told you I should be so, sir—I knew it. The—the—tremor of my passion entirely takes away my presence of mind.

SIR ANTHONY. But it don't take away your voice, fool, does it? Go up, and speak to her directly!

[CAPTAIN ABSOLUTE makes signs to MRS. MALAPROP to leave them together.]

MRS. MALAPROP. Sir Anthony, shall we leave them together? (Aside to LYDIA) Ah! you stubborn little vixen!

SIR ANTHONY. Not yet, ma'am, not yet! —(Aside to CAPTAIN ABSOLUTE) What the devil are you at? unlock your jaws, sirrah, or——

ABSOLUTE (aside). Now Heaven send she may be too sullen to look round! I must disguise my voice. (Draws near LYDIA and speaks in a low hoarse tone)

[2] affluence: influence.

Will not Miss Languish lend an ear to the mild accents of true love? Will not——

SIR ANTHONY. What the devil ails the fellow? Why don't you speak out?—not stand croaking like a frog in a quinsy!

ABSOLUTE. The—the—excess of my awe, and my—my—modesty, quite choke me!

SIR ANTHONY. Ah! your modesty again! I'll tell you what, Jack, if you don't speak out directly, and glibly too, I shall be in such a rage! Mrs. Malaprop, I wish the lady would favor us with something more than a side-front.

[MRS. MALAPROP *seems to chide* LYDIA.]

ABSOLUTE (*aside*). So all will out, I see! (*Goes up to* LYDIA, *speaks softly*) Be not surprised, my Lydia, suppress all surprise at present.

LYDIA (*aside*). Heavens! 'tis Beverley's voice! Sure he can't have imposed on Sir Anthony too! (*Looks round by degrees, then starts up*) Is this possible?—my Beverley! How can this be?—my Beverley?

ABSOLUTE. Ah! 'tis all over. (*Aside*)

SIR ANTHONY. Beverley!—the devil—Beverley! What can the girl mean? This is my son, Jack Absolute.

MRS. MALAPROP. For shame, hussy! for shame! your head runs so on that fellow, that you have him always in your eyes! Beg Captain Absolute's pardon directly.

LYDIA. I see no Captain Absolute, but my loved Beverley!

SIR ANTHONY. Zounds! the girl's mad! Her brain's turned by reading.

MRS. MALAPROP. O' my conscience, I believe so! What do you mean by Beverley, hussy? You saw Captain Absolute before today; there he is—your husband that shall be.

LYDIA. With all my soul, ma'am—when I refuse my Beverley——

SIR ANTHONY. Oh! she's as mad as Bedlam![1] Or has this fellow been playing us a rogue's trick! Come here, sirrah, who

---

[1] **Bedlam:** a London hospital for the insane.

the devil are you?

ABSOLUTE. Faith, sir, I am not quite clear myself; but I'll endeavor to recollect.

SIR ANTHONY. Are you my son or not? Answer for your mother, you dog, if you won't for me.

MRS. MALAPROP. Ay, sir, who are you? O mercy! I begin to suspect!

ABSOLUTE (*aside*). Ye powers of impudence, befriend me!—(*Aloud*) Sir Anthony, most assuredly I am your wife's son; and that I sincerely believe myself to be yours also, I hope my duty has always shown. Mrs. Malaprop, I am your most respectful admirer, and shall be proud to add affectionate nephew. I need not tell my Lydia that she sees her faithful Beverley, who knowing the singular generosity of her temper, assumed that name and station, which has proved a test of the most disinterested love, which he now hopes to enjoy in a more elevated character.

LYDIA. So!—there will be no elopement after all! (*Sullenly*)

SIR ANTHONY. Upon my soul, Jack, thou art a very impudent fellow! To do you justice, I think I never saw a piece of more consummate assurance!

ABSOLUTE. Oh, you flatter me, sir—you compliment—'tis my modesty, you know, sir—my modesty that has stood in my way.

SIR ANTHONY. Well, I am glad you are not the dull, insensible varlet you pretended to be, however! I'm glad you have made a fool of your father, you dog—I am. So this was your *penitence,* your *duty* and *obedience!* I thought it was damned sudden! *You never heard their names before,* not you! *What, the Languishes of Worcestershire,* hey? *If you could please me in the affair it was all you desired!* Ah! you dissembling villain! What! (*Pointing to* LYDIA) *She squints, don't she?—a little red-haired girl!*—hey? Why, you hypocritical young rascal! I wonder you a'n't ashamed to hold up your head!

[SCENE 2 CONTINUES ON PAGE 399.]

ENGLISH PAINTING

Reynolds, Gainsborough, and Their Circle

Out of the need for sound instruction in art and for regular exhibitions of pictures grew an important English institution called the Royal Academy. Founded in 1768, its membership was limited at first to forty eminent artists, known as Royal Academicians, but soon thirty Associates were added. The patronage of the king gave great prestige to the Academy and new dignity to the artistic profession.

On prize-giving days, the Academy's first president, Sir Joshua Reynolds, delivered "discourses" which he hoped would be useful in elevating taste. He stressed that in order to learn the "Grand Style," students must borrow from a select group of Old Masters. Reynolds's own admiration for them is reflected in his *Self-Portrait* (PLATE 1). The strong light falling on the face and hands is a compositional device taken from Rembrandt. The elegant pose of the body fits into a triangle, the shape most favored by Raphael and Titian. But Reynolds's deepest veneration was reserved for Michelangelo, the Italian master whose bust we see in the background.

A man of high ambition as well as culture, Reynolds knew all the famous writers of the period, particularly those in the circle of Samuel Johnson. In his portrait of the great man (PLATE 2) Reynolds shows Dr. Johnson's bulky figure looming in the front of the picture, his head tilted quizzically. Physical infirmities account in part for his uncouth appearance; his left eye, for instance, had been blinded by a disease. But beneath such disfigurements was a tender and generous being who was greatly loved by his friends.

John Zoffany painted another kind of portrait. Late eighteenth-century critics frequently praised David Garrick's superb interpretation of Macbeth and the performance of the imposing Hannah Pritchard as Lady Macbeth. In *Garrick and Mrs. Pritchard* (PLATE 3), Zoffany chose the moment in Act II when Macbeth grows pale and distraught as vivid memories of the murders work on him. Despite the actors' frozen attitudes, their facial expressions are so convincing that we can almost hear Lady Macbeth rail:

"Infirm of purpose! Give me the daggers." Notice that the actors wear contemporary costume and that the scene is played inside a murky Gothic palace, whereas Shakespeare's play was set in eleventh-century Scotland.

According to the Royal Academy, scenes of noble human deeds were the proper subject for the highest type of art. But Thomas Gainsborough cared little for such dictates, and in spurning them he did much to introduce landscape into English art. In *John Plampin of Chadacre* (PLATE 4), one of his early works, portraiture and landscape are combined. A gentleman whose family had lived in Suffolk for two centuries, Plampin is shown resting while on a walk along a country road. The pose is so casual that Plampin almost seems a part of his natural surroundings. His torso follows the line of the tree trunk, and his sprawling legs remind us of spreading branches, while their contours repeat the gentle curves of the distant hills.

Gainsborough's later portrait style was more elegant and formal, for despite his distaste for rules, he felt compelled to idealize his subjects to conform with the conventions of British portraiture. In *The Honorable Mrs. Graham* (PLATE 5), a magnificently attired lady stands erect, with her left elbow resting on a pedestal from which two fluted columns rise. According to Reynolds's *Discourses,* such female sitters should be portrayed with the proportions of goddesses in classical statues. So Gainsborough lengthened Mrs. Graham's neck and hands and narrowed her shoulders to make her appear tall and willowy. Notice, too, the marble-like quality of her skin. Yet Mrs. Graham averts her gaze and pouts ever so slightly, as if anxious to be through with the ordeal of posing. An elegant slipper peeps out from beneath her satin dress, adding just the right piquant touch. Like many of Gainsborough's other portraits of the 1770's, this one is distinguished for its light, delicate brushwork: the feathers and ruff around Mrs. Graham's neck, for instance, seem buoyed up by air.

While Gainsborough regretfully turned to more society portraiture as a means of earning a comfortable living, his contemporary Richard Wilson devoted himself entirely to landscape painting, even though this meant a life of poverty. Some of Wilson's landscapes, however, were intended as idealized "portraits" of the estates of wealthy patrons. *Wilton House from the South-East* (PLATE 6), for instance, shows the picturesque surroundings of the seat of the Earls of Pembroke. The light and atmosphere particularly interested Wilson. Human figures are included, but they are only of secondary importance. Even the house, one of four different views painted by Wilson, has been pushed into the background at the side of the composition.

Wilson composed his picture in broad masses of light and shade, some of them reflected in the tranquil pond. Silhouettes of trees and figures stand out in the foreground against the light concentrated in the sky and on the building. Moisture hangs so heavily in the air that we can readily believe the girl needs her parasol as protection from the sun-warmed haze.

PLATE 1. SIR JOSHUA REYNOLDS (1723–1792): *Self-Portrait*. About 1773. Oil on panel, 50 x 40 inches. (Reproduced by permission of the Royal Academy of Arts, London)

PLATE 2. SIR JOSHUA REYNOLDS (1723–1792): *Dr. Johnson*. 1772. Oil on canvas, $29\frac{1}{2}$ x 25 inches. (Reproduced by courtesy of the Trustees, The Tate Gallery, London)

394

PLATE 3. JOHN ZOFFANY (1733–1810): *Garrick and Mrs. Pritchard*. About 1776. Oil on canvas, 40 x 50 inches. (Garrick Club Collection, London)

PLATE 4. THOMAS GAINSBOROUGH (1727–1788): *John Plampin of Chadacre*. 1755. Oil
on canvas, 19¾ x 23¾ inches. (Reproduced by courtesy of the Trustees, The National Gallery,
London)

PLATE 5. THOMAS GAINSBOROUGH (1727–1788): *The Honorable Mrs. Graham*. 1775–76. Oil on canvas, 92 x 59½ inches. (The National Gallery of Scotland, Edinburgh)

PLATE 6. RICHARD WILSON (1714–1782): *Wilton House from the South-East*. About 1758–60. Oil on canvas, 39 x 56¾ inches. (Collection of Mr. and Mrs. Paul Mellon)

[CONTINUED FROM PAGE 390]

ABSOLUTE. 'Tis with difficulty, sir. I am confused—very much confused, as you must perceive.

MRS. MALAPROP. O Lud! Sir Anthony! —a new light breaks in upon me!—hey!— how! what! captain, did you write the letters then? What—am I to thank you for the elegant compilation[1] of *an old weather-beaten she-dragon*—hey? O mercy! Was it you that reflected on my parts of speech?

ABSOLUTE. Dear sir, my modesty will be overpowered at last if you don't assist me. I shall certainly not be able to stand it!

SIR ANTHONY. Come, come, Mrs. Malaprop, we must forget and forgive; odds life; matters have taken so clever a turn all of a sudden, that I could find in my heart to be so good-humored! and so gallant! hey! Mrs. Malaprop!

MRS. MALAPROP. Well, Sir Anthony, since you desire it, we will not anticipate the past—so mind, young people—our retrospection will be all to the future.[2]

SIR ANTHONY. Come, we must leave them together; Mrs. Malaprop, they long to fly into each other's arms, I warrant! Jack, isn't the cheek as I said, hey?—and the eye, you rogue?—and the lip, hey? Come, Mrs. Malaprop, we'll not disturb their tenderness—theirs is the time of life for happiness! "Youth's the season made for joy—"[3] (*Sings*)—hey!—Odds life! I'm in such spirits, I don't know what I could not do! Permit me, ma'am (*Gives his hand to* MRS. MALAPROP) Tol-de-rol—'gad, I should like to have a little fooling myself— Tol-de-rol! de-rol.

[*Exit, singing and handing* MRS. MALAPROP; LYDIA *sits sullenly in her chair*.]

[1] **compilation:** appellation.
[2] **anticipate . . . future:** She has reversed the meanings of *anticipate* and *retrospection*.
[3] **Youth's . . . joy:** the first line in John Gay's *The Beggar's Opera*, then very popular.

ABSOLUTE (*aside*). So much thought bodes me no good. (*Aloud*) So grave, Lydia!

LYDIA. Sir!

ABSOLUTE (*aside*). So!—egad! I thought as much!—that damned monosyllable has froze me! (*Aloud*) What, Lydia, now that we are as happy in our friends' consent as in our mutual vows——

LYDIA. Friends' consent indeed! (*Peevishly*)

ABSOLUTE. Come, come, we must lay aside some of our romance—a little wealth and comfort may be endured after all. And for your fortune, the lawyers shall make such settlements as——

LYDIA. Lawyers! I hate lawyers!

ABSOLUTE. Nay, then, we will not wait for their lingering forms, but instantly procure the license, and——

LYDIA. The license! I hate license!

ABSOLUTE. Oh, my love! be not so unkind!—thus let me entreat——(*Kneeling*)

LYDIA. Psha!—what signifies kneeling, when you know I must have you?

ABSOLUTE (*rising*). Nay, madam, there shall be no constraint upon your inclinations, I promise you. If I have lost your heart—I resign the rest—(*Aside*) 'Gad, I must try what a little spirit will do.

LYDIA (*rising*). Then, sir, let me tell you, the interest you had there was acquired by a mean, unmanly imposition, and deserves the punishment of fraud. What, you have been treating me like a child! humoring my romance! and laughing, I suppose, at your success!

ABSOLUTE. You wrong me, Lydia, you wrong me—only hear——

LYDIA. So, while I fondly imagined we were deceiving my relations, and flattered myself that I should outwit and incense them all—behold my hopes are to be crushed at once, by my aunt's consent and approbation—and I am myself the only dupe at last! (*Walking about in a heat*) But here, sir, here is the picture— Beverley's picture—(*Taking a miniature from her bosom*) which I have worn, night and day, in spite of threats and entreaties! There, sir *(Flings it to him),* and be assured I throw the original from my heart as easily.

ABSOLUTE. Nay, nay, ma'am, we will not differ as to that. Here *(Taking out a picture),* here is Miss Lydia Languish. What a difference! Ay, there is the heavenly assenting smile that first gave soul and spirit to my hopes! Those are the lips which sealed a vow, as yet scarce dry in Cupid's calendar! And there the half-resentful blush that would have checked the ardor of my thanks! Well, all that's past?—all over indeed! There, madam—in beauty, that copy is not equal to you, but in my mind its merit over the original, in being still the same, is such—that—I cannot find it my heart to part with it. *(Puts it up again)*

LYDIA *(softening).* 'Tis your own doing, sir—I—I, I suppose you are perfectly satisfied.

ABSOLUTE. O, most certainly—sure, now, this is much better than being in love! —ha! ha! ha!—there's some spirit in this! What signifies breaking some scores of solemn promises: all that's of no consequence, you know. To be sure people will say that miss don't know her own mind, but never mind that! Or, perhaps, they may be ill-natured enough to hint, that the gentleman grew tired of the lady and forsook her—but don't let that fret you.

LYDIA. There is no bearing his insolence. *(Bursts into tears)*

[*Reenter* MRS. MALAPROP *and* SIR ANTHONY ABSOLUTE.]

MRS. MALAPROP. Come, we must interrupt your billing and cooing awhile.

LYDIA. This is worse than your treachery and deceit, you base ingrate! *(Sobbing)*

SIR ANTHONY. What the devil's the matter now? Zounds! Mrs. Malaprop, this is the oddest billing and cooing I ever heard! But what the deuce is the meaning of it? I am quite astonished!

ABSOLUTE. Ask the lady, sir.

MRS. MALAPROP. O mercy! I'm quite

analyzed,[1] for my part! Why, Lydia, what is the reason of this?

LYDIA. Ask the gentleman, ma'am.

SIR ANTHONY. Zounds! I shall be in a frenzy! Why, Jack, you are not come out to be anyone else, are you?

MRS. MALAPROP. Ay, sir, there's no more trick, is there? You are not like Cerberus,[2] three gentlemen at once, are you?

ABSOLUTE. You'll not let me speak—I say the lady can account for this much better than I can.

LYDIA. Ma'am, you once commanded me never to think of Beverley again—there is the man—I now obey you: for, from this moment, I renounce him forever. *(Exit.)*

MRS. MALAPROP. O mercy! and miracles! what a turn here is—why, sure, captain, you haven't behaved disrespectfully to my niece?

SIR ANTHONY. Ha! ha! ha!—ha! ha! ha! —now I see it. Ha! ha! ha!—now I see it—you have been too lively, Jack.

ABSOLUTE. Nay, sir, upon my word——

SIR ANTHONY. Come, no lying, —I'm sure 'twas so.

MRS. MALAPROP. O Lud! Sir Anthony! O fy, captain!

ABSOLUTE. Upon my soul, ma'am——

SIR ANTHONY. Come, no excuse, Jack; why, your father, you rogue, was so before you! The blood of the Absolutes was always impatient. Ha! ha! ha! poor little Lydia! why, you've frightened her, you dog, you have.

ABSOLUTE. By all that's good, sir——

SIR ANTHONY. Zounds! say no more, I tell you, Mrs. Malaprop shall make your peace. You must make his peace, Mrs. Malaprop: you must tell her 'tis Jack's way—tell her 'tis all our ways—it runs in the blood of our family! Come away, Jack. Ha! ha! ha! Mrs. Malaprop—a young villain! *(Pushing him out)*

MRS. MALAPROP. O! Sir Anthony! O fy, captain. *(Exeunt severally.)*

---

[1] **analyzed:** paralyzed.
[2] **Cerberus:** the three-headed watchdog of the underworld.

SCENE 3. *The North Parade.*

[*Enter* SIR LUCIUS O'TRIGGER.]

SIR LUCIUS. I wonder where this Captain Absolute hides himself! Upon my conscience! These officers are always in one's way in love affairs: I remember I might have married Lady Dorothy Carmine, if it had not been for a little rogue of a major, who ran away with her before she could get a sight of me! And I wonder too what it is the ladies can see in them to be so fond of them—unless it be a touch of the old serpent in 'em, that makes the little creatures be caught, like vipers, with a bit of red cloth. Ha! isn't this the captain coming?—faith it is! There is a probability of succeeding about that fellow that is mighty provoking! Who the devil is he talking to? (*Steps aside*)

[*Enter* CAPTAIN ABSOLUTE.]

ABSOLUTE (*aside*). To what fine purpose I have been plotting! a noble reward for all my schemes, upon my soul!—a little gypsy! I did not think her romance could have made her so damned absurd either. 'Sdeath, I never was in a worse humor in my life! I could cut my own throat or any other person's with the greatest pleasure in the world!

SIR LUCIUS. Oh, faith! I'm in the luck of it. I never could have found him in a sweeter temper for my purpose—to be sure I'm just come in the nick! Now to enter into conversation with him, and so quarrel genteelly. (*Goes up to* CAPTAIN ABSOLUTE) With regard to that matter, captain, I must beg leave to differ in opinion with you.

ABSOLUTE. Upon my word, then, you must be a very subtle disputant—because, sir, I happened just then to be giving no opinion at all.

SIR LUCIUS. That's no reason. For, give me leave to tell you, a man may think an untruth as well as speak one.

ABSOLUTE. Very true, sir; but if a man never utters his thoughts, I should think they might stand a chance of escaping controversy.

SIR LUCIUS. Then, sir, you differ in opinion with me, which amounts to the same thing.

ABSOLUTE. Hark'ee, Sir Lucius; if I had not before known you to be a gentleman, upon my soul, I should not have discovered it at this interview: for what you can drive at, unless you mean to quarrel with me, I cannot conceive!

SIR LUCIUS. I humbly thank you, sir, for the quickness of your apprehension. (*Bowing*) You have named the very thing I would be at.

ABSOLUTE. Very well, sir; I shall certainly not balk your inclinations. But I should be glad you would be pleased to explain your motives.

SIR LUCIUS. Pray, sir, be easy; the quarrel is a very pretty quarrel as it stands; we should only spoil it by trying to explain it. However, your memory is very short, or you could not have forgot an affront you passed on me within this week. So, no more, but name your time and place.

ABSOLUTE. Well, sir, since you are so bent on it, the sooner the better; let it be this evening—here, by the Spring Gardens. We shall scarcely be interrupted.

SIR LUCIUS. Faith! that same interruption in affairs of this nature shows very great ill breeding. I don't know what's the reason, but in England if a thing of this kind gets wind, people make such a pother, that a gentleman can never fight in peace and quietness. However, if it's the same to you, I should take it as a particular kindness if you'd let us meet in King's-Mead-Fields, as a little business will call me there about six o'clock, and I may despatch both matters at once.

ABSOLUTE. 'Tis the same to me exactly. A little after six, then, we will discuss this matter more seriously.

SIR LUCIUS. If you please, sir; there will be very pretty small-sword light, though it won't do for a long shot. So that matter's settled, and my mind's at ease! (*Exit.*)

[*Enter* FAULKLAND.]

ABSOLUTE. Well met! I was going to look for you. O Faulkland! All the demons of spite and disappointment have conspired against me! I'm so vexed, that if I had not the prospect of a resource in being knocked o' the head by and by, I should scarce have spirits to tell you the cause.

FAULKLAND. What can you mean? Has Lydia changed her mind? I should have thought her duty and inclination would now have pointed to the same object.

ABSOLUTE. Ay, just as the eyes do of a person who squints: when her love-eye was fixed on me, t'other, her eye of duty, was finely obliqued: but when duty bid her point that the same way, off t'other turned on a swivel and secured its retreat with a frown!

FAULKLAND. But what's the resource you——

ABSOLUTE. Oh, to wind up the whole, a good-natured Irishman here has—(*Mimicking* SIR LUCIUS) begged leave to have the pleasure of cutting my throat; and I mean to indulge him—that's all.

FAULKLAND. Prithee, be serious!

ABSOLUTE. 'Tis fact, upon my soul! Sir Lucius O'Trigger—you know him by sight—for some affront, which I am sure I never intended, has obliged me to meet him this evening at six o'clock: 'tis on that account I wished to see you; you must go with me.

FAULKLAND. Nay, there must be some mistake, sure. Sir Lucius shall explain himself, and I dare say matters may be accommodated. But this evening did you say? I wish it had been any other time.

ABSOLUTE. Why? there will be light enough: there will (as Sir Lucius says) be very pretty small-sword light, though it will not do for a long shot. Confound his long shots.

FAULKLAND. But I am myself a good deal ruffled by a difference I have had with Julia. My vile tormenting temper has made me treat her so cruelly that I shall not be myself till we are reconciled.

ABSOLUTE. By heavens! Faulkland, you don't deserve her!

[*Enter* SERVANT, *gives* FAULKLAND *a letter, and exit.*]

FAULKLAND. Oh, Jack! this is from Julia. I dread to open it! I fear it may be to take a last leave—perhaps to bid me return her letters, and restore——Oh, how I suffer for my folly!

ABSOLUTE. Here, let me see. (*Takes the letter and opens it*) Ay, a final sentence, indeed!—'tis all over with you, faith!

FAULKLAND. Nay, Jack, don't keep me in suspense!

ABSOLUTE. Hear then—(*Reads*) *As I am convinced that my dear Faulkland's own reflections have already upbraided him for his last unkindness to me, I will not add a word on the subject. I wish to speak with you as soon as possible. Yours ever and truly.* JULIA. There's stubbornness and resentment for you! (*Gives him the letter*) Why, man, you don't seem one whit happier at this!

FAULKLAND. O yes, I am; but—but—

ABSOLUTE. Confound your buts! you never hear anything that would make another man bless himself, but you immediately damn it with a but!

FAULKLAND. Now, Jack, as you are my friend, own honestly—don't you think there is something forward, something indelicate, in this haste to forgive? Women should never sue for reconciliation: that should always come from us. They should retain their coldness till wooed to kindness; and their pardon, like their love, should "not unsought be won." [1]

ABSOLUTE. I have not patience to listen to you! thou'rt incorrigible! so say no more on the subject. I must go to settle a few matters. Let me see you before six, remember, at my lodgings. A poor industrious devil like me, who have toiled and drudged and plotted to gain my ends, and am at last disappointed by other people's folly, may in pity be allowed to swear and grumble a little; but a captious skeptic in love, a slave to fretfulness and whim,

[1] **"not . . . won":** In Milton's *Paradise Lost* (Book VIII, lines 502–03), Adam speaks of the newly created Eve—"Her virtue, and the conscience of her worth,/That would be wooed, and not unsought be won . . ."

who has no difficulties but of his own creating, is a subject more fit for ridicule than compassion! (*Exit.*)

FAULKLAND. I feel his reproaches; yet I would not change this too exquisite nicety for the gross content with which he tramples on the thorns of love! His engaging me in this duel has started an idea in my head, which I will instantly pursue. I'll use it as the touchstone of Julia's sincerity and disinterestedness. If her love proves pure and sterling ore, my name will rest on it with honor; and once I've stamped it there, I lay aside my doubts for ever! But if the dross of selfishness, the alloy of pride, predominate, 'twill be best to leave her as a toy for some less cautious fool to sigh for! (*Exit.*)

FOR STUDY AND DISCUSSION

1. Bob Acres' servant, David, introduced late in Act III, plays an important role in Act IV, Scene 1. Why do you think Sheridan introduced David so late in the play? What does David contribute to the plot? to the theme of the play? Contrast David with Absolute's servant, Fag.

2. In what ways is the scene between Jack Absolute and Bob Acres parallel to that between Jack and Mrs. Malaprop (Act III, Scene 3)? Throughout the play there is a great deal of hocus-pocus with letters. Recall how many letters are misdirected or misreceived. Why is the device of the messenger-borne letter an excellent one for use in this play?

3. In Act IV, Scene 2, Jack Absolute finally meets Lydia in his own person—as Jack Absolute. What theatrical devices does Sheridan use to dramatize the clash between Jack as himself and as Beverley?

4. Sir Anthony shows mixed reactions upon learning of his son's deception. What is his initial reaction? When his reaction changes, does the change seem natural or forced? Explain your answer.

5. In Scene 3, Jack Absolute is faced with two rivals and two duels. What is ironic about this situation? Why does he regard only one of the duels seriously?

FOR COMPOSITION

In *The Rivals* Sheridan plays a name game that is only one step removed from the old morality-play device of naming characters as abstractions—for example, Everyman, Justice, Vice, Beauty, Death. Sheridan is subtler than this, but not much: one character is called Absolute and another is Malaprop; one lives at Blunderbuss Hall and another at Clod Hall. Point out the advantages and disadvantages of this device, giving other examples from *The Rivals*. Tell why you think the device is not much used by modern writers.

ACT V

SCENE 1. JULIA's *dressing room.*

[JULIA *discovered alone.*]

JULIA. How this message has alarmed me! what dreadful accident can he mean? why such charge to be alone? O Faulkland—how many unhappy moments—how many tears have you cost me.

[*Enter* FAULKLAND.]

JULIA. What means this?—why this caution, Faulkland?

FAULKLAND. Alas! Julia, I am come to take a long farewell.

JULIA. Heavens! what do you mean?

FAULKLAND. You see before you a wretch, whose life is forfeited. Nay, start not! The infirmity of my temper has drawn all this misery on me. I left you fretful and passionate—an untoward accident drew me into a quarrel—the event [1] is that I must fly this kingdom instantly. O Julia, had I been so fortunate as to have called you mine entirely, before this mischance had fallen on me, I should not so deeply dread my banishment!

JULIA. My soul is oppressed with sorrow at the nature of your misfortune: had these adverse circumstances arisen from a less fatal cause, I should have felt strong comfort in the thought that I could now chase from your bosom every doubt of the warm sincerity of my love. My heart has long known no other guardian—I now entrust my person to your honor—we will

[1] **event:** outcome.

fly together. When safe from pursuit, my father's will may be fulfilled—and I receive a legal claim to be the partner of your sorrows, and tenderest comforter. Then on the bosom of your wedded Julia, you may lull your keen regret to slumbering, while virtuous love, with a cherub's hand, shall smooth the brow of upbraiding thought and pluck the thorn from compunction.

FAULKLAND. O Julia! I am bankrupt in gratitude! But the time is so pressing, it calls on you for so hasty a resolution. Would you not wish some hours to weigh the advantages you forego and what little compensation poor Faulkland can make you beside his solitary love?

JULIA. I ask not a moment. No, Faulk-land, I have loved you for yourself: and if I now, more than ever, prize the solemn engagement which so long has pledged us to each other, it is because it leaves no room for hard aspersions on my fame and puts the seal of duty to an act of love. But let us not linger. Perhaps this delay——

FAULKLAND. 'Twill be better I should not venture out again till dark. Yet am I grieved to think what numberless distresses will press heavy on your gentle disposition!

JULIA. Perhaps your fortune may be forfeited by this unhappy act. I know not whether 'tis so; but sure that alone can never make us unhappy. The little I have will be sufficient to support us; and exile never should be splendid.

FAULKLAND. Ay, but in such an abject state of life, my wounded pride perhaps may increase the natural fretfulness of my temper, till I become a rude, morose companion, beyond your patience to endure. Perhaps the recollection of a deed my conscience cannot justify may haunt me in such gloomy and unsocial fits, that I shall hate the tenderness that would relieve me, break from your arms, and quarrel with your fondness!

JULIA. If your thoughts should assume so unhappy a bent, you will the more want some mild and affectionate spirit to watch over and console you, one who, by bearing your infirmities with gentleness and resignation, may teach you so to bear the evils of your fortune.

FAULKLAND. Julia, I have proved you to the quick! and with this useless device I throw away all my doubts. How shall I plead to be forgiven this last unworthy effect of my restless, unsatisfied disposition?

JULIA. Has no such disaster happened as you related?

FAULKLAND. I am ashamed to own that it was pretended; yet in pity, Julia, do not kill me with resenting a fault which never can be repeated: but sealing, this once, my pardon, let me tomorrow, in the face of Heaven, receive my future guide and monitress and expiate my past folly by years of tender adoration.

JULIA. Hold, Faulkland!—that you are free from a crime, which I before feared to name, Heaven knows how sincerely I rejoice! These are tears of thankfulness for that! But that your cruel doubts should have urged you to an imposition that has wrung my heart gives me now a pang more keen than I can express.

FAULKLAND. By Heavens! Julia——

JULIA. Yet hear me. My father loved you, Faulkland! And you preserved the life that tender parent gave me; in his presence I pledged my hand—joyfully pledged it—where before I had given my heart. When, soon after, I lost that parent, it seemed to me that Providence had, in Faulkland, shown me whither to transfer, without a pause, my grateful duty, as well as my affection; hence I have been content to bear from you what pride and delicacy would have forbid me from another. I will not upbraid you by repeating how you have trifled with my sincerity——

FAULKLAND. I confess it all! yet hear——

JULIA. After such a year of trial, I might have flattered myself that I should not have been insulted with a new probation of my sincerity, as cruel as unnecessary! I now see it is not in your nature to be content or confident in love. With this conviction—I never will be yours. While I had hopes that my persevering attention and unreproaching kindness might in time reform your temper, I should have been happy to have gained a dearer influence over you; but I will not furnish you with a licensed power to keep alive an incorrigible fault, at the expense of one who never would contend with you.

FAULKLAND. Nay, but, Julia, by my soul and honor, if after this——

JULIA. But one word more. As my faith has once been given to you, I never will barter it with another. I shall pray for your happiness with the truest sincerity; and the dearest blessing I can ask of Heaven to send you will be to charm you from that unhappy temper, which alone has prevented the performance of our solemn engagement. All I request of you is that you will yourself reflect upon this infirmity, and when you number up the many true delights it has deprived you of, let it not be your least regret that it lost you the love of one who would have followed you in beggary through the world! (Exit.)

FAULKLAND. She's gone—forever! There was an awful resolution in her manner that riveted me to my place. O fool! dolt! barbarian! Cursed as I am, with more imperfections than my fellow-wretches, kind Fortune sent a heaven-gifted cherub to my aid, and, like a ruffian, I have driven her from my side! I must now haste to my appointment. Well, my mind is turned for such a scene. I shall wish only to become a principal in it, and reverse the tale my cursed folly put me upon forging here. O Love!—tormentor! —fiend!—whose influence, like the moon's, acting on men of dull souls, makes idiots of them, but meeting subtler spirits, betrays their course, and urges sensibility to madness! (Exit.)

[Enter LYDIA and MAID.]

MAID. My mistress, ma'am, I know, was here just now—perhaps she is only in the next room. (Exit.)

LYDIA. Heigh-ho! Though he has used me so, this fellow runs strangely in my head. I believe one lecture from my grave cousin will make me recall him. (Reenter JULIA.) O Julia, I have come to you with such an appetite for consolation. Lud! child, what's the matter with you? You have been crying! I'll be hanged if that Faulkland has not been tormenting you.

JULIA. You mistake the cause of my uneasiness! Something has flurried me a little. Nothing that you can guess at. (Aside) I would not accuse Faulkland to a sister!

LYDIA. Ah! whatever vexations you may have, I can assure you mine surpass them. You know who Beverley proves to be?

JULIA. I will now own to you, Lydia, that Mr. Faulkland had before informed me of the whole affair. Had young Absolute been the person you took him for, I should not have accepted your confidence on the subject without serious endeavor to counteract your caprice.

LYDIA. So, then, I see I have been deceived by everyone! But I don't care— I'll never have him.

JULIA. Nay, Lydia——

LYDIA. Why, is it not provoking? when I thought we were coming to the prettiest distress imaginable, to find myself made a mere Smithfield bargain [1] of at last! There, had I projected one of the most sentimental elopements!—so becoming a disguise!—so amiable a ladder of ropes! Conscious moon—four horses—Scotch parson [2]—with such surprise to Mrs. Malaprop—and such paragraphs in the newspapers! Oh, I shall die with disappointment!

JULIA. I don't wonder at it!

LYDIA. Now—sad reverse—what have I to expect, but, after a deal of flimsy preparation, with a bishop's license, and my aunt's blessing, to go simpering up to the altar; or perhaps be cried three times

[1] **Smithfield bargain:** marriage for money.
[2] **Scotch parson:** Couples frequently eloped to Scotland.

in a country church, and have an unmannerly fat clerk ask the consent of every butcher in the parish [1] to join John Absolute and Lydia Languish, spinster! Oh that I should live to hear myself called spinster!

JULIA. Melancholy, indeed!

LYDIA. How mortifying to remember the dear delicious shifts I used to be put to to gain half a minute's conversation with this fellow! How often have I stole forth, in the coldest night in January, and found him in the garden, stuck like a dripping statue! There would he kneel to me in the snow and sneeze and cough so pathetically! he shivering with cold and I with apprehension! and while the freezing blast numbed our joints, how warmly would he press me to pity his flame and glow with mutual ardor! Ah, Julia, that was something like being in love.

JULIA. If I were in spirits, Lydia, I should chide you only by laughing heartily at you; but it suits more the situation of my mind, at present, earnestly to entreat you not to let a man, who loves you with sincerity, suffer that unhappiness from your caprice, which I know too well caprice can inflict.

LYDIA. O Lud! what has brought my aunt here?

[*Enter* MRS. MALAPROP, FAG, *and* DAVID.]

MRS. MALAPROP. So! so! here's fine work!—here's fine suicide, parricide, and simulation [2] going on in the fields! And Sir Anthony not to be found to prevent the antistrophe! [3]

JULIA. For Heaven's sake, madam, what's the meaning of this?

MRS. MALAPROP. That gentleman can tell you—'twas he enveloped [4] the affair to me.

LYDIA. Do, sir, will you, inform us? (*To* FAG)

FAG. Ma'am, I should hold myself very deficient in every requisite that forms the man of breeding if I delayed a moment to give all the information in my power to a lady so deeply interested in the affair as you are.

LYDIA. But quick! quick, sir!

FAG. True, ma'am, as you say, one should be quick in divulging matters of this nature; for should we be tedious, perhaps while we are flourishing on the subject, two or three lives may be lost!

LYDIA. O patience!—do, ma'am, for Heaven's sake! tell us what is the matter?

MRS. MALAPROP. Why, murder's the matter! slaughter's the matter! killing's the matter!—but he can tell you the perpendiculars. [5]

LYDIA. Then, prithee, sir, be brief.

FAG. Why, then, ma'am, as to murder—I cannot take upon me to say—and as to slaughter or manslaughter, that will be as the jury finds it.

LYDIA. But who, sir—who are engaged in this?

FAG. Faith, ma'am, one is a young gentleman whom I should be very sorry anything was to happen to—a very pretty behaved gentleman! We have lived much together, and always on terms.

LYDIA. But who is this? who? who? who?

FAG. My master, ma'am—my master—I speak of my master.

LYDIA. Heavens! What, Captain Absolute!

MRS. MALAPROP. Oh, to be sure, you are frightened now!

JULIA. But who are with him, sir?

FAG. As the rest, ma'am, this gentleman can inform you better than I.

JULIA. Do speak, friend. (*To* DAVID)

[1] **cried . . . parish:** The banns of marriage were announced three times from the church pulpit. Anyone knowing any reason why the marriage should not take place was to come forward and register the objection ("ask the consent of every butcher in the parish"). Lydia considers the whole business unromantic.

[2] **parricide . . . simulation:** homicide and dissimulation.

[3] **antistrophe:** catastrophe.

[4] **enveloped:** unfolded, revealed.

[5] **perpendiculars:** particulars, details.

DAVID. Look'ee, my lady—by the mass! There's mischief going on. Folks don't use to meet for amusement with firearms, firelocks, fire engines, fire screens, fire office, and the devil knows what other crackers beside! This, my lady, I say, has an angry savor.

JULIA. But who is there beside Captain Absolute, friend?

DAVID. My poor master—under favor for mentioning him first. You know me, my lady—I am David—and my master of course is, or was, Squire Acres. Then comes Squire Faulkland.

JULIA. Do, ma'am, let us instantly endeavor to prevent mischief.

MRS. MALAPROP. O fy! it would be very inelegant in us: we should only participate [1] things.

DAVID. Ah! do, Mrs. Aunt, save a few lives—they are desperately given, believe me. Above all, there is that bloodthirsty Philistine, Sir Lucius O'Trigger.

MRS. MALAPROP. Sir Lucius O'Trigger? O mercy! have they drawn poor little dear Sir Lucius into the scrape? Why how you stand, girl! You have no more feeling than one of the Derbyshire putrefactions! [2]

LYDIA. What are we to do, madam?

MRS. MALAPROP. Why, fly with the utmost felicity,[3] to be sure, to prevent mischief! Here, friend, you can show us the place?

FAG. If you please, ma'am, I will conduct you. David, do you look for Sir Anthony. (Exit DAVID.)

MRS. MALAPROP. Come, girls! this gentleman will exhort [4] us. Come, sir, you're our envoy [5]—lead the way, and we'll precede.[6]

FAG. Not a step before the ladies for the world!

[1] **participate**: precipitate.
[2] **Derbyshire putrefactions**: petrifactions (strange rock formations in Derbyshire).
[3] **felicity**: facility.
[4] **exhort**: escort.
[5] **envoy**: convoy.
[6] **precede**: proceed, follow.

MRS. MALAPROP. You're sure you know the spot?

FAG. I think I can find it, ma'am; and one good thing is, we shall hear the report of the pistols as we draw near, so we can't well miss them; never fear, ma'am, never fear. (Exeunt, he talking.)

SCENE 2. *The South Parade.*

[*Enter* CAPTAIN ABSOLUTE, *putting his sword under his greatcoat.*]

ABSOLUTE. A sword seen in the streets of Bath would raise as great an alarm as a mad dog. How provoking this is in Faulkland—never punctual! I shall be obliged to go without him at last. Oh, the devil! here's Sir Anthony! how shall I escape him? (*Muffles up his face and takes a circle to go off.*)

[*Enter* SIR ANTHONY ABSOLUTE.]

SIR ANTHONY. How one may be deceived at a little distance! Only that I see he don't know me, I could have sworn that was Jack! Hey! Gad's life! it is. Why, Jack, what are you afraid of? Hey—sure I'm right. Why, Jack, Jack Absolute! (*Goes up to him*)

ABSOLUTE. Really, sir, you have the advantage of me: I don't remember ever to have had the honor. My name is Saunderson, at your service.

SIR ANTHONY. Sir, I beg your pardon—. I took you—hey?—why, zounds! It is —Stay—(*Looks up to his face*) So, so— your humble servant, Mr. Saunderson! Why, you scoundrel, what tricks are you after now?

ABSOLUTE. Oh, a joke, sir, a joke! I came here on purpose to look for you, sir.

SIR ANTHONY. You did! well, I am glad you were so lucky: but what are you muffled up so for?—what's this for?—hey?

ABSOLUTE. 'Tis cool, sir, isn't it?— rather chilly somehow: but I shall be late —I have a particular engagement.

SIR ANTHONY. Stay! Why, I thought you were looking for me? Pray, Jack, where is't you are going?

ABSOLUTE. Going, sir?

SIR ANTHONY. Ay, where are you going?

ABSOLUTE. Where am I going?

SIR ANTHONY. You unmannerly puppy!

ABSOLUTE. I was going, sir, to—to—to —to Lydia—sir, to Lydia—to make matters up if I could; and I was looking for you, sir, to—to—

SIR ANTHONY. To go with you, I suppose. Well, come along.

ABSOLUTE. Oh! zounds! no, sir, not for the world! I wished to meet with you, sir—to—to—to—You find it cool, I'm sure, sir—you'd better not stay out.

SIR ANTHONY. Cool—not at all. Well, Jack—and what will you say to Lydia?

ABSOLUTE. Oh, sir, beg her pardon, humor her—promise and vow: but I detain you, sir—consider the cold air on your gout.

SIR ANTHONY. Oh, not at all!—not at all! I'm in no hurry. Ah! Jack, you youngsters, when once you are wounded here— (*Putting his hand to* CAPTAIN ABSOLUTE'S *breast*) Hey! what the deuce have you got here?

ABSOLUTE. Nothing, sir—nothing.

SIR ANTHONY. What's this?—here's something damned hard.

ABSOLUTE. Oh, trinkets, sir! trinkets!— a bauble for Lydia.

SIR ANTHONY. Nay, let me see your taste. (*Pulls his coat open, the sword falls*) Trinkets! a bauble for Lydia! Zounds! sirrah, you are not going to cut her throat, are you?

ABSOLUTE. Ha! ha! ha! I thought it would divert you, sir, though I didn't mean to tell you till afterward.

SIR ANTHONY. You didn't? Yes, this is a very diverting trinket, truly!

ABSOLUTE. Sir, I'll explain to you. You know, sir, Lydia is romantic, devilish romantic, and very absurd of course: now, sir, I intend, if she refuses to forgive me, to unsheath this sword, and swear—I'll fall upon its point, and expire at her feet!

SIR ANTHONY. Fall upon a fiddlestick's end! Why, I suppose it is the very thing that would please her. Get along, you fool!

ABSOLUTE. Well, sir, you shall hear of my success—you shall hear. *O Lydia! forgive me, or this pointed steel*—says I.

SIR ANTHONY. *O, booby! stay away and welcome*—says she. Get along! and damn your trinkets!

[*Exit* CAPTAIN ABSOLUTE. *Enter* DAVID, *running*.]

DAVID. Stop him! stop him! Murder! Thief! Fire! Stop fire! Stop fire! O Sir Anthony—call! call! bid'm stop! Murder! Fire!

SIR ANTHONY. Fire! Murder! Where?

DAVID. Oons! he's out of sight! and I'm out of breath for my part! O Sir Anthony, why didn't you stop him? why didn't you stop him?

SIR ANTHONY. Zounds! the fellow's mad! Stop whom? stop Jack?

DAVID. Ay, the captain, sir!—there's murder and slaughter——

SIR ANTHONY. Murder!

DAVID. Ay, please you, Sir Anthony, there's all kinds of murder, all sorts of slaughter to be seen in the fields: there's fighting going on, sir—bloody sword-and-gun fighting!

SIR ANTHONY. Who are going to fight, dunce?

DAVID. Everybody that I know of, Sir Anthony: everybody is going to fight, my poor master, Sir Lucius O'Trigger, your son, the captain——

SIR ANTHONY. Oh, the dog! I see his tricks. Do you know the place?

DAVID. King's-Mead-Fields.

SIR ANTHONY. You know the way?

DAVID. Not an inch; but I'll call the mayor—aldermen—constables—church—wardens—and beadles—we can't be too many to part them.

SIR ANTHONY. Come along—give me your shoulder! We'll get assistance as we go—the lying villain! Well, I shall be in such a frenzy! So this was the history of his trinkets! I'll bauble him! (*Exeunt.*)

SCENE 3. *King's-Mead-Fields.*

[*Enter* SIR LUCIUS O'TRIGGER *and* ACRES *with pistols.*]

ACRES. By my valor! Then, Sir Lucius, forty yards is a good distance. Odds levels and aims! I say it is a good distance.

SIR LUCIUS. Is it for muskets or small field-pieces? Upon my conscience, Mr. Acres, you must leave those things to me. Stay now—I'll show you. (*Measures paces along the stage*) There now, that is a very pretty distance—a pretty gentleman's distance.

ACRES. Zounds! we might as well fight in a sentry box! I tell you, Sir Lucius, the farther he is off, the cooler I shall take my aim.

SIR LUCIUS. Faith! then I suppose you would aim at him best of all if he was out of sight!

ACRES. No, Sir Lucius; but I should think forty or eight and thirty yards——

SIR LUCIUS. Pho! pho! nonsense! three or four feet between the mouths of your pistols is as good as a mile.

ACRES. Odds bullets, no!—by my valor! there is no merit in killing him so near; do, my dear Sir Lucius, let me bring him down at a long shot—a long shot, Sir Lucius, if you love me.

SIR LUCIUS. Well, the gentleman's friend and I must settle that. But tell me now, Mr. Acres, in case of an accident, is there any little will or commission I could execute for you?

ACRES. I am much obliged to you, Sir Lucius, but I don't understand——

SIR LUCIUS. Why, you may think there's no being shot at without a little risk—and if an unlucky bullet should carry a quietus [1] with it—I say it will be no time to be bothering you about family matters.

ACRES. A quietus!

SIR LUCIUS. For instance, now—if that should be the case—would you choose to be pickled and sent home? Or would it be the same to you to lie here in the

___
[1] **quietus:** release from life.

Abbey? I'm told there is very snug lying in the Abbey.

ACRES. Pickled! Snug lying in the Abbey! Odds tremors! Sir Lucius, don't talk so!

SIR LUCIUS. I suppose, Mr. Acres, you never were engaged in an affair of this kind before?

ACRES. No, Sir Lucius, never before.

SIR LUCIUS. Ah! that's a pity!—there's nothing like being used to a thing. Pray now, how would you receive the gentleman's shot?

ACRES. Odd files! I've practiced that —there, Sir Lucius—there. (*Puts himself in an attitude*) A side-front, hey? Odd! I'll make myself small enough? I'll stand edgeways.

SIR LUCIUS. Now—you're quite out— for if you stand so when I take my aim—— (*Leveling at him*)

ACRES. Zounds! Sir Lucius—are you sure it is not cocked?

SIR LUCIUS. Never fear.

ACRES. But—but—you don't know— it may go off of its own head!

SIR LUCIUS. Pho! be easy. Well, now if I hit you in the body, my bullet has a double chance—for if it misses a vital part of your right side, t'will be very hard if it don't succeed on the left!

ACRES. A vital part.

SIR LUCIUS. But, there—fix yourself so—(*Placing him*)—let him see the broadside of your full front—there—now a ball or two may pass clean through your body and never do any harm at all.

ACRES. Clean through me—a ball or two clean through me!

SIR LUCIUS. Ay—may they—and it is much the genteelest attitude into the bargain.

ACRES. Look'ee! Sir Lucius—I'd just as lieve be shot in an awkward posture as a genteel one; so, by my valor! I will stand edgeways.

SIR LUCIUS (*looking at his watch*). Sure they don't mean to disappoint us. Hah! —no, faith—I think I see them coming.

ACRES. Hey!—what!—coming!

SIR LUCIUS. Ay. Who are those yonder getting over the stile?

ACRES. There are two of them indeed! —well—let them come—hey, Sir Lucius! —we—we—we—we—won't run.

SIR LUCIUS. Run!

ACRES. No—I say—we won't run, by my valor!

SIR LUCIUS. What the devil's the matter with you?

ACRES. Nothing—nothing—my dear friend—my dear Sir Lucius—but I—I—I don't feel quite so bold, somehow, as I did.

SIR LUCIUS. O fy!—consider your honor.

ACRES. Ay—true—my honor. Do, Sir Lucius, edge in a word or two every now and then about my honor.

SIR LUCIUS. Well, here they're coming. (*Looking*)

ACRES. Sir Lucius—if I wa'n't with you, I should almost think I was afraid. If my valor should leave me! Valor will come and go.

SIR LUCIUS. Then pray keep it fast, while you have it.

ACRES. Sir Lucius—I doubt [1] it is going —yes—my valor is certainly going! It is sneaking off! I feel it oozing out as it were at the palms of my hands!

SIR LUCIUS. Your honor—your honor. Here they are.

ACRES. O mercy—now—that I was safe at Clod Hall! or could be shot before I was aware!

[*Enter* FAULKLAND *and* CAPTAIN ABSOLUTE.]

SIR LUCIUS. Gentlemen, your most obedient. Hah!—what, Captain Absolute! So, I suppose, sir, you are come here, just like myself—to do a kind office, first for your friend—then to proceed to business on your own account.

ACRES. What, Jack!—my dear Jack! —my dear friend!

ABSOLUTE. Hark'ee. Bob, Beverley's at hand.

[1] **I doubt:** I think; I fear.

SIR LUCIUS. Well, Mr. Acres—I don't blame your saluting the gentleman civilly. (*To* FAULKLAND) So, Mr. Beverley, if you'll choose your weapons, the captain and I will measure the ground.

FAULKLAND. My weapons, sir!

ACRES. Odds life! Sir Lucius, I'm not going to fight Mr. Faulkland; these are my particular friends.

SIR LUCIUS. What, sir, did you not come here to fight Mr. Acres?

FAULKLAND. Not I, upon my word, sir.

SIR LUCIUS. Well, now, that's mighty provoking! But I hope, Mr. Faulkland, as there are three of us come on purpose for the game, you won't be so cantankerous as to spoil the party by sitting out.

ABSOLUTE. O pray, Faulkland, fight to oblige Sir Lucius.

FAULKLAND. Nay, if Mr. Acres is so bent on the matter——

ACRES. No, no, Mr. Faulkland; I'll bear my disappointment like a Christian. Look'ee, Sir Lucius, there's no occasion at all for me to fight; and if it is the same to you, I'd as lieve let it alone.

SIR LUCIUS. Observe me, Mr. Acres—I must not be trifled with. You have certainly challenged somebody—and you came here to fight him. Now, if that gentleman is willing to represent him—I can't see, for my soul, why it isn't just the same thing.

ACRES. Why no—Sir Lucius—I tell you, 'tis one Beverley I've challenged— a fellow, you see, that dare not show his face! If he were here, I'd make him give up his pretensions directly!

ABSOLUTE. Hold, Bob—let me set you right—there is no such man as Beverley in the case. The person who assumed that name is before you; and as his pretensions are the same in both characters, he is ready to support them in whatever way you please.

SIR LUCIUS. Well, this is lucky. Now you have an opportunity——

ACRES. What, quarrel with my dear friend, Jack Absolute? Not if he were fifty Beverleys! Zounds! Sir Lucius, you would not have me so unnatural.

SIR LUCIUS. Upon my conscience, Mr. Acres, your valor has oozed away with a vengeance!

ACRES. Not in the least! Odds backs and abettors! I'll be your second with all my heart—and if you should get a quietus, you may command me entirely. I'll get you snug lying in the Abbey here, or pickle you and send you over to Blunderbuss Hall, or anything of the kind, with the greatest pleasure.

SIR LUCIUS. Pho! pho! you are little better than a coward.

ACRES. Mind, gentlemen, he calls me a coward; coward was the word, by my valor!

SIR LUCIUS. Well, sir?

ACRES. Look'ee, Sir Lucius, 'tisn't that I mind the word coward—coward may be said in joke. But if you had called me a poltroon, odds daggers——

SIR LUCIUS. Well, sir?

ACRES. I should have thought you a very ill-bred man.

SIR LUCIUS. Pho! you are beneath my notice.

ABSOLUTE. Nay, Sir Lucius, you can't have a better second than my friend Acres. He is a most determined dog—called in the country, Fighting Bob. He generally kills a man a week—don't you, Bob?

ACRES. Ay—at home!

SIR LUCIUS. Well, then, captain, 'tis we must begin—so come out, my little counselor—(Draws his sword) and ask the gentleman whether he will resign the lady without forcing you to proceed against him?

ABSOLUTE. Come on then, sir—(Draws) since you won't let it be an amicable suit, here's my reply.

[Enter SIR ANTHONY ABSOLUTE, DAVID, MRS. MALAPROP, LYDIA, and JULIA.]

DAVID. Knock 'em all down, sweet Sir Anthony; knock down my master in particular; and bind his hands over to their good behavior!

SIR ANTHONY. Put up, Jack, put up, or I shall be in a frenzy—how came you in a duel, sir?

ABSOLUTE. Faith, sir, that gentleman can tell you better than I; 'twas he called on me, and you know, sir, I serve his majesty.

SIR ANTHONY. Here's a pretty fellow; I catch him going to cut a man's throat, and he tells me he serves his majesty! Zounds! sirrah, then how durst you draw the king's sword against one of his subjects?

ABSOLUTE. Sir! I tell you, that gentleman called me out without explaining his reasons.

SIR ANTHONY. Gad! sir, how came you to call my son out without explaining your reasons?

SIR LUCIUS. Your son, sir, insulted me in a manner which my honor could not brook.

SIR ANTHONY. Zounds! Jack, how durst you insult the gentleman in a manner which his honor could not brook?

MRS. MALAPROP. Come, come, let's have no honor before ladies—Captain Absolute, come here—How could you intimidate us so? Here's Lydia has been terrified to death for you.

ABSOLUTE. For fear I should be killed, or escape, ma'am?

MRS. MALAPROP. Nay, no delusions [1] to the past—Lydia is convinced; speak, child.

SIR LUCIUS. With your leave, ma'am, I must put in a word, here: I believe I could interpret the young lady's silence. Now mark——

LYDIA. What is it you mean, sir?

SIR LUCIUS. Come, come, Delia, we must be serious now—this is no time for trifling.

LYDIA. 'Tis true, sir; and your reproof bids me offer this gentleman my hand, and solicit the return of his affections.

ABSOLUTE. O! my little angel, say you so? Sir Lucius, I perceive there must be

___
[1] delusions: allusions.

some mistake here with regard to the affront which you affirm I have given you. I can only say that it could not have been intentional. And as you must be convinced that I should not fear to support a real injury—you shall now see that I am not ashamed to atone for an inadvertency—I ask your pardon. But for this lady, while honored with her approbation, I will support my claim against any man whatever.

SIR ANTHONY. Well said, Jack, and I'll stand by you, my boy.

ACRES. Mind, I give up all my claim—I make no pretensions to anything in the world; and if I can't get a wife without fighting for her, by my valor! I'll live a bachelor.

SIR LUCIUS. Captain, give me your hand: an affront handsomely acknowledged becomes an obligation; and as for the lady, if she chooses to deny her own handwriting, here——(*Takes out letters*)

MRS. MALAPROP. O, he will dissolve [1] my mystery! Sir Lucius, perhaps there's some mistake—perhaps I can illuminate—— [2]

SIR LUCIUS. Pray, old gentlewoman, don't interfere where you have no business. Miss Languish, are you my Delia or not?

LYDIA. Indeed, Sir Lucius, I am not. (*Walks aside with* CAPTAIN ABSOLUTE)

MRS. MALAPROP. Sir Lucius O'Trigger —ungrateful as you are—I own the soft impeachment—pardon my blushes, I am Delia.

SIR LUCIUS. You Delia—pho! pho! be easy.

MRS. MALAPROP. Why, thou barbarous vandyke [3]—those letters are mine. When you are more sensible of my benignity—perhaps I may be brought to encourage your addresses.

SIR LUCIUS. Mrs. Malaprop, I am extremely sensible of your condescension; and whether you or Lucy have put this

---

[1] **dissolve**: solve.
[2] **illuminate**: elucidate.
[3] **vandyke**: vandal.

trick on me, I am equally beholden to you. And, to show you I am not ungrateful, Captain Absolute, since you have taken that lady from me, I'll give you my Delia into the bargain.

ABSOLUTE. I am much obliged to you, Sir Lucius; but here's my friend, Fighting Bob, unprovided for.

SIR LUCIUS. Hah! little Valor—here, will you make your fortune?

ACRES. Odds wrinkles! No. But give me your hand, Sir Lucius, forget and forgive; but if ever I give you a chance of picking me again, say Bob Acres is a dunce, that's all.

SIR ANTHONY. Come, Mrs. Malaprop, don't be cast down—you are in your bloom yet.

MRS. MALAPROP. O Sir Anthony—men are all barbarians. (*All retire but* JULIA *and* FAULKLAND.)

JULIA (*aside*). He seems dejected and unhappy—not sullen; there was some foundation, however, for the tale he told me—O woman! how true should be your judgment, when your resolution is so weak!

FAULKLAND. Julia! how can I sue for what I so little deserve? I dare not presume—yet Hope is the child of Penitence.

JULIA. Oh! Faulkland, you have not been more faulty in your unkind treatment of me than I am now in wanting inclination to resent it. As my heart honestly bids me place my weakness to the account of love, I should be ungenerous not to admit the same plea for yours.

FAULKLAND. Now I shall be blessed indeed.

SIR ANTHONY (*coming forward*). What's going on here? So you have been quarreling too, I warrant? Come, Julia, I never interfered before; but let me have a hand in the matter at last. All the faults I have ever seen in my friend Faulkland seemed to proceed from what he calls the delicacy and warmth of his affection for you. There, marry him directly, Julia; you'll find he'll mend surprisingly! (*The rest come forward.*)

SIR LUCIUS. Come, now I hope there is no dissatisfied person, but what is content; for as I have been disappointed myself, it will be very hard if I have not the satisfaction of seeing other people succeed better.

ACRES. You are right, Sir Lucius. So, Jack, I wish you joy. Mr. Faulkland the same. Ladies, come now, to show you I'm neither vexed nor angry, odds tabors and pipes! I'll order the fiddles in half an hour to the New Rooms—and I insist on your all meeting me there.

SIR ANTHONY. 'Gad! sir, I like your spirit; and at night we single lads will drink a health to the young couples, and a husband to Mrs. Malaprop.

FAULKLAND. Our partners are stolen from us, Jack—I hope to be congratulated by each other—yours for having checked in time the errors of an ill-directed imagination, which might have betrayed an innocent heart; and mine, for having, by her gentleness and candor, reformed the unhappy temper of one, who by it made wretched whom he loved most, and tortured the heart he ought to have adored.

ABSOLUTE. Well, Jack, we have both tasted the bitters, as well as the sweets of love; with this difference only, that you always prepared the bitter cup for yourself, while I——

LYDIA. Was always obliged to me for it, hey! Mr. Modesty? But come, no more of that—our happiness is now as unalloyed as general.

JULIA. Then let us study to preserve it so: and while Hope pictures to us a flattering scene of future bliss, let us deny its pencil those colors which are too bright to be lasting. When hearts deserving happiness would unite their fortunes, Virtue would crown them with an unfading garland of modest hurtless flowers; but ill-judging Passion will force the gaudier rose into the wreath, whose thorn offends them when its leaves are dropped!

[*Exeunt omnes.*]

FOR STUDY AND DISCUSSION

1. Is the dueling scene an effective climax to the play? Why or why not? At the end of the play do you feel that all the threads of the plot have been satisfactorily tied up, or are some left hanging? Explain your answer.

2. Some readers see Faulkland as a modern man, haunted by too much self-analysis. To what extent do you agree with this view? In addition to his actions throughout the play, consider Julia's remarks in her long speech in Act I, Scene 2.

3. Bob Acres, as an outsider to the established society of Malaprops and Absolutes, is sometimes considered a superfluous character. What point about eighteenth-century English society does his presence make? Do you consider this point essential to the plot or theme of *The Rivals?* Explain.

4. Sheridan introduces a minor plot with Mrs. Malaprop's love, as Delia, for Sir Lucius. Do you think Sheridan develops this plot enough? When the two characters finally confront each other, how fully does the playwright capitalize on the comic possibilities of the scene?

5. Why do you think the play's final speech was assigned to Julia? Is this conclusion in keeping with the tone of the play? Explain.

6. Do you think *The Rivals* would be an effective stage play for a modern audience? Are its assumptions still valid? If so, why?

FOR COMPOSITION

1. A minor theme throughout *The Rivals* is the idea of heroics and mock-heroics. Write an essay in which you discuss Sheridan's attitude toward heroism as shown through the four men who meet at King's-Mead-Fields.

2. A modern critic has written: "The pleasure that men take in comedy arises from their feeling of superiority to the persons involved in the comic action."

Select a scene from *The Rivals* which you find most enjoyably comic. In a brief composition analyze that scene in the light of the above statement on comedy. Explain whether this statement completely defines the pleasure you derive from the scene you have chosen. If so, demonstrate your point with specific examples from the scene. If you do not agree, explain how you would define the source of the pleasure you derive from comedy.

THOMAS GRAY
(1716–1771)

Although in his day Thomas Gray was considered England's foremost poet, he turned down the position of poet laureate. He is remembered today chiefly as the author of "Elegy Written in a Country Churchyard" and as the poet who represents the transition from classical to Romantic literature in England.

Gray was the only surviving child in a family of eight. By keeping shop, his mother earned the money to send him through Eton and Cambridge. After a three-year Continental tour with his former classmate and fellow writer, Horace Walpole, Gray settled in cloistered bachelor retirement at Cambridge, where he was a scholar of classical literature, a well-liked don, and a poet in residence. He enjoyed the quiet life of a Cambridge professor. On one occasion, however, a practical joke so shattered his nerves and disrupted the "noiseless tenor" of his ways that he moved to another of Cambridge's several colleges—a change which for him was a cataclysmic upheaval.

Although Gray's life was placid, his poetry was venturesome. Without discarding what he believed was good in the old, neoclassic tradition, he explored new and unfamiliar areas in poetry. His use of personification, high-flown allusions, and conventional poetic diction are representative of his ties to the earlier style. But while Pope reflected fashionable city tastes, Gray, like Wordsworth and other Romantic poets, turned to country life and humble people for inspiration. He dealt in honest and homely emotion and brought back into poetry the use of the first-person singular, considered a barbarism by eighteenth-century norms, which dictated suppression of the ego and concealment of emotion. Not only Gray's treatment of nature, but his interest in the past, in Celtic and Norse folklore and simple, primitive cultures, was a foreshadowing of themes that would find their fullest expression in the Romantic movement of the nineteenth century.

A painstaking writer, Gray produced few poems. It took him nine years to complete "Elegy Written in a Country Churchyard." Though his verse form varies only slightly from Pope's, in its personal tone and emotional expressions on life and death, his poetry reveals a Romantic spirit. Johnson may have thought Gray dull, but most readers agreed with General Wolfe, who before the battle of Quebec in 1763, said of the "Elegy": "I would rather be the author of those lines than take Quebec."

Elegy Written in a Country Churchyard

The curfew tolls the knell of parting day,
    The lowing herd wind slowly o'er the lea,
The plowman homeward plods his weary way,
    And leaves the world to darkness and to me.

Now fades the glimmering landscape on the sight,   5
    And all the air a solemn stillness holds,
Save where the beetle wheels his droning flight,
    And drowsy tinklings lull the distant folds;

Save that from yonder ivy-mantled tower
    The moping owl does to the moon complain   10
Of such, as wandering near her secret bower,
    Molest her ancient solitary reign.

Beneath those rugged elms, that yew tree's shade,
    Where heaves the turf in many a moldering heap,
Each in his narrow cell forever laid,   15
    The rude forefathers of the hamlet sleep.

The breezy call of incense-breathing morn,
    The swallow twittering from the straw-built shed,
The cock's shrill clarion, or the echoing horn,°
    No more shall rouse them from their lowly bed.   20

For them no more the blazing hearth shall burn,
    Or busy housewife ply her evening care:
No children run to lisp their sire's return,
    Or climb his knee the envied kiss to share.

Oft did the harvest to their sickle yield,   25
    Their furrow oft the stubborn glebe° has broke;
How jocund did they drive their team afield!
    How bowed the woods beneath their sturdy stroke!

Let not ambition mock their useful toil,
    Their homely joys, and destiny obscure;   30
Nor grandeur hear with a disdainful smile,
    The short and simple annals of the poor.

The boast of heraldry,° the pomp of power,
    And all that beauty, all that wealth e'er gave,
Awaits alike the inevitable hour.   35
    The paths of glory lead but to the grave.

19. **horn:** the horn of the hunter.   26. **glebe:** ground.   33. **The boast of heraldry:** Heraldry is the study of family coats of arms; hence, this phrase refers to the pride of having a noble family.

Nor you, ye proud, impute to these the fault,
    If memory o'er their tomb no trophies raise,
Where through the long-drawn aisle and fretted vault°
    The pealing anthem swells the note of praise.   40

Can storied urn° or animated° bust
    Back to its mansion call the fleeting breath?
Can honor's voice provoke° the silent dust,
    Or flatt'ry soothe the dull cold ear of Death?

Perhaps in this neglected spot is laid   45
    Some heart once pregnant with celestial fire;
Hands, that the rod of empire might have swayed,
    Or waked to ecstasy the living lyre.

But knowledge to their eyes her ample page
    Rich with the spoils of time did ne'er unroll;   50
Chill penury repressed their noble rage,
    And froze the genial° current of the soul.

Full many a gem of purest ray serene,
    The dark unfathomed caves of ocean bear;
Full many a flower is born to blush unseen,   55
    And waste its sweetness on the desert air.

Some village Hampden° that with dauntless breast
    The little tyrant of his fields withstood,
Some mute inglorious Milton here may rest,
    Some Cromwell guiltless of his country's blood.   60

The applause of listening senates to command,
    The threats of pain and ruin to despise,
To scatter plenty o'er a smiling land,
    And read their history in a nation's eyes,°

Their lot forbade: nor circumscribed alone   65
    Their growing virtues, but their crimes confined;
Forbade to wade through slaughter to a throne,
    And shut the gates of mercy on mankind,

The struggling pangs of conscious truth to hide,
    To quench the blushes of ingenuous shame,
Or heap the shrine of luxury and pride   70
    With incense kindled at the Muse's flame.

---

    39. **fretted vault:** church roof ornamented by elaborate design.   41. **storied urn:** an urn inscribed with pictures that tell the story of the deceased.   **animated:** lifelike.   43. **provoke:** arouse.   52. **genial:** warm or living.   57. **Hampden:** a landowner whose resistance to one of the tax assessments of Charles I made the matter of unjust taxes a public issue.   61–64. This whole stanza is the object of *forbade* in the first line of the next stanza.

Far from the madding° crowd's ignoble strife,
   Their sober wishes never learned to stray;
Along the cool sequestered vale of life   75
   They kept the noiseless tenor° of their way.

Yet ev'n these bones from insult to protect,
   Some frail memorial still erected nigh,
With uncouth rhymes and shapeless sculpture decked,
   Implores the passing tribute of a sigh.   80

Their name, their years, spelt by the unlettered Muse,
   The place of fame and elegy supply;
And many a holy text around she strews,
   That teach the rustic moralist to die.

For who to dumb forgetfulness a prey,   85
   This pleasing anxious being e'er resigned,
Left the warm precincts of the cheerful day,
   Nor cast one longing lingering look behind?

On some fond breast the parting soul relies,
   Some pious drops the closing eye requires;   90
Ev'n from the tomb the voice of nature cries,
   Ev'n in our ashes live their wonted fires.

For thee,° who mindful of the unhonored dead
   Dost in these lines their artless tale relate;
If chance, by lonely contemplation led,   95
   Some kindred spirit shall inquire thy fate,

Haply some hoary-headed swain may say,
   "Oft have we seen him at the peep of dawn
Brushing with hasty steps the dews away,
   To meet the sun upon the upland lawn.   100

"There at the foot of yonder nodding beech
   That wreathes its old fantastic roots so high,
His listless length at noontide would he stretch,
   And pore upon the brook that babbles by.

"Hard by yon wood, now smiling as in scorn,   105
   Muttering his wayward fancies he would rove,
Now drooping, woeful wan, like one forlorn,
   Or crazed with care, or crossed in hopeless love.

"One morn I missed him on the customed hill,
   Along the heath and near his favorite tree,   110
Another came; nor yet beside the rill,
   Nor up the lawn, nor at the wood was he;

---

73. **madding:** wild, furious. 76. **tenor** (ten'ər): even course. 93. **thee:** Gray himself.

"The next, with dirges due in sad array
 Slow through the church-way path we saw him borne.
Approach and read (for thou canst read)° the lay,   115
 Graved on the stone beneath yon aged thorn."°

THE EPITAPH

Here rests his head upon the lap of earth
 A youth to fortune and to fame unknown.
Fair science frowned not on his humble birth,°
 And melancholy marked him for her own.   120

Large was his bounty, and his soul sincere,
 Heaven did a recompense as largely send;
He gave to misery all he had, a tear;
 He gained from Heaven ('twas all he wished) a friend.

No farther seek his merits to disclose,   125
 Or draw his frailties from their dread abode,
(There they alike in trembling hope repose)
 The bosom of his Father and his God.

115. **thou canst read:** In the eighteenth century, many country people were unable to read.
116. **thorn:** hawthorn.   119. **Fair . . . birth:** His humble birth had not prevented his having a good education.

FOR STUDY AND DISCUSSION

1. The "Elegy" falls into clear-cut divisions of thought. What stanzas would you include in each of these first three divisions: (a) the setting; (b) the imagined life of the villagers; (c) death, the common end of all, rich and poor? Into what four divisions would you divide the rest of the poem? How would you describe each division? How do all the divisions relate to each other to form a unified whole?

2. Would the poem have been weaker or stronger if it had ended before the epitaph? Explain your answer.

3. To what extent does this poem echo Donne's "Meditation XVII" (page 207)?

4. How does the "Elegy" compare with Pope's "Rape of the Lock" in rhyme scheme, stanza division, subject matter, and tone? What new elements are apparent in the later poem?

THE ELEGY

The term *elegy,* first used to describe any serious meditative poem, regardless of theme, is now used to refer to a lyric poem that laments the death of a particular person. This it does in a restrained, dignified, and formal manner. Tennyson's *In Memoriam* (page 591), for

instance, is one of the most famous elegies in English literature. The term is used in a broader sense to describe Gray's "Elegy," which laments the passing of all people.

Note how Gray uses details to establish the mood of his poem. How does his use of imagery contribute to his restrained expression of sorrow? What effect does he achieve with the verbs *tolls, wind, plods, fades,* and *lull* (lines 1–8)?

INVERSION

The technique of inversion consists of reversing the normal English word order (subject, verb, object) of a sentence. As with other poetic devices, inversion should not be used for its own sake, but should have a definite relation to the thought and feeling of the poem, reinforcing a significant idea or emphasizing the dominant mood. If this relationship is not clear, inversion will result in artificiality and distortion. Inversion is effectively employed in Gray's "Elegy." Note, for example, lines 5–6:

"Now fades the glimmering landscape on the
    sight,
 And all the air a solemn stillness holds . . ."

Cite other examples of inversion in this poem.

ROBERT BURNS
(1759–1796)

Tired and hungry, a traveler arrived one night at an inn in the heart of the Burns country. The place was alive with lights and laughter. When the traveler knocked, he got no answer. He tried shouting and banging, and finally resorted to the colorful rhetoric of an outraged Scotsman. Finally a window opened and a servant peered out and explained, "Oh, sir, Bobbie Burns is ben." When the celebrated Bobbie Burns was "ben" (within), it was understood that no one else should expect attention.

Even to this day "Bobbie Burns" is a magic name, one which kindles the loyalty and pride of his countrymen. Burns, the oldest of seven children, was born near Ayr, in southwestern Scotland, in a two-room cottage his father had built with his own hands. Although the family's poverty made possible only a meager education, Burns, according to Thomas Carlyle, "was fortunate in his father—a man of thoughtful, intense character . . . valuing knowledge, possessing some, and open-minded for more." It was from his father that Burns received most of his learning and his avid love for books. He supplemented his formal schooling by reading the Bible, *The Spectator*, and Pope's poems. His mother taught him old Scottish songs and stories, which he later turned into his best poems. He poured over small volumes of ballads "when driving my cart or walking to labor, song by song, verse by verse." His early life as a plowboy, he wrote, combined "the cheerless gloom of a hermit with the unceasing moil of a galley slave"; but his recollections of this life in his poetry, and particularly his love songs, reveal that his youth was not all toil and moil.

Burns developed into a handsome young man, but his wild ways and his verse satirizing local dignitaries made many enemies. At twenty-six—his father dead, the farm a failure, and his romance with Jean Armour blocked by her angry father— Burns was ready to flee to Jamaica to start a new life. To raise money for his passage, friends helped him to publish his first volume of poetry, called *Poems: Chiefly in Scottish Dialect* (1786). It was an immediate success. One contemporary claimed that "the country murmured of him from sea to sea . . . old and young, grave and gay, learned and ignorant, were all alike transported." Canceling his trip to the West Indies, Burns went instead to Edinburgh where he was lionized, but where his peasant roughness soon jarred the refined sensibilities of polite society. When his novelty wore off, he took the £400 received from the publication of an enlarged edition of his book and toured Scotland and northern England collecting ballads. He then returned to his farm, married Jean Armour, and wrote some of his finest poetry. To supplement his meager income, he served as tax collector, a job he nearly lost because of his bold and outspoken advocacy of the principles of the French Revolution. His last years were clouded by fits of depression brought on by ill health, excessive drinking, and financial difficulties, and he died at the early age of thirty-seven. Upon his death, the whole country united to honor him and to contribute to the support of his destitute family. The recognition that had been only fleeting during his brief, unhappy lifetime flowered into lasting fame, and Burns was hailed as the national poet of Scotland.

Burns poured earthy vigor and warm compassion into his lyrics. He was beloved by his country because, in the Scots' own idiom, he exalted and gave new dignity to the simple aspects of national life that had been cherished for centuries. His patriotism, his independent spirit, his impassioned insistence on the worth of the common folk, won him the admiration not only of his contemporaries but of posterity.

Songs

Robert Burns had a rare gift for creating lilting musical effects, and this, combined with his lively sense of humor and his warm and sympathetic understanding of humanity, helped to make him one of the great song writers of English literature. Some of Burns's songs were completely original. Others were inspired by a stanza, a line, or a phrase from one of the many old ballads in Scottish dialect. Many of his songs were set to Scottish airs already in existence; others have since been set to music.

Highland Mary

"Highland Mary" was Mary Campbell, daughter of a Glasgow skipper, and one of several women with whom Burns fell in love. In this poem, written six years after her death in 1786, Burns tenderly recalls their last meeting.

Ye banks, and braes,° and streams around
  The castle o' Montgomery,°
Green be your woods and fair your
  flowers,
  Your waters never drumlie!°
There simmer first unfald her robes,   5
  And there the langest tarry;
For there I took the last fareweel,
  O' my sweet Highland Mary.

How sweetly bloom'd the gay green birk,°
  How rich the hawthorn's blossom,   10
As underneath their fragrant shade
  I clasp'd her to my bosom!
The golden hours on angel wings
  Flew o'er me and my dearie;
For dear to me as light and life,   15
  Was my sweet Highland Mary.

1. **braes:** banks, hillsides. 2. **Montgomery:** Mary Campbell served as a dairymaid in the household of Burns's friend, Gavin Hamilton. 4. **drumlie:** muddy. 9. **birk:** birch.

Wi' monie a vow and lock'd embrace
    Our parting was fu' tender;
And, pledging aft to meet again,
    We tore oursels asunder;   20
But O! fell Death's untimely frost,
    That nipt my flower sae early!
Now green's the sod, and cauld's the clay,
    That wraps my Highland Mary!

O pale, pale now, those rosy lips,   25
    I aft hae kiss'd sae fondly!
And clos'd for ay the sparkling glance,
    That dwalt on me sae kindly!
And moldering now in silent dust,
    That heart that lo'ed me dearly!   30
But still within my bosom's core
    Shall live my Highland Mary.

To a Mouse

ON TURNING HER UP IN HER NEST WITH THE PLOW, NOVEMBER 1785

In spite of their many words of Scottish dialect, the two following poems have
maintained great popularity. One shows Burns's compassion for the displaced
mouse; the other reveals his sense of irony and humor. Both contain lines frequently quoted because of their pithy, homely philosophy.

Wee, sleekit,° cowrin', tim'rous beastie,
O, what a panic's in thy breastie!
Thou need na start awa sae hasty
    Wi' bickering brattle!°
I wad be laith° to rin an' chase thee   5
    Wi' murd'rin pattle!°

I'm truly sorry man's dominion
Has broken nature's social union,
And justifies that ill opinion
    Which makes thee startle   10
At me, thy poor, earthborn companion,
    An' fellow mortal!

I doubt na, whyles,° but thou may thieve;
What then? poor beastie, thou maun live!
A daimen icker in a thrave°   15
    'S a sma' request;
I'll get a blessin' wi' the lave,°
    An' never miss 't!

Thy wee bit housie, too, in ruin!
It's silly wa's° the win's are strewin'!   20
An' naething, now, to big° a new ane,
    O' foggage° green!
An' bleak December's winds ensuin',
    Baith snell° an' keen!

Thou saw the fields laid bare and waste,
An' weary winter comin' fast,   26
An' cozie here, beneath the blast,
    Thou thought to dwell,
Till crash! the cruel coulter° passed
    Out through thy cell.   30

That wee bit heap o' leaves an' stibble
Has cost thee mony a weary nibble!
Now thou's turn'd out, for a' thy trouble,
    But house or hald,°
To thole° the winter's sleety dribble   35
    An' cranreuch° cauld!

But, Mousie, thou art no thy lane°
In proving foresight may be vain;
The best laid schemes o' mice an' men
    Gang aft agley,°   40
An' lea'e us nought but grief an' pain,
    For promis'd joy.

Still thou art blest, compared wi' me,
The present only toucheth thee;
But och! I backward cast my e'e   45
    On prospects drear!
An' forward, though I canna see,
    I guess an' fear!

1. **sleekit:** sleek. 4. **bickering brattle:** hasty scamper. 5. **laith** (lāth): loath, reluctant.
6. **pattle:** plowstaff. 13. **whyles:** at times. 15. **A daimen . . . thrave:** an occasional head of
grain in a bundle. 17. **lave:** rest. 20. **silly wa's:** weak walls. 21. **big:** build. 22. **foggage:**
herbage. 24. **snell:** sharp. 29. **coulter** (kōl'tər): plow. 34. **But . . . hald:** without a dwelling
place. 35. **thole:** endure. 36. **cranreuch** (krən'rəkh): hoarfrost. 37. **no thy lane:** not alone.
40. **Gang aft agley** (ə·glē'): oft go astray.

To a Louse

Ha! wh' are ye gaun, ye crowlin' ferlie!°
Your impudence protects you sairly;°
I canna say but ye strunt° rarely,
    Owre gauze and lace;
Though faith! I fear ye dine but sparely
    On sic a place.   6

Ye ugly, creepin', blastit wonner,°
Detested, shunned by saunt an' sinner!
How dare ye set your fit° upon her,
    Sae fine a lady?   10
Gae somewhere else, and seek your din-
    ner
    On some poor body.

Swith, in some beggar's haffet squattle;°
There ye may creep, and sprawl, and
    sprattle°
Wi' ither kindred jumping cattle,   15
    In shoals and nations;
Where horn nor bane° ne'er dare unsettle
    Your thick plantations.

Now haud ye there,° ye're out o' sight,
Below the fatt'rels,° snug an' tight;   20
Na, faith ye yet! ye'll no be right
    Till ye've got on it,
The very tapmost tow'ring height
    O' Miss's bonnet.

My sooth! right bauld ye set your nose
    out,   25
As plump and gray as onie grozet;°
O for some rank mercurial rozet,°
    Or fell red smeddum!°
I'd gie you sic a hearty dose o't,
    Wad dress your droddum!°   30

I wad na been surprised to spy
You on an auld wife's flannen toy;°
Or aiblins some bit duddie boy,°
    On's wyliecoat;°
But Miss's fine Lunardi!° fie,   35
    How daur ye do 't?

O Jenny, dinna toss your head,
An' set your beauties a' abroad!°
Ye little ken what cursèd speed
    The blastie's makin'!   40
Thae winks and finger ends,° I dread,
    Are notice takin'!

O wad some Pow'r the giftie gie us
To see oursels as ithers see us!
It wad frae mony a blunder free us,   45
    And foolish notion:
What airs in dress an' gait wad lea'e us,
    And e'en devotion!

---

1. **crowlin' ferlie** (fer'li): crawling wonder.
2. **sairly:** greatly. 3. **strunt:** strut. 7. **blastit wonner:** blasted wonder. 9. **fit:** foot. 13. **Swith . . . squattle:** Be off with you! Sprawl in some beggar's temple. 14. **sprattle:** struggle. 17. **horn nor bane:** comb nor poison. 19. **haud ye there:** stay where you are. 20. **fatt'rels:** ribbon ends. 26. **onie grozet** (groz'it): any gooseberry. 27. **rozet:** rosin. 28. **smeddum:** powder. 30. **Wad . . . droddum:** would put an end to you.

32. **flannen toy:** flannel headdress. 33. **Or . . . boy:** or perhaps on some little ragged boy. 34. **wyliecoat** (wī'lē·kōt'): flannel vest. 35. **Lunardi:** a bonnet named for an aeronaut of that day, probably with winglike ribbons. 38. **abread:** abroad. 41. **Thae . . . ends:** Those people winking and pointing.

A Man's a Man for A' That

Burns wrote this poem in the 1790's, at the time when the French Revolution was arousing strong feelings among the British. An early, clear democratic note, this poem was a significant one in the eighteenth century.

Is there, for honest poverty,
  That hings his head, an' a' that?
The coward slave, we pass him by,
  We dare be poor for a' that!
    For a' that, an' a' that,   5
      Our toils obscure, an' a' that;
    The rank is but the guinea's stamp;°
      The man's the gowd° for a' that.

What tho' on hamely fare we dine,
  Wear hodden-gray,° an' a' that;   10
Gie fools their silks, and knaves their
      wine,
  A man's a man for a' that.
    For a' that, an' a' that,
      Their tinsel show, an' a' that;
    The honest man, though e'er sae poor,
      Is king o' men for a' that.   16

Ye see yon birkie,° ca'd a lord,
  Wha struts, an' stares, an' a' that;
Tho' hundreds worship at his word,
  He's but a coof° for a' that.   20

For a' that, an' a' that,
  His riband, star,° an' a' that,
The man o' independent mind,
  He looks and laughs at a' that.

A prince can mak' a belted knight,   25
  A marquis, duke, an' a' that;
But an honest man's aboon° his might,
  Guid faith he mauna fa' that!°
    For a' that, an' a' that,
      Their dignities, an' a' that,   30
    The pith o' sense, an' pride o' worth,
      Are higher rank than a' that.

Then let us pray that come it may,
  As come it will for a' that,
That sense and worth, o'er a' the earth, 35
  May bear the gree,° an' a' that.
    For a' that, an' a' that,
      It's coming yet, for a' that,
    That man to man, the warld o'er,
      Shall brothers be for a' that.   40

7. **guinea's stamp:** an imprint stamped on gold coins. 8. **gowd:** gold. 10. **hodden-gray:** coarse cloth. 17. **birkie:** fellow. 20. **coof:** fool.

22. **riband, star:** insignia of titles and honors. 27. **aboon:** above. 28. **he . . . that:** he can't make that. 36. **bear the gree:** take the prize.

FOR STUDY AND DISCUSSION

1. In "Highland Mary" Burns uses contrast for effect. What is the main contrast, and what natural images are used to enforce this contrast?

2. "To a Mouse" and "To a Louse" are companion poems in several respects, but most strikingly in the author's use of homely subjects in homely situations to frame universal truths. In each case the truth is double-edged. Does Burns think the plans of "mice and men" are, in general, comparable? Does he really think we would be happier if we could see ourselves as others see us? Explain.

3. What is Burns's point in "A Man's a Man for A' That"? How does this poem reveal the new democratic spirit that was emerging in the eighteenth century? What ideas and customs are challenged in the poem?

FOR COMPOSITION

1. Write a fully developed paragraph using the following statement as your starting point: "Although in many ways Johnson and Burns were poles apart as people and as writers, the spirit that animates Burns's poem "A Man's a Man for A' That" is similar to the spirit behind Johnson's "Letter to Lord Chesterfield."

2. "In the annals of English literature, Burns is a kind of anomaly. He defies classification. He stands apart in isolated individuality. . . . The preceding English poetry of the eighteenth century did not give any prognostication of the possibility of anyone resembling him." Write a comment on two or three of Burns's poems, showing the extent to which they illustrate the above statement. Defend your commentary by comparing Burns's poems with other eighteenth-century poems you have read.

WILLIAM BLAKE
(1757–1827)

One of William Blake's earlier biographers called him the "most spiritual of artists." The description still stands. Matter-of-fact objectors have called Blake mad; in recent years critics, while admitting his eccentricity, have elevated him as a major prophet—not only of the Romantic movement, but of the revolt against the mechanical tyranny of the modern world. It is said that Blake is only negatively related to the eighteenth century. Yet both as a revolutionary and a mystic, Blake was in his lonely way a child of his time. His revolt was against the intellectual patternmaking of the eighteenth century. His achievement—unrecognized in his own time—was a breakthrough into the Romantic movement.

Blake received little formal education, but his father, a poor tradesman, kept him well supplied with books and prints of great paintings. At the age of ten, Blake expressed a desire to be a painter and was sent to drawing school and then apprenticed to an engraver. It was during this period that he first began experimenting with verse, thus embarking upon the two separate careers that he would eventually make one. As a child, Blake had strangely intense religious experiences. He once reported seeing a tree filled with angels and, on another occasion, he saw the prophet Ezekiel under a tree in a field. To Blake the next world was as real as this one. Seeing God at his window was not, for him, unusual. Solitary by ordinary standards, Blake was surrounded from within by his own visitors. His devoted wife once said, "I have very little of Mr. Blake's company. He is always in Paradise."

Blake's trade as an engraver was an important means of livelihood, for his pictures and his poetry were not widely accepted during his lifetime. His talent for sketching is seen in his illustrations not only of his own poems but of specially decorated editions of Milton's *Paradise Lost,* Dante's *Divine Comedy,* and the Book of Job. All his life Blake devoted himself to expressing his mystical faith and his visions of a heavenly world. His concern, in both art and poetry, was to represent eternal things in terms of earthly symbols.

"Without contraries," wrote Blake, "there is no progression." His life and work are a confusion of contraries: infinite patience and painstaking workmanship in the dawn of the Industrial Age; the damning of "mind-forged manacles" in an age of rules; emotion in an age of reason; other-worldly presences involved in this world's work; genius called madness. His *Songs of Innocence* and *Songs of Experience,* two fanciful works which appealed so much to later Romantic poets, are also studies in contrast. In these two works, this great poet of contraries pointed out the need for both childhood's innocence and the wisdom—however painful and disillusioning—gained by experience. *Songs of Innocence* and *Songs of Experience,* though not appreciated until some fifty years after his death, contain some of the most beautiful lyrics in the English language.

The greatness of Blake lies less, perhaps, in his apocalyptic outlook than in his mastery, in art and verse, of an extreme and moving simplicity. William Wordsworth commented perceptively on this extraordinary artist and writer when he noted: "There is something in the madness of this man which interests me more than the sanity of Lord Byron or Walter Scott."

The Lamb

Little Lamb, who made thee?
Dost thou know who made thee?
Gave thee life, and bid thee feed,
By the stream and o'er the mead;
Gave thee clothing of delight,   5
Softest clothing, woolly, bright;
Gave thee such a tender voice,
Making all the vales rejoice?
Little Lamb, who made thee?
Dost thou know who made thee?   10

Little Lamb, I'll tell thee,
Little Lamb, I'll tell thee:
He is callèd by thy name,
For He calls Himself a Lamb,
He is meek, and He is mild;   15
He became a little child.
I a child, and thou a lamb,
We are callèd by His name.
Little Lamb, God bless thee!
Little Lamb, God bless thee!   20

The Tiger

Tiger, tiger, burning bright
In the forest of the night,
What immortal hand or eye
Could frame thy fearful symmetry?

In what distant deeps or skies   5
Burnt the fire of thine eyes?
On what wings dare he aspire?
What the hand dare seize the fire?

And what shoulder, and what art,
Could twist the sinews of thy heart?   10
When thy heart began to beat,
What dread hand forged thy dread feet?

What the hammer? What the chain?
In what furnace was thy brain?
What the anvil? What dread grasp   15
Dared its deadly terrors clasp?

When the stars threw down their spears,
And watered heaven with their tears,
Did He smile his work to see?
Did He who made the lamb make thee?

Tiger, tiger, burning bright   21
In the forest of the night,
What immortal hand or eye
Dare frame thy fearful symmetry?

The Clod and the Pebble

"Love seeketh not itself to please,
   Nor for itself hath any care,
But for another gives its ease,
   And builds a Heaven in Hell's despair."

So sung a little Clod of Clay,   5
   Trodden with the cattle's feet,
But a Pebble of the brook
   Warbled out these meters meet:

"Love seeketh only Self to please,
   To bind another to its delight,   10
Joys in another's loss of ease,
   And builds a Hell in Heaven's despite."

STANZAS FROM *Milton*

And did those feet in ancient time
   Walk upon England's mountains green?
And was the holy Lamb of God
   On England's pleasant pastures seen?

And did the Countenance Divine   5
   Shine forth upon our clouded hills?
And was Jerusalem builded here
   Among these dark Satanic mills?°

Bring me my bow of burning gold!
   Bring me my arrows of desire!   10
Bring me my spear! O clouds, unfold!
   Bring me my chariot of fire!

I will not cease from mental fight,
   Nor shall my sword sleep in my hand,
Till we have built Jerusalem   15
   In England's green and pleasant land.

8. **dark . . . mills:** symbolic, to Blake, of the materialism of English society.

Frontispiece of *Songs of Innocence* (1789), written and printed by William Blake.

FOR STUDY AND DISCUSSION

1. "The Lamb" is one of the poems in Blake's *Songs of Innocence*. Who is speaking to whom in the poem? How does the identity of the speaker determine the diction (choice and arrangement of words), the style, and the tone of the poem? To what extent is the poem an illustration of the Bible's assurance that we must become as little children to enter into the kingdom of heaven?

2. How is the voice that speaks in "The Tiger" different from the voice in "The Lamb"? Why do you think the questions in "The Lamb" receive answers while those in "The Tiger" go unanswered? What do the unanswered questions imply about the "immortal hand" that created the tiger? The creation of the tiger is pictured in an extended metaphor in stanzas 3 and 4. Is the metaphor appropriate? effective? Explain your answer by discussing the specific words used to depict the special kind of creation Blake refers to.

3. In line 6 of "The Clod and the Pebble" Blake describes the clod as "trodden with the cattle's feet." How does this detail help to explain the clod's attitude toward love? Show the extent to which the third stanza derives its force from repetition, with variation of wording and phrasing, of the first stanza. Substitute for *Love* in lines 1 and 9 another word or phrase that defines precisely the kind of love described. Which concept of love do you think better expresses Blake's own view?

4. Jerusalem was considered the ideal city of the Jews in exile. Show how Blake has used this idea symbolically in "Stanzas from *Milton*." In line 1, whose feet are referred to? Why is the imperative "Bring me" repeated in each line of the third stanza? Are the weapons called for appropriate to the purpose stated in the last two lines? How well do the last two stanzas answer the questions asked in the first two stanzas?

SYMBOLISM

Because a symbol implies a meaning beyond its surface meaning, it can serve both to clarify the idea of a poem and to give it added dimensions. Like a metaphor, a symbol suggests a relationship between two objects. Symbols are often derived from conventional relationships familiar to and readily identifiable by most readers. Night, for example, often symbolizes death or evil; white stands for purity; the owl, for wisdom; the lion, for courage.

Although Blake's lamb and tiger can be thought of as real animals, their function as symbols should be emphasized. The lamb is used as a symbol of the innocence of childhood, the tiger mainly as a symbol of the fearful power of worldly experience. Point out lines in both poems in which the lamb and the tiger are pictured as animals and as symbols.

FOR COMPOSITION

1. Basing your answer on your comprehension of the two poems "The Lamb" and "The Tiger," define fully the terms *innocence* and *experience* as you think Blake must have meant his readers to understand them.

2. When Blake combined his *Songs of Innocence* and *Songs of Experience* in one volume, he gave as a subtitle "Showing the Two Contrary States of the Human Soul." Blake's hero, Milton, in his poems "L'Allegro" and "Il Penseroso," also showed two contrary states of the human soul. In a brief essay, compare Blake's contrary states with those of Milton.

THE GROWTH OF THE ENGLISH LANGUAGE

The Eighteenth Century

During most of the eighteenth century, the English were strongly concerned with rules, form, and "correctness" in the use of language. The century began with a revival of interest in the idea of establishing an English Academy to set up official standards for the language, as the French Academy was attempting to do for the French language. Several leading writers of the time—including Defoe, Addison, and Swift—were interested in seeing such an Academy founded, and they wrote articles giving urgent reasons why it was needed.

Swift's ideas on the subject were especially influential. He wanted to see the language improved—but he wanted even more to see it protected from further change. "What I have most at heart," he wrote, "is, that some method be thought on for ascertaining and fixing our language for ever . . . For I am of opinion, it is better a language should not be wholly perfect, than that it should be perpetually changing."

This attitude was notably different from the attitude that had been expressed in the Royal Society's resolution in 1664 (see page 267). The members of the Royal Society had taken it for granted that language changed, but they had not wanted to halt this process—on the contrary, they had wanted to encourage further development. What accounted for the change in opinion that had taken place by the beginning of the eighteenth century? For one thing, the English no longer felt that their own language was inferior to others (particularly to Latin) for purposes of serious writing. But there was an even more important reason why Swift and his contemporaries feared further changes in the language. They were keenly aware that a great national literature had been produced in England during the past century and a half, and they were afraid that if the language kept on changing, soon all of this literature would be dead and lost. Alexander Pope expressed this conviction in *An Essay on Criticism,* where he said:

"Short is the date, alas! of modern
   rhymes . . .
Our sons their fathers' failing language
   see,
And such as Chaucer is shall Dryden be."

Of course, we know that Pope's gloomy prediction about the future of the language has not come true. Approximately three centuries have now passed since the time that Dryden wrote, and Dryden's language—except for an occasional word or two—is still as clear to twentieth-century readers as it was to readers of Dryden's own day.

But why is it that Pope and Swift and other respectable thinkers of the Age of Reason turned out to be wrong about the path of development that the language was following? One answer is that these men had no way of estimating the powerful influence that the written form of the language was coming to exert. Until the end of the Middle Ages, the written language had never had much effect on the kind of English that was used by the population as a whole—simply because most people had not been able to read or write. The introduction of the printing press in 1485 changed this situation by making inexpensive reading matter widely available. By Shakespeare's time, a century after the introduction of printing, probably about half the population of London could read and write. By the time of Pope and Swift, the literacy rate for the middle and upper classes in England was close to 100 percent.

Instead of being exposed only to the English spoken by their own circle of acquaintances, people were now being exposed continually to English that had been written by professional writers. Since the standard written form of the language was regarded as the "best" form or the "correct" form, educated people tended to give up local usages which differed from standard usage. Thus the influence of the written language acted to curb changes that might otherwise have taken wide hold in the spoken language.

The schools also began to exert an important influence on the language. Prior to 1700, most schools had concentrated on the teaching of Latin and had paid little attention to English. During the course of the eighteenth century, however, the teaching of English gradually became the basis of most elementary schooling. Many of the rules of spelling, grammar, and usage that were first set forth in eighteenth-century schoolbooks became a traditional part of the school curriculum and have continued to be taught and enforced up to the present day. In fact, the schools have probably done a far more effective job of preserving the language from change than any official Academy could have hoped to do.

The fact that the basic grammatical system and the basic vocabulary of English have not changed essentially since 1700 does not mean, however, that no changes at all have taken place. While the influence of the written language tends to keep old words and expressions from dropping out of the language, it also speeds the acceptance of new words and expressions. A new term that appears in a few newspaper and magazine articles can become part of the vocabulary of millions of people within a matter of days. Thus today's English vocabulary is indeed different from the vocabulary of Swift's time, but the difference is due almost entirely to the addition of new words and new meanings—not, as Swift had feared, to decay and loss of the old words.

FOR STUDY AND DISCUSSION

1. Another kind of language change that was not very much affected by the influence of the written language was change in pronunciation. Evidence that many changes in pronunciation have taken place during the past two hundred and fifty years can be found by examining the rhymes in an early eighteenth-century poem such as Pope's *Rape of the Lock* (page 304). Since "half-rhymes" were frowned on, we can assume that the following two couplets both ended with full rhymes according to Pope's pronunciation:

"Here Britain's statesmen oft the fall foredoom
Of foreign tyrants and of nymphs at home . . ."

"At omber singly to decide their doom:
And swells her breast with conquests yet to come . . ."

What can you conclude about the pronunciation of *doom, home,* and *come* in the early eighteenth century? Can you find other couplets in this poem that contain rhyme words which no longer rhyme today?

2. Although Defoe's *Journal of the Plague Year* pretended to be an eyewitness account written by a Londoner of the 1660's, an observant reader could probably tell that the language of the *Journal* resembled the language of the 1720's much more than it did the language of the 1660's. Following are two short excerpts from Samuel Pepys' diary, which really was written in the 1660's, and two matching excerpts from Defoe's *Journal.* By looking at the italicized expressions, you should be able to tell which excerpt in each pair is by Pepys and which is by Defoe. Remember that Defoe's language is likely to be closer to modern speech.

a. (1) "I *did ask* him where he learned that immodest garb . . ."
   (2) "I *asked* how long it had lain there . . ."
b. (1) "they *did not know*"
   (2) "so as we *know not* . . ."

THE ENGLISH NOVEL

It is hard to decide exactly what a novel is. It is of course prose fiction, but not all pieces of prose fiction can be reasonably classed as novels. For example, Swift's *Gulliver's Travels* (1726), which is equally successful as a savage satire on humanity and as a story for children, is prose fiction, but nobody would call it a novel. Is *Robinson Crusoe* (1719), Defoe's masterpiece, a novel, or is it simply a tale of adventure? Where do we draw the line between adventure tales, fantasies, romances, science fiction, and novels? It is difficult to decide, but at least we can agree that in the novel proper we are concerned with men and women who are related to some sort of society in a fairly realistic fashion. A story about monsters living at the back of the moon would not be a novel. We can say, then, that a novel is a prose narrative that offers us imaginary characters and events usually set in some particular and recognizable society.

MAJOR PERIODS OF THE ENGLISH NOVEL

The novel was a comparatively late arrival in English literature; Italy, Spain, and France produced what we are entitled to call novels long before England did. The Elizabethans, for example, found it easy to tell a story in dramatic form for the stage, but could not manage prose fiction. But once English literature really got hold of the novel, in the eighteenth century, it became famous for its fiction and influenced writers in many different countries. From the middle of the eighteenth century onward, more and more English novels were written and read; but in this literary form, like others (the drama is a striking example), there was a mysterious ebb and flow of greatness. Excellent English novels have been published continually during the last two hundred years, but some are better than others. We might say that English fiction reached its highest level in three separate periods—roughly, 1740–1770, 1840–1890, and 1905–1930. It is during these years especially that we find English novelists of genius producing acknowledged masterpieces. Now let us take a look at them.

DEFOE: PIONEER IN FICTION

A word first, though, about Daniel Defoe, whose best-known book, *Robinson Crusoe,* appeared in 1719. Defoe was an important originator of realism in English fiction. He had to be realistic because while actually creating fiction—though usually with some basis of fact—he was pretending to offer his readers memoirs and autobiographies. Many authors have claimed to be important novelists when they have been mere journalists, but in Defoe we have a journalist who was secretly a storyteller of quite remarkable talent. And just because his stories had to seem solidly real, he did some valuable pioneer work for English fiction. His best characters, after his famous shipwrecked sailor, are raffish types like Moll Flanders and Captain Singleton.

FOUR EIGHTEENTH-CENTURY NOVELISTS

The 1740–1770 group of English novelists consists of Samuel Richardson, Henry Fielding, Laurence Sterne, and Tobias Smollett. After Richardson, a smug little man and a retired printer, was commissioned to do a book of letters which readers could use as samples, he contrived a novel in the form of letters

Left, "Partridge Interrupting Tom Jones's Protestations to Lady Bellaston," an illustration by Thomas Rowlandson (1791) for the novel *Tom Jones*. Right, Henry Fielding, author of *Tom Jones*.

about a virtuous serving girl, Pamela, who repulsed her master until he consented to marry her. Though *Pamela* (1740) is often referred to as the first English novel, it was Richardson's second and much longer novel, *Clarissa Harlowe,* also written in letter form, that became the rage not only in England but all over the continent. This narrative-in-letters method is entirely unreal, at least as Richardson used it (for his chief characters would be spending twelve hours a day writing letters). However, it has the great advantage, which Richardson made use of very artfully, of giving in turn everybody's points of view, thoughts, feelings, hopes, and fears. The hothouse sentimentality and piety of these novels are not to our taste today, but Richardson's reputation in his own time was tremendous, and he undoubtedly had a great deal of influence on the development of fiction.

Henry Fielding, a very different type of man, detested Richardson and all his works. It was like a dog looking at a cat. Fielding came from an old landed family, lived riotously, and then took to writing to earn a living, finally becoming a city magistrate—a very good one too.

His masterpiece is *Tom Jones* (1749), which is both a magnificent panorama of eighteenth-century life and the expression, unusual in the novel, of a powerful incisive intellect, quick to observe all the ironies, absurdities, and hypocrisies of social life. Nineteenth-century critics considered Fielding one of the great masters of the novel, but during the last fifty years he has been somewhat neglected and undervalued.

Laurence Sterne's reputation has had a different history. He was enormously popular in his own time. Later his faults of taste and manner alienated many critics, but now he is warmly praised again. One reason for this is that his highly original method, ruthlessly cutting out everything that is not essential to our understanding of a character and a situation, is very "modern," like his extremely artful, intimate, and conversational style. His humor is "modern" too, but not his sentiment, which is too often forced and false. *Tristram Shandy* (1760), his masterpiece, is a wonderful study of a family in which nobody understands anybody else.

Tobias Smollett, a Scot who had been a surgeon's mate in the navy, wrote long novels crammed with rough humor and knockabout incidents. He had a very solid reputation for some fifty years after his death and had considerable influence upon Dickens in the latter's earlier years. But now Smollett is no longer regarded as one of the great eighteenth-century masters. Nor is Oliver Goldsmith, who wrote only one novel, read as often as he used to be. *The Vicar of Wakefield* (1766), though charming in its humor and sentiment, tells a story that is too obviously contrived.

JANE AUSTEN AND WALTER SCOTT

Between the two peaks of 1740–1770 and 1840–1890 come two important novelists, Jane Austen (1775–1817) and Sir Walter Scott (1771–1832). Jane Austen, with her very acute and exquisitely perceptive sense of character and scene, has probably never been equaled within her deliberately limited range. Her novels are classics of the art of fiction, and once enjoyed they are our friends for life. Scott is a curious case, for in his own time, when he had stupendous success and very wide influence as author of medieval romances such as *Ivanhoe* (1819), he was thought to be not so much a novelist as a historical romancer. In point of fact, however, he has many weaknesses as a historical romancer and a good deal of enduring strength and appeal as a novelist. His finest stories are those with an eighteenth-century background.

MASTERS OF NINETEENTH-CENTURY FICTION

The 1840–1890 group begins with Charles Dickens (1812–70), one of the acknowledged world masters of fiction. Dickens began to write in a slapdash, improvising way, mixing glorious fun with unreal melodrama; then he gradually planned his work more and more and, while keeping his inimitable humor, filled his writings with a searching criticism of mid-Victorian society. He was a strange, divided man, but for the art of fiction he had a blazing genius. William Makepeace Thackeray (1811–63) had no such genius, but he had great qualities of his own: a wide knowledge of social life, a wonderful eye and ear for character and scene, and an easy narrative style that could rise to passages of great force and beauty. These qualities are perhaps found at their best in *Vanity Fair*, although many critics consider his historical novel, *Esmond,* his masterpiece.

Left, Charles Dickens. Right, New York's farewell to Dickens after his American tour (1867).

Anthony Trollope (1815–82), who was one of Thackeray's most enthusiastic admirers, is less distinguished in style and lacks Thackeray's flashes of insight, but his solid novels about mid-Victorian churchmen and politicians, after being almost forgotten, are once more being widely read and appreciated.

The chief women in this group are Charlotte Brontë (1816–55), who brought an intense and strongly personal realism into fiction; her sister, Emily (1818–48), whose *Wuthering Heights* (1847) is hardly a novel at all in the ordinary sense but rather an impassioned and symbolic prose poem; and Marian Evans (1819–80), who wrote under the name of George Eliot. The latter was a deeply serious woman with a good intellect as well as a sound knowledge of English provincial life; her very solid virtues are found at their best in *Middlemarch* (1871), which thoroughly analyzes a certain type of society and which is one of the best examples in English of a highly organized novel.

George Meredith (1828–1909) and Thomas Hardy (1840–1928) both preferred their poetry to their fiction, although they wrote many long novels. They are both philosophical novelists, making their fiction express certain ideas about life. But whereas Meredith is a high-spirited if rather affected comic-romantic, Hardy is broodingly pessimistic, at his best when his characters are rustic types surrounded by the heaths and vales of the author's native "Wessex," (see page 630). With them may be mentioned Robert Louis Stevenson (1850–94), who died too young—at forty-four—to fulfill completely all his promise, but who has retained his hold on successive generations of readers by the romantic zest of his narrative and a curious charm of style.

BROADENED HORIZONS

Before we reach the next high table-land of the English novel, 1905–1930, we must note that during the intervening

"Mrs. Rawdon's Departure from Paris." An illustration by William Makepeace Thackeray for his novel *Vanity Fair*.

period, from 1890 onward, English prose fiction suddenly began to travel to very distant places. Before this time, from Richardson to Hardy, every major novel, except for a few chapters here and there, had been concerned with the British scene. Now came a much wider sweep. Stevenson began it with his tales of the South Seas. Then Rudyard Kipling (1865–1936) arrived from India, W. H. Hudson (1841–1922) from South America, and Joseph Conrad (1852–1924) from worldwide travels. The last, a Pole by birth who became a captain in the British merchant marine, is the most important of these three as a novelist. Conrad is often thought to be simply a romantic storyteller just because he shows us so many sailors and ships in far-off places. However, he is really a novelist who happens to be indifferent to the usual social themes but one who is deeply concerned with character, with behavior in moments of great stress, and with the fundamental nature of human life and destiny. These themes he often treats in a symbolical way, as poets are apt to do, so that in reading Conrad we must always try to be aware of depths of meaning below the surface of the narrative.

SOCIOLOGICAL NOVELISTS

The beginning of the 1905–1930 period shows us three very successful English writers who might be described as "sociological" novelists. By this we mean that their chief concern is with society itself—its organization, outlook, values, and tone. H. G. Wells (1866–1946), Arnold Bennett (1867–1931), and John Galsworthy (1867–1933), the three writers in question, are far from being alike either as men or as writers, but in their fiction they all have a sociological foundation in common.

Wells, the most brilliant, never thought of himself as a literary artist (though he was), and made no secret of the fact that he made use of the novel as a critic of society. But his genius in the creation of character and scene often triumphs over his sociology, as in *Mr. Polly* (1910) and *Tono-Bungay* (1909). Arnold Bennett's fiction is varied and uneven, but the best of it is a solidly realistic record of the society he knew as a boy in that provincial region known, because it was the center of the pottery industry, as "The Potteries." There is, however, in Bennett an easy, unforced charm as well as a solid realism, which he learned from French novelists during the years he lived in France. Bennett's masterpiece is *The Old Wives' Tale* (1908).

John Galsworthy made his reputation in Britain before World War I, not only through his novels, which were sharply critical studies of the property-owning class to which he himself belonged, but also through his realistic and well-constructed plays. It was, however, with the publication of *The Forsyte Saga* (1906–21) that he achieved during the 1920's a world-wide body of admiring readers who felt that his wide social range, his honest criticism of his own class, his deep compassion, his essential English-ness, made him the representative English novelist of his time. He was the first English writer of fiction after Kipling to be awarded the Nobel prize.

Although Galsworthy achieved international fame after World War I, he, Wells, and Bennett really belong to the period that ended in 1914, at the outbreak of that war. And here it must be remembered that for Britain the war lasted over four years, killed nearly a million young men, and caused an unimaginable amount of suffering and grief. Because these years 1914–1918 represent a break in the history of the English novel, we shall pause here to take a wider view of the writing, publishing, and reading of fiction.

GROWING POPULARITY OF THE NOVEL

During most of the nineteenth century, novels of any importance were originally published in three volumes and at prices that only wealthier readers and libraries could afford to pay. Dickens and Thackeray, however, brought out most of their novels first in what were called "parts," that is, in separate installments published every month. Cheap one-volume editions began to be published chiefly for the benefit of railroad travelers. Then, in the 1890's, enterprising publishers brought out one-volume editions of new novels, at a quarter of the price of the old three-volume editions. Libraries could now afford to buy more copies; ordinary readers became novel-buyers; and the trade in fiction increased enormously.

All manner of readers were now catered to by all manner of novelists specializing in humorous stories, or historical romances, or tales of crime and detection, like the famous Sherlock Holmes stories by Arthur Conan Doyle (1859–1930). Many of these popular novelists were excellent craftsmen—for example, the humorist, W. W. Jacobs (1863–1943). By 1914 the output of fiction in London was so large that lesser known but really excellent writers like Maurice Hewlett (1861–1923), George Moore (1852–

1933), and William de Morgan (1839–1917) cannot be considered in this chronicle. And in the years just before the war, a group of young novelists, including Compton Mackenzie (1883–1972), Frank Swinnerton (1884–   ), and Hugh Walpole (1884–1941), arrived on the scene. But the big names were still Wells, Bennett, Galsworthy—all of them, as we have seen, sociological novelists.

TWENTIETH-CENTURY NOVELISTS

Now what the war did was to remove the interest of the more literary critics of fiction from the sociological novel and to fix that interest on novels and novelists of a very different kind. Instead of looking outward toward society itself, these new novelists tended to look inward and describe what was happening in the minds of their characters. So Virginia Woolf (1882–1941), one of these new novelists and a very brilliant woman, could attack Bennett because he did not seem to her to bring any illusion of life into the novel. (But this was true only from her own point of view, and if a Bennett novel is weak in its inward life, a Virginia Woolf novel is weak in its outward life—in the relation of its characters to society.) Literary fashion in London, following a general European movement, now insisted that fiction, to be of any significance, should explore the depths and recesses of personality, revealing an unending stream of impressions, feelings, and thoughts, and showing us fewer people if necessary, but telling us everything about them.

A master of this method, which he finally carried to an extreme that lies outside the novel proper, was James Joyce (1882–1941). His genius, especially in *Ulysses* (1922), cannot be questioned, but his stature and influence as a novelist have been wildly overestimated. Joyce is best regarded as a kind of humorous prose-poet with an astonishing passion for and knowledge of language—a master of words.

E. M. Forster (1879–1970) published most of his novels before World War I, but his finest novel, *A Passage to India* (1924), did not arrive until the twenties, and he stands quite apart from the older sociological novelists. His work is easier to enjoy than to describe. He cares nothing for a broad picture of human society. His own point of view shapes and colors all his novels, and he tries—as a rule very successfully—to give the reader certain supremely important, all-revealing moments in the lives of his characters. There is a kind of magic in Forster at his best, but he can also be oddly improbable and unconvincing.

Virginia Woolf, as we have seen, believed that the significant modern novel should reflect the inner life of its characters, and with this aim in mind, she made several difficult, subtle, and not always successful experiments. But in novels like *To the Lighthouse* (1927) and *Between the Acts* (1941), she succeeds triumphantly, creating fiction of deep human interest and strange beauty. Elsewhere, character and situation almost seem to vanish, and her work seems more like that of a prose poet than that of a real novelist.

There can be no doubt that D. H. Lawrence (1885–1930), especially in his earlier work, was a real novelist. He too looks inward, but not to show us a stream of impressions as Virginia Woolf does, but to explore those mysterious areas of feeling of which we are hardly conscious but which can strongly influence our lives. Lawrence was certainly a man of genius, and his writing reveals a marvelously sensitive feeling for nature and a gift for description.

Younger novelists who made their first appearance in the twenties are Aldous Huxley (1894–1963), who succeeds in fiction by sheer intelligence but who is really more a philosophical essayist than a novelist proper; Evelyn Waugh (1903–1966), who in his first two stories, *Decline and Fall* (1928) and *Vile Bodies* (1930), achieved something very rare

—namely a new kind of humor that quickly became fashionable and much imitated; and Graham Greene (1904–), whose best work is concerned with good and evil and who is haunted by a feeling of guilt that many of his readers cannot help sharing. Among the women novelists first published during this decade were Elizabeth Bowen (1899–1973), Rosamund Lehmann (1903–), and Ivy Compton-Burnett (1892–1969).

THE CONTEMPORARY SCENE

We made 1930 the outside limit of this third important period in English fiction. This date, which might be pushed forward a few years without doing any harm, does not imply that after 1930 there was a sharp decline in the standard of new English fiction. Good novelists—as for example, Joyce Cary (1888–1957), Liam O'Flaherty (1896–), and C. P. Snow (1905–)—were bringing out excellent new work. But it is difficult not to feel that sometime not long after 1930 much of the earlier excitement about the English novel began to subside. Most of the experiments had already been made. The inner life had been explored and recorded up to a point beyond which fiction would become unreadable. Novels were being written and read, but the form itself seemed to lose its primary importance. Moreover, as the various dictators in Europe became ever more powerful and menacing, political events and books dealing with those events attracted more and more attention. Fiction has always been at its best during comparatively peaceful eras, and this period, which ended with World War II, was anything but peaceful.

English fiction (see also page 799) has produced some good new names and good new work since the second World War. Angus Wilson (1913–), Iris Murdoch (1919–), William Golding (1911–), Alan Sillitoe (1928–), Pamela Hansford Johnson (1912–), and Anthony Burgess (1917–) are some of these names. The craftsmanship, the writing, are on a high level. But this contemporary fiction lacks size and weight, profound originality, and the kind of urgency that makes the novel seem important. These shortcomings may be due to a change of attitude in the reading public itself, for it will be found that it is precisely at those times when people are passionately eager to read fiction—as they were, for example, during the middle years of the nineteenth century, not only in England but all over Europe and in America—that the novel reaches toward greatness.

Finally, it must be understood that much excellent fiction has made its appearance outside Britain, in the various dominions of the British Commonwealth. From Canada we have had the successful novels about the Whiteoaks family by Mazo de la Roche; regional fiction by F. P. Grove, Thomas Raddall, W. O. Mitchell; Morley Callaghan's stories of city life; Hugh McLennan's novels; and well-written lighter fiction by Robertson Davies. Nadine Gordimer (1925–), Alan Paton (1903–), and Doris Lessing (1919–) have all written well about Africa. Australia, which is increasingly productive in fiction, has given us novelists like Katherine Susannah Pritchard, Kylie Tennant, and Henry Handel Richardson, whose trilogy of novels, *Richard Mahony,* is outstanding. Among the most vigorous and powerful of the newer Australian novelists is Patrick White. New Zealand writers of fiction include the famous short-story writer Katherine Mansfield, Jane Mander, and Robin Hyde, who died before he could become widely known outside his own country. The peasant life of India has found its way into the stories of Mulk Raj Anand, and now George Lamming's books are bringing the West Indies into the ever-widening panorama of Commonwealth life. It is impossible, however, to do even the barest justice to the fiction of these Commonwealth writers in a brief survey.

J.B.P.

THE ROMANTIC AGE

(1800–1837)

ROMANCE, Romantic, Romanticism—we shall be always coming across these terms, but they are very hard to define. They have in fact been given quite different meanings by people at different times. But clearly we cannot introduce the Romantic Age without some idea of what it means to be Romantic and what kind of writing belongs to Romanticism.

THE CHARACTERISTICS OF ROMANTICISM

From what we know already about the spirit of the eighteenth century, especially in its earlier, more confident, and classical period we can surmise that Romanticism will be its opposite. Romanticism will be the other side— the hidden and suppressed side, the formerly unfashionable and frowned- upon side—bursting out, breaking through.

Therefore if one side—one spirit, really—is reasonable, calm, and smugly confident, the other will be unreasonable or irrational, agitated, dubious, and troubled. If one side likes company, the other will love solitude. If one side flourishes only in cities, then the other will not only want the country but also the least inhabited parts of the country—the mountains, the forests, the desert. If one side believes in a highly civilized and artificial style of life, the other will turn away from it in disgust and praise all that is simple, natural, even primitive. If one side believes there is no mystery left in the universe, the other will see mystery everywhere—in a flower, a tree, a cloud, a star. If one side stresses traditional forms in its writing, the other will want to experiment with new and untried forms. If the writing of one side is a kind of public performance concerning itself with what we have in common,

Jean-Jacques Rousseau

the writing of the other will be intensely private and individualistic. And so it goes on.

This "other" side which is breaking through is Romanticism. And though the breakthrough was inevitable sooner or later, it came sooner than it might have otherwise, owing to the extraordinary influence of one eighteenth-century man of genius, Jean-Jacques Rousseau (1712–1778), a Swiss who lived and worked mostly in France. It is impossible to overestimate the influence of Rousseau, who denounced with passionate eloquence everything the eighteenth century believed in and hurried on both the French Revolution and the whole Romantic movement. Almost everything in this movement can be found, much earlier, in Rousseau. All the English Romantics read him with enthusiasm, at least when they were young. Rousseau, however, was so far from being a balanced human being that the last years of his life were threatened and then darkened by insanity. But then the Romanticism he so largely helped to create was itself unbalanced. It was one-sided, just as the earlier eighteenth-century attitude of mind was one-sided in the opposite fashion. It was as if a pendulum had been set in motion, taking writers from one extreme to the other.

Balanced people look neither entirely outward nor entirely inward; they consider both the outer world and their own inner world. Sometimes they want society; at other times they prefer solitude, enjoying in turn both the city and the quiet countryside. They do not believe that everything is a mystery, but they also refuse to believe that nothing is a mystery. Shakespeare and nearly all the earlier great writers were balanced people of this sort. They were quite unlike the writers of the Romantic Age, who were one-sidedly correcting something that had itself been too one-sided.

It should be noted that Romanticism was a European movement, though it did not succeed in all countries at the same time. It appeared first in

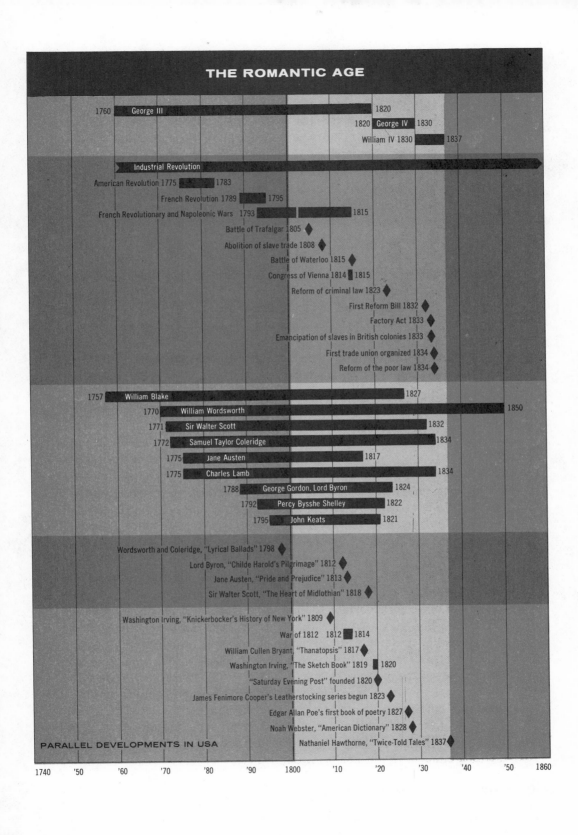

THE ROMANTIC AGE

1760 George III 1820
1820 George IV 1830
William IV 1830 1837

Industrial Revolution
American Revolution 1775 1783
French Revolution 1789 1795
French Revolutionary and Napoleonic Wars 1793 1815
Battle of Trafalgar 1805
Abolition of slave trade 1808
Battle of Waterloo 1815
Congress of Vienna 1814 1815
Reform of criminal law 1823
First Reform Bill 1832
Factory Act 1833
Emancipation of slaves in British colonies 1833
First trade union organized 1834
Reform of the poor law 1834

1757 William Blake 1827
1770 William Wordsworth 1850
1771 Sir Walter Scott 1832
1772 Samuel Taylor Coleridge 1834
1775 Jane Austen 1817
1775 Charles Lamb 1834
1788 George Gordon, Lord Byron 1824
1792 Percy Bysshe Shelley 1822
1795 John Keats 1821

Wordsworth and Coleridge, "Lyrical Ballads" 1798
Lord Byron, "Childe Harold's Pilgrimage" 1812
Jane Austen, "Pride and Prejudice" 1813
Sir Walter Scott, "The Heart of Midlothian" 1818

Washington Irving, "Knickerbocker's History of New York" 1809
War of 1812   1812   1814
William Cullen Bryant, "Thanatopsis" 1817
Washington Irving, "The Sketch Book" 1819   1820
"Saturday Evening Post" founded 1820
James Fenimore Cooper's Leatherstocking series begun 1823
Edgar Allan Poe's first book of poetry 1827
Noah Webster, "American Dictionary" 1828
PARALLEL DEVELOPMENTS IN USA
Nathaniel Hawthorne, "Twice-Told Tales" 1837

1740   '50   '60   '70   '80   '90   1800   '10   '20   '30   '40   '50   1860

Germany, then in England, then in Russia and elsewhere, and then, belatedly but brilliantly, in France as late as 1830. Its main influence on both North and South America was later still. In Britain some writers displayed what we would call Romantic characteristics as early as the 1760's, and some poets—notably Robert Burns and William Blake—were, in the last decades of the eighteenth century, writing in a predominantly Romantic way. But it was in 1798, the date of the publication of Wordsworth's and Coleridge's *Lyrical Ballads*, that Romanticism became the main influence in English literature. By the mid-1830's, when Queen Victoria began her reign, most of the major Romantic poets except Wordsworth had died.

THE LIMITED INFLUENCE OF ROMANTICISM

There is another important point that must be made. We have called this the *Romantic Age*, but what we really mean is the *Romantic Age in English literature*. For the age itself, outside literature, was not "romantic." The Prince Regent (who reigned in the place of his father, George III, who had gone insane); William Pitt, the Prime Minister; and the Duke of Wellington, who commanded the British forces—these men were not Romantics. It was only the poets and their friends and some of the younger people who could be said to belong to the Romantic movement. The politicians, bankers, merchants, soldiers, editors, even most of the literary critics, remained quite untouched by Romanticism.

Now this is important because it is new. In the time of Queen Elizabeth it was not simply the poets who were Elizabethan in spirit; almost everybody was. In the days of Queen Anne the writers shared the outlook, morals, manners, and tastes of the society for which they wrote. But now in the Romantic Age we arrive at a very different state of things. It is only the comparatively small literary part of society that belongs to Romanticism. And this means, in effect, that literature no longer occupies a central position in society. What is being written by the most gifted people of the age no longer expresses what most people are thinking and feeling, as it did in former ages.

The loss of a central position for literature signals our arrival in the modern world. For nowadays it never occurs to us that the poet is typical, the person who is speaking for everybody. Poets seem to us now the odd and exceptional people, who speak mainly for themselves. We should be surprised if newspaper editors, in time of national crisis, hurried to discover and print the opinion of poets. If leaders of political parties spent most of their evenings in the company of poets, they would soon be considered too eccentric to be fit for political leadership. Yet if the poet, the person with unusual depth of insight and feeling, is not speaking for our society, then something is wrong either with our poetry or our society.

The political events of this period, 1800–37, cannot be ignored. They played an important part in the development of the English literature of the time. Revolutionary France, compelled to fight to defend its very existence, badly needed a commander capable of organizing victory. It found one in Napoleon Bonaparte, an astonishing military and organizing genius, one of the greatest commanders of all time, though unscrupulous and the victim of unresting ambition. Unable to invade Britain because his navy was destroyed by Lord Nelson at the Battle of Trafalgar (1805), Napoleon proceeded to conquer most of Western Europe and organize its resources to aid him in his ceaseless struggle against Britain, his most determined and formidable enemy.

Although emperor, with unlimited powers, Napoleon was in some respects still a man of the French Revolution, inheriting some of its liberating ideas, which were already triumphant in America. The Whigs in Britain recognized this fact and were in favor of trying to come to terms with Napoleon. But the Tories, who saw in him a threat to their political and social system, carried the country. Making full use of the invasion scare and allying themselves with the despotic monarchies in Europe, they finally succeeded in defeating Napoleon in 1815 at the Battle of Waterloo. The Congress of Vienna, which met to settle the political problems of Europe, attempted to achieve stability by restoring the absolute monarchies as they had existed before the French Revolution and devising a system, called the "Concert of Europe," for preserving the peace. The Concert of Europe was successful in securing a long period of peace for Europe. But, in its

The Battle of Trafalgar. A contemporary etching by Clarkson Stanfield.

attempt to turn back the clock by removing all traces of liberating influence and discouraging further reform, the Congress was a triumph of reaction.

As it was abroad, so it was at home in Britain, which was held fast in the grip of reactionary and shortsighted Toryism. Liberal opinions were dangerous, any spirited expression of them being liable to drive a writer into exile or into a prison. [One of the minor Romantics, the poet and essayist Leigh Hunt (1784–1859), was sentened to two years' imprisonment for calling the Prince Regent, among other things, "a fat Adonis."] Meetings of laborers, shockingly overworked and underpaid, were broken up by the army. There were riots and much popular agitation for reform. At the end of the period the Whigs passed the First (or "Great") Reform Bill (1832), which helped to abolish the worst inequalities in Parliamentary representation by increasing the number of those eligible to vote. Further reforms— measures against child labor, measures to lighten prison sentences, improve education, broaden freedom of the press, and abolish the slave trade—were also made. Until these reforms had been achieved, however, England was an uncomfortable place for any outspoken lover of liberty.

THE ROMANTICS AS CHAMPIONS OF FREEDOM

The older Romantic poets, William Wordsworth (1770–1850), Samuel Taylor Coleridge (1772–1834), and Robert Southey (1774–1843), were eager revolutionaries in their youth. With many other Romantics, they believed in individual liberty and the human family and sympathized with those who rebelled against injustice and tyranny. Later, when the France they had admired became Napoleon's empire and Britain herself seemed to be in danger, they renounced these early views and followed what was more or less the Tory line. Wiiliam Hazlitt (1778–1830), the finest critic and essayist of the age, was a passionate anti-Tory and Radical—he wrote a biography of Napoleon chiefly to defy official and popular opinion —and though he greatly admired Wordsworth and Coleridge, he never ceased to denounce them as renegades to the cause of freedom.

Among the younger poets, George Gordon, Lord Byron (1788–1824), was famous throughout Europe as a champion of liberty, and Percy Bysshe Shelley (1792–1822) was an out-and-out revolutionary with a special brand of anarchy all his own. John Keats (1795–1821) was not politically minded, but, because he was one of the young Romantics, he was viciously attacked in the *Quarterly Review,* the chief organ of Tory literary opinion. Indeed, this attack was so savage and outrageous that many people believed that it was the cause of his severe illness and early death. We know this to be untrue, however, for Keats was already a victim of tuberculosis and, in fact, faced this attack in a cheerful, mature fashion.

The stupidy and savagery of much of its criticism represent an important feature of this Romantic Age. Reviewers like William Gifford (1756–1826) and John Wilson Croker (1780–1857) were inflamed against the Romantics by two different sets of prejudices. One was literary, for these men still had eighteenth-century ideas about literature and really did not begin to understand what Romantic poetry was trying to do. With them the "breakthrough" described earlier never took place. They wanted tame public verses from people who were writing intensely emotional poetry inspired by their inner lives. The other set of prejudices was political in origin, for these reviewers were all hidebound Tories who regarded the Romantics as dangerous liberals, radicals, and revolutionaries.

ROMANTIC INTEREST IN THE PAST

Tory Romanticism is possible, however, and a writer like Sir Walter Scott (1771–1832) is an outstanding example of it. Oddly enough, in view of the fact that Scott was accepted as an outstanding figure of the whole European Romantic movement, this levelheaded Scots lawyer was not really a true Romantic. The inner world did not break through to him. There is nothing of Rousseau's influence here. Scott was really an eighteenth-century man who, as you can tell from novels such as *Ivanhoe, The Talisman,* and *The Heart of Midlothian,* happened to have a great love of the past in its more picturesque aspects.

Although the true Romantic poets, from Coleridge to Keats, appeared to be always writing about the past, they had not in fact the solid interest in it that Scott had and that historians and antiquaries and archeologists have. This is an important point without which Romanticism cannot be properly understood. Scott wrote about the Middle Ages because he was genuinely interested in the Middle Ages. But the real Romantic poets and storytellers all over Europe who began to give their poems and stories a medieval background were not so much turning to the past as deliberately turning away from the outward scene of their own time. What they wanted to explore was their own inner world of dream and desire, of mysterious hopes and fears; in order to separate this inner world from the ordinary outer world, to make it all different, they used a kind of medieval dreamland. Their poems and tales are not really *about* the Middle Ages but are concerned with their own inner selves.

The Romantics made frequent use of rather vague medieval settings mainly because the Middle Ages of their imagination were so entirely different from the complicated and rather ugly industrial society which was growing up and all around them. The earlier times were simpler and more picturesque and, what was more important, they seemed more *magical*. But the medieval spirit as such was not essential to Romanticism. Any setting that was strange, remote in time or space, served its purpose.

Mining scene of the 1840's. In their choice of subject matter, many Romantics reacted against the dehumanizing effects of the Industrial Revolution.

Thus Shelley and Keats turned to Greek mythology, giving a new significance to ancient figures of legend. Byron and lesser poets like Thomas Moore (1779–1852) made use of the people and landscapes of what we now call the Near and Middle East. If Wordsworth, who was not at all a typical Romantic, was able to stay at home a good deal, that was because he had made his home in the north of England in the heart of the Lake District, at that time not often visited and not easily accessible. In any case, Wordsworth was not concerned with immediate effects of picturesque strangeness. He wanted to brood over the real, outward scene, though always some remote aspect of it far removed from the effects of the Industrial Revolution, so that at last the outer world and his inner world fused together, so to speak, making one whole. It is usually this process that his best poems describe so magnificently. Where other Romantic poets ransack mythology, legend, or folk beliefs for enchantment, Wordsworth waits for the sound of the cuckoo in spring to transform the real world into a magical place.

THE IDEALIZING OF WOMEN

Again, in Romanticism women can hardly ever be simply fellow creatures seeking a lasting relationship, a meaningful life, a home, and children; instead, they must be strange and magical. So Romantic love poetry is not addressed to real women. It is filled with mysterious beings—nymphs, water sprites, Oriental queens and princesses, savage gypsy girls—in fact, with any beautiful feminine creatures who could not possibly live next door. This does not mean that the Romantics were indifferent to ordinary girls and women; far from it. What they were doing was dramatizing and overemphasizing the aspects of real womanhood that appear strange and magical to a man's inner life. The Romantics pictured women in the same way that even the girl next door might appear in the inner world of dream of a boy who falls in love with her. And all this was instinctively understood by the feminine readers of the Romantic poets and storytellers. Some of these enthusiastic readers might have felt that they themselves were not unlike the nymphs, water sprites, Oriental princesses, and gypsy girls described.

ROMANTIC MELANCHOLY

Because it is itself one-sided, never moving toward a balance between the outer and inner worlds, between what is real and what we feel ought to be real, Romanticism always tends, as it loses itself in the inner dream world, to find existence less and less satisfying. This is why poets such as Wordsworth are always praising the lost kingdom of childhood, where dream and reality are not yet separated. The real, outward world remains obstinately itself, refusing to be shaped and colored by what the Romantic feels. So the literature of Romanticism, as we can easily discover in the poetry of this age, is filled with melancholy and regret and hopelessly unsatisfied longing. This mood is more characteristic of the young than of the old, who ought to know better and arrive at some balance. It is significant that Coleridge stopped writing poetry as he grew older; that Wordsworth, except for a few occasional flashes, wrote dull and dutiful verses in his later years.

ROMANTICISM IN LITERATURE

The Romantic Age in English literature, though glorious for what it achieved, was unusually strong in some forms of writing and curiously weak in others. Though most of the poets wrote verse dramas, the wonderful command of the theater that the Elizabethans had was not recaptured. We are often told that if only poets would write for the theater our drama would be great again, but this is too simple. To succeed on the stage poets must be dramatists too. There must also be an audience like the one the

This wood engraving by Thomas Bewick (1753–1828) reveals the artist's love of nature and fine technique. Bewick's work illustrated many books of this period.

Elizabethans had, eager to respond to what the true dramatic poet offers them. Even if Shelley and Keats had lived long enough to write poetic drama, the necessary audience still might have been missing. As it was, the Romantic poets were at their wonderful best in lyrical poetry and, as a good second best, they often succeeded with narrative poetry too.

The age also was not uniformly successful in its prose forms. Its fiction as a whole was inferior to that of the eighteenth century or that of the Victorian Age. The truth is, the novel in a grand scale demands a background of a fairly settled society. This stability the Regency, with its wars and invasion scares, its deep political divisions and unrest, its rapid transformation of a rural into an industrial society, could not offer. There was, however, an increasing output of popular fiction—either Gothic tales of mystery and horror such as Horace Walpole's *The Castle of Otranto* or sentimental and satirical novels about fashionable society—that might have helped to lay a foundation for the greater fiction that was to come.

Although this age can show no masterpieces of biography and history to equal Boswell's *Life of Johnson* and Gibbon's *Decline and Fall of the Roman Empire,* in the personal essay, written with an intimacy and force that the eighteenth-century essay never achieved, the Romantic Age was triumphant. William Hazlitt and Charles Lamb (1775–1834) were its two masters, with Thomas De Quincey (1785–1859), Leigh Hunt, and others not too far behind. These men were critics too—Romantic critics to keep pace with the Romantic poets. Their criticism, unlike that of the eighteenth century, was not so much cold judgment on behalf of society, but was essentially personal and intimate, suggesting first-class talk among friends about books and authors. Here Hazlitt, offering a wide range of criticism from Shakespeare onwards, was the master, but Lamb too did valuable service, especially in his selections from and notes on the lesser Elizabethan and Jacobean dramatists. Finally, in his numerous notes, Coleridge was perhaps the most subtle and profound critic of this or any other age.

The Romantic period was particularly rich in fascinating characters, in and out of literature. There was William Cobbett (1763–1835), who, in his *Rural Rides,* was equally forthright in both his admiration and denunciation of the English scene. There was Shelley's witty friend, Thomas Love Peacock (1785–1866), who, as we can judge from *Nightmare Abbey,* wrote novels like nobody else's. There was Sidney Smith (1771–1845), clergyman, humorist, wit, reformer—a rich character. This age is crammed with remarkable characters, and fortunately it is equally rich in journals, memoirs, and diaries that reveal these characters to us. Whole libraries of works have been concerned with this period. It provides a never-ending feast for the literary historian, the critic, and the student of human nature. Any reader who falls under its spell will discover in it a lifelong fascination and charm.

J.B.P.

WILLIAM WORDSWORTH
(1770–1850)

When we read Milton's *Paradise Lost* it is clear to us that Milton thought of nature chiefly as the scene on which God's purposes were exhibited. But the scientists of the seventeenth century changed all this. People became admiring spectators of the activity of forces such as that described in Newton's law of gravitation. Nature, as the new theories of the natural scientists represented it, seemed a great mechanism. Some people took an optimistic view of the meaning of this mechanism, but those who did not think reason a completely satisfactory means of dealing with human experience were less optimistic. It was hard to feel that human beings had a significant place in this universe. The Frenchman Pascal, a seventeenth-century scientist and religious thinker, wrote: "The silence of these infinite spaces frightens me."

William Wordsworth tried to give us an assured place in nature once more. In *Tintern Abbey* he writes of "the burthen of the mystery," "the heavy and the weary weight of this unintelligible world." How lift that burden? How dissolve that mystery? These are the questions Wordsworth explored. His answers are not those of a philosopher, but those of a poet. He hopes that the experience of reading his poems will convince us that our relation to nature is itself natural and not dependent on scientific theories.

People of Wordsworth's day were not prepared to believe that poetry had the power to make us feel our relation to nature in a new way. They felt that poetry ought to "gratify certain known habits of association." The words and phrases used, the subjects treated, and the emotions aroused were expected to conform to the standard practice of the day. Wordsworth was altogether sure that this practice was wrong and profoundly misleading. "The burthen of the mystery" was only intensified by such trivial poetry.

The young Wordsworth did not come to this conclusion without a struggle. Only after he had realized the barrenness of reason alone, a theory that disregarded human feelings altogether, did he turn to his memories of his boyhood and youth for examples of a different kind of food for feeling and thought: the life of simple people in a world conditioned by sun and shower and by objects of natural beauty. In this world, it seemed to him, morality itself was a natural product of our relations to one another: the fundamental relations of mother to child, wife to husband, neighbor to neighbor, and humankind in general to the animals and the fields which offered sustenance.

The word *growth* is highly significant for all of Wordsworth's work. It is a mistake to think of him as a "nature poet" if we mean by that an admirer of the landscape. He is rather the poet who chronicles our growth—our natural growth. Only in this way could Wordsworth convey his conviction that we are as intimately at home in nature as is the plant in the soil.

Wordsworth had a lively and moving sense of how we come to realize our world, how it becomes real to us. This is something that we are likely to take for granted. Yet when we were infants we literally did not know where our bodies left off and the world began, what would give us pleasure and what would burn, and so on. We learn these things and then we forget that we have not always known them. Wordsworth wanted to give an account of growth which would suggest the conditions of the whole process, from "the babe" who "leaps up on his mother's arm" to something as complicated as a poet.

In the Preface to *Lyrical Ballads,* Wordsworth says that the poet should use a "selection of the language really used by men." Since Wordsworth here refers to the language of those who live in the country, this idea is a tricky one to apply. This famous statement of Wordsworth's is taken to mean that only the uneducated country folks' speech can be used as a model. Wordsworth considered "the mind of man as naturally the mirror of the fairest and most interesting properties of our nature." That mirror, Wordsworth felt, is least distorted in rural communities where country folk live, and where, therefore, our feelings and moral beliefs are most directly responsive to natural conditions. We do not, of course, have to believe in this theory ourselves in order to enjoy Wordsworth's poetry.

What poetic styles and devices did Wordsworth find appropriate to these particular aims? It is obvious that the ballad tradition would be attractive to him, since it was so close to the voice of the common people. A number of the poems in *Lyrical Ballads* employ ballad forms very skillfully. Wordsworth also wrote very great sonnets which are closer to the rhythms of actual speech than those of his great predecessors in the form. But the most familiar, longer Wordsworth poems, such as *Tintern Abbey,* have a leisurely, reflective tone and are written in blank verse. Awareness of the relation between form and content in Wordsworth emerges from even a casual consideration of his imagery. Wordsworth seldom describes only how something *looks*. In reading this poet, you will find that you are much more aware of how things *are*. To say this is to say that Wordsworth is the poet of human experience—of how human beings come to think and feel as they do.

THE LIFE OF WILLIAM WORDSWORTH

William Wordsworth grew up in the Lake District, the beautiful region of lakes, streams, mountains, and waterfalls in northwestern England, where he was born in 1770. One of five children of a lawyer who managed the estate of a nobleman, young Wordsworth did not enjoy family life for very long. Upon the death of his mother, when he was seven years old, the family was broken up, and Wordsworth and one of his three brothers were sent away to school near the shores of Lake Windermere. There in the midst of his "dear native regions" he came to know and love the world of nature. Many of his youthful experiences there are described in *The Prelude,* one of his important long poems.

During his college days at Cambridge University, Wordsworth took a memorable walking tour in France, Switzerland, and Italy. After graduating in 1791, he toured Wales and then once again visited France. There he fell in love with Annette Vallon, the daughter of a French surgeon, and also became deeply involved in the

Dove Cottage, Wordsworth's home in Grasmere, as it appeared in about 1805.

cause of the French Revolution. His disapproving family cut off his allowance, and thus eventually forced him to return home.

By 1793, mainly in an attempt to raise money, Wordsworth had published two volumes of verse, which though favorably reviewed, did not sell. Unable that year to return to France and Annette because of the outbreak of war between France and England, Wordsworth, opposed to his country's war with France, was among those who supported the French Revolution. Later, feeling that the Revolution had fallen short of its early ideals, he became disenchanted with the radical democratic ideas of his day.

Wordsworth led a rather vagrant life until 1795, when the legacy of a friend enabled him to set up housekeeping, with his sister Dorothy as companion. At about this time, he met the poet Samuel Taylor Coleridge, who became one of his closest friends and who also had a considerable influence on his work. Coleridge, together with Dorothy, helped to rouse Wordsworth from his mood of despair over the French Revolution, and the three became close friends. In 1797, the Wordsworths moved to Somerset to be near Coleridge. In the following year, the two poets published *Lyrical Ballads* (see page 504), a collection of poetry which marks the beginning of the English Romantic movement.

In 1798, the Wordsworths and Coleridge visited Germany. Upon their return to England in the following year, Dorothy and Wordsworth moved to Grasmere in the Lake District, where the poet was to spend the rest of his life. In 1802, Wordsworth married Mary Hutchinson, and for the next five years he enjoyed a period of high creativity, during which he produced such important poems as *Ode: Intimations of Immortality from Recollections of Early Childhood*. Although he wrote distinguished verse thereafter, it did not have the brilliance of his earlier work. In 1813, Wordsworth accepted a government post (much to the disillusionment of some of his more radical admirers) and bought Rydal Mount, near Grasmere, his last home. There, surrounded by a group of congenial literary friends, he lived with his wife and sister. In 1843, at the age of seventy-three, he was made poet laureate. When he died seven years later, he was buried in the little churchyard at Grasmere.

Lines Written in Early Spring

I heard a thousand blended notes,
While in a grove I sate reclined,
In that sweet mood when pleasant
    thoughts
Bring sad thoughts to the mind.

To her fair works did Nature link   5
The human soul that through me ran;
And much it grieved my heart to think
What man had made of man.

Through primrose tufts, in that green
    bower,
The periwinkle trailed its wreaths;   10
And 'tis my faith that every flower
Enjoys the air it breathes.

The birds around me hopped and played,
Their thoughts I cannot measure;
But the least motion which they made, 15
It seemed a thrill of pleasure.

The budding twigs spread out their fan,
To catch the breezy air;
And I must think, do all I can,
That there was pleasure there.   20

If this belief from heaven be sent,
If such be Nature's holy plan,
Have I not reason to lament
What man has made of man?

COMMENTARY

In "Lines Written in Early Spring" the poet experiences a succession of feelings: he is caught up in a harmony of sounds, sights, and movements in this springtime scene; and then, by a natural transition, he thinks of those whose lives are *not* touched or ordered by the harmonies of nature. Cite lines which illustrate both.

Wordsworth reveals the activity in the scene before him. How, for example, does the use of the verb *trailed* in the third quatrain (four-line stanza) help him to do this? Find other verbs in the following two stanzas that reveal activity in the scene.

How might we describe the state of those men who have a bad effect on themselves and their fellows (see lines 7–8, 23–24)? Since Wordsworth doesn't tell us what this effect is, we can only be aware of the writer's state of mind and realize that theirs is not the same—and probably quite contrary.

The grove in which the poet sits is bursting with life; how does he show that he shares that life? Remember that you are looking for human responses to the scene. Your answer might well begin with the statement of faith in lines 11–12 and 19–20. These lines indicate that the poet's activity is that of voicing his faith. When, he implies, we are cut off from nature, when we cannot take pleasure in the beauty of spring, we are out of tune as human beings.

Wordsworth believed that, in finding pleasure in nature, we are acknowledging the beauty of the universe. At one point he states that this acknowledgment "is a task light and easy to him who looks on the world in a spirit of love." Furthermore, he saw in the awareness of pleasure a testimony to the "native and naked dignity of man." As you read the following poems, look for examples of Wordsworth's sense of *pleasure,* of his looking on the world in a spirit of love. In which literary work in this book does our assurance of dignity come through an awareness of pain rather than pleasure?

The Tables Turned

Up! up! my Friend, and quit your books;
Or surely you'll grow double.
Up! up! my Friend, and clear your looks;
Why all this toil and trouble?

The sun, above the mountain's head,   5
A freshening luster mellow
Through all the long green fields has spread,
His first sweet evening yellow.

Books! 'tis a dull and endless strife;
Come, hear the woodland linnet,   10
How sweet his music! on my life,
There's more of wisdom in it.

And hark! how blithe the throstle sings!
He, too, is no mean preacher;
Come forth into the light of things;   15
Let Nature be your teacher.

She has a world of ready wealth,
Our minds and hearts to bless—
Spontaneous wisdom breathed by health,
Truth breathed by cheerfulness.   20

One impulse from a vernal wood
May teach you more of man,
Of moral evil and of good,
Than all the sages can.

Sweet is the lore that Nature brings;   25
Our meddling intellect
Misshapes the beauteous forms of things—
We murder to dissect.

Enough of Science and of Art;
Close up those barren leaves;   30
Come forth, and bring with you a heart
That watches and receives.

In another poem, a friend reproaches Wordsworth for sitting on an old gray stone and dreaming his time away instead of reading. In "The Tables Turned" (page 451), the poet counterattacks. The most famous line in all Wordsworth, "One impulse from a vernal wood . . ." is hardly a complete account of his beliefs, as we shall see in discussing later poems. Yet it is true that those who cannot observe can learn nothing from their world; they act blindly, they see things through others' eyes, and their thought can hardly mean much because it is not based on their own experience. We must trust others to tell us when Napoleon died or how to program a computer, but we had better make our own judgments about nature, love, morality, music, and painting.

Composed upon Westminster Bridge

Earth has not anything to show more fair:
Dull would he be of soul who could pass by
A sight so touching in its majesty:
This city now doth, like a garment, wear
The beauty of the morning; silent, bare, 5
Ships, towers, domes, theaters, and temples lie
Open unto the fields, and to the sky;
All bright and glittering in the smokeless air.
Never did sun more beautifully steep
In his first splendor, valley, rock, or hill; 10
Ne'er saw I, never felt, a calm so deep!
The river glideth at his own sweet will:
Dear God! the very houses seem asleep;
And all that mighty heart is lying still!

COMMENTARY

Without all its smoke and bustle, London emerges in this poem both as splendidly shaped to human purposes and as beautiful as any natural landscape. The morning light in which the city lies banishes that "fretful stir" felt "amid the many shapes/ Of joyless daylight" in "Tintern Abbey" (page 472, lines 51–52). In this happy situation the city's "mighty heart," whose pulses mark out the life of England, is calm because all the many hearts which make up its daily life have been brought into a peaceful harmony in sleep.

Can you defend the statement that the key to the emotional power of this sonnet lies in the line, "A sight so touching in its majesty"? You might begin by referring to the kind of sight usually thought of as touching (puppies tumbling in the grass, a child taking its first steps, and so on) as compared with the majesty of the metropolis. Wordsworth's success may then be said to lie in coupling these apparent incompatibles.

London, 1802

Milton! thou should'st be living at this hour;
England hath need of thee; she is a fen°
Of stagnant water; altar, sword, and pen,
Fireside, the heroic wealth of hall and bower,°
Have forfeited their ancient English dower   5
Of inward happiness. We are selfish men;
Oh! raise us up, return to us again;
And give us manners, virtue, freedom, power.
Thy soul was like a Star, and dwelt apart;
Thou hadst a voice whose sound was like the sea;   10
Pure as the naked heavens, majestic, free,
So didst thou travel on life's common way,
In cheerful godliness; and yet thy heart
The lowliest duties on herself did lay.

2. **fen:** a bog.   4. **hall and bower:** a reference to Anglo-Saxon times when the hall and bower were the main rooms in the large houses of various tribes.

COMMENTARY

"London, 1802" tells us something about the character of those "sad thoughts" which break in upon the poet in "Lines Written in Early Spring" (page 450, lines 3–4). In "London. 1802" Wordsworth's distress over conditions in England at the opening of the century is made explicit. Greatly disappointed at the outcome of the French Revolution (in 1802 Napoleon was elected Consul for life), he was also troubled by what seemed to him a betrayal of the English heritage of freedom and virtue, here represented by Milton.

We usually think of a hero as one who acts with splendid courage in some public emergency, such as a fire or a battle. In this sonnet Wordsworth is concerned not with such public acts, but with the social and moral conditions which nourish heroism. What are they? Begin by considering the emphasis on "inward happiness" in line 6 and the comparison of Milton's powers to sea and sky in lines 10–11.

What particular experiences in Milton's life do you think Wordsworth had in mind?

Are the conditions mentioned in this sonnet true of our own time? Explain your answer.

The World Is Too Much with Us

The world is too much with us; late and soon,
Getting and spending, we lay waste our powers;
Little we see in Nature that is ours;
We have given our hearts away, a sordid boon!°
This sea that bares her bosom to the moon;   5
The winds that will be howling at all hours,
And are upgathered now like sleeping flowers;
For this, for everything, we are out of tune;
It moves us not.—Great God! I'd rather be
A Pagan suckled in a creed outworn;   10
So might I, standing on this pleasant lea,
Have glimpses that would make me less forlorn;
Have sight of Proteus° rising from the sea;
Or hear old Triton° blow his wreathèd horn.

4. **boon** (bo͞on): a favor asked or granted.   13. **Proteus** (prō′tē·əs) and **Triton** (trīt′n: line 14)
were sea gods in Greek mythology.

COMMENTARY

Although "The World Is Too Much with Us" is more directly associated in feeling with "Lines Written in Early Spring" than with "London, 1802," the voices heard in these two poems are quite distinct. The sonnet is majestic, as if it had been written for public use, while the "Lines" have a tone of quiet, inward reflection.

Note that the "sad thoughts" of the "Lines" are in part explained by the sonnet. The "world" is, of course, the world of dusty, daily business—the world of human affairs. In giving our hearts to the pursuit of profit, we have made ourselves less valuable than the pagans, for whom the world was peopled by powers—gods whose presences were daily felt. Here again the point is that those who do not respond to nature are betraying their own humanity, for Wordsworth feels that in knowing the winds, the sea, the "pleasant lea," we find ourselves.

To a Skylark (1825)

Ethereal minstrel! pilgrim of the sky!
  Dost thou despise the earth where cares abound?
Or, while the wings aspire, are heart and eye
  Both with thy nest upon the dewy ground?
Thy nest which thou canst drop into at will,   5
Those quivering wings composed, that music still!
Leave to the nightingale her shady wood;
  A privacy of glorious light is thine;
Whence thou dost pour upon the world a flood
  Of harmony, with instinct more divine;   10
Type of the wise who soar, but never roam;
True to the kindred points of heaven and home!

COMMENTARY

Compare "To a Skylark" (above) with the sonnet, "London, 1802" (page 453). Do you think the relation between Milton's greatness and "inward happiness" is akin to that between the skylark's aspiring flight and his heartfelt love of his nest? Discuss, citing lines from each poem.

She Dwelt Among the Untrodden Ways

She dwelt among the untrodden ways
  Beside the springs of Dove;°
A maid whom there were none to praise,
  And very few to love.

A violet by a mossy stone   5
  Half-hidden from the eye!
—Fair as a star, when only one
  Is shining in the sky.

She lived unknown, and few could know
  When Lucy ceased to be;   10
But she is in her grave, and, oh,
  The difference to me!

2. **Dove:** a river in the English Midlands.

COMMENTARY

This is one of the five "Lucy poems," which center upon an imaginary girl of the English countryside. It is very beautiful and teasingly simple. Since we know that the pathos of loss is a universal emotion, we may be puzzled to discover how Wordsworth managed to give it a uniquely memorable form in these twelve lines. How is the pathos intensified by the ways in which the poem establishes Lucy's aloneness? How is it further intensified by the sudden introduction, through the last word in the poem, of the person who has suffered the loss? What do the two comparisons of the second quatrain, taken together, suggest about Lucy?

Strange Fits of Passion Have I Known

Strange fits of passion have I known:
And I will dare to tell,
But in the lover's ear alone,
What once to me befell.

When she I loved looked everyday   5
Fresh as a rose in June,
I to her cottage bent my way,
Beneath an evening moon.

Upon the moon I fixed my eye,
All over the wide lea;   10
With quickening pace my horse drew nigh
Those paths so dear to me.

And now we reached the orchard plot;
And, as we climbed the hill,
The sinking moon to Lucy's cot   15
Came near, and nearer still.

In one of those sweet dreams I slept,
Kind Nature's gentle boon!
And all the while my eyes I kept
On the descending moon.   20

My horse moved on; hoof after hoof
He raised, and never stopped:
When down behind the cottage roof,
At once, the bright moon dropped.

What fond and wayward thoughts will slide   25
Into a lover's head!
"O mercy!" to myself I cried,
"If Lucy should be dead!"

A Slumber Did My Spirit Seal

A slumber did my spirit seal;
  I had no human fears:
She seemed a thing that could not feel
  The touch of earthly years.

No motion has she now, no force;
  She neither hears nor sees;
Rolled round in earth's diurnal course,
  With rocks, and stones, and trees.

COMMENTARY

STRANGE FITS OF PASSION
HAVE I KNOWN

These twenty-eight lines appear very simple when you first read them. Yet their effect is the result of a very deliberate artistry which plays the idea of motion, activity, life, against the idea of stillness, stoppage, arrest, death. In the third quatrain, there are two kinds of motion, and the innocent reader is quite unaware of their fateful meaning. There is the evening moon, and there is the horse, whose pace quickens as he approaches a familiar resting place. How does the very sound and pace of the fourth quatrain suggest something ominous?

In the fifth quatrain, we are made aware that the lover is enjoying a pleasant fantasy or dream, which involves no consciousness of time or motion. Meanwhile, his eye is on the sinking moon. This double consciousness of his fantasy and the movement of the moon becomes single and terrified in the sixth quatrain. Again the effect is secured by the movement of the verse. Compare the second quatrain with the sixth in this respect. How does the beat of the horse's hoofs enter in?

Notice that in the last two quatrains there is a parallelism between the disappearance of the moon behind the cottage (lines 23–24) and the thought that "slides" into the lover's head. How is death suggested by movement in the poem?

Now answer the same question about "A Slumber Did My Spirit Seal," another of the Lucy poems (see above).

A SLUMBER DID MY SPIRIT SEAL

This poem is probably the last of the so-called Lucy poems. The question about the relation of motion and death in the two poems may be answered in various ways, but one might first compare the fantasy of stanza five in "Strange Fits of Passion Have I Known" with the whole of the first stanza in the poem quoted above. Here are two instances describing the lover's view of his beloved and the tie that unites them as timeless ("I had no human fears"). And in both instances death is associated, by contrast, with motion and with activity that terminates: mortality. The fact that the conventional association of death is with stillness, not movement, accounts for the extraordinary effect of the last two lines of "A Slumber Did My Spirit Seal."

Resolution and Independence

Wordsworth wrote of this poem: "This old man I met a few hundred yards from my cottage; and the account of him is taken from his own mouth."

1

There was a roaring in the wind all night;
The rain came heavily and fell in floods;
But now the sun is rising calm and bright;
The birds are singing in the distant woods;
Over his own sweet voice the stock dove broods;   5
The jay makes answer as the magpie chatters;
And all the air is filled with pleasant noise of waters.

2

All things that love the sun are out-of-doors;
The sky rejoices in the morning's birth;
The grass is bright with raindrops; on the moors   10
The hare is running races in her mirth;
And with her feet she from the plashy earth
Raises a mist, that, glittering in the sun,
Runs with her all the way, wherever she doth run.

3

I was a traveler then upon the moor,   15
I saw the hare that raced about with joy;
I heard the woods and distant waters roar,
Or heard them not, as happy as a boy;
The pleasant season did my heart employ;
My old remembrances went from me wholly;   20
And all the ways of men, so vain and melancholy.

4

But, as it sometimes chanceth, from the might
Of joy in minds that can no further go,
As high as we have mounted in delight
In our dejection do we sink as low;   25
To me that morning did it happen so;
And fears and fancies thick upon me came;
Dim sadness—and blind thoughts, I knew not, nor could name.

5

I heard the skylark warbling in the sky,
And I bethought me of the playful hare: 30
Even such a happy child of earth am I;
Even as these blissful creatures do I fare;
Far from the world I walk, and from all care;
But there may come another day to me—
Solitude, pain of heart, distress, and poverty.   35

6

My whole life I have lived in pleasant thought,
As if life's business were a summer mood;
As if all needful things would come unsought
To genial faith, still rich in genial good;
But how can he expect that others should   40
Build for him, sow for him, and at his call
Love him, who for himself will take no heed at all?

7

I thought of Chatterton,° the marvelous boy,
The sleepless soul that perished in his pride;
Of him° who walked in glory and in joy   45
Following his plow, along the mountainside:
By our own spirits are we deified;
We poets in our youth begin in gladness,
But thereof come in the end despondency and madness.

8

Now, whether it were by peculiar grace,   50
A leading from above, a something given,
Yet it befell, that, in this lonely place,
When I with these untoward thoughts had striven,
Beside a pool bare to the eye of Heaven
I saw a man before me unawares: 55
The oldest man he seemed that ever wore gray hairs.

9

As a huge stone is sometimes seen to lie
Couched on the bald top of an eminence;
Wonder to all who do the same espy,
By what means it could thither come, and whence;   60
So that it seems a thing endued with sense;
Like a sea beast crawled forth, that on a shelf
Of rock or sand reposeth, there to sun itself;

10

Such seemed this man, not all alive nor dead,
Nor all asleep—in his extreme old age;   65
His body was bent double, feet and head
Coming together in life's pilgrimage;
As if some dire constraint of pain, or rage
Of sickness felt by him in times long past,
A more than human weight upon his frame had cast.   70

43. **Chatterton:** Thomas Chatterton (1752–1770), a promising young poet who committed suicide at the age of seventeen.   45. **him:** Robert Burns.

11

Himself he propped, limbs, body, and pale face,
Upon a long gray staff of shaven wood;
And, still as I drew near with gentle pace,
Upon the margin of that moorish flood
Motionless as a cloud the old man stood,   75
That heareth not the loud winds when they call
And moveth all together, if it move at all.

12

At length, himself unsettling, he the pond
Stirred with his staff, and fixedly did look
Upon the muddy water, which he conned,   80
As if he had been reading in a book;
And now a stranger's privilege I took,
And, drawing to his side, to him did say,
"This morning gives us promise of a glorious day."

13

A gentle answer did the old man make,   85
In courteous speech which forth he slowly drew;
And him with further words I thus bespake,
"What occupation do you there pursue?
This a lonesome place for one like you."
Ere he replied, a flash of mild surprise   90
Broke from the sable orbs of his yet vivid eyes,

14

His words came feebly, from a feeble chest,
But each in solemn order followed each,
With something of a lofty utterance dressed—
Choice word and measured phrase, above the reach   95
Of ordinary men; a stately speech;
Such as grave livers do in Scotland use,
Religious men, who give to God and man their dues.

15

He told, that to these waters he had come
To gather leeches,° being old and poor—   100
Employment hazardous and wearisome!
And he had many hardships to endure:
From pond to pond he roamed, from moor to moor;
Housing, with God's good help, by choice or chance,
And in this way he gained an honest maintenance.   105

---

100. **leeches:** bloodsucking worms formerly used for medical purposes.

16

The old man still stood talking by my side;
But now his voice to me was like a stream
Scarce heard; nor word from word could I divide;
And the whole body of the man did seem
Like one whom I had met with in a dream;   110
Or like a man from some far region sent,
To give me human strength, by apt admonishment.

17

My former thoughts returned: the fear that kills;
And hope that is unwilling to be fed;
Cold, pain, and labor, and all fleshly ills;   115
And mighty poets in their misery dead.
Perplexed, and longing to be comforted,
My question eagerly did I renew,
"How is it that you live, and what is it you do?"

18

He with a smile did then his words repeat;   120
And said, that, gathering leeches, far and wide
He traveled, stirring thus above his feet
The waters of the pools where they abide.
"Once I could meet with them on every side,
But they have dwindled long by slow decay;   125
Yet still I persevere, and find them where I may."

19

While he was talking thus, the lonely place,
The old man's shape, and speech—all troubled me;
In my mind's eye I seemed to see him pace
About the weary moors continually,   130
Wandering about alone and silently.
While I these thoughts within myself pursued,
He, having made a pause, the same discourse renewed.

20

And soon with this he other matter blended,
Cheerfully uttered, with demeanor kind,   135
But stately in the main; and when he ended,
I could have laughed myself to scorn to find
In that decrepit man so firm a mind.
"God," said I, "be my help and stay secure;
I'll think of the leech gatherer on the lonely moor!"   140

COMMENTARY

In the first three verse paragraphs the poet is wholly absorbed in a scene in which everything seems to be rejoicing after the passage of a storm. The singing birds, the pleasantly flowing waters, and the playful hare, which creates a cloud of light-shot vapor as it runs—all seem expressions of a joy common to nature and familiar to the poet. Suddenly, as in "Lines Written in Early Spring," he is overcome by "dim sadness," though he cannot tell what he is afraid of. He reflects that he has "lived in pleasant thought," happily and "far . . . from all care." He has, in fact (note the title of the poem) been *dependent* upon the hope of unending joy. The fate of poets like Thomas Chatterton and Robert Burns, who abandoned themselves to the glory of the world and came to miserable ends, seems like a forecast of the poet's own future.

Poets are not like cats. A cat doesn't like or trust you any more than your gestures and behavior tell him he can; a cat is always prepared for trouble. But poets reach beyond the surface and allow themselves to feel very deeply what is outside of them; they take the emotional risk of feeling what other things are like. The consequence is that they may at moments lose that firm sense of themselves that usually protects us from anxiety. The poet of this poem frightens himself by becoming so absorbed in the joyous scene before him that he cannot tell where he himself leaves off and the world begins. He swings to the other extreme and is beset by unreasonable fear.

The old man appears as if in answer. He is very strange. To the poet he has all the strangeness of an apparition. He is like a huge stone or a sea beast. When the poet questions him, he learns that the old man follows a hard and laborious calling. The old man goes on talking, but the poet is hardly aware of his words. He is absorbed in an almost reverent sense of what the old man means. To the poet, the leech gatherer has become a mighty symbol of courage and endurance—a tremendous natural fact which banishes the poet's fear.

In *The Prelude,* his long autobiographical poem, Wordsworth tells us repeatedly that as we grow up we are disciplined by both joy and fear. We know from this poem, too, that the poet has learned from his swing from great joy to fear. He has been shown "human strength by apt admonishment" through the steadfastness of the old leech gatherer.

Why does Wordsworth compare the old man to a stone? Why does this suggest the further comparison to a sea beast? What qualities implied by these things are contrasted with the poet's state of mind just before he meets the old man?

[WILLIAM WORDSWORTH CONTINUES ON PAGE 471.]

ENGLISH PAINTING

Early Romanticism:
Science and Nature

The late eighteenth-century paintings shown in the following pages suggest two ways in which English artists strengthened their interest in familiar subject matter: by taking part in scientific inquiry, and by searching ordinary scenes at home and abroad for the beautiful or picturesque.

At first glance you might guess that *Phaeton and Pair* (PLATE 1) was the work of an artist whose reputation depended entirely on the portrayal of well-to-do patrons. But notice that the lady and gentleman have relatively little importance in this picture, and that their name is not even included in the title. The artist, George Stubbs, seems to have been more interested in the details of the carriage—and still more in the matched pair of black horses, whose elegant contours are emphasized so clearly that they seem to be closer to us than the carriage. In fact, though Stubbs painted many portraits, he was at heart a scientist and the author of an important work called *The Anatomy of the Horse.*

In about 1755 Stubbs returned from a journey to the Mediterranean with lively impressions of an incident like the one represented in *White Horse Frightened by a Lion* (PLATE 2). We do not know whether he actually witnessed such an encounter during a visit to Morocco or whether he merely studied a work of classical sculpture exhibited at Rome. In any case, he later painted the horse and the lion several times, showing various stages of the lion's attack. In this picture the dark landscape suggests danger but serves also to make the white horse stand out as the main focal point of the picture. He pulls up short with his mane blowing forward, his nostrils wide, and his muscles tense. To find a model for the lion's head, Stubbs probably went to a London menagerie.

Experiment with the Air Pump (PLATE 3), by Joseph Wright of Derby, represents another sort of biological investigation. The experimenter, repeating an earlier inquiry to determine the amount of air needed for birds to live, has placed a live bird in a closed glass vessel and pumped the air out. The older men look intent and thoughtful, and the young girls show humane concern. The drama of this life-and-death scene is heightened by Wright's reliance upon artificial illumination. A single candle on the table, behind a glass bowl, lights the clustered faces but hardly penetrates the surrounding darkness.

Horses in a Stable (PLATE 4), George Morland's painting of an ostler and two overworked horses in quite an ordinary setting, shows less scientific curiosity than idyllic feeling. Morland spent many of his days in stables, where he could always find congenial companions. With friends who cared less about art than about horse races and prize fights, his conduct frequently took a riotous turn, and his debts grew very heavy. But his paintings of familiar English scenes, instead of suggesting thriftlessness or disillusionment, tend to be mellow and sentimental. The gently luminous colors in this picture are characteristic of his work; and the ostler, like most of Morland's common men, looks admirably sturdy and industrious. Notice, too, the spiky, random brushstroke used for the hay and the smoother, broader strokes in the wall and the ostler's shirt.

John Crome, who painted *Hay Barges on the Yare* (PLATE 5), lived all his life in the provincial city of Norwich. Apprenticed to a coach- and sign-painter, he received very little formal education, but he had access to local picture collections, from which he taught himself a great deal about landscape by copying paintings by Gainsborough, his more famous contemporary. Crome found practically all the subject matter he needed for his pictures in the countryside and on the rivers near Norwich, where he would make sketches on the spot, later using them as a basis for more finished pictures he painted in the studio. In *Hay Barges on the Yare,* most of the composition is sky, with clouds billowing from the horizon, while the river, wide in the front plane, narrows back into the distance. Sails dotted along the river show us its winding path. Notice that the banks of the river show few details, appearing merely as bands of dark or light colors. The viewpoint shown here suggests that Crome himself may have been floating peacefully in a boat while he composed this picture.

For Richard Parkes Bonington, who as a boy moved to France with his parents and received artistic training in Paris, familiar settings were not English but Continental. He liked to develop a French coastal scene as a naturally horizontal composition, or to work out the simple masses of light and shade and rich color in an urban Italian scene. To paint *Column of St. Mark* (PLATE 6), he took a position outside the Doge's Palace in Venice. On the waterfront, between the palace and the old library, stand two granite pillars honoring the patrons of the city, the nearer one holding the winged lion of St. Mark. Bonington's picture is mainly an exercise in composing with strong verticals. The thin horizontal line of clouds at the top of the painting prevents the columns from giving the impression that they might rocket out of view.

PLATE 1. GEORGE STUBBS (1724–1806): *Phaeton and Pair*. 1787. Oil on wood, 32½ x 40 inches. (Reproduced by courtesy of the Trustees, The National Gallery, London)

PLATE 2. GEORGE STUBBS (1724–1806): *White Horse Frightened by a Lion.* 1760's. Oil on canvas, 40 x 50 inches. (Walker Art Gallery, Liverpool, England)

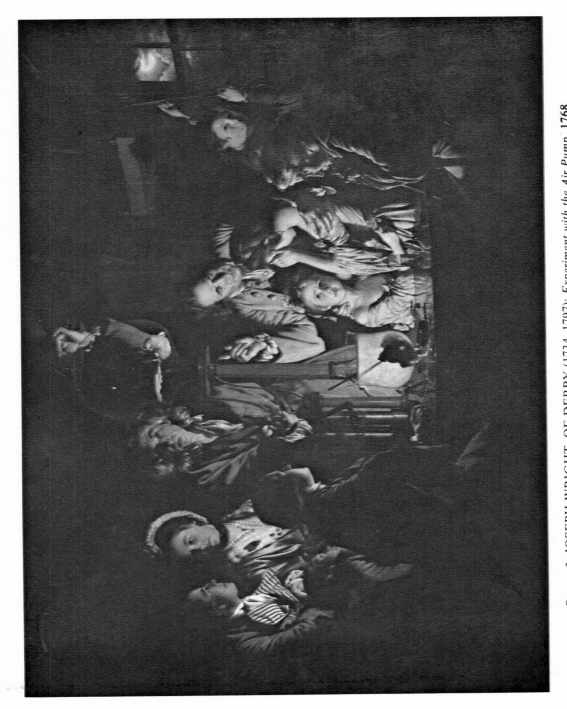

PLATE 3. JOSEPH WRIGHT, OF DERBY (1734–1797): *Experiment with the Air Pump*. **1768.** Oil on canvas, 72 x 96 inches. (Reproduced by courtesy of the Trustees, The Tate Gallery, London)

467

PLATE 4. GEORGE MORLAND (1763–1804): *Horses in a Stable*. 1791. Oil on canvas, 34 x 46 inches. (Victoria and Albert Museum, London, Crown Copyright)

PLATE 5. Attributed to JOHN CROME (1768–1821): *Hay Barges on the Yare*. Oil on canvas, 30½ x 40 inches. (Philadelphia Museum of Art, Wilstach Collection)

469

PLATE 6. RICHARD PARKES BONINGTON (1802–1828): *Column of St. Mark.* 1826. Oil on canvas, 18 x 14¾ inches. (Reproduced by courtesy of the Trustees, The Tate Gallery, London)

Lines Composed a Few Miles
Above Tintern Abbey

Five years have passed; five summers, with the length
Of five long winters! and again I hear
These waters, rolling from their mountain springs
With a soft inland murmur.—Once again
Do I behold these steep and lofty cliffs,   5
That on a wild secluded scene impress
Thoughts of more deep seclusion; and connect
The landscape with the quiet of the sky.
The day is come when I again repose
Here, under this dark sycamore, and view   10
These plots of cottage ground, these orchard tufts,
Which at this season, with their unripe fruits,
Are clad in one green hue, and lose themselves
'Mid groves and copses. Once again I see
These hedgerows, hardly hedgerows, little lines   15
Of sportive wood run wild: these pastoral farms,
Green to the very door; and wreaths of smoke
Sent up, in silence, from among the trees!
With some uncertain notice, as might seem
Of vagrant dwellers in the houseless woods,   20
Or of some hermit's cave, where by his fire
The hermit sits alone.
                              These beauteous forms,
Through a long absence, have not been to me
As is a landscape to a blind man's eye;
But oft, in lonely rooms, and 'mid the din   25
Of towns and cities, I have owed to them
In hours of weariness, sensations sweet,
Felt in the blood, and felt along the heart;
And passing even into my purer mind,
With tranquil restoration:—feelings, too,   30
Of unremembered pleasure: such, perhaps,
As have no slight or trivial influence
On that best portion of a good man's life,
His little, nameless, unremembered acts
Of kindness and of love. Nor less, I trust,   35
To them I may have owed another gift,
Of aspect more sublime; that blessed mood
In which the burthen of the mystery,
In which the heavy and the weary weight
Of all this unintelligible world,   40
Is lightened—that serene and blessed mood,
In which the affections gently lead us on,
Until, the breath of this corporeal frame°
And even the motion of our human blood

43. **corporeal** (kôr·pôr′ē·əl) **frame:** the body.

Almost suspended, we are laid asleep 45
In body, and become a living soul;
While with an eye made quiet by the power
Of harmony, and the deep power of joy,
We see into the life of things.
                              If this
Be but a vain belief, yet, oh! how oft— 50
In darkness and amid the many shapes
Of joyless daylight; when the fretful stir
Unprofitable, and the fever of the world,
Have hung upon the beatings of my heart—
How oft, in spirit, have I turned to thee, 55
O sylvan° Wye!° thou wanderer through the woods,
How often has my spirit turned to thee!
    And now, with gleams of half-extinguished thought,
With many recognitions dim and faint,
And somewhat of a sad perplexity, 60
The picture of the mind revives again;
While here I stand, not only with the sense
Of present pleasure, but with pleasing thoughts
That in this moment there is life and food
For future years. And so I dare to hope, 65
Though changed, no doubt, from what I was when first
I came among these hills; when like a roe
I bounded o'er the mountains, by the sides
Of the deep rivers, and the lonely streams,
Wherever nature led—more like a man 70
Flying from something that he dreads, than one
Who sought the thing he loved. For nature then
(The coarser pleasures of my boyish days,
And their glad animal movements all gone by)
To me was all in all.—I cannot paint 75

56. **sylvan:** wooded. **Wye** (wī): a river in Monmouthshire, Wales.

What then I was. The sounding cataract
Haunted me like a passion; the tall rock,
The mountain, and the deep and gloomy wood,
Their colors and their forms, were then to me
An appetite; a feeling and a love,   80
That had no need of a remoter charm,°
By thought supplied, nor any interest
Unborrowed from the eye. That time is past,
And all its aching joys are now no more,
And all its dizzy raptures. Not for this   85
Faint° I, nor mourn nor murmur; other gifts
Have followed; for such loss, I would believe,
Abundant recompense. For I have learned
To look on nature, not as in the hour
Of thoughtless youth; but hearing oftentimes   90
The still, sad music of humanity,
Nor harsh nor grating, though of ample power
To chasten and subdue. And I have felt
A presence that disturbs me with the joy
Of elevated thoughts; a sense sublime   95
Of something far more deeply interfused,
Whose dwelling is the light of setting suns,
And the round ocean and the living air,
And the blue sky, and in the mind of man;
A motion and a spirit, that impels   100
All thinking things, all objects of all thought,
And rolls through all things. Therefore am I still
A lover of the meadows and the woods
And mountains; and of all that we behold
From this green earth; of all the mighty world   105
Of eye, and ear—both what they half create,
And what perceive; well pleased to recognize
In nature and the language of the sense,
The anchor of my purest thoughts, the nurse,
The guide, the guardian of my heart, and soul   110
Of all my moral being.
                          Nor perchance,
If I were not thus taught, should I the more
Suffer my genial spirits to decay;
For thou art with me here upon the banks
Of this fair river; thou my dearest Friend,   115
My dear, dear Friend; and in thy voice I catch
The language of my former heart, and read
My former pleasures in the shooting lights
Of thy wild eyes. Oh! yet a little while
May I behold in thee what I was once,   120
My dear, dear Sister! and this prayer I make,
Knowing that Nature never did betray
The heart that loved her; 'tis her privilege,

81. **remoter charm:** an attraction apart from the scene itself.   86. **Faint:** lose heart.

Through all the years of this our life, to lead
From joy to joy; for she can so inform 125
The mind that is within us, so impress
With quietness and beauty, and so feed
With lofty thoughts, that neither evil tongues,
Rash judgments, nor the sneers of selfish men,
Nor greetings where no kindness is, nor all 130
The dreary intercourse of daily life,
Shall e'er prevail against us, or disturb
Our cheerful faith, that all which we behold
Is full of blessings. Therefore let the moon
Shine on thee in thy solitary walk; 135
And let the misty mountain winds be free
To blow against thee: and, in after years,
When these wild ecstasies shall be matured
Into a sober pleasure; when thy mind
Shall be a mansion for all lovely forms, 140
Thy memory be as a dwelling place
For all sweet sounds and harmonies; oh! then,
If solitude, or fear, or pain, or grief,
Should be thy portion, with what healing thoughts
Of tender joy wilt thou remember me, 145
And these my exhortations! Nor, perchance—
If I should be where I no more can hear
Thy voice, nor catch from thy wild eyes these gleams
Of past existence—wilt thou then forget
That on the banks of this delightful stream 150
We stood together; and that I, so long
A worshiper of Nature, hither came
Unwearied in that service: rather say
With warmer love—oh! with far deeper zeal
Of holier love. Nor wilt thou then forget, 155
That after many wanderings, many years
Of absence, these steep woods and lofty cliffs,
And this green pastoral landscape, were to me
More dear, both for themselves and for thy sake!

COMMENTARY

This moving expression of Wordsworth's faith helps us to share the poet's sense of how his faith had grown over a period of years. To understand the poem it is necessary to see how it is put together. The divisions suggested here are not Wordsworth's; they simply offer a convenient way of approaching the study of the poem.

Lines 1–22. In this section the poet tells us that he is revisiting a secluded scene, the wild beauty of which suggests "Thoughts of more deep seclusion." The scene seems to him a link between a landscape humanized by people's works and a region of untouched nature, a region still further removed from human activity. The direction of his reflection is therefore *away from* humanity and toward a sense of the world which is described in the next section.

Lines 22–49. His visit to this place five years earlier had had two kinds of influence upon the poet. The first of these is moral. Remembering the banks of the Wye, their beauty and their grandeur, he has been saved from pettiness and has been made more loving and generous. But the second kind of influence had no reference to other people; it was a mood of quietness and joy in which the incessant demands of the self were suspended, and the poet felt at one with the world.

Lines 49–57. Perhaps this exalted reverie is based on illusion; whether it is or not, the poet recalls instances when, oppressed by everyday concerns, he has returned in spirit to the wooded banks of the Wye. His reverie passes, and he is once more aware of the scene before his eyes.

Lines 58–111. No wonder the poet is perplexed; he is recognizing that his memories are those of a very different person: the person he was five years ago. He is reassured, not only by the pleasure he is now experiencing, but by the thought that memories of this present occasion will serve him in future years as well (lines 64–65). At the same time, he recalls how dif-

ferent he was upon his first visit to this scene. Then he was a youth rather than a man. The youth had passed the stage of boyhood's "glad animal movements" and had reached adolescence, when nature "To me was all in all." It is clear that Wordsworth is not scolding his adolescent self for being enthusiastic in his love for nature. He could not experience hearing the "still, sad music of humanity" if he had not first experienced being boy, then youth, then man. In his youth, Wordsworth says, the experience of nature was his master ("The sounding cataract/ Haunted me like a passion"). Now the poet is aware that he cannot be at the mercy of his experience. As a man he must direct his own experience. He must move *toward* humankind. This is the key to the difference between lines 22–49 and lines 93–111. The latter passage is once more an account of a sense of union with the whole, but this union now has a different basis; the "presence" which Wordsworth feels gives order to the world is felt not simply in nature but "in the mind of man" as well.

To put this more simply: when one grows up he no longer passively accepts experience. An adult is aware, not only that he is shaped by sights such as the banks of the Wye, but that he also gives such sights both shape and meaning. The youngster who was lost in nature gives way to the man who half creates and half receives, and hears "the still, sad music of humanity."

Describe in your own words the difference between the moods described in lines 22–49 and lines 93–111. Readers of this poem have often said that it was simply about Wordsworth's love of nature. Why, do you think, is this misleading?

Lines 111–59. The fourth section of the poem moves quite logically from an account of Wordsworth's own growth to thoughts and hopes about his sister Dorothy. Does he expect her to pass through the same stages he himself experienced? What is Wordsworth's hope for his sister as she grows older (lines 137–59)?

Ode: Intimations of Immortality
from Recollections of Early Childhood

The child is father of the man;
And I could wish my days to be
Bound each to each by natural piety.*

1

There was a time when meadow, grove, and stream,
The earth, and every common sight,
      To me did seem
      Appareled in celestial light,
The glory and the freshness of a dream.
It is not now as it hath been of yore;   5
      Turn wheresoe'er I may,
      By night or day,
The things which I have seen I now can see no more.

2

      The rainbow comes and goes,   10
      And lovely is the rose,
      The moon doth with delight
Look round her when the heavens are bare;
      Waters on a starry night
      Are beautiful and fair;   15
      The sunshine is a glorious birth;
      But yet I know, where'er I go,
That there hath passed away a glory from the earth.

* The closing lines of Wordsworth's poem "My Heart Leaps Up."

3

Now, while the birds thus sing a joyous song,
  And while the young lambs bound   20
    As to the tabor's sound,
To me alone there came a thought of grief,
A timely utterance gave that thought relief,
  And I again am strong;
The cataracts blow their trumpets from the steep;   25
No more shall grief of mine the season wrong;
I hear the echoes through the mountains throng,
The winds come to me from the fields of sleep,
  And all the earth is gay;
    Land and sea   30
  Give themselves up to jollity,
    And with the heart of May
Doth every beast keep holiday;
    Thou child of joy,
Shout round me, let me hear thy shouts, thou happy   35
    Shepherd boy!

4

Ye blessed creatures, I have heard the call
  Ye to each other make; I see
The heavens laugh with you in your jubilee;
  My heart is at your festival,   40
  My head hath its coronal,°
The fullness of your bliss, I feel—I feel it all.
  Oh evil day! if I were sullen
  While Earth herself is adorning,
    This sweet May morning,   45
  And the children are culling
    On every side,
  In a thousand valleys far and wide,
  Fresh flowers; while the sun shines warm,
And the babe leaps up on his mother's arm: 50
  I hear, I hear, with joy I hear!
  —But there's a tree, of many, one,
A single field which I have looked upon,
Both of them speak of something that is gone;
  The pansy at my feet   55
  Doth the same tale repeat:
Whither is fled the visionary gleam?
Where is it now, the glory and the dream?

5

Our birth is but a sleep and a forgetting;
The soul that rises with us, our life's star,   60

---

41. **coronal:** a garland, here of wild flowers.

Hath had elsewhere its setting,
   And cometh from afar;
Not in entire forgetfulness,
And not in utter nakedness,
But trailing clouds of glory do we come   65
   From God, who is our home;
Heaven lies about us in our infancy!
Shades of the prison house° begin to close
   Upon the growing boy,
But he beholds the light, and whence it flows,   70
   He sees it in his joy;
The youth, who daily farther from the east°
   Must travel, still is Nature's priest,°
   And by the vision splendid
   Is on his way attended;   75
At length the man perceives it die away,
And fade into the light of common day.

6

Earth fills her lap with pleasures of her own;
Yearnings she hath in her own natural kind,
And, even with something of a mother's mind,   80
   And no unworthy aim,
   The homely° nurse doth all she can
To make her foster child, her inmate man,
   Forget the glories he hath known,
And that imperial palace whence he came.   85

7

Behold the child among his newborn blisses,
A six-years' darling of a pygmy size!
See, where 'mid work of his own hand he lies,
Fretted by sallies of his mother's kisses,
With light upon him from his father's eyes!   90
See, at his feet, some little plan or chart,
Some fragment from his dream of human life,
Shaped by himself with newly learnèd art;
   A wedding or a festival,
   A mourning or a funeral;   95
     And this hath now his heart,
   And unto this he frames his song;
     Then will he fit his tongue
To dialogues of business, love, or strife;
   But it will not be long   100
   Ere this be thrown aside,
   And with new joy and pride
The little actor cons° another part,

---

68. **prison house:** worldly existence.   72. **east:** the beginning of his existence, as the beginning of the sun's daily journey.   73. **Nature's priest:** one who feels a spiritual unity with nature. 82. **homely** (archaic): kindly.   103. **cons:** learns.

Filling from time to time his "humorous stage"°
With all the persons, down to palsied age,   105
That life brings with her in her equipage;
   As if his whole vocation
   Were endless imitation.

8

Thou, whose exterior semblance doth belie
   Thy soul's immensity;   110
Thou best philosopher, who yet dost keep
Thy heritage, thou eye among the blind,
That, deaf and silent, read'st the eternal deep,
Haunted forever by the eternal mind—
   Mighty prophet! Seer blest!   115
   On whom those truths do rest,
Which we are toiling all our lives to find,
In darkness lost, the darkness of the grave;
Thou, over whom thy immortality
Broods like the day, a master o'er a slave,   120
A presence which is not to be put by;
Thou little child, yet glorious in the might
Of heavenborn freedom on thy being's height,
Why with such earnest pains dost thou provoke
The years to bring the inevitable yoke,   125
Thus blindly with thy blessedness at strife?
Full soon thy soul shall have her earthly freight,
And custom lie upon thee with a weight,
Heavy as frost, and deep almost as life!

9

   O joy! that in our embers   130
   Is something that doth live,
   That nature yet remembers
   What was so fugitive!
The thought of our past years in me doth breed
Perpetual benediction: not indeed   135
For that which is most worthy to be blessed;
Delight and liberty, the simple creed
Of childhood, whether busy or at rest,
With new-fledged hope still fluttering in his breast:
   Not for these I raise   140
   The song of thanks and praise;
   But for those obstinate questionings
   Of sense and outward things,
   Fallings from us, vanishings;

---

104. **"humorous stage"**: a reference to a famous speech in Shakespeare's *As You Like It,* in which life is compared to a stage and people to actors who, as their lives progress, play various parts. *Humorous* refers to the many humors, or temperaments, of people.

Blank misgivings of a creature   145
Moving about in worlds not realized,
High instincts before which our mortal nature
Did tremble like a guilty thing surprised;
 But for those first affections,
 Those shadowy recollections,   150
 Which, be they what they may,
Are yet the fountain light of all our day,
Are yet a master light of all our seeing;
 Uphold us, cherish, and have power to make
Our noisy years seem moments in the being   155
Of the eternal silence; truths that wake,
 To perish never;
Which neither listlessness, nor mad endeavor,
 Nor man nor boy,
Nor all that is at enmity with joy,   160
Can utterly abolish or destroy!
 Hence in a season of calm weather
 Though inland far we be,
Our souls have sight of that immortal sea
 Which brought us hither,   165
 Can in a moment travel thither,
And see the children sport upon the shore,
And hear the mighty waters rolling evermore.

10

Then sing, ye birds, sing, sing a joyous song!
 And let the young lambs bound   170
 As to the tabor's sound!
We in thought will join your throng,
 Ye that pipe and ye that play,
 Ye that through your hearts today
 Feel the gladness of the May!   175
What though the radiance which was once so bright
Be now forever taken from my sight,

Though nothing can bring back the hour
Of splendor in the grass, of glory in the flower;
   We will grieve not, rather find   180
   Strength in what remains behind;
   In the primal sympathy°
   Which having been must ever be;
   In the soothing thoughts that spring
   Out of human suffering;   185
   In the faith that looks through death,
In years that bring the philosophic mind.

11

And O, ye fountains, meadows, hills, and groves,
Forebode not any severing of our loves!
Yet° in my heart of hearts I feel your might;   190
I only have relinquished one delight
To live beneath your more habitual sway.
I love the brooks which down their channels fret,
Even more than when I tripped lightly as they;
The innocent brightness of a newborn day   195
   Is lovely yet;
The clouds that gather round the setting sun
Do take a sober coloring from an eye
That hath kept watch o'er man's mortality;
Another race hath been, and other palms are won.   200
Thanks to the human heart by which we live,
Thanks to its tenderness, its joys, and fears;
To me the meanest flower that blows can give
Thoughts that do often lie too deep for tears.

182. **primal** sympathy: the original affinity between humans and God. 190. yet: still.

COMMENTARY

Wordsworth added a long prefatory note to this famous poem in which he says four things of particular importance: (1) that he could not as a child believe that he would ever die; (2) that as a child he had fits of "idealism" in which the world around him seemed unreal (this may have happened to you when you awakened from an unaccustomed afternoon nap and found yourself momentarily bewildered—your bearings lost, so to say). He also recalls (3) "that dreamlike vividness and splendor which invests objects of sight in childhood." Finally, he tells us (4) that he has made poetic use of the idea of the Greek philosopher, Plato, that all we learn is remembered bit by bit from an earlier life. To "use" an idea of this sort, however, is not necessarily to adopt it as a belief.

The intricate stanza structure of this poem and the difficulty and fascination of its subject (how is it that "the Child is Father of the Man"?) makes it imperative that the student first of all experience the poem as a spoken work. Read the poem aloud, alone, or to a friend. Unless you can hear it, you can neither take very much pleasure in it or know its effect as a poem.

What are the divisions of the poem? The first two stanzas tell us of the loss of a "glory" from the earth and the third suggests that the sense of loss has been eased by a "timely utterance" (possibly "Resolution and Independence"). We may therefore assume that the poet is reconciled to his loss by the act of writing a poem.

But the fourth stanza, which begins with a declaration of the poet's joyous sympathy with childhood and infancy, suddenly turns back to the sense of loss. Note particularly the change in the verse which takes place in lines 50–51. The fifth stanza, in which is presented the Platonic idea that the soul's knowledge is lost in the "prison house" of the world, makes growing up seem a process of loss rather than gain. The sixth and seventh stanzas powerfully reinforce this impression. But the seventh does something more. It reminds us in a number of ways that our life on earth is that of mortals: our lives are marked out by births, marriages, deaths, seasonal festivals. Therefore, when Wordsworth praises the child's vision in the eighth stanza and asks at the end why he imitates adults, an answer is beginning to appear. That answer is finally given in the ninth stanza.

In the ninth stanza the poet ceases to ask us to mourn over what happens to us as adults. Instead he inverts the perspective and gives thanks for the perceptions of childhood. What is important in children, he says, *does* survive in us as adults, *is* "yet the fountain light of all our day." The important fact is no longer the loss of the special vision of childhood, but the adult's ability to recall it. The consciousness of an adult is that of someone who has been a child. This is part of what it means to grow up. In the earlier stanzas we have undergone the experience of the sense of loss; we now undergo the experience of discovering that this loss was a necessary phase in human development. An adult is not simply an adult, but a human-being-who-was-child-and-is-now-adult. The child is the adult in the sense that the child possesses all the attributes of human consciousness that become manifest when the child becomes an adult. Wordsworth has given us his own grounds for faith in that "natural piety" which connects the child with the adult, a faith that the "babe" who "leaps up on his mother's arm" is responding to something real in the world, a principle of joy which adults prize as a part of their humanity, without (when they understand their own history) mourning because they are no longer infants enjoying the special gifts of infancy.

In the tenth stanza Wordsworth again declares his joy and his determination to "grieve not, rather find/ Strength in what remains behind." He finds strength also in the "soothing thoughts that spring/ Out of human suffering." Here again, we are reminded of the poem "Resolution and Independence."

The poem closes with a restatement of the poet's joy and faith in nature. In lines 197–99, Wordsworth, perhaps thinking of his own death, reflects that in our maturity we see the world in a more sober light than we do in earlier stages of life, and he ends the poem optimistically by affirming his faith in nature and pointing to the philosophic significance he sees in even the most humble flower.

Explain in your own words what Wordsworth means by the apparently contradictory statement that the child is father of the man. Why do you think, almost a century and a half later, this poem may be easier to understand now than it was in Wordsworth's time?

Drawing upon your study of Wordsworth's poetry, summarize this poet's ideas on growth. What to Wordsworth were the special qualities of childhood, of adolescence, of maturity?

What was Wordsworth's concept of the role played by nature in human life?

What was Wordsworth's concept of joy? Answer these questions by citing passages from the poems.

SAMUEL TAYLOR COLERIDGE

(1772–1834)

Coleridge's literary reputation rests on a fairly small group of poems, the chapters in his *Biographia Literaria* presenting his general theory of poetry and his comments on Wordsworth's poems, and his writings on Shakespeare. At various times, he was a great poet, a brilliant critic, and a profound theoretician. He planned great projects, but unfortunately his ambitions were stronger than his resolution, and he completed only a small part of what he planned. Coleridge described his own character as "indolence capable of energies," and his friend the poet Robert Southey wrote of him, "His mind is a perpetual St. Vitus's dance—eternal activity without action." If he had completed everything he had projected or begun, he might be known today as one of the giants of English literature. Even so, he is a far from negligible figure. Coleridge wrote one complete, perfectly realized masterpiece, *The Rime of the Ancient Mariner,* and, along with John Dryden and Matthew Arnold, he is considered one of the three finest poet–critics in the language. His criticism, particularly, with its emphasis on poetry as an activity of the poet–genius and as a means of synthesizing ideas, has had a great influence on subsequent literature.

Samuel Taylor Coleridge was born in Devonshire, the ninth son and fourteenth child of a clergyman. Favored by his parents, he was resented by his older brothers and withdrew to books and to the world of his own imagination. When his father died, he was sent at the age of ten to Christ's Hospital, a famous free school in London. There he formed a lifelong friendship with another student, Charles Lamb. Later, Coleridge attended Cambridge University. But, although he had been a brilliant student at boarding school, the freedom and temptations of Cambridge proved too much for him. After two years, with debts of £150 hanging over his head, he fled from college and enlisted in a cavalry regiment under the name of Silas Tomkyn Comberbacke. As a cavalryman, Coleridge turned out to be a miserable failure. When his brothers bought his discharge, Coleridge and Robert Southey conceived the plan of starting a colony on the Susquehanna River in America, a site they chose because of its poetic name. Like many other of Coleridge's projects, this one was never carried out.

In 1795, Coleridge made the most important friendship of his life when he met his neighbor William Wordsworth, whom he soon after acclaimed as "the best poet of the age." Several years later, the two men collaborated on *Lyrical Ballads* (see page 504), a book of poems that is a milestone in English literature. Coleridge's contributions to this volume were chiefly poems on supernatural subjects. His aim was to secure the reader's "willing suspension of disbelief" and thus make the unreal seem real.

In later life, Coleridge failed to fulfill the promise of his early poetry. His marriage was an unhappy one. He fell in love with Sarah Hutchinson, Wordsworth's sister-in-law, who did not return his love. To ease the pain of his rheumatism, he began to take laudanum, an opium preparation, and soon became an addict. No longer the happy poet with hundreds of potential poems to sing, now only the leaden victim of pain and despair, he expressed his sense of loss in "Dejection: An Ode." "But now afflictions bow me down to earth:/ Nor care I that they rob me of my mirth;/ But oh! each visitation/ Suspends what nature gave me at my birth,/ My shaping spirit of imagination." He turned more and more to criticism, studied German philosophy for a time, and founded a short-lived paper called *The Watchman*. Toward the end of his life, his health weakened greatly, and he lived during his last eighteen years with a London physician. His last years were not inactive, however. As a famed lecturer and literary lion of London, he enjoyed the homage of many younger literary men, among them the American writer and philosopher Ralph Waldo Emerson.

Kubla Khan *

This poem is but a fragment of a gorgeous oriental dream picture. In the summer of 1797, while the poet was reading in Purchas's *Pilgrimage* a description of the palace of Kubla Khan, he fell asleep and dreamed the scene described here. The fantastic quality of his dream has been often attributed to the opium which Coleridge had begun taking during the previous year. On awakening, he wrote hastily until he was interrupted by a visitor; then he found that the rest was forgotten. While the main features came from the book he had been reading, the incomparable imagery and music are his own.

> In Xanadu° did Kubla Khan
> A stately pleasure dome decree,
> Where Alph,° the sacred river, ran
> Through caverns measureless to man
>   Down to a sunless sea.   5
> So twice five miles of fertile ground
> With walls and towers were girdled round;
> And here were gardens bright with sinuous rills,
> Where blossomed many an incense-bearing tree;
> And here were forests ancient as the hills,   10
> Enfolding sunny spots of greenery.

* **Kubla Khan** (kōō′blə kän′): a thirteenth-century ruler, founder of the Mongol dynasty of China. "Khan," or "cham," is equivalent to "King." The proper names in the poem, whether of real or imaginary places, help to create an atmosphere of mystery and romance. 1. **Xanadu** (zan′ə·dōō): a region of Tartary, an indefinite area in Asia and Europe. 3. **Alph:** Perhaps this name is taken from Alpheus, in classical mythology a river god who loved and pursued Arethusa until Diana changed her into a stream. Their waters united in a fountain in Sicily.

But oh! that deep romantic chasm which slanted
Down the green hill athwart a cedarn cover!°
A savage place! as holy and enchanted
As e'er beneath a waning moon was haunted   15
By woman wailing for her demon lover!
And from this chasm, with ceaseless turmoil seething,
As if this earth in fast thick pants were breathing,
A mighty fountain momently was forced,
Amid whose swift half-intermitted burst   20
Huge fragments vaulted like rebounding hail,
Or chaffy grain beneath the thresher's flail;
And mid these dancing rocks at once and ever
It flung up momently the sacred river.
Five miles meandering with a mazy motion   25
Through wood and dale the sacred river ran,
Then reached the caverns measureless to man,
And sank in tumult to a lifeless ocean;
And mid this tumult Kubla heard from far
Ancestral voices prophesying war!   30

    The shadow of the dome of pleasure
    Floated midway on the waves;
    Where was heard the mingled measure
    From the fountain and the caves.
It was a miracle of rare device,   35
A sunny pleasure dome with caves of ice!

    A damsel with a dulcimer°
    In a vision once I saw;
    It was an Abyssinian maid,
    And on her dulcimer she played,   40
    Singing of Mount Abora.°
    Could I revive within me
    Her symphony and song,
To such a deep delight 'twould win me,
That with music loud and long,   45
I would build that dome in air,
That sunny dome! those caves of ice!
And all who heard should see them there,
And all should cry, Beware! Beware!
His flashing eyes, his floating hair!   50
Weave a circle round him thrice,
And close your eyes with holy dread,
For he on honeydew hath fed,
And drunk the milk of Paradise.

---

13. **athwart . . . cover:** across a thick covering of cedar trees.   37. **dulcimer** (dul′sə·mər): a musical instrument having metallic wires played with light hammers. The word means "sweet song," a phrase that well describes its light, delicate tone.   41. **Mount Abora:** not positively identified; probably Amara, a mountain in Abyssinia. On it, according to tradition, was an earthly paradise like Kubla Khan's.

The Rime of the Ancient Mariner

PART I

An ancient Mariner
meeteth three Gallants
bidden to
a wedding feast and
detaineth one.

It is an ancient Mariner,
And he stoppeth one of three.
"By thy long gray beard and glittering eye,
Now wherefore stopp'st thou me?

"The Bridegroom's doors are opened wide,   5
And I am next of kin;
The guests are met, the feast is set;
May'st hear the merry din."

He holds him with his skinny hand;
"There was a ship," quoth he.   10
"Hold off! unhand me, graybeard loon!"
Eftsoons his hand dropped he.

The Wedding Guest is
spellbound by the eye
of the old seafaring
man and constrained
to hear his tale.

He holds him with his glittering eye—
The Wedding Guest stood still,
And listens like a three years' child;   15
The Mariner hath his will.

The Wedding Guest sat on a stone;
He cannot choose but hear;
And thus spake on that ancient man,
The bright-eyed Mariner.   20

"The ship was cheered, the harbor cleared,
Merrily did we drop
Below the kirk,° below the hill,
Below the lighthouse top.

The Mariner tells how
the ship sailed
southward with a good
wind and fair weather
till it reached
the Line.*

"The sun came up upon the left,   25
Out of the sea came he—
And he shone bright, and on the right
Went down into the sea.

"Higher and higher every day,
Till over the mast at noon—"   30
The Wedding Guest here beat his breast,
For he heard the loud bassoon.

23. **kirk:** church.   * **Line:** the equator.

The bride hath paced into the hall,
Red as a rose is she;
Nodding their heads before her goes   35
The merry minstrelsy.

The Wedding Guest heareth the bridal music; but the Mariner continueth his tale.

The Wedding Guest he beat his breast,
Yet he cannot choose but hear;
And thus spake on that ancient man,
The bright-eyed Mariner.   40

"And now the Storm blast came, and he
Was tyrannous and strong.
He struck with his o'ertaking wings,
And chased us south along.

The ship driven by a storm toward the South Pole.

"With sloping masts and dipping prow,   45
As who pursued with yell and blow
Still treads the shadow of his foe,
And forward bends his head,
The ship drove fast, loud roared the blast,
And southward aye we fled.   50

"And now there came both mist and snow,
And it grew wondrous cold;
And ice, mast-high, came floating by,
As green as emerald.

"And through the drifts° the snowy clifts°   55
Did send a dismal sheen;
Nor shapes of men nor beasts we ken—
The ice was all between.

The land of ice, and of fearful sounds, where no living thing was to be seen.

"The ice was here, the ice was there,
The ice was all around;   60
It cracked and growled, and roared and howled
Like noises in a swound!

"At length did cross an Albatross,
Thorough° the fog it came;
As if it had been a Christian soul,   65
We hailed it in God's name.

Till a great sea bird, called the Albatross, came through the snow fog, and was received with great joy and hospitality.

"It ate the food it n'er had eat,°
And round and round it flew.
The ice did split with a thunder fit;
The helmsman steered us through!   70

---

55. **drifts**: mist. **clifts**: icebergs. 64. **Thorough**: through. 67. **eat**: pronounced et, old form of *eaten*.

And lo!
the Albatross proveth
a bird of good omen,
and followeth the ship
as it returned
northward
through fog and
floating ice.

"And a good south wind sprung up behind;
The albatross did follow,
And every day, for food or play,
Came to the mariners' hollo!

"In mist or cloud, on mast or shroud,°   75
It perched for vespers° nine;
Whiles all the night, through fog-smoke white,
Glimmered the white moonshine."

*The ancient Mariner
inhospitably killeth
the pious bird
of good omen.*

"God save thee, ancient Mariner!
From the fiends, that plague thee thus!—   80
Why look'st thou so?"°—"With my crossbow
I shot the Albatross!

PART II

"The Sun now rose upon the right,
Out of the sea came he,
Still hid in mist, and on the left   85
Went down into the sea.

"And the good south wind still blew behind,
But no sweet bird did follow,
Nor any day for food or play
Came to the mariners' hollo!   90

*His shipmates cry out
against the ancient
Mariner for killing
the bird of good luck.*

"And I had done a hellish thing,
And it would work 'em woe;
For all averred, I had killed the bird
That made the breeze to blow.
Ah wretch! said they, the bird to slay,   95
That made the breeze to blow!

*But when the fog
cleared off, they justify
the same, and thus
make themselves
accomplices in
the crime.*

*The fair breeze
continues; the ship
enters the Pacific
Ocean, and sails
northward, even till
it reaches the Line.*

"Nor dim nor red, like God's own head,
The glorious Sun uprist;°
Then all averred, I had killed the bird
That brought the fog and mist.   100
'Twas right, said they, such birds to slay,
That bring the fog and mist.

"The fair breeze blew, the white foam flew,
The furrow° followed free;
We were the first that ever burst   105
Into that silent sea.

75. **shroud:** rope of the rigging. 76. **vespers:** evenings. 79–81. **God . . . so":** The wedding guest says this. 98. **uprist:** arose. 104. **furrow:** wake of the ship.

"Down dropped the breeze, the sails dropped down,
'Twas sad as sad could be;
And we did speak only to break
The silence of the sea!   110

*The ship hath been
suddenly becalmed.*

"All in a hot and copper sky,
The bloody Sun, at noon,
Right up above the mast did stand,
No bigger than the Moon.

"Day after day, day after day,   115
We stuck, nor breath nor motion;
As idle as a painted ship
Upon a painted ocean.

*And the Albatross
begins to be avenged.*

"Water, water, everywhere,
And all the boards did shrink;   120
Water, water, everywhere,
Nor any drop to drink.

"The very deep did rot; O Christ!
That ever this should be!
Yea, slimy things did crawl with legs   125
Upon the slimy sea.

*A spirit had followed
them: one of the
invisible inhabitants of
this planet, neither
departed souls nor
angels. They are very
numerous, and there is
no climate or element
without one or more.*

"About, about, in reel and rout°
The death fires° danced at night;
The water, like a witch's oils,
Burnt green and blue and white.   130

"And some in dreams assurèd were
Of the Spirit that plagued us so;
Nine fathom deep he had followed us
From the land of mist and snow.

*The shipmates, in
their sore distress,
would fain throw the
whole guilt on the
ancient Mariner, in
sign whereof they hang
the dead sea bird
round his neck.*

"And every tongue, through utter drought,   135
Was withered at the root;
We could not speak, no more than if
We had been choked with soot.

"Ah! welladay! what evil looks
Had I from old and young!   140
Instead of the cross, the Albatross
About my neck was hung.

127. **rout:** tumultuous crowd. 128. **death fires:** St. Elmo's fires, a luminous charge of
electricity sometimes appearing on a ship's rigging or masts. Superstitious sailors believed
it to be an omen of disaster.

PART III

"There passed a weary time. Each throat
Was parched, and glazed each eye.
A weary time! a weary time!   145
How glazed each weary eye,
When looking westward, I beheld
A something in the sky.

The ancient Mariner
beholdeth a sign
in the element
afar off.

"At first it seemed a little speck,
And then it seemed a mist;   150
It moved and moved, and took at last
A certain shape, I wist.°

"A speck, a mist, a shape, I wist!
And still it neared and neared;
As if it dodged a water sprite,   155
It plunged and tacked and veered.

At its nearer approach
it seemeth him to be
a ship, and at a dear
ransom he freeth his
speech from the bonds
of thirst.

"With throats unslaked, with black lips baked,
We could nor laugh nor wail;
Through utter drought all dumb we stood!
I bit my arm, I sucked the blood,   160
And cried, A sail! A sail!

"With throats unslaked, with black lips baked,
Agape they heard me call;
Gramercy!° they for joy did grin,

A flash of joy.   And all at once their breath drew in,   165
As they were drinking all.

And horror follows.
For can it be a ship
that comes onward
without wind or tide?

"See! see! (I cried) she tacks no more!
Hither to work us weal;°
Without a breeze, without a tide,
She steadies with upright keel!   170

"The western wave was all aflame.
The day was well-nigh done!
Almost upon the western wave
Rested the broad bright Sun;
When that strange shape drove suddenly   175
Betwixt us and the Sun.

It seemeth him
but the skeleton
of a ship.

"And straight the Sun was flecked with bars,
(Heaven's Mother send us grace!)
As if through a dungeon grate he peered
With broad and burning face.   180

152. **wist:** knew.   164. **Gramercy** (grə·mûr′sē): great thanks.   168. **work us weal:** help us.

"Alas! (thought I, and my heart beat loud)
How fast she nears and nears!
Are those her sails that glance in the Sun,
Like restless gossameres?°

And its ribs are seen
as bars on the face
of the setting Sun. The
Specter-Woman and
her Death mate, and
no other on board
the skeleton ship.

"Are those her ribs through which the Sun   185
Did peer, as through a grate?
And is that Woman all her crew?
Is that a Death? and are there two?
Is Death that woman's mate?

Like vessel, like crew!

"Her lips were red, her looks were free,°   190
Her locks were yellow as gold.
Her skin was as white as leprosy,
The Nightmare Life-in-Death was she,
Who thicks man's blood with cold.

Death and
Life-in-Death have
diced for the ship's
crew, and she
(the latter) winneth
the ancient Mariner.

"The naked hulk alongside came,   195
And the twain were casting dice;
'The game is done! I've won! I've won!'
Quoth she, and whistles thrice.

No twilight
within the courts
of the Sun.

"The Sun's rim dips; the stars rush out;
At one stride comes the dark;   200
With far-heard whisper, o'er the sea,
Off shot the specter bark.

At the rising of
the Moon,

"We listened and looked sideways up!
Fear at my heart, as at a cup,
My lifeblood seemed to sip!   205
The stars were dim, and thick the night,
The steersman's face by his lamp gleamed white;
From the sails the dew did drip—
Till clomb° above the eastern bar
The hornèd° Moon, with one bright star   210
Within the nether tip.

One after another,

"One after one, by the star-dogged Moon,
Too quick for groan or sigh,
Each turned his face with a ghastly pang,
And cursed me with his eye,   215

His shipmates
drop down dead.

"Four times fifty living men,
(And I heard nor sigh nor groan)
With heavy thump, a lifeless lump,
They dropped down one by one.

184. **gossameres:** floating webs. Coleridge changed the spelling of *gossamers* to rhyme with *nears*.   190. **free:** wild.   209. **clomb:** climbed.   210. **hornèd:** crescent.

But Life-in-Death
begins her work on
the ancient Mariner.
"The souls did from their bodies fly—
They fled to bliss or woe!
And every soul, it passed me by,
Like the whizz of my crossbow!"

220

PART IV

*The Wedding Guest
feareth that a Spirit
is talking to him.*

"I fear thee, ancient Mariner!
I fear thy skinny hand!
And thou art long, and lank, and brown,
As is the ribbed sea sand.

225

"I fear thee and thy glittering eye,
And thy skinny hand, so brown."—

*But the ancient
Mariner assureth him
of his bodily life, and
proceedeth to relate
his horrible penance.*

"Fear not, fear not, thou Wedding Guest!
This body dropped not down.

230

"Alone, alone, all, all alone,
Alone on a wide, wide sea!
And never a saint took pity on
My soul in agony.

235

*He despiseth the
creatures of the calm.*

"The many men, so beautiful!
And they all dead did lie;
And a thousand thousand slimy things
Lived on! and so did I.

*And envieth that they
should live, and so
many lie dead.*

"I looked upon the rotting sea,
And drew my eyes away;
I looked upon the rotting deck,
And there the dead men lay.

240

"I looked to heaven, and tried to pray;
But or° ever a prayer had gushed,
A wicked whisper came, and made
My heart as dry as dust.

245

"I closed my lids, and kept them close,
And the balls like pulses beat;
For the sky and the sea, and the sea and the sky
Lay like a load on my weary eye,
And the dead were at my feet.

250

*But the curse liveth
for him in the eye
of the dead men.*

"The cold sweat melted from their limbs,
Nor rot nor reek did they;
The look with which they looked on me
Had never passed away.

255

245. **or:** before.

In his loneliness and
fixedness he yearneth
toward the journeying
Moon, and the stars
that still sojourn, yet
still move onward: and
everywhere the blue
sky belongs to them,
and is their appointed
rest, and their native
country and their own
natural homes—
which they enter
unannounced, as lords
that are certainly
expected; and yet
there is a silent joy
at their arrival.

"An orphan's curse would drag to hell
A spirit from on high;
But oh! more horrible than that
Is a curse in a dead man's eye!   260
Seven days, seven nights, I saw that curse,
And yet I could not die.

"The moving Moon went up the sky,
And nowhere did abide;
Softly she was going up,   265
And a star or two beside—

"Her beams bemocked the sultry main,°
Like April hoarfrost spread;
But where the ship's huge shadow lay,
The charmèd water burnt alway   270
A still and awful red.

By the light of the
Moon he beholdeth
God's creatures of
the great calm.

"Beyond the shadow of the ship,
I watched the water snakes.
They moved in tracks of shining white,
And when they reared, the elfish light   275
Fell off in hoary flakes.

"Within the shadow of the ship
I watched their rich attire;
Blue, glossy green, and velvet black,
They coiled and swam, and every track   280
Was a flash of golden fire.

Their beauty and
their happiness.

He blesseth them
in his heart.

"Oh happy living things! no tongue
Their beauty might declare.
A spring of love gushed from my heart,
And I blessed them unaware;   285
Sure my kind saint took pity on me,
And I blessed them unaware.

The spell begins
to break.

"The selfsame moment I could pray;
And from my neck so free
The Albatross fell off, and sank   290
Like lead into the sea.

PART V

"O sleep! it is a gentle thing,
Beloved from pole to pole!
To Mary Queen the praise be given!
She sent the gentle sleep from Heaven,   295
That slid into my soul.

267. **main:** sea.

*By grace of the holy
Mother the ancient
Mariner is refreshed
with rain.*

"The silly° buckets on the deck,
That had so long remained,
I dreamt that they were filled with dew;
And when I awoke, it rained.   300

"My lips were wet, my throat was cold,
My garments all were dank;
Sure I had drunken in my dreams,
And still my body drank.

"I moved, and could not feel my limbs;   305
I was so light—almost
I thought that I had died in sleep,
And was a blessèd ghost.

*He heareth sounds
and seeth strange
sights and commotions
in the sky and
the elements.*

"And soon I heard a roaring wind.
It did not come anear;
But with its sound it shook the sails,   310
That were so thin and sere.°

"The upper air burst into life!
And a hundred fire flags sheen,°
To and fro they were hurried about!   315
And to and fro, and in and out,
The wan stars danced between.°

"And the coming wind did roar more loud,
And the sails did sigh like sedge;°
And the rain poured down from one black cloud;   320
The moon was at its edge.

297. **silly:** empty; useless.   312. **sere:** dried up.   314. **fire flags sheen:** bright lightning
flashes.   313–17. **"The upper . . . between:** The Mariner is witnessing the aurora australis or
southern lights.   319. **sedge:** tall rushes.

494   THE ROMANTIC AGE

"The thick black cloud was cleft, and still
The Moon was at its side;
Like waters shot from some high crag,
The lightning fell with never a jag,   325
A river steep and wide.

"The loud wind never reached the ship,
Yet now the ship moved on!
Beneath the lightning and the Moon
The dead men gave a groan.   330

"They groaned, they stirred, they all uprose,
Nor spake, nor moved their eyes;
It had been strange, even in a dream,
To have seen those dead men rise.

"The helmsman steered, the ship moved on;   335
Yet never a breeze upblew;
The mariners all 'gan work the ropes,
Where they were wont° to do;
They raised their limbs like lifeless tools—
We were a ghastly crew.   340

"The body of my brother's son
Stood by me, knee to knee:
The body and I pulled at one rope,
But he said nought to me."

"I fear thee, ancient Mariner!"   345
"Be calm, thou Wedding Guest!
'Twas not those souls that fled in pain,
Which to their corses° came again,
But a troop of spirits blest;

"For when it dawned—they dropped their arms,   350
And clustered round the mast;
Sweet sounds rose slowly through their mouths,
And from their bodies passed.

"Around, around, flew each sweet sound,
Then darted to the Sun;   355
Slowly the sounds came back again,
Now mixed, now one by one.

"Sometimes adropping from the sky
I heard the skylark sing;
Sometimes all little birds that are,   360
How they seemed to fill the sea and air
With their sweet jargoning!°

338. **wont:** accustomed. 348. **corses:** corpses. 362. **jargoning:** singing.

"And now 'twas like all instruments,
Now like a lonely flute;
And now it is an angel's song,
That makes the heavens be mute.   365

"It ceased; yet still the sails made on
A pleasant noise till noon,
A noise like of a hidden brook
In the leafy month of June,   370
That to the sleeping woods all night
Singeth a quiet tune.

"Till noon we quietly sailed on,
Yet never a breeze did breathe;
Slowly and smoothly went the ship,   375
Moved onward from beneath.

The lonesome Spirit   "Under the keel nine fathom deep,
from the South Pole   From the land of mist and snow,
carries on the ship   The Spirit slid; and it was he
as far as the Line,   That made the ship to go.   380
in obedience to the   The sails at noon left off their tune,
angelic troop, but still And the ship stood still also.
requireth vengeance.

"The Sun, right up above the mast,
Had fixed her to the ocean;
But in a minute she 'gan stir,   385
With a short uneasy motion—
Backward and forward half her length
With a short uneasy motion.

"Then like a pawing horse let go,
She made a sudden bound;   390
It flung the blood into my head,
And I fell down in a swound.

The Polar Spirit's   "How long in that same fit I lay,
fellow demons, the   I have not to declare;
invisible inhabitants   But ere my living life returned,
of the element, take   I heard, and in my soul discerned,   395
part in his wrong;   Two voices in the air.
and two of them relate,
one to the other, that   " 'Is it he?' quoth one, 'Is this the man?
penance long and   By him who died on cross,
heavy for the ancient   With his cruel bow he laid full low
Mariner hath been   The harmless Albatross.   400
accorded to the Polar
Spirit, who returneth   " 'The Spirit who bideth by himself
southward.   In the land of mist and snow,
                           He loved the bird that loved the man
                           Who shot him with his bow.'   405

"The other was a softer voice,
As soft as honeydew;
Quoth he, 'The man hath penance done,
And penance more will do.'

PART VI

First Voice

" 'But tell me, tell me! speak again,   410
Thy soft response renewing—
What makes that ship drive on so fast?
What is the ocean doing?'

Second Voice

" 'Still as a slave before his lord,
The ocean hath no blast;   415
His great bright eye most silently
Up to the Moon is cast—

" 'If he may know which way to go;
For she guides him smooth or grim.
See, brother, see! how graciously   420
She looketh down on him.'

First Voice

" 'But why drives on that ship so fast,
Without or wave or wind?'

Second Voice

" 'The air is cut away before,
And closes from behind.   425

" 'Fly, brother, fly! more high, more high!
Or we shall be belated;
For slow and slow that ship will go,
When the Mariner's trance is abated.'

"I woke, and we were sailing on   430
As in a gentle weather;
'Twas night, calm night, the Moon was high;
The dead men stood together.

"All stood together on the deck,
For a charnel dungeon° fitter;   435
All fixed on me their stony eyes,
That in the Moon did glitter.

435. **charnel dungeon:** burial vault.

The Mariner hath been cast into a trance, for the angelic power causeth the vessel to drive northward faster than human life could endure.

The supernatural motion is retarded; the Mariner awakes, and his penance begins anew.

"The pang, the curse, with which they died,
Had never passed away;
I could not draw my eyes from theirs,   440
Nor turn them up to pray.

"And now this spell was snapped; once more
I viewed the ocean green,
The curse is   And looked far forth, yet little saw
finally expiated.   Of what had else been seen—   445

"Like one, that on a lonesome road
Doth walk in fear and dread,
And having once turned round, walks on,
And turns no more his head;
Because he knows a frightful fiend   450
Doth close behind him tread.

"But soon there breathed a wind on me,
Nor sound nor motion made;
Its path was not upon the sea,
In ripple or in shade.   455

"It raised my hair, it fanned my cheek
Like a meadow gale of spring—
It mingled strangely with my fears,
Yet it felt like a welcoming.

"Swiftly, swiftly flew the ship,   460
Yet she sailed softly too;
Sweetly, sweetly blew the breeze—
On me alone it blew.

And the ancient   "Oh! dream of joy! is this indeed
Mariner beholdeth   The lighthouse top I see?   465
his native country.   Is this the hill? Is this the kirk?
Is this mine own countree?

"We drifted o'er the harbor bar,
And I with sobs did pray—
O let me be awake, my God!   470
Or let me sleep alway.

"The harbor bay was clear as glass,
So smoothly it was strewn!°
And on the bay the moonlight lay,
And the shadow of the Moon.   475

473. **strewn:** spread.

"The rock shone bright, the kirk no less,
That stands above the rock;
The moonlight steeped in silentness
The steady weathercock.

"And the bay was white with silent light   480
Till, rising from the same,
Full many shapes, that shadows were,
In crimson colors came.

"A little distance from the prow
Those crimson shadows were;   485
I turned my eyes upon the deck—
Oh, Christ, what saw I there!

"Each corse lay flat, lifeless and flat,
And, by the holy rood!
A man all light, a seraph°-man   490

On every corse there stood.

"This seraph band, each waved his hand;
It was a heavenly sight!
They stood as signals to the land,
Each one a lovely light;   495

"This seraph band, each waved his hand;
No voice did they impart—
No voice; but oh! the silence sank
Like music on my heart.

"But soon I heard the dash of oars,   500
I heard the Pilot's cheer;
My head was turned perforce away,
And I saw a boat appear.

"The Pilot and the Pilot's boy,
I heard them coming fast;   505
Dear Lord in Heaven! it was a joy
The dead men could not blast.

"I saw a third—I heard his voice;
It is the Hermit good!
He singeth loud his godly hymns   510
That he makes in the wood.
He'll shrieve° my soul, he'll wash away
The Albatross's blood.

490. **seraph:** angel.   512. **shrieve** (shrēve): absolve from sin.

PART VII

The Hermit of
the wood

"This Hermit good lives in that wood
Which slopes down to the sea.
How loudly his sweet voice he rears!   515
He loves to talk with mariners
That come from a far countree.

"He kneels at morn, and noon, and eve—
He hath a cushion plump;
It is the moss that wholly hides   520
The rotted old oak stump.

"The skiff boat neared; I heard them talk,
'Why, this is strange, I trow!
Where are those lights so many and fair,   525
That signal made but now?'

Approacheth the ship
with wonder.

" 'Strange, by my faith!' the Hermit said—
'And they answered not our cheer!°
The planks looked warped! and see those sails,
How thin they are and sere!   530
I never saw aught like to them,
Unless perchance it were

" 'Brown skeletons of leaves that lag
My forest brook along,
When the ivy tod° is heavy with snow,   535
And the owlet whoops to the wolf below,
That eats the she-wolf's young.'

" 'Dear Lord! it hath a fiendish look'—
(The Pilot made reply)
'I am afeared'—'Push on, push on!'   540
Said the Hermit cheerily.

"The boat came closer to the ship,
But I nor spake nor stirred;
The boat came close beneath the ship,
And straight° a sound was heard.   545

The ship
suddenly sinketh.

"Under the water it rumbled on,
Still louder and more dread;
It reached the ship, it split the bay;
The ship went down like lead.

The ancient Mariner
is saved
in the Pilot's boat.

"Stunned by that loud and dreadful sound,   550
Which sky and ocean smote,
Like one that hath been seven days drowned

528. **cheer:** call, hail.   535. **ivy tod:** ivy bush.   545. **straight:** immediately.

My body lay afloat;
But swift as dreams, myself I found
Within the Pilot's boat.   555

"Upon the whirl, where sank the ship,
The boat spun round and round;
And all was still, save that the hill
Was telling of the sound.

"I moved my lips—the Pilot shrieked   560
And fell down in a fit;
The holy Hermit raised his eyes,
And prayed where he did sit.

"I took the oars; the Pilot's boy,
Who now doth crazy go,   565
Laughèd loud and long, and all the while
His eyes went to and fro.
'Ha! ha!' quoth he, 'full plain I see,
The Devil knows how to row.'

"And now, all in my own countree,   570
I stood on the firm land!
The Hermit stepped forth from the boat,
And scarcely he could stand.

" 'O shrieve me, shrieve me, holy man!'
The Hermit crossed his brow.   575
'Say quick,' quoth he, 'I bid thee say—
What manner of man art thou?'

"Forthwith this frame of mine was wrenched
With a woeful agony,
Which forced me to begin my tales;   580
And then it left me free.

"Since then, at an uncertain hour,
That agony returns;
And till my ghastly tale is told,
This heart within me burns.   585

SAMUEL TAYLOR COLERIDGE   501

"I pass, like night, from land to land;
I have strange power of speech;
That moment that his face I see
I know the man that must hear me;
To him my tale I teach.   590

"What loud uproar bursts from that door!
The wedding guests are there;
But in the garden bower the bride
And bridemaids singing are;
And hark the little vesper bell,   595
Which biddeth me to prayer!

"O Wedding Guest! this soul hath been
Alone on a wide, wide sea;
So lonely 'twas, that God himself
Scarce seemèd there to be.   600

"O sweeter than the marriage feast,
'Tis sweeter far to me,
To walk together to the kirk
With a goodly company!—

"To walk together to the kirk,   605
And all together pray,
While each to his great Father bends,
Old men, and babes, and loving friends,
And youths and maidens gay!

And to teach by   "Farewell, farewell; but this I tell   610
his own example   To thee, thou Wedding Guest!
love and reverence   He prayeth well, who loveth well
to all things that   Both man and bird and beast.
God made and
loveth.

"He prayeth best, who loveth best
All things both great and small;   615
For the dear God who loveth us,
He made and loveth all."

The Mariner, whose eye is bright,
Whose beard with age is hoar,
Is gone; and now the Wedding Guest   620
Turned from the bridegroom's door.

He went like one that hath been stunned,
And is of sense forlorn;
A sadder and a wiser man,
He rose the morrow morn.   625

KUBLA KHAN

1. How is this poem like a dream? Which lines, in your opinion, most powerfully stir the imagination? How do sound and rhythm contribute to your experience of the poem?

2. At what point in the poem do you think Coleridge was interrupted? Explain your answer. Do you think this poem can be understood as a fragment, or can it be read as a unified poem, though one that falls far short of Coleridge's original plan? In answering this question, consider whether lines 37–54 provide a successful conclusion.

THE RIME OF THE ANCIENT MARINER

1. The accounts of the Wedding Guest's reactions in Parts I and VII serve as a kind of frame for the Mariner's tale. What does this frame contribute to the poem? To what extent does the presence of the Wedding Guest influence your own reactions to the poem? Why?

2. Why does the Mariner call the slaying of the albatross a "hellish" thing? In answering, consider especially lines 65—66.

3. Contrast the two figures that cast dice for the Mariner in Part III. How do they deepen the significance of the Mariner's crime?

4. What had to die within the Mariner before he could be saved? Which lines show his clinging to evil ways—his turning to hate instead of love? Why couldn't he pray? What does the word *unaware* in line 285 reveal about the Mariner's salvation? How does the conversation between the two spirits in Parts V and VI deepen your understanding of his salvation?

5. Read aloud the lines in Part VII that sum up the theme of the poem. Coleridge once admitted that such a pat, explicit statement was a weakness in the poem. Do you agree? Explain. Find at least five other lines in the poem that point to this theme and make it more than simply a moral tag at the end of the poem.

6. Describe the atmosphere of the poem. Cite words, phrases, and vivid images that contribute to the atmosphere. What does the use of supernatural incidents contribute?

THE LITERARY BALLAD

The Rime of the Ancient Mariner is a literary ballad. That is, it is an imitation by a highly conscious and sophisticated poet of the form and devices of the old English and Scottish folk ballad (page 35). The poem is more than simply an imitation, however. Coleridge has used the older form creatively and written a poem that is all his own.

What similarities does *The Ancient Mariner* have to the ballads on pages 36–38? In what ways does the poem depart from the folk ballad? To what extent do Coleridge's departures depend on the fact that he was writing a much longer poem than most folk ballads and wished to avoid monotony?

DEVICES OF SOUND

Coleridge's poems are notable for their use of sound to heighten emotion or deepen meaning, thus influencing the reader's reaction. Among other devices of sound, the following three devices are used in *The Ancient Mariner* and "Kubla Khan":

Internal rhyme. Rhyme which occurs within a poetic line, as in "The guests are *met,* the feast is *set.*"

Alliteration. The repetition of initial consonant sounds, as in "*D*own *d*ropped the breeze, the breeze *d*ropped *d*own."

Assonance. The repetition of vowel sounds, as in "So tw*i*ce f*i*ve m*i*les of fert*i*le ground."

Find three examples of the use of each device of sound in the two poems. What does the use of these devices add to the poem in each case?

LANGUAGE AND VOCABULARY

To evoke the medieval folk ballads, Coleridge made deliberate use of archaic words in *The Rime of the Ancient Mariner.* For example, *wist* (line 152) is the past tense of the verb *wit,* meaning *to know.* (*Wit* survives today only as a noun.) Consult an unabridged dictionary to explain the meaning and origin of the following old words: *eftsoons* (line 12); *ken* (line 57); *swound* (line 62); *rood* (line 489); *trow* (524). What does the use of such words add to the poem?

FOR COMPOSITION

Write a composition in which you describe the means Coleridge employs in *The Rime of the Ancient Mariner* to induce what he calls a "willing suspension of disbelief." Do you think Coleridge is successful in inducing such a suspension? Explain.

Wordsworth, Coleridge, and the Lyrical Ballads

According to Coleridge, the plan for the *Lyrical Ballads* (1798)—the book that caused a revolution in English poetry—arose from a series of conversations between himself and Wordsworth. "The thought suggested itself . . . that a series of poems might be composed of two sorts. In the one, the incidents and agents were to be, in part at least, supernatural . . . For the second class, subjects were to be chosen from ordinary life; the characters and incidents were to be such as will be found in every village and its vicinity where there is a meditative and feeling mind to seek after them or to notice them when they present themselves."

Coleridge was to write the first kind of poem, as exemplified by *The Rime of the Ancient Mariner*. His verse was to make the unfamiliar credible: though his poems were to present the supernatural, they were to possess some semblance of truth in order to produce "that willing suspension of disbelief for the moment, which constitutes poetic faith." Wordsworth, on the other hand, was to write the poems about ordinary rural life, presenting them with a freshness and intensity that would make the familiar seem new. As it happened, Wordsworth was much more productive than Coleridge, and most of the twenty-three poems in the published volume were his. It was Wordsworth's poetic practice in this collection that excited attention and aroused controversy. In the second edition of the *Lyrical Ballads* (1800), Wordsworth added a preface which presented the theory behind his practice.

Near the end of the eighteenth century, the language of poetry had become very artificial. Many poets believed that they were not being properly poetic if they did not use what was considered special "poetic" language. For example, a poet, instead of using the word *fish,* would use a flowery phrase such as *the finny tribe.* Wordsworth's theory, and his practice, rescued poetry from such artificiality. As befit his theme of exalting rural life and the common man, he used language that resembled the plain, unadorned English of ordinary conversation. "It can safely be affirmed," Wordsworth wrote, "that there neither is, nor can be, any essential difference between the language of prose and metrical composition." The language of his own poetry, he stated, was "as far as possible, in a selection of language really used by men," but given greater intensity by the use of meter and rhyme. Thus, as a poet, Wordsworth considered himself "a man speaking to men." He acknowledged, however, that the poet is "endowed with a more lively sensibility, more enthusiasm and tenderness, . . . [with] a greater knowledge of human nature and a more comprehensive soul than are supposed to be common among mankind; . . . [the poet is] a man who rejoices more than other men in the spirit of life that is in him . . ."

CHARLES LAMB
(1775–1834)

There are few English writers who have such a reputation for personal charm as Charles Lamb, and few whose charm is so apparent in their writings. As a man, Lamb had a talent for friendship; Wordsworth, Coleridge, Robert Southey, Leigh Hunt, and William Hazlitt were among his circle. He was also a great conversationalist, as is evident in his essays. Many readers have adopted him as a kind of friend, an author who speaks to them directly and is interesting primarily not for what he says but for the manner in which he says it and for what that manner reveals of the man. Temporarily Lamb's enthusiasms—for old books and old china, for the theater and good food, for friendship and the life around him—become the reader's enthusiasms, shared before an open fire of a quiet evening. And when Lamb is pensive, the reader becomes correspondingly thoughtful.

The son of a lawyer's clerk, Charles Lamb was born in London and was always more at home in the city than in the country. When he visited Wordsworth and Coleridge in the Lake District, he admitted that he missed London and was eager to return. Once he wrote Wordsworth, "I have passed all my days in London, until I have formed as many and intense local attachments as any of you mountaineers can have done with dead nature. The lighted shops of the Strand and Fleet Street, the innumerable trades, tradesmen and customers, coaches, wagons, playhouses . . . life awake if you awake, at all hours of the night, the crowds, the very dirt and mud, the sun shining upon houses and pavements, the print shops, the old book stalls . . . coffeehouses, steams of soups from kitchens, the pantomimes, London itself a pantomime and a masquerade. The wonder of these sights impels me into nightwalks about her crowded streets, and I often shed tears in the motley Strand from fullness of joy at so much life."

Lamb worked as an accountant in the East India House for thirty-three years. Finally, much to his delight, he was retired at two thirds of his salary, an event he describes in his essay, "The Superannuated Man." Once, when someone asked him what he had written, he pointed to the row of ledgers on his desk and whimsically added that they were all manuscript copies of his works. Lamb tried his hand at several kinds of writing. He wrote a number of charming poems, including "The Old Familiar Faces," but did not think that his gifts lay in that direction: "I am a dab at prose; poetry I leave to my betters." He wrote several plays. When one of them was hissed at its only performance, Lamb amiably rose and hissed along with the rest of the audience.

Lamb's *Essays of Elia* first appeared in 1820, and they became enormously popular. It is on these essays that Lamb's reputation chiefly rests. The essay, with its changes of mood and its interplay of subject and personality, proved the perfect form for his talents. Lamb is generally regarded as the finest personal essayist in English. Although between the lines of some of the essays the tragedies of Lamb's life dimly appear, cries of bitterness never threaten to overwhelm these works.

One of Lamb's greatest responsibilities was his sister Mary, who was subject to fits of mental illness. During one of Mary's happier periods, she and her brother collaborated on a children's book, *Tales from Shakespeare*. When Lamb was twenty-one, Mary stabbed their mother to death. For a short time, she was committed to an asylum, but was released through the influence of friends and Lamb's promise to guard her. For the rest of his life, he cared for his sister, sending her to an institution when her malady recurred, and resuming their companionable life together when she had recovered. Because he feared that the family insanity was hereditary, Lamb never married. After his retirement, he and Mary moved to a country house near London where, nine years later, he died.

Dream Children: A Reverie

CHILDREN LOVE to listen to stories about their elders, when *they* were children; to stretch their imagination to the conception of a traditionary great-uncle, or grandame, whom they never saw. It was in this spirit that my little ones crept about me the other evening to hear about their great-grandmother Field,[1] who lived in a great house in Norfolk (a hundred times bigger than that in which they and papa lived) which had been the scene (so at least it was generally believed in that part of the country) of the tragic incidents which they had lately become familiar with from the ballad of the "Children in the Wood." Certain it is that the whole story of the children and their cruel uncle was to be seen fairly carved out in wood upon the chimney piece of the great hall,

the whole story down to the Robin Redbreasts;[2] till a foolish rich person pulled it down to set up a marble one of modern invention in its stead, with no story upon it. Here Alice put out one of her dear mother's looks, too tender to be called upbraiding.

Then I went on to say how religious and how good their great-grandmother Field was, how beloved and respected by everybody, though she was not indeed the mistress of this great house, but had only the charge of it (and yet in some respects she might be said to be the mistress of it too) committed to her by the owner, who preferred living in a newer and more fashionable mansion which he had purchased somewhere in the adjoining county; but still she lived in it in a manner as if it had been her own and kept up the dignity of the great house in a sort while she lived, which afterward came to decay and was nearly pulled down, and all its old ornaments stripped and carried away to the owner's other house, where they were set up and looked as awkward as if someone were to carry away the old tombs they had seen lately at the Abbey, and stick them

---

[1] **great-grandmother Field:** a reference to Mary Field, Lamb's grandmother, a housekeeper at a country home in Hertfordshire.

[2] **Robin Redbreasts:** At the end of the ballad, the robins cover the bodies of the children with leaves.

up in Lady C.'s tawdry gilt drawing room. Here John smiled, as much as to say, "that would be foolish indeed."

And then I told how, when she came to die, her funeral was attended by a concourse of all the poor, and some of the gentry too, of the neighborhood for many miles round, to show their respect for her memory, because she had been such a good and religious woman; so good indeed that she knew all the Psaltery[1] by heart, ay, and a great part of the Testament besides. Here little Alice spread her hands.[2]

Then I told what a tall, upright, graceful person their great-grandmother Field once was; and how in her youth she was esteemed the best dancer—here Alice's little right foot played an involuntary movement, till, upon my looking grave, it desisted—the best dancer, I was saying, in the county, till a cruel disease, called a cancer, came, and bowed her down with pain; but it could never bend her good spirits, or make them stoop, but they were still upright, because she was so good and religious.

Then I told how she was used to sleep by herself in a lone chamber of the great lone house; and how she believed that an apparition of two infants was to be seen at midnight gliding up and down the great staircase near where she slept, but she said, "those innocents would do her no harm"; and how frightened I used to be, though in those days I had my maid to sleep with me, because I was never half so good or religious as she; and yet I never saw the infants. Here John expanded all his eyebrows and tried to look courageous.

Then I told how good she was to all her grandchildren, having us to the great house in the holidays, where I in particular used to spend many hours by myself in gazing upon the old busts of the Twelve Caesars that had been Emperors of Rome, till the old marble heads would seem to live again,

or I to be turned into marble with them; how I never could be tired with roaming about that huge mansion, with its vast empty rooms, with their worn-out hangings, fluttering tapestry, and carved oaken panels, with the gilding almost rubbed out —sometimes in the spacious old-fashioned gardens, which I had almost to myself, unless when now and then a solitary gardening man would cross me—and how the nectarines and peaches hung upon the walls without my ever offering to pluck them because they were forbidden fruit, unless now and then—and because I had more pleasure in strolling about among the old melancholy-looking yew trees, or the firs, and picking up the red berries, and the fir apples,[3] which were good for nothing but to look at—or in lying about upon the fresh grass with all the fine garden smells around me—or basking in the orangery,[4] till I could almost fancy myself ripening too along with the oranges and the limes in that grateful warmth—or in watching the dace that darted to and fro in the fishpond, at the bottom of the garden, with here and there a great sulky pike hanging midway down the water in silent state, as

---

[1] **Psaltery** (sôl′tər·ē): Psalms of David, as they appear in the Book of Common Prayer.
[2] **spread her hands:** a gesture of surprise.

[3] **fir apples:** fir cones.
[4] **orangery:** a building or other protected place used for growing oranges in a mild climate.

if it mocked at their impertinent friskings —I had more pleasure in these busy-idle diversions than in all the sweet flavors of peaches, nectarines, oranges, and suchlike common baits for children. Here John slyly deposited back upon the plate a bunch of grapes, which, not unobserved by Alice, he had meditated dividing with her, and both seemed willing to relinquish them for the present as irrelevant.

Then, in somewhat a more heightened tone, I told how, though their great-grand-mother Field loved all her grandchildren, yet in an especial manner she might be said to love their uncle, John L———,[1] because he was so handsome and spirited a youth, and a king to the rest of us; and, instead of moping about in solitary corners, like some of us, he would mount the most mettlesome horse he could get, when but an imp no bigger than themselves, and make it carry him half over the county in a morning, and join the hunters when there were any out—and yet he loved the old great house and gardens too, but had too much spirit to be always pent up within their boundaries—and how their uncle grew up to man's estate as brave as he was handsome, to the admiration of every-body, but of their great-grandmother Field most especially; and how he used to carry

me upon his back when I was a lame-footed boy—for he was a good bit older than me—many a mile when I could not walk for pain; and how in after life he be-came lame-footed too, and I did not al-ways (I fear) make allowances enough for him when he was impatient and in pain, nor remember sufficiently how consider-ate he had been to me when I was lame-footed; and how when he died, though he had not been dead an hour, it seemed as if he had died a great while ago, such a dis-tance there is betwixt life and death; and how I bore his death as I thought pretty well at first, but afterward it haunted and haunted me; and though I did not cry or take it to heart as some do, and as I think he would have done if I had died, yet I missed him all day long, and knew not till then how much I had loved him. I missed his kindness, and I missed his crossness, and wished him to be alive again to be quarreling with him (for we quarreled sometimes) rather than not have him again, and was as uneasy without him as he, their poor uncle, must have been when the doctor took off his limb.[2] Here the children fell a-crying, and asked if their little mourning which they had on was not for uncle John, and they looked up and prayed me not to go on about their uncle, but to tell them some stories about their pretty dead mother.

---

[1] **John L———:** John Lamb, Charles Lamb's elder brother who died shortly before this essay was written. His lameness, mentioned later, was due to an injury.

[2] **doctor . . . limb:** an imaginary detail.

Then I told how for seven long years, in hope sometimes, sometimes in despair, yet persisting ever, I courted the fair Alice W———n;[1] and, as much as children could understand, I explained to them what coyness, and difficulty, and denial, meant in maidens—when suddenly, turning to Alice, the soul of the first Alice looked out at her eyes with such a reality or representment[2] that I became in doubt which of them stood there before me, or whose that bright hair was; and while I stood gazing, both the children gradually grew fainter to my view, receding, and still receding, till nothing at last but two mournful features were seen in the uttermost distance, which, without speech, strangely impressed upon me the effects of speech: "We are not of Alice, nor of thee, nor are we children at all. The children of Alice call Bartrum father. We are nothing; less than nothing, and dreams. We are only what might have been, and must wait upon the tedious shores of Lethe[3] millions of ages before we have existence and a name"—and immediately awaking, I found myself quietly seated in my bachelor armchair, where I had fallen asleep with the faithful Bridget unchanged by my side—but John L. (or James Elia) was gone forever.

---

[1] **Alice W———n:** Alice Winterton, probably Ann Simmons, whom Lamb loved when he was a young man. She married a Mr. Bartrum.

[2] **representment:** portrayal, picturing.

[3] **Lethe** (lē'thē): in Greek mythology, the river of forgetfulness.

FOR STUDY AND DISCUSSION

1. This essay is a blend of fact and fiction. Which details are factual? which fictitious? Aside from the use of fact, how does this essay differ from a short story?

2. What details does Lamb use in this essay to make John and Alice seem like real children?

3. Do you think the conclusion to this essay is effective? Does the revelation at the end seem merely a cheap, clever effect or did it deepen the meaning of the essay? Explain.

What does this essay reveal about Lamb's attitude toward the world of reality and the world of imagination?

4. Describe the tone and style of this essay. What does the repeated use of the phrase "Then I told" contribute to the tone? Rewrite one of the long sentences of the essay into a series of shorter sentences. If similar stylistic changes were made throughout, how would the effect of the essay be changed?

THE FAMILIAR ESSAY

The familiar, or informal, essay is characterized by its relaxed style, its conversational tone, and its wide range of subject matter. You have already encountered the informal essays of Addison and Steele (pages 286–95). The French essayist Montaigne said that in writing an essay, "It is myself that I portray." This is true not only of Montaigne but of most familiar essayists. No form of writing reveals more about the personality of a writer than the familiar essay.

Charles Lamb is generally considered the finest familiar essayist in English. What impression of Lamb's personality do you get from this essay? How do Lamb's choice of details and his style help to convey this impression? After reading this essay, do you think you would like to have known Lamb personally? Why or why not?

LANGUAGE AND VOCABULARY

At one point in the essay, Lamb uses adjectives in a unique way. In the phrase "busy-idle diversions," he has combined two adjectives with exactly opposite meanings by hyphenating them. Explain the meaning of this phrase. Why do you think Lamb wrote "busy-idle diversions" instead of "diversions that keep idle people busy"? What kind of situations can you think of that might account for the use of the following phrases: *sad-happy occasion, harsh-kind remark.* Invent a similar phrase and show how it might be used in a sentence.

FOR COMPOSITION

Write a familiar essay in which you, like Lamb, hold a conversation with the reader. Choose any subject you desire, but present it in your own, personal style.

GEORGE GORDON, LORD BYRON

(1788–1824)

Throughout the nineteenth century, Lord Byron's name was a watchword for a certain kind of Romantic personality perhaps more common in literature than in life. Like the hero of his play *Manfred,* Byron seemed a dashing, mysterious figure exhibiting a fascinating kind of self-destructive energy, wandering the face of the earth in expiation for some unnamed sin, and rebelling against fate to the end. Years after Byron's death, Matthew Arnold (page 618) wrote of him, "He taught us little, but our soul/ Had *felt* him like the thunder's roll./ With shivering heart the strife we saw/ Of passion with eternal law;/ And yet with reverential awe/ We watched the fount of fiery life/ Which served for that Titanic strife." To the twentieth century, Byron seems a far more complex and more interesting figure than the human volcano that the nineteenth century made of him. We are aware not only of his fiery, destructive qualities but also of his elegance and worldliness, his wit and his genuine devotion to the cause of liberty. And the poetry that modern students of Byron find most interesting are not the early works which made him a romantic legend, but the later comic and satirical poems—*Beppo, The Vision of Judgment,* and, above all, *Don Juan*—which reveal the many-sided person he really was.

Byron's father, a spendthrift army captain called "Mad Jack" Byron, died when the boy was three years old. His mother was emotional, unstable, and tyrannical. She resented the family's poverty but prized their noble ancestry. At times she overindulged her son, but she also railed at him and taunted him for his clubfoot, his one physical blemish. At the age of ten, he inherited his great-uncle's estate, Newstead Abbey. He was given a good education, and at twenty-one was by birthright seated in the House of Lords.

Byron's literary career began at eighteen while he was at Cambridge. His first volume of verse was attacked and ridiculed by the influential literary quarterly *Edinburgh Review.* The indignant poet retaliated with a biting satire, "English Bards and Scotch Reviewers." After two years of touring on the continent, he produced the first two cantos of an astounding travelogue, *Childe Harold's Pilgrimage,* written in the difficult Spenserian stanza. After its publication Byron said, "I awoke one morning to find myself famous." Later he wrote many long poems, often in the form of poetic dramas with lonely, romantic, mysterious heroes, who all suggest Byron himself. He was now at the height of his popularity, a celebrity throughout Europe, more famous even than the well-known Walter Scott.

But after a few years the attitude of the public changed. Whispers of Byron's love affairs and his unconventional behavior were increasing; his wife left him after a year of marriage. Angered and embittered by the public's censure and unsettled as always, he left England forever. He wandered from one place to another on the Continent, and for a time joined Shelley's little group in Italy. His restless life ended with a generous and noble act. Greece was fighting to gain independence from Turkey. This conflict aroused Byron's strong instincts to champion the oppressed, and he gave both his money and his entire effort to the cause. He became an officer in the Greek army, and though he wished to die in battle, he fell ill in the little Greek town of Missolonghi and died of a fever at the age of thirty-six.

It was toward the end of his life that Byron turned more and more to a different kind of poetry than the romantic tales that had made him famous. Modeled on Italian comic poetry, these later poems reflected not only Byron's passionate side but also his worldliness and common sense. Unlike most Romantic poets, Byron was an admirer of Dryden and Pope. Like these earlier poets, he attacked folly and bad writing and, above all, dullness. His masterpiece, *Don Juan,* is in one sense a satiric commentary on the Byronic legend. Less tidy than the work of the neoclassic poets, it is like a talk with a brilliant conversationalist who, even when he is most rambling and uneven, commands your attention by the force of his personality.

She Walks in Beauty

She walks in beauty, like the night
  Of cloudless climes and starry skies;
And all that's best of dark and bright
  Meet in her aspect° and her eyes:
Thus mellowed to that tender light   5
  Which heaven to gaudy day denies.

One shade the more, one ray the less,
  Had half impaired the nameless grace
Which waves in every raven tress,
  Or softly lightens o'er her face;
Where thoughts serenely sweet express   10
  How pure, how dear their dwelling place.

And on that cheek, and o'er that brow,
  So soft, so calm, so eloquent,
The smiles that win, the tints that glow,
  But tell of days in goodness spent,   15
A mind at peace with all below,
  A heart whose love is innocent!

4. **aspect:** countenance.

Sonnet on Chillon *

In the summer of 1816, Byron visited the castle of Chillon, a fortress on the banks of Lake Geneva, near Montreux, Switzerland. There, in the sixteenth century, François de Bonnivard, a patriot of Geneva, was imprisoned for six years because of his religious and political opinions.

Eternal Spirit of the chainless Mind!
Brightest in dungeons, Liberty! thou art,
For there thy habitation is the heart—
The heart which love of thee alone can bind;
And when thy sons to fetters are consigned— 5
To fetters, and the damp vault's dayless gloom,
Their country conquers with their martyrdom,
And Freedom's fame finds wings on every wind.
Chillon! thy prison is a holy place,
And thy sad floor an altar—for 'twas trod, 10
Until his very steps have left a trace
Worn, as if thy cold pavement were a sod,
By Bonnivard!—May none those marks efface!
For they appeal from tyranny to God.

  * **Chillon** (shē·yôn′).

Stanzas Written on the Road Between Florence and Pisa *

Oh, talk not to me of a name great in story—
The days of our youth are the days of our glory;
And the myrtle and ivy° of sweet two-and-twenty
Are worth all your laurels,° though ever so plenty.

What are garlands and crowns to the brow that is wrinkled? 5
'Tis but a dead flower with May dew besprinkled:
Then away with all such from a head that is hoary!
What care I for the wreaths that can *only* give glory?

Oh Fame!—if I e'er took delight in thy praises,
'Twas less for the sake of thy high-sounding phrases 10
Than to see the bright eyes of the dear one discover
She thought that I was not unworthy to love her.

There chiefly I sought thee, *there* only I found thee;
Her glance was the best of the rays that surround thee;
When it sparkled o'er aught that was bright in my story, 15
I knew it was love, and I felt it was glory.

  * **Pisa** (pē′zä). 3. **myrtle . . . ivy:** Myrtle, an evergreen plant, was sacred to Venus, goddess of love. Ivy, an evergreen vine, was sacred to Bacchus, god of revelry. 4. **laurels:** Laurel leaves were used by the ancient Greeks for crowns (wreaths) to honor the winners of athletic games and other contests.

Don Juan

FROM CANTO I

Don Juan (don Jōō′un), Byron's comic masterpiece, is considered one of the great long poems in English. The main character is a legendary figure whose only occupation is to woo beautiful women. In various stories and plays and in *Don Giovanni,* a famous opera by Mozart, Don Juan is depicted as a thoroughly immoral person who will do anything to win a woman's love. In Byron's poem, Juan is an innocent young man who, because of his extreme handsomeness, finds himself involved, usually against his will, in many embarrassing situations.

Don Juan does not move in a straight line but meanders in many directions. Again and again Byron departs from his story to comment on politics, relations between men and women, other poets, and the social vices, follies, and absurdities of his time. In the third canto of *Don Juan,* Byron apologizes for his digressions from the main thread of his story: "I must own/ If I have any fault, it is digression,/ Leaving my people to proceed alone,/ While I soliloquize beyond expression. . . ." Most admirers of *Don Juan* agree that without the digressions, it would be a far inferior poem.

One of Byron's most frequent targets in *Don Juan* and in other poems is a trio of Romantic poets of an older generation—Wordsworth, Coleridge, and Robert Southey. Byron disliked these men not only because he thought they were bad poets but also because he considered them political renegades, men who had turned away from the republicanism of their youth to support the conservative cause. The stanzas that follow are from the first of the sixteen cantos of the poem that Byron completed before his death.

> My poem's epic, and is meant to be
>   Divided in twelve books; each book containing,
> With love, and war, a heavy gale at sea,
>   A list of ships, and captains, and kings reigning,
> New characters; the episodes are three: 5
>   A panoramic view of hell's in training,
> After the style of Virgil and of Homer,
> So that my name of Epic's no misnomer.°

> All these things will be specified in time,
>   With strict regard to Aristotle's rules,°   10
> The *Vade Mecum*° of the true sublime,
>   Which makes so many poets, and some fools:
> Prose poets like blank verse, I'm fond of rhyme,
>   Good workmen never quarrel with their tools;
> I've got new mythological machinery,   15
> And very handsome supernatural scenery.

8. **my . . . misnomer:** Traditionally, an epic poem, such as Homer's *Odyssey,* was supposed to contain all the elements Byron names. 10. **Aristotle's rules:** The rule holding that a tragedy should observe the unities of time, place, and action is popularly attributed to Aristotle, although Aristotle discusses only unity of action in his critical work, the *Poetics.* 11. *Vade Mecum:* handbook.

There's only one slight difference between
  Me and my epic brethren gone before,
And here the advantage is my own, I ween°
  (Not that I have not several merits more,   20
But this will more peculiarly be seen);
  They so embellish, that 'tis quite a bore
Their labyrinth of fables to thread through,
Whereas this story's actually true.

If any person doubt it, I appeal   25
  To history, tradition, and to facts,
To newspapers, whose truth all know and feel,
  To plays in five, and operas in three acts;
All these confirm my statement a good deal,
  But that which more completely faith exacts   30
Is, that myself, and several now in Seville,
Saw Juan's last elopement with the devil.°

If ever I should condescend to prose,
  I'll write poetical commendments, which
Shall supersede beyond all doubt all those   35
  That went before; in these I shall enrich
My text with many things that no one knows,
  And carry precept to the highest pitch:
I'll call the work "Longinus o'er a Bottle,
Or, Every Poet his *own* Aristotle."°   40

Thou shalt believe in Milton, Dryden, Pope;°
  Thou shalt not set up Wordsworth, Coleridge, Southey;
Because the first is crazed beyond all hope,
  The second drunk, the third so quaint and mouthy:
With Crabbe° it may be difficult to cope,   45
  And Campbell's Hippocrene° is somewhat drouthy:
Thou shalt not steal from Samuel Rogers,° nor
Commit—flirtation with the muse of Moore.°

Thou shalt not covet Mr. Sotheby's° Muse,
  His Pegasus,° nor anything that's his;   50
Thou shalt not bear false witness like "the Blues"—°
  (There's one, at least, is very fond of this);

---

19. **ween** (archaic): think.   32. **devil:** in several plays about Don Juan, he meets his end by being dragged off to Hell by the devil.   39–40. **"Longinus . . . Aristotle":** Longinus's *On the Sublime* and Aristotle's *Poetics* were regarded as two basic critical works in ancient Greece and Rome.   41. **Thou . . . Pope:** Byron often defended Dryden and Pope against his Romantic contemporaries.   45. **Crabbe:** George Crabbe (1754–1832), author of the poem *The Village*. 46. **Campbell's Hippocrene** (hip'ə·krēn): that is, Campbell's fountain of inspiration. Thomas Campbell (1777–1844) was a minor Romantic poet.   47. **Samuel Rogers:** Rogers (1763–1855), like Crabbe and Campbell, was a minor poet of the Romantic period and a friend of Byron. 48. **Moore:** Thomas Moore (1779–1852), a poet and friend of Byron.   49. **Sotheby:** William Sotheby (1757–1833), the translator of Homer and Virgil.   50. **Pegasus:** the winged horse of classical mythology, a symbol of poetic inspiration.   51. **"the Blues":** that is, bluestockings; a term applied to pedantic lady intellectuals, among whom Byron included his wife.

Thou shalt not write, in short, but what I choose:
    This is true criticism, and you may kiss—
Exactly as you please, or not,—the rod;   55
But if you don't, I'll lay it on, by G—d!

If any person should presume to assert
    This story is not moral, first, I pray,
That they will not cry out before they're hurt,
    Then that they'll read it o'er again, and say   60
(But, doubtless, nobody will be so pert),
    That this is not a moral tale, though gay;
Beside, in Canto Twelfth, I mean to show
The very place where wicked people go.

If, after all, there should be some so blind   65
    To their own good this warning to despise,
Let by some tortuosity of mind,
    Not to believe my verse and their own eyes,
And cry that they "the moral cannot find,"
    I tell him, if a clergyman, he lies;   70
Should captains the remark, or critics, make,
They also lie too—under a mistake.

The public approbation I expect,
    And beg they'll take my word about the moral,
Which I with their amusement will connect   75
    (So children cutting teeth receive a coral);
Meantime they'll doubtless please to recollect
    My epical pretensions to the laurel:
For fear some prudish readers should grow skittish,
I've bribed my grandmother's review—the British.   80

I sent it in a letter to the Editor,
    Who thanked me duly by return of post—
I'm for a handsome article his creditor;
    Yet, if my gentle Muse he please to roast,
And break a promise after having made it her,   85
    Denying the receipt of what it cost,
And smear his page with gall instead of honey,
All I can say is—that he had the money.

I think that with this holy new alliance
    I may ensure the public, and defy   90
All other magazines of art or science,
    Daily, or monthly or three monthly; I
Have not essayed to multiply their clients,
    Because they tell me 'twere in vain to try,
And that the Edinburgh Review and Quarterly°   95
Treat a dissenting author very martyrly.

95. **Edinburgh Review and Quarterly:** Whig and Tory periodicals, respectively; both journals were hostile to Byron.

"*Non ego hoc ferrem calida juventâ*
    Consule Planco,"° Horace said, and so
Say I; by which quotation there is meant a
    Hint that some six or seven good years ago   100
(Long ere I dreamt of dating from the Brenta)°
    I was most ready to return a blow,
And would not brook at all this sort of thing
In my hot youth—when George the Third was King.

But now at thirty years my hair is grey—   105
    (I wonder what it will be like at forty?
I thought of a peruke° the other day—)
    My heart is not much greener; and, in short, I
Have squandered my whole summer while 'twas May,
    And feel no more the spirit to retort; I   110
Have spent my life, both interest and principal,
And deem not, what I deemed, my soul invincible.

No more—no more—Oh! never more on me
    The freshness of the heart can fall like dew,
Which out of all the lovely things we see   115
    Extracts emotions beautiful and new;
Hived in our bosoms like the bag o' the bee.
    Think'st thou the honey with those objects grew?
Alas! 'twas not in them, but in thy power
To double even the sweetness of a flower.   120

No more—no more—Oh! never more, my heart,
    Canst thou be my sole world, my universe!
Once all in all, but now a thing apart,
    Thou canst not be my blessing or my curse:
The illusion's gone for ever, and thou art   125
    Insensible, I trust, but none the worse,
And in thy stead I've got a deal of judgment,
Though heaven knows how it ever found a lodgment.

My days of love are over; me no more
    The charms of maid, wife, and still less of widow,
Can make the fool of which they made before—   130
    In short, I must not lead the life I did do;
The credulous hope of mutual minds is o'er,
    The copious use of claret is forbid too,
So for a good old-gentlemanly vice,
I think I must take up with avarice.   135

97–98. *"Non . . . Planco":* "I should not have tolerated this in the heat of my youth when Plancus was consul" (Horace, *Odes*).   101. **Brenta:** that is, long before I started dating my letters as written from near Brenta, a river near Venice.   107. **peruke:** wig.

Ambition was my idol, which was broken
   Before the shrines of Sorrow, and of Pleasure;
And the two last have left me many a token
   O'er which reflection may be made at leisure;   140
Now, like Friar Bacon's brazen head, I've spoken,
   "Time is, Time was, Time's past:"°—a chymic° treasure
Is glittering youth, which I have spent betimes—
My heart in passion, and my head on rhymes.

What is the end of fame? 'tis but to fill   145
   A certain portion of uncertain paper:
Some liken it to climbing up a hill,
   Whose summit, like all hills, is lost in vapor;
For this men write, speak, preach, and heroes kill,
   And bards burn what they call their "midnight taper,"   150
To have, when the original is dust,
A name, a wretched picture, and worst bust.

What are the hopes of man? Old Egypt's King
   Cheops° erected the first pyramid
And largest, thinking it was just the thing   155
   To keep his memory whole, and mumm hid:
But somebody or other rummaging,
   Burglariously broke his coffin's lid.
Let not a monument give you or me hopes,
Since not a pinch of dust remains of Cheops.   160

But I, being fond of true philosophy,
   Say very often to myself, "Alas!
All things that have been born were born to die,
   And flesh (which Death mows down to hay) is grass;
You've passed your youth not so unpleasantly.   165
   And if you had it o'er again—'twould pass—
So thank your stars that matters are no worse,
And read your Bible, sir, and mind your purse."

But for the present, gentle reader! and
   Still gentler purchaser! the bard—that's I—   170
Must, with permission, shake you by the hand,
   And so your humble servant, and good-by!
We meet again, if we should understand
   Each other; and if not, I shall not try
Your patience further than by this short sample—   175
'Twere well if others followed my example.

141–42. **Friar Bacon's . . . Time's past:** a legendary speaking head of brass, made by Friar Bacon, says these words in Robert Greene's play *Friar Bacon and Friar Bungay* (1594).
142. **chymic** (kĭm′ĭk): counterfeit; archaic for *chemic* and suggestive of alchemy or magic.
154. **Cheops** (chŏps).

"Go, little book, from this my solitude!
    I cast thee on the waters—go thy ways!
And if, as I believe, thy vein be good,
    The world will find thee after many days."°   180
When Southey's read, and Wordsworth understood,
    I can't help putting in my claim to praise—
The four first rhymes are Southey's, every line:
For God's sake, reader! take them not for mine!

177–80. **"Go . . . days"**: The lines are from Southey's "Epilogue to the Lay of the Laureate."

FOR STUDY AND DISCUSSION

SHORT POEMS

1. In "She Walks in Beauty," how specifically is the woman described? Do you think the poem would be better or worse if it were more specific? Explain your answer.

2. Explain the basic paradox in "Sonnet on Chillon." How can liberty be at its brightest in a dark dungeon? Why is the prison called a "holy place"? Into how many parts would you divide this sonnet? What kind of sonnet is it? (See page 89.)

3. In "Stanzas Written on the Road Between Florence and Pisa," what is the meaning of the fifth line? Explain the different uses of the words *love* and *glory* in this poem. Read part of the poem aloud. What sound does its rhythm suggest to you?

DON JUAN

1. What do you learn about Byron's views on poets, on critics, on literary journals such as the *Edinburgh Review,* on love, on fame, and on growing old? Where does he seem to be joking? Where does he seem serious?

2. Two of the chief characteristics of *Don Juan* are its sudden changes of subject and of mood. Cite two examples of each kind of change.

3. Examine carefully one of the stanzas in the selection from Canto I. Describe the rhyme scheme. How does the rhyming in the last two lines give force to the stanza? Cite examples of strange or unexpected rhymes in this selection. How do these rhymes help give the poem a comic effect?

4. Unlike most Romantic poets, Byron was an admirer of Pope. What comparisons can you make between this poem and "The Rape of the Lock"?

THE SONG

A song is a short lyric poem expressing a simple but intense emotion. A good part of a song's intensity is due to its pronounced rhythm and its musical sound. Some songs are written specifically to be set to music. Other songs are later set to music by composers who admire their inherent musical qualities.

"She Walks in Beauty" has been set to music. Do you think this was a good poem to set to music? Why or why not? Compare this poem with the ballad "Get Up and Bar the Door" (page 37). How do the sound and rhythm of the two poems differ? Are these differences appropriate to the different meanings of the two poems? Explain. In "She Walks in Beauty," what combinations of vowel and consonant seem particularly musical?

FOR COMPOSITION

1. What attitudes toward other people does Byron reveal in *Don Juan?* What human qualities did Byron consider most deserving of derision and contempt? Support your answer with specific examples from the poem.

2. Contrast the Byron you meet in *Don Juan* with the Byron of the short poems. Which Byron seems more romantic? which more attractive? which more interesting? Give reasons for your answers.

PERCY BYSSHE SHELLEY

(1792–1822)

Shelley is perhaps the most controversial of the Romantic poets. He has been praised as one of the purest, most intense, and most musical poets who wrote in English. He has been attacked as a poet whose emotions too often get the better of his reason and whose poetry is too full of strident self-pity. It seems impossible to be indifferent to Shelley's poems. While he has been a favorite target of a number of modern critics, modern scholars have shown that he was a far more orderly and sensible thinker than may sometimes appear. One distinguished critic, I. A. Richards, has praised Shelley's poetry for being at its best a brilliant revelation that could be accomplished by no other arrangement of words or images.

Like his friend Byron, Shelley rebelled against British upper-class society. His reaction against the conventions of the society into which he was born began at Eton. There the older boys goaded this gentle-looking, imaginative boy by chasing him with mud balls and branding him "Mad Shelley." The conflict continued at Oxford, where he was expelled for writing a pamphlet, "On the Necessity of Atheism." He antagonized his wealthy father by eloping at nineteen with a sixteen-year-old girl, Harriet Westbrook. A few years later he fell in love with the beautiful and talented Mary Godwin, daughter of William Godwin, whose home was a center for the political radicals and free thinkers of London. Harriet, then only twenty-one, drowned herself in despair. Shelley and Mary were then married.

Two years later they moved to Italy. Byron joined them for a time, and together with other English friends they formed a small, congenial colony. Here, in the short space of four years, Shelley produced his best poetry. Not long before his thirtieth birthday, while he and a friend were crossing the Gulf of Leghorn in Shelley's small yacht, the *Don Juan*, a raging storm arose. Both Shelley and his companion were drowned. When their bodies were later washed ashore, Shelley's friends burned them on a great funeral pyre on the beach. Byron swam far out to sea to watch the flames that marked the end of his fellow exile.

Shelley had an innate gentleness and sweetness of disposition. He was a generous and loyal friend, an idealist who never lost faith in the power of love and good will. His fellow poet Walter Savage Landor wrote of him that he "possessed all the delicate feelings of a gentleman, all the discrimination of a scholar, and united, in just degree, the ardor of the poet with the patience and forbearance of the philosopher." Like Byron, he was passionately devoted to the idea of personal freedom. He believed that if people were granted freedom and learned to love each other they could then live together peaceably. If not, humankind was condemned to a hypo-critical observance of social conventions, a hypocrisy that could lead in the end only to hatred and self-destruction.

Shelley was a prolific writer. His long poems—*Adonais* (an elegy on the death of Keats) and *Prometheus Unbound*—are intense pleas for freeing the human spirit from the conditions of life that enchain it. His short lyrics are rhythmical master-pieces in which Shelley sings, with apparent ease, of the ideas and emotions that possessed him and evoked from him a rich flow of words and images.

Ozymandias *

I met a traveler from an antique land
Who said: "Two vast and trunkless legs of stone
Stand in the desert. . . . Near them, on the sand,
Half sunk, a shattered visage lies, whose frown,
And wrinkled lip, and sneer of cold command   5
Tell that its sculptor well those passions read
Which yet survive, stamped on these lifeless things,
The hand that mocked them, and the heart that fed;
And on the pedestal these words appear;
'My name is Ozymandias, king of kings;   10
Look on my works, ye Mighty, and despair!'
Nothing beside remains. Round the decay
Of that colossal wreck, boundless and bare
The lone and level sands stretch far away."

* **Ozymandias** (oz'i·man'di·əs): another version of the Egyptian name Rameses. The king referred to in the poem is Rameses II, a great builder of palaces and temples who ruled Egypt during the thirteenth century B.C., and who left a number of statues of himself.

Ode to the West Wind

Shelley wrote of this poem that it "was conceived and chiefly written in a wood that skirts the Arno, near Florence [Italy], and on a day when that tempestuous wind, whose temperature is at once mild and animating, was collecting the vapors which pour down the autumnal rains. They began, as I foresaw, at sunset with a violent tempest of hail and rain, attended by that magnificent thunder and lightning peculiar to the Cisalpine regions."

I

O wild West Wind, thou breath of Autumn's being,
Thou, from whose unseen presence the leaves dead
Are driven, like ghosts from an enchanter fleeing,

Yellow, and black, and pale, and hectic red,　　　　　　　　　5
Pestilence-stricken multitudes: O thou,
Who chariotest to their dark wintry bed

The wingèd seeds, where they lie cold and low,
Each like a corpse within its grave, until
Thine azure sister of the Spring° shall blow

Her clarion° o'er the dreaming earth, and fill　　　　　　　10
(Driving sweet buds like flocks to feed in air)
With living hues and odors plain and hill:

Wild Spirit, which art moving everywhere;
Destroyer and preserver; hear, oh, hear!

II

Thou on whose stream, 'mid the steep sky's commotion,　　15
Loose clouds like earth's decaying leaves are shed,
Shook from the tangled boughs of Heaven and Ocean,

Angels° of rain and lightning: there are spread
On the blue surface of thine aëry surge,
Like the bright hair uplifted from the head　　　　　　　　20

Of some fierce Maenad,° even from the dim verge
Of the horizon to the zenith's° height,
The locks of the approaching storm. Thou dirge

Of the dying year, to which this closing night
Will be the dome of a vast sepulcher,　　　　　　　　　　25
Vaulted with all thy congregated might

Of vapors, from whose solid atmosphere
Black rain, and fire, and hail will burst: oh, hear!

9. **sister . . . Spring:** south wind. 10. **clarion:** a trumpet with a pure, clear tone. 18. **Angels:** messengers (from the Greek *angelos*). 21. **Maenad** (mē´nad): a priestess of Bacchus, "fierce" because she engaged in wild and frenzied ceremonies in honor of the god. 22. **zenith:** the point in the heavens directly overhead.

III

Thou who didst waken from his summer dreams
The blue Mediterranean, where he lay,   30
Lulled by the coil of his crystàlline streams,

Beside a pumice° isle in Baiae's bay,°
And saw in sleep old palaces and towers
Quivering within the wave's intenser day,

All overgrown with azure moss and flowers   35
So sweet, the sense faints picturing them! Thou
For whose path the Atlantic's level powers°

Cleave themselves into chasms, while far below
The sea-blooms and the oozy woods which wear
The sapless foliage of the ocean, know   40

Thy voice and suddenly grow gray with fear,
And tremble and despoil themselves: oh, hear!

IV

If I were a dead leaf thou mightest bear;
If I were a swift cloud to fly with thee;
A wave to pant beneath thy power, and share   45

The impulse of thy strength, only less free
Than thou, O uncontrollable! If even
I were as in my boyhood, and could be

The comrade of thy wanderings over Heaven,
As then, when to outstrip thy skyey speed   50
Scarce seemed a vision;° I would ne'er have striven

As thus with thee in prayer in my sore need.
Oh, lift me as a wave, a leaf, a cloud!
I fall upon the thorns of life! I bleed!

A heavy weight of hours has chained and bowed   55
One too like thee: tameless, and swift, and proud.

V

Make me thy lyre,° even as the forest is:
What if my leaves are falling like its own!
The tumult of thy mighty harmonies

---

32. **pumice** (pum'əs): formed from lava. **Baiae's** (bā'yəz) **bay,** near Naples, is close to nearly extinct volcanoes which still rumble and erupt occasionally. The area was famous as a resort of the ancient Romans. 37. **level powers:** surfaces. 51. **vision:** that is, something impossible to attain. 57. **lyre:** Aeolian lute, or wind harp, which makes musical sounds when the wind blows through it.

Will take from both a deep, autumnal tone,　　　　　60
Sweet though in sadness. Be thou, Spirit fierce,
My spirit! Be thou me, impetuous one!

Drive my dead thoughts over the universe
Like withered leaves to quicken a new birth!
And, by the incantation of this verse,　　　　　65

Scatter, as from an unextinguished hearth
Ashes and sparks, my words among mankind!
Be through my lips to unawakened earth

The trumpet of a prophecy! O Wind,
If Winter comes, can Spring be far behind?　　　　70

A Lament

This poem and the one that follows were written in the last two years of Shelley's life and published in *Posthumous Poems* (1824), two years after his death.

O world! O life! O time!
On whose last steps I climb,
　　Trembling at that where I had stood before;
When will return the glory of your prime?
　　No more—oh, nevermore!　　　　　5

Out of the day and night
A joy has taken flight;
　　Fresh spring, and summer, and winter hoar,
Move my faint heart with grief, but with delight
　　No more—oh, nevermore!　　　　10

A Dirge

Rough wind, that moanest loud
Grief too sad for song;
Wild wind, when sullen cloud
　　Knells all the night long;
Sad storm, whose tears are vain,　　　　　5
Bare woods, whose branches strain,
Deep caves and dreary main,
　　Wail, for the world's wrong!

To a Skylark

Shelley thought of the skylark, one of the most melodious of songbirds and one of the few birds to sing in flight, as nature's poet. Of the origin of this poem, Mary Shelley wrote: "It was on a beautiful summer evening, while wandering along the lanes whose myrtle hedges were the bowers of the fireflies, that we heard the caroling of the skylark which inspired one of the most beautiful of his poems."

> Hail to thee, blithe spirit!
>   Bird thou never wert,
> That from heaven, or near it,
>   Pourest thy full heart
> In profuse strains of unpremeditated art.   5
>
> Higher still and higher
>   From the earth thou springest
> Like a cloud of fire;
>   The blue deep thou wingest,
> And singing still dost soar, and soaring ever singest. 10
>
> In the golden lightning
>   Of the sunken sun,
> O'er which clouds are bright'ning,
>   Thou dost float and run;
> Like an unbodied joy whose race is just begun.   15
>
> The pale purple even°
>   Melts around thy flight;
> Like a star of heaven
>   In the broad daylight
> Thou art unseen, but yet I hear thy shrill delight,   20
>
> Keen as are the arrows
>   Of that silver sphere,°
> Whose intense lamp narrows
>   In the white dawn clear,
> Until we hardly see, we feel that it is there.   25

16. **even:** evening.   22. **silver sphere:** the morning star.

All the earth and air
   With thy voice is loud,
As, when night is bare,
   From one lonely cloud
The moon rains out her beams, and heaven is overflowed.   30

What thou art we know not;
   What is most like thee?
From rainbow clouds there flow not
   Drops so bright to see,
As from thy presence showers a rain of melody.   35

Like a poet hidden
   In the light of thought,
Singing hymns unbidden,
   Till the world is wrought
To sympathy with hopes and fears it heeded not;   40

Like a highborn maiden
   In a palace tower,
Soothing her love-laden
   Soul in secret hour
With music sweet as love, which overflows her bower;   45

Like a glowworm golden
   In a dell of dew,
Scattering unbeholden
   Its aerial hue
Among the flowers and grass, which screen it from the view;   50

Like a rose embowered
   In its own green leaves,
By warm winds deflowered,°
   Till the scent it gives
Makes faint with too much sweet those heavy-wingèd thieves;   55

Sound of vernal showers
   On the twinkling grass,
Rain-awakened flowers,
   All that ever was
Joyous, and clear, and fresh, thy music doth surpass.   60

Teach us, sprite or bird,
   What sweet thoughts are thine;
I have never heard
   Praise of love or wine
That panted forth a flood of rapture so divine.   65

53. **deflowered:** fully opened.

    Chorus Hymeneal,°
      Or triumphal chant,
    'Matched with thine, would be all
      But an empty vaunt,°
A thing wherein we feel there is some hidden want.   70

    What objects are the fountains°
      Of thy happy strain?
    What fields, or waves, or mountains?
      What shapes of sky or plain?
What love of thine own kind? what ignorance of pain?   75

    With thy clear keen joyance
      Languor cannot be;
    Shadow of annoyance
      Never came near thee;
Thou lovest, but ne'er knew love's sad satiety.   80

    Waking or asleep,
      Thou of death must deem°
    Things more true and deep
      Than we mortals dream,
Or how could thy notes flow in such a crystal stream?   85

    We look before and after,
      And pine for what is not;
    Our sincerest laughter
      With some pain is fraught;
Our sweetest songs are those that tell of saddest thought.   90

    Yet if° we could scorn
      Hate, and pride, and fear;
    If we were things born
      Not to shed a tear,
I know not how thy joy we ever should come near.   95

    Better than all measures
      Of delightful sound
    Better than all treasures
      That in books are found,
Thy skill to poet were,° thou scorner of the ground!   100

    Teach me half the gladness
      That thy brain must know,
    Such harmonious madness
      From my lips would flow,
The world should listen then, as I am listening now.   105

---

66. Chorus Hymeneal (hī′mə·nē′əl): marriage chant. Hymen was the Greek god of marriage.
69. vaunt: ostentatious display. **71. fountains:** sources, or inspiration. **82. deem:** know.
91. if: even if. **100. were:** would be.

OZYMANDIAS

1. Explain line 8 of the poem. What is ironic about lines 10–11? This poem is unusual in that it makes a point entirely through implication and not at all through a direct statement. What point is made?

2. Describe the rhyme scheme of this sonnet. Would you classify this poem as an English or an Italian sonnet, or as neither? Give reasons for your answer.

ODE TO THE WEST WIND

1. What are the three dominant images in the first three parts of the poem? How does the effect of the wind on each of these elements in nature bear out Shelley's characterization of the wind as "destroyer and preserver"?

2. To what does the poet compare himself in the fourth part of the poem? Line 54 has often been criticized by modern critics as showing too much self-pity. Do you agree with this criticism, or do you think that the feeling of the line is justified by the violent descriptions that precede it? Explain.

3. What does Shelley ask of the wind in the last part of the poem? How do the comparisons in lines 63–67 support his plea? Does the last line of the poem suggest hope or resignation? Explain.

4. Study carefully the interlocking rhyme scheme. *Interlocking* means that the middle rhyme of each triplet becomes the first and third rhyme of the next triplet: *aba, bcb,* and so on. This is an old form called *terza rima,* derived from Italian poetry. What effect is gained by the interlocking rhymes? How does the sentence structure of the poem help to support this effect? (Do the sentences usually end at the end of a line or at the end of a stanza?) How does the couplet that ends each section help complete the section's meaning?

5. An ode is a lyric poem characterized by noble feeling and dignity of style. Does this poem live up to the description of an ode? Explain.

A LAMENT and A DIRGE

1. In terms of feeling, what do these two poems have in common with "Ode to the West Wind"? How do these poems differ from the ode?

2. Which of these two poems seems to you the more despairing? Why? Which seems to give you a more satisfactory statement of despair? Give reasons for your answer.

TO A SKYLARK

1. What divisions of thought can you find in this poem? Cite the line which ends each division.

2. To what different things does Shelley compare the skylark? What qualities do all these things have in common with the bird? Why are they less lovely to the poet than the bird is?

3. What do you learn from this poem about Shelley's attitude toward poets and toward his own poetry?

4. Describe the stanza form of this poem in terms of rhyme scheme, meter, and line length. Notice that, unlike the stanzas in "Ode to the West Wind," each stanza in this poem is a self-contained grammatical unit. (In reading the poem aloud, you would pause after each stanza.) Explain why this stanza form is appropriate to the subject of the poem (a songbird). Consider especially the effect of the long graceful sweep of the final line of each stanza.

FIGURATIVE LANGUAGE

Both "Ode to the West Wind" and "To a Skylark" depend heavily on figures of speech for their effectiveness. Find examples of the use of *simile, metaphor,* and *personification* in these poems. Explain how each example enriches the poem's meaning or contributes to its mood, or both.

FOR COMPOSITION

1. Compare Wordsworth's poem "To a Skylark" (page 455) with Shelley's poem. Show the differences between the attitudes toward a skylark in the two poems. Consider especially that Shelley addresses his skylark as "thou scorner of the ground" (line 100, page 526), while Wordsworth describes the skylark as "Type of the wise who soar, but never roam;/ True to the kindred points of heaven and home!" (lines 11–12).

2. In *Defence of Poetry,* Shelley defined a poem as "the very image of life expressed in its eternal truth." Discuss in a composition whether or not Shelley's own poems—or, a single one of the poems that you have read here—live up to this definition. Before examining the poems, be sure to explain what Shelley means by "image" and "eternal truth."

JOHN KEATS
(1795–1821)

The place of Keats among the English Romantics may be suggested in a brief discussion of his relation to his great contemporaries, Byron and Shelley, and the towering members of the older generation of Romantics, Wordsworth and Coleridge. In the course of the present century, Wordsworth and Keats have come to be considered the most important of the Romantic poets and Coleridge the founder of modern criticism in English, although he is felt to have matched the accomplishment of the other two in a few poems. It is easy to explain the lessened esteem for Byron. His poetry does not, as T. S. Eliot suggested, give us a fresh sense of the possibilities of the language; words do not seem to glow anew in his handling of them. And his particular virtue—the power of a man of the world to deal in a witty and commanding way with society—is one that our age prizes less than others. Also, Byron cannot match Shelley or the other three in technical accomplishment or the intrinsic interest of the poetic forms he creates. Less admiration has come to Shelley in the last two generations, partly no doubt because his pure revolutionary ardor in behalf of liberty and the imagination doesn't have the same power as it did in times past. To many young people today, Keats and Wordsworth are more interesting than Shelley, perhaps because both poets struggled (in quite different ways) to find within themselves, rather than in society, values which would guarantee the worth of their ambitions both as men and poets.

Keats committed himself to the writing of poetry when he was very young. Because he died at the early age of twenty-six, it is difficult to compare his achievement with that of Wordsworth, for example, who did nothing worth remembering until he was twenty-seven years old. Wordsworth was conscious when he began his important work that he must break old molds; Keats first gave himself to poetry and only afterwards discovered the problems peculiar to the poets of his age. Perhaps the chief of these is best illustrated by a comparison with Milton. Milton had been able to assume that the poet could, or at least should, speak for society. Neither the first nor the second generation of Romantics was able to make this assumption. Keats was both excited and challenged by the awareness that his age was rich in talent, and he was sympathetic with the radicalism that was almost universal among those who had that talent. Keats came to see that his sense of himself as a poet would have to be based on some such foundation as the young Wordsworth had found in his relation to nature. Neither the examples provided by Spenser, Milton, or Shakespeare, nor the images of human nature and destiny to be found in the Greek myths, were sufficient for him. Much of the excitement of Keats's short life lies in his brilliant attempts to solve this problem, which was not simply the problem of the kind of poetry possible in his age, but the problem of realizing whatever powers he had—the problem of achieving an identity.

But Keats had no wish to write poetry that would serve only as a reflection of his own personality, as many of his contemporaries did. Instead, he wanted to minimize his own presence in the poem and emphasize the subject matter. With his rich and imaginative powers of description and his ability to see to the heart of things, Keats sought to translate the life and objects around him into striking images that conveyed the essence of his insight. In his poetry, as in his life, he constantly struggled to see and describe life as he understood it to be.

That Keats's struggle was a fruitful one is revealed in the poetry you will read in the following pages. But we cannot separate his sense of his own problem and of the problems of his age from his fresh grasp of the possibilities of the language. Keats stands unmatched, even by Coleridge, as the greatest innovator in the use of English from Milton's time to his own, and he is a writer whose imaginative range makes comparisons with Shakespeare inevitable. His brilliance in inventing and adapting poetic forms fully matches the demands he made on his imagination; what he had the impulse to say he found a way to say. What he could have done had he lived out a normal span is one of the most teasing of unanswerable questions.

THE LIFE OF JOHN KEATS

John Keats was of humble origin. The eldest of four children, he lost his father, the keeper of a livery stable, when he was nine, and his mother died of tuberculosis when he was fifteen. Keats became deeply interested in English poetry while still in school, where he tried to imitate Spenser and where he undertook to translate Virgil's *Aeneid*. On becoming an orphan Keats left school and shortly thereafter was apprenticed to an apothecary-surgeon in London. Although he later became qualified to practice medicine, he turned instead to poetry.

Keats's first volume of poetry appeared in 1817. During the summer of that year, he devoted himself to the writing of *Endymion,* a poem of 4,000 lines which he thought of as a test of his powers. Although his first volume went largely unnoticed save by the poet and critic Leigh Hunt and his friends, and *Endymion* got some scathing reviews, Keats did not falter, but continued to write and publish his poetry.

The following year, 1818, was a crucial one for Keats. His youngest brother, Tom, fell ill and then died of tuberculosis, the disease that had killed their mother. That same year, before Tom's death, Keats himself contracted an ominous sore throat while on a walking tour of Scotland. While nursing his brother, Keats composed the long poem *Hyperion,* an extraordinary advance over *Endymion*. Between the autumn of 1818 and September 1819, Keats also composed most of the shorter works by which he is remembered. In 1818, too, Keats fell in love with Fanny Brawne, a young neighbor. There followed months of illness and deep discouragement, intensified by his struggle to give up Fanny. When his case was desperate, Keats set sail for the warmer climate of Italy with a young artist, Joseph Severn, as companion. Only a few months after his arrival there, he died in Rome in February 1821, at the age of twenty-six.

On First Looking into Chapman's Homer

When Keats was about twenty-one he borrowed a translation of Homer by George Chapman, an Elizabethan poet. With an old friend, he sat up till daylight reading it, "Keats shouting with delight as some passage of special energy struck his imagination." The next morning his friend found this sonnet on his breakfast table.

Much have I traveled in the realms of gold,
And many goodly states and kingdoms seen;
Round many western islands have I been
Which bards in fealty to Apollo° hold.
Oft of one wide expanse had I been told   5
That deep-browed Homer ruled as his demesne;°
Yet did I never breathe its pure serene°
Till I heard Chapman speak out loud and bold.
Then felt I like some watcher of the skies
When a new planet swims into his ken;   10
Or like stout Cortez° when with eagle eyes
He stared at the Pacific—and all his men
Looked at each other with a wild surmise—
Silent, upon a peak in Darien.°

4. **Apollo:** the Greek god of poetry and music.   6. **demesne** (di·mān′, but here di·mēn′): domain.   7. **serene:** air.   11. **Cortez** (kôr·tez′): It was Balboa, not Cortez, who discovered the Pacific Ocean.   14. **Darien** (dâr·ē·en′): the eastern part of the Isthmus of Panama.

COMMENTARY

This sonnet, composed in October 1816, was a stirring sign that England had a great new poet. Keats knew no Greek, and his first glimpse of Homer's poem in the translation by the Elizabethan poet, Chapman, excited him deeply. In a letter dated February 1818, Keats wrote that a poem's "touches of beauty should never be half-way, thereby making the reader breathless instead of content: the rise, the progress, the setting of imagery should like the sun come natural to him—shine over him and set soberly, although in magnificence leaving him in the luxury of twilight . . ." One of the remarkable things about this sonnet is its "rise," "progress," and "setting." The two opening lines have a conversational directness; they are followed by two lines which make clear that the poet is speaking of the realms of the imagination rather than of the earth. Lines 5–8 focus attention on one specific "realm," Chapman's translation of Homer.

The last six lines of the sonnet are one exquisitely managed sentence, moving to a climax of emotion and then diminishing, or "setting," in the final line. In this case the "setting" is both an exquisite conclusion to the verbal music of the sonnet and a climactic dramatization of Keats's wonder. Notice how the passionate absorption of the imagined explorers comes sharply into focus with the use of the word *silent*. Notice how that same word furnishes a climax to the march of sounds in the poem, and how the sounds following this word give the line a gradually subsiding effect, like the setting of the sun.

FOR STUDY AND DISCUSSION

1. What seems contradictory about Keats's use of the word *silent* when you consider its ordinary meaning?
2. List the uses of "s" and "z" sounds in the last six lines. What effect do they have?
3. Substitute the word *moves* for *swims* in line 10, and *strange* for *wild* in line 13. How do these substitutions change the effect of the poem?

When I Have Fears

When I have fears that I may cease to be
Before my pen has gleaned my teeming brain,
Before high-pilèd books, in charactery,°
Hold like rich garners the full-ripened grain;
When I behold, upon the night's starred face,5
Huge cloudy symbols of a high romance,
And think that I may never live to trace
Their shadows, with the magic hand of chance;°
And when I feel, fair creature of an hour,
That I shall never look upon thee more,10
Never have relish in the fairy power
Of unreflecting love—then on the shore
Of the wide world I stand alone, and think
Till love and fame to nothingness do sink.

3. **charactery:** handwriting.　8. **chance:** inspiration.

COMMENTARY

This sonnet has a high proportion of lines that oblige the reader to pause at the end. Only a few lines vary this effect of regularity, most notably lines 12 and 13, which, with their long open vowels (in *shore, wide world, alone*), provide a change of pace and underline the emotional climax of these lines.

FOR STUDY AND DISCUSSION

Describe the progress in thought in the three quatrains. Is there a progression of emotion also? Explain. How does the variation from the Shakespearean sonnet (see lines 12–13) call attention to the meaning of the poem?

Bright Star! Would I Were Steadfast as Thou Art

Bright star! would I were steadfast as thou art—
Not in lone splendor hung aloft the night
And watching, with eternal lids apart,
Like nature's patient, sleepless Eremite,°
The moving waters at their priestlike task5
Of pure ablution round earth's human shores,
Or gazing on the new soft-fallen mask
Of snow upon the mountains and the moors—
No—yet still steadfast, still unchangeable,
Pillowed upon my fair love's ripening breast,10
To feel forever its soft fall and swell,
Awake forever in a sweet unrest,
Still, still to hear her tender-taken breath,
And so live ever—or else swoon to death.

4. **Eremite** (er'ə·mīt): a religious recluse; a hermit.

COMMENTARY

In "Bright Star!" (page 531), the lover declares that he wants, not the isolation, but the steadfastness of the star. Gradually, it becomes clear that he is also fighting off the thought that lovers die. The two comparisons between the lover's situation and that of the star bring out a familiar difference between men and stars: the star looks down on new-fallen snow which has a whiteness which, by an old poetic convention, the lover attributes to his beloved. But lovers are not hermits, as the poet terms the star: they are in fact completely bound up with another person, the beloved.

The poet acknowledges this difference' by adding the report of another sense, hearing, which is not attributed to the star. In a "sweet unrest" he imagines himself listening to the breathing of his love. Thereupon the fact of which we have all along been half-conscious jumps out at us: the star doesn't change, it isn't displaced. Instead it is the lover who is losing himself, drowning himself in what he sees and feels. To lose one's identity—is that not to die? At the end of the poem, the poet seeks not solitariness or steadfastness but a kind of momentary death, the loss of his identity in his beloved.

FOR STUDY AND DISCUSSION

1. Study the first eight lines of the poem. Why do you think Keats goes to such lengths to explain the ways in which he does *not* want to be like the star? What mood is suggested by the comparisons with the sea and the snow-capped mountains?

2. Of the three sonnets by Keats which you have just read, which moves you most? Which do you think is the best sonnet? Explain.

Ode to a Nightingale

Keats wrote this poem in the spring of 1819. The death of Keats's younger brother Tom, which had occurred the previous December, is referred to in the third stanza.

My heart aches, and a drowsy numbness pains
   My sense, as though of hemlock° I had drunk,
Or emptied some dull opiate to the drains
   One minute past, and Lethe-wards° had sunk;
'Tis not through envy of thy happy lot,   5
   But being too happy in thine happiness—
      That thou, light-wingèd Dryad° of the trees,
         In some melodious plot
Of beechen green, and shadows numberless,
   Singest of summer in full-throated ease.   10

O for a draught of vintage! that hath been
   Cooled a long age in the deep-delvèd earth,
Tasting of Flora° and the country green,
   Dance, and Provençal° song, and sunburnt mirth!

---

2. **hemlock:** a poison. 4. **Lethe-wards:** toward the Greek river of forgetfulness, whose waters prepared the good to enter the bliss of the Elysian Fields. 7. **Dryad:** a wood nymph. 13. **Flora:** goddess of flowers. 14. **Provençal** (prō'vən·säl'): pertaining to Provence in southern France, home of the medieval troubadours.

O for a beaker full of the warm South,   15
  Full of the true, the blushful Hippocrene,°
    With beaded bubbles winking at the brim,
      And purple-stainèd mouth;
  That I might drink, and leave the world unseen,
    And with thee fade away into the forest dim;   20

Fade far away, dissolve, and quite forget
  What thou among the leaves hast never known,
The weariness, the fever, and the fret
  Here, where men sit and hear each other groan;
Where palsy shakes a few, sad, last gray hairs;   25
  Where youth grows pale and specter-thin, and dies;
    Where but to think is to be full of sorrow
      And leaden-eyed despairs;
  Where Beauty cannot keep her lustrous eyes
    Or new Love pine at them beyond tomorrow.   30

Away! away! for I will fly to thee,
  Not charioted by Bacchus and his pards,°
But on the viewless° wings of Poesy,
  Though the dull brain perplexes and retards:
Already with thee! tender is the night,   35
  And haply the Queen Moon is on her throne,
    Clustered around by all her starry Fays;°
      But here there is no light,
Save what from heaven is with the breezes blown
  Through verdurous glooms and winding mossy ways.   40

---

    16. **Hippocrene** (hip′ə·krēn): a fountain on Mount Helicon, sacred to the Muses.   32. **Bacchus** (bak′əs) . . . **pards:** The god of wine rode in a chariot drawn by leopards.   33. **viewless:** invisible.   37. **Fays:** fairies.

I cannot see what flowers are at my feet,
Nor what soft incense hangs upon the boughs,
But, in embalmèd° darkness, guess each sweet
Wherewith the seasonable month endows
The grass, the thicket, and the fruit tree wild;   45
White hawthorn, and the pastoral eglantine;
Fast fading violets covered up in leaves;
And mid-May's eldest child,
The coming musk rose, full of dewy wine,
The murmurous haunt of flies on summer eves.   50

Darkling° I listen; and, for many a time
I have been half in love with easeful Death,
Called him soft names in many a musèd rhyme,
To take into the air my quiet breath;
Now more than ever seems it rich to die,   55
To cease upon the midnight with no pain,
While thou art pouring forth thy soul abroad
In such an ecstasy!
Still wouldst thou sing, and I have ears in vain—
To thy high requiem become a sod.   60

Thou wast not born for death, immortal Bird!
No hungry generations tread thee down;
The voice I hear this passing night was heard
In ancient days by emperor. and clown;
Perhaps the selfsame song that found a path   65
Through the sad heart of Ruth,° when, sick for home,
She stood in tears amid the alien corn;
The same that ofttimes hath
Charmed magic casements, opening on the foam
Of perilous seas, in fairylands forlorn.   70

Forlorn! the very word is like a bell
To toll me back from thee to my sole self!
Adieu! the fancy cannot cheat so well
As she is famed° to do, deceiving elf.
Adieu! adieu! thy plaintive anthem fades   75
Past the near meadows, over the still stream,
Up the hillside; and now 'tis buried deep
In the next valley glades.
Was it a vision, or a waking dream?
Fled is that music—Do I wake or sleep?   80

43. **embalmèd:** balmy.   51. **Darkling:** in the dark.   66. **Ruth:** According to the Bible (Ruth 2:1–23), the widow Ruth left her home and journeyed to Judah where she worked in the corn (wheat) fields.   74. **famed:** reported.

[COMMENTARY ON "ODE TO A NIGHTINGALE" FOLLOWS ON PAGE 543.]

ENGLISH PAINTING

Early English Watercolorists

In the latter half of the eighteenth century, English artists discovered new possibilities in watercolor. For the rendering of solid forms on a large scale, they continued to use oil paints, which are thick and opaque. But for smaller pictures of a wide variety of subjects—supernatural visions, vignettes of everyday life, landscapes—they often preferred the thinner, transparent quality of watercolor.

William Blake, painter and poet, believed in the reality of his extraordinary visions and created a mythology of his own. Original though he was, he supplemented his imagination by using what he had learned as a young engraver about the art of earlier times. From medieval manuscripts he learned to love the page written and illuminated by hand; from Italian paintings, particularly Michelangelo's, he learned to admire the grandeur of the human figure.

The Ancient of Days (PLATE 1), represents one of Blake's favorite subjects. Painted as the frontispiece of his book *Europe, a Prophecy* (1794), this little picture confines in a geometrical pattern the figure of the Creator, shown with compasses in hand, imposing order on the universe. According to Blake, the measuring and bounding of the Infinite was not an act of benevolence. In his mind the Creator was identified with a white-bearded power whom he named Urizen (from a Greek work meaning "to fix a limit"), and whom he thought of as standing for reason, restraint, and law, in opposition to imagination, freedom, and love.

Thomas Rowlandson's genius, which was concerned entirely with things of this world, was of a different order. His characteristic attitude was a hearty appreciation of the flow of life in town and country. His eye for the comic sometimes led him into caricature—that is to say, into deliberate exaggeration of an outstanding feature, like a pointed nose or a fat paunch, for ludicrous or grotesque effect. *Jealousy, The Rival* (PLATE 2) has the air of a comedy by Sheridan. The belle at the harpsichord monopolizes the attention of two gallant soldiers. The other young lady, whose sewing box hints at less showy talents, has only a dog in attendance. She has her scissors in hand and looks as if she wants to use them as a weapon!

In *Reading the Will* (PLATE 3), Rowlandson caricatures a family lawyer and shows the selfishly interested parties gathered around the coffin of someone who had money. The lucky heir appears to be a jovial but irresponsible-looking sportsman whose hounds are playing around his boots. The parson tries to pacify the disappointed father brandishing his cudgel in a rage, while a maid looks after the lady who has fainted.

The earliest English watercolorists generally drew their pictures in black or gray and added the colors later. Both Blake and Rowlandson used this method and sometimes even strengthened the lines in their finished works. At about the turn of the century, landscape artists adopted a new technique. Trying to capture effects of light at various times of day, in all kinds of weather, they suppressed unnaturally sharp lines and worked from the start with *areas of color*. Painting in watercolor is like brushing water on damp paper—except that, of course, the water is colored. If two washes of different colors are placed side by side when both are wet, the edges will blend softly. If one color is placed on top of another that has already dried, the first color will show through the second.

Thomas Girtin's *Kirkstall Abbey* (PLATE 4), a Yorkshire scene, is remarkable both as a composition and as the expression of a mood. Although it is seen at a distance, just off-center in a broad expanse of river, meadow, and woodland, the ruined tower is unmistakably the focal point of this painting. It looms higher than anything else and breaks the almost level horizon. But Girtin had other, subtler ways of drawing our attention to it. He leads us inward by the flattened zigzags made by the river bank and the edges of the meadows; then upward from the middle of the open-ended oval formed by the two bands of dark foliage; and up and down between the dip in the clouds and the nearest, lightest stretch of the river. In other bits of the ruins, in the minute figures approaching the white gate, the main vertical shape is unobtrusively echoed. The feeling is of stillness at evening, solitude, and the grandeur of a structure centuries old.

John Sell Cotman, who brought artistic distinction to his native city of Norwich, showed less concern for poetical effects than for the essential shapes of things and for the patterning of masses. In his watercolor *Greta Bridge* (PLATE 5), Cotman treated the bridge's span and the building as starkly simple patterns of light against the dark foliage.

Samuel Palmer's watercolor, *Cornfield by Moonlight with Evening Star* (PLATE 6), has a quality reminiscent of Blake's visions. In 1826 Palmer went to live in Kent with a band of artists who called themselves "The Ancients" and chose as their watchwords "Poetry and Sentiment." The concluding verses of Psalm 65, which Palmer loved, suggest the state of mind in which he painted this picture: "And the little hills rejoice on every side. The pastures are clothed with flocks; the valleys also are covered with corn; they shout for joy, they also sing."

PLATE 1. WILLIAM BLAKE (1757–1827): *The Ancient of Days.* 1794. Watercolor, 9¼ x 6⅝ inches. (Whitworth Art Gallery, University of Manchester, England)

PLATE 2. THOMAS ROWLANDSON (1756–1827): *Jealousy, The Rival.* 1803. Watercolor, $9\frac{1}{4}$ x $12\frac{1}{8}$ inches. (Boston Public Library)

PLATE 3. THOMAS ROWLANDSON (1756–1827): *Reading the Will.* Watercolor, 8 x 9¼ inches. (Boston Public Library)

539

PLATE 4. THOMAS GIRTIN (1775–1802): *Kirkstall Abbey*. 1800–01. Watercolor, 12 x 20⅛ inches. (Victoria and Albert Museum, London. Crown Copyright)

PLATE 5. JOHN SELL COTMAN (1782–1842): *Greta Bridge*. About 1804. Watercolor. 9 x 13 inches. (The British Museum, London)

541

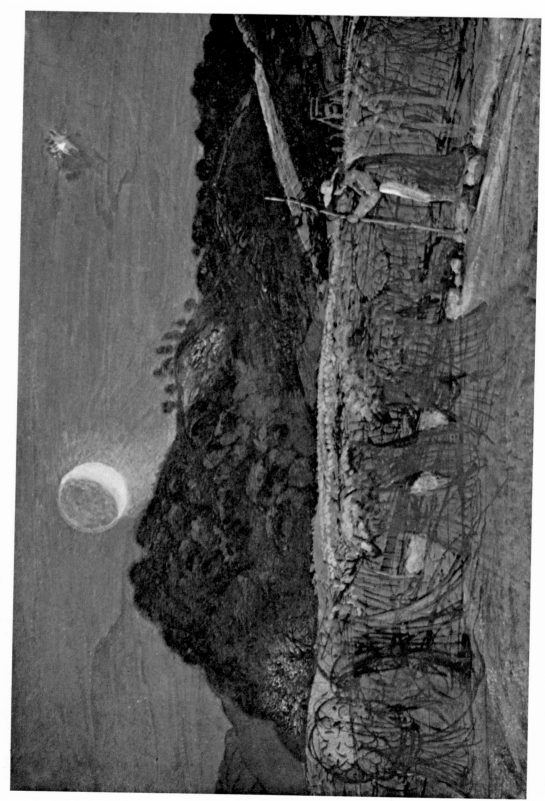

PLATE 6. SAMUEL PALMER (1805–1881): *Cornfield by Moonlight with Evening Star.* About 1830. Watercolor with gouache and pen, 8¼ x 12 inches. (Reproduced by courtesy of Sir Kenneth Clark, C.H., K.C.B.)

COMMENTARY

The term *ode* was applied in the Romantic period to a lyric of praise to a person, a divinity, or even an abstract quality, as in Wordsworth's "Ode to Duty." In Keats's hands it became almost a drama, not a drama with distinct characters, but rather the vehicle of an internal debate between ideal and actual experience.

In "Ode to a Nightingale" (page 532), Keats's choice of a central symbol, the song of the nightingale, dictates his treatment: the nightingale is shifting; it is heard, retreats, and is followed. The bird is immortal only in the sense that its song does not vary from generation to generation. The song is a recurring delight. In the first stanza, the poet is overcome by the song and almost loses himself, so powerful is its effect. In the second stanza he imagines a drink that might take him out of himself completely and carry him off into the nightingale's retreat. The third stanza turns back to the sadness of the world, in which youth dies (as had Keats's brother Tom a few months before the poem was written). The poet's attempted flight from that world takes another form in the fourth stanza—not a liquor, an external thing, but "poesy," is to free him. At this point the poem takes an unexpected turn, almost a somersault, for after proclaiming that the poet is "Already with thee!"—as if he could at a leap join mortal hopes to an eternal being, "a Queen Moon"—he falls back into a world of time and change, a world in which "there is no light" (line 38).

The wood in which the poet finds himself in the fifth stanza is one in which flowers bloom and die and seasons come and go. There he is conscious of his mortality, and is drawn by the fantasy of dying to the nightingale's music. The poem continues, carried by its own emotional logic: the earlier attempts to escape into the regions of the nightingale's song have of course been impossible to a creature who dies. In the sixth stanza, Keats imagines a death which is an ecstatic conclusion, but then acknowledges that if he were dead the song would go unheard. His inability to associate the bird's song with death leads to the sequence of attitudes expressed in the last two stanzas.

FOR STUDY AND DISCUSSION

1. How is the nightingale's symbolic significance widened in the seventh stanza?

2. At the end of the seventh stanza, the "fairylands" are described as "forlorn." What response does this word arouse in the last stanza?

3. How may this ode be read as a poem in which the self has an adventure, an adventure of the imagination? Do you find this reading more satisfying than a purely intellectual interpretation of the poem in terms of its "message"? Why or why not?

4. Describe the stanza form of this poem in terms of rhythm, line length, and rhyme scheme.

Ode on a Grecian Urn

Though there are several large urns among the fine Greek collection at the British Museum, no one of these could have served as an exact model for Keats's poem. In fact, much scholarly research has failed to uncover any urn with just such scenes as he describes. Keats's picture is a composite one, put together from typical Greek carvings he had seen. He shows us a clear picture of one side of the urn in the first three stanzas and of the other side in the fourth stanza.

Thou still unravished bride of quietness,
    Thou foster child of silence and slow time,
Sylvan historian, who canst thus express
    A flowery tale more sweetly than our rhyme:
What leaf-fringed legend haunts about thy shape   5
    Of deities or mortals, or of both,
        In Tempe° or the dales of Arcady?°
What men or gods are these? What maidens loath?
    What mad pursuit? What struggle to escape?
        What pipes and timbrels?° What wild ecstasy?   10

Heard melodies are sweet, but those unheard
    Are sweeter; therefore, ye soft pipes, play on;
Not to the sensual ear, but, more endeared,
    Pipe to the spirit ditties of no tone.
Fair youth, beneath the trees, thou canst not leave   15
    Thy song, nor ever can those trees be bare;
        Bold Lover, never, never canst thou kiss,
Though winning near the goal—yet, do not grieve;
    She cannot fade, though thou hast not thy bliss,
        Forever wilt thou love, and she be fair!   20

7. **Tempe** (tem′pē): a lovely valley in Thessaly, Greece. **Arcady** (är′kə·dē): a picturesque region of Greece, characterized by its beauty and by the contentment of those who dwelt there.
10. **timbrels:** tambourines.

Ah, happy, happy boughs! that cannot shed
  Your leaves, nor ever bid the Spring adieu;
And, happy melodist, unwearièd,
  Forever piping songs forever new;
More happy love! more happy, happy love!   25
  Forever warm and still to be enjoyed,
    Forever panting, and forever young;
All breathing human passion far above,
  That leaves a heart high-sorrowful and cloyed,
    A burning forehead, and a parching tongue.   30

Who are these coming to the sacrifice?
  To what green altar, O mysterious priest,
Lead'st thou that heifer lowing at the skies,
  And all her silken flanks with garlands dressed?
What little town by river or sea shore,   35
  Or mountain-built with peaceful citadel,
    Is emptied of this folk, this pious morn?
And, little town, thy streets for evermore
  Will silent be; and not a soul to tell
    Why thou art desolate, can e'er return.   40

O Attic° shape! Fair attitude! with brede°
  Of marble men and maidens overwrought,
With forest branches and the trodden weed;
  Thou, silent form, dost tease us out of thought
As doth eternity. Cold° Pastoral.   45
  When old age shall this generation waste,
    Thou shalt remain, in midst of other woe
Than ours, a friend to man, to whom thou say'st,
  "Beauty is truth, truth beauty"—that is all
    Ye know on earth, and all ye need to know.   50

41. **Attic:** pertaining to Attica, a state in ancient Greece. **brede:** embroidery. 45. **Cold:** that is, immortal.

COMMENTARY

The urn is a visible shape testifying to the miracle of art—it makes the perishable imperishable. This poem is more sharply focused than the "Ode to a Nightingale" for two reasons: first, it has to do with something specifically seen and described; and second, what the poet sees engraved on the urn are images of human life. The puzzle of the relationship between a creature who is born and dies and an unchanging beauty is sharply put.

The poem is not a philosopher's statement about the contrast between human mortality and beauty's immortality. It does not resolve the contradiction Keats sees. Rather it is an account of his experience of that contradiction. The inner debate takes a form unlike that in "Ode to a Nightingale." That poem explores the ways we can achieve a relationship to the imperishable beauty of the bird's song.

But here the poet is faced with the wonder of something we have made which is not itself alive. As the critic Cleanth Brooks has written: "The love depicted on the urn remains warm and young because it is not human flesh at all but cold ancient marble."

These lovers who will never lose what they can never gain—that little town we are led to imagine as emptied by the procession; the whole spectacle of the urn, a "Cold Pastoral," a moment of warm fleshly life embowered in green which has become marble—leads to this conclusion:

"When old age shall this generation waste,
  Thou shalt remain, in midst of other woe
Than ours, a friend to man, to whom thou say'st,
  'Beauty is truth, truth beauty'—that is all
Ye know on earth, and all ye need to know."

Critics have found good reason to differ about these lines. Several critics have labeled as absolute nonsense the assertion that all we need know is "Beauty is truth, truth beauty." It is possible to interpret the last line and a half of the poem as referring to the entire preceding sentence beginning with line 46 ("When old age shall . . ."). In this interpretation it is the poet who addresses us, telling us that other sufferers will have the same relation to the urn, to immortal beauty, as we do, and that they too may have a chance to find that region in which the urn's speech is true.

In the fourth stanza of "Ode to a Nightingale" the poet cries, "Already with thee!" and all that precedes that moment in the poem encourages us to believe that he has reached a region of light and is assured of a place in that eternal realm—only to tumble down into the warm darkness of life again. The parallel moment in "Ode on a Grecian Urn" appears to come in the urn's imagined speech, "Beauty is truth, truth beauty." What we "need to know" is that even in darkness and suffering we can hear the voice of an unchanging beauty.

FOR STUDY AND DISCUSSION

1. Why does the poet call the urn a "foster child of silence and slow time" (line 2)? Why is it contradictory to call the urn an historian? Can you justify doing so?

2. In what sense are "unheard" melodies sweeter (lines 11–12)?

3. In your own words, give a clear picture of the two scenes on the urn, showing what is happening at the moment the artist has caught and preserved the action.

4. In imagining a little town from which the members of the procession have come (line 35), Keats is making a new use of the urn. How would you describe this use?

5. The last stanza withdraws our attention from the figures of the procession and focuses it on the urn. Is the urn what the poem is really about?

6. Keats wrote odes *to* a nightingale and *on* an urn. Why do you think he used different prepositions in the titles to these poems?

FOR COMPOSITION

1. Keats is regarded as one of the most masterful poets in English, second only to Shakespeare in his magical use of sound and sensuous imagery to convey an impression or mood. In a brief composition, examine at least five examples of Keats's use of sound and imagery. Point out what makes these examples effective poetry. Finally, consider why Keats's use of sound and images is especially appropriate to the subjects of his poems: the joy and beauty of art and literature, the enchantment of song, the lure and fear of death.

2. In a letter, Keats stated, "A poet is the most unpoetical of anything in existence, because he has no identity—he is continually . . . filling some other body—the sun, the moon, the sea, and men and women, who are creatures of impulse, are poetical, and have about them an unchangeable attribute. The poet has none, no identity—he is certainly the most unpoetical of God's creatures." Explain what Keats means here by "unpoetical." Then discuss whether or not what Keats has written is a good guide to reading his poetry. Support your case with examples from his poems.

THE GROWTH OF THE ENGLISH LANGUAGE

The Romantic Age

With the start of the Romantic period, the attitude of English writers toward their language underwent a remarkable change. During the previous three centuries—ever since the start of the Modern English period about 1500—writers had been concentrating on developing a literary language that would be different from everyday speech: grander, more eloquent, and more impressive. The writers of the Elizabethan period had reshaped the literary language by borrowing foreign words and by coining new expressions and figures of speech. The writers of the seventeenth century developed a prose style that could bear the weight of the most serious and complex ideas. Then the writers of the eighteenth century, fairly well satisfied with the condition of the literary language, devoted themselves to smoothing out minor irregularities and to developing a formal, polished, "correct" style of expression. Unfortunately, some eighteenth-century writers had been so convinced that the literary English of their own day represented the final perfection of the language that they had looked down scornfully on all other kinds of English. The English of earlier periods seemed to them primitive and imperfect: even Shakespeare was deemed a "very irregular writer" and a poor example for the young. As for the spoken language, eighteenth-century purists had little use for it at all. They ridiculed the conversation of fashionable society because it allowed contractions, slang, and neologisms (new words); and they regarded the dialect speech of the common people merely as evidence of childish ignorance on the part of the speakers.

The poets and novelists of the Roman-
tic period reacted against this narrow view of language. It seemed to them that eighteenth-century literary English, careful and elegant though it might be, had often proved limited and artificial. Deliberately rejecting the literary style of the immediate past, they looked for inspiration to sources that eighteenth-century purists had scorned—the literature of the Elizabethan period, the language of folk ballads, the speech of everyday life. Coleridge employed the techniques and some of the archaic language of the old ballads in *The Rime of the Ancient Mariner*. Wordsworth tried to capture the simplicity and directness of rural speech in his poetry. Sir Walter Scott put archaic English into the mouth of his hero in *Ivanhoe* and Scottish dialect into the mouth of his heroine in *The Heart of Midlothian*. Byron, in *Don Juan* (page 513), annoyed the conservative critics of his day by writing in a racy conversational style and introducing fashionable slang into his lines.

The appearance of "nonliterary" English in so many literary works marked a turning point in the history of the written language. The earlier ideal of creating a lofty literary English, different in style from spoken English, was overthrown. Since the beginning of the nineteenth century, written English has become progressively less formal and closer to the spoken language. This change has affected not just the work of professional writers, but all the writing that each of us does— even our letterwriting. [To see an example of what English letterwriting was like at the height of the formal era, in the eighteenth century, turn back to Samuel Johnson's letter to Lord Chesterfield (page 335). In the "Letters to the Editor" column of a current newspaper you can probably find a letter written in a similar spirit of anger and disgust. What stylistic differences can you point out between this present-day letter and Dr. Johnson's letter?]

Meanwhile, other events were taking place in the early nineteenth century which made it quite clear that the language was still changing and growing. English-speaking colonists had by now settled in many parts of the world, and the language spoken in some of these places, particularly in North America, was beginning to show clear differences from the language of the British Isles. Before 1750, American speech had probably sounded much the same as British speech, except for the Indian place-names and frontier slang that sprinkled American conversation. By 1800, however, differences in pronunciation and even in the written language had begun to appear. For instance, during the last half of the eighteenth century, speakers in England had come to use an "ah" sound in words like *path, ask, glass,* and *chance.* Most speakers in the newly independent United States were uninfluenced by the British fashion and continued to pronounce these words with the "flat *a*" sound heard in *cat* and *man.* Thus arose one of the first and most noticeable differences between the British accent and the American accent, a difference that persists to the present day.

Differences between British and American spelling also arose during this period. Most of these differences can be traced to the influence of one man, Noah Webster, the author of the first American dictionary of English. Webster had long been interested in spelling reform, and he had come to the conclusion that it would be both convenient and practical to use simplified spellings for certain words—for instance, *honor* instead of *honour, wagon* instead of *waggon, medieval* instead of *mediaeval.* He therefore incorporated these spellings in his dictionary, and the widespread popular acceptance of this dictionary eventually established the new forms as the regular American spellings.

Although these spelling differences were minor ones, they forced upon readers' attention the fact that even standard written English could no longer be viewed as a uniform language. An English person could not pick up a book printed in the United States without becoming aware that the book was in a language which, while perfectly comprehensible, was just a little different from his own.

FOR STUDY AND DISCUSSION

1. One feature of eighteenth-century literary language to which writers of the Romantic period particularly objected was the use of elaborate and roundabout ways of expressing simple ideas. Following are two pairs of excerpts from poetry. The excerpts in each pair express approximately the same idea: one is from mid-eighteenth-century poetry and the other from poetry of the Romantic period. You should be able to tell which is which, and to point out the specific expressions in each excerpt that helped you to form your judgment.

a. (1) "The birds are singing in the distant woods . . ."
   (2) " . . . Every Corpse
       Deep-tangled, Tree irregular, and Bush
       Bending with dewy Moisture, o'er the Heads
       Of the coy Quiristers [1] that lodge within,
       Are prodigal of Harmony."
b. (1) And redning Phoebus lifts his golden Fire . . .
   (2) But now the sun is rising calm and bright . . .

2. The excerpts immediately above are printed with the original spelling and capitalization. What specific differences from modern spelling and capitalization can you point out? Do these differences tend to occur chiefly in the excerpts you identified as being from eighteenth-century poetry? Would you say that English habits of spelling and capitalization probably changed between the middle of the eighteenth century and the beginning of the nineteenth century? Explain.

[1] **Quiristers:** choristers, choir singers.

THE VICTORIAN AGE

(1837–1900)

VICTORIA, daughter of the Duke of Kent, one of the sons of George III, succeeded her uncle, William IV, in 1837 when she was a girl of eighteen. She died in 1901 a fabulous old lady, having celebrated her Jubilee in 1887 and her Diamond Jubilee in 1897. These two Jubilees, marking Victoria's fiftieth and sixtieth anniversaries on the throne, were celebrated with enormous pomp and ceremony and represented the British Empire at its height.

BRITAIN UNDER QUEEN VICTORIA

Queen Victoria was extremely popular in the opening years of her reign and during her marriage to the Prince Consort, Albert of Saxe-Coburg, a minor German prince. Prince Albert was very earnest, conscientious, and industrious, but perhaps too German in manner and outlook to please all the British of his day. After the early death of her adored Albert, in 1861, Victoria remained in mourning for years and virtually retired from public life. This led to some unpopularity, and several prominent radicals during the next twenty years did not hesitate to declare themselves in favor of Britain's becoming a republic. But the two Jubilees, her return to public life, and the great courage of the little old lady (who insisted upon visiting Ireland although there was danger of her assassination by Irish republicans) brought Victoria's reign to a close in a blaze of popularity. She was not a clever woman like the great Elizabeth I and was limited in her tastes and outlook, but she had character and a great sense of public duty and responsibility, and was perhaps the best possible monarch for nineteenth-century Britain.

Queen Victoria, Prince Albert, and their family.

During most of Victoria's reign, Britain held the position of world leadership now occupied by the United States. The saying that "the sun never sets on the British Empire" was not just a flamboyant boast; it was literal truth. Britain, the center of a vast empire which included Canada, Australia, New Zealand, India, South Africa, and many other parts of Africa and Asia, was in those years the wealthiest, the most industrialized, and the most powerful country in the world. Her military power did not rest on her army, which was much smaller than the armies of France, Germany, and Russia, but on her navy, which was so much stronger than any other that it acted as a kind of police force throughout the world. Though frequently engaged in small colonial wars and punitive expeditions, Britain all during this time kept clear of any major wars on the scale of the American War Between the States or the Franco-Prussian War of 1870–71.

SCIENTIFIC AND MATERIAL PROGRESS

The great wealth and unequaled productiveness of Victorian Britain were due to the fact that she was still ahead in the Industrial Revolution and had a world market for Lancashire cotton goods, Yorkshire woolens, and the metal products of Birmingham and Sheffield. London was the financial capital of the world, the center of banking, insurance, shipping, and so on. Most of the railroads that were being built outside Western Europe and the United States were financed by British capital and organized by British engineers. The Great Exhibition of 1851 held at the glass-and-steel Crystal Palace in London was the first great world's fair and represented British commerce and industry at its height.

During these years industrial cities and towns grew like mushrooms, and the country was covered by an intricate network of railroads. The steam press made newspapers cheap and easily available. With factories being built everywhere, the number of jobs increasing, and public health finally gaining attention, population figures went leaping upward. Science and invention also progressed. The Victorian age is studded with the names of great inventors and innovators: from Michael Faraday (1791–1867), the blacksmith's son who invented electromagnetic machinery, to Charles Darwin, whose exposition of the theory of evolution in *The Origin of Species* (1859) turned the western world into two camps—one scientific, the other religious.

Britain's massive contribution to modern civilization belongs mainly to this Victorian period. This is not surprising. The Victorians were astoundingly self-confident, and with this confidence came tremendous energy. Ready to sweep aside all obstacles and to undertake anything anywhere, the Victorians were convinced beyond doubt that they were the representatives of progress and civilization and that wherever they went benefits must follow them. The typical Victorians in England and the typical modern Americans have much in common. There is, however, one important difference. The Americans, coming from a social democracy with a tradition of friendly neighborliness, expect to be liked wherever they go in the world and are disappointed when they are not. The Victorians in England, generally members of a ruling class cool and reserved in its manner, did not expect to be liked, did not care a rap whether they were or not. Liked or disliked, the Victorians' effect on their country—and, indeed, on the whole world—was such that the world changed more, in many different ways, during Victoria's reign than it had in the long centuries from William the Conqueror through William IV, Victoria's immediate predecessor.

The Great Exhibition of 1851 represented British commerce and industry at its height.

The typical Victorian outlook is well expressed in the essays of Thomas Babington Macaulay (1800–1859), the most popular historian of the mid-Victorian period, and in the verse that Alfred, Lord Tennyson (1809–1892), wrote in his official capacity as Victoria's Poet Laureate. Macaulay was a Whig who believed that the "Glorious Revolution" of 1688, which bloodlessly created a constitutional monarchy, and the Reform Bill of 1832, which increased the number of voters, were the greatest political triumphs of humanity. With such examples of wisdom to follow, together with all the material improvements that the age, led by Britain, was devising, the world had only to be sensible to assure itself forever of peace, prosperity, and progress. Macaulay's influence was enormous and, in spite of all the catastrophes of the present century, there are still people who believe more or less that Macaulay was right.

The thought expressed in Tennyson's official verse (actually his weakest verse, though it rarely fails in craftsmanship) follows the same pattern as Macaulay's. The world, it implied, with Britain serving as a shining example, is surely, if slowly, getting better and better. In this official verse Tennyson, apparently forcing himself to be almost as insensitively and blindly optimistic as Macaulay, tends to override his own deep worry about the conflict between religion and science. But the real Tennyson, a magnificent poet, breaks through in finer works—those of a belated Romantic. This poetry is steeped in longing and regret and dreamy melancholy, often expressed in lines of the most exquisite and haunting beauty. It is not when he is celebrating Victoria as Queen-Empress or offering Britain's "broadening freedom" as an example to the world that Tennyson is a magical poet. His magical appeal shines through when he is writing about the aging Ulysses or the lotus-eaters or the dark sorrows of Guinevere and Lancelot.

PROTESTS AGAINST VICTORIAN OPTIMISM

Indeed, Victorian literature as a whole represents a protest: a protest against the Victorianism of Macaulay and of Tennyson in his official mood, a protest against all that is characteristic of the self-confidence, complacency, and optimism of the age. For there is another side to the bright medal this period awarded itself. This is true even on the lowest material level. A country is not a commercial firm, to be judged by the amount of trade it does or by its balance sheets and profits. To be sure, it cannot exist without business enterprise just as it cannot exist without water, but a country is something more than so much business. A country is the home of millions of people. If it is a good home, if people are enjoying satisfactory lives, then the country is really prospering and making genuine progress. This—not the total amount of trade or the annual financial profit—is the real test.

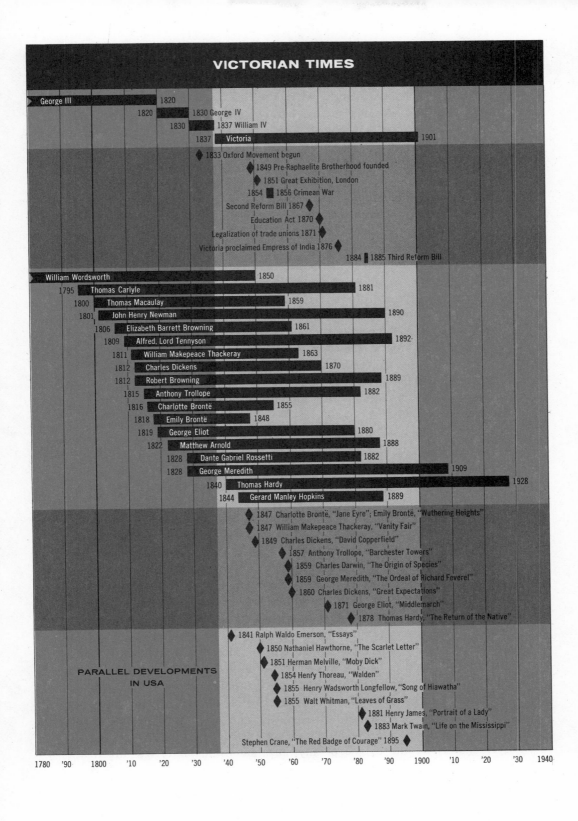

VICTORIAN TIMES

George III | 1820
1820 | 1830 George IV
1830 | 1837 William IV
1837 | Victoria | 1901

1833 Oxford Movement begun
1849 Pre-Raphaelite Brotherhood founded
1851 Great Exhibition, London
1854 ■ 1856 Crimean War
Second Reform Bill 1867
Education Act 1870
Legalization of trade unions 1871
Victoria proclaimed Empress of India 1876
1884 ■ 1885 Third Reform Bill

William Wordsworth | 1850
1795 | Thomas Carlyle | 1881
1800 | Thomas Macaulay | 1859
1801 | John Henry Newman | 1890
1806 | Elizabeth Barrett Browning | 1861
1809 | Alfred, Lord Tennyson | 1892
1811 | William Makepeace Thackeray | 1863
1812 | Charles Dickens | 1870
1812 | Robert Browning | 1889
1815 | Anthony Trollope | 1882
1816 | Charlotte Brontë | 1855
1818 | Emily Brontë | 1848
1819 | George Eliot | 1880
1822 | Matthew Arnold | 1888
1828 | Dante Gabriel Rossetti | 1882
1828 | George Meredith | 1909
1840 | Thomas Hardy | 1928
1844 | Gerard Manley Hopkins | 1889

1847 Charlotte Brontë, "Jane Eyre"; Emily Brontë, "Wuthering Heights"
1847 William Makepeace Thackeray, "Vanity Fair"
1849 Charles Dickens, "David Copperfield"
1857 Anthony Trollope, "Barchester Towers"
1859 Charles Darwin, "The Origin of Species"
1859 George Meredith, "The Ordeal of Richard Feverel"
1860 Charles Dickens, "Great Expectations"
1871 George Eliot, "Middlemarch"
1878 Thomas Hardy, "The Return of the Native"

1841 Ralph Waldo Emerson, "Essays"
1850 Nathaniel Hawthorne, "The Scarlet Letter"
1851 Herman Melville, "Moby Dick"
1854 Henry Thoreau, "Walden"

PARALLEL DEVELOPMENTS IN USA

1855 Henry Wadsworth Longfellow, "Song of Hiawatha"
1855 Walt Whitman, "Leaves of Grass"
1881 Henry James, "Portrait of a Lady"
1883 Mark Twain, "Life on the Mississippi"
Stephen Crane, "The Red Badge of Courage" 1895

1780 '90 1800 '10 '20 '30 '40 '50 '60 '70 '80 '90 1900 '10 '20 '30 1940

Now, although Victorian Britain was increasing its trade and getting richer every year, the great mass of industrial workers, crammed into the dark, ugly towns of the Midlands and the North, led appalling lives working in factories and mines from dawn to dusk—not only men but women and children as well—for wages that barely kept them alive. Industrial England was so horrible that more than one foreign visitor compared it to hell. The countryside was blackened and ruined to produce wealth that vanished and reappeared elsewhere as country mansions, parklike estates, houses in London, and extravagant, fashionable living. This difference was so marked that Benjamin Disraeli (1804–1881), an outstanding Prime Minister of the day, declared that the English were divided into "two nations."

Securely situated above this dark mass of industrial workers toiling to keep themselves alive was a large and growing middle class. It was from this class that the Victorian writers, especially the novelists, drew most of their readers. Indeed, when we think of ordinary Victorian life, we think of it in terms of this segment of society, picturing to ourselves some comfortable middle-class family, with a servant or two, sitting around the drawing-room fire. Too many of the people belonging to this class were typically Victorian in the bad sense; that is, they were smugly complacent, prudish, hypocritical, disinclined to disturb themselves over people less fortunate than they. It was these middle-class Victorians whom Charles Dickens (1812–1870), although he began with a prejudice in their favor, finally came to detest and to satirize savagely.

"ANTI-VICTORIAN" LITERATURE

Good writers are sensitive men and women; it is not easy for them to pretend that all is well when they see quite clearly that all is not well. Furthermore, they are easily angered by the pretense of people who deliberately shut their eyes and close their minds so that they can continue to feel cozy, comfortable, and piously optimistic. Typical Victorians had much to be proud of, for the achievements of this age were beyond question and there was genuine and steady progress in many directions. However, they also undoubtedly had a bad habit of ignoring what was unpleasant and might make them feel uncomfortable. It is against this complacent attitude that much of Victorian literature protested sharply. A great deal of Victorian literature is really anti-Victorian literature in the sense that it angrily denies what was thought to be true by newspaper editors, popular clergymen, self-congratulating businessmen, speechmaking politicians and officials, and second-rate writers trying to please their readers. When the smiling question went up: "Are we all happy?" the great writers said "No!"

Thomas Carlyle (1795–1881) was a historian who said "No" over and over again, refusing to accept anything that even faintly resembled Ma-

**BRITAIN
1800-1900**

ATLANTIC
OCEAN

SCOTLAND

NORTH SEA

Edinburgh• 1

LAKE
DISTRICT **2**
•Grasmere

YORKSHIRE
•York

IRISH SEA

3•Haworth
LANCASHIRE
•Manchester
•Liverpool
ENGLAND

Dublin• **4**

IRELAND

Newstead Abbey• **5**

MIDLANDS

Birmingham•

6•Rugby

7•Cambridge

WALES

Tintern Abbey• **9**

8•Oxford

London• **11**

Bristol•
•Bath

Chatham• **12**

Dover•

Nether Stowey• **10**

Winchester• **15**   **13**
14• •Field Place
Haslemere

•Portsmouth

Dorchester• **16**

ISLE OF WIGHT

ATLANTIC

OCEAN

ENGLISH CHANNEL

FRANCE

1 Carlyle and Scott attended university here. 2 Home of Wordsworth, 1799–1850. 3 Home of the Brontës. 4 Newman was university rector and Hopkins professor of Greek here. 5 Family estate of Lord Byron; his burial place is nearby at Hucknall Torkard. 6 Well-known school where Matthew Arnold studied and taught. 7 University attended by Wordsworth, Coleridge, Byron, Macaulay, Thackeray, and Tennyson. 8 Shelley and Hopkins studied here; Newman and Arnold studied and taught here. 9 Impressive ruins near which Wordsworth wrote his well-known ode. 10 Wordsworth and Coleridge lived here while preparing "Lyrical Ballads." 11 Literary and cultural center. Coleridge, Keats, Lamb, Dickens, Thackeray, Macaulay, Carlyle, Rossetti, and Browning lived and worked here. 12 Childhood home of Charles Dickens. 13 Birthplace of Shelley. 14 Tennyson and George Eliot lived near here. 15 Last home of Jane Austen, whose tomb is in Winchester Cathedral. 16 The "Casterbridge" of Thomas Hardy's "Wessex" novels.

THE VICTORIAN AGE   555

caulay's cheerful conclusions. He believed that the society of his time was moving steadily from bad to worse, that its belief in its own progress was nonsensical, and that a true civilization based chiefly on trade and profit was impossible. John Stuart Mill (1806–1873), the liberal philosopher and economist, also had his doubts. John Ruskin (1819–1900), who was considered an excellent art critic, became a social critic upon observing the predominant spirit of his age.

Following Carlyle in spirit, Ruskin pointed out that the real test of a community is not how much wealth it produces but what kind of people it produces. And, following Ruskin, William Morris (1834–1896), who himself combined various skills in handicrafts with his writing, condemned the whole industrial age for its ugliness, its mean products, and its joyless work. Samuel Butler (1835–1902), a highly original satirist, turned upside down and inside out everything the Victorians held sacred, from family life to banking. Even an author of hugely successful light operas, W. S. Gilbert (1836–1911), was constantly and often very sharply satirical.

But, after all, these men were Victorians too, products of the same age, and must therefore be allowed this very valuable faculty of self-criticism. Here again there is some likeness between the Victorians and the Americans of our day, who through their writers so often attack their own complacency and are so often able to laugh at themselves. It is when such criticism is forbidden, when rebellious writers are silenced, that a society is in real danger. But this did not happen in Victorian Britain.

MAJOR WRITERS OF THE AGE

The chief Victorian novelists were also social critics and did not hesitate to show much of contemporary society in a very unfavorable light. Charles Dickens, the master of the social novelists, is increasingly critical—and indeed almost despairing—as his fiction comes closer and closer to reality. William Makepeace Thackeray (1811–1863) launches attack after attack upon the snobbery and bad social values of the time. George Eliot (1819–1880), herself a radical, is essentially a social critic. And later, George Meredith (1828–1909), in a spirit of sharp mockery, and Thomas Hardy (1840–1928), in his slow, brooding, ironic and tragic fashion, turn fiction into an instrument of philosophical social criticism. Even the easy-going Anthony Trollope (1815–1882) can show us society, whether parsons or politicians are in the foreground, in terms of unsavory intrigues and power plots. And lesser novelists such as Charles Reade, Charles Kingsley, and Benjamin Disraeli almost turn their novels into what we would now call "social propaganda."

The poets reacted against this central complacent Victorianism in another fashion. Tennyson, as we have seen, turned out official verse in the prevailing mood of optimism, but when he was writing to please himself he became a wistful, melancholy Romantic. Robert (1812–1889) and Elizabeth Barrett (1806–1861) Browning did not even live in England, and Browning, though capable of writing very sharply about his own time, preferred on the whole to escape into Renaissance Italy. Algernon Charles Swinburne (1837–1909) in his productive and successful earlier years was an out-and-out rebel who scandalized everybody. George Meredith and Thomas Hardy, who condensed into their poetry the interpretations of life that also shaped their fiction, were also alien to most Victorian thought and feeling. William Morris and Dante Gabriel Rossetti (1828–1882), a painter and one of the founders of the Pre-Raphaelite Brotherhood, were defiant Romantics who paid no tribute to their age.

Like Morris, Rossetti was obviously glad to use his art to escape from his age. Indeed, this was the reason behind his founding of the Pre-Raphaelite Brotherhood in 1849. This association of painters and writers was, in essence, a protest movement, a reaction against the unsettling influences which the Industrial Revolution had had on England socially, economically, and artistically. The Pre-Raphaelite Brotherhood consisted originally of seven young painters and sculptors who wished to revive the purity of color, exactness of form, and simplicity of subject that they felt existed in painting before the time of the Italian Renaissance painter Raphael. From the Brotherhood's primary concern with art developed a parallel concern with literature. Although it existed as a closely knit group for only a few years, the influence of the Brotherhood and its short-lived periodical, *The Germ*, was considerable, strengthening the whole protest movement. (There is some irony in the fact that perhaps the best-known Pre-Raphaelite pictures, with their legendary subjects and medieval backgrounds, were bought by wealthy manufacturers in Birmingham and Manchester.) The group was dominated and its influence extended by Rossetti, its most gifted member and strongest personality. In addition to Rossetti and his sister Christina, William Morris, John Ruskin, and Swinburne were each, at one time or another, with the Brotherhood.

Apart from this common protest against Victorian smugness and hypocrisy, the major writers of the age have little in common. We have seen how the eighteenth-century writers, especially during the early years of the century, formed a compact group which shared the same outlook and held the same values. Later, the Romantics, though by no means a compact group, were at least members of the same general literary movement. But now, in the Victorian age, writers do not seem to be moving together in any particular direction. Not only is it impossible to say that there is a Victorian movement, but it is also difficult to agree that there is a definitely Victorian manner or style. The major Victorian writers cannot be criticized as a literary group; they are individualistic almost to the point of eccentricity.

"FAMILY" LITERATURE

At the same time, however, the Victorian reading public as a whole had certain tastes which writers respected or defied according to their desire for popularity. The middle-class Victorians, who made up the bulk of the reading public, had a very definite liking for what may be called "family" literature. There was a good deal of reading aloud in the evenings and, even when this custom was not observed, parents preferred books that could be read and enjoyed by the whole family. This meant, first, that it was impossible for novelists with a large public, like Dickens and Thackeray, to be as frank as they wished to be or as novelists have been during the past fifty years. But that was not all. A popular novelist was expected to provide something for each member of the family—something pathetic for Mother, dramatic for Father, sentimental for the girls, comic for the boys. A popular Victorian novel was like a Christmas hamper intended for the whole family.

EDUCATION AND REFORM

Victorian writers did not restrict their protests to words. John Stuart Mill, Thomas Macaulay, and William Morris, for example, were all active politically. Matthew Arnold, although a poet, was also a critic of the education of his day and an inspector of schools for thirty-five years. The spread of popular education was one of the best features of the Victorian age. It took several forms. The most important dates from 1870, when the government authorized the creation of "board schools" (the equivalent then of American public schools) for elementary education. It was not until 1890, however, that free elementary education was established in England. At the same time, the needs of older students were being met by the establishment in London, Manchester, and elsewhere of colleges which afterward became universities. University extension lectures, in which scholars appointed by the older universities gave courses of lectures to groups of ordinary citizens, came into existence. There was also a strong and successful movement to remove education from the control of the Church of England—from the level of Oxford and Cambridge down to that of the elementary schools.

Although much was wrong in British society, much was being done to correct wrongs. The Reform Bills of 1832, 1867, and 1884–85 gradually spread the right to vote, and within ten years after Victoria's death England was a democracy. In 1833 there were Parliamentary acts both to emancipate slaves throughout the British Empire and to protect factory workers. The Corn Laws, which made food too expensive for the poor, were repealed in 1846. Trade (labor) unions were legalized in 1871. During Victoria's reign the number of crimes demanding the death penalty was reduced from 438 to 2, and private execution replaced the brutal public spectacle. Most of the reforms were wrung from a reluctant establishment and were preceded by constant outcry from enlightened writers. The year 1843, for example, was notable for the publication in popular magazines of two poems condemning the factory system—"The Cry of the Children" by Elizabeth Barrett Browning and "The Song of the Shirt" by Thomas Hood (1799–1845).

In the shape of the Oxford Movement, begun in 1833, reform also reached into the Church of England. Led by John Henry Newman (1801–1890), an Anglican priest, this movement sought to achieve reform not so much by introducing new elements into the church as by returning to the conceptions and authority of the medieval church. Newman and his colleagues carried on their campaign mainly through sermons and a series of controversial tracts which were published over a period of eight years. Though the movement ended with Newman changing his religious allegiance from the Anglican to the Roman Catholic Church, it nonetheless challenged the Church of England—officials and lay members alike—to re-evaluate its position on many of its most important principles.

VICTORIAN TASTES

It must be understood that what is typically "Victorian" really belongs to the years 1837–77, the first forty years of the period. The late Victorian period—the 1880's and 1890's—is quite different from the early and mid-Victorian periods. These later Victorians lived in a larger world and in a

Elections in England (1852). The Reform Bills gradually spread the right to vote.

more sophisticated fashion than did the earlier Victorians. Rudyard Kipling (1865–1936), who was already famous when he was in his twenties, introduced readers to this larger world through his tales and ballads of British India. He was essentially the poet and storyteller of the spirit of the new imperialism, the pride in controlling and managing a vast empire, which flourished between 1880 and 1914. The sophistication of the late Victorian period is well represented by Oscar Wilde (1854–1900), whose masterful comedy, *The Importance of Being Earnest,* is still frequently produced. When, however, we refer to the taste of the time, it is not these later Victorians but the earlier Victorians that we have in mind.

These earlier Victorians were remarkable for two things, the first of which is a preoccupation with disease and death so strong that we consider it morbid. In characteristically Victorian fiction and verse, we cannot escape from the sickroom, the death bed, and the cemetery. It is true that, because they had large families and many children died young, Victorians saw far more of death than we do now, except of course in war. But even allowing for this, the Victorian taste for fatal illnesses, lingering death, funerals, and graveyards remains extraordinary. Victorians seem to have enjoyed having a good cry, and novelists anxious to please their public, like the early Dickens with his Little Nell and poor Paul Dombey, did not hesitate to set their tears flowing. Tough public men, who seem to have been unmoved by all the appalling sights of real life, would often spend an evening weeping over these pathetic chapters.

On the other hand, the Victorians had an even stronger desire to laugh. Victorian literature is crammed, from Dickens on, with comic scenes and characters, some of them among the finest in English literature. The readers of the day had a special taste, which is very English as well as being Victorian, for the literature of sheer absurdity and wild nonsense. In this spirit the Rev. Charles L. Dodgson (1832–1898), an Oxford mathematics tutor hiding himself behind the pen name "Lewis Carroll," produced masterpieces of elaborate and fascinating absurdity in the famous *Alice in Wonderland, Through the Looking Glass,* and *The Hunting of the Snark.* Edward Lear (1812–1888), the artist, and W. S. Gilbert of operetta fame were also original and fertile in this field, and behind them were dozens of lesser humorists, many of them still worth reading today.

Illness and death; comic characters and nonsense; a new realism in fiction; a fading, wistful Romanticism in verse; science and industry triumphant, thus encouraging complacency and a confident belief in unchecked progress —against these, gradual reform; the doubts, protests, and often savage social criticism of the writers, each of them, however, going his or her own way: such is the richly varied, immensely productive, strangely contradictory Victorian age.

J.B.P.

THOMAS CARLYLE

(1795–1881)

Carlyle was a gloomy and austere man, perhaps with good reason. As a youngster he struggled against severe poverty, and for most of his life he was plagued by illness, difficulties which undoubtedly contributed to his sharp temper and harsh disposition. Carlyle's contemporaries often found him forbidding as a personality, and modern readers may feel the same way about his prose style, which can be characterized as explosive, jagged, and restless, marked by fits and starts, but in total effect extremely powerful.

Carlyle's father, a stonemason and farmer with nine children, was determined that, despite the family's lack of means, his brilliant son should study for the ministry. Young Thomas, then fourteen years old, walked the hundred miles from his home to enroll at Edinburgh University. He read widely, came to know French and German literature, and was strongly influenced in his thinking by the German poet Goethe and the German philosopher Kant. From his Calvinist upbringing and his broad reading, Carlyle fashioned his own system of thought, which included beliefs in a cyclical theory of history, in a supernatural force brooding over and commanding the universe, and in personal conduct determined by self-denial. A reformer, he was much concerned with the political, economic, and social problems of his time, and advocated solutions which were denounced as radical.

In London in 1826, Carlyle married Jane Welsh, who reluctantly agreed to live on her isolated farm in the Scottish countryside. There Carlyle finished work on his spiritual autobiography, *Sartor Resartus,* which he had begun some years earlier after passing through a physical and mental crisis. In 1834 the Carlyles returned to London and established a home in Cheyne Row, which became a center for the most important literary and intellectual figures of the time. This house has been preserved as a national shrine.

After completing *Sartor Resartus,* Carlyle spent some three years working on his history of the French Revolution, generally considered his most important work. It is not now highly regarded as an impartial and accurate history, but it endures because of the strength of the writing, which powerfully conveys the thought and emotions of that turbulent period. As Carlyle said, this work came "flamingly from the heart." It was a great success and encouraged Carlyle to go on to further expositions of history, philosophy, and commentary on current problems. In *Heroes and Hero-Worship* he developed in detail his idea that history should be seen as a process furthered by the actions of great men who embody divine revelations. History, for Carlyle, is always "the essence of innumerable biographies." He amplified this concept in two significant biographies. One, on Oliver Cromwell, the Puritan dictator, did much to rehabilitate the character and achievements of the Lord Protector. The other important biography, *The History of Frederick the Great of Prussia,* was Carlyle's last major work. Although it has passages of great power and was considered a masterpiece in its time, it is now largely neglected.

In spite of his gruff and thorny exterior, Carlyle had the power to make warm friends among those who recognized his sincerity and genius. Dickens, Thackeray, Tennyson, and John Stuart Mill greatly admired him, and when Ralph Waldo Emerson first went to Europe, his most earnest desire was to meet Carlyle. They became close friends and their association helped to win for each a reading public and enduring reputation in the other's country.

The Fall of the Bastille

The near-tragic circumstance connected with Carlyle's writing of *The French Revolution* is one of the most famous anecdotes in English literature. Carlyle had given the nearly completed manuscript to his friend, the economist and philosopher John Stuart Mill. A servant in Mill's household accidentally used the sheets to start a fire one morning. Carlyle had kept no copy and at first could not recall any of his writing. After spending a week reading novels to calm his mind, he laboriously rewrote the work. When Mill offered Carlyle £200 as compensation for the accident, Carlyle accepted only £100, just to tide him over the period spent rewriting what had been burned.

The following selection from *The French Revolution* illustrates Carlyle's unique and curious style. Its broken, exclamatory sentences and the descriptions of strong emotions give the reader the feeling of experiencing the excitement of the scene at first hand.

The gloomy Bastille (bas·tēl') prison, surrounded by a moat, had stood since the fourteenth century at one of the gates of Paris. With its long history of unjust imprisonments and forgotten prisoners, it had become a symbol of the oppressions of the French monarchy. July 14, the anniversary of its destruction in 1789, became the annual celebration of French independence—Bastille Day.

THE BASTILLE is besieged! On, then, all Frenchmen that have hearts in your bodies! Roar with all your throats of cartilage and metal, ye sons of liberty; stir spasmodically whatsoever of utmost faculty is in you, soul, body, or spirit, for it is the hour! Smite thou, Louis Tournay, cartwright of the Marais,[1] old soldier of the Régiment Dauphiné;[2] smite at that outer drawbridge chain, though the fiery hail whistles around thee! Never, over nave[3] or felloe,[4] did thy ax strike such a stroke. Down with it, man; down with it to Orcus;[5] let the whole accursed edifice sink thither, and tyranny be swallowed up forever! Mounted, some say, on the roof of the guardroom, some "on bayonets stuck into joints of the wall," Louis Tournay smites, brave Aubin Bonnemère[6] (also an old soldier) seconding him. The chain yields, breaks; the huge drawbridge slams down, thundering. Glorious! and yet, alas! it is still but the outworks. The eight grim towers with their invalide[7] musketry, their paving stones and

[1] **Marais** (mä·rā'): a manufacturing quarter of Paris.
[2] **Régiment Dauphiné** (rā·zhē·män' dō·fē·nā'): regiment of the Dauphin, or king's son.
[3] **nave:** the hub of a wheel.
[4] **felloe:** a segment of the rim of a wooden wheel.
[5] **Orcus:** in Roman mythology, the home of the dead; the underworld.
[6] **Bonnemère** (bôn·mer').
[7] **invalide** (ản·va·lēd'): veteran (originally, a wounded soldier).

cannon mouths, still soar aloft intact; ditch yawning impassable, stonefaced; the inner drawbridge with its *back* toward us; the Bastille is still to take!...

Paris, wholly, has got to the acme of its frenzy, whirled all ways by panic madness. At every street barricade there whirls, simmering, a minor whirlpool, strengthening the barricade, since God knows what is coming; and all minor whirlpools play distractedly into that grand fire maelstrom [1] which is lashing round the Bastille.

And so it lashes and roars. Cholat,[2] the wine merchant, has become an impromptu cannoneer. See Georget,[3] of the marine service, fresh from Brest,[4] play the King of Siam's cannon. Singular (if we were not used to the like). Georget lay last night taking his ease at his inn; the King of Siam's cannon also lay, knowing nothing of *him* for a hundred years; yet now, at the right instant, they have got together, and discourse eloquent music; for, hearing what was toward, Georget sprang from the Brest diligence,[5] and ran. Gardes Françaises,[6] also, will be here with real artillery. Were not the walls so thick! Upward from the esplanade, horizontally from all neighboring roofs and windows, flashes one irregular deluge of musketry, without effect. The invalides lie flat, firing comparatively at their ease from behind stone; hardly through portholes show the tip of a nose. We fall, shot, and make no impression!

Let conflagration rage of whatsoever is combustible! Guardrooms are burnt, invalides messrooms. A distracted "peruke-maker with two fiery torches" is for burning "the saltpeters of the arsenal," had not a woman run screaming, had not

a patriot, with some tincture of natural philosophy, instantly struck the wind out of him (butt of musket on pit of stomach), overturned barrels, and stayed the devouring element. A young, beautiful lady seized, escaping, in these outer courts, and thought, falsely, to be De Launay's [7] daughter, shall be burned in De Launay's sight; she lies, swooned, on a paillasse; [8] but, again, a patriot—it is brave Aubin Bonnemère, the old soldier —dashes in, and rescues her. Straw is burnt; three cartloads of it, hauled hither, go up in white smoke, almost to the choking of patriotism itself; so that Elie had, with singed brows, to drag back one cart, and Réole, the "gigantic haberdasher," another. Smoke as of Tophet,[9] confusion as of Babel,[10] noise as of the crack of doom!

Blood flows, the aliment of new madness. The wounded are carried into houses of the Rue Cerisaie; [11] the dying leave their last mandate not to yield till the accursed stronghold fall. And yet, alas! how fall? The walls are so thick! Deputations, three in number, arrive from the Hôtel-de-Ville.[12] . . . These wave their town flag in the arched gateway, and stand, rolling their drum, but to no purpose. In such crack of doom De Launay cannot hear them, dare not believe them; they return, with justified rage, the whew of lead still singing in their ears. What to do? The firemen are here, squirting with their fire pumps on the invalides' cannon to wet the touchholes; they unfortunately cannot squirt so high, but produce only clouds of spray. Individuals of classical knowledge propose *catapults*. Santerre, the sonorous brewer of the suburb Saint-Antoine, advises rather that the place be fired

---

[1] **maelstrom** (māl'strəm): a whirlpool off the northwest coast of Norway; used figuratively, any turmoil of resistless movement or influence.

[2] **Cholat** (shō·lä').

[3] **Georget** (zhôr·zhā').

[4] **Brest**: a naval station in northwest France.

[5] **diligence** (dē·lē·zhäns'): stagecoach.

[6] **Gardes Françaises** (gärd frän·sez'): French guards, that is, the regular troops of the French army.

[7] **De Launay** (de·lō·nā'): a governor of the Bastille: slain after its capture.

[8] **paillasse** (pal·yas'): a straw mattress.

[9] **Tophet** (tō'fet): a place near Jerusalem used for burning sacrifices and, later, refuse.

[10] **Babel** (bā'bəl): a confusion of many voices; from the Tower of Babel (Genesis 11:9).

[11] **Rue Cerisaie** (rü ser·ē·sā') : a street in Paris.

[12] **Hôtel-de-Ville** (ô·tel·de·vēl') : City Hall.

by "a mixture of phosphorus and oil of turpentine spouted up through forcing pumps." O Spinola-Santerre,[1] has thou the mixture *ready?* Every man his own engineer! And still the fire deluge abates not; even women are firing, and Turks—at least one woman (with her sweetheart) and one Turk. Gardes Françaises have come; real cannon, real cannoneers. Usher Maillard is busy; half-pay Elie, half-pay Hulin, rage in the midst of thousands.

How the great Bastille clock ticks (inaudible) in its inner court, there, at its ease, hour after hour; as if nothing special, for it or the world, were passing! It tolled one when the firing began, and is now pointing toward five, and still the firing slakes not. Far down in their vaults, the seven prisoners hear muffled din as of earthquakes; their turnkeys answer vaguely.

Woe to thee, De Launay, with thy poor hundred invalides! . . .

What shall De Launay do? One thing only De Launay could have done—what he said he would do. Fancy him sitting, from the first, with lighted taper, within arm's length of the powder magazine; motionless, like an old Roman senator, or bronze lamp holder; coldly apprising all manner of men, by a slight motion of his eye, what his resolution was. Harmless he sat there, while unharmed; but the king's fortress, meanwhile, could, might, would, or should in nowise be surrendered, save to the king's messengers; one old man's life is worthless, so it be lost with honor; but think, ye brawling *canaille,*[2] how will it be when a whole Bastille springs skyward? In such statuesque, taper-holding attitude, one fancies De Launay might have left Thuriot, the red clerks of the Basoche, curé[3] of St.

Stephen, and all the tagrag and bobtail of the world, to work their will.

And yet, withal, he could not do it. . . . Distracted he hovers between two—hopes in the middle of despair; surrenders not his fortress; declares that he will blow it up, seizes torches to blow it up, and does not blow it. Unhappy old De Launay, it is the death agony of the Bastille and thee! Jail, jailoring, and jailor, all three, such as they may have been, must finish.

For four hours now has the world bedlam roared; call it the world chimera[4] blowing fire! The poor invalides have sunk under their battlements, or rise only with reversed muskets; they have made a white flag of napkins, go beating the chamade,[5] or seeming to beat, for one can hear nothing. The very Swiss at the portcullis[6] look weary of firing, disheartened in the fire deluge; a porthole at the drawbridge is opened, as by one that would speak. See Huissier Maillard, the shifty man! On his plank, swinging over the abyss of that stoned ditch, plank resting on parapet, balanced by weight of patriots, he hovers perilous—such a dove toward such an ark! Deftly, thou shifty usher; one man already fell and lies smashed, far down there against the masonry! Usher Maillard falls not; deftly, unerringly, he walks, with outspread palm. The Swiss holds a paper through the porthole; the shifty usher snatches it and returns. Terms of surrender: Pardon, immunity to all! Are they accepted? *"Foi d'officier* (on the word of an officer)," answers half-pay Hulin, or half-pay Elie—for men do not agree on it—"they are!" Sinks the drawbridge, Usher Maillard bolting it when down; rushes in the living deluge; the Bastille is fallen!

Victoire! La Bastille est prise![7]

---

[1] **Spinola-Santerre** (spi·nō′lá-sán·târ′): Santerre, a leader of the Parisian Revolutionary mob, is likened to General Spinola, who captured a fortress in Holland in 1625.

[2] *canaille* (kə·nä′y′): the vulgar multitude; the mob.

[3] **curé** (kyo͞o·rā′): parish priest.

[4] **chimera** (kī·mēr′ə): a mythical fire-breathing animal.

[5] **chamade** (shə·mäd′): a drum or trumpet signal for a parley.

[6] **Swiss . . . portcullis:** The French hired Swiss mercenaries as guards. The portcullis was an iron grating at the entrance.

[7] Victory! The Bastille is taken!

Midas

Inspired by the recent publication of a medieval manuscript, Carlyle wrote *Past and Present* in 1843 in a few weeks' time. He contrasted the achievements of a twelfth-century English abbot with the irresponsible actions of the early Victorian authorities. The following selection, the first chapter of the book, reflects Carlyle's passionate concern for the hardships of the oppressed. It is a call to the English to make order out of chaos and to rescue their people from the outrageous harm that threatened them. Although Carlyle sympathized with the poor, he also had an innate distaste for the democratic system. Carlyle looked to the "Captains of Industry" for the wise guidance necessary to improve burdensome social conditions.

THE CONDITION of England, on which many pamphlets are now in the course of publication, and many thoughts unpublished are going on in every reflective head, is justly regarded as one of the most ominous, and withal one of the strangest, ever seen in this world. England is full of wealth, of multifarious produce, supply for human want in every kind; yet England is dying of inanition. With unabated bounty the land of England blooms and grows; waving with yellow harvests; thick-studded with workshops, industrial implements, with fifteen millions of workers, understood to be the strongest, the cunningest and the willingest our earth ever had; these men are here; the work they have done, the fruit they have realized is here, abundant, exuberant on every hand of us: and behold, some baleful fiat as of enchantment has gone forth, saying, "Touch it not, ye workers, ye master workers, ye master idlers;[1] none of you can touch it, no man of you

shall be the better for it; this is enchanted fruit!" On the poor workers such fiat falls first, in its rudest shape; but on the rich master workers too it falls; neither can the rich master idlers, nor any richest or highest man escape, but all are like to be brought low with it, and made 'poor' enough, in the money sense or a far fataler one.

Of these successful skillful workers some two millions, it is now counted, sit in workhouses, Poor Law prisons, or have "outdoor relief" flung over the wall to them—the workhouse Bastille[2] being filled to bursting, and the strong Poor Law broken asunder by a stronger. They sit there, these many months now; their hope of deliverance as yet small. In workhouses, pleasantly so-named, because work cannot be done in them. Twelve hundred thousand workers in England alone; their cunning right hand lamed, lying idle in their sorrowful bosom; their hopes, outlooks, share of this fair world, shut in by narrow walls. They sit there, pent up, as in a kind of horrid enchantment; glad to be imprisoned and enchanted, that they may not perish starved. The picturesque tourist, in a sunny autumn day, through this bounteous realm of England, descries the union workhouse on his path. "Passing by the workhouse of St. Ives in Huntingdonshire, on a bright day last autumn," says the picturesque tourist, "I saw sitting on wooden benches, in front of their Bastille and within their ringwall and its railings, some half-hundred or more of these men. Tall robust figures, young mostly or of middle age; of honest countenance, many of them thoughtful and even intelligent-looking men. They sat there, near by one another; but in a kind of torpor, especially in a silence, which was very striking. In silence: for, alas, what word was to be said? An earth all lying round crying, Come and till me, come and reap

[1] **master idlers:** the landowning aristocracy, whose wealth accumulated without effort.

[2] **workhouse Bastille:** Carlyle's name for the houses in which the poor were sheltered under the Poor Law of 1834. The food and lodging were miserable deliberately to keep the poor from staying in them any longer than necessary.

me—yet we here sit enchanted! In the eyes and brows of these men hung the gloomiest expression, not of anger, but of grief and shame and manifold inarticulate distress and weariness; they returned my glance with a glance that seemed to say, 'Do not look at us. We sit enchanted here, we know not why. The sun shines and the earth calls; and, by the governing powers and impotences of this England, we are forbidden to obey. It is impossible, they tell us!' There was something that reminded me of Dante's Hell [1] in the look of all this; and I rode swiftly away."

So many hundred thousands sit in workhouses: and other hundred thousands have not yet got even workhouses; and in thrifty Scotland itself, in Glasgow or Edinburgh City, in their dark lanes, hidden from all but the eye of God, and of rare benevolence the minister of God, there are scenes of woe and destitution and desolation, such as, one may hope, the sun never saw before in the most barbarous regions where men dwelt. Competent witnesses, the brave and humane Dr. Alison,[2] who speaks what he knows, whose noble healing art in his charitable hands becomes once more a truly sacred one, report these things for us: these things are not of this year, or of last year, have no reference to our present state of commercial stagnation, but only to the common state. Not in sharp fever-fits, but in chronic gangrene of this kind is Scotland suffering. A Poor Law, any and every Poor Law, it may be observed, is but a temporary measure; an anodyne, not a remedy: Rich and poor, when once the naked facts of their condition have come into collision, cannot long subsist together on a mere Poor Law. True enough—and yet, human beings cannot be left to die! Scotland too, till something better come, must have a Poor Law, if Scotland is not to be a byword among the nations. O, what a waste is there; of noble and thrice-noble national virtues; peasant stoicisms, heroisms; valiant manful habits, soul of a nation's worth, which all the metal of Potosi [3] cannot purchase back; to which the metal of Potosi, and all you can buy with *it,* is dross and dust!

Why dwell on this aspect of the matter? It is too indisputable, not doubtful now to any one. Descend where you will into the lower class, in town or country, by what avenue you will, by factory inquiries, agricultural inquiries, by revenue returns, by mining–laborer committees, by opening your own eyes and looking, the same sorrowful result discloses itself: you have to admit that the working body of this rich English nation has sunk or is fast sinking into a state, to which, all sides of it considered, there was literally never any parallel. At Stockport Assizes [4] —and this too has no reference to the present state of trade, being of date prior to that—a mother and a father are arraigned and found guilty of poisoning three of their children to defraud a "burial society" [5] of some £3 8s. due on the death of each child: they are arraigned, found guilty; and the official authorities, it is whispered, hint that perhaps the case is not solitary, that perhaps you had better not probe farther into that department of things. This is in the autumn of 1841; the crime itself is of the previous year or season. "Brutal savages, degraded Irish," mutters the idle reader of newspapers; hardly lingering on this incident. Yet it is an incident worth lingering on; the depravity, savagery and degraded Irishism [6] being never so well admitted. In the British land, a human mother and father, professing the Christian religion, had done this thing; they, with their Irishism and necessity and savagery,

---

[1] **Dante's Hell:** *The Inferno* of Dante's *The Divine Comedy.*

[2] **Dr. Alison:** William Pulteney Alison, M.D. (1790–1859), advocate of legal relief of the poor in Scotland.

[3] **Potosi:** silver-mining district in Bolivia.

[4] **Stockport Assizes:** periodical court session at Stockport, a cotton-mill town.

[5] **"burial society":** cheap insurance groups which provided the poor with decent burials.

[6] **Irishism:** a distinctively Irish phrase or action.

had been driven to do it. Such instances are like the highest mountain apex emerged into view; under which lies a whole mountain region and land, not yet emerged. A human mother and father had said to themselves, What shall we do to escape starvation? We are deep sunk here, in our dark cellar; and help is far. Yes, in the Ugolino hunger-tower stern things happen; best-loved little Gaddo [1] fallen dead on his father's knees! The Stockport mother and father think and hint: Our poor little starveling Tom, who cries all day for victuals, who will see only evil and not good in this world: if he were out of misery at once; he well dead, and the rest of us perhaps kept alive? It is thought, and hinted; at last it is done. And now Tom being killed, and all spent and eaten, is it poor little starveling Jack that must go, or poor little starveling Will? What a committee of ways and means!

In starved sieged cities, in the uttermost doomed ruin of old Jerusalem fallen under the wrath of God, it was prophesied and said, "The hands of the pitiful women have sodden [2] their own children," The stern Hebrew imagination could conceive no blacker gulf of wretchedness; that was the ultimatum of degraded God-punished man. And we here, in modern England, exuberant with supply of all kinds, besieged by nothing if it be not by invisible enchantments, are we reaching that? How come these things? Wherefore are they, wherefore should they be?

Nor are they of the St. Ives workhouses, of the Glasgow lanes, and Stockport cellars, the only unblessed among us. This successful industry of England, with its plethoric wealth, has as yet made nobody rich; it is an enchanted wealth, and belongs yet to nobody. We might ask, Which of us has it enriched? We can spend thousands where we once spent hundreds; but can purchase nothing good with them. In poor and rich, instead of noble thrift and plenty, there is idle luxury alternating with mean scarcity and inability. We have sumptuous garnitures for our life, but have forgotten to *live* in the middle of them. It is an enchanted wealth; no man of us can yet touch it. The class of men who feel that they are truly better off by means of it, let them give us their name!

Many men eat finer cookery, drink dearer liquors—with what advantage they can report, and their doctors can: but in the heart of them, if we go out of the dyspeptic stomach, what increase of blessedness is there? Are they better, beautifuler, stronger, braver? Are they even what they call "happier"? Do they look with satisfaction on more things and human faces in this God's earth; do more things and human faces look with satisfaction on them? Not so. Human faces gloom discordantly, disloyally on one another. Things, if it be not mere cotton and iron things, are growing disobedient to man. The master worker is enchanted, for the present, like his workhouse workman; clamors, in vain hitherto, for a very simple sort of "liberty": the liberty "to buy where he finds it cheapest, to sell where he finds it dearest." With guineas jingling in every pocket, he was no whit richer; but now, the very guineas threatening to vanish, he feels that he is poor indeed. Poor master worker! And the master unworker, is not he in a still fataler situation? Pausing amid his game preserves, with awful eye, as he well may! Coercing fifty-pound tenants; [3] coercing, bribing, cajoling; "doing what he likes with his own." His mouth full of loud futilities and arguments to prove the excellence of his Corn Law; [4] and in his heart the blackest misgiving, a desperate half-consciousness that his excellent Corn Law is *in*defensible,

---

[1] **Ugolino . . . Gaddo:** In *The Inferno*, Ugolino, starving to death, ate his dead son Gaddo.

[2] **sodden:** boiled.

[3] **fifty-pound tenants:** persons paying the minimum rent necessary for the right to vote.

[4] **Corn Law:** This law imposed a duty on imported grain and resulted in high prices for bread, the staple of the diet.

that his loud arguments for it are of a kind to strike men too literally *dumb*.

To whom, then, is this wealth of England wealth? Who is it that it blesses; makes happier, wiser, beautifuler, in any way better? Who has got hold of it, to make it fetch and carry for him, like a true servant, not like a false mock-servant; to do him any real service whatsoever? As yet no one. We have more riches than any nation ever had before; we have less good of them than any nation ever had before. Our successful industry is hitherto unsuccessful; a strange success if we stop here! In the midst of plethoric plenty, the people perish; with gold walls and full barns, no man feels himself safe or satisfied. Workers, master workers, unworkers, all men, come to a pause; stand fixed, and cannot farther. Fatal paralysis spreading inwards, from the extremities, in St. Ives workhouses, in Stockport cellars, through all limbs, as if towards the heart itself. Have we actually got enchanted, then; accursed by some God?

Midas [1] longed for gold, and insulted the Olympians. He got gold, so that whatsoever he touched became gold —and he, with his long ears, was little the better for it. Midas had misjudged the celestial music-tones; Midas had insulted Apollo and the gods: the gods gave him his wish, and a pair of long ears, which also were a good appendage to it. What a truth in these old fables!

[1] **Midas:** a figure in Greek mythology who was granted his wish that everything he touched would turn to gold. He nearly starved to death because even his food and drink became gold. Another story tells that he insulted Apollo and the angry god furnished Midas with asses' ears.

FOR STUDY AND DISCUSSION

THE FALL OF THE BASTILLE

1. Carlyle offers no extended description of the appearance of the Bastille or of the exact cause of its surrender. Yet by the end of this selection you know much about this important event. How does Carlyle achieve this? Do you think his method is more effective than using a straight narrative would be? Explain.

2. What is the attitude of the mob toward the aristocrats? Be sure to account in your answer for the episode of the lady rescued by Bonnemère. What do you learn about mob psychology? Does Carlyle describe the citizens as a mob, or does he attempt to distinguish the individuals involved? Does Carlyle show sympathy with either side? Support your answers with specific references.

3. Read again the section on De Launay (page 564). Although Carlyle does not give a complete description of the prison governor, the reader comes to know much about him. What kind of man was he? Do you think Carlyle was completely unsympathetic to De Launay's predicament?

MIDAS

1. Several times in this selection Carlyle refers to an "enchantment" that lies across England. Find these references and explain their relation to Carlyle's main point. Do you think this is an appropriate image for the situations described? Support your opinion.

2. Look up the doctrine of *laissez-faire* in a dictionary or encyclopedia. What is the relationship between this economic doctrine and the state of England in Carlyle's essay? Why does Carlyle insist that the country's wealth has made no one rich? What sort of wealth does he think a nation should have?

3. What do the stories about Midas have to do with the selection as whole? Has Carlyle made the most effective use of them by placing them at the end of his chapter?

FOR COMPOSITION

1. A careful modern historian might dispute Carlyle's handling of the fall of the Bastille. Use a good encyclopedia or a scholarly history of the French Revolution for other accounts of this crucial event. Then write a short composition analyzing the qualities and shortcomings of Carlyle's treatment. If you can, make a judgment of the comparative value of the two selections.

2. Using the myths about Midas as your theme, write a composition relating their significance to your own times just as Carlyle employed them to comment on the Victorian era. If you believe that the Midas stories have no bearing on modern America, justify your opinion in an essay.

THOMAS BABINGTON MACAULAY
(1800–1859)

Carlyle and Macaulay are often paired as two of the greatest writers of prose in the Victorian Age. They were both men who had made up their minds on many issues of the day. But while Carlyle scolded and exhorted, Macaulay seemed to have such bland confidence that he never needed to raise his voice. Macaulay's assurance followed the almost instantaneous popular success of his writings and the public esteem earned by meritorious service to the realm. His best-known sentences are studded with absolutes and superlatives: "We hold that the most wonderful and splendid proof of genius is a great poem produced in a civilized age"; "An acre in Middlesex is better than a principality in Utopia"; "We know no spectacle so ridiculous as the British public in one of its periodical fits of morality." Even when contradicting his own liking for axiomatic statements he is absolute: "Nothing is so useless as a general maxim."

Appropriately enough, Macaulay was a child prodigy. Before he was eight years old he had composed a *Compendium of Universal History* and a verse-romance in the style of Sir Walter Scott. Not long after, the boy finished a great work in blank verse: *Fingal, a Poem in Twelve Books.* His public career as a writer began with a sensational success, an essay on John Milton published in 1825 in the *Edinburgh Review.* He continued to write for the *Review* and remained for many years the bulwark of that journal's popularity. On the strength of his essay on Milton, Macaulay was lionized by society. In 1830, he entered Parliament, where he spoke brilliantly in behalf of the Reform Bill to extend suffrage and where he championed the cause of Negro slaves in the British colonies. A few years later, Macaulay was appointed to the council which administered British rule in India, and he served in that country for four years. He did much to liberalize British authority in India, to draft the Indian penal code, and to inaugurate a national education system.

On returning to England, he again entered Parliament and was given a seat in the cabinet. In 1842 he published the *Lays of Ancient Rome,* among them the famous "Horatius," which remained a staple of schoolroom verse well into the twentieth century. A book of Macaulay's essays followed in 1843, and he gradually began to leave his active public involvements to concentrate on his writing, most notably the *History of England.*

Macaulay had planned his great *History* to cover the century and a half from the accession of James II (1685) to his own time. But his meticulous research and careful composition, and his occasional ventures into public affairs, prevented his completing the project. In fifteen years of work he managed to recount little more than fifteen years of history. Despite its incompleteness, however, the *History* was a tremendous best seller. It was widely translated and brought the author more than $150,000 in royalties, but twice that amount was lost to him by the inadequate copyright laws of the day, which prevented his receiving royalties from sales in America. Macaulay's enormous success can be attributed in part to his intimate knowledge of his audience, the steadily advancing middle class. They both believed that they were living in the best of all possible worlds, and that the history of their country was "eminently the history of physical, of moral, and of intellectual improvement."

In August 1857 the great historian and public servant was raised to the nobility and titled Baron Macaulay of Rothley, Lord Macaulay. Two years later he died and was buried with many honors in Westminster Abbey.

Macaulay's career is marked by honesty, industry, perseverance, and a devotion to public welfare. He was sometimes criticized for his lack of deep insight into human problems, his middle-class prejudices, and his apparent inability to see all sides of a question. A Prime Minister of his own party is said to have remarked: "I wish I were as cocksure of any one thing as Tom Macaulay is of everything."

London Streets

Because of his rare gift for vividly re-creating personalities and incidents, Macaulay achieved in his *History of England* what he set out to accomplish—to make history more interesting. "I shall not be satisfied," he wrote to a friend, "unless I produce something which shall for a few days supersede the last fashionable novel on the tables of young ladies." His intention was also furthered by his close attention to accuracy. His contemporary, the novelist William Makepeace Thackeray, noted that "Macaulay reads twenty books to write one sentence and travels one hundred miles to make a line of description." The London described in the following selections remained much the same throughout the late seventeenth and eighteenth centuries.

THE POSITION of London, relatively to the other towns of the empire, was, in the time of Charles II, far higher than at present. For at present the population of London is little more than six times the population of Manchester or of Liverpool. In the days of Charles II the population of London was more than seventeen times the population of Bristol or of Norwich. It may be doubted whether any other instance can be mentioned of a great kingdom in which the first city was more than seventeen times as large as the second. There is reason to believe that in 1685 London had been, during about half a century, the most populous capital in Europe. The inhabitants, who are now at least nineteen hundred thousand, were then probably little more than half a million. . . .

We should greatly err if we were to suppose that any of the streets and squares then bore the same aspect as at present. The great majority of the houses, indeed, have, since that time, been wholly, or in great part, rebuilt. If the most fashionable parts of the capital could be placed before us, such as they then were, we should be disgusted by their squalid appearance, and poisoned by their noisome atmosphere. In Covent Garden a filthy and noisy market was held close to the dwellings of the great. Fruit women screamed, carters fought, cabbage stalks and rotten apples accumulated in heaps at the thresholds of the Countess of Berkshire and of the Bishop of Durham.

The center of Lincoln's Inn Fields [1] was an open space where the rabble congregated every evening, within a few yards of Cardigan House and Winchester House, to hear mountebanks harangue, to see bears dance, and to set dogs at oxen. Rubbish was shot [2] in every part of the area. Horses were exercised there. The beggars were as noisy and importunate as in the worst-governed cities of the Continent. A Lincoln's Inn mumper [3] was a proverb. The whole fraternity knew the arms and liveries of every charitably disposed grandee in the neighborhood, and, as soon as his lordship's coach and six appeared, came hopping and crawling in crowds to persecute him. These disorders lasted, in spite of many accidents, and of some legal proceedings, till, in the reign of George II, Sir Joseph Jekyll, Master of the Rolls, was knocked down and nearly killed in the middle of the square. Then at length palisades were set up and a pleasant garden laid out.

Saint James' Square [4] was a receptacle for all the offal and cinders, for all the dead cats and dead dogs of Westminster.[5] At one time a cudgel player [6] kept the ring there. At another time an impudent squatter settled himself there, and built a shed for rubbish under the windows of the gilded saloons in which the first magnates of the realm, Norfolk, Ormond, Kent, and Pembroke, gave banquets and balls. It was not till these nuisances had lasted through a whole generation, and till much had been written about them, that the inhabitants applied to Parliament for permission to put up rails, and to plant trees.

When such was the state of the region inhabited by the most luxurious portion of society, we may easily believe that the

A London street of the seventeenth century.

great body of the population suffered what would now be considered as insupportable grievances. The pavement was detestable; all foreigners cried shame upon it. The drainage was so bad that in rainy weather the gutters soon became torrents. Several facetious poets have commemorated the fury with which these black rivulets roared down Snow Hill and Ludgate Hill, bearing to Fleet Ditch a vast tribute of animal and vegetable filth from the stalls of butchers and greengrocers. This flood was profusely thrown to right and left by coaches and carts. To keep as far from the carriage road as possible was therefore the wish of every pedestrian. The mild and timid gave the wall. The bold and athletic took it. If two roisterers met, they cocked their hats in each other's faces and pushed each other about till the weaker was shoved toward the kennel.[7] If he was a mere bully he sneaked off, muttering that he should find a time. If he was pugnacious, the encounter probably ended in a duel behind Montague House.[8]

The houses were not numbered. There would indeed have been little advantage in numbering them; for of the coachmen,

[1] **Lincoln's Inn Fields:** the largest square in London, surrounded by lawyers' offices and old mansions.

[2] **shot:** dumped.

[3] **mumper:** a beggar and impostor.

[4] **Saint James' Square:** later a fashionable district.

[5] **Westminster:** the section of London where the government houses are located.

[6] **cudgel player:** a man skilled in defending himself with cudgel or staff.

[7] **kennel:** street gutter.

[8] **Montague** (mon'tȧ·gyōo) **House:** a government building in Whitehall.

chairmen,[1] porters, and errand boys of London, a very small proportion could read. It was necessary to use marks which the most ignorant could understand. The shops were therefore distinguished by painted or sculptured signs, which gave a gay and grotesque aspect to the streets. The walk from Charing Cross to Whitechapel lay through an endless succession of Saracens' Heads, Royal Oaks, Blue Bears, and Golden Lambs, which disappeared when they were no longer required for the direction of the common people.

When the evening closed in, the difficulty and danger of walking about London became serious indeed. The garret windows were opened and pails were emptied, with little regard to those who were passing below. Falls, bruises, and broken bones were of constant occurrence. For, till the last year of the reign of Charles II, most of the streets were left in profound darkness. Thieves and robbers plied their trade with impunity; yet they were hardly so terrible to peaceable citizens as another class of ruffians. It was a favorite amusement of dissolute young gentlemen to swagger by night about the town, breaking windows, upsetting sedans, beating quiet men, and offering rude caresses to pretty women. Several dynasties of these tyrants had, since the Restoration, domineered over the streets. The Muns and Tityre Tus had given place to the Hectors, and the Hectors had been recently succeeded by the Scourers. At a later period rose the Nicker, the Hawcubite, and the yet more dreaded name of Mohawk. The machinery for keeping the peace was utterly contemptible. There was an act of Common Council which provided that more than a thousand watchmen should be constantly on the alert in the city, from sunset to sunrise, and that every inhabitant should take his turn of duty. But this act was negligently executed. Few of those who were summoned left their homes; and those few generally found it more agreeable to tipple in alehouses than to pace the streets.

[1] **chairmen:** men who carried the sedan chairs.

London Coffeehouses

THE COFFEEHOUSE must not be dismissed with a cursory mention. It might indeed at that time have been not improperly called a most important political institution. No Parliament had sat for years. The municipal council of the city had ceased to speak the sense of the citizens. Public meetings, harangues, resolutions, and the rest of the modern machinery of agitation had not yet come into fashion. Nothing resembling the modern newspaper existed. In such circumstances the coffeehouses were the chief organs through which the public opinion of the metropolis vented itself.

The first of these establishments had been set up, in the time of the Commonwealth, by a Turkey merchant, who had acquired among the Mohammedans a taste for their favorite beverage. The convenience of being able to make appointments in any part of the town, and of being able to pass evenings socially at a very small charge, was so great that the fashion spread fast. Every man of the upper or middle class went daily to his coffeehouse to learn the news and to discuss it. Every coffeehouse had one or more orators to whose eloquence the crowd listened with admiration, and who soon became what the journalists of our own time have been called, a fourth Estate of the realm. The court had long seen with uneasiness the growth of this new power in the state. An attempt had been made, during Danby's [2] administration, to close the coffeehouses. But men of all parties missed their usual places of resort so much that there was an universal outcry. The government did not venture, in opposition to a feeling so strong and general, to enforce a regulation of which the legality might well be ques-

[2] **Danby:** Thomas Osborn, Lord Danby: Lord Treasurer under Charles II.

tioned. Since that time ten years had elapsed, and during those years the number and influence of the coffeehouses had been constantly increasing. Foreigners remarked that the coffeehouse was that which especially distinguished London from all other cities; that the coffeehouse was the Londoner's home, and that those who wished to find a gentleman commonly asked, not whether he lived in Fleet Street or Chancery Lane, but whether he frequented the Grecian or the Rainbow. Nobody was excluded from these places who laid down his penny at the bar. Yet every rank and profession, and every shade of religious and political opinion, had its own headquarters. There were houses near Saint James' Park where fops congregated, their heads and shoulders covered with black or flaxen wigs, not less ample than those which are now worn by the Chancellor and by the Speaker of the House of Commons. The wig came from Paris; and so did the rest of the fine gentleman's ornaments, his embroidered coat, his fringed gloves, and the tassel which upheld his pantaloons. The conversation was in that dialect which, long after it had ceased to be spoken in fashionable circles, continued, in the mouth of Lord Foppington,[1] to excite the mirth of theaters. The atmosphere was like that of a perfumer's shop. Tobacco in any other form than that of richly scented snuff was held in abomination. If any clown, ignorant of the usages of the house, called for a pipe, the sneers of the whole assembly and the short answers of the waiters soon convinced him that he had better go somewhere else. Nor, indeed, would he have had far to go. For, in general, the coffeerooms reeked with tobacco like a guardroom; and strangers sometimes expressed their surprise that so many people should leave their own firesides to sit in the midst of eternal fog and stench.

Nowhere was the smoking more constant than at Will's. That celebrated house,

Engraving showing a London coffeehouse of the early eighteenth century.

situated between Covent Garden and Bow Street, was sacred to polite letters. There the talk was about poetical justice and the unities of place and time. There was a faction for Perrault[2] and the moderns, a faction for Boileau[3] and the ancients. One group debated whether *Paradise Lost* ought not to have been in rhyme. To another an envious poetaster demonstrated that *Venice Preserved*[4] ought to have been hooted from the stage. Under no roof was a greater variety of figures to be seen. There were earls in stars and garters, clergymen in cassocks and bands,

[1] **Foppington:** a character in *The Relapse,* by Vanbrugh; he pronounced "Lord" as "Lard."

[2] **Perrault** (pe·rō'): French writer (1628–1703); member of the French Academy.

[3] **Boileau** (bwȧ'lō'): French satirist and critic (1636–1711); member of the French Academy. He and Perrault disputed the merits of ancient and modern literature.

[4] *Venice Preserved:* a play by Thomas Otway (1652–1685). It was revived in London in 1953.

pert Templars,[1] sheepish lads from the universities, translators and index makers in ragged coats of frieze. The great press was to get near the chair where John Dryden sat. In winter that chair was always in the warmest nook by the fire; in summer it stood in the balcony. To bow to the Laureate and to hear his opinion of Racine's[2] last tragedy or of Bossu's[3] treatise on epic poetry was thought a privilege. A pinch from his snuffbox was an honor sufficient to turn the head of a young enthusiast. There were coffeehouses where the first medical men might be consulted. Doctor John Radcliffe, who in the year 1685 rose to the largest practice in London, came daily, at the hour when the Exchange was full, from his house in Bow Street, then a fashionable part of the capital, to Garaway's, and was to be found, surrounded by surgeons and apothecaries, at a particular table. There were Puritan coffeehouses where no oath was heard, and where lank-haired men discussed election and reprobation through their noses; Jew coffeehouses where dark-eyed money-changers from Venice and from Amsterdam greeted each other; and Popish coffeehouses where, as good Protestants believed, Jesuits planned, over their cups, another great fire, and cast silver bullets to shoot the King.

These gregarious habits had no small share in forming the character of the Londoner of that age. He was, indeed, a different being from the rustic Englishman. There was not then the intercourse which now exists between the two classes. Only very great men were in the habit of dividing the year between town and country. Few esquires came to the capital thrice in their lives. Nor was it yet the practice of all citizens in easy circumstances to breathe the fresh air of the fields and woods during some weeks of every summer. A cockney, in a rural village, was stared at as much as if he had intruded

A London scene of the seventeenth century.

into a kraal[4] of Hottentots. On the other hand, when the Lord of a Lincolnshire or Shropshire manor appeared in Fleet Street, he was as easily distinguished from the resident population as a Turk or a lascar.[5] His dress, his gait, his accent, the manner in which he stared at the shops, stumbled into the gutters, ran against the porters, and stood under the waterspouts, marked him out as an excellent subject for the operations of swindlers and banterers. Bullies jostled him into the kennel. Hackney coachmen splashed him from head to foot. Thieves explored with perfect security the huge pockets of his horseman's coat, while he stood entranced by the splendor of the Lord Mayor's show. Money droppers, sore from the cart's tail,[6] introduced themselves to him, and appeared to him the most honest, friendly gentlemen that he had ever seen. Painted women, the refuse of Lewkner Lane and Whetstone Park, passed themselves on him for countesses and maids of honor. If he asked his way to Saint James', his informants sent him to Mile End.[7] If he

[1] **Templars:** lawyers and law students, who resided in the Temple.

[2] **Racine** (rä´sēn´): French poet (1639–1699).

[3] **Bossu** (bô´sü´): French critic (1631–1680).

[4] **kraal** (kräl): a stockaded village of South African natives.

[5] **lascar:** East Indian sailor.

[6] **Money droppers . . . tail:** cheats, who had been tied to a cart and whipped through the streets.

[7] **Mile End:** a poor district in the east end of London.

went into a shop, he was instantly discerned to be a fit purchaser of everything that nobody else would buy, of second-hand embroidery, copper rings, and watches that would not go. If he rambled into any fashionable coffeehouse, he became a mark for the insolent derision of fops and the grave waggery of Templars. Enraged and mortified, he soon returned to his mansion, and there, in the homage of his tenants and the conversation of his boon companions, found consolation for the vexations and humiliations which he had undergone. There he was once more a great man and saw nothing above himself except when at the assizes [1] he took his seat on the bench, near the Judge, or when at the muster of the militia he saluted the Lord Lieutenant.

[1] **assizes** (ə·sīz′ez): sessions of the county court.

FOR STUDY AND DISCUSSION

1. Would you say that Macaulay writes condescendingly about seventeenth-century London? Does he find things to admire in London of that day? Do you think Macaulay has a balanced, or impartial, approach to his subject matter?

2. What social conditions in seventeenth-century London promoted the popularity of the coffeehouses? What later conditions may have contributed to their passing? Coffeehouses have had a minor vogue in modern America. What reasons can you give for their fashion? What might Macaulay have thought of them?

STYLE

Style is everything that concerns a writer's technique and mode of expression: sentence structure, choice of words, use of details, the amount and kind of description, tone, and so on. Writers express themselves in the ways that seem most natural to them. Consciously or unconsciously, writing will reflect personality and individuality as well as thoughts, opinions, and message. A good style is distinguished by clarity and a harmonious relationship between thought and language— that is, between what the writers say and the way in which they say it. The writers' words should not only communicate exactly what they want to say, but they should also convey attitude. Writers must be aware of connotations in a word which are not appropriate to the subject and which therefore should be avoided. The very choice of subject matter and the writers' attitude toward it is also a basic aspect of style.

Basing your judgments on the selections in this book, compare the styles of Carlyle and Macaulay. Do you find their styles appropriate to their subject matter? Explain. How do the styles used in these selections differ from the styles of other historical material with which you are familiar? Both Macaulay's and Carlyle's styles reveal a good deal about the writers themselves. What do you think was Macaulay's attitude toward history? How does his attitude differ from Carlyle's?

LANGUAGE AND VOCABULARY

The spelling of a word may often mislead you as to its meaning. In "London Streets" Macaulay uses the words *impunity* and *noisome*. If you did not already know the meaning of these words, you might rightly guess that *impunity* means "freedom from punishment" and is related to the word *punitive*. But it would be wrong to assume that *noisome* is related to *noise*. It is really related to the word *annoyance*. Look up the definitions of the following words whose spelling and form can also be deceptive: *dissemble, blandish, contentious, flagrant, factitious, meretricious.*

Macaulay writes that several *facetious* poets have written about the bad drainage system of old London. The context might lead you to think that *facetious* means "indignant," but this is not the case. Although it was a subject that perhaps warranted indignation, Macaulay is saying that the poets took a flippant or jesting attitude toward the matter.

In discussing the struggle for the wall (page 571), Macaulay uses the word *bully* in a way that may surprise you: "If he was a mere bully he sneaked off, muttering that he should find a time." We usually think of a bully as one who terrorizes weaker people. But there is another aspect to the meaning of the word as Macaulay uses it here. A bully was primarily a quarrelsome person but one who was more insolent than courageous. In the last paragraph of the selection on coffeehouses, Macaulay uses the word more as we understand it: "Bullies jostled him into the kennel."

JOHN HENRY NEWMAN

(1801–1890)

In an age in which religious faith often seemed to be at odds with scientific learning, John Henry Newman was one of the many Victorians who experienced a religious crisis. In his case the crisis was largely personal as well as spiritual, but because of Newman's influence as a religious leader, his personal views shook the entire nation.

Newman was born into a well-to-do Anglican family. His spiritual nature was evident at an early age. When he was fifteen years old he underwent an "inward conversion," believing that he had been "elected to eternal glory." The effects of this conversion lasted throughout his life. It had an authenticity that overshadowed the real world—as he later wrote in his autobiography: "I still am more certain [of it] than that I have hands and feet." Newman proceeded along the set path of Anglican education, chiefly at Oxford University, and became a teacher and clergyman. When a difference of opinion with a superior led to his resignation from his first important post, he went on a tour of the Mediterranean to consolidate his views. During this tour he wrote the famous hymn known as "Lead, Kindly Light." He was still strongly Protestant in his thinking, but uncertainties were stirring below the surface. Toward the end of his trip, he fell ill of a fever in Sicily. As he related many years afterward: "I sat down on my bed and began to sob bitterly. My servant, who had acted as my nurse, asked what ailed me. I could only answer, 'I have a work to do in England.' "

The "work to do in England" turned out to be his support of the Tractarian movement, promoted by a group of Anglican churchmen who were attempting to redefine the relationship of the Church of England to Roman Catholicism. Newman became the leading figure of this movement and wrote a prodigious number of pamphlets questioning the Protestant position. The last of these tracts brought Anglicanism so close to Roman Catholicism that the series was suppressed by the Bishop of Oxford. Newman was now "on his deathbed as regards membership with the Anglican Church." Pondering this crucial issue, he withdrew from all his positions and retired with a small group of followers to an improvised monastery. Two years later, half his years spent, he formally converted to Roman Catholicism. As the prime minister at the time said, "England reeled under the shock."

Newman shortly became a priest, and his natural ability led to important posts within the Roman Catholic Church. One of these was as rector of a newly established Catholic university in Dublin. Although his success in this position was limited by local opposition, he thought deeply about the educational process. The results of his thinking were embodied in a series of lectures, later published as *The Idea of a University,* from which the following selections are taken.

Because of his conversion, Newman labored under a cloud and gradually fell into obscurity as far as most of the English were concerned. This obscurity might have continued had not an Anglican churchman published a slur on Newman's truthfulness. Newman seized the opportunity to explain his life and actions and began to publish an autobiography, *Apologia pro vita sua (A Defense of His Life),* which brought him much acclaim from all factions. It not only succeeded in turning the tide of adverse public opinion, but assured him a permanent position in the ranks of outstanding English writers. More than a valuable religious memoir, the *Apologia* is one of the great revelations of one man's intellectual development.

John Henry Newman typified the personal earnestness of the Victorians. He found his answers through much soul searching and a marked break with his own past, a break that he believed was a reunion with the mainstream of religious history. Late in life Newman was created a cardinal of the Roman Catholic Church. Since then the respect accorded him as a Catholic intellectual has remained firm.

In the portions of the university lectures printed here, the high standards that Newman wished an educated gentleman to attain are set forth in his best lecturing style—a gracefully clear and assertive one.

The Educated Man

A UNIVERSITY is not a birthplace of poets or of immortal authors, of founders of schools, leaders of colonies, or conquerors of nations. It does not promise a generation of Aristotles or Newtons, of Napoleons or Washingtons, of Raphaels or Shakespeares, though such miracles of nature it has before now contained within its precincts. Nor is it content on the other hand with forming the critic or the experimentalist, the economist or the engineer, though such too it includes within its scope. But a university training is the great ordinary means to a great but ordinary end; it aims at raising the intellectual tone of society, at cultivating the public mind, at purifying the national taste, at supplying true principles to popular enthusiasm and fixed aims to popular aspiration, at giving enlargement and sobriety to the ideas of the age, at facilitating the exercise of political power, and refining the intercourse of private life. It is education which gives a man a clear conscious view of his own opinions and judgments, a truth in developing them, an eloquence in expressing them, and a force in urging them. It teaches him to see things as they are, to get right to the point, to disentangle a skein of thought, to detect what is sophistical, and to discard what is irrelevant. It prepares him to fill any post with credit, and to master any subject with facility. It shows him how to accommodate himself to others, how to throw himself into their state of mind, how to bring before them his own, how to influence them, how to come to an understanding with them, how to bear with them. He is at home in any society, he has common ground with every class; he knows when to speak and when to be silent; he is able to converse, he is able to listen; he can ask a question pertinently, and gain a lesson seasonably, when he has nothing to impart himself; he is ever ready, yet never in the way; he is a pleasant companion, and a comrade you can depend upon; he knows when to be serious and when to trifle, and he has a sure tact which enables him to trifle with gracefulness and to be serious with effect. He has the repose of mind which lives in itself, while it lives in the world, and which has resources for its happiness at home when it cannot go abroad. He has a gift which serves him in public and supports him in retirement, without which good fortune is but vulgar, and with which failure and disappointment have a charm.

The Gentleman

IT IS ALMOST a definition of a gentleman to say he is one who never inflicts pain. This description is both refined and, as far as it goes, accurate. He is mainly occupied in merely removing the obstacles which hinder the free and unembarrassed action of those about him, and he concurs with their movements rather than takes the initiative himself. His benefits may be considered as parallel to what are called comforts or conveniences in arrangements of a personal nature; like an easy chair or a good fire, which do their part in dispelling cold and fatigue, though nature provides both means of rest and animal heat without them. The true gentleman in like manner carefully avoids whatever may cause a jar or a jolt in the minds of those with whom he is cast—all clashing of opinion, or collision of feeling, all restraint, or suspicion, or gloom, or resentment; his great concern being to make everyone at their ease and at home. He has his eyes on all his company; he is tender toward the bashful, gentle toward the distant, and merciful toward the absurd; he can recollect to whom he is speaking; he guards against unreasonable allusions or topics which may irritate; he is seldom prominent in conversation, and never wearisome. He makes light of favors while he does them, and seems to

be receiving when he is conferring. He never speaks of himself except when compelled, never defends himself by a mere retort; he has no ears for slander or gossip, is scrupulous in imputing motives to those who interfere with him, and interprets everything for the best. He is never mean or little in his disputes, never takes unfair advantage, never mistakes personalities or sharp sayings for arguments, or insinuates evil which he dare not say out. From a long-sighted prudence, he observes the maxim of the ancient sage, that we should ever conduct ourselves toward our enemy as if he were one day to be our friend. He has too much good sense to be affronted at insults, he is too well employed to remember injuries, and too indolent to bear malice. He is patient, forbearing, and resigned, on philosophical principles; he submits to pain because it is inevitable, to bereavement because it is irreparable, and to death because it is his destiny. If he engages in controversy of

any kind, his disciplined intellect preserves him from the blundering discourtesy of better, perhaps, but less-educated minds, who, like blunt weapons, tear and hack, instead of cutting clean, who mistake the point in argument, waste their strength on trifles, misconceive their adversary, and leave the question more involved than they find it. He may be right or wrong in his opinion, but he is too clearheaded to be unjust; he is as simple as he is forcible and as brief as he is decisive. Nowhere shall we find greater candor, consideration, indulgence; he throws himself into the minds of his opponents; he accounts for their mistakes. He knows the weakness of human reason as well as its strength, its province and its limits. If he be an unbeliever, he will be too profound and large-minded to ridicule religion or to act against it; he is too wise to be a dogmatist or fanatic in his infidelity. He respects piety and devotion; he even supports institutions as venerable, beautiful, or useful, to which he does not assent; he honors the ministers of religion, and it contents him to decline its mysteries without assailing or denouncing them. He is a friend of religious toleration, and that not only because his philosophy has taught him to look on all forms of faith with an impartial eye, but also from the gentleness and effeminacy of feeling which is the attendant on civilization.

FOR STUDY AND DISCUSSION

1. What are the chief characteristics of a gentleman according to Newman's definition? Can a person be a great man and still not be a gentleman? Conversely, can a person be a gentleman and not be a great man?

2. Which characteristics of Newman's gentleman would also be appropriate to a lady? What requirements would you add?

3. Do you find any similarities of phrasing or idea in these two selections? any sharp differences? Do you think Newman's definitions limit the possibilities of personal achievement? What do you think Newman would say about the modern tendency to free the individual personality from all confinements?

LANGUAGE AND VOCABULARY

While some words can connote only one thing, others often assume a number of meanings, depending upon the context in which they are used. Explain the meaning of the following words taken from Newman's essay.

"a university training is the great *ordinary* means to a great but *ordinary* end; it aims at . . . giving enlargement and *sobriety* to the ideas of the age . . ."

"He has the *repose* of mind which lives in itself, while it lives in the world . . ."

"He makes *light* of favors while he does them . . ."

"He is never *mean* or *little* in his disputes . . ."

"he is too well *employed* to remember injuries . . ."

FOR COMPOSITION

1. Write a composition analyzing Newman's criteria of education. Whether you agree or disagree, give good reasons for your opinion. Do you feel that your education is helping you to develop all of these qualities? If so, how? Can you think of other aspects of education that Newman has not covered?

2. Bearing in mind what Newman says about the proper function of education, examine each of the following stated or implied concepts of education. Then explain why you think Newman would agree wholly, in part, or whether he would disagree with each:

The purpose of an education is to enable a person to live a life rather than to earn a living.

"What I want, you know," said Mr. Tulliver, "what I want is to give Tom a good eddication; an eddication as'll be a bread to him." (George Eliot, *The Mill on the Floss*)

On one occasion Aristotle was asked how much educated men were superior to those uneducated: "As much," said he, "as the living are to the dead."

"Human history becomes more and more a race between education and catastrophe." (H. G. Wells, *The Outline of History*)

"It was in making education not only common to all, but in some sense compulsory on all, that the destiny of the free republics of America was practically settled." (James Russell Lowell, *New England Two Centuries Ago*)

ALFRED, LORD TENNYSON

(1809–1892)

The modern poet T. S. Eliot has said, "Tennyson is a great poet for reasons that are perfectly clear. He has three qualities which are seldom found together except in the greatest poets: abundance, variety, and complete competence." The six large volumes of his *Collected Works* testify to Tennyson's abundance, as does the fact that he continued to produce distinguished poetry for more than fifty years. His variety is evident in the diversity of both his poetic forms and his subject. He wrote lyrics, dramatic monologues, plays, long narrative poems, elegies, and allegories. He treated subjects drawn from classical myth and Arthurian legend, from the history of the English Renaissance and from the life of his own times; he wrote poems about politics, war, science, religion, and immortality. His complete competence is suggested by his mastery of many different kinds of meter and by the compelling music of much of his poetry. Tennyson once remarked that he knew the metrical weight of every English word except "scissors." His skill in manipulating sounds in his poetry bears out his remark.

Underlying all of Tennyson's abundance and variety is a unity provided by his poetic temper and by the conflicting themes of doubt and faith, of dreamy melancholy and responsible action that run through his poetry. Tennyson is the great English poet of nostalgia—of longing for something far away or long ago. He is one of the few poets who has succeeded in representing in poetry those feelings of loss and sorrow that well up in the mind but that are too formless to have a name. He makes the experience of spiritual solitude and religious doubt a living reality in his poems, and he depicts the enchantments and dangers that accompany the life of the imagination cut off from ordinary things and existing only in a world of gorgeous dreams and hazy emotions.

Although Tennyson fully felt the pull toward the subjective life, toward solitude and dreams, he also wanted to cast off his melancholy and irresolution and, through rigorous discipline of his emotions, achieve a life of significant action for social good. Again and again the poetry of Tennyson moves from a dreamlike longing to an assertion of responsibility and self-control. If we knew only the nostalgic side of Tennyson, he might well seem like a caricature of the popular idea of a Romantic poet—always swooning in the moonlight. If we knew only the assertive, dutiful side, he might seem merely stuffy and self-righteous. But the two sides of Tennyson exist together. Out of their conflict Tennyson created a poetry that depicts the struggle every person must undergo to reconcile the claims of the private and public self.

The fourth of twelve children, Alfred Tennyson was born in the Lincolnshire village of Somersby, where his father was rector. As a boy, Tennyson had considerable liberty to browse among books, produce amateur theatricals, and, above all, take "long walks at night-time" and roam among the "large fields, gray hillsides, and noble-towered churches" of the Lincolnshire countryside. Tennyson's early love of the natural world endured throughout his life, and his skill in describing nature became one of his chief attractions for Victorian readers. Most of Tennyson's education took place at home under the supervision of his father, and by the age of fifteen he was already familiar with much of English and classical literature.

Tennyson and several of his brothers and sisters wrote verse while they were still children. In 1827 Tennyson and his brother Charles published anonymously *Poems by Two Brothers*. Written mostly in imitation of Byron and Sir Walter Scott, these poems were received with mild praise. A year later both brothers went to Trinity College, Cambridge, where Tennyson, rebelling particularly against having to study mathematics, gained little from formal academic instruction. His real education began when he was invited to join "The Apostles," a debating club devoted to problems of religion and political liberty. Tennyson formed the most intense emotional relationship of his life in his friendship with a college friend, Arthur Henry Hallam, who, Tennyson later said, was "as near perfection as a mortal man could be." Himself awkward, rustic, and shy, Tennyson was overwhelmed by Hallam's gaiety, charm, and urbanity. In 1830 the two traveled together to the Continent to deliver money to Portuguese revolutionists, and Hallam became engaged to Tennyson's sister Emily. In the same year, Tennyson published his *Poems, Chiefly Lyrical*, which reflects the Apostles' idea that the poet should be a sage and prophet. His Cambridge friends were delighted, but the critical reception was not enthusiastic.

When he left Cambridge in 1831 without taking a degree, there began a dark period in Tennyson's life that was to last for more than a decade. After his father's death, he had to take on the burden of family affairs. Although his *Poems* of 1832 included such fine works as "The Lady of Shalott" and "The Lotos-Eaters," the reviews were so violently abusive that he did not publish again for ten years. In 1833 he was shattered by the news of Hallam's sudden death in Vienna. Three years later, he became engaged to Emily Sellwood, but was too poor to marry her until fourteen years had elapsed. The Tennyson of these years was "a man solitary and sad, carrying a bit of chaos about him." In 1842 he lost all his money through speculation, collapsed, and was for several months under the care of a physician.

But 1842 was also a turning point in Tennyson's life. That year his two-volume *Poems* was published, and his popularity began to rise. In 1845 he was given a government pension, and two years later he published his long narrative poem *The Princess*, which contains some of his most memorable lyrics. The year 1850 was a decisive point in Tennyson's life: he was made poet laureate, married Emily Sellwood, and published his greatest work, *In Memoriam*, a long elegy on the death of his friend Hallam. For the next forty-two years he was without question the leading poet of his time, popular with ordinary readers and highly respected in literary circles. He worked steadily at his art, producing a series of closet dramas, many fine short lyrics, and the elaborate narratives of King Arthur's Round Table that make up *Idylls of the King*. The crowning honor of his life came in 1883, when he was made a peer. Even as an old man he was a striking figure—"a great black, shaggy man"—who looked the part of a poet.

The Lady of Shalott

In his boyhood Tennyson was fascinated by
the stories of King Arthur's knights, and it was
natural for him to turn to them later as subjects
for poetry. The twelve metrical tales included
in *Idylls of the King* were composed over a
period of twenty-six years (1859–85). But long
before that time, in 1832, the poet had written
this legend of the Lady of Shalott.

PART I

On either side the river lie
Long fields of barley and of rye,
That clothe the wold° and meet the sky;
And through the field the road runs by
   To many-towered Camelot;°   5
And up and down the people go,
Gazing where the lilies blow
Round an island there below,
   The island of Shalott.

Willows whiten,° aspens quiver,   10
Little breezes dusk and shiver
Through the wave that runs forever
By the island in the river
   Flowing down to Camelot.
Four gray walls, and four gray towers, 15
Overlook a space of flowers,
And the silent isle embowers
   The Lady of Shalott.

By the margin, willow-veiled,
Slide the heavy barges° trailed   20
By slow horses; and unhailed
The shallop° flitteth silken-sailed
   Skimming down to Camelot.
But who hath seen her wave her hand?
Or at the casement seen her stand?   25
Or is she known in all the land
   The Lady of Shalott?

Only reapers, reaping early
In among the bearded barley,
Hear a song that echoes cheerly   30
From the river winding clearly
   Down to towered Camelot:
And by the moon the reaper weary,
Piling sheaves in uplands airy,
Listening, whispers, "'Tis the fairy   35
   Lady of Shalott,"

PART II

There she weaves by night and day
A magic web with colors gay.
She has heard a whisper say,
A curse is on her if she stay   40
   To look down to Camelot.
She knows not what the curse may be,
And so she weaveth steadily,
And little other care hath she,
   The Lady of Shalott.   45

And moving through a mirror clear
That hangs before her all the year,
Shadows of the world appear.
There she sees the highway near
   Winding down to Camelot: 50
There the river eddy whirls,
And there the surly village churls,°
And the red cloaks of market girls,
   Pass onward from Shalott.

---

3. **wold:** an open stretch of rising ground.
5. **Camelot:** a mysterious city where King Arthur
and his knights held court in medieval romances.
10. **whiten:** Leaves turned by the breeze show
their white undersides. 20. **barges:** roomy, flat-
bottomed freight boats; here drawn by horses along
the river banks. 22. **shallop:** a light pleasure boat.

52. **churls:** country folk.

Sometimes a troop of damsels glad,   55
An abbot on an ambling pad,°
Sometimes a curly shepherd lad,
Or long-haired page in crimson clad,
   Goes by to towered Camelot: 59
And sometimes through the mirror blue
The knights come riding two and two:
She hath no loyal knight and true,
   The Lady of Shalott.

But in her web she still delights
To weave the mirror's magic sights,   65
For often through the silent nights
A funeral, with plumes and lights
   And music, went to Camelot:
Or when the moon was overhead,
Came two young lovers lately wed;   70
"I am half sick of shadows," said
   The Lady of Shalott.

PART III

A bow-shot from her bower eaves,
He rode between the barley sheaves,
The sun came dazzling through the
   leaves,   75
And flamed upon the brazen greaves°
   Of bold Sir Lancelot.
A red-cross knight° forever kneeled
To a lady in his shield,
That sparkled on the yellow field,   80
   Beside remote Shalott.

The gemmy° bridle glittered free,
Like to some branch of stars we see
Hung in the golden Galaxy.°
The bridle bells rang merrily   85
   As he rode down to Camelot:
And from his blazoned baldric° slung,
A mighty silver bugle hung,
And as he rode his armor rung,
   Beside remote Shalott.   90

56. **pad:** an easy-paced riding horse.
76. **greaves:** armor for the legs below the knees.
78. **red-cross knight:** a symbol of St. George, patron saint of England. He slew the dragon and thus saved a maiden from sacrifice. 82. **gemmy:** studded with jewels. 84. **Galaxy:** the Milky Way, a pathway of myriad stars stretching across the middle heavens. 87. **blazoned baldric:** a decorated belt worn diagonally across the chest.

All in the blue unclouded weather
Thick-jeweled shone the saddle leather,
The helmet and the helmet feather
Burned like one burning flame together
   As he rode down to Camelot.   95
As often through the purple night,
Below the starry clusters bright,
Some bearded meteor, trailing light,
   Moves over still Shalott.   99

His broad clear brow in sunlight glowed;
On burnished hoofs his war horse trode;
From underneath his helmet flowed
His coal-black curls as on he rode,
   As he rode down to Camelot.
From the bank and from the river   105
He flashed into the crystal mirror,
"Tirra lirra," by the river
   Sang Sir Lancelot.

She left the web, she left the loom,   109
She made three paces through the room,
She saw the water lily bloom,
She saw the helmet and the plume,
   She looked down to Camelot.
Out flew the web and floated wide;
The mirror cracked from side to side;
"The curse is come upon me," cried   116
   The Lady of Shalott.

In the stormy east wind straining,
The pale yellow woods were waning,
The broad stream in his banks com-
plaining,   120
Heavily the low sky raining
  Over towered Camelot;
Down she came and found a boat
Beneath a willow left afloat,   124
And round about the prow she wrote
  The Lady of Shalott.

And down the river's dim expanse—
Like some bold seër in a trance,
Seeing all his own mischance—
With a glassy countenance   130
  Did she look to Camelot.
And at the closing of the day
She loosed the chain, and down she lay;
The broad stream bore her far away,
  The Lady of Shalott.   135

Lying, robed in snowy white
That loosely flew to left and right—
The leaves upon her falling light—
Through the noises of the night
  She floated down to Camelot: 140
And as the boathead wound along
The willowy hills and fields among,
They heard her singing her last song,
  The Lady of Shalott.

Heard a carol, mournful, holy,   145
Chanted loudly, chanted lowly,
Til her blood was frozen slowly,
And her eyes were darkened wholly,
  Turned to towered Camelot.
For ere she reached upon the tide   150
The first house by the waterside,
Singing in her song she died,
  The Lady of Shalott.

Under tower and balcony,
By garden wall and gallery,   155
A gleaming shape she floated by,
Dead-pale between the houses high,
  Silent into Camelot.

Out upon the wharves they came
Knight and burgher,° lord and dame,   160
And round the prow they read her name,
  The Lady of Shalott.

Who is this? and what is here?
And in the lighted palace near
Died the sound of royal cheer;   165
And they crossed themselves for fear,
  All the knights at Camelot:
But Lancelot mused a little space;
He said, "She has a lovely face;
God in his mercy lend her grace,   170
  The Lady of Shalott."

160. **burgher:** citizen.

COMMENTARY

Although "The Lady of Shalott" is a narrative poem of some length, it has qualities suggesting a lyric that could be set to music. The fifth and ninth lines of every stanza serve as refrains, with only minor variations in wording. The rhythm is heavy and regular. The rhymes are very audible, even insistent, partly because the first four lines of each stanza all rhyme on the same sound (e.g., *lie, rye, sky, by* in the first stanza). The sixth, seventh, and eighth lines also rhyme on a single sound (in the first stanza, *go, blow,* and *below*), while the short refrain lines use "Camelot" and "Shalott" as rhyme words in all the stanzas except two.

The musical quality of this poem has sometimes been criticized for being intrusive and calling too much attention to itself, but it is surely appropriate to the romantic legend that the poem recounts. In "The Lady of Shalott" Tennyson's lifelong interest in "the haunted region of Celtic romance" combines with his interest in what a modern critic calls "the predicament of a mind trying to free itself from a web of fantasy." The medieval tale is used to present a distinctively modern problem: the plight of the dedicated artist who must, because of temperament and the nature of the work, experience life and emotion secondhand. Thus the Lady sits endlessly weaving her magic web and sees the world only in the reflections cast in the mirror before her.

Tennyson himself said that the key to the poem's meaning lay in the closing lines of Part II: "'I am half sick of shadows,' said/ The Lady of Shalott." And he said of the poem as a whole: "The new-born love for something, for someone in the wide world from which she has been so long excluded, takes her out of the region of shadows into that of realities." When the Lady sees the image of two young lovers in her mirror, she becomes "half sick of shadows." After seeing the dazzling vision of Sir Lancelot, she turns from the web and the mirror, and for the first time looks down to Camelot. As Tennyson says, she turns from shadows to realities. But the awakening is a fatal one. The curse of the web and the mirror may have imprisoned the Lady in isolation, but when she leaves them she goes to her death.

FOR STUDY AND DISCUSSION

1. What is the main subject of each part of "The Lady of Shalott"? Why do you think Tennyson constructed this poem in four parts?

2. How is the entrance of Lancelot in Part III prepared for in Part II? Explain the pathos of Lancelot's words in the last stanza of the poem.

3. Sir Lancelot appears in bright sunlight, and everything about him is dazzling, glittering, burnished, flamelike—from his "gemmy bridle" to his "blazoned baldric." Why is this so? Cite examples to show how the imagery of flaming and shining things that dominates Part III contrasts with the imagery of the other three parts of the poem.

*Ulysses**

In this poem Tennyson draws his subject from ancient Greek sources. Ulysses, the famous hero of many adventures in the *Odyssey,* is pictured years after the time described in that epic. To Tennyson's generation this poem symbolized the constant striving onward and upward of the civilized person. It is said that "Ulysses" was the deciding factor in the government's decision to give Tennyson a pension.

It little profits that an idle king,
By this still hearth, among these barren crags,
Matched with an aged wife, I mete and dole°
Unequal laws° unto a savage race,
That hoard, and sleep, and feed, and know not me.   5
I cannot rest from travel; I will drink
Life to the lees. All times I have enjoyed
Greatly, have suffered greatly, both with those
That loved me, and alone; on shore, and when
Through scudding drifts the rainy Hyades°   10
Vexed the dim sea. I am become a name;
For always roaming with a hungry heart

* **Ulysses** (yōō·lis′ez). 3. **mete and dole:** measure and give out. 4. **Unequal laws:** unfair laws. The people were not civilized enough to be governed by the kind of laws Ulysses approved. 10. **Hyades** (hī′ə·dēz): stars in the constellation Taurus, supposed to bring rain.

Much have I seen and known—cities of men
And manners, climates, councils, governments, .
Myself not least, but honored of them all—   15
And drunk delight of battle with my peers,
Far on the ringing plains of windy Troy.
I am a part of all that I have met;
Yet all experience is an arch wherethrough
Gleams that untraveled world whose margin fades   20
Forever and forever when I move.
How dull it is to pause, to make an end,
To rust unburnished, not to shine in use!
As though to breathe were life! Life piled on life
Were all too little, and of one to me   25
Little remains; but every hour is saved
From that eternal silence, something more,
A bringer of new things; and vile it were
For some three suns to store and hoard myself,
And this gray spirit yearning in desire   30
To follow knowledge like a sinking star,
Beyond the utmost bound of human thought.
    This is my son, mine own Telemachus,
To whom I leave the scepter and the isle—°
Well-loved of me, discerning to fulfill   35
This labor, by slow prudence to make mild
A rugged people, and through soft degrees
Subdue them to the useful and the good.
Most blameless is he, centered in the sphere
Of common duties, decent not to fail   40
In offices of tenderness, and pay
Meet adoration to my household gods,
When I am gone. He works his work, I mine.

    There lies the port; the vessel puffs her sail;
There gloom the dark, broad seas. My mariners,
Souls that have toiled, and wrought, and thought with me—   45
That ever with a frolic welcome took
The thunder and the sunshine, and opposed
Free hearts, free foreheads—you and I are old;
Old age hath yet his honor and his toil.   50
Death closes all; but something ere the end,
Some work of noble note, may yet be done,
Not unbecoming men that strove with Gods.
The lights begin to twinkle from the rocks;
The long day wanes; the slow moon climbs; the deep   55
Moans round with many voices. Come, my friends,
'Tis not too late to seek a newer world.
Push off, and sitting well in order smite

34. **isle:** Ulysses' kingdom was Ithaca, an island off the west coast of Greece. Telemachus (tə·lem′ə·kəs), a youth in the *Odyssey*, is now a mature man, well suited to rule the kingdom.

The sounding furrows; for my purpose holds
To sail beyond the sunset, and the baths   60
Of all the western stars, until I die.
It may be that the gulfs will wash us down;
It may be we shall touch the Happy Isles,°
And see the great Achilles,° whom we knew.
Though much is taken, much abides; and though   65
We are not now that strength which in old days
Moved earth and heaven, that which we are, we are—
One equal temper of heroic hearts,
Made weak by time and fate, but strong in will
To strive, to seek, to find, and not to yield.   70

63. **Happy Isles:** the place where heroes went after death. 64. **Achilles** (ə·kil′ēz): the Greek hero of the Trojan War, in which Ulysses had taken part before his long series of adventures on the return journey.

COMMENTARY

Tennyson is reported to have said of "Ulysses" that it "gives the feeling about the need of going forward and braving the struggle of life perhaps more simply than anything in *In Memoriam,*" and that it "was written under the sense of loss and all that had gone by, but that still life must be fought out to the end."

"Ulysses" was occasioned by Tennyson's need to urge himself onward after the overwhelming grief of Arthur Hallam's death. Out of his youthful sorrow, Tennyson created the resolute speech of the aged Ulysses. Sometimes there is a lack of harmony between the assertions of the speaker in the poem and the slow movement of the blank verse. Matthew Arnold once observed that the lines

"Yet all experience is an arch where-
    through
Gleams that untraveled world whose
    margin fades
Forever and forever when I move."

take as much time to read as a whole book of the *Odyssey.* Although the poem's attitude toward experience is vigorous and forward-looking, the movement of the verse suggests a melancholy yearning. Thus there is a conflict between the forcefulness of Ulysses' speech and the often retarded or suspended movement of the verse. This conflict is by no means a weakness, for it helps establish the central emotion of the poem—a combination of high resolve with a melancholy sense of diminished powers. Remember that this voyage into the unknown is undertaken by the old, not by the young; it begins at twilight, not dawn. Although Ulysses never wavers in his desire to set out, he well knows that "We are not now that strength which in old days / Moved earth and heaven . . ."

FOR STUDY AND DISCUSSION

1. Review the chief incidents in the career of Ulysses after the Trojan War was over. Who was his "aged wife"?

2. What, according to the poem (see lines 33–42), does Tennyson consider to be the duties of a good ruler?

3. How would you characterize the philosophy of this poem? Does the poem say that life is easy? How may the last line be described as a summary of the entire poem? Do you find the poem's optimism convincing? Why or why not?

Break, Break, Break

Break, break, break,
  On thy cold gray stones, O Sea!
And I would that my tongue could utter
  The thoughts that arise in me.

Oh, well for the fisherman's boy,   5
  That he shouts with his sister at play!
Oh, well for the sailor lad,
  That he sings in his boat on the bay!

And the stately ships go on
  To their haven under the hill;   10
But oh, for the touch of a vanished hand,
  And the sound of a voice that is still!

Break, break, break,
  At the foot of thy crags, O Sea!
But the tender grace of a day that is dead   15
  Will never come back to me.

COMMENTARY

Like "Ulysses" and *In Memoriam*, this poem was inspired by the death of Arthur Hallam; it was "made in a Lincolnshire lane at 5 o'clock in the morning between blossoming hedges." The unending rush of the sea against the rocks suggests that the sea is the timeless source and end of all being; it includes everything. The shouts of the children at play, the sailor's song, and the ships moving to a safe harbor all suggest security and joy at being alive. These joyous sights and sounds contrast with the monotonous pounding of the sea and with the silent voice and vanished hand of the poet's memories. Filled with sad memories of "a day that is dead," the poet nevertheless does not lose himself entirely in melancholy reverie. He is able to see his memories objectively in relation both to the eternity of the sea and the momentary joys of living.

FOR STUDY AND DISCUSSION

1. Some critics have objected that lines 9–10 are irrelevant to the main theme of the poem. Can you justify Tennyson's inclusion of these lines?

2. Read the poem aloud. What variations in rhythm can you find?

Flower in the Crannied Wall

Flower in the crannied wall,
I pluck you out of the crannies,
I hold you here, root and all, in my hand,
Little flower—but *if* I could understand
What you are, root and all, and all in all,   5
I should know what God and man is.

COMMENTARY

This poem was so popular with readers of Tennyson's time that a statue of Tennyson holding a flower was erected in the Lincoln cathedral yard. Into the poem's few lines, Tennyson has packed his theory that every natural thing is a sign of all the laws governing the universe. If we only knew enough, we would see that every flower is a revelation of divine purpose. The poem affirms the unity of God, nature, and human life.

FOR STUDY AND DISCUSSION

1. Why do you think Tennyson wrote this poem about a flower growing in a wall rather than one growing in the fields?
2. Read the poem aloud. Does it move quickly or slowly? How is the rhythm appropriate to the poem's thought and feeling?

Tears, Idle Tears

Tears, idle tears, I know not what they mean,
Tears from the depth of some divine despair
Rise in the heart, and gather to the eyes,
In looking on the happy autumn fields,
And thinking of the days that are no more.   5

Fresh as the first beam glittering on a sail,
That brings our friends up from the underworld,
Sad as the last which reddens over one
That sinks with all we love below the verge;
So sad, so fresh, the days that are no more.   10

Ah, sad and strange as in dark summer dawns
The earliest pipe of half-awakened birds
To dying ears, when unto dying eyes
The casement slowly grows a glimmering square;
So sad, so strange, the days that are no more.   15

Dear as remembered kisses after death,
And sweet as those by hopeless fancy feigned
On lips that are for others; deep as love,
Deep as first love, and wild with all regret;
O Death in Life, the days that are no more.   20

ALFRED, LORD TENNYSON   589

COMMENTARY

This poem is one of the short songs that are set in Tennyson's long narrative poem, *The Princess*. Tennyson said: "The passion of the past, the abiding in the transient, was expressed in 'Tears, Idle Tears,' which was written at Tintern Abbey." Like Wordsworth's "Lines Composed a Few Miles Above Tintern Abbey" (page 471), Tennyson's poem is about the past that lives on within us, sometimes almost submerged in forgetfulness, sometimes welling up in vivid memories charged with emotion. It evokes the elusive mixture of feelings that are inspired by "thinking of the days that are no more."

The tears are called "idle" because they do not seem to be evoked by anything specific. They can be explained only in a series of apparently contradictory metaphors. The first stanza contrasts the "tears" with the "happy autumn fields"; it opposes the grief-filled sense of the lost past to the happiness of the present. In the second stanza, memories of the past are both "fresh" and "sad"; these memories give joy because they seem to bring back lost friends, but they are also sad because the poet knows that the friends have actually sunk "below the verge" and cannot be recalled. In the third stanza the memories themselves are as clear as the early song of birds and as bright as a sunlit casement, but the poet cannot grasp them. His power of remembering fades in the same way that powers of perception fade away in "dying ears" and "dying eyes." In the last stanza, memories are "dear," "sweet," and "deep," precious and deeply rooted in the poet's being. But they are also "wild with all regret." In memory, the past comes very near, but it is always just out of reach. It is loved, but it can also inspire a frenzied sense of loss.

FOR STUDY AND DISCUSSION

1. Why do you think Tennyson describes the despair in line 2 as "divine"?

2. The "underworld" of line 7 refers both to the Southern Hemisphere and to the underworld of the shades in classical antiquity. Which sense of the word has greater meaning here? Why?

3. What is twice called "sad and strange" in stanza 3? Why are these words appropriate?

4. Explain the term "Death in Life" in the last line of the poem.

5. Tennyson said of this poem, "Few know that it is a blank verse lyric." Most of Tennyson's lyrics employ rhyme. Why do you think Tennyson used blank verse for this lyric?

FROM *In Memoriam*

By common consent the three greatest elegies in English literature are Milton's "Lycidas," on Edward King, a college friend drowned before the completion of his studies; Shelley's *Adonais*, on John Keats; Tennyson's *In Memoriam*, on Arthur Hallam. The similarity in the situations that called forth these elegies is apparent. Each poem mourns a young man of great talent cut off before he is able to fulfill the promise of his youth. However, *In Memoriam* differs from the others in two respects. The personal tie between Tennyson and Hallam was the strongest friendship of the three. Besides being warm college friends, they had traveled together, and Hallam was engaged to Tennyson's sister.

In Memoriam is a series of 131 short meditations on the meaning of life and death. Written through seventeen years of thought and spiritual struggle, it has, in T. S. Eliot's words, "only the unity and continuity of a diary. . . ." but, Eliot adds, "It is a diary of which we have to read every word." *In Memoriam* represents Tennyson's most mature poetry. Tennyson regarded this work as so intensely personal that he did not plan to publish it. Finally, at the urging of his wife, he published the poem anonymously in 1850.

PROEM

Strong Son of God, immortal Love,
  Whom we, that have not seen thy face,
  By faith, and faith alone, embrace,
Believing where we cannot prove;

Thine are these orbs of light and shade; 5
  Thou madest Life in man and brute;
  Thou madest Death; and lo, thy foot
Is on the skull which thou hast made.

Thou wilt not leave us in the dust;
  Thou madest man, he knows not why,
  He thinks he was not made to die; 11
And thou hast made him; thou art just.

Thou seemest human and divine,
  The highest, holiest manhood, thou;
  Our wills are ours, we know not how;
Our wills are ours, to make them thine.

Our little systems have their day; 17
  They have their day and cease to be;
  They are but broken lights° of thee,
And thou, O Lord, art more than they. 20

We have but faith; we cannot know;
  For knowledge is of things we see;
  And yet we trust it comes from thee,
A beam in darkness; let it grow.

Let knowledge grow from more to more,
  But more of reverence in us dwell; 26
  That mind and soul, according well,
May make one music as before,

But vaster. We are fools and slight;
  We mock thee when we do not fear; 30
  But help thy foolish ones to bear;
Help thy vain worlds to bear thy light.°

Forgive what seemed my sin° in me;
  What seemed my worth° since I began;
  For merit lives from man to man, 35
And not from man, O Lord, to thee.

Forgive my grief for one removed,
  Thy creature, whom I found so fair.
  I trust he lives in thee, and there
I find him worthier to be loved. 40

Forgive these wild and wandering cries,
  Confusions of a wasted youth;
  Forgive them where they fail in truth,
And in thy wisdom make me wise.

II

Old yew, which graspest at the stones
  That name the underlying dead,
  Thy fibers net the dreamless head,
Thy roots are wrapped about the bones.

The seasons bring the flower again, 5
  And bring the firstling° to the flock;
  And in the dusk of thee the clock°
Beats out the little lives of men.

PROEM: 19. **broken lights:** colored or prismatic lights; the partial truth obtainable in this world. 32. **light:** the perfect truth. 33. **sin:** mourning for the dead. 34. **worth:** devotion to the memory of Hallam. Tennyson asks forgiveness for both his grief and his devotion.
II: 6. **firstling:** firstborn. 7. **clock:** the clock on the church tower.

O, not for thee the glow, the bloom,
  Who changest not in any gale,   10
  Nor branding summer suns avail
To touch thy thousand years of gloom;

And gazing on thee, sullen tree,
  Sick for° thy stubborn hardihood,
  I seem to fail from out my blood   15
And grow incorporate into thee.

VII

Dark house,° by which once more I stand
  Here in the long unlovely street,
  Doors, where my heart was used to beat
So quickly, waiting for a hand,

A hand that can be clasp'd no more—   5
  Behold me, for I cannot sleep,
  And like a guilty thing I creep
At earliest morning to the door.

He is not here; but far away
  The noise of life begins again,   10
  And ghastly thro' the drizzling rain
On the bald street breaks the blank day.

14. **for:** with desire for.
VII: 1. **Dark house:** the Hallam house in London.

XXVII

I envy not in any moods
  The captive void of noble rage,
  The linnet born within the cage,
That never knew the summer woods;

I envy not the beast that takes   5
  His license in the field of time,
  Unfettered by the sense of crime,
To whom a conscience never wakes;

Nor, what may count itself as blest,
  The heart that never plighted troth   10
  But stagnates in the weeds of sloth;
Nor any want-begotten rest.

I hold it true, whate'er befall;
  I feel it, when I sorrow most;
  'Tis better to have loved and lost   15
Than never to have loved at all.

LIV

Oh, yet we trust that somehow good
  Will be the final goal of ill,
  To pangs of nature, sins of will,
Defects of doubt, and taints of blood;°

That nothing walks with aimless feet;   5
  That not one life shall be destroyed,
  Or cast as rubbish to the void,
When God hath made the pile complete;

That not a worm is cloven in vain;
  That not a moth with vain desire   10
  Is shriveled in a fruitless fire,
Or but subserves another's gain.

Behold, we know not anything;
  I can but trust that good shall fall
  At last—far off—at last, to all,   15
And every winter change to spring.

So runs my dream; but what am I?
  An infant crying in the night;
  An infant crying for the light;
And with no language but a cry.   20

LIV: 3–4. Four kinds of ills are specified: physical, moral, spiritual, and inherited.

COMMENTARY

T. S. Eliot has described *In Memoriam* as "unique": "it is a long poem made by putting together lyrics which have only the unity and continuity of a diary, the concentrated diary of a man confessing himself." The body of the poem is divided into four main sections, each separated from the other by three Christmas lyrics that mark the end of each of the first three years after Hallam's death. The first section deals with despair, the second with doubt, the third with hope, and the last with reconciliation to Hallam's death and the achievement of faith. However, within this general scheme, the poet's moods often alternate, moving backward and forward between doubt and faith.

PROEM

Though the Proem comes first in the poem, it was the last part to be composed and represents the point at which Tennyson had arrived by the end of the poem rather than the point from which he set out. Thus its celebration of faith in God's beneficence is somewhat misleading, since faith is what Tennyson achieved throughout the years of writing the poem, not what he began with. Faith for Tennyson does not follow from argument, demonstration, or the evidence of the senses. Instead it involves an intuitive leap into the unknown, a trust that the "beam in darkness" "comes from thee." It is therefore a difficult achievement, for what the mind knows is not always in accord with what the soul feels, and mere knowledge may be at odds with true wisdom. The split between mind and soul can be healed only by a greater knowledge that is governed by reverence for the nature of people and God. The poet concludes the Proem with a plea for forgiveness for his failure to accept Hallam's death as God's will and his lack of trust that "he lives in thee."

II. OLD YEW, WHICH GRASPEST AT THE STONES

The poet addresses the old yew standing in a graveyard, its roots grasping at the gravestones and at the skulls and bones beneath. A long-lived evergreen traditionally associated with mourning, the yew is a fitting symbol for the poet's grief and his longing for powers of endurance. Unchanged by the seasons and by the passage of time, the yew seems to stand outside the whole cycle of birth, growth, and death. Its "thousand years of gloom" is a kind of immortality. The poet, afflicted by his own weakness and faltering, is "Sick for thy stubborn hardihood." In the last two lines, the poet sinks into a dreamlike reverie and, losing consciousness of his distinctively human identity, feels his self dissolving out of his own body and blending with the yew.

The yew serves as a visual equivalent for the poet's emotion, yet Tennyson never distorts the nature of the tree. He sees it primarily as a physical object and never explicitly attributes to it human moods or emotions. All the words that describe the yew can have a double meaning. Thus "dusk" and "gloom" can refer both to the deep shade cast by the tree's dense, dark foliage and to the poet's sorrowful mood. "Sullen" and "stubborn" both seem to refer primarily to human qualities, but "sullen" has the secondary meaning of "unyielding" when applied to natural objects, and "stubborn" has the secondary meaning of "hard, stiff, rigid."

VII. DARK HOUSE, BY WHICH ONCE MORE I STAND

A contemporary of Tennyson's wrote a poem on the death of Hallam which, superficially at least, is very much like "Dark house, by which once more I stand":

"I thought, how should I see him first,
How should our hands first meet,
Within his room, upon the stairs,—
At the corner of the street?

I thought, where should I hear him
  first,
How catch his greeting tone,—
And thus I went up to his door,
And they told me he was gone!"

Though these verses have the same setting and some of the same images as Tennyson's poem, they are merely a prosaic statement of the writer's disappointment. Tennyson's poem, on the other hand, evokes the whole picture of the dark house and the long, empty street, and makes the reader feel the emotion of the mourner. Standing at early dawn, in the drizzling rain, before the dark house in which Hallam once lived, the poet himself is almost as ghostly as the "hand that can be clasp'd no more." Himself haunted by memories of Hallam, he is almost haunting the house of mourning. In the last stanza, daylight and the noises of the awakening city break in on the trancelike reverie of the poet: the world of daylight and the living seems jarringly ugly and strange to the poet mourning the dead.

XXVII. I ENVY NOT IN ANY MOODS

The lines " 'Tis better to have loved and lost/ Than never to have loved at all" are so commonly quoted that people have almost forgotten what they mean. The first three stanzas present three kinds of experience that the poet says "I envy not." The "captive void of noble rage" and the linnet in the cage represent those who passively live out narrow, constricted lives. The "beast" "whom a conscience never wakes" is the mere animal in us who satisfies appetites but never develops a moral sense. The "heart" that "stagnates in the weeds of sloth" represents a life without emotional ties to others and consequently without emotional power. Love, even at its most painful, is better than these three kinds of apathy and unconsciousness. The last two often-quoted lines affirm full consciousness, moral alertness, and emotional responsiveness to experience. Even though they can

cause suffering, these are superior to the comforts offered by ignorance, animal appetite, and emotional sloth.

LIV. OH, YET WE TRUST THAT SOMEHOW GOOD

In the first three stanzas the poet expresses his trust that good will "somehow" come out of the physical, moral, intellectual, and inherited ills of the world; that life is not without purpose; that death is not without meaning. Stanzas 4 and 5 show the weakening of this trust into a sense of ignorance and helplessness. In the fourth stanza, the verbs become weaker—"we know not," "I can but trust." In the last stanza, the trust that evil will turn to good becomes a "dream," and language becomes an infant's "cry" dissolving into mere sounds of fright and anguish when confronted with the apparently purposeless suffering of the world.

This lyric exemplifies one of the most remarkable characteristics of *In Memoriam:* the constant struggle between faith and doubt that makes the poem such a striking spiritual testament.

FOR STUDY AND DISCUSSION

1. Cite lines in the Proem that express faith in God's wisdom. Cite lines that show a distrust of human intellect. Cite lines that express a desire for a union between the intellect and the soul. Judging from this lyric, how close do you think Tennyson was to achieving such a union? Explain.

2. In the second lyric ("Old yew . . ."), what do the words *graspest, net,* and *wrapped* suggest about the yew? In the last stanza, the poet feels himself becoming a part of the tree. Do you think he derives comfort from this feeling? Why or why not? What is the mood of this stanza? (Consider especially the use of the words *sullen, stubborn,* and *fail.*)

3. In the seventh lyric ("Dark house . . ."), why does the poet compare himself to a "guilty thing" in the second stanza? In the third stanza, does "far away" modify "He" or "noise" or both? What effect is gained by the alliteration (repetition of *b* sounds) in the last line?

4. In the twenty-seventh lyric ("I envy not . . ."), what are the moral implications of the words *license, crime,* and *conscience* used in connection with the "beast" in the second stanza? In line 11, what emotion is suggested by the use of the words *stagnates, weeds,* and *sloth?* In your opinion, does the declaration in line 14 add conviction to or detract from the final two lines of the lyric?

5. In the fifty-fourth lyric ("Oh, yet we trust . . ."), what picture of the world is suggested by the words *aimless, destroyed, rubbish, void,* and *pile* in stanza 2? What about this lyric suggests that Tennyson was troubled by the new scientific doctrines derived from evolutionary theories, such as the "struggle for existence" and "survival of the fittest"?

6. How may *In Memoriam* be regarded as an inner drama depicting the conflict within one man? Several critics have stated that *In Memoriam* is a powerful poem, not because of its statements of affirmation, but because of its moments of doubt and despair. Do you agree? Why or why not? Which of the lyrics seemed to you most powerful? Give reasons for your choice.

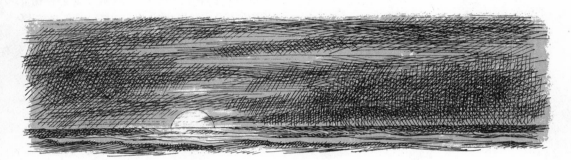

Crossing the Bar

Sunset and evening star,
    And one clear call for me!
And may there be no moaning° of the bar,
    When I put out to sea,

But such a tide as moving seems asleep,   5
    Too full for sound and foam,
When that which drew from out the boundless deep
    Turns again home.

Twilight and evening bell,
    And after that the dark!   10
And may there be no sadness of farewell,
    When I embark;

For though from out our bourne° of Time and Place
    The flood may bear me far,
I hope to see my Pilot face to face   15
    When I have crossed the bar.

3. **moaning:** It is a popular belief that the ebbing tide moans when a death has occurred.
13. **bourne:** bounded territory, referring here to earthly life. Compare with "the boundless deep" (of eternity), line 7.

COMMENTARY

Tennyson wrote this poem at the age of eighty-one, after a serious illness. Three years later, a few days before his death, he said to his son, "Mind you put 'Crossing the Bar' at the end of all editions of my poems." This request has been honored in all of the many editions of Tennyson's poems. As befits a poem intended to be the poet's final utterance, this one is full of indirect echoes and contrasts with Tennyson's earlier poetry. The "sunset and evening star" of the first stanza suggest the sunset and twilight in which Ulysses prepares to set out on his voyage to the unknown. But while Ulysses is voyaging to new earthly experience, "Crossing the Bar" is about the voyage to death. The silence of the sea in the first two stanzas is in contrast to the sea's monotonous thunder in "Break, Break, Break" and its surging restlessness in "Ulysses." And the call for "no sadness of farewell" recalls and contrasts with the profound sadness of "Tears, Idle Tears," when the ship "sinks with all we love beneath the verge."

The poem is a quiet and reverent acceptance of death. In the first two stanzas the images are largely the concrete physical ones of sunset and twilight and the silent flowing of the tide out to sea. In the third and fourth stanzas, the spiritual bearing of the images becomes increasingly explicit, and the language becomes more abstract and symbolizes a spiritual rather than a physical voyage. Thus the speaker is to be carried by the tide of death "from out our bourne of Time and Place" to meet the divine "Pilot," who was explained by Tennyson as "That Divine and Unseen Who is always guiding us."

FOR STUDY AND DISCUSSION

1. "Crossing the Bar" has been praised as a poem in which every image can be seen to have a double meaning. Explain the double meanings of the images in the first two stanzas.

2. Contrast Tennyson's attitude toward approaching death with that of Keats in "When I Have Fears" and Shelley in "A Lament." To what extent, in your opinion, does the difference in attitude depend on the relative ages of these poets when they died?

FOR COMPOSITION

1. Write a composition in which you agree or disagree with the following statement about Tennyson from the biographical introduction: "He makes the experience of spiritual solitude and religious doubt a living reality in his poems, and he depicts the enchantments and dangers that accompany the life of the imagination cut off from ordinary things and existing only in a world of gorgeous dreams and hazy emotions." Support your position with examples from Tennyson's poetry.

2. T. S. Eliot has written of *In Memoriam* that it can "justly be called a religious poem, but for another reason than that which made it seem religious to Tennyson's contemporaries. It is not religious because of the quality of its faith, but because of the quality of its doubt. Its faith is a poor thing, but its doubt is a very intense experience."

Write a composition in which you test Eliot's opinion by comparing Tennyson's expressions of faith with that of earlier writers such as John Donne and John Milton. Which expressions seem to you more heartfelt and profound? Finally, explain how a poem can be considered religious by presenting doubt as "a very intense experience."

ROBERT BROWNING
(1812–1889)

In his own time, as a modern critic says of Robert Browning, "his poetry and presence had become the very symbols of heartiness, courage, and faith." Today he is sometimes criticized for being a shallow optimist, a poet who refused to face up to the presence of evil and misery in the world. If optimism is accepted as a major characteristic of Browning's poetry, then the word *optimism* must be given a deeper meaning than usual. As often as not, Browning's poems end with collapse of the will, defeat of good by evil forces, or the sweeping away of everything, good and bad, by death. Fascinated by abnormal states of mind, even by madness, Browning did not always look on the bright side of things.

But if optimism can be seen as something more profound than the mere refusal to face evil, then this word can help to define Browning's fundamental way of meeting experience. Browning approaches even the most grotesque characters and the most obscure regions of the mind with a confident openness. Assured of his own strong sanity and his powers of assimilating experience, Browning takes an athletic delight in grappling with the dark forces of human nature, not to destroy them, but to reveal them. He relishes even the failures, misfits, villains, and madmen who appear in his poems, because they exhibit the infinite variety of human experience. Everything in his poetry takes on a touch of vitality and splendor—even weeds and rocks and snails. If optimism can be taken to mean confidence in one's own powers and delight in the variety and energy of the world, then Browning is an optimist. Much of his power as a poet comes from his ability to submerge himself imaginatively in psychological darkness and then represent what he has discovered there in firmly controlled and coherent works of art.

As a living influence on poetry, Browning is more important today for his contribution to the language and craft of poetry than for his "message." He was endlessly resourceful in the invention of new stanza patterns and in creating novel metrical combinations. He brought poetic language back into touch with the toughness, vigor, and hard concreteness of speech, and showed anew the poetic uses of harsh, rough sounds and rhythms. His development of the dramatic monologue opened up for later poets a way of exploring the subjective life without giving up the immediacy and concreteness of dramatic form. And finally he brought back into English poetry something of the compression of thought, the pleasure in contradiction and sudden shifts that John Donne had introduced two centuries earlier.

Robert Browning was born in Camberwell, a comfortable, semirural suburb only three miles from central London and "a half hour's green walk" from Dulwich and its then famous art gallery, where he first encountered the Renaissance Italian paintings that were to become one of his lifelong enthusiasms. Although Browning's father spent his days as an official of the Bank of England, he was more interested in art, scholarship, and book collecting than in business. Browning was educated largely at home by his father, who tutored him in Latin and Greek, and by special tutors from whom he learned French, Italian, and music. More important, he read widely, filling his mind with a large store of miscellaneous learning as well as reading the "standard authors" every educated man was expected to know.

Browning began his literary career early: he wrote and deposited under a sofa cushion his first poem "when I could not have been five years old." At twenty-one, he published his first volume, *Pauline,* a thinly veiled autobiographical poem in which he unwittingly revealed himself as an arrogant and self-absorbed adolescent. The severe, accurate criticism that the philosopher John Stuart Mill leveled at the poem is thought to have pushed Browning toward the dramatic monologue and away from poems of self-revelation. During early manhood, Browning lived the life of a young literary man about town, moving in literary and theatrical circles and composing plays and long poems. Between 1841 and 1846 he produced the remarkable series of poetic pamphlets *Bells and Pomegranates* (including the much anthologized *Pippa Passes),* but he had to wait for general recognition until 1868, when *The Ring and the Book* securely established him alongside Tennyson as the leading poet of the Victorian age.

When, in January of 1845, Browning wrote an enthusiastic letter of appreciation to Elizabeth Barrett (page 615) after reading her *Poems,* he took the first step in the most famous of literary romances. Six years older than Browning and considerably more famous than he, Elizabeth Barrett was an invalid who lived in prisonlike seclusion under the domination of a maniacally patriarchal father. After much negotiation by letter, Browning finally met Elizabeth Barrett in May 1845. For the next sixteen months Browning courted Elizabeth Barrett with flowers, visits, and, above all, letters. Convinced that she was a dying woman and that her father would never permit her to marry, Elizabeth Barrett shied away from personal involvement. But Browning swept aside objection after objection, and finally in the autumn of 1846 they were secretly married and eloped to Italy.

For the next sixteen years the Brownings lived in Italy, mostly in Florence, writing, reading, studying pictures, entertaining visiting Englishmen and Americans, and championing the cause of Italian independence. They were almost ideally happy. Browning accepted without bitterness the fact that his wife's *Aurora Leigh* went through edition after edition while his own *Men and Women* was coldly received except by a few scattered young men, mostly in the universities. This sunny period in Browning's life ended with the death of his wife in June 1861, soon after which he returned to London. There he set to work producing *Dramatis Personnae* and his 21,000-line masterpiece, *The Ring and the Book.* His fame had been slowly growing, and after the appearance of *The Ring and the Book* he became a social lion, dining out so often that Tennyson sarcastically predicted that Browning would die in his dinner jacket. Browning Societies were organized throughout England to praise the poet and to explain his more obscure works. Despite occasional literary squabbles, Browning's later life was full of satisfaction—fame, money, friendship, and the sense of an achieved career. He even had the pleasure of seeing a final collected edition of his work in sixteen volumes before he died at the age of seventy-two.

Home Thoughts, from Abroad

Oh, to be in England
Now that April's there,
And whoever wakes in England
Sees, some morning, unaware,
That the lowest boughs and the brushwood sheaf   5
Round the elm tree bole° are in tiny leaf,
While the chaffinch° sings on the orchard bough
In England—now!

And after April, when May follows,
And the whitethroat° builds, and all the swallows!   10
Hark, where my blossomed pear tree in the hedge
Leans to the field and scatters on the clover
Blossoms and dewdrops—at the bent spray's edge—
That's the wise thrush! he sings each song twice over,
Lest you should think he never could recapture   15
The first fine careless rapture!
And though the fields look rough with hoary dew,
All will be gay when noontide wakes anew
The buttercups, the little children's dower
—Far brighter than this gaudy melon flower!   20

---

6. **bole:** tree trunk. 7. **chaffinch:** a common European songbird. 10. **whitethroat:** a European warbler.

COMMENTARY

This poem is a good example of Browning's craftsmanship as a poet. The poem consists of two stanzas, one of eight and one of twelve lines. It is written in trochees—the metrical foot in which a stressed syllable is followed by an unstressed syllable, as in *Óh, tŏ bé ĭn Éng-lănd*. Browning worked here with a regular meter and a rhyme scheme, but within this form, he permitted himself a large degree of freedom. The number of syllables in each line varies from four to eleven. The sentence structure is colloquial—closer to the loose patterns of spoken English than to the close-knit patterns of formal prose. The sentences are full of exclamations, interruptions, and unexpected shifts in sentence structure. The freely varied line length and colloquial syntax combine to give an impression of energy, rapid movement, and freedom.

FOR STUDY AND DISCUSSION

1. Find three examples of the "exclamations, interruptions, and unexpected shifts in sentence structure" referred to in the Commentary. Do you think that the "energy, rapid movement, and freedom" referred to above make the emotion of the poem seem more, or less, convincing? Explain.

2. Where does the last line of the poem suggest that Browning is at the time of writing? (You may wish to consult the biography for a clue.)

Home Thoughts, from the Sea

Nobly, nobly Cape Saint Vincent to the northwest died away;
Sunset ran, one glorious blood-red, reeking into Cadiz Bay;
Bluish 'mid the burning water, full in face Trafalgar lay;
In the dimmest northeast distance dawned Gibraltar grand and gray;
"Here and here did England help me: how can I help England?"—say,   5
Whoso turns as I, this evening, turns to God to praise and pray,
While Jove's planet° rises yonder, silent over Africa.

7. **Jove's planet:** Jupiter, an evening star.

COMMENTARY

Even though this poem is very short and presents an emotion—gratitude to one's country—not usually considered very complex, it is more complicated and condensed than its companion piece, "Home Thoughts, from Abroad." The setting is the waters southwest of the southern Spanish coast, which Browning passed through while on a voyage to Italy and where Britain had three of her greatest naval victories. In Cadiz Bay the Spanish fleets that threatened England were defeated by Drake in 1586, and again by Essex and Raleigh in 1596. Then, in the early nineteenth century, during the Napoleonic wars, Lord Nelson defeated the Spanish fleet off Cape Saint Vincent. Later at nearby Trafalgar he met his death after a famous victory over the combined French and Spanish fleets. Gibraltar is the great British naval stronghold on the southern tip of Spain which the English have long regarded as a first line of defense, a kind of sentinel over the Mediterranean.

These places evoke feelings for the greatness of the poet's country and the almost legendary heroism of Nelson. Further, the places themselves have a sublime appearance: Cape Saint Vincent dies away "nobly, nobly"; Gibraltar is "grand and gray"; the scene is bathed in the light of a "glorious sunset" and then in the splendor of the rising planet Jupiter. Thus a feeling for the majesty and immensity of nature is blended with patriotism and the awe inspired by great heroism. The poet turns to "praise and pray" while "Jove's planet" rises silently over Africa. The poem captures a sublime experience: the awe that we feel before immensity in national greatness, in human heroism, and in nature.

FOR STUDY AND DISCUSSION

1. Notice that the poet's question "how can I help England?" remains unanswered. How would the effect of the poem differ if this question had been answered explicitly?

2. Does this poem, like "Home Thoughts, from Abroad" (page 599), give an impression of rapidity and energy? How does the rhythm of the poem contribute to its mood?

My Last Duchess

This poem is perhaps the most popular of Browning's dramatic monologues.
The scene is in the castle of the Duke of Ferrara, an arrogant Italian nobleman of
the Renaissance period. The duke is showing a painting of his first wife to an envoy
who has been sent to arrange the details of a second marriage.

That's my last Duchess painted on the wall,
Looking as if she were alive; I call
That piece a wonder, now; Fra Pandolf's° hands
Worked busily a day, and there she stands.
Will 't please you sit and look at her? I said   5
"Fra Pandolf" by design, for never read
Strangers like you that pictured countenance,
The depth and passion of its earnest glance,
But to myself they turned (since none puts by
The curtain I have drawn for you, but I)   10
And seemed as they would ask me, if they durst,
How such a glance came there; so, not the first
Are you to turn and ask thus. Sir, 'twas not
Her husband's presence only, called that spot
Of joy into the Duchess' cheek: perhaps   15
Fra Pandolf chanced to say, "Her mantle laps
Over my lady's wrist too much," or, "Paint
Must never hope to reproduce the faint
Half flush that dies along her throat"; such stuff
Was courtesy, she thought, and cause enough   20
For calling up that spot of joy. She had
A heart . . . how shall I say? . . . too soon made glad,
Too easily impressed; she liked whate'er
She looked on, and her looks went everywhere.
Sir, 'twas all one! My favor at her breast,   25
The dropping of the daylight in the West,
The bough of cherries some officious fool
Broke in the orchard for her, the white mule
She rode with round the terrace—all and each
Would draw from her alike the approving speech,   30
Or blush, at least. She thanked men—good; but thanked
Somehow . . . I know not how . . . as if she ranked
My gift of a nine-hundred-year-old name
With anybody's gift. Who'd stoop to blame
This sort of trifling? Even had you skill   35
In speech—which I have not—to make your will
Quite clear to such an one, and say, "Just this
Or that in you disgusts me; here you miss
Or there exceed the mark"—and if she let
Herself be lessoned so, nor plainly set   40

3. **Fra Pandolf:** an imaginary monk and painter of the Italian Renaissance period. "Fra"
means "Brother."

Her wits to yours, forsooth, and made excuse
—E'en then would be some stooping, and I choose
Never to stoop. Oh, sir, she smiled, no doubt,
Whene'er I passed her; but who passed without
Much the same smile? This grew; I gave commands;   45
Then all smiles stopped together. There she stands
As if alive. Will 't please you rise? We'll meet
The company below, then. I repeat,
The Count your Master's known munificence
Is ample warrant that no just pretense   50
Of mine for dowry will be disallowed;
Though his fair daughter's self, as I avowed
At starting, is my object. Nay, we'll go
Together down,° sir! Notice Neptune,° though,
Taming a sea horse, thought a rarity,   55
Which Claus of Innsbruck° cast in bronze for me.

53–54. **we'll . . . down:** The envoy, out of respect, has dropped behind the duke, who calls him forward to a position of equality.   54. **Neptune:** the Greek god of the sea.   56. **Claus of Innsbruck:** an imaginary sculptor.

COMMENTARY

"My Last Duchess" is one of the earliest and most famous of Browning's dramatic monologues. Written in an age which saw an immense expansion of his-torical knowledge, it reflects Browning's lifelong study of the history of the Renaissance. The Renaissance was for Browning not only a historical age but also a kind of symbol of a life of extreme passions, violence, and heightened awareness —a kind of life that contrasted strikingly with the ordinary realities and emotional flatness of the Victorian era. In a Renaissance setting Browning could depict life on a grander and more intense plane than a contemporary setting would permit.

The dramatic monologue is related to the soliloquy used in Shakespeare's plays. In the Shakespearean soliloquy the speaker addresses himself or herself (and the audience), usually in a moment of self-exploration; the soliloquy may begin in fury or violent self-reproach, but it is also an effort toward self-definition. In the dramatic monologue, the speaker addresses someone in a speech that may sound as if it were taken out of a play. The speaker does not, like Macbeth, strive for self-definition; rather he or she more or less unwittingly reveals an inner being by what is said. The external action need not be very striking or remarkable in any way; its purpose is to provide an occasion for the speaker to reveal self. Thus the dramatic monologue is a device for giving dramatic form to the subjective life, not of the poet, but of a created character.

The reader of a dramatic monologue must make a series of inferences about the situation presented in the poem and about the character of the speaker. The reader must envision the scene and the relation of the speaker to whomever is being addressed, and must infer the motives behind the speech. Why does the Duke choose to tell the Count's emissary about his last Duchess? Does he assume that the emissary will share his point of view? Or is his speech a calculated display of ruthlessness to warn the Count of what his daughter must expect? Is the Duke half-mad with pride, or is he making a carefully planned move in his negotiations for a new marriage?

Aside from the immediate motives for the speech, we must also infer the essential character of the Duke and his Duchess from what is said. The Duchess is characterized by a gentle joyousness, an open responsiveness to all life. The "spot of joy" and "faint/ Half-flush that dies along

her throat" represent a spontaneous vitality that torments the Duke, whose fundamental objection to his first wife appears to be that she was too fully alive. He can be content only when he has reduced her to an unmoving work of art that can be hung on the wall. The Duke's arrogance and self-love are expressed in his possessiveness about his wife, his works of art, his ancient name, and the dowry that his new wife will bring. Beyond that, he is obsessed with notions of form and decorum; he worships the rules and observances of life at the expense of life itself.

Thus the poem is more than simply a representation of the psychological peculiarities of a Renaissance Italian duke. The Duke represents rigidity, worship of possessions and forms, and the egoism that wants to reduce other people to mere things and possessions. In her responsiveness, the Duchess has a freedom of spirit that arouses all the Duke's underlying hatred of any life that cannot be reduced to an instrument of his will.

FOR STUDY AND DISCUSSION

1. Answer the questions posed in the third paragraph of the Commentary, finding lines in the poem to justify your answers. What picture of the Duke emerges from your answers?

2. What do you think is the Duke's purpose in concluding his speech by pointing out a bronze cast by Claus of Innsbruck? What does this detail reveal about his character?

3. The Duke mentions his own lack of "skill in speech." Do you think he lacks such skill? Explain. Why, in your opinion, does he claim that he lacks it?

4. Why do you think the Duke is vague about what happened to the Duchess (lines 45–46)? What do you think happened to her?

5. Contrast Browning's use of the iambic pentameter couplet with Pope's heroic couplet in *The Rape of the Lock*. Pope's couplets are especially suitable for pithy, witty poetry. Do you think Browning's couplets are equally suitable in this poem? Are you as aware of the rhyming words in Browning's poem as in Pope's? Explain.

The Lost Leader

Just for a handful of silver he left us,
    Just for a riband to stick in his coat—
Found the one gift of which fortune bereft us,
    Lost all the others she lets us devote;
They, with the gold to give, doled him out silver,   5
    So much was theirs who so little allowed:
How all our copper had gone for his service!
    Rags—were they purple, his heart had been proud!
We that had loved him so, followed him, honored him,
    Lived in his mild and magnificent eye,   10
Learned his great language, caught his clear accents,
    Made him our pattern to live and to die!
Shakespeare was of us, Milton was for us,
    Burns, Shelley, were with us,—they watch from their graves!
He alone breaks from the van° and the freemen,   15
    —He alone sinks to the rear and the slaves!

We shall march prospering—not through his presence;
    Songs may inspirit us—not from his lyre;
Deeds will be done—while he boasts his quiescence,
    Still bidding crouch whom the rest bade aspire: 20
Blot out his name, then, record one lost soul more,
    One task more declined, one more footpath untrod,
One more devils'-triumph and sorrow for angels,
    One wrong more to man, one more insult to God!
Life's night begins: let him never come back to us!   25
    There would be doubt, hesitation and pain,
Forced praise on our part—the glimmer of twilight,
    Never glad confident morning again!
Best fight° on well, for we taught him—strike gallantly,
    Menace our heart ere we master his own;   30
Then let him receive the new knowledge and wait us,
    Pardoned in heaven, the first by the throne!

15. **van:** vanguard of the army of liberalism.   29. **Best fight:** [He had] best fight.

COMMENTARY

Though in his later life Browning was reluctant to talk about the source of this poem, it was certainly written about Wordsworth. In 1842 Wordsworth accepted a civil list pension, and a year later he accepted the poet laureateship. Thus in the first stanza the "handful of silver" may stand for the pension, and the "riband to stick in his coat" for the laureateship. In Browning's eyes, these two acts signified that Wordsworth had betrayed the liberalism of his youth and sunk from being a defender of the people to being a servant of the monarchy. Like Byron and Shelley before him, Browning regarded the increasing conservatism of the older generation of Romantics—Wordsworth, Coleridge, and Southey—as treason both to the cause of poetry and to the cause of humanity: an unhistorical but perfectly natural view.

The first stanza begins with an echo of Judas's betrayal of Christ for thirty pieces of silver and moves through a series of sharply opposed terms such as "silver"–"copper," "found"–"lost," "rib-and"–"rags" to the climactic contrast of "van"–"rear" and "freeman"–"slaves." In the middle of the stanza, the lines memorializing the leader's past greatness employ verbs asserting love, elevation, a sense of shared purpose, and imitation of a pattern of greatness:

> "We that had *loved* him so, *followed*
> him, *honored* him,
> *Lived* in his mild and magnificent
> eye,
> *Learned* his great language, *caught*
> his clear accents,
> *Made* him our pattern to live and
> to die!"

The second stanza begins with defiant acceptance of betrayal and then abandons the leader as a "lost soul" who can never return to the fold but may at last be pardoned in heaven.

The poem can be read as moving from a lament at betrayal to an acceptance of that betrayal and thence to a final pardon and reconciliation beyond the grave. It can also be read as a poem of vigorous denunciation in which the lost leader becomes almost a Satan who has committed a deadly sin and is cast out of the church of poetry.

FOR STUDY AND DISCUSSION

1. To whom does "us" in line 1 refer? Find other lines in the poem to support your answer.
2. Cite words in the second stanza that give it a military tone. In what fight are "we" engaged?
3. Which of the readings of the poem given at the end of the Commentary seems to you the more convincing? Why?

Prospice *

Fear death?—to feel the fog in my throat,
 The mist in my face,
When the snows begin, and the blasts denote
 I am nearing the place,
The power of the night, the press of the storm,   5
 The post of the foe;
Where he stands, the Arch Fear in a visible form,
 Yet the strong man must go;
For the journey is done and the summit attained,
 And the barriers fall,   10
Though a battle's to fight ere the guerdon be gained
 The reward of it all.
I was ever a fighter, so—one fight more,
 The best and the last!
I would hate that death bandaged my eyes, and forbore,   15
 And bade me creep past.

* *Prospice* (prō·spik′ē): look forward (Latin).

No! let me taste the whole of it, fare like my peers,
    The heroes of old,
Bear the brunt, in a minute pay glad life's arrears
    Of pain, darkness, and cold.   20
For sudden the worst turns the best to the brave,
    The black minute's at end,
And the elements' rage, the fiend-voices° that rave,
    Shall dwindle, shall blend,
Shall change, shall become first a peace out of pain,   25
    Then a light, then thy breast,
O thou soul of my soul! I shall clasp thee again,
    And with God be the rest!

23. **fiend-voices:** This term refers to a legend that, as the soul leaves the body, fiends try to snatch it away from the powers of light.

COMMENTARY

This poem was probably written in 1861, a few months after Elizabeth Barrett Browning's death. Browning on one occasion had translated Dante's words on his heroine Beatrice: "Thus I believe, thus I affirm, thus I am certain it is, that from this life I shall pass to another, there, where the lady lives of whom my soul was enamoured." Although the lady of "Prospice" appears only in the final three lines of the poem, she is clearly the goal of the journey and the prize of the battle with death.

The poem affirms Christian faith in immortality and a belief in the continuation of earthly love in another life. It takes the form of a pilgrimage or journey toward death, a heroic battle, a sudden bursting through darkness and cold into peace and light. Death is not seen as slow dissolution or loss of consciousness, but as a heroic climax in which human courage and power of resistance are brought into play. The extended metaphor of the experience of dying is that of a warrior (similar to the warriors in Norse or Saxon poetry) laying siege to the "post of the foe," the "Arch Fear." This is not Keats's "easeful death" (page 534), but a "black minute" that calls forth a supreme effort in an inevitably unsuccessful struggle with death.

FOR STUDY AND DISCUSSION

1. How do the images of fog, mist, and snow in the first three lines of the poem prepare you for the "fiend-voices" in line 23?

2. Contrast Browning's reaction to death in "Prospice" with Tennyson's in "Crossing the Bar." Would you say that Browning's reaction is in keeping with his character? Why? Explain in terms of what you have learned about Browning from reading his poems.

FOR COMPOSITION

Like Browning's "My Last Duchess," Tennyson's "Ulysses" is a famous dramatic monologue of the Victorian period. Compare the two poems in a brief composition in which you consider the following points: Which poem presents a more interesting character? Which poem is the more musical? Which poem depends more on direct statement? which on implication? Does either poem give you the impression that the poet was more concerned with creating a symbol than a convincing character? Explain.

Constable and Turner

Before 1750, British artists concentrated largely on portraiture. As we have seen, Wilson, Gainsborough, and a number of watercolorists then contributed to a new taste for landscape. The full flowering of this development, however, came later, in the first half of the nineteenth century, when landscape attracted two revolutionary but very different types of painters, John Constable and Joseph Mallord William Turner.

Constable avoided the sensational or exotic, turning instead to humble motifs—especially the peaceful valley of the Stour River, which runs through his native Suffolk. Here he painted scenes familiar to him from boyhood. *Willy Lott's House, Near Flatford Mill* (PLATE 1) is a small sketch of a cottage on the Stour owned by an old farmer who, like Constable, had rarely been away from home. Ordinarily, artists executed the landscape portions of their pictures in the studio, but Constable painted this study of Willy Lott's house directly from nature. Delighted with the sparkling light on the bush, he used dabs of pure white to re-create this dappled effect.

Willy Lott's house appears again in Constable's famous picture, *The Haywain* (PLATE 2). *The Haywain* is less bold than the many small sketches Constable had made for it. In the one of Willy Lott's house, for instance, light and shade are summarized in broad strokes; whereas in the final painting, details are clearer but the bold brushstrokes of the sketch are smoothed over. Constable tried to compromise between the spontaneity of his sketches and the qualities of "finish" needed to satisfy public taste and win official recognition. *The Haywain* was exhibited in 1821, but Constable's treatment of his subject was considered too realistic and factual: it lacked the kind of idealization demanded by the Royal Academy, which also disapproved of the looseness of his brushwork. Consequently, Constable was not elected a full Academician until eight years before his death. Yet, when *The Haywain* was exhibited three years later in Paris, it won great acclaim and later influenced the French Impressionists.

Like his contemporary William Wordsworth, Constable persuades us to enjoy quiet, pastoral scenes. In *Wivenhoe Park, Essex* (PLATE 3), a wooden fence and a line of grazing cows lead into the picture. Two white swans and a boating party claim our attention; then we are attracted to the far left edge of the lake where the diagonal edge of the clouds leads to the upper right corner. We can sense the movement of light and shadow as the clouds blow across the sky, and we can see that Constable has emphasized similarities in the shapes of the clouds and the trees. The house of General Rebow, who commissioned this painting, stands half-hidden in the center of the background.

While Constable's inspiration came almost entirely from actual scenes in nature, Turner's was often literary. When *The Slave Ship* (PLATE 4) was first exhibited in 1840, it was accompanied by a quotation from Turner's own poem, "The Fallacies of Hope":

> "Yon angry setting sun and fierce-edged clouds
> Declare the typhoon's coming.
> Before it sweeps your decks, throw overboard
> The dead and dying—ne'er heed their chains . . ."

Turner probably derived his subject from a description of a typhoon in *Seasons,* a well-known eighteenth-century poem by James Thomson. All the details of the poem are in Turner's painting: slave ship, turbulent sea and sky, bodies in the water, chained legs floating (contrary to the laws of nature!), and the sea bloodied by terrifying sea-monsters that devour the slaves.

In this imaginary scene, Turner composes mainly with color. Facing the setting sun, he has painted a white-yellow vertical of light that cuts through the sky and the water. Midway across the painting runs a horizontal layer of the same hue—perhaps the horizon-line, though it is impossible to tell where the sky begins and the water ends. The burst of light at the intersection of these two shafts forms the focal point of the composition.

When Turner sent *Burning of the Houses of Parliament* (PLATE 5) to be exhibited in 1836, it was said to have been "a mere dab of several colors . . . like chaos before the creation." The day before the exhibition opened, however, Turner worked on the canvas steadily to complete it as we see it here. To exploit the dramatic possibilities of light and color in this holocaust which had taken place two years earlier, Turner painted the scene as if he were seeing it at night, but critics pointed out that the light was so bright as to make night more like day. The intense red-orange of the flames is balanced by the blue-green sky and by the dark, silhouetted figures who watch as the buildings burn to the ground. Westminster Bridge seems the only solid object. The smoke and flame, which are reflected in the water, blend with the air, and the colors diffuse into one another.

Turner particularly loved Venice for its delicate pastel colors and moisture-laden air. In a watercolor of *The Approach to Venice: Sunset* (PLATE 6), color, light, and moisture fuse into tinted mists. These drifting veils transform the scene into a fairy-city, a never-never land of delicate, pearly colors.

PLATE 1. JOHN CONSTABLE (1776–1837): *Willy Lott's House, Near Flatford Mill*. About 1810–15? Oil on paper, $9\frac{1}{2}$ x $7\frac{1}{8}$ inches. (Victoria and Albert Museum, London. Crown Copyright)

PLATE 2. JOHN CONSTABLE (1776–1837): *The Haywain*. 1821. Oil on canvas. 50¾ x 73 inches.
(Reproduced by courtesy of the Trustees, The National Gallery, London)

610

PLATE 3. JOHN CONSTABLE (1776–1837): *Wivenhoe Park, Essex.* 1816. Oil on canvas, 22 x 29¾ inches. (National Gallery of Art, Washington, D.C., Widener Collection)

PLATE 4. JOSEPH MALLORD WILLIAM TURNER (1775–1851): *The Slave Ship*. 1840. Oil on canvas. 34¾ x 48 inches. (Courtesy. Museum of Fine Arts. Boston. Harry Lillie Pierce Residuary Fund)

PLATE 5. JOSEPH MALLORD WILLIAM TURNER (1775–1851): *Burning of the Houses of Parliament.* About 1835. Oil on canvas. $36\frac{1}{4}$ x $48\frac{1}{2}$ inches. (Philadelphia Museum of Art. McFadden Collection)

PLATE 6. JOSEPH MALLORD WILLIAM TURNER (1775–1851): *The Approach to Venice: Sunset.* 1840. Watercolor, 9 x 12½ inches. (The British Museum, London).

ELIZABETH BARRETT BROWNING

(1806–1861)

The death of a brother and a back injury seemed to destine Elizabeth Barrett to permanent restriction to her London room under the eye of her dictatorial father, until the poet Robert Browning rescued her through a secret courtship, marriage, and escape to Italy. There the Brownings lived happily for many years. Their constant devotion and deep love is clearly reflected in their correspondence and has made the story of their love almost legendary. Robert Browning's constancy and admiration brought to his wife a renewed vigor and strength that lasted until her death and provided an inspiration for much of her writing. Because of the mild climate and the couple's growing passion for Italy, the Brownings, together with their only son, continued to live there until Elizabeth's death in 1861.

As a child, Elizabeth never had any formal schooling, but she managed to learn Greek, Latin, and modern foreign languages from her brother's tutor. Soon she began writing imitations of her favorite poets. Her father encouraged her literary activity, even to the extent of printing her epic on the battle of Marathon when she was only twelve years old. During her enforced retreat from the world she continued to write and soon came to achieve popular acceptance. Before Elizabeth and Browning met, she was a better-known poet than he. In fact, on the death of Wordsworth, the Poet Laureate, she had been suggested as a successor to the laureateship. Twentieth-century judgment places her well below her husband, but the fame of her *Sonnets from the Portuguese* seems secure.

At the time of their publication, *Sonnets from the Portuguese,* in which the following three poems appear, was perhaps the best example of a true sonnet sequence since Elizabethan times. Elizabeth Barrett wrote the forty-four sonnets during Browning's courtship, but she did not show them to him until after their marriage. She slipped them into his pocket one day and told him to destroy them if he did not like them. Browning, however, insisted on their publication, commenting later: "I dared not reserve to myself the finest sonnets in any language since Shakespeare." Because of the private nature of these poems, a deliberately misleading title was affixed to them. Elizabeth had intended to call them *Sonnets Translated from the Bosnian.* But Robert's nickname for his wife led to the final choice: Mrs. Browning's admiration for one of the classic poets of Portugal and an early love poem of hers based on this poet's life had resulted in Robert calling Elizabeth "the little Portugee."

Sonnet 1

I thought once how Theocritus° had sung
Of the sweet years, the dear and wished-for years,
Who each one in a gracious hand appears
To bear a gift for mortals, old or young:
And, as I mused it in his antique tongue,   5
I saw, in gradual vision through my tears,
The sweet, sad years, the melancholy years,
Those of my own life, who by turns had flung
A shadow across me. Straightway I was 'ware,
So weeping, how a mystic Shape did move   10
Behind me, and drew me backward by the hair,
And a voice said in mastery, while I strove, . . .
"Guess now who holds thee?"—"Death," I said. But, there,
The silver answer rang . . . "Not Death, but Love."

1. **Theocritus:** Greek pastoral poet of the third century, B.C.

Sonnet 14

If thou must love me, let it be for nought
Except for love's sake only. Do not say,
"I love her for her smile—her look—her way
Of speaking gently—for a trick of thought
That falls in well with mine, and certes° brought   5
A sense of pleasant ease on such a day"—
For these things in themselves, Belovèd, may
Be changed, or change for thee—and love, so wrought.
May be unwrought so. Neither love me for
Thine own dear pity's wiping my cheeks dry—   10
A creature might forget to weep, who bore
Thy comfort long, and lose thy love thereby!
But love me for love's sake, that evermore
Thou may'st love on, through love's eternity.

5. **certes:** certainly.

Sonnet 43

How do I love thee? Let me count the ways.
I love thee to the depth and breadth and height
My soul can reach, when feeling out of sight
For the ends of Being and ideal Grace.
I love thee to the level of every day's   5
Most quiet need, by sun and candlelight.

I love thee freely, as men strive for Right;
I love thee purely, as they turn from Praise.
I love thee with the passion put to use
In my old griefs, and with my childhood's faith.   10
I love thee with a love I seemed to lose
With my lost saints—I love thee with the breath,
Smiles, tears, of all my life!—and, if God choose,
I shall but love thee better after death.

FOR STUDY AND DISCUSSION

1. What evidence can you find in these three sonnets to indicate that they were written by a woman or that the speaker had been ill or an invalid? Does the presence or lack of such evidence detract from the effectiveness of the poetry? Give reasons for your opinion.

2. Chart the rhyme scheme of the three sonnets. Is it the pattern of the Petrarchan or of the Shakespearean sonnet? Now examine the movement of thought through the sonnets. Is their structure Petrarchan or Shakespearean? Or neither? Does the difference between the rhyme scheme and the expected structure affect your response to the poems?

3. Note the effective use of repetition in each sonnet—in Sonnet 1, the repeated words in lines 2 and 7, in Sonnet 14, the repeated words in lines 1 and 2, in lines 8 and 9, in lines 12–14; in Sonnet 43, the repetition of "I love thee." How do these repetitions contribute to the emotional force of the poems?

4. Compare Mrs. Browning's concept of love with that revealed in the sonnets of Shakespeare (pages 106–08), and in the Marlowe and Raleigh poems (page 92). These different attitudes may reflect more than the individual feelings of the poets. Can you suggest and analyze other elements, such as the social and cultural forces of the periods, which may reinforce the different concepts of love?

EMOTION IN POETRY

Wordsworth wrote: "Poetry is the spontaneous overflow of powerful feelings." For these feelings to arouse a proper response in the reader, their expression must be appropriate to the situation that evoked them in the poet. If the intensity of the emotion expressed is excessive, the poem will be flawed by sentimentality, and the poet will be considered effusive, or "gushing." If the emotion is inappropriately understated, the poem may not communicate enough to the reader. A balance between sentiment and reserve, between overstatement and understatement, is crucial to a work of quality.

The sonnets of Elizabeth Barrett Browning are considered by many to be the most genuine and the most skilled expressions of love in English literature. These critics point to the emotional unity of her poems, to her sensitivity in choosing the exact words and details necessary to convey the complexity of her feelings. Others think that the feelings in these sonnets are overexpressed, that her poems attempt to communicate more emotion than is appropriate to the means, or that the poet has not set forth sufficient concrete details to support her feelings. Form your own opinion on these questions with special attention to Sonnet 43.

Your consideration may be helped by a comparison with Sonnet 73 (page 107) by Shakespeare, who is also addressing a loved one. How does the emotion conveyed in this sonnet differ from that in Mrs. Browning's? Compare the effectiveness of the metaphors in establishing the speakers' situations and in reinforcing the dominant feelings of the poems. Compare the last two lines of each sonnet. Are the thoughts and feelings conveyed in these concluding lines appropriate to the rest of each poem? Do you think that the emotion expressed in either of these poems is excessive, understated, or well balanced? Explain.

MATTHEW ARNOLD
(1822–1888)

In his prose Matthew Arnold inveighed long and hard against Victorian materialism. He urged his generation to a reverence for culture, to a "pursuit of our total perfection by means of getting to know . . . the best that has been thought and said in the world." His name is inevitably associated with the intellectual ideal of "sweetness and light." He opposed the period's "Philistinism," one of his catchwords, which referred to vulgar concern for material things. But the mechanical age had its revenge in an ironic way: Arnold died of a heart attack suffered while chasing a trolley car in Liverpool.

A poet and critic, Arnold was the son of a famous father, Dr. Thomas Arnold, historian and rigorous headmaster of Rugby School, one of the most notable boys' schools in Victorian England. Following family traditions, Matthew attended Rugby and Oxford. He later began his teaching career at Rugby and, through his father, developed an interest in education. The meaning and content of education were a common concern of many Victorians, but Arnold was the only major writer who became a professional educator. For thirty-five years he led a busy life as government inspector of schools and was especially well known in his day for his reports on European school systems, which he studied in his work as foreign assistant commissioner on education.

Despite the stress of his official duties, Arnold found time to begin his literary career as a poet. He published his first volume in 1849, and three more volumes followed in the next six years. Then there was a long silence. The next and last book of verse to appear was *New Poems* (1867), which included "Dover Beach" (see page 620).

Much of Arnold's poetry is tinged with sadness and pessimism, traceable often to the change (for the worse, he thought) in the cultural climate brought on by the scientific revolution. His attitude reflects the confusion caused by religious doubt and by the criticism of all the certainties upon which men had built their faith. In an early poem he characterized himself well as "Wandering between two worlds, one dead,/ The other powerless to be born."

Perhaps because of the cool reception of his poetry, or, more likely, because of the exhaustion of his lyric gift, Arnold turned in the early 1860's to the writing of prose. His first works in this mode were essays of literary criticism, and he did much to turn English thinking in this area away from personal reactions and extraneous concerns to "disinterestedness" and "high seriousness" as the first requirements for the consideration of great literature.

Arnold's later writings dealt almost exclusively with social, cultural, and theological criticism. He attacked the complacency of the times, urged universal attention to higher values, and rejected social schemes which concentrated merely on the improvement of material welfare.

In Arnold's verse there is always a clear and simple beauty, reminiscent of the Greek poetry in which he was widely read. The two lyrics which follow reflect the themes most often found in his poetry: his pessimism and desire for assurance, his feeling of isolation from others, and his despair over a world that had lost its foundation of faith.

Self-Dependence

Weary of myself, and sick of asking
What I am, and what I ought to be,
At this vessel's prow I stand, which bears me
Forwards, forwards, o'er the starlit sea.

And a look of passionate desire   5
O'er the sea and to the stars I send:
"Ye who from my childhood up have calmed me,
Calm me, ah, compose me to the end!

"Ah, once more," I cried, "ye stars, ye waters,
On my heart your mighty charm renew;   10
Still, still let me, as I gaze upon you,
Feel my soul becoming vast like you!"

From the intense, clear, star-sown vault of heaven,
Over the lit sea's unquiet way,
In the rustling night air came the answer: 15
"Wouldst thou *be* as these are? *Live* as they.

"Unaffrighted by the silence round them,
Undistracted by the sights they see,
These demand not that the things without° them
Yield them love, amusement, sympathy.   20

"And with joy the stars perform their shining,
And the sea its long moon-silvered roll;
For self-poised they live, nor pine with noting
All the fever of some differing soul.

19. **without:** outside.

"Bounded by themselves, and unregardful   25
In what state God's other works may be,
In their own tasks all their powers pouring,
These attain the mighty life you see."

O air-born voice! long since, severely clear,
A cry like thine in mine own heart I hear: 30
"Resolve to be thyself; and know that he,
Who finds himself, loses his misery!"

Dover Beach

The sea is calm tonight.
The tide is full, the moon lies fair
Upon the Straits°—on the French coast, the light
Gleams, and is gone; the cliffs of England stand,
Glimmering and vast, out in the tranquil bay.   5
Come to the window, sweet is the night air!
Only, from the long line of spray
Where the sea meets the moon-blanched sand,
Listen! you hear the grating roar
Of pebbles which the waves suck back, and fling,   10
At their return, up the high strand,
Begin, and cease, and then again begin,
With tremulous cadence slow, and bring
The eternal note of sadness in.

Sophocles° long ago   15
Heard it on the Aegean,° and it brought
Into his mind the turbid ebb and flow
Of human misery; we
Find also in the sound a thought,
Hearing it by this distant northern sea.   20

The Sea of Faith
Was once, too, at the full, and round earth's shore
Lay like the folds of a bright girdle furled;
But now I only hear
Its melancholy, long, withdrawing roar,
Retreating to the breath   25
Of the night wind down the vast edges drear
And naked shingles° of the world.

3. **Straits:** the Strait of Dover, the narrow body of water lying between England and the
Continent.   15. **Sophocles** (sof'ə·klēz): an Athenian writer (496?—406 B.C.), one of the three
greatest tragedians in the golden age of Greek drama.   16. **Aegean** (i·jē'ən): an arm of the
Mediterranean Sea, between Greece and Asia Minor.   28. **shingles:** shores of large coarse
gravel, common in England.

Ah, love, let us be true
To one another! for the world, which seems   30
To lie before us like a land of dreams,
So various, so beautiful, so new,
Hath really neither joy, nor love, nor light,
Nor certitude, nor peace, nor help for pain;
And we are here as on a darkling plain   35
Swept with confused alarms of struggle and flight,
Where ignorant armies clash by night.

FOR STUDY AND DISCUSSION

SELF–DEPENDENCE

1. Does the speaker in this poem give sufficient details of the cause of his unhappiness? If not, are you convinced that his despondency is warranted?

2. What effect do the repetitions of words in lines 4 and 11 have on the movement of the poem? Do you think these repetitions harmonize with the speaker's state of mind? Give reasons for your opinion.

3. Does the poem offer any clues to the source of the "air-born voice"? What are these clues? Does the vagueness of the source affect the speaker's response to the message? Does it affect your own response? Explain your answer.

4. Do you think the last two lines provide an adequate answer to the personal problem posed in the first two lines of the poem? Define the problem and the answer in your own words.

DOVER BEACH

1. How does the rhythm created here by irregular meter and lines of varying length contribute to the dominant tone of the poem? Can you find other poetic devices that reinforce the tone?

2. Arnold makes effective transitions between stanzas 1 and 2 and between stanzas 2 and 3. Explain these transitions and trace the developments of the new thoughts introduced in the second and third stanzas.

3. Has the poet supported his image of the "sea of faith" by reference to the action of the real ocean? Are there other aspects of the activity of the sea that the poet has not mentioned? Why do you think he has not included them?

4. In "Self-Dependence" and "Dover Beach" Arnold has attempted to communicate the Victorian sense of uneasiness, an element of the time as typical as its often-noted complacency. Do you think the poet was successful in this attempt? Are the poems entirely pessimistic? Do you find any notes of hope in them? Do you find Arnold's consolation adequate to contemporary problems? Explain.

FOR COMPOSITION

1. In 1884, Ralph Waldo Emerson in an essay entitled "Self-Reliance" wrote: "What I must do is all that concerns me, not what the people think . . . Nothing can bring you peace but yourself." Referring to specific lines in "Self-Dependence," write a paragraph comparing Emerson's thoughts to those expressed by Arnold. What, according to these two writers, is the basis for achieving self-dependence or self-reliance?

2. For John Donne "No man is an island, entire of itself; every man is a piece of the continent, a part of the main." For Arnold everyone is "enisled" in the sea of life, one's shore separated from every other shore by "the unplumbed, salt, estranging sea."

Here are two views of our relation to other people: one from the beginning of the seventeenth century, the other dating from the Victorian era. In a brief composition, discuss how each of these statements reveals its author to be a spokesman for his own time.

DANTE GABRIEL ROSSETTI

(1828–1882)

Dante Gabriel Rossetti, who thought of himself more as a painter than a poet, achieved greatness as both a painter and a poet. In these arts his desire was to "encourage the simplicity of nature in all things." In the visual arts he furthered this aim not only in his own paintings and frescoes: at the age of twenty he was the prime mover in the founding of the Pre-Raphaelite Brotherhood, a group of early Victorian artists opposed to the contemporary conventions in art and literature. The Brotherhood sought to return to the clarity of form and detail which they believed had prevailed in the work of Italian artists before the sophisticated influence of Raphael. The improvement of morals and the elevation of emotions was also a professed goal of the Pre-Raphaelites. The Brotherhood had little popular success until John Ruskin, the great Victorian art critic, gave them his full support. Although the group later formally disbanded, individual members went on to flourish. Rossetti was one of those whose reputation was assured.

The poet–painter was the son of an Anglo-Italian mother and an Italian father, who was exiled because of his struggle to free Italy from Austrian rule. The three other children in the family were also writers; one of the sisters, Christina, was a highly acclaimed poet. Dante Gabriel published some of his early work in the Pre-Raphaelite magazine, *The Germ,* writing under the influence of Robert Browning and Edgar Allan Poe. In 1850 Rossetti met Elizabeth Siddal, a salesgirl in a hat shop who became the favorite model of the Brotherhood. Rossetti and Elizabeth entered into a stormy engagement which lasted some nine years. They finally married, but Elizabeth's tuberculosis and her distress at her husband's changeable and neurotic nature brought the union to a quick end. She died after two years, apparently a suicide. Rossetti was heartbroken and, in a great romantic gesture, buried his unpublished manuscripts with her. He later had second thoughts about his work, and had his friends disinter the poems. When they were published they came under violent attack, in a magazine article titled "The Fleshly School of Poetry." The combination of Elizabeth's tragic death and public abuse of his work affected Rossetti's mind. He suffered hallucinations and thought himself the victim of persecution. He became addicted to pain-relieving drugs, but was lucid enough at times to continue his work. His last volume of poetry was published in the year before his death.

This last volume, *Ballads and Sonnets,* contained an expanded version of Rossetti's most important poetic work, "The House of Life." Although often called a sonnet sequence, it is not technically one: no connected story is told. Much of it is inspired by Rossetti's relationship with Elizabeth Siddal and reflects the desperation and mysticism of that experience. "Silent Noon," which follows below, is from this series and is an appropriate example of Rossetti's idea of the poetic form he used: "A sonnet is a moment's monument—/ Memorial from the Soul's eternity/ To one dead deathless hour."

Silent Noon

Your hands lie open in the long fresh grass,
The finger points look through like rosy blooms;
Your eyes smile peace. The pasture gleams and glooms
'Neath billowing skies that scatter and amass.
All round our nest, far as the eye can pass,   5
Are golden kingcup fields with silver edge
Where the cow parsley skirts the hawthorn hedge.
'Tis visible silence, still as the hourglass.
Deep in the sun-searched growths the dragonfly
Hangs like a blue thread loosened from the sky—   10
So this winged hour is dropped to us from above.
Oh! clasp we to our hearts, for deathless dower,
This close-companioned inarticulate hour
When twofold silence was the song of love.

Spring

Soft-littered is the new year's lambing fold,
And in the hollowed haystack at its side
The shepherd lies o' nights now, wakeful-eyed
At the ewes' travailing call through the dark cold.
The young rooks cheep 'mid the thick caw o' the old: 5
And near unpeopled streamsides, on the ground,
By her spring-cry the moor hen's nest is found,
Where the drained floodlands flaunt their marigold,
Chill are the gusts to which the pastures cower,
And chill the current where the young reeds stand   10
As green and close as the young wheat on land:
Yet here the cuckoo and the cuckoo flower
Plight to the heart Spring's perfect imminent hour
Whose breath shall soothe you like your dear one's hand.

The Woodspurge

The wind flapped loose, the wind was still,
Shaken out dead from tree and hill;
I had walked on at the wind's will—
I sat now, for the wind was still.

Between my knees my forehead was—   5
My lips, drawn in, said not Alas!
My hair was over in the grass,
My naked ears heard the day pass.

My eyes, wide open, had the run
Of some ten weeds to fix upon;   10
Among those few, out of the sun,
The woodspurge flowered, three cups in one.

From perfect grief there need not be
Wisdom or even memory:
One thing then learned remains to me,   15
The woodspurge has a cup of three.

FOR STUDY AND DISCUSSION

1. In "Silent Noon" the primary goal of the poet is to convey a sense of deep silence. Do you think that the clarity of detail and the specifically named objects contribute to the mood of the poem? Give reasons for your opinion.

2. Nearly every line of "Spring" uses the same poetic device. What is this device and how does it contribute to the musical quality of the poem? Do you find the use of this device excessive in this poem? Give reasons for your answer.

3. Has spring actually come in this poem, or does the title refer to what is about to happen? Which word in line 13 supports your answer?

4. In "The Woodspurge," although the speaker does not reveal his grief until the last stanza, earlier in the poem he does offer details that suggest his state of mind. What clues in stanzas 1 and 2 hint at his state of mind?

5. Has the speaker learned anything significant from his grief? What would you say is the theme of the poem?

GERARD MANLEY HOPKINS
(1844–1889)

It would be easy to claim that Hopkins was a typical Victorian writer. He dabbled in poetry as a child and studied at the Oxford college where Matthew Arnold was professor of poetry. He fell under the influence of the Tractarian movement (see page 576), and when he decided to convert to Roman Catholicism, it was Cardinal Newman who received him into that faith. But despite these links to the period's great names, Hopkins the poet was essentially unknown to his time. It was not until nearly thirty years after his death that his poems were published. Ironically, this delayed exposure may have been the best thing that could have happened. The few who knew his poems during his lifetime were put off by them. They objected to their oddity, their obscurity, their experimentalism. But published as they were in the midst of the poetic ferment of the twentieth century, they came as a revelation. Hopkins was soon claimed as one of the great "ancestors" of modern poetry, and his influence is still evident in today's verse. In 1931 a critic wrote of Hopkins: "He has left us only ninety poems—but so essential that they will color and convert the development of English poetry for many decades to come."

Two years after his conversion, Hopkins joined the Jesuit order and burned all his early poems. It was not until seven years later that he resumed writing. He eventually became a priest and was sent to do missionary work in the slums of Liverpool. Sensitive by nature and shocked by the vicious conditions of the slums, he soon retreated to a church in Oxford and then to a professorship of Greek in Dublin. He died in that city of typhoid fever, the great killer of the nineteenth-century poor.

The intensity of Hopkins's inner life is amply reflected in his poetry. A sense of great pressure is always communicated: the reader experiences a rush of images and alliterations, words necessary to syntax are discarded if they impede the surge of rhythm and language, thoughts are compressed and then stretched to the breaking point. But the seeming haste of the poetry is under strict control, and it must be read slowly and carefully to understand its resonance. Through it all Hopkins aims at one important goal: to display the individual nature of every creature and thing—the *inscape,* as Hopkins called it. In glorifying the inscape in everything, the poet is exalting God. Despite the idiosyncrasies of his technique, Hopkins's themes are universal and eternal.

Pied Beauty

Glory be to God for dappled things—
  For skies of couple-color as a brinded cow;
    For rose-moles all in stipple upon trout that swim;
Fresh-firecoal chestnut-falls; finches' wings;
    Landscape plotted and pieced—fold, fallow, and plow;   5
    And all trades, their gear and tackle and trim.

All things counter, original, spare, strange;
    Whatever is fickle, freckled (who knows how?)
    With swift, slow; sweet, sour; adazzle, dim;
He fathers-forth whose beauty is past change: 10
        Praise him.

God's Grandeur

The world is charged with the grandeur of God.
  It will flame out, like shining from shook foil;°
  It gathers to a greatness, like the ooze of oil
Crushed. Why do men then now not reck his rod?°
Generations have trod, have trod, have trod;   5
  And all is seared with trade; bleared, smeared with toil;
  And wears man's smudge and shares man's smell: the soil
Is bare now, nor can foot feel, being shod.

And for all this, nature is never spent;
  There lives the dearest freshness deep down things;   10
And though the last lights off the black West went
  Oh, morning, at the brown brink eastward, springs—
Because the Holy Ghost over the bent
  World broods with warm breast and with ah! bright wings.

2. **foil:** tinfoil, or tinsel. 4. **reck his rod:** heed God's authority.

The Cuckoo

Repeat that, repeat,
Cuckoo, bird, and open ear wells, heart-springs, delightfully sweet,
With a ballad, with a ballad, a rebound
Off trundled timber and scoops of the hillside ground, hollow hollow hollow
    ground:
The whole landscape flushes on a sudden at a sound.　　　　　　　　　5

Thou Art Indeed Just, Lord

Thou art indeed just, Lord, if I contend
With thee; but, sir, so what I plead is just.
Why do sinners' ways prosper? and why must
Disappointment all I endeavor end?
Wert thou my enemy, O thou my friend,　　　　　　　　　　5
How wouldst thou worse, I wonder, than thou dost
Defeat, thwart me? Oh, the sots and thralls of lust
Do in spare hours more thrive than I that spend,
Sir, life upon thy cause. See, banks and brakes°
Now, leavèd how thick! lacèd they are again　　　　　　　　10
With fretty chervil, look, and fresh wind shakes
Them; birds build—but not I build; no, but strain,
Time's eunuch, and not breed one work that wakes.
Mine, O thou lord of life, send my roots rain.

9. **brakes:** clumps of ferns.

FOR STUDY AND DISCUSSION

PIED BEAUTY

1. The image in the first part of line 4 is conveyed in very compressed language. Can you rearrange the words in this image and supply the additional words necessary to clarify the thought? (It may help you to know that a chestnut has a green husk which cracks open to show a reddish nut.) Find other instances of compressed syntax in this poem.

2. The first line and the last two lines announce the source of all the "pied beauty" which inspires Hopkins. How is God's beauty different from that of the natural world? In which lines are human works introduced? How does the appearance of these works reinforce what Hopkins finds in nature?

3. In the first stanza Hopkins concentrates on the multicolored variation of things. What new element of variation is mentioned in line 8? How is the idea implied in the word *counter* (line 7) developed in the next two lines? Explain the contrast between "past change" and the "fickle" quality of nature.

GOD'S GRANDEUR

1. The word *charged* is developed in the two images in lines 2 and 3. Explain how this word is used in two different senses in these images. Use an unabridged dictionary to check the appropriate meanings of *charge*.

2. Lines 5–8, showing the contamination of the world, are a strong contrast to the opening lines. What is the source of this con-

tamination? Is the contamination purely physical, or are emotions and attitudes involved too? Account in your answer for the statement "nor can foot feel, being shod."

3. The sestet of this sonnet returns to the ideas put forth in the opening lines of the octave. How does the word *spent* relate to the images of lines 2 and 3? Which line in the sestet shows that "man's smudge" has affected only the surface of the world? Look again at the first part of line 9. Do you interpret it to mean "because of all this" or "despite all this"? Explain your answer.

4. Where in the sestet does Hopkins suggest the "bright wings" of the Holy Ghost? How has Hopkins used nature in these lines to establish the image of the wings? Is the natural phenomenon described in lines 11 and 12 possible?

THE CUCKOO

1. "The Cuckoo," like most of Hopkins's poems, appeals more strongly to the ear than the eye. In which lines does the use of alliteration contribute to the musical quality of the poem?

2. The sound of the poem clearly reflects the song of the cuckoo. What poetic device does Hopkins use to mimic the cuckoo's song? In which lines is this most apparent?

3. Do you think Hopkins was a casual or a close observer of nature? What effect does he say the bird's singing has on the landscape? What does "rebound" mean in line 3? What is meant by "trundled" in line 4?

THOU ART INDEED JUST, LORD

1. What is the cause of the speaker's complaint? How does the speaker's attitude toward other people and toward nature reinforce his complaint? What is his relationship with God?

2. Read the poem aloud and then contrast the rhythms and syntax of lines 5–8 with those of lines 9–11. How do these contrasts contribute to the mood of the poem?

3. How does the last image of the poem ("send my roots rain") contrast with the view of nature given in lines 9–12? Where else does figurative language support the idea of barrenness?

4. Review the devices characteristic of Anglo-Saxon poetry as described on page 11. Do you find any similarities between these devices and those employed by Hopkins?

Has Hopkins changed or adapted any of the Anglo-Saxon techniques for his own purposes? Explain, giving examples from the three Hopkins poems.

5. Besides adopting certain Anglo-Saxon techniques, Hopkins made several innovations of his own. Perhaps it may be said that each innovation alone is not especially significant, but that in combination the reader feels a powerful new force in Hopkins's poetry. Among his personal devices are the use of familiar words in original and unusual contexts, the revival of words no longer commonly used, startling combinations of language, and the elimination of prepositions, conjunctions, and relative pronouns. Where in the four poems you have just read do you encounter these techniques? Cite an example of each one and explain how it contributes to the total effect of the poem.

SPRUNG RHYTHM

Hopkins's fascination with rhythm led to his popularization of a metrical system resembling natural speech and called *sprung rhythm*. As Hopkins himself explained his technique, "It consists in scanning by accents alone or stresses alone, so that a foot may be one strong syllable or it may be many light and one strong." Conventional poetic rhythm consists of a number of metrical feet each having a fixed number of stressed and unstressed syllables. Sprung rhythm differs from conventional rhythm in that it is not concerned with the number of syllables in a foot. The flexibility of sprung rhythm allows any kind of foot to follow any other. However, Hopkins most frequently used a foot consisting of a single stressed syllable or dactyls and trochees; that is, a stressed syllable followed by one or two unstressed syllables: And for all/ this/ na ture is/ nev er/ spent. It is not unusual in one of Hopkins's poems to find the startling combination of a number of stressed syllables followed by a succession of unstressed syllables.

Scan the first stanza of the poem "Pied Beauty," placing the stresses where you think they should fall. Are there an equal number of stresses in each line? What else besides verse stress contributes to the rhythm of this poem? Is the rhythm in keeping with the main thought and feeling of the poem? Explain.

THOMAS HARDY

(1840–1928)

The pessimistic element of Victorian sensibility reached its fullest voice in the work of Thomas Hardy. Carlyle had charged the social and economic system with do-nothingism, Newman had urged a return to traditional religion, and Arnold had nagged at rampant materialism. Hardy's complaint was simpler and yet transcendent. He lamented the workings of the universe.

Hardy's was a timeless pessimism, which did not stem directly from the difficulties of the age. He agreed with Sophocles that "not to have been born is best," and he had harsh words for contemporary Pollyannas: "I believe, indeed, that a good deal of the robustious, swaggering optimism of recent literature is at bottom cowardly and insincere." To be sure, he believed that things would improve, and he worked in small ways to help them along. But he was pitiless in declaring that the world was ill made. God and Nature were equally indifferent to the strivings and values of people. Fate, the great law of life, was inevitably and inexorably incompatible with human desires for happiness, and the individual had little hope in fulfilling plan or purpose.

Surprisingly, this "last of the great Victorians" lived a long and seemingly happy life. He was trained to be a church architect, but his heart was always in his writing. Most of his early work was poetry, but he had no success in selling his verse. Gradually he turned to the writing of fiction. He produced novels at a steady rate, almost one a year, and each was a solid improvement over the last. Among his distinguished works are *The Return of the Native, The Mayor of Casterbridge, Far from the Madding Crowd, Tess of the d'Urbervilles,* and *Jude the Obscure.* This work continued until 1895, when he returned to his first love, poetry, disregarding the achievement of his fiction.

From 1904 to 1908 Hardy published various parts of a long dramatic poem, *The Dynasts.* Although it was written apparently to show England's part in the Napoleonic wars, this vast epic is actually a complex study of human destiny, a reflection of the thinking of the modern world, just as Milton's *Paradise Lost* reflects the thinking of the seventeenth century. With the publication of this work, Hardy's reputation as a poet was at once established. For the rest of his life he worked only in verse, the dark themes of his fiction prevailing in his poetry as well. His poems are compressed, intellectual, individualistic, and careless of pictorial beauty or music. The voice of twentieth-century poetry began to be heard.

In this last period Hardy's reputation as a man of letters was tremendous, and his death was an occasion for international mourning. His ashes were buried in

Westminster Abbey, but in accordance with his wishes his heart was removed and buried in his parish churchyard in Dorsetshire. Significantly, on the day of his death he asked his wife to read to him one of the darkest quatrains of *The Rubaiyat:*

"Oh Thou, who Man of Baser Earth didst make,
　And ev'n with Paradise devise the Snake,
　　For all the Sin wherewith the Face of Man
　Is blackened—Man's forgiveness give—and take!"

That Hardy was equally concerned in his short stories as in his novels and poems with the part that chance, or fate, plays in people's lives is evident in "The Three Strangers," which follows. The setting of this story is the remote and windswept downs of "Wessex," a name Hardy used for the six southwest counties of England, including his native Dorset. The sense of specific place is always strong in Hardy's fiction and poetry. Here his rich use of local color acquaints us with a rural celebration—with the mead-drinking, the singing and dancing, the Wessex dialect, and the homely philosophy of the people.

The Three Strangers

AMONG THE FEW features of agricultural England which retain an appearance but little modified by the lapse of centuries may be reckoned the high, grassy and furzy downs, coombs,[1] or ewe-leases, as they are indifferently called, that fill a large area of certain counties in the south and southwest. If any mark of human occupation is met with hereon, it usually takes the form of the solitary cottage of some shepherd.

Fifty years ago such a lonely cottage stood on such a down, and may possibly be standing there now. In spite of its loneliness, however, the spot, by actual measurement, was not more than five miles from a county town. Yet that affected it little. Five miles of irregular up-

land, during the long inimical seasons, with their sleets, snows, rains, and mists, afford withdrawing space enough to isolate a Timon[2] or a Nebuchadnezzar;[3] much less, in fair weather, to please that less repellent tribe, the poets, philosophers, artists, and others who "conceive and meditate of pleasant things."

Some old earthen camp or barrow,[4] some clump of trees, at least some starved fragment of ancient hedge is usually taken advantage of in the erection of these forlorn dwellings. But, in the present case, such a kind of shelter has been disregarded. Higher Crowstairs, as the house was called, stood quite detached and undefended. The only reason for its precise situation seemed to be the crossing of two footpaths at right angles hard by, which may have crossed there and thus for a good five hundred years. Hence the house was exposed to the elements on all sides. But, though the wind

---

[1] **coombs** (kōōms): open uplands.

[2] **Timon** (tī'mən): a Greek of the fifth century who hated people and preferred to live in a cave.

[3] **Nebuchadnezzar** (neb'yōō·kəd·nez'ər): a Babylonian king who went to live in the fields when he became insane.

[4] **barrow**: a hill or mound, often an ancient burial ground.

up here blew unmistakably when it did blow, and the rain hit hard whenever it fell, the various weathers of the winter season were not quite so formidable on the coomb as they were imagined to be by dwellers on low ground. The raw rimes [1] were not so pernicious as in the hollows, and the frosts were scarcely so severe. When the shepherd and his family who tenanted the house were pitied for their sufferings from the exposure, they said that upon the whole they were less inconvenienced by "wuzzes and flames" (hoarses and phlegms) than when they had lived by the stream of a snug neighboring valley.

The night of March 28, 182–, was precisely one of the nights that were wont to call forth these expressions of commiseration. The level rainstorm smote walls, slopes, and hedges like the clothyard shafts of Senlac [2] and Crécy. [3] Such sheep and outdoor animals as had no shelter stood with their buttocks to the winds; while the tails of little birds trying to roost on some scraggy thorn were blown inside-out like umbrellas. The gable-end of the cottage was stained with wet, and the eavesdroppings flapped against the wall. Yet never was commiseration for the shepherd more misplaced. For that cheerful rustic was entertaining a large party in glorification of the christening of his second girl.

The guests had arrived before the rain began to fall, and they were all now assembled in the chief or living room of the dwelling. A glance into the apartment at eight o'clock on this eventful evening would have resulted in the opinion that it was as cozy and comfortable a nook as could be wished for in boisterous weather. The calling of its inhabitant was proclaimed by a number of highly polished sheep crooks without stems that were hung ornamentally over the fireplace, the curl of each shining crook varying from the antiquated type engraved in the patriarchal pictures of old family Bibles to the most approved fashion of the last local sheep fair. The room was lighted by half a dozen candles having wicks only a trifle smaller than the grease which enveloped them, in candlesticks that were never used but at high-days, holy-days, and family feasts. The lights were scattered about the room, two of them standing on the chimney piece. This position of candles was in itself significant. Candles on the chimney piece always meant a party.

On the hearth, in front of a backbrand to give substance, blazed a fire of thorns, that crackled "like the laughter of the fool."

Nineteen persons were gathered here. Of these, five women, wearing gowns of various bright hues, sat in chairs along the wall; girls shy and not shy filled the window-bench; four men, including Charley Jake, the hedge carpenter, Elijah New, the parish clerk, and John Pitcher, a neighboring dairyman, the shepherd's father-in-law, lolled in the settle; a young man and maid, who were blushing over tentative *pour-parlers* [4] on a life companionship, sat beneath the corner cupboard; and an elderly engaged man of fifty or upward moved restlessly about from spots where his betrothed was not to the spot where she was. Enjoyment was pretty general, and so much the more prevailed in being unhampered by conventional restrictions. Absolute confidence in each other's good opinion begat perfect ease, while the finishing stroke of manner, amounting to a truly princely serenity, was lent to the majority by the absence of any expression or trait denoting that they wished to get on in the world, enlarge their minds, or do any

---

[1] **rimes** (rīms): white frost.

[2] **Senlac:** hill near Hastings in southeastern England where the Normans defeated the Saxons in 1066.

[3] **Crécy** (krā·sē'): town in northern France where English archers defeated the French in 1346 during the Hundred Years War between France and England. The *clothyard shafts* referred to are the yard-long arrows of the English archers.

[4] *pour-parlers* (pōōr'pàr'lāz'): informal discussions (French).

eclipsing thing whatever—which nowadays so generally nips the bloom and bonhomie [1] of all except the two extremes of the social scale.

Shepherd Fennel had married well, his wife being a dairyman's daughter from a vale at a distance, who brought fifty guineas in her pocket—and kept them there, till they should be required for ministering to the needs of a coming family. This frugal woman had been somewhat exercised as to the character that should be given to the gathering. A sit-still party had its advantages; but an undisturbed position of ease in chairs and settles was apt to lead on the men to such an unconscious deal of toping [2] that they would sometimes fairly drink the house dry. A dancing party was the alternative; but this, while avoiding the foregoing objection on the score of good drink, had a counterbalancing disadvantage in the matter of good victuals, the ravenous appetites engendered by the exercise causing immense havoc in the buttery. Shepherdess Fennell fell back upon the intermediate plan of mingling short dances with short periods of talk and singing, so as to hinder any ungovernable rage in either. But this scheme was entirely confined to her own gentle mind: the shepherd himself was in the mood to exhibit the most reckless phases of hospitality.

The fiddler was a boy of those parts, about twelve years of age, who had a wonderful dexterity in jigs and reels, though his fingers were so small and short as to necessitate a constant shifting for the high notes, from which he scrambled back to the first position with sounds not of unmixed purity of tone. At seven the shrill tweedle-dee of this youngster had begun, accompanied by a booming ground-bass from Elijah New, the parish clerk, who had thoughtfully brought with him his favorite musical instrument, the serpent. [3] Dancing was instantaneous,

Mrs. Fennel privately enjoining the players on no account to let the dance exceed the length of a quarter of an hour.

But Elijah and the boy, in the excitement of their position, quite forgot the injunction. Moreover, Oliver Giles, a man of seventeen, one of the dancers, who was enamored of his partner, a fair girl of thirty-three rolling years, had recklessly handed a new crown-piece to the musicians, as a bribe to keep going as long as they had muscle and wind. Mrs. Fennel, seeing the steam begin to generate on the countenances of her guests, crossed over and touched the fiddler's elbow and put her hand on the serpent's mouth. But they took no notice, and fearing she might lose her character of genial hostess if she were to interfere too markedly, she retired and sat down helpless. And so the dance whizzed on with cumulative fury, the performers moving in their planetlike courses, direct and retrograde, from apogee to perigee, [4] till the hand of the well-kicked clock at the bottom of the room had traveled over the circumference of an hour.

While these cheerful events were in course of enactment within Fennel's pastoral dwelling, an incident having considerable bearing on the party had occurred in the gloomy night without. Mrs. Fennel's concern about the growing fierceness of the dance corresponded in point of time with the ascent of a human figure to the solitary hill of Higher Crowstairs from the direction of the distant town. This personage strode on through the rain without a pause, following the little-worn path which, further on in its course, skirted the shepherd's cottage.

It was nearly the time of full moon, and on this account, though the sky was lined with a uniform sheet of dripping cloud, ordinary objects out of doors were readily visible. The sad, wan light revealed the lonely pedestrian to be a man of sup-

---

[1] **bonhomie** (bô·nô·mē′): good nature (French).

[2] **toping**: drinking.

[3] **serpent**: an obsolete bass wind instrument of the trumpet type.

[4] **apogee . . . perigee:** the points at which the orbit of a planet is, respectively, farthest from and nearest to the earth.

ple frame; his gait suggested that he had somewhat passed the period of perfect and instinctive agility, though not so far as to be otherwise than rapid of motion when occasion required. At a rough guess, he might have been about forty years of age. He appeared tall, but a recruiting sergeant, or other person accustomed to the judging of men's heights by the eye, would have discerned that this was chiefly owing to his gauntness, and that he was not more than five-feet-eight or nine.

Notwithstanding the regularity of his tread, there was caution in it, as in that of one who mentally feels his way; and despite the fact that it was not a black coat nor a dark garment of any sort that he wore, there was something about him which suggested that he naturally belonged to the black-coated tribes [1] of men. His clothes were of fustian,[2] and his boots hobnailed, yet in his progress he showed not the mud-accustomed bearing of hobnailed and fustianed peasantry.

By the time that he had arrived abreast of the shepherd's premises the rain came down, or rather came along, with yet more determined violence. The outskirts of the little settlement partially broke the force of wind and rain, and this induced him to stand still. The most salient of the shepherd's domestic erections was an empty sty at the forward corner of his hedgeless garden, for in these latitudes the principle of masking the homelier features of your establishment by a conventional frontage was unknown. The traveler's eye was attracted to this small building by the pallid shine of the wet slates that covered it. He turned aside, and, finding it empty, stood under the pent-roof for shelter.

While he stood, the boom of the serpent within the adjacent house, and the lesser strains of the fiddler, reached the spot as an accompaniment to the surging hiss of the flying rain on the sod, its louder beating on the cabbage leaves of the garden, on the eight or ten beehives just discernible by the path, and its dripping from the eaves into a row of buckets and pans that had been placed under the walls of the cottage. For at Higher Crowstairs, as at all such elevated domiciles, the grand difficulty of housekeeping was an insufficiency of water; and a casual rainfall was utilized by turning out, as catchers, every utensil that the house contained. Some queer stories might be told of the contrivances for economy in suds and dishwaters that are absolutely necessitated in upland habitations during the droughts of summer. But at this season there were no such exigencies; a mere acceptance of what the skies bestowed was sufficient for an abundant store.

At last the notes of the serpent ceased and the house was silent. This cessation of activity aroused the solitary pedestrian from the reverie into which he had elapsed, and, emerging from the shed, with an apparently new intention, he walked up the path to the house door. Arrived here, his first act was to kneel down on a large stone beside the row of vessels, and to drink a copious draught from one of them. Having quenched his thirst, he rose and lifted his hand to knock, but paused with his eye upon the panel. Since the dark surface of the wood revealed absolutely nothing, it was evident that he must be mentally looking through the door, as if he wished to measure thereby all the possibilities that a house of this sort might include, and how they might bear upon the question of his entry.

In his indecision he turned and surveyed the scene around. Not a soul was anywhere visible. The garden path stretched downward from his feet, gleaming like the track of a snail; the roof of the little well (mostly dry), the well-cover, the top rail of the garden gate, were varnished with the same dull liquid glaze; while, far away in the vale, a faint whiteness of more than usual ex-

---

[1] **black-coated tribes:** middle class.
[2] **fustian:** a type of coarse cotton.

tent showed that the rivers were high in the meads. Beyond all this winked a few bleared lamplights through the beating drops—lights that denoted the situation of the county town from which he had appeared to come. The absence of all notes of life in that direction seemed to clinch his intentions, and he knocked at the door.

Within, a desultory chat had taken the place of movement and musical sound. The hedge carpenter was suggesting a song to the company, which nobody just then was inclined to undertake, so that the knock afforded a not unwelcome diversion.

"Walk in!" said the shepherd, promptly.

The latch clicked upward, and out of the night our pedestrian appeared upon the door mat. The shepherd arose, snuffed two of the nearest candles, and turned to look at him.

Their light disclosed that the stranger was dark in complexion and not unprepossessing as to feature. His hat, which for a moment he did not remove, hung low over his eyes, without concealing that they were large, open, and determined, moving with a flash rather than a glance round the room. He seemed pleased with his survey, and, baring his shaggy head, said, in a rich, deep voice: "The rain is so heavy, friends, that I ask leave to come in and rest awhile."

"To be sure, Stranger," said the shepherd. "And faith, you've been lucky in choosing your time, for we are having a bit of a fling for a glad cause—though, to be sure, a man could hardly wish that glad cause to happen more than once a year."

"Nor less," spoke up a woman. "For 'tis best to get your family over and done with, as soon as you can, so as to be all the earlier out of the fag o't."

"And what may be this glad cause?" asked the stranger.

"A birth and christening," said the shepherd.

The stranger hoped his host might not be made unhappy either by too many or too few of such episodes and, being invited by a gesture to a pull at the mug, he readily acquiesced. His manner, which, before entering, had been so dubious, was now altogether that of a careless and candid man.

"Late to be traipsing athwart this coomb—hey?" said the engaged man of fifty.

"Late it is, Master, as you say—I'll take a seat in the chimney corner, if you have nothing to urge against it, Ma'am; for I am a little moist on the side that was next the rain."

Mrs. Shepherd Fennel assented, and made room for the self-invited comer, who, having got completely inside the chimney corner, stretched out his legs and arms with the expansiveness of a person quite at home.

"Yes, I am rather cracked in the vamp,"[1] he said freely, seeing that the eyes of the shepherd's wife fell upon his boots, "and I am not well fitted either. I have had some rough times lately, and have been forced to pick up what I can get in the way of wearing, but I must find a suit better fit for working days when I reach home."

"One of hereabouts?" she inquired.

"Not quite that—further up the country."

"I thought so. And so be I; and by your tongue you come from my neighborhood."

"But you would hardly have heard of me," he said quickly. "My time would be long before yours, Ma'am, you see."

This testimony to the youthfulness of his hostess had the effect of stopping her cross-examination.

"There is only one thing more wanted to make me happy," continued the newcomer, "and that is a little baccy, which I am sorry to say I am out of."

"I'll fill your pipe," said the shepherd.

"I must ask you to lend me a pipe likewise."

---

[1] **vamp:** the part of a shoe above the sole and in front of the ankle seam.

"A smoker, and no pipe about 'ee?"

"I have dropped it somewhere on the road."

The shepherd filled and handed him a new clay pipe, saying, as he did so, "Hand me your baccy-box—I'll fill that too, now I am about it."

The man went through the movement of searching his pockets.

"Lost that too?" said his entertainer, with some surprise.

"I am afraid so," said the man with some confusion. "Give it to me in a screw of paper." Lighting his pipe at the candle with a suction that drew the whole flame into the bowl, he resettled himself in the corner and bent his looks upon the faint steam from his damp legs, as if he wished to say no more.

Meanwhile the general body of guests had been taking little notice of this visitor by reason of an absorbing discussion in which they were engaged with the band about a tune for the next dance. The matter being settled, they were about to stand up when an interruption came in the shape of another knock at the door.

At sound of the same the man in the chimney corner took up the poker and began stirring the brands as if doing it thoroughly were the one aim of his existence; and a second time the shepherd said, "Walk in!" In a moment another man stood upon the straw-woven door mat. He too was a stranger.

This individual was one of a type radically different from the first. There was more of the commonplace in his manner, and a certain jovial cosmopolitanism sat upon his features. He was several years older than the first arrival, his hair being slightly frosted, his eyebrows bristly, and his whiskers cut back from his cheeks. His face was rather full and flabby, and yet it was not altogether a face without power. A few grog-blossoms marked the neighborhood of his nose. He flung back his long drab greatcoat, revealing that beneath it he wore a suit of cinder-gray shade throughout, large heavy seals, of some metal or other that would take a polish, dangling from his fob as his only personal ornament. Shaking the water drops from his low-crowned glazed hat, he said, "I must ask for a few minutes' shelter, comrades, or I shall be wetted to my skin before I get to Casterbridge."

"Make yourself at home, Master," said the shepherd, perhaps a trifle less heartily than on the first occasion. Not that Fennel had the least tinge of niggardliness in his composition; but the room was far from large, spare chairs were not numerous, and damp companions were not altogether desirable at close quarters for the women and girls in their bright-colored gowns.

However, the second comer, after taking off his greatcoat, and hanging his hat on a nail in one of the ceiling-beams as if he had been specially invited to put it there, advanced and sat down at the table. This had been pushed so closely into the chimney corner, to give all available room to the dancers, that its inner edge grazed the elbow of the man who had ensconced himself by the fire; and thus the two strangers were brought into close companionship. They nodded to each other by way of breaking the ice of unacquaintance, and the first stranger handed his neighbor the family mug— a huge vessel of brown ware, having its upper edge worn away like a threshold by the rub of whole generations of thirsty lips that had gone the way of all flesh, and bearing the following inscription burnt upon its rotund side in yellow letters:

THERE IS NO FUN
UNTIL i CUM.

The other man, nothing loth,[1] raised the mug to his lips, and drank on, and on, and on—till a curious blueness overspread the countenance of the shepherd's wife, who had regarded with no little surprise the first stranger's free offer to

___
[1] **nothing loth:** not reluctant.

the second of what did not belong to him to dispense.

"I knew it!" said the toper to the shepherd with much satisfaction. "When I walked up your garden before coming in, and saw the hives all of a row, I said to myself, 'Where there's bees there's honey, and where there's honey there's mead.' But mead of such a truly comfortable sort as this I really didn't expect to meet in my older days." He took yet another pull at the mug, till it assumed an ominous elevation.

"Glad you enjoy it!" said the shepherd warmly.

"It is goodish mead," assented Mrs. Fennel, with an absence of enthusiasm which seemed to say that it was possible to buy praise for one's cellar at too heavy a price. "It is trouble enough to make—and really I hardly think we shall make any more. For honey sells well, and we ourselves can make shift with a drop o' small mead and metheglin [1] for common use from the comb-washings."

"Oh, but you'll never have the heart!" reproachfully cried the stranger in cinder-gray, after taking up the mug a third time and setting it down empty. "I love mead, when 'tis old like this, as I love to go to church o' Sundays, or to relieve the needy any day of the week."

"Ha, ha, ha!" said the man in the chimney corner, who, in spite of the taciturnity induced by the pipe of tobacco, could not or would not refrain from this slight testimony to his comrade's humor.

Now the old mead of those days, brewed of the purest first-year or maiden honey, four pounds to the gallon—with its due complement of white of eggs, cinnamon, ginger, cloves, mace, rosemary, yeast, and processes of working, bottling, and cellaring—tasted remarkably strong; but it did not taste so strong as it actually was. Hence presently, the stranger in cinder-gray at the table, moved

by its creeping influence, unbuttoned his waistcoat, threw himself back in his chair, spread his legs, and made his presence felt in various ways.

"Well, well, as I say," he resumed, "I am going to Casterbridge, and to Casterbridge I must go. I should have been almost there by this time; but the rain drove me into your dwelling, and I'm not sorry for it."

"You don't live in Casterbridge?" said the shepherd.

"Not as yet; though I shortly mean to move there."

"Going to set up in trade, perhaps?"

"No, no," said the shepherd's wife. "It is easy to see that the gentleman is rich, and don't want to work at anything."

The cinder-gray stranger paused, as if to consider whether he would accept that definition of himself. He presently rejected it by answering. "Rich is not quite the word for me, Dame. I do work, and I must work. And even if I only get to Casterbridge by midnight I must begin work there at eight tomorrow morning. Yes, het or wet, blow or snow, famine or sword, my day's work tomorrow must be done."

"Poor man! Then, in spite o'seeming, you be worse off than we," replied the shepherd's wife.

"'Tis the nature of my trade, men and maidens. 'Tis the nature of my trade more than my poverty. . . . But really and truly I must up and off, or I shan't get a lodging in the town." However, the speaker did not move, and directly added, "There's time for one more draught of friendship before I go; and I'd perform it at once if the mug were not dry."

"Here's a mug o' small," said Mrs. Fennel. "Small, we call it, though to be sure 'tis only the first wash o' the combs."

"No," said the stranger, disdainfully. "I won't spoil your first kindness by partaking o' your second."

"Certainly not," broke in Fennel. "We don't increase and multiply every day, and I'll fill the mug again." He went away

---

[1] **small mead and metheglin:** weaker forms of mead.

to the dark place under the stairs where the barrel stood. The shepherdess followed him.

"Why should you do this?" she said, reproachfully, as soon as they were alone. "He's emptied it once, though it held enough for ten people; and now he's not contented wi' the small, but must needs call for more o' the strong! And a stranger unbeknown to any of us. For my part, I don't like the look o' the man at all."

"But he's in the house, my honey; and 'tis a wet night, and a christening. Daze it, what's a cup of mead more or less? There'll be plenty more next bee-burning."

"Very well—this time, then," she answered, looking wistfully at the barrel. "But what is the man's calling, and where is he one of, that he should come in and join us like this?"

"I don't know. I'll ask him again."

The catastrophe of having the mug drained dry at one pull by the stranger in cinder-gray was effectually guarded against this time by Mrs. Fennel. She poured out his allowance in a small cup, keeping the large one at a discreet distance from him. When he had tossed off his portion the shepherd renewed his inquiry about the stranger's occupation.

The latter did not immediately reply, and the man in the chimney corner, with sudden demonstrativeness, said, "Anybody may know my trade—I'm a wheelwright."

"A very good trade for these parts," said the shepherd.

"And anybody may know mine—if they've the sense to find it out," said the stranger in cinder-gray.

"You may generally tell what a man is by his claws," observed the hedge carpenter, looking at his own hands. "My fingers be as full of thorns as an old pincushion is of pins."

The hands of the man in the chimney corner instinctively sought the shade, and he gazed into the fire as he resumed his pipe. The man at the table took up the hedge carpenter's remark, and added smartly, "True; but the oddity of my trade is that, instead of setting a mark upon me, it sets a mark upon my customers."

No observation being offered by anybody in elucidation of this enigma, the shepherd's wife once more called for a song. The same obstacles presented themselves as at the former time—one had no voice, another had forgotten the first verse. The stranger at the table, whose soul had now risen to a good working temperature, relieved the difficulty by exclaiming that, to start the company, he would sing himself. Thrusting one thumb into the armhole of his waistcoat, he waved the other hand in the air, and, with an extemporizing gaze at the shining sheep-crooks above the mantelpiece, began:

"O my trade it is the rarest one,
    Simple shepherds all—
My trade is a sight to see;
For my customers I tie, and take them
    up on high,
And waft 'em to a far countree!"

The room was silent when he had finished the verse—with one exception, that of the man in the chimney corner, who at the singer's word, "Chorus!" joined him in a deep bass voice of musical relish:

"And waft 'em to a far countree!"

Oliver Giles, John Pitcher the dairyman, the parish clerk, the engaged man of fifty, the row of young women against the wall, seemed lost in thought not of the gayest kind. The shepherd looked meditatively on the ground, the shepherdess gazed keenly at the singer, and with some suspicion; she was doubting whether this stranger were merely singing an old song from recollection, or was composing one there and then for the occasion. All were as perplexed at the obscure revelation as the guests at Belshazzar's Feast,[1] except

[1] All . . . Belshazzar's Feast: According to the Old Testament, writing appeared on the wall prophesying the destruction of Babylonia.

the man in the chimney corner, who quietly said, "Second verse, stranger," and smoked on.

The singer thoroughly moistened himself from his lips inward, and went on with the next stanza as requested:

"My tools are but common ones,
        Simple shepherds all—
    My tools are no sight to see:
    A little hempen string, and a post
        whereon to swing,
    Are implements enough for me!"

Shepherd Fennel glanced round. There was no longer any doubt that the stranger was answering his question rhythmically. The guests one and all started back with suppressed exclamations. The young woman engaged to the man of fifty fainted halfway, and would have proceeded, but finding him wanting in alacrity for catching her she sat down trembling.

"Oh, he's the——!" whispered the people in the background, mentioning the name of an ominous public officer. "He's come to do it! 'Tis to be at Casterbridge jail tomorrow—the man for sheepstealing—the poor clockmaker we heard of, who used to live away at Shottsford and had no work to do—Timothy Summers, whose family were astarving, and so he went out of Shottsford by the highroad, and took a sheep in open daylight, defying the farmer and the farmer's wife and the farmer's lad, and every man jack among 'em. He" (and they nodded toward the stranger of the deadly trade) "is come from up the country to do it because there's not enough to do in his own county-town, and he's got the place here now our own countryman's dead; he's going to live in the same cottage under the prison wall."

The stranger in cinder-gray took no notice of this whispered string of observations, but again wetted his lips. Seeing that his friend in the chimney corner was the only one who reciprocated his joviality in any way, he held out his cup toward that appreciative comrade, who also held out his own. They clinked together, the

eyes of the rest of the room hanging upon the singer's actions. He parted his lips for the third verse; but at that moment another knock was audible upon the door. This time the knock was faint and hesitating.

The company seemed scared; the shepherd looked with consternation toward the entrance, and it was with some effort that he resisted his alarmed wife's deprecatory glance, and uttered for the third time the welcoming words, "Walk in!"

The door was gently opened, and another man stood upon the mat. He, like those who had preceded him, was a stranger. This time it was a short, small personage, of fair complexion, and dressed in a decent suit of dark clothes.

"Can you tell me the way to——?" he began: when, gazing round the room to observe the nature of the company among whom he had fallen, his eyes lighted on the stranger in cinder-gray. It was just at the instant when the latter, who had thrown his mind into his song with such a will that he scarcely heeded the interruption, silenced all whispers and inquiries by bursting into his third verse:

"Tomorrow is my working day,
        Simple shepherds all—
    Tomorrow is a working day for me:
    For the farmer's sheep is slain, and lad
        who did it ta'en,
        And on his soul may God ha'
            merc-y!"

The stranger in the chimney corner, waving cups with the singer so heartily that his mead splashed over the hearth, repeated in his bass voice as before:

"And on his soul may God ha'
    merc-y!"

All this time the third stranger had been standing in the doorway. Finding now that he did not come forward or go on speaking, the guests particularly regarded him. They noticed to their surprise that he stood before them the picture of abject terror—his knees trembling, his hand shaking so violently that the door latch by which he supported himself rattled audibly: his white lips were parted, and his eyes fixed on the merry officer of justice in the middle of the room. A moment more and he had turned, closed the door, and fled.

"What a man can it be?" said the shepherd.

The rest, between the awfulness of their late discovery and the odd conduct of this third visitor, looked as if they knew not what to think, and said nothing. Instinctively they withdrew further and further from the grim gentleman in their midst, whom some of them seemed to take for the Prince of Darkness himself, till they formed a remote circle, an empty space of floor being left between them and him— . . . *circulus, cujus centrum diabolus.*[1] The room was so silent— though there were more than twenty people in it—that nothing could be heard but the patter of the rain against the window-shutters, accompanied by the occasional hiss of a stray drop that fell down the chimney into the fire, and the steady puffing of the man in the corner, who had now resumed his pipe of long clay.

The stillness was unexpectedly broken. The distant sound of a gun reverberated through the air—apparently from the direction of the county town.

"Be jiggered!" cried the stranger who had sung the song, jumping up.

"What does that mean?" asked several.

"A prisoner escaped from the jail— that's what it means."

All listened. The sound was repeated, and none of them spoke but the man in the chimney corner, who said quietly, "I've often been told that in this county they fire a gun at such times; but I never heard it till now."

"I wonder if it is *my* man?" murmured the personage in cinder-gray.

"Surely it is!" said the shepherd involuntarily. "And surely we've zeed him! That little man who looked in at the door

---

[1] *circulus . . . diabolus:* a circle with the devil at its center.

by now, and quivered like a leaf when he zeed ye and heard your song!"

"His teeth chattered, and the breath went out of his body," said the dairyman.

"And his heart seemed to sink within him like a stone," said Oliver Giles.

"And he bolted as if he'd been shot at," said the hedge carpenter.

"True—his teeth chattered, and his heart seemed to sink; and he bolted as if he'd been shot at," slowly summed up the man in the chimney corner.

"I didn't notice it," remarked the hangman.

"We were all awondering what made him run off in such a fright," faltered one of the women against the wall, "and now 'tis explained!"

The firing of the alarm gun went on at intervals, low and sullenly, and their suspicions became a certainty. The sinister gentleman in cinder-gray roused himself. "Is there a constable here?" he asked, in thick tones. "If so, let him step forward."

The engaged man of fifty stepped quavering out from the wall, his betrothed beginning to sob on the back of the chair.

"You are a sworn constable?"

"I be, Sir."

"Then pursue the criminal at once, with assistance, and bring him back here. He can't have gone far."

"I will, Sir, I will—when I've got my staff. I'll go home and get it, and come sharp here, and start in a body."

"Staff!—never mind your staff; the man'll be gone!"

"But I can't do nothing without my staff—can I, William, and John, and Charles Jake? No; for there's the king's royal crown apainted on en in yaller and gold, and the lion and the unicorn, so as when I raise en up and hit my prisoner, 'tis made a lawful blow thereby. I wouldn't 'tempt to take up a man without my staff— no, not I. If I hadn't the law to gie me courage, why, instead o' my taking up him he might take up me!"

"Now, I'm a king's man myself, and can give you authority enough for this," said the formidable officer in gray. "Now then, all of ye, be ready. Have ye any lanterns?"

"Yes—have ye any lanterns?—I demand it!" said the constable.

"And the rest of you able-bodied——"

"Able-bodied men—yes—the rest of ye!" said the constable.

"Have you some good stout staves and pitchforks——"

"Staves and pitchforks—in the name o' the law! And take 'em in yer hands and go in quest, and do as we in authority tell ye!"

Thus aroused, the men prepared to give chase. The evidence was, indeed, though circumstantial, so convincing that but little argument was needed to show the shepherd's guests that after what they had seen it would look very much like connivance if they did not instantly pursue the unhappy third stranger, who could not as yet have gone more than a few hundred yards over such uneven country.

A shepherd is always well provided with lanterns; and, lighting these hastily, and with hurdle-staves in their hands, they poured out of the door, taking a direction along the crest of the hill, away from the town, the rain having fortunately a little abated.

Disturbed by the noise, or possibly by unpleasant dreams of her baptism, the child who had been christened began to cry heartbrokenly in the room overhead. These notes of grief came down through the chinks of the floor to the ears of the women below, who jumped up one by one and seemed glad of the excuse to ascend and comfort the baby, for the incidents of the last half-hour greatly oppressed them. Thus in the space of two or three minutes the room on the ground-floor was deserted quite.

But it was not for long. Hardly had the sound of footsteps died away when a man returned round the corner of the house from the direction the pursuers had taken. Peeping in at the door, and seeing nobody there, he entered leisurely. It was the stranger of the chimney corner, who had gone out with the rest. The motive of his return was shown by his helping himself to a cut piece of skimmer-cake that lay on a ledge beside where he had sat, and which he had apparently forgotten to take with him. He also poured out half a cup more mead from the quantity that remained, ravenously eating and drinking these as he stood. He had not finished when another figure came in just as quietly —his friend in cinder-gray.

"Oh—you here?" said the latter, smiling. "I thought you had gone to help in the capture." And this speaker also revealed the object of his return by looking solicitously round for the fascinating mug of old mead.

"And I thought you had gone," said the other, continuing his skimmer-cake with some effort.

"Well, on second thoughts, I felt there were enough without me," said the first confidentially, "and such a night as it is, too. Besides, 'tis the business o' the Government to take care of its criminals— not mine."

"True; so it is. And I felt as you did, that there were enough without me."

"I don't want to break my limbs running over the humps and hollows of this wild country."

"Nor I neither, between you and me."

"These shepherd people are used to it—simple-minded souls, you know, stirred up to anything in a moment. They'll have him ready for me before the morning, and no trouble to me at all."

"They'll have him, and we shall have saved ourselves all labor in the matter."

"True, true. Well, my way is to Casterbridge; and 'tis as much as my legs will do to take me that far. Going the same way?"

"No, I am sorry to say! I have to get home over there" (he nodded indefinitely to the right), "and I feel as you do, that it is quite enough for my legs to do before bedtime."

The other had by this time finished the mead in the mug, after which, shaking hands heartily at the door, and wishing each other well, they went their several ways.

In the meantime the company of pursuers had reached the end of the hog's-back elevation which dominated this part of the down. They had decided on no particular plan of action; and, finding that the man of the baleful trade was no longer in their company, they seemed quite unable to form any such plan now. They descended in all directions down the hill, and straightway several of the party fell into the snare set by Nature for all misguided midnight ramblers over this part of the cretaceous [1] formation. The "lanchets," or flint slopes, which belted the escarpment at intervals of a dozen yards, took the less cautious ones unawares, and losing their footing on the rubbly steep they slid sharply downward, the lanterns rolling from their hands to the bottom, and there lying on their sides till the horn [2] was scorched through.

When they had again gathered themselves together, the shepherd, as the man who knew the country best, took the lead, and guided them round these treacherous inclines. The lanterns, which seemed rather to dazzle their eyes and warn the fugitive than to assist them in the exploration, were extinguished, due silence was observed; and in this more rational order they plunged into the vale. It was a grassy, briery, moist defile, affording some shelter to any person who had sought it; but the party perambulated it in vain, and ascended on the other side. Here they wandered apart, and after an interval closed together again to report progress. At the second time of closing in they found themselves near a lonely ash, the single tree on this part of the coomb, probably sown there by a passing bird some fifty years before. And here, standing a little to one side of the trunk, as motionless as the trunk itself appeared the man they were in quest of, his outline being well defined against the sky beyond. The band noiselessly drew up and faced him.

"Your money or your life!" said the constable sternly to the still figure.

"No, no," whispered John Pitcher. " 'Tisn't our side ought to say that. That's the doctrine of vagabonds like him, and we be on the side of the law."

"Well, well," replied the constable, impatiently; "I must say something, mustn't I? and if you had all the weight o' this undertaking upon your mind, perhaps you'd say the wrong thing, too! Prisoner at the bar, surrender in the name of the Father—the Crown, I mane!"

The man under the tree seemed now to notice them for the first time, and, giving them no opportunity whatever for exhibiting their courage, he strolled slowly toward them. He was, indeed, the little man, the third stranger; but his trepidation had in a great measure gone.

"Well, travelers," he said, "did I hear you speak to me?"

"You did; you've got to come and be our prisoner at once!" said the constable. "We arrest 'ee on the charge of not biding in Casterbridge jail in a decent proper manner to be hung tomorrow morning. Neighbors, do your duty, and seize the culpet!"

On hearing the charge, the man seemed enlightened and, saying not another word, resigned himself with preternatural civility to the search party, who, with their staves in their hands, surrounded him on all sides and marched him back toward the shepherd's cottage.

It was eleven o'clock by the time they arrived. The light shining from the open door, a sound of men's voices within, proclaimed to them as they approached the house that some new events had arisen in their absence. On entering they discovered the shepherd's living room to be invaded by two officers from Casterbridge jail, and a well-known magistrate who lived at the nearest county seat, intelligence of the escape having become generally circulated.

"Gentlemen," said the constable, "I

---

[1] **cretaceous:** chalky.

[2] **horn:** scraped horn was sometimes used instead of glass in lanterns.

have brought back your man—not without risk and danger; but every one must do his duty! He is inside this circle of able-bodied persons, who have lent me useful aid, considering their ignorance of Crown work. Men, bring forward your prisoner!" And the third stranger was led to the light.

"Who is this?" said one of the officials.

"The man," said the constable.

"Certainly not," said the turnkey; and the first corroborated his statement.

"But how can it be otherwise?" asked the constable. "Or why was he so terrified at sight o' the singing instrument of the law who sat there?" Here he related the strange behavior of the third stranger on entering the house during the hangman's song.

"Can't understand it," said the officer coolly. "All I know is that it is not the condemned man. He's quite a different character from this one; a gauntish fellow, with dark hair and eyes, rather good-looking, and with a musical bass voice that if you heard it once you'd never mistake as long as you lived."

"Why, souls—'twas the man in the chimney corner!"

"Hey—what?" said the magistrate, coming forward after inquiring particulars from the shepherd in the background. "Haven't you got the man after all?"

"Well, Sir," said the constable, "he's the man we were in search of, that's true; and yet he's not the man we were in search of. For the man we were in search of was not the man we wanted, Sir, if you understand my everyday way; for 'twas the man in the chimney corner!"

"A pretty kettle of fish altogether!" said the magistrate. "You had better start for the other man at once."

The prisoner now spoke for the first time. The mention of the man in the chimney corner seemed to have moved him as nothing else could do. "Sir," he said, stepping forward to the magistrate, "take no more trouble about me. The time is come when I may as well speak. I have done nothing; my crime is that the con-

demned man is my brother. Early this afternoon I left home at Shottsford to tramp it all the way to Casterbridge jail to bid him farewell. I was benighted, and called here to rest and ask the way. When I opened the door I saw before me the very man, my brother, that I thought to see in the condemned cell at Casterbridge. He was in this chimney corner; and jammed close to him, so that he could not have got out if he had tried, was the executioner who'd come to take his life, singing a song about it and not knowing that it was his victim who was close by, joining in to save appearances. My brother looked a glance of agony at me, and I know he meant, 'Don't reveal what you see; my life depends on it.' I was so terror-struck that I could hardly stand, and, not knowing what I did, I turned and hurried away."

The narrator's manner and tone had the stamp of truth, and his story made a great impression on all around. "And do you know where your brother is at the present time?" asked the magistrate.

"I do not. I have never seen him since I closed this door."

"I can testify to that, for we've been between ye ever since," said the constable.

"Where does he think to fly to?—what is his occupation?"

"He's a watch-and-clock maker, Sir."

"'A said 'a was a wheelwright—a wicked rogue," said the constable.

"The wheels of clocks and watches he meant, no doubt," said Shepherd Fennel. "I thought his hands were palish for's trade."

"Well, it appears to me that nothing can be gained by retaining this poor man in custody," said the magistrate; "your business lies with the other, unquestionably."

And so the little man was released off-hand; but he looked nothing the less sad on that account, it being beyond the power of magistrate or constable to raze out the written troubles in his brain, for they concerned another whom he regarded with more solicitude than himself. When this was done, and the man had gone his way, the night was found to be so far advanced that it was deemed useless to renew the search before the next morning.

Next day, accordingly, the quest for the clever sheep-stealer became general and keen, to all appearance at least. But the intended punishment was cruelly disproportioned to the transgression, and the sympathy of a great many country-folk in that district was strongly on the side of the fugitive. Moreover, his marvelous coolness and daring in hob-and-nobbing with the hangman, under the unprecedented circumstances of the shepherd's party, won their admiration. So that it may be questioned if all those who ostensibly made themselves so busy in exploring woods and fields and lanes were quite so thorough when it came to the private examination of their own lofts and outhouses.

Stories were afloat of a mysterious figure being occasionally seen in some old overgrown trackway or other, remote from turnpike roads, but when a search was instituted in any of these suspected quarters nobody was found. Thus the days and weeks passed without tidings.

In brief, the bass-voiced man of the chimney corner was never recaptured. Some said that he went across the sea, others that he did not, but buried himself in the depths of a populous city. At any rate, the gentleman in cinder-gray never did his morning's work at Casterbridge, nor met anywhere at all, for business purposes, the genial comrade with whom he had passed an hour of relaxation in the lonely house on the coomb.

The grass has long been green on the graves of Shepherd Fennel and his frugal wife; the guests who made up the christening party have mainly followed their entertainers to the tomb; the baby in whose honor they all had met is a matron in the sere and yellow leaf. But the arrival of the three strangers at the shepherd's that night, and the details connected therewith, is a story as well known as ever in the country about Higher Crowstairs.

The Darkling Thrush

I leant upon a coppice gate
  When Frost was specter-gray,
And Winter's dregs made desolate
  The weakening eye of day.
The tangled vine-stems scored the sky   5
  Like strings of broken lyres,
And all mankind that haunted nigh
  Had sought their household fires.

The land's sharp features seemed to be
  The Century's corpse outleant,   10
His crypt the cloudy canopy,
  The wind his death lament.
The ancient pulse of germ and birth
  Was shrunken hard and dry,
And every spirit upon earth   15
  Seemed fervorless as I.

At once a voice arose among
  The bleak twigs overhead
In a fullhearted evensong
  Of joy illimited;   20
An aged thrush, frail, gaunt, and small,
  In blast-beruffled plume,
Had chosen thus to fling his soul
  Upon the growing gloom.

So little cause for carolings   25
  Of such ecstatic sound
Was written on terrestrial things
  Afar or nigh around,
That I could think there trembled through
  His happy good-night air   30
Some blessèd Hope, whereof he knew
  And I was unaware.

Snow in the Suburbs

Every branch big with it,
Bent every twig with it;
Every fork like a white web-foot;
Every street and pavement mute:
Some flakes have lost their way, and grope back upward, when   5
Meeting those meandering down they turn and descend again.
The palings are glued together like a wall,
And there is no waft of wind with the fleecy fall.

A sparrow enters the tree
Whereon immediately   10
A snow-lump thrice his own slight size
Descends on him and showers his head and eyes.
And overturns him,
And near inurns° him,
And lights on a nether twig, when its brush   15
Starts off a volley of other lodging lumps with a rush.

The steps are a blanched slope,
Up which, with feeble hope,
A black cat comes, wide-eyed and thin;
And we take him in.   20

14. **inurns:** puts in an urn. An urn is a receptacle for the ashes of the dead.

Neutral Tones

We stood by a pond that winter day,
And the sun was white, as though chidden of God,
And a few leaves lay on the starving sod:
    They had fallen from an ash, and were gray.

Your eyes on me were as eyes that rove   5
Over tedious riddles solved years ago;
And some words played between us to and fro
    On which lost the more by our love.

The smile on your mouth was the deadest thing
Alive enough to have strength to die;   10
And a grin of bitterness swept thereby
    Like an ominous bird a-wing. . . .

Since then, keen lessons that love deceives,
And wrings with wrong, have shaped to me
Your face, and the God-curst sun, and a tree,   15
    And a pond edged with grayish leaves.

FOR STUDY AND DISCUSSION
THE THREE STRANGERS

1. Hardy carefully prepares his effects through the use of precise description and sometimes through the use of irony. What effect on subsequent happenings do each of the following details have?

   a. The house "stood quite detached and undefended. The only reason for its precise situation seemed to be the crossing of two footpaths."

   b. "The level rainstorm smote walls, slopes, and hedges."

   c. "That cheerful rustic was entertaining a large party in glorification of the christening of his second girl."

   d. "the absence of any expression or trait denoting that they wished to get on in the world, enlarge their minds, or do any eclipsing thing whatever . . ."

   e. "Now the old mead of these days . . . tasted remarkably strong; but it did not taste so strong as it actually was."

2. How do the guests of the Fennels amuse themselves on the joyous occasion of the christening party? What elements of local color can you find throughout the story?

THOMAS HARDY   645

3. How does Hardy create interest in the first stranger as he begins to ascend the solitary hill of Higher Crowstairs? What impression does he make on the guests?

4. The second stranger was "one of a type radically different from the first." Compare the two. Why does Mrs. Fennel dislike him? How does he arouse the curiosity of the guests? Hardy reveals this stranger's identity in an oblique manner. Does this device enrich the story, or would a straight exposition have been more effective? Give reasons for your opinion.

5. The guests are quick to conclude that the third stranger is the escaped prisoner. At this point in the story, do you have any reason to suspect either of the other two strangers? What effect does Hardy achieve by introducing the long silence after the stranger leaves?

6. At what point in the story did you first recognize the hangman and the prisoner? Does the revelation of their identities come at the same time? Point out phrases and sentences in which Hardy prepares you to rejoice at the escape of the condemned man.

7. How does the adventure of the escaped prisoner exemplify Hardy's view of human life as subject to the indifferent forces of chance and circumstance?

8. What part does fate play in the story? How does it affect the lives of the chief characters? What connection is there between irony and fate in this story?

9. Hardy's work is frequently marked by subtle touches of humor. Give some examples of the use of humor in this story. Do you think Hardy introduced these lighter moments simply for amusement, or might he have had another purpose? Explain.

THE DARKLING THRUSH

1. This poem was written on the last day of the nineteenth century, and there is an obvious reference to the occasion in line 10. Do you think that Hardy limits his theme to the specific situation, or does he express more universal concerns? What other feelings might be expressed at the end of one century and the beginning of another?

2. Has the poet supplied sufficient detail to establish his bleak mood? What part does the thrush play in developing the mood? Might the sharp description in lines 21–22 refer to anything or anyone else besides the bird? Give reasons for your opinion.

3. Is the poet warranted in claiming that the thrush had "so little cause for carolings"? What effect is gained by the great contrast between the "little cause" and the "joy illimited" (line 20)? In line 29 the poet says "I could think" rather than "I did think." How does this tentative statement contribute to the mood of the poem?

4. In "Dover Beach" (page 620) Matthew Arnold is similarly inspired by nature. Compare the outlook on life expressed in Arnold's poem with that in Hardy's.

SNOW IN THE SUBURBS

1. What effect is gained by Hardy's use of the word *it* instead of *snow* in lines 1–2? Where else in the poem is a pronoun repeated in a similar way?

2. On the surface, this poem is simply narrative and descriptive. Yet a strong emotional impact is communicated. How is this achieved? Does the poet's choice of specific detail from all those observable in a snowstorm aid in conveying his feelings? Explain.

3. Important figures in this little scene are revealed only in the last stanza. How does the delayed introduction affect the mood of the poem? What would have been lost if the poet had introduced all the figures at the beginning?

NEUTRAL TONES

1. What is the situation described by the speaker in the first three stanzas? The fourth stanza shows that the incident occurred in the past. Would you say that the poem is addressed to an absent person? Why or why not?

2. What part does nature play in the episode? Has God's curse also fallen on the two characters? What does the image of "tedious riddles" contribute to the tone of the poem? The last stanza shows that the speaker has often been reminded of the difficult day of the past. Might this lead you to think that the "riddles" were not really solved? Explain.

3. The title "Neutral Tones" might be taken as descriptive of the color effects of the three poems by Hardy which you have just read. But this lack of color contrast does not destroy the sharp pictorial effects Hardy achieves. Explain how the poet forms clear pictures in his work without using bright color images.

4. In all three Hardy poems a bird or the image of a bird plays a central part. Compare and contrast the role of the birds in establishing the themes and reinforcing the moods of the poems.

ENGLISH PAINTING

The Pre-Raphaelites

In 1848 a group of young English artists, rebelling against the conventionality of instruction given in the Royal Academy schools, undertook a "return to nature." Instead of painting idealized forms in nonexistent settings, they wanted to work from living models in recognizably real places, paying scrupulous attention to details and using the bright colors of nature. Enthusiasm from the Italian painters who worked before the time of Raphael (1483–1520) led them to call themselves the Pre-Raphaelite Brotherhood, or "P.R.B."

Three of the seven original members of the Brotherhood gained fame as painters: William Holman Hunt, John Everett Millais, and Dante Gabriel Rossetti. Their friends Ford Madox Brown and Arthur Hughes painted "Pre-Raphaelitish" pictures, but never formally joined the Brotherhood, which lasted only about five years. A second band of young artists, brought together by Rossetti in 1857, were likewise known as Pre-Raphaelites. Among them were William Morris, later a distinguished designer and craftsman, and Edward Coley Burne-Jones.

Pre-Raphaelitism was markedly literary. The typical Pre-Raphaelite picture tells a story and requires "reading." Sometimes the story has to do with contemporary life; sometimes it derives from the Bible, an old legend, poem, or play. We are expected to observe every detail and to respond to clues supplied by the picture's title. The Pre-Raphaelites also wrote verse and prose, and frequently composed sonnets to accompany their paintings. Only Rossetti and Morris won high reputations as poets, but others of their circle produced many volumes of letters and memoirs.

Painting from nature, the Pre-Raphaelites worked in two different directions—some toward photographic realism, some toward the effect of dream-visions. Look, for example, at PLATE 1. When in 1852 a sculptor-member of the P.R.B. left England for Australia, Ford Madox Brown, thinking of his friend's severance from all that was familiar and of the uncertainties to be faced in a strange land, was moved to paint *The Last of England* (PLATE 1). Working mostly out-of-doors on dull, chilly days, and using himself and his wife as models, Brown tried to catch realistically the effect of details impressed upon the mind in a time of emotional stress. Note, for instance, that the wife holds in her left hand the hand of an infant.

Rossetti, who was committed all his life to a quest for love and beauty, showed less interest in actuality than in romantic imaginings and treated real things as if he had seen them in visions. *The Day Dream* (PLATE 2) portrays a Pre-Raphaelite "stunner," Mrs. William Morris, sitting in the sycamore tree in Rossetti's garden. As a sonnet by the artist explains, she is deep in reverie; she has forgotten her book and dropped a sprig of honeysuckle. It is as if Rossetti had seen this daydreamer not with waking eyes, but in a dream of his own; not ensconced in the real, familiar tree, but enclosed in an intricate floral pattern suggestive of tapestry.

Burne-Jones likewise moved from the real to the unreal. His friend Morris had retold in his poem *The Earthly Paradise* the story of Perseus: how Perseus slew the Gorgon whose terrifying head, seen directly, turned men to stone, and how Perseus rescued Andromeda from a sea-monster. For a series of pictures based on the legend, Burne-Jones made many life-studies and sketches of armor; but he showed little concern with reality in the finished paintings. In *The Baleful Head* (PLATE 3) Perseus displays the Gorgon's head to Andromeda by holding it over a well in which they see only the reflection. The effect is of a memory of far away and long ago.

Millais treated in a far more realistic manner a scene we hear about but never see in *Hamlet*. At the end of Act IV, the Queen tells how Ophelia fell in the river and floated downstream, singing, borne up for a time by her clothes. As a background for his *Ophelia* (PLATE 4), Millais chose a spot under some willows in a hayfield by the river Ewell. So accurate was his rendering of the flowers and plants that a botanist used the painting as illustration for a lecture.

When Arthur Hughes's painting *Home from the Sea* (PLATE 5) was first exhibited, its title was *A Mother's Grave*. Hughes had no literary source for this painting; he simply imagined a situation in which a sailor-lad is grief-stricken on learning of the loss suffered during his long absence. The setting for Hughes's picture, however, is real, for Hughes painted the churchyard at Chingford, Essex. He added the boy a year later, in 1857. For the boy's sister, Hughes posed his own wife, including her as a needed contrast to the horizontals of the boy's body and the church.

While Millais was painting the background for *Ophelia*, his friend Holman Hunt worked at the same place on *The Hireling Shepherd*, a picture intended as a rebuke to pastors who neglect their flocks. For a patron who could not afford a replica of it, Hunt undertook a new painting—*The Strayed Sheep* (PLATE 6). Not merely a rebuke, this painting is at the same time a study of sunlight near a cliff-edge of Fairlight Downs on England's southern coast, and a reminder of the words in the Anglican Prayer Book: "We have erred and strayed from thy ways like lost sheep."

PLATE 1. FORD MADOX BROWN (1821–1893): *The Last of England*. 1852–55. Oil on canvas, almost circular, 32½ x 29½ inches. (Birmingham Museum and Art Gallery, England)

PLATE 2. DANTE GABRIEL ROSSETTI (1828–1882): *The Day Dream*. 1880. Oil on canvas, 62½ x 36½ inches. (Victoria and Albert Museum, London, Crown Copyright)

PLATE 3. SIR EDWARD COLEY BURNE-JONES (1833–1898): *The Baleful Head*, number 8 in the series *The Legend of Perseus*. 1884–88. Oil on canvas, 61 x 51 inches. (Gallery of Modern Art, New York, The Huntington Hartford Collection)

PLATE 4. SIR JOHN EVERETT MILLAIS (1829–1896): *Ophelia.* 1852. Oil on canvas, $29\frac{1}{2}$ x 44 inches. (Reproduced by courtesy of the Trustees, The Tate Gallery, London)

PLATE 5. ARTHUR HUGHES (1832–1915): *Home from the Sea*. 1863. Oil on wood panel. 20 x 25¾ inches. (By courtesy of the Ashmolean Museum. Oxford. England)

654

THE GROWTH OF THE ENGLISH LANGUAGE

The Victorian Age

When Victoria ascended the throne in 1837, her country was already in the midst of a period of great social and economic upheaval. Great Britain, which only two centuries earlier had been a tiny island country on the fringes of European civilization, had now become the most powerful nation in the world and the governing center of a vast colonial empire. Many English who might formerly have spent their lives quietly in the towns where they had been born now found themselves assigned to the far corners of the earth as government officials or as soldiers. Even for those who did stay at home, life was no longer the same. The Industrial Revolution had begun; factories were springing up everywhere, cities were growing rapidly, railways were extending over the countryside. The English way of life was changing rapidly, and these changes were reflected in the language and literature.

The English who saw service in outlying parts of the British Empire returned home with a new vocabulary of exotic terms, some of which quickly made their way into the standard vocabulary of the language. Names of African animals became familiar words—*aardvark, bushbuck, eland, gnu*. Australia and New Zealand also contributed animal names—*cassowary, kangaroo, kookaburra, wallaby*. And in India, the largest territory under British rule, thousands of English became accustomed to living in *bungalows*, sleeping on *cots*, sipping *punch* on *verandahs*, eating *curry*, and traveling through the *jungle*. (All the italicized words come from native languages of India.)

Meanwhile, in England itself, the vocabulary of modern science and technology was taking shape. An "engine," in eighteenth-century England, had been any kind of tool or device; in nineteenth-century England, it began to assume its present-day meaning of a machine that converts energy into mechanical force. The arrival of the steam engine was marked by the appearance of new terms such as *piston valve, drive shaft, steamship*, and *steamroller*. During the last half of the century, many words associated with electrical power put in their first appearance: *dynamo, ampere, ohm, volt, watt*.

At the same time that the scientific and technological vocabulary was expanding rapidly, other specialized vocabularies were beginning to shrink and fall into disuse. When the stagecoach gave way to the railroad, for instance, terms like *postillion, splinter bar*, and *swingle* began to disappear from common speech. A little later, with the coming of the automobile, almost all horse-drawn vehicles vanished from the scene; and with them went an enormous group of specialized terms. Everyone today knows the difference between a *sports car*, a *taxi*, a *trailer truck*, and a *bus*. But how many people could distinguish between a *victoria*, a *hackney*, a *dray*, and a *tallyho?*

The writers of the Victorian period were keenly aware that they were living in a time of change. On the whole, they found the changes disturbing and unsettling. They had good reason for looking on modern developments with a gloomy eye: among the most visible signs of "progress" were ugly factory districts, growing urban slums, and an ever-increasing stream of cheap, shoddy manufactured items. Some writers, such as Carlyle, spoke out directly against the ugliness and the suffering they saw in contemporary life (see "Midas," page 565). But many others, especially the poets, reacted by turning away from modern civilization and concentrating on pleasant rural scenes or on a romantically idealized past. It was left for twentieth-century writers to adopt urban life as their theme; few nineteenth-century English writers felt quite at home in the city streets. To some extent, therefore, the language of Victorian literature is the language of a vanishing country life or of a vanished past. Many modern readers owe to Tennyson their familiarity with medieval terms such as *greaves* and *baldric* (see "The Lady of Shalott," page 582), and they owe to Hardy their familiarity with certain rural English dialects (see the dialogue in "The Three Strangers," page 630).

The love of the past that was so strong an element in Victorian thought was often combined, however, with an equally strong passion for scientific accuracy. One of the aspects of the past that particularly fascinated Victorian thinkers was the history of language. During the seventeenth and eighteenth centuries, the little research that had been done into Old English and Middle English had been based mainly on guesswork. Nineteenth-century researchers, however, began to go systematically through collections of old manuscripts, classifying and comparing them in minute detail. Scholarly societies devoted to the study of language history were formed: the Philological Society was founded in 1842, the Early English Text Society in 1864, the Chaucer Society in 1868.

Perhaps the greatest single product of nineteenth-century language scholarship was the *Oxford English Dictionary,* a dictionary that traces the origin of hundreds of thousands of English words, giving the date when each word was first found in English writing and showing the development of new meanings by giving definitions and carefully dated quotations. The preparation of this dictionary was an immense task. Work on it was begun in 1857, and by the time the first volume appeared in 1884, approximately a thousand readers and editors had given their time to the project. The complete twelve-volume dictionary took more than seventy years to finish.

FOR STUDY AND DISCUSSION

1. Using a dictionary that gives etymologies (word origins), look up the following words and find out from which language each of them entered the English language. All are terms that were acquired from far-reaching parts of the British Empire. From which specific part of the world did each of them come?

bangle	gingham	parian
cooey	loot	polo
dinghy	nirvana	thug

2. Find out whether there is a set of the *Oxford English Dictionary* available in a local library. (You might find an older edition under the title *A New English Dictionary;* this will serve your purpose just as well.) If you find a set, read the Historical Introduction near the beginning of the first volume, and prepare a brief report, answering one of the following questions:

a. What led up to the Philological Society's decision to prepare a dictionary based on historical principles?

b. Who were the chief editors involved with work on the dictionary over the years? What did each of these editors accomplish?

c. Exactly how were the entry slips prepared?

3. Using either the *Oxford English Dictionary (New English Dictionary)* or the *Shorter Oxford English Dictionary,* look up the following words and find the date given for the first recorded appearance of the word in English writing. The *Shorter Oxford English Dictionary* is an abridged version available in many libraries which may not have the unabridged multi-volume set. What does the date given for the word's first appearance tell you about the historical development of science or technology?

aeronaut	gasoline	pasteurize
automobile	hydroelectric	radium
bacterium	ion	X rays

THE TWENTIETH CENTURY

(1900–   )

THIS AGE of ours represents the triumph of science, invention, technology, and social welfare. We travel faster and faster, farther and farther. We are able to invent machines that do more and more of our work for us. By means of public health services and the use of antibiotics and other new drugs we have been able to save countless millions of lives that would have been lost in any former age. The mass of people in Western Europe and North America are better fed, better housed, better clothed, and better educated than they—or anyone else—have ever been before. On all this, and much more besides, the twentieth century can congratulate itself.

But there is another side to the picture, and unless we take a look at it we cannot understand our age or the literature it has produced. This century has already witnessed the two most destructive and terrible wars in all history, and it is not yet out of danger of a third world war which would destroy our whole civilization. Science has saved many lives; but with two thirds of the world's inhabitants continually threatened by starvation, it has not yet found the way to produce enough food for the tremendously rapidly increasing population of the earth. It may be important to travel through space to the moon and beyond, but it is even more important to insure somehow that all the people on this planet are adequately fed, housed, and clothed, and that they have at least a chance of good health and attaining a good education.

In this age, three important things have happened to Britain. First, she has had to face two ruinous wars. These have cost her lives, chiefly of young men, that she could ill spare. They have also caused the destruction of much property; and, in order to pay for the wars, Britain has had to relinquish many of the investments abroad that in the nineteenth century had made

London the financial capital of the world. Second, Britain has lost the dominant position in world politics that she had during the nineteenth century and now must accept third place, behind the United States and the Soviet Union. And third—a gain now instead of a loss—first through the Liberal Party, then through the Labor Party, Britain not only has achieved full political democracy but also has raised the standard of living and finally created a welfare state.

The effects on Britain of the two world wars have been great—just how great is sometimes difficult for Americans to grasp, for to Americans they were much shorter and much less crippling than they were to the British.

In Europe, World War I began in August 1914 and continued to November 1918. During that time almost a million young Britons were killed. The slaughter was terrible, especially during the battle of the Somme, which began in July 1916. Since many battalions had been recruited largely from single cities, after which they were named, these cities were plunged at once into mourning when their battalions were mowed down by machine guns. The effect of these ghastly casualties was powerful and lasting, both on surviving soldiers themselves—poets like Siegfried Sassoon (1886–1967) and Robert Graves (1895–)—and on the civilians at home. There was a grim contrast between the rousing patriotic speeches of the leaders at home and the slaughter in the trenches of France. A certain optimism—the nineteenth-century conviction that progress must forever continue, which can also be found in such twentieth-century writers as George Bernard Shaw (1856–1950) and H. G. Wells (1867–1946)—vanished from Britain.

From 1919 onward, many of the younger writers turned in disgust from public affairs and, much influenced by writers abroad, moved from a concern with people in society to a concern with the inner world of the mind. Whatever was associated with the world before the war was condemned or ignored because it was that world that had produced the war. Even such rebels against prewar society as Shaw and Wells never recovered the popularity among "advanced" young writers and critics that they had had before 1914.

THE NEW WRITING

Literature now had a much narrower base. It was regarded as something that could appeal only to a very small minority, the cultured few. The old idea that literature could be enjoyed by almost everybody who could read did not survive into the 1920's, which was very much a period of new writing that might be called "highbrow" and "precious." The work of these writers—T. S. Eliot (1888–1965), James Joyce (1882–1941), Virginia Woolf (1882–1941), for example—was often difficult and deliberately obscure. If

BRITAIN
1900 to Present

ATLANTIC OCEAN

SCOTLAND

•Edinburgh

NORTH SEA

IRISH SEA

•York

Dublin •**1**

IRELAND

•Liverpool •Manchester

ENGLAND

2•Nottingham

•Birmingham

3•Ludlow

7•Cambridge

WALES

Gloucester•**5**

8
6•Oxford •Ayot St. Lawrence

4•Laugharne

London•**9**

Abinger•**10**   Canterbury•**11**

12•Lewes

ATLANTIC

OCEAN

ENGLISH CHANNEL

FRANCE

1 Birthplace of G. B. Shaw, W. B. Yeats, James Joyce, and Sean O'Faolain. Site of Abbey (Irish National) Theater, where Frank O'Connor was librarian.   **2** D. H. Lawrence grew up in a mining town near here and taught school here for a time. **3** A. E. Housman was born near here in the county of Shropshire, the setting of most of his poetry. **4** Home of Dylan Thomas.   **5** Evelyn Waugh lived many years at Stinchcombe, near here.   **6** Housman, T. S. Eliot, Aldous Huxley, Graham Greene, and Evelyn Waugh studied here; Stephen Spender and "new school" of poets met here.   **7** E. M. Forster attended university and Housman was professor of Latin here.   **8** Long-time home of George Bernard Shaw.   **9** Katherine Mansfield attended university here. Home of Eliot, Spender, Greene, George Orwell, and Virginia Woolf, in whose home the "Bloomsbury Group" gathered.   **10** Long-time home of E. M. Forster.   **11** Joseph Conrad settled near here after his retirement from the merchant marine.   **12** Country home of Virginia Woolf, where she died.

ordinary people could not understand such writing, then so much the worse for ordinary people, who, anyhow, had plenty of rubbish to amuse them. This was the more extreme literary attitude during the 1920's.

One reason for this defiant and rather conceited attitude was the enormous development throughout the 1920's and 1930's—and, indeed, down to this day—of what are generally referred to as "mass media." These are the popular press, including both newspapers and magazines, with large circulations; films, radio, and, of course more recently, television. All these were held to be the enemies of real literature. Young creative writers felt themselves in danger of being overwhelmed by these mass media, so they had to keep a long way off and do something very different. If so much was being made easily acceptable to the ordinary public, then real literature, not meant for such people, could afford to be difficult, could even glory in its difficulty.

There were, of course, other writers whose work was less affected by the war and the disillusionment that it bred. Joseph Conrad (1857–1924), E. M. Forster (1879–1970), and Katherine Mansfield (1888–1923), whose careers as writers of fiction began well before the war and ended shortly after it, exercised much influence on later writers—Conrad by his deep concern with our inner nature, Forster and Mansfield by their subtle treatments of personal relationships. Among poets, William Butler Yeats (1865–1939) progressed from a dreamy kind of romanticism in the 1890's to highly disciplined, intellectual verse in the 1920's and 1930's, while A. E. Housman (1859–1936) assured his fame with a small number of ex-

Winston Churchill and his victory sign helped buoy spirits during World War II.

During World War II, much of the Battle of Britain was fought in the London skies.

quisitely polished lyrics. An important novelist, contemporary with Joyce and Virginia Woolf but markedly different in his approach, was D. H. Lawrence (1885–1930).

WORLD WAR II

In Europe World War II lasted from 1939 to 1945. During most of 1940 and much of 1941, Britain was alone facing Hitler, who launched bombing attacks on London and many other English cities in the hope of so weakening the country that it could be invaded successfully. The destruction of property in this war was staggering but the loss of life among the armed forces was less than in the previous war, though the civilian casualties, those killed or severely wounded in air raids, numbered about 250,000. There was nothing like the growing disillusionment and bitterness of the first war, if only because few illusions remained when the war began. Indeed, many of us feel that the spirit of the British was higher during World War II than it had been before or has been since. A large share of the credit for this must go to Winston Churchill, Prime Minister from 1940 to 1945, whose inspired leadership helped buoy the country and its allies when the going was hardest.

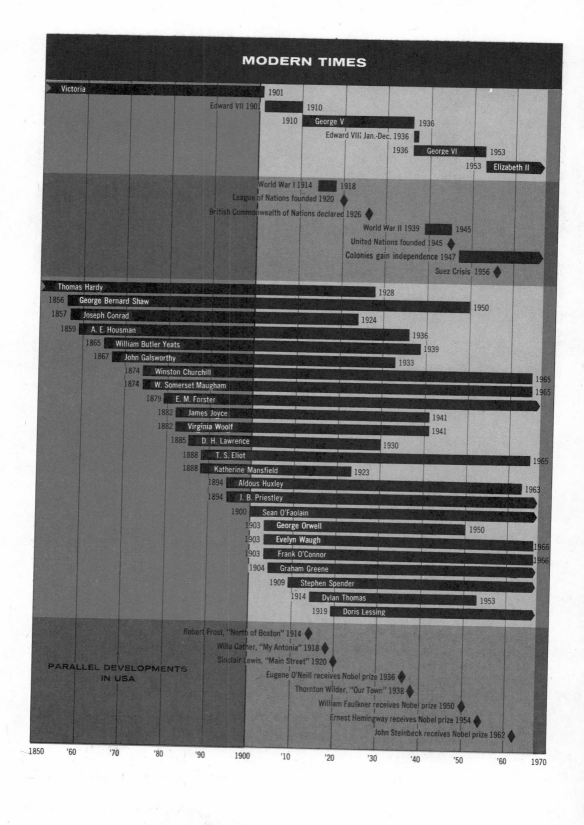

MODERN TIMES

Victoria | 1901
Edward VII 1901 | 1910
1910 | George V | 1936
Edward VIII Jan.-Dec. 1936
1936 | George VI | 1953
1953 | Elizabeth II

World War I 1914 | 1918
League of Nations founded 1920 ◆
British Commonwealth of Nations declared 1926 ◆
World War II 1939 | 1945
United Nations founded 1945 ◆
Colonies gain independence 1947
Suez Crisis 1956 ◆

Thomas Hardy | 1928
1856 | George Bernard Shaw | 1950
1857 | Joseph Conrad | 1924
1859 | A. E. Housman | 1936
1865 | William Butler Yeats | 1939
1867 | John Galsworthy | 1933
1874 | Winston Churchill | 1965
1874 | W. Somerset Maugham | 1965
1879 | E. M. Forster
1882 | James Joyce | 1941
1882 | Virginia Woolf | 1941
1885 | D. H. Lawrence | 1930
1888 | T. S. Eliot | 1965
1888 | Katherine Mansfield | 1923
1894 | Aldous Huxley | 1963
1894 | J. B. Priestley
1900 | Sean O'Faolain
1903 | George Orwell | 1950
1903 | Evelyn Waugh | 1966
1903 | Frank O'Connor | 1966
1904 | Graham Greene
1909 | Stephen Spender
1914 | Dylan Thomas | 1953
1919 | Doris Lessing

PARALLEL DEVELOPMENTS IN USA

Robert Frost, "North of Boston" 1914 ◆
Willa Cather, "My Antonia" 1918 ◆
Sinclair Lewis, "Main Street" 1920 ◆
Eugene O'Neill receives Nobel prize 1936 ◆
Thornton Wilder, "Our Town" 1938 ◆
William Faulkner receives Nobel prize 1950 ◆
Ernest Hemingway receives Nobel prize 1954 ◆
John Steinbeck receives Nobel prize 1962 ◆

1850 | '60 | '70 | '80 | '90 | 1900 | '10 | '20 | '30 | '40 | '50 | '60 | 1970

Because the mood of Britain in World War II was so different from that of World War I, the later war did not have a comparable effect on young writers. In World War II there was, however, a tremendous demand for good reading and theater, for music and the visual arts. It was during the war that what is now called the British Arts Council was born. By dispensing government grants to worthy nonprofit cultural projects that otherwise would be unable to exist, this organization has done much to encourage the arts in Britain.

FROM EMPIRE TO COMMONWEALTH

It was after World War II that a movement which had long been underway reached its climax—namely, the transformation of the British Empire into the Commonwealth of Nations. This is not merely a change of name: it indicates that the lands once governed by Britain have become independent, self-governing nations, now tied to Britain only by bonds of tradition and, in most cases, language. This status had been achieved as early as 1867 by Canada, followed in the first decade of the twentieth century by Australia, New Zealand, and South Africa, and in 1921 by the Irish Free State. The establishment of the Irish Free State, including all of Ireland except six northern counties that remained tied to Great Britain, resolved, for the most part, a very long and often bitter struggle that had frequently involved many Irish literary figures, most notably William Butler Yeats. The two decades immediately following World War II saw the triumph of movements for national independence in almost every other part of what had been the British Empire—the most important by far being the independence of India in 1947 as the two separate states of India and Pakistan. Since that time, almost all of the former British colonies in other parts of Asia, in Africa, and in the West Indies have become independent. Most have chosen to remain within the Commonwealth, although none is required to do so.

People who have a prejudice against Britain often sneer at her for "losing her Empire," but this is to misjudge the more liberal British attitude toward her former possessions. The more liberal and progressive idea was always that Britain had been holding these territories in trust for their inhabitants, who when they were ready to govern themselves should be encouraged to do so. Many brutal and stupid things were done in the name of the British Empire, and such things have always been denounced by the more enlightened British themselves. But the idea behind the Commonwealth—that of gradually bringing new states and nations into existence, capable of holding their own in the modern world—is fit companion to the ideas that inspired the American Declaration of Independence.

No doubt in earlier years Britain's colonial possessions were exploited for commercial purposes and were financially beneficial to Britain. Today the heavily taxed Britons find themselves helping to run these areas at a financial loss. Not only are they still responsible for their protection (adding to the size and cost of army, navy, and air force), but they must also subsidize their development into economically strong nations. Moreover, the more prosperous members of the Commonwealth have no financial responsibility to Britain herself. Canada, one of the wealthiest members of the Commonwealth, is not even within the "sterling area" (that is, those countries using British currency in international exchange), but has her own dollar currency. The ties between Britain and the Commonwealth are in fact more sentimental than economic or political. Nevertheless, in each of the two world wars the then independent Commonwealth members hastened to support Britain with men and materials as well as with financial assistance.

BRITAIN SINCE WORLD WAR II

At the same time that the Empire was being transformed into the Commonwealth, far-reaching changes were also taking place at home. Most notable was the continuing demand for extensive social legislation—unemployment and health insurance, pensions, and the like. The first social legislation had been enacted before World War I and other programs were initiated in the years between the wars.

A most extensive program of social and economic legislation was put through by the Labor Party in the years 1945–51. It included the nationalization of several important industries, such as mining and the railroads, and the establishment of the National Health Service, under which every Briton may receive medical care at virtually no cost. Through these and other programs the government has taken over a large share of the responsibility for the health, employment, housing, education, and pensions of the great mass of the population. Although taxes have risen considerably in order to pay for these programs, they are very little higher than those of the United States and lower than those of most nations of the European continent.

Since World War II Britain's greatest problems have been economic, for reasons largely unconnected with the welfare program. Because British industry has had difficulty modernizing and expanding at the same rates achieved by industry in other countries, British exports have encountered increasingly serious competition from the United States and Europe. This is a far more serious problem for Britain than it would be for most other countries, for Britain must import large quantities of food in order to feed her population, and these can be paid for only by exporting industrial goods. As a result, Britain has had several financial crises, during which the government has had to take severe steps to limit consumer spending. Thus, while the standard of living is higher than ever before, there is an underlying uncertainty in the country that has affected its morale in many, sometimes very subtle, ways. The national morale has also been affected by Britain's inability to influence world affairs to the extent to which she had been accustomed.

Although there is much activity together with a fairly high level of accomplishment in postwar British writing, there is still a disappointing lack of really outstanding figures. The giants are slow to arrive. But this may have something to do with the public mind, for, as we have already seen, it is when some form of literature (like the drama in the Elizabethan Age, the novel in the Victorian) is exciting and important to people in general that great work is achieved. A public that is more concerned about "television personalities" than it is about authors is in no condition to nourish great literature.

Fiction has been declining steadily. There are various good reasons for this: interest in television, the growth of paperback publishing, the vast number of novel readers who borrow books from the free libraries. Meanwhile, though paperbacks have helped many serious readers who could not afford hardcover editions, it is generally not good modern writers but sensational bad writers who benefit most from paperbacks. Moreover, as magazines find it hard to compete with paperback books, it is increasingly difficult for good writers to find a likely publisher for their short stories, poems, and essays.

However, the Arts Council has been receiving a far larger government grant than it used to, with the result that subsidies to theaters, new playwrights, poets, and novelists have increased in number and are far more generous. The British Broadcasting Corporation increasingly provides to dramatists and poets and a limited number of critics an opportunity to reach a large public. On the other hand, many promising new writers, finding it impossible to live on the meager rewards of publication, are lured into working for television and radio almost exclusively, and they are therefore soon lost to the printed word.

Much of the twentieth century has been a time of war, both hot and cold war, and for Britain it has been a time of declining national fortune. But in the midst of uncertainty, in seeking answers to the problems they face, people still put their thoughts on paper. And so the English literary tradition, one of the greatest the world has known, continues to express the hopes, fears, and ideals of its people.

J.B.P.

JOSEPH CONRAD
(1857–1924)

Two facts have long obscured the full meaning of Conrad's work: first, the fact that he did not learn to speak and write English until he was twenty-one; and, second, the fact that his early work centered on the sea and the exotic regions of the Far East. Both of these facts are of importance, but the attempts of Conrad's early critics to use one or both of them to define the nature of his achievement were misleading. That the young Polish man learned English is less interesting than that he used it to achieve a new kind of fiction in English; that he excelled at describing the sights, sounds, and smells of Malaysia, or the absorbing craft of the sea and the lonely trials of command, is less important than that he discovered our common humanity in these unfamiliar settings.

In one of his prefaces Conrad describes the writer's calling in this way:

"He [the writer] speaks to our capacity for delight and wonder, to the sense of mystery surrounding our lives; to our sense of pity, and beauty, and pain; to the latent feeling of fellowship with all creation—and to the subtle but invincible conviction of solidarity that knits together the loneliness of innumerable hearts, to the solidarity in dreams, in joy, in sorrow, in aspirations, in illusions, in hope, in fear, which binds men to each other, which binds together all humanity— the dead to the living, and the living to the unborn."

Conrad here insists on a community based on aspiration, illusion, and dream. A number of important writers at the end of the nineteenth century tried to find some basis outside the state and outside organized religion for defining our common humanity and for creating a bond which might hold people together. For Conrad the ideal of the nation–state lay in the past. He found a kind of bond, a partial order, in the code of the sea which bound officers and men in a network of defined responsibilities to each other, to their passengers, and to the vessel.

Conrad did more than discover a usable code of conduct, a bond between people. In his novels he measured this code against the pressures of Western civilization in his time. In some of his works he may, in fact, to a superficial reader, seem more concerned with the pressures of civilization than with the code. In *Heart of Darkness,* he deals with the merciless exploitation of Africans in the Belgian Congo. In *Nostromo,* he exposes the weakness of commercial interests. But underlying these works as well as such masterpieces as *Victory, The Secret Agent,* and *Lord Jim,* there is always Conrad's greatest theme: the way in which our dreams of ourselves work either to join us with, or cut us off from, humanity. In the process of exploring this theme, he is to an extent one of the finest modern psychological novelists. He penetrates the obscure places of the human heart and shows how life is wrecked or sustained by dreams and illusions. In Conrad, however, the psychological as well as the social is subordinated to a basic concern with "the truth, manifold and one" about people and the world they inhabit and shape. Conrad has no very happy view of this adventure of dream and reality. Almost always he remains the stern shipmaster of souls: act on your dream you must, he says, but take good care that it reaches out to include others, otherwise you will lose your humanity.

THE LIFE OF JOSEPH CONRAD

Josef Teodor Conrad Nalecz Korzeniowski was born in Russian Poland in December 1857. He was the son of a nobleman, a Polish patriot, whose efforts to liberate his country from Russia led in 1862 to his exile with his wife and son. Conrad's mother died in 1865 of the hardships she had to endure in their bleak Russian home. Her young son was then sent to live with his maternal uncle, Tadeusz Bobrowski, with whom he remained for two years. He then rejoined his father, who had been permitted to move closer to home, first to Lemberg in Galicia, and then to the city of Cracow. The desolate father and son were both in fragile health, and they buried themselves in books. Apollo Korzeniowski, Conrad's father, translated from the works of Shakespeare and Victor Hugo, and looked, as did most of the cultivated Poles of his day, to France and England for cultural enlightenment. In 1869 he died, and Conrad's uncle Tadeusz again became responsible for the slight, emotional youngster. For some years thereafter Conrad was educated by a tutor, with whom he made a European tour in 1873.

In 1874 Tadeusz gave in to an extraordinary request. His ward wished to become a seaman. The firm, practical, and affectionate guardian apprenticed him to a banking and shipping company in Marseilles. There Conrad learned seamanship in voyages to the West Indies. In 1877 and 1878, on a small vessel of which he was part owner, he was involved in smuggling arms to the forces of a pretender to the Spanish throne. In the latter year, having lost all his money and perhaps (no one knows) having had an unhappy love affair, he shot himself in the chest. (He later made up a tale about a duel to account for this episode.) The faithful uncle Tadeusz cared for him, and in the same year Conrad shipped out on a British vessel for the first time. Until 1894, he was to serve as seaman and officer on British ships with only occasional intervals ashore.

From 1889 until its publication in 1895, Conrad spent all his leisure moments on the manuscript of his first novel, *Almayer's Folly*. He had become a British subject in 1886, the year in which he had also become a licensed ship's captain. In the year following the publication of his first book he married an Englishwoman and became a householder and the head of a family. But with marriage he did not achieve tranquillity. He was a nervous, irritable, passionate man, who labored long agonized hours at his desk, was in constant need of money, and never received full public recognition during the years when he did his best work. When recognition finally came in the form of an offer of knighthood, Conrad refused it. He died in 1924.

The Lagoon

THE WHITE MAN, leaning with both arms over the roof of the little house in the stern of the boat, said to the steersman:

"We will pass the night in Arsat's clearing. It is late."

The Malay only grunted, and went on looking fixedly at the river. The white man rested his chin on his crossed arms and gazed at the wake of the boat. At the end of the straight avenue of forests cut by the intense glitter of the river, the sun appeared unclouded and dazzling, poised low over the water that shone smoothly like a band of metal. The forests, somber and dull, stood motionless and silent on each side of the broad stream. At the foot of big, towering trees, trunkless nipa palms rose from the mud of the bank, in bunches of leaves enormous and heavy, that hung unstirring over the brown swirl of eddies. In the stillness of the air every tree, every leaf, every bough, every tendril of creeper and every petal of minute blossoms seemed to have been bewitched into an immobility perfect and final. Nothing moved on the river but the eight paddles that rose flashing regularly, dipped together with a single splash, while the steersman swept right and left with a periodic and sudden flourish of his blade describing a glinting semicircle above his head. The churned-up water frothed alongside with a confused murmur. And the white man's canoe, advancing upstream in the short-lived disturbance of its own making, seemed to enter the portals of a land from which the very memory of motion had forever departed.

The white man, turning his back upon the setting sun, looked along the empty and broad expanse of the sea reach. For the last three miles of its course the wandering, hesitating river, as if enticed irresistibly by the freedom of an open horizon, flows straight into the sea, flows straight to the east—to the east that harbors both light and darkness. Astern of the boat the repeated call of some bird, a cry discordant and feeble, skipped along over the smooth water and lost itself before it could reach the other shore in the breathless silence of the world.

The steersman dug his paddle into the stream, and held hard with stiffened arms, his body thrown forward. The water gurgled aloud; and suddenly the long straight reach seemed to pivot on its center, the forests swung in a semicircle, and the slanting beams of sunset touched the broadside of the canoe with a fiery glow, throwing the slender and distorted shadows of its crew upon the streaked glitter of the river. The white man turned to look ahead. The course of the boat had been altered at right angles to the stream, and the carved dragonhead on its prow was pointing now at a gap in the fringing bushes of the bank. It glided through, brushing the overhanging twigs, and disappeared from the river like some slim and amphibious creature leaving the water for its lair in the forests.

The narrow creek was like a ditch: tortuous, fabulously deep; filled with gloom under the thin strip of pure and shining blue of the heaven. Immense trees soared up, invisible behind the festooned draperies of creepers. Here and there, near the glistening blackness of the water, a twisted root of some tall tree showed among the tracery of small ferns, black and dull, writhing and motionless, like an arrested snake. The short words of the paddlers reverberated loudly between the thick and somber walls of vegetation. Darkness oozed out from between the trees, through the tangled maze of the creepers, from behind the great fantastic and unstirring leaves; the darkness, mysterious and invincible; the darkness scented and poisonous of impenetrable forests.

The men poled in the shoaling water. The creek broadened, opening out into a wide sweep of a stagnant lagoon. The forests receded from the marshy bank, leaving a level strip of bright green, reedy grass to frame the reflected blueness of the sky. A fleecy pink cloud drifted high above, trailing the delicate coloring of its image under the floating leaves and the silvery blossoms of the lotus. A little house, perched on high piles, appeared black in the distance. Near it, two tall nibong palms that seemed to have come out of the forests in the background leaned slightly over the ragged roof, with a suggestion of sad tenderness and care in the droop of their leafy and soaring heads.

The steersman, pointing with his paddle, said, "Arsat is there. I see his canoe fast between the piles."

The polers ran along the sides of the boat glancing over their shoulders at the end of the day's journey. They would have preferred to spend the night somewhere else than on this lagoon of weird aspect and ghostly reputation. Moreover, they disliked Arsat, first as a stranger, and also because he who repairs a ruined house, and dwells in it, proclaims that he is not afraid to live amongst the spirits that haunt the places abandoned by mankind. Such a man can disturb the course of fate by glances or words; while his familiar ghosts are not easy to propitiate by casual wayfarers upon whom they long to wreak the malice of their human master. White men care not for such things, being unbelievers and in league with the Father of Evil, who leads them unharmed through the invisible dangers of this world. To the warnings of the righteous they oppose an offensive pretense of disbelief. What is there to be done?

So they thought, throwing their weight on the end of their long poles. The big canoe glided on swiftly, noiselessly, and smoothly, toward Arsat's clearing, till, in a great rattling of poles thrown down, and the loud murmurs of "Allah be praised!" it came with a gentle knock against the crooked piles below the house.

The boatmen with uplifted faces shouted discordantly, "Arsat! O Arsat!" Nobody came. The white man began to climb the rude ladder giving access to the bamboo platform before the house. The juragan[1] of the boat said sulkily, "We will cook in the sampan,[2] and sleep on the water."

"Pass my blankets and the basket," said the white man curtly.

He knelt on the edge of the platform to receive the bundle. Then the boat shoved off, and the white man, standing up, confronted Arsat, who had come out through the low door of his hut. He was a man young, powerful, with broad chest and muscular arms. He had nothing on but his sarong.[3] His head was bare. His big, soft eyes stared eagerly at the white man, but his voice and demeanor were composed as he asked, without any words of greeting:

"Have you medicine, Tuan?"[4]

"No," said the visitor in a startled tone. "No. Why? Is there sickness in the house?"

"Enter and see," replied Arsat, in the same calm manner, and turning short round, passed again through the small doorway. The white man, dropping his bundles, followed.

In the dim light of the dwelling he made out on a couch of bamboos a woman stretched on her back under a broad sheet of red cotton cloth. She lay still, as if dead; but her big eyes, wide open, glittered in the gloom, staring upward at the slender rafters, motionless and unseeing. She was in a high fever, and evidently un-

[1] **juragan:** native leader or captain.
[2] **sampan:** flat-bottomed boat used in river and harbor traffic.
[3] **sarong:** skirt or kilt worn by both sexes in the Malay Peninsula.
[4] **Tuan:** term of respect, like *Sir,* used by natives to white men.

conscious. Her cheeks were sunk slightly, her lips were partly open, and on the young face there was the ominous and fixed expression—the absorbed, contemplating expression of the unconscious who are going to die. The two men stood looking down at her in silence.

"Has she been long ill?" asked the traveler.

"I have not slept for five nights," answered the Malay in a deliberate tone. "At first she heard voices calling her from the water and struggled against me who held her. But since the sun of today rose she hears nothing—she hears not me. She sees nothing. She sees not me—me!"

He remained silent for a minute, then asked softly:

"Tuan, will she die?"

"I fear so," said the white man, sorrowfully. He had known Arsat years ago, in a far country in times of trouble and danger, when no friendship is to be despised. And since his Malay friend had come unexpectedly to dwell in the hut on the lagoon with a strange woman, he had slept many times there, in his journeys up and down the river. He liked the man who knew how to keep faith in council and how to fight without fear by the side of his white friend. He liked him—not so much perhaps as a man likes his favorite dog—but still he liked him well enough to help and ask no questions, to think sometimes vaguely and hazily in the midst of his own pursuits about the lonely man and the long-haired woman with audacious face and triumphant eyes, who lived together hidden by the forests—alone and feared.

The white man came out of the hut in time to see the enormous conflagration of sunset put out by the swift and stealthy shadows that, rising like a black and impalpable vapor above the treetops, spread over the heaven, extinguishing the crimson glow of floating clouds and the red brilliance of departing daylight. In a few moments all the stars came out above the intense blackness of the earth, and the great lagoon gleaming suddenly with reflected lights resembled an oval patch of night sky flung down into the hopeless and abysmal night of the wilderness. The white man had some supper out of the basket, then collecting a few sticks that lay about the platform, made up a small fire, not for warmth, but for the sake of the smoke, which would keep off the mosquitoes. He wrapped himself in the blankets and sat with his back against the reed wall of the house, smoking thoughtfully.

Arsat came through the doorway with noiseless steps and squatted down by the fire. The white man moved his outstretched legs a little.

"She breathes," said Arsat in a low voice, anticipating the expected question. "She breathes and burns as if with a great fire. She speaks not; she hears not—and burns!"

He paused for a moment, then asked in a quiet, incurious tone:

"Tuan . . . will she die?"

The white man moved his shoulders uneasily and uttered in a hesitating manner:

"If such is her fate."

"No, Tuan," said Arsat, calmly. "If such is my fate. I hear, I see, I wait. I remember . . . Tuan, do you remember the old days? Do you remember my brother?"

"Yes," said the white man. The Malay rose suddenly and went in. The other, sitting still outside, could hear the voice in the hut. Arsat said: "Hear me! Speak!" His words were succeeded by a complete silence. "O Diamelen!" he cried suddenly. After that cry there was a deep sigh. Arsat came out and sank down again in his old place.

They sat in silence before the fire. There was no sound within the house, there was no sound near them; but far away on the lagoon they could hear the voices of the boatmen ringing fitful and distinct on the calm water. The fire in the bow of the sampan shone faintly in the distance with a hazy red glow. Then it died out. The voices ceased. The land and the water slept invisible, unstirring, and mute. It was as though there had been nothing left in the world but the glitter of stars streaming, ceaseless and vain, through the black stillness of the night.

The white man gazed straight before him into the darkness with wide-open eyes. The fear and fascination, the inspiration and the wonder of death—of death near, unavoidable, and unseen, soothed the unrest of his race and stirred the most indistinct, the most intimate of his thoughts. The ever-ready suspicion of evil, the gnawing suspicion that lurks in our hearts, flowed out into the stillness round him—into the stillness profound and dumb, and made it appear untrustworthy and infamous, like the placid and impenetrable mask of an unjustifiable violence. In that fleeting and powerful disturbance of his being, the earth, enfolded in the starlight peace, became a shadowy country of inhuman strife, a battlefield of phantoms terrible and charming, august or ignoble, struggling ardently for the possession of our helpless hearts. An unquiet and mysterious country of inextinguishable desires and fears.

A plaintive murmur rose in the night; a murmur saddening and startling, as if the great solitudes of surrounding woods had tried to whisper into his ear the wisdom of their immense and lofty indifference. Sounds hesitating and vague floated in the air round him, shaped themselves slowly into words; and at last flowed on gently in a murmuring stream of soft and monotonous sentences. He stirred like a man waking up and changed his position slightly. Arsat, motionless and shadowy, sitting with bowed head under the stars, was speaking in a low and dreamy tone:

"... for where can we lay down the heaviness of our trouble but in a friend's heart? A man must speak of war and of love. You, Tuan, know what war is, and you have seen me in time of danger seek death as other men seek life! A writing may be lost; a lie may be written; but what the eye has seen is truth and remains in the mind!"

"I remember," said the white man, quietly. Arsat went on with mournful composure:

"Therefore I shall speak to you of love. Speak in the night. Speak before both night and love are gone—and the eye of day looks upon my sorrow and my shame; upon my blackened face; upon my burnt-up heart."

A sigh, short and faint, marked an almost imperceptible pause, and then his words flowed on, without a stir, without a gesture.

"After the time of trouble and war was over and you went away from my country in the pursuit of your desires, which we, men of the islands, cannot understand, I and my brother became again, as we had been before, the swordbearers of the Ruler. You know we were men of family, belonging to a ruling race, and more fit than any to carry on our right shoulder the emblem of power. And in the time of prosperity Si Dendring showed us favor, as we, in time of sorrow, had showed to him the faithfulness of our courage. It was a time of peace. A time of deer hunts and cockfights; of idle talks and foolish squabbles between men whose bellies are full and weapons are rusty. But the sower watched the young rice shoots grow up without fear, and the traders came and went, departed lean and returned fat into the river of peace. They brought news, too. Brought lies and truth mixed together, so that no man knew when to rejoice and when to be sorry. We heard from them about you also. They had seen you here and had seen you there. And I was glad to hear, for I remembered the stirring times, and I always remembered you, Tuan, till the time came when my eyes could see nothing in the past, because they had looked upon the one who is dying there—in the house."

He stopped to exclaim in an intense whisper, "O Mara bahia! O Calamity!" then went on speaking a little louder:

"There's no worse enemy and no better friend than a brother, Tuan, for one brother knows another, and in perfect knowledge is strength for good or evil. I loved my brother. I went to him and told him that I could see nothing but one face, hear nothing but one voice. He told me: 'Open your heart so that she can see what is in it—and wait. Patience is wisdom. Inchi Midah may die or our Ruler may throw off his fear of a woman!' . . . I waited. . . . You remember the lady with the veiled face, Tuan, and the fear of our Ruler before her cunning and temper. And if she wanted her servant, what could I do? But I fed the hunger of my heart on short glances and stealthy words. I loitered on the path to the bathhouses in the daytime, and when the sun had fallen behind the forest I crept along the jasmine hedges of the women's courtyard. Unseeing, we spoke to one another through the scent of flowers, through the veil of leaves, through the blades of long grass that stood still before our lips; so great was our prudence, so faint was the murmur of our great longing. The time passed swiftly . . . and there were whispers among women—and our enemies watched —my brother was gloomy, and I began to think of killing and of a fierce death. . . . We are of a people who take what they want—like you whites. There is a time when a man should forget loyalty and respect. Might and authority are given to rulers, but to all men is given love and strength and courage. My brother said, 'You shall take her from their midst. We are two who are like one.' And I answered, 'Let it be soon, for I find no warmth in sunlight that does not shine upon her.' Our time came when the Ruler and all the great people went to the mouth of the river to fish by torchlight. There were hundreds of boats, and on the white sand, between the water and the forests, dwellings of leaves were built for the households of the Rajahs. The smoke of cooking fires was like a blue mist of the evening, and many voices rang in it joyfully. While they were making the boats ready to beat up the fish, my brother came to me and said, 'Tonight!' I looked to my weapons, and when the time came our canoe took its place in the circle of boats carrying the torches. The lights blazed on the water, but behind the boats there was darkness. When the shouting began and the excitement made them like mad we dropped out. The water swallowed our fire, and we floated back to the shore that was dark with only here and there the glimmer of embers. We could hear the talk of slave girls among the sheds. Then we found a place deserted and silent. We waited there. She came. She came running along the shore, rapid and leaving no trace, like a leaf driven by the wind into the sea. My brother said gloomily, 'Go and take her; carry her into our boat.' I lifted her in my arms. She panted. Her heart was beating against my breast. I said, 'I take you from those people. You came to the cry of my heart, but my arms take you into my boat against the will of the great!' 'It is right,' said my brother. 'We are men who take what we want and can hold it against many. We should have taken her in daylight.' I said, 'Let us be off'; for since she was in my boat I began to think of our Ruler's many men. 'Yes. Let us be off,' said my brother. 'We are cast out and this boat is our country now —and the sea is our refuge.' He lingered with his foot on the shore, and I entreated him to hasten, for I remembered the strokes of her heart against my breast and thought that two men cannot withstand a hundred. We left, paddling downstream close to the bank; and as we passed by the creek where they were fishing, the great shouting had ceased, but the murmur of voices was loud like the humming of insects flying at noonday. The boats floated, clustered together, in the red light of torches, under a black roof of smoke; and men talked of their sport. Men that boasted, and praised, and jeered—men that would have been our friends in the morning, but on that night were already our enemies. We paddled swiftly past. We had not more friends in the country of our birth. She sat in the middle of the canoe with covered face; silent as she is now; unseeing as she is now—and I had no regret at what I was leaving because I could hear her breathing close to me—as I can hear her now."

He paused, listened with his ear turned to the doorway, then shook his head and went on:

"My brother wanted to shout the cry of challenge—one cry only—to let the people know we were freeborn robbers who trusted our arms and the great sea. And again I begged him in the name of our love to be silent. Could I not hear her breathing close to me? I knew the pursuit would come quick enough. My brother loved me. He dipped his paddle without a splash. He only said, 'There is half a man in you now—the other half is in that woman. I can wait. When you are a whole man again, you will come back with me here to shout defiance. We are sons of the same mother.' I made no answer. All my strength and all my spirit were in my hands that held the paddle—for I longed to be with her in a safe place beyond the reach of men's anger and of women's spite. My love was so great that I thought it could guide me to a country where death was unknown, if I could only escape from Inchi Midah's fury and from our Ruler's sword. We paddled with haste, breathing through our teeth. The blades bit deep into the smooth water. We passed out of the river; we flew in clear channels among the shallows. We skirted the black coast; we skirted the sand beaches where the sea speaks in whispers to the land; and the gleam of white sand flashed back past our boat, so swiftly she ran upon the water. We spoke not. Only once I said, 'Sleep, Diamelen, for soon you may want all your strength.' I heard the sweetness of her voice, but I never turned my head. The sun rose and still we went on. Water fell from my face like rain from a cloud. We flew in the light and heat. I never looked back, but I knew that my brother's eyes, behind me, were looking steadily ahead, for the boat went as straight as a bush-

man's dart when it leaves the end of the sumpitan.[1] There was no better paddler, no better steersman than my brother. Many times, together, we had won races in that canoe. But we never had put out our strength as we did then—then, when for the last time we paddled together! There was no braver or stronger man in our country than my brother. I could not spare the strength to turn my head and look at him, but every moment I heard the hiss of his breath getting louder behind me. Still he did not speak. The sun was high. The heat clung to my back like a flame of fire. My ribs were ready to burst, but I could no longer get enough air into my chest. And then I felt I must cry out with my last breath, 'Let us rest!' ... 'Good!' he answered; and his voice was firm. He was strong. He was brave. He knew not fear and no fatigue.... My brother!"

A murmur powerful and gentle, a murmur vast and faint; the murmur of trembling leaves, of stirring boughs, ran through the tangled depths of the forests, ran over the starry smoothness of the lagoon, and the water between the piles lapped the slimy timber once with a sudden splash. A breath of warm air touched the two men's faces and passed on with a mournful sound—a breath loud and short like an uneasy sigh of the dreaming earth.

Arsat went on in an even, low voice.

"We ran our canoe on the white beach of a little bay close to a long tongue of land that seemed to bar our road; a long wooded cape going far into the sea. My brother knew that place. Beyond the cape a river has its entrance, and through the jungle of that land there is a narrow path. We made a fire and cooked rice. Then we lay down to sleep on the soft sand in the shade of our canoe, while she watched. No sooner had I closed my eyes than I heard her cry of alarm. We leaped up. The sun was halfway down the sky al-

---

[1] **sumpitan:** a kind of blowgun for discharging a dart, used by natives of Borneo and adjacent islands.

ready, and coming in sight in the opening of the bay we saw a prau [1] manned by many paddlers. We knew it at once; it was one of our Rajah's praus. They were watching the shore, and saw us. They beat the gong, and turned the head of the prau into the bay. I felt my heart become weak within my breast. Diamelen sat on the sand and covered her face. There was no escape by sea. My brother laughed. He had the gun you had given him, Tuan, before you went away, but there was only a handful of powder. He spoke to me quickly: 'Run with her along the path. I shall keep them back, for they have no firearms, and landing in the face of a man with a gun is certain death for some. Run with her. On the other side of that wood there is a fisherman's house—and a canoe. When I have fired all the shots I will follow. I am a great runner, and before they can come up we shall be gone. I will hold out as long as I can, for she is but a woman —that can neither run nor fight, but she has your heart in her weak hands.' He dropped behind the canoe. The prau was coming. She and I ran, and as we rushed along the path I heard shots. My brother fired—once—twice—and the booming of the gong ceased. There was silence behind us. That neck of land is narrow. Before I heard my brother fire the third shot I saw the shelving shore, and I saw the water again; the mouth of a broad river. We crossed a grassy glade. We ran down to the water. I saw a low hut above the black mud, and a small canoe hauled up. I heard another shot behind me. I thought, 'That is his last charge.' We rushed down to the canoe; a man came running from the hut, but I leaped on him, and we rolled together in the mud. Then I got up, and he lay still at my feet. I don't know whether I had killed him or not. I and Diamelen pushed the canoe afloat. I heard yells behind me, and I saw my brother run across the glade. Many men were bound-

ing after him. I took her in my arms and threw her into the boat, then leaped in myself. When I looked back I saw that my brother had fallen. He fell and was up again, but the men were closing round him. He shouted, 'I am coming!' The men were close to him. I looked. Many men. Then I looked at her. Tuan, I pushed the canoe! I pushed it into deep water. She was kneeling forward looking at me, and I said, 'Take your paddle,' while I struck the water with mine. Tuan, I heard him cry. I heard him cry my name twice; and I heard voices shouting, 'Kill! Strike!' I never turned back. I heard him calling my name again with a great shriek, as when life is going out together with the voice— and I never turned my head. My own name!... My brother! Three times he called—but I was not afraid of life. Was she not there in that canoe? And could I not with her find a country where death is forgotten—where death is unknown!"

The white man sat up. Arsat rose and stood, an indistinct and silent figure above the dying embers of the fire. Over the lagoon a mist drifting and low had crept, erasing slowly the glittering images of the stars. And now a great expanse of white vapor covered the land: it flowed cold and gray in the darkness, eddied in noiseless whirls round the tree trunks and about the platform of the house, which seemed to float upon a restless and impalpable illusion of a sea. Only far away the tops of the trees stood outlined on the twinkle of heaven, like a somber and forbidding shore—a coast deceptive, pitiless and black.

Arsat's voice vibrated loudly in the profound peace.

"I had her there! I had her! To get her I would have faced all mankind. But I had her—and——"

His words went out ringing into the empty distances. He paused and seemed to listen to them dying away very far— beyond help and beyond recall. Then he said quietly:

"Tuan, I loved my brother."

[1] **prau:** swift Malayan vessel with sharp prow and stern, which can sail equally well prow or stern first.

A breath of wind made him shiver. High above his head, high above the silent sea of mist the drooping leaves of the palms rattled together with a mournful and expiring sound. The white man stretched his legs. His chin rested on his chest, and he murmured sadly without lifting his head:

"We all love our brothers."

Arsat burst out with an intense whispering violence:

"What did I care who died? I wanted peace in my own heart."

He seemed to hear a stir in the house—listened—then stepped in noiselessly. The white man stood up. A breeze was coming in fitful puffs. The stars shone paler as if they had retreated into the frozen depths of immense space. After a chill gust of wind there were a few seconds of perfect calm and absolute silence. Then from behind the black and wavy line of the forests a column of golden light shot up into the heavens and spread over the semicircle of the eastern horizon. The sun had risen. The mist lifted, broke into drifting patches, vanished into thin flying wreaths; and the unveiled lagoon lay, polished and black, in the heavy shadows at the foot of the wall of trees. A white eagle rose over it with a slanting and ponderous flight, reached the clear sunshine and appeared dazzlingly brilliant for a moment, then, soaring higher, became a dark and motionless speck before it vanished into the blue as if it had left the earth forever. The white man, standing gazing upward before the doorway, heard in the hut a confused and broken murmur of distracted words ending with a loud groan. Suddenly Arsat stumbled out with outstretched hands, shivered, and stood still for some time with fixed eyes. Then he said:

"She burns no more."

Before his face the sun showed its edge above the treetops, rising steadily. The breeze freshened; a great brilliance burst upon the lagoon, sparkled on the rippling water. The forests came out of the clear shadows of the morning, became distinct, as if they had rushed nearer—to stop short in a great stir of leaves, of nodding boughs, of swaying branches. In the merciless sunshine the whisper of unconscious life grew louder, speaking in an incomprehensible voice round the dumb darkness of that human sorrow. Arsat's eyes wandered slowly, then stared at the rising sun.

"I can see nothing," he said half aloud to himself.

"There is nothing," said the white man, moving to the edge of the platform and waving his hand to his boat. A shout came faintly over the lagoon and the sampan began to glide toward the abode of the friend of ghosts.

"If you want to come with me, I will wait all the morning," said the white man, looking away upon the water.

"No, Tuan," said Arsat softly. "I shall not eat or sleep in this house, but I must first see my road. Now I can see nothing—see nothing! There is no light and no peace in the world; but there is death—death for many. We are sons of the same mother—and I left him in the midst of enemies; but I am going back now."

He drew a long breath and went on in a dreamy tone:

"In a little while I shall see clear enough to strike—to strike. But she has died, and . . . now . . . darkness."

He flung his arms wide open, let them fall along his body, then stood still with unmoved face and stony eyes, staring at the sun. The white man got down into his canoe. The polers ran smartly along the sides of the boat, looking over their shoulders at the beginning of a weary journey. High in the stern, his head muffled up in white rags, the juragan sat moody, letting his paddle trail in the water. The white man, leaning with both arms over the grass roof of the little cabin, looked at the shining ripple of the boat's wake. Before the sampan passed out of the lagoon into the creek he lifted his eyes. Arsat had not moved. He stood lonely in the searching sunshine; and he looked beyond the great light of a cloudless day into the darkness of a world of illusions.

COMMENTARY

How simply we can summarize the action of this story! Arsat's brother has been killed in helping him to escape their homeland with Diamelen. When she dies he realizes that while she lived his tie to her had bound him to live, no matter how or where. Now that she is dead a profounder tie obliges him to die in order to avenge his brother. If you like the story you may well exclaim: "There is much more to it than that!" This "more" which eludes a simple summary is the additional burden of feeling that results from actually reading the story. This comes from what we may call "frames," the different perspectives from which the reader is led to look at the story's simple sequence of events.

The first and most obvious frame is the consciousness of the white man, a witness from another culture moving in a world not his own. In the consciousness of the white man, all the things which are familiar to his paddlers for him add up to total strangeness. In this foreigner's mind, the world he is moving through is a *whole*. We seldom see anything this way unless we are far from our own home. Descriptive passages in the first part of the story add to the effect of strangeness: "The narrow creek was like a ditch: tortuous, fabulously deep; filled with gloom under the thin strip of pure and shining blue of the heaven. Immense trees soared up, invisible behind the festooned draperies of creepers. Here and there, near the glistening blackness of the water, a twisted root of some tall tree showed among the tracery of small ferns, black and dull, writhing and motionless, like an arrested snake."

The second frame is the disconnection (what critics call the "alienation") of Arsat himself, living as he does in a world in which he is an impious intruder. He disregards the spirits of those now dead who have lived in the house on the lagoon. The paddlers think of him as cut off from them altogether. His isolation intensifies the terrible plight he is in: the woman for whom he had sacrificed his brother's life is dying, and she is his whole world.

A third, more general, frame is the cosmic view behind the story—the sense of people as strangers moving through a mysterious country toward an unknown end. The white man has this sense as he looks into the darkness while Diamelen is dying: "In that fleeting and powerful disturbance of his being, the earth, enfolded in the starlight peace, became a shadowy country of inhuman strife, a battlefield of phantoms terrible and charming, august or ignoble, struggling ardently for the possession of our helpless hearts." Placed against such a view, simple virtues such as loyalty become supremely important—as our only surety, our defense against our own weaknesses and against our fear that the world is only an illusion.

FOR STUDY AND DISCUSSION

1. "There is half a man in you now—the other half is in that woman. I can wait. When you are a whole man again, you will come back with me here to shout defiance. We are sons of the same mother." Use this passage to analyze Arsat's moral obligations.

2. Cite the crucial passage in the story which shows Arsat failing his obligations. How does the white man's comment, "We all love our brothers," frame this episode?

3. What use does Conrad make of the great stillness at the opening of the story?

4. Both the white man and Arsat are alienated from their countries and their people. Does the white man's alienation seem self-imposed? What is the relationship of the two men? Does the white man's attitude toward Arsat seem somewhat detached? If so, how does this attitude further illustrate the cosmic, or universal, theme of Conrad's story?

5. Divide the story into episodes, describing briefly what happens in each. What effect on the reader is each meant to produce?

6. Choose a single episode and study Conrad's use of adjectives in that episode to discover how often he tells you what to feel, and how often he creates a situation or picture which inspires your feeling.

7. Explain why, in your opinion, Conrad chose to call his story "The Lagoon."

Il Conde

A Pathetic Tale

"Vedi Napoli E Poi Mori." *

THE FIRST TIME we got into conversation was in the National Museum in Naples, in the rooms on the ground floor containing the famous collection of bronzes from Herculaneum and Pompeii: [1] that marvelous legacy of antique art whose delicate perfection has been preserved for us by the catastrophic fury of a volcano.

He addressed me first, over the celebrated Resting Hermes which we had been looking at side by side. He said the right things about that wholly admirable piece. Nothing profound. His taste was natural rather than cultivated. He had obviously seen many fine things in his life and appreciated them: but he had no jargon of a dilettante or the connoisseur. A hateful tribe. He spoke like a fairly intelligent man of the world, a perfectly unaffected gentleman.

We had known each other by sight for some few days past. Staying in the same hotel—good, but not extravagantly up-to-date—I had noticed him in the vestibule going in and out. I judged he was an old and valued client. The bow of the hotel keeper was cordial in its deference, and he acknowledged it with familiar courtesy.

For the servants he was *Il Conde*. There was some squabble over a man's parasol —yellow silk with white lining sort of thing—the waiters had discovered abandoned outside the dining-room door. Our gold-laced doorkeeper recognized it and I heard him directing one of the lift boys to run after *Il Conde* with it. Perhaps he was the only Count staying in the hotel, or perhaps he had the distinction of being *the* Count *par excellence,* [2] conferred upon him because of his tried fidelity to the house.

Having conversed at the Museo— [3] (and by the by he had expressed his dislike of the busts and statues of Roman emperors in the gallery of marbles: their faces were too vigorous, too pronounced for him)—having conversed already in the morning I did not think I was intruding when in the evening, finding the dining room very full, I proposed to share his little table. Judging by the quiet urbanity of his consent he did not think so either. His smile was very attractive.

He dined in an evening waistcoat and a "smoking" [4] (he called it so) with a black tie. All this of very good cut, not new— just as these things should be. He was, morning or evening, very correct in his dress. I have no doubt that his whole existence had been correct, well ordered and conventional, undisturbed by startling events. His white hair brushed upwards off a lofty forehead gave him the air of an idealist, of an imaginative man. His white mustache, heavy but carefully trimmed and arranged, was not unpleasantly tinted a golden yellow in the middle. The faint scent of some very good perfume, and of good cigars (that last an odor quite remarkable to come upon in Italy) reached me across the table. It was in his eyes that his age showed most. They were a little weary with creased eyelids. He must have been sixty or a couple of years more. And he was communicative. I would not

---

* *"Vedi ... Mori"*: "See Naples and Die." An Italian compliment to the beauty of Naples, meaning that a person is supposed to die content after having seen the beautiful city.

[1] **Herculaneum** (hûr′kyə·lā′nē·əm) **and Pompeii** (pom·pā′): ancient cities near Naples that were buried by an eruption of Vesuvius in A.D. 79.

[2] *par excellence* (pär·ek′sə·läns): excellent beyond comparison.

[3] **Museo** (myo͞o·sā′ō): museum.

[4] **"smoking"**: smoking jacket.

go so far as to call it garrulous—but distinctly communicative.

He had tried various climates, of Abbazia,[1] of the Riviera,[2] of other places, too, he told me, but the only one which suited him was the climate of the Gulf of Naples. The ancient Romans, who, he pointed out to me, were men expert in the art of living, knew very well what they were doing when they built their villas on these shores, in Baiae, in Vico, in Capri.[3] They came down to this seaside in search of health, bringing with them their trains of mimes[4] and flute players to amuse their leisure. He thought it extremely probable that the Romans of the higher classes were specially predisposed to painful rheumatic affections.

This was the only personal opinion I heard him express. It was based on no special erudition. He knew no more of the Romans than an average informed man of the world is expected to know. He argued from personal experience. He had suffered himself from a painful and dangerous rheumatic affection till he found relief in this particular spot of southern Europe.

This was three years ago, and ever since he had taken up his quarters on the shores of the gulf, either in one of the hotels in Sorrento[5] or hiring a small villa in Capri. He had a piano, a few books: picked up transient acquaintances of a day, week, or month in the stream of travelers from all Europe. One can imagine him going out for his walks in the streets and lanes, becoming known to beggars, shopkeepers, children, country people; talking amiably over the walls to the contadini[6]—and coming back to his rooms or his villa to sit before the piano, with his white hair brushed up on his thick orderly mustache "to make a little music for myself." And, of course, for a change there was Naples near by—life, movement, animation, opera. A little amusement, as he said, is necessary for health. Mimes and flute players, in fact. Only unlike the magnates of ancient Rome, he had no affairs of the city to call him away from these moderate delights. He had no affairs at all. Probably he had never had any grave affairs to attend to in his life. It was a kindly existence, with its joys and sorrows regulated by the course of Nature—marriages, births, deaths—ruled by the prescribed usages of good society and protected by the State.

He was a widower; but in the months of July and August he ventured to cross the Alps for six weeks on a visit to his married daughter. He told me her name. It was that of a very aristocratic family. She had a castle—in Bohemia,[7] I think. This is as near as I ever came to ascertaining his nationality. His own name, strangely enough, he never mentioned. Perhaps he thought I had seen it on the published list. Truth to say, I never looked. At any rate, he was a good European—he spoke four languages to my certain knowledge—and a man of fortune. Not of great fortune, evidently and appropriately. I imagine that to be extremely rich would have appeared to him improper, outré[8]—too blatant altogether. And obviously, too, the fortune was not of his making. The making of a fortune cannot be achieved without some roughness. It is a matter of temperament. His nature was too kindly for strife. In the course of conversation he mentioned his estate quite by the way, in reference to that painful and alarming rheumatic affection. One year, staying incautiously beyond the Alps as late as the middle of September, he had been laid up for three months in that lonely country house with

---

[1] **Abbazia** (äb′bä·tsē′ä): a village in Yugoslavia noted for its mild climate.

[2] **Riviera** (riv′ē·âr′ə): a resort area on the southern coast of France.

[3] **Baiae** (bā′ē), **Vico** (vē′kō), **Capri** (kä′prē): Roman beach resorts.

[4] **mimes** (mīmz): actors who specialize in pantomime.

[5] **Sorrento** (sôr·ren′tō): a port city in Italy, on the Bay of Naples.

[6] **contadini** (côn·tä·dē′nē): small landowners.

[7] **Bohemia:** an area in Czechoslovakia.

[8] *outré* (ōō·trā′): exaggerated, bizarre.

no one but his valet and the caretaking couple to attend to him. Because, as he expressed it, he "kept no establishment there." He had only gone for a couple of days to confer with his land agent. He promised himself never to be so imprudent in the future. The first weeks of September would find him on the shores of his beloved gulf.

Sometimes in traveling one comes upon such lonely men, whose only business is to wait for the unavoidable. Deaths and marriages have made a solitude round them, and one really cannot blame their endeavors to make the waiting as easy as possible. As he remarked to me, "At my time of life freedom from physical pain is a very important matter."

It must not be imagined that he was a wearisome hypochondriac. He was really much too well bred to be a nuisance. He had an eye for the small weaknesses of humanity. But it was a good-natured eye. He made a restful, easy, pleasant companion for the hours between dinner and bedtime. We spent three evenings together, and then I had to leave Naples in a hurry to look after a friend who had fallen seriously ill in Taormina.[1] Having nothing to do, *Il Conde* came to see me off at the station. I was somewhat upset, and his idleness was always ready to take a kindly form. He was by no means an indolent man.

He went along the train peering into the carriages for a good seat for me, and then remained talking cheerily from below. He declared he would miss me that evening very much and announced his intention of going after dinner to listen to the band in the public garden, the Villa Nazionale. He would amuse himself by hearing excellent music and looking at the best society. There would be a lot of people, as usual.

I seem to see him yet—his raised face with a friendly smile under the thick mustaches, and his kind, fatigued eyes.

---

[1] **Taormina** (tä´ōr·mē´nä): a town on the eastern coast of Sicily.

As the train began to move, he addressed me in two languages: first in French, saying *"Bon voyage";* then, in his very good, somewhat emphatic English, encouragingly, because he could see my concern: "All will—be—well—yet!"

My friend's illness having taken a decidedly favorable turn, I returned to Naples on the tenth day. I cannot say I had given much thought to *Il Conde* during my absence, but entering the dining room I looked for him in his habitual place. I had an idea he might have gone back to Sorrento to his piano and his books and his fishing. He was great friends with all the boatmen, and fished a good deal with lines from a boat. But I made out his white head in the crowd of heads, and even from a distance noticed something unusual in his attitude. Instead of sitting erect, gazing all round with alert urbanity, he drooped over his plate. I stood opposite him for some time before he looked up, a little wildly, if such a strong word can be used in connection with his correct appearance.

"Ah, my dear sir! Is it you?" he greeted me. "I hope all is well."

He was very nice about my friend. Indeed, he was always nice, with the niceness of people whose hearts are genuinely humane. But this time it cost him an effort. His attempts at general conversation broke down into dullness. It occurred to me he might have been indisposed. But before I could frame the inquiry he muttered:

"You find me here very sad."

"I am sorry for that," I said. "You haven't had bad news, I hope?"

It was very kind of me to take an interest. No. It was not that. No bad news, thank God. And he became very still as if holding his breath. Then, leaning forward a little, and in an odd tone of awed embarrassment, he took me into his confidence.

"The truth is that I have had a very—a very—how shall I say?—abominable adventure happen to me."

The energy of the epithet was sufficiently startling in that man of moderate feelings and toned-down vocabulary. The word *unpleasant* I should have thought would have fitted amply the worst experience likely to befall a man of his stamp. And an adventure, too. Incredible! But it is in human nature to believe the worst; and I confess I eyed him stealthily, wondering what he had been up to. In a moment, however, my unworthy suspicions vanished. There was a fundamental refinement of nature about the man which made me dismiss all idea of some more or less disreputable scrape.

"It is very serious. Very serious." He went on, nervously. "I will tell you after dinner, if you will allow me."

I expressed my perfect acquiescence by a little bow, nothing more. I wished him to understand that I was not likely to hold him to that offer, if he thought better of it later on. We talked of indifferent things, but with a sense of difficulty quite unlike our former easy, gossipy intercourse. The hand raising a piece of bread to his lips, I noticed, trembled slightly. This symptom, in regard to my reading of the man, was no less than startling.

In the smoking room he did not hang back at all. Directly we had taken our usual seats he leaned sideways over the arm of his chair and looked straight into my eyes earnestly.

"You remember," he began, "that day you went away? I told you then I would go to the Villa Nazionale to hear some music in the evening."

I remembered. His handsome old face, so fresh for his age, unmarked by any trying experience, appeared haggard for an instant. It was like the passing of a shadow. Returning his steadfast gaze, I took a sip of my black coffee. He was systematically minute in his narrative, simply in order, I think, not to let his excitement get the better of him.

After leaving the railway station, he had an ice and read the paper in a café. Then he went back to the hotel, dressed for dinner, and dined with a good appetite. After dinner he lingered in the hall (there were chairs and tables there) smoking his cigar; talked to the little girl of the Primo Tenore [1] of the San Carlo theatre, and exchanged a few words with that "amiable lady," the wife of the Primo Tenore. There was no performance that evening, and these people were going to the Villa also. They went out of the hotel. Very well.

At the moment of following their example—it was half-past nine already—he remembered he had a rather large sum of money in his pocketbook. He entered, therefore, the office and deposited the greater part of it with the bookkeeper of the hotel. This done, he took a carozella [2] and drove to the seashore. He got out of the cab and entered the villa on foot from the Largo di Vittoria end.

He stared at me very hard. And I understood then how really impressionable he was. Every small fact and event of that evening stood out in his memory as if endowed with mystic significance. If he did not mention to me the color of the pony which drew the carozella, and the aspect of the man who drove, it was a mere oversight arising from his agitation, which he repressed manfully.

He had then entered the Villa Nazionale from the Largo di Vittoria end. The Villa Nazionale is a public pleasure-ground laid out in grass plots, bushes, and flowerbeds between the houses of the Riviera di Chiaja and the waters of the bay. Alleys of trees, more or less parallel, stretch its whole length—which is considerable. On the Riviera di Chiaja side the electric tramcars run close to the railings. Between the garden and the sea is the fashionable drive, a broad road bordered by a low wall, beyond which the Mediterranean splashes with gentle murmurs when the weather is fine.

As life goes on late at night in Naples, the broad drive was all astir with a brilliant swarm of carriage lamps moving in pairs, some creeping slowly, others run-

[1] **Primo Tenore** (prē′mō ten·ôr′ə): the leading tenor in an opera company.
[2] **carozella** (cä·rō·zel′à): carriage.

ning rapidly under the thin, motionless line of electric lamps defining the shore. And a brilliant swarm of stars hung above the land humming with voices, piled up with houses, glittering with lights—and over the silent flat shadows of the sea.

The gardens themselves are not very well lit. Our friend went forward in the warm gloom, his eyes fixed upon a distant luminous region extending nearly across the whole width of the Villa, as if the air had glowed there with its own cold, bluish, and dazzling light. This magic spot, behind the black trunks of trees and masses of inky foliage, breathed out sweet sounds mingled with bursts of brassy roar, sudden clashes of metal, and grave, vibrating thuds.

As he walked on, all these noises combined together into a piece of elaborate music whose harmonious phrases came persuasively through a great disorderly murmur of voices and shuffling of feet on the gravel of that open space. An enormous crowd immersed in the electric light, as if in a bath of some radiant and tenuous fluid shed upon their heads by luminous globes, drifted in its hundreds round the band. Hundreds more sat on chairs in more or less concentric circles, receiving unflinchingly the great waves of sonority that ebbed out into the darkness. The Count penetrated the throng, drifted with it in tranquil enjoyment, listening and

looking at the faces. All people of good society: mothers with their daughters, parents and children, young men and young women all talking, smiling, nodding to each other. Very many pretty faces, and very many pretty toilettes. There was, of course, a quantity of diverse types: showy old fellows with white mustaches, fat men, thin men, officers in uniforms; but what predominated, he told me, was the South Italian type of young man, with a colorless, clear complexion, red lips, jet-black little mustache and liquid black eyes so wonderfully effective in leering or scowling.

Withdrawing from the throng, the Count shared a little table in front of the café with a young man of just such a type. Our friend had some lemonade. The young man was sitting moodily before an empty glass. He looked up once, and then looked down again. He also tilted his hat forward. Like this——

The Count made the gesture of a man pulling his hat down over his brow, and went on:

"I think to myself: he is sad; something is wrong with him; young men have their troubles. I take no notice of him, of course. I pay for my lemonade, and go away."

Strolling about in the neighborhood of the band, the Count thinks he saw twice that young man wandering alone in the crowd. Once their eyes met. It must have

been the same young man, but there were so many there of that type that he could not be certain. Moreover, he was not very much concerned except in so far that he had been struck by the marked, peevish discontent of that face.

Presently, tired of the feeling of confinement one experiences in a crowd, the Count edged away from the band. An alley, very somber by contrast, presented itself invitingly with its promise of solitude and coolness. He entered it, walking slowly on till the sound of the orchestra became distinctly deadened. Then he walked back and turned about once more. He did this several times before he noticed that there was somebody occupying one of the benches.

The spot being midway between two lampposts, the light was faint.

The man lolled back in the corner of the seat, his legs stretched out, his arms folded and his head drooping on his breast. He never stirred, as though he had fallen asleep there, but when the Count passed by next time he had changed his attitude. He sat leaning forward. His elbows were propped on his knees, and his hands were rolling a cigarette. He never looked up from that occupation.

The Count continued his stroll away from the band. He returned slowly, he said. I can imagine him enjoying to the full, but with his usual tranquillity, the balminess of this southern night and the sounds of music softened delightfully by the distance.

Presently, he approached for the third time the man on the garden seat, still leaning forward with his elbows on his knees. It was a dejected pose. In the semi-obscurity of the alley his high shirt collar and his cuffs made small patches of vivid whiteness. The Count said that he had noticed him getting up brusquely as if to walk away, but almost before he was aware of it the man stood before him asking in a low, gentle tone whether the signore would have the kindness to oblige him with a light.

The Count answered this request by a polite "Certainly," and dropped his hands with the intention of exploring both pockets of his trousers for the matches.

"I dropped my hands," he said, "but I never put them in my pockets. I felt a pressure there——"

He put the tip of his finger on a spot close under his breastbone, the very spot of the human body where a Japanese gentleman begins the operations of the hara-kiri, which is a form of suicide following upon dishonor, upon an intolerable outrage to the delicacy of one's feelings.

"I glance down," the Count continued in an awestruck voice, "and what do I see? A knife! A long knife——"

"You don't mean to say," I exclaimed, amazed, "that you have been held up like this in the Villa at half-past ten o'clock, within a stone's throw of a thousand people!"

He nodded several times, staring at me with all his might.

"The clarionet," he declared solemnly, "was finishing his solo, and I assure you I could hear every note. Then the band crashed *fortissimo*,[1] and that creature rolled its eyes and gnashed its teeth hissing at me with the greatest ferocity, 'Be silent! No noise or——' "

I could not get over my astonishment.

"What sort of knife was it?" I asked stupidly.

"A long blade. A stiletto—perhaps a kitchen knife. A long narrow blade. It gleamed. And his eyes gleamed. His white teeth, too. I could see them. He was very ferocious. I thought to myself: 'If I hit him he will kill me.' How could I fight with him? He had the knife and I had nothing. I am nearly seventy, you know, and that was a young man. I seemed even to recognize him. The moody young man at the café. The young man I met in the crowd. But I could not tell. There are so many like him in this country."

This distress of that moment was reflected in his face. I should think that physically he must have been paralyzed

---

[1] *fortissimo* (fôr·tēs′sē·mō): very loud.

by surprise. His thoughts, however, remained extremely active. They ranged over every alarming possibility. The idea of setting up a vigorous shouting for help occurred to him, too. But he did nothing of the kind, and the reason why he refrained gave me a good opinion of his mental self-possession. He saw in a flash that nothing prevented the other from shouting, too.

"That young man might in an instant have thrown away his knife and pretended I was the aggressor. Why not? He might have said I attacked him. Why not? It was one incredible story against another! He might have said anything—bring some dishonoring charge against me—what do I know? By his dress he was no common robber. He seemed to belong to the better classes. What could I say? He was an Italian—I am a foreigner. Of course, I have my passport, and there is our consul—but to be arrested, dragged at night to the police office like a criminal!"

He shuddered. It was in his character to shrink from scandal, much more than from mere death. And certainly for many people this would have always remained —considering certain peculiarities of Neapolitan [1] manners—a deucedly queer story. The Count was no fool. His belief in the respectable placidity of life having received this rude shock, he thought that now anything might happen. But also a notion came into his head that this young man was perhaps merely an infuriated lunatic.

This was for me the first hint of his attitude toward this adventure. In his exaggerated delicacy of sentiment he felt that nobody's self-esteem need be affected by what a madman may choose to do to one. It became apparent, however, that the Count was to be denied that consolation. He enlarged upon the abominably savage way in which that young man rolled his glistening eyes and gnashed his white teeth. The band was going now through a slow movement of solemn bray-

ing by all the trombones, with deliberately repeated bangs of the big drum.

"Nothing," answered the Count. "I let my hands hang down very still. I told him quietly I did not intend making a noise. He snarled like a dog, then said in an ordinary voice:

"'Vostro portofolio.'" [2]

"So I naturally," continued the Count —and from this point acted the whole thing in pantomime. Holding me with his eyes, he went through all the motions of reaching into his inside breast pocket, taking out a pocketbook, and handing it over. But that young man, still bearing steadily on the knife, refused to touch it.

He directed the Count to take the money out himself, received it into his left hand, motioned the pocketbook to be returned to the pocket, all this being done to the sweet trilling of flutes and clarionets sustained by the emotional drone of the hautboys. And the "young man," as the Count called him, said: "This seems very little."

"It was, indeed, only 340 or 360 lire," the Count pursued. "I had left my money in the hotel, as you know. I told him this was all I had on me. He shook his head impatiently and said:

"'Vostro orologio.'" [3]

The Count gave me the dumb show of pulling out his watch, detaching it. But, as it happened, the valuable gold half-chronometer he possessed had been left at a watchmaker's for cleaning. He wore that evening (on a leather guard) the Waterbury fifty-franc thing he used to take with him on his fishing expeditions. Perceiving the nature of this booty, the well-dressed robber made a contemptuous clicking sound with his tongue like this, "Tse-Ah!" and waved it away hastily. Then, as the Count was returning the disdained object to his pocket, he demanded with a threateningly increased pressure of the knife on the epigastrium, by way of reminder:

[1] **Neapolitan:** characteristic of Naples.

[2] "**Vostro portofolio**'": your billfold.
[3] "**Vostro orologio**'": your watch.

" 'Vostri anelli.' " [1]

"One of the rings," went on the Count, "was given me many years ago by my wife; the other is the signet ring of my father. I said 'No. *That* you shall not have!' "

Here the Count reproduced the gesture corresponding to that declaration by clapping one hand upon the other, and pressing both thus against his chest. It was touching in its resignation. "That you shall not have," he repeated firmly, and closed his eyes, fully expecting—I don't know whether I am right in recording that such an unpleasant word had passed his lips—fully expecting to feel himself being—I really hesitate to say—being disembowelled by the push of the long, sharp blade resting murderously against the pit of his stomach—the very seat, in all human beings, of anguishing sensations.

Great waves of harmony went on flowing from the band.

Suddenly the Count felt the nightmarish pressure removed from the sensitive spot. He opened his eyes. He was alone. He had heard nothing. It is probable that "the young man" had departed, with light steps, some time before, but the sense of the horrid pressure had lingered even after the knife had gone. A feeling of weakness came over him. He had just time to stagger to the garden seat. He felt as though he had held his breath for a long time. He sat all in a heap, panting with the shock of the reaction.

The band was executing, with immense bravura, the complicated finale. It ended with a tremendous crash. He heard it unreal and remote, as if his ears had been stopped, and then the hard clapping of a thousand, more or less, pairs of hands, like a sudden hail-shower passing away. The profound silence which succeeded recalled him to himself.

A tramcar resembling a long glass box, wherein people sat with their heads strongly lighted, ran along swiftly within sixty yards of the spot where he had been

robbed. Then another rustled by, and yet another going the other way. The audience about the band had broken up, and were entering the alley in small conversing groups. The Count sat up straight and tried to think calmly of what had happened to him. The vileness of it took his breath away again. As far as I can make it out he was disgusted with himself. I do not mean to say with his behavior. Indeed, if his pantomimic rendering of it for my information was to be trusted, it was simply perfect. No, it was not that. He was not ashamed. He was shocked at being the selected victim, not of robbery so much as of contempt. His tranquillity had been wantonly desecrated. His lifelong, kindly nicety of outlook had been defaced.

Nevertheless, at that stage, before the iron had time to sink deep, he was able to argue himself into comparative equanimity. As his agitation calmed down somewhat, he became aware that he was frightfully hungry. Yes, hungry. The sheer emotion had made him simply ravenous. He left the seat and, after walking for some time, found himself outside the gardens and before an arrested tramcar, without knowing very well how he came there. He got in as if in a dream, by a sort of instinct. Fortunately he found in his trouser pocket a copper to satisfy the conductor. Then the car stopped, and as everybody was getting out he got out, too. He recognized the Piazza San Ferdinando, but apparently it did not occur to him to take a cab and drive to the hotel. He remained in distress on the Piazza like a lost dog, thinking vaguely of the best way of getting something to eat at once.

Suddenly he remembered his twenty-franc piece. He explained to me that he had that piece of French gold for something like three years. He used to carry it about with him as a sort of reserve in case of accident. Anybody is liable to have his pocket picked—a quite different thing from a brazen and insulting robbery.

---

[1] " *Vostri anelli* ": your rings.

The monumental arch of the Galleria Umberto faced him at the top of a noble flight of stairs. He climbed these without loss of time, and directed his steps toward the Café Umberto. All the tables outside were occupied by a lot of people who were drinking. But as he wanted something to eat, he went inside into the café, which is divided into aisles by square pillars set all round with long looking glasses. The Count sat down on a red plush bench against one of these pillars, waiting for his risotto.[1] And his mind reverted to his abominable adventure.

He thought of the moody, well-dressed young man with whom he had exchanged glances in the crowd around the bandstand, and who, he felt confident, was the robber. Would he recognize him again? Doubtless. But he did not want ever to see him again. The best thing was to forget this humiliating episode.

The Count looked round anxiously for the coming of his risotto, and, behold! to the left against the wall—there sat the young man. He was alone at a table, with a bottle of some sort of wine or syrup and a carafe of iced water before him. The smooth olive cheeks, the red lips, the little jet-black mustache turned up gallantly, the fine black eyes a little heavy and shaded by long eyelashes, that peculiar expression of cruel discontent to be seen only in the busts of some Roman emperors—it was he, no doubt at all. But that was a type. The Count looked away hastily. The young officer over there reading a paper was like that, too. Same type. Two young men farther away playing draughts[2] also resembled——

The Count lowered his head with the fear in his heart of being everlastingly haunted by the vision of that young man. He began to eat his risotto. Presently he heard the young man on his left call the waiter in a bad-tempered tone.

At the call, not only his own waiter, but two other idle waiters belonging to a quite different row of tables, rushed toward him with obsequious alacrity, which is not the general characteristic of the waiters in the Café Umberto. The young man muttered something and one of the waiters walking rapidly to the nearest door called out into the Galleria: "Pasquale! O! Pasquale!"

Everybody knows Pasquale, the shabby old fellow who, shuffling between the tables, offers for sale cigars, cigarettes, picture postcards, and matches to the clients of the café. He is in many respects an engaging scoundrel. The Count saw the gray-haired, unshaven ruffian enter the café, the glass case hanging from his neck by a leather strap, and, at a word from the waiter, make his shuffling way with a sudden spurt to the young man's table. The young man was in need of a cigar with which Pasquale served him fawningly. The old peddler was going out, when the Count, on a sudden impulse, beckoned to him.

Pasquale approached, the smile of deferential recognition combining oddly with the cynical searching expression of his eyes. Leaning his case on the table, he lifted the glass lid without a word. The Count took a box of cigarettes and, urged by a fearful curiosity, asked as casually as he could:

"Tell me, Pasquale, who is that young signor sitting over there?"

The other bent over his box confidentially.

"That, *Signor Conde*," he said, beginning to rearrange his wares busily and without looking up, "that is a young *Cavaliere*[3] of a very good family from Bari.[4] He studies in the University here, and is the chief, *capo*, of an association of young men—of very nice young men."

He paused, and then, with mingled discretion and pride of knowledge, murmured the explanatory word "Camorra"[5] and shut down the lid. "A very powerful

---

[1] **risotto** (rē·sō′tō): rice cooked with gravy or mushrooms.

[2] **draughts** (drafts): checkers.

[3] *Cavaliere* (ka·və·lē·âr′ə): nobleman, or gentleman.

[4] **Bari** (bä′rē): a province of Apulia, Italy.

[5] **"Camorra"** (kä·môr′rä): a secret society.

Camorra," he breathed out. "The professors themselves respect it greatly . . . *una lira e cinquanti centesimi,*[1] *Signor Conde.*"

Our friend paid with the gold piece. While Pasquale was making up the change, he observed that the young man, of whom he had heard so much in a few words, was watching the transaction covertly. After the old vagabond had withdrawn with a bow, the Count settled with the waiter and sat still. A numbness, he told me, had come over him.

The young man paid, too, got up, and crossed over, apparently for the purpose of looking at himself in the mirror set in the pillar nearest to the Count's seat. He was dressed all in black with a dark green bow tie. The Count looked round, and was startled by meeting a vicious glance out of the corners of the other's eyes. The young *Cavaliere* from Bari (according to Pasquale; but Pasquale is, of course, an accomplished liar) went on arranging his tie, settling his hat before the glass, and meantime he spoke just loud enough to be heard by the Count. He spoke through his teeth with the most insulting venom of contempt and gazing straight into the mirror.

"Ah! So you had some gold on you— you old liar—you old *birba*—you *furfante!*[2] But you are not done with me yet."

The fiendishness of his expression vanished like lightning, and he lounged out of the café with a moody, impassive face.

The poor Count, after telling me this last episode, fell back trembling in his chair. His forehead broke into perspiration. There was a wanton insolence in the spirit of this outrage which appalled even me. What it was to the Count's delicacy I won't attempt to guess. I am sure that if he had been not too refined to do such a blatantly vulgar thing as dying

from apoplexy in a café, he would have had a fatal stroke there and then. All irony apart, my difficulty was to keep him from seeing the full extent of my commiseration. He shrank from every excessive sentiment, and my commiseration was practically unbounded. It did not surprise me to hear that he had been in bed a week. He had got up to make his arrangements for leaving Southern Italy for good and all.

And the man was convinced that he could not live through a whole year in any other climate!

No argument of mine had any effect. It was not timidity, though he did say to me once: "You do not know what a Camorra is, my dear sir. I am a marked man." He was not afraid of what could be done to him. His delicate conception of his dignity was defiled by a degrading experience. He couldn't stand that. No Japanese gentleman, outraged in his exaggerated sense of honor, could have gone about his preparations for hara-kiri with greater resolution. To go home really amounted to suicide for the poor Count.

There is a saying of Neapolitan patriotism, intended for the information of foreigners, I presume: " See Naples and then die." *Vedi Napoli e poi mori.* It is a saying of excessive vanity, and everything excessive was abhorrent to the nice moderation of the poor Count. Yet, as I was seeing him off at the railway station, I thought he was behaving with singular fidelity to its conceited spirit. *Vedi Napoli! . . .* He had seen it! He had seen it with startling thoroughness—and now he was going to his grave. He was going to it by the *train de luxe* of the International Sleeping Car Company, *via* Trieste and Vienna. As the four long, somber coaches pulled out of the station I raised my hat with the solemn feeling of paying the last tribute of respect to a funeral *cortège.*[3] *Il Conde's* profile, behind the lighted pane of glass—*Vedi Napoli e poi mori!*

---

[1] *una . . . centesimi:* the price of the cigarettes.

[2] *birba* (bir′bà) *. . . furfante* (fûr·fan′tē): rascal, rogue.

[3] *cortège* (kôr·tezh′): procession.

COMMENTARY

"Il Conde" was written in 1907 and published the following year. At that time it seemed to many Europeans that they had finally achieved a society in which war was impossible, and that they could now progress in an orderly manner toward perfection, wiping out hunger, injustice, and violence along the way. This story is like a prophecy, a forecast of all the violence, public and private, which was to cut across the protected calm of Europe in the half-century to follow.

Il Conde and the young man who robs him are at different ends of the civilized spectrum: the Count is, if anything, over-civilized; the young man is violent, almost a savage. The story deals not only with the contrast between their different conceptions of life but also with the inevitable conflict between these two conceptions. The narrator explains that Il Conde does not like the busts of the Roman emperors. "Their faces were too vigorous, too pronounced for him." But the violence of these emperors was a part of their greatness. They were concerned not simply with building gardens and palaces filled with "mimes and flute players." They built something much larger, a great empire, a complexly ordered society. At the end of the story, Il Conde unexpectedly meets the violent young man at the Café Umberto. He is reminded both of all the young men of Naples who have olive cheeks, red lips, and little jet-black mustaches and also of "that peculiar expression of cruel discontent to be seen only in the busts of some Roman emperors." The Count himself is the end result of the kind of society such emperors have built. If bitterness and violence are somehow bound up with empire-building, it may also be true that a man like Il Conde, no longer capable of building empires, will inevitably find himself confronted with a terrible and seemingly meaningless violence.

FOR STUDY AND DISCUSSION

1. "His tranquillity had been wantonly desecrated." Explain how this sentence is a clue to what happens to the Count.

2. How does Conrad use the music in the park to enforce the meaning of the robbery?

3. What is the importance to the story of the saying "See Naples and die?" In how many ways might the saying be interpreted? Explain.

4. Does the Count ever show bravery in the story? Of what importance is his bravery to the story's theme? (Is his bravery very effective against the young man?)

5. How does the Count react when he learns that the young man is said to be a member of a band (Camorra)? How is the fact that the young man is revealed to be acting as part of a larger group related to the theme of the story?

6. The implied destruction of the Count is symbolic of the disintegration of the social order that insulated people—such as Il Conde—from the harsh realities of the world. How did Il Conde's reaction to the robbery reflect the attitudes of his fading social class?

7. How is the narrator used to frame this story? (For a discussion of framing, see page 676.) How would the effect of this story be different if it were told directly from the Count's point of view?

8. Compare "Il Conde" with "The Lagoon." Which story tries more obviously to build up atmosphere? Which story relies more on adjectives and adverbs to build up an effect? Which story do you think presents more interesting, or more complex, characters? Which story do you prefer? Why?

FOR COMPOSITION

1. In a preface, Conrad wrote, "My task, which I am trying to achieve, is, by the power of the written word, to make you hear, to make you feel—it is, before all, to make you *see*." Citing relevant passages from the stories you have just read, show how Conrad achieves his task.

2. The biographical introduction states that Conrad's most persistent concern is with "the way in which each man's dream of himself works either to join him with, or cut him off from, his fellows." Explore the way this concern is developed in the stories you have read.

A. E. HOUSMAN
(1859–1936)

Despite the small number of poems he published, A. E. Housman was hailed in his lifetime as the chief writer of lyric poetry since the death of Tennyson. His reputation was founded on *A Shropshire Lad,* a volume containing sixty-three simple lyrics. This collection was published in 1896, when Housman was thirty-seven. Twenty-six years later, he published *Last Poems,* an even smaller collection. A third volume, *More Poems,* was published by his brother Laurence after Housman's death. The poems in his first volume, by which he won his reputation, were supposed to be the songs and meditations of a young man, a farm lad of Shropshire. Housman said, "The Shropshire Lad is an imaginary figure, with something of my own temper and view of life." Many of the poems are tinged with a gentle melancholy. They show a deep awareness of life's grim realities, but subjects that might have been an occasion for harsh music in the hands of a poet like Thomas Hardy are tempered by the careful simplicity and melody of Housman's verse. Housman wrote of his poetry: "They say my verse is sad: no wonder; / Its narrow measure spans / Tears of eternity, and sorrow, / Not mine, but man's."

By profession, Housman was a gifted and eminent classical scholar. For most of his life, he was a professor of legendary formidability, holding first the chair of Latin at University College of the University of London and later a corresponding chair at Cambridge University. Much of his scholarly labor was devoted to the preparation of an edition of the works of Manilius, an obscure Latin poet of small reputation. Housman seems to have had a perverse appreciation of Manilius's dullness. As a scholar he was a savage controversialist and wrote a number of papers attacking other scholars that are remarkable for their irony and invective. As a man, he was painfully shy and hid behind an air of aloofness. Wilfred Blunt, the poet, wrote of him that he "would, I think, be quite silent if he were allowed to be."

But Housman's poems make it clear that beneath the savage and aloof scholar there was someone else, a man from the country who made smooth, beautiful songs out of his pain. It is this Housman who continues to win the admiration and sympathy of many readers. Sometimes, however, readers who are charmed by Housman's music fail to notice the sting behind the beauty. In an important lecture he gave on *The Name and Nature of Poetry,* he declared that poetry ought to have a physical effect on the reader, a sensation akin to love or fear. Housman's best poems have precisely this effect.

Loveliest of Trees

Loveliest of trees, the cherry now
Is hung with bloom along the bough,
And stands about the woodland ride°
Wearing white for Eastertide.

Now, of my three score years and ten, 5
Twenty will not come again,
And take from seventy springs a score,
It only leaves me fifty more.

And since to look at things in bloom
Fifty springs are little room, 10
About the woodlands I will go
To see the cherry hung with snow.

3. **ride:** a road intended for horseback travel.

When I Was One-and-Twenty

When I was one-and-twenty
    I heard a wise man say,
"Give crowns and pounds and guineas,
    But not your heart away;
Give pearls away and rubies 5
    But keep your fancy free."
But I was one-and-twenty,
    No use to talk to me.

When I was one-and-twenty
    I heard him say again, 10
"The heart out of the bosom
    Was never given in vain;
'Tis paid with sighs a plenty
    And sold for endless rue."
And I am two-and-twenty, 15
    And oh, 'tis true, 'tis true.

To an Athlete Dying Young

The time you won your town the race
We chaired you through the marketplace;
Man and boy stood cheering by,
And home we brought you shoulder-high.

Today, the road all runners come, 5
Shoulder-high we bring you home,
And set you at your threshold down,
Townsman of a stiller town.

Smart lad, to slip betimes away
From fields where glory does not stay, 10
And early though the laurel grows
It withers quicker than the rose.

Eyes the shady night has shut
Cannot see the record cut,
And silence sounds no worse than cheers
After earth has stopped the ears: 16

Now you will not swell the rout
Of lads that wore their honors out,
Runners whom renown outran
And the name died before the man. 20

So set, before its echoes fade,
The fleet foot on the sill of shade,
And hold to the low lintel up
The still-defended challenge cup.

And round that early-laureled head 25
Will flock to gaze the strengthless dead,
And find unwithered on its curls
The garland briefer than a girl's.

A. E. HOUSMAN   689

With Rue My Heart Is Laden

With rue my heart is laden
    For golden friends I had,
For many a rose-lipt maiden
    And many a lightfoot lad.

By brooks too broad for leaping   5
    The lightfoot boys are laid;
The rose-lipt girls are sleeping
    In fields where roses fade.

FOR STUDY AND DISCUSSION

1. How old is the speaker of "Loveliest of Trees"? Why is it particularly appropriate for him to look at the cherry trees at this time? What do you think the snow in the last line might symbolize?

2. What has the young man of "When I Was One-and-Twenty" learned in a year? What do you think has happened to him? Housman has a reputation for being able to compress much meaning into a few lines of poetry. Do you think this poem bears out his reputation? Explain.

3. In "To an Athlete Dying Young," what two processions are contrasted? What final race has the athlete won, according to the poem? Why does the poet call the athlete "Smart lad"? Explain the attitude that underlies this poem. (In answering this question, consider the title of the poem. Does the title lead you to expect a lament for the athlete? Is the poem actually a lament?)

4. "With Rue My Heart Is Laden" is the shortest of these four poems by Housman. Is it the least meaningful? Explain. What meanings arise out of the contrasts in the second stanza? *Contrast* is one of Housman's most important devices. Discuss the use of contrast in all of these poems by Housman.

5. After reading these four poems, how would you describe the predominant theme of Housman's poetry? How does each of the four poems reflect this theme?

6. Notice that Housman uses a ballad measure in two of these poems. Are these poems ballads? How do they conform to the definition of a lyric poem? What do these poems gain from the ballad form? In what way are Housman's poems similar to folk poetry (such as the folk ballads on pages 35–38)?

FOR COMPOSITION

Housman's poetry has been said to reveal "a bitter but fearless philosophy." Write a composition in which you agree or disagree with this statement. Support your case with examples from Housman's poems.

WILLIAM
BUTLER YEATS
(1865–1939)

Born a good poet, William Butler Yeats in middle age grappled with his poetic personality and technique and acquired the feeling and the skill to die a great one. He deserves a special place in literary history for turning British poetry away from a decadent and limiting concern with pure beauty and forcing it to deal with the personal, moral, and spiritual problems of the modern world. As Wordsworth had done a century before, Yeats brought poetry into touch with the language and the preoccupations of the modern world.

Yeats was an Irishman of English descent who was brought up among the legends and magical fancies of the west coast of Ireland. He was the grandson and great-grandson of clergymen, but his immediate family centered on his father— a painter who was more or less pressed for money most of the time, who moved between Dublin and London where Willie, as his family called him, attended school. During his summers in Sligo, Yeats discovered his vocations, first art, then poetry; there also he determined to make himself a leader in the Irish Nationalist movement.

Yeats was an arch-Romantic at first. His mind was deeply tinged by the mysticism of Blake, the passionate activity of Shelley, and the aestheticism of the Pre-Raphaelites. By the time he moved to London in 1887, his ambition was to lead his century out of the materialism of modern living into a pure world of the imagination. He wanted to make the Irish people in particular conscious of their past and aware of the possibilities of a better future. By the age of thirty-five, he had found a niche for himself, partly through love of Maud Gonne, a beautiful woman who was also a fierce Irish Nationalist, and partly through helping Lady Gregory, another enthusiast of Irish legend, to found an Irish National Theater. Maud Gonne fostered Yeats's revolutionary enthusiasms; Lady Gregory damped them down by tying his practical ability to forming and directing the Abbey Players. After returning to Ireland in 1896, Yeats more or less abandoned the writing of poetry for ten years and devoted himself largely to drama and the theater.

Had Yeats abandoned poetry for good, he would be remembered today as the writer of beautiful and melancholy lyrics, richly sensuous in vocabulary and stemming directly from nineteenth-century influences such as those of Rossetti and William Morris. Some critical essays might be remembered, and a handful of plays that were more literary than dramatic. But a remarkable change was taking place. Yeats was working to toughen his poetry, to make it more vital, more modern, a poetry shaken by the great spiritual problems of the age. He was working also to simplify his style, to bring his poetry closer to the rhythms of everyday speech and still make it sing. He strove to write poems that would be "as cold and passionate as the dawn."

Yeats's final style did not crystallize until 1928, when he published *The Tower*. But already in 1910—with the publication of his collection *The Green Helmet*—the enervating influence of the 1890's was broken. English poetry, still dominated by memories of Tennyson and Swinburne and caught in a convention which esteemed prettiness above strength, and regularity above enterprise, was about to be revived. The process would come to involve a fresh minting of language, a fresh extension of poetic interests, a fresh ear for new rhythms. It was not to be carried through by Yeats alone. His younger friend Ezra Pound, and later, T. S. Eliot, Edith Sitwell, and W. H. Auden, among others, would play an essential part. But it was Yeats who was the first great liberator, not as a theorist but as an example.

Throughout his poetic career, Yeats searched for the means to unify his experience of the world and gain for his poems a central illuminating vision, one that would lie at the core of all experience and pull together the thousand separate fragments of everyday life.

Despite his mysticism, Yeats had strong ties with the life around him. He was involved, although with misgivings, in the Irish struggle for independence, and he became a senator in the Irish Free State. In 1923, he was awarded the Nobel prize for literature. As time passed, he became a national sage. Having, up to the age of fifty, earned no more from his writing than one thousand dollars in a good year, he was suddenly accepted everywhere as the chief living poet writing in English. During the last ten years of his life, he lived much abroad. It was on the French Riviera that he died in January 1939.

The British poet Edwin Muir has defined the source of Yeats's poetry as "A magnificent temperament associated with a magnificent style." And now, in retrospect, it is clear that among his chief claims to fame must stand the fact that everything about him was of splendid size. He aspired, successfully, to be a full man, copious in output, various, unafraid of the world or himself, a man of ample appetite. In one of his autobiographical volumes, *Dramatis Personae,* he wrote: "No art can conquer the people alone—the people are conquered by an ideal of art upheld by authority." Yeats himself was perfectly ready to supply both the authority and the art.

Today it is no longer the fashion to don a mantle—as Yeats did—or to strike an attitude and speak out of the assurance that, however few the elect, we are inevitably among them ourselves. It is the measure of Yeats's triumph that nobody has successfully questioned his right to stand among the aristocrats of poetry.

When You Are Old

When you are old and gray and full of sleep,
And nodding by the fire, take down this book,
And slowly read, and dream of the soft look
Your eyes had once, and of their shadows deep;

How many loved your moments of glad grace,   5
And loved your beauty with love false or true;
But one man loved the pilgrim soul in you,
And loved the sorrows of your changing face.

And bending down beside the glowing bars,
Murmur, a little sadly, how Love fled   10
And paced upon the mountains overhead
And hid his face amid a crowd of stars.

The Wild Swans at Coole*

The trees are in their autumn beauty,
The woodland paths are dry,
Under the October twilight the water
Mirrors a still sky;
Upon the brimming water among the stones   5
Are nine-and-fifty swans.

The nineteenth autumn has come upon me
Since I first made my count;
I saw, before I had well finished,
All suddenly mount   10
And scatter wheeling in great broken rings
Upon their clamorous wings.

I have looked upon those brilliant creatures,
And now my heart is sore.
All's changed since I, hearing at twilight,   15
The first time on this shore,
The bell-beat of their wings above my head,
Trod with a lighter tread.

Unwearied still, lover by lover,
They paddle in the cold   20
Companionable streams or climb the air;
Their hearts have not grown old;
Passion or conquest, wander where they will,
Attend upon them still.

But now they drift on the still water   25
Mysterious, beautiful;
Among what rushes will they build,
By what lake's edge or pool
Delight men's eyes when I awake some day
To find they have flown away?   30

* **Coole** (ko͞ol'): the estate of Yeats's friend and fellow dramatist Lady Gregory, whom Yeats often visited.

WILLIAM BUTLER YEATS   **693**

An Irish Airman Foresees His Death

This poem concerns an Irish volunteer in England's Royal Flying Corps, which fought against Germany in World War I.

I know that I shall meet my fate
Somewhere among the clouds above;
Those that I fight I do not hate,
Those that I guard I do not love;°
My country is Kiltartan Cross,   5
My countrymen Kiltartan's poor,°
No likely end could bring them loss
Or leave them happier than before.
Nor law, nor duty bade me fight,
Nor public men, nor cheering crowds,   10
A lonely impulse of delight
Drove to this tumult in the clouds;
I balanced all, brought all to mind,
The years to come seemed waste of breath,
A waste of breath the years behind   15
In balance with this life, this death.

3–4. **Those . . . love:** Ireland was still under English rule in World War I. The hatred of the Irish was directed at their rulers rather than against Germany. 6. **Kiltartan's poor:** the poor of Ireland.

Sailing to Byzantium

Byzantium (now Istanbul) was founded by the Greeks in the seventh century B.C., and later was the capital of the Eastern Roman Empire. To Yeats Byzantium was a symbol of the timeless, spiritual world of art as opposed to the natural, physical world of growth and change.

1

That is no country for old men. The young
In one another's arms, birds in the trees
—Those dying generations—at their song,
The salmon-falls, the mackerel-crowded seas
Fish, flesh, or fowl, commend all summer long   5
Whatever is begotten, born, and dies.
Caught in that sensual music all neglect
Monuments of unaging intellect.

An aged man is but a paltry thing,
A tattered coat upon a stick, unless   10
Soul clap its hands and sing, and louder sing
For every tatter in its mortal dress,
Nor is there singing school but studying
Monuments of its own magnificence;
And therefore I have sailed the seas and come   15
To the holy city of Byzantium.

3

O sages standing in God's holy fire
As in the gold mosaic of a wall,°
Come from the holy fire, perne in a gyre,°
And be the singing-masters of my soul.   20
Consume my heart away; sick with desire
And fastened to a dying animal
It knows not what it is; and gather me
Into the artifice of eternity.

4

Once out of nature I shall never take   25
My bodily form from any natural thing,
But such a form as Grecian goldsmiths make
Of hammered gold and gold enameling
To keep a drowsy Emperor awake;
Or set upon a golden bough to sing   30
To lords and ladies of Byzantium
Of what is past, or passing, or to come.

18. **gold . . . wall:** like the figures on the walls of the Church of Hagia Sophia (Holy Wisdom) in Byzantium. 19. **perne . . . gyre:** whirl around in a spiral motion. For Yeats, such spinning (perning) symbolized the basic cycle of life and history.

FOR STUDY AND DISCUSSION

WHEN YOU ARE OLD

1. What is the speaker trying to tell his love? How does he contrast himself to other lovers? What does he mean by "pilgrim soul" and "the sorrows of your changing face"?

2. What is the eventual fate of this love? What lines indicate this? Explain the last line of the poem.

THE WILD SWANS AT COOLE

1. What season of the year is being described? what time of day? Why are the season and time of day important to this poem?

2. How does the speaker feel when he sees the swans? What do the swans symbolize to

him? (In answering, notice expecially lines 23–24.)

3. Why are the swans "mysterious"? Of what importance is their mystery to the poem?

AN IRISH AIRMAN FORESEES HIS DEATH

1. What do you learn about the airman and his countrymen? Explain lines 7–8. For what reasons is the airman *not* fighting?

2. What does the airman mean by "A lonely impulse of delight" (line 11)? How does the word *lonely* imply a contrast with what he has said in the preceding lines? Why is this word especially appropriate to a fighter pilot (particularly during World War I)?

3. What "balance" does the airman strike in the last four lines of the poem? Explain line 14.

4. Notice how the poem moves from specific details to far-reaching ideas. What is the emotional effect of this progression?

SAILING TO BYZANTIUM

1. What country is referred to in the first stanza of the poem? How is this country contrasted to Byzantium? Find two phrases in the first stanza that express this contrast.

2. In the second stanza, how does the poet describe his own situation? To what does he compare himself? How, according to Yeats, can he "sail" to Byzantium?

3. The third stanza is an invocation to the "sages" of Byzantium. Do you think this stanza is addressed to actual people? Why or why not? To what or whom might it be addressed? Why does Yeats ask the sages to "consume my heart away"? Explain the phrase "artifice of eternity."

4. Why in the fourth stanza does the poet wish to be reincarnated as an artificial bird? The activities of the bird may seem rather trivial. In describing these activities, what comment is the poet making about the nature of art and poetry? (Is he saying, for example, that these are trivial occupations?) To what previous line can the last line of the poem be contrasted? Explain the contrast.

5. "Sailing to Byzantium" may seem a strange, difficult poem at first reading. Yet it is regarded by many readers as one of the greatest poems written in English during the twentieth century. Reread it several times. Think of it as a work of art created by a poet who is deeply troubled by the prospect of old age and death. What can you find in the poem that so many readers have found so moving?

SYMBOLS AND THE SYMBOLIST MOVEMENT

A *symbol* is an image used to stand for an idea. By using symbols, writers can make a general idea vivid and specific. They can charge an otherwise neutral concept with emotion and, since a symbol tends to suggest other symbols, can give ideas an evocative quality they would otherwise lack.

Much twentieth-century poetry relies heavily upon symbols. The two most influential modern British poets—William Butler Yeats and T. S. Eliot—were themselves deeply influenced by the French Symbolist movement. French Symbolist poets such as Baudelaire, Mallarmé, and Rimbaud wrote musically evocative poems that usually suggested ideas rather than stated them directly. Yeats used symbols in his poems as a path to an inner vision, a complex system which he described in his book *A Vision* and which he hoped would be a unifying core for his poetry. In an essay on "The Symbolism of Poetry," Yeats asserted that the power of poetry comes chiefly from symbols, both emotional symbols "that evoke emotions alone" and intellectual symbols "that evoke ideas alone or ideas mingled with emotions." Calling for a rejection from a direct discussion of intellectual and moral issues in poetry, Yeats wrote:

"If people were to accept the theory that poetry moves us because of its symbolism, what change should one look for in the manner of our poetry? A return to the way of our fathers, a casting out of descriptions of nature for the sake of nature, of the moral law for the sake of the moral law, a casting out of all anecdotes and of that brooding over scientific opinion that so often extinguished the central flame in Tennyson.... With this change of substance, this return to imagination, this understanding of the laws of art ... would come a change of style ... we would seek out those wavering, meditative, organic rhythms, which are the embodiment of the imagination, that neither desires nor hates, because it has done with time, and only wishes to gaze upon some reality, some beauty ..."

Cite the examples of the use of symbols in "Sailing to Byzantium." To what extent, in your opinion, does the emotional power of this poem rely on use of symbols? How do symbols give this poem a visionary quality, a sense that Yeats was looking through an immediate situation to something deeper and eternal?

FOR COMPOSITION

1. Using several of Yeats's poems as examples, write a composition in which you discuss the use of symbols in poetry. You may also wish to use poems such as Shelley's "Ode to the West Wind" and Blake's "The Tiger."

2. Compare the themes of "Sailing to Byzantium" and Keats's "Ode on a Grecian Urn," considering the following point: To what extent is one poem obviously the work of a young man and the other the work of a man growing old? Refer specifically to passages in the two poems to support your discussion.

E. M. FORSTER

(1879–1970)

In 1939, on the eve of World War II and only a year before Winston Churchill was to tell the English "I have nothing to offer but blood, toil, tears, and sweat," E. M. Forster wrote a quiet essay that began "I do not believe in belief." To some readers, Forster's essay "What I Believe" may have seemed un-English. Forster drew away from the moral absolutes that were important to many Britons. Defending the small virtues, he wrote. "Tolerance, good temper, and sympathy—they are what matter really, and if the human race is not to collapse, they must come to the front before long." He offered no overwhelming faith that could sustain people through a long struggle. Instead he noted, "I believe in an aristocracy. . . . Not an aristocracy of power, based upon rank and influence, but an aristocracy of the sensitive, the considerate, and the plucky. Its members are to be found in all nations and classes, and all through the ages, and there is a secret understanding between them when they meet. They represent the true human tradition, the one permanent victory of our race over cruelty and chaos. . . . They are sensitive for others as well as for themselves, they are considerate without being fussy, their pluck is not swankiness but the power to endure, and they can take a joke." It took considerable bravery for Forster to declare his disbelief in large ideas and his belief in small decencies. It is a bravery that, together with his considerable artistry, marks most of Forster's writing.

As well as being a distinguished essayist, Edward Morgan Forster, in the opinion of many readers, is one of the finest English novelists. While he did not write a novel after the 1920's, two of his novels—*Howards End* and especially *A Passage to India*—are regarded as modern classics. Since *A Passage to India,* almost all of his published works have been essays. These, like his novels, display a complex moral awareness and a graceful, sensitive style that is one of the finest in modern literature.

Forster was born in the town of Tonbridge in Kent. Growing to manhood, he was horrified by the narrow-mindedness and indifference to art and culture of middle-class England. As he grew older and began to travel, his attitudes toward the English were confirmed. Under all his work lies a hatred of hypocrisy and convention, an aspiration toward a free, honest life. Forster was in the lucky position of having just enough money to make him independent. A man of few and simple tastes, he devoted himself to his friends, most of whom were associated with Cambridge University and had studied under the philosopher G. E. Moore, a man whose teachings had a great influence on Forster and others. Later Forster and his friends—among them Virginia Woolf (page 712); Lytton Strachey, the biographer; and Roger Fry, the art critic—became known as the "Bloomsbury Group," after a section of London where some of them lived. The men and women of the circle were known for their interest in literary and artistic experiments, their creativity, and their rejection of Victorian values.

For a while Forster was a secretary to an Indian prince, an experience which he put to fine use in *A Passage to India,* his best-known novel. A stay in Egypt during World War I led to two delightful short books about the city of Alexandria. Having lost his home in Abinger, England, during World War II, he moved to King's College, Cambridge. There he established himself as a wise counselor and a philosophic companion to people of all ages, beliefs, and racial backgrounds. His own interests were wide. He was an excellent musician, a charming talker, and a master of the natural human response.

Forster's remedies for the ills of the world may seem a little too simple today. In his essays, he advises us to shun dogmatism, to be kind and loyal, to keep our private integrity no matter what pressures may be put upon us. These maxims may seem a little thin in times of crisis, when we need something more to resist oppression. Nothing however can detract from the wit and charm with which Forster defends and exemplifies his position.

Notes on the English Character

FIRST NOTE. I had better let the cat out of the bag at once and record my opinion that the character of the English is essentially middle-class. There is a sound historical reason for this, for, since the end of the eighteenth century, the middle classes have been the dominant force in our community. They gained wealth by the Industrial Revolution, political power by the Reform Bill of 1832; they are connected with the rise and organization of the British Empire; they are responsible for the literature of the nineteenth century. Solidity, caution, integrity, efficiency, lack of imagination, hypocrisy. These qualities characterize the middle classes in every country, but in England they are national characteristics also, because only in England have the middle classes been in power for one hundred and fifty years. Napoleon, in his rude way, called us "a nation of shopkeepers." We prefer to call ourselves "a great commercial nation"— it sounds more dignified—but the two phrases amount to the same. Of course there are other classes: there is an aristocracy, there are the poor. But it is on the middle classes that the eye of the critic rests—just as it rests on the poor in Russia and on the aristocracy in Japan. Russia is symbolized by the peasant or by the factory worker; Japan by the samurai;[1] the national figure of England is Mr. Bull with his top hat, his comfortable clothes, his substantial stomach, and his substantial balance at the bank. Saint George may caper on banners and in the speeches of politicians, but it is John Bull who delivers the goods. And even Saint George—if Gibbon[2] is correct—wore a top hat once; he was an army contractor and supplied

[1] **samurai** (sam'oo·rī): In feudal Japan, the samurai were a special class of warriors.

[2] **Gibbon** (gib'ən): Edward Gibbon, an English historian (1737–1794).

indifferent bacon. It all amounts to the same in the end.

SECOND NOTE. Just as the heart of England is the middle classes, so the heart of the middle classes is the public school [1] system. This extraordinary institution is local. It does not even exist all over the British Isles. It is unknown in Ireland, almost unknown in Scotland (countries excluded from my survey), and though it may inspire other great institutions—Aligarh,[2] for example, and some of the schools in the United States—it remains unique, because it was created by the Anglo-Saxon middle classes, and can flourish only where they flourish. How perfectly it expresses their character—far better, for instance, than does the university, into which social and spiritual complexities have already entered. With its boardinghouses, its compulsory games, its system of prefects and fagging,[3] its insistence on good form and on *esprit de corps*,[4] it produces a type whose weight is out of all proportion to its numbers.

On leaving his school, the boy either sets to work at once—goes into the army or into business, or emigrates—or else proceeds to the university, and after three or four years there enters some other profession—becomes a barrister,[5] doctor, civil servant, schoolmaster, or journalist. (If through some mishap he does not become a manual worker or an artist.) In all these careers his education, or the absence of it, influences him. Its memories influence him also. Many men look back on their school days as the happiest of their lives. They remember with regret that golden time when life, though hard, was not yet complex; when they all worked together and thought together, so far as they thought at all; when they were taught that school is the world in miniature, and believed that no one can love his country who does not love his school. And they prolong that time as best they can by joining their Old Boys' society;[6] indeed, some of them remain Old Boys and nothing else for the rest of their lives. They attribute all good to the school. They worship it. They quote the remark that "the battle of Waterloo [7] was won on the playing fields of Eton." It is nothing to them that the remark is inapplicable historically and was never made by the Duke of Wellington, and that the Duke of Wellington was an Irishman. They go on quoting it because it expresses their sentiments; they feel that if the Duke of Wellington didn't make it he ought to have, and if he wasn't an Englishman he ought to have been. And they go forth into a world that is not entirely composed of public school men or even of Anglo-Saxons, but of men who are as various as the sands of the sea; into a world of whose richness and subtlety they have no conception. They go forth into it with well-developed bodies, fairly developed minds, and undeveloped hearts. And it is this undeveloped heart that is largely responsible for the difficulties of Englishmen abroad. An undeveloped heart—not a cold one. The difference is important, and on it my next note will be based.

For it is not that the Englishman can't feel—it is that he is afraid to feel. He has been taught at his public school that feeling is bad form. He must not express great joy or sorrow, or even open his mouth too wide when he talks—his pipe might fall out if he did. He must bottle up his emotions, or let them out only on a very special occasion.

Once upon a time (this is an anecdote) I went for a week's holiday on the Continent with an Indian friend. We both enjoyed ourselves and were sorry when

---

[1] **public school:** corresponds to the American private school. English grammar schools correspond to our public schools.

[2] **Aligarh** (al'i·gûr'): a school in the city of Aligarh, India.

[3] **fagging:** a system wherein underclassmen run errands and do chores for upperclassmen.

[4] *esprit de corps* (es·prē'də kôr'): group spirit, such as "school spirit."

[5] **barrister:** lawyer.

[6] **Old Boys' society:** alumni organization.

[7] **battle of Waterloo:** a decisive battle in English history in which the Duke of Wellington defeated the forces of Napoleon.

the week was over, but on parting our behavior was absolutely different. He was plunged in despair. He felt that because the holiday was over all happiness was over until the world ended. He could not express his sorrow too much. But in me the Englishman came out strong. I reflected that we should meet again in a month or two, and could write in the interval if we had anything to say; and under these circumstances I could not see what there was to make a fuss about. It wasn't as if we were parting forever or dying. "Buck up," I said, "do buck up." He refused to buck up, and I left him plunged in gloom.

The conclusion of the anecdote is even more instructive. For when we met the next month our conversation threw a good deal of light on the English character. I began by scolding my friend. I told him that he had been wrong to feel and display so much emotion upon so slight an occasion; that it was inappropriate. The word "inappropriate" roused him to fury. "What?" he cried. "Do you measure out your emotions as if they were potatoes?" I did not like the simile of the potatoes, but after a moment's reflection I said, "Yes, I do; and what's more, I think I ought to. A small occasion demands a little emotion, just as a large occasion demands a great one. I would like my emotions to be appropriate. This may be measuring them like potatoes, but it is better than slopping them about like water from a pail, which is what you did." He did not like the simile of the pail. "If those are your opinions, they part us forever," he cried, and left the room. Returning immediately, he added: "No—but your whole attitude toward emotion is wrong. Emotion has nothing to do with appropriateness. It matters only that it shall be sincere. I happened to feel deeply. I showed it. It doesn't matter whether I ought to have felt deeply or not."

This remark impressed me very much. Yet I could not agree with it, and said that I valued emotion as much as he did, but used it differently; if I poured it out

on small occasions I was afraid of having none left for the great ones, and of being bankrupt at the crises of life. Note the word "bankrupt." I spoke as a member of a prudent middle-class nation, always anxious to meet my liabilities. But my friend spoke as an Oriental, and the Oriental has behind him a tradition, not of middle-class prudence, but of kingly munificence and splendor. He feels his resources are endless, just as John Bull feels his are finite. As regards material resources, the Oriental is clearly unwise. Money isn't endless. If we spend or give away all the money we have, we haven't any more, and must take the consequences, which are frequently unpleasant. But, as regards the resources of the spirit, he may be right. The emotions may be endless. The more we express them, the more we may have to express.

"True love in this differs from gold and clay,
    That to divide is not to take away,"

says Shelley. Shelley, at all events, believes that the wealth of the spirit is endless; that we may express it copiously, passionately, and always; and that we can never feel sorrow or joy too acutely.

In the above anecdote, I have figured as a typical Englishman. I will now descend from that dizzy and somewhat unfamiliar height, and return to my business of note-taking. A note on the *slowness* of the English character. The Englishman appears to be cold and unemotional because he is really slow. When an event happens, he may understand it quickly enough with his mind, but he takes quite a while to feel it. Once upon a time a coach, containing some Englishmen and some Frenchmen, was driving over the Alps. The horses ran away, and as they were dashing across a bridge the coach caught on the stonework, tottered, and nearly fell into the ravine below. The Frenchmen were frantic with terror: they screamed and gesticulated and flung themselves about, as Frenchmen would. The Englishmen sat quite calm. An hour later the coach drew up at an inn to change horses, and by that time the situations were exactly reversed. The Frenchmen had forgotten all about the danger, and were chattering gaily; the Englishmen had just begun to feel it, and one had a nervous breakdown and was obliged to go to bed. We have here a clear physical difference between the two races—a difference that goes deep into character. The Frenchmen responded at once; the Englishmen responded in time. They were slow and they were also practical. Their instinct forbade them to throw themselves about in the coach, because it was more likely to tip over if they did. They had this extraordinary appreciation of *fact* that we shall notice again and again. When a disaster comes, the English instinct is to do what can be done first, and to postpone the feeling as long as possible. Hence they are splendid at emergencies. No doubt they are brave—no one will deny that—but bravery is partly an affair of the nerves, and the English nervous system is well equipped for meeting a physical emergency. It acts promptly and feels slowly. Such a combination is fruitful, and anyone who possesses it has gone a long way toward being brave. And when the action is over, then the Englishman can feel.

There is one more consideration—a most important one. If the English nature is cold, how is it that it has produced a great literature and a literature that is particularly great in poetry? Judged by its prose, English literature would not stand in the first rank. It is its poetry that raises it to the level of Greek, Persian, or French. And yet the English are supposed to be so unpoetical. How is this? The nation that produced the Elizabethan drama and the Lake Poets[1] cannot be a cold, unpoetical nation. We can't get fire out of ice. Since literature always rests upon national character, there must be in the English nature hidden springs of fire to produce the fire we see. The warm sympathy, the romance, the imagination, that we look for in Englishmen whom we meet, and too often vainly look for, must exist in the nation as a whole, or we could not have this outburst of national song. An undeveloped heart—not a cold one.

The trouble is that the English nature is not at all easy to understand. It has a great air of simplicity, it advertises itself as simple, but the more we consider it, the greater the problems we shall encounter. People talk of the mysterious East, but the West also is mysterious. It has depths that do not reveal themselves at the first gaze. We know what the sea looks like from a distance: it is of one color, and level, and obviously cannot contain such creatures as fish. But if we look into the sea over the edge of a boat, we see a dozen colors, and depth below depth, and fish swimming in them. That sea is the English character—apparently imperturbable and even. The depths and the colors are the English romanticism and the English sensitiveness—we do not expect to find such things, but they exist. And—to continue my metaphor—the fish are the English emotions, which are always trying to get up to the surface, but don't quite know how. For the most part we see them moving far below, distorted and obscure. Now and then they succeed and we exclaim, "Why, the Englishman has emotions! He actually can feel!" And occasionally we see that beautiful creature the flying fish, which rises out of the water altogether into the air and the sunlight. English literature is a flying fish. It is a sample of the life that goes on day after day beneath the surface; it is a proof that beauty and emotion exist in the salt, inhospitable sea.

And now let's get back to terra firma.[2] The Englishman's attitude toward criticism will give us another starting point. He is not annoyed by criticism. He listens or not as the case may be, smiles and passes on, saying, "Oh, the fellow's

---

[1] **Lake Poets:** Coleridge, Wordsworth, and Southey, who lived for a while in the Lake District in northwestern England.

[2] **terra firma:** solid ground.

E. M. FORSTER   701

jealous"; "Oh, I'm used to Bernard Shaw; monkey tricks don't hurt me." It never occurs to him that the fellow may be accurate as well as jealous, and that he might do well to take the criticism to heart and profit by it. It never strikes him—except as a form of words—that he is capable of improvement; his self-complacency is abysmal. Other nations, both Oriental and European, have an uneasy feeling that they are not quite perfect. In consequence they resent criticism. It hurts them; and their snappy answers often mask a determination to improve themselves. Not so the Englishman. He has no uneasy feeling. Let the critics bark. And the "tolerant humorous attitude" with which he confronts them is not really tolerant, because it is insensitive, and not really humorous, because it is bounded by the titter and the guffaw.

Turn over the pages of *Punch*.[1] There is neither wit, laughter, nor satire in our national jester—only the snigger of a suburban householder who can understand nothing that does not resemble himself. Week after week, under Mr. Punch's supervision, a man falls off his horse, or a colonel misses a golf ball, or a little girl makes a mistake in her prayers. Week

after week ladies show not too much of their legs, foreigners are deprecated, originality condemned. Week after week a bricklayer does not do as much work as he ought and a futurist does more than he need. It is all supposed to be so good-tempered and clean; it is also supposed to be funny. It is actually an outstanding example of our attitude toward criticism: the middle-class Englishman, with a smile on his clean-shaven lips, is engaged in admiring himself and ignoring the rest of mankind. If, in those colorless pages, he came across anything that really was funny—a drawing by Max Beerbohm,[2] for instance —his smile would disappear, and he would say to himself, "The fellow's a bit of a crank," and pass on.

This particular attitude reveals such insensitiveness as to suggest a more serious charge: is the Englishman altogether indifferent to the things of the spirit? Let us glance for a moment at his religion—not, indeed, at his theology, which would not merit inspection, but at the action on his daily life of his belief in the unseen. Here again his attitude is practical. But an innate decency comes out: he is thinking of others rather than of himself. Right conduct is his aim. He asks of his religion that

---

[1] ***Punch:*** a well-known humorous and satirical weekly.

[2] **Max Beerbohm:** an English essayist and caricaturist (1872–1956).

The British laugh at themselves in this cartoon from *Punch*. Entitled "A Noble Sportsman," its caption reads: "Mr. Tyms hired a mount with the staghounds, but quickly came to the conclusion that it was a brutal shame to chase the poor deer up and down those horrible banks."

it shall make him a better man in daily life; that he shall be more kind, more just, more merciful, more desirous to fight what is evil and to protect what is good. No one could call this a low conception. It is, as far as it goes, a spiritual one. Yet—and this seems to me typical of the race—it is only half the religious idea. Religion is more than an ethical code with a divine sanction. It is also a means through which man may get into direct connection with the divine, and, judging by history, few Englishmen have succeeded in doing this. We have produced no series of prophets, as has Judaism or Islam.[1] We have not even produced a Joan of Arc, or a Savonarola.[2] We have produced few saints. In Germany the Reformation was due to the passionate conviction of Luther. In England it was due to a palace intrigue.[3] We can show a steady level of piety, a fixed determination to live decently according to our lights—little more.

Well, it is something. It clears us of the charge of being an unspiritual nation. That facile contrast between the spiritual East and the materialistic West can be pushed too far. The West also is spiritual. Only it expresses its belief, not in fasting and visions, not in prophetic rapture, but in the daily round, the common task. An incomplete expression, if you like. I agree. But the argument underlying these scattered notes is that the Englishman is an incomplete person. Not a cold or an unspiritual one. But undeveloped, incomplete.

I have suggested earlier that the English are sometimes hypocrites, and it is now my duty to develop this rather painful subject. Hypocrisy is the prime charge that is always brought against us. The Germans are called brutal, the Spanish cruel, the Americans superficial, and so on; but we are *perfide Albion*,[4] the island of hypocrites, the people who have built up an Empire with a Bible in one hand, a pistol in the other, and financial concessions in both pockets. Is the charge true? I think it is; but while making it we must be quite clear as to what we mean by hypocrisy. Do we mean *conscious* deceit? Well, the English are comparatively guiltless of this; they have little of the Renaissance villain about them. Do we mean *unconscious* deceit? Muddle-headedness? Of this I believe them to be guilty. When an Englishman has been led into a course of wrong action, he has nearly always begun by muddling himself. A public school education does not make for mental clearness, and he possesses to a very high degree the power of confusing his own mind. We have seen this tendency at work in the domain of theology; how does it work in the domain of conduct?

Jane Austen[5] may seem an odd authority to cite, but Jane Austen has, within her limits, a marvelous insight into the English mind. Her range is limited, her characters never attempt any of the more scarlet sins. But she has a merciless eye for questions of conduct, and the classical example of two English people muddling themselves before they embark upon a wrong course of action is to be found in the opening chapters of *Sense and Sensibility*. Old Mr. Dashwood has just died. He has been twice married. By his first marriage he has a son, John; by his second marriage three daughters. The son is well off; the young ladies and their mother—for Mr. Dashwood's second wife survives him—are badly off. He has called his son to his deathbed and has solemnly adjured him to provide for the second family. Much moved, the young man promises, and mentally decides to give each of his sisters a thousand pounds; and then the comedy begins. For he announces his

---

[1] **Islam:** the Moslem religion.

[2] **Savonarola** (sav′ə·nə·rō′lə): an Italian monk (1452–1498), a political and religious reformer, who was burned as a heretic.

[3] **due . . . intrigue:** Henry VIII (1491–1547) initiated the break between England and the Church of Rome when the Pope refused to grant him a divorce from Catherine of Aragon.

[4] ***perfide Albion:*** false England; Albion (al′bē·ən) is an ancient name for England still retained in poetry.

[5] **Jane Austen:** English novelist (1775–1817).

generous intention to his wife, and Mrs. John Dashwood by no means approves of depriving their own little boy of so large a sum. The thousand pounds are accordingly reduced to five hundred. But even this seems rather much. Might not an annuity to the stepmother be less of a wrench? Yes—but though less of a wrench it might be more of a drain, for "she is very stout and healthy, and scarcely forty." An occasional present of fifty pounds will be better, "and will, I think, be amply discharging my promise to my father." Or, better still, an occasional present of fish. And in the end nothing is done, nothing; the four impecunious ladies are not even helped in the moving of their furniture.

Well, are the John Dashwoods hypocrites? It depends upon our definition of hypocrisy. The young man could not see his evil impulses as they gathered force and gained on him. And even his wife, though a worse character, is also self-deceived. She reflects that old Mr. Dashwood may have been out of his mind at his death. She thinks of her own little boy—and surely a mother ought to think of her own child. She has muddled herself so completely that in one sentence she can refuse the ladies the income that would enable them to keep a carriage and in the next can say that they will not be keeping a carriage and so will have no expenses. No doubt men and women in other lands can muddle themselves, too, yet the state of mind of Mr. and Mrs. John Dashwood seems to me typical of England. They are slow—they take time even to do wrong; whereas people in other lands do wrong quickly.

There are national faults as there are national diseases, and perhaps one can draw a parallel between them. It has always impressed me that the national diseases of England should be cancer and consumption—slow, insidious, pretending to be something else; while the diseases proper to the South should be cholera and plague, which strike at a man when he is perfectly well and may leave him a corpse by evening. Mr. and Mrs. John Dashwood are moral consumptives. They collapse gradually without realizing what the disease is. There is nothing dramatic or violent about their sin. You cannot call them villains.

Here is the place to glance at some of the other charges that have been brought against the English as a nation. They have, for instance, been accused of treachery, cruelty, and fanaticism. In these charges I have never been able to see the least point, because treachery and cruelty are conscious sins. The man knows he is doing wrong, and does it deliberately, like Tartuffe [1] or Iago.[2] He betrays his friend because he wishes to. He tortures his prisoners because he enjoys seeing the blood flow. He worships the Devil because he prefers evil to good. From villainies such as these the average Englishman is free. His character, which prevents his rising to certain heights, also prevents him from sinking to these depths. Because he doesn't produce mystics he doesn't produce villains either; he gives the world no prophets, but no anarchists, no fanatics —religious or political.

Of course there are cruel and treacherous people in England—one has only to look at the police courts—and examples of public infamy can be found, such as the Amritsar massacre.[3] But one does not look at the police courts or the military mind to find the soul of any nation; and the more English people one meets the more convinced one becomes that the charges as a whole are untrue. Yet foreign critics often make them. Why? Partly because they fix their eyes on the criminal classes, partly because they are annoyed with certain genuine defects in the English character, and in their irritation throw in

[1] **Tartuffe** (tär·to͞of'): a hypocrite in Molière's comedy *Tartuffe* who swindles his benefactor.
[2] **Iago** (ē·ä′gō): the villain in Shakespeare's *Othello,* who deceives Othello and makes him think that his wife has been unfaithful.
[3] **Amritsar massacre:** During a riot in 1919 in Amritsar (um·rit′sər), India, British soldiers fired into a crowd and killed nearly 400 people.

cruelty in order to make the problem simpler. Moral indignation is always agreeable, but nearly always misplaced. It is indulged in both by the English and by the critics of the English. They all find it great fun. The drawback is that while they are amusing themselves the world becomes neither wiser nor better.

The main point of these notes is that the English character is incomplete. No national character is complete. We have to look for some qualities in one part of the world and others in another. But the English character is incomplete in a way that is particularly annoying to the foreign observer. It has a bad surface—self-complacent, unsympathetic, and reserved. There is plenty of emotion further down, but it never gets used. There is plenty of brain power, but it is more often used to confirm prejudices than to dispel them. With such an equipment the Englishman cannot be popular. Only I would repeat: there is little vice in him and no real coldness. It is the machinery that is wrong.

I hope and believe myself that in the next twenty years we shall see a great change, and that the national character will alter into something that is less unique but more lovable. The supremacy of the middle classes is probably ending. What new element the working classes will introduce one cannot say, but at all events they will not have been educated at public schools. And whether these notes praise or blame the English character—that is only incidental. They are the notes of a student who is trying to get at the truth and would value the assistance of others. I believe myself that the truth is great and that it shall prevail. I have no faith in official caution and reticence. The cats are all out of their bags, and diplomacy cannot recall them. The nations *must* understand one another, and quickly; and without the interposition of their governments, for the shrinkage of the globe is throwing them into one another's arms. To that understanding these notes are a feeble contribution—notes on the English character as it has struck a novelist.

FOR STUDY AND DISCUSSION

1. In his first paragraph Forster writes: "Napoleon, in his rude way, called us 'a nation of shopkeepers.' We prefer to call ourselves 'a great commercial nation' . . ." The only distinction between the two phrases mentioned by Forster is that one "sounds more dignified." Are there any other distinctions between these phrases? If so, what are they? Why do you think Forster says that "the two phrases amount to the same"?

2. In this essay Forster pays his respects to the English public schools, schools which are actually private preparatory schools for boys. What are Forster's feelings about these schools? How does he convey his feelings?

3. Forster uses three anecdotes: the tale of his week's holiday with an Indian friend; the account of the Englishmen and the Frenchmen driving together over the Alps; the episode from Jane Austen's *Sense and Sensibility*. What point or points about the English character does each of these incidents illustrate? Why is each of the incidents an effective illustration?

4. Forster develops an analogy between the sea and the English character. What paradox is he trying to account for by using this metaphor? How does he employ the various elements of the sea to clarify the point he is making?

5. The author says that the "tolerant humorous attitude" with which the English confront criticism is not really humorous or tolerant. What is his explanation for this? What does he mean by the phrase "because it is bounded by the titter and the guffaw"?

6. Near the conclusion of the essay, Forster states that in the English "there is little vice . . . and no real coldness. It is the machinery that is wrong." What does he mean by "machinery"? What details in the essay support this statement?

7. Reread the quotations from the essay "What I Believe" on page 697. How do these quotations deepen your understanding of Forster's remarks about the English? By what standards does Forster judge the English people?

8. What aim does Forster's essay have in common with Goldsmith's *Citizen of the World* (page 350) and Swift's *Gulliver's Travels* (page 313)? In what ways do the method, tone, and style Forster uses to achieve this aim differ from theirs?

KATHERINE MANSFIELD
(1888–1923)

Katherine Mansfield performed for the English short story what the great Russian writer Anton Chekhov performed for the European story. In 1911, when she began to write the stories that made her famous, readers expected short stories to be "well made" with cleverly devised plots that had a beginning, middle, and end; with characters about whom readers could feel that they knew almost everything; often with tricky but logically constructed endings, as in the short stories of O. Henry. Miss Mansfield took the opposite course. As far as possible, she directed herself to the untidiness of real life. She became a mistress of small gestures, tiny fragments of significance, intuitive moments. She hardly ever told a story from A to Z, but took its inner core as her theme. The truth of a situation was immensely important to her. She was very conscious of the lies that human beings tell to protect themselves, and attempted in her stories to carry the reader past these lies. Giving an intense sense of participation in life, she showed a concern with essentials only, a deep appreciation of situations that seem ordinary only on the surface. Her style, with its quick strokes and its shifting evocative quality, is an instrument that conveys almost perfectly her special sense of life.

Katherine Mansfield's real name was Kathleen Beauchamp. Born of a wealthy family in Wellington, New Zealand, she studied in London as a young girl and later settled there after an unhappy return home. An attack of tuberculosis forced her to go to Germany to recuperate, and here she began to write stories. In England once again, she married the editor and critic J. Middleton Murry and became known as a literary reviewer and story writer. But appreciation of her work came too late for her to enjoy. Constantly ill, she spent most of her last years trying to regain her health in the warmer climates of Italy and France, where she died at an early age.

Behind her, Katherine Mansfield left three volumes that are particularly notable: *The Garden Party* and *The Dove's Nest,* which contain some of her best short stories; and her *Journal,* which reveals her aims and methods as a writer and is a legacy to all short-story writers who followed her. Almost all her writing, whether fiction or nonfiction, reveals her special personality. In a memoir her husband described her as "spontaneous as no other human being I have ever met. She seemed to adjust herself to life as a flower adjusts itself to the earth and to the sun. She suffered greatly, she delighted greatly; but her suffering and her delight were never partial, they filled the whole of her."

A Cup of Tea

ROSEMARY FELL was not exactly beautiful. No, you couldn't have called her beautiful. Pretty? Well, if you took her to pieces . . . But why be so cruel as to take anyone to pieces? She was young, brilliant, extremely modern, exquisitely well dressed, amazingly well read in the newest of the new books, and her parties were the most delicious mixture of the really important people and . . . artists— quaint creatures, discoveries of hers, some of them too terrifying for words, but others quite presentable and amusing.

Rosemary had been married two years. She had a duck of a boy. No, not Peter— Michael. And her husband absolutely adored her. They were rich, really rich, not just comfortably well off, which is odious and stuffy and sounds like one's grandparents. But if Rosemary wanted to shop she would go to Paris as you and I would go to Bond Street.[1] If she wanted to buy flowers, the car pulled up at that perfect shop in Regent Street, and Rosemary inside the shop just gazed in her dazzled, rather exotic way, and said: "I want those and those and those. Give me four bunches of those. And that jar of roses. Yes, I'll have all the roses in the jar. No, no lilac. I hate lilac. It's got no shape." The attendant bowed and put the lilac out of sight, as though this was only too true; lilac was dreadfully shapeless. "Give me those stumpy little tulips. Those red and white ones." And she was followed to the car by a thin shopgirl staggering under an immense white paper armful that looked like a baby in long clothes. . . .

One winter afternoon she had been buying something in a little antique shop in Curzon Street. It was a shop she liked. For one thing, one usually had it to oneself. And then the man who kept it was ridiculously fond of serving her. He beamed whenever she came in. He clasped his hands; he was so gratified he could scarcely speak. Flattery, of course. All the same, there was something . . .

"You see, madam," he would explain in his low respectful tones, "I love my things. I would rather not part with them than sell them to someone who does not appreciate them, who has not that fine feeling which is so rare. . . ." And, breathing deeply, he unrolled a tiny square of blue velvet and pressed it on the glass counter with his pale fingertips.

Today it was a little box. He had been keeping it for her. He had shown it to nobody as yet. An exquisite little enamel box with a glaze so fine it looked as though it had been baked in cream. On the lid a minute creature stood under a flowery tree, and a more minute creature still had her arms around his neck. Her hat, really no bigger than a geranium petal, hung from a branch; it had green ribbons. And there was a pink cloud like a watchful cherub floating above their heads. Rosemary took her hands out of her long gloves. She always took off her gloves to examine such things. Yes, she liked it very much. She loved it; it was a great duck. She must have it. And, turning the creamy box, opening and shutting it, she couldn't help noticing how charming her hands were against the blue velvet. The shopman, in some dim cavern of his mind, may have dared to think so too. For he took a pencil, leaned over the counter, and his pale bloodless fingers crept timidly towards those rosy, flashing ones, as he murmured gently: "If I may venture to point out to madam, the flowers on the little lady's bodice."

"Charming!" Rosemary admired the flowers. But what was the price? For a moment the shopman did not seem to hear. Then a murmur reached her. "Twenty-eight guineas, madame."

[1] **Bond Street:** a London street known for its fashionable shops.

"A Cup of Tea" from *The Short Stories of Katherine Mansfield*, copyright 1923, 1937 by Alfred A. Knopf, Inc.; renewed 1951 by John Middleton Murry. Reprinted by permission of the publishers.

"Twenty-eight guineas." Rosemary gave no sign. She laid the little box down; she buttoned her gloves again. Twenty-eight guineas. Even if one is rich . . . She looked vague. She stared at a plump teakettle like a plump hen above the shopman's head, and her voice was dreamy as she answered: "Well, keep it for me—will you? I'll . . ."

But the shopman had already bowed as though keeping it for her was all any human being could ask. He would be willing, of course, to keep it for her forever.

The discreet door shut with a click. She was outside on the step, gazing at the winter afternoon. Rain was falling, and with the rain it seemed the dark came too, spinning down like ashes. There was a cold bitter taste in the air, and the new-lighted lamps looked sad. Sad were the lights in the houses opposite. Dimly they burned as if regretting something. And people hurried by, hidden under their hateful umbrellas. Rosemary felt a strange pang. She pressed her muff to her breast; she wished she had the little box, too, to cling to. Of course, the car was there. She'd only to cross the pavement. But still she waited. There are moments, horrible moments in life, when one emerges from shelter and looks out, and it's awful. One oughtn't to give way to them. One ought to go home and have an extra-special tea. But at the very instant of thinking that, a young girl, thin, dark, shadowy—where had she come from?—was standing at Rosemary's elbow and a voice like a sigh, almost like a sob, breathed: "Madam, may I speak to you a moment?"

"Speak to me?" Rosemary turned. She saw a little battered creature with enormous eyes, someone quite young, no older than herself, who clutched at her coat collar with reddened hands and shivered as though she had just come out of the water.

"M-madam," stammered the voice, "Would you let me have the price of a cup of tea?"

"A cup of tea?" There was something simple, sincere in that voice; it wasn't in the least the voice of a beggar. "Then have you no money at all?" asked Rosemary.

"None, madam," came the answer.

'How extraordinary!" Rosemary peered through the dusk, and the girl gazed back at her. How more than extraordinary! And suddenly it seemed to Rosemary such an adventure. It was like something out of a novel by Dostoevsky, this meeting in the dusk. Supposing she took the girl home? Supposing she did do one of those things she was always reading about or seeing on the stage, what would happen? It would be thrilling. And she heard herself saying afterwards to the amazement of her friends: "I simply took her home with me," as she stepped forward and said to that dim person beside her: "Come home to tea with me."

The girl drew back startled. She even stopped shivering for a moment. Rosemary put out a hand and touched her arm. "I mean it," she said, smiling. And she felt how simple and kind her smile was. "Why won't you? Do. Come home with me now in my car and have tea."

"You—you don't mean it, madam," said the girl, and there was pain in her voice.

"But I do," cried Rosemary. "I want you to. To please me. Come along."

The girl put her fingers to her lips and her eyes devoured Rosemary. "You're—you're not taking me to the police station?" she stammered.

"The police station!" Rosemary laughed out. "Why should I be so cruel? No, I only want to make you warm and to hear —anything you care to tell me."

Hungry people are easily led. The footman held the door of the car open, and a moment later they were skimming through the dusk.

"There!" said Rosemary. She had a feeling of triumph as she slipped her hand through the velvet strap. She could have said, "Now I've got you," as she gazed at the little captive she had netted. But of course she meant it kindly. Oh, more than kindly. She was going to prove to this girl that—wonderful things did happen in life, that—fairy godmothers were real, that—rich people had hearts, and that women *were* sisters. She turned impulsively, saying: "Don't be frightened. After all, why shouldn't you come back with me? We're both women. If I'm the more fortunate, you ought to expect . . ."

But happily at that moment, for she didn't know how the sentence was going to end, the car stopped. The bell was rung, the door opened, and with a charming, protecting, almost embracing movement, Rosemary drew the other into the hall. Warmth, softness, light, a sweet scent, all those things so familiar to her she never even thought about them, she watched that other receive. It was fascinating. She was like the little rich girl in her nursery with all the cupboards to open, all the boxes to unpack.

"Come, come upstairs," said Rosemary, longing to begin to be generous. "Come up to my room." And, besides, she wanted to spare this poor little thing from being stared at by the servants; she decided as they mounted the stairs she would not even ring for Jeanne, but take off her things by herself. The great thing was to be natural!

And "There!" cried Rosemary again, as they reached her beautiful big bedroom with the curtains drawn, the fire leaping on her wonderful lacquer furniture, her gold cushions and the primrose and blue rugs.

The girl stood just inside the door; she seemed dazed. But Rosemary didn't mind that.

"Come and sit down," she cried, dragging her big chair up to the fire, "in this comfy chair. Come and get warm. You look so dreadfully cold."

"I daren't, madam," said the girl, and she edged backwards.

"Oh, please"—Rosemary ran forward —"you mustn't be frightened, you mustn't, really. Sit down, and when I've taken off my things we shall go into the next room and have tea and be cozy. Why are you afraid?" And gently she half pushed the thin figure into its deep cradle.

But there was no answer. The girl stayed just as she had been put, with her hands by her sides and her mouth slightly open. To be quite sincere, she looked rather stupid. But Rosemary wouldn't acknowledge it. She leaned over her, saying: "Won't you take off your hat? Your pretty hair is all wet. And one is so much more comfortable without a hat, isn't one?"

There was a whisper that sounded like "Very good, madam," and the crushed hat was taken off.

"Let me help you off with your coat, too," said Rosemary.

The girl stood up. But she held on to the chair with one hand and let Rosemary pull. It was quite an effort. The other scarcely helped her at all. She seemed to stagger like a child, and the thought came and went through Rosemary's mind that if people wanted helping they must respond a little, just a little, otherwise it became very difficult indeed. And what was she to do with the coat now? She left it on the floor, and the hat too. She was just going to take a cigarette off the mantelpiece when the girl said quickly, but so lightly and strangely: "I'm very sorry, madam, but I'm going to faint. I shall go off, madam, if I don't have something."

"Good heavens, how thoughtless I am!" Rosemary rushed to the bell.

"Tea! Tea at once! And some brandy immediately!"

The maid was gone again, but the girl almost cried out. "No, I don't want no brandy. I never drink brandy. It's a cup of tea I want, madam." And she burst into tears.

It was a terrible and fascinating moment. Rosemary knelt beside her chair.

"Don't cry, poor little thing," she said.

"Don't cry." And she gave the other her lace handkerchief. She really was touched beyond words. She put her arm round those thin, birdlike shoulders.

Now at last the other forgot to be shy, forgot everything except that they were both women, and gasped out: "I can't go on no longer like this. I can't bear it. I shall do away with myself. I can't bear no more."

"You shan't have to. I'll look after you. Don't cry any more. Don't you see what a good thing it was that you met me? We'll have tea and you'll tell me everything. And I shall arrange something. I promise. *Do* stop crying. It's so exhausting. Please!"

The other did stop just in time for Rosemary to get up before the tea came. She had the table placed between them. She plied the poor little creature with everything, all the sandwiches, all the bread and butter, and every time her cup was empty she filled it with tea, cream and sugar. People always said sugar was so nourishing. As for herself she didn't eat; she smoked and looked away tactfully so that the other should not be shy.

And really the effect of that slight meal was marvelous. When the tea table was carried away a new being, a light, frail creature with tangled hair, dark lips, deep, lighted eyes, lay back in the big chair in a kind of sweet languor, looking at the blaze. Rosemary lit a fresh cigarette; it was time to begin.

"And when did you have your last meal?" she asked softly.

But at that moment the door handle turned.

"Rosemary, may I come in?" It was Philip.

"Of course."

He came in. "Oh, I'm so sorry," he said, and stopped and stared.

"It's quite all right," said Rosemary smiling. "This is my friend, Miss——"

"Smith, madam," said the languid figure, who was strangely still and unafraid.

"Smith," said Rosemary. "We are going to have a little talk."

"Oh, yes," said Philip. "Quite," and his eye caught sight of the coat and hat on the floor. He came over to the fire and turned his back to it. "It's a beastly afternoon," he said curiously, still looking at that listless figure, looking at its hands and boots, and then at Rosemary again.

"Yes, isn't it?" said Rosemary enthusiastically. "Vile."

Philip smiled his charming smile. "As a matter of fact," said he, "I wanted you to come into the library for a moment. Would you? Will Miss Smith excuse us?"

The big eyes were raised to him, but Rosemary answered for her. "Of course she will." And they went out of the room together.

"I say," said Philip, when they were alone. "Explain. Who is she? What does it all mean?"

Rosemary, laughing, leaned against the door and said: "I picked her up in Curzon Street. Really. She's a real pickup. She asked me for the price of a cup of tea, and I brought her home with me."

"But what on earth are you going to do with her?" cried Philip.

"Be nice to her," said Rosemary quickly. "Be frightfully nice to her. Look after her. I don't know how. We haven't talked yet. But show her—treat her—make her feel——"

"My darling girl," said Philip, "you're quite mad, you know. It simply can't be done."

"I knew you'd say that," retorted Rosemary. "Why not? I want to. Isn't that a reason? And besides, one's always reading about these things. I decided——"

"But," said Philip slowly, and he cut the end of a cigar, "she's so astonishingly pretty."

"Pretty?" Rosemary was so surprised that she blushed. "Do you think so? I—I hadn't thought about it."

"Good Lord!" Philip struck a match "She's absolutely lovely. Look again, my child. I was bowled over when I came into your room just now. However . . . I think you're making a ghastly mistake. Sorry, darling, if I'm crude and all that. But let me know if Miss Smith is going to dine with us in time for me to look up *The Milliner's Gazette.*"

"You absurd creature!" said Rosemary, and she went out of the library, but not back to her bedroom. She went to her writing room and sat down at her desk. Pretty! Absolutely lovely! Bowled over! Her heart beat like a heavy bell. Pretty! Lovely! She drew her cheque book towards her. But no, cheques would be no use, of course. She opened a drawer and took out five pound notes, looked at them, put two back, and holding the three squeezed in her hand, she went back to her bedroom.

Half an hour later Philip was still in the library, when Rosemary came in.

"I only wanted to tell you," said she, and she leaned against the door again and looked at him with her dazzled exotic gaze, "Miss Smith won't dine with us tonight."

Philip put down the paper. "Oh, what's happened? Previous engagement?"

Rosemary came over and sat down on his knee. "She insisted on going," said she, "so I gave the poor little thing a present of money. I couldn't keep her against her will, could I?" she added softly.

Rosemary had just done her hair, darkened her eyes a little, and put on her pearls. She put up her hands and touched Philip's cheeks.

"Do you like me?" said she, and her tone, sweet, husky, troubled him.

"I like you awfully," he said, and he held her tighter. "Kiss me."

There was a pause.

Then Rosemary said dreamily, "I saw a fascinating little box today. It cost twenty-eight guineas. May I have it?"

Philip jumped her on his knee. "You may, little wasteful one," said he.

But that was not really what Rosemary wanted to say.

"Philip," she whispered, and she pressed his head against her bosom, "am I *pretty?*"

FOR STUDY AND DISCUSSION

1. What does Rosemary Fell think of herself? What attitude do you think the author wishes you to take toward this character? List some of the details that help establish this attitude.

2. When Rosemary invites the girl home, she smiles at her. "And she felt how simple and kind her smile was." What is the irony in this sentence? Find three other ironic sentences in the story. Why, in your opinion, is an ironic approach appropriate to Rosemary Fell?

3. Describe Rosemary's relationship to Philip. How do you think the incident involving the girl has changed their relationship? In your opinion, will the incident have any permanent effect on Rosemary's character? Why or why not?

4. Reread the first paragraph of the story. Does this paragraph have new significance now that you have read the entire story? Explain.

5. Rosemary reflects, "There are moments, horrible moments in life, when one emerges from shelter and looks out, and it's awful." To what extent, in your opinion, is this reflection related to the theme of "A Cup of Tea?"

6. Katherine Mansfield was interested in "the moment of direct feeling when we are most ourselves and least personal." How does the story you have just read reveal this interest? What do you think she meant by "when we are most ourselves and least personal"? How might this remark be related to the way she presents her characters?

FOR COMPOSITION

1. The psychoanalyst Carl Jung has said: "There is no coming to consciousness without pain." Write a composition in which you show how this statement might be applied to the heroine of "A Cup of Tea"—and perhaps to an experience in your own life as well.

2. Contrast Katherine Mansfield's "A Cup of Tea" with Thomas Hardy's "The Three Strangers" (page 630). Hardy's story and Miss Mansfield's story reveal different conceptions of the short story in terms of plot, character development, tone, and style. In your composition, consider one critic's comment that Miss Mansfield's work reveals "an endless stalking of feelings, perceptions, language...."

VIRGINIA WOOLF
(1882–1941)

To the outside observer, Virginia Woolf was an exceptionally lucky being. She was born into a brilliant and loving home; she was beautiful; she had a devoted husband who spent much of his time fostering her talent; her friends were the most intelligent Londoners of her day; and by early middle age she was hailed by them as the most original novelist (apart from James Joyce) in an age of ardent experiment. Beneath this surface, however, she had constantly to fight a mental instability which led to several severe breakdowns and eventual suicide at the age of fifty-nine. A penetrating critic herself, she was painfully sensitive to the criticism of others. Because she needed, and received, shelter from the harshness of life in order to preserve her sanity, her talent became too rarified, too narrow in range, ever to flower into the genius expected of her.

Latent genius, however, she undoubtedly possessed, and once or twice in her work, it rose to the surface. *The Waves,* a poetic statement rather than a novel, stands out as a truly remarkable creation. More conventional in form, the novels *To the Lighthouse* and *Mrs. Dalloway,* the better essays in the two volumes of *The Common Reader,* and *A Room of One's Own,* a short defense of women's rights, have lost none of their freshness.

What made her fiction distinctive was its attempt to go beyond what she regarded as the tyranny of plot, to get close to life as it is actually experienced. "Look within and life, it seems, is very far from being 'like this' [that is, like the conventional novel]. Examine for a moment an ordinary mind on an ordinary day. The mind receives myriad impressions—trivial, fantastic, evanescent, or engraved with the sharpness of steel . . . life is a luminous halo, a semitransparent envelope surrounding us from the beginning of consciousness to the end. Is it not the task of the novelist to convey this varying, this unknown and uncircumscribed spirit . . .?" To approach the experience of life, she often employed the "stream-of-consciousness" technique (see page 718) in her novels. Although she did not invent this technique, she refined and brightened by her own wit and observation the procedure by which the characters of a novel reveal themselves through their unspoken thoughts. She was an insightful writer, whose method was to assemble in language of great poetic force tiny fragments of perception. She tried, as far as possible, to catch each moment as it passed rather than to thrust her characters into the contrivances of a plot.

Virginia Woolf was the daughter of Sir Leslie Stephen, an eminent Victorian scholar, critic, and writer. Throughout her life, she moved in the company of highly intelligent and articulate writers, artists, critics, and philosophers. Her father's first wife was the daughter of the novelist William Makepeace Thackeray, and Virginia herself married a keenly intelligent writer, Leonard Woolf. Her elder sister, Vanessa, was an excellent painter who married the eminent art critic Clive Bell. Roger Fry, whose biography she wrote, and whose insights as a critic of painting did much to revolutionize British taste by introducing the work of the Post-Impressionists, was a close friend. So were John Maynard Keynes, the economist; Lytton Strachey, the biographer; Bertrand Russell, the philosopher; and E. M. Forster, the novelist. Bound together by a common outlook, working and living in the Bloomsbury section of London, the Woolfs and some of their friends were known as the "Bloomsbury Group," a remarkable intellectual circle.

Inevitably, spared from close contact with "ordinary" people, Mrs. Woolf's writing grew less and less concerned with ordinary life and concentrated more and more on moments of great subtlety and sensitivity. Her friend E. M. Forster characterized her as "a poet who wants to write something as near to a novel as possible." She recorded her own anxieties and frustrations in a journal, part of which was posthumously published as *A Writer's Diary*. After her death, it became fashionable to emphasize her faults as a writer—her inability to create exciting plots or to draw strong, distinctive characters—at the expense of her virtues. But, as time passes, it is likely that she will again be discovered, not as a great novelist, but as a rare spirit who, in her own delicate fashion, has enlarged our knowledge of the human heart.

The New Dress

Mabel had her first serious suspicion that something was wrong as she took her cloak off and Mrs. Barnet, while handing her the mirror and touching the brushes and thus drawing her attention, perhaps rather markedly, to all the appliances for tidying and improving hair, complexion, clothes, which existed on the dressing table, confirmed the suspicion—that it was not right, not quite right, which growing stronger as she went upstairs and springing at her with conviction as she greeted Clarissa Dalloway, she went straight to the far end of the room, to a shaded corner where a looking glass hung and looked. No! It was not *right*. And at once the misery which she always tried to hide,

the profound dissatisfaction—the sense she had had, ever since she was a child, of being inferior to other people—set upon her, relentlessly, remorselessly, with an intensity which she could not beat off, as she would when she woke at night at home, by reading Borrow[1] or Scott;[2] for oh these men, oh these women, all were thinking—"What's Mabel wearing? What a fright she looks! What a hideous new dress!"—their eyelids flickering as they came up and then their lids shutting rather tight. It was her own appalling inadequacy; her cowardice; her mean, water-sprinkled blood that depressed her. And at once the whole of the room where, for ever so many hours, she had planned with the little dressmaker how it was to go, seemed sordid, repulsive; and her own drawing room so shabby, and herself, going out, puffed up with vanity as she touched the letters on the hall table and

[1] **Borrow:** George Henry Borrow, English writer (1803–1881).
[2] **Scott:** Sir Walter Scott. Scottish novelist and poet (1771–1832).

said, "How dull!" to show off—all this now seemed unutterably silly, paltry, and provincial. All this had been absolutely destroyed, shown up, exploded, the moment she came into Mrs. Dalloway's drawing room.

What she had thought that evening when, sitting over the teacups, Mrs. Dalloway's invitation came, was that, of course, she could not be fashionable. It was absurd to pretend it even—fashion meant cut, meant style, meant thirty guineas at least—but why not be original? Why not be herself, anyhow? And, getting up, she had taken that old fashion book of her mother's, a Paris fashion book of the time of the Empire, and had thought how much prettier, more dignified, and more womanly they were then, and so set herself—oh, it was foolish—trying to be like them, pluming herself in fact, upon being modest and old-fashioned and very charming, giving herself up, no doubt about it, to an orgy of self-love, which deserved to be chastised, and so rigged herself out like this.

But she dared not look in the glass. She could not face the whole horror—the pale yellow, idiotically old-fashioned silk dress with its long skirt and its high sleeves and its waist and all the things that looked so charming in the fashion book, but not on her, not among all these ordinary people. She felt like a dressmaker's dummy standing there, for young people to stick pins into.

"But, my dear, it's perfectly charming!" Rose Shaw said, looking her up and down with that little satirical pucker of the lips which she expected—Rose herself being dressed in the height of the fashion, precisely like everybody else, always.

We are all like flies trying to crawl over the edge of the saucer, Mabel thought, and repeated the phrase as if she were crossing herself, as if she were trying to find some spell to annul this pain, to make this agony endurable. Tags of Shakespeare, lines from books she had read ages ago, suddenly came to her when she was in agony, and she repeated them over and over again. "Flies trying to crawl," she repeated. If she could say that over often enough and make herself see the flies, she would become numb, chill, frozen, dumb. Now she could see flies crawling slowly out of a saucer of milk with their wings stuck together; and she strained and strained (standing in front of the looking glass, listening to Rose Shaw) to make herself see Rose Shaw and all the other people there as flies, trying to hoist themselves out of something, or into something, meager, insignificant, toiling flies. But she could not see them like that, not other people. She saw herself like that— she was a fly, but the others were dragonflies, butterflies, beautiful insects, dancing, fluttering, skimming, while she alone dragged herself up out of the saucer. (Envy and spite, the most detestable of the vices, were her chief faults.)

"I feel like some dowdy, decrepit, horribly dingy old fly," she said, making Robert Haydon stop just to hear her say that, just to reassure herself by furbishing up a poor weak-kneed phrase and so showing how detached she was, how witty, that she did not feel in the least out of anything. And, of course, Robert Haydon answered something quite polite, quite insincere, which she saw through instantly, and said to herself, directly he went (again from some book), "Lies, lies, lies!" For a party makes things either much more real, or much less real, she thought; she saw in a flash to the bottom of Robert Haydon's heart; she saw through everything. She saw the truth. *This* was true, this drawing room, this self, and the other false. Miss Milan's little workroom was really terribly hot, stuffy, sordid. It smelled of clothes and cabbage cooking; and yet, when Miss Milan put the glass in her hand, and she looked at herself with the dress on, finished, an extraordinary bliss shot through her heart. Suffused with light, she sprang into existence. Rid of cares and wrinkles, what she had dreamed of herself was there—a beautiful woman. Just for a second (she had not dared look longer, Miss Milan wanted to know about the length of the skirt), there looked at her, framed in the scrolloping mahogany, a gray-white, mysteriously smiling, charming girl, the core of herself, the soul of herself; and it was not vanity only, not only self-love that made her think it good, tender, and true. Miss Milan said that the skirt could not well be longer; if anything the skirt, said Miss Milan, puckering her forehead, considering with all her wits about her, must be shorter; and she felt, suddenly, honestly, full of love for Miss Milan, much, much fonder of Miss Milan than of anyone in the whole world, and could have cried for pity that she should be crawling on the floor with her mouth full of pins, and her face red and her eyes bulging—that one human being should be doing this for another, and she saw them all as human beings merely, and herself going off to her party, and Miss Milan pulling the cover over the canary's cage, or letting him pick a hempseed from between her lips, and the thought of it, of this side of human nature and its patience and its endurance and its being content with such miserable, scanty, sordid little pleasures filled her eyes with tears.

And now the whole thing had vanished. The dress, the room, the love, the pity, the scrolloping looking glass, and the canary's cage—all had vanished, and here she was in a corner of Mrs. Dalloway's drawing room, suffering tortures, woken wide awake to reality.

But it was all so paltry, weak-blooded, and petty-minded to care so much at her age with two children, to be still so utterly dependent on people's opinions and not have principles or convictions, not to be able to say as other people did, "There's Shakespeare! There's death! We're all weevils in a captain's biscuit"—or whatever it was that people did say.

She faced herself straight in the glass; she pecked at her left shoulder; she issued out into the room, as if spears were thrown at her yellow dress from all sides. But instead of looking fierce or tragic, as Rose Shaw would have done—Rose would have looked like Boadicea [1]—she looked foolish and self-conscious, and simpered like a schoolgirl and slouched across the room, positively slinking, as if she were a beaten mongrel, and looked at a picture, an engraving. As if one went to a party to look at a picture! Everybody knew why she did it—it was from shame, from humiliation.

"Now the fly's in the saucer," she said to herself, "right in the middle, and can't get out, and the milk," she thought, rigidly staring at the picture, "is sticking its wings together."

"It's so old-fashioned," she said to Charles Burt, making him stop (which by itself he hated) on his way to talk to someone else.

She meant, or she tried to make herself think that she meant, that it was the picture and not her dress that was old-fashioned. And one word of praise, one word of affection from Charles would have made all the difference to her at the moment. If he had only said, "Mabel, you're looking charming tonight!" it would have changed her life. But then she ought to have been truthful and direct. Charles said nothing of the kind, of course. He was malice itself. He always saw through one, especially if one were feeling particularly mean, paltry, or feeble-minded.

"Mabel's got a new dress!" he said, and the poor fly was absolutely shoved into the middle of the saucer. Really, he would like her to drown, she believed. He had no heart, no fundamental kindness, only a veneer of friendliness. Miss Milan was much more real, much kinder. If only one could feel that and stick to it always. "Why," she asked herself—replying to Charles much too pertly, letting him see that she was out of temper, or "ruffled" as he called it ("Rather ruffled?" he said and went on to laugh at her with some woman over there)—"Why," she asked herself, "can't I feel one thing always, feel

[1] **Boadicea** (bō′ad·ə·sē′ə): a British queen who in A.D. 62 poisoned herself after suffering defeat by the Romans.

quite sure that Miss Milan is right, and Charles wrong and stick to it, feel sure about the canary and pity and love and not be whipped all round in a second by coming into a room full of people?" It was her odious, weak, vacillating character again, always giving at the critical moment and not being seriously interested in conchology, etymology, botany, archeology, cutting up potatoes and watching them fructify like Mary Dennis, like Violet Searle.

Then Mrs. Holman, seeing her standing there, bore down upon her. Of course a thing like a dress was beneath Mrs. Holman's notice, with her family always tumbling downstairs or having the scarlet fever. Could Mabel tell her if Elmthorpe was ever let for August and September? Oh, it was a conversation that bored her unutterably!—it made her furious to be treated like a house agent or a messenger boy, to be made use of. Not to have value, that was it, she thought, trying to grasp something hard, something real, while she tried to answer sensibly about the bathroom and the south aspect and the hot water to the top of the house; and all the time she could see little bits of her yellow dress in the round looking glass which made them all the size of boot-buttons or tadpoles; and it was amazing to think how much humiliation and agony and self-loathing and effort and passionate ups and downs of feeling were contained in a thing the size of a threepenny bit. And what was still odder, this thing, this Mabel Waring, was separate, quite disconnected; and though Mrs. Holman (the black button) was leaning forward and telling her how her eldest boy had strained his heart running, she could see her, too, quite detached in the looking glass, and it was impossible that the black dot, leaning forward, gesticulating, should make the yellow dot, sitting solitary, self-centered, feel what the black dot was feeling, yet they pretended.

"So impossible to keep boys quiet"— that was the kind of thing one said.

And Mrs. Holman, who could never get enough sympathy and snatched what little there was greedily, as if it were her right (but she deserved much more for there was her little girl who had come down this morning with a swollen knee-joint), took this miserable offering and looked at it suspiciously, grudgingly, as if it were a half-penny when it ought to have been a pound and put it away in her purse, must put up with it, mean and miserly though it was, times being hard, so very hard; and on she went, creaking, injured Mrs. Holman, about the girl with the swollen joints. Ah, it was tragic, this greed, this clamor of human beings, like a row of cormorants,[1] barking and flapping their wings for sympathy—it was tragic, could one have felt it and not merely pretended to feel it!

But in her yellow dress tonight she could not wring out one drop more; she wanted it all, all for herself. She knew (she kept on looking into the glass, dipping into that dreadfully showing up blue pool) that she was condemned, despised, left like this in a backwater, because of her being like this a feeble, vacillating creature; and it seemed to her that the yellow dress was a penance which she had deserved, and if she had been dressed like Rose Shaw, in lovely, clinging green with a ruffle of swansdown, she would have deserved that; and she thought that there was no escape for her—none whatever. But it was not her fault altogether, after all. It was being one of a family of ten; never having money enough, always skimping and paring; and her mother carrying great cans, and the linoleum worn on the stair edges, and one sordid little domestic tragedy after another—nothing catastrophic, the sheep farm failing, but not utterly; her eldest brother marrying beneath him but not very much—there was no romance, nothing extreme about them all. They petered out respectably in seaside resorts; every watering place had one of her aunts even now asleep in some lodging with the front windows not

[1] **cormorants:** large, web-footed aquatic birds.

quite facing the sea. That was so like them—they had to squint at things always. And she had done the same—she was just like her aunts. For all her dreams of living in India, married to some hero like Sir Henry Lawrence, some empire builder (still the sight of a native in a turban filled her with romance), she had failed utterly. She had married Hubert, with his safe, permanent underling's job in the Law Courts, and they managed tolerably in a smallish house without proper maids and hash when she was alone or just bread and butter, but now and then—Mrs. Holman was off, thinking her the most dried up, unsympathetic twig she had ever met, absurdly dressed, too, and would tell everyone about Mabel's fantastic appearance—now and then, thought Mabel Waring, left alone on the blue sofa, punching the cushion in order to look occupied, for she would not join Charles Burt and Rose Shaw, chattering like magpies and perhaps laughing at her by the fireplace—now and then, there did come to her delicious moments, reading the other night in bed, for instance, or down by the sea on the sand in the sun at Easter—let her recall it—a great tuft of pale sand grass standing all twisted like a shock of spears against the sky, which was blue like a smooth china egg, so firm, so hard, and then the melody of the waves—"Hush, hush," they said, and the children's shouts paddling—yes, it was a divine moment, and there she lay, she felt, in the hand of the Goddess who was the world; rather a hard-hearted, but very beautiful Goddess, a little lamb laid on the altar (one did think these silly things, and it didn't matter so long as one never said them). And also with Hubert sometimes she had quite unexpectedly—carving the mutton for Sunday lunch, for no reason, opening a letter, coming into a room—divine moments, when she said to herself (for she would never say this to anybody else), "This is it. This has happened. This is it!" And the other way about it was equally surprising—that is, when everything was arranged—music, weather, holidays, every

reason for happiness was there—then nothing happened at all. One wasn't happy. It was flat, just flat, that was all.

Her wretched self again, no doubt! She had always been a fretful, weak, unsatisfactory mother, a wobbly wife, lolling about in a kind of twilight existence with nothing very clear or very bold, or more one thing than another, like all her brothers and sisters, except perhaps Herbert— they were all the same poor water-veined creatures who did nothing. Then in the midst of this creeping, crawling life, suddenly she was on the crest of a wave. That wretched fly—where had she read the story that kept coming into her mind about the fly and the saucer?—struggled out. Yes, she had those moments. But now that she was forty, they might come more and more seldom. By degrees she would cease to struggle any more. But that was deplorable! That was not to be endured! That made her feel ashamed of herself!

She would go to the London Library tomorrow. She would find some wonderful, helpful, astonishing book, quite by chance, a book by a clergyman, by an American no one had ever heard of; or she would walk down the Strand and drop, accidentally, into a hall where a miner was telling about the life in the pit, and suddenly she would become a new person. She would be absolutely transformed. She would wear a uniform; she would be called Sister Somebody; she would never give a thought to clothes again. And for ever after she would be perfectly clear about Charles Burt and Miss Milan and this room and that room; and it would be always, day after day, as if she were lying in the sun or carving the mutton. It would be it!

So she got up from the blue sofa, and the yellow button in the looking glass got up too, and she waved her hand to Charles and Rose to show them she did not depend on them one scrap, and the yellow button moved out of the looking glass, and all the spears were gathered into her breast as she walked towards Mrs. Dalloway and said, "Good night."

"But it's too early to go," said Mrs. Dalloway, who was always so charming.

"I'm afraid I must," said Mabel Waring. "But," she added in her weak, wobbly voice which only sounded ridiculous when she tried to strengthen it, "I have enjoyed myself enormously."

"I have enjoyed myself," she said to Mr. Dalloway, whom she met on the stairs.

"Lies, lies, lies!" she said to herself, going downstairs, and "Right in the saucer!" she said to herself as she thanked Mrs. Barnet for helping her and wrapped herself round and round and round in the Chinese cloak she had worn these twenty years.

FOR STUDY AND DISCUSSION

1. How would you describe Mabel's relationship to the other people at the party? Does she "belong"? Why or why not?

2. How does what you learn of Mabel's past explain her behavior at the party? Why do you think this information is given so late in the story?

3. There are repeated references to Mabel's enjoyment of reading. Why does she turn to books? What satisfaction does she find in them?

4. What do you learn of Mrs. Dalloway, Rose Shaw, Robert Haydon, Miss Milan, and the other people at the party? Do they emerge as distinct individuals? Why or why not?

5. A simile involving a "fly trying to crawl over the edge of the saucer" occurs with variations several times in the story. Describe the variations. What is the significance of this simile in the story?

6. Cite at least three references to mirrors in "The New Dress." Why do mirrors play such an important role in this story?

7. In Shakespeare's *Hamlet,* the hero says, "There's nothing good or bad but thinking makes it so." How may this statement be applied to Mabel Waring?

THE STREAM–OF–CONSCIOUSNESS TECHNIQUE

Twentieth-century writers such as Virginia Woolf and James Joyce (page 727) have tried not merely to describe how characters might think; they have also attempted to present a record of their consciousness—that is, the stream of the characters' thoughts as they are thinking them. For example, in her novel *Mrs. Dalloway,* Virginia Woolf records the consciousness of Clarissa Dalloway as she thinks about a party she is giving:

"But to go deeper, beneath what people said (and these judgments, how superficial, how fragmentary they are!) in her own mind now, what did it mean to her, this thing she called life? Oh, it was very queer. Here was So-and-so in South Kensington; someone up in Bayswater; and someone else, say, in Mayfair [districts of London]. And she felt continuously a sense of their existence; and she felt a waste; and she felt what a pity; and she felt if only they could be brought together; so she did it. And it was an offering; to combine, to create, but to whom?"

Notice that the author does not try to be especially clear. Instead, she follows the mind wherever it goes, seeking to give an impression of spontaneity rather than order.

1. Find passages in "The New Dress" that employ the stream-of-consciousness technique. Do the sentences follow one another logically? If not, what relationship do they have to one another?

2. In terms of sentence order and the kinds of sentences used, compare a passage in "The New Dress" with a passage in "The Lagoon" (page 668) which describes the white man's thoughts as he looks at the sky. Compare the two passages.

FOR COMPOSITION

In her essay "Mr. Bennett and Mrs. Brown," Virginia Woolf states that the fiction writer's central concern is with character, the mysteries of the human personality. Using as an example an old lady she calls Mrs. Brown, the author goes on to show what an elusive, complex person Mrs. Brown is and describes her own attempt to capture the reality of this character: "And to have got what I meant, I should have had to go back and back and back; to experiment with one thing and another; to try this sentence and that, referring each word to my vision [of Mrs. Brown], matching it as exactly as possible." Discuss "The New Dress" as an attempt to capture the reality of Mabel Waring. What means does Mrs. Woolf use to present this character? To what extent does she succeed in creating a convincing character? Give reasons for your opinions.

ENGLISH PAINTING

Impressionism and Its Aftermath

For the last hundred years the most exciting developments in painting have originated in France. The French Impressionists had won a following in England by 1885; the Post-Impressionists created a stir at the first London exhibition of their works in 1910. Many English artists, after studying in Paris, sketching villages from Brittany to Provence, or serving as official war artists in World War I, have looked upon France as their second country. But English artists, despite their respect for French painters and their fond regard for France, have remained thoroughly English. Most of them have been highly independent, especially in their attitudes toward the Royal Academy. For artistic training, they have favored instead the Slade School in London; for new artists' societies—again, in opposition to the Academy—they have chosen such plain English names as "New English Art Club" (1885) and "London Group" (1914). Though they have watched Continental movements like Cubism and Futurism, they have always kept in mind the artistic achievements of their own compatriots, and they have continued to find their subjects in the English surroundings which they know best. As a matter of course, they have shown keen interest in English poetry and the London stage.

Walter Richard Sickert, who was known as an English Impressionist, sought out studios in humble neighborhoods and probed the lives of ordinary people. He relished the popular entertainment provided by singers, comedians, and acrobats in the London music halls. See, for example, *The Old Bedford* (PLATE 1). Stagelight plays on the ornate gallery and on faces in an audience of ordinary people caught up in a theatrical illusion.

Among the younger painters whom Sickert met in London around the turn of the century was Augustus John, then a student at the Slade. John's work, though criticized by some as unbeautiful or unfinished, had already gained praise for its strength. In 1907 he stayed at Coole Park, Lady Gregory's house in Ireland, to do a portrait of the poet William Butler Yeats, a painter's son with art school training, who wrote that John's sketches were "all powerful ugly gypsy things." Fourteen years later, to his own surprise, John was elected an Associate of the Royal Academy. At about this time he painted a more mature portrait of Yeats (PLATE 2) which showed him as he was not long before becoming a senator of the Irish Free State and a Nobel prizewinner.

One of John's friends in the London Group was Wyndham Lewis, a painter and writer who in 1914 became a spokesman for the modernist movement in art. The age of the merely representational, he argued, had ended with Impressionism; the time had come to clarify significant form by seeing through the very essence of things. In the 1915 number of his "Vorticist" review, *Blast*, Lewis published two poems by T. S. Eliot. Friendship between the two men continued, and in 1938 Lewis painted a portrait of T. S. Eliot (PLATE 3), which the Royal Academy rejected from its Summer Exhibition. It was widely assumed that this rigorously simplified and geometrically patterned portrait was "too modern" for the ultra-conservative Academy jury.

Paul Nash, when he entered the Slade in 1910, drew like a Pre-Raphaelite, but when he painted the devastation of war in Belgium, he seemed to be a "modernist" fascinated by lines and angles. After the war, he allied himself with the great English landscape tradition by cultivating his sense of place and by working mainly in watercolor. Like Lewis, however, Nash looked beyond the immediately visible. Convinced that every place has its own magic "implicated in its own design," he experimented first with Cubist patterns and later, during the 1930's, with surrealist visions. *Landscape of the Megaliths* (PLATE 4) originated in Nash's recollection of the mysterious stones and mounds erected about 1900 B.C. near Avebury, Wiltshire, but it might be a scene on a distant planet where life had just begun.

Victor Pasmore's *Evening, Hammersmith (Chiswick Reach)* (PLATE 5), suggestive of air heavy with dampness, delicately contrasts the linear sharpness of the trees with the softness of verdure, river, and sky. Painted beside the Thames in 1943, but reminiscent of works by the Impressionists, it seems to contradict Lewis's announcement that representational art was dead. For a few years just before World War II, Pasmore and his colleagues of the Euston Road School turned for inspiration to Sickert and his American master, Whistler, a famous painter of Thames nocturnes. But the age demanded something newer, and Pasmore soon abandoned the Whistlerian manner and started to produce austerely geometrical abstract designs.

According to the title, the subject of Stanley Spencer's *Swan Upping* (PLATE 6) is the annual rounding-up of swans on the Thames and nicking of their beaks with their owner's mark. This time something out of the ordinary is happening, or about to happen. The stylized forms, arranged in a clear-cut, bold composition, seem unreal and very still. Mysteriously, the woman carrying cushions looks less English than Tahitian, and the clouds in the sky and the looks passing between the man and the woman on the bridge create tension such as one may feel before a summer storm.

720

PLATE 1. WALTER RICHARD SICKERT (1860–1942): *The Old Bedford*. 1897. Oil on canvas, 30 x 23¾ inches. (Walker Art Gallery, Liverpool, England)

PLATE 2. AUGUSTUS JOHN (1878–1961): *Portrait of Yeats*. 1930. Oil on canvas, 48 x 30 inches. (Reproduced by courtesy of the Glasgow Art Gallery and Museum, Scotland)

PLATE 3. WYNDHAM LEWIS (1884–1957): *Portrait of T. S. Eliot*. 1938. Oil on canvas, $52\frac{1}{2}$ x $33\frac{1}{2}$ inches. (Durban Museum and Art Gallery, South Africa)

PLATE 4. PAUL NASH (1889–1946): *Landscape of the Megaliths*. 1937. Watercolor, $19\frac{3}{4}$ x $29\frac{3}{4}$ inches. (Albright-Knox Art Gallery, Buffalo, Room of Contemporary Art Fund)

PLATE 5. VICTOR PASMORE (1908–): *Evening, Hammersmith (Chiswick Reach)*. 1943. Oil on canvas. 34 x 47$\frac{1}{4}$ inches. (National Gallery of Canada, Ottawa)

PLATE 6. STANLEY SPENCER (1892–1959): *Swan Upping*. 1914–19. Oil on canvas, 58 x 45½ inches. (Reproduced by courtesy of the Trustees, The Tate Gallery, London)

726

JAMES JOYCE
(1882–1941)

During the nineteenth century, England gave a somewhat grudging and uncertain approval to the abilities of contemporary foreign writers. But today when modern literature is spoken of, the term is naturally understood to refer to literary works in several languages and implies that great works in any one of these languages have been built, in part, upon an awareness and appreciation of literature in other tongues.

James Joyce, whose work is at once intensely local and universal, is a striking instance of this interdependence. He attributed his most famous innovation in fictional method to a Frenchman, Edouard Dujardin, and he ransacked the world's languages and literatures for his own purposes, yet he never wrote anything of consequence which did not deal with his native Dublin and his life there. He is known for six works: a book of poems, a play, and four other works of far larger scope. These four comprise *Dubliners* (1914), *A Portrait of the Artist as a Young Man* (1916), *Ulysses* (1922), and *Finnegans Wake* (1939). Before we turn to *Dubliners* (the volume of short stories from which the following selection is drawn), we must glance at the other three books. *A Portrait of the Artist* is much more directly autobiographical than the others, although its hero, Stephen Dedalus, is a "young man" on whom the writer looks back with sometimes ironical detachment. This young man renounces his family and country and sets out to "encounter the reality of experience and to forge in the smithy of my soul the uncreated conscience of my race." In French, *conscience* means "consciousness," and, if we combine this meaning with the English meaning, we arrive at a notion of Joyce's ambition. He named his hero after Daedalus, the legendary Greek inventor who designed the labyrinth of Crete, was imprisoned to protect its secret, and then made wings to escape. Stephen Dedalus similarly escapes from Ireland and takes flight, only to penetrate every secret of the labyrinth of Irish consciousness from afar and to judge all he has known.

Dubliners and *A Portrait of the Artist* do not present the difficulties of *Ulysses,* a work which reflects the consciousness of its characters in a literal sense: that is, the book is composed of the characters' internal monologues. This device, often referred to as "stream of consciousness" (see page 718), is the innovation which Joyce said he had found in Dujardin. Although the use of the "stream of consciousness" was a radical shift in fictional technique, the aim of *Ulysses* was newer still. *Ulysses* is told chiefly through the consciousness of its principal figure, Leopold Bloom. Bloom's consciousness is made to embrace not only the multitudinous details of the life of the city of Dublin on just one day—June 16, 1904—but the whole human journey from birth to grave. In this novel Joyce attempts to embody the significance of all human history, the meaning of the family, of manhood and womanhood, war, politics, and human achievement of every sort, but preeminently the achievements of those artists who have found in words the means of binding us to others and to our world. Words are Joyce's obsession, his delight, the source of his power. So wonderfully are words used by this great artificer that the whole world of Dublin springs up out of their sounds, colors, reverberations, and linkages with each other. Almost nothing is *seen* in this book. We hear, rather, torrents of words which flow out into rivers of meaning. To organize this flow and to show how all time coils back upon itself, making history instantaneous and continuous, Joyce uses the story of the wanderings of the classical hero Ulysses as a kind of mythical shorthand to underscore the eternal significance of the contemporary episodes in his work.

The content of *Dubliners, A Portrait of the Artist,* and *Ulysses* is in a sense all the same: Joyce's childhood and youth in Dublin. It is no surprise, therefore, to learn that his final achievement, *Finnegans Wake,* is also based on Dublin. In this book, however, the artificer is no longer content with existing words; he takes apart, combines, and rebuilds words into a pattern of meanings that no single language alone (but all languages taken together) affords. Joyce was a linguist who for many years earned his living by teaching English to foreigners. He knew Latin, Italian, French, German, and numerous other tongues, and in this final work drew upon all his knowledge. The effect of his melting down and building up language cannot be fully described here, for a characteristic Joycean sentence in *Finnegans Wake* is like an echoing corridor with rooms branching from it, all reverberating with the most splendid and complicated puns ever made. Word-play, puns, the use of sounds to enforce meaning (onomatopoeia)—these are just a suggestion of the allusive and musical uses of language achieved in this book.

One brief example may indicate the density of nuance and the concentration of attention necessary to appreciate Joyce's imaginative use of language in *Finnegans Wake.* In the famous "Anna Livia Plurabelle" chapter, two washerwomen are doing the laundry on the banks of Dublin's river Liffey. The chapter consists solely of their dialogue and musings. These lines occur: "Wring out the clothes! Wring in the dew! Godavari, vert the showers!" The first two sentences reveal the laundresses' occupation at the same time that they parody Tennyson's phrases from *In Memoriam:* "Ring out the old, ring in the new." In the third sentence, "Godavari" means "God of Eire (Ireland)" and is also the name of a river in India. "Vert" is French for "green" and is short for "avert" in English. The showers would ruin the laundry but would also make the grass green. Thus these lines represent a fairly typical yoking of literary allusion, religion, human activity, the cycles of nature, time, and history, and the continual flowing of the world's water, the great primal element. (Joyce attempted to name all the rivers of the world in this book, usually in puns as in "Godavari" here.) Devices such as these, used to build layer upon layer of meanings, will keep readers busy for a long time, hunting among the byways of scholastic philosophy, Dublin newspapers, American comic strips, geographical atlases, Joyce's own life in Trieste, Zurich, and Paris, and a hundred other places.

As *Ulysses* is an account of one day, so *Finnegans Wake* is the account of a night, or rather a night dreamed by a man in whose consciousness all recorded history finds a meaning and a home. To further exemplify Joyce's celebrated use of language, it is interesting to note that *wake* is not only the Irish term for funeral, but a part of the verb to *awaken.* Thus the novel is concerned with the death and rebirth of Finnegan, builder of cities and a Dublin bricklayer; a compound of all the heroes of myth. So full of riddles, allusions, and ambiguities is this book that it is hard to imagine reading it all with ease and pleasure. Yet if it is not quite a *funferal* (one of Joyce's puns which suggests a funeral *and* a joyous celebration, "fun for all"), it is nevertheless a tremendous performance, a book about everything.

It can be charged that Joyce's achievement is limited by the private and often obscure techniques of narrative which he developed, and by what amounts to an obsession with words and their manipulation. But despite this limitation, Joyce's accomplishment cannot otherwise be faulted. Among the monuments of twentieth-century literature in English, his work conveys most and is most comprehensive.

THE LIFE OF JAMES JOYCE

Joyce wrote in 1921: "For myself, I always write about Dublin, because if I can get to the heart of Dublin I can get to the heart of all the cities of the world. In the particular is contained the universal." These sentences reveal not only Joyce's devotion to his lifelong subject, but another important aspect of his own background. The terms *particular* and *universal* are central to the scholastic philosophy (derived from medieval Catholic thought) which he studied in two excellent Jesuit schools as a child. Although Joyce's attention to his education was responsible, effective, and orderly, his home life was a chaos—perhaps a fruitful chaos since he survived it and made much of it in his work. One may also say that Joyce spent most of his adult life trying to make sense of an environment which must have been hard for a youngster to endure or understand. His father, John Joyce, who had inherited some property, frittered it away. The family kept moving to meaner quarters, and the father, who was jovial, savage, extravagantly affectionate, and brutal by turns, was more likely to come home drunk than with food for his family. John Joyce had been devoted to Charles Stewart Parnell, the advocate of Irish freedom, and his betrayal and death affected both the elder Joyce and his son James deeply.

Joyce's mother tried to hold the large family together. Her oldest son, James, was deeply dependent on her, and he defined growing up as the business of breaking free from her. After his mother's death, he finally fled Dublin for good, in the company of Nora Barnacle, the beautiful and maternal woman who was to become his wife. The mileposts in the years that followed are the names of the cities in which Joyce successively lived, the publication of the books over which he labored for years, the gradual deterioration of his always poor eyesight, and the names of the patrons who gave him the financial freedom which he needed to write. Joyce acquired his first patron himself by getting his steady, responsible brother, Stanislaus, to share (and help support) his household in Trieste where he had settled as a teacher of English at the Berlitz School. On the surface his life seemed to be one of improvidence very much like his father's, but in fact it was wholly centered on his writing. Many of his pupils were charmed by him and helped him in various ways. World War I forced him to Switzerland, where he remained until he was able to move to Paris in 1920. Here he lived through the triumphant period of the publication of *Ulysses*. Driven again to Switzerland by the Nazi occupation of France, he died in 1941, nearly blind and almost worn out by a combination of hard work and hard living. Joyce lived in an atmosphere of conspiracy at times. He was quick to feel insulted and equally quick to return defiance to the world. At other times he was full of gaiety and a delightful companion. But, in reviewing his troubled life, the most vivid picture is that of a man fiercely guarding his talent and doing the work that he knew he alone could do.

Araby

NORTH RICHMOND STREET, being blind,[1] was a quiet street except at the hour when the Christian Brothers' School set the boys free. An uninhabited house of two stories stood at the blind end, detached from its neighbors in a square ground. The other houses of the street, conscious of decent lives within them, gazed at one another with brown imperturbable faces.

The former tenant of our house, a priest, had died in the back drawing room. Air, musty from having been long enclosed, hung in all the rooms, and the waste room behind the kitchen was littered with old useless papers. Among these I found a few paper-covered books, the pages of which were curled and damp: *The Abbot,* by Walter Scott, *The Devout Communicant* and *The Memoirs of Vidocq.*[2] I liked the last best because its leaves were yellow. The wild garden behind the house contained a central apple tree and a few straggling bushes under one of which I found the late tenant's rusty bicycle pump. He had been a very charitable priest; in his will he had left all his money to institutions and the furniture of his house to his sister.

When the short days of winter came dusk fell before we had well eaten our dinners. When we met in the street the houses had grown somber. The space of sky above us was the color of everchanging violet and toward it the lamps of the street lifted their feeble lanterns. The cold air stung us and we played till our bodies glowed. Our shouts echoed in the silent street. The career of our play brought us through the dark muddy lanes behind the houses where we ran the gauntlet of the rough tribes from the cottages, to the back doors of the dark dripping gardens where odors arose from the ashpits, to the dark odorous stables where a coachman smoothed and combed the horse or shook music from the buckled harness. When we returned to the street, light from the kitchen windows had filled the areas. If my uncle was seen turning the corner we hid in the shadow until we had seen him safely housed. Or if Mangan's sister came out on the doorstep to call her brother in to his tea we watched her from our shadow peer up and down the street. We waited to see whether she would remain or go in and, if she remained, we left our shadow and walked up to Mangan's steps resignedly. She was waiting for us, her figure defined by the light from the half-opened door. Her brother always teased her before he obeyed and I stood by the railings looking at her. Her dress swung as she moved her body and the soft rope of her hair tossed from side to side.

Every morning I lay on the floor in the front parlor watching her door. The blind was pulled down to within an inch of the sash so that I could not be seen. When she came out on the doorstep my heart leaped. I ran to the hall, seized my books and followed her. I kept her brown figure always in my eye and, when we came near the point at which our ways diverged, I quickened my pace and passed her. This happened morning after morning. I had never spoken to her, except for a few casual words, and yet her name was like a summons to all my foolish blood.

Her image accompanied me even in places the most hostile to romance. On Saturday evenings when my aunt went marketing I had to go to carry some of the parcels. We walked through the flaring streets, jostled by drunken men and bargaining women, amid the curses of laborers, the shrill litanies of shopboys who stood on guard by the barrels of pigs'

[1] **blind:** a dead-end street.

[2] ***The Abbot . . . Vidocq:*** a historical romance, a religious manual, and the reminiscences of a French adventurer, respectively.

cheeks, the nasal chanting of streetsingers, who sang a *come-all-you* about O'Donovan Rossa,[1] or a ballad about the troubles in our native land. These noises converged in a single sensation of life for me: I imagined that I bore my chalice safely through a throng of foes. Her name sprang to my lips at moments in strange prayers and praises which I myself did not understand. My eyes were often full of tears (I could not tell why) and at times a flood from my heart seemed to pour itself out into my bosom. I thought little of the future. I did not know whether I would ever speak to her or not or, if I spoke to her, how I could tell her of my confused adoration. But my body was like a harp and her words and gestures were like fingers running upon the wires.

One evening I went into the back drawing room in which the priest had died. It was a dark rainy evening and there was no sound in the house. Through one of the broken panes I heard the rain impinge upon the earth, the fine incessant needles of water playing in the sodden beds. Some distant lamp or lighted window gleamed below me. I was thankful that I could see so little. All my senses seemed to desire to veil themselves and, feeling that I was about to slip from them, I pressed the palms of my hands together until they trembled, murmuring: *"O love! O love!"* many times.

At last she spoke to me. When she addressed the first words to me I was so confused that I did not know what to answer. She asked me was I going to *Araby*.[2] I forgot whether I answered yes or no. It would be a splendid bazaar, she said she would love to go.

"And why can't you?" I asked.

While she spoke she turned a silver bracelet round and round her wrist. She could not go, she said, because there would be a retreat [3] that week in her con-

vent. Her brother and two other boys were fighting for their caps and I was alone at the railings. She held one of the spikes, bowing her head towards me. The light from the lamp opposite our door caught the white curve of her neck, lit up her hair that rested there and, falling, lit up the hand upon the railing. It fell over one side of her dress and caught the white border of a petticoat, just visible as she stood at ease.

"It's well for you," she said.

"If I go," I said, "I will bring you something."

What innumerable follies laid waste my waking and sleeping thoughts after that evening! I wished to annihilate the tedious intervening days. I chafed against the work of school. At night in my bedroom and by day in the classroom her image came between me and the page I strove to read. The syllables of the word *Araby* were called to me through the silence in which my soul luxuriated and cast an Eastern enchantment over me. I asked for leave to go to the bazaar on Saturday night. My aunt was surprised and hoped it was not some Freemason [4] affair. I answered few questions in class. I watched my master's face pass from amiability to sternness; he hoped I was not beginning to idle. I could not call my wandering thoughts together. I had hardly any patience with the serious work of life which, now that it stood between me and my desire, seemed to me child's play, ugly monotonous child's play.

On Saturday morning I reminded my uncle that I wished to go to the bazaar in in the evening. He was fussing at the hallstand, looking for the hat brush, and answered me curtly:

"Yes, boy, I know."

As he was in the hall I could not go into the front parlor and lie at the window. I left the house in bad humor and walked slowly toward the school. The air was pitilessly raw and already my heart misgave me.

---

[1] *come-all-you* ... **Rossa:** a street ballad about an Irish hero.

[2] *Araby:* a bazaar in Oriental style.

[3] **retreat:** secluded religious exercises, here held at the convent school.

[4] **Freemason:** a fraternal society, thought to be anti-Catholic.

When I came home to dinner my uncle had not yet been home. Still it was early. I sat staring at the clock for some time and, when its ticking began to irritate me, I left the room. I mounted the staircase and gained the upper part of the house. The high cold empty gloomy rooms liberated me and I went from room to room singing. From the front window I saw my companions playing below in the street. Their cries reached me weakened and indistinct and, leaning my forehead against the cool glass, I looked over at the dark house where she lived. I may have stood there for an hour, seeing nothing but the brown-clad figure cast by my imagination, touched discreetly by the lamplight at the curved neck, at the hand upon the railings and at the border below the dress.

When I came downstairs again I found Mrs. Mercer sitting at the fire. She was an old garrulous woman, a pawnbroker's widow, who collected used stamps for some pious purpose. I had to endure the gossip of the tea table. The meal was prolonged beyond an hour and still my uncle did not come. Mrs. Mercer stood up to go: she was sorry she couldn't wait any longer, but it was after eight o'clock and she did not like to be out late, as the night air was bad for her. When she had gone I began to walk up and down the room, clenching my fists. My aunt said:

"I'm afraid you may put off your bazaar for this night of Our Lord."

At nine o'clock I heard my uncle's latchkey in the halldoor. I heard him talking to himself and heard the hallstand rocking when it had received the weight of his overcoat. I could interpret these signs. When he was midway through his dinner I asked him to give me the money to go to the bazaar. He had forgotten.

"The people are in bed and after their first sleep now," he said.

I did not smile. My aunt said to him energetically:

"Can't you give him the money and let him go? You've kept him late enough as it is."

My uncle said he was very sorry he had forgotten. He said he believed in the old saying: "All work and no play makes Jack a dull boy." He asked me where I was going and, when I had told him a second time he asked me did I know *The Arab's Farewell to His Steed*.[1] When I left the kitchen he was about to recite the opening lines of the piece to my aunt.

I held a florin [2] tightly in my hand as I strode down Buckingham Street toward the station. The sight of the streets thronged with buyers and glaring with gas recalled to me the purpose of my journey. I took my seat in a third-class carriage of a deserted train. After an intolerable delay the train moved out of the station slowly. It crept onward among ruinous houses and over the twinkling river. At Westland Row Station a crowd of people pressed to the carriage doors; but the porters moved them back, saying that it was a special train for the bazaar. I remained alone in the bare carriage. In a few minutes the train drew up beside an improvised wooden platform. I passed out on to the road and saw by the lighted dial of a clock that it was ten minutes to ten. In front of me was a large building which displayed the magical name.

I could not find any sixpenny entrance and, fearing that the bazaar would be closed, I passed in quickly through a turnstile, handing a shilling to a weary-looking man. I found myself in a big hall girdled at half its height by a gallery. Nearly all the stalls were closed and the greater part of the hall was in darkness. I recognized a silence like that which pervades a church after a service. I walked into the center of the bazaar timidly. A few people were gathered about the stalls which were still open. Before a curtain, over which the words *Café Chantant* [3] were written in colored lamps, two men were counting money on a salver. I listened to the fall of the coins.

[1] *The Arab's Farewell to His Steed:* a popular sentimental poem of the nineteenth century.

[2] **florin:** a two-shilling coin.

[3] *Café Chantant:* a café with musical entertainment.

Remembering with difficulty why I had come I went over to one of the stalls and examined porcelain vases and flowered tea sets. At the door of the stall a young lady was talking and laughing with two young gentlemen. I remarked their English accents and listened vaguely to their conversation.

"O, I never said such a thing!"

"O, but you did!"

"O, but I didn't!"

"Didn't she say that?"

"Yes. I heard her."

"O, there's a . . . fib!"

Observing me the young lady came over and asked me did I wish to buy anything. The tone of her voice was not encouraging; she seemed to have spoken to me out of a sense of duty. I looked humbly at the great jars that stood like eastern guards at either side of the dark entrance to the stall and murmured:

"No, thank you."

The young lady changed the position of one of the vases and went back to the two young men. They began to talk of the same subject. Once or twice the young lady glanced at me over her shoulder.

I lingered before her stall, though I knew my stay was useless, to make my interest in her wares seem the more real. Then I turned away slowly and walked down the middle of the bazaar. I allowed the two pennies to fall against the sixpence in my pocket. I heard a voice call from one end of the gallery that the light was out. The upper part of the hall was now completely dark.

Gazing up into the darkness I saw myself as a creature driven and derided by vanity; and my eyes burned with anguish and anger.

COMMENTARY

Joyce came to manhood in an Ireland full of the stirrings of the Irish Renaissance, whose most notable figures were W. B. Yeats, George Moore, Lady Gregory, and J. M. Synge. Ireland was at this time trying rather self-consciously to achieve a sense of national identity, and, as part of this endeavor, an attempt was made to revive Gaelic as a national language. Believing this movement would separate Ireland further from the mainstream of European culture, Joyce was resolutely against it. He thought it superficial and sentimental and preferred to tell the bitter truth about Dublin, and since for him this involved telling the truth about growing up there, he planned *Dubliners* very carefully to reflect the grim reality of Irish life. However, the stories in *Dubliners* reveal a certain lyricism as well: the wild cry of youth is in the book, muted but always seeking an escape from ugliness. Joyce said of this collection of short stories that it was written "for the most part in a style of scrupulous meanness." This does not apply to certain passages in "Araby," but it is a good way to note the historical position of *Dubliners,* for this book marks a sharp break with the techniques of nineteenth-century fiction. Each word and phrase has a precise function; incident and plot are minimized; the author does not seem to be manipulating characters and emotions; form and theme are intimately connected. Lyricism springs not only out of the promise that youth offers us all, but out of a strong sense of the power of art to shape a world no matter how wretched and shabby it may be. This power enables Joyce ultimately to triumph over the meanness which betrays itself in the impoverished emotions and the cadences of speech which are so faithfully recorded in *Dubliners.*

"Araby" is a story which evokes response because it puts so clearly before us the disproportion between our passionate dreams as children and the world which denies those dreams. It may be pointed out that the dream of this story was in one way realized. The child who bore his chalice "safely through a throng of foes" is also the young artist conscious of the vessel of his powers which he must guard. But the movement of the story is not to such a symbolic conclusion. The little boy makes a brave offer of a present to the girl, and he succeeds in his effort to visit the bazaar with the mysterious and wonderful name. But all ends in dull and meaningless talk as the hall is darkened; no trace of the exotic lingers. The splendid bazaar is simply a place that is closing, a place where small boys aren't welcome. "Araby" vanishes, and the child is beset by "anguish and anger."

The uncle in this story is a version of Joyce's own father; there actually was such an oriental bazaar in Dublin; one of the houses in which Joyce lived was on North Richmond Street; and there was in fact such a girl, the sister of Joyce's friend—but it is astonishing how little all this matters. What does matter is the power to order and choose out of the welter of the past. Only that power turns the past to rich account.

FOR STUDY AND DISCUSSION

1. Although the first two paragraphs may seem to have little to do with the main concerns of the story, important details of setting and personality are offered here. How does the description of North Richmond Street and its houses convey the emotional life of the inhabitants? What do the priest's books reveal about him? Was the priest really "charitable?" Do you think Joyce used this word ironically?

2. How does his trip to the market with his aunt contribute to the boy's feeling of separation from real life?. Which words in this paragraph reinforce the contrast between Dublin life and the boy's desire for romance? Do you think the boy's romantic ardor is excessive? Why might Joyce have deliberately exaggerated the boy's emotions? Do you find this exaggeration in the ending of the story also? Explain.

3. The first line of direct dialogue is "And why can't you?" Discuss the significance of this question to Mangan's sister. What other characters in the story are prevented from finding splendor in their lives? the boy? the dead priest? the boy's uncle? Explain how Joyce reveals the restrictions in the lives of these three characters.

4. Mrs. Mercer, the "old garrulous woman," is one of the few figures named in the story. Why do you think she is introduced, and what is the point of reporting her conversation? The aunt at first discourages the boy and then urges her husband to give him the money. How do you account for this changeableness? Do you think she really understands the boy? How does the uncle reflect the meanness of Dublin life?

5. The most extended conversation in the story is that of the shopgirl and the two young gentlemen at the bazaar. What contrast is achieved between this dialogue and the boy's fervent longings? Why do you think the boy does not buy a present for Mangan's sister? Is he intimidated by the shopgirl, or does he realize the futility of his desire for romance? Cite specific lines from the story to support your answer.

D. H. LAWRENCE
(1885–1930)

It was the triumph of D. H. Lawrence, and his misfortune, that he refused so adamantly to join "the club" of contemporary writers. Lawrence was born in a village in the industrial midlands of England. His father was a coal miner and his mother a schoolteacher. By birth and education he was therefore a man apart from the typical writer of the early twentieth century, who was very unlikely to be of working-class stock. By the time Lawrence's first book, *The White Peacock,* was published in 1911, he had begun to glory in his apartness, an attitude reinforced by his elopement the following year with Frieda von Richthofen, the German-born wife of a Nottingham professor.

From 1912 until his death from tuberculosis in 1930, the Lawrences spent most of their time abroad: in Italy, in Australia, and New Mexico. Their relationship was a stormy one. Lawrence always felt uneasy in conventional surroundings. Before World War I he had been accepted by the English social and literary world as a budding genius, but friendship with him required a degree of patience that not all his would-be helpers were able to sustain. There was a permanently adolescent streak in his nature which found satisfaction in rows, reconciliations, and infidelities, real and imagined. But his temperament went hand in hand with a powerful imagination and a prose style which, if humorless, beautifully matched the blunt and challenging situations into which he liked to plunge his fictional characters.

All his life Lawrence sought a Utopia, an ideally civilized community in which he could live with a few chosen followers. His dislike of British puritanism and snobbery, as he saw it, made him bitterly dislike his own country. He thought for a time that he had found what he sought in Queensland, Australia, and in Taos, New Mexico. But as time passed, his deteriorating health made him always harder to satisfy.

Although two of his novels caused many people to dismiss Lawrence as immoral, it would be quite wrong to dismiss Lawrence as a cranky, disreputable writer. Those of his contemporaries who knew him well never accepted his view of himself as a tiger; they considered him a sick man living on his nerves. But they, like posterity, were forced to acknowledge the fineness of his best short stories, such as "The Prussian Officer," and his best novels, among which *Women in Love* and *The Plumed Serpent* are outstanding. Lawrence was also a more than ordinarily skillful writer of free verse, with an acute understanding of animals and a warmly sensuous view of nature. Artifice was as abhorrent to him as convention. He liked to think himself a child of the Mediterranean dawn—as a child of the Italy of the Etruscans, who preceded the coming of the Romans. In more primitive man Lawrence attempted to find the wholeness and balance which he felt had been lost by civilization.

In addition to his strikingly original fiction and poetry, Lawrence wrote some remarkable travel books, such as *Sea and Sardinia* and *Twilight in Italy*. When he chose, he also could be a refreshingly original critic. His *Studies in Classical American Literature* remains one of the best unprofessorial pieces of critical writing to be published in this century. Perhaps his most attractive book is the posthumous collection of his *Letters,* edited by Aldous Huxley. It confirms his claim to be one of the most influential leaders of a movement which took English writing out of Queen Victoria's shadow and into a world of modern interests, techniques, and honesties.

Snake

A snake came to my water trough
On a hot, hot day, and I in pajamas for the heat,
To drink there.

In the deep, strange-scented shade of the great dark carob tree
I came down the steps with my pitcher   5
And must wait, must stand and wait, for there he was at the trough before
   me.

He reached down from a fissure in the earth-wall in the gloom
And trailed his yellow-brown slackness soft-bellied down, over the edge
   of the stone trough
And rested his throat upon the stone bottom,
And where the water had dripped from the tap, in a small clearness,   10
He sipped with his straight mouth,
Softly drank through his straight gums, into his slack long body,
Silently.

Someone was before me at my water trough,
And I, like a second comer, waiting.
                                     15

He lifted his head from his drinking, as cattle do,
And looked at me vaguely, as drinking cattle do,
And flickered his two-forked tongue from his lips, and mused a moment,
And stooped and drank a little more,
Being earth-brown, earth-golden from the burning bowels of the earth   20
On the day of Sicilian July, with Etna smoking.

The voice of my education said to me
He must be killed,
For in Sicily the black, black snakes are innocent, the gold are venomous.

And voices in me said, If you were a man 25
You would take a stick and break him now, and finish him off.

But must I confess how I liked him,
How glad I was he had come like a guest in quiet, to drink at my water trough
And depart peaceful, pacified, and thankless,
Into the burning bowels of this earth? 30

Was it cowardice, that I dared not kill him?
Was it perversity, that I longed to talk to him?
Was it humility, to feel so honored?
I felt so honored.

And yet those voices: 35
If you were not afraid, you would kill him!

And truly I was afraid, I was most afraid,
But even so, honored still more
That he should seek my hospitality
From out the dark door of the secret earth. 40

He drank enough
And lifted his head, dreamily, as one who has drunken,
And flickered his tongue like a forked night on the air, so black,
Seeming to lick his lips,
And looked around like a god, unseeing, into the air, 45
And slowly turned his head,
And slowly, very slowly, as if thrice adream,
Proceeded to draw his slow length curving round
And climb again the broken bank of my wall-face.

And as he put his head into that dreadful hole, 50
And as he slowly drew up, snake-easing his shoulders, and entered farther,
A sort of horror, a sort of protest against his withdrawing into that horrid
    black hole,
Deliberately going into the blackness, and slowly drawing himself after,
Overcame me now his back was turned.

I looked around, I put down my pitcher, 55
I picked up a clumsy log
And threw it at the water trough with a clatter.

I think I did not hit him,
But suddenly that part of him that was left behind convulsed in undignified
    haste,
Writhed like lightning, and was gone 60
Into the black hole, the earth-lipped fissure in the wall-front,
At which, in the intense still noon, I stared with fascination.

And immediately I regretted it.
I thought how paltry, how vulgar, what a mean act!
I despised myself and the voices of my accursed human education.   65

And I thought of the albatross,
And I wished he would come back, my snake.

For he seemed to me again like a king,
Like a king in exile, uncrowned in the underworld,
Now due to be crowned again.   70

And so, I missed my chance with one of the lords
Of life.
And I have something to expiate;
A pettiness.

The Rocking-horse Winner

THERE WAS a woman who was beautiful, who started with all the advantages, yet she had no luck. She married for love, and the love turned to dust. She had bonny children, yet she felt they had been thrust upon her, and she could not love them. They looked at her coldly, as if they were finding fault with her. And hurriedly she felt she must cover up some fault in herself. Yet what it was that she must cover up she never knew. Nevertheless, when her children were present, she always felt the center of her heart go hard. This troubled her, and in her manner she was all the more gentle and anxious for her children, as if she loved them very much. Only she herself knew that at the center of her heart was a hard little place that could not feel love, no, not for anybody. Everybody else said of her: "She is such a good mother. She adores her children." Only she herself, and her children themselves, knew it was not so. They read it in each other's eyes.

There were a boy and two little girls. They lived in a pleasant house, with a garden, and they had discreet servants, and felt themselves superior to anyone in the neighborhood.

Although they lived in style, they felt always an anxiety in the house. There was never enough money. The mother had a small income, and the father had a small income, but not nearly enough for the social position which they had to keep up. The father went in to town to some office. But though he had good prospects, these prospects never materialized. There was always the grinding sense of the shortage of money, though the style was always kept up.

At last the mother said: "I will see if *I* can't make something." But she did not know where to begin. She racked her brains, and tried this thing and the other, but could not find anything successful. The failure made deep lines come into her face. Her children were growing up, they would have to go to school. There must be more money, there must be more money. The father, who was always very handsome and expensive in his tastes, seemed as if he never *would* be able to do anything worth doing. And the mother,

"The Rocking-horse Winner" from *The Complete Short Stories of D. H. Lawrence,* Vol. III. Copyright 1933 by the Estate of D. H. Lawrence, © 1961 by Angelo Ravagli and C. M. Weekley, Executors of the Estate of Frieda Lawrence Ravagli. Reprinted by permission of The Viking Press.

who had a great belief in herself, did not succeed any better, and her tastes were just as expensive.

And so the house came to be haunted by the unspoken phrase: *There must be more money! There must be more money!* The children could hear it all the time, though nobody said it aloud. They heard it at Christmas, when the expensive and splendid toys filled the nursery. Behind the shining modern rocking horse, behind the smart doll's house, a voice would start whispering: "There *must* be more money! There *must* be more money!" And the children would stop playing, to listen for a moment. They would look into each other's eyes, to see if they had all heard. And each one saw in the eyes of the other two that they too had heard. "There *must* be more money! There *must* be more money!"

It came whispering from the springs of the still-swaying rocking horse, and even the horse, bending his wooden, champing head, heard it. The big doll, sitting so pink and smirking in her new pram, could hear it quite plainly, and seemed to be smirking all the more self-consciously because of it. The foolish puppy, too, that took the place of the teddy bear, he was looking so extraordinarily foolish for no other reason but that he heard the secret whisper all over the house: "There *must* be more money!"

Yet nobody ever said it aloud. The whisper was everywhere, and therefore no one spoke it. Just as no one ever says: "We are breathing!" in spite of the fact that breath is coming and going all the time.

"Mother," said the boy Paul one day, "why don't we keep a car of our own? Why do we always use uncle's, or else a taxi?"

"Because we're the poor members of the family," said the mother.

"But why *are* we, mother?"

"Well—I suppose," she said slowly and bitterly, "it's because your father has no luck."

The boy was silent for some time.

"Is luck money, mother?" he asked rather timidly.

"No, Paul. Not quite. It's what causes you to have money."

"Oh!" said Paul vaguely. "I thought when Uncle Oscar said *filthy lucker,* it meant money."

"Filthy lucre does mean money," said the mother. "But it's lucre, not luck."

"Oh!" said the boy. "Then what *is* luck, mother?"

"It's what causes you to have money. If you're lucky you have money. That's why it's better to be born lucky than rich. If you're rich, you may lose your money. But if you're lucky, you will always get more money."

"Oh! Will you? And is father not lucky?"

"Very unlucky, I should say," she said bitterly.

The boy watched her with unsure eyes.

"Why?" he asked.

"I don't know. Nobody ever knows why one person is lucky and another unlucky."

"Don't they? Nobody at all? Does *nobody* know?"

"Perhaps God. But He never tells."

"He ought to, then. And aren't you lucky either, mother?"

"I can't be, if I married an unlucky husband."

"But by yourself, aren't you?"

"I used to think I was, before I married. Now I think I am very unlucky indeed."

"Why?"

"Well—never mind! Perhaps I'm not really," she said.

The child looked at her, to see if she meant it. But he saw, by the lines of her mouth, that she was only trying to hide something from him.

"Well, anyhow," he said stoutly, "I'm a lucky person."

"Why?" said his mother, with a sudden laugh.

He stared at her. He didn't even know why he had said it.

"God told me," he asserted, brazening it out.

"I hope He did, dear!" she said, again with a laugh, but rather bitter.

"He did, mother!"

"Excellent!" said the mother, using one of her husband's exclamations.

The boy saw she did not believe him; or, rather, that she paid no attention to his assertion. This angered him somewhat, and made him want to compel her attention.

He went off by himself, vaguely, in a childish way, seeking for the clue to "luck." Absorbed, taking no heed of other people, he went about with a sort of stealth, seeking inwardly for luck. He wanted luck, he wanted it, he wanted it. When the two girls were playing dolls in the nursery, he would sit on his big rocking horse, charging madly into space, with a frenzy that made the little girls peer at him uneasily. Wildly the horse careered, the waving dark hair of the boy tossed, his eyes had a strange glare in them. The little girls dared not speak to him.

When he had ridden to the end of his mad little journey, he climbed down and stood in front of his rocking horse, staring fixedly into its lowered face. Its red mouth was slightly open, its big eye was wide and glassy-bright.

"Now!" he would silently command the snorting steed. "Now, take me to where there is luck! Now take me!"

And he would slash the horse on the neck with the little whip he had asked Uncle Oscar for. He *knew* the horse could take him to where there was luck, if only he forced it. So he would mount again, and start on his furious ride, hoping at last to get there. He knew he could get there.

"You'll break your horse, Paul!" said the nurse.

"He's always riding like that! I wish he'd leave off!" said his elder sister Joan.

But he only glared down on them in silence. Nurse gave him up. She could make nothing of him. Anyhow he was growing beyond her.

One day his mother and his Uncle Oscar came in when he was on one of his furious rides. He did not speak to them.

"Hallo, you young jockey! Riding a winner?" said his uncle.

"Aren't you growing too big for a rocking horse? You're not a very little boy any longer, you know," said his mother.

But Paul only gave a blue glare from his big, rather close-set eyes. He would speak to nobody when he was in full tilt. His mother watched him with an anxious expression on her face.

At last he suddenly stopped forcing his horse into the mechanical gallop, and slid down.

"Well, I got there!" he announced fiercely, his blue eyes still flaring, and his sturdy long legs straddling apart.

"Where did you get to?" asked his mother.

"Where I wanted to go," he flared back at her.

"That's right, son!" said Uncle Oscar. "Don't you stop till you get there. What's the horse's name?"

"He doesn't have a name," said the boy.

"Gets on without all right?" asked the uncle.

"Well, he has different names. He was called Sansovino last week."

"Sansovino, eh? Won the Ascot.[1] How did you know his name?"

"He always talks about horse races with Bassett," said Joan.

The uncle was delighted to find that his small nephew was posted with all the racing news. Bassett, the young gardner, who had been wounded in the left foot in the war and had got his present job through Oscar Cresswell, whose batman[2] he had been, was a perfect blade of the "turf."[3] He lived in the racing events, and the small boy lived with him.

Oscar Cresswell got it all from Bassett.

"Master Paul comes and asks me, so I can't do more than tell him, sir," said Bassett, his face terribly serious, as if he were speaking of religious matters.

[1] **Ascot:** a famous English horse race.
[2] **batman:** an officer's servant in the British army.
[3] **turf:** racetrack.

"And does he ever put anything on a horse he fancies?"

"Well—I don't want to give him away—he's a young sport, a fine sport, sir. Would you mind asking him himself? He sort of takes a pleasure in it, and perhaps he'd feel I was giving him away sir, if you don't mind."

Bassett was serious as a church.

The uncle went back to his nephew and took him off for a ride in the car.

"Say, Paul, old man, do you ever put anything on a horse?" the uncle asked.

The boy watched the handsome man closely.

"Why, do you think I oughtn't to?" he parried.

"Not a bit of it! I thought perhaps you might give me a tip for the Lincoln."

The car sped on into the country, going down to Uncle Oscar's place in Hampshire.

"Honor bright?" said the nephew.

"Honor bright, son!" said the uncle.

"Well, then, Daffodil."

"Daffodil! I doubt it, sonny. What about Mirza?"

"I only know the winner," said the boy. "That's Daffodil."

"Daffodil, eh?"

There was a pause. Daffodil was an obscure horse comparatively.

"Uncle!"

"Yes, son?"

"You won't let it go any further, will you? I promised Bassett."

"Bassett be damned, old man! What's he got to do with it?"

"We're partners. We've been partners from the first. Uncle, he lent me my first five shillings, which I lost. I promised him, honor bright, it was only between me and him; only you gave me that ten-shilling note I started winning with, so I thought you were lucky. You won't let it go any further, will you?"

The boy gazed at his uncle from those big, hot, blue eyes, set rather close together. The uncle stirred and laughed uneasily.

"Right you are, son! I'll keep your tip private. Daffodil, eh? How much are you putting on him?"

"All except twenty pounds," said the boy. "I keep that in reserve."

The uncle thought it a good joke.

"You keep twenty pounds in reserve, do you, you young romancer? What are you betting, then?"

"I'm betting three hundred," said the boy gravely. "But it's between you and me, Uncle Oscar! Honor bright?"

The uncle burst into a roar of laughter.

"It's between you and me all right, you young Nat Gould," [1] he said, laughing. "But where's your three hundred?"

"Bassett keeps it for me. We're partners."

"You are, are you! And what is Bassett putting on Daffodil?"

"He won't go quite as high as I do, I expect. Perhaps he'll go a hundred and fifty."

"What, pennies?" laughed the uncle.

"Pounds," said the child, with a surprised look at his uncle. "Bassett keeps a bigger reserve than I do."

Between wonder and amusement Uncle Oscar was silent. He pursued the matter no further, but he determined to take his nephew with him to the Lincoln races.

"Now, son," he said, "I'm putting twenty on Mirza, and I'll put five for you on any horse you fancy. What's your pick?"

"Daffodil, uncle."

"No, not the fiver on Daffodil!"

"I should if it was my own fiver," said the child.

"Good! Good! Right you are! A fiver for me and a fiver for you on Daffodil."

The child had never been to a race meeting before, and his eyes were blue fire. He pursed his mouth tight, and watched. A Frenchman just in front had put his money on Lancelot. Wild with excitement, he flayed his arms up and down, yelling *Lancelot! Lancelot!* in his French accent.

Daffodil came in first, Lancelot second,

---

[1] **Nat Gould:** a famous authority on horse racing.

Mirza third. The child, flushed and with eyes blazing, was curiously serene. His uncle brought him four five-pound notes, four to one.

"What am I to do with these?" he cried, waving them before the boy's eyes.

"I suppose we'll talk to Bassett," said the boy. "I expect I have fifteen hundred now; and twenty in reserve; and this twenty."

His uncle studied him for some moments.

"Look here, son!" he said. "You're not serious about Bassett and that fifteen hundred, are you?"

"Yes, I am. But it's between you and me, uncle. Honor bright!"

"Honor bright all right, son! But I must talk to Bassett."

"If you'd like to be a partner, uncle, with Bassett and me, we could all be partners. Only, you'd have to promise, honor bright, uncle, not to let it go beyond us three. Bassett and I are lucky, and you must be lucky, because it was your ten shillings I started winning with. . . ."

Uncle Oscar took both Bassett and Paul into Richmond Park for an afternoon, and there they talked.

"It's like this, you see, sir," Bassett said. "Master Paul would get me talking about racing events, spinning yarns, you

know, sir. And he was always keen on knowing if I'd made or if I'd lost. It's about a year since, now, that I put five shilling on Blush of Dawn for him—and we lost. Then the luck turned, with that ten shillings he had from you, that we put on Singhalese. And since that time, it's been pretty steady, all things considering. What do you say, Master Paul?"

"We're all right when we're sure," said Paul. "It's when we're not quite sure that we go down."

"Oh, but we're careful then," said Bassett.

"But when are you *sure?*" smiled Uncle Oscar.

"It's Master Paul, sir," said Bassett, in a secret, religious voice. "It's as if he had it from heaven. Like Daffodil, now, for the Lincoln. That was as sure as eggs."

"Did you put anything on Daffodil?" asked Oscar Cresswell.

"Yes, sir. I made my bit."

"And my nephew?"

Bassett was obstinately silent, looking at Paul.

"I made twelve hundred, didn't I, Bassett? I told uncle I was putting three hundred on Daffodil."

"That's right," said Bassett, nodding.

"But where's the money?" asked the uncle.

"I keep it safe locked up, sir. Master Paul he can have it any minute he likes to ask for it."

"What, fifteen hundred pounds?"

"And twenty! And *forty,* that is, with the twenty he made on the course."

"It's amazing!" said the uncle.

"If Master Paul offers you to be partners, sir, I would, if I were you; if you'll excuse me," said Bassett.

Oscar Cresswell thought about it.

"I'll see the money," he said.

They drove home again, and sure enough, Bassett came round to the garden house with fifteen hundred pounds in notes. The twenty pounds reserve was left with Joe Glee, in the Turf Commission deposit.

"You see, it's all right, uncle, when I'm

sure! Then we go strong, for all we're worth. Don't we Bassett?"

"We do that, Master Paul."

"And when are you sure?" said the uncle, laughing.

"Oh, well, sometimes I'm *absolutely* sure, like about Daffodil," said the boy; "and sometimes I have an idea; and sometimes I haven't even an idea, have I, Bassett? Then we're careful, because we mostly go down."

"You do, do you! And when you're sure, like about Daffodil, what makes you sure, sonny?"

"Oh, well, I don't know," said the boy uneasily. "I'm sure, you know, uncle; that's all."

"It's as if he had it from heaven, sir," Bassett reiterated.

"I should say so!" said the uncle.

But he became a partner. And when the Leger was coming on, Paul was "sure" about Lively Spark, which was a quite inconsiderable horse. The boy insisted on putting a thousand on the horse, Bassett went for five hundred, and Oscar Cresswell two hundred. Lively Spark came in first, and the betting had been ten to one against him. Paul had made ten thousand.

"You see," he said, "I was absolutely sure of him."

Even Oscar Cresswell had cleared two thousand.

"Look here, son," he said, "this sort of thing makes me nervous."

"It needn't, uncle! Perhaps I shan't be sure again for a long time."

"But what are you going to do with your money?" asked the uncle.

"Of course," said the boy, "I started it for mother. She said she had no luck, because father is unlucky, so I thought if *I* was lucky, it might stop whispering."

"What might stop whispering?"

"Our house. I *hate* our house for whispering."

"What does it whisper?"

"Why—why"—the boy fidgeted—"why, I don't know. But it's always short of money, you know, uncle."

"I know it, son, I know it."

"You know people send mother writs,[1] don't you, uncle?"

"I'm afraid I do," said the uncle.

"And then the house whispers, like people laughing at you behind your back. It's awful, that is! I thought if I was lucky . . ."

"You might stop it," added the uncle.

The boy watched him with big blue eyes, that had an uncanny cold fire in them, and he said never a word.

"Well, then!" said the uncle. "What are we doing?"

"I shouldn't like mother to know I was lucky," said the boy.

"Why not, son?"

"She'd stop me."

"I don't think she would."

"Oh!"—and the boy writhed in an odd way—"I *don't* want her to know, uncle."

"All right, son! We'll manage it without her knowing."

They managed it very easily. Paul, at the other's suggestion, handed over five thousand pounds to his uncle, who deposited it with the family lawyer, who was then to inform Paul's mother that a relative had put five thousand pounds into his hands, which sum was to be paid out a thousand pounds at a time, on the mother's birthday, for the next five years.

"So she'll have a birthday present of a thousand pounds for five successive years," said Uncle Oscar. "I hope it won't make it all the harder for her later."

Paul's mother had her birthday in November. The house had been "whispering" worse than ever lately, and, even in spite of his luck, Paul could not bear up against it. He was very anxious to see the effect of the birthday letter, telling his mother about the thousand pounds.

When there were no visitors, Paul now took his meals with his parents, as he was beyond the nursery control. His mother went into town nearly every day. She had discovered that she had an odd knack of sketching furs and dress materials, so she

---

[1] **writ:** a court order stating that unless certain bills are paid, legal action will have to be taken.

worked secretly in the studio of a friend who was the chief "artist" for the leading drapers. She drew the figures of ladies in furs and ladies in silk and sequins for the newspaper advertisements. This young woman artist earned several thousand pounds a year, but Paul's mother only made several hundreds, and she was again dissatisfied. She so wanted to be first in something, and she did not succeed, even in making sketches for drapery advertisements.

She was down to breakfast on the morning of her birthday. Paul watched her face as she read her letters. He knew the lawyer's letter. As his mother read it, her face hardened and became more expressionless. Then a cold, determined look came on her mouth. She hid the letter under the pile of others, and said not a word about it.

"Didn't you have anything nice in the post for your birthday, mother?" said Paul.

"Quite moderately nice," she said, her voice cold and absent.

She went away to town without saying more.

But in the afternoon Uncle Oscar appeared. He said Paul's mother had had a long interview with the lawyer, asking if the whole five thousand could not be advanced at once, as she was in debt.

"What do you think, uncle?" said the boy.

"I leave it to you, son."

"Oh, let her have it, then! We can get some more with the other," said the boy.

"A bird in the hand is worth two in the bush, laddie!" said Uncle Oscar.

"But I'm sure to *know* for the Grand National; or the Lincolnshire; or else the Derby. I'm sure to know for *one* of them," said Paul.

So Uncle Oscar signed the agreement, and Paul's mother touched the whole five thousand. Then something very curious happened. The voices in the house suddenly went mad, like a chorus of frogs on a spring evening. There were certain new furnishings, and Paul had a tutor. He was

really going to Eton, his father's school, in the following autumn. There were flowers in the winter, and a blossoming of the luxury Paul's mother had been used to. And yet the voices in the house, behind the sprays of mimosa and almond blossom, and from under the piles of iridescent cushions, simply trilled and screamed in a sort of ecstasy: "There *must* be more money! Oh-h-h; there *must* be more money. Oh, now, now-w! Now-w-w-w— there *must* be more money!—more than ever! More than ever!"

It frightened Paul terribly. He studied away at his Latin and Greek with his tutors. But his intense hours were spent with Bassett. The Grand National had gone by: he had not "known," and had lost a hundred pounds. Summer was at hand. He was in agony for the Lincoln. But even for the Lincoln he didn't "know," and he lost fifty pounds. He became wild-eyed and strange, as if something were going to explode in him.

"Let it alone, son! Don't you bother about it!" urged Uncle Oscar. But it was as if the boy couldn't really hear what his uncle was saying.

"I've got to know for the Derby! I've got to know for the Derby!" the child reiterated, his big blue eyes blazing with a sort of madness.

His mother noticed how overwrought he was.

"You'd better go to the seaside. Wouldn't you like to go now to the seaside, instead of waiting? I think you'd better," she said, looking down at him anxiously, her heart curiously heavy because of him.

But the child lifted his uncanny blue eyes.

"I couldn't possibly go before the Derby, mother!" he said. "I couldn't possibly!"

"Why not?" she said, her voice becoming heavy when she was opposed. "Why not? You can still go from the seaside to see the Derby with your Uncle Oscar, if that's what you wish. No need for you to wait here. Besides, I think you care too much about these races. It's a bad sign. My family has been a gambling family, and you won't know till you grow up how much damage it has done. But it has done damage. I shall have to send Bassett away, and ask Uncle Oscar not to talk racing to you, unless you promise to be reasonable about it; go away to the seaside and forget it. You're all nerves!"

"I'll do what you like, mother, so long as you don't send me away till after the Derby," the boy said.

"Send you away from where? Just from this house?"

"Yes," he said, gazing at her.

"Why, you curious child, what makes you care about this house so much, suddenly? I never knew you loved it."

He gazed at her without speaking. He had a secret within a secret, something he had not divulged, even to Bassett or to his Uncle Oscar.

But his mother, after standing undecided and a little bit sullen for some moments, said:

"Very well, then! Don't go to the seaside till after the Derby, if you don't wish it. But promise me you won't let your nerves go to pieces. Promise you won't think so much about horse racing and *events,* as you call them!"

"Oh, no," said the boy casually. "I won't think much about them, mother. You needn't worry. I wouldn't worry, mother, if I were you."

"If you were me and I were you," said his mother, "I wonder what we *should* do!"

"But you know you needn't worry, mother, don't you?" the boy repeated.

"I should be awfully glad to know it," she said wearily.

"Oh, well, you *can,* you know. I mean, you *ought* to know you needn't worry," he insisted.

"Ought I? Then I'll see about it," she said.

Paul's secret of secrets was his wooden horse, that which had no name. Since he was emancipated from a nurse and a nursery governess, he had had his rocking horse removed to his own bedroom at the top of the house.

"Surely, you're too big for a rocking horse!" his mother had remonstrated.

"Well, you see, mother, till I can have a *real* horse, I like to have *some* sort of animal about," had been his quaint answer.

"Do you feel he keeps you company?" she laughed.

"Oh, yes! He's very good, he always keeps me company, when I'm there," said Paul.

So the horse, rather shabby, stood in an arrested prance in the boy's bedroom.

The Derby was drawing near, and the boy grew more and more tense. He hardly heard what was spoken to him, he was very frail, and his eyes were really uncanny. His mother had sudden strange seizures of uneasiness about him. Sometimes, for half-an-hour, she would feel a sudden anxiety about him that was almost anguish. She wanted to rush to him at once, and know he was safe.

Two nights before the Derby, she was at a big party in town, when one of her rushes of anxiety about her boy, her first born, gripped her heart till she could hardly speak. She fought with the feeling, might and main, for she believed in common sense. But it was too strong. She had to leave the dance and go downstairs to telephone to the country. The children's nursery governess was terribly surprised and startled at being rung up in the night.

"Are the children all right, Miss Wilmot?"

"Oh, yes, they are quite all right."

"Master Paul? Is he all right?"

"He went to bed as right as a trivet. Shall I run up and look at him?"

"No," said Paul's mother reluctantly. "No! Don't trouble. It's all right. Don't sit up. We shall be home fairly soon." She did not want her son's privacy intruded upon.

"Very good," said the governess.

It was about one o'clock when Paul's mother and father drove up to their house. All was still. Paul's mother went to her room and slipped off her white fur cloak. She had told her maid not to wait up for her. She heard her husband downstairs, mixing a whisky-and-soda.

And then, because of the strange anxiety at her heart, she stole upstairs to her son's room. Noiselessly she went along the upper corridor. Was there a faint noise? What was it?

She stood, with arrested muscles, outside his door, listening. There was a strange, heavy, and yet not loud noise. Her heart stood still. It was a soundless noise, yet rushing and powerful. Something huge, in violent, hushed motion. What was it? What in God's name was it? She ought to know. She felt that she knew the noise. She knew what it was.

Yet she could not place it. She couldn't say what it was. And on and on it went, like a madness.

Softly, frozen with anxiety and fear, she turned the door handle.

The room was dark. Yet in the space near the window, she heard and saw something plunging to and fro. She gazed in fear and amazement.

Then suddenly she switched on the light, and saw her son, in his green pajamas, madly surging on the rocking horse. The blaze of light suddenly lit him up, as he urged the wooden horse, and lit her up, as she stood, blonde, in her dress of pale green and crystal, in the doorway.

"Paul!" she cried. "Whatever are you doing?"

"It's Malabar!" he screamed, in a powerful, strange voice. "It's Malabar!"

His eyes blazed at her for one strange and senseless second, as he ceased urging his wooden horse. Then he fell with a crash to the ground, and she, all her tormented motherhood flooding upon her, rushed to gather him up.

But he was unconscious, and unconscious he remained, with some brain fever. He talked and tossed, and his mother sat stonily by his side.

"Malabar! It's Malabar! Bassett, Bassett, I *know!* It's Malabar!"

So the child cried, trying to get up and urge the rocking horse that gave him his inspiration.

"What does he mean by Malabar?" asked the heart-frozen mother.

"I don't know," said the father stonily.

"What does he mean by Malabar?" she asked her brother Oscar.

"It's one of the horses running for the Derby," was the answer.

And, in spite of himself, Oscar Cresswell spoke to Bassett, and himself put a thousand on Malabar: at fourteen to one.

The third day of the illness was critical: they were waiting for a change. The boy, with his rather long, curly hair, was tossing ceaselessly on the pillow. He neither slept nor regained consciousness, and his eyes were like blue stones. His mother sat, feeling her heart had gone, turned actually into a stone.

In the evening, Oscar Cresswell did not come, but Bassett sent a message, saying could he come up for one moment, just one moment? Paul's mother was very angry at the intrusion, but on second thought she agreed. The boy was the same. Perhaps Bassett might bring him to consciousness.

The gardener, a shortish fellow with a little brown mustache, and sharp little brown eyes, tiptoed into the room, touched his imaginary cap to Paul's mother, and stole to the bedside, staring with glittering, smallish eyes, at the tossing, dying child.

"Master Paul!" he whispered. "Master

Paul! Malabar came in first all right, a clean win. I did as you told me. You've made over seventy thousand pounds, you have; you've got over eighty thousand. Malabar came in all right, Master Paul."

"Malabar! Malabar! Did I say Malabar, mother? Did I say Malabar? Do you think I'm lucky, mother? I knew Malabar, didn't I? Over eighty thousand pounds! I call that lucky, don't you, mother? Over eighty thousand pounds! I knew, didn't I know I knew? Malabar came in all right. If I ride my horse till I'm sure, then I tell you, Bassett, you can go as high as you like. Did you go for all you were worth, Bassett?"

"I went a thousand on it, Master Paul."

"I never told you, mother, that if I can ride my horse, and *get there* then I'm absolutely sure—oh, absolutely! Mother, did I ever tell you? I *am* lucky!"

"No, you never did," said the mother.

But the boy died in the night.

And even as he lay dead, his mother heard her brother's voice saying to her: "My God, Hester, you're eighty-odd thousand to the good, and a poor devil of a son to the bad. But, poor devil, poor devil, he's best gone out of a life where he rides his rocking horse to find a winner."

FOR STUDY AND DISCUSSION

SNAKE

1. How does the poet make the snake seem a distinct individual? Do you think that Lawrence tried to make the snake seem human? Or did he try to oppose the snake's qualities to human qualities?

2. What does the speaker mean by the "voices of his education"? How do these voices create a conflict within the speaker? How is the conflict resolved?

3. Why, in your opinion, does the speaker describe the snake as kingly in lines 68–70? Explain the reference to the "underworld." What associations is this word meant to call up?

4. Explain the reference to the albatross in line 66. (You may wish to review Coleridge's *The Rime of the Ancient Mariner,* especially lines 273–87 about water snakes.) What similarity is there between the Mariner's feeling about the water snakes and the speaker's attitude toward the snake? In what way is the situation of the speaker like that of Coleridge's Mariner?

THE ROCKING-HORSE WINNER

1. What details in the story explain Paul's desperate eagerness to win money for his mother?

2. What words and phrases are most frequently used to characterize Paul and his behavior? Why do you think Paul's eyes are frequently described?

3. Why, at the conclusion of the story, can the uncle appreciate more fully than anyone else what has happened?

4. Do you think Lawrence succeeds in making credible Paul's odd gift of "knowing"? What clues tell you that the story is meant to be taken as a fantasy? Why are so many realistic details included?

5. What do the voices in the house represent? What reasons can you give for the voices going "mad"?

6. Irony is an important element in this story. What irony do you detect in Bassett's words "It's as if he had it from heaven"? When Paul refuses to go to the seashore, what irony is there in his mother's words, "Why, you curious child, what makes you care about this house so much, suddenly? I never knew you loved it." How are Paul's last words to his mother ironic? How does the mother's definition of luck appear ironic in the light of what happens?

7. What does this story tell you about the features of English society that Lawrence detested? Do you think Lawrence's criticism of English society can be applied to our own society? Explain.

FOR COMPOSITION

1. Perhaps like the speaker in "Snake," you have had an experience with an animal which led you to see your own actions in a new light. Write an account of such an experience; or, if you like, write a fictional story about such an experience.

2. *Luck* and *lucky* are key terms in "The Rocking-horse Winner." Study the different occasions in which these words are used. Show how the meaning of the word develops throughout the story until Paul's last words, "I *am* lucky." What significance does the repeated use of these words add to the story?

T. S. ELIOT
(1888–1965)

   If one figure had to be named as the pivotal leader among writers in English during the first half of the twentieth century, it would be T. S. Eliot—not simply because he was a great poet, a great critic, a fine playwright, and a far-reaching influence on others, but also because he combined these qualities with a singularly powerful and integrated personality. Like Matthew Arnold (page 618) in the 1870's, Eliot became the conscience of his generation, deliberately fitting himself for this role, which he summed up in a celebrated phrase when he defined his beliefs as "Anglo-Catholic in religion, classicist in literature, and royalist in politics."

   If Eliot's attitude was not exactly a fashionable one, nobody has been able to dismiss him as a reactionary cultural force. When Eliot began to publish verse at the age of twenty-six, his first few readers were generally shocked by what they took to be a dry, overclever, revolutionary use of language and syntax. Fifty years later, when his name was surrounded by an air of majesty unique in his time, that same verse still had a contemporary ring to it. Today he seems the spokesman of an age in which men, feeling themselves barren because of their doubt, searched feverishly for an experience of faith.

   Eliot was born in St. Louis, Missouri, attended Harvard University, and subsequently the Sorbonne in Paris and Oxford University in England. World War I caught him in England, where he worked for a time in Lloyd's Bank, married, and finally settled for good in a country which his ancestor had left for Massachusetts in 1670. In the 1920's he joined the London publishing house which later became Faber and Faber, and in 1927 he adopted British citizenship. The history of his remaining years is the history of his art and reputation. He evaded publicity and deliberately cultivated a shy aloofness, lightened by an almost absurdly youthful sense of humor.

   What Eliot achieved was an exact expression for the spiritual disease of the twentieth century. After the unquenchable optimism of the Victorian Age had burned itself out in the world war of 1914, a period of intense questioning began. One by one, what had seemed established certainties were questioned; a society which had appeared both stable and progressive for over a century broke into fragments. Eliot's classic expression of the temper of his age is *The Waste Land,* a poem which, despite its extreme difficulty, brought him immediate fame. "The Hollow Men" published two years after *The Waste Land* is almost as powerful an expression of an age of doubt that longs in despair for belief. In the early 1920's Eliot's attitude toward the world was negative. He watched it carefully and hated what he saw. He cultivated an ironic, detached, corrosive manner in his poetry, and when he wrote prose, it was with the didactic purpose of turning his readers away from what he considered the self-indulgence of the Romantics and toward the sterner splendors of Elizabethan drama and seventeenth-century metaphysical poetry (see page 209). He wished to discourage the easy acceptance of popular favorites like Milton or Shelley in order to make room for neglected masters like John Donne.

Little by little Eliot's negative attitude toward society changed. Close study of Dante brought him to consider traditional Christianity as the one chance of finding a still center in the midst of chaos. His poem *Ash Wednesday,* written following his confirmation in 1927 in the Church of England, was a significant step in this direction. But the final expression of a long process of thought took place ten years later when he wrote *Four Quartets.* These poems were published in 1943 and conclude his major work as a poet not on an affirmative note but with a new serenity of outlook.

In the latter part of his life, Eliot turned more and more to playwriting and to the writing of essays and books discussing social and religious themes, notably *Notes Toward a Definition of Culture* and *The Aims of Education.* It was his aim to revitalize poetic drama, to write plays that would seem perfectly natural to audiences although the characters were speaking poetry. One of his modern plays, *The Cocktail Party,* had a long run both in London and New York, but his best-known play, *Murder in the Cathedral* (page 754), is closest to traditional poetic drama.

As a poet, Eliot is above all an intellectual, one who has put much hard thinking into his verse and who demands an equal amount of thought from the reader. He can encompass poignant feeling when he chooses, but his habitual choice is to establish an exact equation between feeling and thought. Eliot's poetry stands at the opposite end of some of the poems of the Romantics in which the meaning becomes hazy because it is carried along on waves of gorgeous sound and compelling rhythm. Some of his poems are difficult because the links between the ideas have been suppressed. Consequently, the reader must study these poems carefully to piece together into a logical sequence the seemingly isolated statements.

It would be hard to overemphasize Eliot's influence on other writers. The spectacle of Eliot's somewhat somber, dedicated life, lived quite consciously as an exercise in control and enrichment of sensibility, may have seemed uncomfortably austere to many, but it stood out as an instance of classical dignity in a shapeless society. Although he wrote comparatively little and rarely mixed with literary people, Eliot may be said to have changed the direction of modern writing more sharply than any of his contemporaries. He changed it in the direction of precision and complexity, and of wide-ranging reference, so that the entire human history is brought into his poetry. And he moved it toward deep but highly controlled emotion—emotion, as some of his poems imply, that is much too serious to be stated in consciously "poetic" language.

Preludes

I

The winter evening settles down
With smell of steaks in passageways.
Six o'clock.
The burnt-out ends of smoky days.
And now a gusty shower wraps   5
The grimy scraps
Of withered leaves about your feet
And newspapers from vacant lots;
The showers beat
On broken blinds and chimney pots,   10
And at the corner of the street
A lonely cab-horse steams and stamps.
And then the lighting of the lamps.

II

The morning comes to consciousness
Of faint stale smells of beer   15
From the sawdust-trampled street
With all its muddy feet that press
To early coffee stands.
With the other masquerades
That time resumes,   20
One thinks of all the hands
That are raising dingy shades
In a thousand furnished rooms.

III

You tossed a blanket from the bed,
You lay upon your back, and waited;   25
You dozed, and watched the night re-
    vealing

The thousand sordid images
Of which your soul was constituted;
They flickered against the ceiling.
And when all the world came back   30
And the light crept up between the
    shutters
And you heard the sparrows in the gutters,
You had such a vision of the street
As the street hardly understands;
Sitting along the bed's edge, where   35
You curled the papers from your hair,
Or clasped the yellow soles of feet
In the palms of both soiled hands.

IV

His soul stretched tight across the skies
That fade behind a city block,   40
Or trampled by insistent feet
At four and five and six o'clock;
And short square fingers stuffing pipes,
And evening newspapers, and eyes
Assured of certain certainties,   45
The conscience of a blackened street
Impatient to assume the world.

I am moved by fancies that are curled
Around these images, and cling:
The notion of some infinitely gentle   50
Infinitely suffering thing.

Wipe your hand across your mouth, and
    laugh;
The worlds revolve like ancient women
Gathering fuel in vacant lots.

The Hollow Men

In his poem *The Waste Land,* now considered a modern classic, Eliot compared the modern world to a desert, a place where nothing grows. In "The Hollow Men," Eliot continued to explore the dilemma of modern people, whose experience lacks a central unifying meaning because they live without real faith.

Mistah Kurtz—he dead.
*A penny for the Old Guy.**

I

We are the hollow men
We are the stuffed men
Leaning together
Headpiece filled with straw. Alas!
Our dried voices, when   5
We whisper together
Are quiet and meaningless
As wind in dry grass
Or rats' feet over broken glass
In our dry cellar   10

Shape without form, shade without
    color,
Paralyzed force, gesture without motion;

Those who have crossed
With direct eyes, to death's other Kingdom
Remember us—if at all—not as lost   15
Violent souls, but only
As the hollow men
The stuffed men.

II

Eyes I dare not meet in dreams
In death's dream kingdom   20
These do not appear:
There, the eyes are
Sunlight on a broken column
There, is a tree swinging
And voices are   25
In the wind's singing
More distant and more solemn
Than a fading star.

Let me be no nearer
In death's dream kingdom   30
Let me also wear
Such deliberate disguises
Rat's coat, crowskin, crossed staves
In a field
Behaving as the wind behaves   35
No nearer—

Not that final meeting
In the twilight kingdom

* **Mistah Kurtz:** a character in Joseph Conrad's *Heart of Darkness* who goes to Africa with the idea of reforming the natives but, because of his own inner weakness, is instead corrupted by the primitive environment. All his base instincts are aroused, and he is eventually destroyed by the horror of what he has become. **A . . . Guy:** A cry used by children on Guy Fawkes Day when, in England they carry stuffed effigies of Fawkes and beg for handouts to buy firecrackers. Fawkes was a traitor who in 1605 unsuccessfully attempted to blow up the Houses of Parliament.

III

This is the dead land
This is cactus land   40
Here the stone images
Are raised, here they receive
The supplication of a dead man's hand°
Under the twinkle of a fading star.

Is it like this   45
In death's other kingdom
Waking alone
At the hour when we are
Trembling with tenderness
Lips that would kiss   50
Form prayers to broken stone.

IV

The eyes are not here
There are no eyes here
In this valley of dying stars
In this hollow valley   55
This broken jaw of our lost kingdoms

In this last of meeting places
We grope together
And avoid speech
Gathered on this beach of the tumid river

Sightless, unless   61
The eyes reappear
As the perpetual star
Multifoliate rose
Of death's twilight kingdom   65
The hope only
Of empty men.

41–43. **Here . . . hand:** Men pray *(supplication)*
to outworn tradition *(stone images).*

V

Here we go round the prickly pear
Prickly pear prickly pear
Here we go round the prickly pear   70
At five o'clock in the morning.

Between the idea
And the reality
Between the motion
And the act   75
Falls the Shadow
    For Thine is the Kingdom

Between the conception
And the creation
Between the emotion   80
And the response
Falls the Shadow
     Life is very long

Between the desire
And the spasm   85
Between the potency
And the existence
Between the essence
And the descent
Falls the Shadow   90
    For Thine is the Kingdom
For Thine is
Life is
For Thine is the

This is the way the world ends   95
This is the way the world ends
This is the way the world ends
Not with a bang but a whimper.

PRELUDES

1. A prelude is something that precedes or introduces something else. In music, the word often refers to a brief piano piece. The most famous musical preludes are those by the Romantic composer Frederic Chopin. How are these meanings of the word related to Eliot's poem? How does the association with Chopin's romantic music lend a note of irony to the title? Is there an element of romantic yearning and hope in the poem?

2. Describe the images found in the poem. How do these images express the poet's attitude toward modern life? In discussing this attitude, consider especially lines 33–34.

3. In lines 39, who does "His" refer to? How is this line related to lines 50–51? How is the simile in the last two lines related to lines 48–51?

4. Can "Preludes" best be described as a group of related poems or as a single poem in four parts? Explain. If you think it is a single poem, describe the relation of the parts to each other. Where does the poem reach an emotional climax?

5. Consider the rhythm of the poem. Most of the lines are basically iambic tetrameter. Which lines vary from this pattern? What are the effects of the variations? The poem also employs irregular rhyme. Point out some of these rhymes. Why do you think the poet excluded rhyme from the last three lines of the poem?

THE HOLLOW MEN

1. Study the epigraphs to the poem. In what ways are the hollow men like the effigy of Guy Fawkes? Find and explain lines that develop this idea. (Consider especially lines 11–12.) "A penny for the Old Guy" refers not only to Guy Fawkes but also to Charon, the ferryman of the river Styx, one of the five rivers of the underworld in classical legend. (In classical legend, coins were placed on the eyes of the dead so they would be able to pay Charon for passage across the Styx to Hades.) Find references to the legend of Charon in the poem.

2. What images are used to evoke the situation of the hollow men? Explain the emotional effect of these images.

3. What does the phrase "death's other Kingdom" (line 14) imply about this life? Whose eyes are the hollow men afraid to meet? Why? Lines 29–38 reveal that these men are afraid to die. Why do they fear death and feel the need to assume disguises? How is the imagery of lines 31–34 related to the idea of the Guy Fawkes effigy?

4. In lines 45–51, what is it that "we" desire? What frustrates this desire and causes the men to pray fearfully, to "Form prayers to broken stone"?

5. In Part IV, it is revealed that the men will remain "sightless," (ineffectual) "unless/ The eyes reappear." What is the only hope of these men? How does the reference to the star help make the meaning of this section clear? (In answering this question, consider Eliot's religious concerns.)

6. What nursery rhyme is parodied in Part V? How does the parody gain intensity in the last four lines of the poem? What is the "Shadow" that repeatedly falls between desire and fulfillment? What are the men attempting unsuccessfully to do in lines 93–94? The last line of the poem is one of Eliot's most often-quoted lines. Why do you think it is so easily remembered?

7. One of Eliot's basic poetic devices is to introduce references from all of Western culture to relate his poetry not simply to the thoughts of one person but to the basic dilemmas of a society. Find four references in this poem to literature, legend, folk sayings, and so forth. Explain how these references deepen the poem's significance.

FOR COMPOSITION

Eliot has commented that Tennyson's *In Memoriam* may be considered a religious poem not because of the quality of its faith but because of the quality of its despair (see page 596). Write a short composition in which you discuss how this comment may be applied to the poems by Eliot himself that you have studied.

Murder in the Cathedral

When T. S. Eliot began to write *Murder in the Cathedral* in 1935, he had already gained a reputation as the foremost poet of his generation. Twice before he had turned his hand to the drama. In 1926 and 1927 he had published two fragments of *Sweeney Agonistes,* a play dealing with the emptiness and terror of the modern world, a world without faith. Although *Sweeney Agonistes* was never completed, it is occasionally produced on the stage and, when skillfully performed, is an exciting, disturbing theatrical experience. Then, in 1934, a pageant to promote the building of churches in London gave Eliot the opportunity to write more poetry for the theater. While the basic plan for the pageant, called *The Rock,* was devised by its producer, E. Martin Browne, Eliot (in Mr. Browne's words) "created . . . a series of Choruses which contain some of his finest dramatic poetry, and [he] was rewarded by hearing large audiences . . . receive its humor with delight and its lyricism with exaltation." In these choruses, Eliot dealt once more with the emptiness of a world without religious faith, but now he set against that emptiness the presence of a living God and of a religion and church embodying a faith in God and reviving human awareness of God's presence.

> "You have seen the house built, you have seen it adorned
> By one who came in the night, it is now dedicated to GOD.
> It is now a visible church, one more light set on a hill
> In a world confused and dark and disturbed by portents of fear."

For Eliot, only a living faith, a constant reaching for the universal, absolute God, could give meaning to life. In 1935, the opportunity came to embody his beliefs in a full-length play. Because of the success of *The Rock,* the Friends of Canterbury Cathedral requested the poet to write a play for their annual festival. As the event has been described by Mr. Browne, who again served as producer, the play received eight performances "in a medieval hall of great discomfort, seating less than five hundred people. . . ." *Murder in the Cathedral* has since been performed many times, but it is well to remember that it was originally written to be performed in a cathedral. Just as this play is best seen in a religious setting, so it is best read when the reader provides a similar setting in the mind. The play can be understood as an exploration of a number of relationships: between spiritual and civil authority; between the common people and their civil and spiritual leaders; between one man, a saint, and his king, his Church, and God. Ultimately, the play is about the relationship of God to each person.

As the subject of his drama, Eliot chose the martyrdom of St. Thomas à Becket, the Archbishop of Canterbury who, in A.D. 1170 gave his life to defend the rights of the Church. The son of a prosperous London merchant,

Becket was educated in London and Paris and served as clerk to an important London official. When he was twenty-four, he joined the household of Theobald, Archbishop of Canterbury, the chief prelate of England. During his years as a member of Theobald's staff, Becket showed such a talent for administration that in 1154 he was named Archdeacon of Canterbury. Later the same year, on Theobald's recommendation, King Henry II appointed Becket Chancellor of England. In the years Becket served as chief administrative official of the nation, he impressed almost everyone as a thoroughly admirable choice for the post—tactful, energetic, superbly able. In a military campaign against France, he distinguished himself both as a warrior on the field and as the negotiator of a peace settlement. In that time there was a fairly constant struggle between Church and state. The Church fought to retain its prerogatives. The King strove to strengthen his authority over all parts and classes of the nation. As King Henry's intimate friend, Becket put the rights of the King well before the rights of the Church. When Theobald died, Henry had Becket appointed Archbishop of Canterbury.

But if the King expected his friend to strengthen the royal power and weaken religious authority, he was mistaken. Becket was not eager to be an archbishop. When he did accept, however, he made it clear that he was no longer the King's loyal servant but a prince of the Church. Against Henry's wishes, he resigned his post as Chancellor. Zealously he defended the Church against royal encroachment. By 1164, Becket's position in England was so difficult that he fled to France. There he continued to influence the English Church through wide powers granted him by the Pope. In 1170, Henry offended Becket by having the heir-apparent crowned by the Archbishop of York, a deliberate infringement of the Archbishop of Canterbury's right to perform this ceremony. Henry, wishing to avoid a papal interdiction, a prohibition that excludes a person from the rites of the Church and is almost as serious as an excommunication, therefore became reconciled with Becket and allowed the prelate to return to England. Before crossing the English Channel, however, the Archbishop gave a further demonstration of the Church's power. He suspended the bishops who had been involved in the coronation ceremony. News of the suspension reached England before Becket. Henry was furious. Four knights, interpreting Henry's angry words as a command, set out for Canterbury. On Christmas Day, 1170, the Archbishop publicly excommunicated his enemies. Four days later, the martyrdom of St. Thomas à Becket took place in Canterbury Cathedral.

As you read the first part of *Murder in the Cathedral*, you will notice that there are few references to a particular period in history and little attempt to give the impression most plays try to give—of specific people living at a specific time. The outward action of the play is almost as formal as a religious ceremony. The important events take place in Becket's mind. Through poetry, Eliot attempts the difficult, almost impossible, task of dramatizing the thoughts and feelings of a saint, one who finds union with God. As you read this play, pay special attention to its inward action: the reasoning and perceptions that prompt Becket to his course of action, the decisions he makes, and, just as important, the decisions he refuses to make.

Murder in the Cathedral

PART I

Characters

A CHORUS OF WOMEN OF CANTERBURY   ARCHBISHOP THOMAS BECKET
THREE PRIESTS OF THE CATHEDRAL   FOUR TEMPTERS
A MESSENGER   ATTENDANTS

The Scene is the Archbishop's Hall on December 2nd, 1170.

CHORUS. Here let us stand, close by the cathedral. Here let us wait.
    Are we drawn by danger? Is it the knowledge of safety, that draws our feet
    Toward the cathedral? What danger can be
    For us, the poor, the poor women of Canterbury?° What tribulation
    With which we are not already familiar? There is no danger   5
    For us, and there is no safety in the cathedral. Some presage of an act
    Which our eyes are compelled to witness, has forced our feet
    Toward the cathedral. We are forced to bear witness.

    Since golden October declined into somber November
    And the apples were gathered and stored, and the land became brown sharp
       points of death in a waste of water and mud,   10
    The New Year waits, breathes, waits, whispers in darkness.
    While the laborer kicks off a muddy boot and stretches his hand to the fire,
    The New Year waits, destiny waits for the coming.
    Who has stretched out his hand to the fire and remembered the Saints at
       All Hallows,°
    Remembered the martyrs and saints who wait? And who shall   15
    Stretch out his hand to the fire, and deny his master? who shall be warm
    By the fire, and deny his master?

    Seven years and the summer is over,
    Seven years since the Archbishop° left us,
    He who was always kind to his people.
    But it would not be well if he should return.   20
    King rules or barons rule;
    We have suffered various oppression,
    But mostly we are left to our own devices,
    And we are content if we are left alone.
    We try to keep our households in order;   25
    The merchant, shy and cautious, tries to compile a little fortune,
    And the laborer bends to his piece of earth, earth-color, his own color,

---

4. **Canterbury:** city in the county of Kent in southeastern England; the ecclesiastical center of England.   14. **All Hallows:** November 1; also known as All Saints' Day, on which all saints and martyrs are commemorated.   19. **Archbishop:** Thomas à Becket, Archbishop of Canterbury (1162–1170).

Murder in the Cathedral by T. S. Eliot. Copyright 1935 by Harcourt Brace Jovanovich, Inc.; copyright © 1963 by T. S. Eliot. Reprinted by permission of the publishers and Faber and Faber Ltd.

Preferring to pass unobserved.
Now I fear disturbance of the quiet seasons: 30
Winter shall come bringing death from the sea,
Ruinous spring shall beat at our doors,
Root and shoot shall eat our eyes and our ears,
Disastrous summer burn up the beds of our streams
And the poor shall wait for another decaying October.   35
Why should the summer bring consolation
For autumn fires and winter fogs?
What shall we do in the heat of summer
But wait in barren orchards for another October?
Some malady is coming upon us. We wait, we wait,   40
And the saints and martyrs wait, for those who shall be martyrs and saints.
Destiny waits in the hand of God, shaping the still unshapen:
I have seen these things in a shaft of sunlight.
Destiny waits in the hand of God, not in the hands of statesmen
Who do, some well, some ill, planning and guessing,   45
Having their aims which turn in their hands in the pattern of time.
Come, happy December, who shall observe you, who shall preserve you?
Shall the Son of Man be born again in the litter° of scorn?
For us, the poor, there is no action,
But only to wait and to witness.   50

                        [*Enter* PRIESTS.]

FIRST PRIEST. Seven years and the summer is over.
        Seven years since the Archbishop left us.

SECOND PRIEST. What does the Archbishop do, and our Sovereign Lord the Pope°
        With the stubborn King° and the French King°
        In ceaseless intrigue, combinations,   55
        In conference, meetings accepted, meetings refused,
        Meetings unended or endless
        At one place or another in France?

THIRD PRIEST. I see nothing quite conclusive in the art of temporal government,
        But violence, duplicity and frequent malversation.°   60

___

48. **litter:** a reference to the hay in the manger where Jesus was born.   53. **Pope:** Alexander III,
Pope (1159–1181).   54. **King:** Henry II, who ruled England 1154–1189.   **French King:** Louis VII,
who ruled 1137–1180.   60. **malversation:** misconduct in a public office.

King rules or barons rule:
The strong man strongly and the weak man by caprice.
They have but one law, to seize the power and keep it,
And the steadfast can manipulate the greed and lust of others,
The feeble is devoured by his own.   65

FIRST PRIEST. Shall these things not end
   Until the poor at the gate
   Have forgotten their friend, their Father in God, have forgotten
   That they had a friend?

[Enter MESSENGER.]

MESSENGER. Servants of God, and watchers of the temple,   70
   I am here to inform you, without circumlocution:
   The Archbishop is in England, and is close outside the city.
   I was sent before in haste
   To give you notice of his coming, as much as was possible,
   That you may prepare to meet him.   75

FIRST PRIEST. What, is the exile ended, is our Lord Archbishop
   Reunited with the King? what reconciliation
   Of two proud men?

THIRD PRIEST.   What peace can be found
   To grow between the hammer and the anvil?

SECOND PRIEST.   Tell us,
   Are the old disputes at an end, is the wall of pride cast down   80
   That divided them? Is it peace or war?

FIRST PRIEST.   Does he come
   In full assurance, or only secure
   In the power of Rome, the spiritual rule,
   The assurance of right, and the love of the people?

MESSENGER. You are right to express a certain incredulity.   85
   He comes in pride and sorrow, affirming all his claims,
   Assured, beyond doubt, of the devotion of the people,
   Who receive him with scenes of frenzied enthusiasm,
   Lining the road and throwing down their capes,
   Strewing the way with leaves and late flowers of the season.   90
   The streets of the city will be packed to suffocation,
   And I think that his horse will be deprived of its tail,
   A single hair of which becomes a precious relic.
   He is at one with the Pope, and with the King of France,
   Who indeed would have liked to detain him in his kingdom: 95
   But as for our King, that is another matter.

FIRST PRIEST. But again, is it war or peace?

MESSENGER.   Peace, but not the kiss of peace.
   A patched-up affair, if you ask my opinion.
   And if you ask me, I think the Lord Archbishop
   Is not the man to cherish any illusions,   100

Or yet to diminish the least of his pretensions.
If you ask my opinion, I think that this peace
Is nothing like an end, or like a beginning.
It is common knowledge that when the Archbishop
Parted from the King, he said to the King,   105
My Lord, he said, I leave you as a man
Whom in this life I shall not see again.
I have this, I assure you, on the highest authority;
There are several opinions as to what he meant,
But no one considers it a happy prognostic.   110

                      [*Exit.*]

FIRST PRIEST. I fear for the Archbishop, I fear for the Church,
I know that the pride bred of sudden prosperity
Was but confirmed by bitter adversity.
I saw him as Chancellor, flattered by the King,
Liked or feared by courtiers, in their overbearing fashion,   115
Despised and despising, always isolated,
Never one among them, always insecure;
His pride always feeding upon his own virtues,
Pride drawing sustenance from impartiality,
Pride drawing sustenance from generosity,   120
Loathing power given by temporal devolution,°
Wishing subjection to God alone.
Had the King been greater, or had he been weaker
Things had perhaps been different for Thomas.

SECOND PRIEST. Yet our lord is returned. Our lord has come back to his own
    again.   125
We have had enough of waiting, from December to dismal December.
The Archbishop shall be at our head, dispelling dismay and doubt.
He will tell us what we are to do, he will give us our orders, instruct us.
Our Lord is at one with the Pope, and also the King of France.
We can lean on a rock, we can feel a firm foothold   130
Against the perpetual wash of tides of balance of forces of barons and
    landholders.
The rock of God is beneath our feet. Let us meet the Archbishop with
    cordial thanksgiving:
Our lord, our Archbishop returns. And when the Archbishop returns
Our doubts are dispelled. Let us therefore rejoice,
I say rejoice, and show a glad face for his welcome.   135
I am the Archbishop's man. Let us give the Archbishop welcome!

THIRD PRIEST. For good or ill, let the wheel turn.
The wheel has been still, these seven years, and no good.
For ill or good, let the wheel turn.
For who knows the end of good or evil?   140
Until the grinders cease
And the door shall be shut in the street,
And all the daughters of music shall be brought low.

121. **temporal devolution:** the transfer of authority by a political power.

CHORUS. Here is no continuing city, here is no abiding stay.
Ill the wind, ill the time, uncertain the profit, certain the danger.   145
O late late late, late is the time, late too late, and rotten the year;
Evil the wind, and bitter the sea, and gray the sky, gray gray gray.
O Thomas, return, Archbishop; return, return to France.
Return. Quickly. Quietly. Leave us to perish in quiet.
You come with applause, you come with rejoicing, but you come bringing
    death into Canterbury: 150
A doom on the house, a doom on yourself, a doom on the world.

We do not wish anything to happen.
Seven years we have lived quietly,
Succeeded in avoiding notice,
Living and partly living.   155
There have been oppression and luxury,
There have been poverty and license,
There has been minor injustice.
Yet we have gone on living,
Living and partly living.   160
Sometimes the corn has failed us,
Sometimes the harvest is good,
One year is a year of rain,
Another a year of dryness,
One year the apples are abundant,   165
Another year the plums are lacking.
Yet we have gone on living,
Living and partly living.
We have kept the feasts, heard the masses,
We have brewed beer and cider,   170
Gathered wood against the winter,
Talked at the corner of the fire,
Talked at the corners of streets,
Talked not always in whispers,
Living and partly living.   175
We have seen births, deaths and marriages,
We have had various scandals,
We have been afflicted with taxes,
We have had laughter and gossip,
Several girls have disappeared   180
Unaccountably, and some not able to.
We have all had our private terrors,
Our particular shadows, our secret fears.
But now a great fear is upon us, a fear not of one but of many,
A fear like birth and death, when we see birth and death alone   185
In a void apart. We
Are afraid in a fear which we cannot know, which we cannot face, which
    none understands,
And our hearts are torn from us, our brains unskinned like the layers of
    an onion, our selves are lost lost
In a final fear which none understands. O Thomas Archbishop,
O Thomas our Lord, leave us and leave us be, in our humble and tarnished

frame of existence, leave us; do not ask us   190
To stand to the doom on the house, the doom on the Archbishop, the doom on the world.
Archbishop, secure and assured of your fate, unaffrayed among the shades, do you realize what you ask, do you realize what it means
To the small folk drawn into the pattern of fate, the small folk who live among small things,
The strain on the brain of the small folk who stand to the doom of the house, the doom of their lord, the doom of the world?
O Thomas, Archbishop, leave us, leave us, leave sullen Dover, and set sail for France. Thomas our Archbishop still our Archbishop even in France. Thomas Archbishop, set the white sail between the gray sky and the bitter sea, leave us, leave us for France.   195

SECOND PRIEST: What a way to talk at such a juncture!
You are foolish, immodest and babbling women.
Do you not know that the good Archbishop
Is likely to arrive at any moment?
The crowds in the streets will be cheering and cheering,   200
You go on croaking like frogs in the treetops:
But frogs at least can be cooked and eaten.
Whatever you are afraid of, in your craven apprehension,
Let me ask you at the least to put on pleasant faces,
And give a hearty welcome to our good Archbishop.   205

[*Enter* THOMAS.]

THOMAS. Peace. And let them be, in their exaltation.
They speak better than they know, and beyond your understanding.
They know and do not know, what it is to act or suffer.
They know and do not know, that action is suffering
And suffering is action. Neither does the agent suffer   210
Nor the patient act. But both are fixed
In an eternal action, an eternal patience
To which all must consent that it may be willed
And which all must suffer that they may will it,
That the pattern may subsist, for the pattern is the action   215
And the suffering, that the wheel may turn and still
Be forever still.

SECOND PRIEST. O my Lord, forgive me, I did not see you coming,
Engrossed by the chatter of these foolish women.
Forgive us, my Lord, you would have had a better welcome   220
If we had been sooner prepared for the event.
But your Lordship knows that seven years of waiting,
Seven years of prayer, seven years of emptiness,
Have better prepared our hearts for your coming,
Than seven days could make ready Canterbury.   225
However, I will have fires laid in all your rooms
To take the chill off our English December,
Your Lordship now being used to a better climate.
Your Lordship will find your rooms in order as you left them.

THOMAS. And will try to leave them in order as I find them.   230
    I am more than grateful for all your kind attentions.
    These are small matters. Little rest in Canterbury
    With eager enemies restless about us.
    Rebellious bishops, York, London, Salisbury,°
    Would have intercepted our letters,   235
    Filled the coast with spies and sent to meet me
    Some who hold me in bitterest hate.
    By God's grace aware of their prevision
    I sent my letters on another day,
    Had fair crossing, found at Sandwich°   240
    Broc, Warenne, and the Sheriff of Kent,
    Those who had sworn to have my head from me.
    Only John, the Dean of Salisbury,
    Fearing for the King's name, warning against treason,
    Made them hold their hands. So for the time   245
    We are unmolested.

FIRST PRIEST.   But do they follow after?

THOMAS. For a little time the hungry hawk
    Will only soar and hover, circling lower,
    Waiting excuse, pretense, opportunity.
    End will be simple, sudden, God-given.   250
    Meanwhile the substance of our first act
    Will be shadows, and the strife with shadows.
    Heavier the interval than the consummation.
    All things prepare the event. Watch.

                    [*Enter* FIRST TEMPTER.]

FIRST TEMPTER. You see, my Lord, I do not wait upon ceremony: 255
    Here I have come, forgetting all acrimony,
    Hoping that your present gravity
    Will find excuse for my humble levity
    Remembering all the good time past.
    Your Lordship won't despise an old friend out of favor?   260
    Old Tom, gay Tom, Becket of London,
    Your Lordship won't forget that evening on the river
    When the King, and you and I were all friends together?
    Friendship should be more than biting Time can sever.
    What, my Lord, now that you recover   265
    Favor with the King, shall we say that summer's over
    Or that the good time cannot last?
    Fluting in the meadows, viols° in the hall,
    Laughter and apple blossom floating on the water,
    Singing at nightfall, whispering in chambers,   270
    Fires devouring the winter season,
    Eating up the darkness, with wit and wine and wisdom!

234. **York, London, Salisbury:** the bishops who have been excommunicated.   240. **Sandwich:** a
city on the coast of southeastern England.   268. **viols:** stringed instruments.

Now that the King and you are in amity,
Clergy and laity may return to gaiety,
Mirth and sportfulness need not walk warily.   275

THOMAS. You talk of seasons that are past. I remember
Not worth forgetting.

TEMPTER.   And of the new season.
Spring has come in winter. Snow in the branches
Shall float as sweet as blossoms. Ice along the ditches
Mirror the sunlight. Love in the orchard   280
Send the sap shooting. Mirth matches melancholy.

THOMAS. We do not know very much of the future
Except that from generation to generation
The same things happen again and again.
Men learn little from others' experience.   285
But in the life of one man, never
The same time returns. Sever
The cord, shed the scale. Only
The fool, fixed in his folly, may think
He can turn the wheel on which he turns.   290

TEMPTER. My Lord, a nod is as good as a wink.
A man will often love what he spurns.
For the good times past, that are come again
I am your man.

THOMAS.   Not in this train
Look to your behavior. You were safer   295
Think of penitence and follow your master.

TEMPTER. Not at this gait!
If you go so fast, others may go faster.
Your Lordship is too proud!
The safest beast is not the one that roars most loud,   300
This was not the way of the King our master!
You were not used to be so hard upon sinners
When they were your friends. Be easy, man!
The easy man lives to eat the best dinners.
Take a friend's advice. Leave well alone,   305
Or your goose may be cooked and eaten to the bone.

THOMAS. You come twenty years too late.

TEMPTER. Then I leave you to your fate.
I leave you to the pleasures of your higher vices,
Which will have to be paid for at higher prices.   310
Farewell, my Lord, I do not wait upon ceremony,
I leave as I came, forgetting all acrimony,
Hoping that your present gravity
Will find excuse for my humble levity.
If you will remember me, my Lord, at your prayers,   315
I'll remember you at kissing-time below the stairs.

THOMAS. Leave-well-alone, the springtime fancy,
So one thought goes whistling down the wind.
The impossible is still temptation.
The impossible, the undesirable,   320
Voices under sleep, waking a dead world,
So that the mind may not be whole in the present.

[*Enter* SECOND TEMPTER.]

SECOND TEMPTER. Your Lordship has forgotten me, perhaps. I will remind you.
We met at Clarendon, at Northampton,
And last at Montmirail, in Maine.° Now that I have recalled them,   325
Let us but set these not too pleasant memories
In balance against other, earlier
And weightier ones: those of the Chancellorship.
See how the late ones rise! You, master of policy
Whom all acknowledged, should guide the state again.   330

THOMAS. Your meaning?

TEMPTER.   The Chancellorship that you resigned
When you were made Archbishop—that was a mistake
On your part—still may be regained. Think, my Lord,
Power obtained grows to glory,
Life lasting, a permanent possession.   335
A templed tomb, monument of marble.
Rule over men reckon no madness.

THOMAS. To the man of God what gladness?

TEMPTER.   Sadness
Only to those giving love to God alone.
Shall he who held the solid substance   340
Wander waking with deceitful shadows?
Power is present. Holiness hereafter.

THOMAS. Who then?

TEMPTER.   The Chancellor. King and Chancellor.
King commands. Chancellor richly rules.
This is a sentence not taught in the schools.   345
To set down the great, protect the poor,
Beneath the throne of God can man do more?
Disarm the ruffian, strengthen the laws,
Rule for the good of the better cause,
Dispensing justice make all even,   350
Is thrive on earth, and perhaps in heaven.

THOMAS. What means?

TEMPTER.   Real power
Is purchased at price of a certain submission.

324–25. **Clarendon, Northampton, Maine:** Clarendon, a parish in southern England; Northampton, a county in central England; Maine, an ancient province in western France.

Your spiritual power is earthly perdition.
Power is present, for him who will wield.   355

THOMAS. Who shall have it?

TEMPTER.   He who will come.

THOMAS. What shall be the month?

TEMPTER.   The last from the first.

THOMAS. What shall we give for it?

TEMPTER.   Pretense of priestly power.

THOMAS. Why should we give it?

TEMPTER.   For the power and the glory.

THOMAS. No!

TEMPTER.   Yes! Or bravery will be broken,   360
Cabined in Canterbury, realmless ruler,
Self-bound servant of a powerless Pope,
The old stag, circled with hounds.

THOMAS. No!

TEMPTER.   Yes! men must maneuver. Monarchs also,
Waging war abroad, need fast friends at home.   365
Private policy is public profit;
Dignity still shall be dressed with decorum.

THOMAS. You forget the bishops
Whom I have laid under excommunication.

TEMPTER. Hungry hatred   370
Will not strive against intelligent self-interest.

THOMAS. You forget the barons. Who will not forget
Constant curbing of petty privilege.

TEMPTER. Against the barons
Is King's cause, churl's° cause, Chancellor's cause.   375

THOMAS. No! shall I, who keep the keys
Of heaven and hell, supreme alone in England,
Who bind and loose, with power from the Pope,
Descend to desire a punier power?
Delegate to deal the doom of damnation,   380
To condemn kings, not serve among their servants,
Is my open office. No! Go.

TEMPTER. Then I leave you to your fate.
Your sin soars sunward, covering kings' falcons.

THOMAS. Temporal power, to build a good world,   385
To keep order, as the world knows order.

375. **churl:** peasant.

Those who put their faith in worldly order
Not controlled by the order of God,
In confident ignorance, but arrest disorder,
Make it fast, breed fatal disease,   390
Degrade what they exalt. Power with the King—
I *was* the King, his arm, his better reason.
But what was once exaltation
Would now be only mean descent.

[*Enter* THIRD TEMPTER.]

THIRD TEMPTER. I am an unexpected visitor.

THOMAS.   I expected you.   395

TEMPTER. But not in this guise, or for my present purpose.

THOMAS. No purpose brings surprise.

TEMPTER.   Well, my Lord,
I am no trifler, and no politician.
To idle or intrigue at court
I have no skill. I am no courtier.   400
I know a horse, a dog, a wench;
I know how to hold my estates in order,
A country-keeping lord who minds his own business.
It is we country lords who know the country
And we who know what the country needs.   405
It is our country. We care for the country.
We are the backbone of the nation.
We, not the plotting parasites
About the King. Excuse my bluntness:
I am a rough straightforward Englishman.   410

THOMAS. Proceed straight forward.

TEMPTER.   Purpose is plain.
Endurance of friendship does not depend
Upon ourselves, but upon circumstance.
But circumstance is not undetermined.
Unreal friendship may turn to real
But real friendship, once ended, cannot be mended.   415
Sooner shall enmity turn to alliance.
The enmity that never knew friendship
Can sooner know accord.

THOMAS.   For a countryman
You wrap your meaning in as dark generality
As any courtier.   420

TEMPTER.   This is the simple fact!
You have no hope of reconciliation
With Henry the King. You look only
To blind assertion in isolation.
That is a mistake.

THOMAS.   O Henry, O my King!

TEMPTER.   Other friends   425
     May be found in the present situation.
     King in England is not all-powerful;
     King is in France, squabbling in Anjou;°
     Round him waiting hungry sons.°
     We are for England. We are in England.   430
     You and I, my Lord, are Normans.°
     England is a land for Norman
     Sovereignty. Let the Angevin
     Destroy himself, fighting in Anjou.
     He does not understand us, the English barons.   435
     We are the people.

THOMAS. To what does this lead?

TEMPTER.   To a happy coalition
     Of intelligent interests.

THOMAS.   But what have you—
     If you do speak for barons—

TEMPTER.   For a powerful party
     Which has turned its eyes in your direction—   440
     To gain from you, your Lordship asks.
     For us, Church favor would be an advantage,
     Blessing of Pope powerful protection
     In the fight for liberty. You, my Lord,
     In being with us, would fight a good stroke   445
     At once, for England and for Rome,
     Ending the tyrannous jurisdiction
     Of king's court over bishop's court,
     Of king's court over baron's court.

THOMAS. Which I helped to found.

TEMPTER.   Which you helped to found.   450
     But time past is time forgotten.
     We expect the rise of a new constellation.

THOMAS. And if the Archbishop cannot trust the King,
     How can he trust those who work for King's undoing?

TEMPTER. Kings will allow no power but their own;   455
     Church and people have good cause against the throne.

THOMAS. If the Archbishop cannot trust the Throne,
     He has good cause to trust none but God alone.
     I ruled once as Chancellor
     And men like you were glad to wait at my door.   460

---

428. **Anjou** (an′jo͞o): a former province in western France.   429. **sons:** Henry's four sons, Richard, Geoffrey, Henry, and John, were selfish, ruthless men who conspired together against their father. 431. **Normans:** from the old province of Normandy in northern France.

Not only in the court, but in the field
And in the tilt-yard I made many yield.
Shall I who ruled like an eagle over doves
Now take the shape of a wolf among wolves?
Pursue your treacheries as you have done before: 465
No one shall say that I betrayed a king.

TEMPTER. Then, my Lord, I shall not wait at your door.
And I well hope, before another spring
The King will show his regard for your loyalty.

THOMAS. To make, then break, this thought has come before,   470
The desperate exercise of failing power.
Samson in Gaza° did no more.
But if I break, I must break myself alone.

[*Enter* FOURTH TEMPTER.]

FOURTH TEMPTER. Well done, Thomas, your will is hard to bend.
And with me beside you, you shall not lack a friend.   475

THOMAS. Who are you? I expected
Three visitors, not four.

TEMPTER. Do not be surprised to receive one more.
Had I been expected, I had been here before.
I always precede expectation.

THOMAS.   Who are you?   480

TEMPTER. As you do not know me, I do not need a name,
And, as you know me, that is why I come.
You know me, but have never seen my face.
To meet before was never time or place.

THOMAS. Say what you come to say.

TEMPTER.   It shall be said at last.   485
Hooks have been baited with morsels of the past.
Wantonness is weakness. As for the King,
His hardened hatred shall have no end.
You know truly, the King will never trust
Twice, the man who has been his friend.   490
Borrow use cautiously, employ
Your services as long as you have to lend.
You would wait for trap to snap
Having served your turn, broken and crushed.
As for barons, envy of lesser men   495
Is still more stubborn than king's anger.
Kings have public policy, barons private profit,
Jealousy raging possession of the fiend.
Barons are employable against each other;
Greater enemies must kings destroy.   500

472. **Samson in Gaza:** Samson, having been blinded by the Philistines, loosened the pillars that
supported their temple at Gaza, thus destroying both his enemies and himself.

THOMAS. What is your counsel?

TEMPTER.   Fare forward to the end.
    All other ways are closed to you
    Except the way already chosen.
    But what is pleasure, kingly rule,
    Or rule of men beneath a king,   505
    With craft in corners, stealthy stratagem,
    To general grasp of spiritual power?
    Man oppressed by sin, since Adam fell—
    You hold the keys of heaven and hell.
    Power to bind and loose: bind, Thomas, bind,   510
    King and bishop under your heel.
    King, emperor, bishop, baron, king:
    Uncertain mastery of melting armies,
    War, plague, and revolution,
    New conspiracies, broken pacts;   515
    To be master or servant within an hour,
    This is the course of temporal power.
    The Old King shall know it, when at last breath,
    No sons, no empire, he bites broken teeth.
    You hold the skein: wind, Thomas, wind   520
    The thread of eternal life and death.
    You hold this power, hold it.

THOMAS.   Supreme, in this land?

TEMPTER. Supreme, but for one.

THOMAS.   That I do not understand.

TEMPTER. It is not for me to tell you how this may be so;
    I am only here, Thomas, to tell you what you know.   525

THOMAS. How long shall this be?

TEMPTER. Save what you know already, ask nothing of me.
    But think, Thomas, think of glory after death.
    When king is dead, there's another king,
    And one more king is another reign.   530
    King is forgotten, when another shall come:
    Saint and Martyr rule from the tomb.
    Think, Thomas, think of enemies dismayed,
    Creeping in penance, frightened of a shade;
    Think of pilgrims, standing in line   535
    Before the glittering jeweled shrine,
    From generation to generation
    Bending the knee in supplication,
    Think of the miracles, by God's grace,
    And think of your enemies, in another place.   540

THOMAS. I have thought of these things.

TEMPTER.   That is why I tell you.
    Your thoughts have more power than kings to compel you.

You have also thought, sometimes at your prayers.
Sometimes hesitating at the angles of stairs,
And between sleep and waking, early in the morning,   545
When the bird cries, have thought of further scorning.
That nothing lasts, but the wheel turns,
The nest is rifled, and the bird mourns;
That the shrine shall be pillaged, and the gold spent,
The jewels gone for light ladies' ornament.   550
When miracles cease, and the faithful desert you.
And men shall only do their best to forget you.
And later is worse, when men will not hate you
Enough to defame or to execrate you,
But pondering the qualities that you lacked   555
Will only try to find the historical fact.
When men shall declare that there was no mystery
About this man who played a certain part in history.

THOMAS. But what is there to do? What is left to be done?
Is there no enduring crown to be won?   560

TEMPTER. Yes, Thomas, yes; you have thought of that too.
What can compare with glory of Saints
Dwelling forever in presence of God?
What earthly glory, of king or emperor,
What earthly pride, that is not poverty   565
Compared with richness of heavenly grandeur?
Seek the way of martyrdom, make yourself the lowest
On earth, to be high in heaven.
And see far off below you, where the gulf is fixed,
Your persecutors, in timeless torment,   570
Parched passion, beyond expiation.

THOMAS.   No!
Who are you, tempting with my own desires?
Others have come, temporal tempters,
With pleasure and power at palpable price.
What do you offer? What do you ask?   575

TEMPTER. I offer what you desire. I ask
What you have to give. Is it too much
For such a vision of eternal grandeur?

THOMAS. Others offered real goods, worthless
But real. You only offer   580
Dreams to damnation.

TEMPTER.   You have often dreamt them.

THOMAS. Is there no way, in my soul's sickness,
Does not lead to damnation in pride?
I well know that these temptations
Mean present vanity and future torment.   585
Can sinful pride be driven out

Only by more sinful? Can I neither act nor suffer
Without perdition?

TEMPTER. You know and do not know, what it is to act or suffer.
You know and do not know, that action is suffering,   590
And suffering action. Neither does the agent suffer
Nor the patient act. But both are fixed
In an eternal action, an eternal patience
To which all must consent that it may be willed
And which all must suffer that they may will it,   595
That the pattern may subsist, that the wheel may turn and still
Be forever still.

CHORUS. There is no rest in the house. There is no rest in the street.
I hear restless movement of feet. And the air is heavy and thick.
Thick and heavy the sky. And the earth presses up against our feet.   600
What is the sickly smell, the vapor? The dark green light from a cloud on
   a withered tree? The earth is heaving to parturition of issue of hell. What
   is the sticky dew that forms on the back of my hand?

THE FOUR TEMPTERS. Man's life is a cheat and a disappointment;
All things are unreal,
Unreal or disappointing:
The Catherine wheel,° the pantomime cat,   605
The prizes given at the children's party,
The prize awarded for the English Essay,
The scholar's degree, the statesman's decoration.
All things become less real, man passes
From unreality to unreality.   610
This man is obstinate, blind, intent
On self-destruction.
Passing from deception to deception,
From grandeur to grandeur to final illusion,
Lost in the wonder of his own greatness,   615
The enemy of society, enemy of himself.

THE THREE PRIESTS. O Thomas my Lord do not fight the intractable tide,
Do not sail the irresistible wind; in the storm,
Should we not wait for the sea to subside, in the night
Abide the coming of day, when the traveler may find his way,   620
The sailor lay course by the sun?

CHORUS, PRIESTS *and* TEMPTERS *(alternately).*

   C. Is it the owl that calls, or a signal between the trees?
   P. Is the windowbar made fast, is the door under lock and bolt?
   T. Is it rain that taps at the window, is it wind that pokes at the door?
   C. Does the torch flame in the hall, the candle in the room?   625
   P. Does the watchman walk by the wall?
   T. Does the mastiff prowl by the gate?
   C. Death has a hundred hands and walks by a thousand ways.

605. **Catherine wheel:** a firework similar to a pinwheel. An allusion to the attempt to torture
St. Catherine on a spiked wheel.

P. He may come in the sight of all, he may pass unseen unheard.

T. Come whispering through the ear, or a sudden shock on the skull.   630

C. A man may walk with a lamp at night, and yet be drowned in a ditch.

P. A man may climb the stair in the day, and slip on a broken step.

T. A man may sit at meat, and feel the cold in his groin.

CHORUS. We have not been happy, my Lord, we have not been too happy.
    We are not ignorant women, we know what we must expect and not ex-
      pect.   635
    We know of oppression and torture,
    We know of extortion and violence,
    Destitution, disease,
    The old without fire in winter,
    The child without milk in summer,   640
    Our labor taken away from us,
    Our sins made heavier upon us.
    We have seen the young man mutilated,
    The torn girl trembling by the millstream.
    And meanwhile we have gone on living,   645
    Living and partly living,
    Picking together the pieces,
    Gathering faggots at nightfall,
    Building a partial shelter,
    For sleeping, and eating and drinking and laughter.   650

    God gave us always some reason, some hope; but now a new terror has
      soiled us, which none can avert, none can avoid, flowing under our feet
      and over the sky;
    Under doors and down chimneys, flowing in at the ear and the mouth and
      the eye.
    God is leaving us, God is leaving us, more pang, more pain than birth or
      death.
    Sweet and cloying through the dark air
    Falls the stifling scent of despair;   655
    The forms take shape in the dark air:
    Puss-purr of leopard, footfall of padding bear,
    Palm-pat of nodding ape, square hyena waiting
    For laughter, laughter, laughter. The Lords of Hell are here.
    They curl round you, lie at your feet, swing and wing through the dark
      air.   660
    O Thomas Archbishop, save us, save us, save yourself that we may be
      saved;
    Destroy yourself and we are destroyed.

THOMAS. Now is my way clear, now is the meaning plain:
    Temptation shall not come in this kind again.
    The last temptation is the greatest treason: 665
    To do the right deed for the wrong reason.
    The natural vigor in the venial sin
    Is the way in which our lives begin.
    Thirty years ago, I searched all the ways
    That lead to pleasure, advancement and praise.   670

Delight in sense, in learning and in thought,
Music and philosophy, curiosity,
The purple bullfinch in the lilac tree,
The tilt-yard° skill, the strategy of chess,
Love in the garden, singing to the instrument,   675
Were all things equally desirable.
Ambition comes when early force is spent
And when we find no longer all things possible.
Ambition comes behind and unobservable.
Sin grows with doing good. When I imposed the King's law   680
In England, and waged war with him against Toulouse,°
I beat the barons at their own game. I
Could then despise the men who thought me most contemptible,
The raw nobility, whose manners matched their fingernails.
While I ate out of the King's dish   685
To become servant of God was never my wish.
Servant of God has chance of greater sin
And sorrow, than the man who serves a king.
For those who serve the greater cause may make the cause serve them,
Still doing right: and striving with political men   690
May make that cause political, not by what they do
But by what they are. I know
What yet remains to show you of my history
Will seem to most of you at best futility,
Senseless self-slaughter of a lunatic,   695
Arrogant passion of a fanatic.
I know that history at all times draws
The strangest consequence from remotest cause.
But for every evil, every sacrilege,
Crime, wrong, oppression and the axe's edge,   700
Indifference, exploitation, you, and you,
And you, must all be punished. So must you.
I shall no longer act or suffer, to the sword's end.
Now my good Angel, whom God appoints
To be my guardian, hover over the swords' points.   705

674. **tilt-yard:** area where jousting was practiced.   681. **Toulouse** (tōō·lōōz′): a former province
in southern France.

COMMENTARY

T. S. Eliot's bold experiments, probably more than the work of any other poet, have determined the characteristic qualities of modern poetry in English. As a poetic innovator, Eliot was as thoughtful as he was bold. He pondered the kinds of effects he wished to create, and, rather than rejecting all poetic traditions, he drew heavily on the work of a number of poets before him, particularly on nineteenth-century French poets and sixteenth- and seventeenth-century English poets. In trying to create a contemporary poetic drama, Eliot was similarly bold and thoughtful. He rejected the realistic tradition of the modern theater, a tradition which assumes that a stage is merely a room in which people looking like ourselves speak in colloquial prose. One of his aims was to restore *poetic* drama to the eminent place it had once held in the theater. But, as he stated, poetry must not be simply a useless embellishment of a play. "From this it follows that no play should be written in verse for which prose is *dramatically* adequate." The subject of the drama must give full opportunities for the subtlety, power, and illumination that poetry can provide.

In fashioning *Murder in the Cathedral,* his first full-length poetic drama, Eliot drew on two dramatic traditions which are not usually influential in the modern theater: that of ancient Greek tragedy and that of the medieval morality play. Both kinds of plays are concerned with religion and religious observances. Scholars believe that Greek tragedies had their origins in various religious rituals. The morality plays of the Middle Ages were performed in churches to teach moral lessons.

From Greek tragedy, Eliot (like many dramatists before him) drew on the concept of a noble character, the *protagonist,* who moves through three stages: (1) *purpose,* the phase in which the protagonist decides to perform a significant action; (2) *passion* or suffering, in which the protagonist experiences the emotional consequences of the decision; (3) *perception,* in which the protagonist perceives the ultimate implications of the action and thus gains insight into the nature of the universe. A *chorus,* a group of men or women in a subservient position to the protagonist, serves as a link between the protagonist and the audience.

From the medieval morality play, Eliot drew the idea of using dramatic means to teach a moral lesson. In the best-known morality play, *Everyman,* the protagonist is summoned by Death to meet and be judged by his Maker. Beseeching characters with names such as Beauty, Knowledge, and Wealth to accompany him, Everyman discovers that these are false

friends who desert him. Only Good Deeds is willing to accompany him on the journey and testify on his behalf at his judgment. Like Good Deeds and Wealth, a number of Eliot's characters also have allegorical significance. The four tempters could appropriately be renamed Pleasure, Temporal Power, and so forth. But unlike the morality plays, *Murder in the Cathedral* does not teach a simple lesson. Its moral content is complex and difficult to understand. As we attempt to analyze it, keep in mind the devices from older theatrical traditions that Eliot uses to point up the moral and intellectual content of his drama; allegorical characters, a protagonist progressing from purpose to passion to perception, and a chorus establishing a relationship between the protagonist and the audience or reader.

The play begins with a speech by the chorus of poor women describing the condition of the nation. After Becket's departure seven years before, the State was triumphant over the Church. ("King rules or barons rule.") But life goes on; time passes as before; the seasons change. Now the world seems on the brink of a great event, an event which will connect people, who move on the level of time, with a Being who exists outside of time; that is, the eternal God. God, not humans, controls the shape of events:

"Destiny waits in the hands of God, not in the hands of statesmen
Who do, some well, some ill, planning and guessing,
Having their aims which turn in their hands in the pattern of time."

People are limited by existing in and being controlled by time. The opposition between time and timelessness is crucial to much of Eliot's work. When Thomas enters, he develops this idea in a symbol that appears frequently in Eliot's poetry: the turning of a wheel. Most people move on the rim of the wheel, on the level of time. They are born, marry, grow old, and die without ever achieving a consciousness of life as anything greater than the flow of time. But some, like Thomas, seek to move beyond the level of time to the still point at the center of the wheel where time and timelessness intersect and they experience the eternal presence of God. Much of the difficulty of Eliot's later poetry stems from his attempts to express this profound, extremely difficult idea.

When Thomas makes his entrance, he has already reached the phase of *purpose*. He has made his decision to uphold the rights of the Church and defy the King. But behind his decision is a consciousness of a timeless Presence beyond temporal events. Thomas's actions are therefore part of a larger "eternal action, an eternal patience/ To which all must consent that it may be willed/ And which all must suffer that they may will it. . . ."

Passion, or suffering, the second stage of Part I, begins with the coming of the tempters. The first tempter's speech is light and witty. He offers Thomas temporal pleasures: "Fluting in the meadows, viols in the hall,/ Laughter and apple blossom floating on the water,/ Singing at nightfall, whispering in chambers,/ Fires devouring the winter season./ Eating up the darkness, with wit and wine and wisdom!" But Thomas is unmoved by his temptation. He has matured past the point where he can be seriously attracted by such pleasures: "Men learn little from others' experience./ But in the life of one man, never/ The same time returns." He knows that "the mind may not be whole in the present." A person cannot be completely fulfilled on the temporal level.

The second tempter offers Thomas temporal power: "You, master of policy/ Whom all acknowledged, should guide the state again." But Thomas knows that such power is puny compared with God's power, of which he is the instrument: "No! shall I, who keep the keys/ Of heaven and hell, supreme alone in England,/ Who bind and loose, with power from the Pope,/ Descend to desire a punier power?"

The third tempter represents the barons, who resent the King's encroachments on their power. Having the appearance of a bluff honest man who has the nation's good at heart, he offers Thomas the opportunity to be part of a coalition against the King. But Thomas knows that the barons are to be trusted even less than the king: "And if the Archbishop cannot trust the King,/ How can he trust those who work for King's undoing? . . . No one shall say that I betrayed a king."

Since the first three tempters were expected, Thomas was prepared for them. It is the final unexpected tempter who poses a real threat to the Archbishop's purpose. The temptation he offers is glory: "What can compare with glory of Saints/ Dwelling forever in presence of God?" By consciously bringing about his own martyrdom, Thomas would be setting his own will against that of God. He would be acting not as God's instrument but as the instrument of his own vanity. In pain and despair, Thomas cries out to the tempter, "No!/ Who are you, tempting with my own desires?" And he asks, "Can I neither act nor suffer/ Without perdition?" Ominously, to show how closely he mirrors Thomas's thoughts and desires, the tempter answers in words that are almost exactly the same as Thomas's earlier words (lines 208–17). "You know and do not know, what it is to act or suffer./ You know and do not know, that action is suffering,/ And suffering action." These lines reflect the difficulty of moving beyond the temporal level, of acting not simply as an instrument of one's own will but of the will of God. How can people make a decision and know that they are fulfilling not merely the pattern of their own desires but one that is deeper and timeless so that "the pattern may subsist, that the wheel may turn and still/ Be forever still."

The hour of Thomas's agony is upon him. He suffers torments of doubt, unsure whether in his obstinacy against the King he is acting as the servant of God or merely as a proud official. Thomas's suffering is not portrayed directly. Instead it is implied in the speeches of the chorus, tempters, and the priests (lines 598–662). When Thomas speaks once again (line

663), he has gone beyond the stage of passion to the stage of perception:

"Now is my way clear, now is the
    meaning plain:
Temptation shall not come in this kind
    again.
The last temptation is the greatest
    treason:
To do the right deed for the wrong
    reason. . . .
I shall no longer act or suffer, to the
    sword's end.
Now my good Angel, whom God ap-
    points
To be my guardian, hover over the
    swords' points."

Thomas has reached a point of consciousness that few of us achieve. He is completely reconciled to the pattern of events and no longer wishes to force his own will on them. He is beyond both action and suffering, which are of time, of this world. He has achieved the awareness of a saint, a level of consciousness where it is extremely difficult for the priests, the chorus, and the audience to follow. The remainder of the play will be devoted to exploring and clarifying this level and relating it to the everyday world of struggle and suffering, authority and rebellion, violence and order, that the chorus and priests, audience and readers inhabit.

FOR STUDY AND DISCUSSION

1. How is the season of the year during which the play takes place appropriate to the action of the play? Cite lines referring to the season. What significance is given to the season by these lines?

2. How is the setting of the play indicated? Who fills the audience in on the background of Becket's past? Is this device reminiscent of anything you have previously encountered in drama?

3. The speeches of the messenger (see lines 85–110) prepare for the entrance of the Archbishop. How does the messenger describe Thomas? Is the tone of his speeches respectful or ironic? What clues does he give to Thomas's state of mind? In answering this

question, consider especially the lines, "He comes in pride and sorrow, affirming all his claims" and "if you ask me, I think the Lord Archbishop/ Is not the man to cherish any illusions,/ Or yet to diminish the least of his pretensions."

4. Describe the relationship of the priests to the chorus and to the Archbishop. What is the dramatic function of the priests? If they were dropped from Part I, would the play suffer? Why?

5. The chorus speaks of "the small folk drawn into the pattern of fate, the small folk who live among small things,/ The strain on the brain of the small folk who stand to the doom of the house, the doom of their lord, the doom of the world" (lines 193–94). When the priests chide these "foolish, immodest and babbling women," Thomas appears and tells the priests, "They speak better than they know, and beyond your understanding" (line 207). What do the women know that the priests do not? How is this knowledge related to the theme of the play?

6. What does critic John Peter mean when he says that the tempters are simply "objectified facets of his [Becket's] own consciousness"? Why do you think Eliot chose to portray Thomas's mental torment indirectly— through speeches by the priests, tempters, and chorus—instead of giving Thomas a long soliloquy about the ordeal he was undergoing?

7. "The true martyr is he who has . . . lost his will in the will of God, and who no longer desires anything for himself, not even the glory of being a martyr." In discussing this passage from the Interlude (page 777), one critic says: "The dramatic problem is, of course, that the more perfect the saint's self-surrender, the more difficult it is to keep him a real man since it is by our weaknesses that we are most human." In your opinion, is it possible to feel pity for Thomas? Or is he too perfect to command our sympathies as a human being? To support your answer, give reasons based on a careful reading of Part I.

8. Why does Thomas find it fairly easy to resist the first three tempters and not the fourth? What conflict of motives is revealed? How do the following lines spoken by the chorus influence Becket and enable him to resolve his inner struggle: "O Thomas Archbishop, save us, save us, save yourself that we may be saved;/ Destroy yourself and we are destroyed."

INTERLUDE

"Glory to God in the highest, and on earth peace to men of good will." *The fourteenth verse of the second chapter of the Gospel according to Saint Luke.* In the Name of the Father, and of the Son, and of the Holy Ghost. Amen.

Dear children of God, my sermon this Christmas morning will be a very short one. I wish only that you should meditate in your hearts the deep meaning and mystery of our masses of Christmas Day. For whenever Mass is said, we reenact the Passion and Death of Our Lord; and on this Christmas Day we do this in celebration of His Birth. So that at the same moment we rejoice in His coming for the salvation of men, and offer again to God His Body and Blood in sacrifice, oblation and satisfaction for the sins of the whole world. It was in this same night that has just passed, that a multitude of the heavenly host appeared before the shepherds at Bethlehem, saying "Glory to God in the highest, and on earth peace to men of good will"; at this same time of all the year that we celebrate at once the Birth of Our Lord and His Passion and Death upon the Cross. Beloved, as the World sees, this is to behave in a strange fashion. For who in the World will both mourn and rejoice at once and for the same reason? For either joy will be overborne by mourning, or mourning will be cast out by joy; so it is only in these our Christian mysteries that we can rejoice and mourn at once for the same reason. Now think for a moment about the meaning of this word "peace." Does it seem strange to you that the angels should have announced Peace, when ceaselessly the world has been stricken with War and the fear of War? Does it seem to you that the angelic voices were mistaken, and that the promise was a disappointment and a cheat?

Reflect now, how Our Lord Himself spoke of Peace. He said to His disciples, "My peace I leave with you, my peace I give unto you." Did He mean peace as we think of it: the kingdom of England at peace with its neighbors, the barons at peace with the King, the householder counting over his peaceful gains, the swept hearth, his best wine for a friend at the table, his wife singing to the children? Those men His disciples knew no such things: they went forth to journey afar, to suffer by land and sea, to know torture, imprisonment, disappointment, to suffer death by martyrdom. What then did He mean? If you ask that, remember then that He said also, "Not as the world gives, give I unto you." So then, He gave to His disciples peace, but not peace as the world gives.

Consider also one thing of which you have probably never thought. Not only do we at the feast of Christmas celebrate at once Our Lord's Birth and His Death: but on the next day we celebrate the martyrdom of His first martyr, the blessed Stephen. Is it an accident, do you think, that the day of the first martyr follows immediately the day of the Birth of Christ? By no means. Just as we rejoice and mourn at once, in the Birth and in the Passion of Our Lord; so also, in a smaller figure, we both rejoice and mourn in the death of martyrs. We mourn, for the sins of the world that has martyred them; we rejoice, that another soul is numbered

T. S. ELIOT   777

among the Saints in Heaven, for the glory of God and for the salvation of men.

Beloved, we do not think of a martyr simply as a good Christian who has been killed because he is a Christian: for that would be solely to mourn. We do not think of him simply as a good Christian who has been elevated to the company of the Saints: for that would be simply to rejoice: and neither our mourning nor our rejoicing is as the world's is. A Christian martyrdom is never an accident, for Saints are not made by accident. Still less is a Christian martyrdom the effect of a man's will to become a Saint, as a man by willing and contriving may become a ruler of men. A martyrdom is always the design of God, for His love of men, to warn them and to lead them, to bring them back to His ways. It is never the design of man; for the true martyr is he who has become the instrument of God, who has lost his will in the will of God, and who no longer desires anything for himself, not even the glory of being a martyr. So thus as on earth the Church mourns and rejoices at once, in a fashion that the world cannot understand; so in Heaven the Saints are most high, having made themselves most low, and are seen, not as we see them, but in the light of the Godhead from which they draw their being.

I have spoken to you today, dear children of God, of the martyrs of the past, asking you to remember especially our martyr of Canterbury, the blessed Archbishop Elphege; because it is fitting, on Christ's birthday, to remember what is that Peace which He brought; and because, dear children, I do not think I shall ever preach to you again; and because it is possible that in a short time you may have yet another martyr, and that one perhaps not the last. I would have you keep in your hearts these words that I say, and think of them at another time. In the Name of the Father, and of the Son, and of the Holy Ghost. Amen.

PART II

Characters

ARCHBISHOP THOMAS BECKET   THREE PRIESTS
CHORUS OF WOMEN OF CANTERBURY   FOUR KNIGHTS
ATTENDANTS

The first scene is in the Archbishop's Hall, the second scene is in the Cathedral, on December 29th, 1170.

CHORUS. Does the bird sing in the South?
    Only the seabird cries, driven inland by the storm.
    What sign of the spring of the year?
    Only the death of the old: not a stir, not a shoot, not a breath.
    Do the days begin to lengthen?   5
    Longer and darker the day, shorter and colder the night.
    Still and stifling the air: but a wind is stored up in the East.
    The starved crow sits in the field, attentive; and in the wood
    The owl rehearses the hollow note of death.

What signs of a bitter spring?   10
The wind stored up in the East.
What, at the time of the birth of Our Lord, at Christmastide,
Is there not peace upon earth, good will among men?
The peace of this world is always uncertain, unless men keep the peace
    of God.
And war among men defiles this world, but death in the Lord renews it,   15
And the world must be cleaned in the winter, or we shall have only
A sour spring, a parched summer, an empty harvest.
Between Christmas and Easter what work shall be done?
The ploughman shall go out in March and turn the same earth
He has turned before, the bird shall sing the same song.   20
When the leaf is out on the tree, when the elder and may
Burst over the stream, and the air is clear and high,
And voices trill at windows, and children tumble in front of the door,
What work shall have been done, what wrong
Shall the bird's song cover, the green tree cover, what wrong   25
Shall the fresh earth cover? We wait, and the time is short
But waiting is long.

[*Enter the* FIRST PRIEST *with a banner of St. Stephen borne before him. The lines
sung are in italics.*]

FIRST PRIEST. Since Christmas a day: and the day of St. Stephen, First Martyr.
    Princes moreover did sit, and did witness falsely against me.
    A day that was always most dear to the Archbishop Thomas.   30
    And he kneeled down and cried with a loud voice:
    Lord, lay not this sin to their charge.
    Princes moreover did sit.

[*Introit* of St. Stephen is heard. Enter the* SECOND PRIEST, *with a banner of St.
John the Apostle borne before him.*]

SECOND PRIEST. Since St. Stephen a day: and the day of St. John the Apostle.
    In the midst of the congregation he opened his mouth.   35
    That which was from the beginning, which we have heard,
    Which we have seen with our eyes, and our hands have handled
    Of the word of life; that which we have seen and heard
    Declare we unto you.
    In the midst of the congregation.   40

[*Introit of St. John is heard. Enter the* THIRD PRIEST, *with a banner of the Holy
Innocents borne before him.*]

THIRD PRIEST. Since St. John the Apostle° a day: and the day of the Holy Inno-
    cents.°
    Out of the mouth of very babes, O God.
    As the voice of many waters, of thunder, of harps,
    They sung as it were a new song.

---

* **Introit:** part of the Mass.   41. **St. John the Apostle:** The commemoration of St. John is on December 27.   **day ... Innocents:** December 28, the commemoration of Herod's slaughter of the children.

The blood of thy saints have they shed like water,   45
And there was no man to bury them. Avenge, O Lord,
The blood of thy saints. In Rama,° a voice heard, weeping.
Out of the mouth of very babes, O God!

[*The* PRIESTS *stand together with the banners behind them.*]

FIRST PRIEST. Since the Holy Innocents a day: the fourth day from Christmas.

THE THREE PRIESTS. *Rejoice we all, keeping holy day.*   50

FIRST PRIEST. As for the people, so also for himself, he offereth for sins.
He lays down his life for the sheep.

THE THREE PRIESTS. *Rejoice we all, keeping holy day.*

FIRST PRIEST.   Today?

SECOND PRIEST. Today, what is today? For the day is half gone.

FIRST PRIEST. Today, what is today? But another day, the dusk of the year.   55

SECOND PRIEST. Today, what is today? Another night, and another dawn.

THIRD PRIEST. What day is the day that we know that we hope for or fear for?
Every day is the day we should fear from or hope from. One moment
Weighs like another. Only in retrospection, selection,
We say, that was the day. The critical moment   60
That is always now, and here. Even now, in sordid particulars
The eternal design may appear.

[*Enter the* FOUR KNIGHTS. *The banners disappear.*]

FIRST KNIGHT. Servants of the King.

FIRST PRIEST.   And known to us.
You are welcome. Have you ridden far?

FIRST KNIGHT. Not far today, but matters urgent   65
Have brought us from France. We rode hard,
Took ship yesterday, landed last night,
Having business with the Archbishop.

SECOND KNIGHT. Urgent business.

THIRD KNIGHT.   From the King.

SECOND KNIGHT. By the King's order.

FIRST KNIGHT.   Our men are outside.   70

FIRST PRIEST. You know the Archbishop's hospitality.
We are about to go to dinner.
The good Archbishop would be vexed
If we did not offer you entertainment
Before your business. Please dine with us.   75
Your men shall be looked after also.
Dinner before business. Do you like roast pork?

48. **Rama** (rä′mə): a Hindu deity.

FIRST KNIGHT. Business before dinner. We will roast your pork
    First, and dine upon it after.

SECOND KNIGHT. We must see the Archbishop.

THIRD KNIGHT.   Go, tell the Archbishop   80
    We have no need of his hospitality.
    We will find our own dinner.

FIRST PRIEST (to attendant). Go, tell His Lordship.

FOURTH KNIGHT.   How much longer will you keep us waiting?
                   [Enter THOMAS.]

THOMAS (to PRIESTS). However certain our expectation
    The moment foreseen may be unexpected   85
    When it arrives. It comes when we are
    Engrossed with matters of other urgency.
    On my table you will find
    The papers in order, and the documents signed.
    (To KNIGHTS) You are welcome, whatever your business may be.   90
    You say, from the King?

FIRST KNIGHT.   Most surely from the King.
    We must speak with you alone.

THOMAS (to PRIESTS).   Leave us then alone.
    Now what is the matter?

FIRST KNIGHT.   This is the matter.

THE THREE KNIGHTS. You are the Archbishop in revolt against the King; in
    rebellion to the King and the law of the land;
    You are the Archbishop who was made by the King; whom he set in your
    place to carry out his command.   95
    You are his servant, his tool, and his jack,°
    You wore his favors on your back,
    You had your honors all from his hand; from him you had the power, the
    seal and the ring.
    This is the man who was the tradesman's son: the backstairs brat who was
    born in Cheapside;°
    This is the creature that crawled upon the King; swollen with blood and
    swollen with pride.   100
    Creeping out of the London dirt,
    Crawling up like a louse on your shirt,
    The man who cheated, swindled, lied; broke his oath and betrayed his
    King.

THOMAS. This is not true.
    Both before and after I received the ring   105
    I have been a loyal subject to the King.
    Saving my order,° I am at his command,
    As his most faithful vassal in the land.

96. **jack:** a doer of odd jobs.   99. **Cheapside:** an unfashionable section of London.   107. **order:**
responsibilities as Archbishop.

FIRST KNIGHT. Saving your order! let your order save you—
    As I do not think it is like to do.
    Saving your ambition is what you mean,
    Saving your pride, envy and spleen.   110

SECOND KNIGHT. Saving your insolence and greed.
    Won't you ask us to pray to God for you, in your need?

THIRD KNIGHT. Yes, we'll pray for you!

FIRST KNIGHT.   Yes, we'll pray for you!   115

THE THREE KNIGHTS. Yes, we'll pray that God may help you!

THOMAS. But, gentlemen, your business
    Which you said so urgent, is it only
    Scolding and blaspheming?

FIRST KNIGHT.   That was only
    Our indignation, as loyal subjects.   120

THOMAS. Loyal? To whom?

FIRST KNIGHT.   To the King!

SECOND KNIGHT.   The King!

THIRD KNIGHT. The King!

THE THREE KNIGHTS.   God bless him!

THOMAS. Then let your new coat of loyalty be worn
    Carefully, so it get not soiled or torn.
    Have you something to say?

FIRST KNIGHT.   By the King's command.   125
    Shall we say it now?

SECOND KNIGHT.   Without delay,
    Before the old fox is off and away.

THOMAS.   What you have to say
    By the King's command—if it be the King's command—
    Should be said in public. If you make charges,
    Then in public I will refute them.

FIRST KNIGHT.   No! here and now!   130

[*They make to attack him, but the priests and attendants return and quietly interpose themselves.*]

THOMAS. Now and here!

FIRST KNIGHT. Of your earlier misdeeds I shall make no mention.
    They are too well known. But after dissension
    Had ended, in France, and you were endued
    With your former privilege, how did you show your gratitude? 135
    You had fled from England, not exiled
    Or threatened, mind you; but in the hope

Of stirring up trouble in the French dominions.
You sowed strife abroad, you reviled
The King to the King of France, to the Pope,   140
Raising up against him false opinions.

SECOND KNIGHT. Yet the King, out of his charity,
And urged by your friends, offered clemency,
Made a pact of peace, and all dispute ended
Sent you back to your See° as you demanded.   145

THIRD KNIGHT. And burying the memory of your transgressions
Restored your honors and your possessions.
All was granted for which you sued:
Yet how, I repeat, did you show your gratitude?

FIRST KNIGHT. Suspending those who had crowned the young prince,   150
Denying the legality of his coronation.

SECOND KNIGHT. Binding with the chains of anathema.

THIRD KNIGHT. Using every means in your power to evince°
The King's faithful servants, every one who transacts
His business in his absence, the business of the nation.   155

FIRST KNIGHT. These are the facts.
Say therefore if you will be content
To answer in the King's presence. Therefore were we sent.

THOMAS. Never was it my wish
To uncrown the King's son, or to diminish   160
His honor and power. Why should he wish
To deprive my people of me and keep me from my own
And bid me sit in Canterbury, alone?
I would wish him three crowns rather than one,
And as for the bishops, it is not my yoke   165
That is laid upon them, or mine to revoke.
Let them go to the Pope. It was he who condemned them.

FIRST KNIGHT. Through you they were suspended.

SECOND KNIGHT.   By you be this amended.

THIRD KNIGHT. Absolve them.

FIRST KNIGHT.   Absolve them.

THOMAS.   I do not deny
That this was done through me. But it is not I   170
Who can loose whom the Pope has bound.
Let them go to him, upon whom redounds
Their contempt toward me, their contempt toward the Church shown.

FIRST KNIGHT. Be that as it may, here is the King's command:
That you and your servants depart from this land.   175

---

145. **See:** local seat from which the bishop exercises authority.   153. **evince:** overcome, vanquish.

THOMAS. If that *is* the King's command, I will be bold
        To say: seven years were my people without
        My presence; seven years of misery and pain.
        Seven years a mendicant on foreign charity
        I lingered abroad: seven years is no brevity.   180
        I shall not get those seven years back again.
        Never again, you must make no doubt,
        Shall the sea run between the shepherd and his fold.

FIRST KNIGHT. The King's justice, the King's majesty,
        You insult with gross indignity;   185
        Insolent madman, whom nothing deters
        From attainting his servants and ministers.

THOMAS. It is not I who insult the King,
        And there is higher than I or the King.
        It is not I, Becket from Cheapside,   190
        It is not against me, Becket, that you strive.
        It is not Becket who pronounces doom,
        But the Law of Christ's Church, the judgment of Rome.

FIRST KNIGHT. Priest, you have spoken in peril of your life.

SECOND KNIGHT. Priest, you have spoken in danger of the knife.   195

THIRD KNIGHT. Priest, you have spoken treachery and treason.

THE THREE KNIGHTS. Priest! traitor, confirmed in malfeasance.

THOMAS. I submit my cause to the judgment of Rome.
        But if you kill me, I shall rise from my tomb
        To submit my cause before God's throne.   200

                        [*Exit.*]

FOURTH KNIGHT. Priest! monk! and servant! take, hold, detain,
        Restrain this man, in the King's name.

FIRST KNIGHT. Or answer with your bodies.

SECOND KNIGHT.   Enough of words.

THE FOUR KNIGHTS. We come for the King's justice, we come with swords.

                        [*Exeunt.*]

CHORUS. I have smelt them, the death-bringers, senses are quickened   205
        By subtile forebodings; I have heard
        Fluting in the nighttime, fluting and owls, have seen at noon
        Scaly wings slanting over, huge and ridiculous. I have tasted
        The savor of putrid flesh in the spoon. I have felt
        The heaving of earth at nightfall, restless, absurd. I have heard 210
        Laughter in the noises of beasts that make strange noises: jackal, jackass,
            jackdaw; the scurrying noise of mouse and jerboa;° the laugh of the loon,
            the lunatic bird. I have seen

        211. **jerboa:** rodents.

Gray necks twisting, rat tails twining, in the thick light of dawn. I have eaten
Smooth creatures still living, with the strong salt taste of living things under sea; I have tasted
The living lobster, the crab, the oyster, the whelk and the prawn;° and they live and spawn in my bowels, and my bowels dissolve in the light of dawn. I have smelt
Death in the rose, death in the hollyhock, sweet pea, hyacinth, primrose and cowslip. I have seen   215
Trunk and horn, tusk and hoof, in odd places;
I have lain on the floor of the sea and breathed with the breathing of the sea anemone, swallowed with ingurgitation of the sponge. I have lain in the soil and criticized the worm. In the air
Flirted with the passage of the kite, I have plunged with the kite and cowered with the wren. I have felt
The horn of the beetle, the scale of the viper, the mobile hard insensitive skin of the elephant, the evasive flank of the fish. I have smelt
Corruption in the dish, incense in the latrine, the sewer in the incense, the smell of sweet soap in the woodpath, a hellish sweet scent in the woodpath, while the ground heaved. I have seen   220
Rings of light coiling downward, descending
To the horror of the ape. Have I not known, not known
What was coming to be? It was here, in the kitchen, in the passage,
In the mews° in the barn in the byre° in the marketplace
In our veins our bowels our skulls as well   225
As well as in the plottings of potentates
As well as in the consultations of powers.
What is woven on the loom of fate
What is woven in the councils of princes
Is woven also in our veins, our brains,   230
Is woven like a pattern of living worms
In the guts of the women of Canterbury.

I have smelt them, the death-bringers; now is too late
For action, too soon for contrition.
Nothing is possible but the shamed swoon   235
Of those consenting to the last humiliation.
I have consented, Lord Archbishop, have consented.
Am torn away, subdued, violated,
United to the spiritual flesh of nature,
Mastered by the animal powers of spirit,   240
Dominated by the lust of self-demolition,
By the final utter uttermost death of spirit,
By the final ecstasy of waste and shame,
O Lord Archbishop, O Thomas Archbishop, forgive us, forgive us, pray for us that we may pray for you, out of our shame.

[*Enter* THOMAS.]

214. **whelk and prawn:** shellfish.   224. **mews** (my$\overline{oo}$z): stables.   **byre** (bīr): cow barn.

THOMAS. Peace, and be at peace with your thoughts and visions.   245
    These things had to come to you and you to accept them.
    This is your share of the eternal burden,
    The perpetual glory. This is one moment,
    But know that another
    Shall pierce you with a sudden painful joy   250
    When the figure of God's purpose is made complete.
    You shall forget these things, toiling in the household,
    You shall remember them, droning by the fire,
    When age and forgetfulness sweeten memory
    Only like a dream that has often been told   255
    And often been changed in the telling. They will seem unreal.
    Humankind cannot bear very much reality.

                        [*Enter* PRIESTS.]

PRIESTS (*severally*). My Lord, you must not stop here. To the minster.°
    Through the cloister.° No time to waste. They are coming back, armed.
        To the altar, to the altar.

THOMAS. All my life they have been coming, these feet. All my life   260
    I have waited. Death will come only when I am worthy,
    And if I am worthy, there is no danger.
    I have therefore only to make perfect my will.

PRIESTS. My Lord, they are coming. They will break through presently.
    You will be killed. Come to the altar.   265
    Make haste, my Lord. Don't stop here talking. It is not right.
    What shall become of us, my Lord, if you are killed; what shall become
        of us?

THOMAS. Peace! be quiet! remember where you are, and what is happening;
    No life here is sought for but mine,
    And I am not in danger: only near to death.   270

PRIESTS. My Lord, to vespers!° You must not be absent from vespers. You must
    not be absent from the divine office. To vespers. Into the cathedral!

THOMAS. Go to vespers, remember me at your prayers.
    They shall find the shepherd here; the flock shall be spared.
    I have had a tremor of bliss, a wink of heaven, a whisper,
    And I would no longer be denied; all things   275
    Proceed to a joyful consummation.

PRIESTS. Seize him! force him! drag him!

THOMAS. Keep your hands off!

PRIESTS. To vespers! Hurry.

[*They drag him off. While the* CHORUS *speak, the scene is changed to the
    cathedral.*]

———————————————————

258. **minster:** cathedral.   259. **cloister** (klois′tər): a covered walk along the inside walls of a church
courtyard.   271. **vespers:** late afternoon or evening worship service.

CHORUS *(while a* Dies Iræ* *is sung in Latin by a choir in the distance)*. Numb the
    hand and dry the eyelid,   280
    Still the horror, but more horror
    Than when tearing in the belly.

    Still the horror, but more horror
    Than when twisting in the fingers,
    Than when splitting in the skull.   285

    More than footfall in the passage,
    More than shadow in the doorway,
    More than fury in the hall.

    The agents of hell disappear, the human, they shrink and dissolve
    Into dust on the wind, forgotten, unmemorable; only is here   290
    The white flat face of Death, God's silent servant,
    And behind the face of Death the Judgment
    And behind the Judgment the Void, more horrid than active shapes of hell;
    Emptiness, absence, separation from God;
    The horror of the effortless journey, to the empty land   295
    Which is no land, only emptiness, absence, the Void,
    Where those who were men can no longer turn the mind
    To distraction, delusion, escape into dream, pretense,
    Where the soul is no longer deceived, for there are no objects, no tones,
    No colors, no forms to distract, to divert the soul   300
    From seeing itself, foully united forever, nothing with nothing,
    Not what we call death, but what beyond death is not death,
    We fear, we fear. Who shall then plead for me,
    Who intercede for me, in my most need?

* *Dies Iræ:* literally, Day of Wrath; a Latin hymn for Judgment Day, sung at requiem masses.

Dead upon the tree, my Savior,
Let not be in vain Thy labor;
Help me, Lord, in my last fear.

Dust I am, to dust am bending,
From the final doom impending
Help me, Lord, for death is near.

[*In the cathedral.* THOMAS *and* PRIESTS.]

PRIESTS. Bar the door. Bar the door.
    The door is barred.
    We are safe. We are safe.
    They dare not break in.
    They cannot break in. They have not the force.
    We are safe. We are safe.

THOMAS. Unbar the doors! throw open the doors!
    I will not have the house of prayer, the church of Christ,
    The sanctuary, turned into a fortress.
    The Church shall protect her own, in her own way, not
    As oak and stone; stone and oak decay,
    Give no stay, but the Church shall endure.
    The church shall be open, even to our enemies. Open the door!

PRIEST. My Lord! these are not men, these come not as men come, but
    Like maddened beasts. They come not like men, who
    Respect the sanctuary, who kneel to the Body of Christ,
    But like beasts. You would bar the door
    Against the lion, the leopard, the wolf or the boar,
    Why not more
    Against beasts with the souls of damned men, against men
    Who would damn themselves to beasts. My Lord! My Lord!

THOMAS. You think me reckless, desperate and mad.
    You argue by results, as this world does,
    To settle if an act be good or bad.
    You defer to the fact. For every life and every act
    Consequence of good and evil can be shown.
    And as in time results of many deeds are blended
    So good and evil in the end become confounded.
    It is not in time that my death shall be known;
    It is out of time that my decision is taken
    If you call that decision
    To which my whole being gives entire consent.
    I give my life
    To the Law of God above the Law of Man.
    Unbar the door! unbar the door!
    We are not here to triumph by fighting, by stratagem, or by resistance,
    Not to fight with beasts as men. We have fought the beast
    And have conquered. We have only to conquer
    Now, by suffering. This is the easier victory.
    Now is the triumph of the Cross, now
    Open the door! I command it. OPEN THE DOOR!

[*The door is opened. The* KNIGHTS *enter, slightly tipsy.*]

PRIESTS. This way, my Lord! Quick. Up the stair. To the roof. To the crypt.
Quick. Come. Force him.

KNIGHTS.　　　Where is Becket, the traitor to the King?
　　　　　　　Where is Becket, the meddling priest?　　　　　　　355
　　　Come down Daniel° to the lions' den,
　　　　　Come down Daniel for the mark of the beast.

　　　Are you washed in the blood of the Lamb?
　　　　Are you marked with the mark of the beast?
　　　Come down Daniel to the lions' den,　　　　　　　　　　360
　　　　Come down Daniel and join in the feast.

　　　Where is Becket the Cheapside brat?
　　　　Where is Becket the faithless priest?
　　　Come down Daniel to the lions' den,
　　　　Come down Daniel and join in the feast.　　　　　　365

THOMAS. It is the just man who
Like a bold lion, should be without fear.
I am here.
No traitor to the King. I am a priest,
A Christian, saved by the blood of Christ,　　　　　　370
Ready to suffer with my blood.
This is the sign of the Church always,
The sign of blood. Blood for blood.
His blood given to buy my life,
My blood given to pay for His death,　　　　　　375
My death for His death.

FIRST KNIGHT. Absolve all those you have excommunicated.

SECOND KNIGHT. Resign the powers you have arrogated.

THIRD KNIGHT. Restore to the King the money you appropriated.

FIRST KNIGHT. Renew the obedience you have violated.　　　　　380

THOMAS. For my Lord I am now ready to die,
That His Church may have peace and liberty.
Do with me as you will, to your hurt and shame;
But none of my people, in God's name,
Whether layman or clerk, shall you touch.　　　　　385
This I forbid.

KNIGHTS. Traitor! traitor! traitor!

THOMAS. You, Reginald, three times traitor you:
Traitor to me as my temporal vassal,
Traitor to me as your spiritual lord,　　　　　　390
Traitor to God in desecrating His Church.

FIRST KNIGHT. No faith do I owe to a renegade,
And what I owe shall now be paid.

---

356. **Daniel:** a Hebrew prophet who was thrown into a den of lions by his Babylonian captors for
not obeying an official decree.

THOMAS. Now to Almighty God, to the Blessed Mary ever Virgin, to the blessed John the Baptist, the holy apostles Peter and Paul, to the blessed 395 martyr Denys, and to all the Saints, I commend my cause and that of the Church.

[*While the* KNIGHTS *kill him, we hear the* CHORUS.]

Clear the air! clean the sky! wash the wind! take stone from stone and wash them.

The land is foul, the water is foul, our beasts and ourselves defiled with blood.

A rain of blood has blinded my eyes. Where is England? Where is Kent? Where is Canterbury? 400

O far far far far in the past; and I wander in a land of barren boughs: if I break them, they bleed; I wander in a land of dry stones: if I touch them they bleed.

How how can I ever return, to the soft quiet seasons?

Night stay with us, stop sun, hold season, let the day not come, let the spring not come.

Can I look again at the day and its common things, and see them all smeared with blood, through a curtain of falling blood?

We did not wish anything to happen. 405
We understood the private catastrophe,
The personal loss, the general misery,
Living and partly living;
The terror by night that ends in daily action,
The terror by day that ends in sleep; 410
But the talk in the marketplace, the hand on the broom,
The nighttime heaping of the ashes,
The fuel laid on the fire at daybreak,
These acts marked a limit to our suffering.
Every horror had its definition, 415
Every sorrow had a kind of end:
In life there is not time to grieve long.
But this, this is out of life, this is out of time,
An instant eternity of evil and wrong.
We are soiled by a filth that we cannot clean, united to supernatural vermin, 420

It is not we alone, it is not the house, it is not the city that is defiled,
But the world that is wholly foul.
Clear the air! clean the sky! wash the wind! take the stone from the
stone, take the skin from the arm, take the muscle from the bone, and
wash them. Wash the stone, wash the bone, wash the brain, wash the
soul, wash them wash them!

[*The* KNIGHTS, *having completed the murder, advance to the front of the stage
and address the audience.*]

FIRST KNIGHT. We beg you to give us your attention for a few moments. We
know that you may be disposed to judge unfavorably of our action.   425
You are Englishmen, and therefore you believe in fair play: and when
you see one man being set upon by four, then your sympathies are all
with the underdog. I respect such feelings, I share them. Nevertheless,
I appeal to your sense of honor. You are Englishmen, and therefore will
not judge anybody without hearing both sides of the case. That is in   430
accordance with our long-established principle of Trial by Jury. I am not
myself qualified to put our case to you. I am a man of action and not of
words. For that reason I shall do no more than introduce the other
speakers, who, with their various abilities, and different points of view,
will be able to lay before you the merits of this extremely complex   435
problem. I shall call upon our eldest member to speak first, my neighbor
in the country: Baron William de Traci.

THIRD KNIGHT. I am afraid I am not anything like such an experienced speaker
as my old friend Reginald Fitz Urse would lead you to believe. But there
is one thing I should like to say, and I might as well say it at once. It   440
is this: in what we have done, and whatever you may think of it, we have
been perfectly disinterested. *(The other* KNIGHTS: "Hear! hear!") *We* are
not getting anything out of this. We have much more to lose than to gain.
We are four plain Englishmen who put our country first. I dare say that
we didn't make a very good impression when we came in just now.   445
The fact is that we knew we had taken on a pretty stiff job; I'll only speak
for myself, but I had drunk a good deal—I am not a drinking man ordinarily—to brace myself up for it. When you come to the point, it does go
against the grain to kill an Archbishop, especially when you have been
brought up in good Church traditions. So if we seemed a bit rowdy,   450
you will understand why it was; and for my part I am awfully sorry about
it. We realized this was our duty, but all the same we had to work ourselves up to it. And, as I said, *we* are not getting a penny out of this. We
know perfectly well how things will turn out. King Henry—God bless
him—will have to say, for reasons of state, that he never meant this   455
to happen; and there is going to be an awful row; and at the best we shall
have to spend the rest of our lives abroad. And even when reasonable
people come to see that the Archbishop *had* to be put out of the way—
and personally I had a tremendous admiration for him—you must have
noticed what a good show he put up at the end—they won't give *us*   460
any glory. No, we have done for ourselves, there's no mistake about that.
So, as I said at the beginning, please give us at least the credit for being
completely disinterested in this business. I think that is about all I have
to say.

FIRST KNIGHT. I think we will all agree that William de Traci has spoken 465
well and has made a very important point. The gist of his argument is this:
that we have been completely disinterested. But our act itself needs more
justification than that; and you must hear our other speakers. I shall
next call upon Hugh de Morville, who has made a special study of state-
craft and constitutional law. Sir Hugh de Morville. 470

SECOND KNIGHT. I should like first to recur to a point that was very well put by
our leader, Reginald Fitz Urse: that you are Englishmen, and therefore
your sympathies are always with the underdog. It is the English spirit of
fair play. Now the worthy Archbishop, whose good qualities I very much
admired, has throughout been presented as the underdog. But is this 475
really the case? I am going to appeal not to your emotions but to your
reason. You are hardheaded sensible people, as I can see, and not to be
taken in by emotional clap-trap. I therefore ask you to consider soberly:
what were the Archbishop's aims? And what are King Henry's aims?
In the answer to these questions lies the key to the problem. 480
  The King's aim has been perfectly consistent. During the reign of the
late Queen Matilda and the irruption of the unhappy usurper Stephen,°
the kingdom was very much divided. Our King saw that the one thing
needful was to restore order: to curb the excessive powers of local government, which were usually exercised for selfish and often for sedi- 485
tious ends, and to reform the legal system. He therefore intended that
Becket, who had proved himself an extremely able administrator—no
one denies that—should unite the offices of Chancellor and Archbishop.
Had Becket concurred with the King's wishes, we should have had an
almost ideal State: a union of spiritual and temporal administration, 490
under the central government. I knew Becket well, in various official relations; and I may say that I have never known a man so well qualified
for the highest rank of the Civil Service. And what happened? The moment that Becket, at the King's instance, had been made Archbishop, he
resigned the office of Chancellor, he became more priestly than the 495
priests, he ostentatiously and offensively adopted an ascetic manner of
life, he affirmed immediately that there was a higher order than that which
our King, and he as the King's servant, had for so many years striven to
establish; and that—God knows why—the two orders were incompatible.
  You will agree with me that such interference by an Archbishop 500
offends the instincts of a people like ours. So far, I know that I have your
approval: I read it in your faces. It is only with the measures we have
had to adopt, in order to set matters to rights, that you take issue. No one
regrets the necessity for violence more than we do. Unhappily, there are
times when violence is the only way in which social justice can be 505
secured. At another time, you would condemn an Archbishop by vote of
Parliament and execute him formally as a traitor, and no one would have
to bear the burden of being called murderer. And at a later time still, even
such temperate measures as these would become unnecessary. But, if
you have now arrived at a just subordination of the pretensions of 510
the Church to the welfare of the State, remember that it is we who took

<hr />

482. **Matilda . . . Stephen:** Matilda was the daughter of Henry I and mother of Henry II. After her
father's death, she fought her cousin, Stephen of Blois, for the succession to the throne.

the first step. We have been instrumental in bringing about the state of affairs that you approve. We have served your interests; we merit your applause; and if there is any guilt whatever in the matter, you must share it with us.   515

FIRST KNIGHT. Morville has given us a great deal to think about. It seems to me that he has said almost the last word, for those who have been able to follow his very subtle reasoning. We have, however, one more speaker, who has I think another point of view to express. If there are any who are still unconvinced, I think that Richard Brito, coming as he does of a fam-   520 ily distinguished for its loyalty to the Church, will be able to convince them. Richard Brito.

FOURTH KNIGHT. The speakers who have preceded me, to say nothing of our leader, Reginald Fitz Urse, have all spoken very much to the point. I have nothing to add along their particular lines of argument. What I have   525 to say may be put in the form of a question: *Who killed the Archbishop?* As you have been eyewitnesses of this lamentable scene, you may feel some surprise at my putting it in this way. But consider the course of events. I am obliged, very briefly, to go over the ground traversed by the last speaker. While the late Archbishop was Chancellor, no one,   530 under the King, did more to weld the country together, to give it the unity, the stability, order, tranquillity, and justice that it so badly needed. From the moment he became Archbishop, he completely reversed his policy; he showed himself to be utterly indifferent to the fate of the country, to be, in fact, a monster of egotism. This egotism grew upon him,   535 until it became at last an undoubted mania. I have unimpeachable evidence to the effect that before he left France he clearly prophesied, in the presence of numerous witnesses, that he had not long to live, and that he would be killed in England. He used every means of provocation; from his conduct, step by step, there can be no inference except that   540 he had determined upon a death by martyrdom. Even at the last, he could have given us reason: you have seen how he evaded our questions. And when he had deliberately exasperated us beyond human endurance, he could still have easily escaped; he could have kept himself from us long enough to allow our righteous anger to cool. That was just what he   545 did not wish to happen; he insisted, while we were still inflamed with wrath, that the doors should be opened. Need I say more? I think, with these facts before you, you will unhesitatingly render a verdict of Suicide while of Unsound Mind. It is the only charitable verdict you can give, upon one who was, after all, a great man.   550

FIRST KNIGHT. Thank you, Brito, I think that there is no more to be said; and I suggest that you now disperse quietly to your homes. Please be careful not to loiter in groups at street corners, and do nothing that might provoke any public outbreak.

[*Exeunt* KNIGHTS.]

FIRST PRIEST. O father, father, gone from us, lost to us,   555
How shall we find you, from what far place
Do you look down on us? You now in Heaven,
Who shall now guide us, protect us, direct us?

After what journey through what further dread
Shall we recover your presence? When inherit 560
Your strength? The Church lies bereft,
Alone, desecrated, desolated, and the heathen shall build on the ruins,
Their world without God. I see it. I see it.

THIRD PRIEST. No. For the Church is stronger for this action,
Triumphant in adversity. It is fortified 565
By persecution: supreme, so long as men will die for it.
Go, weak sad men, lost erring souls, homeless in earth or heaven.
Go where the sunset reddens the last gray rock
Of Brittany,° or the Gates of Hercules.
Go venture shipwreck on the sullen coasts 570
Where blackamoors make captive Christian men;
Go to the northern seas confined with ice
Where the dead breath makes numb the hand, makes dull the brain;
Find an oasis in the desert sun,
Go seek alliance with the heathen Saracen,° 575
To share his filthy rites, and try to snatch
Forgetfulness in his libidinous courts,
Oblivion in the fountain by the date tree;
Or sit and bite your nails in Aquitaine.°
In the small circle of pain within the skull 580
You still shall tramp and tread one endless round
Of thought, to justify your action to yourselves,
Weaving a fiction which unravels as you weave,
Pacing forever in the hell of make-believe
Which never is belief: this is your fate on earth 585
And we must think no further of you.

FIRST PRIEST.   O my lord
The glory of whose new state is hidden from us,
Pray for us of your charity.

SECOND PRIEST.   Now in the sight of God
Conjoined with all the saints and martyrs gone before you,
Remember us.

THIRD PRIEST.   Let our thanks ascend
To God, who has given us another Saint in Canterbury. 590

CHORUS (while a Te Deum* is sung in Latin by a choir in the distance). We
praise Thee, O God, for Thy glory displayed in all the creatures of
the earth,
In the snow, in the rain, in the wind, in the storm; in all of Thy creatures,
both the hunters and the hunted.
For all things exist only as seen by Thee, only as known by Thee, all things
exist

569. **Brittany:** an old French province on the English Channel.   575. **Saracen:** Moslem.
579. **Aquitaine** (ak´wə·tān´): a region of southwest France.   * **Te Deum:** a Latin hymn of praise to
God.

Only in Thy light, and Thy glory is declared even in that which denies
Thee; the darkness declares the glory of light.   595
Those who deny Thee could not deny, if Thou didst not exist; and their
denial is never complete, for if it were so, they would not exist.
They affirm Thee in living; all things affirm Thee in living; the bird in the
air, both the hawk and the finch; the beast on the earth, both the wolf and
the lamb; the worm in the soil and the worm in the belly.
Therefore man, whom Thou hast made to be conscious of Thee, must
consciously praise Thee, in thought and in word and in deed.
Even with the hand to the broom, the back bent in laying the fire, the knee
bent in cleaning the hearth, we, the scrubbers and sweepers of Canter-
bury,
The back bent under toil, the knee bent under sin, the hands to the face
under fear, the head bent under grief,   600
Even in us the voices of seasons, the snuffle of winter, the song of spring,
the drone of summer, the voices of beasts and of birds, praise Thee.
We thank Thee for Thy mercies of blood, for Thy redemption by blood.
For the blood of Thy martyrs and saints
Shall enrich the earth, shall create the holy places.
For wherever a saint has dwelt, wherever a martyr has given his blood for
the blood of Christ,
There is holy ground, and the sanctity shall not depart from it   605
Though armies trample over it, though sightseers come with guidebooks
looking over it;
From where the western seas gnaw at the coast of Iona,°
To the death in the desert, the prayer in forgotten places by the broken
imperial column,
From such ground springs that which forever renews the earth
Though it is forever denied. Therefore, O God, we thank Thee   610
Who hast given such blessing to Canterbury.

Forgive us, O Lord, we acknowledge ourselves as type of the common
man,
Of the men and women who shut the door and sit by the fire;
Who fear the blessing of God, the loneliness of the night of God, the sur-
render required, the deprivation inflicted;
Who fear the injustice of men less than the justice of God;   615
Who fear the hand at the window, the fire in the thatch, the fist in the
tavern, the push into the canal,
Less than we fear the love of God.
We acknowledge our trespass, our weakness, our fault; we acknowl-
edge
That the sin of the world is upon our heads; that the blood of the martyrs
and the agony of the saints
Is upon our heads.   620
Lord, have mercy upon us.
Christ, have mercy upon us.
Lord, have mercy upon us.
Blessed Thomas pray for us.

607. **Iona** (ī·ō·nə): a small island of the Inner Hebrides, Scotland.

COMMENTARY

Some readers and audiences have found Thomas's speech (lines 663–705) at the end of Part I rather puzzling and unsatisfying. They have felt that the speech was not a clear statement of the Archbishop's position and intentions, that it left them bewildered and uncertain of what Thomas would do and why. This speech is a greatly condensed account of the progress of Thomas's soul from delight in temporal pleasures, to delight in power, to disillusionment with temporal things, to a transcendence of time—a moment of insight into the level of timelessness and a consequent surrender to God's will. At the end of the speech, Thomas appears to step out of the twelfth century and address a modern audience directly: "I know/ What yet remains to show you of my history/ Will seem to most of you at best futility,/ Senseless self-slaughter of a lunatic,/ Arrogant passion of a fanatic." The remainder of the play is designed to show that Thomas's martyrdom is not the "senseless self-slaughter of a lunatic" and to confront modern audiences and readers with the issues raised by martyrdom.

The Interlude, Thomas's Christmas sermon, helps to clarify his position. As you noticed, the sermon is written in prose rather than verse. Eliot did not wish his audience to respond to the sermon as a poetic speech. "A sermon cast in verse is too unusual an experience for even the most regular churchgoer: nobody would have responded to it as a sermon at all."

The sermon begins with a reminder of the meaning of Christmas as a day both of rejoicing and of mourning, for it is "at this same time of all the year that we celebrate at once the Birth of Our Lord and His Passion and Death upon the Cross." The paradox of joy and mourning at the same time is examined in a discussion of the meaning of peace and the meaning of martyrdom. "Does it seem strange to you," Thomas asks, "that the angels should have announced Peace, when ceaselessly the world has been stricken with War and the fear of War?" The peace which Christ spoke of was not "peace as the world gives," but a release from the world. The death of a martyr is similarly an occasion for mourning and rejoicing. "Just as we rejoice and mourn at once, in the Birth and in the Passion of our Lord; so also, in a smaller figure, we both rejoice and mourn in the death of martyrs. We mourn, for the sins of the world that has martyred them; we rejoice, that another soul is numbered among the Saints in Heaven, for the glory of God and for the salvation of men."

Thomas goes on to clarify his insight into the meaning of martyrdom. "A martyrdom is always the design of God, for His love of men . . . It is never the design of man; for the true martyr is he who has become the instrument of God, who has lost his will in the will of God, and who no longer desires anything for himself, not even the glory of being a martyr." Part II, which follows the sermon, is an exemplification of Thomas's words.

Both the sermon and Part II emphasize the ritualistic quality of the play. A sermon is, of course, part of a religious service. After a troubled speech by the chorus, Part II goes on to speeches by the priests which mark the passage of four days following Christmas Day. After each of the first two speeches, parts of the Mass are inserted, and the whole episode is very much like part of a religious service. The priests are uncertain "what is today." It is, of course, the day of St. Thomas à Becket, the martyr-to-be.

When the knights enter, they accuse Thomas of trying to undermine the king. Thomas answers that he never desired "to diminish/ His honor and power" (lines 160–61) but wishes instead to uphold one "higher than I or the King" (line 189). Later (lines 339–44) he states once more the meaning of his fate:

"It is not in time that my death shall be known;

It is out of time that my decision is
    taken
If you call that decision
To which my whole being gives entire
    consent.
I give my life
To the Law of God above the Law of
    Man."

After the murder of Thomas, which is
enacted ritualistically while the chorus
chants a speech, the knights step forward
and address the audience. Their speeches
are unlike anything that has come before.
During this part of the play, some spectators usually gape in bewilderment,
some giggle uneasily, some stiffen with
tension, but all are surprised by the sudden change in tone. In explaining this
change, Eliot has said: "And in the
speeches of the knights, who are quite
aware that they are addressing an audience of people living eight hundred years
after they themselves are dead, the use of
platform prose [in the style of English
political speeches] is intended of course
to have a special effect: to shock the audience out of their complacency." If the
arguments of the knights seem reasonable
to the audience, then there comes the
shocking realization that the modern
world might have dealt with Becket exactly as did the twelfth century, and that
the issue of temporal power versus spiritual authority is still alive. The final request made by the first knight is one that
the police today might make to a restless mob: "Please be careful not to loiter
in groups at street corners, and do nothing
that might provoke any public outbreak."
It remains for the third priest to sum up
the meaning of Thomas's death:

". . . For the Church is stronger for this
    action,
Triumphant in adversity. It is fortified
By persecution: supreme, so long as
    men will die for it."

But his is not the last word. Always there
are the people, represented by the chorus,
who for the moment have been buoyed
up by the martyrdom, this sign of God's
glory. They must make the inevitable return to the temporal level, the round of
daily and seasonal and yearly events, but
they will remember the extraordinary
event that they have been privileged to
witness and they will make Canterbury
Cathedral a memorial and shrine to that
event. They cannot hope to be lifted now
to the level of timelessness, as Thomas
was, but they are not without hope. They
can pray that God's grace and mercy will
come to them, and that Thomas, their
special saint, will intercede on their behalf.

"Lord, have mercy upon us.
    Christ, have mercy upon us.
    Lord, have mercy upon us.
    Blessed Thomas, pray for us."

Thus this play, written to be performed
in a cathedral and to awaken its audience
to the possibility of an existence beyond
time, and of a loyalty above loyalty to a
nation, ends with a prayer.

FOR STUDY AND DISCUSSION

1. What is the function of the Interlude?
Why is it an appropriate and relevant link between Parts I and II?
2. Thomas says, "Humankind cannot bear
very much reality" (line 257), a line Eliot also
uses in his poem "Burnt Norton." What do
Thomas and Eliot mean by "reality"?
3. E. Martin Browne, who first produced
the play, has written that the chorus "is the
most important single factor in the success of
the play from the author's point of view, and
the most difficult." He refers to the difficulty of
having a group of women speak their lines convincingly in unison and also of the great range
of emotion which the chorus must express.
Cite examples from the play that support or
contradict Mr. Browne's comments.
4. Robert Speaight, who portrayed Becket
at the play's first performances and on many
occasions thereafter, has written of the difficulty of acting the role of Becket in Part I. The
difficulty, he feels, lies in the fact that the
Archbishop seems a stiff and distant figure. In
the sermon, however, Becket, according to
Speaight, becomes "human and approach-
able." Do you agree or disagree? Why?

5. In many productions of *Murder in the Cathedral,* and in accordance with Eliot's intentions, the actors who portray the four tempters also portray the four knights. Do you think this doubling of roles is merely a convenience to avoid the necessity of hiring more actors, or do you think that it adds meaning to the major conflict of the play? Explain.

6. In your opinion, in Part II do the priests remain rather vague figures, as they were in Part I, or do they acquire some individuality? Give examples from the play to support your answer.

7. Does Thomas martyr himself in vain? Explain your answer with specific reference to the final speeches of the priests and the chorus.

8. In addition to an elaborate use of imagery, Eliot relies heavily on metaphor and symbolism to convey his message. Point out the most effective metaphors and explain the specific contribution of each to the play's development. Which symbols recur? How are they used?

9. George Hoellering, the film producer who made the movie version of *Murder in the Cathedral,* asked the author to read through the entire play in a recording studio, so that the actors in the film could use the recording as a guide. As Mr. Hoellering writes, "When toward the end of the play, we came to the speeches in which the . . . knights justify themselves before the crowd, the sound recordist suddenly turned round to Mr. Eliot and, completely forgetting his control switches, said excitedly, 'Aren't they right, sir? What do you think?' Mr. Eliot, needless to say, was highly amused." Do you think that the sound engineer's reaction was a natural one? Why or why not? Do you think Eliot may have intended the speeches to have this effect on some members of the audience? Are the speeches plausible? Are they convincing? Explain. What in the play counterbalances them?

10. Mr. Browne, an experienced theatrical producer, has commented that *Murder in the Cathedral* "is one of the few dramas which have universal validity; it affects an audience in the same way whether in church or theater, village schoolroom or air-raid shelter. . . . Experience shows that this play can always make its impact unless the producer gets in the way." Do you agree or disagree? Give reasons to support your answer. How might a producer get in the way of the play's effectiveness?

11. In writing this play, one of Eliot's intentions was to reestablish the importance of poetic drama. Do you think that he succeeded in demonstrating that poetry is necessary for certain plays, or might *Murder in the Cathedral* have just as well been written in prose? Explain.

12. According to Ashley Dukes, who produced the first London production of *Murder in the Cathedral,* Eliot called the first draft of the play "Fear in the Way." This title is taken from Ecclesiastes 12:5. "Also when they shall be afraid of that which is high, and fears shall be in the way, and the almond tree shall flourish, and the grasshopper shall be a burden, and desire shall fail: because man goeth to his long home, and the mourners go about the streets." This Biblical passage is obviously appropriate to the play because of its concern with death and mourning. However, can you show any deeper relationship between "and fears shall be in the way" and the theme of the play? Cite lines from the play that support your answer.

FOR COMPOSITION

1. Eliot obviously intended his play to have a universal significance and to apply as much to the problems of modern times as to the problems of the twelfth century. Write a composition in which you discuss the extent to which, in your opinion, *Murder in the Cathedral* is relevant to modern problems. What comments might the play lead you to make about totalitarian societies, democratic societies, the rights of the individual, and the position of the Church in the contemporary world?

2. Shakespeare's *Macbeth* and Eliot's *Murder in the Cathedral* are both concerned with the human struggle between love of power and a sense of moral responsibility. Write a composition in which you compare the two treatments of this struggle in its initial stages, development, culmination, and outcome.

3. Write a composition in which you make a detailed examination of the role of the chorus. Show the range of emotions the chorus must express in a variety of kinds of verse. Consider the following questions: To what extent does a reader or an audience identify with the chorus? To what extent does the chorus embody a view of the common people of any country or of humanity in general? Do you agree or disagree with this point of view? Why?

CONTEMPORARY BRITISH WRITING

In contemporary Britain a surprising amount of poetry is being written, far more than is being published. And—this is an excellent development—much of it is being read in public, both on radio and in recitals. Since the death of T. S. Eliot, the poetry most in demand at bookshops has been that of John Betjeman (1906–   ), whose wry nostalgia has a wide appeal, and of course Dylan Thomas (1914–1953), a powerful but isolated figure without much influence on younger poets. Of the older poets still living, Robert Graves is probably the most securely established, and any new poems of his quickly find their way into periodicals. For the next generation of Oxford contemporaries, the deaths of Louis MacNeice (1907–1963) and C. Day Lewis (1904–1972) were great losses, especially as Stephen Spender (1909–   ) is now less active as a poet. Among the best poets on the contemporary scene are Basil Bunting, Charles Causley, Donald Davie, Thom Gunn, Ted Hughes, George MacBeth, R. S. Thomas, and the Irish poets Patrick Kavanagh and Thomas Kinsella. Philip Larkin (1922–   ) is a genuine original poet, deceptively quiet and everyday in subject and manner. John Wain (1925–   ) is also a genuine poet. Finally, as part of the so-called "explosion" in working-class culture, much rough-and-ready verse is being produced, often to be recited in jazz clubs or taverns. It is not poetry, but a poet may come out of it.

Contemporary British fiction, on a serious level, is nearly always well-written, sharply observed, and entertaining, but it lacks both breadth and force and is too often slackly constructed. The death of Evelyn Waugh (1903–1966) was a loss, although most good judges consider his earliest work his best. Graham Greene keeps his hold on reviewers and readers, though his recent writing seems rather tired. And for several good reasons, both C. P. Snow and his wife, Pamela Hansford Johnson, now attract more attention outside the realm of fiction, though their novels are widely read. Some original novelists neither seek nor find a large public but are the subject of an enthusiastic cult, and of these Anthony Powell, William Golding, and Muriel Spark are excellent examples. Angus Wilson, like Waugh and Powell, is a sharp satirist of manners and morals. Iris Murdoch keeps up a steady flow and is always exciting to read—if at times too fantastic to be convincing. Writers who came crashing into the 1950's with immediate successes—notably Kingsley Amis with *Lucky Jim,* John Wain with *Hurry On Down,* and John Braine with *Room at the Top*—have not continued writing with their original flair. Among newer novelists to look out for are Alan Sillitoe and Stan Barstow, who really understand the contemporary industrial society they describe, and Thomas Hinde and John Fowles, who can be both dramatic and deeply symbolic.

The theater in Britain is in a curious position today. While it is supposed to be enjoying a wonderful "renaissance," it is in fact, like the theater elsewhere, suffering from a rapid decline in public patronage and esteem. There is too wide a gap between ordinary and fairly intelligent playgoers and the avant-garde writers and critics. And too many new plays, though they are not without merit, are not theatrically effective. Of the genuinely talented figures of this dubious "renaissance"—playwrights who established reputations in the 1950's—the following may serve as a summary. John Osborne, original and finely eloquent, still suffers from an inability to create drama out of a group of characters: his plays tend to be dramatic monologues. John Arden has great talent, but seems too eccentric in his choice of themes and backgrounds. Arnold Wesker now devotes more of his time and attention to popularizing the arts than to writing plays. Of this generation of dramatists, the most technically efficient and theatrically effective is Harold Pinter, who, if less enigmatic, would be a very fine dramatist indeed. Among the newer playwrights, the following should be noted: Ann Jellicoe, a genuine original and experimenter; Henry Livings, a provincial working-class humorist; David Rudkin, a symbolist with a genuine sense of drama; Alun Owen, highly and deservedly successful on television; Charles Wood, David Turner, Edward Bond, David Campton, satirists who range from the wildly "absurd" to naturalistic studies of provincial society. It is true of almost all the playwrights mentioned here that for one reason or other they are too apt to wander away from the theater to work in films or television. A notable example of this is Robert Bolt, who was tempted away from the theater after the great success of his *A Man for All Seasons*. The trouble possibly is that, although the Arts Council heavily subsidizes fine repertory companies—like the National Theater, the Royal Shakespeare, the Royal Court, and a few provincial companies—the general theatrical activity of the country is far narrower than it used to be, fewer good plays can be seen on tour, and the attempt to turn the young into regular playgoers has so far not succeeded. We can blame television or films or pop music and dancing, but writers and directors and critics must accept some responsibility. The young will still flock to see Shakespeare.

J.B.P.

GEORGE ORWELL
(1903–1950)

George Orwell was a writer who disliked frills, both in life and in art. Pursuing his own brand of integrity, he liked ugly rather than beautiful rooms, worn clothes rather than new ones, and abrupt rather than ingratiating personalities. As a writer he cultivated a beautifully clear prose style and strove to cut out "all stale or mixed images, all prefabricated phrases, needless repetitions, and humbug and vagueness generally." He believed that a muddled style could lead to vague thinking and that precision in both thought and writing was one of the chief defenses against political tyranny. As a writer, his chief concern was to warn against such tyranny. His two most famous books, *Animal Farm* and *Nineteen Eighty-Four,* are both reminders that no country's liberty is ever completely secure. *Animal Farm,* a brilliant fable, traces the downward path of a revolution of animals from the initial decree that "All animals are equal" to the revised version, "All animals are equal, but some are more equal than others." *Nineteen Eighty-Four* is a stern warning, a nightmarish tale of a future in which freedom has lost its meaning. Orwell was a liberal in the British sense, a firm believer in freedom and a hater of tyranny from both right and left. Despite his blunt, sometimes rude manner, he was at heart a most kindly man whose main preoccupation was to save modern civilization from the results of its own follies.

"George Orwell" was the pseudonym adopted by Eric Blair. Born in India, he was sent to boarding school in England at an early age and completed his formal education at Eton. His service with the Imperial Police in Burma led not only to his essay "Shooting an Elephant" but also to a novel, *Burmese Days.* Orwell was born into "the lower upper-middle-class," the term he used to characterize people with upper-middle-class pretensions who lacked the money to live up to these pretensions. As Orwell wrote, "Theoretically you knew how to wear your clothes and how to order a good dinner, although in practice you could never afford to go to a decent tailor or a decent restaurant." Very early and in part because of his Burmese experiences, he turned against the attitudes of mind which might have been expected of him. He chose poverty, a working-class background, and anonymity in preference to the conventional career which a young man of his gifts might have followed. The choice was not easy. Not only did the workers not feel him one of them, but Orwell never fitted into any other level of society. He himself rather humorlessly adopted a degree of protective coloring without being able to hide from himself that he remained an eccentric individual at heart.

In 1936, Orwell was wounded after fighting on the Loyalist side in the Spanish Civil War. He described his war experiences in one of his books, *Homage to Catalonia*. From the middle 1930's on, he constantly wrote novels and essays until ill health undermined him. He became famous only in the 1940's after *Animal Farm* and *Nineteen Eighty-Four*, his greatest success, were published. At the very end of his life he married. Through the kindness of friends he was given a home in the western islands of Scotland to fight the lung illness which finally killed him at the age of forty-six.

Shooting an Elephant

IN MOULMEIN, in lower Burma, I was hated by large numbers of people—the only time in my life that I have been important enough for this to happen to me. I was subdivisional police officer of the town, and in an aimless, petty kind of way an anti-European feeling was very bitter. No one had the guts to raise a riot, but if a European woman went through the bazaars alone somebody would probably spit betel juice over her dress. As a police officer I was an obvious target and was baited whenever it seemed safe to do so. When a nimble Burman tripped me up on the football field and the referee (another Burman) looked the other way, the crowd yelled with hideous laughter. This happened more than once. In the end the sneering yellow faces of young men that met me everywhere, the insults hooted after me when I was at a safe distance, got badly on my nerves. The young Buddhist priests were the worst of all. There were several thousands of them in the town and none of them seemed to have anything to do except stand on street corners and jeer at Europeans.

All this was perplexing and upsetting. For at that time I had already made up my mind that imperialism was an evil thing and the sooner I chucked up my job and got out of it the better. Theoretically—and secretly, of course—I was all for the Burmese and all against their oppressors, the British. As for the job I was doing, I hated it more bitterly than I can perhaps make clear. In a job like that you see the dirty work of Empire at close quarters. The wretched prisoners huddling in the stinking cages of the lock-ups, the gray, cowed faces of the long-term convicts, the scarred buttocks of men who had been flogged with bamboos —all these oppressed me with an intolerable sense of guilt. But I could get nothing into perspective. I was young and ill-educated and I had to think out my problems in the utter silence that is imposed on every Englishman in the East. I did not know that the British Empire is dying, still less did I know that it is a great deal better than the younger empires that are going to supplant it. All I knew was that I was stuck between my hatred of the empire I served and my rage against the evil-spirited little beasts who tried to make my job impossible. With one part of my mind I thought of the British Raj[1] as an unbreakable tyranny, as something clamped down, in *saecula saeculorum*,[2] upon the will of prostrate peoples; with another part I thought that the greatest

[1] **Raj** (räj): government or rule.
[2] *saecula* (sek'yoo·lə) *saeculorum:* forever and ever.

joy in the world would be to drive a bayonet into a Buddhist priest's guts. Feelings like these are the normal by-product of imperialism; ask any Anglo-Indian official, if you can catch him off duty.

One day something happened which in a roundabout way was enlightening. It was a tiny incident in itself, but it gave me a better glimpse than I had had before of the real nature of imperialism—the real motives for which despotic governments act. Early one morning the subinspector at a police station the other end of the town rang me up on the phone and said that an elephant was ravaging the bazaar. Would I please come and do something about it? I did not know what I could do, but I wanted to see what was happening and I got onto a pony and started out. I took my rifle, an old .44 Winchester and much too small to kill an elephant, but I thought the noise might be useful *in terrorem*.[1] Various Burmans stopped me on the way and told me about the elephant's doings. It was not, of course, a wild elephant, but a tame one which had gone "must."[2] It had been chained up, as tame elephants always are when their attack of "must" is due, but on the previous night it had broken its chain and escaped. Its mahout,[3] the only person who could manage it when it was in that state, had set out in pursuit, but had taken the wrong direction and was now twelve hours' journey away, and in the morning the elephant had suddenly reappeared in the town. The Burmese population had no weapons and were quite helpless against it. It had already destroyed somebody's bamboo hut, killed a cow, and raided some fruit stalls and devoured the stock; also it had met the municipal rubbish van and, when the driver jumped out and took to his heels, had turned the van over and inflicted violences upon it.

The Burmese subinspector and some

Indian constables were waiting for me in the quarter where the elephant had been seen. It was a very poor quarter, a labyrinth of squalid huts, thatched with palm leaf, winding all over a steep hillside. I remember it was a cloudy, stuffy morning at the beginning of the rains. We began questioning the people where the elephant had gone and, as usual, failed to get any definite information. That is invariably the case in the East; a story always sounds clear enough at a distance, but the nearer you get to the scene of events the vaguer it becomes. Some of the people said that the elephant had gone in one direction, some said that it had gone in another, some professed not even to have heard of any elephant. I had made up my mind that the whole story was a pack of lies, when I heard yells a little distance away. There was a loud, scandalized cry of "Go away, child! Go away this instant!" and an old woman with a switch in her hand came round the corner of a hut, violently shooing away a crowd of naked children. Some more women followed, clicking their tongues and exclaiming; evidently there was something the children ought not to have seen. I rounded the hut and saw a man's dead

[1] *in terrorem:* in a case of fright.
[2] "**must**": a condition of dangerous frenzy.
[3] **mahout** (mə·hout'): the keeper and driver of an elephant.

body sprawling in the mud. He was an Indian, a black Dravidian [1] coolie, almost naked, and he could not have been dead many minutes. The people said that the elephant had come suddenly upon him round the corner of the hut, caught him with its trunk, put its foot on his back, and ground him into the earth. This was the rainy season and the ground was soft, and his face had scored a trench a foot deep and a couple of yards long. He was lying on his belly with his arms crucified and head sharply twisted to one side. His face was coated with mud, the eyes wide open, the teeth bared and grinning with an unendurable agony. (Never tell me, by the way, that the dead look peaceful. Most of the corpses I have seen looked devilish.) The friction of the great beast's foot had stripped the skin from his back as neatly as one skins a rabbit. As soon as I saw the dead man I sent an orderly to a friend's house nearby to borrow an elephant rifle. I had already sent back the pony, not wanting it to go mad with fright and throw me if it smelt the elephant.

The orderly came back in a few minutes with a rifle and five cartridges, and meanwhile some Burmans had arrived and told us that the elephant was in the paddy fields [2] below, only a few hundred yards away. As I started forward practically the whole population of the quarter flocked out of the houses and followed me. They had seen the rifle and were all shouting excitedly that I was going to shoot the elephant. They had not shown much interest in the elephant when he was merely ravaging their homes, but it was different now that he was going to be shot. It was a bit of fun to them, as it would be to an English crowd; besides they wanted the meat. It made me vaguely uneasy. I had no intention of shooting the elephant—I had merely sent for the rifle to defend myself if necessary—and

it is always unnerving to have a crowd following you. I marched down the hill, looking and feeling a fool, with the rifle over my shoulder and an ever growing army of people jostling at my heels. At the bottom, when you got away from the huts, there was a metaled road and beyond that a miry waste of paddy fields a thousand yards across, not yet plowed but soggy from the first rains and dotted with coarse grass. The elephant was standing eight yards from the road, his left side toward us. He took not the slightest notice of the crowd's approach. He was tearing up bunches of grass, beating them against his knees to clean them, and stuffing them into his mouth.

I had halted on the road. As soon as I saw the elephant I knew with perfect certainty that I ought not to shoot him. It is a serious matter to shoot a working elephant—it is comparable to destroying a huge and costly piece of machinery—and obviously one ought not to do it if it can possibly be avoided. And at that distance, peacefully eating, the elephant

---

[1] **Dravidian** (drə·vid′ē·ən): belonging to an ancient race of India, numerous in the south.

[2] **paddy fields:** rice fields.

looked no more dangerous than a cow. I thought then and I think now that his attack of "must" was already passing off; in which case he would merely wander harmlessly about until the mahout came back and caught him. Moreover, I did not want in the least to shoot him. I decided that I would watch him a little while to make sure that he did not turn savage again, and then go home.

But at that moment I glanced round at the crowd that had followed me. It was an immense crowd, two thousand at the least and growing every minute. It blocked the road for a long distance on either side. I looked at the sea of yellow faces above the garish clothes—faces all happy and excited over this bit of fun, all certain that the elephant was going to be shot. They were watching me as they would watch a conjurer about to perform a trick. They did not like me, but with the magical rifle in my hand I was momentarily worth watching. And suddenly I realized that I would have to shoot the elephant after all. The people expected it of me and I had got to do it; I could feel their two thousand wills pressing me forward irresistibly. And it was at this moment, as I stood there with the rifle in my hands, that I first grasped the hollowness, the futility of the white man's dominion in the East. Here was I, the white man with his gun, standing in front of the unarmed crowd—seemingly the leading actor of the piece; but in reality I was only an absurd puppet pushed to and fro by the will of those yellow faces behind. I perceived in this moment that when the white man turns tyrant it is his own freedom that he destroys. He becomes a sort of hollow, posing dummy, the conventionalized figure of a sahib.[1] For it is the condition of his rule that he shall spend his life in trying to "impress the natives," and so in every crisis he has got to do what the "natives" expect of him. He wears a mask, and his face grows to fit it. I had

[1] **sahib** (sä′ib): native term for a European gentleman.

got to shoot the elephant. I had committed myself to doing it when I sent for the rifle. A sahib has got to act like a sahib; he has got to appear resolute, to know his own mind and do definite things. To come all that way, rifle in hand, with two thousand people marching at my heels, and then to trail feebly away, having done nothing—no, that was impossible. The crowd would laugh at me. And my whole life, every white man's in the East, was one long struggle not to be laughed at.

But I did not want to shoot the elephant. I watched him beating his bunch of grass against his knees, with that preoccupied grandmotherly air that elephants have. It seemed to me that it would be murder to shoot him. At that age I was not squeamish about killing animals, but I had never shot an elephant and never wanted to. (Somehow it always seems worse to kill a large animal.) Besides, there was the beast's owner to be considered. Alive, the elephant was worth at least a hundred pounds; dead, he would only be worth the value of his tusks, five pounds, possibly. But I had got to act quickly. I turned to the experienced-looking Burmans who had been there when we arrived, and asked them how the elephant had been behaving. They all said the same thing; he took no notice of you if you left him alone, but he might charge if you went too close to him.

It was perfectly clear to me what I ought to do. I ought to walk up to within, say, twenty-five yards of the elephant and test his behavior. If he charged, I could shoot; if he took no notice of me, it would be safe to leave him until the mahout came back. But I also knew that I was going to do no such thing. I was a poor shot with a rifle and the ground was soft mud into which one would sink at every step. If the elephant charged and I missed him, I should have about as much chance as a toad under a steam roller. But even then I was not thinking particularly of my own skin, only of the watchful yellow faces behind. For at that moment, with the crowd watching me, I was not afraid in the ordinary sense, as I would have been if I had been alone. A white man mustn't be frightened in front of "natives"; and so, in general, he isn't frightened. The thought in my mind was that if anything went wrong those two thousand Burmans would see me pursued, caught, trampled on, and reduced to a grinning corpse like that Indian up the hill. And if that happened it was quite probable that some of them would laugh. That would never do. There was only one alternative. I shoved the cartridges into the magazine and lay down on the road to get a better aim.

The crowd grew very still, and a deep, low, happy sigh, as of people who see the theater curtain go up at last, breathed from innumerable throats. They were going to have their bit of fun after all. The rifle was a beautiful German thing with cross-hair sights. I did not know then that in shooting an elephant one would shoot to cut an imaginary bar running from earhole to earhole. I ought, therefore, as the elephant was sideways on, to have aimed straight at his earhole; actually I aimed several inches in front of this, thinking the brain would be further forward.

When I pulled the trigger I did not hear the bang or feel the kick—one never does when a shot goes home—but I heard the devilish roar of glee that went up from the crowd. In that instant, in too short a time, one would have thought, even for the bullet to get there, a mysterious, terrible change had come over the elephant. He neither stirred nor fell, but every line of his body had altered. He looked suddenly stricken, shrunken, immensely old, as though the frightful impact of the bullet had paralyzed him without knocking him down. At last, after what seemed a long time—it might have been five seconds, I dare say—he sagged flabbily to his knees. His mouth slobbered. An enormous senility seemed to have settled upon him. One could have imagined him thousands of years old. I fired again into the same spot. At the second shot he did not collapse but climbed with desperate slowness to his feet and stood weakly erect, with legs sagging and head drooping. I fired a third time. That was the shot that did for him. You could see the agony of it jolt his whole body and knock the last remnant of strength from his legs. But in falling he seemed for a moment to rise, for as his hind legs collapsed beneath him he seemed to tower upward like a huge rock toppling, his trunk reaching skywards like a tree. He trumpeted for the first and only time. And then down he came, his belly toward me, with a crash that seemed to shake the ground even where I lay.

I got up. The Burmans were already

racing past me across the mud. It was obvious that the elephant would never rise again, but he was not dead. He was breathing very rhythmically with long rattling gasps, his great mound of a side painfully rising and falling. His mouth was wide open—I could see far down into caverns of pink throat. I waited a long time for him to die, but his breathing did not weaken. Finally I fired my two remaining shots into the spot where I thought his heart must be. The thick blood welled out of him like red velvet, but still he did not die. His body did not even jerk when the shots hit him, the tortured breathing continued without a pause. He was dying, very slowly and in great agony, but in some world remote from me where not even a bullet could damage him further. I felt that I had got to put an end to that dreadful noise. It seemed dreadful to see the great beast lying there, powerless to move and yet powerless to die, and not even to be able to finish him. I sent back for my small rifle and poured shot after shot into his heart and down his throat. They seemed to make no impression. The tortured gasps continued as steadily as the ticking of a clock.

In the end I could not stand it any longer and went away. I heard later that it took him half an hour to die. Burmans were bringing dahs [1] and baskets even before I left, and I was told they had stripped his body almost to the bones by afternoon.

Afterwards, of course, there were endless discussions about the shooting of the elephant. The owner was furious, but he was only an Indian and could do nothing. Besides, legally I had done the right thing, for a mad elephant has to be killed, like a mad dog, if its owner fails to control it. Among the Europeans, opinion was divided. The older men said I was right, the younger men said it was a shame to shoot an elephant for killing a coolie, because an elephant was worth more than any

---

[1] **dahs** (däz): large, heavy knives.

Coringhee [2] coolie. And afterwards I was very glad that the coolie had been killed; it put me legally in the right and gave me a sufficient pretext for shooting the elephant. I often wondered whether any of the others grasped that I had done it solely to avoid looking a fool.

[2] **Coringhee** (kô·rin′gē).

FOR STUDY AND DISCUSSION

1. What impression do you get of Orwell as a young man? To what extent do you think his explanation of his actions given in the last sentence of the essay is true? Give reasons for your answer. Why do you think the death struggle of the elephant is described at such great length?

2. Orwell writes that the incident concerning the elephant "gave me a better glimpse than I had had before of the real nature of imperialism." What do you learn about imperialism from the incident?

3. One important characteristic of this essay is that it is written by an older man looking back on himself as a young man. What is the older Orwell's attitude toward the younger man? In what ways have his ideas and attitudes changed? Cite passages from the essay to support your answer.

4. Study the first two paragraphs of the essay. What do they contribute to the work as a whole? Do you think the essay would be more effective if these paragraphs were omitted? Explain.

5. Irony is an important element in this essay. What is ironic about the central incident of the essay? Explain the irony in the following sentences:

"Theoretically—and secretly, of course—I was all for the Burmese and all against their oppressors . . ." (Page 802.)

"A sahib has got to act like a sahib; he has got to appear resolute, to know his own mind and do definite things." (Page 805.)

"The owner was furious, but he was only an Indian and could do nothing." (Page 807.)

FOR COMPOSITION

Select one sentence from this essay which you think expresses Orwell's basic point better than any other. Write a composition defending your choice.

EVELYN WAUGH
(1903–1966)

There are several reasons for reading the books of Evelyn Waugh. For one, they are consistently entertaining and, at times, hilariously funny. For another, they range widely through fiction, travel, biography, and autobiography. For a third, all have the stamp of Waugh's strong personality. But perhaps the best reason of all, sheer pleasure aside, is that they are models of good writing. Waugh never wastes a word, never misplaces an emphasis. His manner, like that of any good writer, is stamped by his period, but, in his attention to the niceties of expression, it is also timeless.

It is not surprising that Waugh pursued a literary career. His father was a book publisher and a critic and his elder brother, Alec, wrote a best seller before he was twenty. After toying with the idea of becoming an artist and briefly teaching at an uncongenial school, Waugh himself achieved fame at the age of twenty-five with *Decline and Fall,* his first satirical novel.

Vile Bodies and *Black Mischief* followed, each at two-year intervals. Waugh seemed destined to write, one after another, a series of highly satirical, blisteringly comic novels of sophisticated life. In the meantime, however, he became converted to Roman Catholicism. His conversion was partly a matter of theological conviction and partly the result of a search for order, both spiritual and social. At the end of the 1920's Waugh had flinched from the chaos of postwar Europe, and he decided that the prime force of order remaining was the Roman Catholic Church. This conviction greatly influenced his books from that time on and gave his personal eccentricities a social and political turn. After World War II, he emerged almost as a caricature of the country squire, a world-hating, irritable conservative who disapproved of any innovation—whether political, social, or mechanical—and who held up past glory against present dishonor. He once remarked that he did not vote in elections because he did not presume to advise the Queen on her choice of ministers.

Novelists are seldom all of one piece, however, and Waugh is no exception. His books show that as well as nostalgia for an ordered past, he felt an ironic delight in the present. During the war he enlarged his experience of life considerably by serving as an officer in the Marines and in the Commandos. After the war he devoted himself to the life of a writer.

Brideshead Revisited, which appeared in 1945, is usually considered Waugh's masterpiece. It is the most spacious and the least ironic of his books. His own favorite work was *Helena,* a historical novel based on the life of the mother of

Constantine the Great. Many readers, however, prefer *Put Out More Flags,* which gives a wonderfully witty picture of wartime Britain; *Scoop,* a novel based on Waugh's journalistic experience as a special correspondent at the time of the Italian attack on Ethiopia, or a famous short novel, *The Loved One,* which records his wry reaction to the cemetery at Forest Lawn, California. Waugh also wrote a trilogy of war novels—*Men at Arms, Officers and Gentlemen,* and *The End of the Battle*—which add notably to the gallery of sharply observed characters which he accumulated for over thirty-five years.

Bella Fleace Gave a Party

BALLINGAR is four and a half hours from Dublin if you catch the early train from Broadstone Station and five and a quarter if you wait until the afternoon. It is the market town of a large and comparatively well-populated district. There is a pretty Protestant church in 1820 Gothic on one side of the square and a vast, unfinished Catholic cathedral opposite it, conceived in that irresponsible medley of architectural orders that is so dear to the hearts of transmontane [1] pietists. Celtic lettering of a sort is beginning to take the place of the Latin alphabet on the shop fronts that complete the square. These all deal in identical goods in varying degrees of dilapidation; Mulligan's Store, Flannigan's Store, Riley's Store, each sells thick black boots, hanging in bundles, soapy colonial cheese, hardware and haberdashery, oil and saddlery, and each is licensed to sell ale and porter for consumption on or off the premises. The shell of the barracks stands with empty window frames as a monument to emancipation. A typical Irish town.

Fleacetown is fifteen miles from Ballingar, on a direct, uneven road through typical Irish country; vague, purple hills in the far distance and toward them, on one side of the road, fitfully visible among drifting patches of white mist, unbroken miles of bog, dotted with occasional stacks of cut peat. On the other side the ground slopes up to the north, divided irregularly into spare fields by banks and stone walls over which the Ballingar hounds have some of their most eventful hunting. Moss lies on everything; in a rough green rug on the walls and banks, soft green velvet on the timber—blurring the transitions so that there is no knowing where the ground ends and trunk and masonry begin. All the way from Ballingar there is a succession of whitewashed cabins and a dozen or so fair-size farmhouses; but there is no gentleman's house, for all this was Fleace property in the days before the Land Commission. The demesne [2] land is all that belongs to Fleacetown now, and this is let for pasture to neighboring farmers. Only a few beds are cultivated in the walled kitchen garden; the rest has run to rot, thorned bushes barren of edible fruit spreading everywhere among weedy flowers reverting rankly to type. The hothouses have been drafty skeletons for ten years. The great gates set in their Georgian arch are permanently padlocked, the lodges are derelict, and the line of the main drive is only just discernible through the meadows. Access to the house is half a mile farther up through a farm gate, along a track befouled by cattle.

[1] **transmontane:** here, foreign, continental.

"Bella Fleace Gave a Party" from *Mr. Loveday's Little Outing* by Evelyn Waugh. Reprinted by permission of A. D. Peters & Co. Ltd.

[2] **demesne:** the grounds belonging to a residence or landed estate.

But the house itself was in a condition of comparatively good repair; compared, that is to say, with Ballingar House or Castle Boycott or Knode Hall. It did not, of course, set up to rival Gordontown, where the American Lady Gordon had installed electric light, central heating, and a lift, or Mock House or Newhill, which were leased to sporting Englishmen, or Castle Mockstock, since Lord Mockstock married beneath him. These four houses with their neatly raked gravel, bathrooms, and dynamos, were the wonder and ridicule of the country. But Fleacetown, in fair competition with the essentially Irish houses of the Free State, was unusually habitable.

Its roof was intact; and it is the roof which makes the difference between the second and third grade of Irish country houses. Once that goes you have moss in the bedrooms, ferns on the stairs, and cows in the library, and in a very few years you have to move into the dairy or one of the lodges. But so long as he has, literally, a roof over his head, an Irishman's house is still his castle.

Miss Annabel Rochfort-Doyle-Fleace, to give her the full name under which she appeared in books of reference, though she was known to the entire countryside as Bella Fleace, was the last of her family. There had been Fleaces and Fleysers living about Ballingar since the days of Strongbow, and farm buildings marked the spot where they had inhabited a stockaded fort two centuries before the immigration of the Boycotts or Gordons or Mockstocks. A family tree emblazoned by a nineteenth-century genealogist, showing how the original stock had merged with the equally ancient Rochforts and the respectable though more recent Doyles, hung in the billiard room. The present home had been built on extravagant lines in the middle of the eighteenth century, when the family, though enervated, was still wealthy and influential. It would be tedious to trace its gradual decline from fortune; enough to say that it was due to no heroic debauchery. The Fleaces just

got unobtrusively poorer in the way that families do who make no effort to help themselves. In the last generations, too, there had been marked traces of eccentricity. Bella Fleace's mother—an O'Hara of Newhill—had from the day of her marriage until her death suffered from the delusion that she was a Negress. Her brother, from whom she had inherited, devoted himself to oil painting; his mind ran on the simple subject of assassination and before his death he had executed pictures of practically every such incident in history from Julius Caesar to General Wilson.[1] He was at work on a painting, his own murder, at the time of the troubles, when he was, in fact, ambushed and done to death with a shotgun on his own drive.

It was under one of her brother's paintings—Abraham Lincoln in his box at the theater—that Miss Fleace was sitting one colorless morning in November when the idea came to her to give a Christmas party. It would be unnecessary to describe her appearance closely, and somewhat confusing, because it seemed in contradiction to much of her character. She was over eighty, very untidy, and very red; streaky gray hair was twisted behind her head into a horsy bun, wisps hung round her cheeks; her nose was prominent and blue-veined; her eyes pale blue, blank, and mad; she had a lively smile and spoke with a marked Irish intonation. She walked with the aid of a stick, having been lamed many years back when her horse rolled her among loose stones late in a long day with the Ballingar hounds; a tipsy sporting doctor had completed the mischief, and she had not been able to ride again. She would appear on foot when hounds drew the Fleacetown coverts and loudly criticize the conduct of the huntsmen, but every year fewer of her old friends turned out; strange faces appeared.

They knew Bella, though she did not know them. She had become a byword in

[1] **General Wilson:** an English general in World War I who was opposed to the Irish nationalist movement. He was assassinated in 1922 by an Irish extremist.

the neighborhood, a much-valued joke.

"A rotten day," they would report. "We found our fox, but lost it again almost at once. But we saw Bella. Wonder how long the old girl will last. She must be nearly ninety. My father remembers when she used to hunt—went like smoke, too."

Indeed, Bella herself was becoming increasingly occupied with the prospect of death. In the winter before the one we are talking of, she had been extremely ill. She emerged in April, rosy-cheeked as ever, but slower in her movements and mind. She gave instructions that better attention must be paid to her father's and brother's graves, and in June took the unprecedented step of inviting her heir to visit her. She had always refused to see this young man up till now. He was an Englishman, a very distant cousin, named Banks. He lived in South Kensington and occupied himself in the Museum. He arrived in August and wrote long and very amusing letters to all his friends describing his visit, and later translated his experiences into a short story for the *Spectator*. Bella disliked him from the moment he arrived. He had horn-rimmed spectacles and a BBC [1] voice. He spent most of his time photographing the Fleacetown chimney pieces and the molding of the doors. One day he came to Bella bearing a pile of calf-bound volumes from the library.

"I say, did you know you had these?" he asked.

"I did," Bella lied.

"All first editions. They must be extremely valuable."

"You put them back where you found them."

Later, when he wrote to thank her for his visit—enclosing prints of some of his photographs—he mentioned the books again. This set Bella thinking. Why should that young puppy go poking round the house putting a price on everything? She wasn't dead yet, Bella thought. And the more she thought of it, the more repugnant

[1] **BBC:** the British Broadcasting Company. BBC announcers are known for their careful, rather pompous diction.

it became to think of Archie Banks carrying off her books to South Kensington and removing the chimney pieces and, as he threatened, writing an essay about the house for the *Architectural Review*. She had often heard that the books were valuable. Well, there were plenty of books in the library and she did not see why Archie Banks should profit by them. So she wrote a letter to a Dublin bookseller. He came to look through the library, and after a while he offered her twelve hundred pounds for the lot, or a thousand for the six books which had attracted Archie Banks' attention. Bella was not sure that she had the right to sell things out of the house; a wholesale clearance would be noticed. So she kept the sermons and military history which made up most of the collection, the Dublin bookseller went off with the first editions, which eventually fetched rather less than he had given, and Bella was left with winter coming on and a thousand pounds in hand.

It was then that it occurred to her to give a party. There were always several parties given round Ballingar at Christmas time, but of late years Bella had not been invited to any, partly because many of her neighbors had never spoken to her, partly because they did not think she would want to come, and partly because they would not have known what to do with her if she had. As a matter of fact she loved parties. She liked sitting down to supper in a noisy room, she liked dance music and gossip about which of the girls was pretty and who was in love with them, and she liked drink and having things brought to her by men in pink evening coats. And though she tried to console herself with contemptuous reflections about the ancestry of the hostesses, it annoyed her very much whenever she heard of a party being given in the neighborhood to which she was not asked.

So it came about that, sitting with the *Irish Times* under the picture of Lincoln and gazing across the bare trees of the park to the hills beyond, Bella took it into her head to give a party. She rose immediately and hobbled across the room to the bell rope. Presently her butler came into the morning room; he wore the green baize apron in which he cleaned the silver and in his hand he carried the plate brush to emphasize the irregularity of the summons.

"Was it yourself ringing?" he asked.

"It was, who else?"

"And I at the silver!"

"Riley," said Bella with some solemnity, "I propose to give a ball at Christmas."

"Indeed!" said her butler. "And for what would you want to be dancing at your age?" But as Bella adumbrated her idea, a sympathetic light began to glitter in Riley's eye.

"There's not been such a ball in the country for twenty-five years. It will cost a fortune."

"It will cost a thousand pounds," said Bella proudly.

The preparations were necessarily stupendous. Seven new servants were recruited in the village and set to work dusting and cleaning and polishing, clearing out furniture and pulling up carpets. Their industry served only to reveal fresh requirements; plaster moldings, long rotten, crumbled under the featherbrooms; worm-eaten mahogany floorboards came up with the tin tacks; bare brick was disclosed behind the cabinets in the great drawing room. A second wave of the invasion brought painters, paperhangers, and plumbers, and in a moment of enthusiasm Bella had the cornice and the capitals of the pillars in the hall regilded; windows were reglazed, banisters fitted into gaping sockets, and the stair carpet shifted so that the worn strips were less noticeable.

In all these works Bella was indefatigable. She trotted from drawing room to hall, down the long gallery, up the staircase, admonishing the hireling servants, lending a hand with the lighter objects of furniture, sliding, when the time came, up and down the mahogany floor of the drawing room to work in the French chalk. She unloaded chests of silver in the attics, found long-forgotten services of china, went down with Riley into the cellars to count the few remaining and now flat and acid bottles of champagne. And in the evenings when the manual laborers had retired exhausted to their gross recreations, Bella sat up far into the night turning the pages of cookery books, comparing the estimates of rival caterers, inditing long and detailed letters to the agents for dance bands and, most important of all, drawing up her list of guests and addressing the high double piles of engraved cards that stood in her escritoire.[1]

Distance counts for little in Ireland. People will readily drive three hours to pay an afternoon call, and for a dance of such importance no journey was too great. Bella had her list painfully compiled from works of reference, Riley's more up-to-date social knowledge, and her own suddenly animated memory. Cheerfully, in a steady, childish handwriting, she transferred the names to the cards and addressed the envelopes. It was the work of several sittings. Many of those whose names were transcribed were dead or bedridden; some whom she just remembered seeing as small children were reaching retiring age in remote corners of the globe; many of the houses she wrote down were blackened shells, burned during the troubles [2] and never rebuilt; some had "no one living in them, only farmers." But at last, none too early, the last envelope was addressed. A final lap with the stamps and then later than usual she rose from the desk. Her limbs were stiff, her eyes dazzled, her tongue cloyed with the gum of the Free State post office; she felt a little dizzy, but she locked her desk that evening with the knowledge that the most serious part of the work of the party was over. There had been several notable and deliberate omissions from the list.

---

[1] **escritoire** (es′kri·twär′): writing desk.

[2] **the troubles:** a reference to the period following the establishment of the Irish Free State, when the extremists continued the fight for complete independence.

"What's all this I hear about Bella giving a party?" said Lady Gordon to Lady Mockstock. "I haven't had a card."

"Neither have I yet. I hope the old thing hasn't forgotten me. I certainly intend to go. I've never been inside the house. I believe she's got some lovely things."

As the last days approached Bella concentrated more upon her own appearance. She had bought few clothes of recent years, and the Dublin dressmaker with whom she used to deal had shut up shop. For a delirious instant she played with the idea of a journey to London and even Paris, and considerations of time alone obliged her to abandon it. In the end she discovered a shop to suit her, and purchased a very magnificent gown of crimson satin; to this she added long white gloves and satin shoes. There was no tiara, alas! among her jewels, but she unearthed large numbers of bright, nondescript Victorian rings, some chains and lockets, pearl brooches, turquoise earrings, and a collar of garnets.

On the day of the ball she woke early, slightly feverish with nervous excitement, and wiggled in bed till she was called, restlessly rehearsing in her mind every detail of the arrangements. Before noon she had been to supervise the setting of hundreds of candles in the sconces round the ballroom and supper room, and in the three great chandeliers of cut Waterford glass; she had seen the supper tables laid out with silver and glass and stood the massive wine coolers by the buffet; she had helped bank the staircase and hall with chrysanthemums. She had no luncheon that day, though Riley urged her with samples of the delicacies already arrived from the caterer's. She felt a little faint; lay down for a short time, but soon rallied to sew with her own hands the crested buttons on to the liveries of the hired servants.

The invitations were timed for eight o'clock. She wondered whether that would be too early—she had heard tales of parties that began very late—but as the after-noon dragged on unendurably, and rich twilight enveloped the house, Bella became glad that she had set a short term on this exhausting wait.

At six she went up to dress. The hairdresser was there with a bag of thongs and combs. He brushed and coiled her hair and whiffed it up and generally manipulated it until it became orderly and formal and apparently far more copious. She put on all her jewelry and, standing before the cheval glass [1] in her room, could not forbear a gasp of surprise. Then she limped downstairs.

The house looked magnificent in the candlelight. The band was there, the twelve hired footmen, Riley in knee breeches and black silk stockings.

It struck eight. Bella waited. Nobody came.

She sat down on a gilt chair at the head of the stairs, looked steadily before her with her blank, blue eyes. In the hall, in the cloakroom, in the supper room, the hired footmen looked at one another with knowing winks. "What does the old girl expect? No one'll have finished dinner before ten."

At half-past twelve Bella rose from her chair. Her face gave no indication of what she was thinking.

"Riley, I think I will have some supper. I am not feeling altogether well."

She hobbled slowly to the dining room.

"Give me a stuffed quail and a glass of wine. Tell the band to start playing."

The "Blue Danube" waltz flooded the house. Bella smiled approval and swayed her head a little to the rhythm.

"Riley, I am really quite hungry. I've had nothing all day. Give me another quail and some more champagne."

Alone among the candles and the hired footmen, Riley served his mistress with an immense supper. She enjoyed it all.

Presently she rose. "I am afraid there must be some mistake. No one seems to

---

[1] **cheval glass:** a long mirror mounted on horizontal pivots in a frame.

be coming to the ball. It is very disappointing after all our trouble. You may tell the band to go home."

But just as she was leaving the dining room there was a stir in the hall. Guests were arriving. With wild resolution Bella swung herself up the stairs. She must get to the top before the guests were announced. One hand on the banister, one on her stick, pounding heart, two steps at a time. At last she reached the landing and turned to face the company. There was a mist before her eyes and singing in her ears. She breathed with effort, but dimly she saw four figures advancing and heard Riley announce:

"Lord and Lady Mockstock, Sir Samuel and Lady Gordon."

Suddenly the daze in which she had been moving cleared. Here on the stairs were the two women she had not invited—Lady Mockstock, the draper's daughter, Lady Gordon, the American.

She drew herself up and fixed them with her blank, blue eyes.

"I had not expected this honor," she said. "Please forgive me if I am unable to entertain you."

The Mockstocks and the Gordons stood aghast; saw the mad blue eyes of their hostess, her crimson dress; the ballroom beyond, looking immense in its emptiness; heard the dance music echoing through the empty house. The air was charged with the scent of chrysanthemums. And then the drama and unreality of the scene were dispelled. Miss Fleace suddenly sat down, and, holding out her hands to her butler, said, "I don't quite know what's happening."

He and two of the hired footmen carried the old lady to a sofa. She spoke only once more. Her mind was still on the same subject. "They came uninvited, those two . . . and nobody else."

A day later she died.

Mr. Banks arrived for the funeral and spent a week sorting out her effects. Among them he found in her escritoire, stamped, addressed, but unposted, the invitations to the ball.

1. In the first two paragraphs of the story, what contrast is set up between Ballingar and Fleacetown? Which town do you think the author prefers? Why? Of what importance is this contrast to the rest of the story?

2. Characterize Bella Fleace. Do you think that the author intends her to be considered a ridiculous figure, or does he find something admirable about her? Cite details in the story to support your answer. To her neighbors she is "a much-valued joke." What contrast is made between Bella's neighbors, who are part of the modern world, and Bella, who is part of a bygone world? How is this contrast related to the theme of the story?

3. Bella is also contrasted to her heir, Archie Banks. What sort of person is he? Why, in your opinion, does the author have Banks rather than the butler or family lawyer find the unmailed invitations?

4. The climax of the story, the arrival of the Gordons and Mockstocks, may be regarded as another and final confrontation between Bella and the modern world. Of what importance are the Gordons and Mockstocks to the story? What details are given about them to relate them to Bella? Explain the significance of Bella's last words.

5. Bella's house is an important element in the story. What do you learn about this house and its furnishings? What does the house tell you about Bella? What does it tell you about the author's attitude toward his story?

LANGUAGE AND VOCABULARY

Explain how the following italicized words are related to the theme of the story, a theme that grows out of the author's attitude toward the characters and events.

"The great gates set in their Georgian arch are permanently padlocked, the lodges are *derelict* . . ." (Page 809.)

"A family tree *emblazoned* by a nineteenth-century *genealogist* . . ." (Page 810.)

"The present home had been built on extravagant lines in the middle of the eighteenth century, when the family, though *enervated*, was still wealthy and influential." (Page 810.)

"He [the hairdresser] brushed and coiled her [Bella's] hair and whiffed it up and generally manipulated it until it became orderly and formal and apparently far more *copious*." (Page 813.)

SEAN O'FAOLAIN

(1900–   )

The Irish can claim some of the best writers of the twentieth century. First and foremost are three giants: James Joyce, William Butler Yeats, and George Bernard Shaw. Of a later generation are Frank O'Connor, the dramatist Sean O'Casey, and the novelist and short-story writer Sean O'Faolain. There must be something special about the island for it to produce so many fine literary men. It is a small country with a long history, with many traditions and many individualists. Irish writers can arrive at an intimate knowledge of the ways of their country and countrymen and write out of a confidence that such knowledge gives. Also, many Irish writers have a way with the English language. They write musically and with simplicity, and with a gift for turning a phrase that is often the envy of Englishmen and Americans alike.

Sean O'Faolain, one of the best contemporary writers, was born in Cork, the son of a policeman. In reaction to what he regarded as his father's exaggerated respect for English authority, he took up the Irish Republican cause in his teens and joined the Republican Army. But, as he later commented ruefully, "I was never cut out to be either a soldier or a killer." His tastes were bookish rather than explosive. Therefore, when he was twenty-six, he welcomed the chance to accept a Commonwealth Fund Scholarship to Harvard University. After he left Harvard, he taught three years at Boston College. By this time, he had married an Irish teacher whom he had known since boyhood. They contemplated remaining in the United States but concluded that "we belonged to an old, intimate and much-trodden country. . . . We decided that we could live only in Europe, and in Ireland." For several years, O'Faolain taught at St. Mary's College in Middlesex, England. Then he returned to Ireland.

O'Faolain has written novels, short stories, biographies, and travel books. During the last two decades, his reputation has rested chiefly on his short stories. Like his countryman Frank O'Connor, he is regarded as a fine craftsman and, also like O'Connor, he has written a valuable study of the short-story form. At times he has been a controversial figure in his own country, a fighter against orthodoxies who advised that the young Irish "follow my practice, to get out of Ireland as often as possible in order to keep their sense of perspective." The themes of O'Faolain's fiction are firmly rooted in his country, in the conflicts that arise from the clashes between generation and generation, convention and innovation, individual and individual. One of his most recent books is an excellent autobiography, *Vive Moi.*

The Fur Coat

WHEN MAGUIRE became Parliamentary Secretary to the Minister for Roads and Railways his wife wound her arms around his neck, lifted herself on her toes, gazed into his eyes and said, adoringly:

"Now, Paddy, I must have a fur coat."

"Of course, of course, me dear," Maguire cried, holding her out from' him admiringly; for she was a handsome little woman still, in spite of the graying hair and the first hint of a stoop. "Get two fur coats! Switzer's will give us any amount of tick [1] from now on."

Molly sat back into her chair with her fingers clasped between her knees and said chidingly:

"You think I'm extravagant!"

"Indeed, then, I do not. We've had some thin times together and it's about time we had a bit of comfort in our old age. I'd like to see my wife in a fur coat. I'd love to see my wife take a shine out of some of those straps in Grafton Street—painted jades that never lifted a finger for God or man, not to as much as mention the word *Ireland*. By all means get a fur coat. Go down to Switzer's tomorrow morning," he cried with all the innocence of a warm-hearted, inexperienced man, "and order the best fur coat that money can buy."

Molly Maguire looked at him with affection and irritation. The years had polished her hard—politics, revolution, husband in and out of prison, children reared with the help of relatives and Prisoners' Dependents' Funds. You could see the years on her fingertips, too pink, too coarse, and in her diamond-bright eyes.

"Paddy, you big fool, do you know

---

[1] **tick:** credit.

what you'd pay for a mink coat? Not to mention a sable? And not as much as to whisper the word broadtail?"

"Say a hundred quid," [2] said Paddy manfully. "What's a hundred quid? I'll be handling millions of public money from now on. I have to think big."

She replied in her warm Limerick sing-song; sedately and proudly as befitted a woman who had often, in her father's country store, handled thousands of pound notes.

"Do you know, Paddy Maguire, what a really bang-up fur coat could cost you? It could cost you a thousand guineas, [3] and more."

"One thousand guineas? For a coat? Sure, that's a whole year's salary."

"It is."

Paddy drew into himself. "And," he said, in a cautious voice, "is that the kind of coat you had in mind?"

She laughed, satisfied at having taken him off his perch.

"Yerrah, not at all. I thought I might pick up a nice little coat for, maybe, thirty or forty or, at the outside, fifty quid. Would that be too much?"

"Go down to Switzer's in the morning and bring it home on your back."

But, even there, she thought she detected a touch of the bravo, as if he was still feeling himself a great fellow. She let it pass. She said she might have a look around. There was no hurry. She did not bring up the matter again for quite fifteen minutes.

"Paddy! About that fur coat. I sincerely hope you don't think I'm being *vulgar?*"

"How could you be vulgar?"

"Oh, sort of *nouveau riche.* [4] I don't want a fur coat for show-off." She leaned forward eagerly. "Do you know the reason why I want a fur coat?"

---

[2] **quid:** British and Irish slang for a pound, which then was worth about two dollars and eighty cents.

[3] **guineas:** A guinea is worth one pound and one shilling.

[4] *nouveau riche* (n̅o̅o̅′vō′rēsh)· one who has recently become rich.

"To keep you warm. What else?"

"Oh, well, that too, I suppose, yes," she agreed shortly. "But you must realize that from this on we'll be getting asked out to parties and receptions and so forth. And—well—I haven't a rag to wear!"

"I see," Paddy agreed; but she knew that he did not see.

"Look," she explained, "what I want is something I can wear any old time. I don't want a fur coat for grandeur." (This very scornfully.) "I want to be able to throw it on and go off and be as well dressed as anybody. You see, you can wear any old thing under a fur coat."

"That sounds a good idea." He considered the matter as judiciously as if he were considering a memorandum for a projected bypass. She leaned back, contented, with the air of a woman who has successfully laid her conscience to rest.

Then he spoiled it all by asking, "But, tell me, what do all the women do who haven't fur coats?"

"They dress."

"Dress? Don't ye all dress?"

"Paddy, don't be silly. They think of nothing else but dress. I have no time for dressing. I'm a busy housewife and, anyway, dressing costs a lot of money." (Here she caught a flicker in his eye which obviously meant that forty quid isn't to be sniffed at either.) "I mean they have costumes that cost twenty-five pounds. Half a dozen of 'em. They spend a lot of time and thought over it. They live for it. If you were married to one of 'em you'd soon know what it means to dress. The beauty of a fur coat is that you can just throw it on and you're as good as the best of them."

"Well, that's fine! Get the ould coat."

He was evidently no longer enthusiastic. A fur coat, he had learned, is not a grand thing—it is just a useful thing. He drew his briefcase toward him. There was that pier down in Kerry to be looked at. "Mind you," he added, "it'd be nice and warm, too. Keep you from getting a cold."

"Oh, grand, yes, naturally, cozy, yes, all that, yes, yes!"

And she crashed out and banged the door after her and put the children to bed as if she were throwing sacks of turf into a cellar. When she came back he was poring over maps and specifications. She began to patch one of the boy's pajamas. After a while she held it up and looked at it in despair. She let it sink into her lap and looked at the pile of mending beside her.

"I suppose when I'm dead and gone they'll invent plastic pajamas that you can wash with a dishcloth and mend with a lump of glue."

She looked into the heart of the turf fire. A dozen pajamas . . . underwear for the whole house . . .

"Paddy!"

"Huh?"

"The last thing that I want anybody to start thinking is that I, by any possible chance, could be getting grand notions."

She watched him hopefully. He was lost in his plans.

"I can assure you, Paddy, that I loathe —I simply loathe all this modern show-off."

"That's right."

"Those wives that think they haven't climbed the social ladder until they've got a fur coat!"

He grunted at the map of the pier.

"Because I don't care what you or anybody else says, Paddy, there *is* something vulgar about a fur coat. There's no shape to them. Especially musquash. What I was thinking of was black Indian lamb. Of course, the real thing would be ocelot. But they're much too dear. The real ones. And I wouldn't be seen dead in an imitation ocelot."

He glanced sideways from the table. "You seem to know a lot about fur." He leaned back and smiled benevolently. "I never knew you were hankering all this time after a fur coat."

"Who said I'm hankering! I am *not*. What do you mean? Don't be silly. I just want something decent to wear when we go out to a show, or to wear over a dance frock, that's all. What do you mean— hankering?"

"Well, what's wrong with that thing you have with the fur on the sleeves? The shiny thing with the what-do-you-call-'ems—sequins, is it?"

"That! Do you mean *that?* For heaven's sake, don't be talking about what you don't know anything about. I've had *that* for fourteen years. It's like something me grandmother wore at her own funeral."

He laughed. "You used to like it."

"Of course, I liked it when I got it. Honestly, Paddy Maguire, there are times when . . ."

"Sorry, sorry, sorry. I was only trying to be helpful. How much is an ocelot?"

"Eighty-five or ninety—at the least."

"Well, why not?"

"Paddy, tell me honestly. Honestly, now! Do you seriously think that I could put eighty-five pounds on my back?"

With his pencil Maguire frugally drew a line on the map, reducing the pier by five yards, and wondered would the county surveyor let him get away with it.

"Well, the question is: will you be satisfied with the Indian lamb? What color did you say it is? Black? That's a very queer lamb."

Irritably he rubbed out the line. The wretched thing would be too shallow at low water if he cut five yards off it.

"It's dyed. You could get it brown, too," she cried. "You could get all sorts of lamb. Broadtail is the fur of unborn Persian lambs."

That woke him up: the good farmer stock in him was shocked.

"Unborn lambs!" he cried. "Do you mean to say that they . . ."

"Yes, isn't it awful? Honest to Heaven, Paddy, anyone that'd wear broadtail ought to be put in prison. Paddy, I've made up my mind. I just couldn't buy a fur coat. I just won't buy it. That's the end of it."

She picked up the pajamas again and looked at them with moist eyes. He turned to devote his full attention to her problem.

"Molly, darling, I'm afraid I don't understand what you're after. I mean, do you or do you not want a fur coat? I mean, supposing you didn't buy a fur coat, what else could you do?"

"Just exactly what do you mean?"— very coldly.

"I mean, it isn't apparently necessary that you should buy a fur coat. I mean, not if you don't really want to. There must be some other way of dressing besides fur coats? If you have a scunner against[1] fur coats, why not buy something else just as good? There's hundreds of millions of other women in the world and they all haven't fur coats."

"I've told you before that they dress! And I've no time to dress. I've explained all that to you."

Maguire got up. He put his back to the fire, his hands behind him, a judicial look on him. He addressed the room.

"All the other women in the world can't all have time to dress. There must be some way out of it. For example, next month there'll be a garden party up at the President's house. How many of all these women will be wearing fur coats?" He addressed the armchair. "Has Mrs. de Valera[2] time to dress?" He turned and leaned over the turf basket. "Has Mrs. General Mulcahy time to dress? There's ways and means of doing everything." (He shot a quick glance at the map of the pier; you could always knock a couple of feet off the width of it.) "After all, you've told me yourself that you could purchase a black costume for twenty-five guineas. Is that or is that not a fact? Very well then," triumphantly, "why not buy a black costume for twenty-five guineas?"

"Because, you big fathead, I'd have to have shoes and a blouse and hat and gloves and a fur and a purse and everything to match it, and I'd spend far more in the heel of the hunt, and I haven't time for that sort of thing and I'd have to have two or three costumes—Heaven above, I

---

[1] **scunner against:** loathing for.
[2] **Mrs. de Valera:** the wife of Eamon de Valera, premier of Ireland for many years.

can't appear day after day in the same old rig, can I?"

"Good! Good! That's settled. Now, the question is: shall we or shall we not purchase a fur coat? Now! What is to be said for a fur coat?" He marked off the points on his fingers. "Number one: it is warm. Number two: it will keep you from getting cold. Number three . . ."

Molly jumped up, let a scream out of her, and hurled the basket of mending at him.

"Stop it! I told you I don't want a fur coat! And you don't want me to get a fur coat! You're too mean, that's what it is! And, like all the Irish, you have the peasant streak in you. You're all alike, every bloody wan of ye. Keep your rotten fur coat. I never wanted it . . ."

And she ran from the room sobbing with fury and disappointment.

"Mean?" gasped Maguire to himself. "To think that anybody could say that I . . . Mean!"

She burst open the door to sob:

"I'll go to the garden party in a mackintosh. And I hope that'll satisfy you!" and ran out again.

He sat miserably at his table, cold with anger. He murmured the hateful word over and over, and wondered could there be any truth in it. He added ten yards to the pier. He reduced the ten to five, and then, seeing what he had done, swept the whole thing off the table.

It took them three days to make it up. She had hit him below the belt, and they both knew it. On the fourth morning she found a check for a hundred and fifty pounds on her dressing table. For a moment her heart leaped. The next moment it died in her. She went down and put her arms about his neck and laid the check, torn in four, into his hand.

"I'm sorry, Paddy," she begged, crying like a kid. "You're not mean. You never were. It's me that's mean."

"You! Mean?" he said, fondly holding her in his arms.

"No, I'm not mean. It's not that. I just haven't the heart, Paddy. It was knocked out of me donkeys' years ago." He looked at her sadly. "You know what I'm try to say?"

He nodded. But she saw that he didn't. She was not sure that she knew herself. He took a deep, resolving breath, held her out from him by the shoulders, and looked her straight in the eyes. "Molly, tell me the truth. You want this coat?"

"I do. O God, I do!"

"Then go out and buy it."

"I couldn't, Paddy. I just couldn't."

He looked at her for a long time. Then he asked:

"Why?"

She looked straight at him and, shaking her head sadly, she said in a little sobbing voice:

"I don't know."

FOR STUDY AND DISCUSSION

1. At the beginning of the story, Molly says, "Now, Paddy, I must have a fur coat." What does she really mean when she says "must"? What does the use of this word indicate about her?

2. The author comments: "The years had polished her [Molly] hard." Does Molly seem a hard woman as the story progresses? Explain.

3. Describe the stages Molly goes through as she moves to deny herself the coat. What does the coat represent to her?

4. What kind of person is Paddy? What do you learn about him from his dealings with the map and the specifications for the pier?

5. Near the end of the story, the author comments, "It took them three days to make it up. She had hit him below the belt, and they both knew it." In what way did Molly hit Paddy "below the belt"?

FOR COMPOSITION

In his novel *Lord Jim,* Joseph Conrad commented: "It is my belief that no man ever understands his own artful dodges to escape from the grim shadow of self-knowledge." Write a brief composition in which you apply Conrad's statement to the characters in O'Faolain's story, "The Fur Coat."

FRANK
O'CONNOR
(1903–1966)

Frank O'Connor is generally regarded as one of the best short-story writers of the twentieth century. His stories have an outstanding honesty and craftsmanship about them and reveal a deep knowledge of modern Ireland. Like many other Irish, O'Connor was a born storyteller, and he wrote with a refreshing directness and lack of pretension. As a short-story writer, he declared himself a follower of the great Russian writer Anton Chekhov, who, more than anyone else, turned writers away from the neatly plotted, "well-made" story and created the modern short story. O'Connor once wrote that the short story "is the nearest thing one can get to the quality of a pure lyric poem. It doesn't deal with problems; it doesn't have any solutions to offer; it just states the human condition."

Frank O'Connor was the pseudonym adopted by Michael O'Donovan, who was born and grew up in Cork, Ireland. His childhood was the classic childhood of the underprivileged Irish at the turn of the century: the father a laborer, the mother going out to work as a cleaning woman, the child's future darkened by the difficulty of getting an education and by the narrowness of a life in which money is a perpetual problem. Michael O'Donovan did, however, receive an elementary education from the Christian Brothers and contrived by voracious reading to extend that education. Between odd jobs, he managed to make a start as a writer. After spending a year in jail for his political support of the Irish Republican cause, he became a librarian in Cork and in Dublin. For a time he was a director of the Abbey Theater where he worked with William Butler Yeats. Although he collaborated on a number of plays, his main interest was in the short story. Yeats once said that O'Connor was "doing for Ireland what Chekhov did for Russia."

During the last twenty years of his life, O'Connor lived largely in the United States, although he returned periodically to Ireland. He taught at Northwestern University and at Harvard. Most American readers came to know him from his many stories that appeared in *The New Yorker* magazine. Even while he lived in the United States, he continued to write about Ireland. "I prefer to write about Ireland and the Irish people," he said, "merely because I know to a syllable how everything in Ireland can be said." In addition to his plays and poetry, he published critical studies of the short story and the novel and several collections of verse. His autobiography, *An Only Child*—of which "Go Where Glory Waits Thee" is a part—has many of the qualities of his best fiction.

Go Where Glory Waits Thee

Aʟʟ I ever wanted from life was an education. Apart from any liking I may have had for it, I knew it was the key to success. Everyone admitted that. They said you could get nowhere without an education. They blamed their own failure in life on the lack of it. You should learn everything, they said, because it all came in useful—every scrap of it. If Father was no more than a casual laborer and never earned more than fourteen or fifteen shillings a week, that was because he hadn't the education like Mr. Moynihan down the road had it. If Mother was only a charwoman who went out every day to work in the big houses on the river in Cork, it was because she hadn't the education, either. So I knew it was up to me to get the education, and, by the Lord, when I did, things were going to be different in the home. Father would have to treat me with proper respect, and Mother, instead of going out to work, would stay at home and look after me. As for me, I'd look after everybody.

But the difficulty was to get started. It seemed to be extremely hard to get an education, or even—at the level on which we lived—to find out what education was. Education, of course, implied nice manners as opposed to coarse ones—I could see that for myself—and I set out to be a polite and good-living boy, which in the main I was, except when the business of getting an education became too much for me and I had to go to confession and tell the priest that I had been disobedient and rude to my parents. Education was also speaking correctly, and I listened with great admiration to the priest on Sunday and then came home and

imitated him in front of the mirror. But in moments of depression I realized that these were only the things that went with education, not education itself. The priest not only spoke well but he also knew Latin. Latin was clearly a great part of education, so I got Mother to teach me the Latin hymns she knew, like the "Stabat Mater" and the "Ave Maris Stella," and at intervals I had the excited feeling that I really was getting somewhere at last, but those fits of exultation rarely lasted for more than an evening, and I woke next morning with the foreboding that I was never going to get any education.

All that anybody seemed able to tell you about how you got an education was that you should "stick to the books." Now, I didn't have any books, but I did read comics and boys' weeklies, and I stuck to them with great enthusiasm. I don't mean that I didn't enjoy them for their own sakes, for I did. I lived in a sort of social vacuum between the kids of my own class, who had no ambitions to be educated, and the class above ours—policemen and minor officials—whose sons got educated whether they wanted to or not. The latter lived down the Ballyhooley Road, and the boys gathered at night by the gas lamp. Between them, they produced all those indications of a proper education I learned to recognize from the boys' weeklies—a bicycle, or a stamp album, or a real football, or boxing gloves, or a cricket bat, or occasionally even a copy of *The Boy's Own Paper,* which cost sixpence and had halftone illustrations, as compared with the weeklies I could afford, which cost a penny and only had line drawings. To both of those groups I must have seemed a freak—to the poorer kids because I spoke in what probably sounded like an affected accent, and used strange words I had picked up from my reading and didn't even know how to pronounce; to the others because I was only a ragged laney boy who put on airs and tried to force his company on them. So, though I was a fairly normal child who did his best to fit in with others, the others could never fit in with me, and for a lot of the time I had to live in my fantasy. It wasn't such a bad place to live if only the bottom weren't always falling out of it.

There was nothing exclusive about my approach to the world of make-believe—cops and robbers, cowboys and Indians, sailors and pirates—but more than anything else I loved the penny school stories. I don't think they appealed to me for any snobbish reason, for though English boys might recognize that there were remote originals for such schools, and that being given a hundred lines on the day of a cricket match might be a cruel punishment, and that "playing the game" and "keeping a stiff upper lip" were desirable things socially, with me all this was an act of faith. I had never seen or heard of anything in the least resembling an English public school. The appeal of these stories, which has kept them fresh in my mind to this day, was that the characters were getting an education, and I could watch them at it with the certainty that some of the education was bound to brush off on me. If only the authors had identified the particular hundred lines of Latin that the hero was compelled to write out during the last cricket match of the season, how gladly I would have written them for him! As it was, I had to be content with the odd snatches of Latin and French that emerged from the narrative.

But education was hard. To be properly educated, you had to have a father who didn't drink and a mother who didn't work; you had to have long trousers and a short jacket and a top hat; you had to have footballs and cricket bats and shorts and a suit with white trousers, and the best people had uncles who came to the school in racing cars and tipped them five pounds, a sum of money I had never seen all together, so that they could blow it all in the tuckshop [1] and have a feed in the dormitory after dark. The only rich relative I could get certain tidings of was a patrolman in the Chicago police force, known

as Big Tim Fahy. He was a cousin of Mother, and so tall and powerful that Father, who was a six-footer, admitted he felt like a small boy beside him. He had a photograph of him on the sideboard in his uniform, wearing a sword, and the photographs and clippings the Fahys showed us proved that he was highly regarded in Chicago. A man like that would, I thought, go far in the States, and might eventually help me.

Meanwhile, even if you couldn't afford a top hat, you could play cricket with an old piece of board and a raggy ball against a wicket you had chalked on the blank end wall of a block of houses. You could get papers that gave you tips about the Noble Art of Self-Defense and practice a straight left in front of the mirror. You could even abide by the public school code, and not tell lies, or betray a friend when he'd done something wrong, or yell when you got punished in school. All the boys I knew screamed that their wrist was broken and went back to their desks sobbing and nursing their hand between their knees.

I was always fond of heights, and afterward it struck me that reading was only another form of height. It was a way of looking beyond one's own backyard, and seeing into the neighbors'. Our yard—the real one—had a high back wall, and by early afternoon it had made the whole kitchen dark, but when the evening was fine I climbed the door of the outdoor toilet and onto the top of the wall. It was on a level with the respectable terrace behind ours, which had front gardens and a fine view, and there I sat for hours, on terms of relative equality with the policemen and their children, and watched the opposite hillside that fell headlong toward the valley of the city, with its terraces of tall houses and its crest of dark trees. It was all lit up when our little house was in darkness. In the mornings, the first thing I did when I got up was to put a chair under my attic window and push up the window sash to see the same hillside when it was still in shadow and its colors had the stiffness of early-morning light.

---

[1] **tuckshop:** snack shop.

The best place for a good view was the quarry that fell sheer from the neighborhood of the Barrack to the Ballyhooley Road. It was a noisome place, where people dumped their rubbish and gangs of wild kids held stoning matches after school and poor people from lanes around the Barrack poked among the rubbish for treasure; but all that meant nothing to me, and I picked my way through the discarded bully-beef tins and climbed till I found a ledge of rock or a hollow in the quarry face that could be promoted to the rank of a cave, and after carefully placing an old penknife or a heavy stone beside me as a weapon to use against imaginary pursuers, I sat happily surveying the whole neighborhood, from Mayfield Chapel, which rode the extreme top of the hillside on the edge of the open country, to the spire of St. Luke's Church, which lay beneath me, and beyond which, dim in the distance, were the hills at the other side of the River Lee. Lord knows what I should think of it now, but then it seemed to me a wonderful view: the Ballyhooley Road winding up the hill from St. Luke's Cross, with its little houses and their tiny front gardens, and, on the side of the road nearest me, the back yards where the women came to hang out their washing. And all the time the shadow moved with a chill one could almost feel, and the isolated spots of sunlight grew brighter. Up there I felt like some sort of wild bird, secure from everything and observing everything: a horse and cart coming up the road, or a little girl with her skipping rope on the pavement, or an old man staggering along on his stick—all of them unaware of the eagle eyes that watched them from above.

Cork on its hills was full of such spots. Not far from our house was Goulding's Glen, in those days a valley with a stream that led from the clean open country by Ballyvolane to a manure factory in Blackpool where Father worked for a time. It skirted the base of the hill on which the Barrack stood, with the Barrack itself the highest spot, and for hours each day young buglers practiced on the sandy bluff that overlooked the second terrace, known as the Black Patch. Here the British had their rifle range and the local boys played football, and on the third level was the Glen itself, which led from the Big Pond, where we skated in wintertime, past the Mill House, which always looked dank and sinister between its trees, and along by the crimson sluice gates that controlled the factory stream under the steep hills which in those days were still covered in trees. This deep cutting was the first to fill with shadow, and I liked to sit somewhere high up, watching the workmen come home in the evening. Once I began to read, I needed no other landscape for dreaming. It was a pretty dirty hole even then, but for me it contained everything that the books told of—the Rocky Mountains, the Alps, the Castle on the Hill, the

Haunted House, and the playing fields of whichever imaginary school I was then reading about.

But whatever the height, whether that of the storybook or the quarry, the eagle had to descend. Even eagles get cold and hungry, and nobody has taught the human eagle to feed off its own heights. Mother would soon be finished work. At some houses she did half a day, which ended at three o'clock, and for which she was paid ninepence or a shilling, and at others she did a whole day, which did not end till six, and for which she was paid one and sixpence. Depending on the humor of the maid she worked for, I might be allowed to call for her half an hour or so before she was finished work. In one house not only was I admitted to the kitchen after school and given my tea, but—if the family was out or on holiday—I was allowed up to the lumber room in the attic, which was filled with old pamphlets, guidebooks, phrase books in German and French, heavenly old dance programs with tassels and tiny pencils, a number of old school-books, including a French primer, and—greatest treasure of all—a text of the Oberammergau Passion Play, in English and German. It was junk that would have meant nothing to almost anyone else in the world, and indeed the maid eventually let me take my pick of it before she cleared it out, but it filled my mind with ravishing glimpses of how educated people lived, the places they saw, the things they did, and the way they spoke to hotel managers and railway porters. "From which platform does the train start for Köln." "We wish a carriage for nonsmokers." "We have two trunks and five bags." "That is for you, young man." It was only another aspect of the vision I had caught in the master bedrooms. In these rooms there were mirrors in which you could see yourself twice over in profile, silver-handled brushes with engraved designs, and curiously shaped bottles that contained hair oil and scents that I experimented with recklessly when Mother's back was turned. Sometimes since then, when I

stay in such a house, I wonder what small black face has studied itself in the mirror of the dressing table, what grubby little paw has used the silver-handled brushes to rub in the bay rum, and turn round almost expecting to see a tiny figure dash past me down the stairs toward the kitchen.

So I scampered down the quarry face to the snug suburban road, with its gas lamps and smooth pavements, and went to the tram stop at St. Luke's Cross, where I could be sure Mother would not escape me. In the dusk I sat, swinging my legs on the wall that overlooked the church, afraid to look behind me for fear I might grow dizzy, and when a tram came wheezing up the hill and discharged its passengers, I chased the men for cigarette pictures, terrified at the same time that I might miss her, a small, grave figure in a black shawl. Sometimes she had only her day's wages, but occasionally a maid would give her a bit of meat or a slice of apple pie for my supper, and then if she could spare me a penny for a boys' weekly, my day was almost saved. Saved it would be if for any reason Father was working late and we could sit in the dusk over the fire while I explained to her my plans for taking her abroad, and got her to sing for me "Farewell, but Whenever You Welcome the Hour" and "How Dear to Me the Hour When Daylight Dies." She was very fond of "Go Where Glory Waits Thee," and I put up with the rather dull tune for the sake of the words, which were beautiful and held such a personal appeal to myself that I could barely listen to them without tears:

> "Go where glory waits thee,
> But while fame elates thee,
>   Oh, then remember me!
> When the praise thou meetest
> To thine ear is sweetest,
>   Oh, still remember me."

But often it was misery to return from the heights. It wasn't only that I might find Father drunk or quarrelsome, or that the rent collector might turn up and take a shilling of what Mother had earned, or that I might be sent for a loaf of bread and be refused it without the money. It was also that sometimes I ran into some happy group of boys amusing themselves at a lamppost, and, drawn by the clublike atmosphere of the pool of light and the shadowy figures, I tried to join them. Everything went well for a minute or two, till I suddenly said something wrong or used a word no one recognized and the whole group began to jeer me and call me "Four-eyes," and I would realize that once again I had been talking the language of the heights.

The trouble was that I was always a little bit of what I had picked up from whatever source—book or picture or glimpse of a different sort of life—always half in and half out of the world of reality, like Moses descending the mountain, or a dreamer waking. I couldn't see a picture of Robin Hood in a storybook but I had to make myself a long bow out of a curtain pole; and when I got a couple of younger kids to assist me at cricket and stood with a make-believe bat before a make-believe wicket, I was always the Dark Horse of the school, emerging to save its honor when all seemed lost. Once when we were playing cricket in the square in front of our house, a policeman came up the road and the others ran home. I didn't run, though I was as scared as they were. I rested on my hurling stick and waited for him to speak. "What do you mean, playing ball on the public street?" he demanded. "Excuse me," I replied politely. "This is not a public street. This square is private property." The bobby was so surprised at being checked by a small spectacled boy with an imitation cricket bat that he let me get away with it. But it wasn't often I got away with it, and sometimes I got in trouble for being cheeky when all I was doing was acting out a part, and at other times I was accused of being a liar when I was still only half in, half out of the dream and telling the truth as best I could; and then I slunk back in tears to my heights and my loneliness.

I couldn't keep from brooding on suffering and injustice, or from making a fool of myself about them. I don't know what age I was when I heard that a wild and handsome boy up the road, whose father beat him savagely, had run away from home and was being searched for by the police. The story was told in whispers. He would eventually be found, people said, and sent to the reformatory. That evening I found him myself, lurking in an alleyway, his long face filthy with tears, and begged him to come home. He would not come, and I would not leave him. At last he agreed to come, on condition that I go with him and plead for him. While I knocked at his door, he stood against the wall, his head down. His elder sister opened the door and I made my little speech. She promised to see that he was not punished, and I went home in a glow of exaltation, feeling that I had saved him from a terrible fate—the fate I was always dreading, of finding myself without a mother and a home. I thought that after this he and I might be friends. When we met again, he wouldn't even look at me but turned away with a sneer, and I knew that his father had beaten him again and that it was all my fault. As a protector of the weak I never was worth much.

As a result of this queer existence, half real and half fantastic, I who was always standing up for truth and justice never learned to fight; I who was always winning games for the school when everything seemed lost never learned to play any game; I who was always swimming flooded rivers to escape my pursuers never could swim at all till I was thirty. I never even got to be an acolyte [1] in the parish church or learned to ride a bicycle. The distance between the dream and the reality, between the private and the public personality, was always too great.

By the time I was fourteen or fifteen, it had become altogether clear that education was something I could not afford.

---

[1] **acolyte** (ak′ə·līt): a boy who assists a priest at Mass.

Not that even then I had any intention of giving it up. I was just looking for a job that would enable me to buy the books from which I could pick up the education myself. So with the rest of the unemployed I went to the newsroom of the Carnegie Library, where on wet days the central heating warmed the perished bodies in the broken boots and made the dirty rags steam and smell. I read carefully through the advertisements and applied for every job that demanded "a smart boy." Sometimes, as a sort of bonus from Providence, I found a new number of *The Times Literary Supplement, The Spectator, The New Statesman,* or *The Studio* free, and I sat there and read reviews of books I would never be able to read and discussions of paintings I would never see, but usually some hungry old man would have toppled asleep over it and I was cheated. The real out-of-works always favored the high-class magazines, at which they were not likely to be disturbed. After a while, I got up and went out and wandered aimlessly round town till hunger or darkness or rain sent me home.

When it became clear that I would never be a priest, Mother's only ambition was for me to become a clerk: someone who would wear a white collar and be called "Mister." Knowing no better but always willing, I went to the Technical School and the School of Commerce at night to learn arithmetic, bookkeeping, and shorthand–typing. Of bookkeeping all I remember is a saying quoted approvingly on the first page of our textbook: "In business there is no such thing as an out-and-out free gift." And the very first thing I was asked to type in the School of Commerce threw me into a fresh fever, for it was Tennyson's "Blow, Bugle, Blow," presented as an example of advanced punctuation. To me it was merely fresh material for fantasy. I also worked hard at a Self-Educator, a big blue book that contained courses in everything, which I had picked up. From my reading I had deduced that German was the real language of culture, and that the

greatest of cultured persons was Goethe, so I read Goethe right through in English and studied German out of the Self-Educator to read him in the original. I also made an attempt to learn Greek, which struck me as a very important cultural medium, but as I had never learned the rudiments of grammar in any language, I didn't get far with Greek.

I got my first job through my confessor, a gentle old priest who regarded me as a very saintly boy, and if innocence and sanctity are related, he was probably not so far wrong. The job was in a pious wholesale drapery business, where every single member of the staff seemed to have been recommended by his confessor, but I hated my immediate boss—a small, smug, smooth, greasy man, who tried hard to teach me that whenever he called my name I was instantly to drop whatever I was doing and reply smartly "Yessir." I never minded dropping whatever I was doing, which was usually folding shirts— the two arms neatly across the breast, as if I were laying out a corpse—and I had no objection to calling anybody "sir," but it was several seconds before my armor of daydreaming was penetrated by any voice from outside, and several seconds more before I realized that it was the voice to which I should reply "Yessir"; so at the end of a fortnight I stopped folding shirts and saying yessir and went home to do some more work at Greek. Then I tried a spell in a chemist's shop that was looking for a smart boy, but I soon discovered that I was only wanted to deliver messages. I have a vivid recollection of the end of this job, with myself, a small boy looking up at a tall counter, and a still taller man, refreshed by a visit to the pub next door, looking down at me pityingly and begging me in a thick Dublin accent to get out of this for my own good. There was an even briefer spell at a job printer's. While I was being shown the ropes, the printer asked me if I could spell and I replied airily "Oh, that's my forte!" which was the sort of language we used on the heights and I saw nothing wrong with it. That evening I met the man who had recommended me to the printer, and he repeated my reply with a good deal of laughter, and I realized that as usual I had made a fool of myself. I was so mortified that I never went back. I was sorry about that because I really was quite good at spelling, and I still think I might have made an excellent typesetter.

I went to the railway as a messenger boy, because I despaired of ever becoming anything better, and besides, though the hours—eight to seven—were cruelly long for a growing boy, the pay was good —a pound a week—and with money like that coming in I could buy a lot of books and get a lot of education. My job was to assist the invoice and claims clerks, bringing in dockets from the warehouse, and going to the warehouse to inquire for missing goods. All transport companies have colossal claims for missing goods, most of which were not really missing at all but lying around forgotten. Whiskey and tobacco were easy to trace, as they had to be loaded into sealed wagons in the presence of one of the old railway policemen, who recorded them in his book. But nobody took much responsibility for other articles, and it depended on the uncertain memory of checkers whether or not you could find out what had happened to them. A friendly checker could often remember a particular consignment, and if he were in really good

humor, find it where it had lain for weeks in a corner, covered by a mountain of fresh merchandise. Usually, nobody remembered anything at all, and you solemnly marked your memorandum or wire with some code word, like "Bison," which signified "Certainly forwarded please say if since received." Back came a wire saying "Moose," meaning that it hadn't been received, and you had to go to the file room, where the dockets were stored, and search through scores of dusty files to find the original docket and the name of the porter or checker who had signed for the goods.

Sheehy and Cremin, the two other tracers, were the sons of railwaymen and protected by their fathers' presence from anything worse than good-natured ragging, but, apart from the patience and kindness of two or three checkers, I had to depend on my wits, which were all but nonexistent. I hated the file room, and when I worked there with Cremin or Sheehy I realized that they found six dockets in the time it took me to find one. I had bad sight, and often failed to see a docket properly, particularly when it was written in the semiliterate scrawl of carters or porters, and even when I should have seen it I was daydreaming, and when I wasn't daydreaming I was harassed by panic, shyness, and ignorance. Sheehy sneered all the time; Cremin sneered only some of the time, because he had a sort of

impatient pity for my stupidity, and occasionally, smiling as I bogged myself deeper in some job I couldn't do, he took it from me with a complacent air and did it himself in a moment.

One of my jobs was to answer the telephone, and I did it with such intensity that I could never hear a word the other person said, and usually I was too ashamed to admit that I hadn't understood. When I did admit it, it was worse, for the person at the other end grew furious—a fatal thing to do with me, as it deprives me of the last shred of my wits. The trouble was that I couldn't believe in the telephone or the messages that came by it. I couldn't believe that the missing goods I was supposed to trace had ever existed, or if they had, that their loss meant anything to anybody. All I could believe in was words. I would read the word "unsophisticated" and at once I would want to know what the Irish for it was. In those days I didn't ask to be a writer. All I wanted was to translate, to feel the unfamiliar become familiar, the familiar take on all the mystery of some dark foreign face one glimpsed in the street.

I had taken a checker's discarded notebook from the railway storeroom and, having patiently rubbed out all the pencil notes, begun a poem book of my own. And though I was stupid, I really did care madly about poetry, good and bad, without understanding why I cared. More even than music it is the universal speech, but it is spoken fluently only by those whose existence is already all aflame with emotion, for then the beauty and order of language are the only beauty and order possible. Above all, it is the art of the boy and girl overburdened by the troubles of their sex and station, for as Jane Austen wistfully noted, poetry can be best appreciated by those who should taste it most sparingly.

It was a strange double life, and small wonder if it comes back to me as hallucination. Each morning when I made my way across the tracks from the passenger station to the goods station, I said good-by to a part of myself, and at seven that evening, when I returned across the dark railway yard and paused in the well-lit passenger station to see the new books in the bookstall, he rejoined me, a boy exactly like myself except that no experience had dinged or dented him.

When my first wretched effort at composition appeared in a boys' paper and word of it got round the office, everyone was astonished, but most of all my boss. Sitting at his high desk with the paper open before him and a frown on his bulgy forehead, he asked, "Did you write this, Native?"

"Yes, sir," I said, feeling sure I had done it again. Everything I did only seemed to get me into fresh trouble.

"Nobody help you?" he asked suspiciously.

"No, sir," I replied warmly, because it looked as though someone else might have fallen under suspicion, and I still hung on to the code of the boys' weeklies and was always prepared to own up sooner than see another suffer.

The frown deepened on his fat face. "Then for God's sake, stick to writing!" he snapped. "You'll never be any good on the Great Southern & Western Railway."

And that, as we used to say in Cork, was one sure five. Looking for models of fine conduct as usual, I had lit on a Left Wing timekeeper, who knew all the Italian operas by heart and made it a point of honor not to take off his cap when speaking to the bosses. Thinking that anyone who knew so much about Italian operas must know the correct thing for other situations, I decided not to take my cap off, either. Even then I should probably have been let off with a reprimand, because my boss realized that I had no self-confidence and went about imitating everybody in the wild hope that I might accidentally strike on the right thing. But with my bad sight, I fell over a handtruck and injured my shin, so that I couldn't walk for weeks. On the railway, bad sight was more serious than bad manners, because it might result in a claim, and transport companies have a thing about claims.

On the Saturday night I was sacked, I read my first paper before the Gaelic League. It was in Irish, and the subject was Goethe. For me, my whole adolescence is summed up in that extraordinary evening—so much that even yet I can't laugh at it in comfort. I didn't know much about Irish, and I knew practically nothing about Goethe, and that little was wrong. In a truly anthropomorphic spirit, I recreated Goethe in my own image and likeness, as a patriotic young fellow who merely wished to revive the German language, which I considered to have been gravely threatened by the use of French. I drew an analogy between the French culture that dominated eighteenth-century Germany and the English culture by which we in Ireland were dominated.

While I was reading, it was suddenly borne in on me that I no longer had a job, or a penny in the world, or even a home I could return to without humiliation, and that the neighbors would say again, as they had so often said before, that I was mad and a good-for-nothing. And I knew they would be right, for here I was committing myself absolutely and publicly to vague words and vaguer impressions. I could barely control my voice, because the words and impressions no longer mattered. All that mattered to me now was the act of faith, the hope that somewhere, somehow I would be able to prove that I was neither mad nor a good-for-nothing, because now I realized that there was no turning back. I had tossed my cap over the wall of life, and I must follow wherever it had fallen.

FOR STUDY AND DISCUSSION

1. The author writes that "for a lot of the time I had to live in my fantasy. It wasn't such a bad place to live if only the bottom weren't always dropping out of it." Cite details from the selection that support this statement.

2. Characterize the boy. Consider his relationship to his mother, his dreams and ambitions, his taste in literature. What do the following sentences tell you about him?

"As a protector of the weak I never was worth much,"

"I got my first job through my confessor, a gentle old priest who regarded me as a very saintly boy, and if innocence and sanctity are related, he was probably not so far wrong."

3. Describe the boy's various jobs. Why does he fail to hold them? What effect do you think these jobs had on his character? What experience of self-realization comes to him as he reads his paper on Goethe? Do you think that, at the end of the essay, he is a stronger person than at the beginning? Explain.

4. One strong element in this selection is its concern with both literal and figurative heights. Cite at least five references to such heights and show how these make the boy's situation more vivid and more poignant. To what are the heights contrasted, either explicitly or implicitly?

5. What was the significance to the boy of the hymn "Go Where Glory Waits Thee"? Why do you think O'Connor chose this as the title for this piece? What does this choice imply about the boy's future? Considering its title, would you characterize this selection as basically sad or cheerful in tone? Explain.

LANGUAGE AND VOCABULARY

Many words that refer to abstract ideas, such as *love, honor,* and *freedom,* can have a variety of meanings that will shift depending on the context in which the words are used. In "Go Where Glory Waits Thee," the word *education* has a number of different meanings for the young Frank O'Connor. Give three different definitions of this word which the boy might have offered. Support these definitions by citing passages from the story. Finally, offer your own definition of the word.

FOR COMPOSITION

As O'Connor tells it, his reading the paper on Goethe was a turning point in his life, not because of any outward event, but because of an experience of self-revelation. Describe a similar experience in your own life.

STEPHEN SPENDER

(1909–   )

Stephen Spender was one of a group of young poets of the 1930's who tried to incorporate the modern world into their poetry. Unlike Yeats and Eliot, who railed at the modern world and saw it as a wasteland or a scene of bloody chaos, these younger poets tried to come to terms with their age and accept it as a time of beauty and order. Thus, in one of his most famous poems, Spender celebrated the beauty of an express train: "Ah, like a comet through flame, she moves entranced/ Wrapt in her music no bird song, no, nor bough/ Breaking with honey buds, shall ever equal."

Like other members of his group, Spender did not strive for a perpetually optimistic note. He was as much concerned with protesting the evils of his time as with proclaiming its beauties. Some of his poems are as much an expression of an unhappy man living in a frustrating period as the work of earlier poets such as Arnold and Hardy. Although Spender tried to accept the age in which he lived, he was honest enough to acknowledge that his attempt was not altogether successful.

At seventeen Stephen Spender had his own printing press and was earning money by printing druggists' labels. Later he used the press to print his own poems. As an adolescent, Spender believed in "pure poetry, an invocation which one understands imperfectly but which is yet expressed exactly . . ." At Oxford—falling under the influence of his friend W. H. Auden and reading writers such as T. S. Eliot, James Joyce, and Ernest Hemingway—Spender's views changed. "I ceased to think of it [poetry] creating a special world in which the poet enjoys Keatsian imaginings shutting out the real world. . . . I believed now that everything which men make and invent is to some degree a symbol of an inner state of consciousness. . . . I began to realize that unpoetic-seeming things were material for poetry. . . . What excited me about the modern movement was the inclusion within new forms of material which seemed ugly, antipoetic, and inhuman . . . [The modern poems and novels] showed me that modern life could be material for art, and that the poet, instead of having to set himself apart from his time, could create out of an acceptance of it."

In addition to poetry, Spender has written a novel, short stories, and a number of books on the situation of the writer in modern society. As a magazine editor, he helped found two important literary journals, *Horizon* and *Encounter*. In 1951, he published an unusually penetrating autobiography, *World Within World*. But it is probably by his poems that he wishes ultimately to be judged. Although some of them, inspired by political events of the 1930's, appear dated today, many of his lyrics are still fresh. At least a handful of these will probably survive as the testament of one sensitive man who struggled to accept his times and could not help remaining at odds with them.

Epilogue to a Human Drama

When pavements were blown up, exposing nerves,
And the gas mains burned blue and gold,
And stucco and brick were pulverized to a cloud
Pungent with smells of mice, dust, garlic, anxiety:
When the reverberant emptied façades   5
Of the West End palaces of commerce
Isolated in a vacuum of silence, suddenly
Cracked and blazed and fell, with the seven-maned
Lions of Wrath licking the stony fragments—

Then the one voice through deserted streets   10
Was the Cassandra° bell which rang and rang and ran
Released at last by Time
To seek those fires that burst through many walls—
Prophetic doom laid bare under the nostrils,
Blood and fire streaming from the stones.   15

London burned with unsentimental dignity
Of resigned kingship: those stores and Churches
Which had glittered century-long in dusty gold
Stood near the throne of domed St. Paul's
Like courtiers round the Royal sainted martyr.   20
August shadows of night
And bursting of concentrated light
Dropped from the skies to paint a final scene
Illuminated agony of frowning stone.
Who then can wonder that every word   25
In burning London, stepped out of a play?

On the stage, there were heroes, maidens, fools,
Victims, a Chorus. The heroes were brave,
The fools spat jokes into the skull of death,
The victims waited with the humble patience   30
Of animals trapped behind a wall
For the pickaxes to break, with light and water.
The Chorus assisted, bringing cups of tea,
Praising the heroes, deploring the morals of the wicked,
Underlining punishment, justifying Doom to Truth.   35

11. **Cassandra** (kə·san′drə): In mythology, a prophetess whose prophecies were not believed.

What I Expected

What I expected was
Thunder, fighting,
Long struggles with men
And climbing.
After continual straining 5
I should grow strong;
Then the rocks would shake
And I should rest long.

What I had not foreseen
Was the gradual day 10
Weakening the will
Leaking the brightness away,
The lack of good to touch
The fading of body and soul
Like smoke before wind 15
Corrupt, unsubstantial.

The wearing of Time,
And the watching of cripples pass
With limbs shaped like questions
In their odd twist, 20
The pulverous grief
Melting the bones with pity,
The sick falling from earth—
These, I could not foresee.

For I had expected always 25
Some brightness to hold in trust,
Some final innocence
To save from dust;
That, hanging solid,
Would dangle through all 30
Like the created poem
Or the dazzling crystal.

Without That Once Clear Aim

Without that once clear aim, the path of flight
To follow for a lifetime through white air,
This century chokes me under roots of night
I suffer like history in Dark Ages, where
Truth lies in dungeons, from which drifts no whisper: 5
We hear of towers long broken off from sight
And tortures and war, in dark and smoky rumor,
But on men's buried lives there falls no light.
Watch me who walk through coiling streets where rain
And fog drown every cry: at corners of day   10
Road drills explore new areas of pain,
Nor summer nor light may reach down here to play.
The city builds its horror in my brain,
This writing is my only wings away.

FOR STUDY AND DISCUSSION

1. What do you learn from "Epilogue to a Human Drama" about London's experience of World War II? In what ways does Spender compare this experience to a play? In a sense, this "Epilogue" is a summing up, a judgment of what has happened in the "human drama." What is the summation and judgment of the poem? (In answering, consider especially lines 27–35.)

2. Contrast what the speaker of "What I Expected" anticipated with what he actually found. Cite images used to give emotional meaning to each statement. It might seem that this poem, after having devoted a stanza to what the speaker expected, might end neatly after describing what he actually found. Yet after two stanzas of such description, the poem returns once again in its final stanza to what the speaker expected. Why, in your opinion, does the poem make such a return? In answering this question, consider the emotional effect of the concluding lines.

3. In "Without That Once Clear Aim," what is it that makes the speaker suffer? What does he mean by "that once clear aim"? What is his only escape? Is this poem an English or an Italian sonnet, or neither? (In your answer, consider how the poem might be divided in terms of content as well as rhyme scheme.)

LANGUAGE AND VOCABULARY

Epilogue and the related words *prologue, dialogue, monologue,* and *decalogue* all have a common root. Discuss how this root combined with different prefixes gives each of these words a different but related meaning.

GRAHAM
GREENE
(1904–   )

Graham Greene is probably the most gifted British storyteller of his generation. Nobody can plan taut, exciting action better than he; nobody possesses a sharper insight into the kinks and fissures of human personality. Adverse critics may accuse him of a morbid interest in the run-down, the second-rate, the pathological, but nobody is likely to question his skill in catching and holding his reader's attention.

From early youth on, Greene developed an individual pattern of living. He has told in an autobiographical essay how, as an adolescent, in order to stimulate a jaded zest for life, he used to play the dangerous game of Russian roulette. By the time he was twenty-three, he had been very briefly a member of the Communist Party; then he became a convert to Roman Catholicism. As a writer, Greene has always shown himself a partisan of extreme states of mind. He has little use for the ordinary or the safe. His special bent as a writer has been to wrest out of unpromising material an unexpected affirmation, a stinging paradox, or an unsuspected nobility.

His first entirely successful novel, *Brighton Rock,* is a case in point. Its central character, Pinkie, is a minor gangster. It is typical of Greene not only to prefer him to those few in the book who represent conventional standards of conduct, but to give him, by virtue of one good action, moral superiority over the upholders of law and order. A verse tag quoted in this book may be taken as a motto for all Greene's work. It signifies that even at the eleventh hour a destiny can be reversed: "Between the stirrup and the ground/ He mercy sought and mercy found." Much of Greene's work has been a prolonged brooding over the eleventh hour: the moment at which a rider, in falling, has time not only to face the reality of his dilemma, but to take a last desperate action.

There is, for example, the priest in Greene's finest novel, *The Power and the Glory,* who, by sacrificing himself to his duty at the last possible moment, buys back a lifetime of personal failure. There is Scobie in *The Heart of the Matter,* struggling to overcome the wreck of a marriage, and Sarah in *The End of the Affair,* attaining a degree of sainthood after renouncing the man who loves her. These are the kinds of men and women who appeal to Greene, and again and again he returns to the struggle they engage in to transcend some crippling weakness.

Greene's novels still appear at regular intervals, often as the result of a journey to some trouble-center currently in the news. *The Quiet American* sprang out of a trip to Indochina; *Our Man in Havana* was inspired by a stay in Cuba; *A Burnt-Out Case* followed a journey into the Congo. *The Comedians* was the result of a trip to

Across the Bridge

THEY SAY he's worth a million," Lucia said. He sat there in the little hot damp Mexican square, a dog at his feet, with an air of immense and forlorn patience. The dog attracted your attention at once; for it was very nearly an English setter, only something had gone wrong with the tail and the feathering. Palms wilted over his head, it was all shade and stuffiness round the bandstand, radios talked loudly in Spanish from the little wooden sheds where they changed your pesos into dollars at a loss. I could tell he didn't understand a word from the way he read his newspaper—as I did myself, picking out the words which were like English ones. "He's been here a month," Lucia said. "They turned him out of Guatemala and Honduras."

You couldn't keep any secrets for five hours in this border town. Lucia had only been twenty-four hours in the place, but she knew all about Mr. Joseph Calloway. The only reason I didn't know about him (and I'd been in the place two weeks) was because I couldn't talk the language any more than Mr. Calloway could. There wasn't another soul in the place who didn't know the story—the whole story of the Halling Investment Trust and the proceedings or extradition. Any man doing dusty business in any of the wooden booths in the town is better fitted by long observation to tell Mr. Calloway's tale

"Across the Bridge" from *Twenty-One Stories* by Graham Greene. Copyright 1947, © renewed 1975 by Graham Greene. Published in England in *Collected Stories* by The Bodley Head and William Heinemann. Reprinted by permission of The Viking Press, and Laurence Pollinger Limited.

than I am, except that I was in—literally— at the finish. They all watched the drama proceed with immense interest, sympathy and respect. For, after all, he had a million.

Every once in a while through the long steamy day, a boy came and cleaned Mr. Calloway's shoes: he hadn't the right words to resist them—they pretended not to know his English. He must have had his shoes cleaned the day Lucia and I watched him at least half a dozen times. At midday he took a stroll across the square to the Antonio Bar and had a bottle of beer, the setter sticking to heel as if they were out for a country walk in England (he had, you may remember, one of the biggest estates in Norfolk). After his bottle of beer, he would walk down between the moneychangers' huts to the Rio Grande and look across the bridge into the United States: people came and went constantly in cars. Then back to the square till lunchtime. He was staying in the best hotel, but you don't get good hotels in this border town: nobody stays in them more than a night. The good hotels were on the other side of the bridge: you could see their electric signs twenty stories high from the little square at night, like lighthouses marking the United States.

You may ask what I'd been doing in so drab a spot for a fortnight. There was no interest in the place for anyone; it was just damp and dust and poverty, a kind of shabby replica of the town across the river: both had squares in the same spots; both had the same number of cinemas. One was cleaner than the other, that was all, and more expensive, much more expensive. I'd stayed across there a couple of nights waiting for a man a tourist bureau said was driving down from Detroit to Yucatan and would sell a place in his car for some fantastically small figure—twenty dollars, I think it was. I don't know if he existed or was invented by the optimistic half-caste in the agency; anyway, he never turned up and so I waited, not much caring, on the cheap side of the river. It didn't much matter; I was living. One day I meant to give up the man from Detroit and go home or go south, but it was easier not to decide anything in a hurry. Lucia was just waiting for a car going the other way, but she didn't have to wait so long. We waited together and watched Mr. Calloway waiting—for God knows what.

I don't know how to treat this story—it was a tragedy for Mr. Calloway, it was poetic retribution, I suppose, in the eyes of the shareholders he'd ruined with his bogus transactions, and to Lucia and me, at this stage, it was pure comedy—except when he kicked the dog. I'm not a sentimentalist about dogs, I prefer people to be cruel to animals rather than to human beings, but I couldn't help being revolted at the way he'd kick that animal—with a hint of cold-blooded venom, not in anger' but as if he were getting even for some trick it had played him a long while ago. That generally happened when he returned from the bridge: it was the only sign of anything resembling emotion he showed. Otherwise he looked a small, set, gentle creature with silver hair and a silver mustache, and gold-rimmed glasses, and one gold tooth like a flaw in character.

Lucia hadn't been accurate when she said he'd been turned out of Guatemala and Honduras; he'd left voluntarily when the extradition proceedings seemed likely to go through and moved north. Mexico is still not a very centralized state, and it is possible to get round governors as you can't get round cabinet ministers or judges. And so he waited there on the border for the next move. That earlier part of the story is, I suppose, dramatic, but I didn't watch it and I can't invent what I haven't seen—the long waiting in anterooms, the bribes taken and refused, the growing fear of arrest, and then the flight—in gold-rimmed glasses—covering his tracks as well as he could, but this wasn't finance and he was an amateur at escape. And so he'd washed up here, under my eyes and Lucia's eyes, sitting all day under the bandstand, nothing to read but a Mexican paper, nothing to do but look across the river at the United States, quite unaware, I suppose, that everyone knew everything about him, once a day kicking his dog. Perhaps in its semi-setter way it reminded him too much of the Norfolk estate—though that too, I suppose, was the reason he kept it.

And the next act again was pure comedy. I hesitate to think what this man worth a million was costing his country as they edged him out from this land and that. Perhaps somebody was getting tired of the business, careless; anyway, they sent across two detectives, with an old photograph. He'd grown his silvery mustache since that had been taken, and he'd aged a lot, and they couldn't catch sight of him. They hadn't been across the bridge two hours when everybody knew that there were two foreign detectives in town looking for Mr. Calloway—everybody knew, that is to say, except Mr. Calloway, who couldn't talk Spanish. There were plenty of people who could have told him in English, but they didn't. It wasn't cruelty, it was a sort of awe and respect: like a bull, he was on show, sitting there mournfully in the plaza with his dog, a magnificent spectacle for which we all had ringside seats.

I ran into one of the policemen in the Bar Antonio. He was disgusted; he had had some idea that when he crossed the bridge life was going to be different, so much more color and sun, and—I suspect —love, and all he found were wide mud streets where the nocturnal rain lay in pools, and mangy dogs, smells and cockroaches in his bedroom, and the nearest to love, the open door of the Academia Comercial, where pretty mestizo [1] girls

[1] **mestizo** (mes·tē'zō): a person of Spanish and Indian blood.

sat all the morning learning to typewrite. Tip-tap-tip-tap-tip—perhaps they had a dream, too—jobs on the other side of the bridge, where life was going to be so much more luxurious, refined and amusing.

We got into conversation; he seemed surprised that I knew who they both were and what they wanted. He said, "We've got information this man Calloway's in town."

"He's knocking around somewhere," I said.

"Could you point him out?"

"Oh, I don't know him by sight," I said.

He drank his beer and thought a while. "I'll go out and sit in the plaza. He's sure to pass sometime."

I finished my beer and went quickly off and found Lucia. I said, "Hurry, we're going to see an arrest." We didn't care a thing about Mr. Calloway, he was just an elderly man who kicked his dog and swindled the poor, and who deserved anything he got. So we made for the plaza; we knew Calloway would be there, but it had never occurred to either of us that the detectives wouldn't recognize him. There was quite a surge of people round the place; all the fruitsellers and bootblacks in town seemed to have arrived together; we had to force our way through, and there in the little green stuffy center of the place, sitting on adjoining seats, were the two plainclothesmen and Mr. Calloway. I've never known the place so silent; everybody was on tiptoe, and the plainclothesmen were staring at the crowd looking for Mr. Calloway, and Mr. Calloway sat on his usual seat staring out over the moneychanging booths at the United States.

"It can't go on. It just can't," Lucia said. But it did. It got more fantastic still. Somebody ought to write a play about it. We sat as close as we dared. We were afraid all the time we were going to laugh. The semi-setter scratched for fleas and Mr. Calloway watched the U.S.A. The two detectives watched the crowd, and the crowd watched the show with solemn

satisfaction. Then one of the detectives got up and went over to Mr. Calloway. That's the end, I thought. But it wasn't, it was the beginning. For some reason they had eliminated him from their list of suspects. I shall never know why.

The man said, "You speak English?"

"I *am* English," Mr. Calloway said.

Even that didn't tear it, and the strangest thing of all was the way Mr. Calloway came alive. I don't think anybody had spoken to him like that for weeks. The Mexicans were too respectful—he was a man with a million—and it had never occurred to Lucia and me to treat him casually like a human being; even in our eyes he had been magnified by the colossal theft and the worldwide pursuit.

He said, "This is rather a dreadful place, don't you think?"

"It is," the policeman said.

"I can't think what brings anybody across the bridge."

"Duty," the policeman said gloomily. "I suppose you are passing through."

"Yes," Mr. Calloway said.

"I'd have expected over here there'd have been—you know what I mean—life. You read things about Mexico."

"Oh, life," Mr. Calloway said. He spoke firmly and precisely, as if to a committee of shareholders. "That begins on the other side."

"You don't appreciate your own country until you leave it."

"That's very true," Mr. Calloway said. "Very true."

At first it was difficult not to laugh, and then after a while there didn't seem to be much to laugh at; an old man imagining all the fine things going on beyond the international bridge. I think he thought of the town opposite as a combination of London and Norfolk—theaters and cocktail bars, a little shooting and a walk round the field at evening with the dog—that miserable imitation of a setter—poking the ditches. He'd never been across, he couldn't know that it was just the same thing over again—even the same layout; only the streets were paved and the hotels had ten more stories, and life was more expensive, and everything was a little bit cleaner. There wasn't anything Mr. Calloway would have called living—no galleries, no bookshops, just *Film Fun* and the local paper, and *Click* and *Focus* and the tabloids.

"Well," said Mr. Calloway, "I think I'll take a stroll before lunch. You need an appetite to swallow the food here. I generally go down and look at the bridge about now. Care to come too?"

The detective shook his head. "No," he said, "I'm on duty. I'm looking for a fellow." And that, of course, gave *him* away. As far as Mr. Calloway could understand, there was only one "fellow" in the world anyone was looking for—his brain had eliminated friends who were seeking their friends, husbands who might be waiting for their wives, all objectives of any search but just the one. The power of elimination was what had made him a financier—he could forget the people behind the shares.

That was the last we saw of him for a while. We didn't see him going into the Botica Paris to get his aspirin, or walking back from the bridge with his dog. He simply disappeared, and when he disappeared, people began to talk, and the detectives heard the talk. They looked silly enough, and they got busy after the very man they'd been sitting next to in the garden. Then they too disappeared. They, as well as Mr. Calloway, had gone to the state capital to see the Governor and the Chief of Police, and it must have been an amusing sight there too, as they bumped into Mr. Calloway and sat with him in the waiting rooms. I suspect Mr. Calloway was generally shown in first, for everyone knew he was worth a million. Only in Europe is it possible for a man to be a criminal as well as a rich man.

Anyway, after about a week the whole pack of them returned by the same train. Mr. Calloway traveled Pullman, and the two policemen traveled in the daycoach. It was evident that they hadn't got their extradition order.

Lucia had left by that time. The car came and went across the bridge. I stood in Mexico and watched her get out at the United States Customs. She wasn't anything in particular but she looked beautiful at a distance as she gave me a wave out of the United States and got back into the car. And I suddenly felt sympathy for Mr. Calloway, as if there were something over there which you couldn't find here, and turning round I saw him back on his old beat, with the dog at his heels.

I said, "Good afternoon," as if it had been all along our habit to greet each other. He looked tired and ill and dusty, and I felt sorry for him—to think of the kind of victory he'd been winning, with so much expenditure of cash and care—the prize this dirty and dreary town, the booths of the money-changers, the awful little beauty parlors with their wicker chairs and sofas looking like the reception rooms of brothels, that hot and stuffy garden by the bandstand.

He replied gloomily, "Good morning," and the dog started to sniff at some ordure and he turned and kicked it with fury, with depression, with despair.

And at that moment a taxi with the two policemen in it passed us on its way to the bridge. They must have seen that kick; perhaps they were cleverer than I had given them credit for, perhaps they were just sentimental about animals, and thought they'd do a good deed, and the rest happened by accident. But the fact remains—those two pillars of the law set about the stealing of Mr. Calloway's dog.

He watched them go by. Then he said, "Why don't you go across?"

"It's cheaper here," I said.

"I mean just for an evening. Have a meal at that place we can see at night in the sky. Go to the theater."

"There isn't a chance."

He said angrily, sucking his gold tooth, "Well, anyway, get away from here." He stared down the hill and up the other side. He couldn't see that that street climbing up from the bridge contained only the same moneychangers' booths as this one.

I said, "Why don't *you* go?"

He said evasively, "Oh—business."

I said, "It's only a question of money. You don't *have* to pass by the bridge."

He said with faint interest, "I don't talk Spanish."

"There isn't a soul here," I said, "who doesn't talk English."

He looked at me with surprise. "Is that so?" he said. "Is that so?"

It's as I have said; he'd never tried to talk to anyone, and they respected him too much to talk to him—he was worth a million. I don't know whether I'm glad or sorry that I told him that. If I hadn't, he might be there now, sitting by the bandstand having his shoes cleaned—alive and suffering.

Three days later his dog disappeared. I found him looking for it, calling it softly and shamefacedly between the palms of the garden. He looked embarrassed. He said in a low angry voice, "I *hate* that dog. The beastly mongrel," and called "Rover, Rover" in a voice which didn't carry five yards. He said, "I bred setters once. I'd have shot a dog like that." It reminded him, I *was* right, of Norfolk, and he lived in the memory, and he hated it for its imperfection. He was a man without a family and without friends, and his only enemy was that dog. You couldn't call the law an enemy; you have to be intimate with an enemy.

Late that afternoon someone told him they'd seen the dog walking across the bridge. It wasn't true, of course, but we didn't know that then—they'd paid a Mexican five pesos to smuggle it across. So all that afternoon and the next Mr. Calloway sat in the garden having his shoes cleaned over and over again, and thinking how a dog could just walk across like that, and a human being, an immortal soul, was bound here in the awful routine of the little walk and the unspeakable meals and the aspirin at the *botica*. That dog was seeing things he couldn't see—that hateful dog. It made him mad—I think literally mad. You must remember the man had been going on for months. He had a million and

he was living on two pounds a week, with nothing to spend his money on. He sat there and brooded on the hideous injustice of it. I think he'd have crossed over one day in any case, but the dog was the last straw.

Next day when he wasn't to be seen I guessed he'd gone across, and I went too. The American town is as small as the Mexican. I knew I couldn't miss him if he was there, and I was still curious. A little sorry for him, but not much.

I caught sight of him first in the only drugstore, having a Coca-Cola, and then once outside a cinema looking at the posters; he had dressed with extreme neatness, as if for a party, but there was no party. On my third time round, I came on the detectives—they were having Coca-Colas in the drugstore, and they must have missed Mr. Calloway by inches. I went in and sat down at the bar.

"Hello," I said, "you still about?" I suddenly felt anxious for Mr. Calloway, I didn't want them to meet.

One of them said, "Where's Calloway?"

"Oh," I said, "he's hanging on."

"But not his dog," he said, and laughed. The other looked a little shocked, he didn't like anyone to *talk* cynically about a dog. Then they got up—they had a car outside.

"Have another?" I said.

"No, thanks. We've got to keep moving."

The man bent close and confided to me, "Calloway's on this side."

"No!" I said.

"And his dog."

"He's looking for it," the other said.

"I'm damned if he is," I said, and again one of them looked a little shocked, as if I'd insulted the dog.

I don't think Mr. Calloway was looking for his dog, but his dog certainly found him. There was a sudden hilarious yapping from the car and out plunged the semi-setter and gambolled furiously down the street. One of the detectives—the sentimental one—was into the car before we got to the door and was off after the dog.

Near the bottom of the long road to the bridge was Mr. Calloway—I do believe he'd come down to look at the Mexican side when he found there was nothing but the drugstore and the cinemas and the paper shops on the American. He saw the dog coming and yelled at it to go home— "home, home, home," as if they were in Norfolk—it took no notice at all, pelting toward him. Then he saw the police car coming and ran. After that, everything happened too quickly, but I think the order of events was this—the dog started across the road right in front of the car, and Mr. Calloway yelled, at the dog or the car, I don't know which. Anyway, the detective swerved—he said later, weakly, at the inquiry, that he couldn't run over a dog, and down went Mr. Calloway, in a mess of broken glass and gold rims and silver hair, and blood. The dog was on to him before any of us could reach him, licking and whimpering and licking. I saw Mr. Calloway put up his hand, and down it went across the dog's neck and the whimper rose to a stupid bark of triumph, but Mr. Calloway was dead—shock and a weak heart.

"Poor old geezer," the detective said, "I bet he really loved that dog," and it's true that the attitude in which he lay looked more like a caress than a blow. I thought it was meant to be a blow, but the detective may have been right. It all seemed to me a little too touching to be true as the old crook lay there with his arm over the dog's neck, dead with his million between the moneychangers' huts, but it's as well to be humble in the face of human nature. He had come across the river for something, and it may, after all, have been the dog he was looking for. It sat there, baying its stupid and mongrel triumph across his body, like a piece of sentimental statuary. The nearest he could get to the fields, ditches, the horizon of his home. It was comic and it was pitiable; but it wasn't less comic because the man was dead. Death doesn't change comedy to tragedy, and if that last gesture was one of affection, I suppose it was only one

more indication of a human being's capacity for self-deception, our baseless optimism that is so much more appalling than our despair.

FOR STUDY AND DISCUSSION

1. Is Calloway's inability to "talk the language" simply a plot device or does it have a deeper significance? Explain.

2. Describe the relationship between Calloway and the dog. Consider especially the sentences, "He was a man without a family and without friends, and his only enemy was that dog. You couldn't call the law an enemy; you have to be intimate with an enemy."

3. Can any incidents in the story be described as comic? If so, what is the importance of this incident to the story? Is the comedy happy or bitter? Explain.

4. What is ironic about Calloway's death? about the detective's remark after the death? Why is Calloway's last action left ambiguous?

5. The narrator remarks, "I don't know how to treat this story—it was a tragedy for Mr. Calloway, it was poetic retribution, I suppose, in the eyes of the shareholders . . . and to Lucia and me, at this stage, it was pure comedy . . ." Would you describe this story as tragedy, comedy, or neither? Explain.

6. In the last sentence of the story, the narrator speaks of "a human being's capacity for self-deception, our baseless optimism that is so much more appalling than our despair." What does he mean? What is the importance of this comment to the story? Can Calloway be viewed as more than simply a dishonest, rather trivial person? How does he reflect the general situation of all human beings, as the narrator views this situation? How does the story's title respect this situation?

7. What kind of person is the narrator? How do you know? Why do you think the author chose this kind of person as a narrator? Does the use of a narrator rob the reader of the chance to make his own discoveries? If so, is this a weakness in the story's technique, or is a narrator necessary to this story?

FOR COMPOSITION

Discuss the narrator's role in making clear the theme of this story. Consider how the story might be different if another narrator— for example, a brash, aggressive salesperson —had told it.

DYLAN THOMAS
(1914–1953)

More than any other poet following W. H. Auden and Stephen Spender, it was Dylan Thomas who returned English poetry to a personal, lyrical romanticism. Auden and his friends wrote poems that were cool, mocking, and jazzy, and that reflected their divided attitude toward the modern world: their desire to belong to it and, at the same time, their distrust of it. Thomas's poems, with their rush of feeling, either ignored the world or took it by storm. His resonant language and evocative images are frequently compressed and personal, and several of his poems are among the most difficult in the English language. Yet many readers, even when they do not fully understand Thomas's poems, find themselves responding to his magnificent use of words and sense of driving emotion. Stephen Spender has called him "a poet obsessed with words, a linguistic genius. . . . His poems have a bardic primitive quality, and at the same time there is superimposed on this an awareness of the discoveries of modern psychology." Some readers feel Thomas was like a high priest or magician, working a spell on the reader through powerful incantations. Thomas's manuscripts reveal that he was a careful craftsman who revised his poems many times to get the effects he wanted. And intensive study of his best poems uncovers, not an impulsive wildness, but a coherent expression of Thomas's personal view of the world: his joy in love and physical beauty, his rage against death, his search for a means of overcoming mortality. Thomas himself said of his poetry, "My poems are written for the love of man and the praise of God—and I'd be a fool if they weren't."

Dylan Thomas was born in Swansea, a seacoast town in Southern Wales. As he records it in *Quite Early One Morning,* he spent a happy childhood in Swansea, a great industrial center surrounded by fine natural scenery. Although he later went to London, he settled once again in Wales in his later years, and the Welsh countryside obviously left its mark on his poetry. His first volume, *Eighteen Poems,* was published in 1934 when he was only twenty. His early work showed wonderful promise. His poems were cloudy but wonderfully alive. Elder poets like Edith Sitwell at once recognized in Thomas's work a distinctive voice and acclaimed him as an important new talent, perhaps a genius. Later poetry was collected in *25 Poems* (1936), *The Map of Love* (1939), and *New Poems* (1943). Although, as he grew older, he wrote fewer and fewer poems—only six in the last six years of his life—his late work shows that he was moving toward a simpler, clearer, more direct poetic language. His *Collected Poems* was published the year before his death.

As well as a poet, Thomas was at various times a reporter, a writer of radio and film scripts, and a lecturer. It was as a reader of poetry, his own and others', that he gained the widest audience for his work. Several times he toured the United States to give readings and lectures. Delivering his poems and his radio play, *Under Milk Wood,* in a deep, resonant voice, he drew large audiences, particularly of college students, who were fascinated not only by his voice but also by his impulsive charm, his wit, and his striking appearance. When he died at thirty-nine, he had already become a legend.

Fern Hill

This poem, about a summer on a Welsh farm, is an echo of Thomas's youth.

Now as I was young and easy under the apple boughs
About the lilting house and happy as the grass was green,
   The night above the dingle° starry,
     Time let me hail and climb
    Golden in the heydays of his eyes,   5
And honored among wagons I was prince of the apple towns
And once below a time I lordly had the trees and leaves
    Trail with daisies and barley
   Down the rivers of the windfall light.

And as I was green and carefree, famous among the barns   10
About the happy yard and singing as the farm was home,
   In the sun that is young once only,
     Time let me play and be
    Golden in the mercy of his means,
And green and golden I was huntsman and herdsman, the calves   15
Sang to my horn, the foxes on the hills barked clear and cold,
    And the sabbath rang slowly
   In the pebbles of the holy streams.

All the sun long it was running, it was lovely, the hay
Fields high as the house, the tunes from the chimneys, it was air   20
   And playing, lovely and watery
    And fire green as grass.
   And nightly under the simple stars
As I rode to sleep the owls were bearing the farm away,
All the moon long I heard, blessed among stables, the nightjars°   25
   Flying with the ricks,° and the horses
    Flashing into the dark.

3. **dingle:** little valley.   25. **nightjars:** a kind of night bird.   26. **ricks:** haystacks.

And then to awake, and the farm, like a wanderer white
With the dew, come back, the cock on his shoulder: it was all
    Shining, it was Adam and maiden,   30
      The sky gathered again
    And the sun grew round that very day.
So it must have been after the birth of the simple light
In the first, spinning place, the spellbound horses walking warm
    Out of the whinnying green stable   35
      On to the fields of praise.

And honored among foxes and pheasants by the gay house
Under the new made clouds and happy as the heart was long,
    In the sun born over and over,
      I ran my heedless ways,   40
    My wishes raced through the house high hay
And nothing I cared, at my sky blue trades, that time allows
In all his tuneful turning so few and such morning songs
    Before the children green and golden
      Follow him out of grace,   45

Nothing I cared, in the lamb white days, that time would take me
Up to the swallow thronged loft by the shadow of my hand,
    In the moon that is always rising,
      Nor that riding to sleep
I should hear him fly with the high fields   50
And wake to the farm forever fled from the childless land
Oh as I was young and easy in the mercy of his means,
    Time held me green and dying
    Though I sang in my chains like the sea.

Do Not Go Gentle into That Good Night

This poem was written when Thomas's father was dying.

Do not go gentle into that good night,
Old age should burn and rave at close of day;
Rage, rage against the dying of the light.

Though wise men at their end know dark is right,
Because their words had worked no lightning they   5
Do not go gentle into that good night.

Good men, the last wave by, crying how bright
Their frail deeds might have danced in a green bay,
Rage, rage against the dying of the light.

Wild men who caught and sang the sun in flight,   10
And learn, too late, they grieved it on its way,
Do not go gentle into that good night.

Grave men, near death, who see with blinding sight
Blind eyes could blaze like meteors and be gay,
Rage, rage against the dying of the light.   15

And you, my father there on the sad height,
Curse, bless, me now with your fierce tears, I pray.
Do not go gentle into that good night.
Rage, rage against the dying of the light.

The Force That Through the Green Fuse Drives

The force that through the green fuse drives the flower
Drives my green age; that blasts the roots of trees
Is my destroyer.
And I am dumb to tell the crooked rose
My youth is bent by the same wintry fever.   5

The force that drives the water through the rocks
Drives my red blood; that dries the mouthing streams
Turns mine to wax.
And I am dumb to mouth unto my veins
How at the mountain spring the same mouth sucks.   10

The hand that whirls the water in the pool
Stirs the quicksand; that ropes the blowing wind
Hauls my shroud sail.
And I am dumb to tell the hanging man
How of my clay is made the hangman's lime.   15

The lips of time leech to the fountain head;
Love drips and gathers, but the fallen blood
Shall calm her sores.
And I am dumb to tell a weather's wind
How time has ticked a heaven round the stars.   20

And I am dumb to tell the lover's tomb
How at my sheet goes the same crooked worm.

FERN HILL

1. What specific scenes and childhood activities are mentioned in the poem? Are they described matter-of-factly and realistically? Support your answer with passages from the poem. What significance does Thomas give these details?

2. What two colors dominate this poem? With what are these colors associated in the poem?

3. How does the mood of the poem change in the last stanza? What details in previous stanzas anticipate this change of mood?

4. Point out details in the poem that have a religious implication. How do these details call up a state of innocence—or of grace— that was the human state before the fall? How does the poet see himself as a child? as a man?

5. "Fern Hill" is full of striking images and memorable sounds. Select lines and phrases that seem to you most effective.

DO NOT GO GENTLE INTO THAT GOOD NIGHT

1. What knowledge does the poet say that "wise men at their end" have gained? good men? wild men? grave men?

2. Point out contrasting images of light and dark. What effect do they have on the poem?

3. Why is the "night" called "good"? Why is the poet's father, then, asked to "rage" against it? Explain why the poet calls on his father to "Curse, bless, me now." What is the emotional effect of the poet's divided attitude toward death?

4. "Do Not Go Gentle" is a *villanelle,* an intricately patterned kind of poem. Note that there are only two rhymes in the poem, and that the first and third lines are used as refrains throughout the rest of the poem. Note also the use of three-line stanzas and the final stanza of four lines, which concludes with the first and third line of the poem. All these are characteristics of a villanelle. Because of its intricate, restrictive pattern, the villanelle form is usually associated with trivial poems designed to display a poet's technical skill. Is "Do Not Go Gentle" a typical villanelle, or does Thomas go beyond the restrictions of the form to write an emotionally powerful work? Explain.

THE FORCE THAT THROUGH THE GREEN FUSE DRIVES

1. Explain the "force" that is the subject of this poem. How does it link the poet to flowers, trees, rocks, and so on?

2. What is meant by "green age" (line 2)? by "the same wintry fever" (line 5)? What is "the same mouth" referred to in line 10? How is time compared to a leech in the fourth stanza?

3. What common subject does this poem share with "Fern Hill"? How do these poems differ in treating this subject?

FOR COMPOSITION

Many of Thomas's poems reveal his concern with our tragic destiny; that is, with the fact that we must lose our youth and vitality and eventually die. Show how this concern is revealed by the poems by Thomas that you have read. In what way do these poems show one man, in several moods, reacting to one major fact of existence? How can Thomas's poems be seen as an attempt to go beyond the limitations of mortality?

DORIS LESSING
(1919–   )

Doris Lessing is one of a number of African authors writing in English who have settled in Europe. A characteristic most of these writers have in common is a deep affection for their own continent coupled with a reluctance to live in it and a sharp eye for its defects. Mrs. Lessing has written that writers brought up in Africa have the advantage of "being at the center of a modern battlefield, part of a society in rapid, dramatic change." But, she notes, being too close to this battlefield, too exposed to the brutalities that are a part of the battle, tends to limit the writer's point of view and dry up the imagination. Therefore, it becomes necessary for African writers to leave their country and gain the perspective which travel and distance give. "I believe that the chief gift from Africa to writers, white and black, is the continent itself, its presence, which for some people is like an old fever, latent always in their blood; or like an old wound throbbing in the bones as the air changes. That is not a place to visit unless one chooses to be an exile ever afterward from an inexplicable majestic silence lying just over the border of memory or of thought. Africa gives you the knowledge that man is a small creature, among other creatures, in a large landscape."

The daughter of British parents, Doris Lessing was born in Persia and grew up in Southern Rhodesia. In 1949 she settled in England. Since living there, she has written a number of novels, many short stories, and some poetry. In her book *In Pursuit of the English,* she gives an absorbing account of her early years in England. Her typical heroine is a frustrated, highly intellectual young woman who struggles, against the inadequacies of her environment, to realize herself. Probably her two most important works are *The Golden Notebook,* her most experimental piece of fiction, and a series of novels known collectively as *Children of Violence.*

Mrs. Lessing is a very conscious, probing writer, greatly preoccupied with social questions. One critic has summed up her work as "enormously lucid sociological journalism." There is a strong didactic streak in her work: not only do her novels explore social questions but they take a very clear stand on them. She is one of the few contemporary fiction writers who have tried to deal seriously with some of the serious questions that vex our civilization. The London *Times* has called her "not only the best woman novelist we have, but one of the most serious and intelligent and honest writers of the whole postwar generation."

Through the Tunnel

GOING to the shore on the first morning of the vacation, the young English boy stopped at a turning of the path and looked down at a wild and rocky bay, and then over to the crowded beach he knew so well from other years. His mother walked on in front of him, carrying a bright striped bag in one hand. Her other arm, swinging loose, was very white in the sun. The boy watched that white, naked arm, and turned his eyes, which had a frown behind them, toward the bay and back again to his mother. When she felt he was not with her, she swung around. "Oh, there you are, Jerry!" she said. She looked impatient, then smiled. "Why, darling, would you rather not come with me? Would you rather——" She frowned, conscientiously worrying over what amusements he might secretly be longing for, which she had been too busy or too careless to imagine. He was very familiar with that anxious, apologetic smile. Contrition sent him running after her. And yet, as he ran, he looked back over his shoulder at the wild bay; and all morning, as he played on the safe beach, he was thinking of it.

Next morning, when it was time for the routine of swimming and sunbathing, his mother said, "Are you tired of the usual beach, Jerry? Would you like to go somewhere else?"

"Oh, no!" he said quickly, smiling at her out of that unfailing impulse of contrition—a sort of chivalry. Yet, walking down the path with her, he blurted out, "I'd like to go and have a look at those rocks down there."

She gave the idea her attention. It was a wild-looking place, and there was no

"Through the Tunnel" from *The Habit of Loving* by Doris Lessing, copyright © 1955, 1957 by Doris Lessing, originally published in *The New Yorker*. Reprinted by permission of Thomas Y. Crowell Company.

one there; but she said, "Of course, Jerry. When you've had enough, come to the big beach. Or just go straight back to the villa, if you like." She walked away, that bare arm, now slightly reddened from yesterday's sun, swinging. And he almost ran after her again, feeling it unbearable that she should go by herself, but he did not.

She was thinking, Of course he's old enough to be safe without me. Have I been keeping him too close? He mustn't feel he ought to be with me. I must be careful.

He was an only child, eleven years old. She was a widow. She was determined to be neither possessive nor lacking in devotion. She went worrying off to her beach.

As for Jerry, once he saw that his mother had gained her beach, he began the steep descent to the bay. From where he was, high up among red-brown rocks, it was a scoop of moving bluish green fringed with white. As he went lower, he saw that it spread among small promontories and inlets of rough, sharp rock, and the crisping, lapping surface showed stains of purple and darker blue. Finally, as he ran sliding and scraping down the last few yards, he saw an edge of white surf and the shallow, luminous movement of water over white sand, and, beyond that, a solid, heavy blue.

He ran straight into the water and began swimming. He was a good swimmer. He went out fast over the gleaming sand, over a middle region where rocks lay like discolored monsters under the surface, and then he was in the real sea—a warm sea where irregular cold currents from the deep water shocked his limbs.

When he was so far out that he could look back not only on the little bay but past the promontory that was between it and the big beach, he floated on the buoyant surface and looked for his mother. There she was, a speck of yellow under an umbrella that looked like a slice of orange peel. He swam back to shore, relieved at being sure she was there, but all at once very lonely.

On the edge of a small cape that marked

the side of the bay away from the promontory was a loose scatter of rocks. Above them, some boys were stripping off their clothes. They came running, naked, down to the rocks. The English boy swam toward them, but kept his distance at a stone's throw. They were of that coast; all of them were burned smooth dark brown and speaking a language he did not understand. To be with them, of them, was a craving that filled his whole body. He swam a little closer; they turned and watched him with narrowed, alert dark eyes. Then one smiled and waved. It was enough. In a minute, he had swum in and was on the rocks beside them, smiling with a desperate, nervous supplication. They shouted cheerful greetings at him; and then, as he preserved his nervous, uncomprehending smile, they understood that he was a foreigner strayed from his own beach, and they proceeded to forget him. But he was happy. He was with them.

They began diving again and again from a high point into a well of blue sea between rough, pointed rocks. After they had dived and come up, they swam around, hauled themselves up, and waited their turn to dive again. They were big boys—men, to Jerry. He dived, and they watched him; and when he swam around to take his place, they made way for him. He felt he was accepted and he dived again, carefully, proud of himself.

Soon the biggest of the boys poised himself, shot down into the water, and did not come up. The others stood about, watching. Jerry, after waiting for the sleek brown head to appear, let out a yell of warning; they looked at him idly and turned their eyes back toward the water. After a long time, the boy came up on the other side of a big dark rock, letting the air out of his lungs in a spluttering gasp and a shout of triumph. Immediately the rest of them dived in. One moment, the morning seemed full of clattering boys; the next, the air and the surface of the water were empty. But through the heavy blue, dark shapes could be seen moving and groping.

Jerry dived, shot past the school of underwater swimmers, saw a black wall of rock looming at him, touched it, and bobbed up at once to the surface, where the wall was a low barrier he could see across. There was no one visible; under him, in the water, the dim shapes of the swimmers had disappeared. Then one, and then another of the boys came up on the far side of the barrier of rock, and he understood that they had swum through some gap or hole in it. He plunged down again. He could see nothing through the stinging salt water but the blank rock. When he came up the boys were all on the diving rock, preparing to attempt the feat again. And now, in a panic of failure, he yelled up, in English, "Look at me! Look!" and he began splashing and kicking in the water like a foolish dog.

They looked down gravely, frowning. He knew the frown. At moments of failure, when he clowned to claim his mother's attention, it was with just this grave, embarrassed inspection that she rewarded him. Through his hot shame, feeling the pleading grin on his face like a scar that he could never remove, he looked up at the group of big brown boys on the rock and shouted, *"Bonjour! Merci! Au revoir! Monsieur, monsieur!"* while he hooked his fingers round his ears and waggled them.

Water surged into his mouth; he choked, sank, came up. The rock, lately weighted with boys, seemed to rear up out of the water as their weight was removed. They were flying down past him, now, into the water; the air was full of falling bodies. Then the rock was empty in the hot sunlight. He counted one, two, three. . . .

At fifty, he was terrified. They must all be drowning beneath him, in the watery caves of the rock! At a hundred, he stared around him at the empty hillside, wondering if he should yell for help. He counted faster, faster, to hurry them up, to bring them to the surface quickly, to drown them quickly—anything rather than the terror of counting on and on into the blue emptiness of the morning. And then, at a hundred and sixty, the water beyond the rock was full of boys blowing like brown whales. They swam back to the shore without a look at him.

He climbed back to the diving rock and sat down, feeling the hot roughness of it under his thighs. The boys were gathering up their bits of clothing and running off along the shore to another promontory. They were leaving to get away from him. He cried openly, fists in his eyes. There was no one to see him, and he cried himself out.

It seemed to him that a long time had passed, and he swam out to where he could see his mother. Yes, she was still there, a yellow spot under an orange umbrella. He swam back to the big rock, climbed up, and dived into the blue pool among the fanged and angry boulders. Down he went, until he touched the wall of rock again. But the salt was so painful in his eyes that he could not see.

He came to the surface, swam to shore and went back to the villa to wait for his mother. Soon she walked slowly up the path, swinging her striped bag, the flushed, naked arm dangling beside her. "I want some swimming goggles," he panted, defiant and beseeching.

She gave him a patient, inquisitive look as she said casually, "Well, of course, darling."

But now, now, now! He must have them this minute, and no other time. He nagged and pestered until she went with him to a shop. As soon as she had bought the goggles, he grabbed them from her hand as if she were going to claim them for herself, and was off, running down the steep path to the bay.

Jerry swam out to the big barrier rock, adjusted the goggles, and dived. The impact of the water broke the rubber-enclosed vacuum, and the goggles came loose. He understood that he must swim down to the base of the rock from the surface of the water. He fixed the goggles tight and firm, filled his lungs, and floated, face down, on the water. Now, he could see. It was as if he had eyes of a different kind—fish eyes that showed everything clear and delicate and wavering in the bright water.

Under him, six or seven feet down, was a floor of perfectly clean, shining white sand, rippled firm and hard by the tides. Two grayish shapes steered there, like long, rounded pieces of wood or slate. They were fish. He saw them nose toward each other, poise motionless, make a dart forward, swerve off, and come around again. It was like a water dance. A few inches above them the water sparkled as if sequins were dropping through it. Fish again—myriads of minute fish, the length of his fingernail, were drifting through the water, and in a moment he could feel the innumerable tiny touches of them against his limbs. It was like swimming in flaked silver. The great rock the big boys had swum through rose sheer out of the white sand—black, tufted lightly with greenish weed. He could see no gap in it. He swam down to its base.

Again and again he rose, took a big chestful of air, and went down. Again and again he groped over the surface of the rock, feeling it, almost hugging it in the desperate need to find the entrance. And then, once, while he was clinging to the black wall, his knees came up and he shot his feet out forward and they met no obstacle. He had found the hole.

He gained the surface, clambered about the stones that littered the barrier rock until he found a big one, and, with this in his arms, let himself over the side of the rock. He dropped, with the weight, straight to the sandy floor. Clinging tight to the anchor of stone, he lay on his side and looked in under the dark shelf at the place where his feet had gone. He could see the hole. It was an irregular, dark gap; but he could not see deep into it. He let go of his anchor, clung with his hands to the edges of the hole, and tried to push himself in.

He got his head in, found his shoulders jammed, moved them in sidewise, and was inside as far as his waist. He could see nothing ahead. Something soft and clammy touched his mouth; he saw a dark frond moving against the grayish rock, and panic filled him. He thought of octopuses, of clinging weed. He pushed himself out backward and caught a glimpse, as he retreated, of a harmless tentacle of seaweed drifting in the mouth of the tunnel. But it was enough. He reached the sunlight, swam to shore, and lay on the diving rock. He looked down into the blue well of water. He knew he must find his way through that cave, or hole, or tunnel, and out the other side.

First, he thought, he must learn to control his breathing. He let himself down into the water with another big stone in his arms, so that he could lie effortlessly on the bottom of the sea. He counted. One, two, three. He counted steadily. He could hear the movement of blood in his chest. Fifty-one, fifty-two. . . . His chest was hurting. He let go of the rock and went up into the air. He saw that the sun was low. He rushed to the villa and found his mother at her supper. She said only "Did you enjoy yourself?" and he said "Yes."

All night the boy dreamed of the water-filled cave in the rock, and as soon as breakfast was over he went to the bay.

That night, his nose bled badly. For hours he had been underwater, learning to hold his breath, and now he felt weak and dizzy. His mother said, "I shouldn't overdo things, darling, if I were you."

That day and the next, Jerry exercised his lungs as if everything, the whole of his life, all that he would become, depended upon it. Again his nose bled at night, and his mother insisted on his coming with her the next day. It was a torment to him to waste a day of his careful self-training, but he stayed with her on that other beach, which now seemed a place for small children, a place where his mother might lie safe in the sun. It was not his beach.

He did not ask for permission, on the following day, to go to his beach. He went, before his mother could consider the complicated rights and wrongs of the matter. A day's rest, he discovered, had improved his count by ten. The big boys had made the passage while he counted a hundred and sixty. He had been counting fast, in his fright. Probably now, if he tried, he could get through that long tunnel, but he was not going to try yet. A curious, most unchildlike persistence, a controlled impatience, made him wait. In the meantime, he lay underwater on the white sand, littered now by stones he had brought down from the upper air, and studied the entrance to the tunnel. He knew every jut and corner of it, as far as it was possible to see. It was as if he already felt its sharpness about his shoulders.

He sat by the clock in the villa when his mother was not near, and checked his time. He was incredulous and then proud to find he could hold his breath without strain for two minutes. The words "two minutes," authorized by the clock, brought close the adventure that was so necessary to him.

In another four days, his mother said casually one morning, they must go home. On the day before they left, he would do it. He would do it if it killed him, he said defiantly to himself. But two days before they were to leave—a day of triumph when he increased his count by fifteen—his nose bled so badly that he turned dizzy and had to lie limply over the big rock like a bit of seaweed, watching the thick red blood flow on to the rock and trickle slowly down to the sea. He was frightened. Supposing he turned dizzy in the tunnel? Supposing he died there, trapped? Supposing—his head went around, in the hot sun, and he almost gave up. He thought he would return to the house and lie down, and next summer, perhaps, when he had another year's growth in him—*then* he would go through the hole.

But even after he had made the decision, or thought he had, he found himself sitting up on the rock and looking down into the water; and he knew that now, this moment, when his nose had only just stopped bleeding, when his head was still sore and throbbing—this was the moment when he would try. If he did not do it now, he never would. He was trembling with fear that he would not go; and he was trembling with horror at that long, long tunnel under the rock, under the sea. Even in the open sunlight, the barrier rock seemed very wide and very heavy; tons of rock pressed down on where he would go. If he died there, he would lie until one day—perhaps not before next year—those big boys would swim into it and find it blocked.

He put on his goggles, fitted them tight, tested the vacuum. His hands were shaking. Then he chose the biggest stone he could carry and slipped over the edge of the rock until half of him was in the cool, enclosing water and half in the hot sun. He looked up once at the empty sky, filled his lungs once, twice, and then sank fast to the bottom with the stone. He let it go and began to count. He took the edges of the hole in his hands and drew himself into it, wriggling his shoulders in sidewise as he remembered he must, kicking himself along with his feet.

Soon he was clear inside. He was in a small rockbound hole filled with yellowish-gray water. The water was pushing him up against the roof. The roof was sharp and pained his back. He pulled himself along with his hands—fast, fast—and used his legs as levers. His head knocked against something; a sharp pain dizzied him. Fifty, fifty-one, fifty-two. . . . He was without light, and the water seemed to press upon him with the weight of rock. Seventy-one, seventy-two. . . . There was no strain on his lungs. He felt like an inflated balloon, his lungs were so light and easy, but his head was pulsing.

He was being continually pressed against the sharp roof, which felt slimy as well as sharp. Again he thought of octopuses, and wondered if the tunnel might be filled with weed that could tangle him. He gave himself a panicky, convulsive kick forward, ducked his head, and swam. His feet and hands moved freely, as if in open water. The hole must have widened out. He thought he must be swimming fast, and he was frightened of banging his head if the tunnel narrowed.

A hundred, a hundred and one. . . . The water paled. Victory filled him. His lungs were beginning to hurt. A few more strokes and he would be out. He was counting wildly; he said a hundred and fifteen, and then, a long time later, a hundred and fifteen again. The water was a clear jewel-green all around him. Then he saw, above his head, a crack running up through the rock. Sunlight was falling through it, showing the clean, dark rock of the tunnel, a single mussel shell, and darkness ahead.

He was at the end of what he could do. He looked up at the crack as if it were filled with air and not water, as if he could put his mouth to it to draw in air. A hundred and fifteen, he heard himself say inside his head—but he had said that long ago. He must go on into the blackness ahead, or he would drown. His head was swelling, his lungs cracking. A hundred and fifteen, a hundred and fifteen pounded through his head, and he feebly clutched at rocks in the dark, pulling himself forward, leaving the brief space of sunlit water behind. He felt he was dying. He was no longer quite conscious. He struggled on in the darkness between lapses into unconsciousness. An immense, swelling pain filled his head, and then the darkness cracked with an explosion of green light. His hands, groping forward, met nothing; and his feet, kicking back, propelled him out into the open sea.

He drifted to the surface, his face turned up to the air. He was gasping like a fish. He felt he would sink now and drown; he could not swim the few feet back to the rock. Then he was clutching it and pulling himself up on to it. He lay face down, gasping. He could see nothing but a red-veined, clotted dark. His eyes must have burst, he thought; they were full of blood. He tore off his goggles and a gout of blood went into the sea. His nose was bleeding, and the blood had filled the goggles.

He scooped up handfuls of water from the cool, salty sea, to splash on his face, and did not know whether it was blood or salt water he tasted. After a time, his heart quieted, his eyes cleared, and he sat up. He could see the local boys diving and playing half a mile away. He did not want them. He wanted nothing but to get back home and lie down.

In a short while, Jerry swam to shore and climbed slowly up the path to the villa. He flung himself on his bed and slept, waking at the sound of feet on the path outside. His mother was coming back. He rushed to the bathroom, thinking she must not see his face with bloodstains, or tearstains, on it. He came out of the bathroom and met her as she walked into the villa, smiling, her eyes lighting up.

"Have a nice morning?" she asked, laying her hand on his warm brown shoulder a moment.

"Oh, yes, thank you," he said.

"You look a bit pale." And then, sharp and anxious, "How did you bang your head?"

"Oh, just banged it," he told her.

She looked at him closely. He was strained; his eyes were glazed-looking. She was worried. And then she said to herself, Oh, don't fuss! Nothing can happen. He can swim like a fish.

They sat down to lunch together.

"Mummy," he said, "I can stay under water for two minutes—three minutes, at least." It came bursting out of him.

"Can you, darling?" she said. "Well, I shouldn't overdo it. I don't think you ought to swim any more today."

She was ready for a battle of wills, but he gave in at once. It was no longer of the least importance to go to the bay.

FOR STUDY AND DISCUSSION

1. Describe the relationship between Jerry and his mother at the beginning of the story. Does it remain the same throughout the story? If not, how does it change?

2. The author writes of Jerry's feelings about the boys on the rocks: "To be with them, of them, was a craving that filled his whole body." At the end of this paragraph, she writes, "He was with them." What does this paragraph suggest about Jerry's previous experience on this vacation? about Jerry's relationship with his mother?

3. Why does swimming through the tunnel become important to Jerry? Describe Jerry's preparations for this ordeal. Why do you think these preparations are described in such detail? At one point, the author writes, "A curious, most unchildlike persistence, a controlled impatience, made him wait." What two words in this sentence do most to describe a change in Jerry?

4. Describe Jerry's passage through the tunnel. Cite details and images that make the reader feel that he too is struggling desperately to get through the tunnel.

5. After Jerry swims through the tunnel, he sees "the local boys diving and playing half a mile away. He did not want them." Why does Jerry's attitude toward the boys change?

6. What is the significance of Jerry carefully washing himself before meeting his mother? What is the significance of his change in attitude in the last paragraph of the story?

7. Can the title of this story have more than a literal meaning? Explain.

FOR COMPOSITION

1. Compare the mother–son relationship in "Through the Tunnel" with that in "The Rocking-horse Winner." Contrast Paul's compulsion with Jerry's. Which story seems to you the more powerful? Why?

2. Just as Jerry passed a self-imposed trial in "Through the Tunnel," so all human beings must endure and pass certain trials as they grow to maturity. Tell about such a trial in your own life, or write a story about a girl or boy enduring such a trial.

THE GROWTH OF THE ENGLISH LANGUAGE

The Twentieth Century

One of the most interesting developments in the English language during the present century has been the swift rise in importance of the spoken language. During previous centuries, the only practical way of communicating with someone at a distance was by writing a letter, and the only practical way of reaching a large audience was through print. Today, however, the spoken word—on the telephone, over public-address systems, on television, and so forth—has become nearly as important as the written word.

In accord with the increasingly important role that spoken English is playing in our lives, the spoken forms of the language have become a subject of increasing interest to language specialists. In the nineteenth century, language research had focused chiefly on the study of historical dialects and on the tracing of language history. Much of what we know about Old English and Middle English, for instance, was first discovered by nineteenth-century researchers. But research into living forms of speech had been largely ignored until the very end of the century. Although this field is therefore still relatively new, many important discoveries have already been made. For example, one of the tasks that researchers are undertaking is the mapping of regional and local dialect areas, both in the British Isles and in the United States. Although this work is far from finished, some interesting results have already come about—for instance, dialect mapping has shed a good deal of light on patterns of historical settlement and migration within the United States.

Twentieth-century writers have taken full advantage of the great range of possibilities offered by the spoken language. Although nineteenth-century writers had also been interested in this aspect of language, the feeling had lingered until the end of the century that informal spoken English was not entirely respectable. For instance, while Wordsworth admired the simplicity and directness of rural speech, he believed that for literary purposes it must be "purified"—by which he seems to have meant that all dialect expressions and any grammatical departures from standard English must be avoided. The language of Wordsworth's poetry may indeed be simple and direct, but it is also unquestionably standard written English, not a country dialect. Dickens also delicately refrained from assigning dialect-speech to his humblest heroes and heroines.

Today the prejudice against nonstandard English in literature has practically disappeared. This is partly due to the concern for realism and accurate detail that marks much of the writing of the present century, but it is due in even greater part to the increasing democratization of society and to the growing belief that an individual's worth does not depend on having been born into the "right" social class. Irish writers were among the first to employ their own spoken English in preference to standard literary English. The poets and playwrights who were associated with the Irish Nationalist movement deliberately tried to free themselves from literary dependence on England. At first, writers like Yeats and J. M. Synge frequently turned to Irish folklore and the Irish peasantry for their themes and their language. Writers of a later generation —James Joyce, Sean O'Faolain, Frank

O'Connor—tended to write directly out of their own experience, using contemporary Irish settings and current speech.

This tendency to write from experience and to develop a written style based on the spoken language has become a characteristic of twentieth-century English literature as a whole. Dylan Thomas's poetry reflects the speech of his native Wales. Hugh McDiarmid and other Scottish poets have revived the old tradition of writing in Scots dialect. Even writers whose own spoken dialect happened to be standard British English, such as Evelyn Waugh and E. M. Forster, proved expert at capturing in writing the nuances of this spoken language.

If the trend toward using spoken dialect in literary works continues, we may soon find ourselves reading works in kinds of English that are now completely unfamiliar to us. English has remained the official language of many countries that were formerly part of the British Empire, in Africa, Asia, the South Pacific, and the Western Hemisphere. Up to the present time, most professional writers in these countries have employed standard literary English, but with political independence there may come assertions of literary independence in many countries similar to the movement that took place in Ireland at the beginning of the century. Folk songs have already given us an idea of the dialect speech of some of these places—for instance, "Waltzing Matilda" from Australia, calypso songs from Trinidad, hand-clapping songs from different parts of Africa.

There are also processes at work, however, that may curb the growth of new varieties of English. The increasing use of the spoken language in public communication, for instance, will probably result in greater standardization of speech. In the British Isles, "BBC English"—the deliberately uniform speech used by speakers on radio and television—is rapidly becoming accepted as the norm for spoken English. In the United States, a similar standardized kind of English,

sometimes called "General **American,**" is used by movie actors and television performers. The increasing ease and speed of travel is also having an effect on spoken dialects. Few people nowadays live all their lives in the same town, or even in the same state or the same part of the country. Thus there are more and more speakers of English who employ "composite dialects" reflecting the speech patterns of the various regions they have lived or traveled in. It is even possible that, as international travel becomes more common, an international composite dialect may arise that may eventually become the standard language of English-speaking people all over the world.

FOR STUDY AND DISCUSSION

1. Although most of the expressions in the following list are now familiar throughout the English-speaking world, each of them was originally a local term used by speakers in a particular part of the British Isles or of the British Empire. In a dictionary that gives etymologies (word origins), look up each expression and find out which part of the world it came from originally.

auld lang syne	trek
pundit	veldt
smithereens	wallah
swagman	whiskey

2. The language is growing at such a rapid rate that no dictionary can keep up with the new words that enter our vocabulary each year. All the terms on the following list have made their appearance within the past decade or two. Some of them are scientific terms; some are terms having to do with national or world events; some are short-lived fad words. See how many of these terms you can find in your dictionary. Then check the copyright date of your dictionary. For each word that you cannot find in your dictionary, try to decide whether the word is not listed because it probably had not come into general use by the time the dictionary was published, or whether the editors may have had other reasons for not including it.

bamboo curtain	heat shield
beatnik	laser beam
DNA	miniskirt
frug	sit-in (*noun*)

Modern British Painters

In twentieth-century art, as we have seen, lifelike representation is less important than the expression of unique visions. Artists have learned how to use line, shape, and color in whatever manner seems best suited to their work, and they often find it necessary to disregard traditional standards of "accurate" drawing and "natural" color.

For example, *The Yellow Man* (PLATE 1), by Christopher Wood, may at first seem childlike. Through the street of a sleeping village on a moonlit night, a mysterious figure stalks with a companion. Their heads are death-like. The central figure wears a sinister black coat; but his tights are bright yellow, the color of the sun and of life, and his smile is benevolent. The houses are not convincing as *real* houses, nor do the figures belong to the everyday world. Rather, this is a surrealistic dream-world, drawn from the subconscious part of the artist's mind. In 1930, when Wood painted this picture, he was at work also on stage and costume designs for a dance production which involved acrobats and other circus figures. Apparently these images haunted him, for they reappeared in *The Yellow Man*, a picture of uncertain meaning but disturbing fascination.

In *Four Grey Sleepers* (PLATE 2), Henry Moore, one of England's most celebrated sculptors, created an image that is as haunting as Wood's painting but far less esoteric. During World War II, when many Londoners took shelter in the subways against the nightly bombings by enemy aircraft, Moore made studies, in two sketchbooks and a hundred larger drawings, of people who had fallen into deep sleep in the underground caverns. In this drawing he sought, with a sculptor's eye, to give the illusion of solid objects with light falling on them. He abstracted and molded the human form into tubular shapes, which he then joined in rhythmical patterns to suggest the companionship of the sleepers. Only the open-mouthed snorer breaks the stonelike immobility of their seemingly eternal rest. Moore's technique, white crayon under watercolor washes and ink, is remarkably effective: the sharp contrast between highlights and shaded areas makes us think of his sculpture.

John Piper saw the effects of war in another way. A series of watercolors commissioned by the British Government in 1942 records the bomb-damage inflicted on the city of Bath. *Somerset Place, Bath* (PLATE 3) shows stately eighteenth-century buildings ravaged by incendiary bombs. The stark composition and dramatic color suggest the influence of work that Piper had been doing in stage design. At the left, the debris is sharply outlined by pen-line. As the facade curves back, details become less distinct. Where bombs seared ornaments away, washes of gray and brown slide down the facade and obliterate details altogether. The dark gray sky intensifies the sense of disaster, and the red-brown of the rubble reminds us that we are looking into an open wound.

In *Sun Setting between the Hills* (PLATE 4), Graham Sutherland shows violence of an unexpected kind: he envisions the hills as great jaws about to devour the sinking sun. Curiously sinister forces often appear in Sutherland's animation of natural objects. What is the spiky, multicolored shape in the foreground of this watercolor? Perhaps, as the blue-green at the base may hint, it is Sutherland's abstraction of a cactus, blackened on one side by the scorching sun. Whatever it is, the form adds new colors to the composition and echoes the craggy rocks and the V-shaped division between the hills. In this sunset, the land is colored more interestingly than the sky. Beams from the sun, a simplified orange ball, reach over the dark hills and turn stretches of sand into a warm yellow. Throughout the picture, the contrast of warm and cool colors suggests a time of day between the hot afternoon and the refreshing evening.

Francis Bacon's painting *Dog* (PLATE 5) shows a dazed, panting animal alone in the center of a red grid—a victim of violence, perhaps accidental. The ragged tracks and the pathetic stance indicate its helpless condition. Has it been hit by a car, or driven into some sort of inescapable trap? In either case, the outcome must be death, which is suggested by the blackness which seems to close in on the victim from above. Bacon derived the dog and the setting from two unlikely and unrelated sources: an early American photograph of a mastiff, and the decoration of a stadium in Nuremberg for a Nazi Party convention. Using these images, he produced a picture of agony which fuses the representational and the abstract.

Ben Nicholson's *Vertical Seconds* (PLATE 6) is altogether nonrepresentational. Colored rectilinear shapes lead in at a slight angle to an upright monochromatic background which looks as if it might be composed of transparent plastic sheets laid one on top of another. The edges are outlined so that we see interlocking shapes. Notice, too, how the various colors depend on one another: for instance, if you block out the red square with your thumb, the composition becomes lifeless. The intensity of the red is balanced by the bright yellow L-shape and by bits of black. This is a picture meant to be enjoyed for the balance of shapes and colors and for its delicate linear quality.

PLATE 1. CHRISTOPHER WOOD (1901–1930): *The Yellow Man*. 1930. Oil on board, 20 x 24 inches. (Reproduced by permission of Mr. Brinsley Ford)

PLATE 2. HENRY MOORE (1898–): *Four Grey Sleepers*. 1941. Pen, ink, watercolor, and chalk, 17 x 20 inches. (Gelsthorpe Art Gallery, Wakefield, England)

PLATE 3. JOHN PIPER (1903–): *Somerset Place, Bath.* 1942. Watercolor, 18 x 29 inches. (Reproduced by courtesy of the Trustees, The Tate Gallery, London)

PLATE 4. GRAHAM SUTHERLAND (1903–   ): *Sun Setting between the Hills.* 1937. Watercolor, $10\frac{11}{16}$ x $14\frac{3}{8}$ inches. (Reproduced by courtesy of Sir Kenneth Clark, C.H., K.C.B.)

PLATE 5. FRANCIS BACON (1910–   ): *Dog*. 1952. Oil on canvas, $78\frac{1}{4}$ x $54\frac{1}{4}$ inches. (Collection, The Museum of Modern Art, New York, William A. M. Burden Fund)

PLATE 6. BEN NICHOLSON (1894–   ): *Vertical Seconds*. 1953. Oil on canvas, 29 x 19 inches. (Reproduced by courtesy of the Trustees, The Tate Gallery, London)

Art and Literature: For Composition

The following composition assignments are based on the fine art in the anthology. The assignments are grouped in the order in which the fine art appears in the anthology.

THE LATE MIDDLE AGES
AND THE RENAISSANCE *(page 111)*

1. One of the major themes of late medieval art and literature was proper behavior according to a formal code in religion, at court, and on the battlefield. We can see this in the idealized heroes and the code of chivalry described in Malory's *Le Morte D'Arthur* (page 69). It is also present in the conventionalized figures of the *Wilton Diptych* (pages 113–14). Referring to the unit introduction, the selection from Malory, and the painting, write a composition discussing the ideals of medieval society that can be inferred from these works. Note, for example, that in the painting the saints tend to dominate the kneeling monarch. In discussing medieval ideals, reread pages 111–12 and consider the symbolic significance of Richard's sponsors and emblematic animal.

2. In contrast to medieval art and literature, Renaissance art and thought focused attention on the individual and took great delight in observing the unique qualities that distinguish one person from another. As we have seen, Chaucer exemplified this tendency to a high degree in *The Canterbury Tales*. The same particularization of detail and interest in psychology marked Renaissance painting, especially as it developed in northern Europe. Look, for example, at Holbein's portraits of Sir Thomas More and King Henry VIII (pages 116 and 117). Which details in these paintings seem to reveal the sitters as individuals with distinct personalities? Study the way in which the figures are placed in the pictures, especially in contrast to those in the *Wilton Diptych*. Which style makes you more aware of the subjects as particular individuals? Support your conclusions with details from the paintings.

EARLY ENGLISH PORTRAITURE *(page 215)*

1. English painting of the Elizabethan age conveyed a spirit of refinement similar in many respects to the courtly poetry of the period. Study the two paintings by Nicholas Hilliard (pages 217 and 218) and write a composition describing the elements that you think express this spirit. Note how the painter's delicate style combines with the gestures of the figures and the symbolic significance of the objects to represent an emotional state. In *A Young Man Among Roses,* for example, what details tell us that the courtier is suffering from unreturned love? Compare the two Hilliard paintings to the poems you have read in this unit, citing passages from works that indicate a similarity of tone.

2. Arriving in England as painter to Charles I, Anthony Van Dyck brought with him a much muted form of the "Grand Manner" of painting practiced on the continent. He was a student of the great Flemish painter, Peter Paul Rubens. Some modern critics have compared Van Dyck's style to that used in the lyrics of poets such as Robert Herrick. They point, for example, to Herrick's precise diction and melodic line in "To the Virgins, to Make Much of Time" (page 225) and note that these elements are similar to Van Dyck's delicate glazes of color and subtle drawing. Yet, the painter and poet are not entirely alike. Study Herrick's poem and Van Dyck's portrait of Charles I (page 219) with an eye to their similarities and differences. Write a composition dealing with the following questions:

   a. King Charles is represented as though he were a courtier about to go for a stroll. Does he seem to you a likely suitor, a possible speaker of Herrick's lines? Why? Cite the qualities in the painting that support your position.

   b. Van Dyck's portrait is rather large and imposing. Aside from this fact, how is Charles I's sense of his own importance conveyed in the painting? How does this contrast with Herrick's use of language? with the purpose of his argument?

3. Van Dyck's style was continued by succeeding generations of English portraitists, although his images of melancholy refinement

were to a large extent abandoned by those who came immediately afterward. We can see this in Robert Walker's portrait of Oliver Cromwell (page 221). This painting can serve as an interesting comparison with the likeness of Charles I. Both are, in a sense, state portraits. Van Dyck's painting is an equestrian portrait, a type of picture that usually shows its subject mounted and, when of a king, in the posture of a commander of troops. In Van Dyck's portrait, though, Charles is dismounted and looks at best like the leading cavalier of the day. Moreover, the painting's play of light and shadow softens the image and gives one a sense of introspection. This portrait is almost an intimate view of the monarch. In contrast to Van Dyck's portrait, the harsh light, stormy background, and military attire of Cromwell make Walker's painting seem like an attempt at Miltonic grandeur. Yet, both canvases adequately project the kind of image their sitters wanted. Citing details from both paintings to support your observations, write a composition describing the personalities that are conveyed by each portrait and explain why the style of each painting is appropriate to the subject portrayed.

WILLIAM HOGARTH (page 319)

1. William Hogarth, like Jonathan Swift, had a profound interest in moral problems. He made satiric thrusts at the foibles of mankind as Swift did in *Gulliver's Travels,* and he used the painter's equivalent of the narrative form as the most effective means to convey his message. So similar are Hogarth and Swift in their ways of seeing human folly and failure that some of Hogarth's paintings could very well illustrate Swift's writings. Indeed, *Chairing the Member* (page 325) might serve as the pictorial equivalent of Flimnap's rope dance described in the selection from *Gulliver's Travels* (page 313). Reread pages 319–20 and study *Calais Gate* (page 322) and the episode from *A Rake's Progress* (page 324). Then write a composition discussing the view you believe Hogarth held of the figures he depicts. Try to imagine Swift's reaction to the same situations shown in the paintings and describe his response.

2. Hogarth turned his back on fashionable portraiture and painted likenesses of common people. Compare, for instance, Hogarth's *The Shrimp Girl* (page 321) and *The Painter's Servants* (page 326) to Anthony Van Dyck's *Charles I of England* (page 219) and Robert Walker's *Oliver Cromwell with His Squire* (page 221). In a brief composition, describe the details in each of these paintings which reveal the differences in social station of the various sitters.

REYNOLDS, GAINSBOROUGH, AND THEIR CIRCLE (page 391)

1. In the latter half of the eighteenth century, English painting, as well as English literature, began to reflect some of the thought and sentiment that was to culminate in Romanticism. Among the major artistic impulses in this direction was a self-conscious allusion to the past. Sometimes this took the form of Reynolds's *Self-Portrait* (page 393), in which the artist not only shows a bust of the Renaissance artist Michelangelo, but also openly borrows composition, lighting, color, and even costuming from Rembrandt van Rijn, the seventeenth-century Dutch painter. More often, though, artists used architectural fragments to refer to historical periods, as in Gainsborough's use of a fluted column to evoke classical antiquity in *The Honorable Mrs. Graham* (page 397). Study the Reynolds and Gainsborough portraits as well as John Zoffany's *Garrick and Mrs. Pritchard* (page 395). How do these paintings use historical references? In a brief composition, explain the function in these paintings of subject, costuming, and setting, in creating contrast between the present and the past.

2. In addition to classical antiquity, nature was another major interest of Romanticism. It was by turning to nature that the Romantics hoped to rediscover genuine feelings and strip away what they felt to be the distortions of civilization. An immediate emotional response to experience was eagerly sought, and the stimulus for this was often found in landscape, which, as with Constable and Turner, was made to express the full range of poetic sensibility. Gainsborough displays the beginnings of the Romantic landscape in both *John Plampin of Chadacre* (page 396) and *The Honorable Mrs. Graham* (page 397). In the portrait of John Plampin the landscape is rather idyllic; in the painting of Mrs. Graham it is almost foreboding. Richard Wilson's *Wilton House from the South-East* (page 398) expresses yet another mood, one very much akin to wistful nostalgia. This painting is not a landscape done for its own sake; it is. dis-

guised as a "portrait of an estate." Study these three works and, in a brief composition, describe those elements that convey the predominant tone of the landscape. For example, how does color serve to create the mood in *John Plampin of Chadacre?* What effect does the sky have in *The Honorable Mrs. Graham?* In what way does the softening of the foliage in the center of *Wilton House from the South-East* contribute to the mood of this painting?

3. As late as the second half of the eighteenth century, portraiture was the dominant genre of English painting. As we have seen above, landscape was introduced at about this time by the back door, so to speak. Reread pages 391–92 and look carefully at the Gainsborough and Wilson paintings. Then write a composition explaining the different roles landscape plays in each of these three paintings. To what degree does each artist use landscape in these paintings? How much of each painting is occupied by the figures and how much by landscape?

EARLY ROMANTICISM: SCIENCE AND NATURE (*page 463*)

1. In the mid-eighteenth century many artists and writers began to look for interesting material in picturesque subjects or dramatic situations. Scenes of violence were a favorite subject, as were exotic lands and times and sentimental views of rustic life. To a large extent such subjects allowed for a more personal approach than had been possible earlier.

In the mid-eighteenth century, writers such as Robert Burns and Thomas Gray, along with the painters represented on pages 465–70, turned away from the urbane universe of Neoclassicism and looked forward to the new approaches and attitudes suggested by the Romantic movement. Study the paintings on pages 465–70 and choose one or two that seem to point toward a Romantic treatment and choice of subject. What qualities in the painting seem Romantic? Note the use of lighting, subject, and mood to create an effect. What sort of effect do you think the artist wished to produce in the paintings you have chosen?

2. Among the conflicting directions of Romanticism were a scientific, hence objective, interest in all natural phenomena and a morbid, hence subjective, fascination with the response to terror. In *White Horse Frightened by a Lion* (page 466) by George Stubbs and *Experiment with the Air Pump* (page 467) by Joseph Wright of Derby, both conflicting impulses are present. After looking carefully at these paintings and rereading pages 463–64, write a composition discussing the elements in the paintings that dramatize fear and horror and reflect scientific curiosity. What sort of lighting is used in both paintings? Where is the center, the point of greatest interest, in both pictures? What are the subjects of the pictures? How much attention is paid to anatomical detail in the paintings?

EARLY ENGLISH WATERCOLORISTS (*page 535*)

In the history of English painting, watercolor has been an extremely popular medium. It lends itself to quick, spontaneous sketches of almost any subject. English artists of the nineteenth century, such as Constable and Turner (see pages 607–14), exploited the medium's potential to the fullest, but at the end of the eighteenth century, when it was relatively new to them, the English artists working in watercolor were stiff and, at times, clumsy. Their works often seem to be tinted drawings and pallid imitations of oil painting.

1. As the eighteenth century ended and the nineteenth century began, English watercolorists gained mastery of the medium, and they used it less as a supplement to drawing and more as an instrument with its own inherent qualities. The paintings on pages 537–42 reflect this development. Study these paintings and the accompanying text on pages 535–36 with a view to describing the increased skill of the watercolorists. For example, what is the effect of the clear design of Cotman's *Greta Bridge* (page 541) and the loose brushwork of Palmer's *Cornfield by Moonlight* (page 542)? How does the technique of these paintings contrast with that in *Jealousy, The Rival,* and *Reading the Will* (pages 538 and 539) by Rowlandson?

2. As pointed out on page 536, the later watercolorists painted directly on paper instead of drawing first. They also paid much more attention to landscape than previously. Directness of painting and interest in landscape are among the main features of Romantic art. What are other characteristics that seem Romantic in the paintings of Thomas Girtin and Samuel Palmer (pages 540 and 542)?

What, for example, is the mood expressed in these paintings?

CONSTABLE AND TURNER (page 607)

Romanticism was so varied and complex a movement that we still have trouble defining it with a single set of terms. Not only did it vary from country to country, it also varied from individual to individual. In England alone there were a large number of Romantic artists and writers, all of whom were markedly different from one another, although several painters seem to have shared a common view with a number of poets. Wordsworth and Constable often appear to have looked at nature from the same vantage point. On the other hand, Coleridge's fascination with hallucinatory images brought him closer to the painter Turner than to his friend Wordsworth.

Most Romantics were not only highly individual, but also at times highly inconsistent, sometimes stressing the value of personal response to such a degree that they did not adhere to a fixed style or theme. For example, Constable's manner of painting was quite varied, as is shown in part by the works reproduced on pages 609–11. His varying styles represent a shifting personal response to the objects he looked at and to such natural phenomena as changing light. Turner, however, remained faithful to a single vision and style throughout his career. He kept his eyes steadily fixed on an inner image, responding only to the changing qualities of his medium. We can see this in the paintings reproduced on pages 612–14.

1. Study the paintings of Constable and Turner in conjunction with the text on pages 607–08. Then write a paragraph on each of the following questions:
   a. How do Constable's paintings differ from one another? For example, what is the difference between the way the trees and land are painted in *Willy Lott's House,* in *The Haywain,* and in *Wivenhoe Park, Essex* (pages 609, 610, and 611)?
   b. What is the effect of Turner's heightened color and very sketchy drawing? How does Turner convert an actual scene, such as the burning Parliament buildings or the view of Venice, into a dreamlike vision?
2. The paintings of John Constable are often compared to the poetry of William Wordsworth. Reread Wordsworth's poetry (pages 450–82) and write a brief composition in which you describe the qualities in the work of these two men which you think relate them to one another.

THE PRE-RAPHAELITES (page 647)

1. Turning away from the fairly rigid rules of their fellow Victorians, the Pre-Raphaelite painters sought inspiration in the artificial gracefulness of fifteenth-century Florentine painters, especially in the work of Sandro Botticelli and Fra Filippo Lippi. This is readily apparent in the carefully designed painting of Ford Madox Brown (page 649), with its emphasis on curvilinear shapes. It is equally visible in the highly patterned, jewel-like surfaces and languid figures painted by Rossetti, Burne-Jones, and Millais (pages 650, 651, and 652). The Pre-Raphaelites' concern with artistic style influenced their view of emotion and nature. How is this influence expressed in their work? Study the paintings on pages 649–54 and reread the text on pages 647–48. Then write a composition discussing the mood, style, and subject matter of the pictures.

2. The Pre-Raphaelites' interest in stylized nature led, in many cases, to an extreme density of detail, which at times seems to overwhelm the picture and certainly affects our response to the subject. In the paintings of Rossetti, Burne-Jones, and Millais (pages 650, 651, and 652), details of foliage, cloth, and hair are often as prominent as the main forms of the figures and are usually shown twisting and turning in a serpentine fashion. In the majority of Pre-Raphaelite paintings and drawings, only the exposed parts of the body serve as areas of relief. What effect does this have on the total image? In a brief composition, compare *The Baleful Head* by Burne-Jones (page 651) to Constable's *Willy Lott's House* (page 609). How does each artist use detail and mass in his painting?

3. The Pre-Raphaelites were poets as well as painters. Compare some of their paintings shown on pages 649–54 to some of the poems in this unit (see pages 582 ff.). Which poems seem to echo the qualities and evoke the same spirit as the paintings? Do not confine yourself to the poems of Rossetti. For example, does *The Lady of Shalott* (page 582) seem a likely subject for a Pre-Raphaelite painting? Explain your answer by referring both to the Rossetti paintings and to Tennyson's poem— or any other paintings and poems in the unit.

IMPRESSIONISM AND ITS AFTERMATH (page 719)

1. Impressionism was a part of the nineteenth century's movement toward realism in art and literature. Most Impressionists favored scenes from the everyday life of ordinary people. Bustling streets, railroads, horse races, picnics, circuses, and music halls were among their preferred subjects. To strengthen the illusion of reality, paintings were sometimes executed as though they were soft-focus snapshots of unposed or unrehearsed occurrences. Walter Sickert's *The Old Bedford* (page 721) has a good deal of this quality. The painting is very much a segment taken directly from life, almost as it might appear in a photograph. Study the painting and write a composition discussing the elements in the picture that contribute to a sense of realism. For example, to what class of society do the people seem to belong? How is this shown in the painting? Note that the people are unself-conscious, in contrast to traditional figures in action, which usually seem contrived or carefully posed, as in Burne-Jones' *The Baleful Head* (page 651).

2. As the twentieth century began, Impressionism gave way to a number of other artistic trends. Artists became increasingly interested in either stylized forms or abstract design and less concerned with the values of nineteenth-century realism. In Augustus John's portrait of W. B. Yeats (page 722), the loose brushwork and color planes of Impressionism are exaggerated, but as yet without too severe a distortion of recognizable forms. Somewhat more distorted, Wyndham Lewis's portrait of T. S. Eliot (page 723) reflects a greater willingness to depart from reality for design purposes. With the passage of time, realism was almost entirely abandoned and forms were distorted or stylized, as in Paul Nash's *Landscape of Megaliths* (page 724) or Stanley Spencer's *Swan Upping* (page 726).

Although much concerned with design problems (line, form, color), the paintings discussed above are not abstractions, but rather variations of the tradition of representing objects the way they appear to the eye. Study the paintings on pages 721–26 and write a composition describing how they appear to you with respect to the realistic conventions of perspective, proportion, form, tone, and color. How do these paintings differ from *The Old Bedford* by Walter Sickert (page 721)? For instance, how does Sickert's representation of figures differ from that of Wyndham Lewis? How do Sickert and Spencer (page 726) differ in the way they indicate detail or use decorative pattern? How is shape and three-dimensional form used differently in Sickert, Lewis, and Spencer?

MODERN BRITISH PAINTERS (page 855)

1. In England, as elsewhere, the formal conventions of abstract art have often been put to an expressive or symbolic use as well as explored for their own sake. Line, color, and shape serve not only to produce pure art, as in Ben Nicholson's *Vertical Seconds* (page 862), but also to evoke a powerful, if not always pleasant, emotion. Avant-garde art, running parallel to modern literature, has contrived many of its images to express a sense of futility or horror. Indeed, at times the poets and painters use despair as the very ground of art. Stephen Spender reveals the stupid brutality of war in "Epilogue to a Human Drama" (page 831), and Francis Bacon's *Dog* (page 861) cringes as one of the "animals trapped behind a wall." Examine this picture closely. What elements in the painting express despair and defeat? Reread page 856 and note Bacon's sources for the picture. What meaning do you think these had for the artist? For that matter, what meaning do you think an injured mastiff used in connection with Nazism would generally have? How is Bacon's idea expressed in the painting?

2. Frequently, modern poets and painters use startling, unexpected relationships to convey their thought or provide new insight into traditional themes. In Section V of *The Hollow Men* (page 752), T. S. Eliot juxtaposes a nursery rhyme, the Lord's Prayer, and an almost primitive chant about reality and perception to express failure and impotence. In like fashion, to impart strong feeling to his landscape in *Sun Setting Between the Hills* (page 860), Graham Sutherland juxtaposes hot against cool colors and raggedly cut shapes of sandy beach against softly rounded masses of rock. Although the subject of the painting—the landscape—is emotionally neutral, the painter has used formal devices such as line, color, and design to produce a powerful emotional effect. In a brief composition, describe what emotional responses you think the artist wanted to evoke. Cite elements in the picture to support your thought.

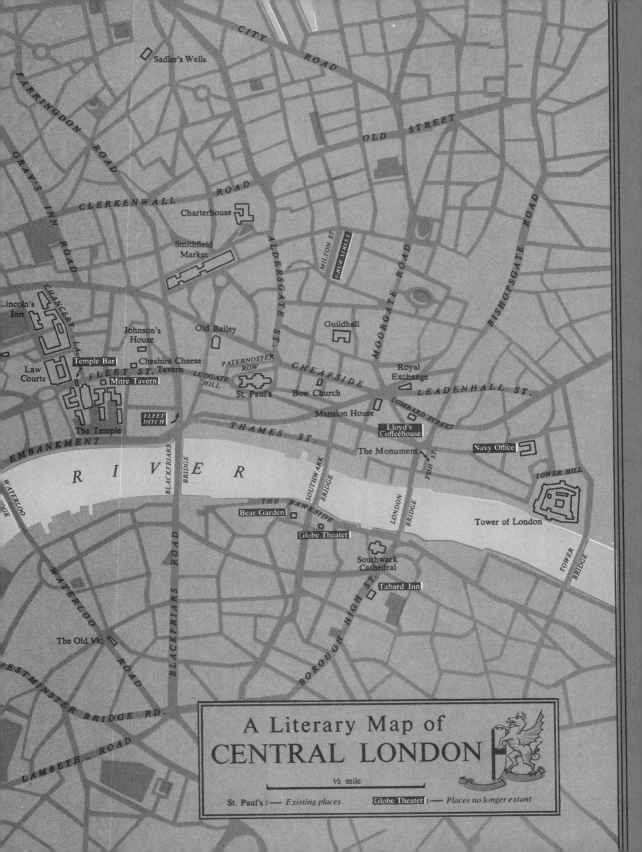

A Literary Map of
CENTRAL LONDON

½ mile

St. Paul's : —— *Existing places*   Globe Theater : —— *Places no longer extant*

THE COMPOSITION AND LANGUAGE PROGRAM

Assignments Based on Selections

All assignments are presented in the anthology under the heading *For Composition*. Numbers in parentheses refer to the numbered items in the text under the heading *For Composition*.

Comparing a modern and an old treatment of a similar theme 11
   "The Seafarer"

Analyzing old and modern concepts of the hero 19
   Beowulf (number 3)

Writing a newspaper reporter's version of a medieval ballad 39
   "Sir Patrick Spens" (number 1)

Comparing several versions of a ballad 39
   "Bonny Barbara Allan" (number 2)

Character sketch in Chaucerian style 62
   Chaucer, *Prologue* to *The Canterbury Tales* (number 2)

Writing a tale based on a common saying 68
   Chaucer, "The Pardoner's Tale"

Evaluating two characters in terms of ideal leader 74
   Malory, *Morte d'Arthur* (number 1)

Essay on medieval literature and society 74
   Malory, *Morte d'Arthur* (number 2)

Writing a Shakespearean sonnet and an analysis of difficulties encountered 108
   Shakespeare, Sonnets (number 2)

Evaluating a character's description of two other characters 179
   Shakespeare, *Macbeth* (number 1)

Essay on flaws causing downfall of Shakespearean characters 179
   Shakespeare, *Macbeth* (number 2)

Rephrasing passages of formal writing in light, modern English 190
   Francis Bacon

Describing main theme of essay and its variations 208
   Donne, "Meditation XVII"

Explaining how poem illustrates the metaphysical conceit 214
   Herbert, "The Collar" (number 2)

Evaluating poet's point of view 214
   Vaughan, "The Retreat" (number 3)

Evaluating a Renaissance concept in terms of medieval life 225
   Robert Herrick

Journal entry giving eye-witness description of event 260
   Samuel Pepys

Using Defoe's techniques to present realistic account of natural disaster 285
   Defoe, *A Journal of the Plague Year*

Writing prospectus for newspaper 295
   Addison and Steele (number 1)

Writing diary entries for twentieth-century "Clarinda" 295
   Addison and Steele (number 2)

Paragraph of commentary supporting or attacking statement by Pope 304
   Alexander Pope

Brief essay developing subject for modern mock epic 311
   Alexander Pope

Analyzing Swift's use of satire 333
   Swift, *Gulliver's Travels* (number 1)

Imaginary scene in which a modern Gulliver initiates King of Brobdingnag into mysteries of modern society 333
   Swift, *Gulliver's Travels* (number 2)

Relating Johnson's letter to Lord Chesterfield to Cardinal Newman's definition of a gentleman 339
   Samuel Johnson

Literary Terms and Techniques

Glossary of Literary Terms

ALEXANDRINE A poetic line consisting of six IAMBIC FEET (*iambic hexameter*). The line is so named because it was used by French poets of the twelfth and thirteenth centuries in poems about Alexander the Great. In English poetry, the SPENSERIAN STANZA, a nine-line stanza, ends with an alexandrine. (See page 303.) Here is an example from Percy Bysshe Shelley's *Adonais*:

Like pageantry of mist on an autumnal stream.

ALLEGORY A tale in verse or prose in which characters, actions, or settings represent abstract ideas or moral qualities. Thus, an allegory is a story with two meanings, a literal meaning and a symbolic meaning. The most famous allegory in English literature is John Bunyan's *The Pilgrim's Progress*, published in 1687. Bunyan's hero, Christian, makes a journey to the Celestial City, during which he meets such characters as Hope, Shame, and Despair.

ALLITERATION The repetition of initial consonant sounds. Although alliteration sometimes appears in prose, it is mainly a poetic device. Like other forms of sound repetition, alliteration in poetry serves two important purposes: it is pleasing to the ear, and it emphasizes the words in which it occurs. Alliteration is a characteristic element of Anglo-Saxon poetry. Here is an example from *Beowulf* (page 12):

Grim and greedy, his grip made ready;
Snatched in their sleep, with savage fury

ALLUSION A reference to a person, a place, an event, or a literary work which a writer expects the reader to recognize and respond to. An allusion may be drawn from history, geography, literature, or religion. An allusion to Greek mythology is found in these lines from Shakespeare's "Sonnet 55" (page 107):

Nor Mars his sword nor war's quick fire shall burn
The living record of your memory.

Through this simple allusion to Mars, the Roman god of war, Shakespeare suggests that not even a powerful and violent god can erase the memory of his beloved.

ANALOGY A comparison made between two things to show the similarities between them. Analogies are often used for illustration (to explain something unfamiliar by comparing it to something familiar) or for argument (to persuade that what holds true for one thing holds true for the thing to which it is compared). Samuel Johnson draws an analogy for the sake of argument in his "Preface to Shakespeare" (page 336), when he compares a work of nature to a work of art:

As among the works of nature no man can properly call a river deep or a mountain high, without the knowledge of many mountains and many rivers; so in the productions of genius, nothing can be styled excellent till it has been compared with other works of the same kind.

ANAPEST A poetic FOOT consisting of two unstressed syllables followed by a stressed syllable ($\smile\smile\,'$). Generally, a poem with *anapestic* meter has a light, tripping sound. The following line from the ballad "Bonny Barbara Allan" (page 36) contains anapests:

Ĭt wăs ĭn ánd ăbóut thĕ Mártĭnmăs tíme

ANECDOTE A very short story that is told to make a point. Anecdotes are often humorous; at times they are jokes. Anecdotes are used in all forms of literature.

ANTAGONIST A person or force opposing the PROTAGONIST in a narrative; a rival of the hero or heroine. Famous antagonists in literature include Professor Moriarty, Sherlock Holmes's antagonist in Arthur Conan Doyle's detective stories, and the monster Grendel, Beowulf's antagonist in the Anglo-Saxon epic poem *Beowulf* (page 12).

ANTITHESIS The balancing of two contrasting ideas, words, phrases, or sentences. An antithesis is often expressed in a BALANCED SENTENCE. (See page 266.) A famous example of antithesis is this line from Alexander Pope's *Essay on Criticism* (page 300):

To err is human, to forgive divine.

APHORISM A concise, pointed statement expressing a wise or clever observation about life. For example:

Silence is the virtue of fools.
Francis Bacon

APOSTROPHE A FIGURE OF SPEECH in which an absent or a dead person, an abstract quality, or something nonhuman is addressed directly. (See page 95.)

Robert Herrick uses an apostrophe when he addresses daffodils in "To Daffodils" (page 224):

Fair daffodils, we weep to see
You haste away so soon.

ASIDE In drama, lines spoken by a CHARACTER in an undertone or directly to the audience. An aside is meant to be heard by the audience, but it is supposedly not heard by the other characters onstage. (See page 133.) Here are some asides from Richard Brinsley Sheridan's *The Rivals* (page 358):

MRS. MALAPROP. Oh! it gives me the hydrostatics to such a degree. I thought she had persisted from corresponding with him; but, behold, this very day I have interceded another letter from the fellow; I believe I have it in my pocket.
ABSOLUTE. Oh, the devil; my last note. (*Aside*)
MRS. MALAPROP. Ay, here it is.
ABSOLUTE. Ay, my note indeed! Oh, the little traitress Lucy. (*Aside*)

ASSONANCE The repetition of vowel sounds, especially in poetry, as in "h*i*gh fl*i*er." (See page 503.) Here is an example of assonance from Alfred, Lord Tennyson's "The Lady of Shalott" (page 582):

An *a*bbot on *a*n *a*mbling p*a*d

ATMOSPHERE The prevailing mood or feeling of a literary work. Atmosphere is often developed, at least in part, through descriptions of SETTING. Such descriptions help to create an emotional climate for the work which serves to establish the reader's expectations and attitudes. For example, in "Across the Bridge" (page 835), Graham Greene develops an atmosphere of decay and boredom with descriptions of the dusty, shabby town where the story is set.

AUTOBIOGRAPHY A person's account of his or her own life. An autobiography is generally written in narrative form and includes some introspection. Autobiographies are distinct from diaries, journals, and letters, which are not unified life stories written for publication. Autobiographies are also different from memoirs, which often deal, at least in part, with public events and important persons other than the author. (See page 348.) An example of an autobiographical essay is George Orwell's "Shooting an Elephant" (page 802).

BALANCED SENTENCE A sentence in which identical or similar grammatical structure is used to express contrasting ideas. (See page 190.) (See also ANTITHESIS.) Here is an example of a balanced sentence from Samuel Johnson's "Preface to Shakespeare" (page 336):

> While an author is yet living we estimate his powers by his worst performance, and when he is dead we rate them by his best.

BALLAD A story told in verse and usually meant to be sung. In many countries, the *folk ballad* was one of the earliest forms of literature. Folk ballads are anonymous because they were transmitted orally from generation to generation and not set down in writing until centuries after they were first sung. The subject matter of folk ballads stems from the everyday life of the common people. The most popular subjects, often tragic ones, are disappointed love, jealousy, revenge, sudden disaster, and deeds of adventure and daring. (See pages 35 and 39.) A later form of ballad is the *literary ballad,* which imitates the style of the folk ballad. (See page 503.) The most famous English literary ballad is Samuel Taylor Coleridge's *The Rime of the Ancient Mariner* (page 486).

BALLAD STANZA A type of stanza of four lines. The first and third lines have four stressed words or syllables; the second and fourth lines have three stresses. The number of unstressed syllables in each line may vary. The second and fourth lines rhyme. Here is a ballad stanza from the Scottish folk ballad "Get Up and Bar the Door" (page 37):

> Then by there came two gentlemen,
> At twelve o'clock at night,
> And they could neither see house nor hall,
> Nor coal nor candlelight.

BIOGRAPHY A detailed account of a person's life written by another person. Biographies in English have taken many different forms since they were first written in medieval times to praise the virtue of saints and to celebrate the feats of heroes. The modern biographer aims at accuracy and usually makes an attempt to interpret the personality of the subject. Details of the social and historical circumstances in which the subject lived are often included. (See page 348.) A famous example of English biography is James Boswell's *The Life of Samuel Johnson* (page 341).

BLANK VERSE Verse written in unrhymed IAMBIC PENTAMETER. Blank verse is the verse form used in some of the greatest English poetry, including that of William Shakespeare and John Milton. (See page 133.) Here is an example from Shakespeare's *Romeo and Juliet:*

> But soft! What light through yonder window breaks?
> It is the east, and Juliet is the sun!
> Arise, fair sun, and kill the envious moon,
> Who is already sick and pale with grief
> That thou her maid art far more fair than she.

CAESURA A break or pause in a line of poetry. (See page 11.) In these lines from Robert Herrick's "The Argument of His Book" (page 224), there are several caesuras, which are indicated by double lines (‖):

> I sing of brooks, ‖ of blossoms, ‖ birds, ‖ and bowers;
> Of April, ‖ May, ‖ of June, ‖ and July flowers.

CANTO A section or division of a long poem. The most famous cantos in literature are those which make up Dante's *Divine Comedy,* a fourteenth-century EPIC. In English poetry, Alexander Pope's *The Rape of the Lock* (page 304) and George Gordon, Lord Byron's *Don Juan* (page 513) are divided into cantos.

CHARACTER A person—or an animal, a thing, or a natural force presented as a person—appearing in a short story, novel, play, or narrative poem. Famous characters from English literature include Hamlet from William Shakespeare's play *Hamlet,* Robinson Crusoe from Daniel Defoe's novel *Robinson Crusoe,* Ebenezer Scrooge from Charles

Dickens's story "A Christmas Carol," Sherlock Holmes from Arthur Conan Doyle's Sherlock Holmes stories, and Rikki-Tikki-Tavi, a mongoose, from Rudyard Kipling's story "Rikki-Tikki-Tavi."

CHARACTERIZATION The personality a character displays; also, the means by which a writer reveals that personality. Generally, a writer develops a character in one or more of the following ways: (1) through the character's actions; (2) through the character's thoughts and speeches; (3) through a physical description of the character; (4) through the opinions others have about the character; (5) through a direct statement about the character telling what the writer thinks of him or her. In "Bella Fleace Gave a Party" (page 809), Evelyn Waugh establishes part of Bella's character through a description of her physical characteristics: her red complexion, gray, streaky hair, pale blue eyes, and lively smile.

CLASSICISM A movement or tendency in art, literature, or music which reflects the principles manifested in the art of ancient Greece and Rome. Classicism emphasizes the traditional and the universal, and places value on reason, clarity, balance, and order. Classicism, with its concern for reason and universal themes, is traditionally opposed to **ROMANTICISM**, which is concerned with emotions and personal themes.

CLIMAX The point of greatest intensity, interest, or suspense in a narrative. The climax usually marks a story's turning point. In William Shakespeare's *Macbeth* (page 119), the climax occurs during the banquet scene in Act III. Macbeth, overcome by guilt and nervousness over the murders of Duncan and Banquo, sees the ghost of Banquo appearing in the banquet hall. This tense moment is the play's turning point. After this moment, events turn against Macbeth and lead to his final downfall. (See page 155.)

COMEDY In general, a literary work which ends happily with a healthy, amicable armistice between the **PROTAGONIST** and society. Comedy is distinct from **TRAGEDY**, which is generally concerned with a protagonist who meets an unhappy or disastrous end. Also, the comic protagonist may be a person of ordinary character and ability, and need not achieve the heroic stature of the protagonist in a tragedy. (See **TRAGIC HERO**.) Comedies are often concerned, at least in part, with exposing human folly, and frequently depict the overthrow of rigid social fashions and customs. Wit, humor, and a sense of festivity are found in many comedies.

COMEDY OF MANNERS A comedy dealing with the social intrigues of a polished and sophisticated society. The humor stems mainly from the characters' violation of social conventions and decorum and from witty dialogue. (See page 357.) A famous comedy of manners is Richard Brinsley Sheridan's *The Rivals* (page 358).

CONCEIT A kind of **METAPHOR** which makes a comparison between two startlingly different things. A conceit may be a brief metaphor, but it usually provides the framework for an entire poem. An especially unusual and intellectual kind of conceit is the *metaphysical conceit,* used by certain seventeenth-century poets such as John Donne. (See page 207.)

CONFLICT A struggle between two opposing forces or **CHARACTERS** in a short story, novel, play, or narrative poem. Conflict can be external or internal, and it can take one of these forms: 1) a person against another person; 2) a person against society; 3) a person against nature; 4) two elements within a person struggling for mastery. Most works of fiction contain two or more of these forms of conflict. In William Shakespeare's *Macbeth* (page 119), for example, there is a conflict within Macbeth (his wish to murder Duncan and become king versus his loyalty to Duncan), and conflicts between Macbeth and other individuals in the play (Lady Macbeth, Banquo, Macduff). Conflict is often an important element in **PLOT** development and provides, among other things, the basis for **SUSPENSE**.

CONNOTATION All the emotions and associations that a word or phrase may arouse. Connotation is distinct from **DENOTATION**, which is the literal or "dictionary" meaning of a word or phrase. For example the word *springtime* literally means that season of the year between the vernal equinox and the summer solstice, but the word usually makes most people think of such things as youth, rebirth, and romance. The word *shroud* literally means a cloth used for burial purposes, or anything that covers or protects. However, most people associate the word *shroud* with death, gloom, darkness, and other unpleasant things.

CONSONANCE The repetition of consonant sounds in the middle or at the ends of words, a device often used in poetry. (See also **ALLITERATION**.) Here is an example of consonance from Thomas Gray's "Elegy Written in a Country Churchyard" (page 415):

And a*ll* the air a so*l*emn sti*ll*ness ho*l*ds

CONTEXT The words and phrases closely surrounding another word or phrase, or the general meaning conveyed by those words or phrases. Context often determines the meaning of a word, as in these examples:

That book has a fascinating *plot*.
I'd like to build a house on that *plot*.

Context is also the situation and circumstances that surround an event; we often speak of a character's action in the *context* of the entire story.

CONTRAST A striking difference between two things. In expository writing, two ideas may be contrasted for clarification and emphasis. In imaginative writing, contrasting settings, characters, and events are often presented for dramatic effect. (See page 690.)

COUPLET Two consecutive lines of poetry that rhyme. A *heroic couplet* is a couplet written in **IAMBIC PENTAMETER**. Alexander Pope is famous for his heroic couplets, such as the following from "Essay on Criticism" (page 300):

Ă pérfĕct júdge wĭll réad eăch wórk ŏf
wít
Wĭth thé saměe spírĭt thát ĭts áuthŏr wrít.

DACTYL A poetic **FOOT** consisting of a stressed syllable followed by two unstressed syllables (ʹ˘˘). Dactyls are often found in nonsense poetry, in children's rhymes, and in advertising jingles. Notice the dactyls in the first of these lines from a nursery rhyme:

Híckŏrў díckŏrў dóck,
Thĕ móuse răn úp thĕ clóck.

DENOTATION The literal or "dictionary" meaning of a word, which is distinct from its **CONNOTATION**. For example, the denotation, or dictionary definition, of the word *star* (as in "movie *star*") is "a prominent actor or actress," but the connotation of the word *star* is that of an actor or actress who is adored by fans and who leads a fascinating and glamorous life.

DÉNOUEMENT (dā·no͞o·män′) From the French word for "unknotting." The dénouement is that part of a play, short story, novel, or narrative poem in which **CONFLICTS** are resolved, or unraveled, and mysteries and secrets connected with the **PLOT** are explained.

DESCRIPTION The type of writing that is concerned with re-creating sensory impressions: sights, sounds, smells, textures, and tastes. Description is one of the major **FORMS OF DISCOURSE**. (See also **NARRATION**, **EXPOSITION**, and **PERSUASION**.) Although descriptions are often written to stand on their own, they are more frequently written to enhance other forms of writing. Here is a piece of description from Charles Lamb's essay, "Dream Children: A Reverie" (page 506):

. . . I had more pleasure in strolling about among the old melancholy-looking yew trees, or the firs, and picking up the red berries, and the fir apples, which were good for nothing but to look at—or in lying about upon the fresh grass. . . .

DEUS EX MACHINA A term meaning "a god from a machine." In some ancient Greek and

Roman plays, a god or goddess would descend from the sky to rescue the hero from an impossible situation. The god's appearance was accomplished by stage machinery: the actor would be lowered from above by ropes. The term *deus ex machina* is now used to refer to any sudden last-minute discovery, rescue, or change of heart that helps resolve a complex situation and bring about a happy ending.

DIALECT The characteristic speech of a particular regional or social group. Dialect differs from standard English in sentence pattern, vocabulary, and pronunciation. Writers use dialect to aid in CHARACTERIZATION and to give their stories a realistic historical or regional quality. Robert Burns wrote many poems in Scottish dialect, including "A Man's a Man for A' That" (page 423), a stanza of which follows:

Ye see yon birkie, ca'd a lord,
Wha' struts, and stares, an' a' that

DIALOGUE A conversation between two or more CHARACTERS in a literary work. Dialogue can be used to make characters come alive, to advance the action, and to establish ATMOSPHERE. Dialogue appears in every form of literature: in short stories, novels, biographies, essays, poems, and plays. Plays are made up almost entirely of dialogue.

DICTION A writer's choice of words, particularly for clarity, effectiveness, and precision. A writer's diction can be formal or informal, abstract or concrete. In choosing "the right word," writers must think of their subject and their audience. Words that are appropriate in informal DIALOGUE would not always be appropriate in a piece of formal writing. (See also CONNOTATION and STYLE.)

DRAMATIC MONOLOGUE A kind of NARRATIVE POEM in which one CHARACTER speaks to one or more listeners whose replies are not given in the poem. The occasion is usually a crucial one in the speaker's life, and the dramatic monologue reveals the speaker's personality as well as the incident that is the subject of the poem. An example of a dramatic monologue is "My Last Duchess" by Robert Browning (page 601). (See page 603.)

DRAMATIC POEM A NARRATIVE POEM in which one or more CHARACTERS speak. Each speaker always addresses a specific listener. This listener may be silent but identifiable, as in a DRAMATIC MONOLOGUE. Or the listener may be another character who carries on a DIALOGUE with the speaker.

ELEGY A poem of mourning, usually over the death of an individual. It may also be a lament over the passing of life and beauty or a meditation on the nature of death. An elegy is a type of LYRIC poem, usually formal in language and structure, and solemn or even melancholy in tone. One of the greatest elegies in English is Alfred, Lord Tennyson's *In Memoriam* (page 591). (See also page 418.)

EPIC A long NARRATIVE POEM telling about the deeds of a great hero and reflecting the values of the society from which it originated. Many epics were drawn from an oral tradition and were transmitted by song and recitation before they were written down. Two of the most famous epics of Western civilization are Homer's *Iliad* and *Odyssey*. The great epic of the Middle Ages is the *Divine Comedy,* by the Italian poet Dante. One of the most famous English epics is John Milton's *Paradise Lost* (page 240).

EPIGRAM A short, witty, pointed statement, often in the form of a poem. (See page 187.) Here is an example from William Shakespeare's *Romeo and Juliet:*

What's in a name? That which we call a rose
By any other name would smell as sweet.

EPITAPH An inscription on a gravestone, or a short poem written in memory of someone who has died. (See page 418.) Many epitaphs are actually EPIGRAMS, or short, witty sayings, and are not intended for serious use as monument inscriptions. Here is an example:

Life is a jest, and all things show it.
I thought so once; but now I know it.
        John Gay, "My Own Epitaph"

EPITHET A descriptive name or phrase used to characterize someone or something, such as "America the Beautiful" or "Catherine the Great." Homer's EPIC the *Odyssey* contains many epithets, such as "wine-dark sea" and "keen-edged sword."

ESSAY A piece of prose writing, usually short, that deals with a subject in a limited way and expresses a particular point of view. An essay is never a comprehensive treatment of a subject (the word comes from a French word, *essai*, meaning "attempt" or "try"). An essay may be serious or humorous, tightly organized or rambling, restrained or emotional. (See page 295.)

The two general classifications of essay are the *informal essay* (also called the *familiar* or *personal essay*) and the *formal essay*. An informal essay is usually brief and is written as if the writer is talking informally to the reader about some topic, using a conversational style and a personal or humorous tone. In an informal essay, the writer might digress from the topic at hand, or express some amusing, startling, or absurd opinions. In general, an informal essay reveals as much about the personality of its author as it does about its subject. In contrast, a formal essay is tightly organized, dignified in style, and serious in tone. Francis Bacon's "Of Wisdom For a Man's Self" (page 189) is an example of a formal essay.

EXAGGERATION Overstatement for emphasis, for added interest, or for humorous effect. (See also HYPERBOLE.) We use exaggeration in many everyday expressions:

The batter hit the ball a mile.
I'm so hungry I could eat a horse.

Exaggeration is a common element of folk tales and tall tales, where heroes perform amazing feats and unbelievable events occur. Exaggeration is often used in SATIRE for humor and emphasis. For example, in his MOCK EPIC, "The Rape of the Lock" (page 304), Alexander Pope uses humorous

exaggeration to describe a great fight between some ladies and gentlemen over the loss of a lock of hair:

"To arms, to arms!" the fierce virago cries,
And swift as lightning to the combat flies.
All side in parties, and begin th' attack;
Fans clap, silks rustle, and tough whalebones crack;
Heroes' and heroines' shouts confus'dly rise,
And bass and treble voices strike the skies.

EXEMPLUM From the Latin, meaning "example." An exemplum is a tale, usually inserted into the text of a sermon, that illustrates a moral principle. "The Pardoner's Tale" (page 63) from Chaucer's *Canterbury Tales* (page 42) is an exemplum; its moral is, greed will lead to an evil end. (See page 68.)

EXPOSITION The kind of writing that is intended primarily to present information. Exposition is one of the major FORMS OF DISCOURSE. (See also NARRATION, DESCRIPTION, and PERSUASION.) Also, exposition is that part of a short story, a novel, a narrative poem, and especially of a play, which helps the reader to understand essential background information. For example, in *Macbeth* (page 119), William Shakespeare provides essential background information, or exposition, in the first two scenes. Before the plot begins to unfold, the audience is informed of the rebellion in Scotland and of the heroic actions of two of the major characters, Macbeth and Banquo. (See page 365.)

FABLE A brief story that is told to present a moral, or practical lesson. The CHARACTERS of fables are often animals who speak and act like human beings.

FALLING ACTION All of the action in a play that follows the CLIMAX, or turning point. In William Shakespeare's *Macbeth* (page 119), for example, the climax occurs in Act III during the banquet scene. Macbeth, nervous and guilty, sees Banquo's ghost appearing in the banquet hall. The action following this intense moment, leading to Macbeth's downfall, is the falling action. (See page 155.)

FARCE A type of COMEDY based on a ridiculous situation, often with STEREOTYPED characters. The humor in a farce is largely slapstick—that is, it often involves crude physical action. The characters in a farce are often the butts of practical jokes: flying cream pies hit them in the face, and beds cave in on them.

FIGURATIVE LANGUAGE Language that is not intended to be interpreted in a literal sense. (See page 527.) William Shakespeare uses figurative language in these lines from Macbeth's famous soliloquy at the end of *Macbeth* (page 119):

> Out, out, brief candle!
> Life's but a walking shadow, a poor player
> That struts and frets his hour upon the stage
> And then is heard no more.

Shakespeare is not saying that life is actually a flickering candle, a shadow, or a nervous actor moving about on a stage. Rather, he is making comparisons between life and these other things, pointing out special similarities between them. By appealing to the imagination, figurative language provides new ways of looking at the world. Figurative language consists of FIGURES OF SPEECH. (See also HYPERBOLE, METAPHOR, METONYMY, OXYMORON, PERSONIFICATION, and SIMILE.)

FIGURE OF SPEECH A word or an expression that is not meant to be interpreted in a literal sense. (See FIGURATIVE LANGUAGE.) The most common kinds of figures of speech —SIMILE, METAPHOR, PERSONIFICATION, and METONYMY—involve a comparison between unlike things. (See also HYPERBOLE and OXYMORON.) Figures of speech are found in many familiar expressions, such as "It's raining cats and dogs" and "You're the apple of my eye."

FLASHBACK A scene in a short story, novel, play, or narrative poem that interrupts the action to show an event that happened at an earlier point in time. Most narratives present events in chronological order—that is, as they occur in time. Sometimes, however, a writer interrupts this natural sequence of events and "flashes back" to tell the reader what happened earlier in the story or in a character's life. Often a flashback takes the form of a character's recollection.

FOOT A unit used to measure the METER, or rhythmic pattern, of a line of poetry. A foot is made up of one stressed syllable and, usually, one or more unstressed syllables. A line of poetry has as many feet as it has stressed syllables. "A Slumber Did My Spirit Seal" (page 457) by William Wordsworth has four feet:

> She seemed a thing that could not feel

There are several patterns of feet in poetry. Wordsworth's line uses IAMBS—that is, feet made up of one unstressed syllable followed by one stressed syllable. (See also ANAPEST, DACTYL, and TROCHEE.)

FORESHADOWING The use of hints, or clues, to suggest what will happen later in a narrative. Writers use foreshadowing to create interest and to build SUSPENSE. Sometimes foreshadowing also prepares the reader for the ending of the story. In Graham Greene's "Across the Bridge" (page 835), the ending of the story is foreshadowed in the fifth paragraph when the NARRATOR refers to Mr. Calloway's story as a tragedy.

FORMS OF DISCOURSE A classification of writing according to the writer's main purpose. Four forms of discourse are DESCRIPTION, NARRATION, EXPOSITION, and PERSUASION.

HEXAMETER A line of poetry made up of six verse FEET. Thus, a hexameter line has six groupings of stressed and unstressed syllables. Here is a hexameter line from Percy Bysshe Shelley's "To a Skylark" (page 524):

> Until we hardly see, we feel that it is there.

HYPERBOLE A FIGURE OF SPEECH using EXAGGERATION, or overstatement, for special effect. Shakespeare uses hyperbole in these lines from *Macbeth* (page 119):

> Will all great Neptune's ocean wash this
> blood
> Clean from my hand?

IAMB A poetic FOOT consisting of an unstressed syllable followed by a stressed syllable (˘ ′). The iamb is the most common metrical unit in English poetry, perhaps because the natural rhythm of the English language tends to be *iambic*. (See page 133.) In the following example from Alfred, Lord Tennyson's "The Eagle," the meter is iambic, and there are four feet in each line.

> The wrinkled sea beneath him crawls;
> He watches from his mountain walls,
> And like a thunderbolt he falls.

IAMBIC PENTAMETER A poetic line consisting of five verse FEET (*penta-* is from a Greek word meaning "five"), with each foot an IAMB—that is, an unstressed syllable followed by a stressed syllable. Iambic pentameter is the most common verse line in English poetry. The following line from William Shakespeare's *Romeo and Juliet* is written in iambic pentameter:

> But soft! What light through yonder win-
> dow breaks?

Unrhymed iambic pentameter is called BLANK VERSE.

IMAGERY Words or phrases that create pictures, or images, in the reader's mind. Images are primarily visual, as in these lines from William Wordsworth's "Ode: Intimations of Immortality from Recollections of Early Childhood" (page 476):

> The rainbow comes and goes,
> And lovely is the rose,
> The moon doth with delight
> Look round her when the heavens are
> bare

Images can appeal to other senses as well: touch, taste, smell, and hearing. The images

in Percy Bysshe Shelley's "A Dirge" (page 523) give the reader a sound impression of a scene:

> Rough wind, that moanest loud
> Grief too sad for song;
> Wild wind, when sullen cloud
>   Knells all the night long;
> Sad storm, whose tears are vain,
> Bare woods, whose branches strain,
> Deep caves and dreary main,
>   Wail, for the world's wrong!

INCREMENTAL REPETITION A device commonly used in BALLADS, in which a STANZA repeats one or more lines from another stanza, but adds a few new details (*increments*) to advance the story. (See page 35.) For example, in these three opening stanzas of the ballad "The Wife of Usher's Well," the second and third stanzas use incremental repetition:

> There lived a wife at Usher's Well,
>   And a wealthy wife was she;
> She had three stout and stalwart sons,
>   And sent them o'er the sea.
>
> They hadna been a week from her,
>   A week but barely ane,
> Whan word came to the carline wife
>   That her three sons were gane.
>
> They hadna been a week from her,
>   A week but barely three,
> Whan word came to the carline wife
>   That her sons she'd never see.

IN MEDIAS RES A Latin phrase meaning "in the middle of things." The term refers to a technique of plunging into the middle of a story and only later using a FLASHBACK to tell what has happened previously. (See page 240.) The most famous examples of this technique are found in some EPICS. Book I of Homer's *Odyssey*, for example, opens ten years after the Trojan War has ended. The goddess Athena is telling Odysseus's son to go to Sparta to inquire about his father, who should have returned home from the war ten years before. Only later, in Book IX, do we hear Odysseus tell about his adventures of the previous ten years. An English epic that begins *in medias res* is John Milton's *Paradise Lost* (page 240).

INVERSION The technique of reversing, or *inverting*, the normal word order (subject, verb, object) of a sentence. For example, an inversion of "I went to the park" is "To the park went I." Writers may use inversion to create a certain tone or to emphasize a particular word or idea. A poet may invert a line so that it fits into a particular METER or RHYME scheme. (See page 418.)

IRONY A CONTRAST or an incongruity between what is stated and what is really meant, or between what is expected to happen and what actually happens. Three kinds of irony are (1) *verbal irony,* in which a writer or speaker says one thing and means something entirely different; (2) *dramatic irony,* in which a reader or an audience perceives something that a character in the story or play does not know (see page 155); (3) *irony of situation,* in which the writer shows a discrepancy between the expected result of some action or situation and its actual result (see page 807).

The character Antony in William Shakespeare's play *Julius Caesar* uses *verbal irony* when he keeps repeating in his funeral oration over Caesar's body: "For Brutus is an honorable man." Antony is a political enemy of Brutus and is actually trying to convince his audience that Brutus is a liar and therefore dishonorable.

Examples of *dramatic irony* are found throughout *Julius Caesar.* For example, the audience of the play knows from history that Caesar will be murdered by members of the Senate, but Caesar himself does not know this. The audience also hears the conspirators actually planning to murder Caesar, but Caesar himself is ignorant of the plot.

An example of *irony of situation* is found in James Joyce's short story "Araby" (page 730). The main character, a romantic young boy, impatiently awaits the night of a bazaar in his neighborhood. He expects it to be exotic and colorful, and hopes to bring back a gift for a neighborhood girl he adores. But on the night of the bazaar, he arrives late only to find that it is empty, dark, and half-closed, and not like what he had expected.

KENNING In Old English poetry, an elaborate phrase that describes persons, things, or events in a METAPHORICAL and indirect way. The Anglo-Saxon EPIC *Beowulf* (page 12) contains many kennings, such as "swanroad" for the sea and "wave-skimmer" for a ship. (See page 11.)

LYRIC A poem, usually a short one, that expresses a speaker's personal thoughts or feelings. The ELEGY, ODE, and SONNET are all forms of the lyric. As its Greek name indicates, a lyric was originally a poem sung to the accompaniment of a lyre, and lyrics to this day have retained a melodic quality. Lyrics may express a range of emotions and reflections: Robert Herrick's "To Daffodils" (page 224) reflects on the brevity of life and the need to live for the moment, while T. S. Eliot's "Preludes" (page 750) observe the sordidness and depression of modern life.

MASQUE An elaborate and spectacular dramatic entertainment that was popular among the English aristocracy in the late sixteenth and early seventeenth centuries. Masques were written as DRAMATIC POEMS and made use of songs, dances, colorful costumes, and startling stage effects. (See page 231.)

MELODRAMA Originally, melodramas were so called because melodies accompanied certain actions (*melos* means "song" in Greek). Also, each character in a melodrama had a theme melody, which was played each time he or she made an appearance on stage. Today we use the term *melodrama* to mean a drama that has STEREOTYPED characters, exaggerated emotions, and a CONFLICT that pits an all-good hero or heroine against an all-evil villain. The good characters always win and the evil ones are always punished.

METAPHOR A FIGURE OF SPEECH that makes a comparison between two things which are basically dissimilar. "Life is a dream," "Life is a vale of tears," and "Life is a hard road" are all examples of metaphor. Unlike a SIMILE, a metaphor does not use a connective word such as *like, as* or *resembles* in making the comparison. (See page 19.)

Many metaphors are implied, or suggested. An *implied metaphor* does not directly state that one thing is another, different thing. Alfred, Lord Tennyson uses an implied metaphor in these lines from "Crossing the Bar" (page 595):

I hope to see my Pilot face to face
  When I have crossed the bar.

By capitalizing the word *Pilot,* the poet implies a comparison between God and the pilot of his ship.

An *extended metaphor* is a metaphor that is extended throughout a poem. In "Crossing the Bar," Tennyson compares death to a voyage at sea, at the end of which he will meet the "Pilot," or God. This comparison is extended throughout the poem.

A *dead metaphor* is a metaphor which has become so commonplace that it seems literal rather than figurative. Some examples are the *foot* of a hill, the *head* of the class, a *point* in time, and the *leg* of a chair.

A *mixed metaphor* is the use of two or more inconsistent metaphors in one expression. When they are examined, mixed metaphors make no sense. Mixed metaphors are often unintentionally humorous: "The storm of protest was nipped in the bud" or "To hold the fort, he'd have to shake a leg."

METER A generally regular pattern of stressed and unstressed syllables in poetry. In these lines from Robert Burns's poem "O, My Luve's like a Red, Red Rose," the stressed syllables are marked (ʹ) and the unstressed syllables are marked (˘):

As fair art thou, my bonnie lass,
  So deep in luve am I;
And I will luve thee still, my dear,
  Till a' the seas gang dry.

For the common metrical patterns, see **ANAPEST, DACTYL, IAMB,** and **TROCHEE.**

METONYMY (mə·tonʹə·mē) A **FIGURE OF SPEECH** in which a part of a thing, or something very closely associated with it, is used to stand for or suggest the thing itself. "Three sails came into the harbor" is an example of metonymy. The word *sails* is used to stand for the ships themselves. Other common examples of metonymy are *crown* to mean a king, *hardhat* to mean a construction worker, and *White House* to mean the President.

William Shakespeare uses metonymy in these lines from his play *Cymbeline.* The words *scepter, learning,* and *physic* stand for the king, the scholar, and the doctor:

The scepter, learning, and physic, must
All follow this, and come to dust.

MOCK EPIC A comic literary form which treats a trivial subject in the grand, heroic style of the **EPIC.** A mock epic is also referred to as a *mock-heroic* poem. (See page 304.) Perhaps the greatest mock epic in English is Alexander Pope's *The Rape of the Lock* (page 304).

MOTIF A recurring feature (such as a name, an image, or a phrase) in a work of literature. A motif generally contributes in some way to the **THEME** of a short story, novel, poem, or play. For example, a motif used by D. H. Lawrence in his story "The Rocking-horse Winner" (page 738) is the word *luck.* The main character of the story, a boy named Paul, discovers that he has the power to predict the winner in a horse race. However, this becomes an ironic kind of luck, for Paul grows obsessed with his power and is finally destroyed by it.

At times, *motif* is used to refer to some commonly used **PLOT** or **CHARACTER** type in literature. The "ugly duckling motif" refers to a plot that involves the transformation of a plain-looking person into a beauty. Two other commonly used motifs are the "Romeo and Juliet motif" (about doomed lovers) and the "Horatio Alger motif" (about the office clerk who becomes the corporation president).

MOTIVATION The reasons, either stated or implied, for a character's behavior. To make a story believable, a writer must provide characters with motivation sufficient to explain what they do. Characters may be motivated by outside events, or they may be motivated by inner needs of fears.

MYTH A story, often about immortals and sometimes connected with religious rituals, that is intended to give meaning to the mysteries of the world.

In myths, the gods and goddesses are usually identified with the immense powers of the universe: in the Greek myths, Zeus is associated with the sky, Hades with the underworld, Poseidon with the sea, Apollo with the sun, Athena with wisdom, Ares with war. But the gods are also given the forms and feelings of human beings. Thus, myths make it possible for people to understand and deal with things that they cannot control and often cannot see.

A body of related myths that is accepted by a people is known as its *mythology*. A mythology tells a people what it is most concerned about: where it came from, who its gods are, what its most sacred rituals are, and what its destiny is.

NARRATION The kind of writing or speaking that tells a story (a *narrative*). Narration is one of the major FORMS OF DISCOURSE. (See also DESCRIPTION, EXPOSITION, and PERSUASION.) Narration may take the form of prose or poetry. A narrative may be book-length, as in a NOVEL or an EPIC, or it may be paragraph-length, as in a FABLE or an ANEC-DOTE. The short stories, narrative poems, and plays in this book are all examples of narration.

NARRATIVE POEM A poem that tells a story. One kind of narrative poem is the EPIC, a long poem which sets forth the heroic ideals of a particular society. *Beowulf* (page 12) is an epic. The BALLAD is another kind of narrative poem. "Bonny Barbara Allan" (page 36) is an example of a ballad.

NARRATOR One who narrates, or tells, a story. A story may be told by a *first-person* narrator, someone who is either a major or minor character in the story. Or a story may be told by a *third-person* narrator, someone who is not in the story at all. (See POINT OF VIEW.)

The word *narrator* can also refer to a character in a drama who guides the audience through the play, often commenting on the action and sometimes participating in it. In Thornton Wilder's play *Our Town*, the Stage Manager serves as the narrator.

NATURALISM An extreme form of REALISM. Naturalistic writers usually depict the sordid side of life and show CHARACTERS who are severely, if not hopelessly, limited by their environment or heredity. James Joyce's "Araby" (page 730) and Graham Greene's "Across the Bridge" (page 835) are examples of naturalistic writing.

NOVEL A book-length fictional prose narrative, having many CHARACTERS and, often, a complex PLOT. Some important English novels are *Tom Jones* by Henry Fielding, *Pride and Prejudice* by Jane Austen, *Great Expectations* by Charles Dickens, and *Ulysses* by James Joyce. (See page 430.)

OCTAVE An eight-line poem or STANZA. Usually the term *octave* refers to the first eight lines of an ITALIAN SONNET. The remaining six lines form a SESTET.

ODE A complex and often lengthy LYRIC poem, written in a dignified, formal style on some lofty or serious subject. Odes are often written for a special occasion, to honor a person or a season, or to commemorate an event. (See page 266.) Some famous odes are William Wordsworth's "Ode: Intimations of Immortality from Recollections of Early Childhood" (page 476), Percy Bysshe Shelley's "Ode to the West Wind" (page 521), and John Keats's "Ode on a Grecian Urn" (page 544).

ONOMATOPOEIA The use of a word whose sound in some degree imitates or suggests its meaning. (See pages 11 and 266.) The names of some birds are onomatopoetic, imitating the cry of the bird named: *cuckoo, whippoorwill, owl, crow, towhee, bobwhite*. Some onomatopoetic words are *hiss, clang, rustle,* and *snap*. In these lines from John Keats's poem "La Belle Dame sans Merci," the word *moan* is onomatopoetic:

> She looked at me as she did love,
> And made sweet *moan*.

OXYMORON A FIGURE OF SPEECH that combines opposite or contradictory ideas or terms, as in "living death," "dear enemy," "sweet sorrow," and "wise fool." An oxymoron suggests a PARADOX, but it does so very briefly, usually in two or three words. (See page 207.)

PARADOX A statement that reveals a kind of truth, although it seems at first to be self-contradictory and untrue. (See pages 95 and 207.) Richard Lovelace included a famous paradox in his poem "To Althea from Prison":

> Stone walls do not a prison make,
>   Nor iron bars a cage;
> Minds innocent and quiet take
>   That for an hermitage.

PARALLELISM The use of phrases, clauses, or sentences that are similar or complementary in structure or in meaning. In Alfred, Lord Tennyson's poem "Sweet and Low," the first and third lines of the first stanza are parallel in structure:

> Sweet and low, sweet and low,
>   Wind of the western sea,
> Low, low, breathe and blow,
>   Wind of the western sea.

Parallelism is used extensively in the psalms in the Bible, where the thought of one line is often repeated with some variation in the next line:

> I will sing unto the Lord as long as I live:
> I will sing praise to my God while I have
>   my being.
>
> Psalm 104

PARODY The humorous imitation of a work of literature, art, or music. A parody often achieves its humorous effect through the use of EXAGGERATION or mockery. In literature, parody can be made of a PLOT, a CHARACTER, a writing STYLE, or a sentiment or THEME. The poet Algernon Charles Swinburne parodies his own verse in a humorous poem called "Nephelidia." Here, Swinburne is mocking a kind of lush verse that makes excessive use of ALLITERATION:

> Pallid and pink as the palm of the flag-flower that flickers with fear of the flies as they float,
> Are the looks of our lovers that lustrously lean from a marvel of mystic, miraculous moonshine

PASTORAL A type of poem which deals in an idealized way with shepherds and rustic life (the word *pastoral* comes from the Latin word for shepherd, *pastor*). (See page 92.) Two pastoral poems are Christopher Mar-

lowe's "The Passionate Shepherd to His Love" and Sir Walter Raleigh's "The Nymph's Reply to the Shepherd" (page 92).

PATHOS The quality in a work of literature or art that arouses the reader's feelings of pity, sorrow, or compassion for a character. The term is usually used to refer to situations in which innocent characters suffer through no fault of their own. An example of a scene with pathos is the scene in Chapter 12 of George Eliot's novel *Silas Marner* in which the child Eppie slips from her dead mother's arms and toddles over the snow to Silas's cottage.

PENTAMETER A poetic line that consists of five verse FEET. (See also BLANK VERSE and IAMBIC PENTAMETER.) The following lines from William Shakespeare's "Sonnet 29" (page 106) are written in pentameter—that is, there are five stressed syllables in each line. The stressed syllables are marked (´), the unstressed (˘):

> When in disgrace with fortune and men's
>   eyes
> I all alone beweep my outcast state.

PERSONIFICATION A FIGURE OF SPEECH in which something nonhuman is given human qualities. (See pages 95 and 239.) In these lines from "Blow, Blow, Thou Winter Wind," William Shakespeare personifies the wind. He addresses it as if it were a person who could consciously act with kindness or unkindness. He also gives it teeth and breath.

> Blow, blow, thou winter wind,
> Thou art not so unkind
>   As man's ingratitude:
> Thy tooth is not so keen,
> Because thou art not seen,
>   Although thy breath be rude.

PERSUASION The type of speaking or writing that is intended to make its audience adopt a certain opinion, or perform an action, or both. Persuasion is one of the major FORMS OF DISCOURSE. (See also NARRATION,

DESCRIPTION, and EXPOSITION.) Modern examples of persuasion include political speeches, television commercials, and newspaper editorials. A good example of persuasive writing is Thomas Carlyle's "Midas" (page 565), in which the author calls on the English people to improve their social conditions:

> To whom, then, is this wealth of England wealth? Who is it that it blesses; makes happier, wiser, beautifuler, in any way better? Who has got hold of it, to make it fetch and carry for him, like a true servant, not like a false mock-servant; to do him any real service whatsoever? As yet no one. We have more riches than any nation ever had before. Our successful industry is hitherto unsuccessful; a strange success if we stop here! In the midst of plethoric plenty, the people perish; with gold walls and full barns, no man feels himself safe or satisfied.

PLOT   The sequence of events or actions in a short story, novel, play, or narrative poem. Plots may be simple or complicated, loosely constructed or close-knit. But every plot is made up of a series of incidents that are related to one another. The most important element of plot is CONFLICT. For example, the plot of James Joyce's short story "Araby" (page 730) could be summarized in this way: A romantic boy idolizes a girl from his neighborhood. He watches her from afar and dreams about her. When an exotic bazaar comes to their neighborhood, he decides to go and bring back a gift for her. He loses interest in all other things and waits impatiently for the night of the bazaar. But on that night the boy's uncle, who must give him money, comes home late. When the boy arrives at the bazaar, he is bitterly disappointed to find it already deserted and nearly closed, and not at all like what he had expected. He sees himself as a vain person, and feels sadness and anger.

POINT OF VIEW   The vantage point from which a narrative is told. There are two basic points of view. (1) In the *first-person* point of view, the story is told by one of the characters in his or her own words. The first-person point of view is limited, since the reader is told only what this character knows and observes. Here is an example of first-person point of view from Jonathan Swift's *Gulliver's Travels* (page 313):

> The King was struck with horror at the description I had given of those terrible engines and the proposal I had made. He was amazed how so impotent and groveling an insect as I (these were his expressions) could entertain such inhuman ideas. . . .

(2) In the *third-person* point of view, the narrator is not a character in the story. The narrator may be an *omniscient,* or "all-knowing," observer who can describe and comment on all the characters and actions in the story. Thomas Hardy's "The Three Strangers" (page 630) is written from a third-person omniscient point of view:

> Shepherdess Fennel fell back upon the intermediate plan of mingling short dances with short periods of talk and singing, so as to hinder any ungovernable rage in either.

On the other hand, the third-person narrator might tell a story from the point of view of only one character in the story, as Virginia Woolf does in "The New Dress" (page 713). All the action in that story is told by the third-person narrator, from the *limited* point of view of Mabel Waring.

PROTAGONIST   The central CHARACTER of a drama, novel, short story, or narrative poem. The protagonist is the character on whom the action centers and with whom the reader sympathizes most. Usually the protagonist strives against an opposing force, or ANTAGONIST, to accomplish something. The protagonist can be either heroic or ordinary, good or bad. For example, Beowulf (page 12) is brave and good. Macbeth (page 119) is noble and honorable at first, but becomes increasingly hateful. Bella Fleace, the protagonist of Evelyn Waugh's "Bella Fleace Gave a Party" (page 809), is elderly and friendless.

PSALM   A song or LYRIC poem in praise of God. The term usually refers to the 150 sacred lyrics in the Book of Psalms in the Bible. "Psalm 8" is found on page 192.

PUN The humorous use of a word or phrase to suggest two or more meanings at the same time. A famous pun on the word *grave* occurs in Shakespeare's *Romeo and Juliet*. Mercutio, who is always joking, is fatally wounded and knows that he does not have long to live. He says, "Ask for me tomorrow, and you shall find me a grave man."

QUATRAIN Usually a stanza or poem of four lines. However, a quatrain may also be any group of four lines unified by a rhyme scheme. Quatrains usually follow an *abab*, *abba,* or *abcb* rhyme scheme. (See pages 39 and 450.) Here is a quatrain from William Wordsworth's "Lines Written in Early Spring" (page 450):

The birds around me hopped and *played,*	*a*
Their thoughts I cannot *measure;*	*b*
But the least motion which they *made,*	*a*
It seemed a thrill of *pleasure.*	*b*

REALISM The attempt in literature and art to represent life as it really is, without sentimentalizing or idealizing it. Realistic writing often depicts the everyday life and speech of ordinary people. This has led, sometimes, to an emphasis on sordid details. (See NATURALISM.)

REFRAIN A word, phrase, line, or group of lines repeated regularly in a poem, usually at the end of each STANZA. Refrains are often used in BALLADS and NARRATIVE POEMS to create a songlike RHYTHM and to help build SUSPENSE. Refrains can also serve to emphasize a particular idea. (See page 35.) A modern example of the use of refrain appears in Dylan Thomas's "Do Not Go Gentle into That Good Night" (page 843).

RHYME The repetition of sounds in two or more words or phrases that appear close to each other in a poem. For example: *river-shiver, song-long, leap-deep.* If the rhyme occurs at the ends of lines, it is called *end rhyme.* Here is an example from William Blake's "The Tiger" (page 425):

In what distant deeps or *skies*
Burnt the fire of thine *eyes?*

On what wings dare he *aspire?*
What the hand dare seize the *fire?*

If the rhyme occurs within a line, it is called *internal rhyme.* Here is an example of internal rhyme from Edmund Spenser's "Sonnet 26" (page 87):

Sweet is the *rose,* but *grows* upon a briar

Approximate rhyme is rhyme in which only the final consonant sounds of the words are identical (as opposed to *exact rhyme*). *Cook-look* is an exact rhyme; *cook-lack* is an approximate rhyme.

A *rhyme scheme* is the pattern of rhymes in a poem. *Interlocking rhyme* is a rhyme scheme in which an unrhymed line in one STANZA forms a rhyme in the following stanza. Interlocking rhyme occurs in an Italian verse form called TERZA RIMA. (See page 527.)

RHYTHM The arrangement of stressed and unstressed syllables into a pattern. Rhythm is most apparent in poetry, though it is part of all good writing. Rhythm often gives a poem a distinct musical quality, as in Samuel Taylor Coleridge's "Kubla Khan" (page 484):

Ĭn Xănădu̅ did Kúblă Khán
Ă státelў pleásŭre dome dĕcree̅
Whĕre Alph, the̅ sácred rivĕr, rán
Through cavĕrns measŭreless to̅ mán

Poets also use rhythm to echo meaning. In these lines from Alfred, Lord Tennyson's "Break, Break, Break" (page 588), the pounding rhythm reinforces the image of waves crashing against the land:

Bréak, bréak, bréak,
Ŏn thў cóld grăy stónes, Ŏ Séa!

RISING ACTION The action of a play that increases tension and builds toward the CLIMAX, or turning point of the play. In William Shakespeare's *Macbeth* (page 119), the climax occurs in Act III during the banquet scene. Macbeth, overcome by nervousness and guilt over the murders of Duncan and

Banquo, sees Banquo's ghost appearing in the banquet hall. At this intense moment, Macbeth is nearly driven insane. The action preceding this climactic moment, including the prophecy of the three witches and the plan and carrying out of the two murders, is the rising action. (See page 155.)

ROMANCE Originally, a term used to describe a medieval tale dealing with the loves and adventures of kings, queens, knights, and ladies, and including unlikely or supernatural happenings. (See page 29.) One of the most famous examples of a romance is the legend of King Arthur and the Knights of the Round Table (page 70). In a more general sense, a romance is any form of imaginative literature that is set in an idealized world and that deals with heroic adventures and battles between good characters and villains or monsters.

ROMANTICISM A movement that flourished in literature, philosophy, music, and art in Western culture during most of the nineteenth century, beginning as a revolt against CLASSICISM. There have been many varieties of Romanticism in many different times and places. Many of the ideas of English Romanticism were first expressed by the poets William Wordsworth (page 447) and Samuel Taylor Coleridge (page 483). Romanticism, essentially, idealizes life. Whereas REALISM attempts to show life as it really is, Romanticism attempts to show life as it should be, or as the writer, reader, or audience would like it to be. Romanticism emphasizes the picturesque, emotional, exotic, and mysterious aspects of life. Romanticism tends to uphold the idea that people are basically good and perfectible. Romanticism also tends to glorify nature, showing that those who live closest to nature and imitate it are the noblest kind of people. (See page 437.)

SATIRE A kind of writing that holds up to ridicule or contempt the weaknesses and wrongdoings of individuals, groups, institutions, or humanity in general. The aim of satirists is to set a moral standard for society, and they attempt to persuade the reader to see their point of view through the force of laughter. (See pages 311 and 333.) The most famous satirical work in English literature is Jonathan Swift's *Gulliver's Travels* (page 313). In the distant land of Brobdingnag, where the people are twelve times as tall as a normal human being, Gulliver is brought before the King to describe the English people. Swift satirizes the English people through the King's response:

> He was perfectly astonished with the historical account I gave him of our affairs during the last century, protesting it was only an heap of conspiracies, rebellions, murders, massacres, revolutions, banishments; the very worst effects that avarice, faction, hypocrisy, perfidiousness, cruelty, rage, madness, hatred, envy, lust, malice, and ambition could produce.

SESTET A six-line poem or STANZA. Usually the term *sestet* refers to the last six lines of an ITALIAN SONNET. The first eight lines of an Italian sonnet form an OCTAVE.

SETTING The time and place in which the events in a short story, novel, play, or narrative poem occur. A setting may serve simply as the physical background of a story, or a skillful writer may use setting to establish a particular ATMOSPHERE, which in turn, contributes to the PLOT and THEME of the story.

SIMILE A comparison made between two things through the use of a specific word of comparison, such as *like, as, than,* or *resembles.* The comparison must be between two essentially unlike things. To say "Susan is like her grandmother" is not to use a simile. But to say "Susan is like a golden flower" is to use a simile. (See page 19.) In "To a Skylark" (page 524), Percy Bysshe Shelley uses a simile to describe the flight of the skylark:

> Higher still and higher
>   From the earth thou springest
> Like a cloud of fire

SOLILOQUY In drama, an extended speech delivered by a character alone onstage. The character reveals his or her innermost thoughts and feelings directly to the audience, as if thinking aloud. (See page 603.) One of the most famous soliloquies in literature occurs at the end of Shakespeare's *Macbeth* (page 119), when Macbeth, near defeat, expresses a bleak and bitter vision of life:

Tomorrow, and tomorrow, and tomorrow,
Creeps in this petty pace from day to day
To the last syllable of recorded time,
And all our yesterdays have lighted fools
The way to dusty death. Out, out, brief
    candle!
Life's but a walking shadow, a poor player
That struts and frets his hour upon the
    stage
And then is heard no more. It is a tale
Told by an idiot, full of sound and fury,
Signifying nothing.

SONG A short LYRIC poem with distinct musical qualities, normally written to be set to music. (See page 518.) "She Walks in Beauty" (page 511) by George Gordon, Lord Byron is a song.

SONNET A fourteen-line LYRIC poem, usually written in rhymed IAMBIC PENTAMETER. Sonnets usually express a single THEME or idea. (See pages 89 and 617.) Sonnets vary in structure and RHYME scheme, but are generally of two types: the *Petrarchan* or *Italian sonnet,* and the *Elizabethan* or *Shakespearean sonnet.*

The Italian sonnet is a form that originated in Italy in the thirteenth century. The Italian sonnet has two parts, an OCTAVE (eight lines) and a SESTET (six lines). Its rhyme scheme is usually *abbaabba, cdecde.* The two parts of the Italian sonnet play off each other in a variety of ways. Sometimes the octave raises a question which the sestet answers. Sometimes the sestet opposes what the octave says, or extends it. The Italian sonnet is often called the Petrarchan sonnet, because the Italian poet Francesco Petrarch used it so extensively. He dedicated more than 300 sonnets to a woman named Laura.

The Shakespearean sonnet consists of three QUATRAINS and a concluding COUPLET, with the rhyme scheme *abab cdcd efef gg.* (See page 89.)

SONNET SEQUENCE A series of SONNETS linked together by subject or THEME. (See

page 89.) William Shakespeare's 154 sonnets comprise the most famous sonnet sequence in English.

SPENSERIAN STANZA A nine-line STANZA with the following rhyme scheme: *ababb-cbcc.* The first eight lines are written in IAMBIC PENTAMETER. The ninth line is written in iambic hexameter and is called an ALEXANDRINE. The Spenserian stanza was invented by Edmund Spenser for his EPIC poem *The Faerie Queene.* (See page 87.) The Spenserian stanza was also used by Robert Burns, John Keats, and Percy Bysshe Shelley.

SPRUNG RHYTHM A term created by the poet Gerard Manley Hopkins to designate a variable kind of poetic meter in which a stressed syllable may be combined with any number of unstressed syllables. Poems with sprung rhythm have an irregular meter and are meant to sound like natural speech. (See page 628.) Here is an example of sprung rhythm from Hopkins's poem "God's Grandeur" (page 626):

The world is charged with the grandeur
    of God.
It will flame out, like shining from
    shook foil

STEREOTYPE A commonplace type of character that appears so often in literature that his or her nature is immediately familiar to the reader. Stereotypes, also called *stock characters,* always look and act the same way and reveal the same traits of character. Examples of stereotypes are the temperamental movie star, the talkative cab driver, the mad scientist, the villain with a waxed mustache, and the wisecracking, hard-boiled private detective.

STREAM-OF-CONSCIOUSNESS The style of writing that attempts to imitate the natural flow of a character's thoughts, feelings, reflections, memories, and mental images, as the character experiences them. The stream-of-consciousness technique enables a writer to delve deeply into a character's psychology and record fully a character's consciousness—not only *what* the character thinks, but also *how* the character thinks. As a record of the spontaneous flow of a character's consciousness, this technique makes no attempt to be logical or even clear. It simply attempts to follow the mind wherever it goes. (See pages 712, 718, and 727.) An example is Virginia Woolf's story "The New Dress" (page 713).

STYLE An author's characteristic way of writing, determined by the choice of words, the arrangement of words in sentences, and the relationship of the sentences to one another. Thus, one author may write long, complex sentences, while another writes short, terse ones. One author may use few adjectives, while another uses many. Style also refers to the particular way in which an author uses IMAGERY, FIGURATIVE LANGUAGE, and RHYTHM. Style is the sum total of qualities and characteristics that distinguish the writings of one writer from those of another. (See page 575.)

SUSPENSE The quality of a story, novel, or drama that makes the reader or audience uncertain or tense about the outcome of events. Suspense makes readers ask, "What will happen next?" or "How will this work out?" and impels them to read on. Suspense is greatest when it focuses attention on a sympathetic character. Thus the most familiar kind of suspense involves a character in mortal danger: hanging from the ledge of a tall building; tied to railroad tracks as a train approaches; or alone in an old house, ascending a staircase to open the attic door. But suspense may simply arise from curiosity, as when a character must make a decision, or seek an explanation for something.

SYMBOL Any object, person, place, or action that has a meaning in itself and that also stands for something larger than itself, such as a quality, an attitude, a belief, or a value. A rose is often a symbol of love and beauty; a skull is often a symbol of death; spring and winter often symbolize youth and old age. (See page 696.)

SYMBOLISM A literary movement which arose in France in the last half of the nineteenth century and which greatly influenced many English writers, particularly poets, of the twentieth century. To the Symbolist poets, an emotion is indefinite and therefore difficult to communicate. Symbolist poets tend to avoid any direct statement of meaning. Instead, they work through emotionally powerful symbols which suggest meaning and MOOD. (See pages 427 and 696.)

TERZA RIMA An Italian verse form consisting of a series of three-line STANZAS in which the middle line of each stanza rhymes with the first and third lines of the following stanza, as follows: *aba bcb cdc*, etc. (See page 527.) Percy Bysshe Shelley's "Ode to the West Wind" (page 521) is written in *terza rima.* Here are the first two stanzas:

O wild West Wind, thou breath of Autumn's *being,*	*a*
Thou, from whose unseen presence the leaves *dead*	*b*
Are driven, like ghosts from an enchanter *fleeing,*	*a*
Yellow, and black, and pale, and hectic *red,*	*b*
Pestilence-stricken multitudes: O *thou,*	*c*
Who chariotest to their dark wintry *bed*	*b*

TETRAMETER A line of poetry made up of four verse FEET. Thus, a tetrameter line has four groupings of stressed and unstressed syllables. Here is an example of tetrameter verse from Alfred, Lord Tennyson's "The Lady of Shalott" (page 582):

Ŏn éither síde thĕ rívĕr líe
Lŏng fíelds ŏf bárlĕy aňd ŏf rýe

THEME The general idea or insight about life that a writer wishes to express in a literary work. All the elements of the literary work—PLOT, SETTING, CHARACTERIZATION, and FIGURATIVE LANGUAGE—contribute to the development of its theme. A simple theme can often be stated in a single sentence. But sometimes a literary work is rich and complex, and a paragraph or even an essay is needed to state the theme. Not all literary works have a controlling theme. For example, the purpose of some simple ghost stories is to frighten the reader, and some detective stories seek only to thrill.

TONE The attitude a writer takes toward his or her subject, characters, or audience. In writing about his childhood in his poem "Fern Hill" (page 842), Dylan Thomas takes a nostalgic tone. In "Preface to Shakespeare" (page 336), Samuel Johnson takes a serious, admiring tone toward a great writer. Tone is found in every kind of writing. It is created through the choice of words and details.

TRAGEDY In general, a literary work in which the PROTAGONIST meets an unhappy or disastrous end. Unlike COMEDY, tragedy depicts the actions of a central character who is usually dignified or heroic. Through a series of events, this main character, or tragic hero or heroine, is brought to a final downfall. The causes of the downfall vary. In traditional dramas, the cause can be fate, a flaw in character, or an error in judgment. In modern dramas, where the tragic figure is often an ordinary individual, the causes range from moral or psychological weakness to the evils of society. The tragic figure, though defeated, usually gains a measure of wisdom or self-awareness. (See page 181.)

TRIMETER A poetic line made up of three verse FEET. Thus, a trimeter line has three groupings of stressed and unstressed syllables. Here is an example of trimeter verse

from Alfred, Lord Tennyson's "Break, Break, Break" (page 588):

Ŏh, wéll fŏr thĕ físhĕrman's bóy,
  Thăt hĕ shóuts wĭth hĭs sístĕr ăt pláy!

TROCHEE A poetic FOOT consisting of a stressed syllable followed by an unstressed syllable. Here is an example of *trochaic* verse from William Blake's "The Tiger" (page 425):

Whát thĕ hámmĕr? Whát thĕ cháin?

VERSE PLAY A drama written mostly or entirely in verse. A character's speech may form an individual poem, and several characters' speeches linked together may form one poem. Verse plays are often written in BLANK VERSE. In this book, William Shakespeare's *Macbeth* (page 119) and T. S. Eliot's *Murder in the Cathedral* (page 756) are verse plays.

VILLANELLE An intricate verse form of French origin, consisting of several three-line stanzas and a concluding four-line stanza. The first and third lines of the first stanza are used as REFRAINS in the succeeding stanzas and as the last two lines of the concluding stanza. Only two rhymes are allowed in a villanelle. (See page 845.) A famous modern villanelle is Dylan Thomas's "Do Not Go Gentle into That Good Night" (page 843).

Exercises in the Text

The page numbers cited in this index indicate the location of the major exercises on the topics listed below.

Index of Fine Art

Glossary

Listed below are words from selections in this book that you will find useful to add to your vocabulary. Proper names and words that are specialized, archaic, or not generally useful are not included in this glossary but have been footnoted, as appropriate, in the text. The pronunciation key is that of the Funk and Wagnalls *Standard College Dictionary* and the definitions are based on those given in the *Standard College Dictionary*.

A

abate (ə·bāt′) To make less; reduce in quantity, value, force, or intensity.

abjure (ab·jŏŏr′) 1. To renounce under oath; forswear. 2. To retract or recant, as an opinion; repudiate.

ablution (ab·lōō′shən) A washing or cleansing, especially of the body; a bath.

abysmal (ə·biz′məl) Unfathomable; immeasurable; extreme.

abyss (ə·bis′) 1. A bottomless gulf; chasm. 2. Any profound depth or void; an *abyss* of shame; the *abyss* of time. 3. The lowest depths of the sea.

accession (ak·sesh′ən) The attainment of an office, dignity, or right.

accolade (ak′ə·lād′, -läd′) An honor; award.

acquiescence (ak′wē·es′əns) Quiet submission; passive consent.

acrimony (ak′rə·mō′nē) Sharpness or bitterness of speech or temper.

acumen (ə·kyōō′mən, ak′yōō-) Quickness of insight or discernment; keenness of intellect.

adamantly (ad′ə·mənt·lē, -mant′-) Stubbornly; unyieldingly.

adjuration (aj′ŏŏ·rā′shən) The act of adjuring; a solemn oath.

adjure (ə·jŏŏr′) To appeal to earnestly.

adroit (ə·droit′) Skillful or ready in the use of bodily or mental power; dexterous; expert.

adulation (aj′ŏŏ·lā′shən) Extravagant and hypocritical praise; servile flattery.

adumbrate (ad·um′brāt, ə·dum′-) To represent the mere shadow of; outline sketchily.

aesthetic (es·thet′ik) Of or having to do with beauty in art, nature, etc.

affinity (ə·fin′ə·tē) A natural attraction or inclination.

affront (ə·frunt′) To insult openly; offend by word or act.

akimbo (ə·kim′bō) With hand on hip and elbow out.

alacrity (ə·lak′rə·tē) Cheerful willingness and promptitude; liveliness.

allegory (al′ə·gor′ē) A narrative veiling a moral or some form of abstract teaching by means of symbolic devices, such as metaphor, personification, etc.

allusion (ə·lōō′zhən) 1. The act of alluding; indirect reference; suggestion. 2. A casual but significant reference.

alms (ämz) A gift or gifts for the poor; charity.

altercation (ôl′tər·kā′shən, al′-) A heated dispute; angry controversy; wrangling.

amalgamate (ə·mal′gə·māt) To unite or combine.

amorphous (ə·môr′fəs) 1. Without definite form or shape. 2. Of no fixed character.

analogy (ə·nal′ə·jē) Agreement or resemblance in certain aspects, as form or function, between otherwise dissimilar things; similarity without identity.

anathema (ə·nath′ə·mə) A formal ecclesiastical ban or curse, excommunicating a person or damning something, as a book or doctrine.

anchorite (ang′kə·rīt) One who has withdrawn from the world for religious reasons; hermit.

animadversion (an′ə·mad·vûr′zhən, -shən) Criticism or censure; a censorious comment or reflection.

annals (an′əlz) 1. A record of events in their chronological order, year by year. 2. History or records in general.

annuity (ə·nōō′ə·tē, -nyōō′-) An allowance or income paid yearly or at specified periods.

anodyne (an′ə·dīn) Anything that relieves pain or soothes.

anomaly (ə·nom′ə·lē) Deviation from rule, type, or form; irregularity.

anonymity (an′ə·nim′ə·tē) An anonymous condition, especially the lack of identification and of an established name.

anthropomorphism (an′thrə·pō·môr′fiz·əm) The ascription of human form or characteristics to a deity, or to any being or thing not human. —**anthropomorphic** *adj.*

antipodes (an·tip′ə·dēz) A place or region on the opposite side of the earth, or its inhabitants.

antithesis (an·tith′ə·sis) 1. In rhetoric, the balancing of two contrasted words, ideas, or phrases against each other. 2. Opposition; contrast.

apocalyptic (ə·pok′ə·lip′tik) Of or of the nature of a revelation.

apostate (ə·pos′tāt, -tit) Guilty of desertion of one's faith, religion, party, or principles; false.

appease (ə·pēz′) To reduce or bring to peace; placate; soothe, as by making concessions or yielding to demands.

appellation (ap′ə·lā′shən) A name or title.

approbation (ap′rə·bā′shən) The act of approving; approval.

archetype (är′kə·tīp) An original or standard pattern or model; a prototype.

ardent (är′dənt) Very eager and enthusiastic; fervent.

PRONUNCIATION: add, āce, câre, pälm; end, ēven; it, īce; odd, ōpen, ôrder; tŏŏk, pōōl; up, bûrn; ə = a in *above*, e in *sicken*, i in *flexible*, o in *melon*, u in *focus*; yōō = u in *fuse*; oil; pout; check; go; ring; thin; this; zh, vision.

arduous (är′jōō·əs) Difficult to do; hard.

arid (ar′id) Dull; dry.

arraign (ə·rān′) *Law* To call into court and cause to answer to an indictment.

arrogate (ar′ə·gāt) To claim or take presumptuously or without right: assume; usurp.

artifice (är′tə·fis) **1.** An ingenious expedient; stratagem; maneuver. **2.** Subtle or deceptive craft; trickery.

ascetic (ə·set′ik) **1.** In the early church, one who renounced social life and comfort for solitude, self-mortification, and religious devotion; a hermit; recluse. **2.** One who leads a very austere and self-denying life.

aspersion (ə·spûr′zhən, -shən) A slandering; defamation.

assess (ə·ses′) To measure; evaluate; assign a value to.

assignation (as′ig·nā′shən) An appointment for meeting, especially a secret or illicit one as made by lovers.

asunder (ə·sun′dər) Apart; into pieces.

audacity (ô·das′ə·tē) Boldness; daring.

august (ô·gust′) Inspiring awe, admiration, or reverence; majestic; imposing.

aura (ôr′ə) A distinctive air or quality enveloping or characterizing a person or thing.

avarice (av′ə·ris) Passion for acquiring and hoarding riches; covetousness; greed.

aver (ə·vur′) To declare confidently as fact; affirm.

avid (av′id) Eager; enthusiastic.

B

bailiff (bā′lif) **1.** A court officer having custody of prisoners under arraignment. **2.** One who oversees an estate for the owner; a steward. **3.** *Brit.* A subordinate magistrate with jurisdiction limited to a certain district or to a certain function, as keeping the peace.

baleful (bāl′fəl) **1.** Hurtful; malignant. **2.** *Archaic* Sorrowful; miserable.

bard (bärd) **1.** A Celtic poet and minstrel. **2.** A poet.

belie (bi·lī′) **1.** To misrepresent; disguise: His clothes *belie* his station. **2.** To prove false; contradict: Her actions *belied* her words.

benison (ben′ə·zən, -sən) A benediction; blessing.

betimes (bi·tīmz′) In good time; early; also, soon.

billow (bil′ō) To rise or roll in waves; swell; surge.

blandish (blan′dish) To wheedle; flatter; cajole.

blaspheme (blas·fēm′) To speak in an impious manner of (God or sacred things).

blatant (blā′tənt) **1.** Offensively loud or noisy. **2.** Obvious.

bombast (bom′bast) Grandiloquent or pompous language.

boor (boor) An awkward, ill-mannered person.

brandish (bran′dish) To wave, shake, or flourish triumphantly, menacingly, or defiantly.

bravura (brə·vyoor′ə) *Music.* A passage requiring dashing and brilliant execution; also, a brilliant style of execution.

brazen (brā′zən) **1.** Made of brass. **2.** Resembling brass in hardness, color, sound, etc. **3.** Impudent; shameless.

brimstone (brim′stōn′) Sulphur.

brook (brook) To put up with; tolerate; usually with the negative: I cannot *brook* such conduct.

buoy (boi, boo′ē) . To hold up; keep afloat.

C

cadence (kād′ns) **1.** Rhythmic or measured flow, as of poetry or oratory. **2.** The measure or beat of music, marching, etc.

cajole (kə·jōl′) To coax with flattery or false promises; wheedle.

calumny (kal′əm·nē) **1.** A false and malicious accusation or report, made to injure another. **2.** Defamation; slander.

candor (kan′dər) **1.** Openness; frankness. **2.** Impartiality; fairness.

canonize (kan′ən·īz) **1.** To place (a deceased person) in the canon of saints; declare to be a saint. **2.** To give or ascribe glory to; glorify.

cant (kant) **1.** The hypocritical expression of pious sentiments; insincere religious or moralistic talk. **2.** Words or phraseology used merely for effect; stock phrases. **3.** Phraseology peculiar to a sect, class, or calling.

captious (kap′shəs) Apt to find fault; disposed to criticize; caviling; carping.

caricature (kar′i·kə·choor) A picture or description in which certain features or qualities are exaggerated so as to produce an absurd effect.

cataclysm (kat′ə·kliz′əm) Any violent upheaval or change, as a war, revolution, etc. —**cataclysmic** *adj.*

catholic (kath′ə·lik) Universal in reach; general.

cavalcade (kav′əl·kād, kav′əl·kād′) A procession of people on horseback, or sometimes in carriages.

chasten (chā′sən) **1.** To discipline by punishment or affliction; chastise. **2.** To moderate; soften; temper.

cherubim (cher′ə·bim, -yə·bim) *Theol.* The second of the nine orders of angels.

choleric (kol′ər·ik) Easily provoked to anger; quick-tempered.

circumscribe (sûr′kəm·skrīb′) **1.** To mark out the limits of; define; especially, to confine within bounds. **2.** To draw a line or figure around; encompass.

circumspect (sur′kəm·spekt) Attentive to everything; watchful in all directions, as against danger or error; cautious; wary.

citadel (sit′ə·dəl, -del) A fortress commanding a city.

clarion (klar′ē·ən) **1.** An obsolete kind of trumpet having a shrill tone. **2.** The sound of a clarion, or any sound resembling it.

cleave (klēv) **1.** To split or sunder, as with ax or wedge. **2.** To stick fast; adhere.

clemency (klem′ən·sē) Mildness of temper, especially toward offenders; leniency; mercy.

cloistered (klois′tərd) Concealed or withdrawn from the world.

cloy (kloi) To gratify beyond desire, especially with richness or sweetness; surfeit.

coalition (kō′ə·lish′ən) An alliance of persons, parties, or states.

coerce (kō·ûrs′) **1.** To compel by force, law, authority, or fear. **2.** To restrain or repress by superior force.

comely (kum′lē) Pleasing; handsome; graceful.

complacent (kəm·plā′sənt) Feeling or showing smugness; satisfaction, especially self-satisfaction.

compunction (kəm·pungk′shən) An uneasiness of mind arising from wrongdoing; a sense of guilt or remorse. —**compunctious** *adj.*

con (kon) To study; commit to memory.

conciliate (kən·sil′ē·āt) To overcome the hostility or suspicion of; secure the friendship of; win over; placate; appease; propitiate.

concourse (kon′kôrs) **1.** A coming together; confluence. **2.** A crowd; throng.

conflagration (kon′flə·grā′shən) A great or extensive fire.

conjecture (kən·jek′chər) To conclude or suppose from incomplete evidence; guess; infer.

connivance (kə·nī′vəns) The act or fact of encouraging or assenting to a wrongdoing by silence or feigned ignorance.

connoisseur (kon′ə·sûr′) One competent to judge critically because of thorough knowledge, especially in matters of art and taste.

consign (kən·sīn′) To forward or deliver, as merchandise, for sale or disposal.

896

consort (*n*. kon'sôrt; *v*. kən·sôrt') *n*. **1**. A husband or wife; spouse. **2**. A companion or partner; mate; also, companionship; company. —*v*. To keep company; associate.

constrain (kən·strān') To compel by physical or moral means; coerce.

consummate (*v*. kon'sə·māt; *adj*. kən·sum'it) *v*. To bring to completion or perfection; achieve. —*adj*. Of the highest degree; perfect; complete.

contend (kən·tend') To strive in competition or rivalry; vie.

contrition (kən·trish'ən) Sincere sorrow for wrongdoing.

conversant (kon'vər·sənt, kən·vûr'-) Well acquainted or familiar, as by study.

coomb (kōōm) *Brit*. A narrow valley.

copious (kō'pi·əs) **1**. Large in quantity; ample. **2**. Abundant; plentiful.

coppice (kop'is) A copse.

copse (kops) A thicket of bushes or small trees.

cordial (kôr'jəl, -dyəl) A liqueur.

corroborate (kə·rob'ə·rāt) To strengthen or support, as conviction; confirm.

corrosive (kə·rō'siv) **1**. Having the power of corroding or eating away. **2**. Having the power to hurt one's feelings, etc.; biting; cutting.

cotillion (kō·til'yən, kə-) A lively, quick dance similar to the quadrille (a square dance).

covert (kuv'ert, kō'vert) A thicket where game is likely to hide.

covetous (kuv'ə·təs) Excessively desirous (of something); avaricious; greedy. —**covetousness** *n*.

coxcomb (koks'kōm') A pretentious and conceited fop.

craven (krā'vən) Conspicuously lacking in courage; cowardly.

credulous (krej'ōō·ləs) Disposed to believe on slight evidence; gullible.

cribbage (krib'ij) A game of cards for two, three, or four players, the score being kept on a small board with rows of holes into which pegs are inserted.

crypt (kript) A chamber or vault, especially one beneath a church, used as a place of burial.

cull (kul) To pick or sort out; select.

cursory (kûr'sər·ē) Rapid and superficial; not thorough.

cynical (sin'i·kəl) Having no belief in the goodness and sincerity of others.

D

darkling (därk'ling) *Poetic* Occurring or being in the dark; dim.

dauntless (dônt'lis, dänt'-) Fearless; intrepid.

dearth (dûrth). Scarcity; lack; famine.

debauchery (di·bô'chər·ē) Gross indulgence of one's sensual appetites.

Decalogue (dek'ə·lôg, -log) The Ten Commandments.

declaim (di·klām') To give a formal, set speech or recitation. —**declamation** (dek'lə·mā'shən) *n*.

decussate (di·kus'āt, dek'ə·sāt) To cross in the form of an X; intersect.

defile (*n*. di·fīl', dē'fīl; *v*. di·fīl') *n*. A long, narrow pass, as between mountains. *v*. To make foul or dirty; pollute.

defray (di·frā') To pay (the costs, expenses, etc.).

deign (dān) To condescend to grant or allow.

delve (delv) **1**. *Archaic & Dial*. To engage in digging, as with a spade. **2**. To make careful investigation; search for information.

demur (di·mûr') To offer objections; take exception.

denunciation (di·nun'sē·ā'shən) Open condemnation of a person or action; an act of denouncing.

deprecate (dep'rə·kāt) To express disapproval of or regret for; plead earnestly against.

derogatory (di·rog'ə·tôr'ē) Meant to lessen the good points or merit of someone or something.

descry (di·skrī') To discover with the eye, as something distant or obscure; discern; detect.

despoil (di·spoil') To strip or deprive of possessions; plunder; rob.

destitute (des'tə·tōōt, -tyōōt) Extremely poor; lacking money even for bare necessities.

desultory (des'əl·tôr'ē) Passing abruptly from one thing to another; disconnected; unmethodical.

devolve (di·volv') To pass to a successor or substitute.

dialogue (dī'ə·lôg, -log) **1**. A conversation in which two or more take part. **2**. The conversation in a play, novel, etc.

didactic (dī·dak'tik, di-) **1**. Intended to instruct; expository. **2**. Morally instructive; preceptive. **3**. Overly inclined to teach or moralize; pedantic.

dilapidation (di·lap'ə·dā'shən) A ruined or decayed condition.

dilettante (dil'ə·tan'tē, -tant') A person interested in a subject superficially or merely for amusement; a dabbler.

diminutive (di·min'yə·tiv) Very small; tiny.

dirge (dûrj) **1**. A song or melody expressing mourning; a lament. **2**. A hymn or choral service at a funeral.

discern (di·sûrn', -zûrn') **1**. To perceive, as with sight or mind; recognize; apprehend. **2**. To recognize as separate and different; discriminate mentally.

discourse (dis'kôrs) Connected communication of thought; continuous expression or exchange of ideas; conversation; talk.

dissemble (di·sem'bəl) **1**. To conceal or disguise the actual nature of (intentions, feelings, etc.); cover up; dissimulate. **2**. To make a false show of; feign: to *dissemble* madness.

distemper (dis·tem'pər) A disorder of the mind or body; illness. —**distempered** *adj*.

diurnal (dī·ûr'nəl) Of, belonging to, or occurring each day; daily.

divers (dī'vərz) **1**. Several. **2**. Various.

divest (di·vest', dī-) **1**. To strip, as of clothes. **2**. To deprive, as of rights or possessions.

dock (dok) To cut off the end of (a tail, etc.), or clip short the tail of. —*n*. A wharf or pier.

docket (dok'it) A tag or label attached to a parcel, listing contents, directions, etc.

dogmatism (dôg'mə·tiz'əm, dog'-) Positive or arrogant assertion, as of opinions, or beliefs. —**dogmatic** *adj*.

don (don) *informal* A tutor or the head of a college in a British university.

dotage (dō'tij) Feebleness of mind as a result of old age; senility.

doughty (dou'tē) Valiant; brave: chiefly humorous.

dour (dōōr, dour) Forbidding and surly; morosely stern; ill-tempered.

dower (dou'ər) A dowry.

drivel (driv'əl) Senseless talk; twaddle. —**driveler** *n*.

dross (drôs) Waste matter; refuse.

dynamo (dī'nə·mō) A generator for the conversion of mechanical energy into electrical energy through the agency of electromagnetic induction.

dyspepsia (dis·pep'shə, -sē·ə) Difficult or painful digestion, usually chronic. —**dyspeptic** *adj*.

PRONUNCIATION: add, āce, câre, pălm; end, ēven; it, īce; odd, ōpen, ôrder; tōŏk, pōōl; up, bûrn; ə = a in *above*, e in *sicken*, i in *flexible*, o in *melon*, u in *focus*; yōō = u in *fuse*; oil; pout; check; go; ring; thin; this; zh, vision.

897

E

eccentric (ek·sen′trik) Odd; peculiar; unusual.

ecclesiastical (i·klē′zē·as′ti·kəl) Having to do with a church.

eclipse (i·klips′) 1. To cause an eclipse of; darken. 2. To obscure the beauty, fame, worth, etc., of; overshadow; surpass. —*n.* The apparent dimming or elimination of light from one heavenly body by another.

edible (ed′ə·bəl) Fit to eat.

edict (ē′dikt) 1. An official decree publicly proclaimed. 2. Any formal command or prohibition.

effusion (i·fyōō′zhən) An outpouring of fervid or unrestrained language, sentiment, etc.

elocution (el′ə·kyōō′shən) The art of public speaking, including vocal delivery and gesture.

elucidate (i·lōō′sə·dāt) To make clear; explain. —**elucidation** *n.*

emblazon (em·blā′zən) To adorn magnificently, especially with heraldic devices; set off in bright colors.

emblem (em′bləm) Something that stands for an idea, belief, nation, or party; symbol.

emulate (em′yə·lāt) To try to equal or surpass.

encroach (in·krōch′) To intrude stealthily or gradually upon the possessions or rights of another; trespass.

endue (in·dōō′, -dyōō′) To provide or endow with some quality, power, etc.

enervate (en′ər·vāt) To sap the strength or vitality of; weaken in body or will.

enigma (i·nig′mə) Anything that puzzles or baffles.

enjoin (in·join′) To order authoritatively and emphatically; direct or command (a person or group) to a course of action, conduct, etc.

enmity (en′mə·tē) Deep-seated unfriendliness accompanied by readiness to quarrel or fight; hostility; antagonism.

epithet (ep′ə·thət) 1. An adjective or other descriptive word or phrase qualifying or used in place of the usual name of a person or thing, as *rosy-fingered* in "the rosy-fingered dawn" or *the Bold* in "Philip the Bold." 2. Loosely, any disparaging name, especially for a person.

epitomize (i·pit′ə·mīz) To be a type of; represent the whole class of.

equity (ek′wə·tē) Fairness or impartiality; justness.

ere (âr) Before.

erratic (i·rat′ik) 1. Not conforming to usual standards; irregular; eccentric. 2. Lacking a fixed or certain course; wandering; straying.

erudition (er′yōō·dish′ən, er·ōō-) Great learning; scholarship.

escarpment (es·karp′mənt) A steep slope or drop; especially, the precipitous face of a line of cliffs.

esplanade (es′plə·nād′, -näd′) 1. A level, open stretch of land, as along a shore, used especially as a roadway or public walk. 2. An open embankment or level area before a fortress, designed to expose attackers to the defenders' fire.

essence (es′əns) 1. That which makes something what it is; that in which the real nature of a thing consists; intrinsic or fundamental nature. 2. An existent being; especially, an immaterial being; spirit.

ethereal (i·thir′ē·əl) 1. Not belonging to earth; celestial; spiritual. 2. Of or existing in the ether or upper regions of the atmosphere or of space.

evanescent (ev′ə·nes′ənt) Passing away, or liable to pass away, gradually or imperceptibly; fleeting.

evocative (i·vok′ə·tiv, -vō′kə-) Tending to evoke.

evoke (i·vōk′) 1. To call or summon forth, as memories. 2. To draw forth or produce (a response, reaction, etc.); elicit.

execrate (ek′sə·krāt) 1. To denounce violently. 2. To detest; abhor.

exhort (ig·zôrt′) To urge by earnest appeal or argument; advise or recommend strongly.

exhortation (eg′zôr·tā′shən, ek′sôr-) That which is said so as to exhort; an earnest plea.

exigency (ek′sə·jən·sē) *Usually pl.* A pressing need or necessity; urgent requirement.

exorbitant (ig·zor′bə·tant) Going beyond usual and proper limits, as in price or demand; excessive; extravagant.

expiate (ek′spē·āt) To atone for; make amends for.

expiation (ek′spē·ā′shən) The act of expiating; atonement.

exponent (ik·spō′nənt) 1. One who or that which represents or symbolizes something: an *exponent* of fair play. 2. One who or that which explains or expounds.

expostulation (ik·spos′chōō·lā′shən) The act of expostulating; earnest argument or remonstrance.

expound (ik·spound′) To set forth in detail; state; declare.

extemporize (ik·stem′pə·rīz) To do, make, compose, or perform with little or no advance preparation; improvise.

extol or **extoll** (ik·stōl′) To praise highly.

extort (ik·stôrt′) To obtain (money, etc.) from a person by violence, threat, oppression, or abuse of authority; wring; wrest. —**extortion** *n.*

F

facile (fas′əl, -il) Requiring little effort; easily achieved or performed; also, showing little expenditure of effort; superficial.

factitious (fak·tish′əs) 1. Not spontaneous; affected. 2. Produced by artificial conditions or standards: a *factitious* demand for a product.

farce (färs) A comedy employing ludicrous or exaggerated effects or situations.

farrier (far′ē·ər) *Brit.* 1. One who shoes horses. 2. A veterinarian, especially one for horses.

fealty (fē′əl·tē) 1. The obligation of fidelity owed to a feudal lord by his vassal or tenant; also, the sworn recognition of this obligation. 2. Faithfulness; loyalty.

feign (fān) 1. To make a false show of; put on a deceptive appearance of. 2. To think up (a false story, a lying excuse, etc.) and give out as true.

fetter (fet′ər) To bind with chains or the like, especially to confine the ankles; shackle.

fiat (fī′at, -ət) A positive and authoritative order or decree.

filial (fil′ē·əl, fil′yəl) Of, pertaining to, or befitting a son or daughter: *filial* devotion.

flagrant (flā′grənt) Openly disgraceful; shockingly bad; notorious; heinous.

flout (flout) To express scorn or contempt for; scoff at; defy with open contempt; mock; jeer. —*n.* A contemptuous or mocking act or remark; gibe; scoff.

fop (fop) A man overly fastidious in dress or deportment; a dandy.

forestall (fôr·stôl′) To hinder, prevent, or guard against in advance.

forswear (fôr·swâr′) To renounce or abandon emphatically or upon oath; swear to give up completely; abjure.

fortitude (fôr′tə·tōōd, -tyōōd) Strength of mind in the face of pain, adversity, or peril; patient and constant courage.

fretwork (fret′wûrk′) Ornamental openwork, usually composed of frets or interlaced parts.

frieze (frēz) 1. A coarse, woolen cloth with a shaggy nap. 2. Any decorative horizontal strip, as along the top of a wall in a room.

fructify (fruk′tə·fī, frōōk′-) To bear fruit.

frugal (frōō′gəl) Avoiding waste; using thrift.

G

garner (gär'nər) A place for storing grain; granary.

garrulous (gar'ə·ləs, -yə-) Given to continual or glib talking; habitually loquacious.

gauntlet (gônt'lit, gänt'-) In medieval armor, a glove covered with metal plates to protect the hand.

genealogist (jē'nē·al'ə·jist) One who traces genealogies or who is a student of genealogy.

genealogy (jē'nē·al'ə·jē, -nē·ol'-) A record or table showing the descent of an individual or family from a certain ancestor.

glean (glēn) **1.** To collect (facts, etc.) by patient effort. **2.** To gather (the leavings) from a field after the crop has been reaped.

gregarious (gri·gâr'ē·əs) Enjoying or seeking the company of others; sociable.

grotto (grot'ō) **1.** A cave. **2.** An artificial cavelike structure, as for a recreational retreat, shrine, etc.

grovel (gruv'əl, grov'-) To act with abject humility; abase oneself, as from fear or servility.

guerdon (gûr'dən) *Poetic* Reward; recompense.

guile (gīl) Treacherous cunning or craft; deceit.

H

hack (hak) **1.** A person who is hired out to do routine or tedious work, especially literary work: drudge. **2.** A horse for hire. —*v.* To cut or chop crudely or irregularly, as with an ax, cleaver, sword, etc.

hackney (hak'nē) **1.** A horse of medium size used for ordinary driving and riding. **2.** A carriage for hire.

harangue (hə·rang') A lengthy, loud and vehement speech; tirade. —*v.* To address in a harangue.

harbinger (här'bin·jər) One who or that which goes before and announces the coming of something; herald.

harridan (har'ə·dən) A hateful old woman; vicious hag.

hautboy (hō'boi, ō'-) An oboe.

hawker (hô'kər) One who peddles goods in the street.

heath (hēth) *Brit.* An area of open land overgrown with heath or coarse herbage.

hie (hī) To hasten; hurry.

hitherto (hith'ər·tōō', hith'ər·tōō') Until this time; up to now.

hoar (hôr) **1.** Having hair that is white or gray with age. **2.** White or grayish white in color; whitened, as with frost.

hypocrisy (hi·pok'rə·sē) The pretense of having feelings or characteristics one does not possess; especially the deceitful assumption of praiseworthy qualities; insincerity.

I

idiosyncrasy (id'ē·ō·sing'krə·sē) A habit, mannerism, mode of expression, etc., peculiar to an individual; personal oddity; quirk.

ignominy (ig'nə·min'ē) **1.** Disgrace or dishonor. **2.** That which causes or merits disgrace; dishonorable quality or conduct.

imbibe (im·bīb') **1.** To drink in; drink. **2.** To take in and retain mentally.

impalpable (im·pal'pə·bəl) **1.** Not capable of being distinguished by the mind; intangible. **2.** Not capable of being perceived by the sense of touch.

impecunious (im'pə·kyōō'nē·əs) Having no money; poor.

impede (im·pēd') To retard or hinder in progress or action; put obstacles in the way of.

impious (im'pē·əs) Lacking in reverence for God; ungodly; blasphemous.

importunity (im'pôr·tōō'nə·tē, -tyōō'-) Persistence in making demands or requests.

impound (im·pound') To seize and hold, or seize and turn over to a court of law.

imprecation (im'prə·kā'shən) A malediction; curse.

impropriety (im'prə·prī'ə·tē) An improper action.

impunity (im·pyōō'nə·tē) Freedom or exemption from punishment, harm, or unpleasant consequence.

inadvertent (in'əd·vûr'tənt) Not exercising due care or consideration; negligent. —**inadvertency** *n.*

inanition (in'ə·nish'ən) **1.** Exhaustion caused by lack of nourishment or inability to assimilate food. **2.** Emptiness.

incantation (in'kan·tā'shən) The uttering or intoning of words or syllables supposed to produce magical results.

inception (in·sep'shən) Beginning, as of an undertaking.

incredulity (in'krə·dōō'lə·tē, -dyōō'-) The quality or state of being disbelieving; doubting; questioning. —**incredulous** *adj.*

indefatigable (in'də·fat'ə·gə·bəl) Not yielding readily to fatigue; tireless; unflagging.

indite (in·dīt') *Archaic* To put into written words; compose; write.

indolent (in'də·lənt) Averse to exertion or work; lazy; idle.

indubitable (in·dōō'bə·tə·bəl, -dyōō'-) Not to be doubted; unquestionable; certain.

inexorable (in·ek'sər·ə·bəl) **1.** Not to be moved by entreaty or persuasion; unyielding. **2.** Unalterable; relentless. —**inexorably** *adv.*

infallible (in·fal'ə·bəl) Exempt from fallacy or error of judgment, as in opinion or statement. —**infallibly** *adv.*

ingenious (in·jēn'yəs) Having inventive and adaptive ability; clever.

ingenuous (in·jen'yōō·əs) **1.** Innocent and simple; naive. **2.** Straightforward; candid; frank.

ingrate (in'grāt) An ungrateful person.

inimical (in·im'i·kəl) **1.** Behaving as an enemy; unfriendly; hostile. **2.** Characterized by harmful opposition; antagonistic: a trend *inimical* to learning.

insidious (in·sid'ē·əs) **1.** Subtly cunning or deceitful; treacherous. **2.** Progressing unnoticeably, but harmfully.

interlocution (in'tər·lō·kyōō'shən) Interchange of speech between two or more people; dialogue.

intermit (in'tər·mit') To stop temporarily or at intervals; pause —**intermission** *n.*

intractable (in·trak'tə·bəl) Not tractable; not easily controlled or guided; stubborn; unruly.

intrinsic (in·trin'sik) Belonging to the real or inner nature of a thing; essential.

inure (in·yōōr') To cause to accept or tolerate by use or exercise; accustom; habituate.

invective (in·vek'tiv) Violent accusation or denunciation; vituperation; abuse.

inveigh (in·vā') To utter vehement censure or invective.

inversion (in·vûr'zhən) The reversing of the normal word order of English.

invincible (in·vin'sə·bəl) Not to be overcome; unconquerable.

irrevocable (i·rev'ə·kə·bəl) Incapable of being revoked or repealed.

irruption (i·rup'shən) A violent incursion; sudden invasion.

PRONUNCIATION: add, āce, câre, pälm; end, ēven; it, īce; odd, ōpen, ôrder; tŏŏk, pōōl; up, bûrn; ə = a in *above*, e in *sicken*, i in *flexible*, o in *melon*, u in *focus*; yōō = u in *fuse*; oil; pout; check; go; ring; thin; ᵗhis; zh, vision.

899

J

jade (jād) To weary or become weary through hard work or overuse; tire. *n.* Either of two hard, translucent minerals, jadeite or nephrite, usually green but sometimes white or variously colored, used as a gemstone.

jocund (jok′ənd, jō′kənd) Having a cheerful, gay disposition or appearance; jovial; glad.

joust (just, joust, jōōst) A formal combat between two mounted knights armed with lances.

judicious (jōō·dish′əs) Having, showing, or using good judgment.

juxtapose (juks′tə·pōz′) To place close together; put side by side. **—juxtaposition** *n.*

K

kaleidoscopic (ke·lī′də·skop′ik) Always changing, as the patterns in a kaleidoscope.

kindred (kin′drid) **1.** Belonging to the same family; related by blood; akin. **2.** Having a like nature or character; similar; cognate; related.

knell (nel) **1.** The tolling of a bell, especially one announcing a death. **2.** An omen of death, extinction, or failure.

L

labyrinth (lab′ə·rinth) **1.** An arrangement or system of winding, intricate passages or paths, as in a building, enclosed garden, park, etc., designed to confuse whoever tries to go through and find the exit; maze. **2.** Any intricate or perplexing set of difficulties, state of affairs, etc.

languor (lang′gər) **1.** Lassitude of body; weakness; fatigue. **2.** A lack of energy or enthusiasm; spiritlessness.

lascivious (lə·siv′ē·əs) **1.** Having or manifesting wanton desires; lustful. **2.** Arousing sensual desires.

latent (lā′tənt) Not visible or apparent, but capable of developing or being expressed; dormant.

lay (lā) **1.** A song, ballad, or narrative poem. **2.** A melody **—***v.* To put or place; especially, to cause to be in a specified place, state, or condition.

lee (lē) Shelter or protection, especially from the wind, provided by any object, barrier, etc.

lees (lēz) Sediment, especially in wine or liquor; dregs.

levity (lev′ə·tē) Conduct or attitude characterized by lack of seriousness; inappropriate gaiety; frivolity.

levy (lev′ē) To impose and collect by authority or force, as a tax, fine, etc. **—***n.* That which is levied, as money or troops.

lexicographer (lek′sə·kog′rə·fər) One who works at writing or compiling a dictionary.

libation (lī·bā′shən) A liquid ceremonially poured out, as in honor of a god; also, the act of pouring such a liquid.

libidinous (li·bid′ə·nəs) Characterized by or inclining toward excesses of sexual desire; lustful.

lilt (lilt) To sing, speak, or move in a cheerful, rhythmic way.

linnet (lin′it) A common fringilline songbird of Europe, the male of which has a crimson breast and crown.

lintel (lin′təl) A horizontal part above the opening of a door or window, supporting the structure above it.

lionize (lī′ə·nīz) To regard as a celebrity; treat as a celebrity.

livery (liv′ər·ē) The uniform worn by servants.

M

magnitude (mag′nə·tōōd, -tyōōd) **1.** Size or extent. **2.** Greatness or importance.

malady (mal′ə·dē) An illness or disease; sickness.

malevolent (mə·lev′ə·lənt) Wishing evil toward others; malicious; ill-disposed. **—malevolence** *n.*

malfeasance (mal·fē′zəns) The performance of some act that is wrongful or that one has specifically contracted not to perform: said usually of official misconduct.

mandarin (man′də·rin) **1.** A member of any of the nine grades of exquisitely well-educated officials of the Chinese Empire. **2.** A powerful person; especially a literary or intellectual arbiter.

mandate (man′dāt) **1.** In politics, an instruction from an electorate to its representative, expressed by the result of an election. **2.** An authoritative command, as of a sovereign; order; charge.

manifest (man′ə·fest) Plainly apparent to sight or understanding; evident; obvious. **—***v.* To reveal; show; display. **—manifestation** *n.*

manifold (man′ə·fōld) Having many and varied forms, types, instances, etc.; multiple.

maxim (mak′sim) A brief statement of a general principle, truth, or rule of conduct.

mead (mēd) **1.** An alcoholic beverage of fermented honey and water to which malt, yeast, and spices are added. **2.** *Poetic* A meadow.

mendicant (mən′də·kənt) A beggar.

meretricious (mer′ə·trish′əs) Artificially and vulgarly attractive.

meritorious (mer′ə·tôr′ē·əs) Deserving reward or praise; having merit.

metaphysical (met′ə·fiz′i·kəl) **1.** Of or pertaining to ultimate reality or basic knowledge. **2.** Beyond or above the physical or the laws of nature; transcendental. **3.** Of or designating certain English poets of the 17th century, including Donne, Herbert, and Crashaw, whose poetry is characterized by complex, intellectual imagery, paradox, and subtlety of thought.

metrical (met′ri·kəl) Of, pertaining to, or characterized by meter; rhythmic.

mettlesome (met′l·səm) Full of spirit; courageous; valiant.

mien (mēn) Manner, bearing, expression, or outward appearance.

minion (min′yən) **1.** A servile favorite or follower: a term of contempt. **2.** *Obs.* Any favorite object.

mitigate (mit′ə·gāt) To make or become milder or less severe.

modulate (moj′ōō·lāt) To regulate or adjust; modify; soften.

moil (moil) Toil; drudgery.

moiré (mwä·rā′) A ribbed fabric, usually silk or rayon, having a wavy or watered pattern; also *moire* (mwär, mōr).

moor (mōōr) A tract of wasteland sometimes covered with heath, often elevated, marshy, and abounding in peat.

morose (mə·rōs′) Ill-humored; sullen; gloomy, as a person, mood, etc.

mortification (mor′tə·fə·kā′shən) A feeling of loss of self-esteem through failure, disappointment, or embarrassment; humiliation; shame.

mote (mōt) A minute particle or speck, especially of dust.

motley (mot′lē) **1.** Made up of diverse elements; heterogeneous: a *motley* crew. **2.** A woolen cloth of mixed colors worn between the 14th and 17th centuries.

mountebank (moun′tə·bangk) **1.** One who sells quack medicines at fairs after drawing a crowd with jokes, tricks, etc. **2.** Any charlatan.

multifarious (mul′tə·fâr′ē·əs) Having great diversity or variety.

multifoliate (mul′ti·fō′lē·āt, -it) Bearing many leaves.

munificent (myōō·nif′ə·sənt) Extraordinarily generous or bountiful; liberal. **—munificence** *n.*

myriad (mir′ē·əd) **1.** A vast indefinite number. **2.** A vast number of persons or things.

900

N

nether (neth′ər) Situated beneath or below.

newt (nōōt, nyōōt) Any of various semiaquatic salamanders, especially of the genus Triturus.

noisome (noi′səm) **1.** Offensive or disgusting, especially in smell; stinking. **2.** Injurious; noxious.

nostalgic (nos·tal′jik) Having or showing a longing for a pleasant happening, condition, or place that is past or far away.

O

obdurate (ob′dyə·rit, -rāt) **1.** Unmoved by or hardened against human feelings or moral influence; hardhearted. **2.** Difficult to handle or manage; intractable; *obdurate materials.*

oblation (ob·lā′shən) The act of offering religious worship, sacrifice, etc., especially in the Eucharist.

oblique (ə·blēk′) **1.** Deviating from the perpendicular or horizontal; slanting; sloping. **2.** Not direct or straightforward in meaning, expression, etc.: *oblique* praise. **—obliquely** *adv.*

obsequious (əb·sē′kwē·əs) Excessively obedient or submissive; sycophantic; servile.

offal (ô′fəl) **1.** The waste parts of a butchered animal. **2.** Rubbish or refuse of any kind.

omniscience (om·nish′əns) Infinite knowledge.

opacity (ō·pas′ə·tē) **1.** The state or quality of being opaque. **2.** Obscurity.

ostensible (os·ten′sə·bəl) Offered as real or genuine; apparent. **—ostensibly** *adv.*

ostentatious (os′tən·tā′shəs) Intended to attract notice; showy.

P

paling (pā′ling) One of a series of upright pales forming a fence.

palisade (pal′ə·sād′) **1.** A barrier or fortification made of strong timbers set in the ground. **2.** An extended cliff or rocky precipice.

paltry (pôl′trē) Having little or no worth or value; trifling; trivial.

panegyric (pan·ə·jir′ik) **1.** A formal public eulogy, either written or spoken. **2.** Elaborate praise; laudation.

paragon (par′ə·gon) A model or pattern of excellence, especially of a specific excellence: a *paragon* of virtue.

parapet (par′ə·pit, -pet) A low wall about the edge of a roof, terrace, bridge, etc.

paraphrase (par′ə·frāz) A restatement of the meaning of a passage, work, etc., as for clarity.

parricide (par′ə·sīd) The killing of a parent.

partisan (pär′tə·zən) One who supports or upholds a party, cause, etc.; especially, an overly zealous adherent or devotee.

parturition (par′tyōō·rish′ən, -chōō-) The act of bringing forth young; delivery; childbirth.

pastoral (pas′tər·əl) Of or pertaining to shepherds, rustics, or rural life.

pathos (pā′thos) The quality, especially in literature or art, that arouses feelings of pity, sorrow, compassion, etc.

patrimony (pat′rə·mō′nē) An inheritance from a father or an ancestor; also, anything inherited.

peat (pēt) **1.** A substance consisting of partially carbonized vegetable material, chiefly mosses, found usually in bogs.

2. A block of this substance, pressed and dried for fuel.

pecuniary (pi·kyōō′nē·er′ē) Consisting of or relating to money.

pedant (ped′ənt) One who makes needless display of learning, or who insists upon the importance of trifling points of scholarship.

pedantry (ped′ən·trē) **1.** Ostentatious display of knowledge. **2.** Undue or slavish adherence to forms or rules.

peer (pir) **1.** An equal, as in natural gifts or in social rank. **2.** An equal before the law. **3.** A noble; especially, a member of a hereditary legislative body.

pendent (pen′dənt) Hanging downward; suspended.

penitent (pen′ə·tənt) Affected by a sense of one's own guilt, and resolved on amendment. **—n.** One who is penitent.

penury (pen′yə·rē) Extreme poverty or want.

perdition (pər·dish′ən) **1.** Eternal damnation; the utter loss of a soul. **2.** The place of eternal damnation; hell.

perfidious (pər·fid′ē·əs) Marked by or guilty of perfidy; treacherous.

perforce (pər·fors′) By or of necessity; necessarily.

pernicious (pər·nish′əs) **1.** Having the power of destroying or injuring; tending to kill or hurt; very injurious; deadly. **2.** Malicious; wicked.

perspicacity (pûr′spə·kas′ə·tē) Keenness in mental penetration or discernment.

perturbation (pûr′tər·bā′shən) The act of agitating and greatly disturbing or the state of being agitated and greatly disturbed.

peruse (pə·rōōz′) To read carefully or attentively.

phlegmatic (fleg·mat′ik) Not easily moved or excited; sluggish; indifferent.

pietism (pī′ə·tiz′əm) **1.** Piety or godliness; devotion as distinguished from insistence on religious creeds or forms. **2.** Affected or exaggerated piety.

pillage (pil′ij) To rob openly, as in war; plunder.

pillory (pil′ə·rē) A framework in which an offender was fastened by the neck and wrists and exposed to public scorn.

pinion (pin′yən) **1.** To bind or hold the arms of (someone) so as to render helpless. **2.** To shackle; confine.

piquant (pē′kənt, -känt, -kwant, pē·känt′) **1.** Lively and charming; interesting. **2.** *Obs.* Stinging; sharp.

plethoric (ple·thôr′ik, pleth′ə·rik) Excessively full; overloaded; turgid; inflated. **—plethora** *n.*

poetaster (pō′it·as′tər) An inferior poet.

poet laureate (lô′rē·it) **1.** In Great Britain, the official poet of the realm, a member of the royal household charged with writing verses for particular occasions. **2.** A poet acclaimed as the most eminent in a locality.

poltroon (pol·trōōn′) A mean-spirited coward; craven; dastard.

porter (por′tər) **1.** A dark brown, heavy, English malt liquor resembling ale. **2.** One who carries travelers' luggage, etc., for hire, as in a hotel or at a railroad station.

posthumous (pos′chōō·məs) **1.** Published after the author's death, as a book. **2.** Arising or continuing after one's death: a *posthumous* reputation.

postilion (pōs·til′yən, pos-) One who guides a team drawing a carriage or other heavy vehicle by riding the near horse when one pair is used or the near horse of the leaders when two or more pairs are used.

potentate (pōt′n·tāt) One having great power or sway; a sovereign.

pother (poth′ər) Excitement mingled with confusion; bustle; full.

prate (prāt) To talk idly and at length; chatter.

PRONUNCIATION: add, āce, câre, pälm; end, ēven; it, īce; odd, ōpen, ôrder; tŏŏk, pōōl; up, bûrn; ə = a in *above,* e in *sicken,* i in *flexible,* o in *melon,* u in *focus;* yōō = u in *fuse;* oil; pout; check; go; ring; thin; this; zh, vision.

precept (prē'sept) A rule prescribing a particular kind of conduct or action.

predilection (prē'də·lek'shən, pred'ə-) A preference or bias in favor of something; a partiality.

prelate (prel'it) An ecclesiastic of high rank, as a bishop, archbishop, etc.

prerogative (pri·rog'ə·tiv) An exclusive and unquestionable right belonging to a person or body of persons; especially, a hereditary or official right.

presage (pres'ij) 1. An indication of something to come; portent; omen. 2. A presentiment; foreboding.

probity (prō'bə·tē, prob'ə-) Virtue or integrity tested and confirmed; strict honesty.

prodigal (prod'ə·gəl) 1. Addicted to wasteful expenditure, as of money, time, or strength; extravagant. 2. Yielding in profusion; bountiful.

progeny (proj'ə·nē) Offspring.

prognostic (prog·nos'tik) A sign of some future occurrence; an omen.

prognostication (prog·nos'tə·kā'shən) A prediction or prophecy.

prolific (prō·lif'ik) Producing results abundantly: a *prolific* writer.

promontory (prom'ən·tôr'ē, -tō'rē) A high point of land extending into the sea; headland.

propitiate (prō·pish'ē·āt) To cause to be favorably disposed; appease; conciliate.

prospectus (prə·spek'təs) A paper containing information of a proposed literary, commercial, or industrial undertaking.

protégé (prō'tə·zhā) A person whose career is guided and protected by someone older or more powerful.

proverbial (prə·vûr'bē·əl) Being the object of general remark, as a typical case; well-known; notorious. **—proverb** *n.*

providence (prov'ə·dəns) The care exercised by God over the universe.

provocation (prov'ə·kā'shən) An incitement to action; stimulus. **—provoke** *v.*

prudent (prōōd'nt) 1. Careful to avoid errors and follow the most politic and profitable course; cautious; worldly-wise. 2. Exercising sound judgment; sagacious; judicious.

pugnacious (pug·nā'shəs) Disposed or inclined to fight; quarrelsome.

pungent (pun'jənt) Causing a sharp pricking, piercing, or acrid effect on the sense of taste or smell; keen; penetrating.

purport (pûr'pôrt) That which is conveyed or suggested to the mind as the meaning or intention; import; significance.

Q

quagmire (kwag'mīr', kwog'-) 1. Marshy ground that gives way under the foot; bog. 2. A difficult situation.

quell (kwel) 1. To put down or suppress by force; extinguish. 2. To quiet; allay, as pain.

quinsy (kwin'zē) A suppurative inflammation of the tonsils.

R

rabid (rab'id) Unreasonably zealous; fanatical; violent.

raillery (rā'lər·ē) Merry jesting or teasing; banter.

rakish (rā'kish) Dashing; jaunty; smart.

rancor (rang'kər) Bitter and vindictive enmity; malice; spitefulness.

rapt (rapt) Engrossed; intent; deeply engaged.

ravage (rav'ij) To hurt or damage severely.

ravening (rav'ən·ing) Seeking eagerly for prey; rapacious.

raze (rāz) 1. To level to the ground; demolish, as a building. 2. *Rare* To scrape or shave off.

rebuke (ri·byōōk') To reprove sharply; reprimand.

recapitulate (rē'kə·pich'ōō·lāt) To review briefly; sum up.

reck (rek) *Archaic* To have a care or thought (for); heed.

recourse (rē'kôrs, ri·kôrs') Resort to or application for help or security.

redound (ri·dound') To have an effect, as by reaction, to the credit, discredit, advantage, etc., of the original agent; return; react; accrue.

redress (ri·dres') To set right, as a wrong, by compensation or by punishment of the wrongdoer; make reparation for.

regimentals (rej'ə·men'təlz). 1. The uniform worn by a regiment. 2. A military uniform.

remission (ri·mish'ən) Discharge from penalty; pardon; deliverance, as from a debt or obligation.

rend (rend) 1. To tear apart forcibly; split; break. 2. To pass through (the air) violently and noisily.

renegade (ren'ə·gād) A traitor; deserter.

repartee (rep'ər·tē', -är-, -tā) A witty or quick reply; a sharp rejoinder.

repast (ri·past') A meal.

repertory (rep'ər·tôr'ē, -tō'rē) A list of songs, plays, operas, or the like, that a person or company is prepared to perform; also, such pieces collectively.

replete (ri·plēt') 1. Full to the uttermost. 2. Abundantly supplied or stocked; abounding.

reprobate (rep'rə·bāt) A depraved or profligate person.

reprobation (rep'rə·bā'shən) The act of reprobating or the condition of being reprobated; censure.

repugnant (ri·pug'nənt) Offensive to taste or feeling; exciting aversion or repulsion.

repulse (ri·puls') Rejection; refusal. **—v.** To drive back; repel, as an attacking force.

requisite (rek'wə·zit) Required by the nature of things or by circumstances; indispensable.

requite (ri·kwīt') To make equivalent return for, as kindness, service, or injury; make up for.

respite (res'pit) Temporary intermission of labor or effort; an interval of rest.

restive (res'tiv) 1. Impatient of control; unruly. 2. Restless; fidgety.

retentive (ri·ten'tiv) Able to remember things easily and accurately.

reticulate (ri·tik'yə·lāt) To make a network of.

retrench (ri·trench') 1. To cut down or reduce; curtail (expenditures). 2. To cut off or away; remove; omit.

retribution (ret'rə·byōō'shən) The act of requiting; especially, impartial infliction of punishment.

retrospection (ret'rə·spek'shən) A looking back upon or recollection of the past; a remembering.

revel (rev'əl) Merrymaking; carousing; noisy festivity.

reverberation (ri·vûr'bə·rā'shən) Resounding and reechoing.

reversion (ri·vûr'zhən, -shən) A return to or toward some former state or condition.

revile (ri·vīl') To assail with abusive or contemptuous language; vilify; abuse.

rhetoric (ret'ə·rik) Showy, high-flown language.

roister (rois'tər) 1. To act in a blustery manner; swagger. 2. To engage in tumultuous merry-making; revel. **—roisterer** *n.*

rout (rout) To defeat disastrously; put to flight. **—n.** A disorderly defeat or flight.

rue (rōō) To feel sorrow or remorse for; regret extremely. **—n.** Sorrowful remembrance; regret.

runic (rōōn'ik) Of or having to do with runes, characters in an early European alphabet.

ruse (rōōz) Some action or trick intended to mislead or deceive.

rustic (rus'tik) One who lives in the country. —*adj.* Typical of or appropriate to country life.

S

sable (sā'bəl) 1. Black, especially as the color of mourning. 2. Made of or having the color of sable fur; dark brown. —*n.* A carnivore of northern Asia and Europe, related to the marten and prized for its valuable fur.

saffron (saf'rən) 1. A deep yellow-orange. 2. An autumn-flowering species of crocus.

sagacity (sə·gas'ə·tē) The quality of being sagacious; discernment and judgment; shrewdness.

sage (sāj) A venerable person of recognized experience, prudence, and foresight; a profoundly wise counselor or philosopher. —*adj.* Characterized by or proceeding from calm, far-seeing wisdom and prudence.

salient (sā'lē·ənt) Standing out prominently; striking; conspicuous.

sally (sal'ē) 1. A rushing forth, as of troops against besiegers; sortie. 2. Any sudden rushing forth.

sanction (sangk'shən) 1. Final and authoritative confirmation; justification or ratification. 2. A provision for securing conformity to law, as by the enactment of rewards or penalties or both; a reward or penalty.

sanguine (sang'gwin) 1. Of buoyant disposition; hopeful; confident; cheerful. 2. Ruddy; robust.

satiety (sə·tī'ə·tē) The state of being satiated; repletion; surfeit.

saturnine (sat'ər·nīn) Having a grave, gloomy, or morose disposition or character; heavy; dull.

scabbard (skab'ərd) A sheath for a weapon, as for a bayonet or a sword.

scathing (skā'thing) Mercilessly severe; blasting; withering.

scoff (skôf) An expression or an object of contempt or derision.

sconce (skons) An ornamental wall bracket for holding a candle or other light.

scrofula (skrof'yə·lə) A tuberculous condition of the lymphatic glands, characterized by enlargement, suppurating abscesses, and cheeselike degeneration.

scruple (skroo'pəl) Doubt or uncertainty regarding a question of moral right or duty; reluctance arising from conscientious disapproval.

sedition (si·dish'ən) 1. Language or conduct directed against public order and the tranquillity of the state. 2. Dissension; revolt. —**seditious** *adj.*

sepulcher (sep'əl·kər) A burial place, especially one found or made in a rock or solidly built of stone; tomb; vault.

sequester (si·kwes'tər) 1. To seclude; withdraw. 2. To place apart; separate.

serge (sûrj) A strong twilled fabric made of wool yarns and characterized by a diagonal rib on both sides of the cloth.

shire (shīr) A territorial division of Great Britain; a county.

shoal (shōl) A shallow place in any body of water.

sinuous (sin'yoo·əs) Characterized by bends, curves, or folds; winding; undulating.

slake (slāk) 1. To quench or satisfy, as thirst or an appetite. 2. To lessen the force or intensity of; cause to subside; quell.

smite (smīt), **smote**, **smitten** To strike (something).

sobriety (sō·brī'ə·tē) 1. Abstinence from intoxicating drink. 2. Moderateness in temper or conduct; sedateness; seriousness.

solicit (sə·lis'it) 1. To ask for earnestly; seek to obtain by persuasion or entreaty. 2. To influence to action; tempt; especially, to entice (one) to an unlawful or immoral act.

solicitude (sə·lis'ə·tood, -tyood) The state of being solicitous; anxiety or concern.

sophistic (sə·fis'tik) Pertaining to a Sophist, sophists, or sophistry.

sophistry (sof'is·trē) Subtly fallacious reasoning or disputation.

sot (sot) A habitual drunkard.

spate (spāt) A sudden or vigorous outpouring, as of words, feeling, etc.

specious (spē'shəs) 1. Apparently good or right, but actually not so; plausible. 2. Pleasing or attractive in appearance, but deceptive.

spleen (splēn) 1. Ill temper; spitefulness; to vent one's spleen. 2. A highly vascular, flattened, ductless organ located on the upper left side of the abdominal cavity, and effecting certain modifications in the blood. 3. This organ regarded as the seat of various emotions.

spurn (spûrn) To scorn; reject with contempt.

squalidly (skwol'id·lē) In a poor, wretched, or degraded manner or condition.

stiletto (sti·let'ō) A small dagger with a slender blade.

stipulate (stip'yə·lāt) To specify as the terms of an agreement, contract, etc.

stoicism (stō'ə·siz'əm) Indifference to pleasure or pain; stoicalness.

strand (strand) 1. A shore or beach; especially, that portion of an ocean shore between high and low tides. 2. Anything plaited or twisted.

subsist (səb·sist') 1. To have existence or reality; continue to exist. 2. To maintain one's existence; manage to live. 3. To continue unchanged; abide.

succor (suk'ər) Help or relief rendered in danger, difficulty, or distress.

suffuse (sə·fyooz') To overspread, as with a vapor, fluid, or color.

sundry (sun'drē) Of an indefinite small number; various; several; miscellaneous.

superannuate (soo'pər·an'yoo·āt) 1. To permit to retire on a pension on account of age or infirmity. 2. To set aside or discard on account of age or infirmity.

supersede (soo'pər·sēd') To take the place of, as by reason of superior worth, right, or appropriateness; replace; supplant.

supplant (sə·plant') To take the place of; displace.

suppliant (sup'lē·ənt) 1. Entreating earnestly and humbly; beseeching. 2. Manifesting entreaty or submissive supplication.

surmise (sər·mīz') A conjecture made on slight evidence; supposition.

surrealist (sə·rē'əl·ist) As conceived, or "seen," by the subconscious mind, not reshaped or "corrected" by reason.

swain (swān) 1. A youthful rustic. 2. A lover.

swarthy (swôr'thē) Having a dark hue; of dark or sunburned complexion; tawny.

sycophant (sik'ə·fənt) A servile flatterer; parasite.

sylph (silf) An imaginary being, mortal but without a soul, living in the air.

sylvan (sil'vən) *Chiefly Poetic* Of, pertaining to, or located in a forest or woods.

syntax (sin'taks) 1. The arrangement and interrelationship of words in phrases and sentences. 2. The branch of linguistics dealing with relationships.

PRONUNCIATION: add, āce, câre, pälm; end, ēven; it, īce; odd, ōpen, ôrder; took, pool; up, bûrn; ə = a in *above*, e in *sicken*, i in *flexible*, o in *melon*, u in *focus*; yoo = u in *fuse*; oil; pout; check; go; ring; thin; this; zh, vision.

903

T

tabloid (tab′loid) A newspaper consisting of sheets one half the size of those in an ordinary newspaper, in which the news is presented by means of pictures and concise reporting.

tabor (tā′bɔr) A small drum or tambourine used to accompany oneself on a pipe or fife.

taciturn (tas′ə·tûrn) Habitually silent or reserved; disinclined to conversation.

taper (tā′pər) 1. A small candle. 2. A burning wick or other light substance giving but feeble illumination. 3. A gradual dimunition of size in an elongated object: the *taper* of a mast.

temerity (tə·mer′ə·tē) Venturesome or foolish boldness; rashness.

temporal (tem′pər·əl) 1. Pertaining to affairs of the present life; earthly. 2. Pertaining or related to time. 3. Temporary; transitory.

tenet (ten′it) An opinion, principle, dogma, etc., that a person or organization believes or maintains as true.

tenor (ten′ər) 1. A settled course or manner of progress. 2. The adult male voice intermediate in range between baritone and countertenor; also a singer having such a voice, or a part to be sung by it.

tenuous (ten′yo͞o·əs) Thin; slim; delicate; also, weak; flimsy; unsubstantial.

terrestrial (tə·res′trē·əl) Of, belonging to, or representing the earth.

theoretical (the′ə·ret′i·kəl) 1. Of, relating to, or consisting of theory. 2. Relating to knowledge or science without reference to its application. 3. Existing only in theory; hypothetical. —**theory** *n*.

thrall (thrôl) A person in bondage; a slave; serf.

tilt (tilt) 1. To cause to rise at one end or side; incline at an angle; slant; lean; tip. 2. A medieval sport in which mounted knights, charging with lances, endeavored to unseat each other. 3. Any similar encounter, as a quarrel or dispute.

titillate (tit′ə·lāt) 1. To cause a tickling sensation in. 2. To excite pleasurably in any way.

torpor (tôr′pər) Complete or partial insensibility; stupor.

tortuous (tôr′cho͞o·əs) 1. Consisting of or abounding in irregular bends or turns; twisting. 2. Not straightforward; devious.

Tory (tôr′ē) 1. A member of an English political party, successor to the Cavaliers and opponent of the Whigs, since about 1832 called the Conservative Party. 2. One who at the period of the American Revolution adhered to the cause of British sovereignty over the colonies.

traipse (trāps) To walk about in an idle or aimless manner.

trammel (tram′əl) To entangle in or as in a snare. —*n*. That which limits freedom or activity; an impediment; hindrance.

transcendent (tran·sen′dənt) 1. Of very high and remarkable degree; surpassing; excelling. 2. *Theol.* Above and beyond the universe; said of God.

transgression (trans·gresh′ən, tranz-) A violation or infringement of a law, command, etc.; especially, a violation of a law regarded as having divine authority; sin.

transmontane (trans·mon′tān) Situated beyond a mountain; tramontane.

triumvirate (trī·um′vər·it, -və·rāt) 1. A group or coalition of three people who unitedly exercise authority or control; government by triumvirs. 2. A group of three; trio.

trivet (triv′it) A three-legged stand for holding cooking vessels in a fireplace, a heated iron, or a hot dish on a table.

tumid (to͞o′mid, tyo͞o′-) 1. Swollen; enlarged, as a part of the body. 2. Inflated or pompous in style; bombastic.

3. Bursting; teeming.

turbid (tûr′bid) 1. Being in a state of confusion. 2. Thick and dense, like heavy smoke or fog.

U

unimpeachable (un′im·pē′chə·bəl) Not to be called into question as regards truth, honesty, etc.; faultless; blameless.

unsavory (un·sā′vər·ē) Morally bad or offensive.

upbraid (up·brād′) To reproach for some wrongdoing; scold or reprove.

urbanity (ûr·ban′ə·tē) The character or quality of being urbane; refined or elegant courtesy.

V

vacillate (vas′ə·lāt) 1. To waver in mind; be irresolute. 2. To sway one way and the other; totter; waver.

valor (val′ər) Intrepid courage, especially in warfare; personal bravery.

varlet (vär′lit) A knave or scoundrel.

vaunt (vônt, vänt) To speak boastfully. —*n*. Boastful assertion or ostentatious display.

venerable (ven′ər·ə·bəl) Meriting or commanding veneration; worthy of reverence: now usually implying age.

venerate (ven′ə·rāt) To look upon or regard with respect and deference; revere.

venial (vē′nē·əl, vēn′yəl) 1. *Theol.* That may be easily pardoned or forgiven: distinguished from *mortal: venial* sin. 2. Excusable; pardonable.

veracity (və·ras′ə·tē) That which is true; truth.

verdant (vûr′dənt) Green with vegetation; covered with grass or green leaves; fresh.

verdure (vûr′jər) The fresh greenness of growing vegetation; also, such vegetation itself.

verisimilitude (ver′ə·si·mil′ə·to͞od, -tyo͞od) 1. Appearance of truth; likelihood. 2. That which resembles truth.

verity (ver′ə·tē) 1. The quality of being correct or true. 2. A true or established statement or principle; a fact; truth.

vernal (vûr′nəl) Belonging to, appearing in, or appropriate to spring.

vicissitude (vi·sis′ə·to͞od, -tyo͞od) *pl.* Irregular changes or variations, as of fortune.

vignette (vin·yet′) A drawing with a background that shades off gradually at the edges.

vindication (vin′də·kā′shən) Justification; defense. —**vindicate** *v*.

vintage (vin′tij) The yield of a vineyard or wine-growing district for one season; also, the wine produced from this yield.

virago (vi·rä′gō, -rā′-, vī-) A noisy, sharp-tongued woman; a scold.

votary (vō′tər·ē) 1. One devoted to some particular worship, pursuit, study, etc. 2. One bound by a vow or promise, as a nun.

vouchsafe (vouch·sāf′) To grant, as with condescension; permit; deign.

W

wanton (won′tən) 1. Unjust; malicious. 2. Extravagant; running to excess; unrestrained. 3. Dissolute; licentious; lustful.

wayward (wā′wərd) 1. Wanting its way; willful; froward. 2. Unexpected or unwished for: a *wayward* fortune.

welter (wel′tər) 1. A rolling movement, as of waves. 2. A commotion; turmoil. —*v*. To roll about; wallow.

whalebone (hwāl′bōn′) **1.** A strip of whalebone, used in stiffening dress bodies, corsets, etc. **2.** The horny substance developed in plates from the upper jaw on either side of the palate of certain whales.

whence (hwens) From what or which place, source, or cause; from which: the place *whence* these sounds arise.

whet (hwet) **1.** To sharpen, as a knife, by friction. **2.** To make more keen or eager; excite; stimulate, as the appetite.

Whig (hwig) In England, a member of a more or less liberal party in the 18th and 19th centuries, opposed to the Tories and later known as the Liberal Party.

whimsical (hwim′zi·kəl) Oddly constituted; fantastic; quaint.

whip (hwip) **1.** One who handles a whip expertly, as a driver. **2.** An instrument consisting of a lash attached to a handle, used for driving draft animals or for administering punishment. —*v.* To strike with a lash, rod, strap, etc.

wrack (rak) **1.** Marine vegetation and floating material cast ashore by the sea, as seaweed or eelgrass. **2.** Ruin; destruction: chiefly in the phrase **wrack and ruin.**

Z

zealous (zel′əs) Filled with or incited by zeal; enthusiastic.

PRONUNCIATION: add, āce, câre, pälm; end, ēven; it, īce; odd, ōpen, ôrder; tŏŏk, pōōl; up, bûrn; ə = a in *above*, e in *sicken*, i in *flexible*, o in *melon*, u in *focus*; yōō = u in *fuse*; oil; pout; check; go; ring; thin; this; zh, vision.

General Index

Names of authors represented in the text appear in small capitals; numbers in italics refer to the pages on which author biographies appear. Titles of selections presented in the text are shown in italics. Other references are shown in regular type.

PICTURE ACKNOWLEDGMENTS

p. 4 (right), The British Museum; p. 40, Fogg Art Museum, Harvard University; pp. 45, 47, 49, 53, 55, 57, The Pierpont Morgan Library; p. 60, Bettmann Archive; p. 73, From *Le Morte D'Arthur* by Sir Thomas Malory as illustrated by Aubrey Beardsley. Published 1927 by E. P. Dutton & Co., Inc. and reproduced with their permission; p. 86, From a portrait at Pembroke College, Cambridge, England, by kind permission of the Master and Fellows of the College; p. 87, New York Public Library Print Room; p. 90, Uffizi Gallery, Florence; pp. 93, 100, National Portrait Gallery, London; pp. 113, 114, 118, John R. Freeman (Photographers) Ltd., London; p. 183, National Portrait Gallery, London; p. 187, New York Public Library Print Room; p. 188, National Portrait Gallery, London; p. 190, Culver Pictures, Inc.; p. 204, National Portrait Gallery, London; p. 213, University Press, Oxford; p. 219, Musées Nationaux; p. 220, John Webb, F.R.P.S., Brompton Studios, London; pp. 221, 222, John R. Freeman (Photographers) Ltd., London; p. 233, Culver Pictures, Inc.; p. 226, National Portrait Gallery, London; p. 229, Harbrace Collection; p. 254, National Portrait Gallery, London; p. 261, Brown Brothers; p. 274, From Robinson and Beard's *The Development of Modern Europe* by courtesy of Ginn and Company; p. 277, Bettmann Archive; p. 281, Culver Pictures, Inc.; p. 284, Bettmann Archive; p. 288 (top left), National Portrait Gallery, London; p. 288 (top right), British Information Services; p. 288 (left), Bettmann Archive; p. 296, Bodleian Library, Oxford; p. 312, National Portrait Gallery, London; p. 321, John R. Freeman (Photographers) Ltd., London; pp. 322, 323, John Webb, F.R.P.S., Brompton Studios, London; pp. 324, 325, 326, John R. Freeman (Photographers) Ltd., London; pp. 334, 340, 349, 356, National Portrait Gallery, London; p. 370, New York Public Library Print Room; pp. 383, 388, New York Public Library Lincoln Center Drama Collection; p. 393, John R. Freeman (Photographers) Ltd., London; p. 394, Vince Finnigan & Associates, Washington, D. C.; p. 396, John R. Freeman (Photographers) Ltd., London; p. 397, Tom Scott, Edinburgh; p. 414, National Portrait Gallery, London; p. 419, Culver Pictures, Inc.; p. 424, National Portrait Gallery, London; pp. 431 (right), 432 (left), 444, Bettmann Archive; p. 447, Harbrace Collection; p. 449, New York Public Library Print Room; p. 465, John R. Freeman (Photographers) Ltd., London; p. 467, John Webb, F.R.P.S., Brompton Studios, London; p. 468, John R. Freeman (Photographers) Ltd., London; p. 470, John Webb, F.R.P.S., Brompton Studios, London; pp. 483, 505, 510, 519, 528, National Portrait Gallery, London; pp. 538, 539, George M. Cushing; pp. 540, 542, John R. Freeman (Photographers) Ltd., London; pp. 550, 551, 559, Culver Pictures, Inc.; p. 561, Harbrace Collection; p. 569, National Portrait Gallery, London; p. 571, Bettmann Archive; p. 573, Radio Times Hulton Picture Library; p. 574, Folger Shakespeare Library; p. 576, Courtesy, Oriel College, Oxford; pp. 580, 597, National Portrait Gallery, London; p. 609, John R. Freeman (Photographers) Ltd., London; p. 615, Culver Pictures, Inc.; p. 618, Bettmann Archive; p. 622, National Portrait Gallery, London; p. 625, University Press, Oxford; p. 629, Culver Pictures, Inc.; pp. 650, 652, John R. Freeman (Photographers) Ltd., London; p. 654, John Webb, F.R.P.S., Brompton Studios, London; p. 660, Culver Pictures, Inc.; p. 661, British Information Services; p. 666, Gernsheim Collection, The University of Texas; p. 688, British Information Service; p. 691, Bettmann Archive; p. 697, British Information Services; p. 702, Culver Pictures, Inc.; p. 706, Wide World Photos; p. 712, British Information Service; p. 724, Sherwin Greenberg, McGranahan & May, Inc., Buffalo; p. 725, John Evans, Ottawa; p. 726, John Webb, F.R.P.S., Brompton Studios, London; p. 727, Culver Pictures, Inc.; p. 735, Bettmann Archive; p. 748, Photo by Angus MacBean; pp. 801, 808, British Information Service; pp. 815, 820, Department of External Affairs, Dublin; pp. 830, 834, British Information Service; p. 841, Photo by Jane Bown, Camera Press, Pix Incorporated, London; p. 846, Camera Press, Pix Incorporated, London; pp. 857, 859, John Webb, F.R.P.S., Brompton Studios, London; pp. 860, 862, John R. Freeman (Photographers) Ltd., London. All maps are Harbrace Maps.

ART CREDITS

ENRICO ARNO. 308, 422, 455, 476, 480, 494, 501, 507, 508, 520, 524, 533, 543, 544, 578, 590, 757, 787, 790

MANNY HALLER. 119, 315, 317, 328, 353, 453, 454, 681, 689, 733, 742, 746, 803, 804, 806, 823, 827

MEL KLAPHOLZ. 224, 461, 472, 474, 588, 592, 595, 600, 602, 645

JAMES AND RUTH MCCREA. 36, 37, 38, 99, 582, 583, 624

E 2
F 3
G 4
H 5
I 6
J 7